StreetSmart
1992 PERTH
STREET DIRECTORY

DOLA
Department of LAND ADMINISTRATION

FOREWORD

I have much pleasure in presenting the 1992 edition of the Department of Land Administration's StreetSmart Street Directory.

In this, the 33rd edition, the usual comprehensive revision of detail and road patterns has been carried out and new information this year includes the much requested depiction of petrol stations on the street maps.

Another long awaited addition to the Directory is the coverage of most of the metropolitan area on two wall maps at scale 1:40 000. Details of these appear on the inside of the front cover.

The content and production of the directory is once again of the highest quality and an invaluable source of information for all Perth motorists.

Acknowledgement is given to the numerous Government bodies and professional organisations who regularly contribute information to the Directory.

HON. DAVID SMITH, M.L.C.
MINISTER FOR LANDS

Although great care has been taken to ensure the accuracy of information, errors may occur. The Department welcomes your co-operation in pointing out any such irregularities. Please direct your information or queries to:

StreetSmart Street Directory
c/o The Manager,
Cartographic Services Branch,
Department of Land Administration,
184 St. Georges Terrace,
Perth, W.A. 6000 or Telephone: (09) 322 2155

For any general enquiries regarding mapping, please contact the:

Central Map Agency
Department of Land Administration,
Central Government Buildings,
Cathedral Avenue,
Perth, W.A. 6000 or Telephone: (09) 323 1344

TO FIND A STREET

1. Turn to page 171, Index to Street Names
2. Look for your street in the alphabetical listing. We will use "Abalone Crescent", Waikiki as an example.
3. Note the reference — Map 145
   Ref. B 3
4. Turn to map 145
5. Trace down from the letter B in the top margin and across from the number 3 in the side margin, keeping between the blue lines. Where the lines meet, a rectangle is formed in which Abalone Crescent will be found.

mbers 13 and 14 is a black box — Joins ... ber of the adjoining map. Note that the numbers in the top margin of map 145 are the same as the numbers in the bottom margin of map 137. This occurs in all common margins between adjoining maps. Thus, "Read Street", which finishes at reference number 13 on map 145, continues from reference number 13 on adjoining map 137.

For more information concerning the use of this directory, please refer to:

page 2 — Contents
page 3 — Explanation of Map Symbols
page 170 — To Find a Street and Relationship to the State Large Scale Series.

USEFUL REFERENCES

Hospitals	Map	Ref.	
Fremantle	1D	C	6
Princess Margaret	72	C	1
Royal Perth	1C	A	3
Sir Charles Gairdner	71	E	6

For other hospitals see "Facilities Guide"

	Map	Ref.	
Perth International Airport	63	D	10
Perth Domestic Airport	63	B	8
Perth Railway Terminal	61	C	10

PRODUCED BY THE CARTOGRAPHIC SERVICES BRANCH, DEPARTMENT OF LAND ADMINISTRATION, PERTH, WESTERN AUSTRALIA.
EDITION 33   CROWN COPYRIGHT RESERVED 1992.
PRINTED BY STATE PRINTING DIVISION, PERTH, WESTERN AUSTRALIA

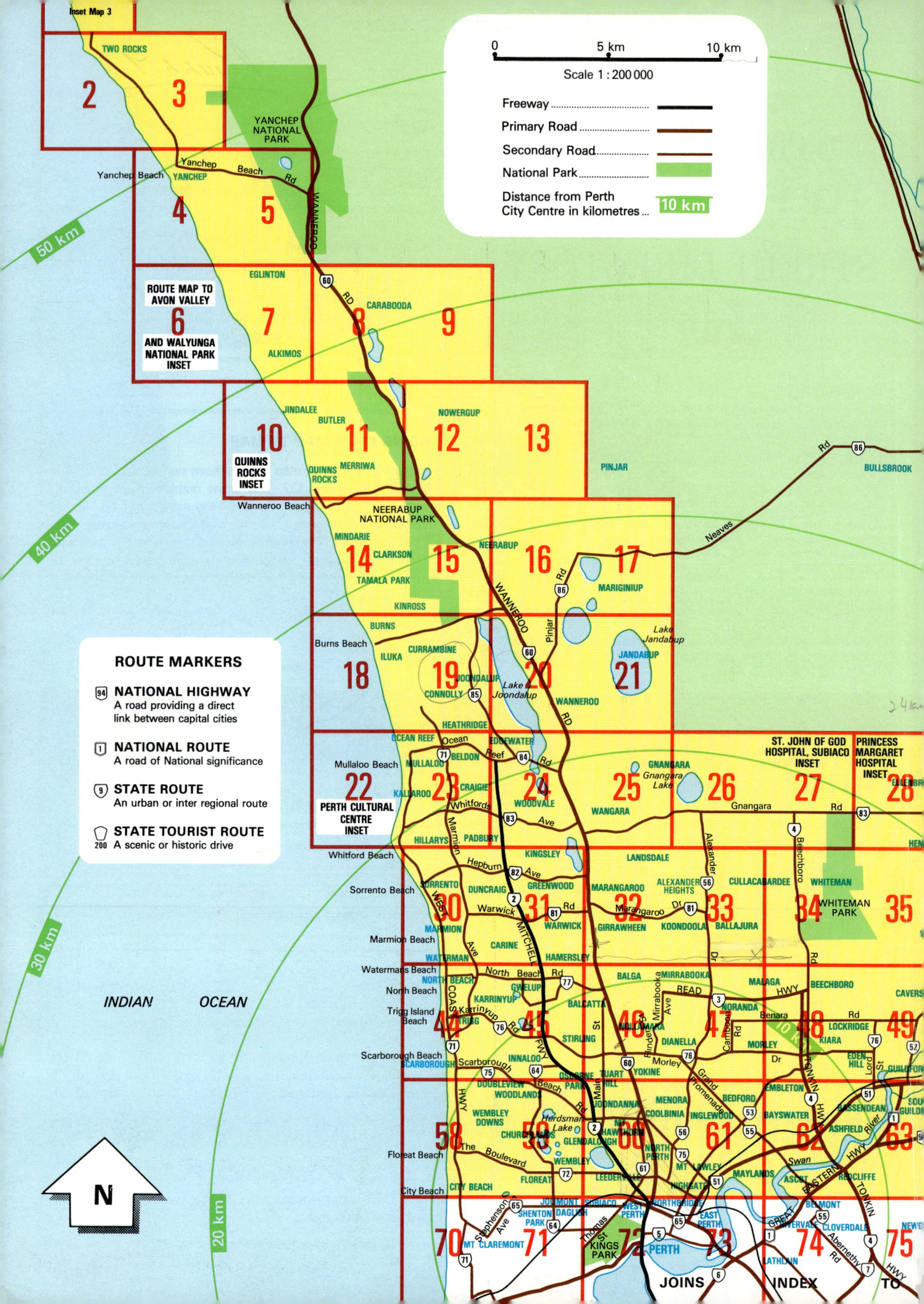

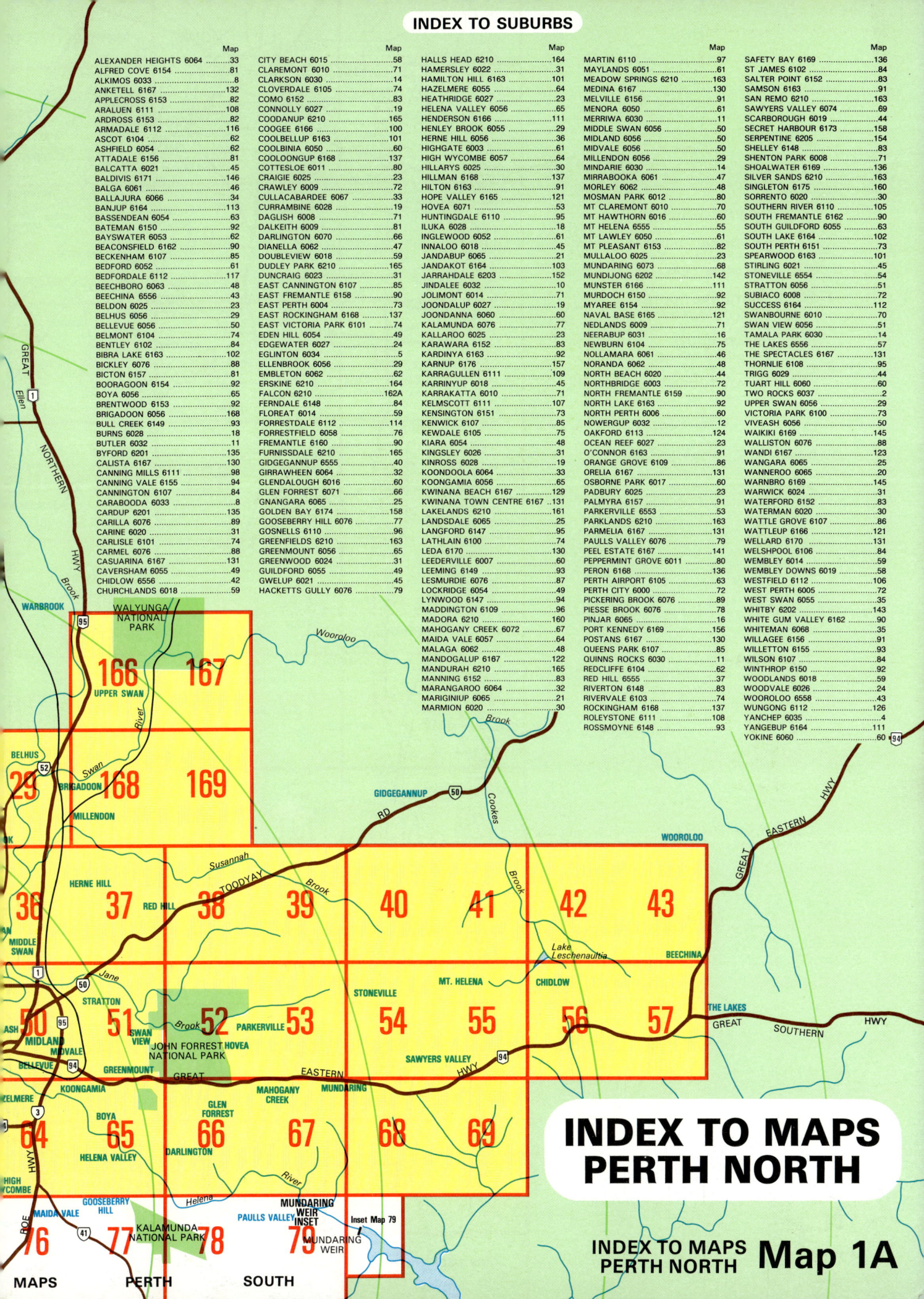

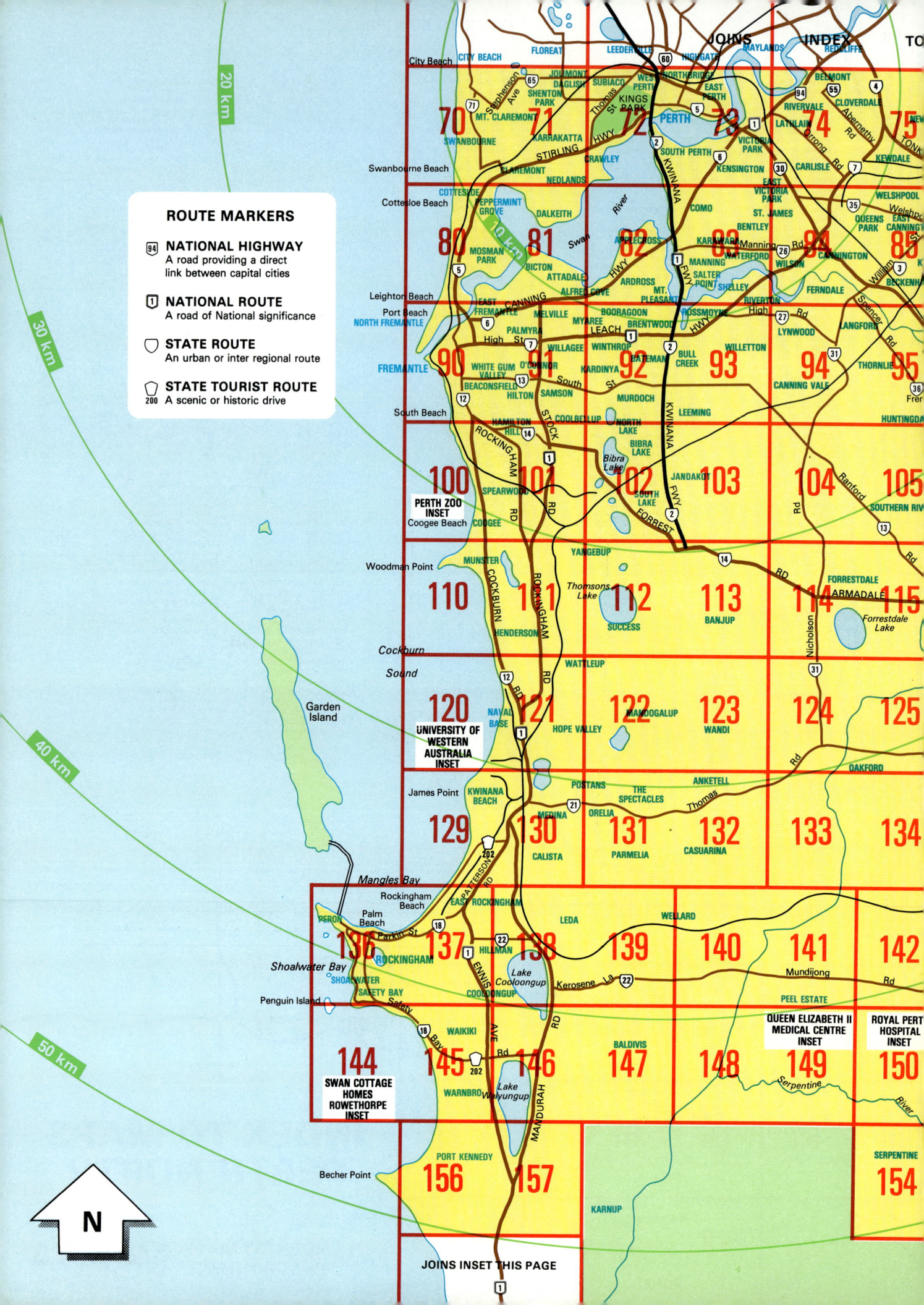

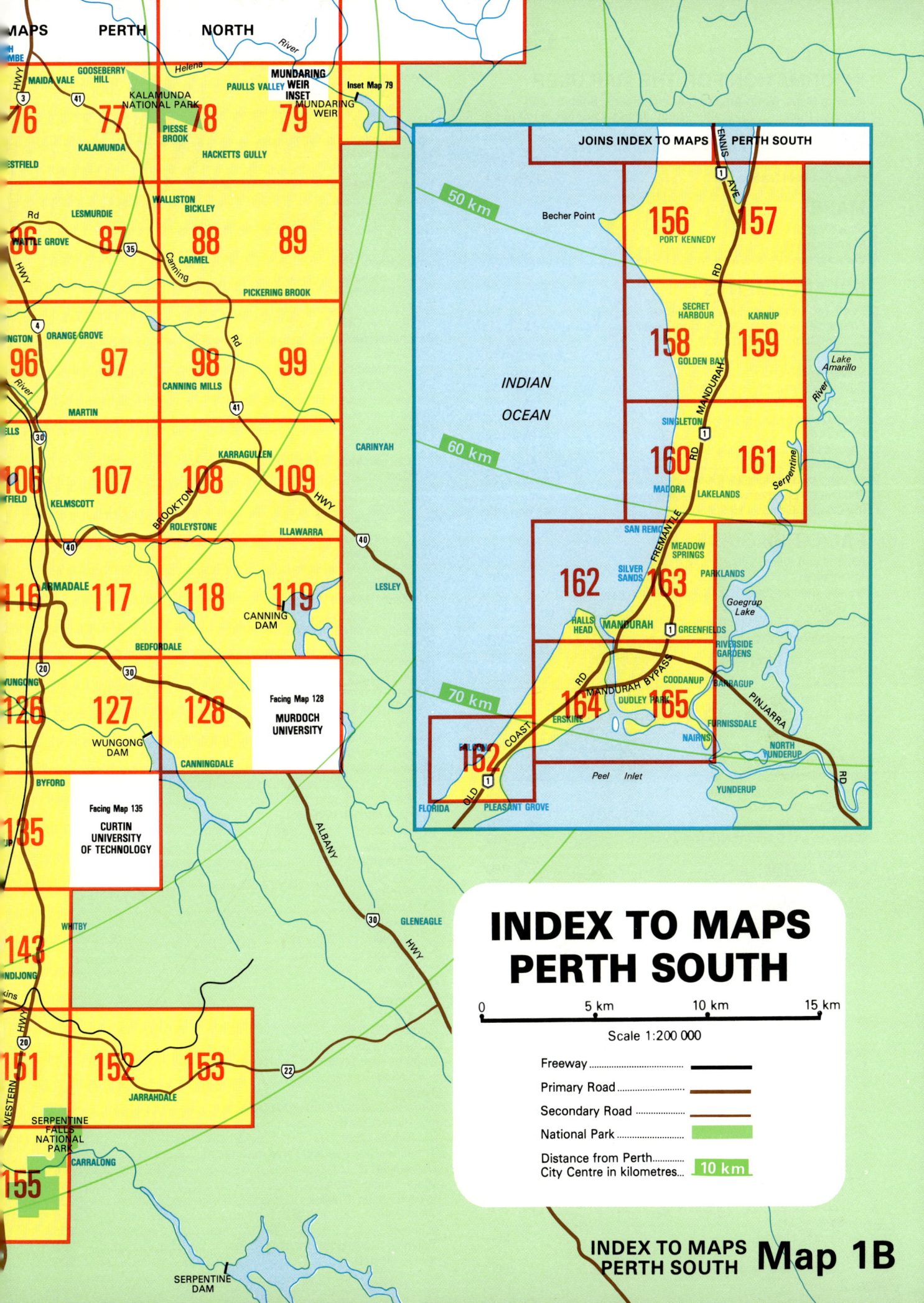

CONTENTS

INFORMATION FOR THE MAP USER

Index to Maps, Metro Area with Arterial Roads, Suburbs and
Distance Radii .... North - Map 1A and South - Map 1B
Explanation of Map Symbols .... Page 3
To Find a Street and Explanation of State Large Scale
Series .... Page 170
Index to Street Names .... Page 171

MAPS

Street Maps .... Maps 2-169
Mundaring Weir .... Inset Map 79
Walyunga and Avon Valley National Parks .... Inset Map 6

ENLARGEMENTS

Perth - with Index to Principal Features .... Map 1C
Fremantle - with Index to Principal Features .... Map 1D
Cultural Centre .... Inset Map 22
Murdoch University .... Facing Map 128
University of W.A. .... Inset Map 120
Curtin University of Technology .... Facing Map 135
Rowethorpe - Home for the Aged .... Inset Map 144
Swan Cottage Homes - Home for the Aged ...... Inset Map 144
Perth Zoo .... Inset Map 100
Princess Margaret Hospital for Children .... Inset Map 28
Royal Perth Hospital .... Inset Map 150
St. John of God Hospital (Subiaco) .... Inset Map 27
The Queen Elizabeth II Medical Centre
(Sir Charles Gairdner Hospital) .... Inset Map 149

FACILITIES GUIDE

Airports and Airline Offices 261
Ambulance 261
Aquatic Centres (see Beaches and Swimming Centres) 261
Art Galleries 283
Beaches and Swimming Centres 261
Blood Donor Clinics 261
Boat Ramps 261
Bowling:
    Lawn 261
    Ten Pin 262
Bus Transfer Stations and Coach Departure Points:
    Bus - Transperth 262
    Coach - Day Tours 262
    Coach - Interstate 262
Caravan Parks 262
Cemeteries and Crematoria 262
Child Care Centres 262
Child Health Centres 264
Churches and Places of Worship 265
Cinemas 295
Colleges of TAFE 269
Community and Recreation Centres 269
Consulates and Legations 269
Croquet Clubs 269
Drive-in Cinemas 295
Education Institutions:
    Administration 269
    Colleges of TAFE 269
    Off Site Pre-Primary Centres 270
    Schools 270
    Special Schools 276
    Universities 276
Ferry Terminals 276
Fire Services:
    Volunteer Fire Stations 276
    W.A. Bush Fires Board Fire Stations 276
    W.A. Fire Brigades Board Permanent 276
Golf Courses:
    Private 276
    Public 276
Government Departments:
    Commonwealth 276
    Local 278
    State 278
Homes for Children 280
Hospitals:
    Casualty or Emergency 280

Hospitals:
    Private 280
    Public 280
Hostels, Y.H.A. 296
Hotels, Taverns and Wine Bars 280
Leisure Centres 286
Libraries 282
Localities, Postcodes and Postal Districts 282
Motels 283
Museums and Art Galleries 283
Nursing, Rest Homes, Hostels and Retirement Communities 284
Off Road Vehicle Areas 286
Ovals, Parks, Reserves and Leisure Centres 286
Police - Stations, Traffic and Licensing Centres 290
Postal Districts, Postcodes and Localities 282
Post Offices (Official) 291
Pre-Primary Centres - Off Site 270
Psychiatric Services:
    Clinics 291
    Extended Care Units 291
    Hospitals 292
    Other Facilities 292
Public Transport (see Bus - Transperth) 262
Racing Tracks:
    BMX 292
    Car and Motorcycle 292
    Dog 292
    Horse 292
    Trotting 292
Railway Stations:
    Country Passenger Stations 292
    Freight Terminals 292
    Perth - Armadale Line 292
    Perth - Fremantle Line 292
    Perth - Midland Line 292
Recreation Centres 269
Religious Establishments 265
Reserves 286
Retirement Communities and Homes 284
Rowing Clubs 295
Rubbish Tips and Baling Plants 292
Schools (see Education Institutions) 270
Sea Rescue Group (Volunteer) 292
Shire Council Offices (see Government, Local) 278
Shopping Centres (Major) 292
Skating Rinks:
    Ice 293
    Roller 293
Sporting Venues (Major):
    Athletics 293
    Baseball 293
    Basketball 293
    Cricket 294
    Cycling 294
    Football 294
    Hockey 294
    Netball 294
    Soccer 294
    Squash 294
    Swimming 294
    Tennis 294
    Water Polo 294
Squash Centres 294
State Emergency Service 294
Suburbs (see Localities, Postcodes and Postal Districts) 282
Swimming Centres 261
Taverns 280
Tennis Clubs and Public Courts:
    Public Courts 294
    Tennis Clubs 294
Theatres, Cinemas and Drive-in Cinemas 295
Universities 276
Water Skiing Areas 295
Weighbridges (Public) 295
Wine Bars 280
Wineries 295
Yachting, Rowing and Angling Clubs 295
Y.H.A. Hostels 296

EXPLANATION OF MAP SYMBOLS

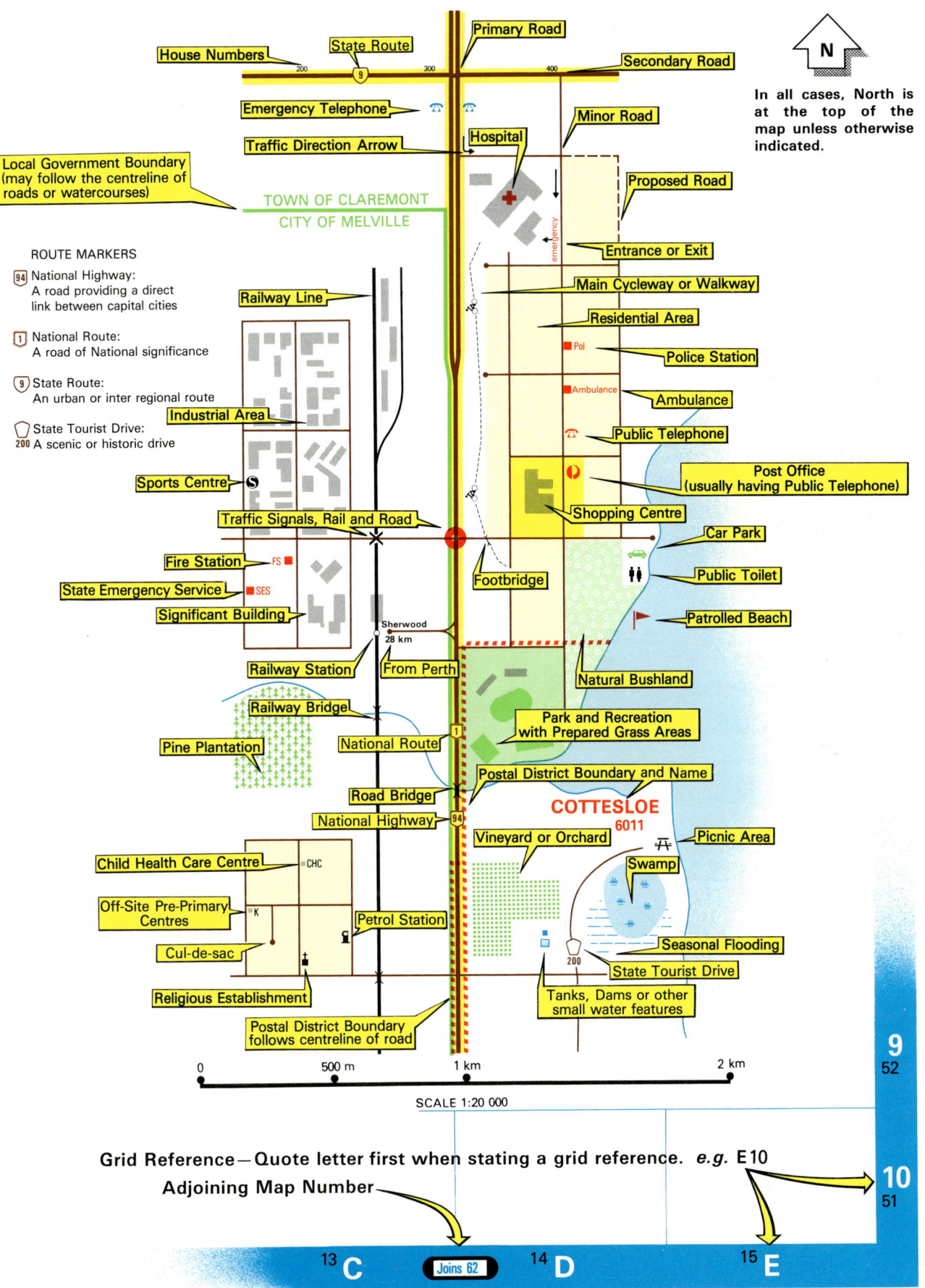

Page 3

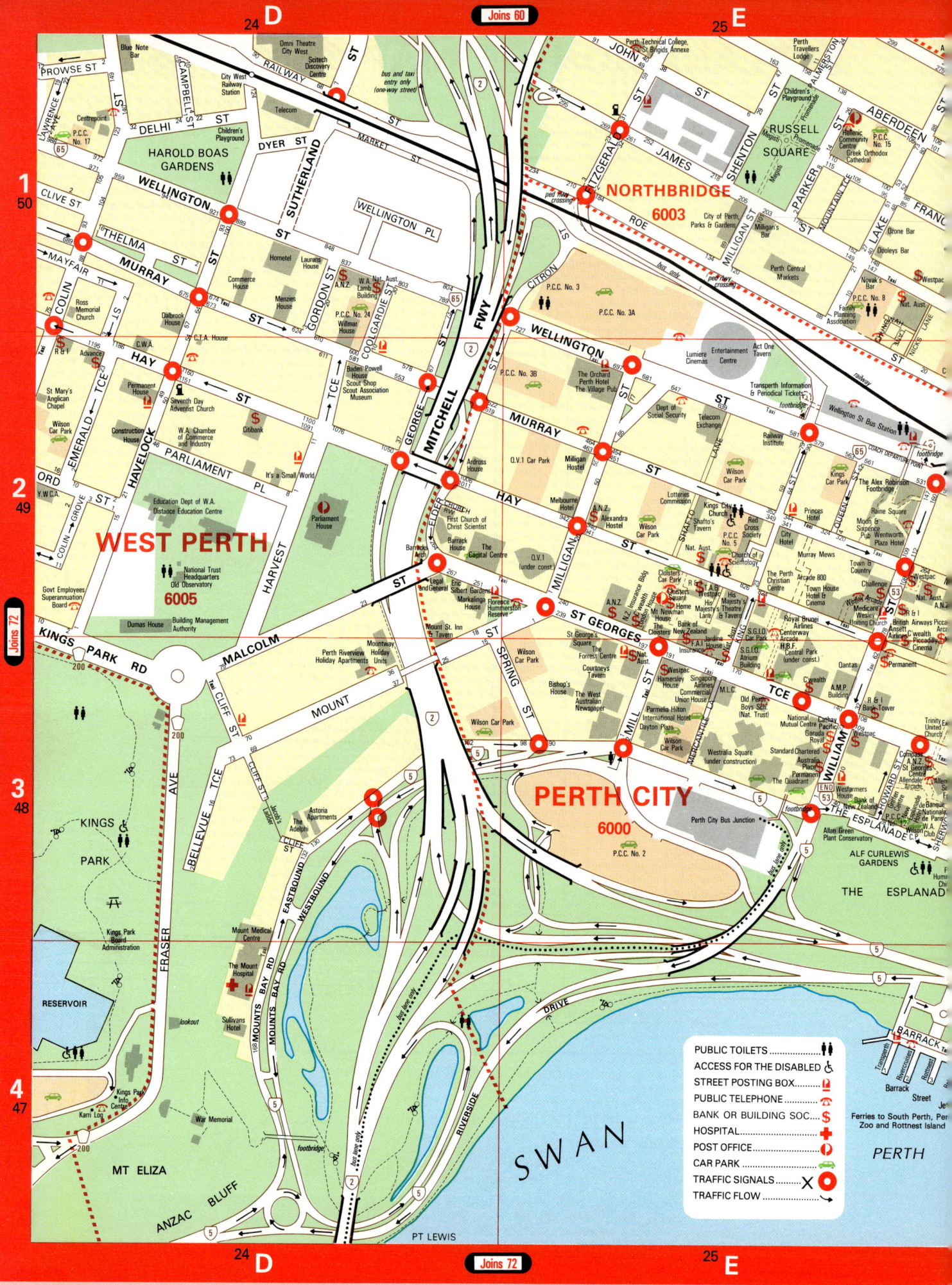

INDEX TO PERTH ENLARGEMENT MAP 1C

PRINCIPAL FEATURES

Aberdeen Hotel A 1
Aberdeen Lodge (Travellers Hostel) A 1
Aboriginal Centre A 1
Aboriginal Child Care Agency B 3
Aboriginal Legal Services A 2
Aboriginal Medical Service B 1
Act One Tavern E 2
Adelphi, The D 3
Advance Bank, 1195 Hay St D 2
A.G.C. House B 4
Ainslie House (R.P.H.) A 3
Air New Zealand (National Aust. Bank Building) A 3
Airways Hotel B 4
Albert Facey House A 2
Alexander Library Building A 1
Alexandra Hostel E 2
Alf Curlewis Gardens E 3
Allan Green Plant Conservatory E 3
Allendale Arcade E 3
Allendale Square E 3
A.M.P. Building E 3
Ansett Airlines, 26 St Georges Tce A 3
Ansett Airlines, Hay St Mall E 3
Anzac House A 3
Arcade 800 E 2
Arcadia Hotel E 1
Archbishop Goody Hostel B 3
Ardross House D 2
Army Museum B 1
Art Gallery of W.A. A 2
Astoria Apartments D 3
Atrium Building E 3
Australia Place E 3
Australian and New Zealand Bank (A.N.Z.), 8 St Georges Tce A 3
Australian and New Zealand Bank (A.N.Z.), 77 St Georges Tce E 3
Australian and New Zealand Bank (A.N.Z.), 198 Adelaide Tce B 4
Australian and New Zealand Bank (A.N.Z.), "Hyatt Centre", Adelaide Tce B 4
Australian and New Zealand Bank (A.N.Z.), 608 Hay St A 3
Australian and New Zealand Bank (A.N.Z.), 940 Hay St E 2
Australian and New Zealand Bank (A.N.Z.), 837 Wellington St D 1
Australian and New Zealand Bank (A.N.Z.), 220 St Georges Tce E 2
Australian and New Zealand Bank (A.N.Z.), 223 William Street A 1
Australian and New Zealand Bank (A.N.Z.), 237 Murray St E 2
Australian Airlines A 3
Australian Broadcasting Corporation B 4
Australian Customs A 1
Australian Bureau of Statistics B 4
Australian Mutual Provident Soc. (A.M.P.) E 3
Australian Post Supply Branch A 2
Australian Red Cross Society Depot A 2
Baden Powell House D 2
Bank of New Zealand E 2
Bank of New Zealand E 3
Banque Nationale de Paris E 3
Baptist Church A 2
Barrack House D 2
Barracks Arch E 2
Barrack Street Jetties E 4
Bible House B 4
Bishop's House E 3
Blind Bowling Club B 4
Blood Donor Centre A 2
Blue Note Bar D 1
Bon Marche Arcade A 3
Brass Monkey Hotel A 1
Brewer House, Trades and Labour Council B 1
Britannia Y.H.A. Hostel A 1
British Airways E 2
Building Management Authority D 2
Bureau of Meteorology B 3
Burt Memorial Hall A 3
Cable House A 3
Carillon Arcade E 3
Carlton Hotel B 3
Cathay Pacific Airways, 111 St Georges Tce E 3
Centerway Arcade E 2
Centrepoint D 1
Central Law Courts A 3
Central Metropolitan College of T.A.F.E. - Perth Campus A 1
Central Metropolitan College of T.A.F.E. - Perth Campus - Art and Design A 1
Central Park Building E 3
C.E.S. Job Centre B 4
Challenge Bank, 95 William St E 2
Challenge Bank, 25 Barrack St A 3
Challenge Bank, City Arcade A 2
Chancery House A 3
Chases Bar A 2
Chateau Commodore Hotel A 3
Children's Court B 2
Chinese Community Centre B 1
Churchills Tavern (Perth Concert Hall) A 3
Church of Christ A 1
Church of Scientology E 2
Cinecentre A 3
Cinema City A 3
Cinema City Arcade A 3
Citibank, 1111 Hay St D 2
Citiplace Community Centre A 2
City Arcade A 2
City Council Library (Council House) A 3
City Hotel E 2
City of Perth, Parks and Gardens E 1
City Waters Lodge A 4
City West D 1
City West Railway Station D 1
Civil Service Association A 3
C.S.A. Credit Union A 3
Claisebrook Railway Station B 2
Claisebrook Junction Tavern B 1
Cloisters Square, The E 2
Colonial Mutual Life Building (C.M.L.) A 3
Commerce House D 1
Commercial Union Building E 3
Commonwealth Bank, 86 Barrack St A 3
Commonwealth Bank, 42 Bennett St B 3
Commonwealth Bank, 726 Hay St E 3
Commonwealth Bank, 86 James St E 1
Commonwealth Bank, Wellington St D 1
Commonwealth Bank, cnr St Georges Tce and Victoria Ave A 3
Commonwealth Bank, State Administration, 150 St Georges Tce E 3
Commonwealth Development Bank of Australia, 1 Forrest Pl A 2
Commonwealth Bank, London House, St Georges Tce E 2
Commonwealth Bank, 214 St Georges Tce E 2
Commonwealth Government Centre A 3
Compass Airlines E 3
Confederation House B 4
Construction House D 2
Country Women's Assoc. (C.W.A.) D 2
Court Hotel A 2
Courtneys Tavern E 2
C.T.A. House D 1
Cultural Centre A 2
Curtin House A 2
Dalbrook House D 1
Dayton Plaza E 3
Dental School B 3
Dept of Administrative Services B 3
Dept of Community Services B 2
Dept of Land Administration A 3
Dept of Social Security E 2
Distance Education Centre D 2
Doogues Arcade A 2
Dooleys Bar E 1
Dumas House D 2
Durack Centre, The A 4
Eastpoint Plaza A 4
Education Dept of W.A. D 2
Entertainment Centre E 2
Environ. Protection Authority A 3
Eric Silbert Gardens D 2
Esplanade, The E 3
Exchange House E 3
Exchange Plaza A 3
F.A.I. Insurance E 3
Fairlanes 10-Pin Bowling B 3
Family Planning Association E 1
Federal and Family Courts A 4
Fenians Pub B 4
Fire Safety Education Centre and Museum A 3
Fire Station, Perth Central A 3
First Church of Christ Scientist D 2
Fisheries Department B 4
Florence Hummerston Child Care E 3
Florence Hummerston Reserve D 2
Forrest Centre E 3
Forrest Chase A 2
Foxy Lady Tavern E 3
Francis Burt Law Centre, The A 3
Freemasons Grand Lodge of W.A. B 4
Garuda Indonesia E 3
Gateway Christian Fellowship A 1
General Post Office (G.P.O.) A 2
Girl Guide Association B 3
Globe Hotel E 2
Government Centre A 3
Government Chemical Laboratories B 4
Government Employees Superannuation Board D 2
Government House and Ballroom A 3
Government Offices B 2
Grand Central Private Hotel A 2
Greek Orthodox Cathedral E 1
Griffin Centre E 3
Grosvenor Hotel B 3
Gurlongga Njininj Children's Centre B 1
Hamersley House E 3
Harold Boas Gardens D 1
Health Department B 2
Health Insurance Fund of W.A. A 2
Hellenic Community Centre E 1
Hickeys Cine Cellars Tavern A 3
His Majesty's Theatre and Tavern E 2
Home Building Society, Adelaide Tce B 4
Home Building Society, Cloisters Square E 2
Home Building Society, Exchange House A 3
Home Building Society, Piccadilly Arcade A 2
Homeswest Centre B 4
Hometel D 1
Horseshoe Bridge A 2
Hospital Benefit Fund Health Centre E 2
Hospital Benefit Fund of W.A. A 3
Hospital Benefit Fund of W.A., Centerway Arcade E 3
Hotel Regatta A 3
Hoyts Cine Centre A 3
Hyatt Centre B 4
Hyatt Regency Perth Hotel B 4
I.B.J. Australia Bank, 37 St Georges Tce A 3
Immigration Department A 3
Industry House B 4
Inntown Hotel, The A 3
International House A 3
It's A Small World D 2
Jack Davis House B 2
Jacob's Ladder D 3
Jardine House E 3
Jewell House B 3
Karrakatta Club E 3
Kimberley Cinema A 3
Kings Ambassador Hotel A 3
Kings City Church E 2
Kings Park D 3
Kings Park Board Administration D 3
Kings Park Information Centre D 4
Kirkman House A 3
Labour Centre A 2
Langley Park B 4
Langley Plaza Hotel B 4
Laurens House D 1
Law Chambers A 3
Law Museum, The A 3
Legal and General D 2
Local Government House B 4
London Court A 3
London House E 2
Loton Park Tennis Club B 1
Lotteries Commission E 2
Lotteries House A 2
Lumiere Cinemas E 2
Madisons Bar D 1
Mangoes Tavern A 3
Marine and Harbours Department A 4

Name	Ref
Malaysian Airlines (Allendale Square)	A 3
Markalinga House	D 2
May Holman Centre	A 3
McIver Railway Station	A 2
McNess Hall	A 3
Medicare	E 2
Medicare	E 3
Melbourne Hotel	E 2
Menzies House	D 1
Mercedes College	A 3
Milligan Hostel	E 2
Milligan's Bar	E 1
Mines Dept	B 4
Ministry of Education	B 2
Miss Maud European Hotel	A 3
M.L.C. Building	E 3
Moon and Sixpence Pub	A 3
Mount Eliza	D 4
Mount Hospital, The	D 4
Mount Medical Centre	D 4
Mount St Inn and Tavern	D 2
Mountway Holiday Units	D 3
Mt Newman House	E 2
Murray Mews	E 2
Museum	A 2
Mutual Life and Citizen's Building (M.L.C.)	E 3
National Australia Bank, 197 Adelaide Tce	B 4
National Australia Bank, 524 Hay St	A 3
National Australia Bank, 860 Hay St	E 2
National Australia Bank, Kirkman House, R.P.H.	A 3
National Australia Bank, 109 James St	E 1
National Australia Bank, cnr King St and St Georges Tce	E 3
National Australia Bank, 813 Wellington St	D 1
National Australia Bank, cnr Mill St and St Georges Tce	E 3
National Australia Bank, 255 Murray St	E 2
National Australia Bank, Piccadilly Square	B 2
National Australia Bank, 16 St Georges Tce	A 3
National Australia Bank, 50 St Georges Tce	A 3
National Australia Bank, Shop 19, Forrest Pl	A 2
National Australia Bank, Forrest Chase	A 2
National Mutual Life Building (N.M.L.)	E 3
National Mutual Centre (N.M.L.) Building	E 3
National Mutual Royal Bank	E 3
National Trust Headquarters	D 2
Natwest	A 4
New Beaufort Hotel	A 1
Newcastle Lodge	A 1
New Church, The	B 4
New Esplanade Hotel	E 3
New Zealand Insurance Building	E 2
Northbridge Post Office	E 1
North Lodge	A 1
Novak's Bar	E 1
Oakleigh Building	A 3
Old Perth Boys School (Nat. Trust)	E 3
Omni Theatre	D 1
Orchard Perth Hotel, The	E 2
Orchestral Shell	A 4
Ozone Bar	E 1
Parkside Motel	B 3
Parliament House	D 2
Parmelia Hilton International Hotel	E 3
Permanent Building Society, cnr William St and Hay St Mall	E 3
Permanent Building Society, 1st Floor, Australia Place	E 3
Permanent House	D 2
Perth Ambassador Hotel	B 4
Perth and Tattersalls Bowling and Recreation Club	B 4
Perth Central Markets	E 1
Perth Chest Clinic	A 3
Perth Christian Centre, The	E 2
Perth City Bus Junction	A 2
Perth City Council House and Library	A 3
Perth City Council Works Dept	E 1
Perth City Mission - City Youth Centre	B 2
Perth City 1 Youth Hostel	A 1
Perth City 3 Youth Hostel	A 1
Perth Community Police Post	A 3
Perth Concert Hall	A 3
Perth Dental Hospital	B 3
Perth Function Centre	A 2
Perth International Hotel	A 3
Perth Institute of Contemporary Art	A 2
Perth Mail Exchange and Post Office	A 1
Perth Oval	B 1
Perth Parkroyal Hotel	B 4
Perth Railway Station	A 2
Perth Riverview Holiday Apartments	D 3
Perth Technical College, St Brigids	E 1
Perth Travellers Lodge	E 1
Piccadilly Bar	B 2
Piccadilly Cinema	E 3
Piccadilly Arcade	E 2
Piccadilly Square	A 2
Playhouse Theatre	A 3
Plaza Arcade	A 3
Police Department	B 3
Police Station	A 2
Primary Industry House	A 4
Princes Hotel	E 2
Public Trust Office	A 3
Public Weighbridge	E 1
Qantas, Central Park	E 3
Quadrant, The	E 3
QV1	E 2
Radio Station 94.5 KY fm	B 4
Radio Station 6PR am	B 4
Radio Station 96 fm	B 3
Railway Institute	E 2
Raine Square	E 2
Red Cross Society	E 2
Red Cross Society, Australian	A 2
Reserve Bank of Australia, 45 St Georges Tce	A 3
Returned Servicemen's League (Anzac House)	A 3
Rod Evans Senior Citizen's Centre	B 4
Ross Memorial Church	D 1
Royal Automobile Club of W.A. (R.A.C.)	B 4
Royal Brunei Airlines	E 2
Royal Perth Hospital	A 3
R. & I. Bank Tower	E 3
Rural and Industries Bank (R. & I.), 54 Barrack St	A 3
Rural and Industries Bank (R. & I.), 148 Adelaide Tce	B 4
Rural and Industries Bank (R. & I.), 257 Adelaide Tce	A 3
Rural and Industries Bank (R. & I.), 288 Hay St	B 3
Rural and Industries Bank (R. & I.), 853 Hay St	E 2
Rural and Industries Bank (R. & I.), James St	E 1
Rural and Industries Bank (R. & I.), 227 Murray St	E 2
Rural and Industries Bank (R. & I.), 92 William St	E 2
Russell Square	E 1
St Andrew's Uniting Church	A 3
St George's Anglican Cathedral	A 3
St George's Centre	E 3
St George's Square	E 3
St John Ambulance Association	A 2
St John Ambulance, East Perth	B 3
St John's Lutheran Church	A 1
St John's Lutheran Church Centre	A 1
St Martin's Arcade	A 3
St Martin's Tower	A 3
St Mary's Roman Catholic Cathedral	A 3
St Mary's Anglican Chapel	D 2
Salvation Army Headquarters	A 1
Salvation Army Hostel, Lentara	A 2
Sassella's Tavern	E 2
Savoy Cinema	A 3
Scitech Discovery Centre	D 1
Scout Shop	D 2
Seventh Day Adventist Church	D 2
Septimus Roe Square	A 1
Shafto's Tavern	E 2
Sheraton Perth Hotel	B 4
Singapore Airlines	E 3
Social Security, Department of	A 2
South African Airways (S.A.A.) Exchange House	E 3
Standard Chartered Bank	E 3
State Energy Commission (Head Office)	A 2
State Energy Commission (Accounts)	A 2
State Government Insurance Commission	A 4
State Government Insurance Office (S.G.I.O.)	E 3
State Government Insurance Office (S.G.I.O.) "Autocheck"	A 2
State Head Office, Telecom Australia	A 2
Stirling Gardens	A 3
Stock Exchange of Perth (Exchange House)	E 3
Sullivans Hotel	D 4
Sunday Times Newspaper	A 2
Supreme Court Gardens	A 4
Supreme Court of W.A.	A 3
Swan Barracks, H.Q. 5th Military District	A 1
Swy Theatre	A 3
Taxation Department, Commonwealth	A 3
Teachers' Union of W.A.	B 4
Telecom	B 3
Telecom Depot	A 2
Telecom Exchange	E 2
Telecom, State Head Office	A 2
Telecom Storage Depot	B 2
The Capital Centre	D 2
The Cathedral Church of St John the Divine	B 1
The Mothers Union	A 3
The Perth Mint	B 3
The Village Pub	E 2
The West Australian Newspaper	E 3
Town and Country, 297 Murray St	E 2
Town and Country, Chancery House	A 3
Town and Country, Airways Hotel	B 4
Town and Country, Hay St Mall	A 3
Town Hall	A 3
Town House Hotel and Cinema	E 2
Tracks Tavern	A 2
Trades and Labour Council	B 1
Transperth Information and Periodical Tickets	E 2
Transperth Training and Development Centre	B 2
Transit Inn Hotel	A 3
Trinity Arcade	E 3
Trinity Uniting Church	E 3
Turkish Community Centre	B 1
United Ancient Order of Druids - Grand Lodge	B 3
Veteran's Affairs	B 4
Victoria Centre	A 3
W.A. Alcohol and Drug Authority	B 2
W.A. Blind Bowling Club	B 4
W.A. Chamber of Commerce and Industry	D 2
W.A. Lamb Building	D 1
W.A. School of Nursing	B 3
W.A. Tourist Centre	A 2
War Memorial	D 4
Wellington Square	B 3
Wellington St Bus Station	E 2
Weld Club	A 3
Weld Square	A 1
Wellington Fair	B 3
Wentworth Plaza Hotel	E 2
Wesfarmers House	E 3
Wesley Arcade	E 2
Wesley Uniting Church	E 2
West Australian Club	E 3
West Australian Rowing Club	A 4
Westpac Bank, 168 Adelaide Tce	B 4
Westpac Bank, cnr Barrack and Murray Sts	A 2
Westpac Bank, Hamersley House	E 3
Westpac Bank, 843 Hay St	E 2
Westpac Bank, Hay St Mall	A 3
Westpac Bank, 116 James St	E 1
Westpac Bank, cnr Pier and Hay Sts	A 3
Westpac Bank, cnr St Georges Tce and Barrack St	A 3
Westpac Bank, cnr Victoria Ave and Adelaide Tce	A 3
Westpac Bank, cnr William and Murray Sts	E 2
Westpac Bank, cnr William St and St Georges Tce	E 3
Westrade Centre	B 2
Westralia Square	E 3
Willmar House	D 1
Y.M.C.A. House	A 2
Y.W.C.A.	D 2
Young Australian League	A 3
Young Men's Christian Association (Y.M.C.A.) Administration	B 3
Youth Hostels Association (Y.H.A.) OF W.A.	E 1
Youth With a Mission	B 3
Ziggy's Bar	A 3

INDEX TO FREMANTLE ENLARGEMENT MAP 1D

PRINCIPAL FEATURES

ABC Child Care Centre .... C 6
Adventure Playground .... C 6
Aquatic Centre .... C 4
Army Barracks .... C 3
Atwell Arcade .... B 5
Australian and New Zealand Bank
 (A.N.Z.), 21 Adelaide St .... C 5
Australian and New Zealand Bank
 (A.N.Z.), William St .... C 5
Australian Wool Corporation .... C 6
Bannister St Mall .... B 5
Birukmarri Gallery .... B 5
British Sailor's Society
 (Flying Angel Club) .... C 3
Bus Station .... C 5
Challenge Bank .... C 5
Chamber of Commerce .... B 5
Cherrys Bar .... C 6
Christian Brothers College .... C 4
Church of Christ .... C 5
Cicerello's Fish Markets .... C 6
Civic Library .... C 5
Clancy's Tavern .... C 4
Commercial Club .... B 5
Commercial Hotel .... B 5
Commonwealth Bank, 88 High St .... B 5
Commonwealth Bank, 56 Adelaide St . C 5
Commonwealth Employment Service .. C 5
Commonwealth Offices .... B 5
Community Education Centre .... C 4
Court House .... C 5
Crane House, 185 High St .... C 5
Customs House .... B 5
Dept of Marine and Harbours .... B 6
Elders Wool Store .... C 4
Esme Fletcher Day Nursery .... C 5
Esplanade Plaza Hotel .... B 6
Esplanade Reserve, The .... B 6
Essex Street Cinemas .... B 6
Federal Hotel .... C 5
Fire Station .... B 5
Fisheries Department .... B 6
Fremantle Bowling Club .... C 4
Fremantle Buffalo Club .... B 5
Fremantle Children's Court .... C 5
Fremantle Children's Service Centre ... C 4
Fremantle Club, The .... B 5
Fremantle College of TAFE Annexe .... B 5
Fremantle Crocodile Park .... B 6
Fremantle Exchange Club
 (Chamber of Commerce Building) ..... B 5
Fremantle Fisherman's Co-op .... B 6
Fremantle Hospital School of Nursing . C 6
Fremantle Hotel .... B 5
Fremantle Lane Arcade .... C 5
Fremantle Malls .... C 5
Fremantle Markets .... C 5

Fremantle Migrant Resource Centre .... C 5
Fremantle Museum and Arts Centre .... C 4
Fremantle Music School .... C 5
Fremantle Oval .... C 5
Fremantle Park .... C 4
Fremantle Port Authority .... B 5
Fremantle Prison .... C 5
Fremantle Prison Museum .... C 5
Fremantle Professional Centre .... C 5
Fremantle Public Hospital .... C 6
Fremantle Railway Station .... B 4
Fremantle Technical College Annexe .. C 6
Fremantle Sports Medicine Centre ...... C 5
Fremantle Tennis Club .... C 4
Fremantle Workers' Club .... B 5
Fremantle Youth Centre .... C 4
F.T.I. Film and T.V. Institute
 and Cinemas .... C 4
General Post Office (G.P.O.) .... B 5
Harbourside Hotel .... C 4
His Lordships Larder Hotel .... B 5
Homeswest Centre .... C 5
Hospital Benefit Fund of W.A. .... B 5
Italian Club .... B 6
Jobcentre C.E.S. .... C 5
Kailis Fish Markets .... B 6
Lance Holt School .... B 5
Legacy House .... C 5
Lombardo's Tavern .... B 6
Marine House .... B 6
Marriage Guidance Council .... C 4
Meals on Wheels .... C 6
Medicare .... C 5
Missions to Seamen,
 Flying Angel Club .... C 3
National Australia Bank,
 cnr Adelaide and Queen Sts .... C 5
National Australia Bank, 96 High St ..... B 5
National Hotel .... B 5
Navy Club .... B 6
Newport Hotel .... B 5
Norfolk Hotel .... C 6
Old Signal Station .... C 3
Orient Hotel .... B 5
Overseas Terminal .... C 4
P. & O. Hotel .... B 5
Park Lodging House, The .... C 5
Pioneer Reserve .... B 5
Police Station .... C 5
Port Cinema .... C 4
Port Manager's Tower .... B 6
Potter's Workshop .... B 6
Princess May Park .... C 4
Proclamation Plaque and Tree .... C 4
Queensgate Cinemas .... C 5
Red Cross Blood Bank .... C 6
Red Shield Centre .... C 5

Returned Servicemen's League Hall ... B 5
Roo on the Roof Guest House .... B 5
Round House .... B 5
Royal Perth Yacht Club
 Fremantle Annexe .... B 6
Rural and Industries Bank
 (R. & I.), Market St .... B 5
Rural and Industries Bank
 (R. & I.), Adelaide St .... C 5
Sail and Anchor Tavern .... C 5
Sails of the Century Museum .... B 5
Samson House Museum .... C 4
St Andrew's Mariners' Chapel
 (Flying Angel Club) .... C 3
St John Ambulance Association .... C 4
St John's Anglican Church .... C 5
St John's Square .... C 5
St Patrick's Church and Hall (R.C.) ...... C 4
St Patrick's Day Care Centre .... C 4
St Patrick's Primary School .... C 5
Scots Presbyterian Church .... C 6
S.E.C. .... C 5
Skye Hospital (Private) .... C 6
South Fremantle Football Club .... C 6
South Terrace Pre-Language Centre
 and Pre-Primary .... C 6
South Terrace Primary School .... C 6
Spare Parts Puppet Theatre .... B 5
Stan Reilly Frail Centre .... C 6
State Government Insurance Office
 (S.G.I.O.) .... C 5
Stella Maris Centre .... C 4
The Cleopatra Hotel .... B 5
The Endeavour Replica .... C 6
The Energy Museum .... C 4
The Esplanade Railway Station .... B 6
The Potters House .... B 5
Tourist Information Office .... C 6
Town Hall and Fremantle City Offices . C 5
Uniting Church .... B 5
Uniting House .... B 6
Victoria Hall .... C 5
Victoria Quay .... B 4
Water Authority .... C 5
Waterside Workers' Federation Office . B 5
Wesley Way Arcade .... B 5
West Australian Maritime Museum ...... B 6
Westgate Mall .... C 5
Westpac Bank, 22 High St .... B 5
Westpac Bank, 9 Adelaide St .... C 5
Westpac Bank, 66 High St .... B 5
Westpac Bank, South Tce .... B 5
Westport Medical Centre .... B 5
Whalers Tunnel .... B 6
Wool Exchange .... C 6

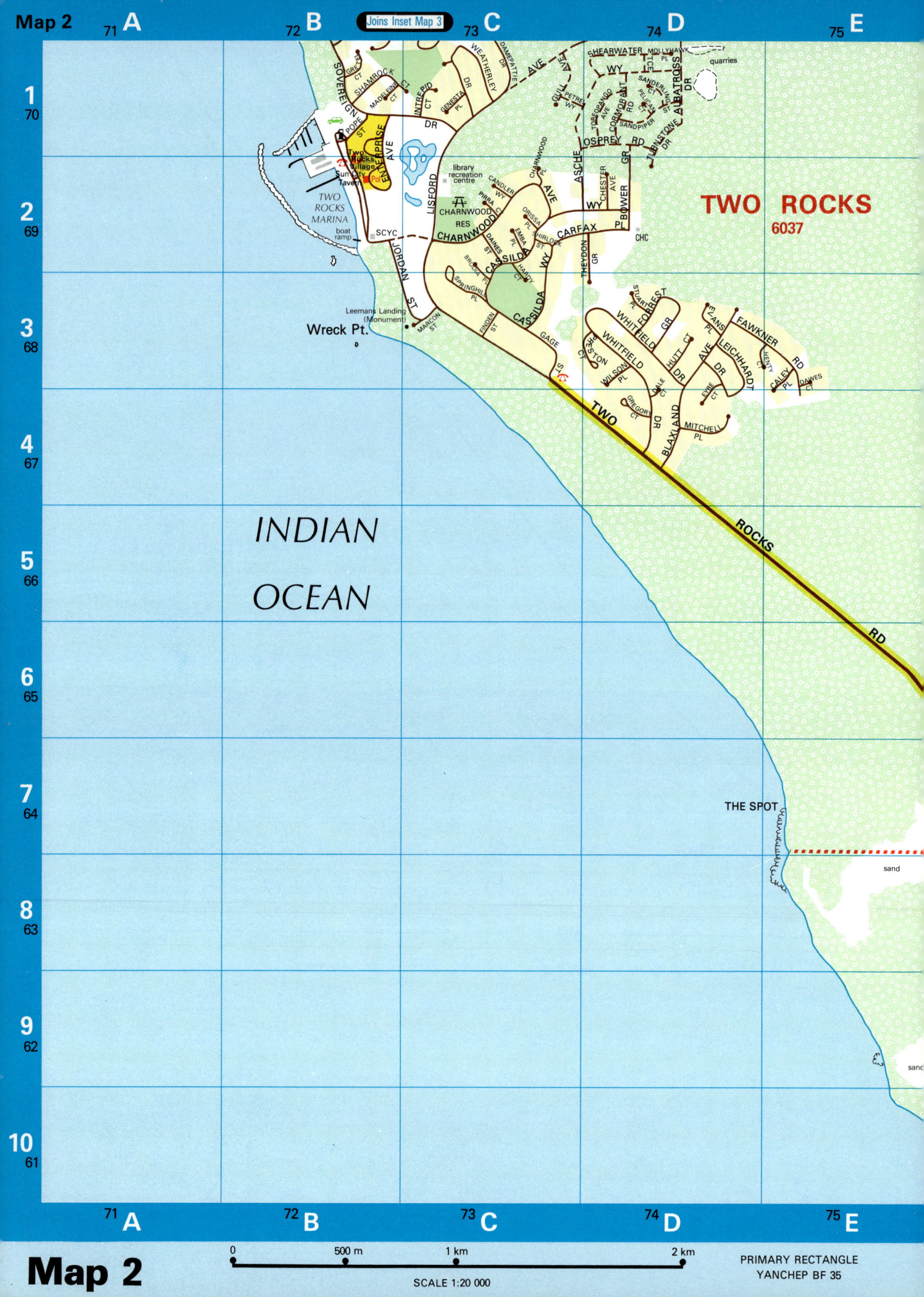

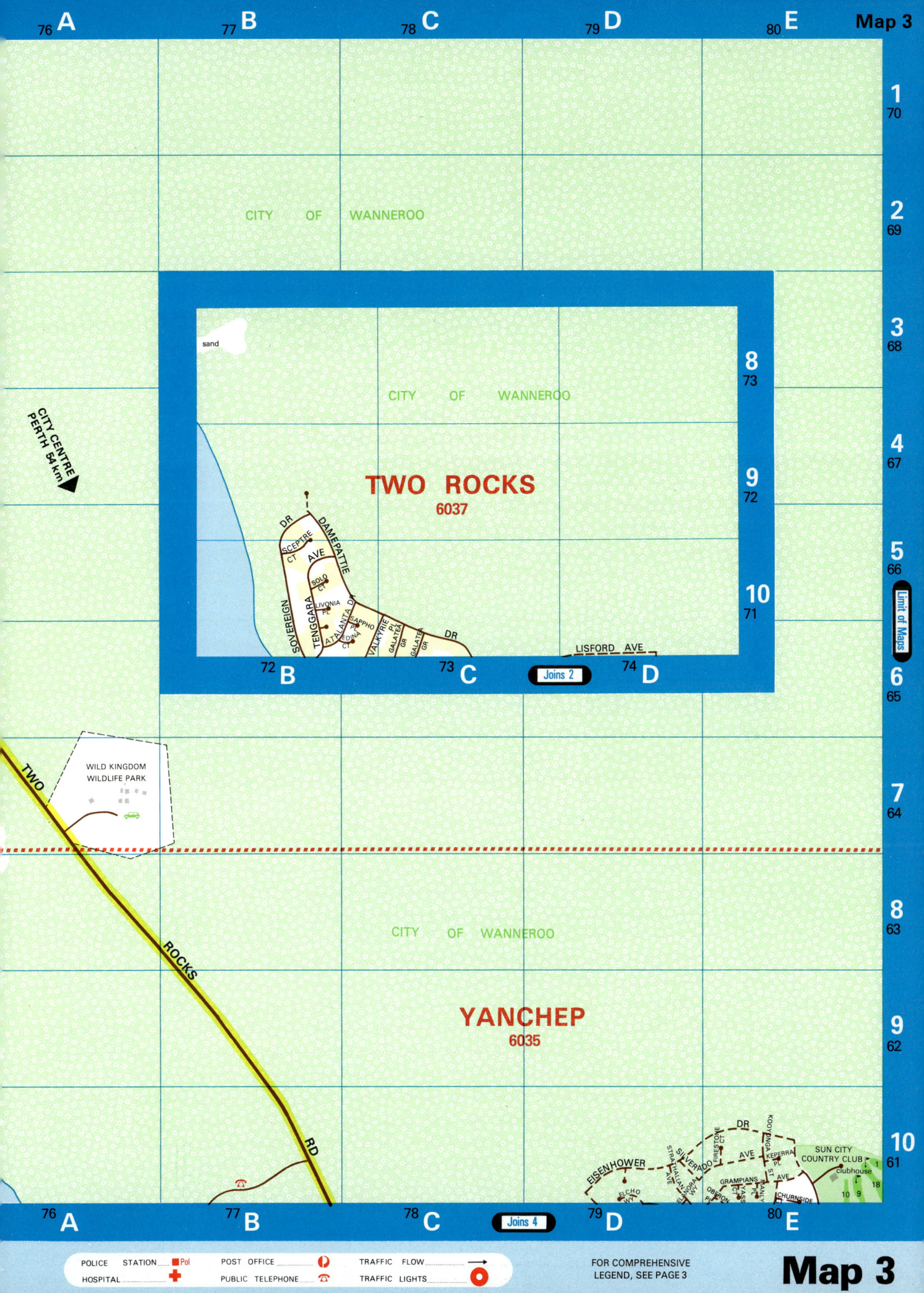

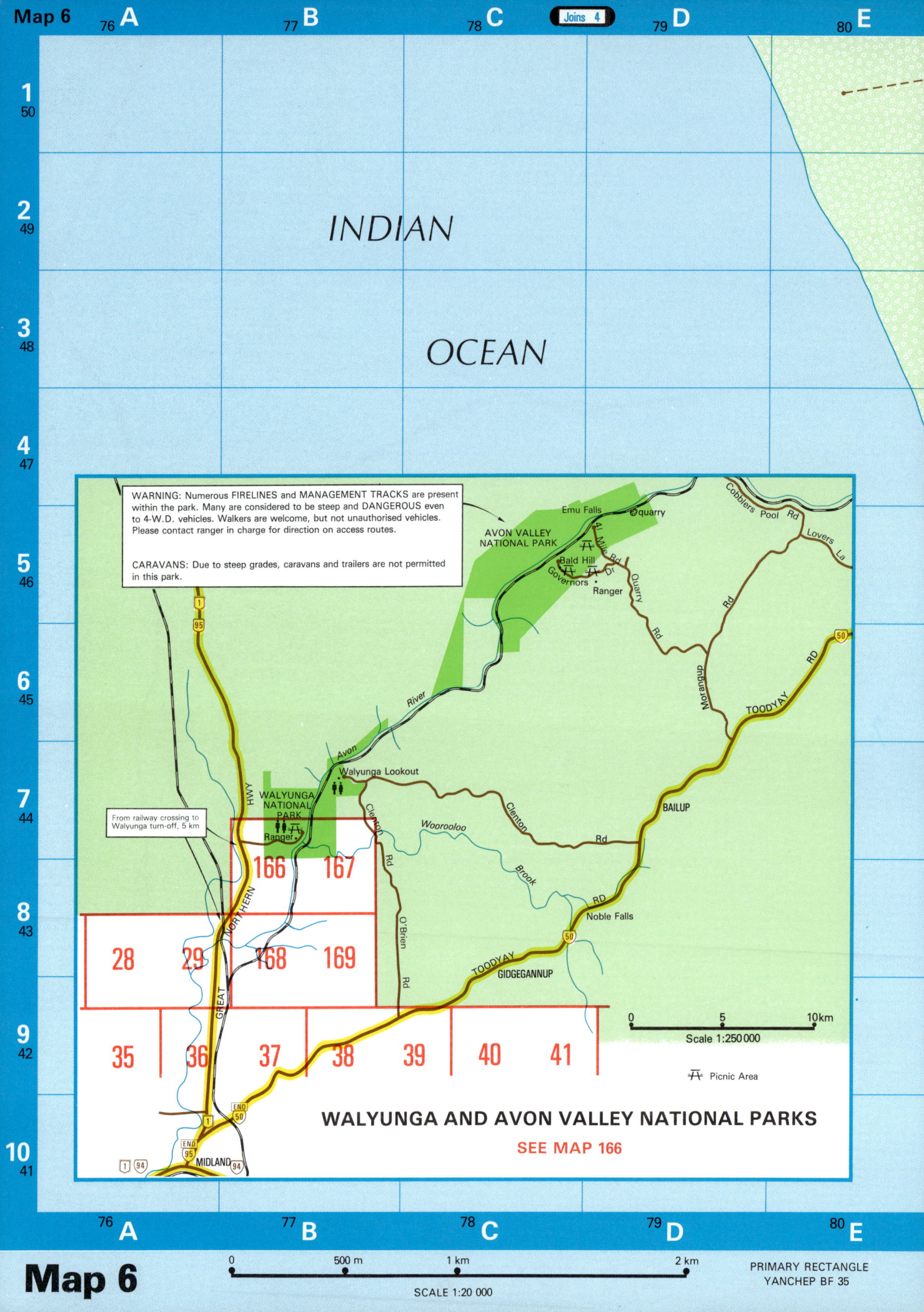

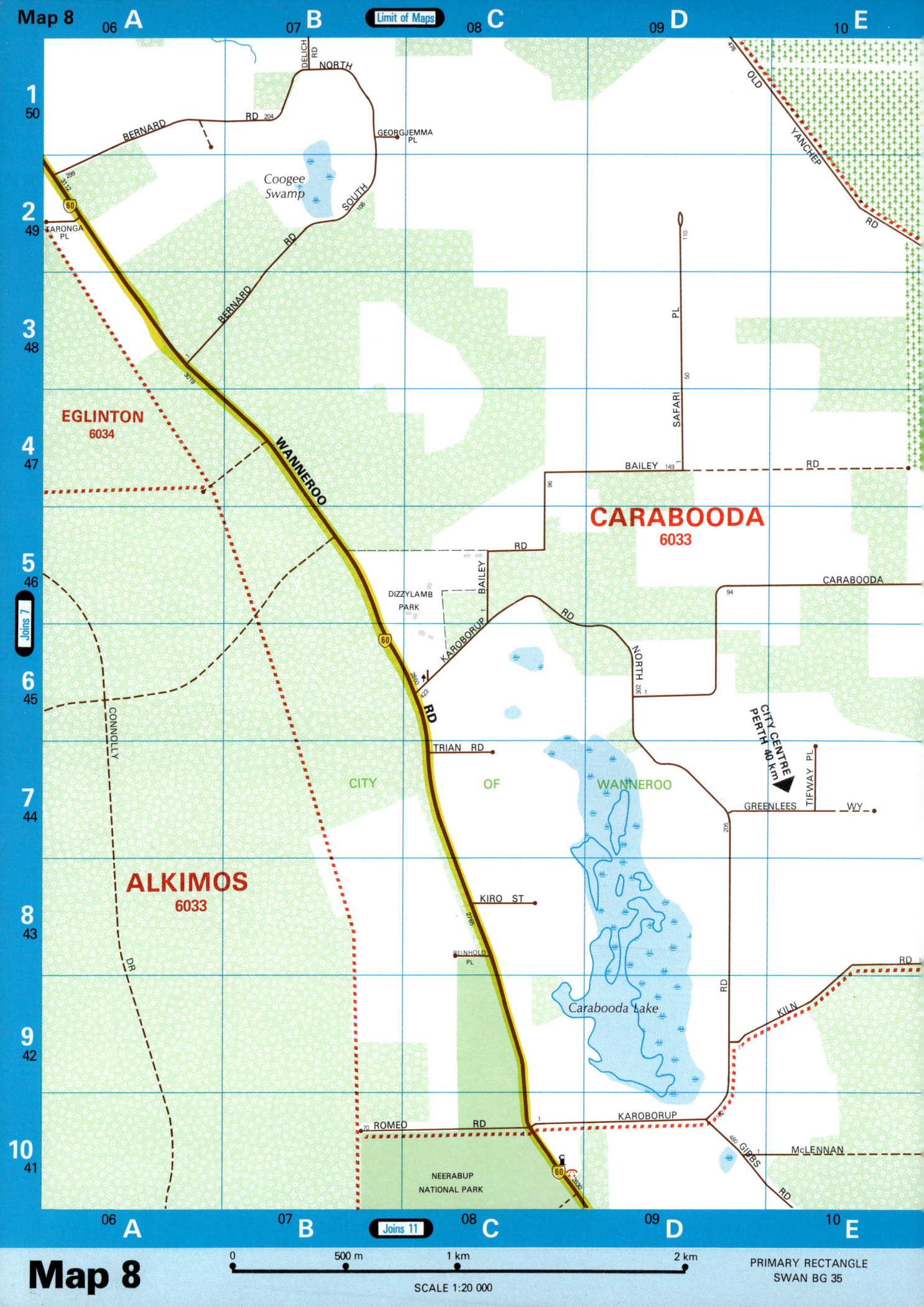

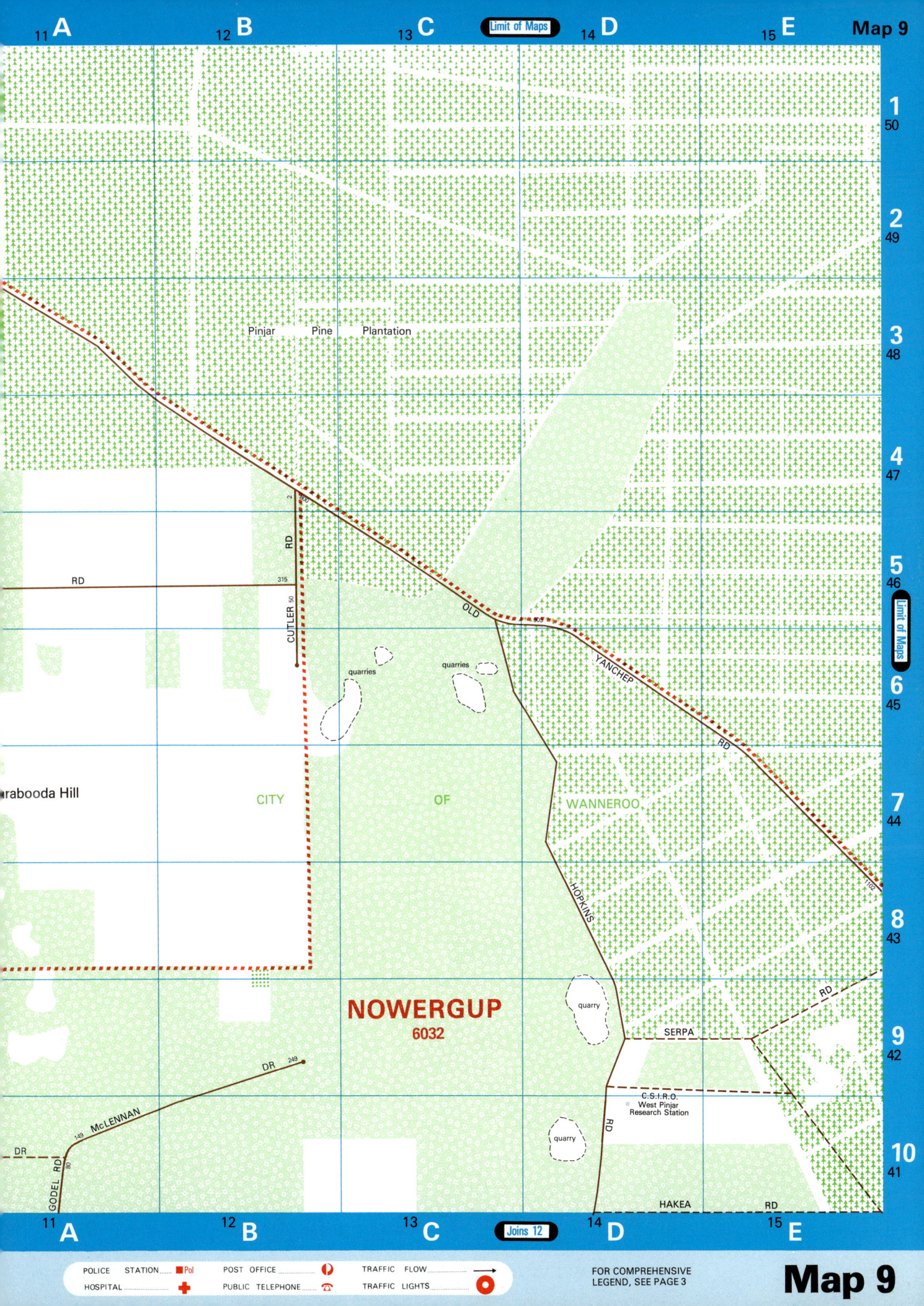

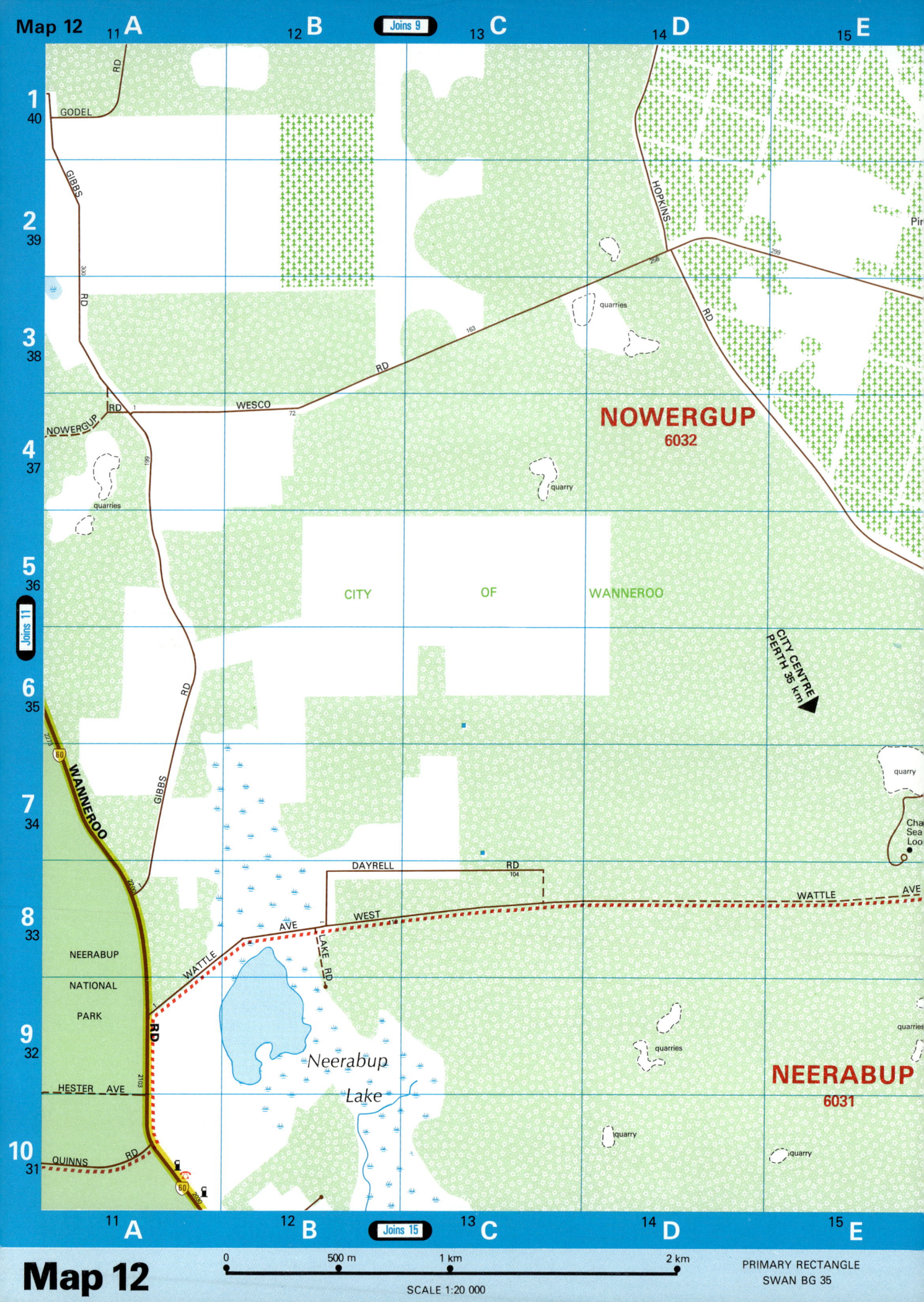

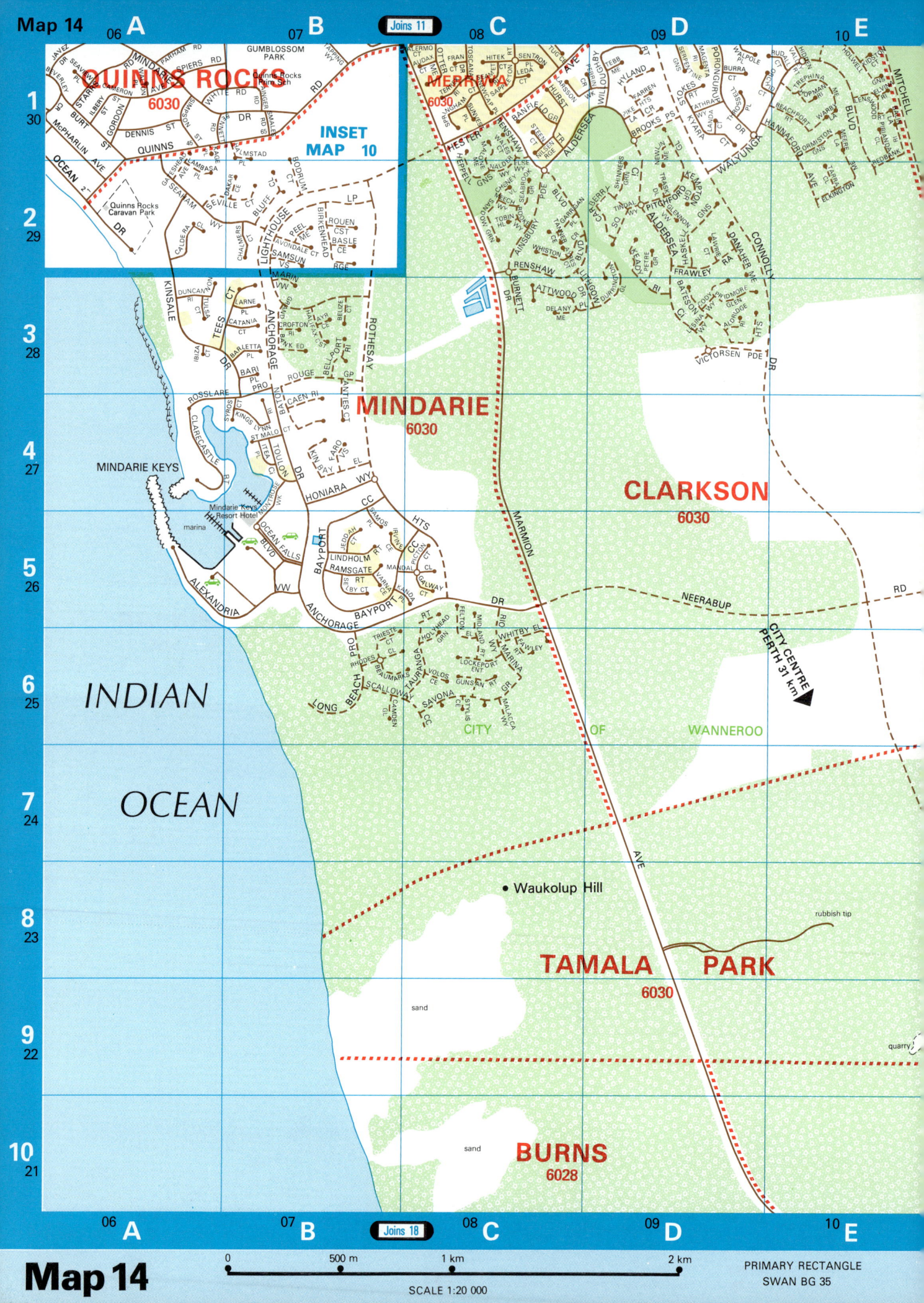

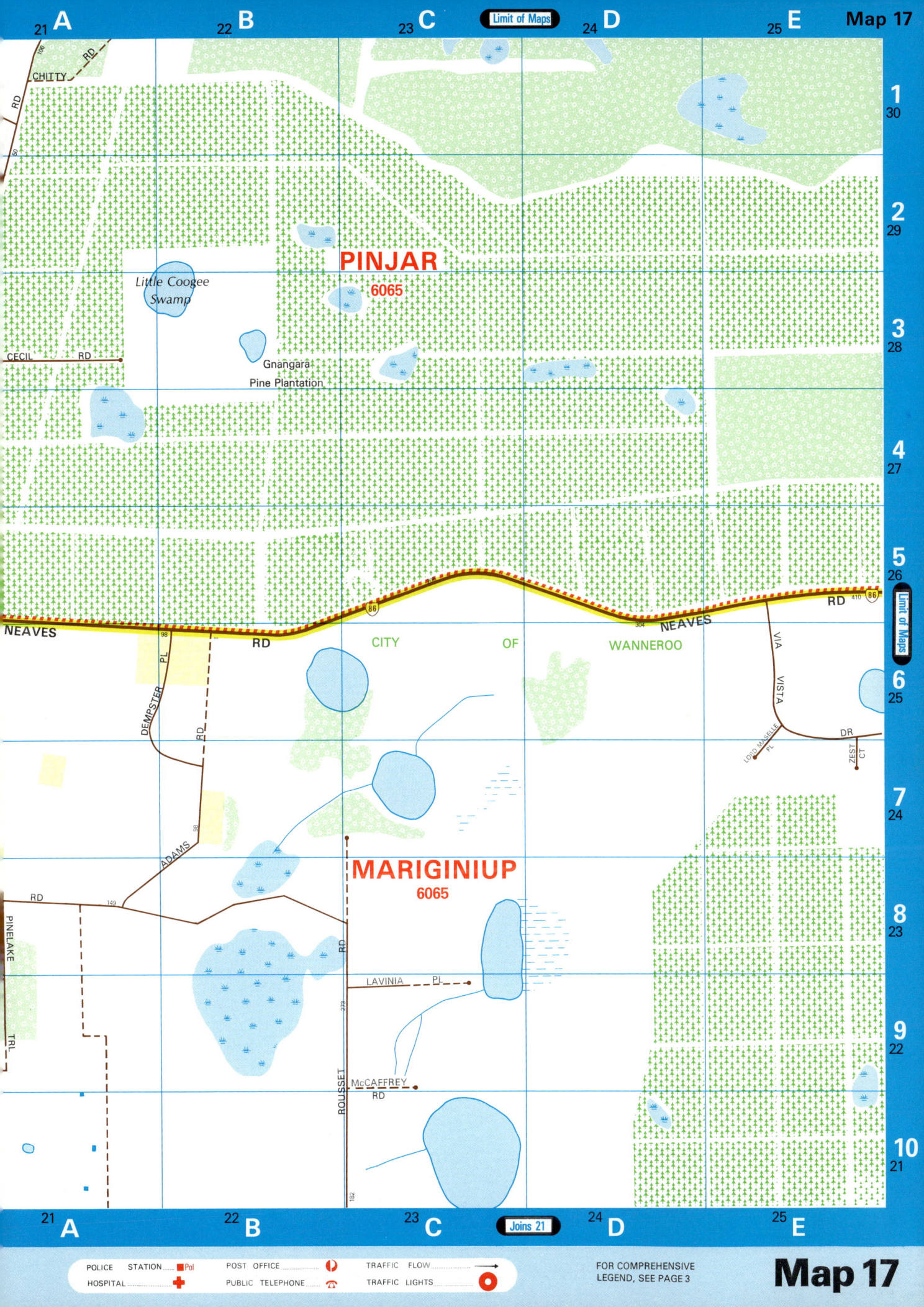

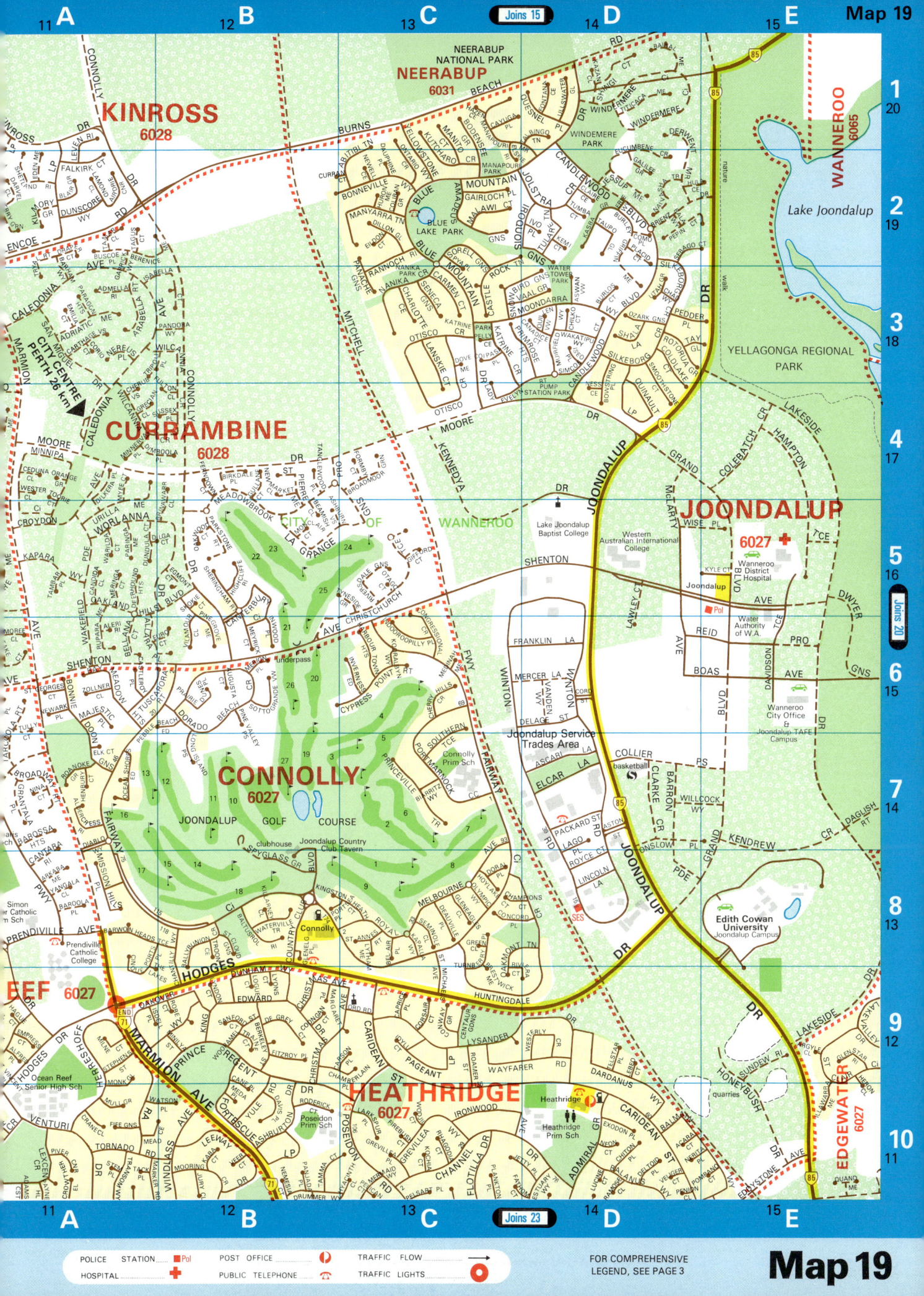

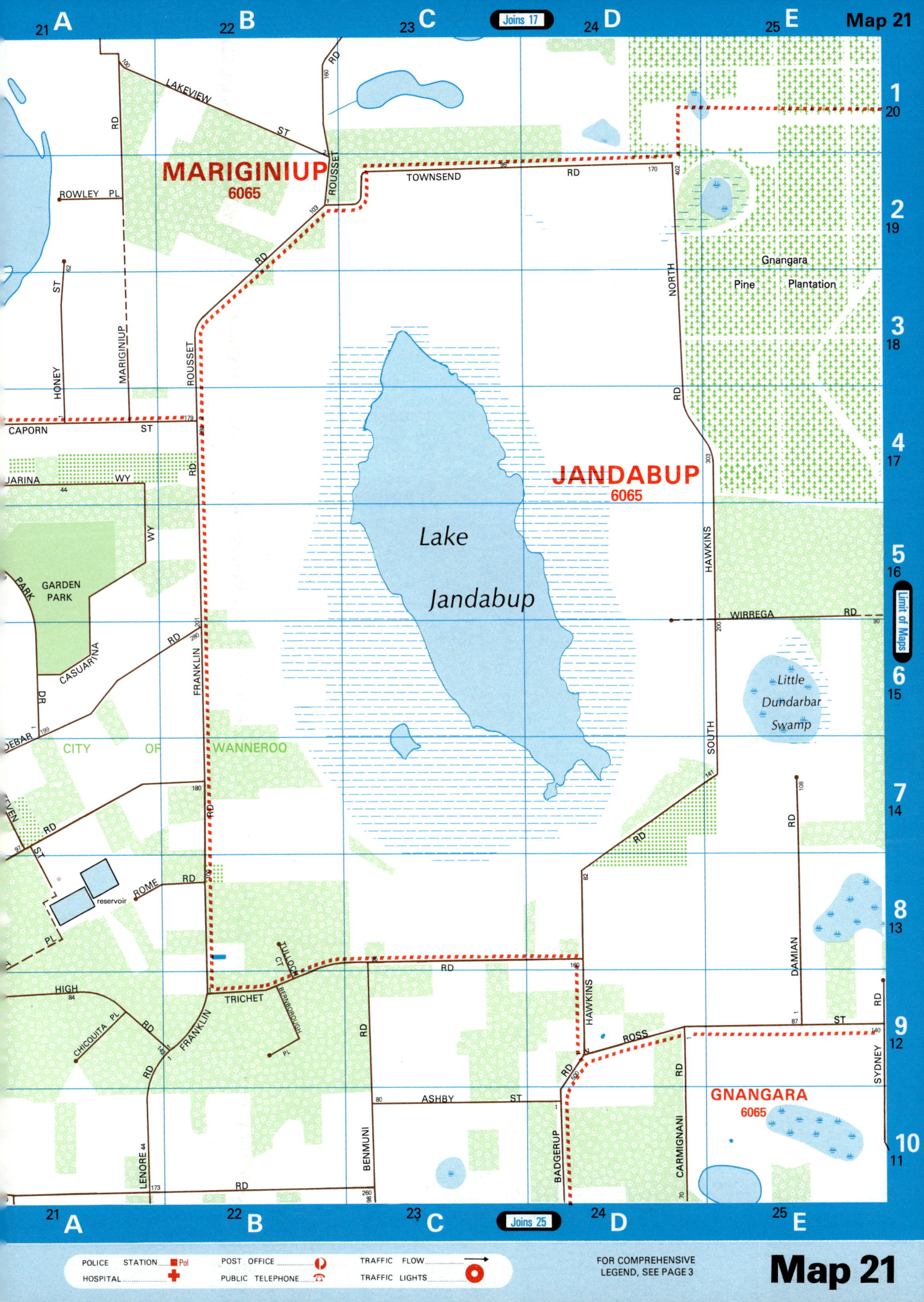

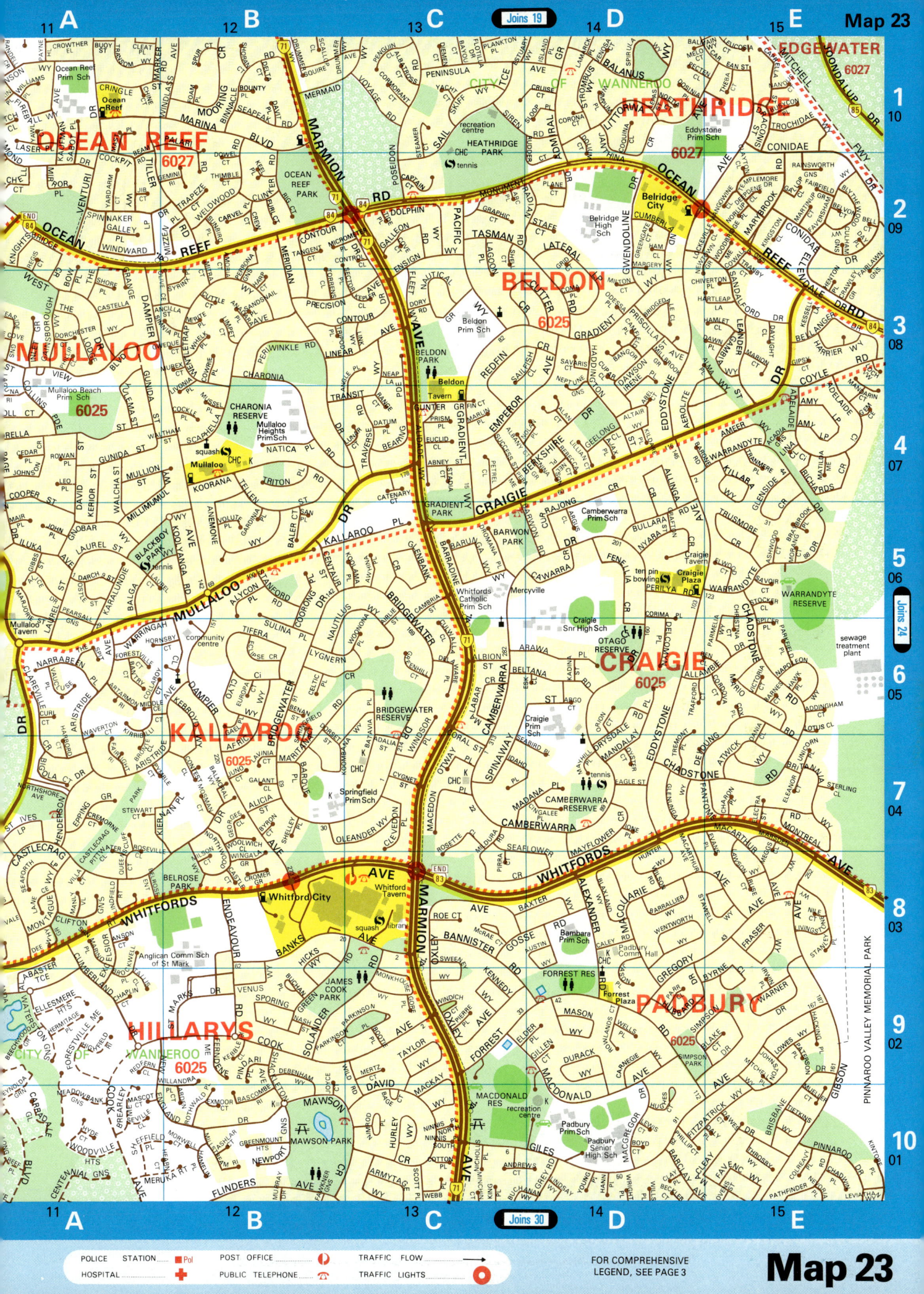

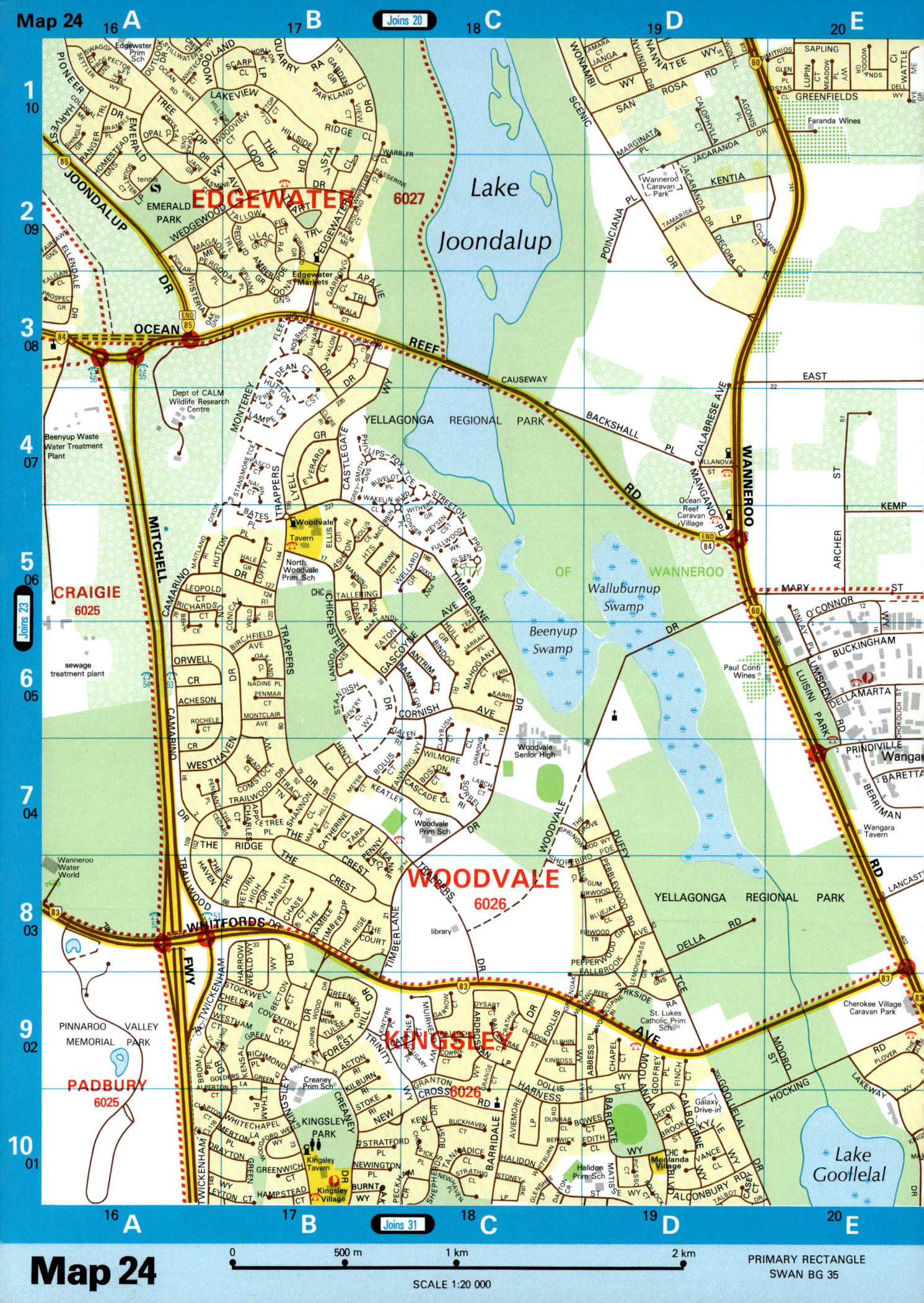

Joins 21

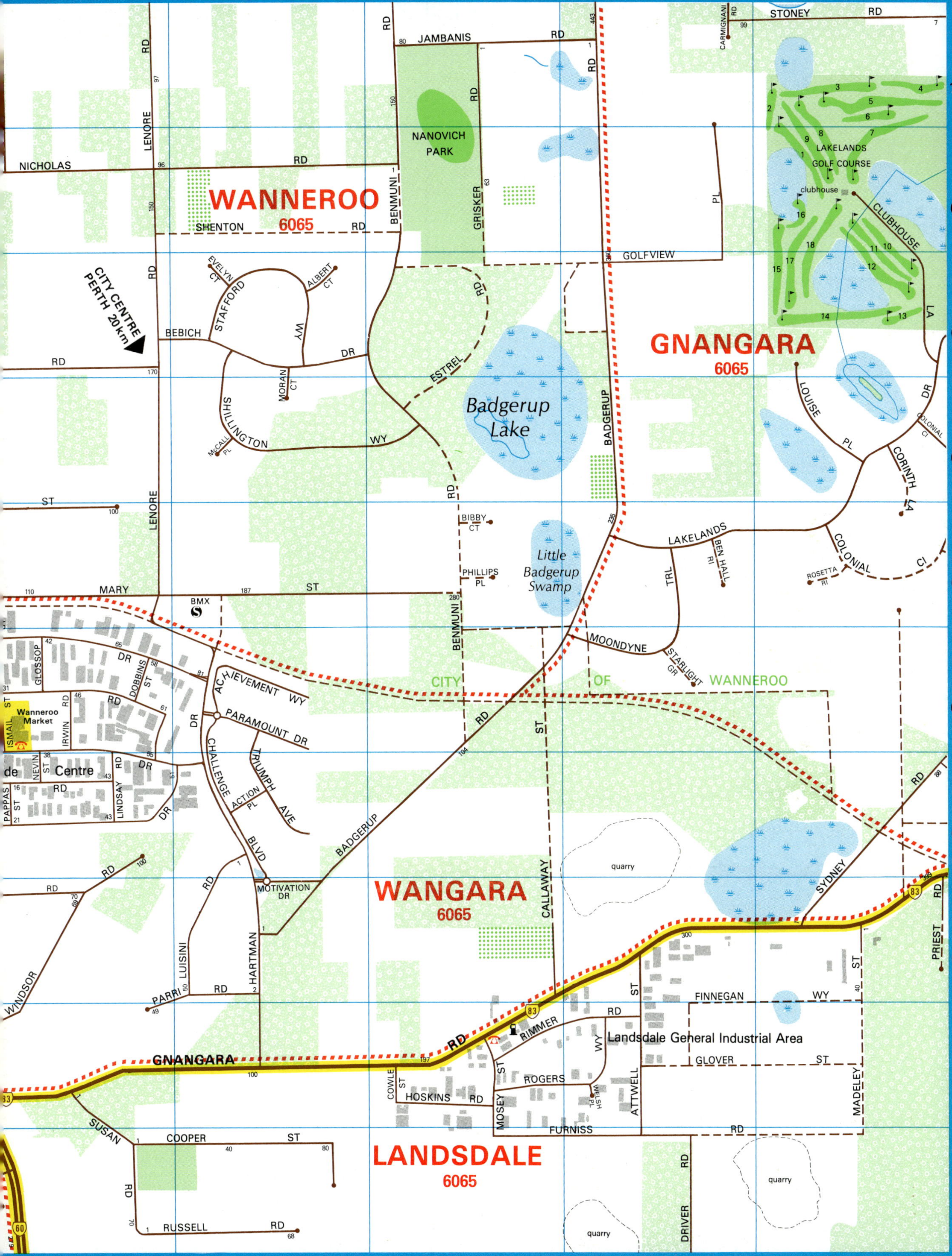

Joins 26

Joins 32

POLICE STATION .... Pol
HOSPITAL ....
POST OFFICE ....
PUBLIC TELEPHONE ....
TRAFFIC FLOW ....
TRAFFIC LIGHTS ....

FOR COMPREHENSIVE LEGEND, SEE PAGE 3

Map 26

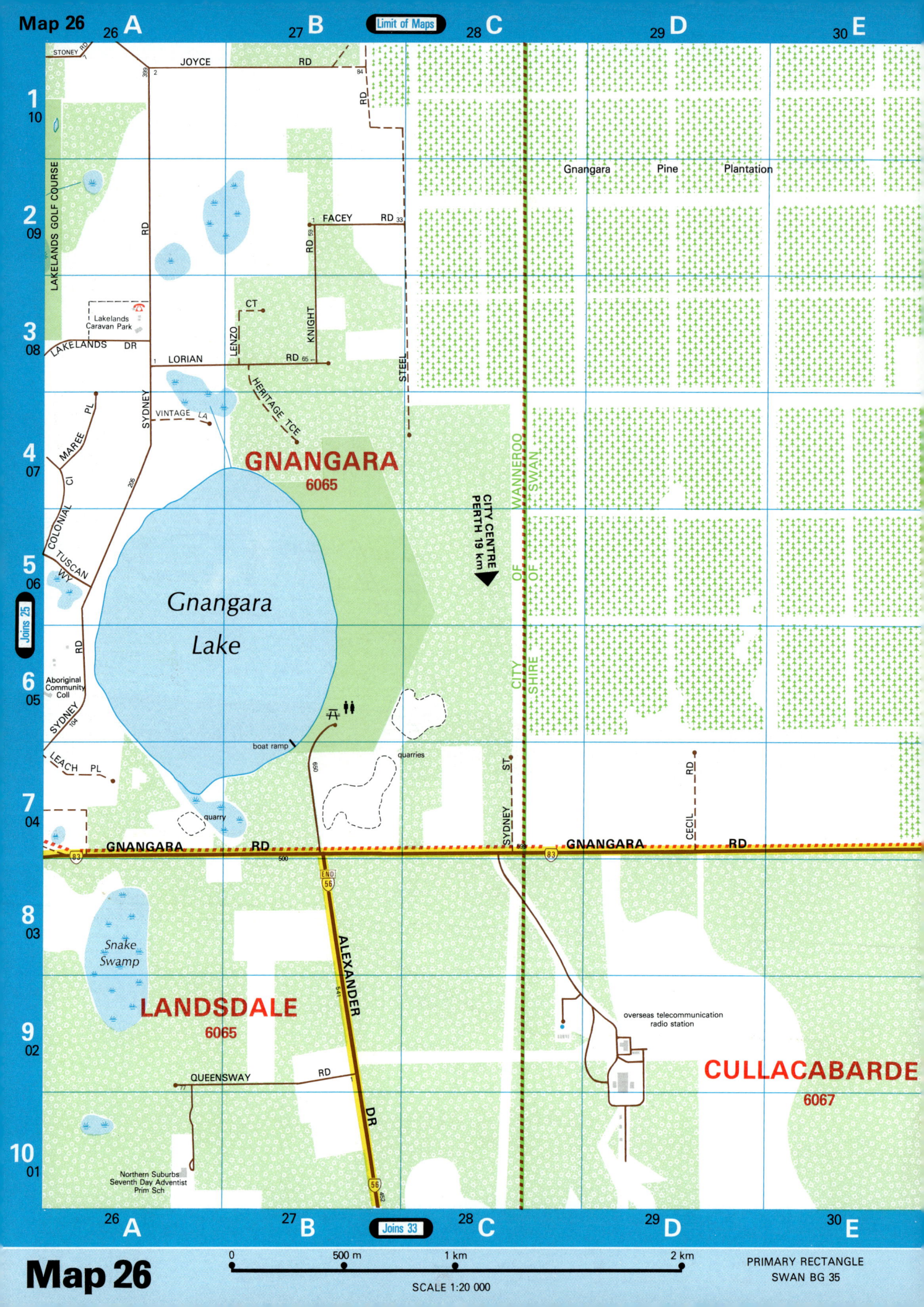

Map 27

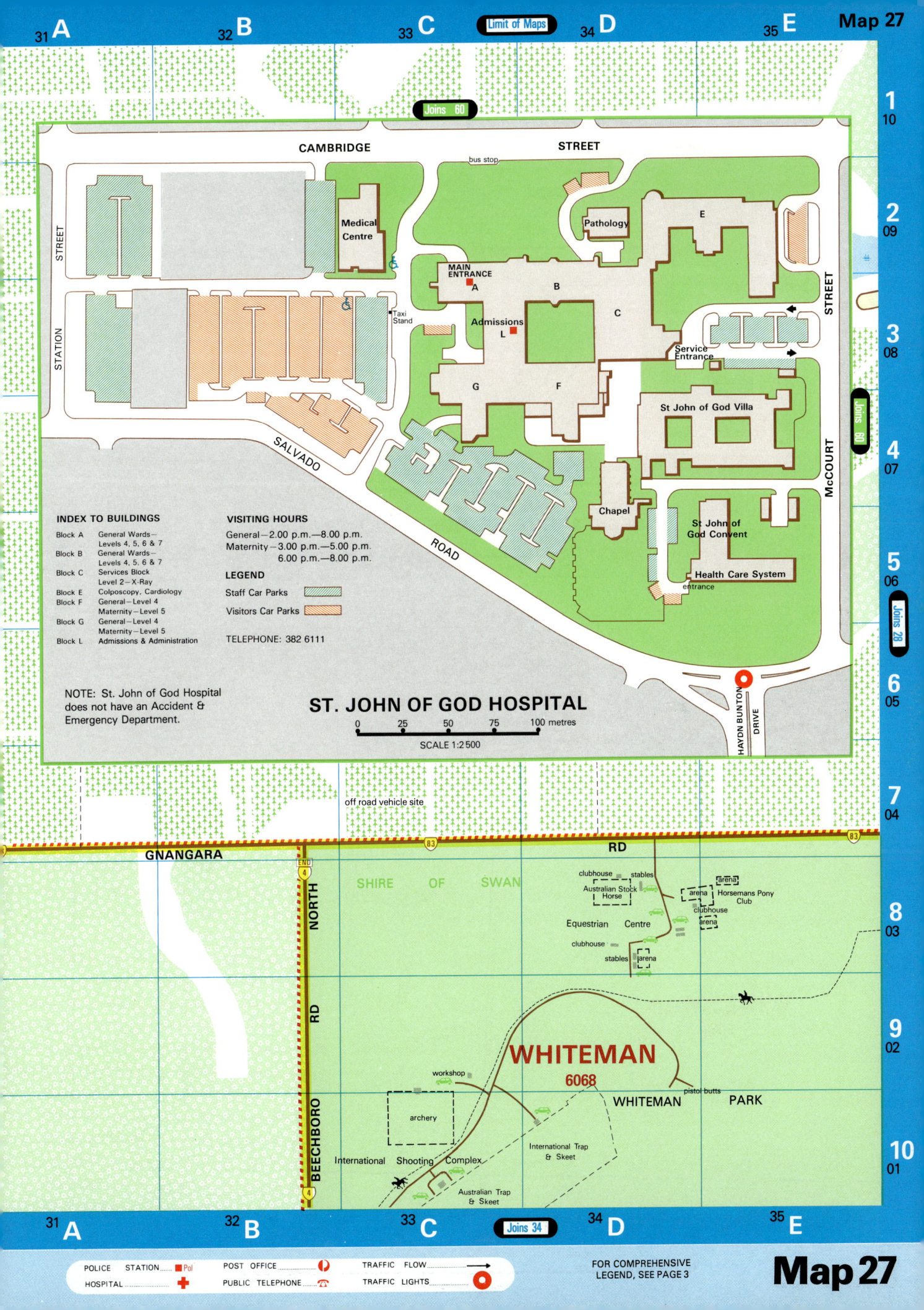

ST. JOHN OF GOD HOSPITAL

INDEX TO BUILDINGS
- Block A — General Wards — Levels 4, 5, 6 & 7
- Block B — General Wards — Levels 4, 5, 6 & 7
- Block C — Services Block Level 2 — X-Ray
- Block E — Colposcopy, Cardiology
- Block F — General — Level 4, Maternity — Level 5
- Block G — General — Level 4, Maternity — Level 5
- Block L — Admissions & Administration

VISITING HOURS
- General — 2.00 p.m.–8.00 p.m.
- Maternity — 3.00 p.m.–5.00 p.m.
- 6.00 p.m.–8.00 p.m.

LEGEND
- Staff Car Parks
- Visitors Car Parks

TELEPHONE: 382 6111

NOTE: St. John of God Hospital does not have an Accident & Emergency Department.

SCALE 1:2 500

Streets/features labeled on map: Cambridge Street, Station Street, Salvado Road, McCourt Street, Haydn Bunton Drive, Gnangara Rd, Beechboro Rd North, Whiteman Park (6068), Shire of Swan, Equestrian Centre, Australian Stock Horse, Horsemans Pony Club, International Shooting Complex, International Trap & Skeet, Australian Trap & Skeet, archery, workshop, pistol butts.

Buildings on hospital campus: Medical Centre, Pathology, Main Entrance (A), Admissions (L), B, C, G, F, E, Service Entrance, St John of God Villa, Chapel, St John of God Convent, Health Care System, Taxi Stand, bus stop.

LEGEND (bottom)
- POLICE STATION — Pol
- HOSPITAL — +
- POST OFFICE
- PUBLIC TELEPHONE
- TRAFFIC FLOW
- TRAFFIC LIGHTS

FOR COMPREHENSIVE LEGEND, SEE PAGE 3

Map 28

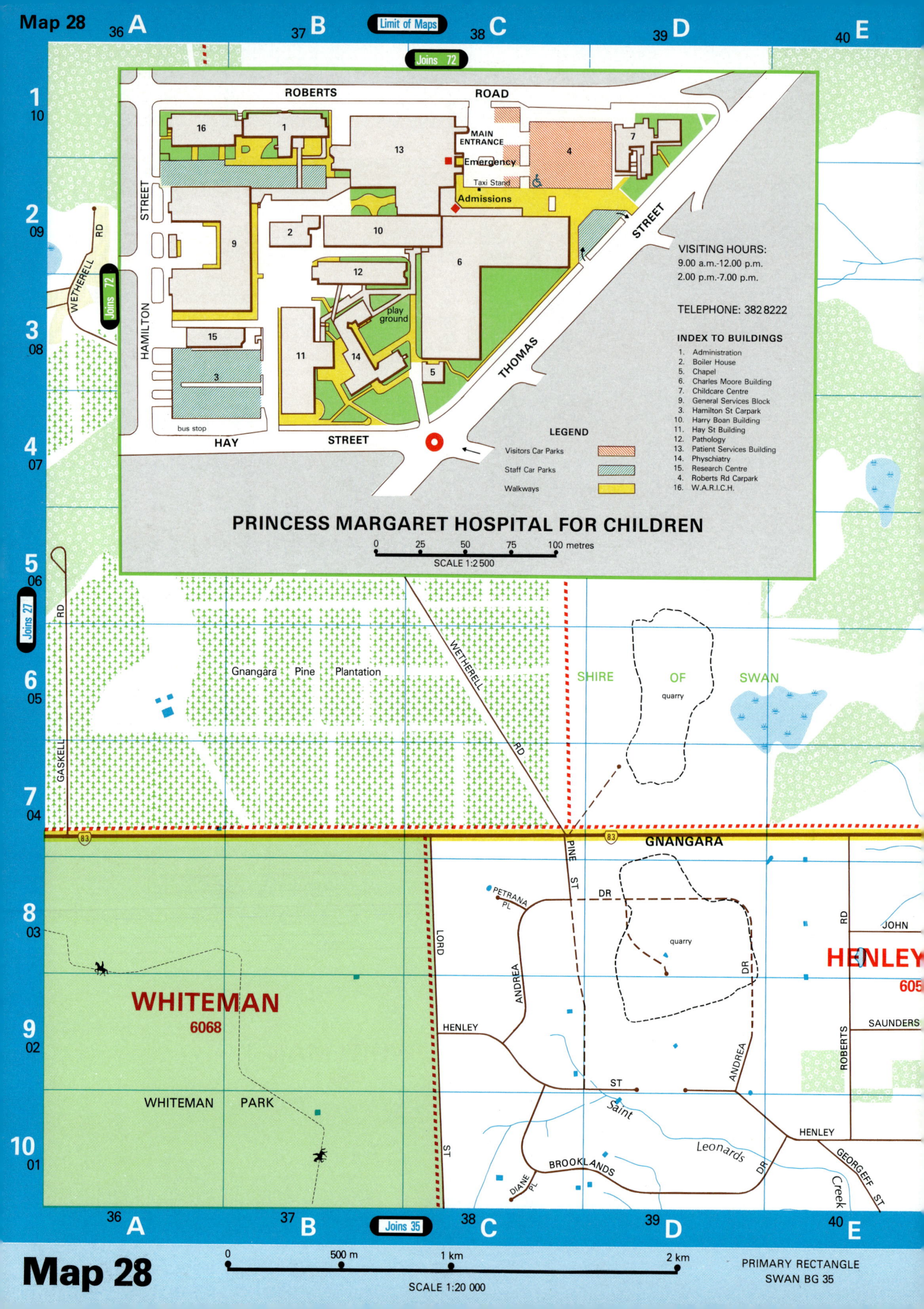

PRINCESS MARGARET HOSPITAL FOR CHILDREN

VISITING HOURS:
9.00 a.m.-12.00 p.m.
2.00 p.m.-7.00 p.m.

TELEPHONE: 382 8222

INDEX TO BUILDINGS
1. Administration
2. Boiler House
5. Chapel
6. Charles Moore Building
7. Childcare Centre
9. General Services Block
3. Hamilton St Carpark
10. Harry Boan Building
11. Hay St Building
12. Pathology
13. Patient Services Building
14. Physchiatry
15. Research Centre
4. Roberts Rd Carpark
16. W.A.R.I.C.H.

LEGEND
- Visitors Car Parks
- Staff Car Parks
- Walkways

SCALE 1:2 500
0 25 50 75 100 metres

WHITEMAN 6068
WHITEMAN PARK

HENLEY 6056

SCALE 1:20 000
0 500 m 1 km 2 km

PRIMARY RECTANGLE
SWAN BG 35

Limit of Maps

Joins 36

POLICE STATION Pol
HOSPITAL
POST OFFICE
PUBLIC TELEPHONE
TRAFFIC FLOW
TRAFFIC LIGHTS

FOR COMPREHENSIVE LEGEND, SEE PAGE 3

Joins 23

Joins 44

0 500 m 1 km 2 km

SCALE 1:20 000

PRIMARY RECTANGLE
PERTH BG 34

Joins 24

16 A 17 B 18 C 19 D 20 E

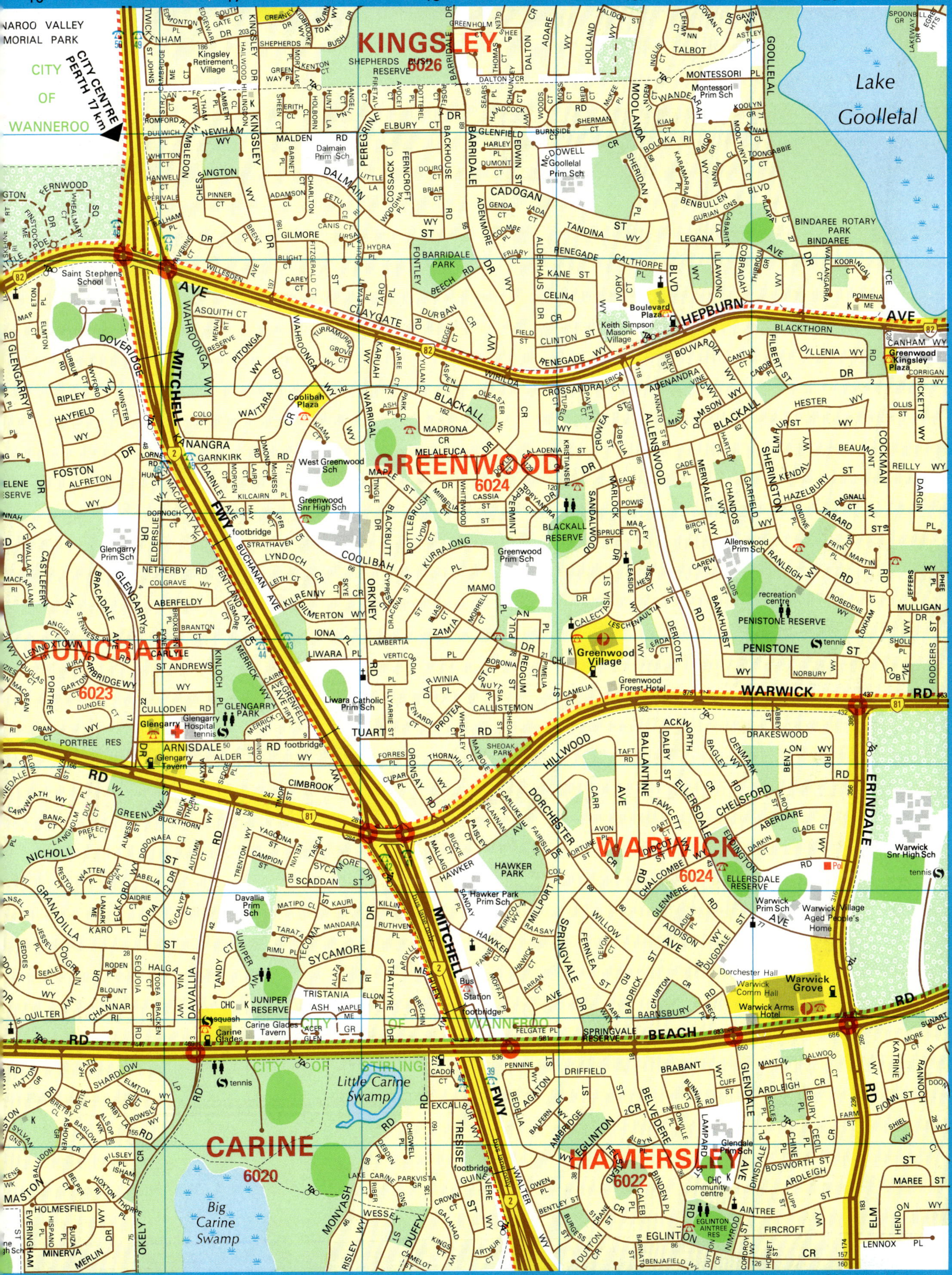

16 A 17 B 18 C 19 D 20 E

1 80 · 2 79 · 3 78 · 4 77 · 5 76 · 6 75 · 7 74 · 8 73 · 9 72 · 10 71

Joins 32

Joins 45

POLICE STATION Pol
HOSPITAL
POST OFFICE
PUBLIC TELEPHONE
TRAFFIC FLOW
TRAFFIC LIGHTS

FOR COMPREHENSIVE LEGEND, SEE PAGE 3

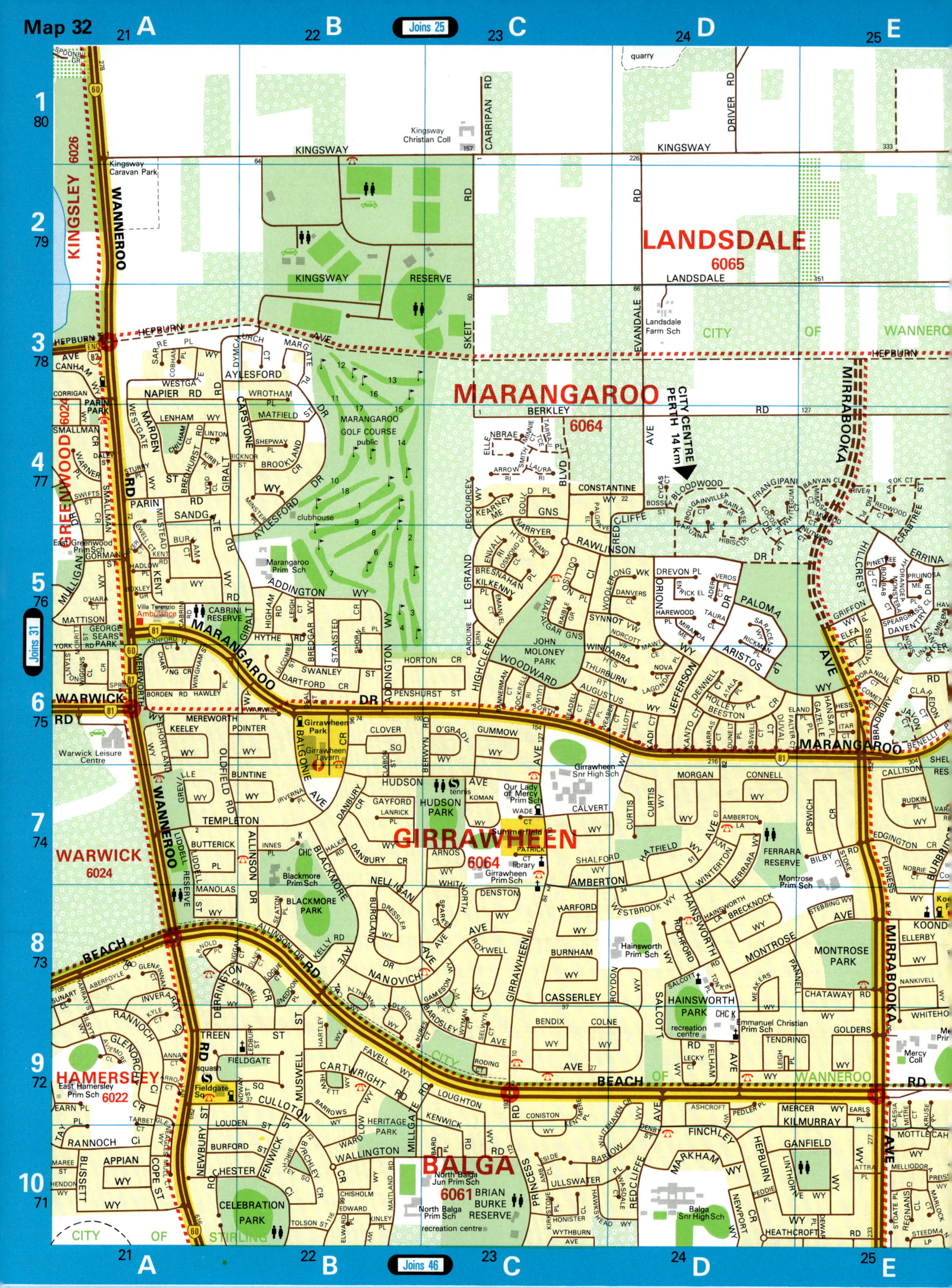

0 500 m 1 km 2 km

SCALE 1:20 000

PRIMARY RECTANGLE
PERTH BG 34

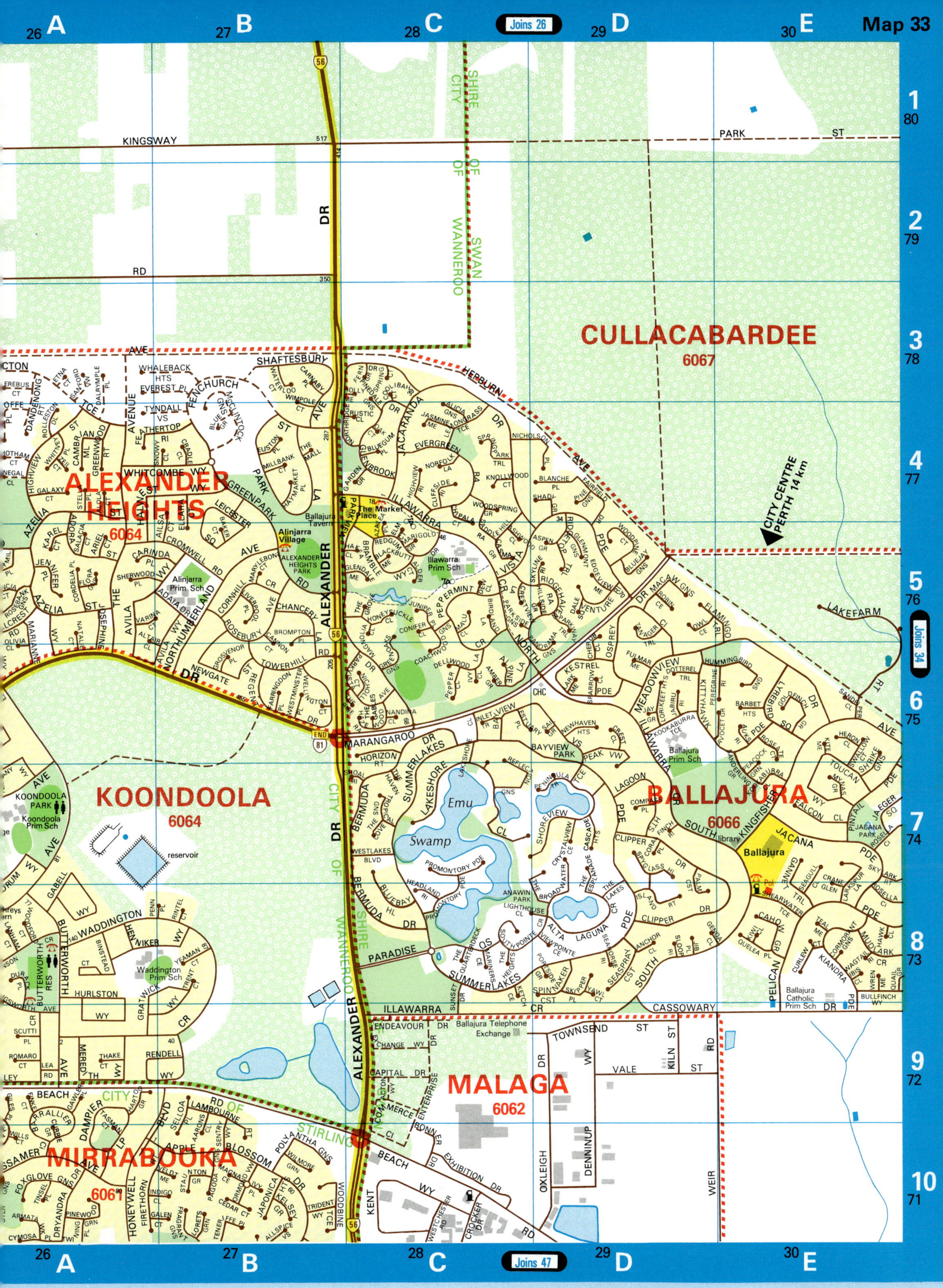

POLICE STATION ... Pol
HOSPITAL
POST OFFICE
PUBLIC TELEPHONE
TRAFFIC FLOW
TRAFFIC LIGHTS

FOR COMPREHENSIVE LEGEND, SEE PAGE 3

Map 34

Map 35

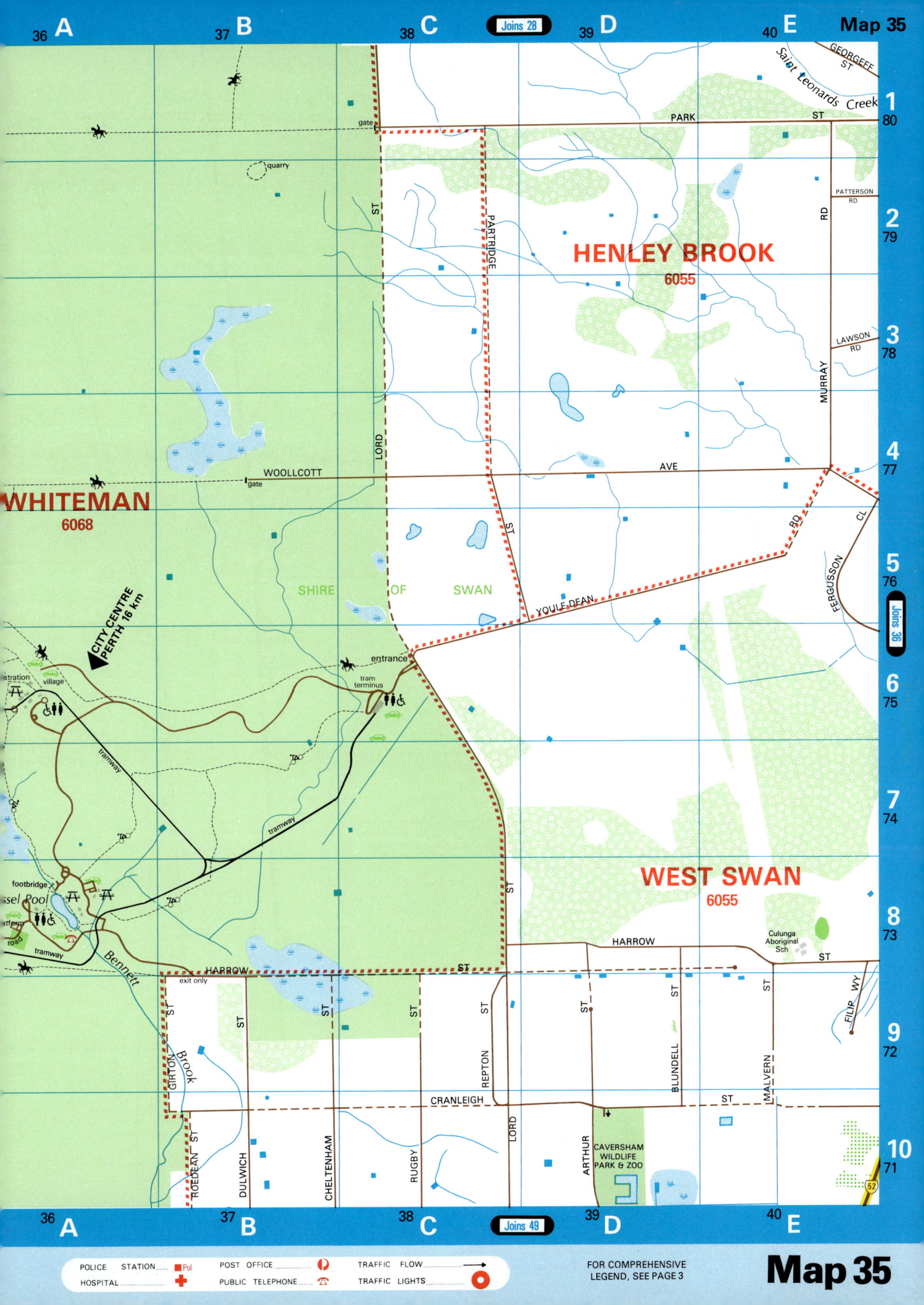

WHITEMAN 6068

HENLEY BROOK 6055

WEST SWAN 6055

SHIRE OF SWAN

CITY CENTRE PERTH 16 km

Saint Leonards Creek

Joins 28
Joins 36
Joins 49

Streets and features:
- GEORGEFF ST
- PARK ST
- PATTERSON RD
- LAWSON RD
- MURRAY RD
- PARTRIDGE ST
- LORD ST
- WOOLLCOTT AVE
- YOULE-DEAN RD
- FERGUSSON CL
- HARROW ST
- BENNETT
- GIRTON ST
- ROEDEAN ST
- DULWICH ST
- CHELTENHAM ST
- RUGBY ST
- REPTON ST
- LORD ST
- ARTHUR ST
- BLUNDELL ST
- MALVERN ST
- FILIP WY
- CRANLEIGH ST

Features: quarry, gate, village, tramway, tram terminus, entrance, footbridge, exit only, Caversham Wildlife Park & Zoo, Culunga Aboriginal Sch

LEGEND:
- POLICE STATION — Pol
- HOSPITAL
- POST OFFICE
- PUBLIC TELEPHONE
- TRAFFIC FLOW
- TRAFFIC LIGHTS

FOR COMPREHENSIVE LEGEND, SEE PAGE 3

Joins 29

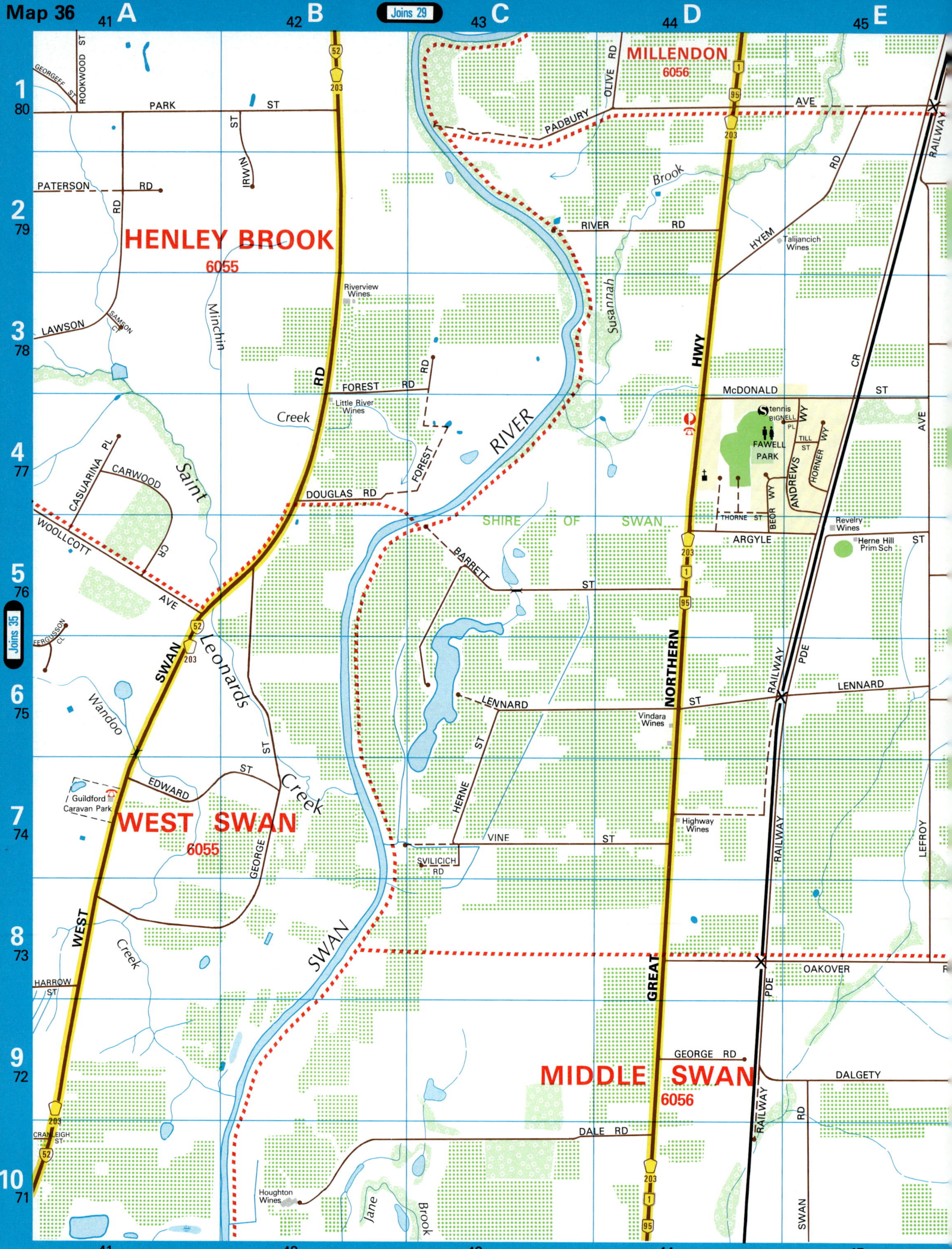

Joins 50

0 500 m 1 km 2 km

SCALE 1:20 000

PRIMARY RECTANGLE
PERTH BG 34

Map 37

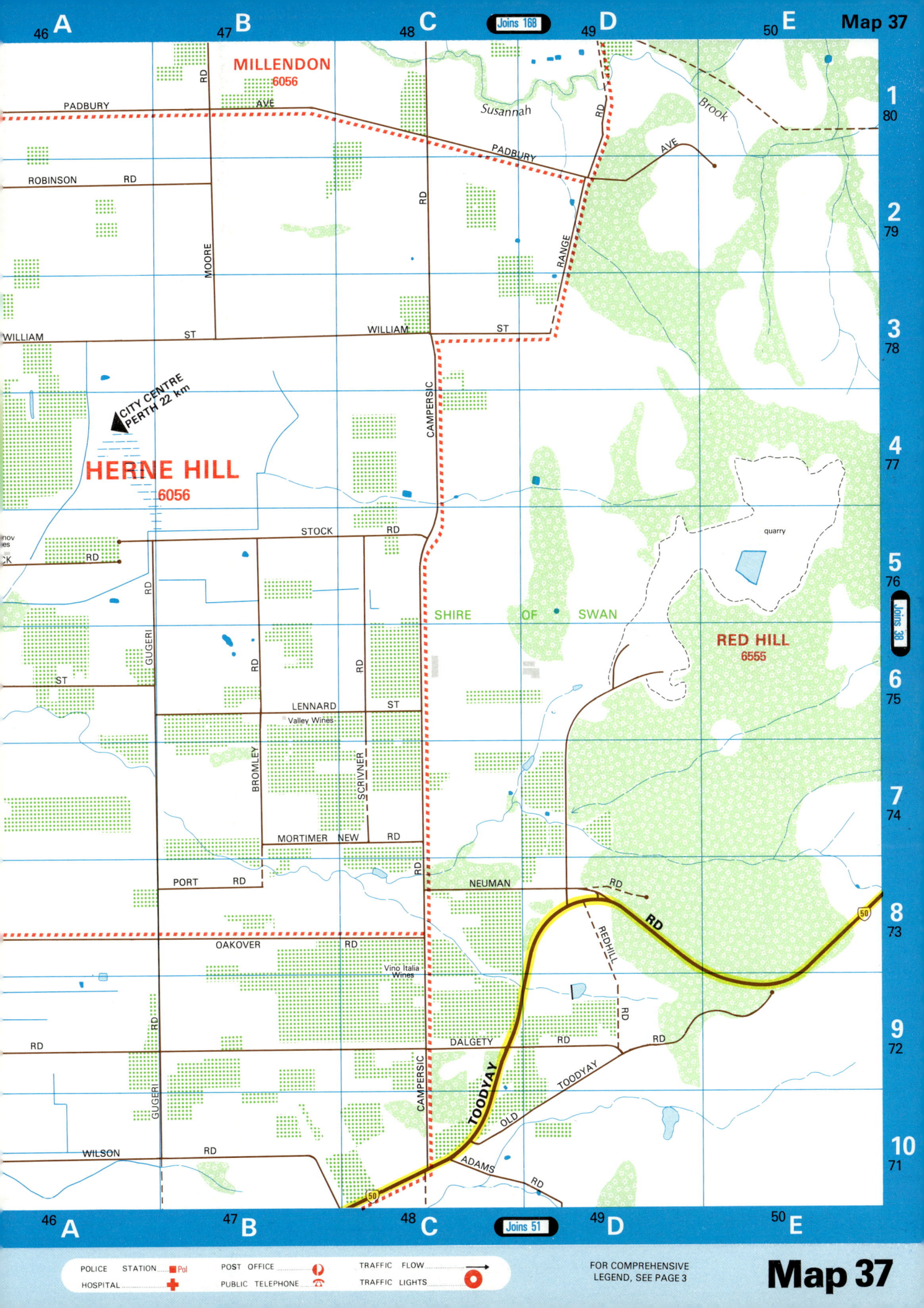

MILLENDON 6056

HERNE HILL 6056

RED HILL 6555

SHIRE OF SWAN

CITY CENTRE PERTH 22 km

Map 38

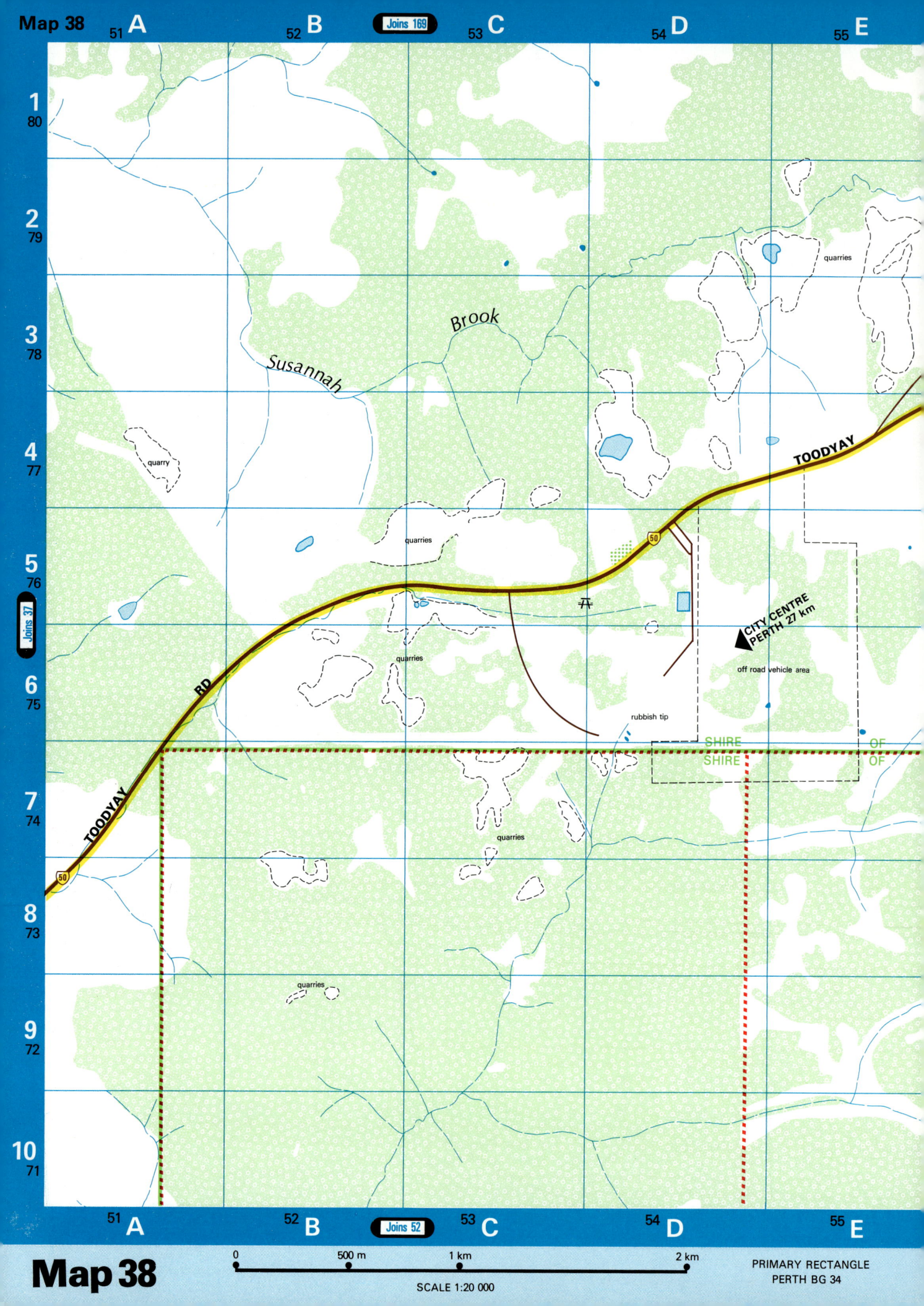

Map 39

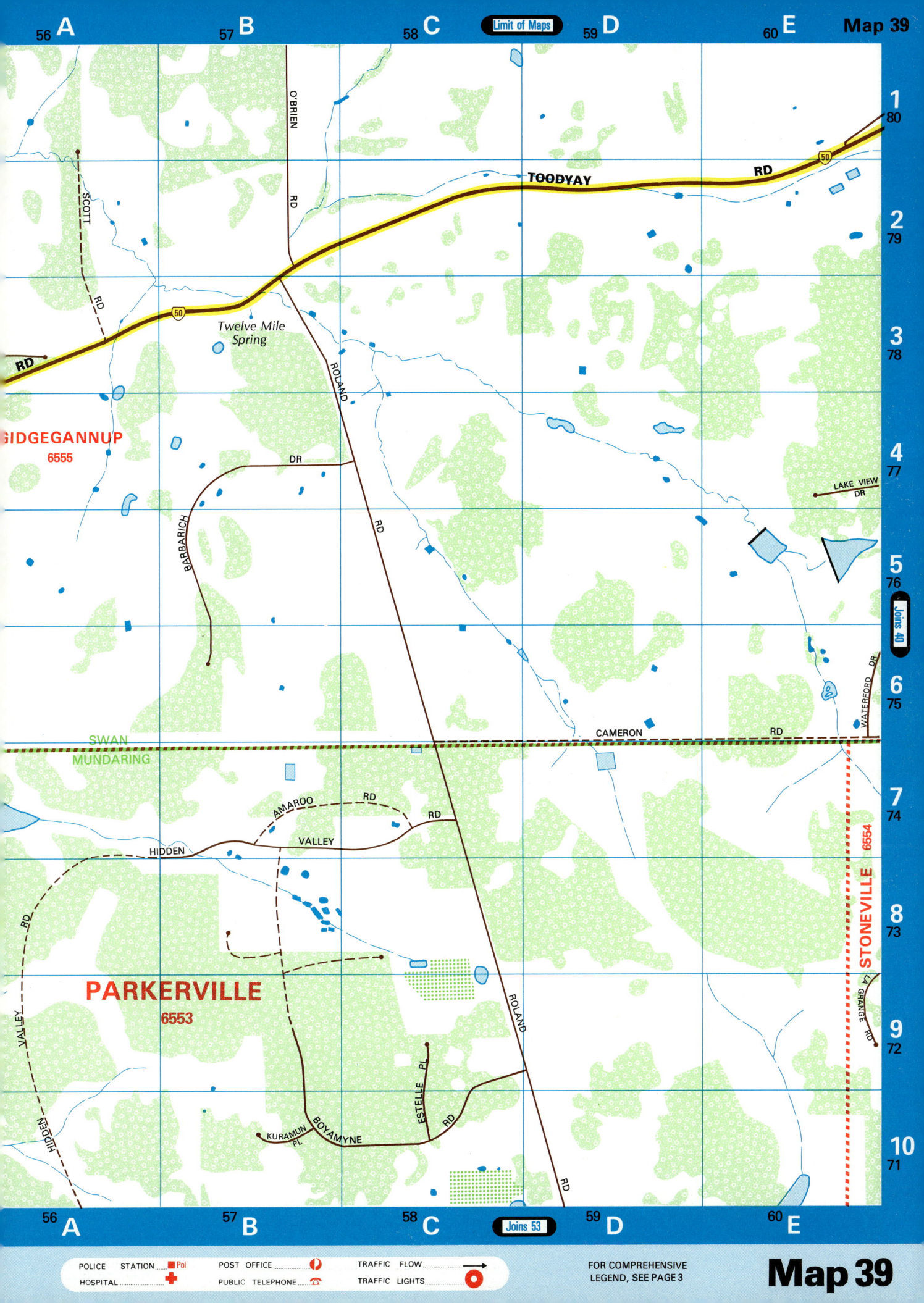

GIDGEGANNUP 6555

Twelve Mile Spring

PARKERVILLE 6553

STONEVILLE 6554

SWAN / MUNDARING

Roads/labels: SCOTT RD, O'BRIEN RD, TOODYAY RD, ROLAND RD, BARBARICH DR, LAKE VIEW DR, WATERFORD DR, CAMERON RD, AMAROO RD, HIDDEN VALLEY RD, ESTELLE PL, BOYAMYNE RD, KURAMUN PL, LA GRANGE RD

Joins 40
Joins 53
Limit of Maps

POLICE STATION — Pol
HOSPITAL
POST OFFICE
PUBLIC TELEPHONE
TRAFFIC FLOW
TRAFFIC LIGHTS

FOR COMPREHENSIVE LEGEND, SEE PAGE 3

Map 39

Map 40

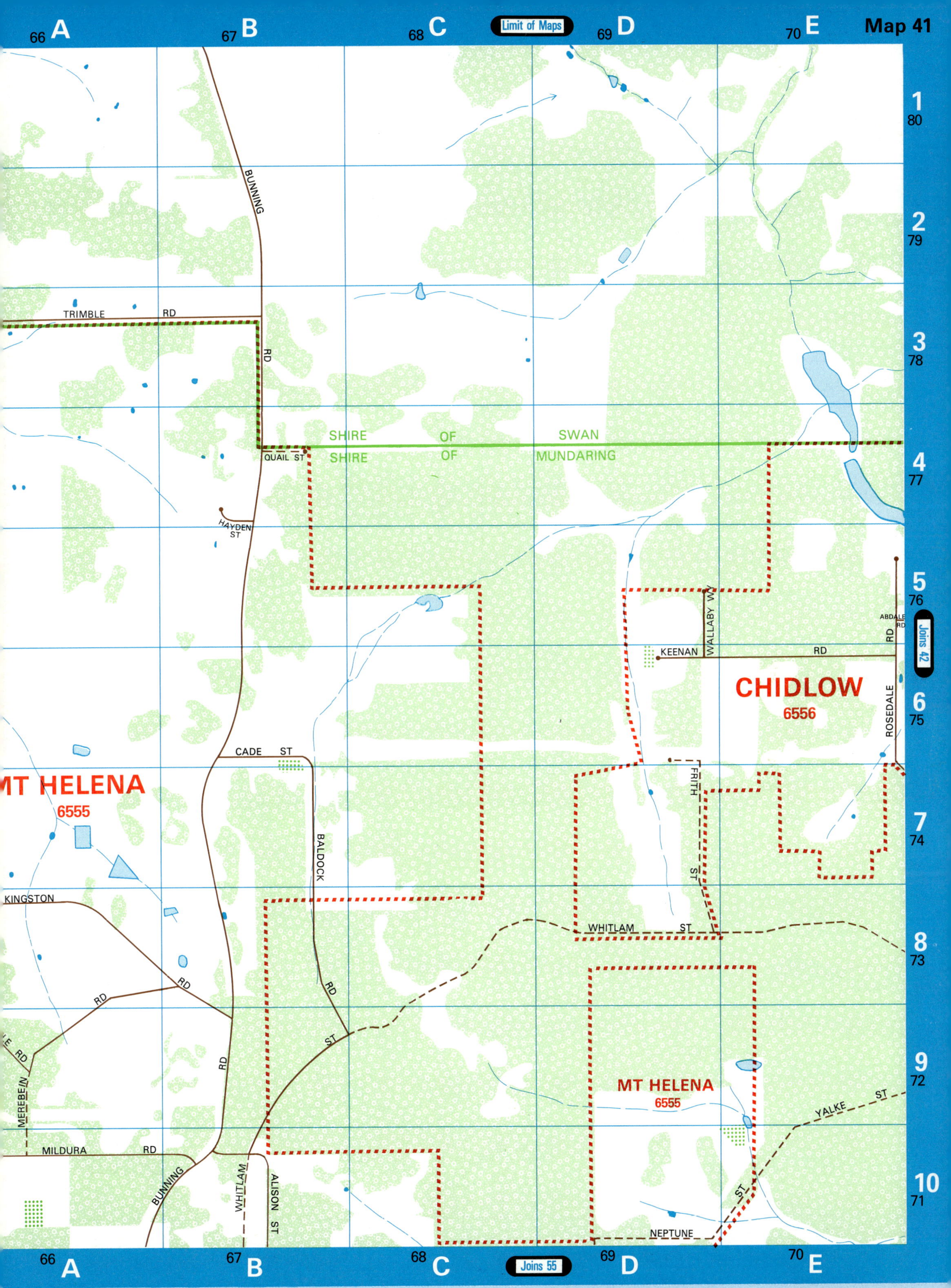
66 A
67 B
68 C
Limit of Maps
69 D
70 E
1
80
2
79
3
78
4
77
5
76
6
75
7
74
8
73
9
72
10
71
BUNNING
TRIMBLE RD
RD
QUAIL ST
SHIRE OF SWAN
SHIRE OF MUNDARING
HAYDEN ST
WALLABY WY
KEENAN RD
ABDALE RD
RD
Joins 42
CHIDLOW
6556
ROSEDALE
CADE ST
MT HELENA
6555
FRITH
ST
BALDOCK
KINGSTON
WHITLAM ST
RD
RD
RD
ST
RD
MEREBEIN
RD
MT HELENA
6555
YALKE ST
MILDURA RD
BUNNING
WHITLAM
ALISON ST
ST
NEPTUNE
66 A
67 B
68 C
Joins 55
69 D
70 E

POLICE STATION Pol
HOSPITAL
POST OFFICE
PUBLIC TELEPHONE
TRAFFIC FLOW
TRAFFIC LIGHTS

FOR COMPREHENSIVE LEGEND, SEE PAGE 3

Map 42

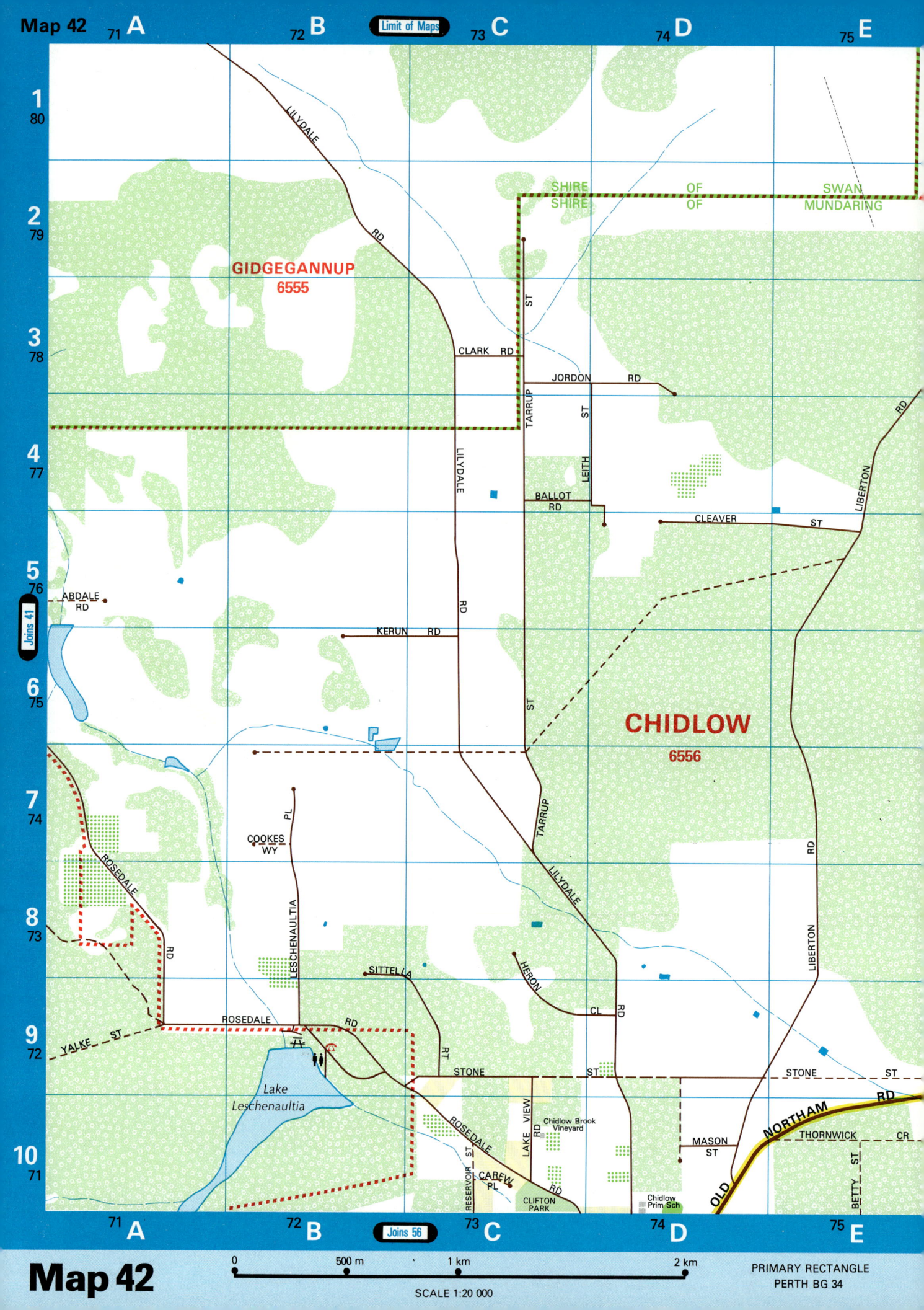

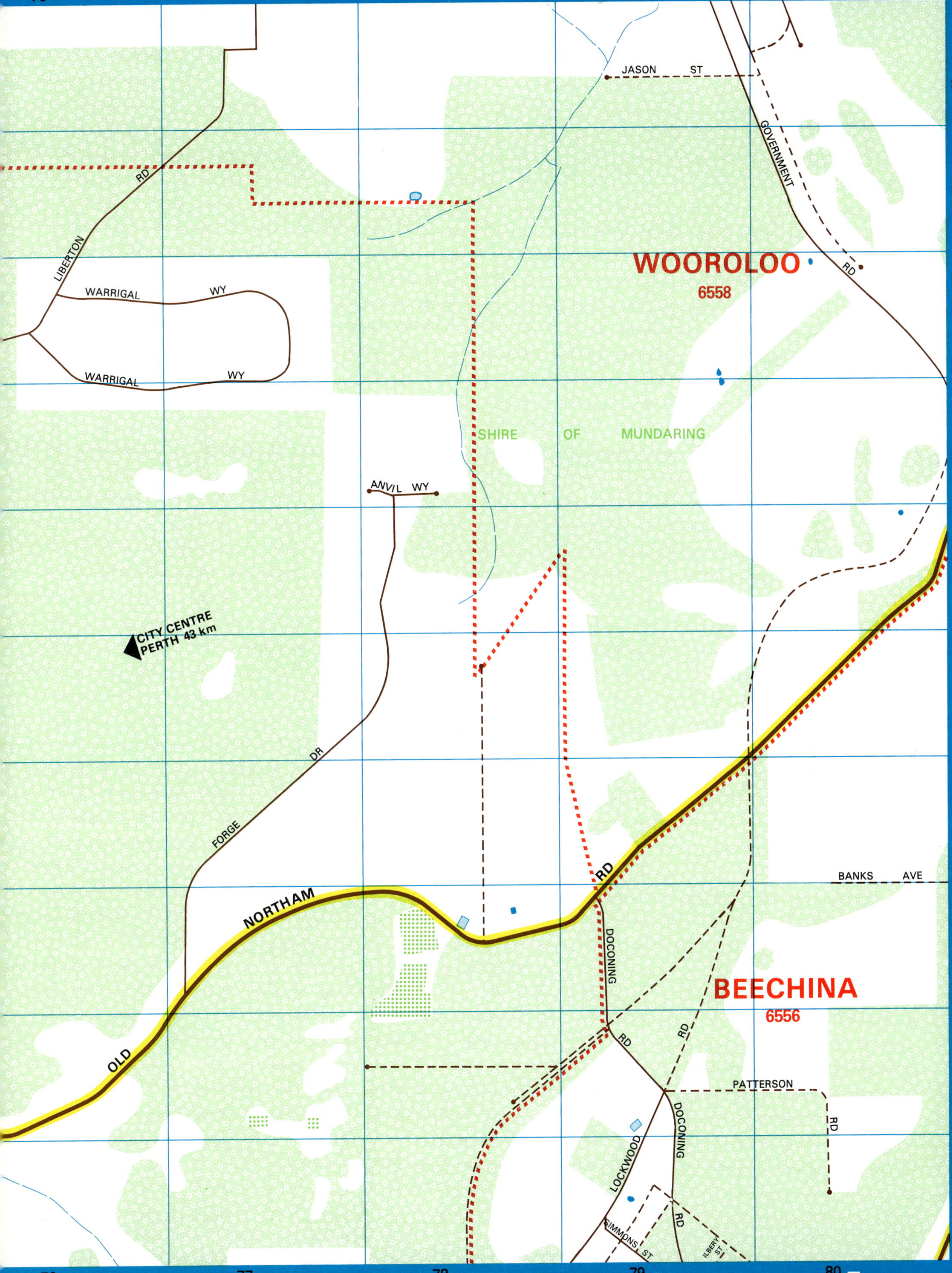

76 A
77 B
78 C
Limit of Maps
79 D
80 E
1 80
2 79
3 78
4 77
5 76
6 75
7 74
8 73
9 72
10 71
Limit of Maps
JASON ST
GOVERNMENT RD
WOOROLOO
6558
LIBERTON RD
WARRIGAL WY
WARRIGAL WY
SHIRE OF MUNDARING
ANVIL WY
CITY CENTRE PERTH 43 km
FORGE DR
OLD NORTHAM RD
BANKS AVE
DOCONING RD
BEECHINA
6556
PATTERSON RD
LOCKWOOD RD
SIMMONS ST
ILBERY ST
76 A
77 B
78 C
Joins 57
79 D
80 E

POLICE STATION Pol
HOSPITAL
POST OFFICE
PUBLIC TELEPHONE
TRAFFIC FLOW
TRAFFIC LIGHTS

FOR COMPREHENSIVE LEGEND, SEE PAGE 3

Map 44

0 | 500 m | 1 km | 2 km

SCALE 1:20 000

PRIMARY RECTANGLE
PERTH BG 34

Joins 31

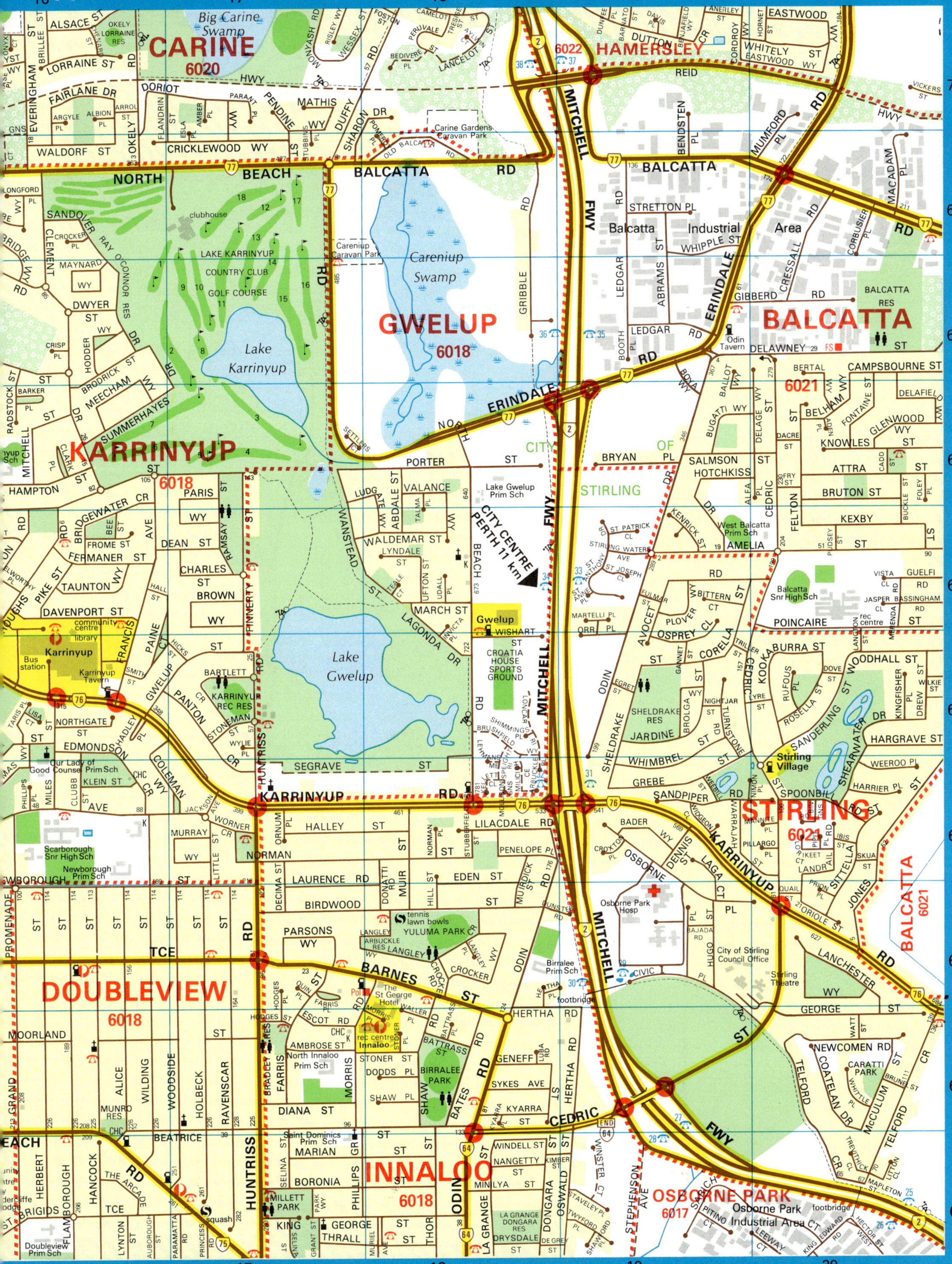

Joins 59

POLICE STATION Pol
HOSPITAL
POST OFFICE
PUBLIC TELEPHONE
TRAFFIC FLOW
TRAFFIC LIGHTS

FOR COMPREHENSIVE LEGEND, SEE PAGE 3

Map 46

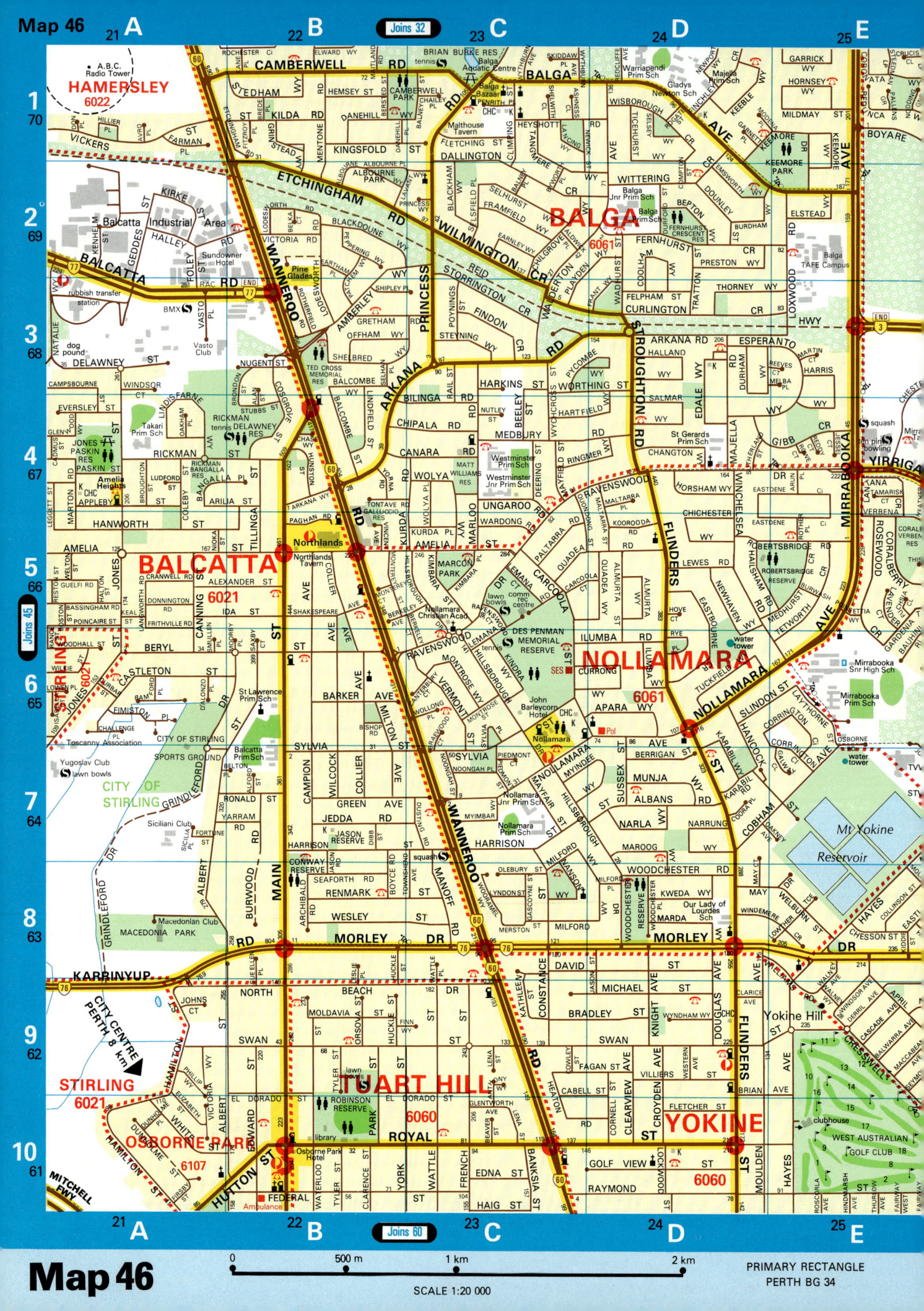

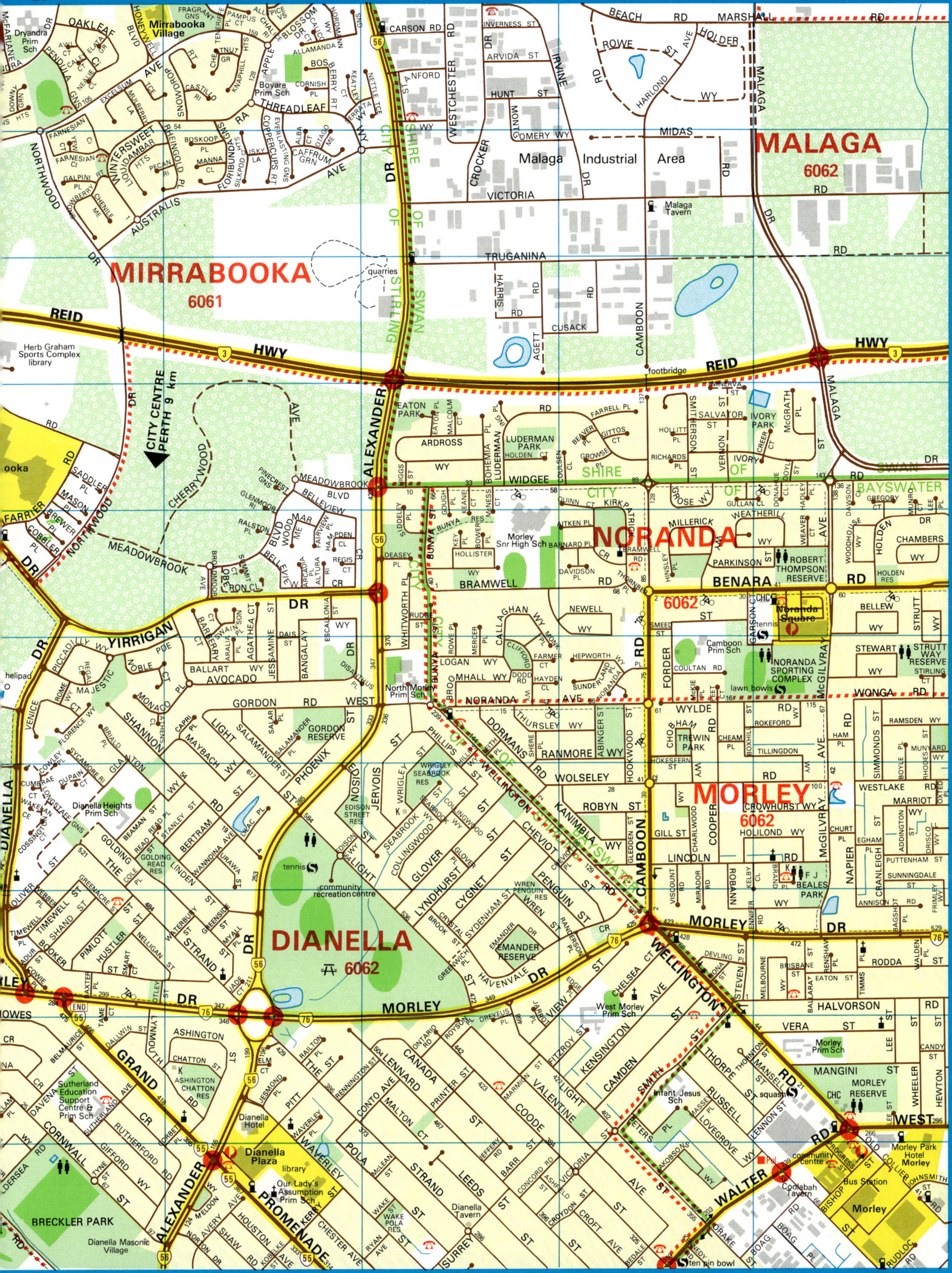

POLICE STATION
HOSPITAL
POST OFFICE
PUBLIC TELEPHONE
TRAFFIC FLOW
TRAFFIC LIGHTS

FOR COMPREHENSIVE LEGEND, SEE PAGE 3

Map 48

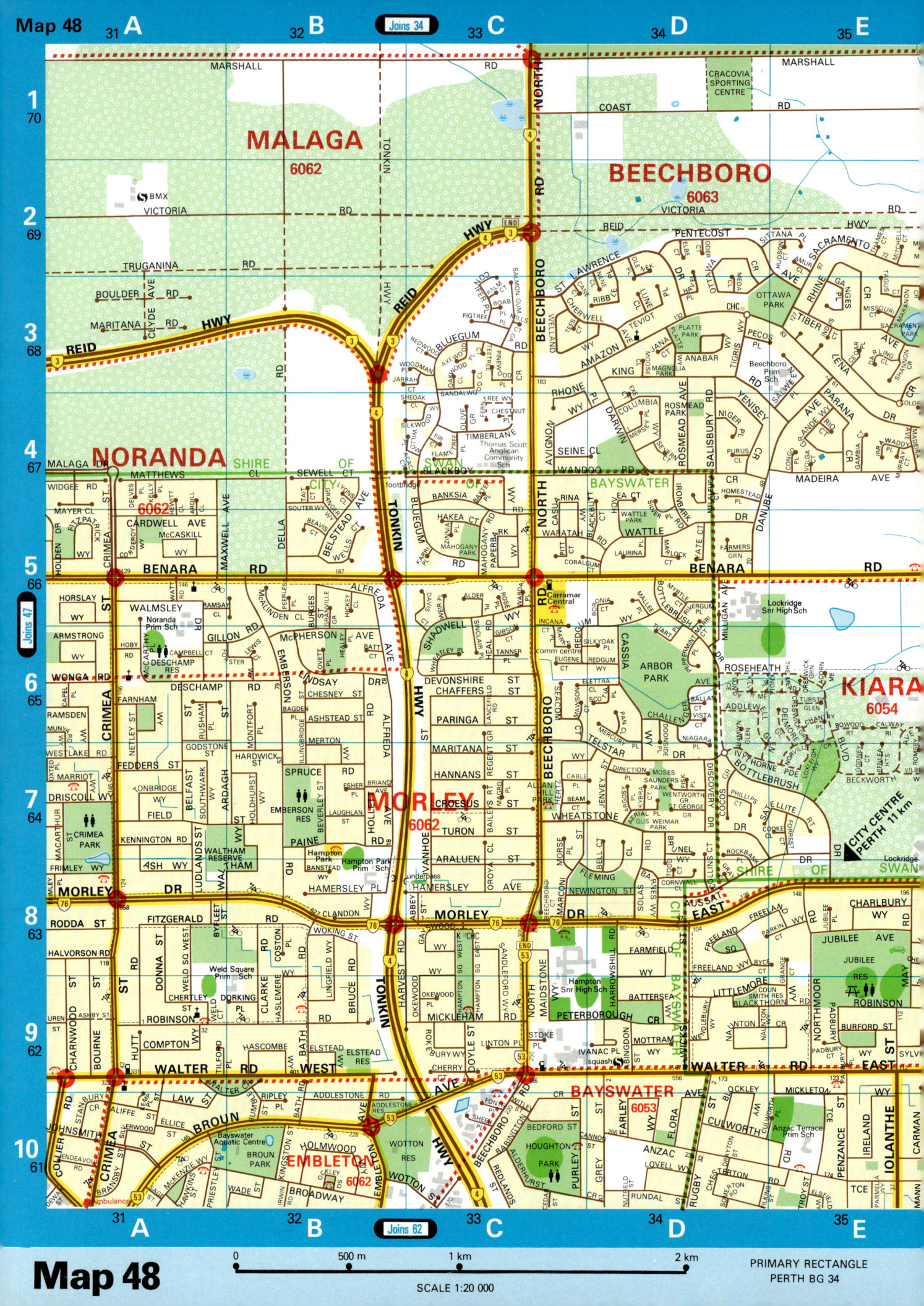

Joins 35

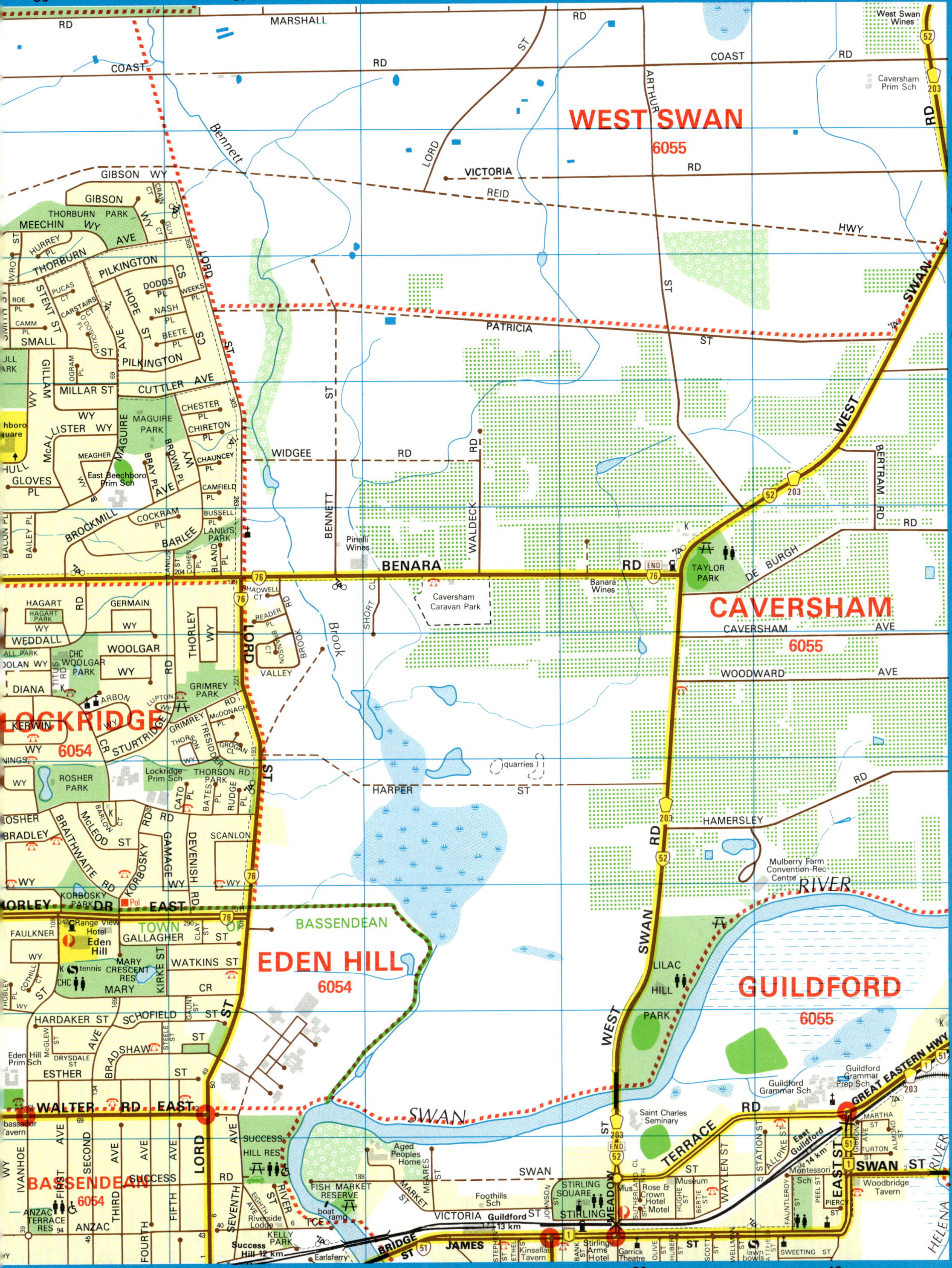

Joins 50

Joins 63

POLICE STATION Pol
HOSPITAL
POST OFFICE
PUBLIC TELEPHONE
TRAFFIC FLOW
TRAFFIC LIGHTS

FOR COMPREHENSIVE LEGEND, SEE PAGE 3

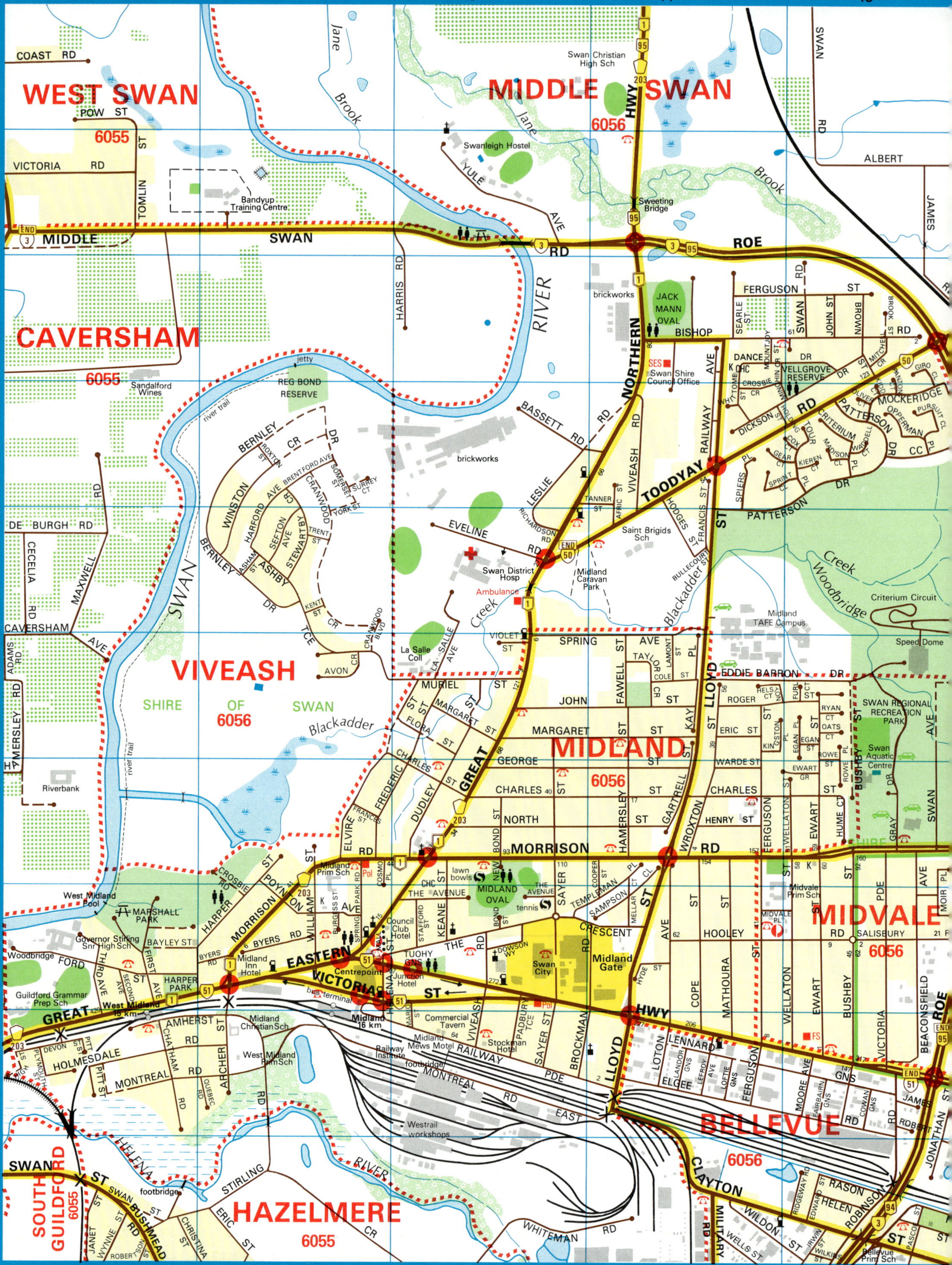

0 500 m 1 km 2 km
SCALE 1:20 000

PRIMARY RECTANGLE
PERTH BG 34

Map 51

Map 52

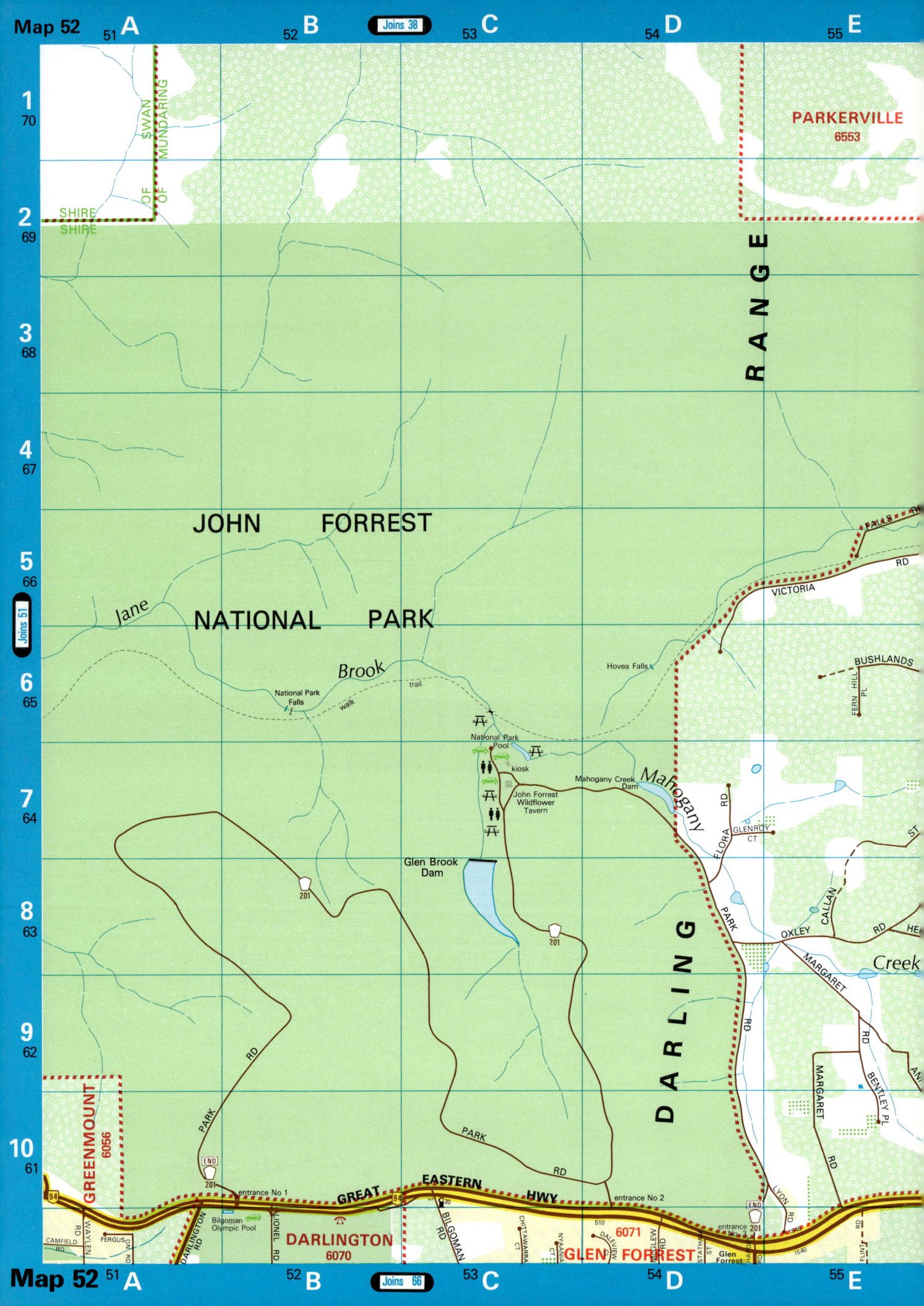

JOHN FORREST NATIONAL PARK

PARKERVILLE 6553

DARLING RANGE

Jane Brook
National Park Falls
walk trail
Hovea Falls
National Park Pool
kiosk
Mahogany Creek Dam
John Forrest Wildflower Tavern
Glen Brook Dam
Mahogany Creek

GREENMOUNT 6056
DARLINGTON 6070
GLEN FORREST 6071

GREAT EASTERN HWY
entrance No 1
entrance No 2
Bilgoman Olympic Pool

FERN HILL BUSHLANDS
FLORA RD
GLENROY CT
OXLEY
CALLAN RD
MARGARET RD
BENTLEY PL
LYON RD
FLINT RD

CAMFIELD RD
WAYLEN RD
FERGUSO
DARLINGTON RD
LIONEL RD
BILGOMAN RD
CHITTAWARRA CT
NYAANA
DALEVIEW
MCLEW
STATHAM ST
Glen Forrest
HAY

PARK RD
Joins 38
Joins 51
Joins 66

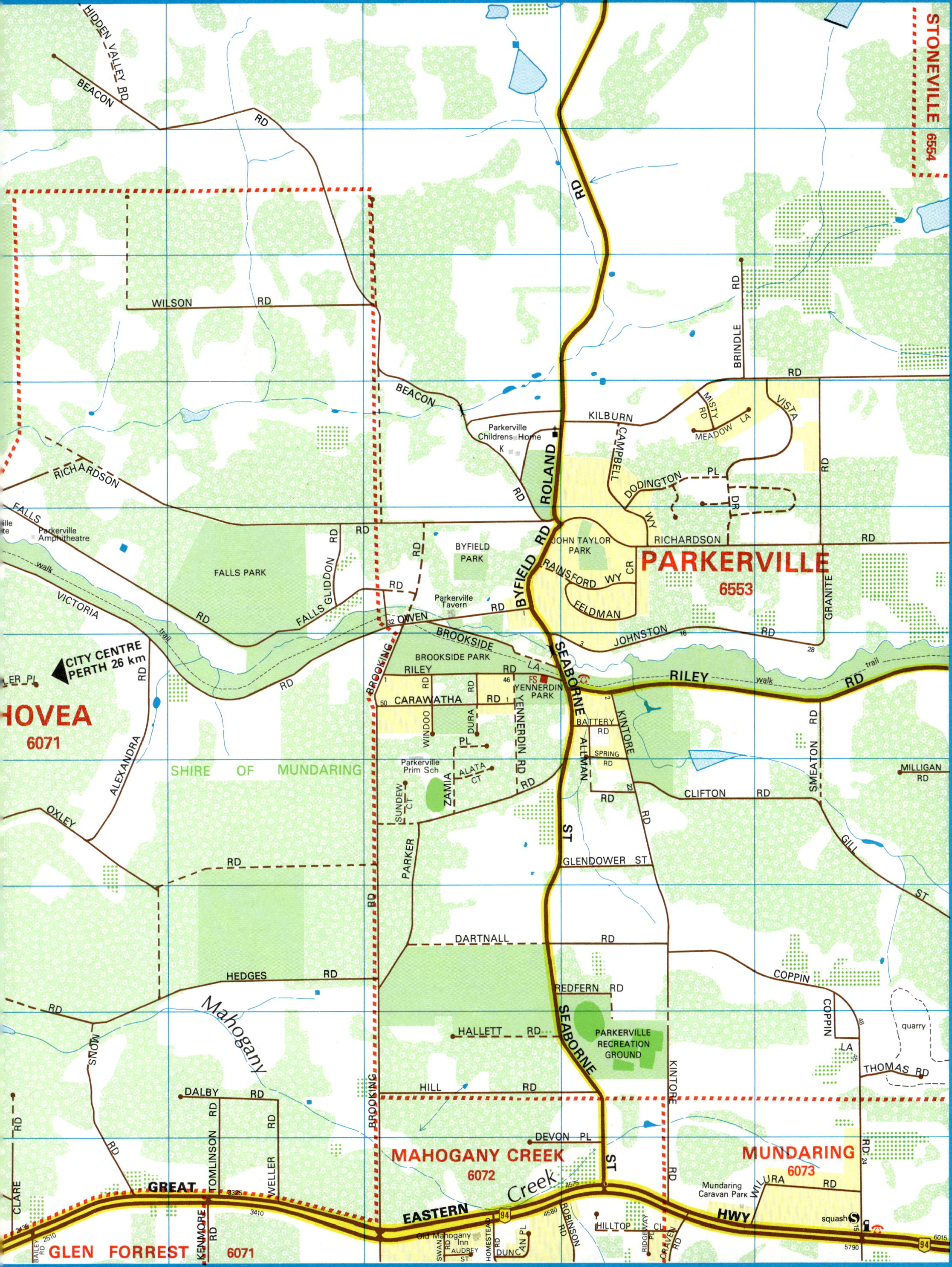

POLICE STATION Pol
HOSPITAL
POST OFFICE
PUBLIC TELEPHONE
TRAFFIC FLOW
TRAFFIC LIGHTS

FOR COMPREHENSIVE LEGEND, SEE PAGE 3

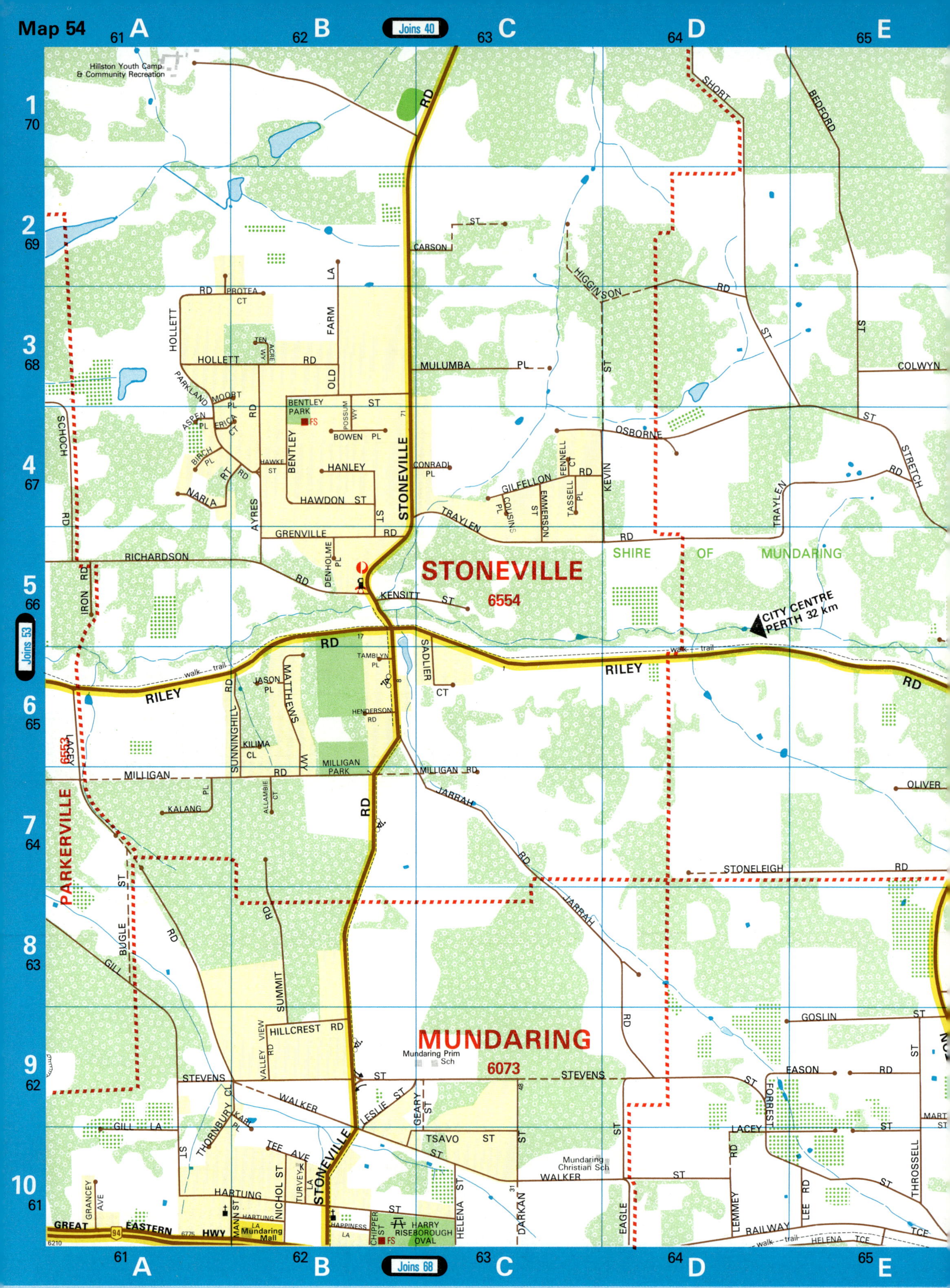

0 500 m 1 km 2 km
SCALE 1:20 000

PRIMARY RECTANGLE
PERTH BG 34

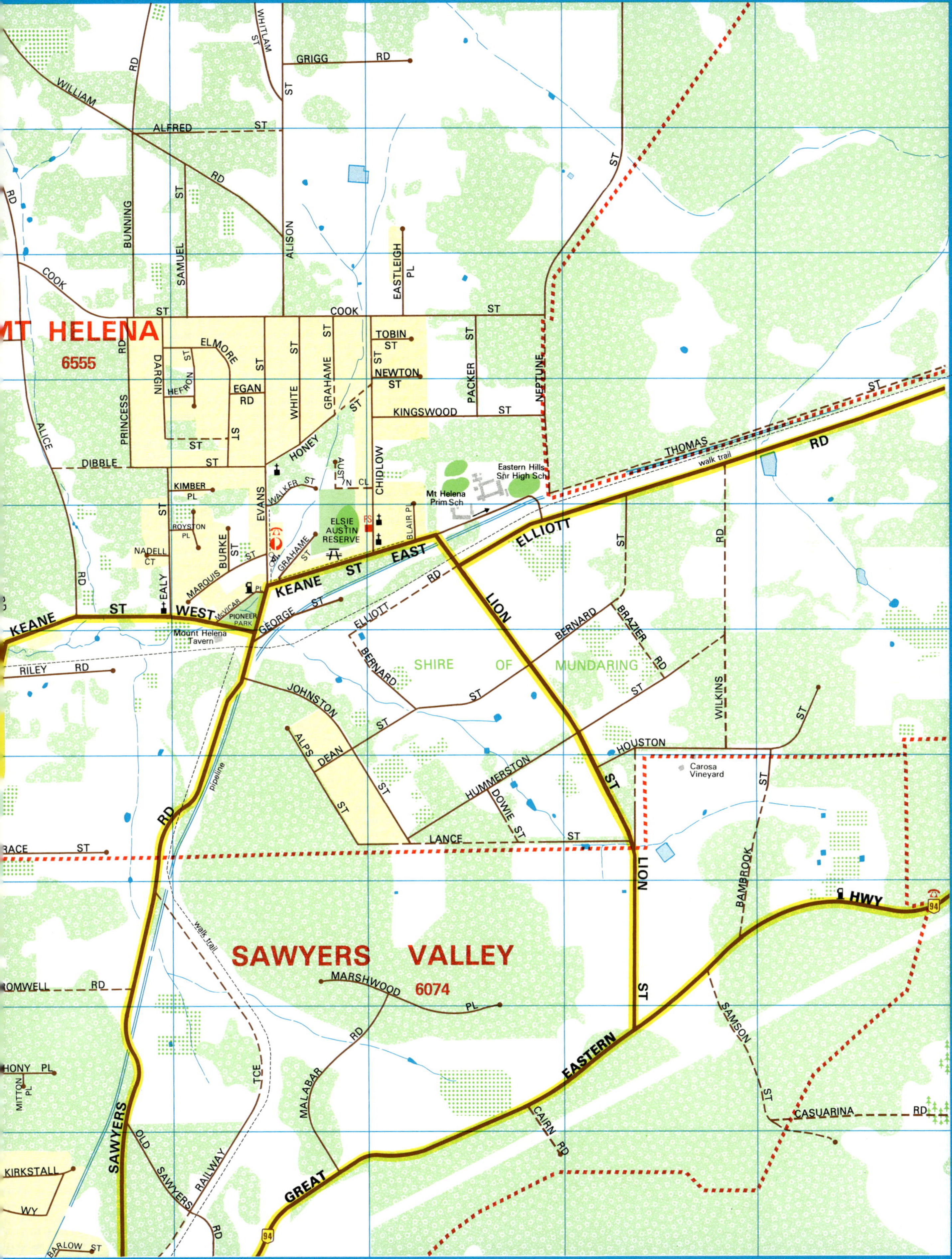

POLICE STATION — Pol
HOSPITAL
POST OFFICE
PUBLIC TELEPHONE
TRAFFIC FLOW
TRAFFIC LIGHTS

FOR COMPREHENSIVE LEGEND, SEE PAGE 3

71 A 72 B Joins 42 73 C 74 D 75 E

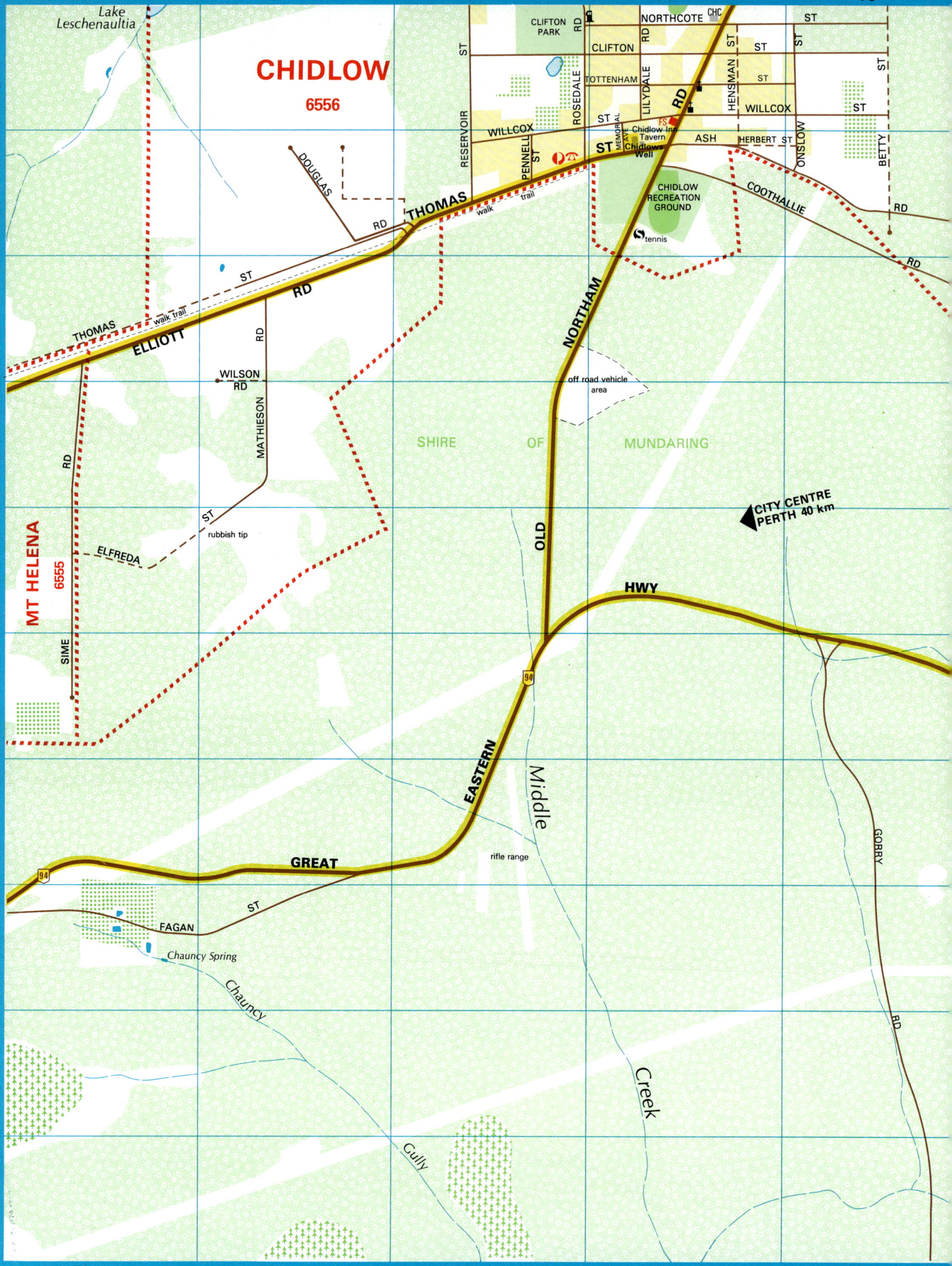

Joins 55

1 70
2 69
3 68
4 67
5 66
6 65
7 64
8 63
9 62
10 61

71 A 72 B Limit of Maps 73 C 74 D 75 E

0 500 m 1 km 2 km

SCALE 1:20 000

PRIMARY RECTANGLE
PERTH BG 34

Map 57

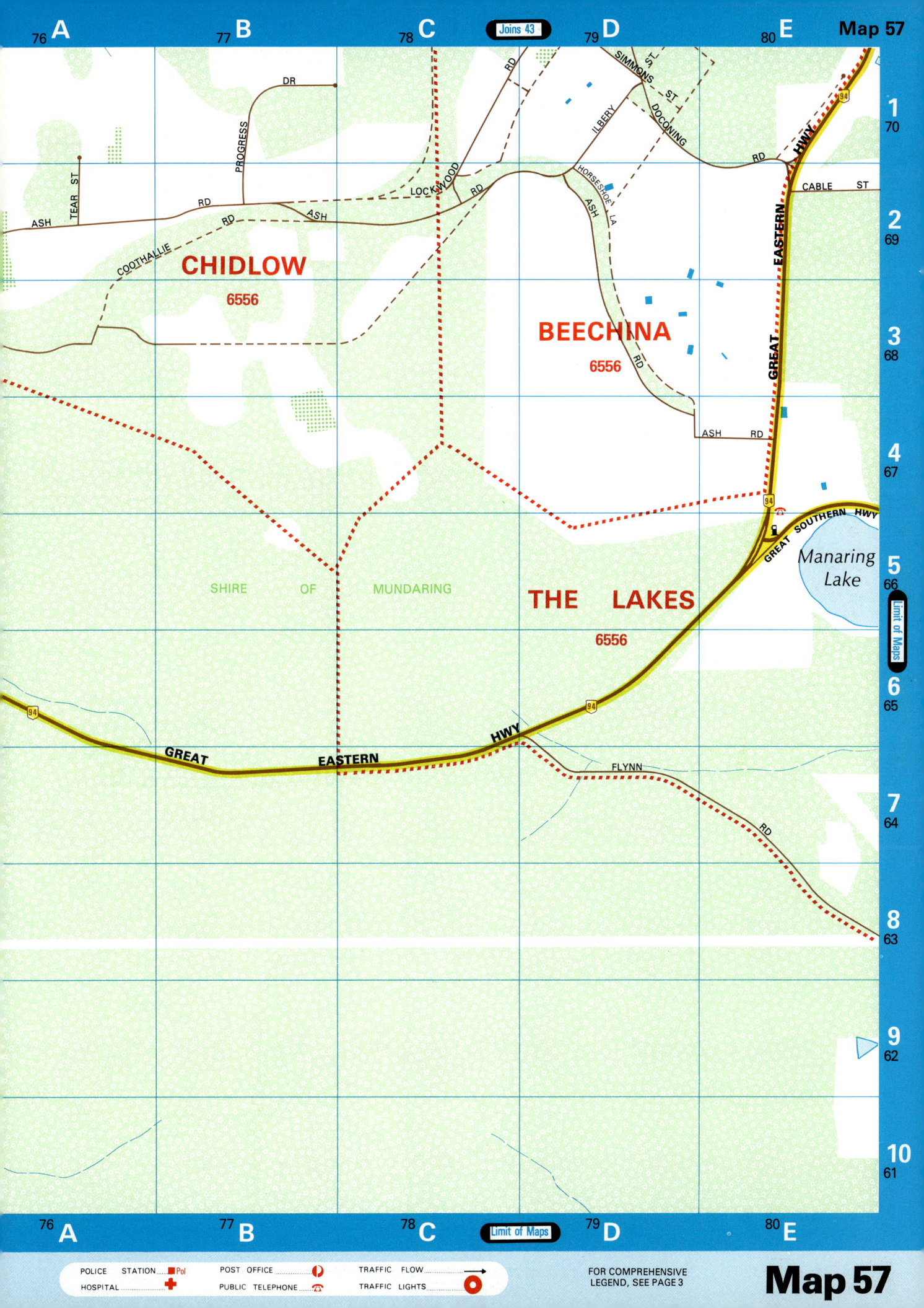

CHIDLOW 6556

BEECHINA 6556

THE LAKES 6556

SHIRE OF MUNDARING

Manaring Lake

Great Eastern Hwy
Great Southern Hwy

Joins 44

Joins 70

SCALE 1:20 000 (0 – 500 m – 1 km – 2 km)

PRIMARY RECTANGLE
PERTH BG 34

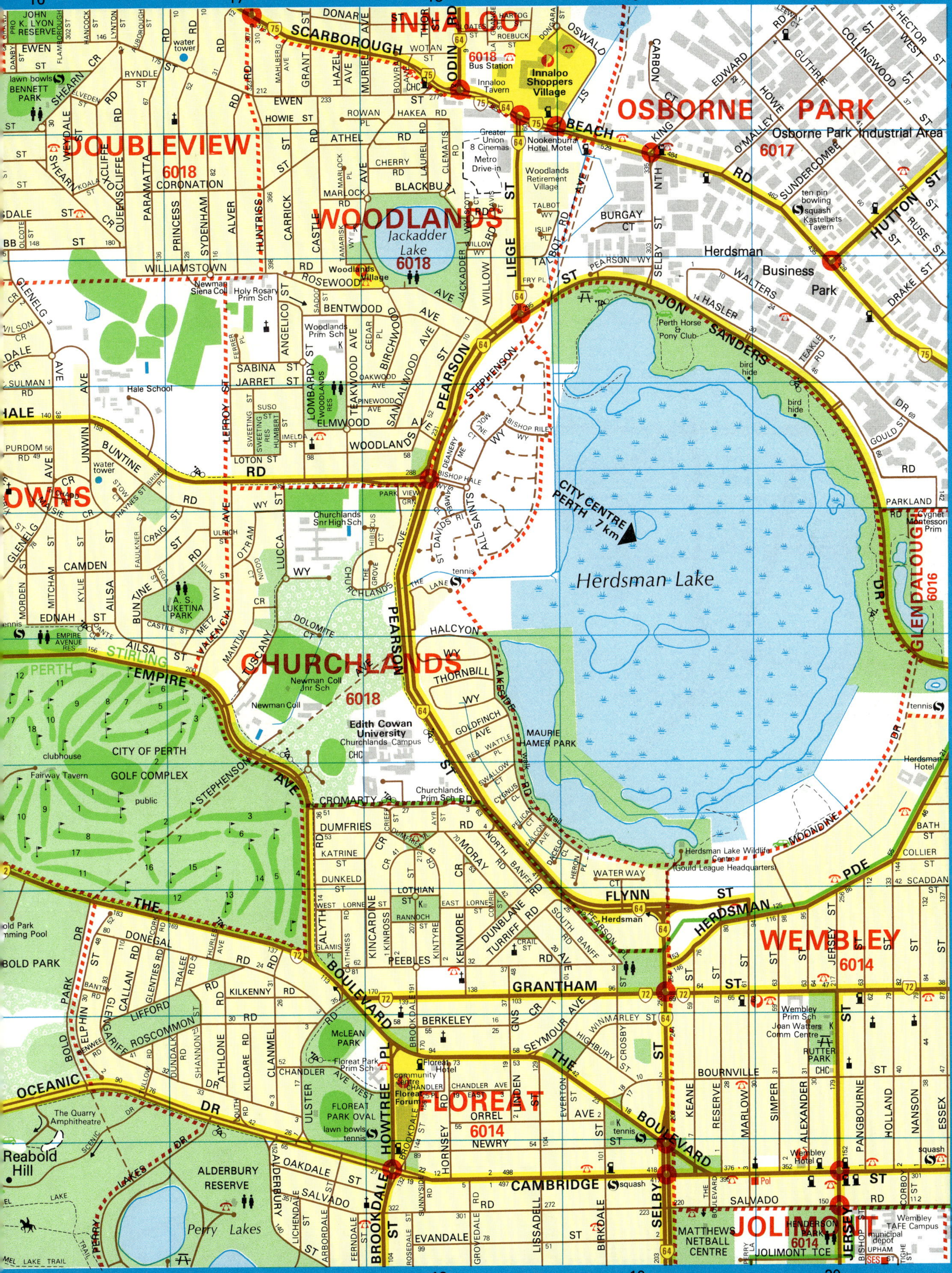

1 60
2 59
3 58
4 57
5 56
6 55
7 54
8 53
9 52
10 51

Joins 60

POLICE STATION Pol — POST OFFICE — TRAFFIC FLOW
HOSPITAL — PUBLIC TELEPHONE — TRAFFIC LIGHTS

FOR COMPREHENSIVE LEGEND, SEE PAGE 3

21 A 22 B Joins 46 23 C 24 D 25 E

21 A 22 B Joins 72 23 C 24 D 25 E

0 500 m 1 km 2 km

SCALE 1:20 000

PRIMARY RECTANGLE
PERTH BG 34

Joins 47

A 26	B 27	C 28	D 29	E 30	

Joins 62

Joins 73

POLICE STATION Pol · HOSPITAL · POST OFFICE · PUBLIC TELEPHONE · TRAFFIC FLOW · TRAFFIC LIGHTS

FOR COMPREHENSIVE LEGEND, SEE PAGE 3

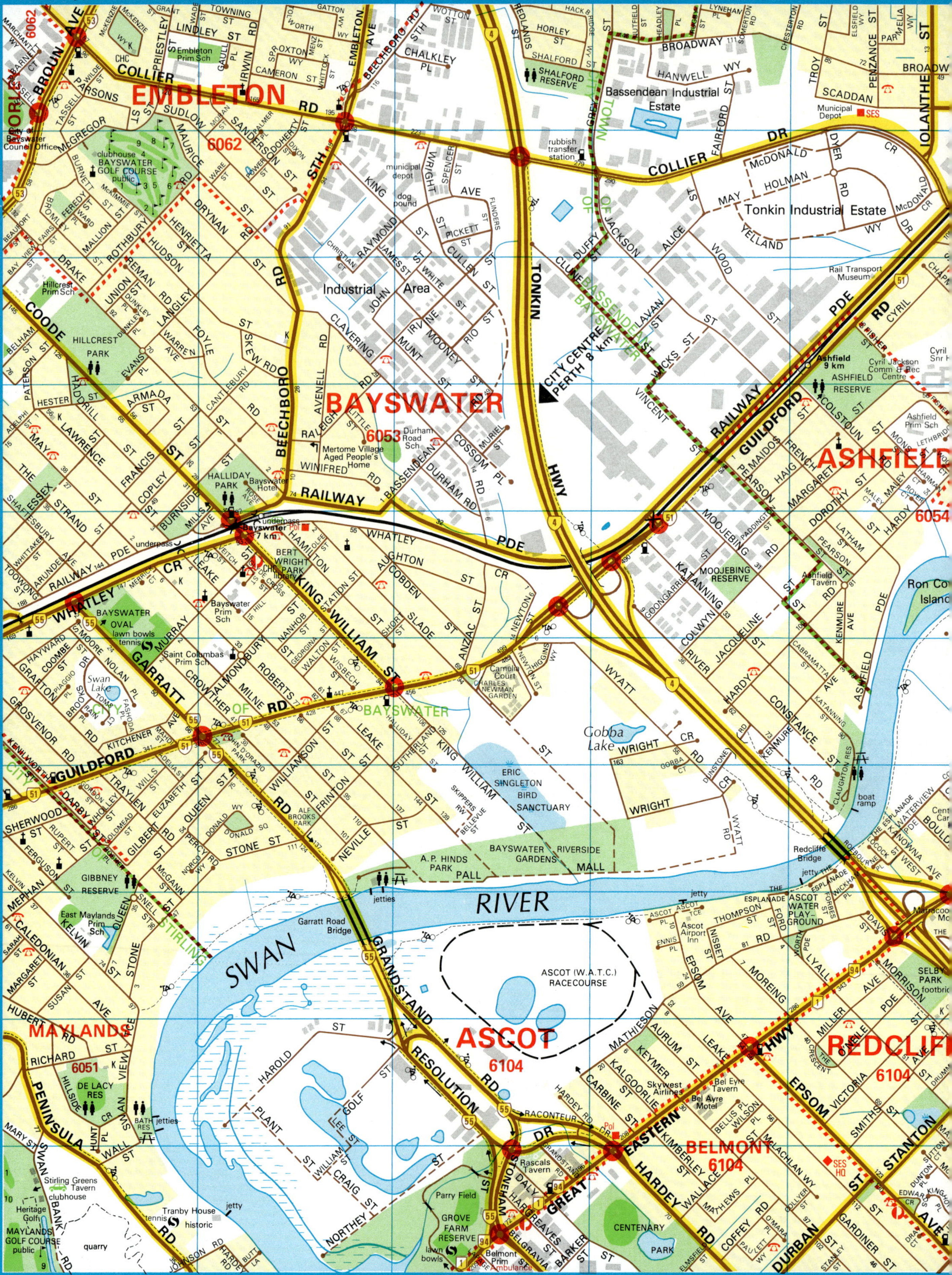

Map 62

0 500 m 1 km 2 km

SCALE 1:20 000

PRIMARY RECTANGLE
PERTH BG 34

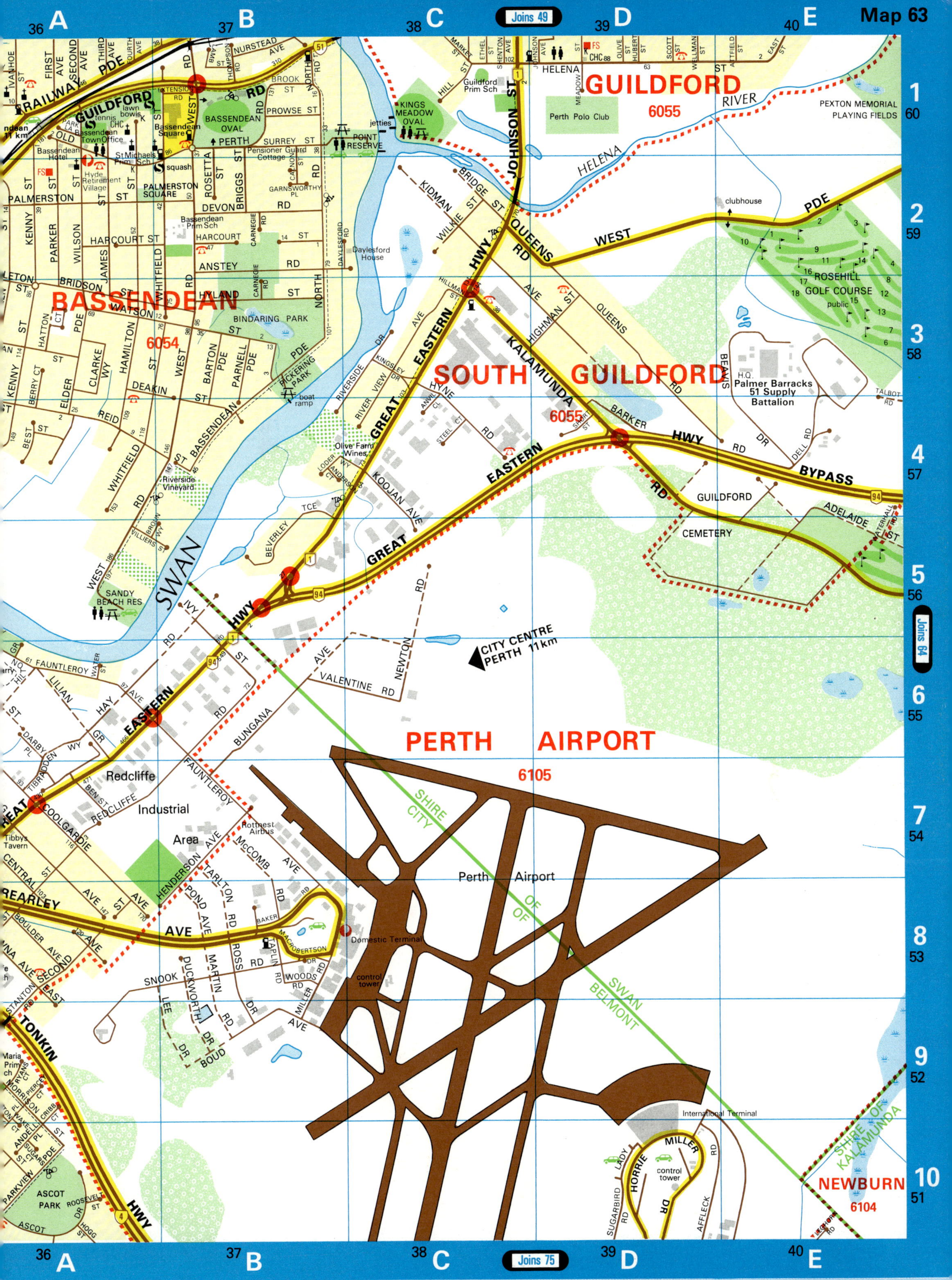
Joins 49
Joins 64
Joins 75
GUILDFORD
6055
BASSENDEAN
6054
SOUTH GUILDFORD
6055
PERTH AIRPORT
6105
NEWBURN
6104
Redcliffe
Industrial
Area
SWAN
RIVER
HELENA
GREAT EASTERN HWY
GREAT EASTERN HWY BYPASS
JOHNSON ST
WEST PDE
QUEENS RD
KALAMUNDA RD
TONKIN HWY
FAUNTLEROY AVE
VALENTINE RD
NEWTON RD
BUNGANA AVE
BELMONT AVE
SECOND AVE
BRIDGE ST
KIDMAN AVE
RIVERSIDE DR
RIVER VIEW AVE
HYNE RD
KOOJAN AVE
BARKER RD
BEAVIS RD
HIGHMAN ST
ADELAIDE ST
GUILDFORD
CEMETERY
Perth Polo Club
KINGS MEADOW OVAL
POINT RESERVE
jetties
PEXTON MEMORIAL PLAYING FIELDS
clubhouse
ROSEHILL GOLF COURSE
public
H.Q. Palmer Barracks
51 Supply Battalion
Daylesford House
Olive Farm Wines
Riverside Vineyard
SANDY BEACH RES
BASSENDEAN OVAL
BINDARING PARK
PICKERING PARK
boat ramp
Bassendean Square
Bassendean Town Office
Bassendean Hotel
Hyde Retirement Village
St Michaels Prim Sch
Bassendean Prim Sch
Guildford Prim Sch
Pensioner Guard Cottage
PALMERSTON SQUARE
CITY CENTRE PERTH 11km
SHIRE OF SWAN
CITY OF BELMONT
SHIRE OF KALAMUNDA
Perth Airport
Domestic Terminal
International Terminal
control tower
Rottnest Airbus
Tibbys Tavern
ASCOT PARK
Maria Prim Sch

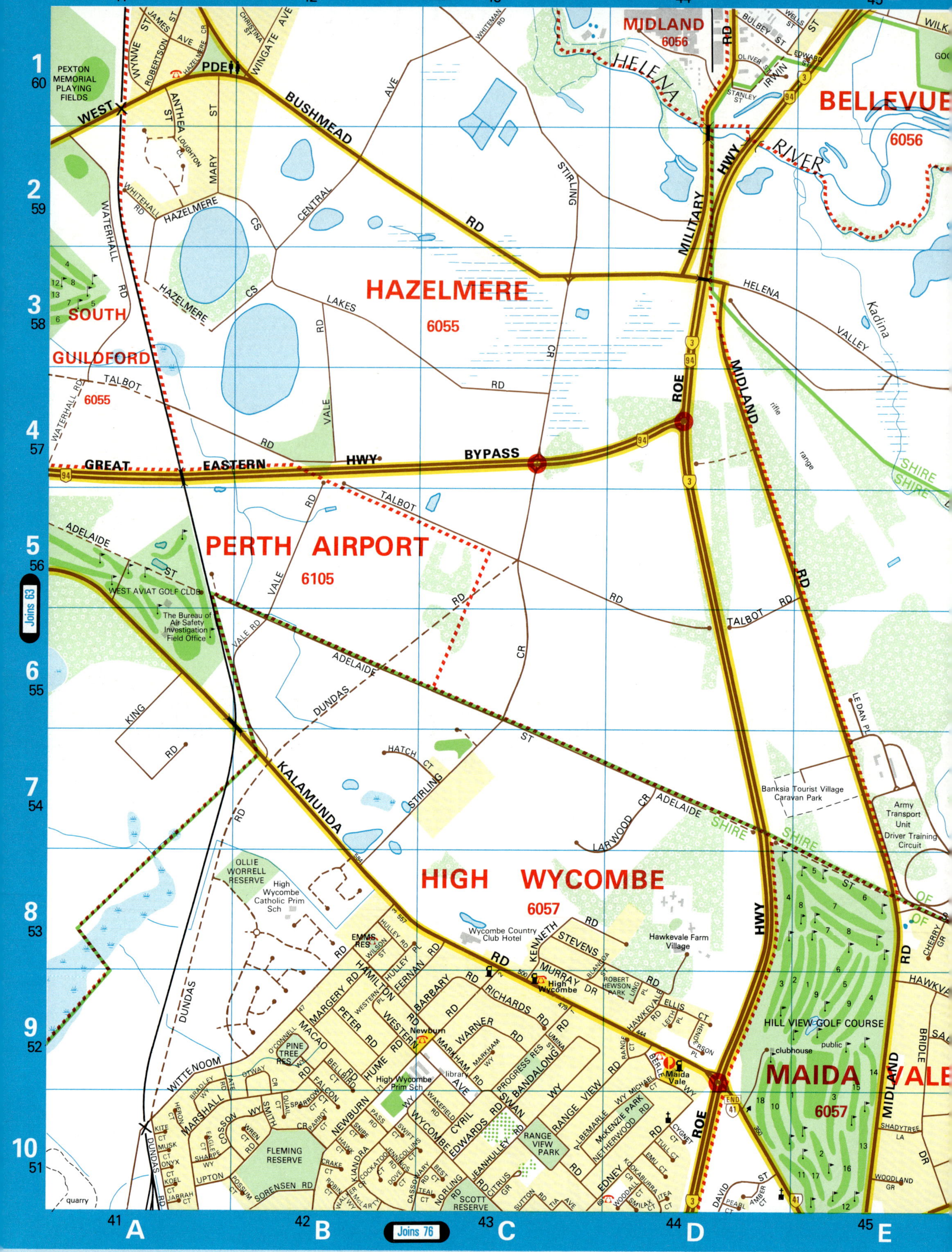

0 500 m 1 km 2 km

SCALE 1:20 000

PRIMARY RECTANGLE
PERTH BG 34

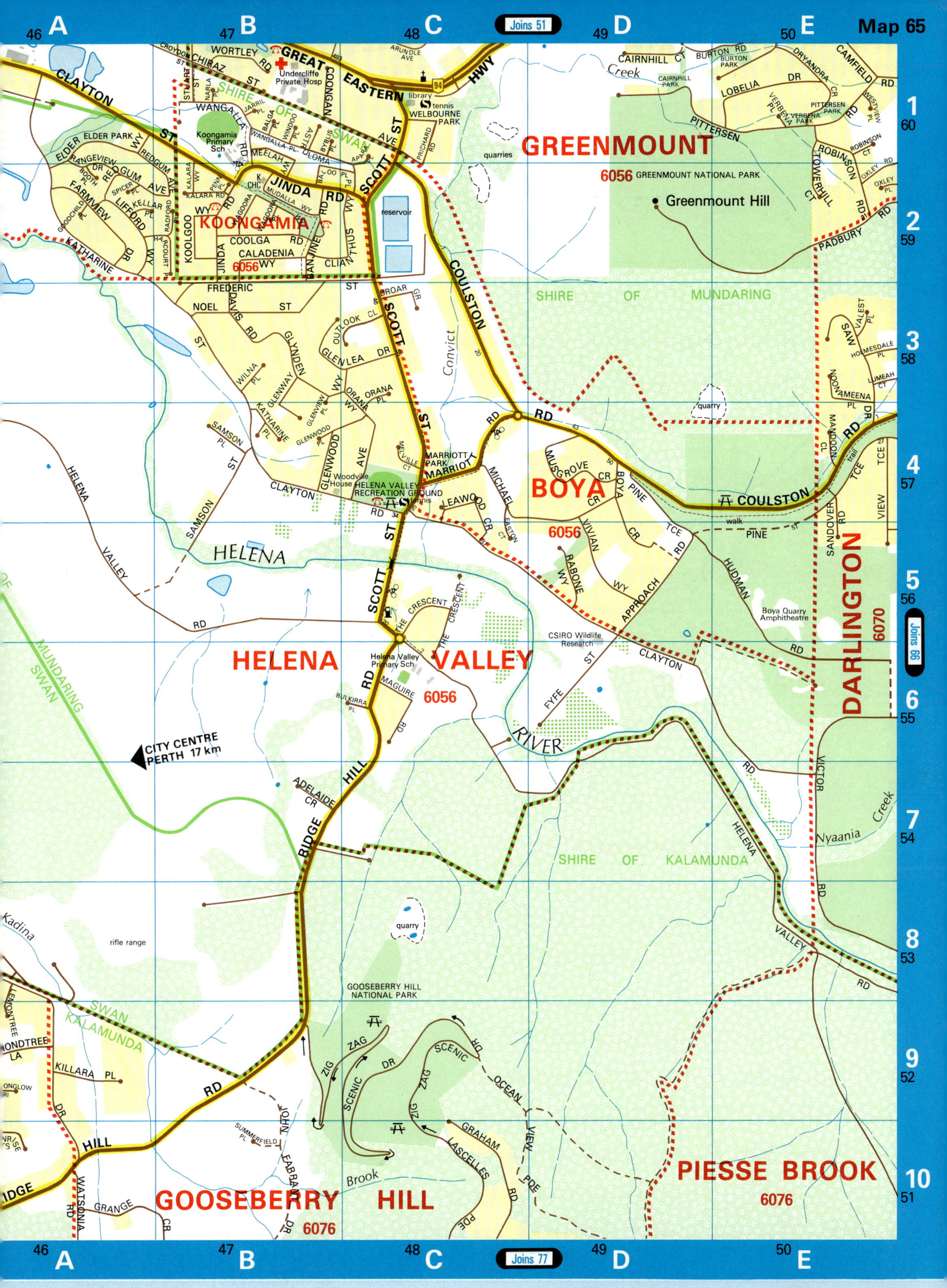
Joins 51
GREENMOUNT
6056
GREENMOUNT NATIONAL PARK
Greenmount Hill
KOONGAMIA
6056
SHIRE OF SWAN
SHIRE OF MUNDARING
GREAT EASTERN HWY
94
Undercliffe Private Hosp
library
tennis
WELBOURNE PARK
Koongamia Primary Sch
quarries
reservoir
CLAYTON ST
ELDER PARK
KATHARINE DR
JINDA RD
SCOTT ST
COULSTON RD
Convict
FREDERIC ST
NOEL ST
MARRIOTT PARK
MARRIOTT
Woodville House
HELENA VALLEY RECREATION GROUND
tennis
BOYA
6056
COULSTON RD
PINE TCE
APPROACH RD
HUDMAN RD
Boya Quarry Amphitheatre
walk
quarry
DARLINGTON
6070
Joins 66
HELENA
VALLEY
6056
HELENA VALLEY RD
HELENA
Helena Valley Primary Sch
CSIRO Wildlife Research
CLAYTON RD
FYFE ST
RIVER
MUNDARING
SWAN
CITY CENTRE PERTH 17 km
RIDGE HILL RD
ADELAIDE CR
SHIRE OF KALAMUNDA
HELENA VALLEY RD
Nyaania Creek
VICTOR RD
Kadina
rifle range
quarry
GOOSEBERRY HILL NATIONAL PARK
SWAN
KALAMUNDA
ZIG ZAG SCENIC DR
OCEAN VIEW PDE
GRAHAM RD
LASCELLES PDE
Brook
HILL RD
KILLARA PL
WATSONIA RD
GRANGE CR
JOHN FARRANT DR
SUMMERFIELD PL
GOOSEBERRY HILL
6076
PIESSE BROOK
6076
Joins 77

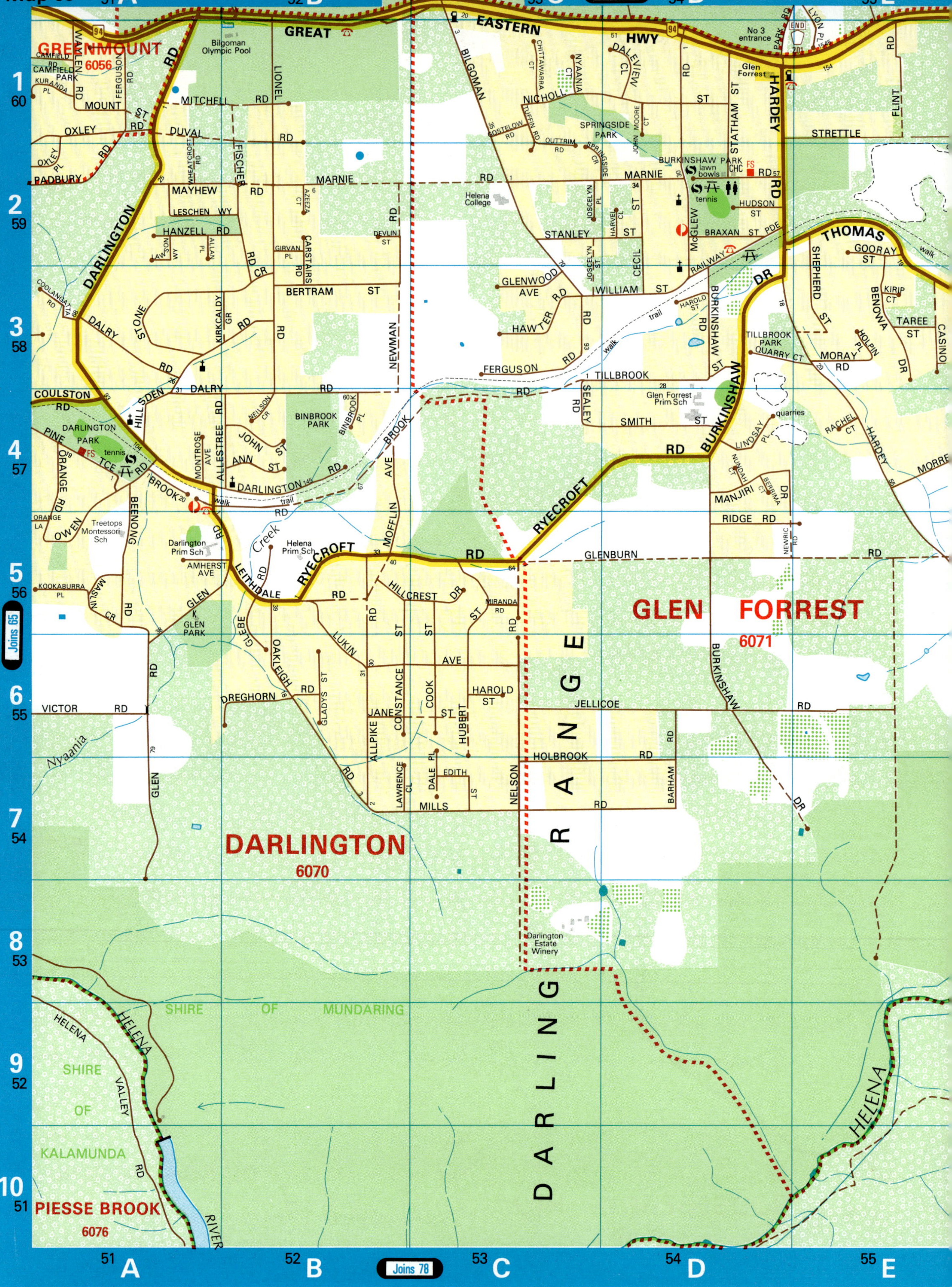

0 500 m 1 km 2 km

SCALE 1:20 000

PRIMARY RECTANGLE
PERTH BG 34

Map 67

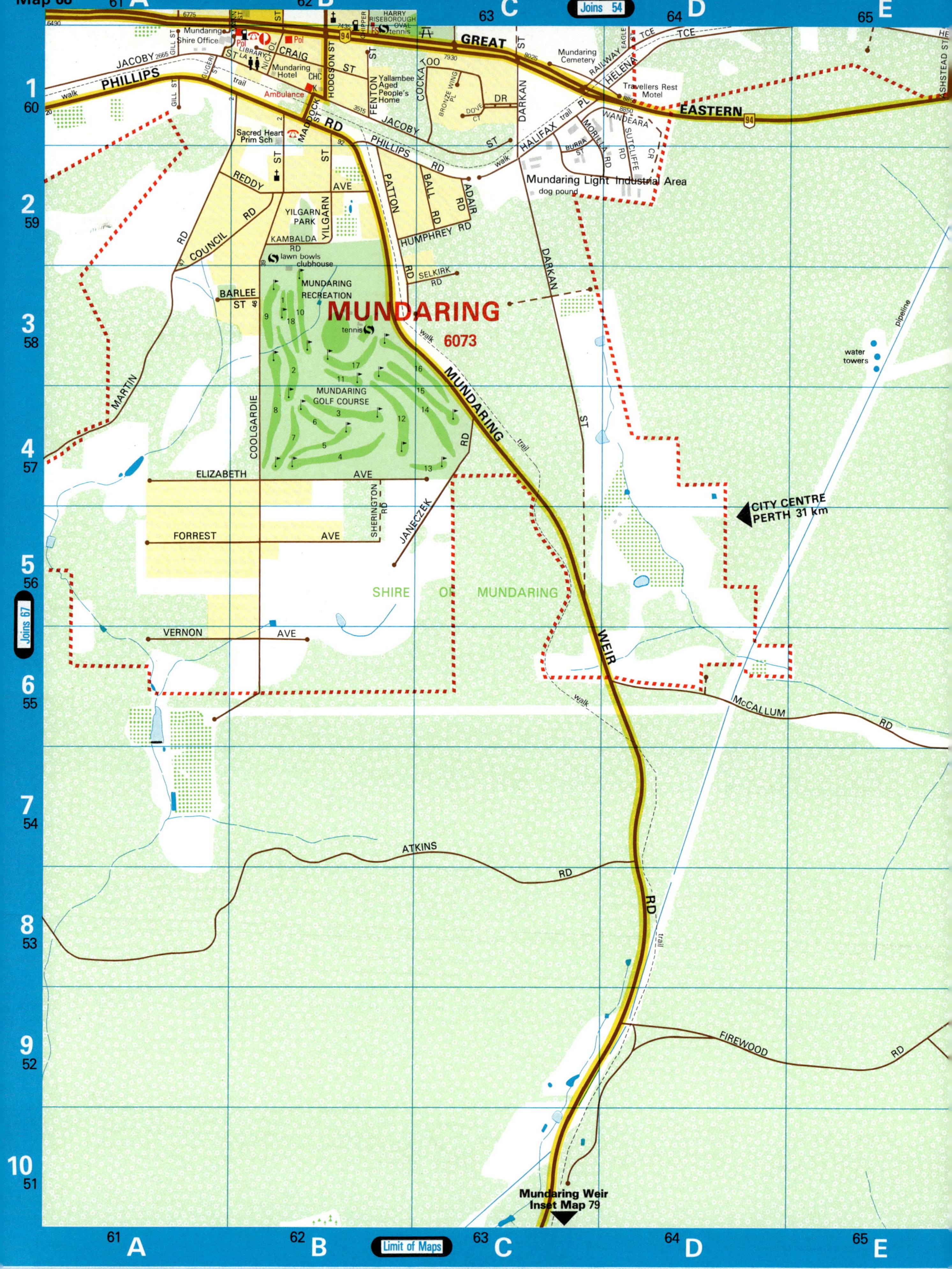

0 500 m 1 km 2 km

SCALE 1:20 000

PRIMARY RECTANGLE
PERTH BG 34

Map 69

SAWYERS VALLEY 6074

SHIRE OF MUNDARING

COLE RD
POISON LEASE RD
FIREWOOD RD
WATSON RD
NORTH RUSHY RD
RUSHY RD

Limit of Maps

POLICE STATION — Pol
HOSPITAL
POST OFFICE
PUBLIC TELEPHONE
TRAFFIC FLOW
TRAFFIC LIGHTS

FOR COMPREHENSIVE LEGEND, SEE PAGE 3

Map 69

Map 70

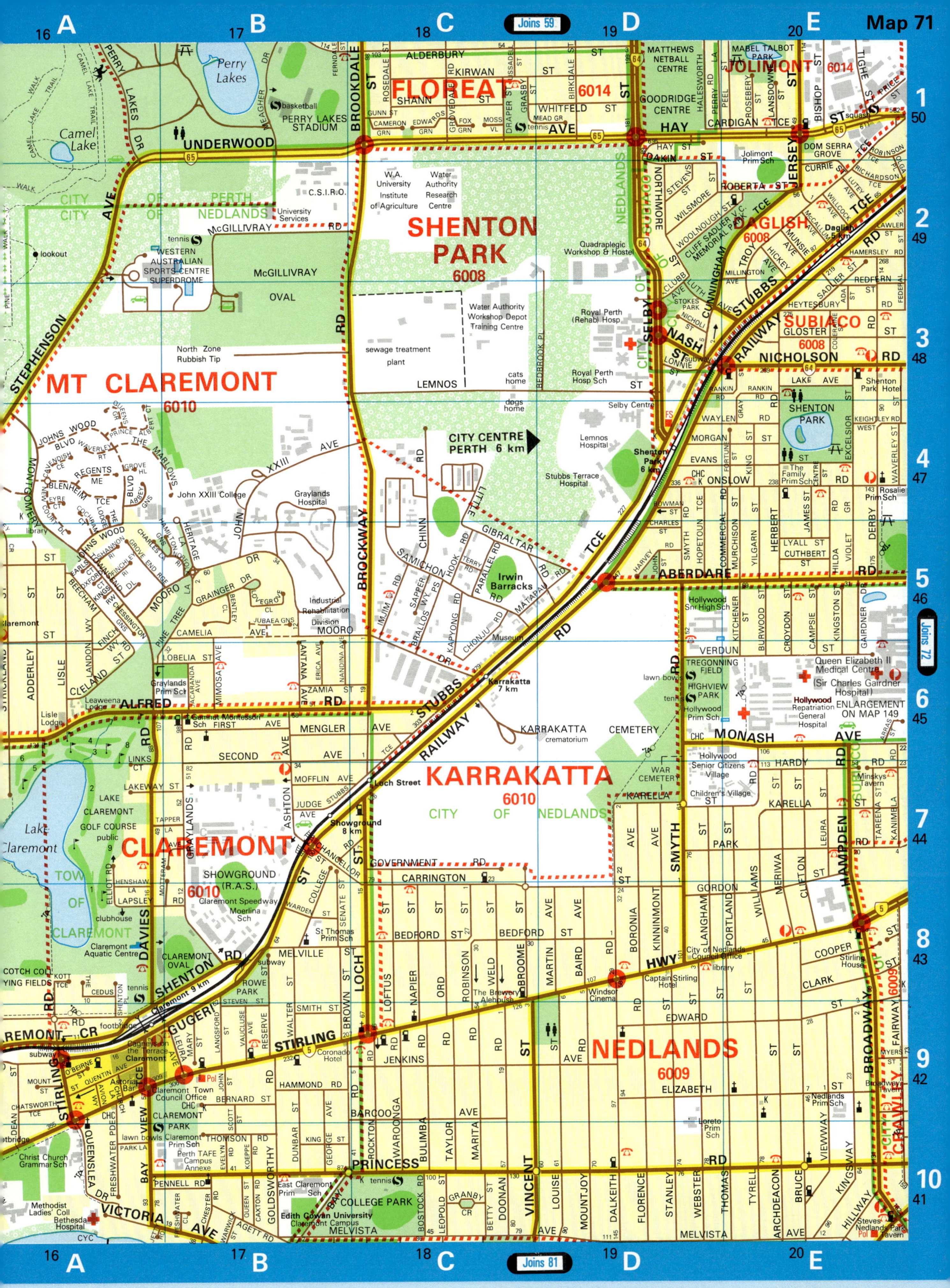
Joins 59
Joins 72
Joins 81
A
B
C
D
E
16
17
18
19
20
1
2
3
4
5
6
7
8
9
10
50
49
48
47
46
45
44
43
42
41
FLOREAT
6014
JOLIMONT
SHENTON PARK
6008
DAGLISH
SUBIACO
MT CLAREMONT
6010
KARRAKATTA
CITY OF NEDLANDS
CLAREMONT
NEDLANDS
6009
CITY OF PERTH
TOWN OF CLAREMONT
Perry Lakes
Camel Lake
Lake Claremont
PERRY LAKES STADIUM
UNDERWOOD AVE
McGILLIVRAY OVAL
WESTERN AUSTRALIAN SPORTS CENTRE SUPERDROME
North Zone Rubbish Tip
C.S.I.R.O.
University Services
W.A. University Institute of Agriculture
Water Authority Research Centre
Water Authority Workshop Depot Training Centre
sewage treatment plant
cats home
dogs home
Quadraplegic Workshop & Hostel
Royal Perth (Rehab) Hosp
Royal Perth Hosp Sch
Selby Centre
Lemnos Hospital
Stubbs Terrace Hospital
CITY CENTRE PERTH 6 km
John XXIII College
Graylands Hospital
Industrial Rehabilitation Division
Irwin Barracks
Museum
Karrakatta 7 km
KARRAKATTA CEMETERY
crematorium
WAR CEMETERY
Queen Elizabeth II Medical Centre (Sir Charles Gairdner Hospital)
ENLARGEMENT ON MAP 149
Hollywood Repatriation General Hospital
Hollywood Snr High Sch
Hollywood Prim Sch
Hollywood Senior Citizens Village
Children's Village
SHENTON PARK
Shenton Park Hotel
The Family Prim Sch
Rosalie Prim Sch
Jolimont Prim Sch
MATTHEWS NETBALL CENTRE
MABEL TALBOT PARK
GOODRIDGE CENTRE
DOM SERRA GROVE
LAKE CLAREMONT GOLF COURSE public
SHOWGROUND (R.A.S.)
Claremont Speedway
Showground 8 km
Loch Street
CLAREMONT OVAL
Claremont Aquatic Centre
Claremont Town Council Office
CLAREMONT PARK
Claremont Prim Sch
Perth TAFE Campus Annexe
Christ Church Grammar Sch
Methodist Ladies' Coll
Bethesda Hospital
COLLEGE PARK
Edith Cowan University Claremont Campus
East Claremont Prim Sch
St Thomas Prim Sch
Coronado Hotel
Captain Stirling Hotel
City of Nedlands Council Office
Windsor Cinema
The Brewery Alehouse
Loreto Prim Sch
Nedlands Prim Sch
Steves Nedlands Park Tavern
Broadway's Tavern
Minskys Tavern
Stirling House
STIRLING HWY
BROCKWAY RD
BROOKDALE ST
SELBY ST
NICHOLSON RD
ABERDARE RD
MONASH AVE
STUBBS TCE
RAILWAY RD
ALFRED RD
PRINCESS RD
VICTORIA AVE
HAMPDEN RD
BROADWAY
CRAWLEY
HAY ST
STEPHENSON AVE
SHENTON RD

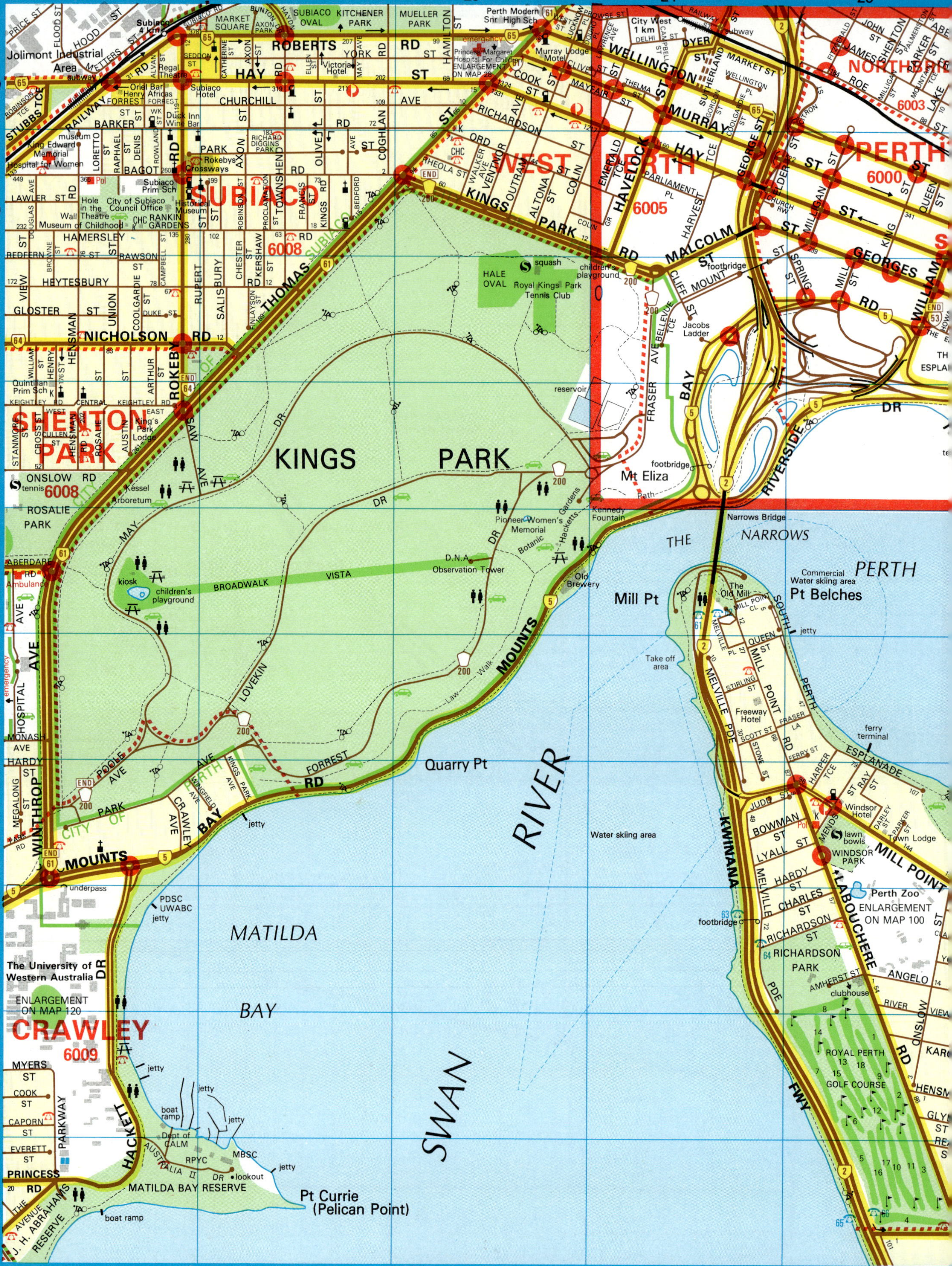

SCALE 1:20 000

0 · 500 m · 1 km · 2 km

PRIMARY RECTANGLE
PERTH BG 34

POLICE STATION — Pol
HOSPITAL
POST OFFICE
PUBLIC TELEPHONE
TRAFFIC FLOW
TRAFFIC LIGHTS

FOR COMPREHENSIVE LEGEND, SEE PAGE 3

Map 74

0 500 m 1 km 2 km

SCALE 1:20 000

PRIMARY RECTANGLE
PERTH BG 34

Joins 63

Joins 76

Joins 85

POLICE STATION Pol	POST OFFICE	TRAFFIC FLOW
HOSPITAL	PUBLIC TELEPHONE	TRAFFIC LIGHTS

FOR COMPREHENSIVE LEGEND, SEE PAGE 3

Joins 64

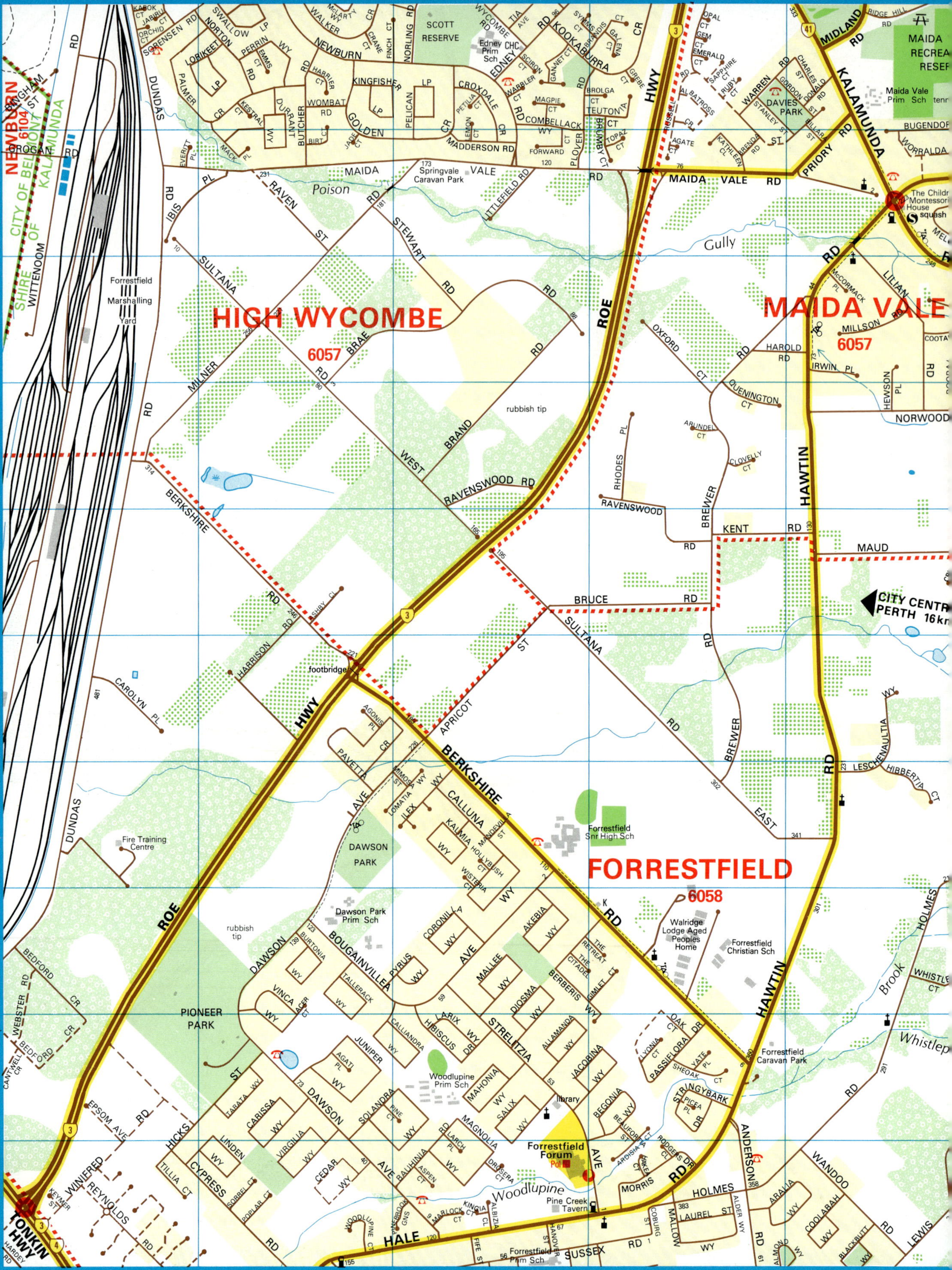

Joins 75

Joins 86

0 500 m 1 km 2 km

SCALE 1:20 000

PRIMARY RECTANGLE
PERTH BG 34

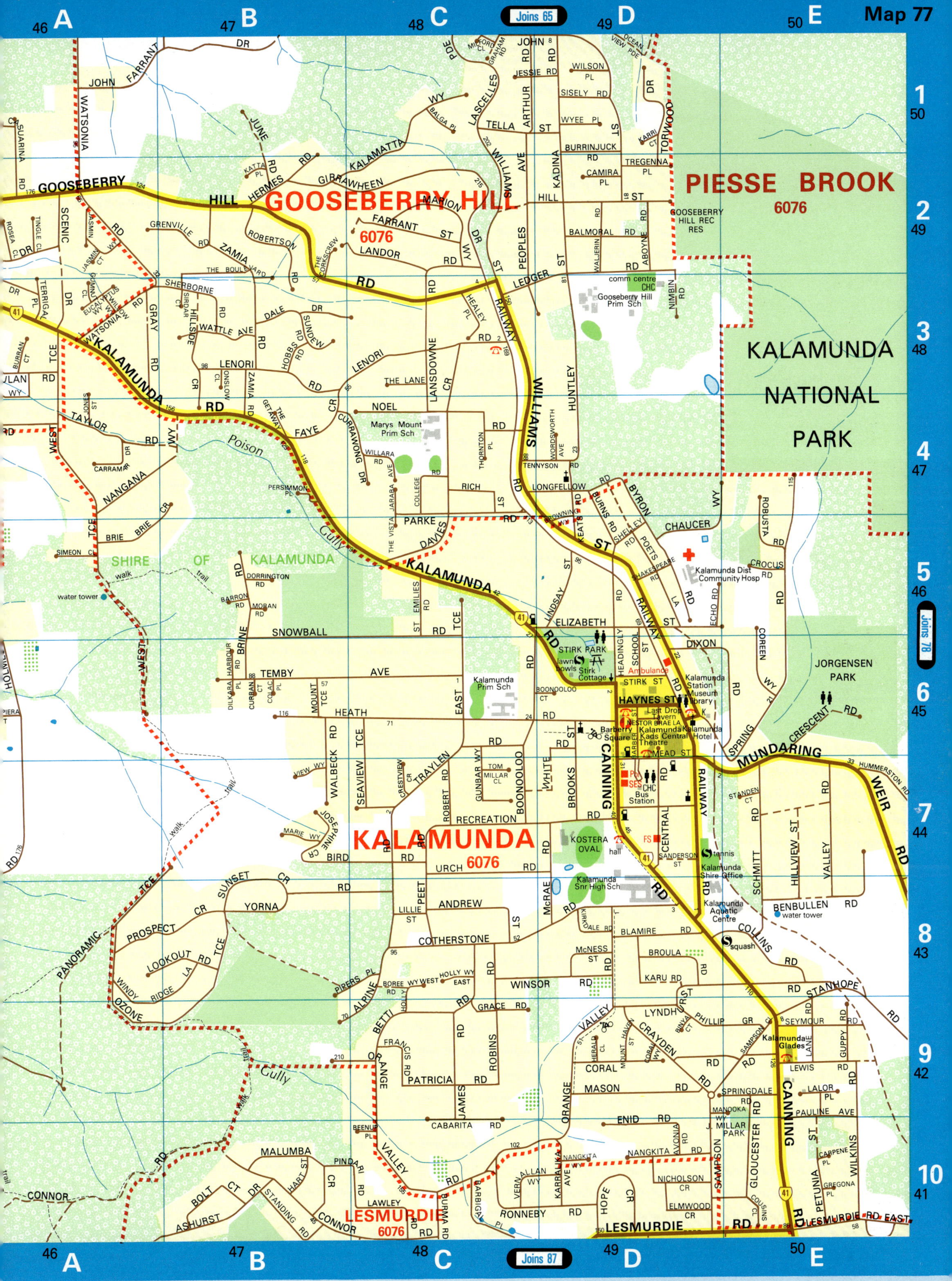

POLICE STATION Pol
HOSPITAL
POST OFFICE
PUBLIC TELEPHONE
TRAFFIC FLOW
TRAFFIC LIGHTS

FOR COMPREHENSIVE LEGEND, SEE PAGE 3

Map 78

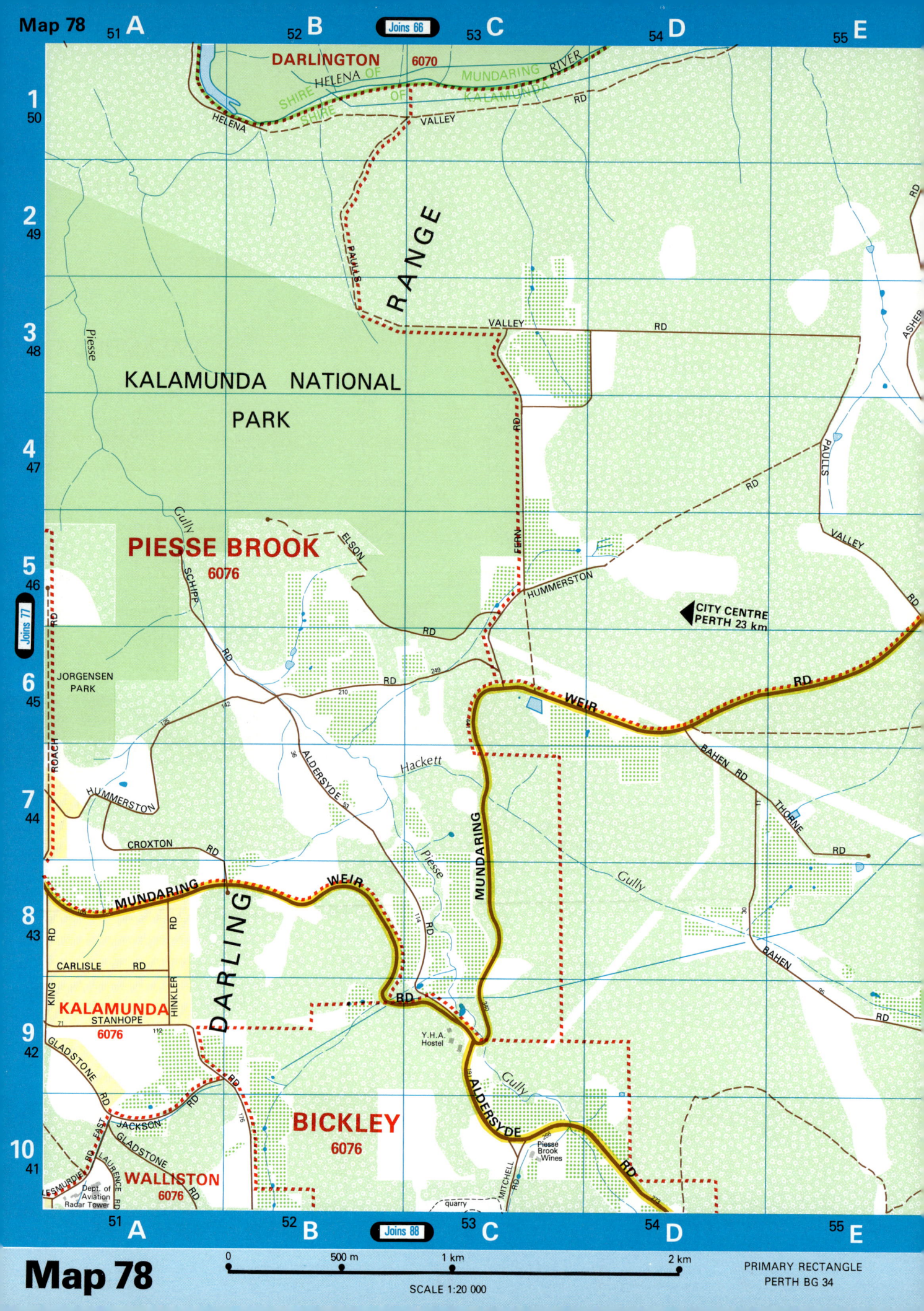

Map 79

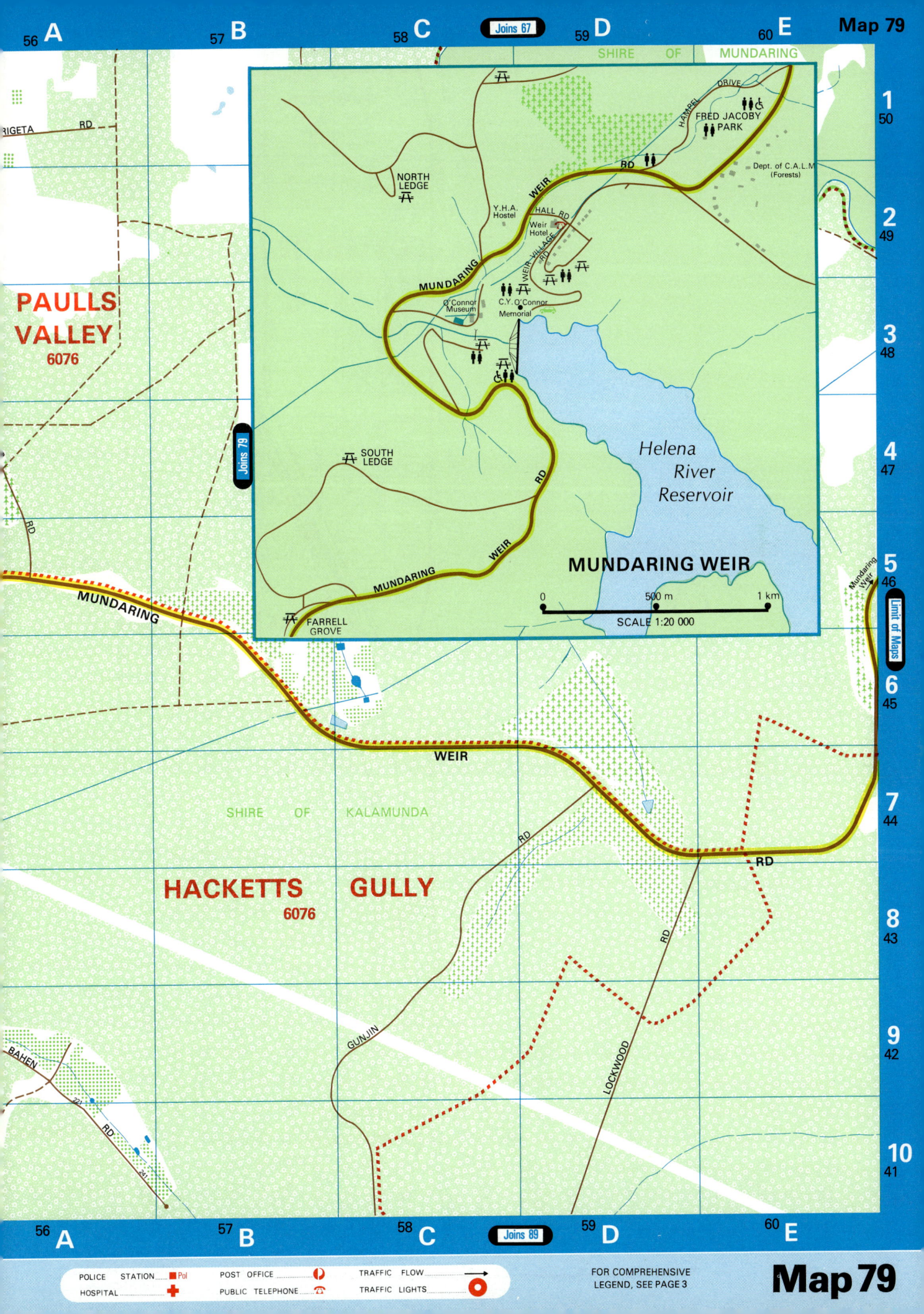

11 A 12 B 13 C 14 D 15 E

1 40
2 39
3 38
4 37
5 36
6 35
7 34
8 33
9 32
10 31

11 A 12 B 13 C 14 D 15 E

0 500 m 1 km 2 km

SCALE 1:20 000

PRIMARY RECTANGLE
PERTH BG 34

Joins 71

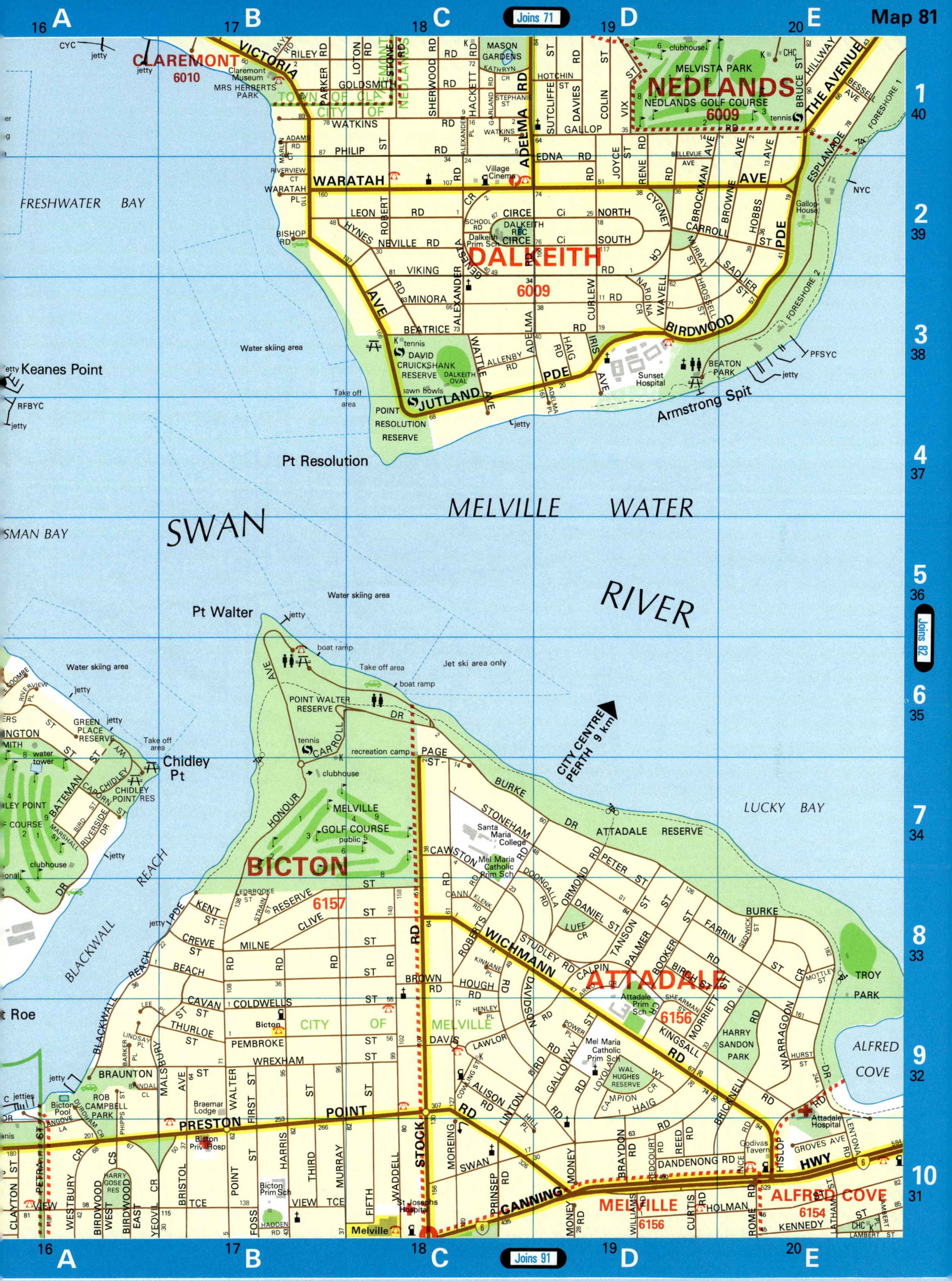

Joins 91

POLICE STATION Pol
HOSPITAL
POST OFFICE
PUBLIC TELEPHONE
TRAFFIC FLOW
TRAFFIC LIGHTS

FOR COMPREHENSIVE LEGEND, SEE PAGE 3

Map 82

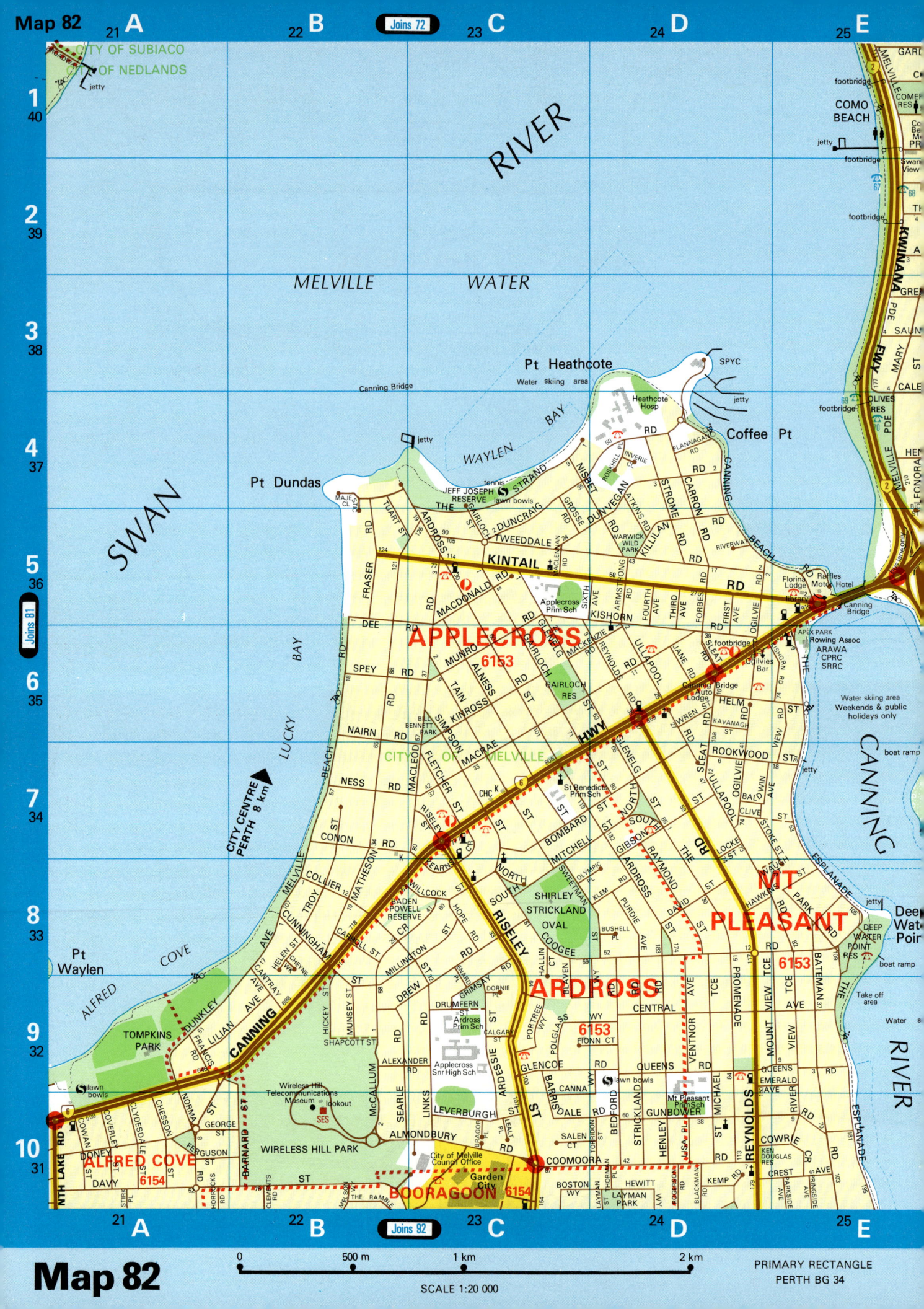

POLICE STATION Pol
HOSPITAL
POST OFFICE
PUBLIC TELEPHONE
TRAFFIC FLOW
TRAFFIC LIGHTS

FOR COMPREHENSIVE LEGEND, SEE PAGE 3

31 A 32 B Joins 74 33 C 34 D 35 E

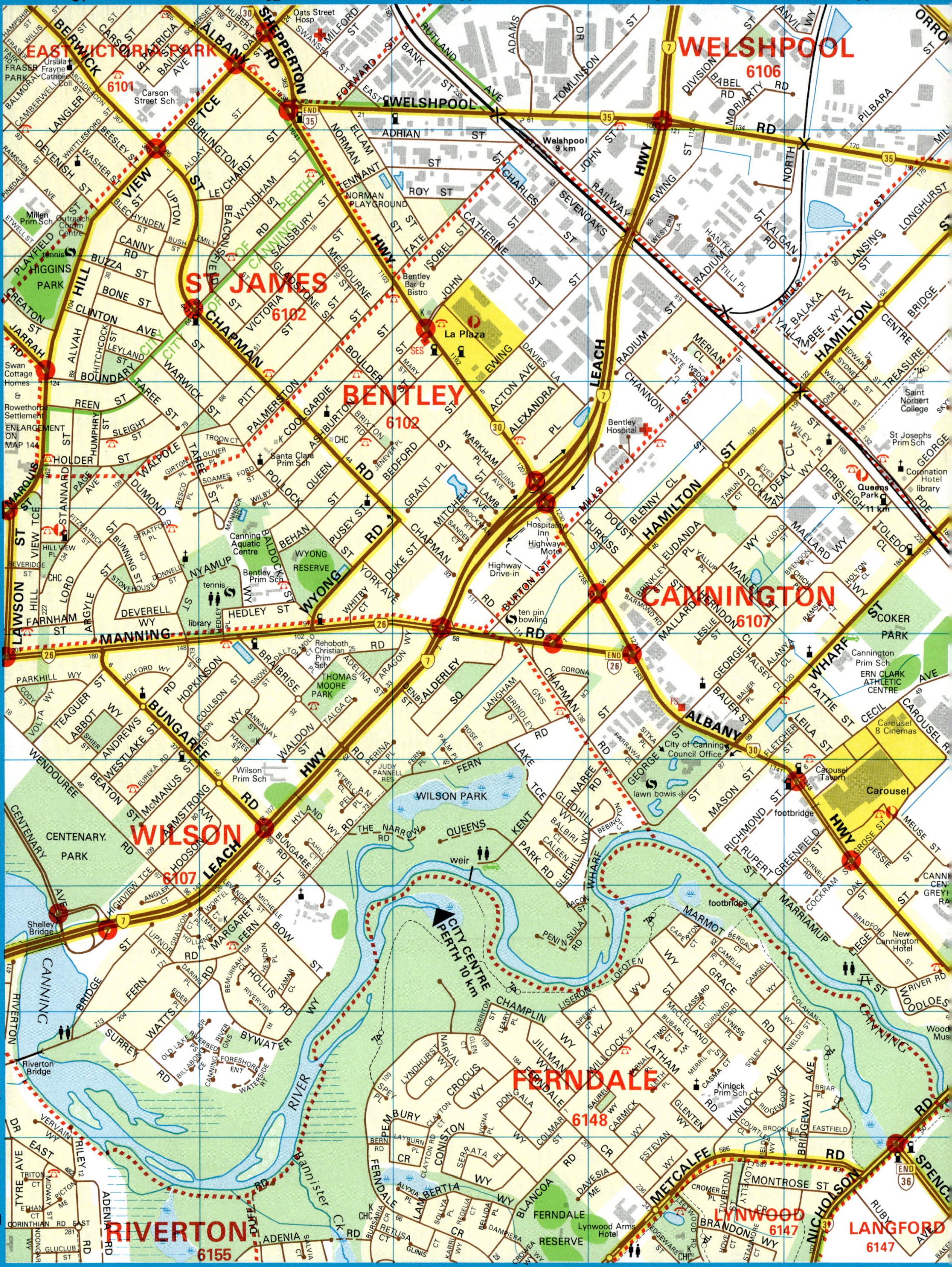

31 A 32 B Joins 94 33 C 34 D 35 E

0 500 m 1 km 2 km

SCALE 1:20 000

PRIMARY RECTANGLE
PERTH BG 34

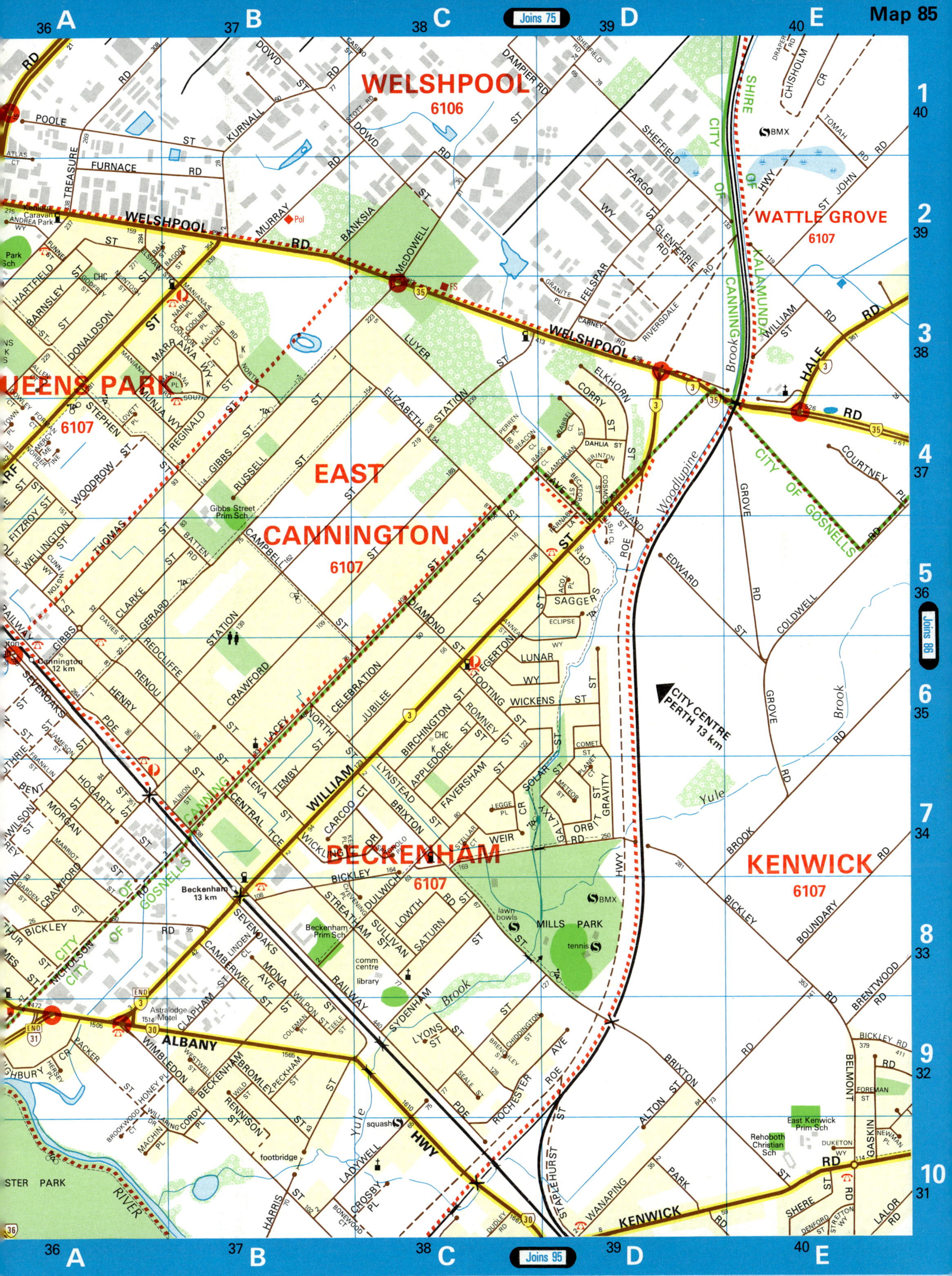

POLICE STATION Pol
HOSPITAL
POST OFFICE
PUBLIC TELEPHONE
TRAFFIC FLOW
TRAFFIC LIGHTS

FOR COMPREHENSIVE LEGEND, SEE PAGE 3

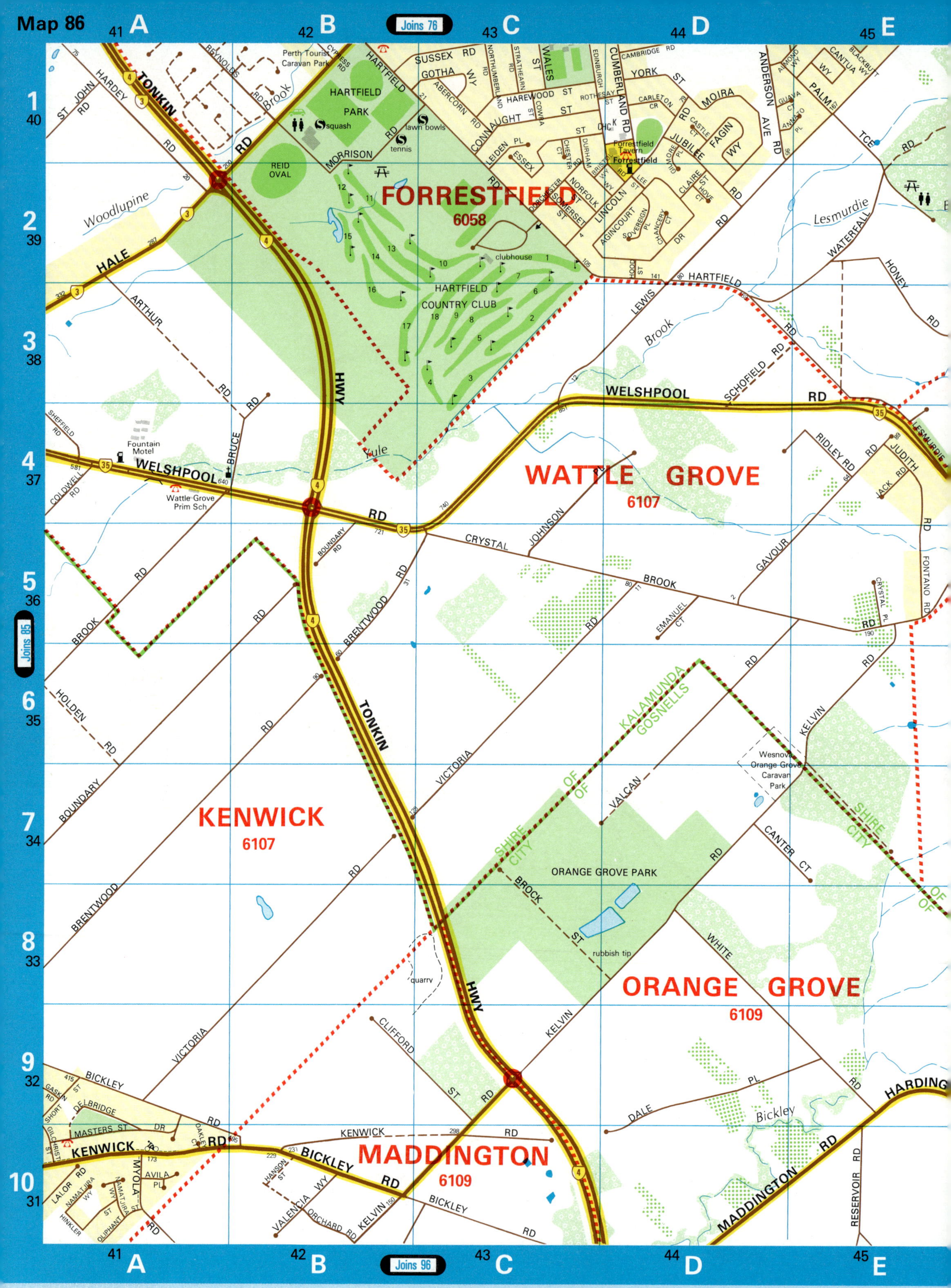

PRIMARY RECTANGLE
PERTH BG 34

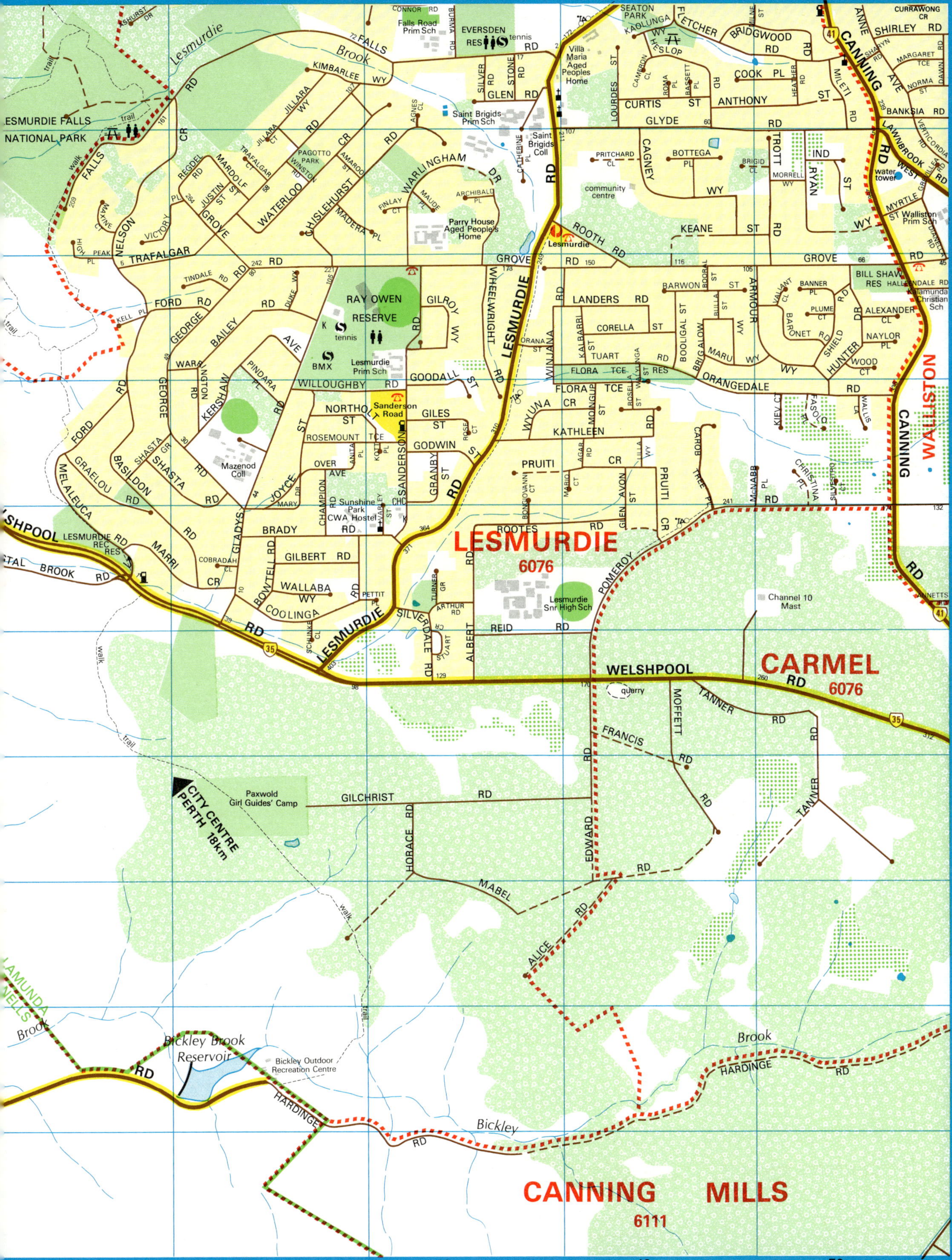

POLICE STATION Pol
HOSPITAL
POST OFFICE
PUBLIC TELEPHONE
TRAFFIC FLOW
TRAFFIC LIGHTS

FOR COMPREHENSIVE LEGEND, SEE PAGE 3

Map 88

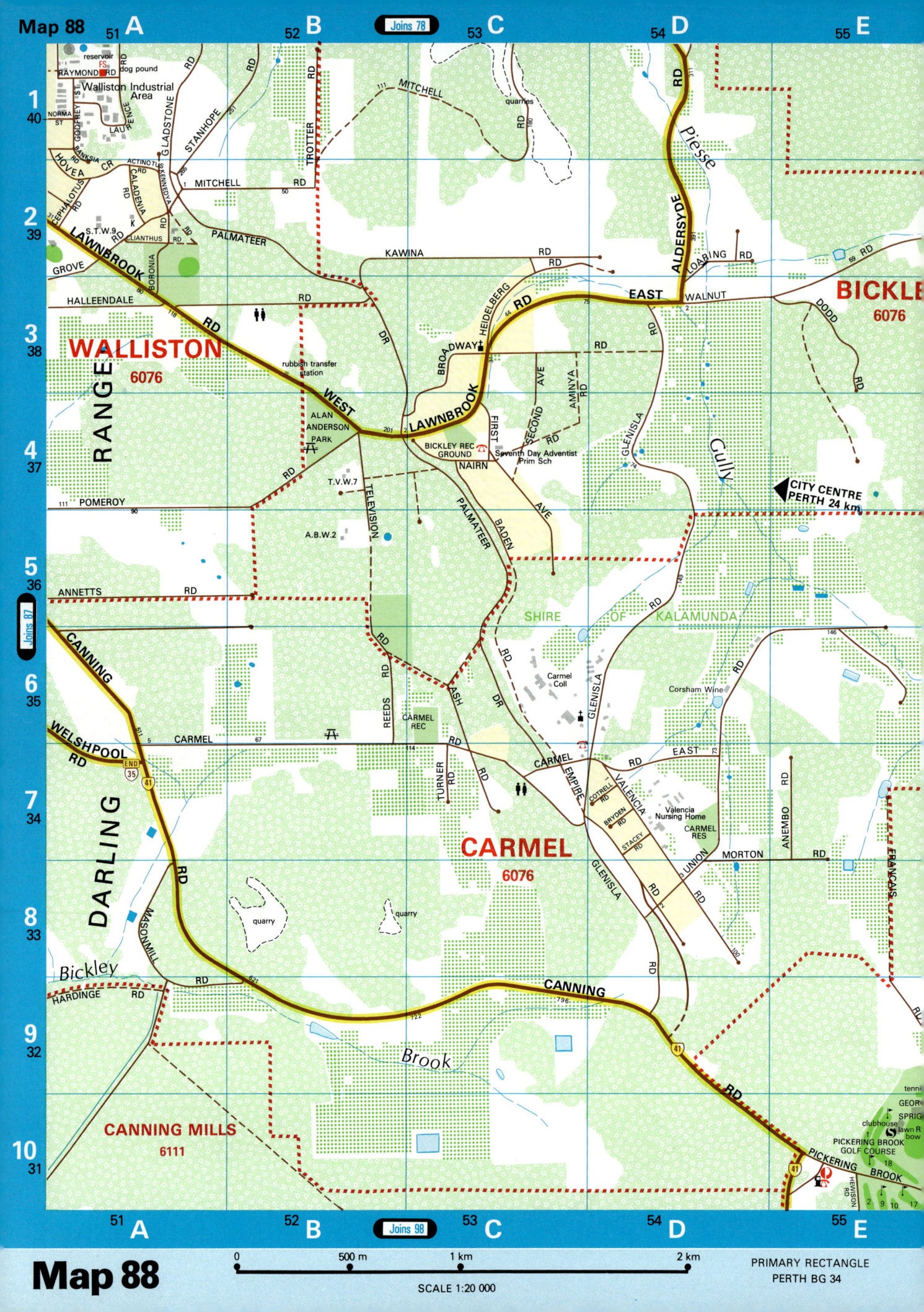

Map 89

HACKETTS GULLY
6076

PICKERING BROOK
6076

SHIRE OF KALAMUNDA

11 A 12 B Joins 80 13 C 14 D 15 E

11 A 12 B Joins 100 13 C 14 D 15 E

0 500 m 1 km 2 km

SCALE 1:20 000

PRIMARY RECTANGLE
PERTH BG 34

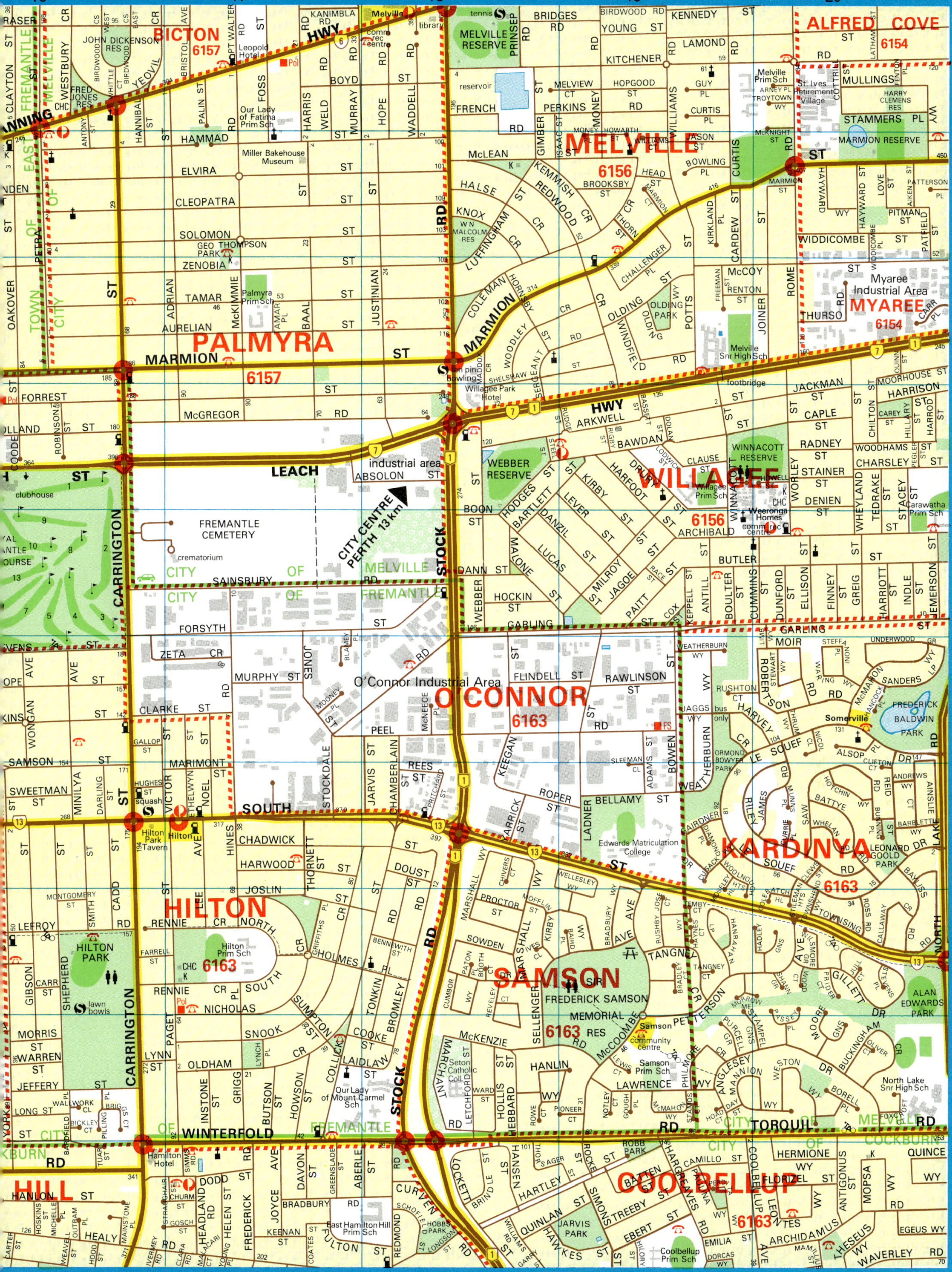

POLICE STATION
HOSPITAL
POST OFFICE
PUBLIC TELEPHONE
TRAFFIC FLOW
TRAFFIC LIGHTS

FOR COMPREHENSIVE LEGEND, SEE PAGE 3

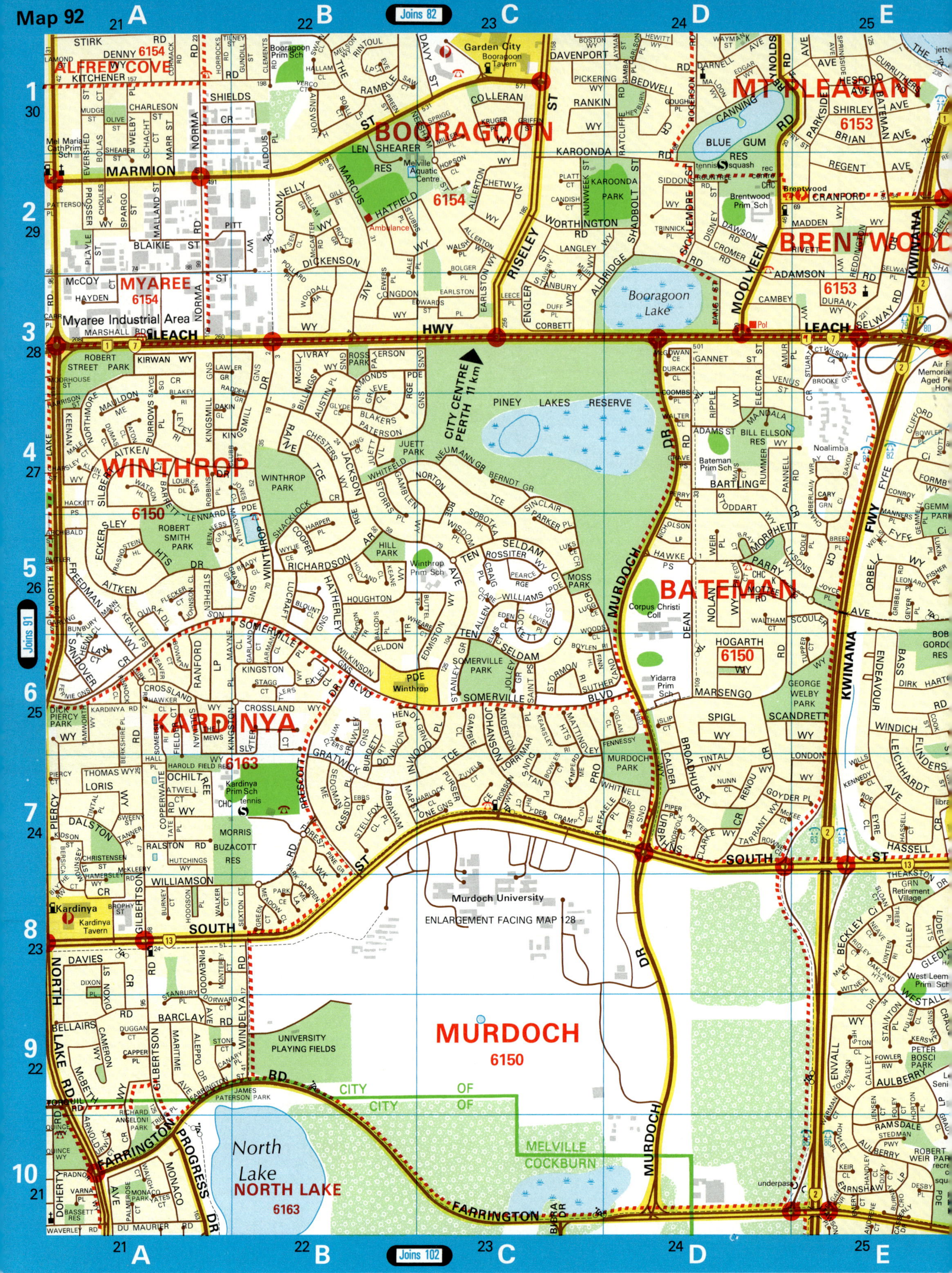

0 500 m 1 km 2 km
SCALE 1:20 000

PRIMARY RECTANGLE
PERTH BG 34

26 A 27 B 28 C Joins 83 29 D 30 E

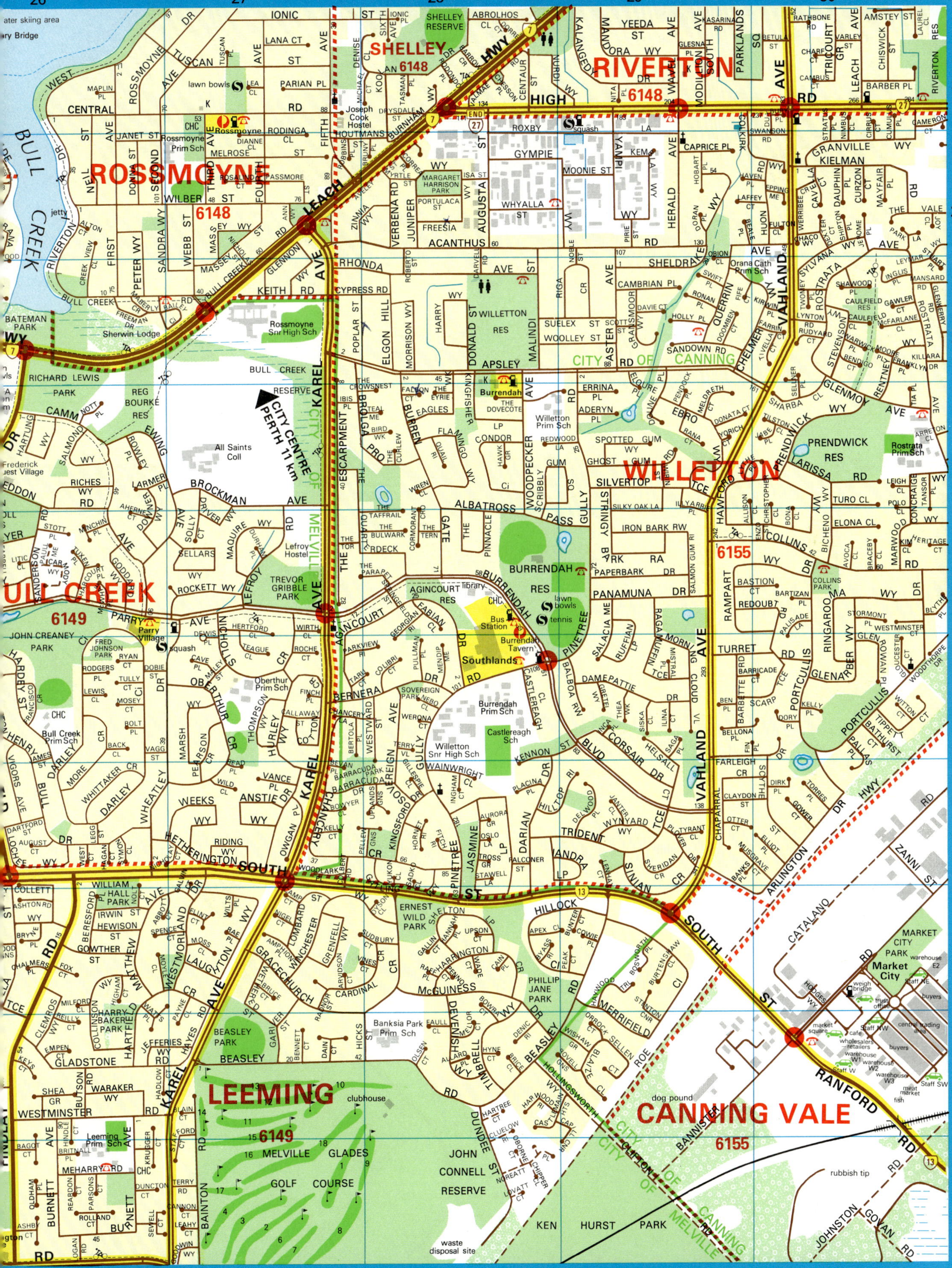

26 A 27 B 28 C Joins 103 29 D 30 E

POLICE STATION Pol
HOSPITAL
POST OFFICE
PUBLIC TELEPHONE
TRAFFIC FLOW
TRAFFIC LIGHTS

FOR COMPREHENSIVE LEGEND, SEE PAGE 3

Joins 84

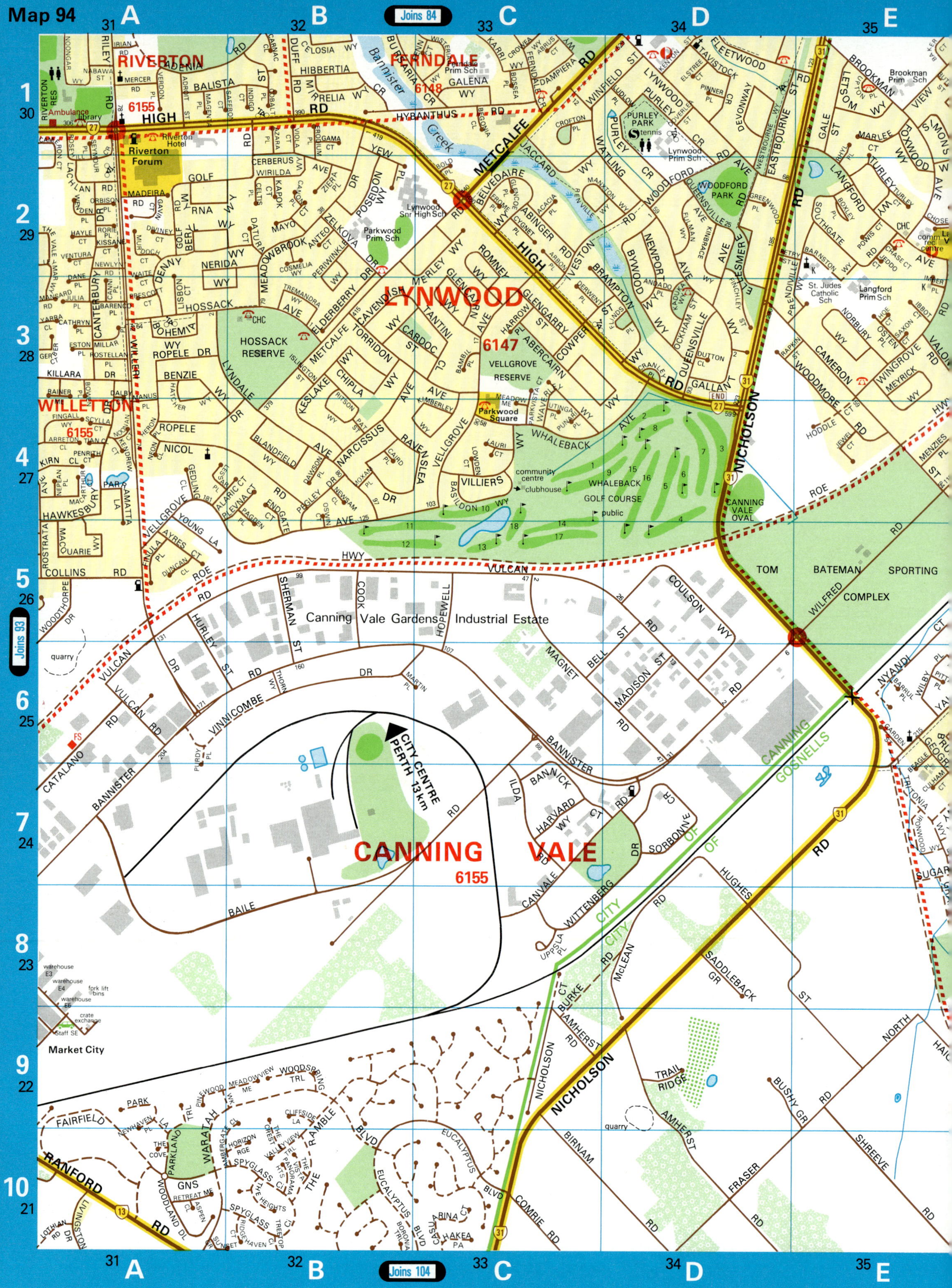

Joins 93

Joins 104

0 500 m 1 km 2 km

SCALE 1:20 000

PRIMARY RECTANGLE
PERTH BG 34

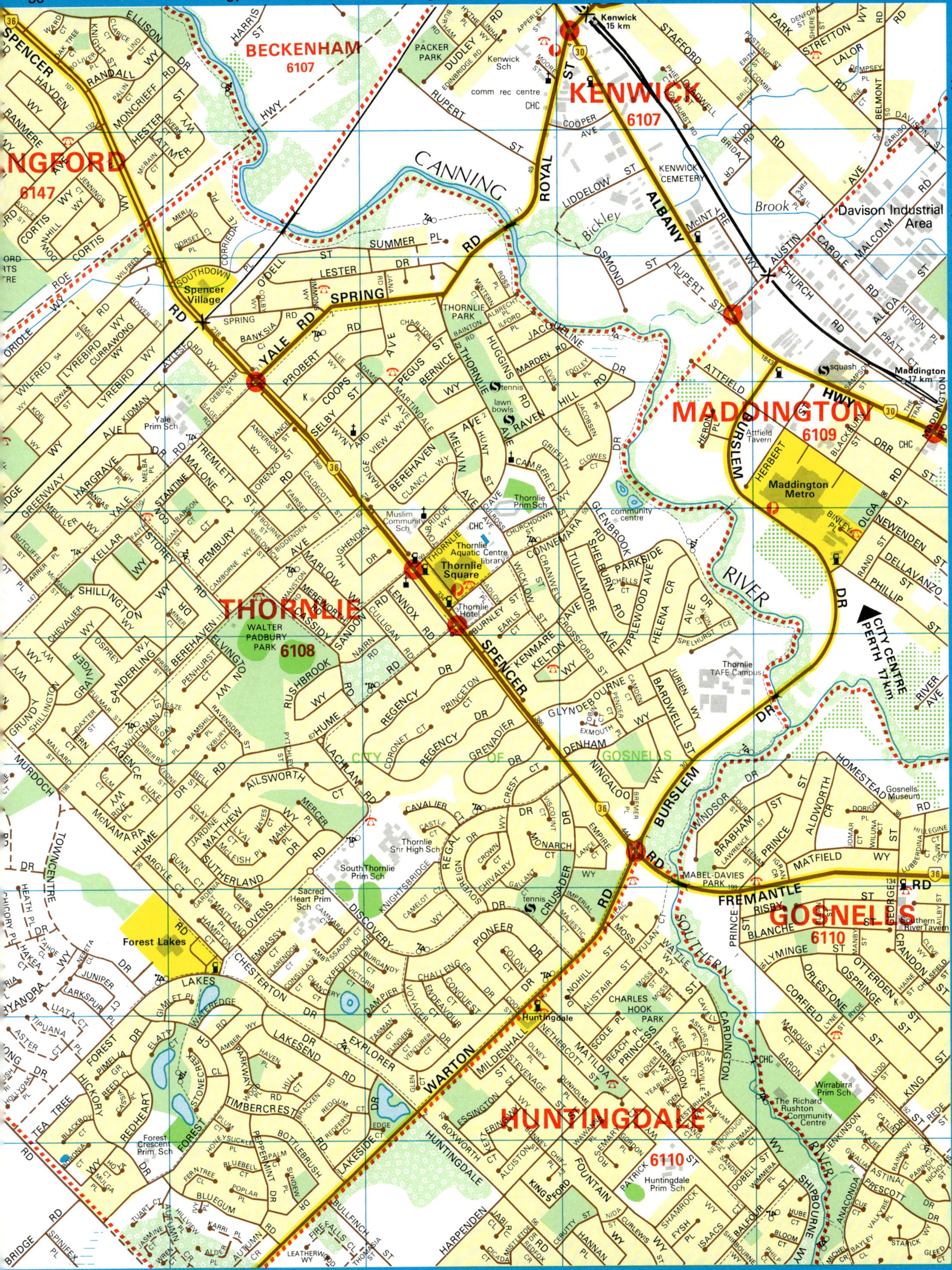

POLICE STATION
HOSPITAL
POST OFFICE
PUBLIC TELEPHONE
TRAFFIC FLOW
TRAFFIC LIGHTS

FOR COMPREHENSIVE LEGEND, SEE PAGE 3

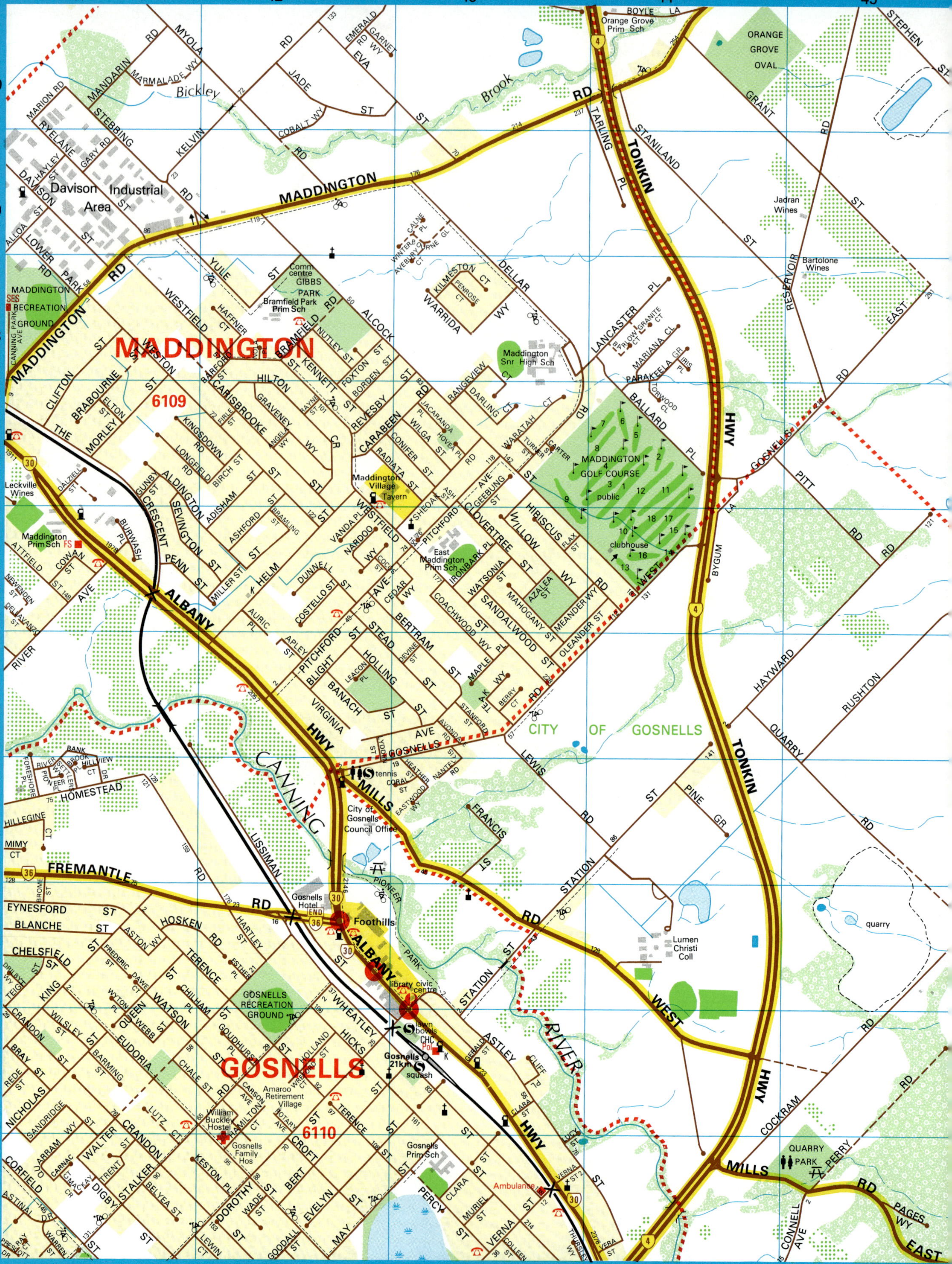

Map 96

0 500 m 1 km 2 km
SCALE 1:20 000

PRIMARY RECTANGLE
PERTH BG 34

Map 97

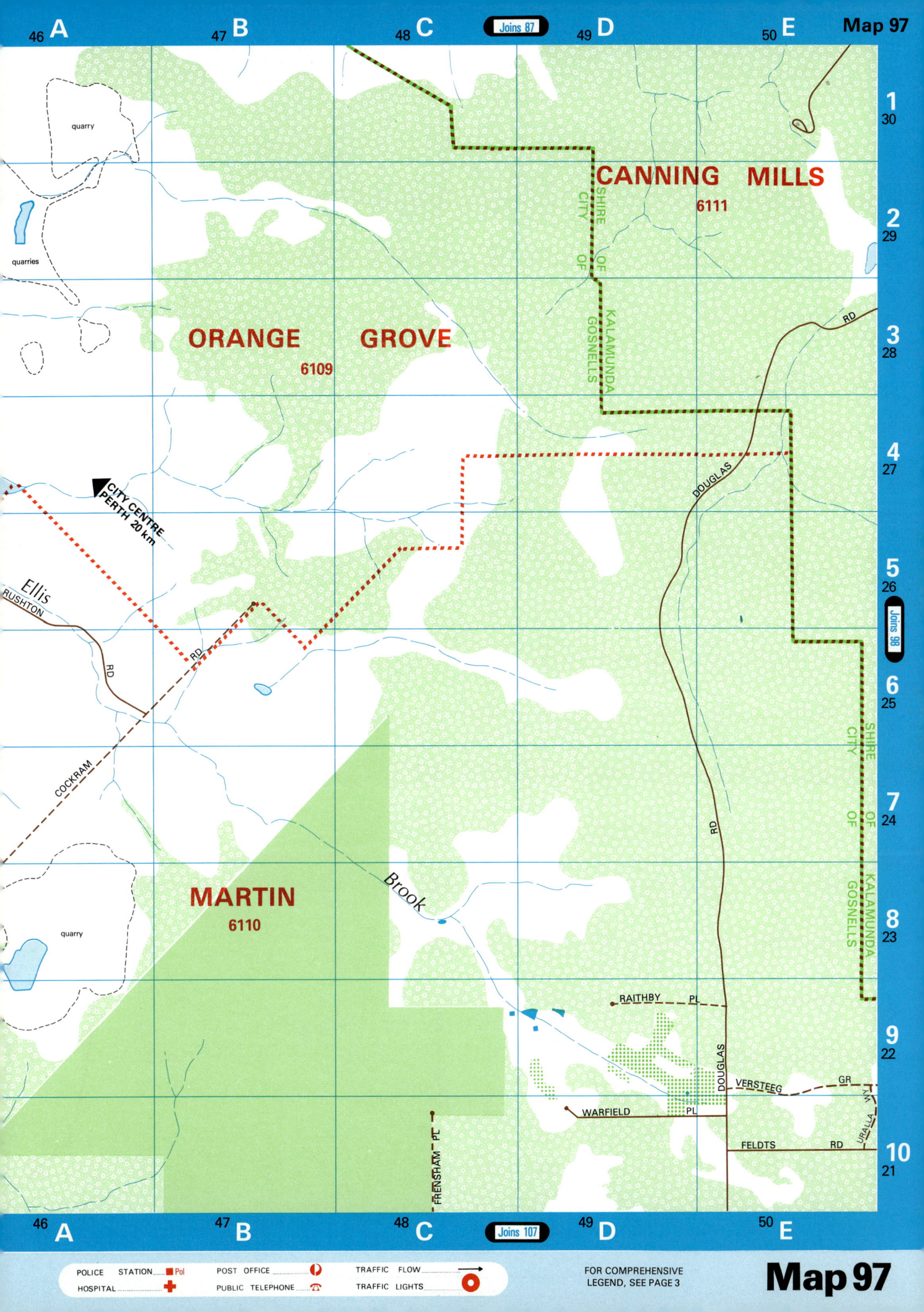

ORANGE GROVE 6109

CANNING MILLS 6111

MARTIN 6110

SHIRE OF KALAMUNDA / CITY OF GOSNELLS

CITY CENTRE PERTH 20 km

Ellis, RUSHTON RD, COCKRAM RD, Douglas Rd, Brook, Raithby Pl, Versteeg Gr, Warfield Pl, Feldts Rd, Uralla Wy, Frensham Pl

Joins 87 (top), Joins 107 (bottom), Joins 98 (right)

POLICE STATION — Pol
HOSPITAL
POST OFFICE
PUBLIC TELEPHONE
TRAFFIC FLOW
TRAFFIC LIGHTS

FOR COMPREHENSIVE LEGEND, SEE PAGE 3

Map 98

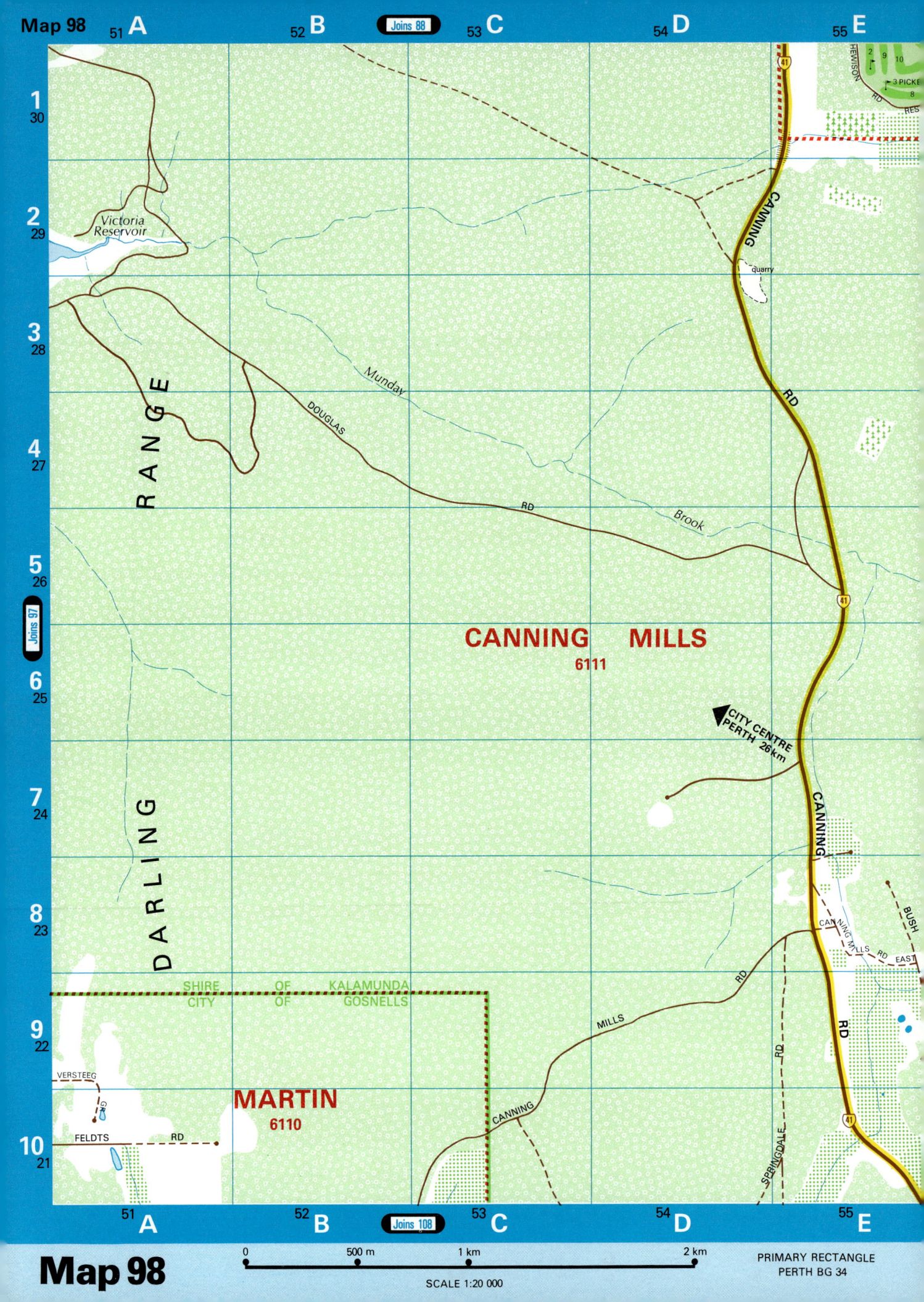

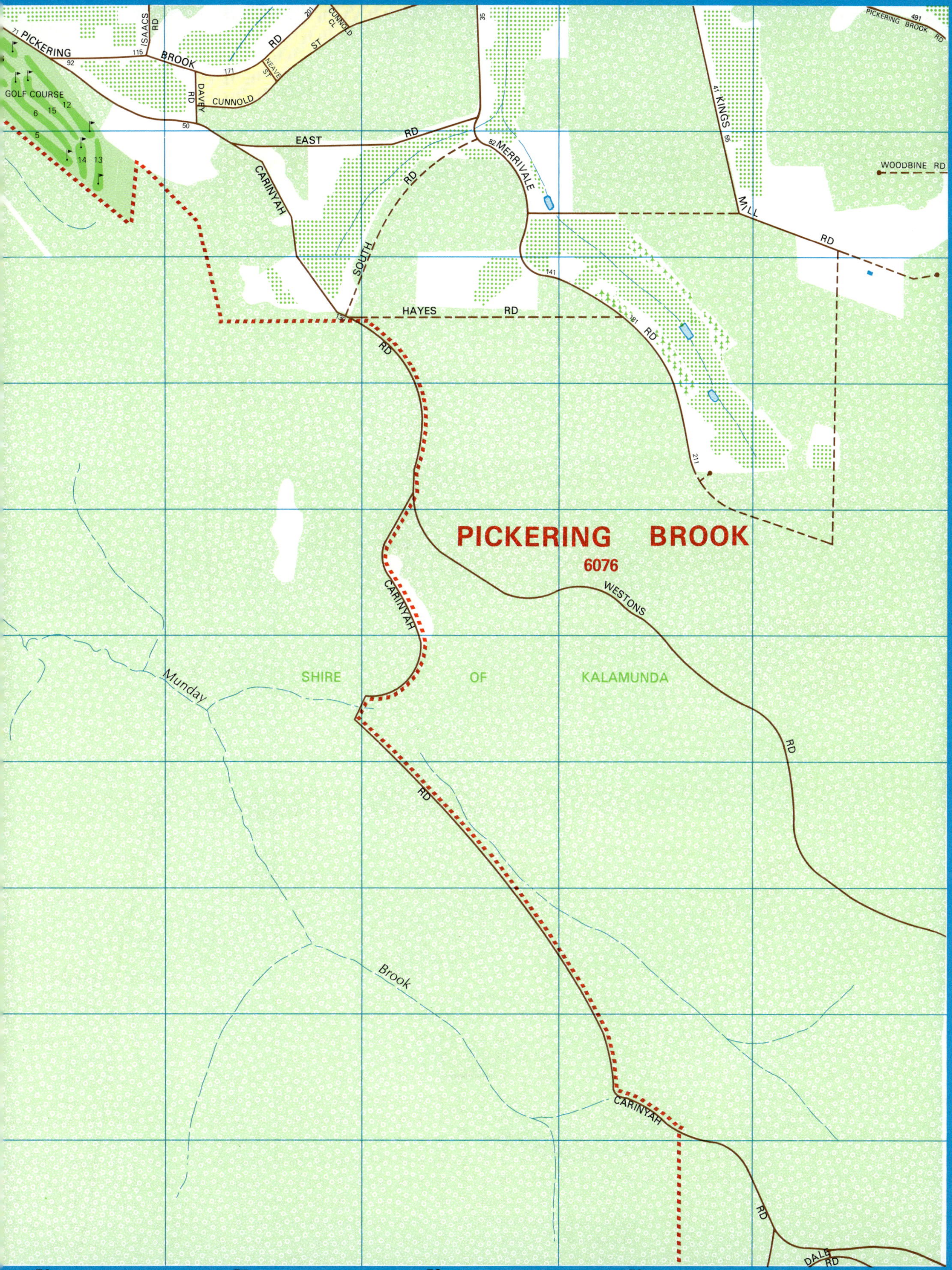
PICKERING BROOK
6076
SHIRE OF KALAMUNDA
PICKERING BROOK RD
ISAACS RD
CUNNOLD RD
CUNNOLD CL
NEAVE ST
DAVEY RD
GOLF COURSE
EAST RD
CARINYAH RD
SOUTH RD
MERRIVALE RD
HAYES RD
KINGS MILL RD
WOODBINE RD
WESTONS RD
DALE RD
Munday Brook
Limit of Maps
1 30
2 29
3 28
4 27
5 26
6 25
7 24
8 23
9 22
10 21

POLICE STATION Pol
HOSPITAL
POST OFFICE
PUBLIC TELEPHONE
TRAFFIC FLOW
TRAFFIC LIGHTS

FOR COMPREHENSIVE LEGEND, SEE PAGE 3

Map 100

31	Baboons	46	Mice
35	Bandicoots	56	Monitors
35	Bats	46	Monkeys
21	Bears	19	Numbats
3	Black Swans	33	Orang-utans
52	Boobies	28	Otters
22	Brown Bear	39	Oryx
36	Bushbirds	4,44	Ostrich
5	Bustards	36	Owls
6	Cassowaries	9,36	Parrots
37	Cape Hunting Dogs	3	Pelicans
38	Cheetah	52	Penguins
33	Chimpanzees	38	Pheasants
9,55	Cockatoos	36	Pigeons
49	Crocodiles	18	Porcupines
8	Deer	35	Possums
50	Dragon Lizards	56	Pythons
3	Ducks	10	Quokkas
13	Echidnas	56	Reptiles
47	Eland	48	Rhinoceros
30	Elephant	12	Rock Wallabies
13	Emu	29	Siamangs
36	Finches	50	Skinks
32,53	Gibbons	21	Sun Bear
43	Giraffe	51	Tahr
40	Hyena	34	Tamarins
2	Jabirus	24	Tigers
13,26	Kangaroos	11	Tortoise Giant
57	Kites	16	Tree Kangaroo
14	Koalas	17	Turtles
13,20	Kookaburras	1	Waterbirds
54	Lemurs	12,27	Wallabies
23	Leopards	27	Wallaroo
25	Lions	41	Zebra
45	Meerkats		

OPENING HOURS:
10.00 a.m. to 5.00 p.m. every day of the year.
tel: 367 7988

The zoo may be reached by Bus Nos. 36 or 38 from St. Georges Terrace, or by ferry from the Barrack Street Jetty.

SCALE 1:4 000

PRIMARY RECTANGLE
PERTH BG 34

SCALE 1:20 000

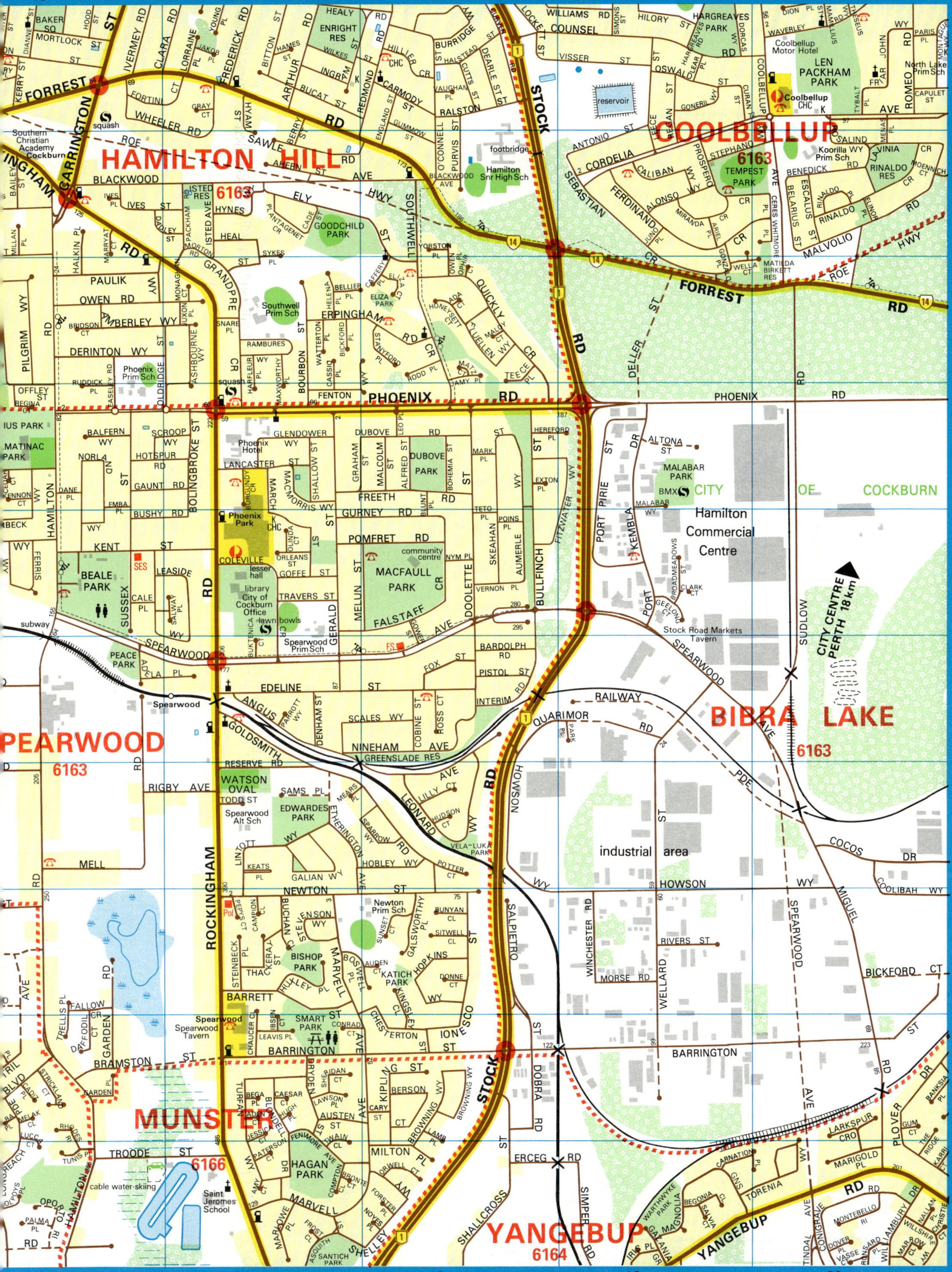

POLICE STATION Pol — HOSPITAL — POST OFFICE — PUBLIC TELEPHONE — TRAFFIC FLOW — TRAFFIC LIGHTS

FOR COMPREHENSIVE LEGEND, SEE PAGE 3

Map 102

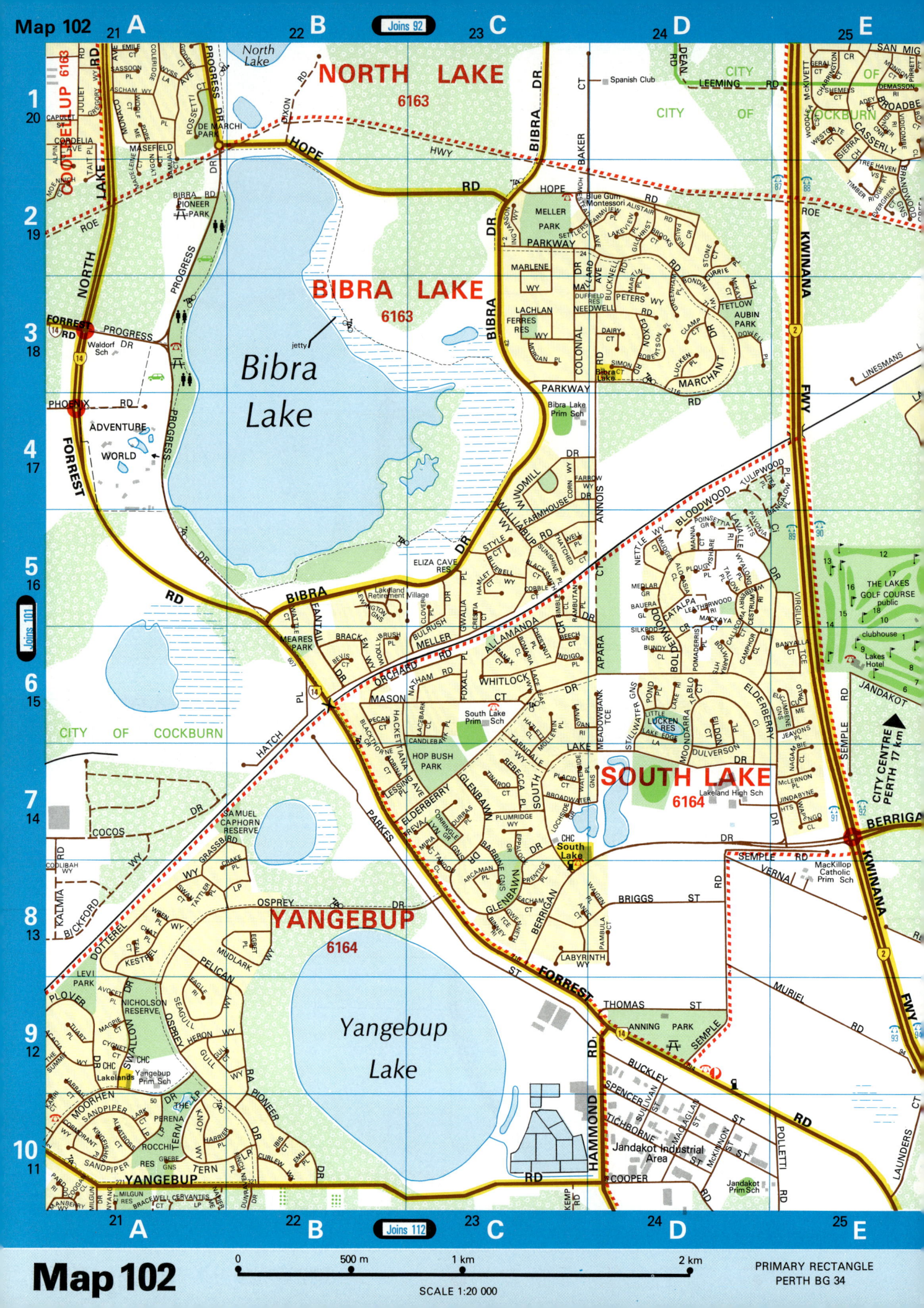

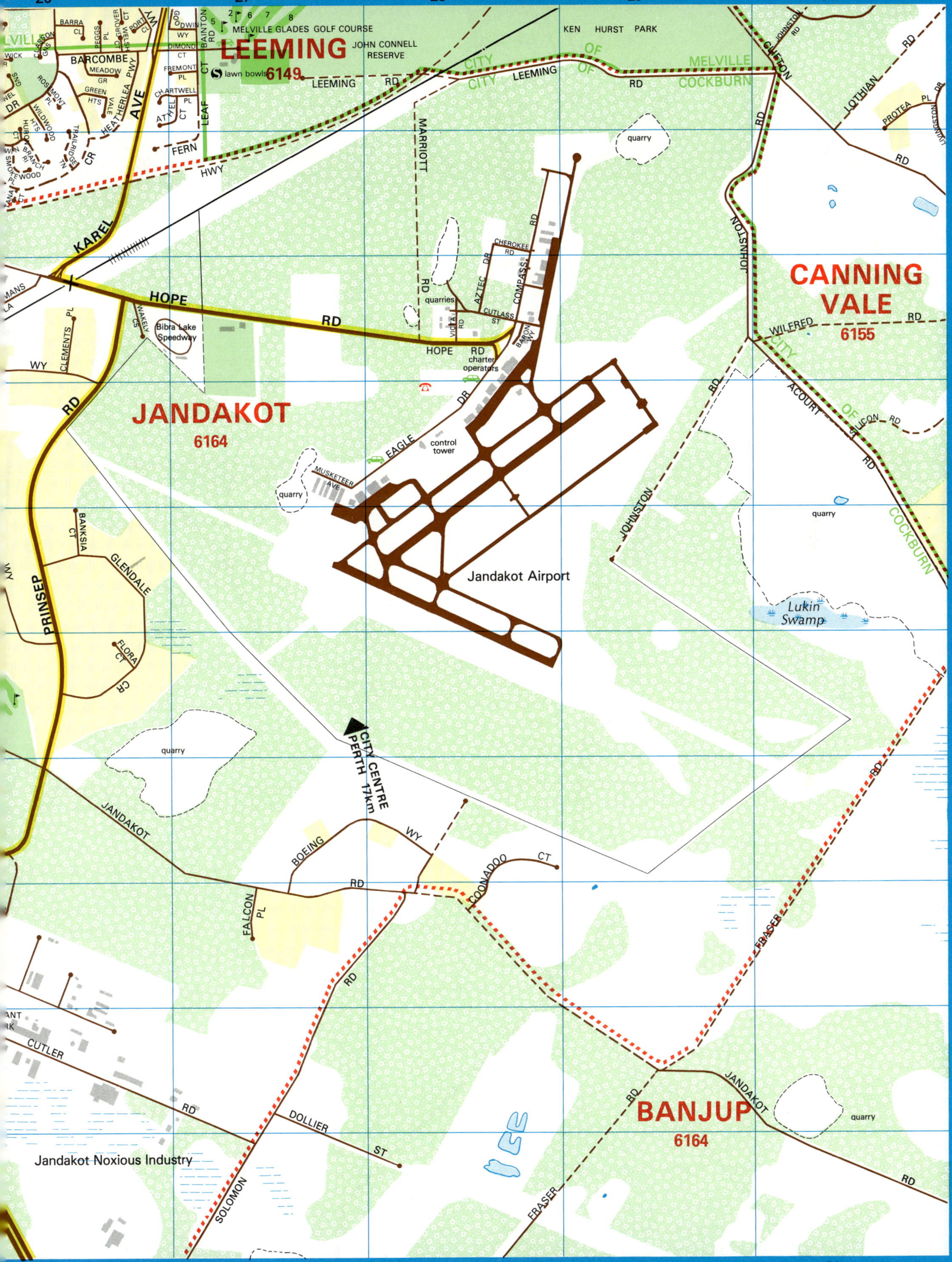

POLICE STATION
HOSPITAL
POST OFFICE
PUBLIC TELEPHONE
TRAFFIC FLOW
TRAFFIC LIGHTS
FOR COMPREHENSIVE LEGEND, SEE PAGE 3

Map 104

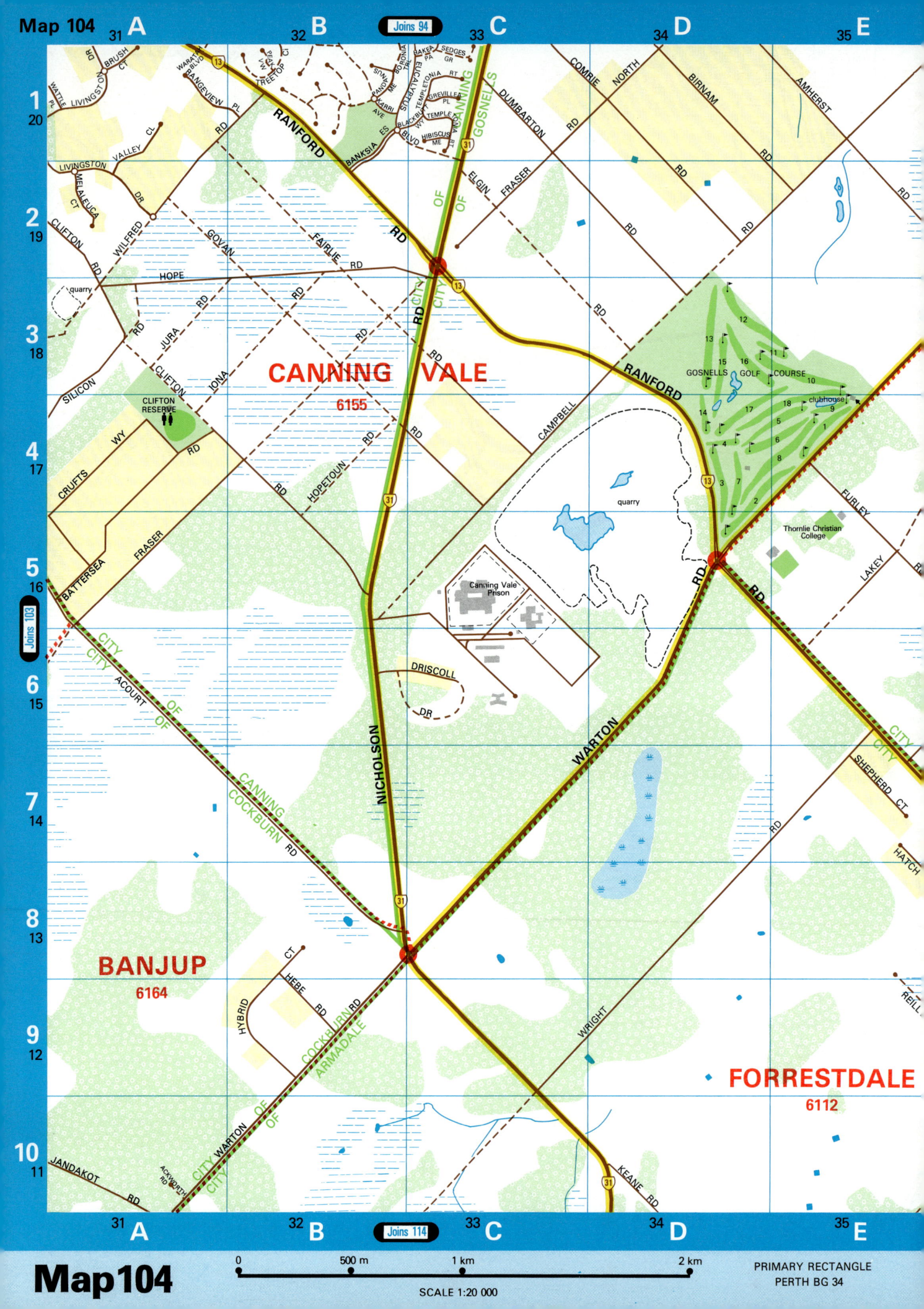

CANNING VALE 6155
BANJUP 6164
FORRESTDALE 6112

PRIMARY RECTANGLE
PERTH BG 34

SCALE 1:20 000

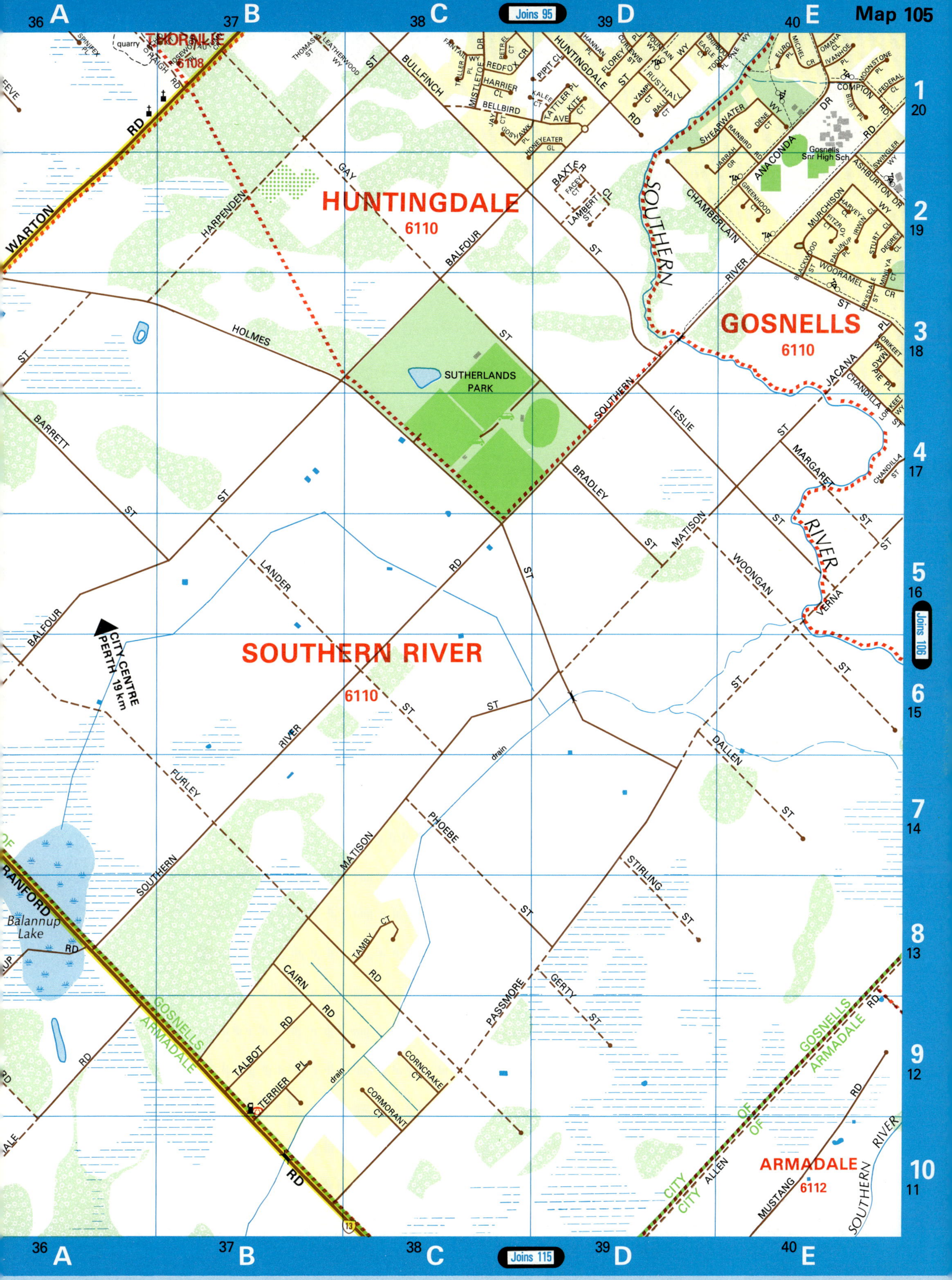

POLICE STATION Pol
HOSPITAL
POST OFFICE
PUBLIC TELEPHONE
TRAFFIC FLOW
TRAFFIC LIGHTS

FOR COMPREHENSIVE LEGEND, SEE PAGE 3

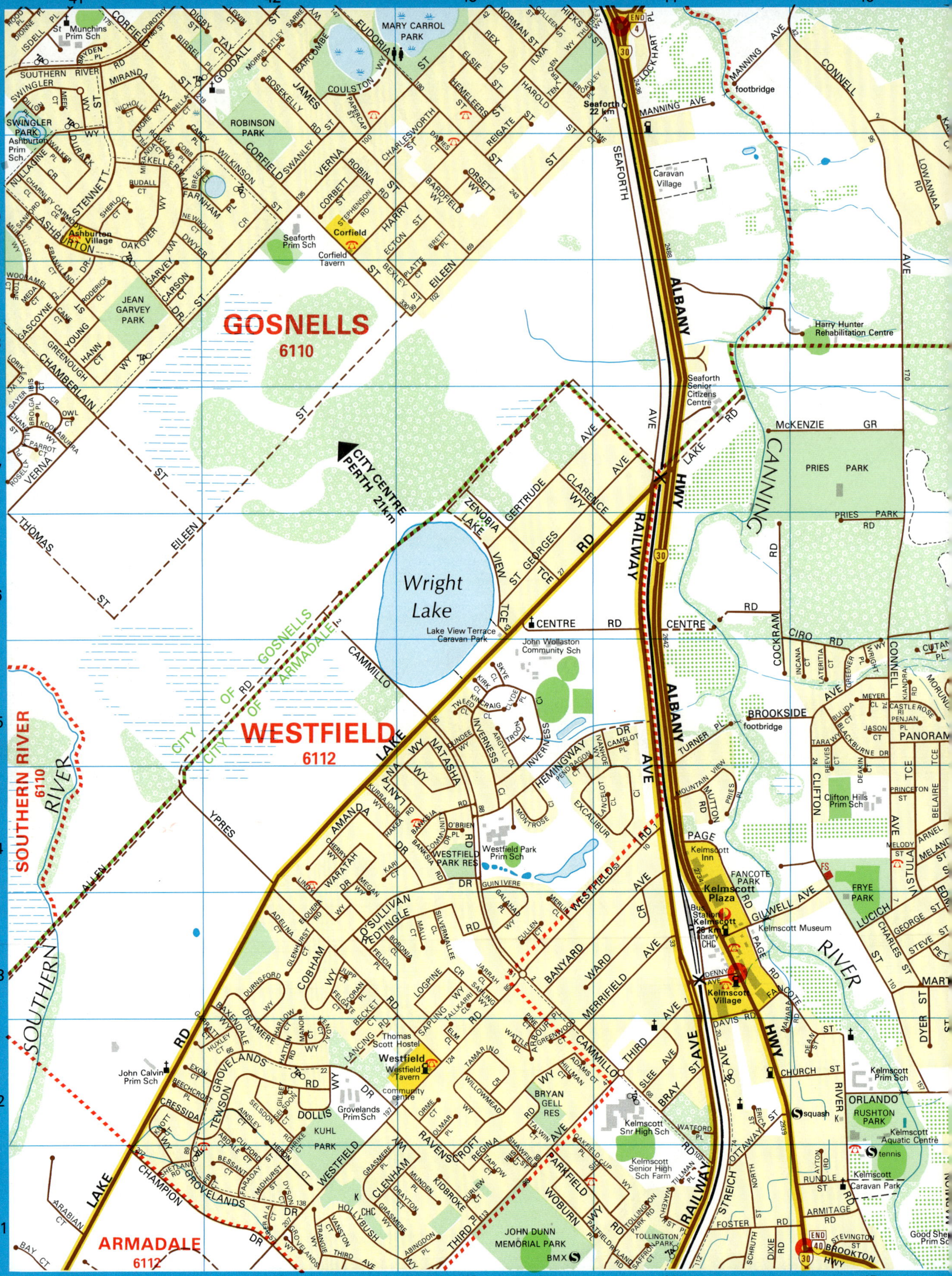

Joins 105

Map 106

0 500 m 1 km 2 km

SCALE 1:20 000

PRIMARY RECTANGLE
PERTH BG 34

Map 107

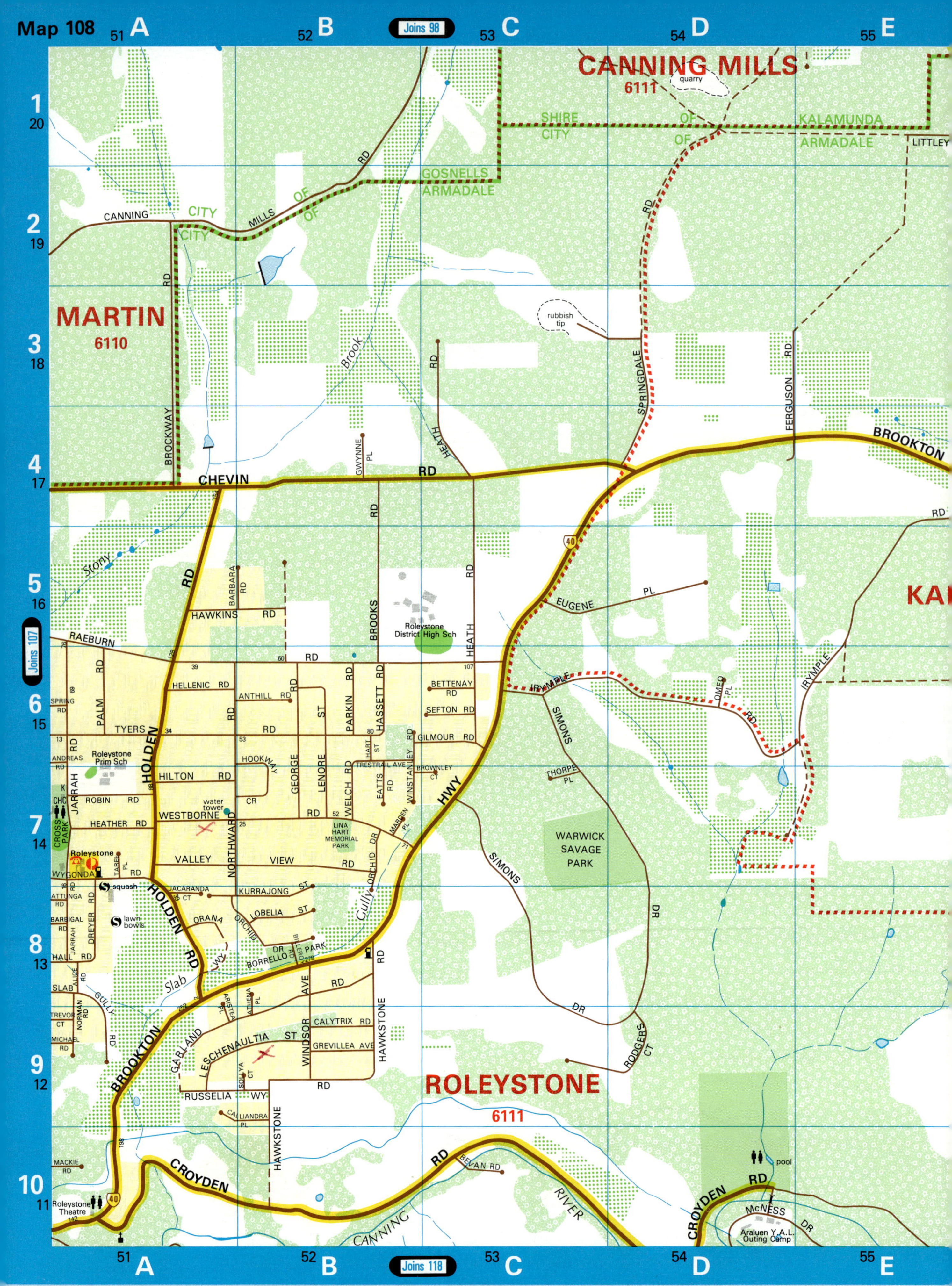

0 500 m 1 km 2 km

SCALE 1:20 000

PRIMARY RECTANGLE
PERTH BG 34

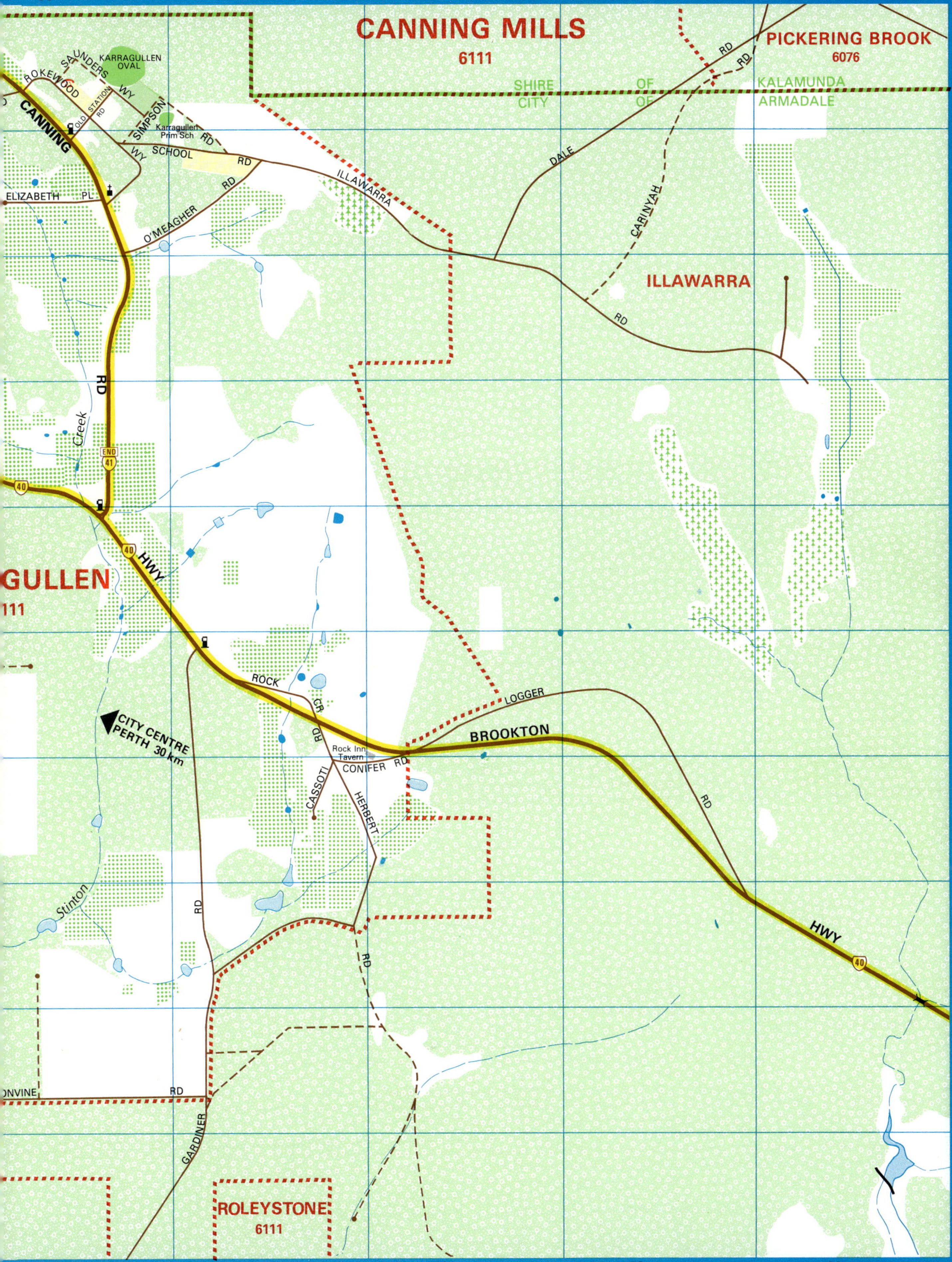

POLICE STATION Pol
HOSPITAL
POST OFFICE
PUBLIC TELEPHONE
TRAFFIC FLOW
TRAFFIC LIGHTS

FOR COMPREHENSIVE LEGEND, SEE PAGE 3

Map 110

COOGEE 6166

MUNSTER 6166

OWEN ANCHORAGE

Woodman Point Recreation Reserve
Woodmans Point Caravan Park
Woodman Point Recreation Camp
CITY CENTRE PERTH 22km

jetty
JBSC
Wapet Groyne
Woodman Pt.
O'KANE CT
WOODMAN POINT VW
JERVOISE BAY CE
CITY OF COCKBURN
boat ramp
CPBA/A
wreck

JERVOISE BAY

COCKBURN SOUND

jetty
groyne
CLARENCE BEACH RD
shipyards
Cockburn Volunteer Sea R
Ship & Dock
offshore construction yard

Joins 100
Joins 120

SCALE 1:20 000
0 — 500 m — 1 km — 2 km

PRIMARY RECTANGLE
PERTH BG 34

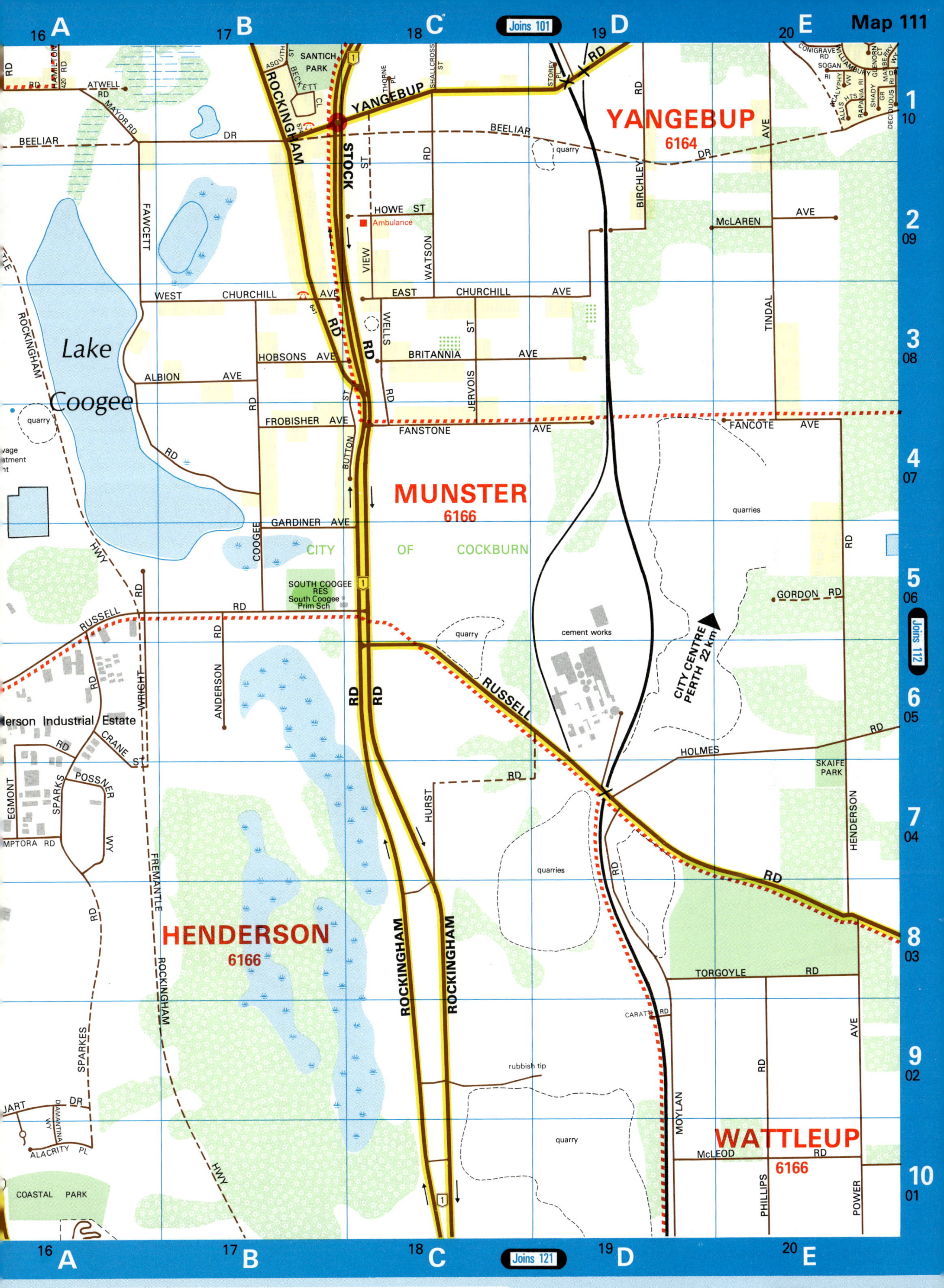

POLICE STATION Pol
HOSPITAL
POST OFFICE
PUBLIC TELEPHONE
TRAFFIC FLOW
TRAFFIC LIGHTS

FOR COMPREHENSIVE LEGEND, SEE PAGE 3

Map 112

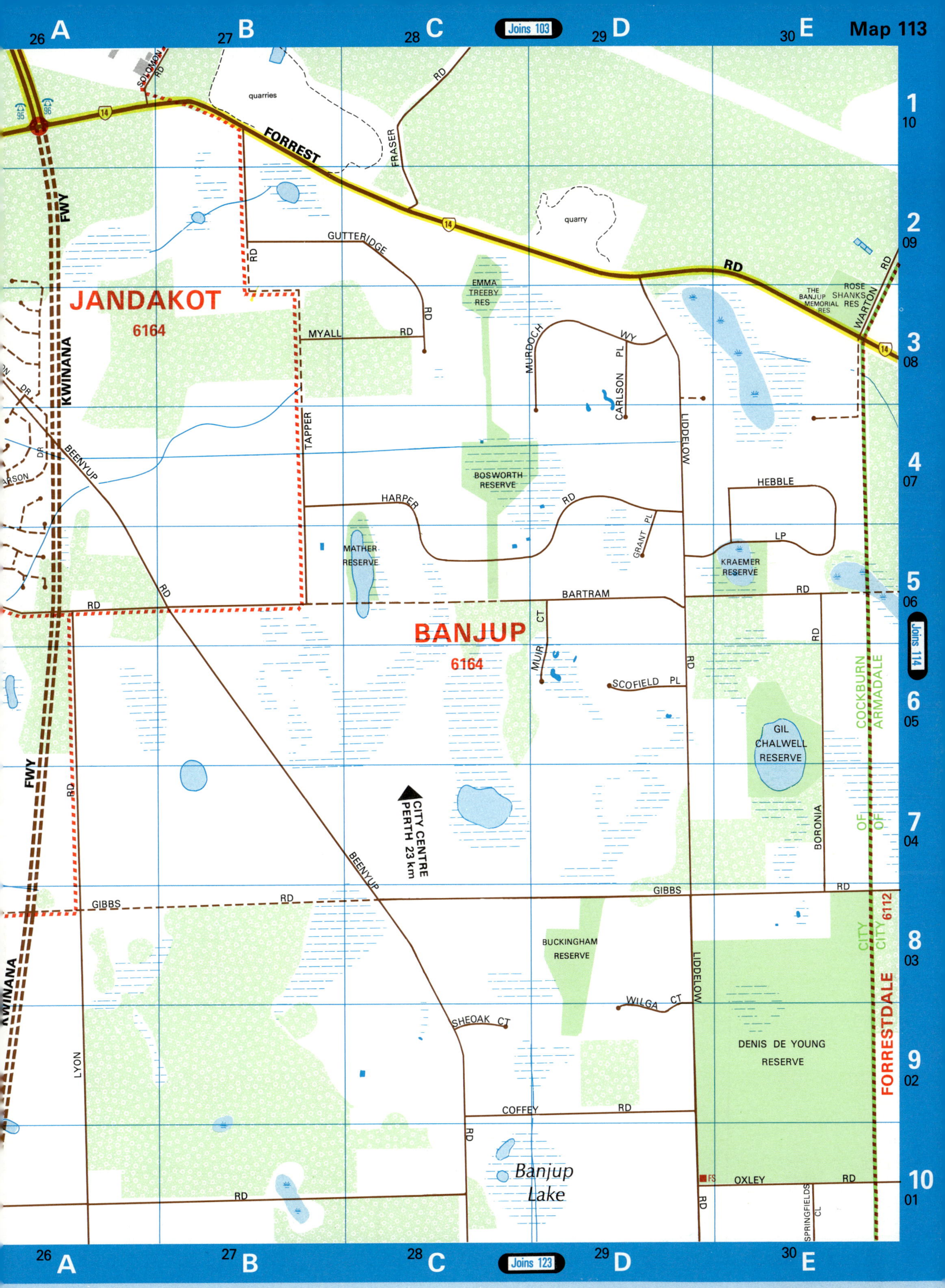

POLICE STATION Pol
HOSPITAL
POST OFFICE
PUBLIC TELEPHONE
TRAFFIC FLOW
TRAFFIC LIGHTS

FOR COMPREHENSIVE LEGEND, SEE PAGE 3

Map 114

BANJUP 6164

FORRESTDALE 6112

Forrestdale Lake

PRIMARY RECTANGLE
PERTH BG 34

SCALE 1:20 000

Map 115

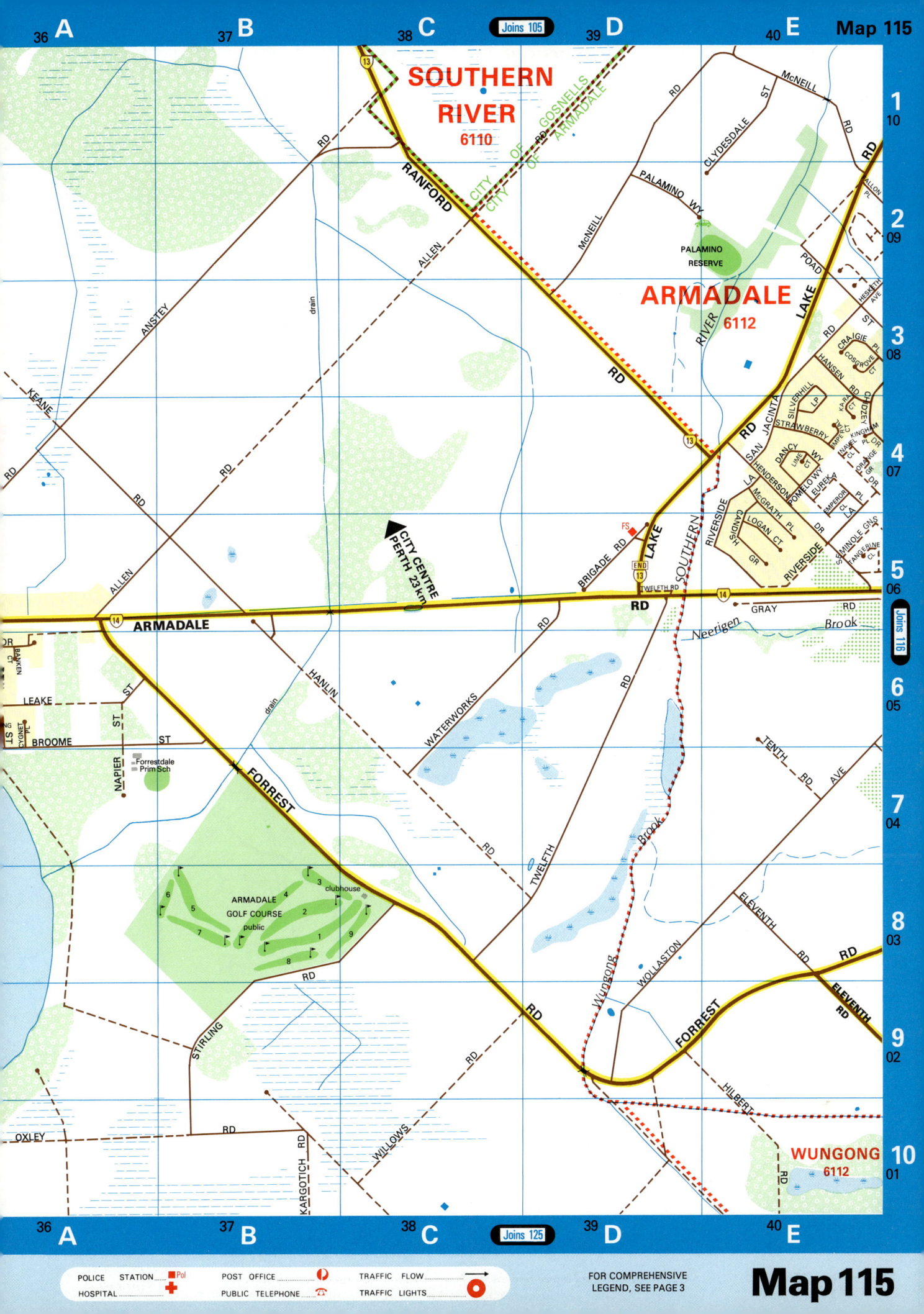

SOUTHERN RIVER 6110
ARMADALE 6112
WUNGONG 6112

Map 116

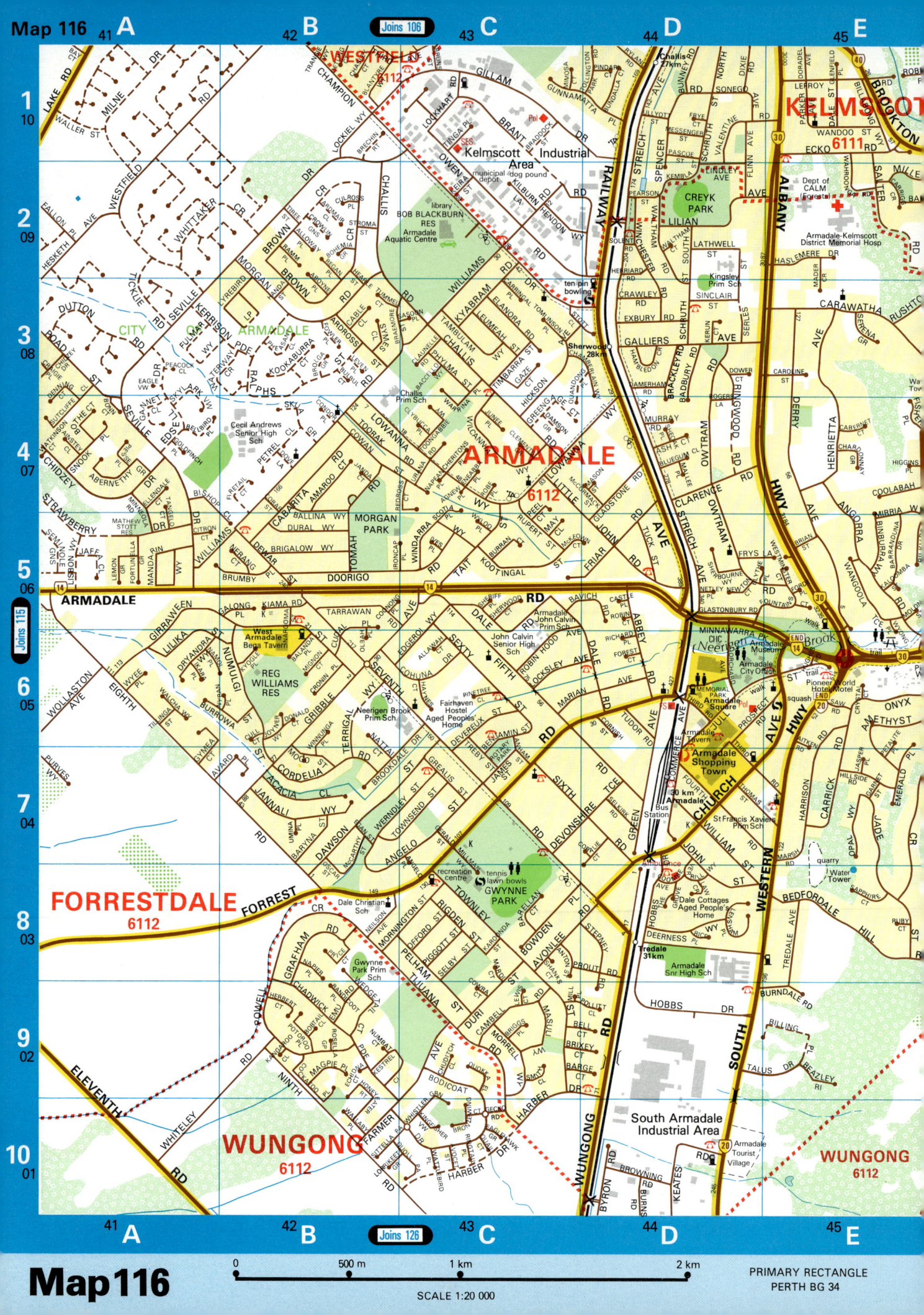

Map 117

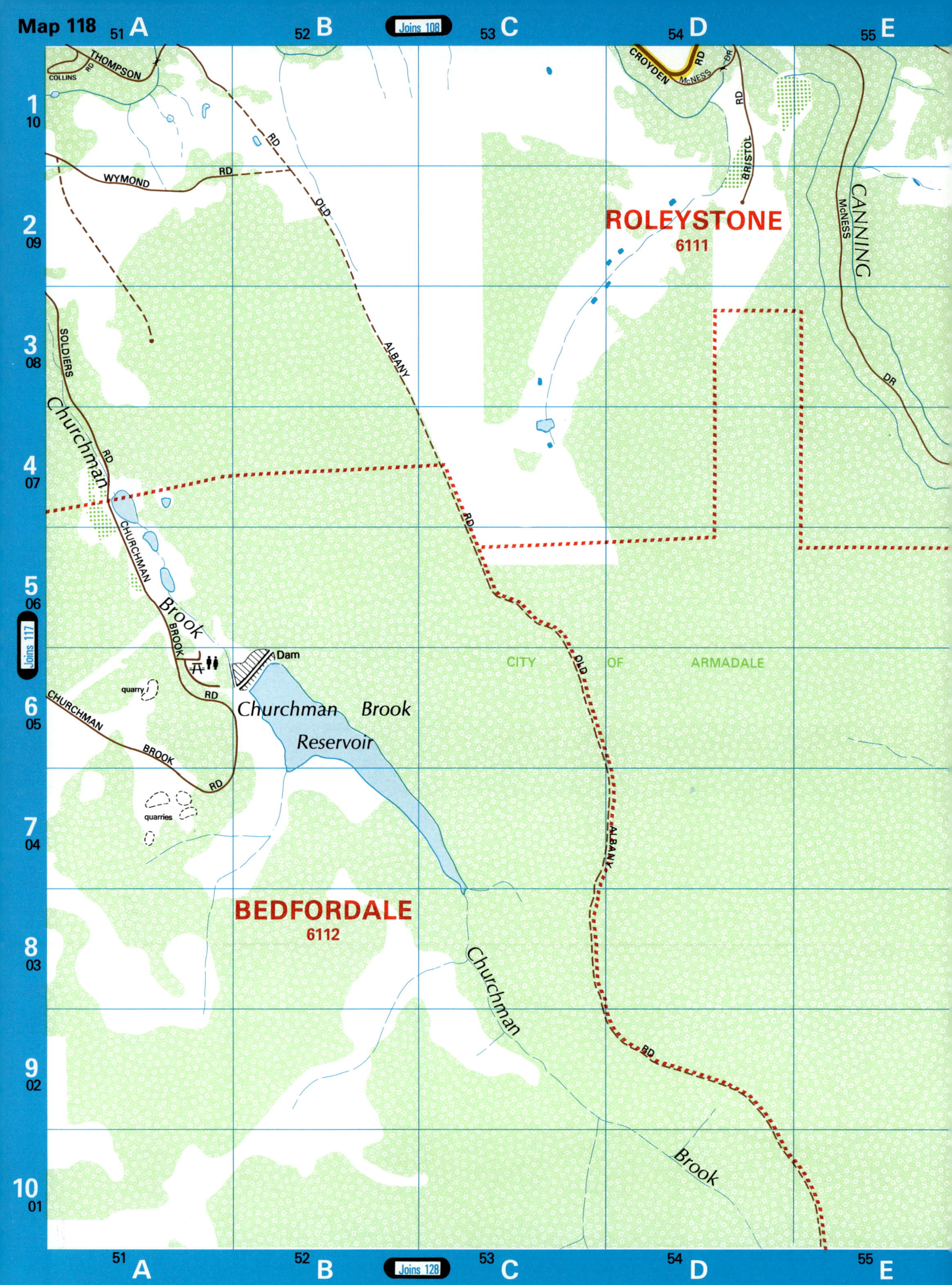

0 500 m 1 km 2 km
SCALE 1:20 000

PRIMARY RECTANGLE
PERTH BG 34

Map 119

Map 120

THE UNIVERSITY OF WESTERN AUSTRALIA

INDEX TO BUILDINGS

Administration	5
Adoption Centre and Legal Aid	54
Agriculture	45
Anatomy	39
Animal House	52
Architecture	3
Arts	27
Biochemistry	44
Biology	49
Biological Sciences Library	46
Bookshop	9
Botany	48
28 Broadway	55
Central Plant	60
Chemistry	41
Child Care Centre	51
Child Study Centre	23
Commerce	33
Computing Centre	24
Dolphin Theatre	10
Economics	33
Education	28
Electrical Engineering	30
Engineering	32
27 Fairway House	31
General Purpose Building	17
3rd General Purpose Building	63
Geography	20
Grounds House	58
Guild	36
Guild Craft Centre	37
Guild Pharmacy	8
Guild Physical Recreation Centre	11
Guild Shop	7
Hackett Coffee Lounge	8
Hackett Hall	7
Human Movement and Recreation Studies	53
Irwin Street Building	59
Law	34
Lawrence Wilson Art Gallery	62
Mathematics	29
Music	12
Music Examinations	18
New Fortune Theatre	22
Octagon Theatre	14
Outdoor Laboratory	61
14/16 Parkway	56
Physics	25
Physiology	43
Psychology	40
Psychology Clinic Unit	57
Radio Station 6UVS F.M.	19
Reid Library	26
Sanders Building	42
Shenton House	38
Social Sciences	35
Soil Science	47
Somerville Auditorium	13
Sunken Garden	4
Swimming Pools and Outdoor Laboratory	61
Tuart House	2
University House	15
Winthrop Hall	6
Workshops	50
Zoology	1

Legend

- Staff and Student Car Parks
- Visitor's Car Park
- Motorcycle Parking
- Administration Building

Scale 1:6000 — 0, 50, 100, 150, 200 metres

15 E

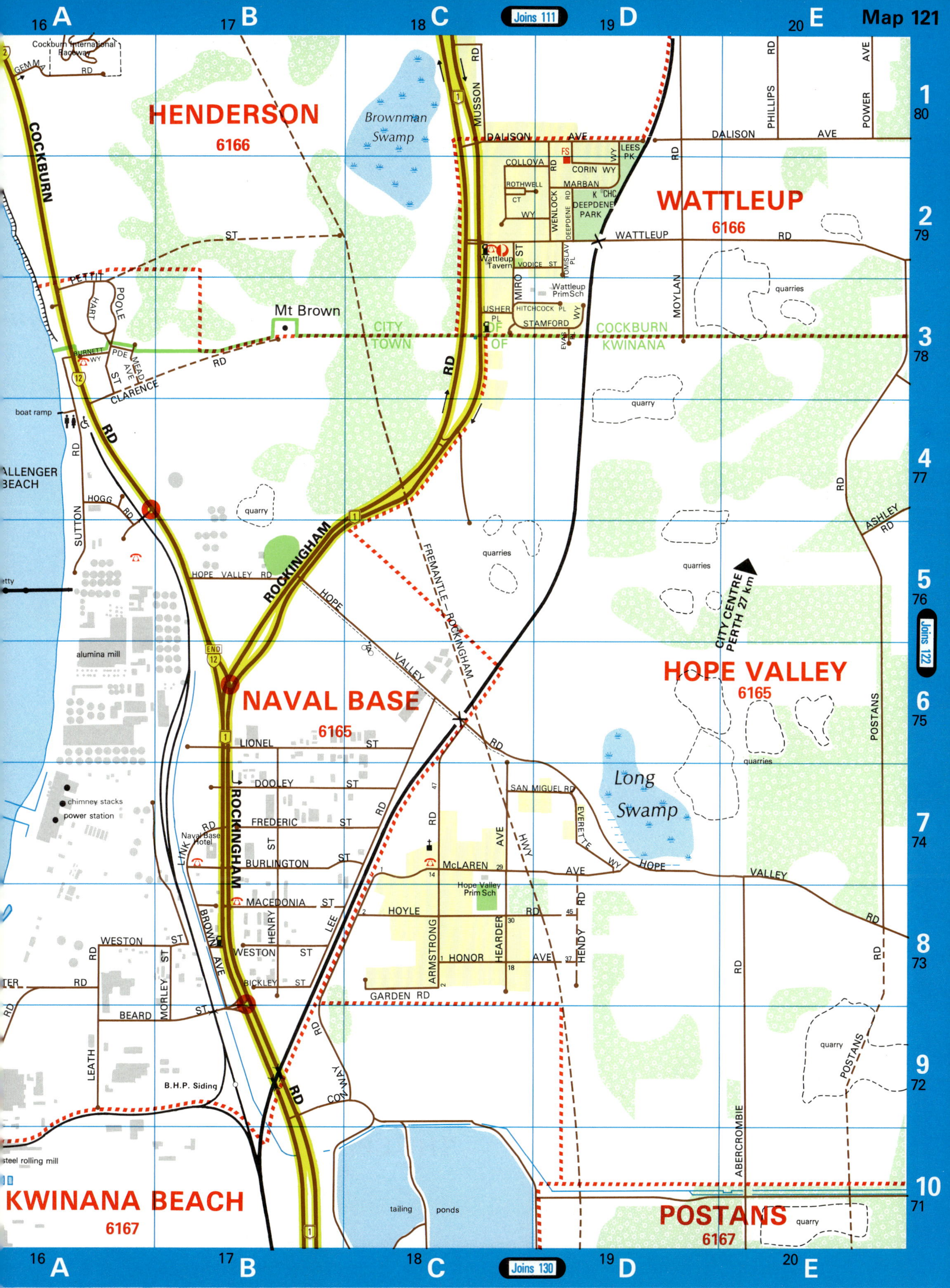
16 A
17 B
18 C
Joins 111
19 D
20 E
1 80
2 79
3 78
4 77
5 76
6 75
7 74
8 73
9 72
10 71
Joins 122
Joins 130
Cockburn International Raceway
GEMMA RD
HENDERSON
6166
COCKBURN RD
Brownman Swamp
MUSSON RD
DALISON AVE
DALISON AVE
PHILLIPS RD
POWER AVE
LEES PK
COLLOVA
CORIN WY
ROTHWELL CT
MARBAN
WY
WENLOCK RD
DEEPDENE RD
DEEPDENE PARK
K CHC
WATTLEUP
6166
WATTLEUP RD
ST
Wattleup Tavern
VODICE ST
OMISLAV PL
Wattleup Prim Sch
MIRO ST
USHER PL
HITCHCOCK PL
STAMFORD
WY
EVANS
MOYLAN RD
quarries
PETTIT
HART
POOLE
Mt Brown
CITY OF COCKBURN
TOWN OF KWINANA
BURNETT WY
PDE
MEAD AVE
ST
CLARENCE RD
RD
boat ramp
quarry
CHALLENGER BEACH
SUTTON RD
HOGG RD
quarry
ROCKINGHAM RD
HOPE VALLEY RD
HOPE VALLEY RD
quarries
quarries
CITY CENTRE PERTH 27 km
ASHLEY RD
RD
jetty
alumina mill
END
12
NAVAL BASE
6165
FREMANTLE–ROCKINGHAM HWY
HOPE VALLEY
6165
POSTANS
LIONEL ST
DOOLEY ST
quarries
SAN MIGUEL RD
chimney stacks
power station
FREDERIC ST
Naval Base Hotel
LINK RD
ROCKINGHAM RD
ST
Long Swamp
EVERETTE WY
ARMSTRONG RD
HEARDER AVE
BURLINGTON ST
McLAREN AVE
HOPE VALLEY RD
MACEDONIA ST
Hope Valley Prim Sch
HOYLE RD
HENDY RD
BROWN AVE
HENRY ST
LEE RD
WESTON ST
WESTON ST
HONOR AVE
MORLEY ST
BICKLEY ST
GARDEN RD
ABERCROMBIE RD
RD
RD
BEARD ST
LEATH RD
quarry
POSTANS
B.H.P. Siding
CONWAY RD
steel rolling mill
tailing ponds
KWINANA BEACH
6167
POSTANS
6167
quarry

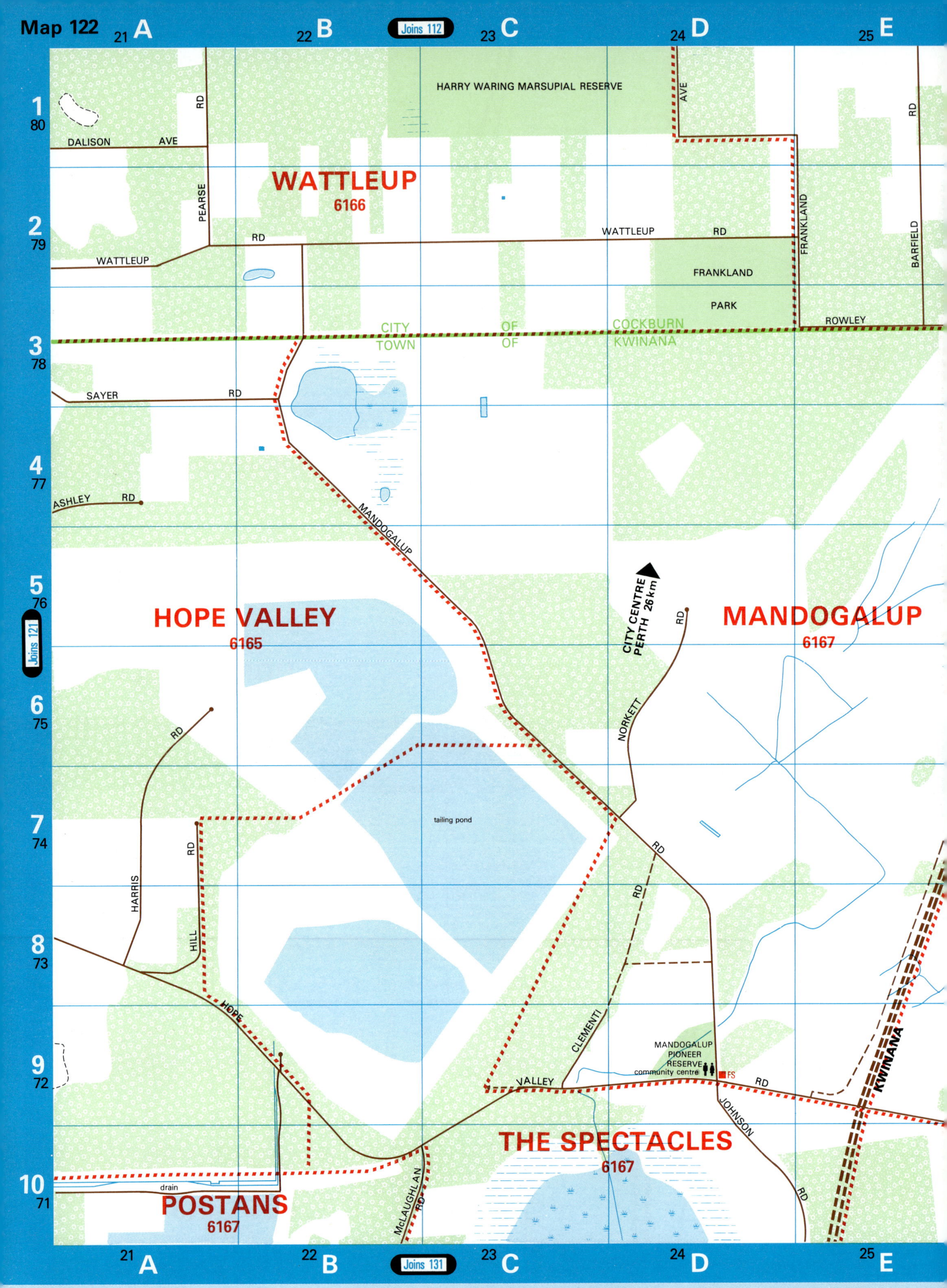

0 500 m 1 km 2 km
SCALE 1:20 000

PRIMARY RECTANGLE
PEEL BG 33

Map 123

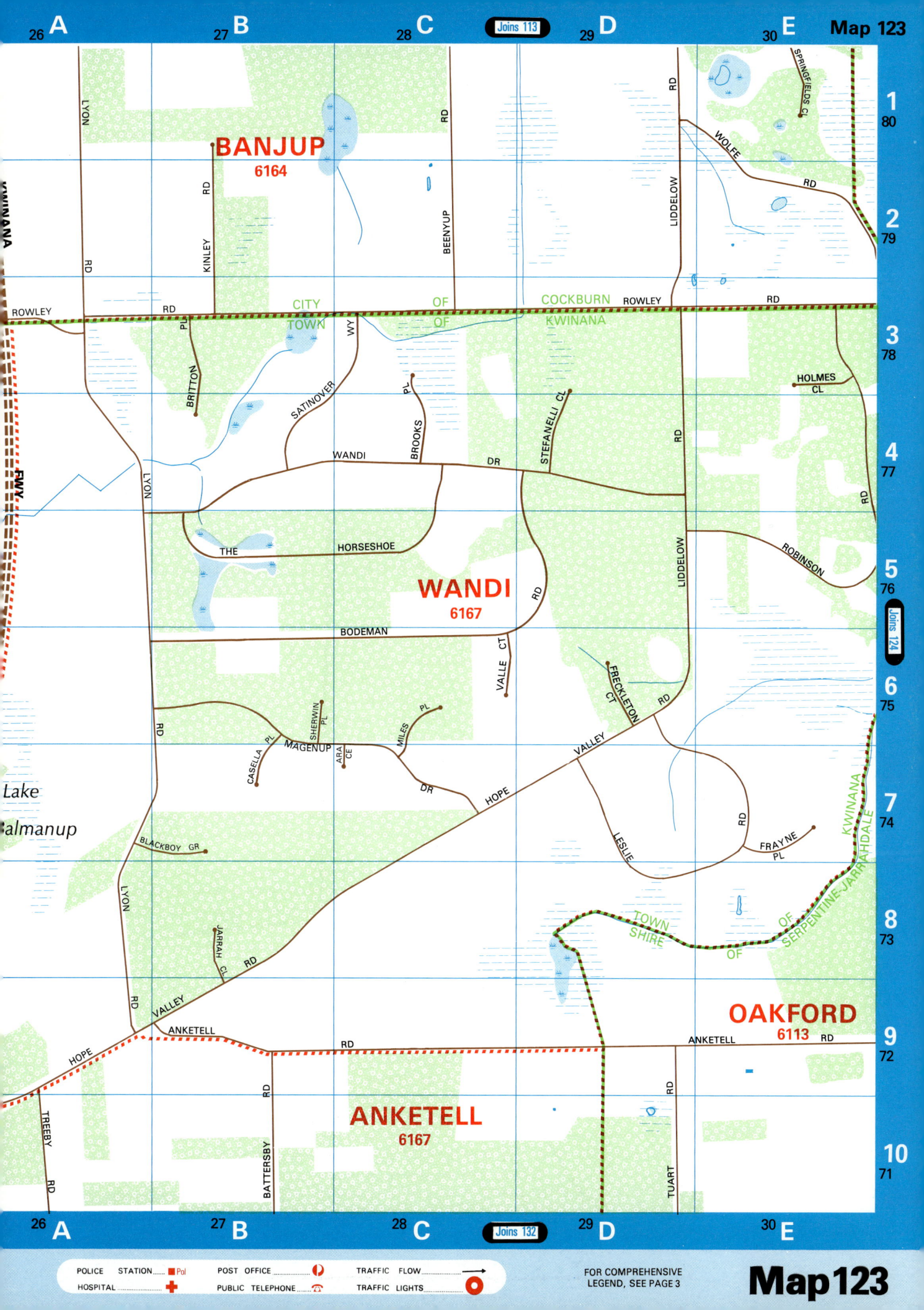

BANJUP 6164

WANDI 6167

OAKFORD 6113

ANKETELL 6167

Lake Balmanup

POLICE STATION	Pol
HOSPITAL	
POST OFFICE	
PUBLIC TELEPHONE	
TRAFFIC FLOW	
TRAFFIC LIGHTS	

FOR COMPREHENSIVE LEGEND, SEE PAGE 3

Map 124

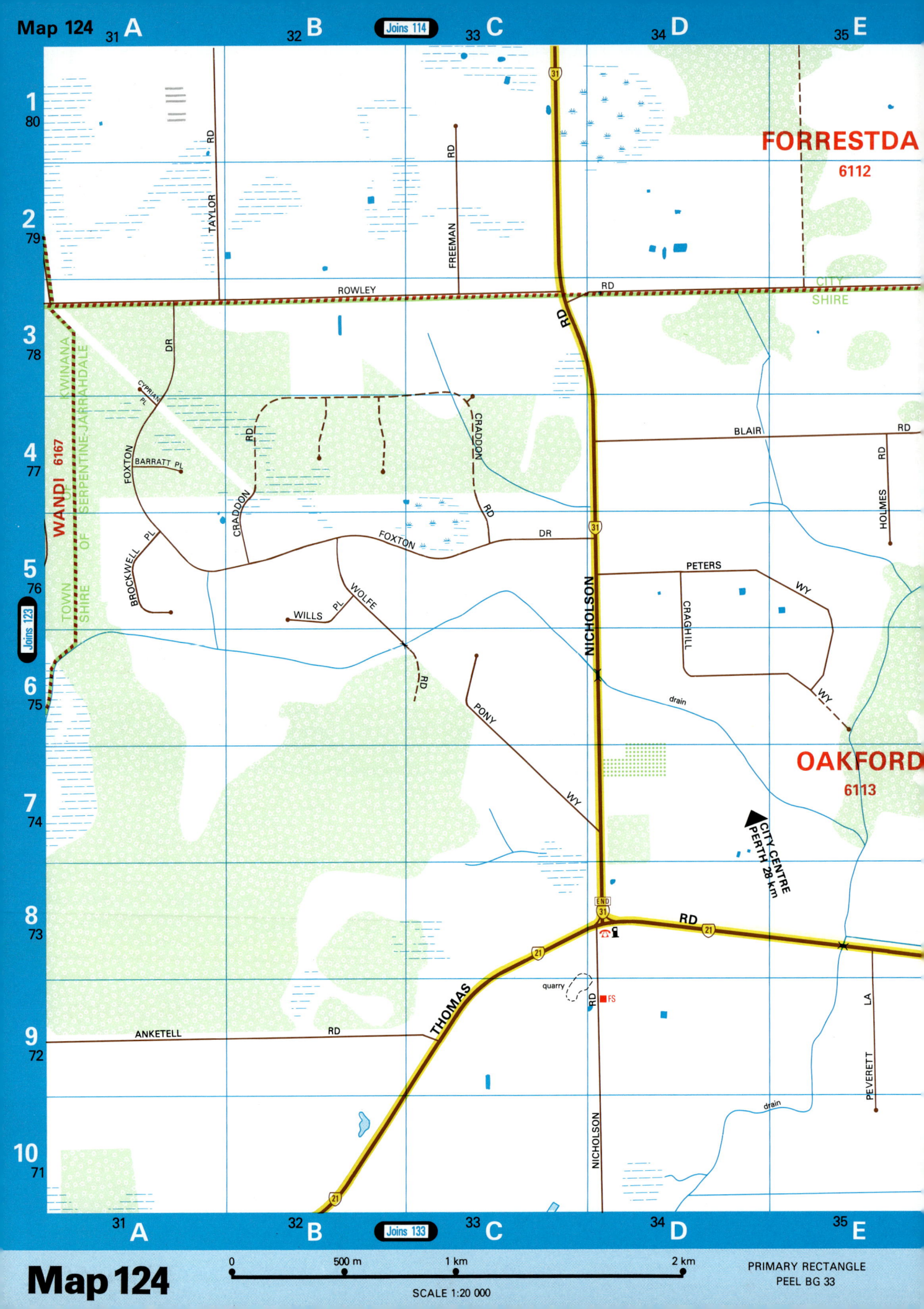

FORRESTDALE 6112

OAKFORD 6113

WANDI 6167

TOWN OF KWINANA / SHIRE OF SERPENTINE-JARRAHDALE

Joins 114 (top)
Joins 133 (bottom)
Joins 123 (left)

Roads and features:
- TAYLOR RD
- FREEMAN RD
- ROWLEY RD
- NICHOLSON RD (31)
- CITY SHIRE
- CYPRIAN PL
- FOXTON DR
- BARRATT PL
- CRADDON RD
- BROCKWELL PL
- WILLS PL
- WOLFE RD
- FOXTON DR
- BLAIR RD
- HOLMES RD
- PETERS WY
- CRAGHILL WY
- drain
- PONY WY
- CITY CENTRE PERTH 28 km
- END 31
- THOMAS RD (21)
- ANKETELL RD
- quarry
- FS
- NICHOLSON RD
- PEVERETT LA
- drain

PRIMARY RECTANGLE
PEEL BG 33

SCALE 1:20 000
0 — 500 m — 1 km — 2 km

Map 125

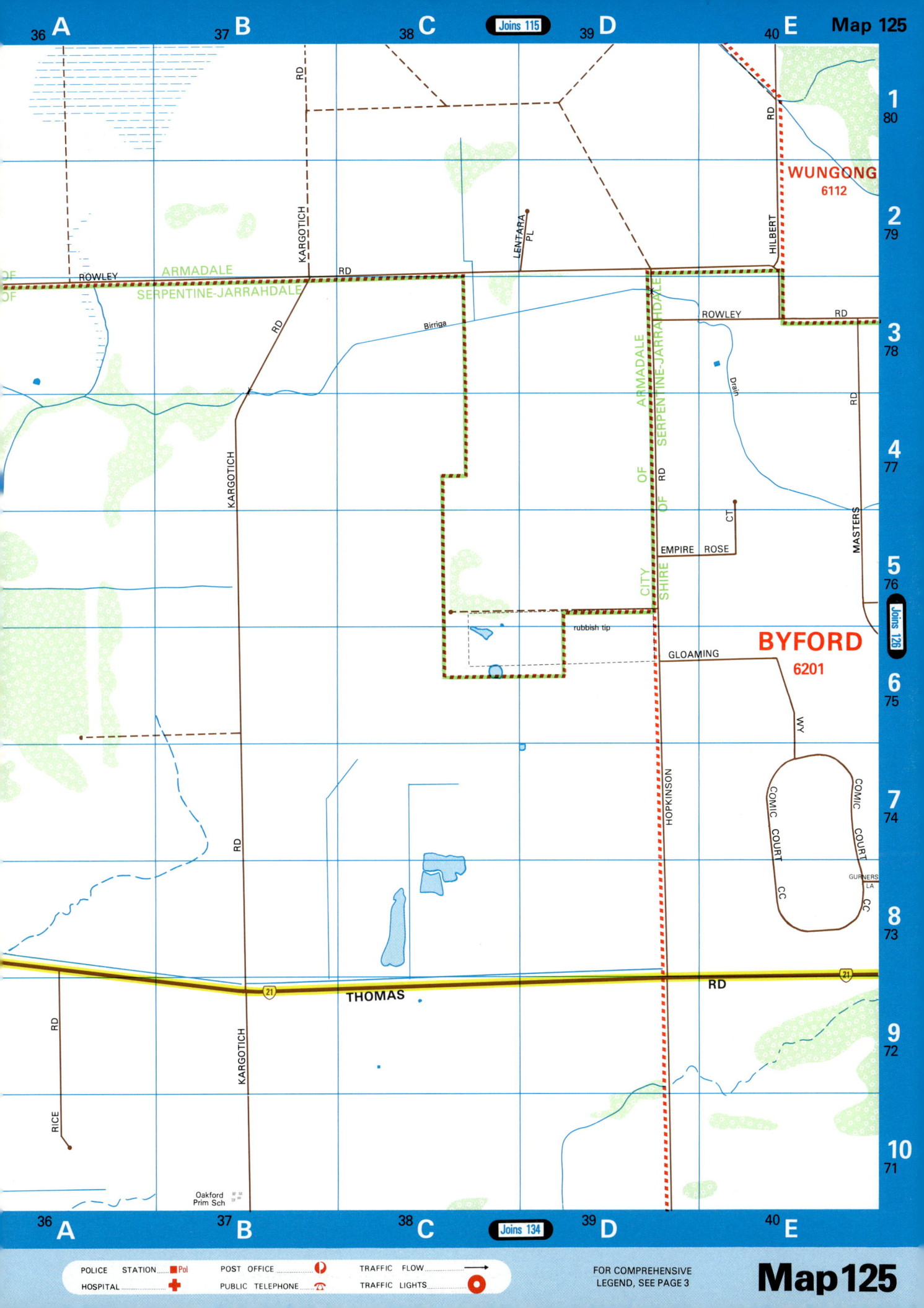

WUNGONG 6112

BYFORD 6201

Joins 116

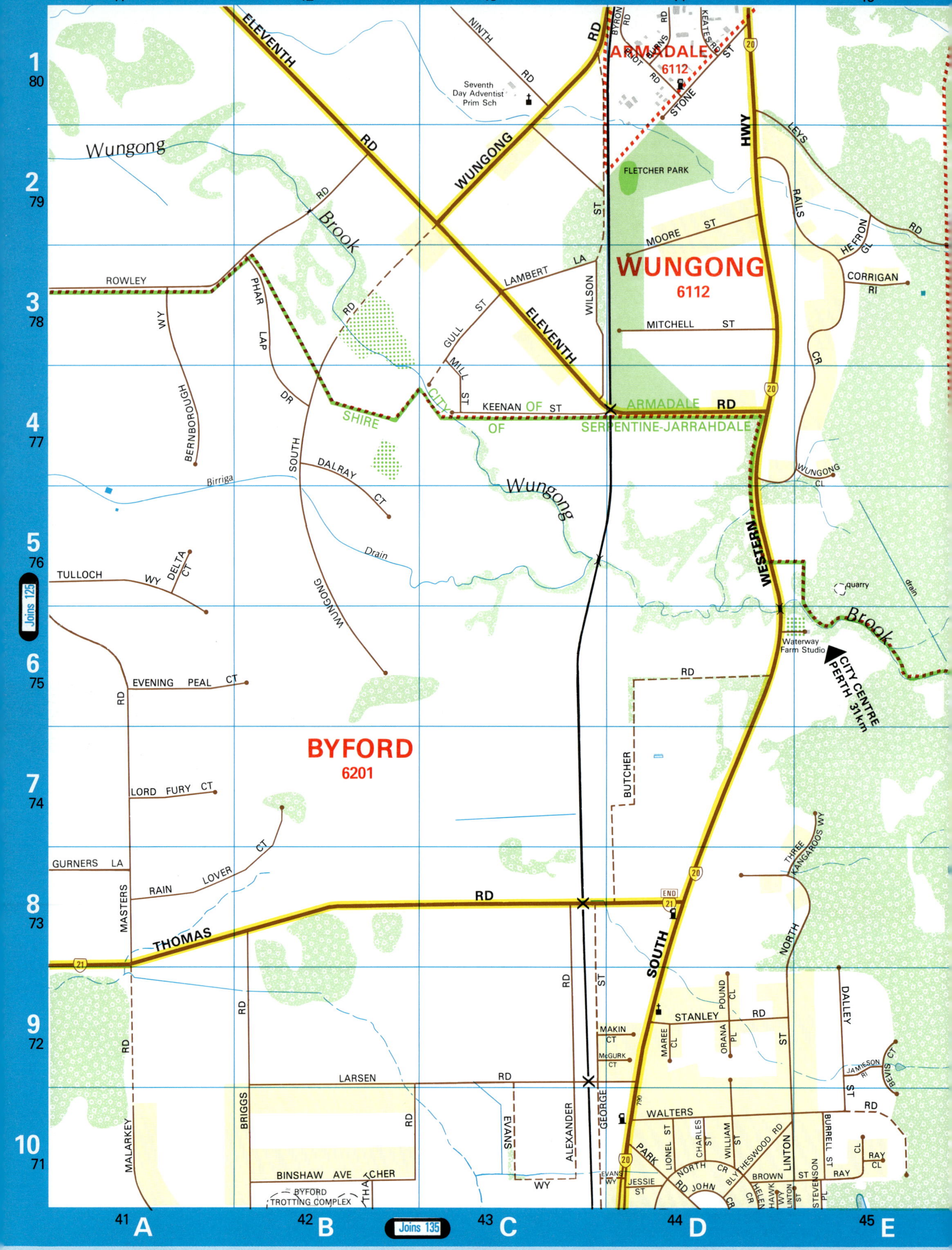

Joins 125

Joins 135

0 500 m 1 km 2 km

SCALE 1:20 000

PRIMARY RECTANGLE
PEEL BG 33

Map 127

BEDFORDALE 6112

BYFORD 6201

Bungendore Park
Emmaus Christian Sch
Wungong Brook
Wungong Dam
Wungong Reservoir
Darling Range

Streets: Waterwheel Rd, Albany Hwy, Howe St, St Vincent St, Nelson St, Blake St, Admiral, Collingwood Rd, Cross Rd, Howard St, Neerigen Brook, Powell Cl, Wallangarra Dr, Otway Pl, Barge Rd, North Rd, Admiral

City of Armadale / Shire of Serpentine-Jarrahdale

Joins 117 / Joins 128 / Limit of Maps

Legend: Police Station (Pol), Hospital, Post Office, Public Telephone, Traffic Flow, Traffic Lights — For comprehensive legend, see page 3

Map 128

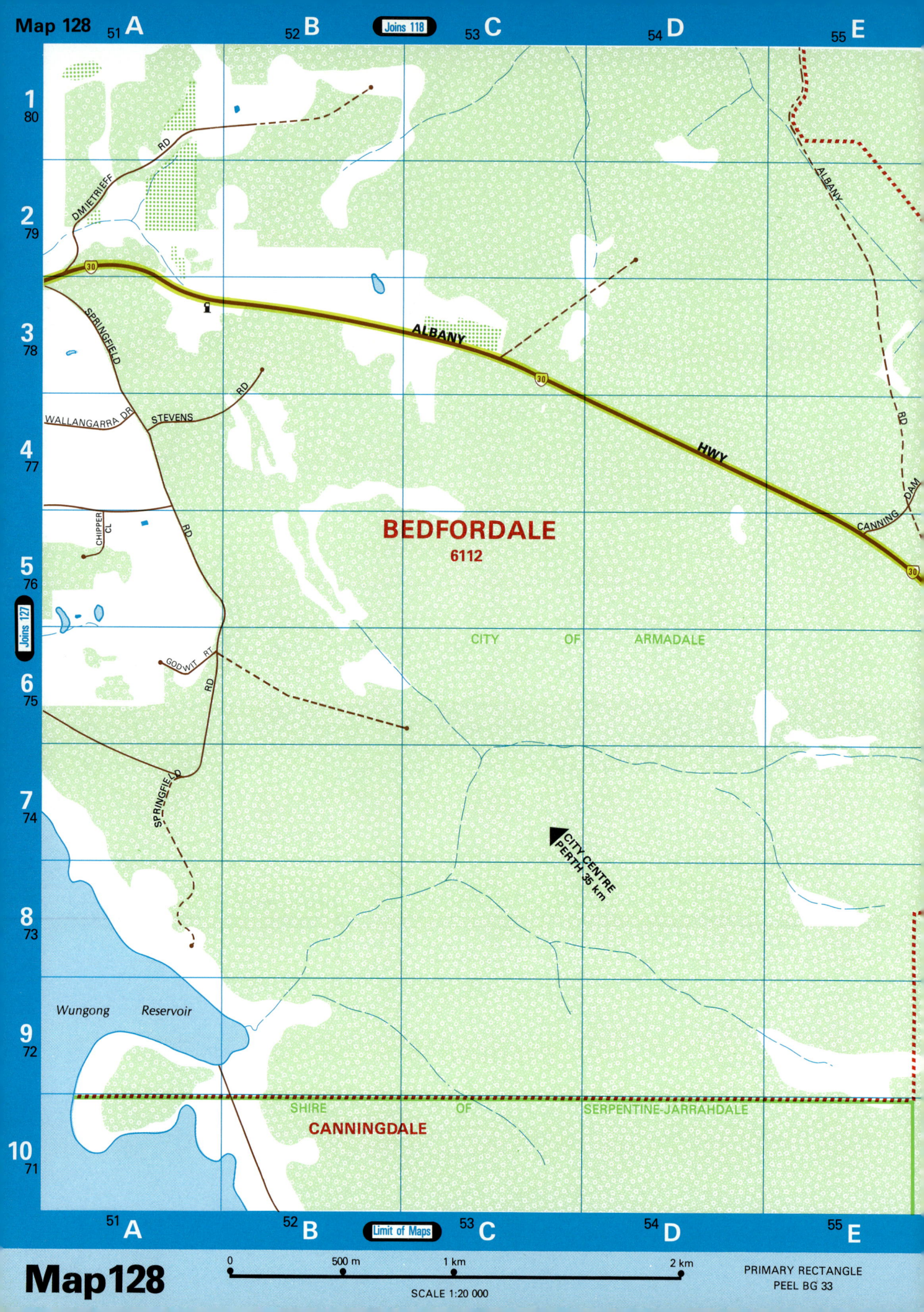

BEDFORDALE 6112

CANNINGDALE

CITY OF ARMADALE

SHIRE OF SERPENTINE-JARRAHDALE

Wungong Reservoir

Joins 118
Joins 127
Joins Limit of Maps

CITY CENTRE PERTH 35 km

Roads and features: DMIETRIEFF RD, SPRINGFIELD RD, WALLANGARRA DR, STEVENS RD, CHIPPER CL, GODWIT RT, ALBANY HWY (30), CANNING DAM RD

SCALE 1:20 000
0 — 500 m — 1 km — 2 km

PRIMARY RECTANGLE
PEEL BG 33

MURDOCH UNIVERSITY

Administration/Admissions Office	1
Administration Building	17
Alcoa Laboratory and Glasshouse	14
Amenities Building	4
Amphitheatre	22
Animal Clinic Paddocks	27
Animal House	25
Animal House Paddocks	26
Animal Resource Centre	32
Battery Project Laboratories	15
Biological Sciences Building	11
Bookshop	4
Cafeteria, Restaurant	4
Chaplain's Office	2
Child Care Centre	21
Computer Services Unit	10
Drama Workshop	19
Economics, Commerce, Law Building	16
Education (School of)	2
Environmental Science Building	9
External Studies Unit	3
Function Centre	23
Gymnasium	18
Humanities (School of)	1
Isolation Animal House	24
Law, Economics, Commerce Building	16
Lecture Theatres 1, 2, 3	7
Library	6
Livestock Manager's House	30
Magro Mol	33
Mathematical & Physical Sciences (School of)	8
Meteorological Garden	31
Murdoch University Energy Research Institute	29
Native Fauna Research Unit	35
Personnel Section	2
Physical Sciences Building	8
Registrar's Office	1
Research & Post-graduate Studies	1
Sciences & Computing Building	10
Senate Suite	5
Social Studies (School of)	3
Squash Courts	20
Student Guild	4
Student Services	3
Veterinary Biology Building	12
Veterinary Clinical Sciences Building	13
Veterinary Hospital	13
Veterinary Farm Research/Storage Buildings	34
Vice-Chancellor's Office	1
West Academic I	3
West Academic II	1
Workshops, Stores and Printery	28

Staff and Student Car Parks
Visitor's Car Parks
NOTE: Visitors may use any parking area if visitor's car parks are full.
Motorcycle Parking
Administration Building

Scale 1:6000

Map 129

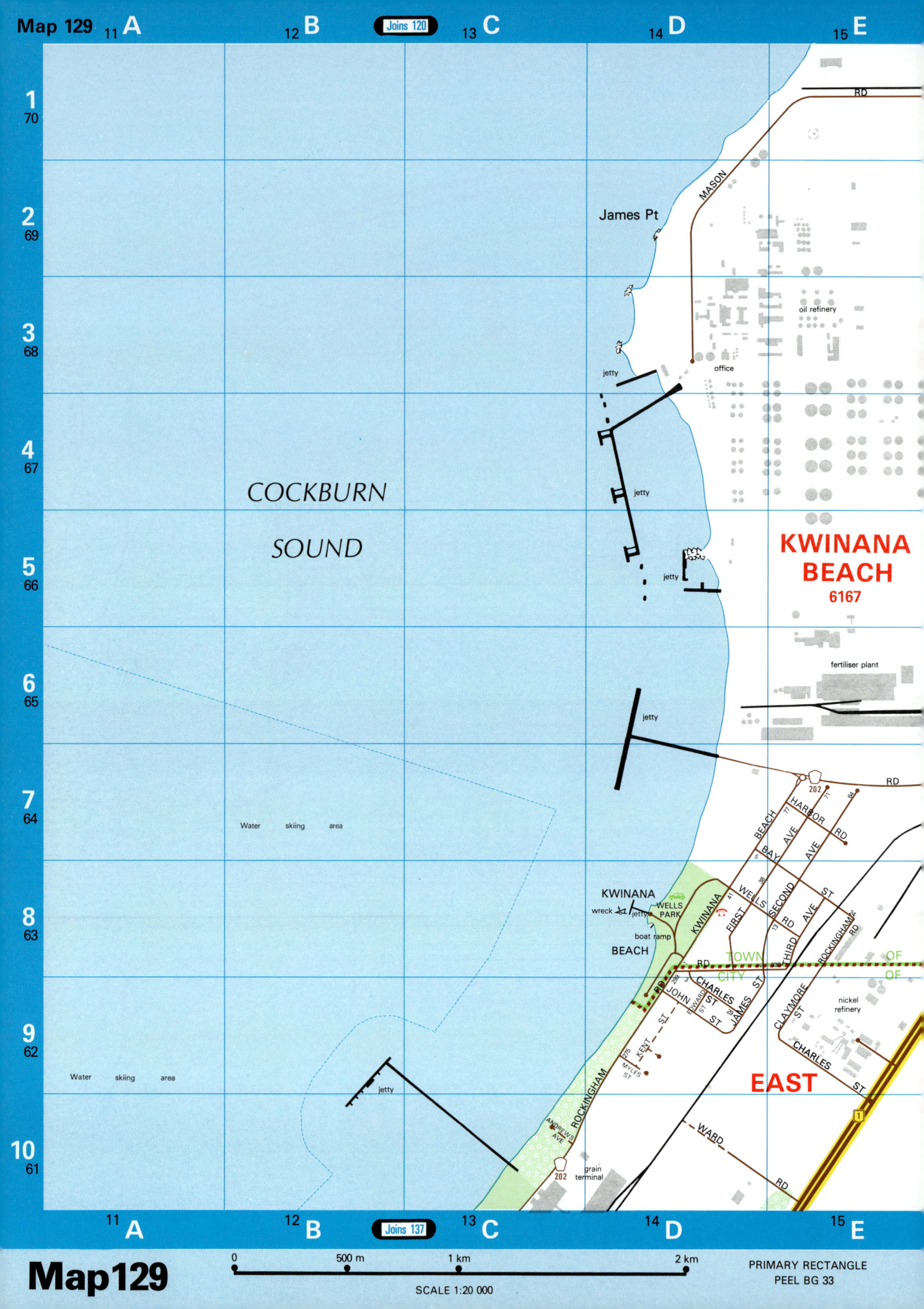

COCKBURN SOUND

James Pt

oil refinery
office
jetty
jetty
jetty

KWINANA BEACH 6167

fertiliser plant

jetty

Water skiing area

202
BEACH RD
BAY AVE
HARBOR AVE
RD

KWINANA
wreck jetty
WELLS PARK
boat ramp
BEACH
KWINANA RD
FIRST
WELLS RD
SECOND AVE
ST
THIRD AVE
ROCKINGHAM RD

TOWN OF
CITY OF

JOHN ST
CHARLES ST
JAMES ST
EDWARD ST
KENT ST
MYLES ST
CLAYMORE ST
CHARLES ST

nickel refinery

EAST

Water skiing area
jetty

ANDREWS AVE
ROCKINGHAM RD
WARD RD
202 grain terminal

SCALE 1:20 000
0 — 500 m — 1 km — 2 km

PRIMARY RECTANGLE
PEEL BG 33

Joins 121

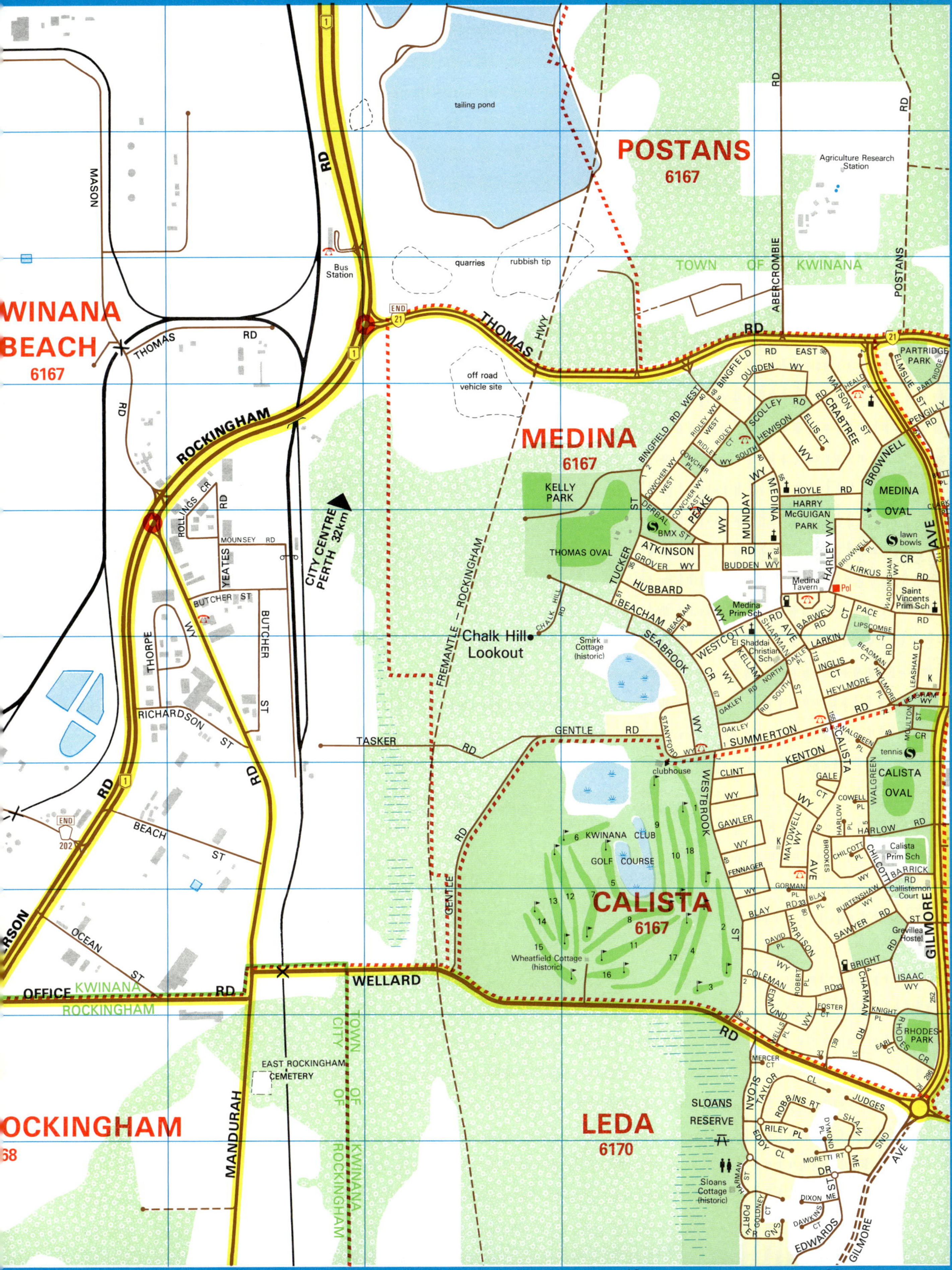

Joins 138

POLICE STATION ...... Pol
HOSPITAL ......
POST OFFICE ......
PUBLIC TELEPHONE ......
TRAFFIC FLOW ......
TRAFFIC LIGHTS ......

FOR COMPREHENSIVE LEGEND, SEE PAGE 3

Map 131

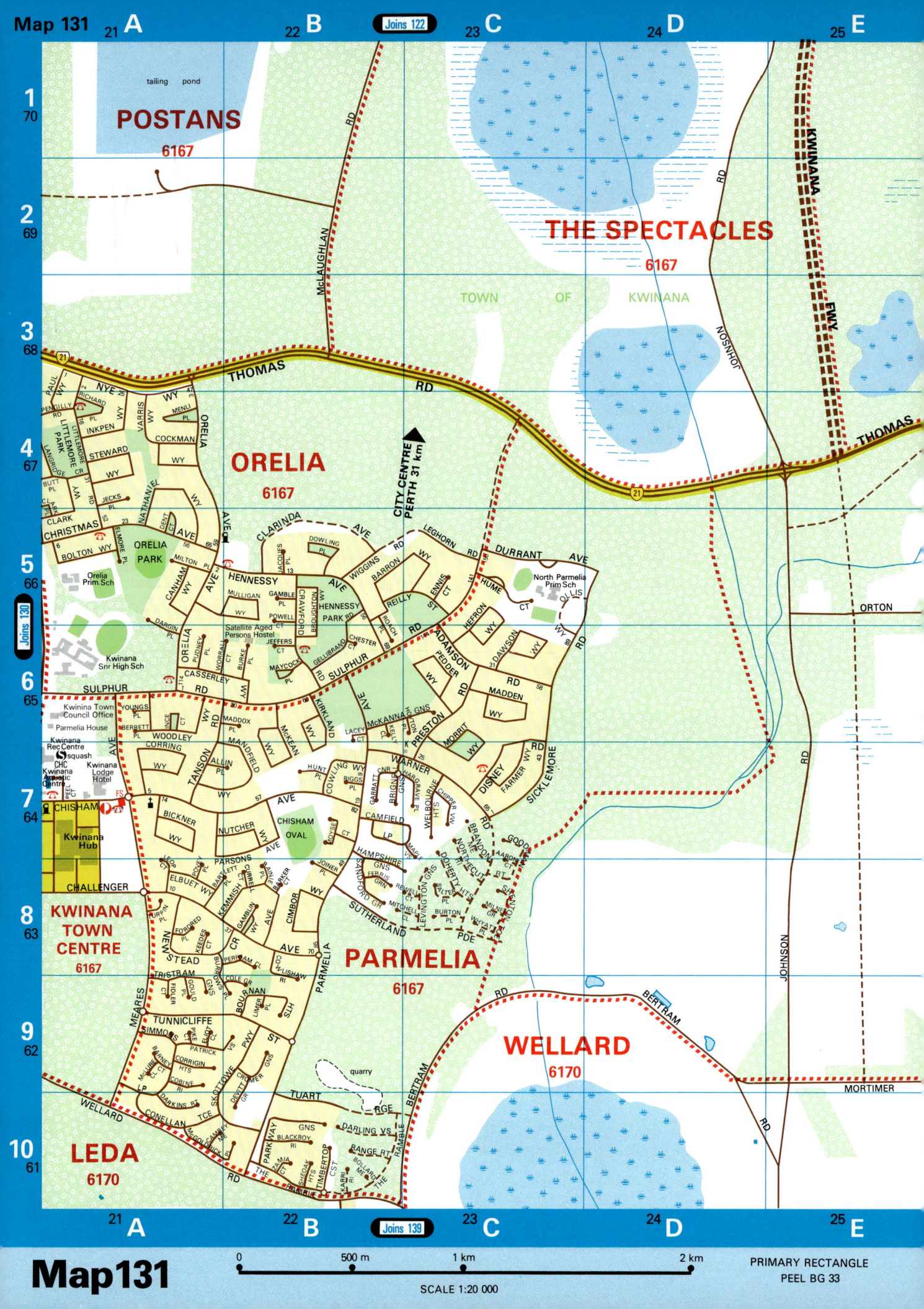

POSTANS 6167

THE SPECTACLES 6167

TOWN OF KWINANA

ORELIA 6167

CITY CENTRE PERTH 31 km

PARMELIA 6167

KWINANA TOWN CENTRE 6167

WELLARD 6170

LEDA 6170

SCALE 1:20 000

PRIMARY RECTANGLE PEEL BG 33

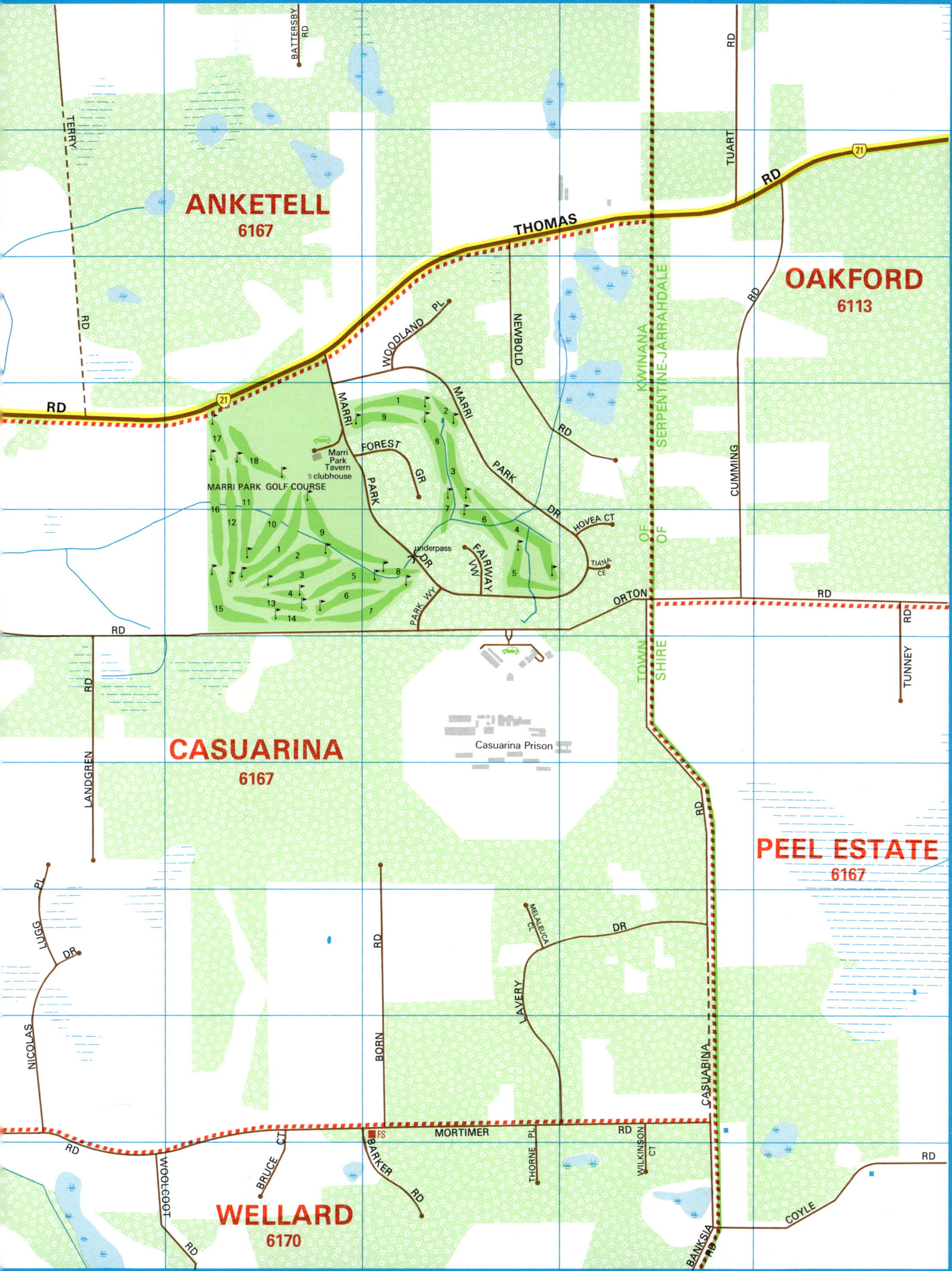

1 70
2 69
3 68
4 67
5 66
6 65
7 64
8 63
9 62
10 61

Joins 133

POLICE STATION Pol	POST OFFICE	TRAFFIC FLOW
HOSPITAL	PUBLIC TELEPHONE	TRAFFIC LIGHTS

FOR COMPREHENSIVE LEGEND, SEE PAGE 3

Map 133

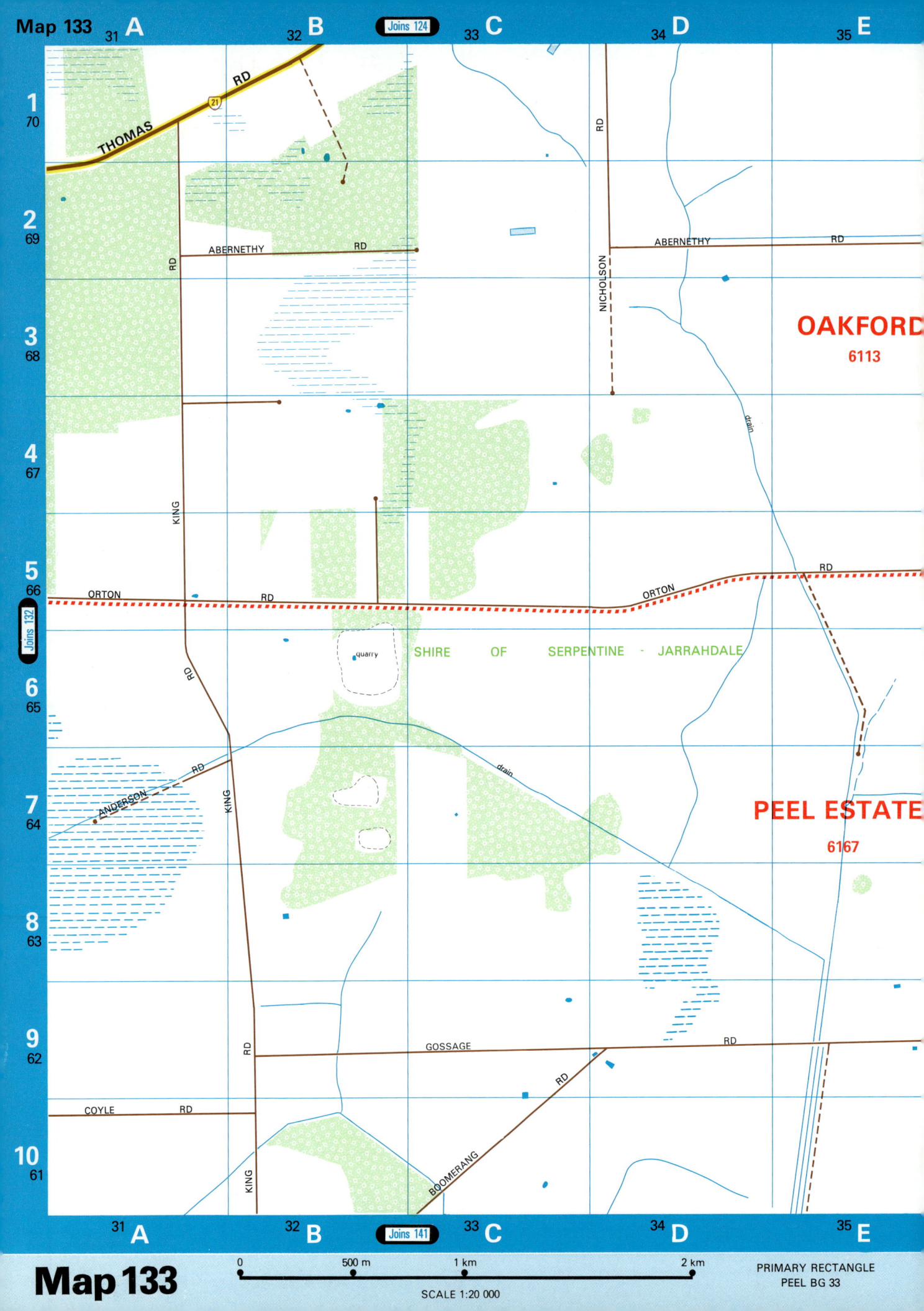

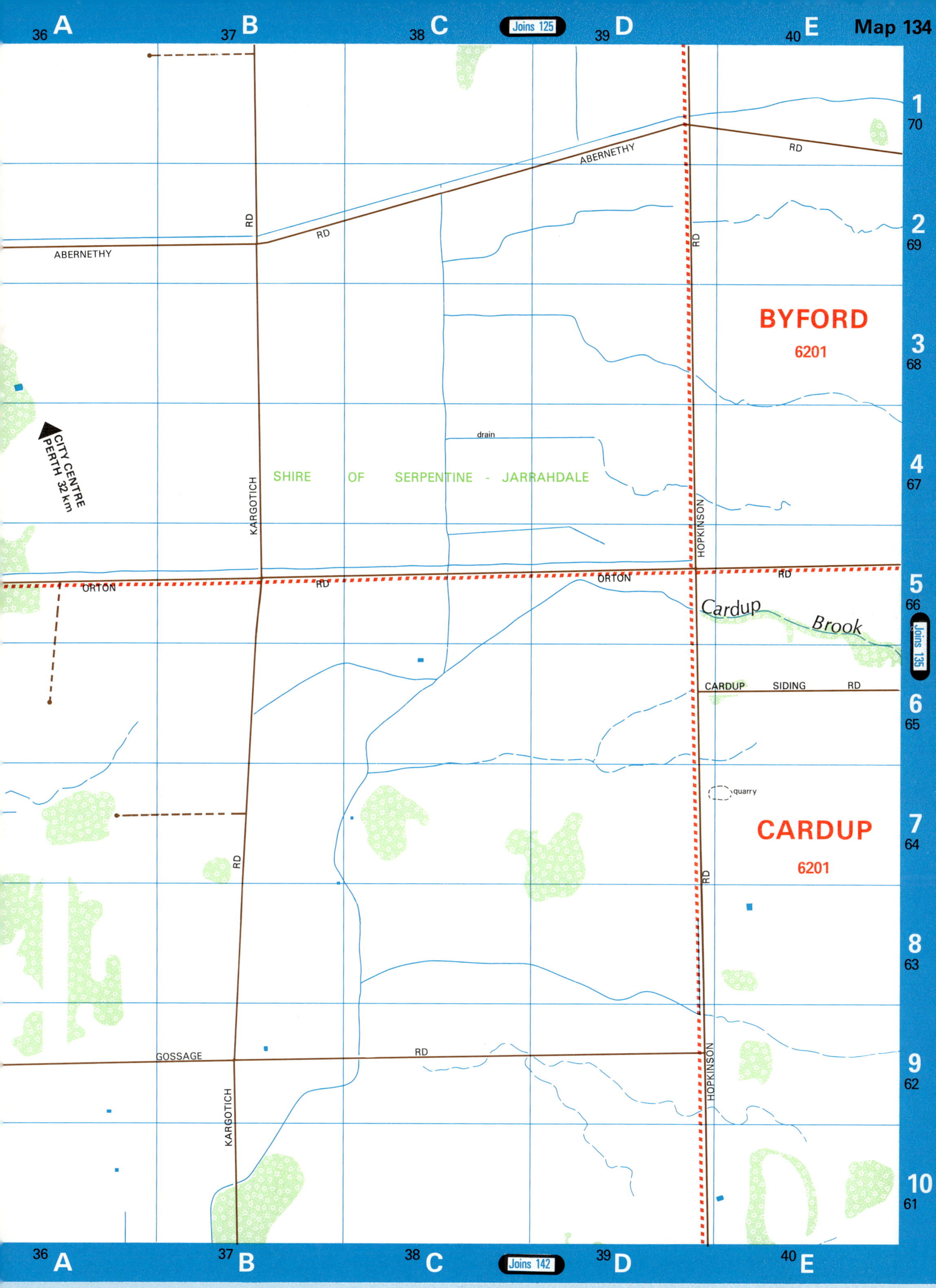
36 A
37 B
38 C
Joins 125
39 D
40 E
1
70
2
69
3
68
4
67
5
66
Joins 135
6
65
7
64
8
63
9
62
10
61
36 A
37 B
38 C
Joins 142
39 D
40 E
ABERNETHY
RD
ABERNETHY
RD
RD
RD
BYFORD
6201
CITY CENTRE
PERTH 32 km
drain
SHIRE OF SERPENTINE - JARRAHDALE
KARGOTICH
HOPKINSON
ORTON
RD
ORTON
RD
Cardup Brook
CARDUP SIDING RD
quarry
CARDUP
6201
RD
RD
GOSSAGE
RD
KARGOTICH
HOPKINSON

POLICE STATION Pol
HOSPITAL
POST OFFICE
PUBLIC TELEPHONE
TRAFFIC FLOW
TRAFFIC LIGHTS

FOR COMPREHENSIVE LEGEND, SEE PAGE 3

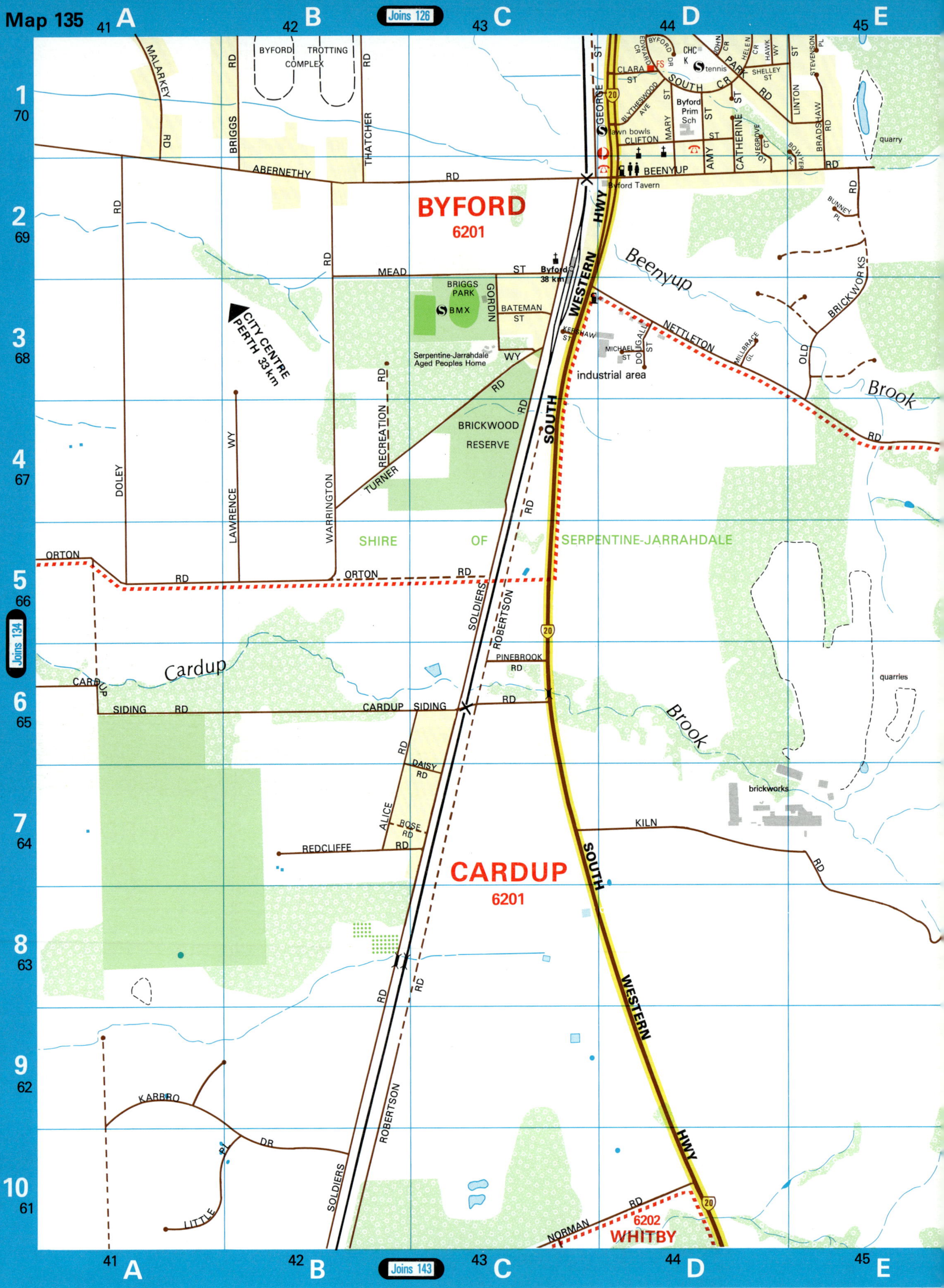

Map 135

0 500 m 1 km 2 km

SCALE 1:20 000

PRIMARY RECTANGLE
PEEL BG 33

CURTIN UNIVERSITY OF TECHNOLOGY

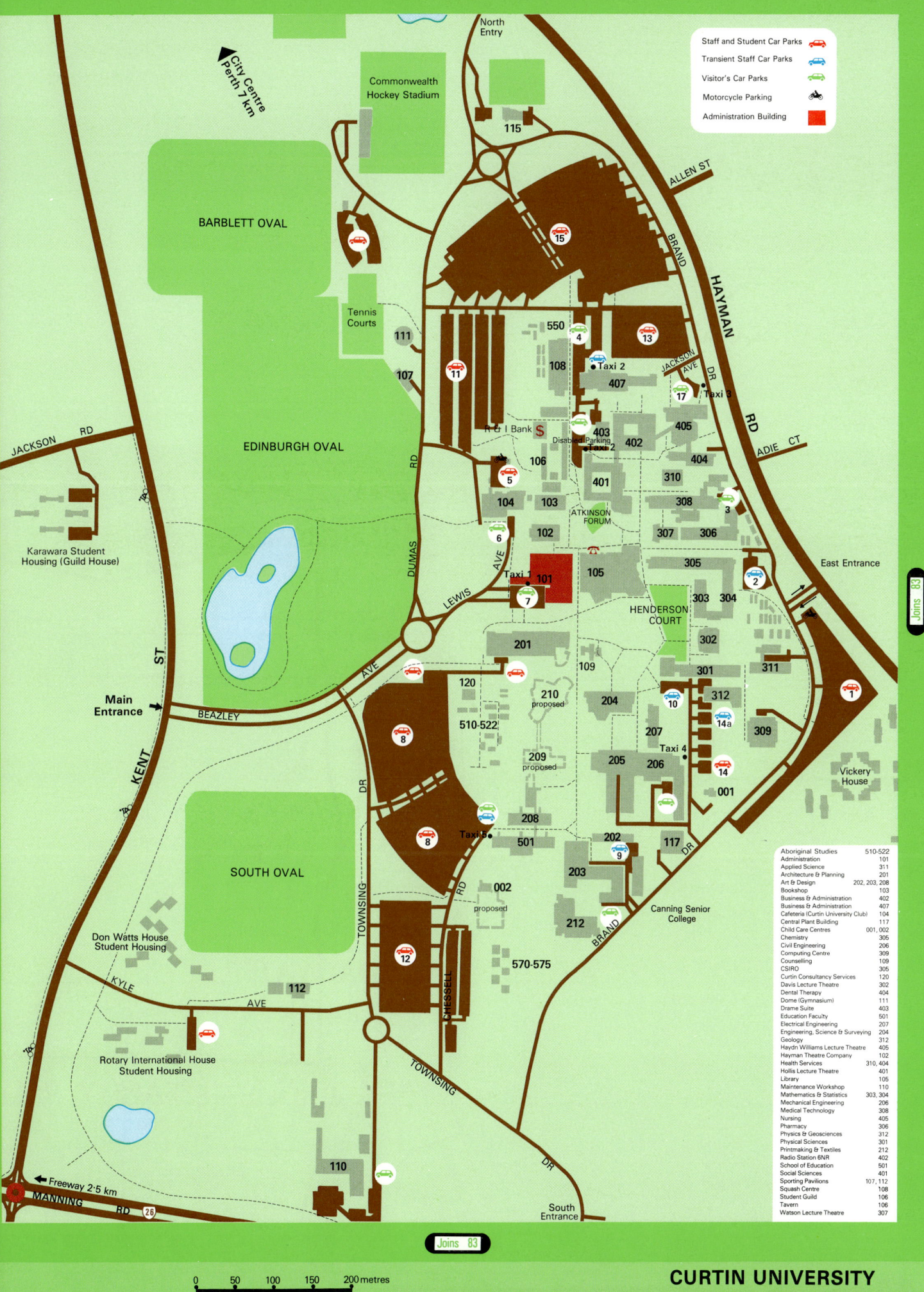

Legend:
- Staff and Student Car Parks
- Transient Staff Car Parks
- Visitor's Car Parks
- Motorcycle Parking
- Administration Building

Building	Number
Aboriginal Studies	510-522
Administration	101
Applied Science	311
Architecture & Planning	201
Art & Design	202, 203, 208
Bookshop	103
Business & Administration	402
Business & Administration	407
Cafeteria (Curtin University Club)	104
Central Plant Building	117
Child Care Centres	001, 002
Chemistry	305
Civil Engineering	206
Computing Centre	309
Counselling	109
CSIRO	305
Curtin Consultancy Services	120
Davis Lecture Theatre	302
Dental Therapy	404
Dome (Gymnasium)	111
Drame Suite	403
Education Faculty	501
Electrical Engineering	207
Engineering, Science & Surveying	204
Geology	312
Haydn Williams Lecture Theatre	405
Hayman Theatre Company	102
Health Services	310, 404
Hollis Lecture Theatre	401
Library	105
Maintenance Workshop	110
Mathematics & Statistics	303, 304
Mechanical Engineering	206
Medical Technology	308
Nursing	405
Pharmacy	306
Physics & Geosciences	312
Physical Sciences	301
Printmaking & Textiles	212
Radio Station 6NR	402
School of Education	501
Social Sciences	401
Sporting Pavilions	107, 112
Squash Centre	108
Student Guild	106
Tavern	106
Watson Lecture Theatre	307

Scale 1:6000 — 0, 50, 100, 150, 200 metres

Joins 83

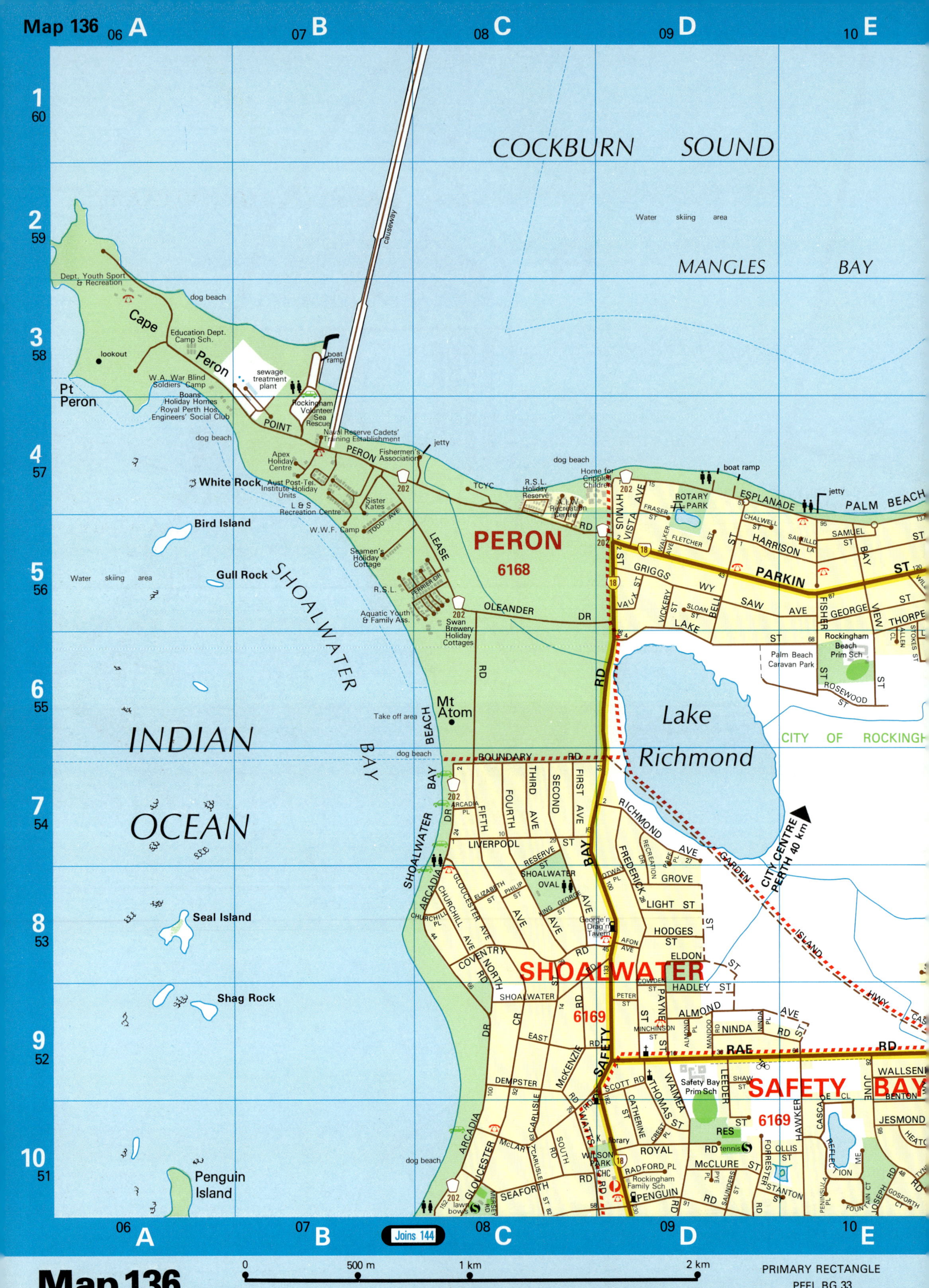

PRIMARY RECTANGLE
PEEL BG 33

POLICE STATION Pol
HOSPITAL
POST OFFICE
PUBLIC TELEPHONE
TRAFFIC FLOW
TRAFFIC LIGHTS

FOR COMPREHENSIVE LEGEND, SEE PAGE 3

Map 138

EAST ROCKINGHAM 6168
ROCKINGHAM 6168
HILLMAN 6168
COOLOONGUP 6168
LEDA 6170

Lake Cooloongup

Rockingham Holiday Village
Rockingham/Kwinana District Hospital
Rockingham Golf Course
quarry
clubhouse

CHESTERFIELD RD
MANDURAH RD
MEAD RD
CROMPTON RD
SAVERY WY
HARGREAVES RD
DAY RD
DIXON RD
LAWSON RD
GARDEN ISLAND HWY
CALUME ST
ST DAY ST
DARILE
MAPLEWOOD PL
OREGON PL
PARK LAND
CUTHBERTSON
ELANORA DR
PAR CT
BIRDIE
LINK
ST ANDREWS WY
CADDY CL
MANDURAH RD
MILLAR RD
KEROSENE
FEILMAN DR
GILMORE AVE

CITY CENTRE PERTH 36 km

TOWN CITY

Joins 130
Joins 137
Joins 148

SCALE 1:20 000
0 – 500 m – 1 km – 2 km

PRIMARY RECTANGLE PEEL BG 33

Map 139

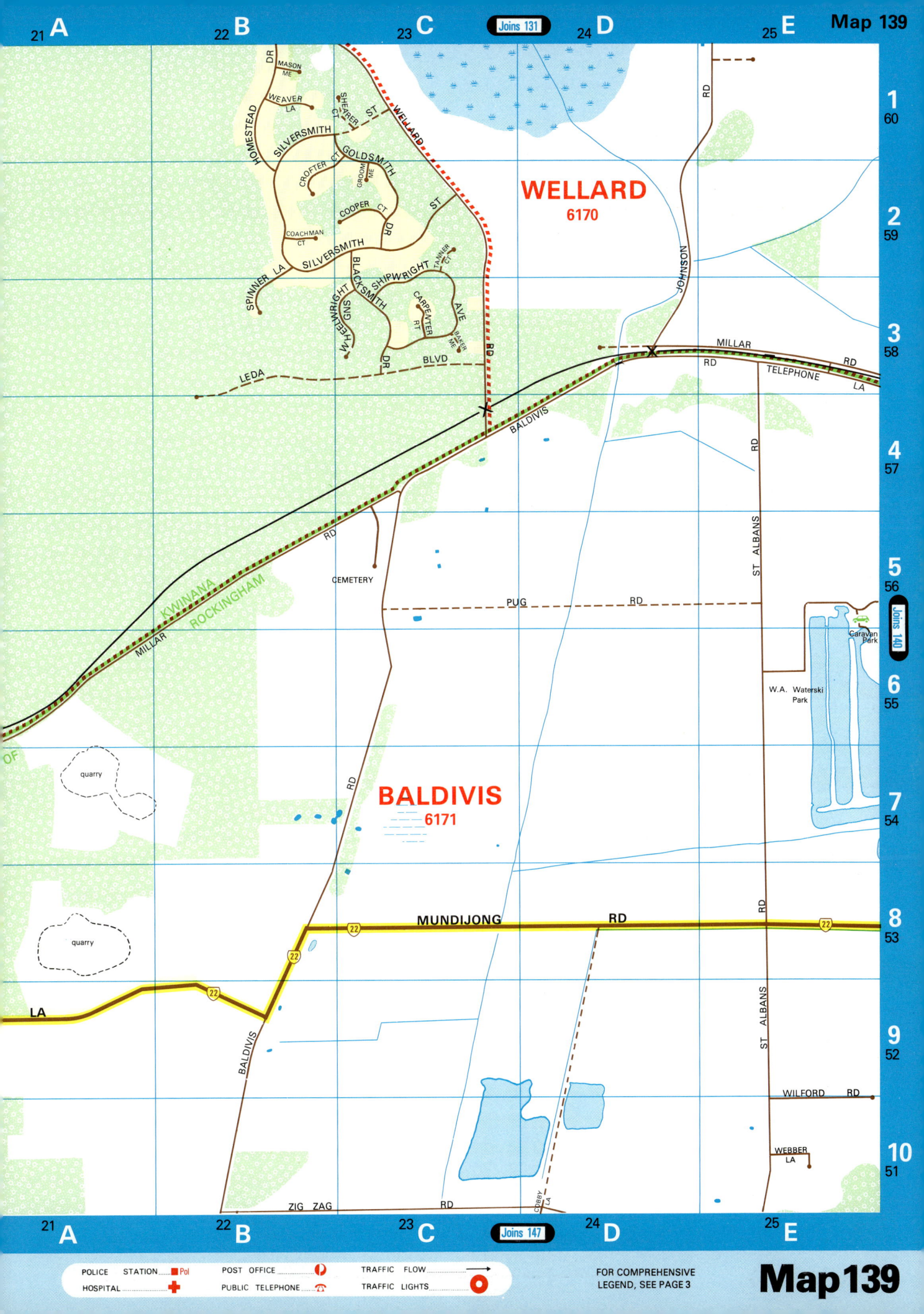

WELLARD 6170

BALDIVIS 6171

Streets and features visible:
- Mason Me, Weaver La, Homestead Dr, Silversmith St, Shearer Ct, Wellard Rd
- Crofter Ct, Goldsmith Dr, Groomer Me
- Coachman Ct, Cooper Ct, Silversmith Dr
- Spinner La, Blacksmith St, Shipwright Ave, Tanner Ct
- Wheelwright Dr, Carpenter Rt, Baxter Me
- Leda Blvd
- Millar Rd, Telephone La
- Kwinana Rockingham Rd
- Baldivis Rd, Johnson Rd
- Cemetery
- Pug Rd
- St Albans Rd
- W.A. Waterski Park, Caravan Park
- Mundijong Rd (Route 22)
- Zig Zag Rd, Cobby La
- Wilford Rd, Webber La
- quarry (x2)

Joins 131 (top), Joins 147 (bottom), Joins 140 (right)

Grid: A21–E25, rows 1–10

Legend: Police Station (Pol), Hospital, Post Office, Public Telephone, Traffic Flow, Traffic Lights

FOR COMPREHENSIVE LEGEND, SEE PAGE 3

26 A
27 B
Joins 132
28 C
29 D
30 E
1 60
2 59
3 58
4 57
5 56
Joins 139
6 55
7 54
8 53
9 52
10 51
CHANDLER CL
CT
ARUNDEL
ALEXANDER
DR
RD
WELLARD
6170
TOWN OF KWINANA
JOLLEY RD
RD
rifle range
BOOMERANG
BANKSIA
BRADDOCK RD
JACKSON
WOOLCOOT
MILLAR RD
RD
BANKSIA
TELEPHONE
LA
DUCKPOND
CITY CENTRE PERTH 37 km
CITY OF ROCKINGHAM
BALDIVIS
6171
RD
22
MUNDIJONG
RD
TELEPHONE
MUNDIJONG
22
RD
RD
LA
WILKINSON
LLOYD
26 A
27 B
Joins 148
28 C
29 D
30 E

0 500 m 1 km 2 km

SCALE 1:20 000

PRIMARY RECTANGLE
PEEL BG 33

31 A
32 B
33 C
Joins 133
34 D
35 E
1 60
2 59
3 58
4 57
5 56
6 55
7 54
8 53
9 52
10 51
Joins 142
BOOMERANG RD
JACKSON RD
BIRD RD
RD
LEIPOLD RD
SHIRE OF SERPENTINE - JARRAHDALE
PEEL ESTATE
6167
KING RD
MUNDIJONG RD
22
LIGHTBODY RD
Joins 149

POLICE STATION Pol
HOSPITAL
POST OFFICE
PUBLIC TELEPHONE
TRAFFIC FLOW
TRAFFIC LIGHTS

FOR COMPREHENSIVE LEGEND, SEE PAGE 3

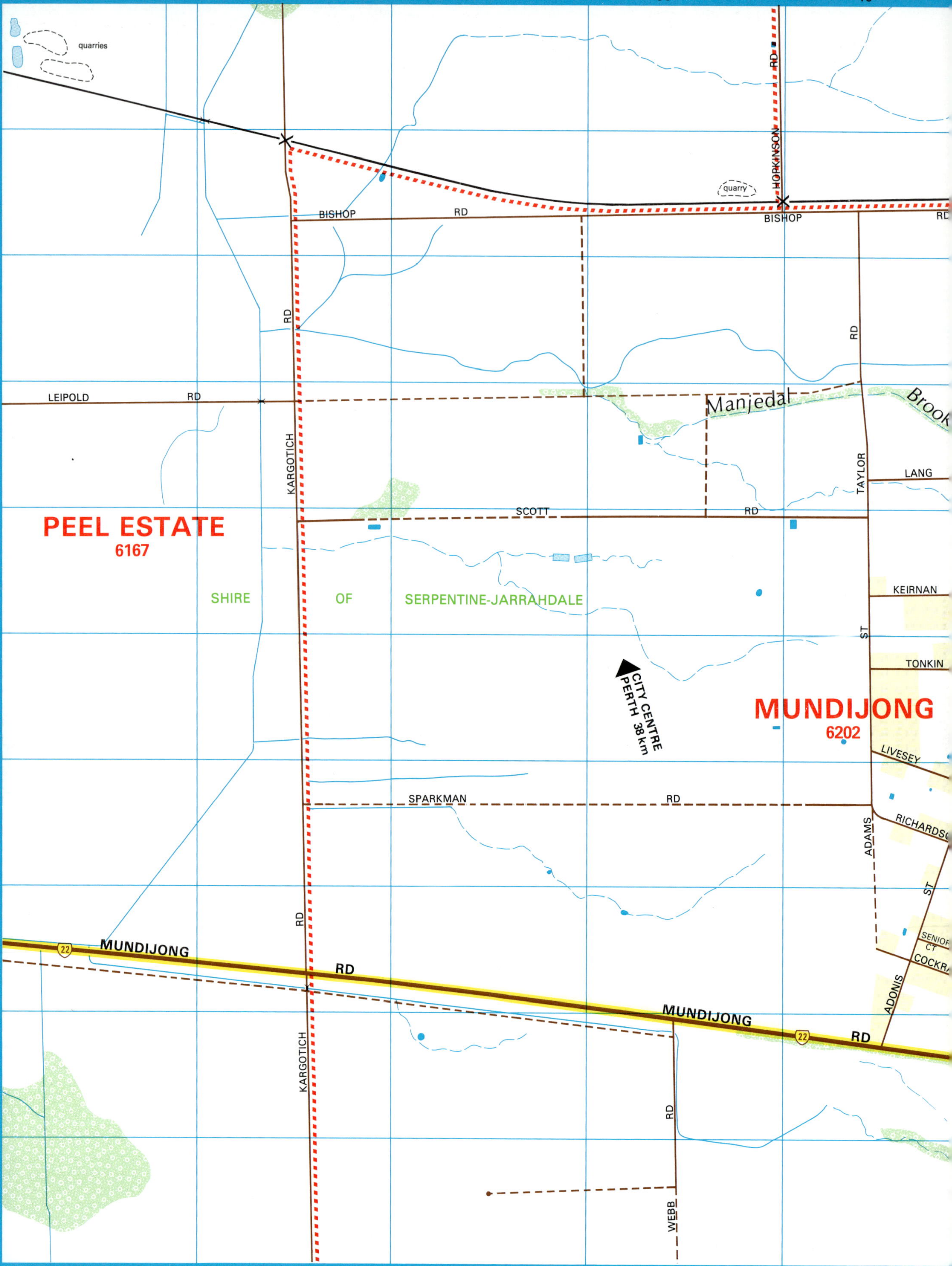
36 A
37 B
Joins 134
38 C
39 D
40 E
1 60
2 59
3 58
4 57
5 56
6 55
7 54
8 53
9 52
10 51
Joins 141
quarries
quarry
HORKINSON RD
BISHOP RD
BISHOP RD
LEIPOLD RD
KARGOTICH RD
Manjedal Brook
TAYLOR RD
LANG
SCOTT RD
PEEL ESTATE
6167
SHIRE OF SERPENTINE-JARRAHDALE
KEIRNAN
ST
TONKIN
CITY CENTRE
PERTH 38 km
MUNDIJONG
6202
LIVESEY
SPARKMAN RD
RICHARDSO
ADAMS ST
SENIOR CT
COCKR
ADONIS
22
MUNDIJONG RD
MUNDIJONG RD
22
KARGOTICH RD
WEBB RD
36 A
37 B
Joins 150
38 C
39 D
40 E

0 500 m 1 km 2 km

SCALE 1:20 000

PRIMARY RECTANGLE
PEEL BG 33

Map 143

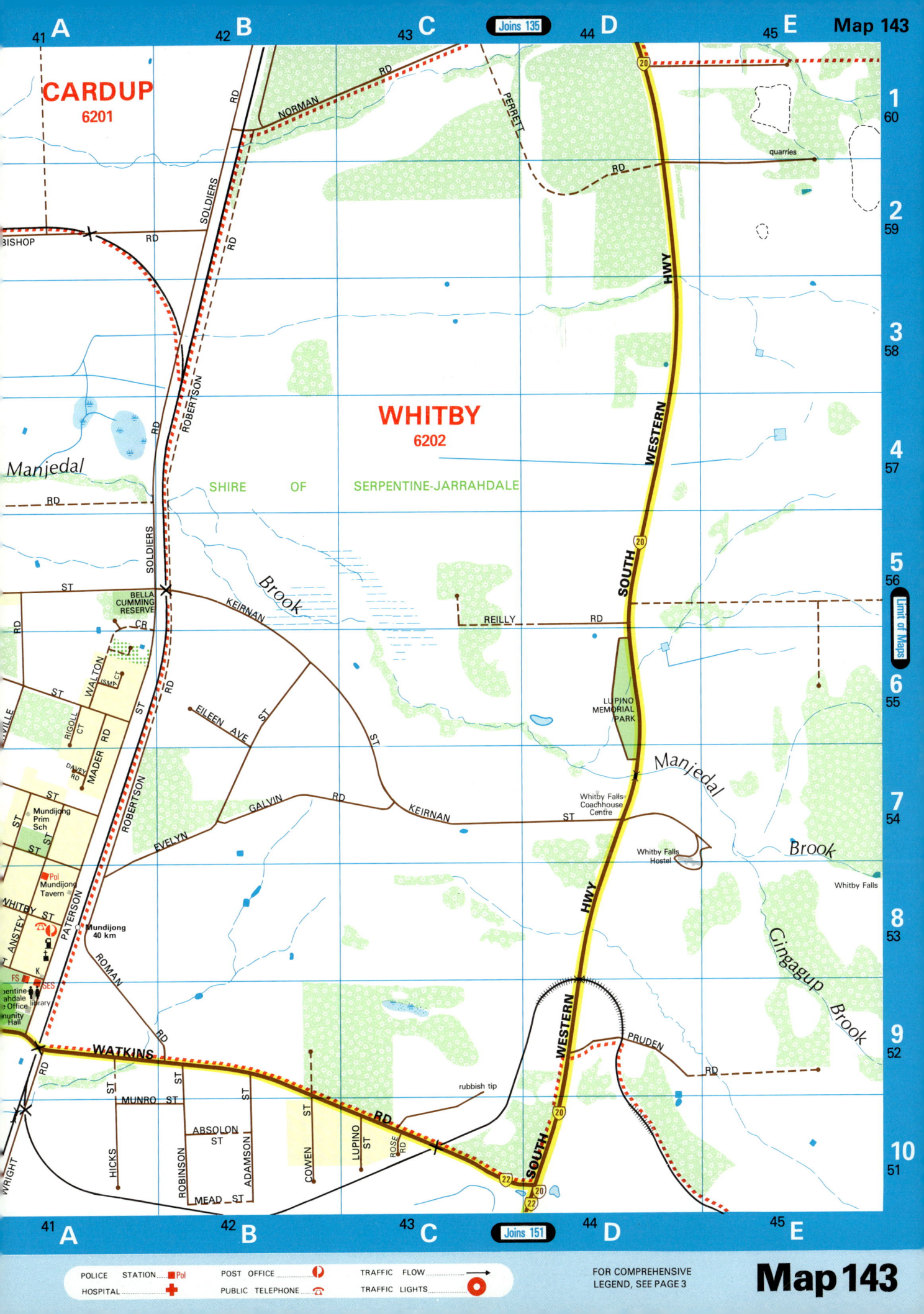

CARDUP 6201

WHITBY 6202

SHIRE OF SERPENTINE-JARRAHDALE

Map 144

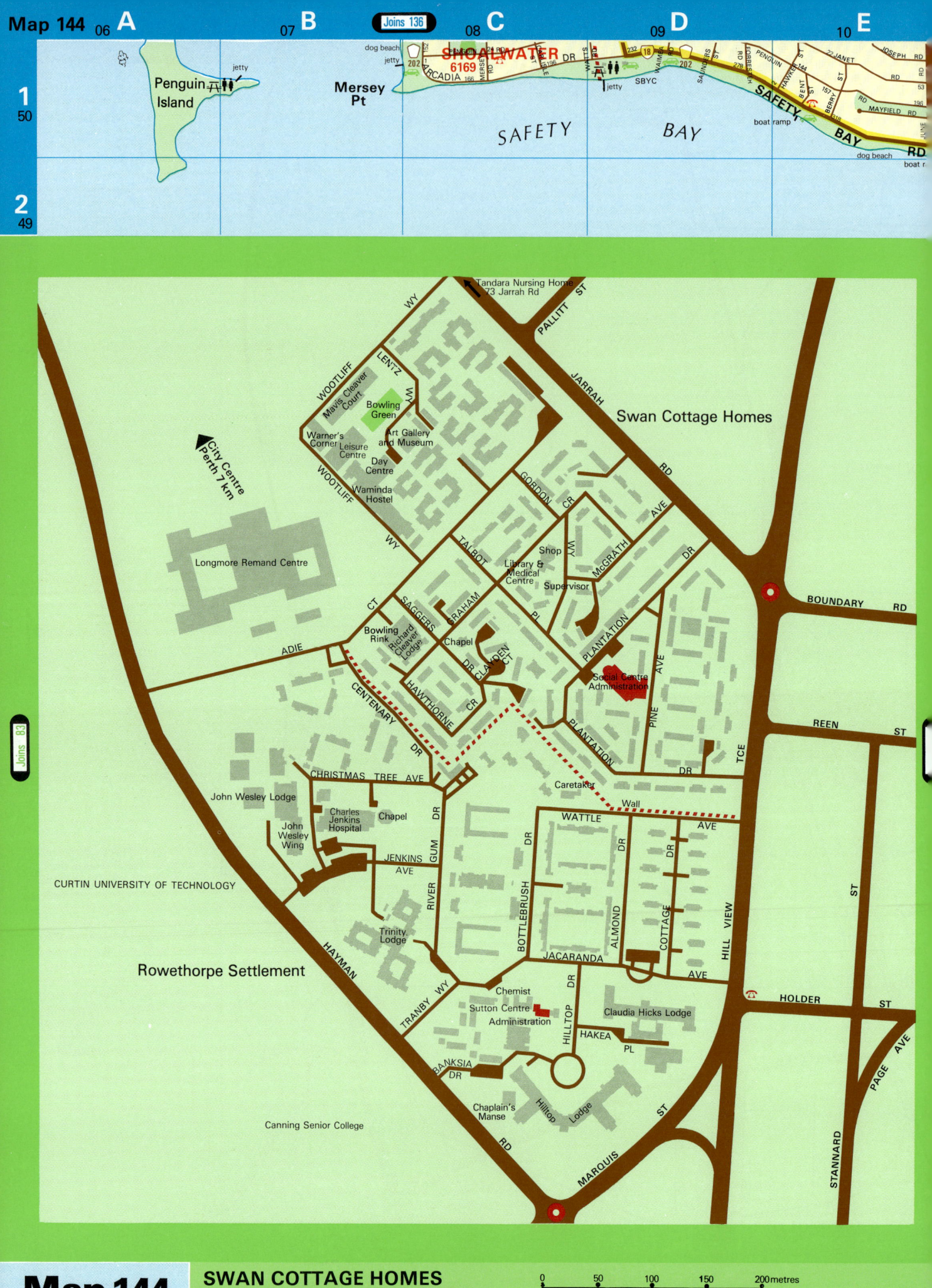

SWAN COTTAGE HOMES
ROWETHORPE SETTLEMENT

POLICE STATION Pol
HOSPITAL
POST OFFICE
PUBLIC TELEPHONE
TRAFFIC FLOW
TRAFFIC LIGHTS

FOR COMPREHENSIVE LEGEND, SEE PAGE 3

Map 146

COOLOONGUP 6168

WAIKIKI 6169

WARNBRO 6169

Lake Walyungup

CITY OF ROCKINGHAM

Tamworth Hill

Lakeside Caravan Park

SAFETY BAY RD
MANDURAH RD
PIKE RD
ENNIS AVE
McDONALD RD
FIFTY RD
EIGHTY RD
CLYDE RD

Joins 138
Joins 157
Joins 145

SCALE 1:20 000
0 — 500 m — 1 km — 2 km

PRIMARY RECTANGLE PEEL BG 33

Map 147

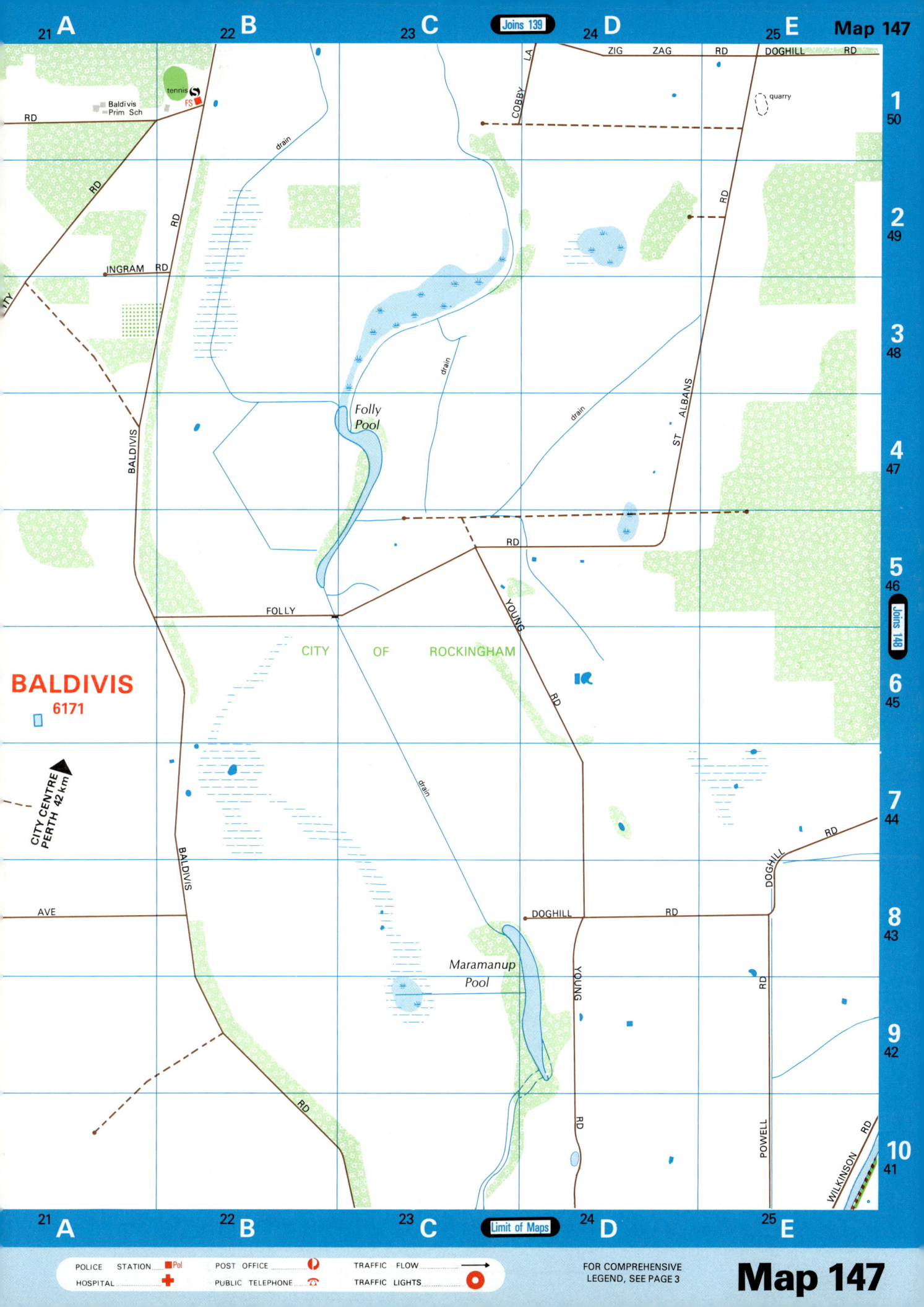

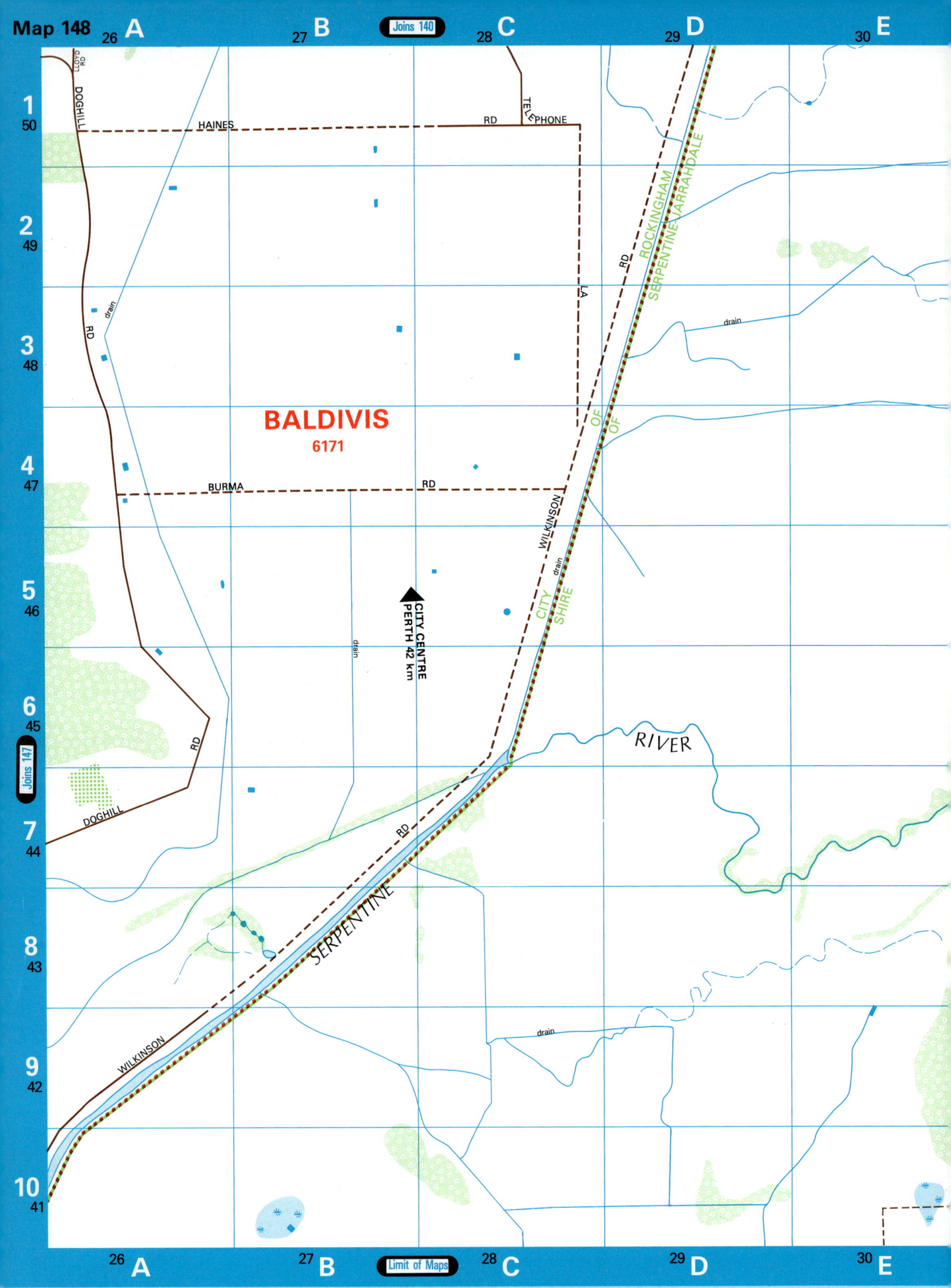

0 500 m 1 km 2 km

SCALE 1:20 000

PRIMARY RECTANGLE
PEEL BG 33

THE QUEEN ELIZABETH II MEDICAL CENTRE
(SIR CHARLES GAIRDNER HOSPITAL)

Scale 1:4 000 (0–120 metres)

INDEX TO BUILDINGS

- A. Lions Eye Institute & Other Research Institutes, S.C.G.H. Departments
- B. S.C.G.H. Oncology & Respiratory Medicine (Wards B8–B12)
- C. S.C.G.H. Geriatric Unit & Extended Care (Wards C14–C18)
- D. S.C.G.H. Psychiatric Unit Ward D20
- E. Outpatient Clinics & S.C.G.H. Administration
- F. S.C.G.H. Radiotherapy Department
- G. S.C.G.H. Main Ward & Theatre Block (Wards GB1–G75)
- H. Central Plant
- J. State Health Laboratory North
- K. State Health Laboratory South
- L. U.W.A. School of Medicine South
- M. U.W.A. School of Medicine North
- N. U.W.A. School of Medicine Library
- P. Lecture Theatres
- Q. Departments of Nursing Staff Development & Nursing Research
- R. Health Dept. of W.A., Radiation Health Branch, U.W.A., N.H.M.R.C. & S.C.G.H. Departments
- S. Anstey House, Residential Staff Clinic
- T. S.C.G.H. Engineering Workshops
- U. Biomedical Engineering & Radiation Health
- V. S.C.G.H. Communications Centre
- W. S.C.G.H. Engineering Workshops
- X. St John Ambulance Depot
- Y. Dangerous Goods Store

PARKING LEGEND

- Visitors Car Parks
- Staff Car Parks
- Special Rights & Disabled Persons Car Parks

VISITING HOURS:

General Wards	7 a.m.–12 noon	3 p.m.–8.30 p.m.
Coronary Care Unit	7 a.m.–12 noon	3 p.m.–8 p.m.
Ward D20 Mon–Fri	12.30 p.m.–2 p.m.	3.30 p.m.–9 p.m.
Weekends	8.30 a.m.–9.30 p.m.	
Intensive Care Unit	By Arrangement	

TELEPHONE: 389 3333

MAIN ENTRANCE — ABERDARE ROAD

PEEL ESTATE 6167

Map 149

Map 150

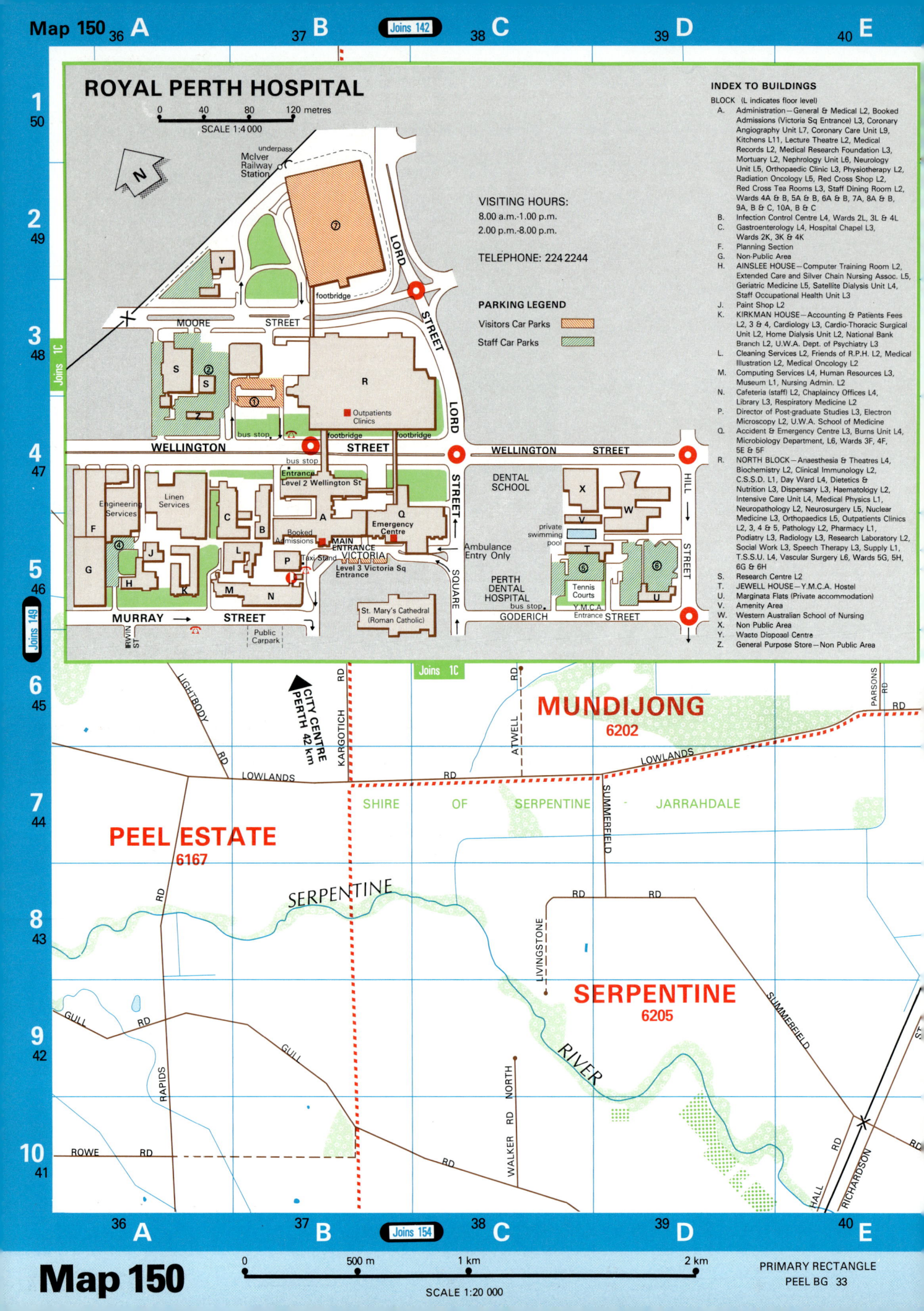

ROYAL PERTH HOSPITAL

SCALE 1:4 000

VISITING HOURS:
8.00 a.m.-1.00 p.m.
2.00 p.m.-8.00 p.m.

TELEPHONE: 224 2244

PARKING LEGEND
- Visitors Car Parks
- Staff Car Parks

INDEX TO BUILDINGS
BLOCK (L indicates floor level)

- **A.** Administration—General & Medical L2, Booked Admissions (Victoria Sq Entrance) L3, Coronary Angiography Unit L7, Coronary Care Unit L9, Kitchens L11, Lecture Theatre L2, Medical Records L2, Medical Research Foundation L3, Mortuary L2, Nephrology Unit L6, Neurology Unit L5, Orthopaedic Clinic L3, Physiotherapy L2, Radiation Oncology L5, Red Cross Shop L2, Red Cross Tea Rooms L3, Staff Dining Room L2, Wards 4A & B, 5A & B, 6A & B, 7A, 8A & B, 9A, B & C, 10A, B & C
- **B.** Infection Control Centre L4, Wards 2L, 3L & 4L
- **C.** Gastroenterology L4, Hospital Chapel L3, Wards 2K, 3K & 4K
- **F.** Planning Section
- **G.** Non-Public Area
- **H.** AINSLEE HOUSE—Computer Training Room L2, Extended Care and Silver Chain Nursing Assoc. L5, Geriatric Medicine L5, Satellite Dialysis Unit L4, Staff Occupational Health Unit L3
- **J.** Paint Shop L2
- **K.** KIRKMAN HOUSE—Accounting & Patients Fees L2, 3 & 4, Cardiology L3, Cardio-Thoracic Surgical Unit L2, Home Dialysis Unit L2, National Bank Branch L2, U.W.A. Dept. of Psychiatry L3
- **L.** Cleaning Services L2, Friends of R.P.H. L2, Medical Illustration L2, Medical Oncology L2
- **M.** Computing Services L4, Human Resources L3, Museum L1, Nursing Admin. L2
- **N.** Cafeteria (staff) L2, Chaplaincy Offices L4, Library L3, Respiratory Medicine L2
- **P.** Director of Post-graduate Studies L3, Electron Microscopy L2, U.W.A. School of Medicine
- **Q.** Accident & Emergency Centre L3, Burns Unit L4, Microbiology Department L6, Wards 3F, 4F, 5E & 5F
- **R.** NORTH BLOCK—Anaesthesia & Theatres L4, Biochemistry L2, Clinical Immunology L2, C.S.S.D. L1, Day Ward L4, Dietetics & Nutrition L3, Dispensary L3, Haematology L2, Intensive Care Unit L4, Medical Physics L1, Neuropathology L2, Neurosurgery L5, Nuclear Medicine L3, Orthopaedics L5, Outpatients Clinics L2, 3, 4 & 5, Pathology L2, Pharmacy L1, Podiatry L3, Radiology L3, Research Laboratory L2, Social Work L3, Speech Therapy L3, Supply L1, T.S.S.U. L4, Vascular Surgery L6, Wards 5G, 5H, 6G & 6H
- **S.** Research Centre L2
- **T.** JEWELL HOUSE—Y.M.C.A. Hostel
- **U.** Marginata Flats (Private accommodation)
- **V.** Amenity Area
- **W.** Western Australian School of Nursing
- **X.** Non Public Area
- **Y.** Waste Disposal Centre
- **Z.** General Purpose Store—Non Public Area

MUNDIJONG 6202

PEEL ESTATE 6167

SHIRE OF SERPENTINE JARRAHDALE

SERPENTINE 6205

SCALE 1:20 000

PRIMARY RECTANGLE
PEEL BG 33

Map 151

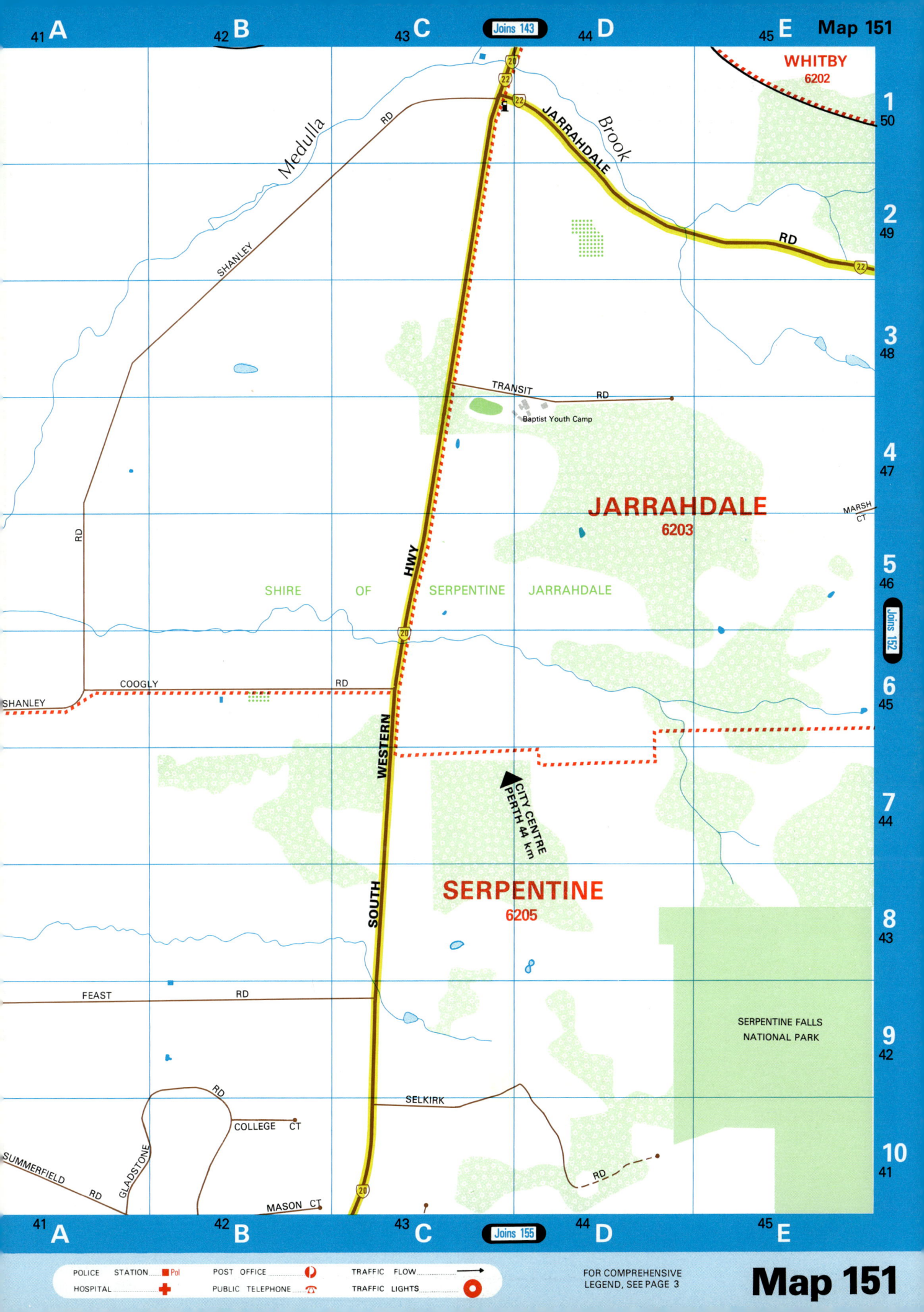

WHITBY 6202

JARRAHDALE 6203

SHIRE OF SERPENTINE JARRAHDALE

SERPENTINE 6205

SERPENTINE FALLS NATIONAL PARK

CITY CENTRE PERTH 44 km

Roads and features: Medulla Rd, Shanley Rd, Jarrahdale Rd, Transit Rd, Baptist Youth Camp, Marsh Ct, Coogly Rd, South Western Hwy, Feast Rd, Selkirk Rd, College Ct, Gladstone Rd, Summerfield Rd, Mason Ct, Jarrahdale Brook

Joins 143 (top) / Joins 155 (bottom) / Joins 152 (right)

Legend: POLICE STATION — Pol | POST OFFICE | TRAFFIC FLOW | HOSPITAL | PUBLIC TELEPHONE | TRAFFIC LIGHTS | FOR COMPREHENSIVE LEGEND, SEE PAGE 3

Map 152

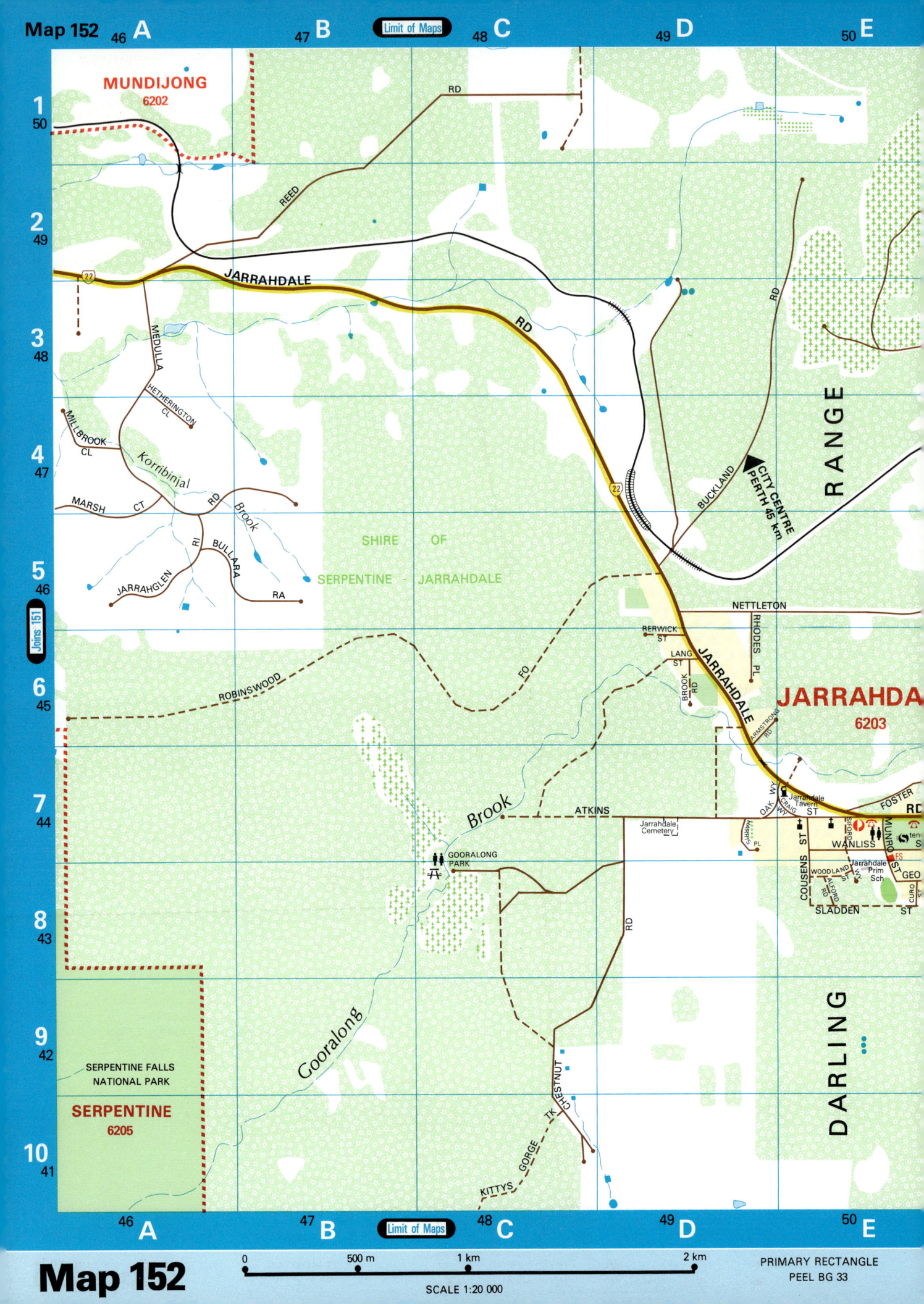

MUNDIJONG 6202

JARRAHDALE 6203

SERPENTINE 6205
Serpentine Falls National Park

Shire of Serpentine - Jarrahdale

Darling Range

Jarrahdale Rd
Reed Rd
Medulla Rd
Hetherington Cl
Millbrook Cl
Marsh Ct
Korribinjal Brook
Jarrahglen Ri
Bullara Ra
Robinswood
Gooralong Brook
Atkins Rd
Gooralong Park
Kittys Gorge Tk
Chestnut Rd
Buckland Rd — City Centre Perth 45 km
Nettleton St
Berwick St
Rhodes Pl
Lang St
Brook Rd
Armstrong Rd
Oak Wy
Craig St
Foster Rd
Jarrahdale Tavern
Harris Pl
Wanliss St
Cousens St
Munro St
Woodland Rd
Sladden St
Jarrahdale Prim Sch
Jarrahdale Cemetery

Joins 151

Scale 1:20 000
0 — 500 m — 1 km — 2 km

PRIMARY RECTANGLE
PEEL BG 33

Map 153

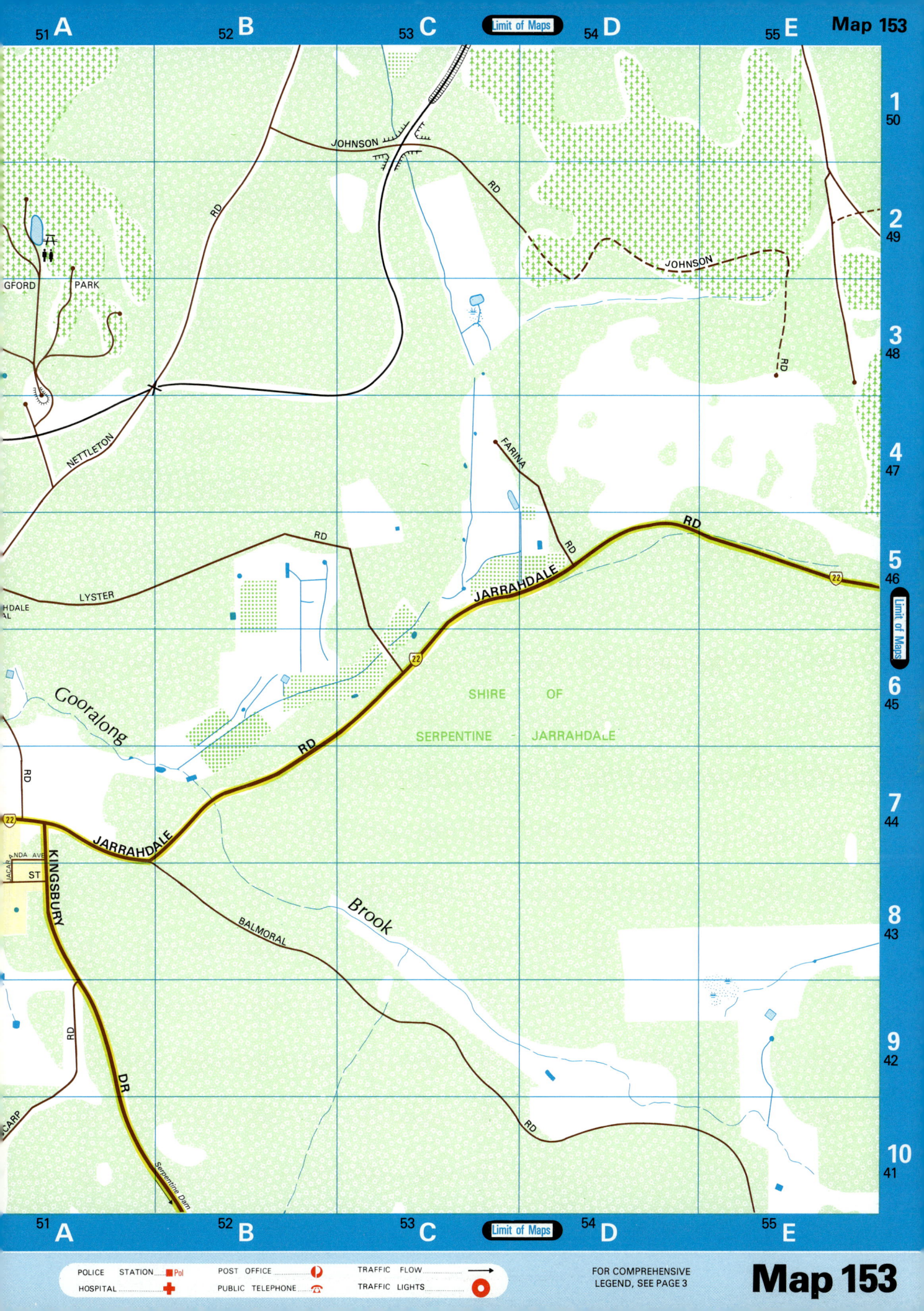

Map 154

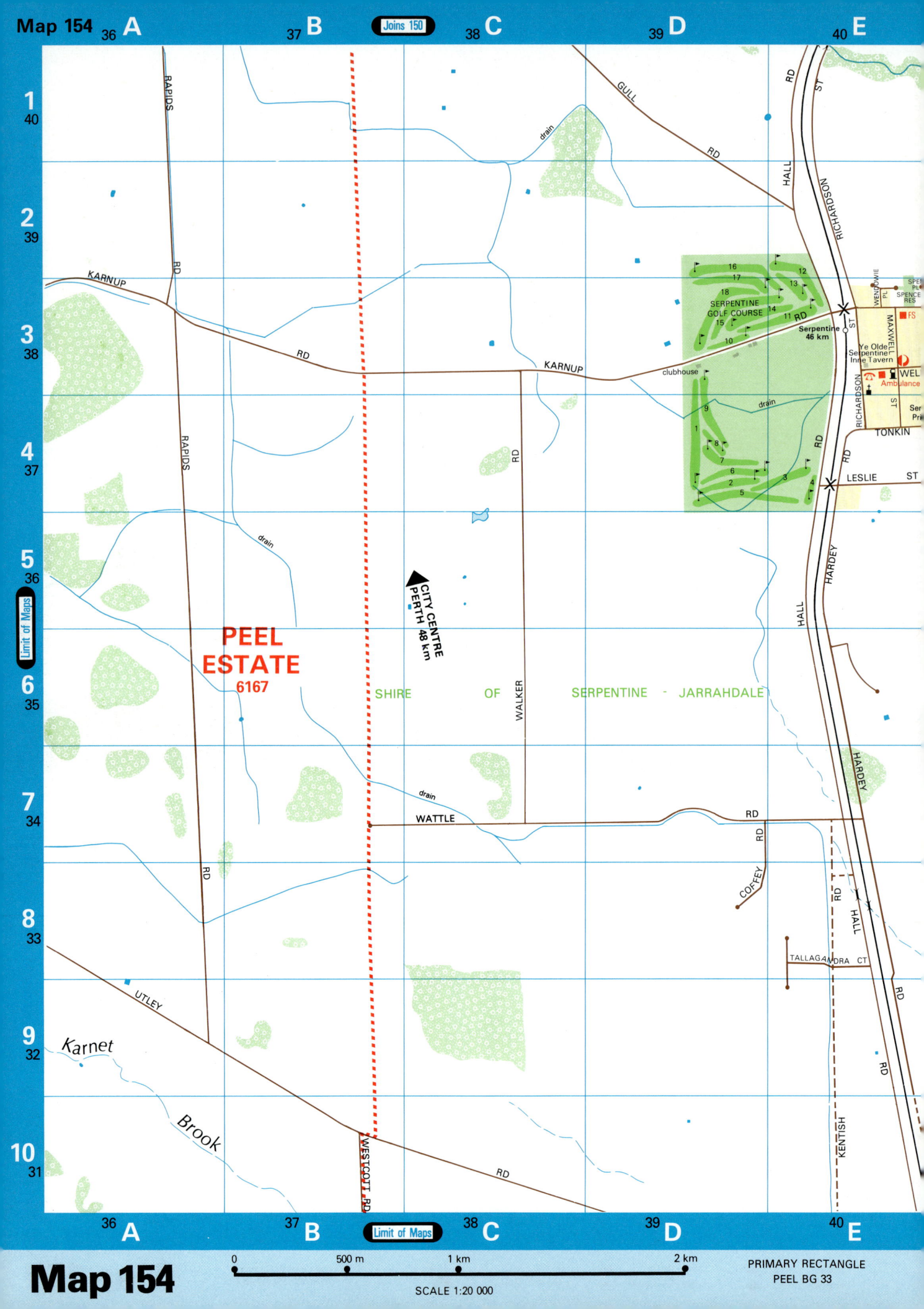

Map 155

Map 156

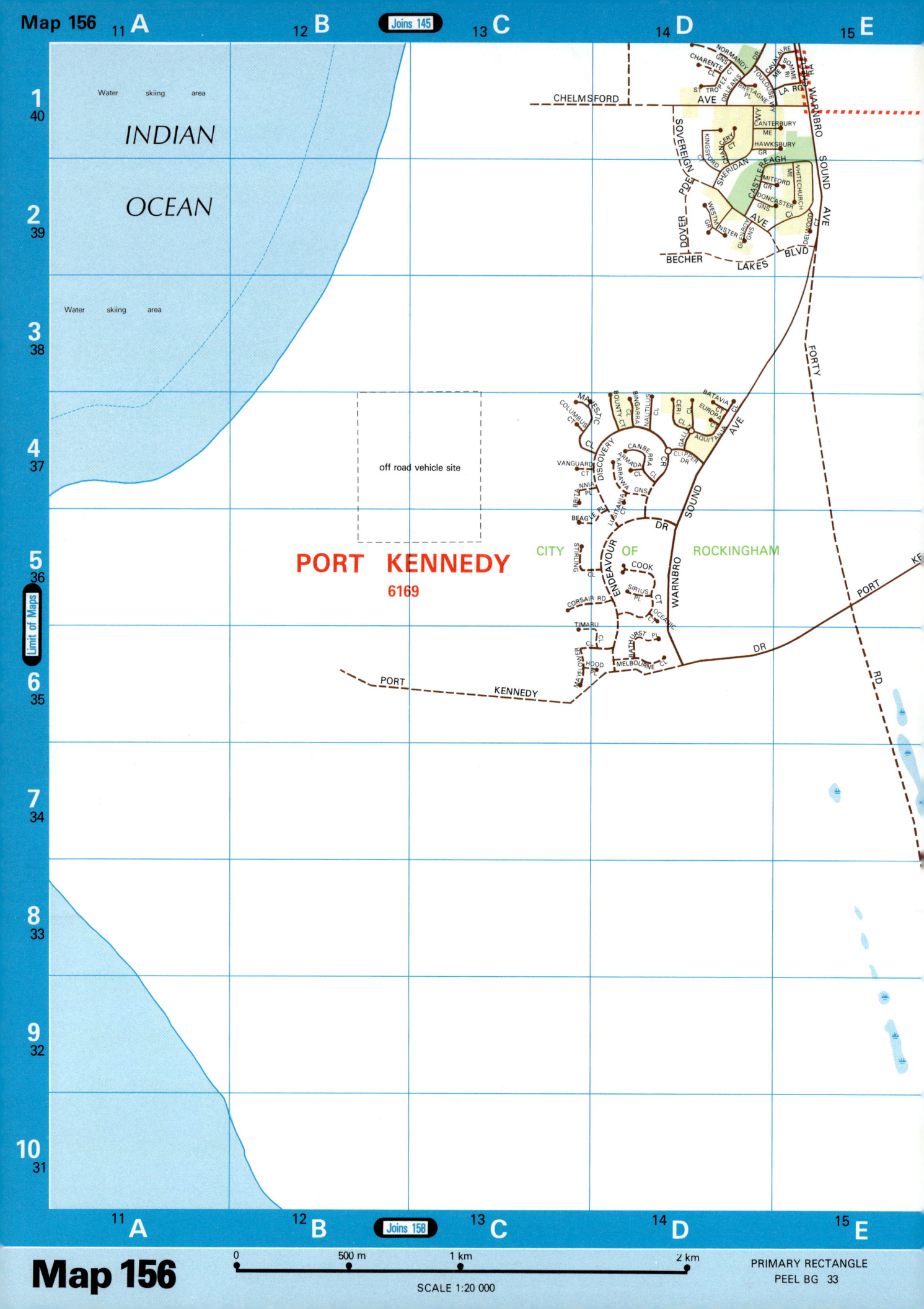

PORT KENNEDY 6169

INDIAN OCEAN

Water skiing area

off road vehicle site

CITY OF ROCKINGHAM

Limit of Maps

Joins 145
Joins 158

SCALE 1:20 000
0 – 500 m – 1 km – 2 km

PRIMARY RECTANGLE PEEL BG 33

Map 157

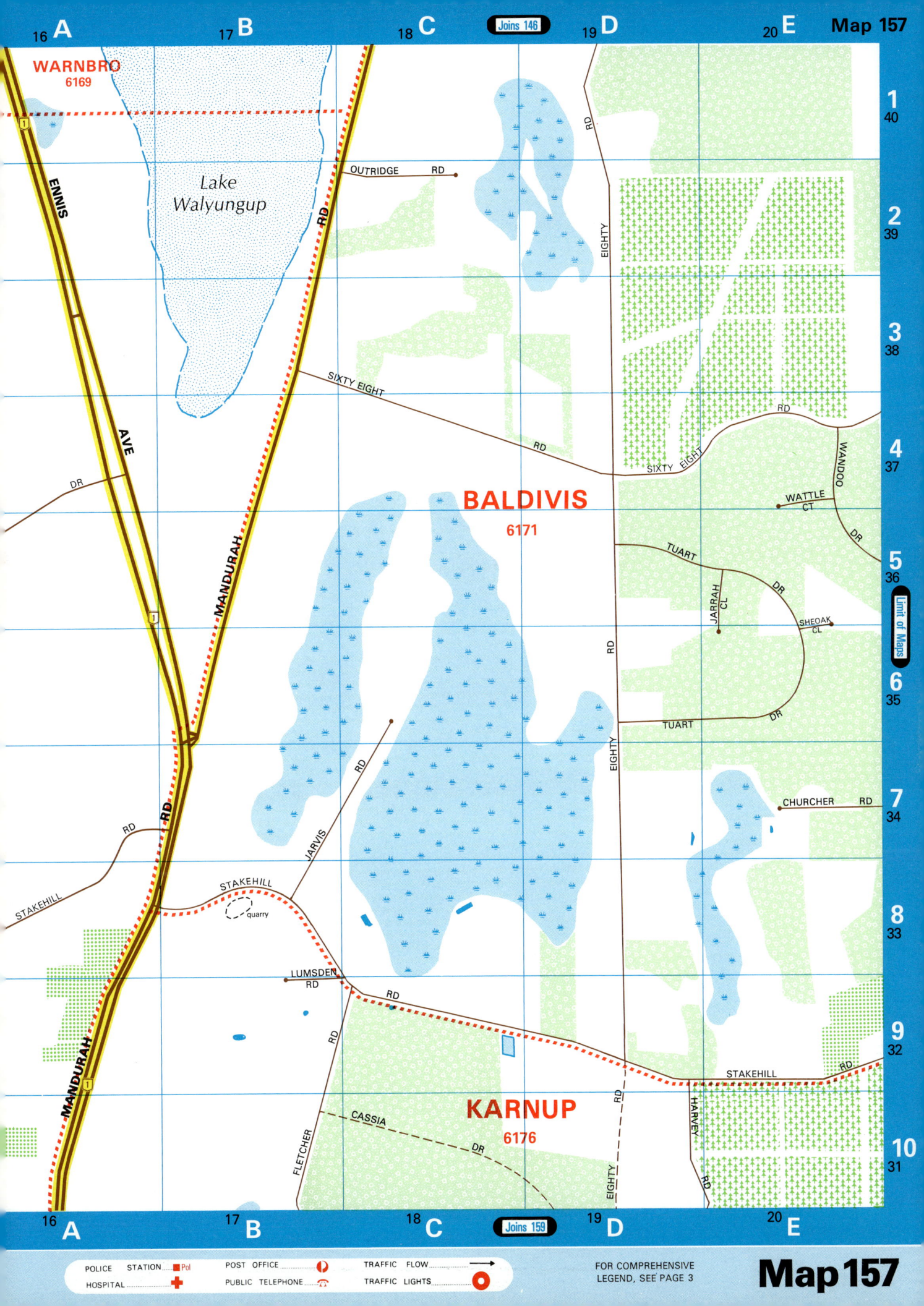

WARNBRO 6169

BALDIVIS 6171

KARNUP 6176

Lake Walyungup

Ennis Ave
Mandurah Rd
Outridge Rd
Sixty Eight Rd
Wandoo Dr
Wattle Ct
Tuart Dr
Jarrah Cl
Sheoak Cl
Eighty Rd
Tuart Dr
Churcher Rd
Jarvis Rd
Stakehill Rd
quarry
Lumsden Rd
Stakehill Rd
Harvey Rd
Fletcher Rd
Cassia Dr
Eighty Rd
Stakehill Rd

Joins 146
Joins 159
Limit of Maps

POLICE STATION ■ Pol
HOSPITAL ✚
POST OFFICE
PUBLIC TELEPHONE
TRAFFIC FLOW →
TRAFFIC LIGHTS ⊙

FOR COMPREHENSIVE LEGEND, SEE PAGE 3

Map 158

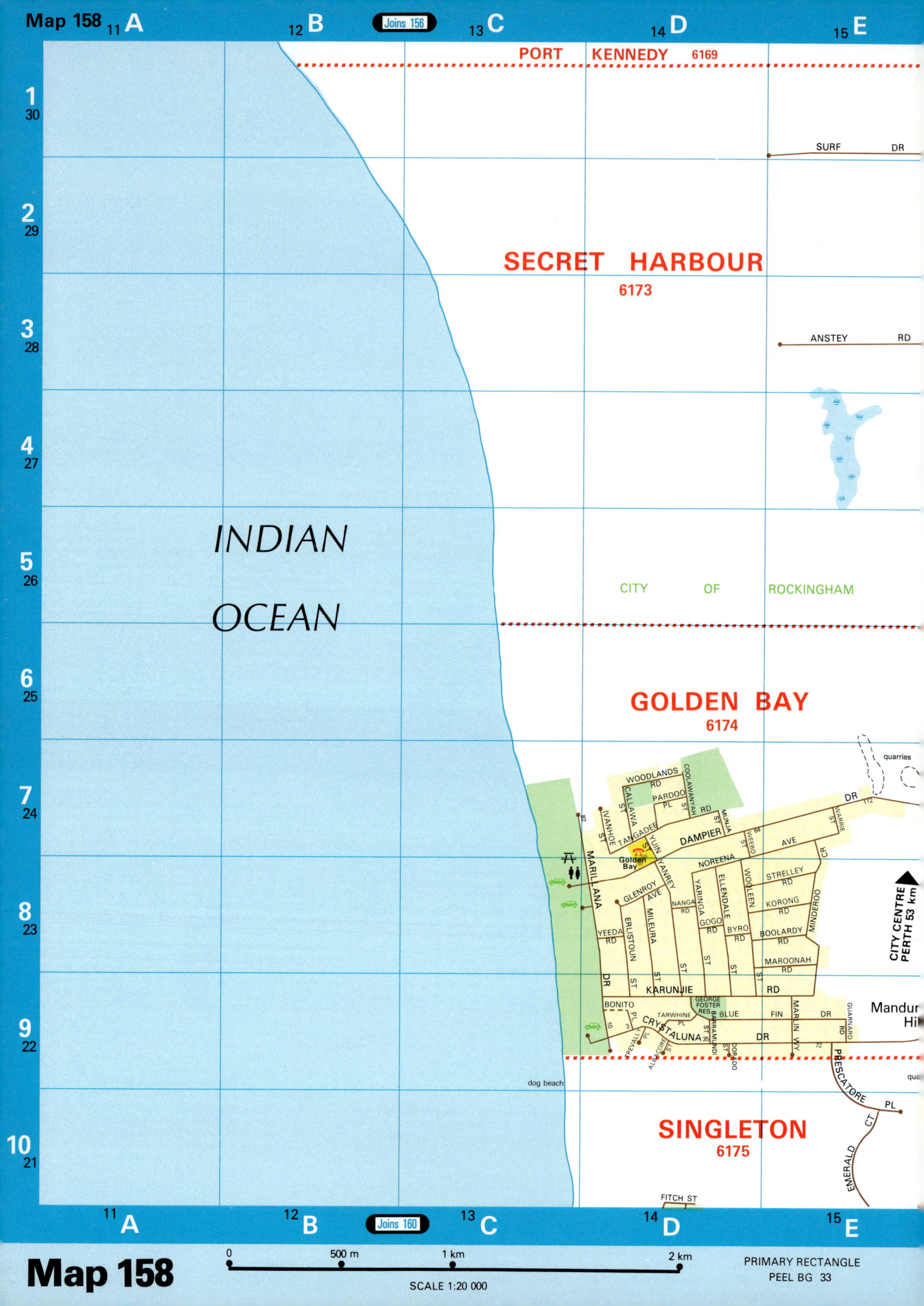

PORT KENNEDY 6169

SECRET HARBOUR 6173

SURF DR

ANSTEY RD

INDIAN OCEAN

CITY OF ROCKINGHAM

GOLDEN BAY 6174

quarries

WOODLANDS RD
COOLAWANYAH
CALLAWA
PARDOO PL
IVANHOE ST
TANGADEE
YUIN
MUNJA ST
MARRIE ST
DAMPIER
WEEBO ST
DR
NOREENA
STRELLEY RD
MARILANA
Golden Bay
YANREY
ELLENDALE
WOOLEEN
CITY CENTRE PERTH 53 km
GLENROY AVE
YARINGA
KORONG RD
NANGA RD
GOGO
BYRO RD
MINDEROO CR
ERLISTOUN
MILEURA
BOOLARDY RD
YEEDA RD
MAROONAH RD
KARUNJIE
BONITO PL
GEORGE FOSTER RES
BLUE FIN DR
MARLIN WY
GUANARD RD
TARWHINE
BARRAMUNDI
Mandur Hi
CRYSTALUNA DR
DORADO RD
ALBACORE
PESCATORE PL
dog beach
EMERALD CT

SINGLETON 6175

FITCH ST

SCALE 1:20 000 0 — 500 m — 1 km — 2 km

PRIMARY RECTANGLE PEEL BG 33

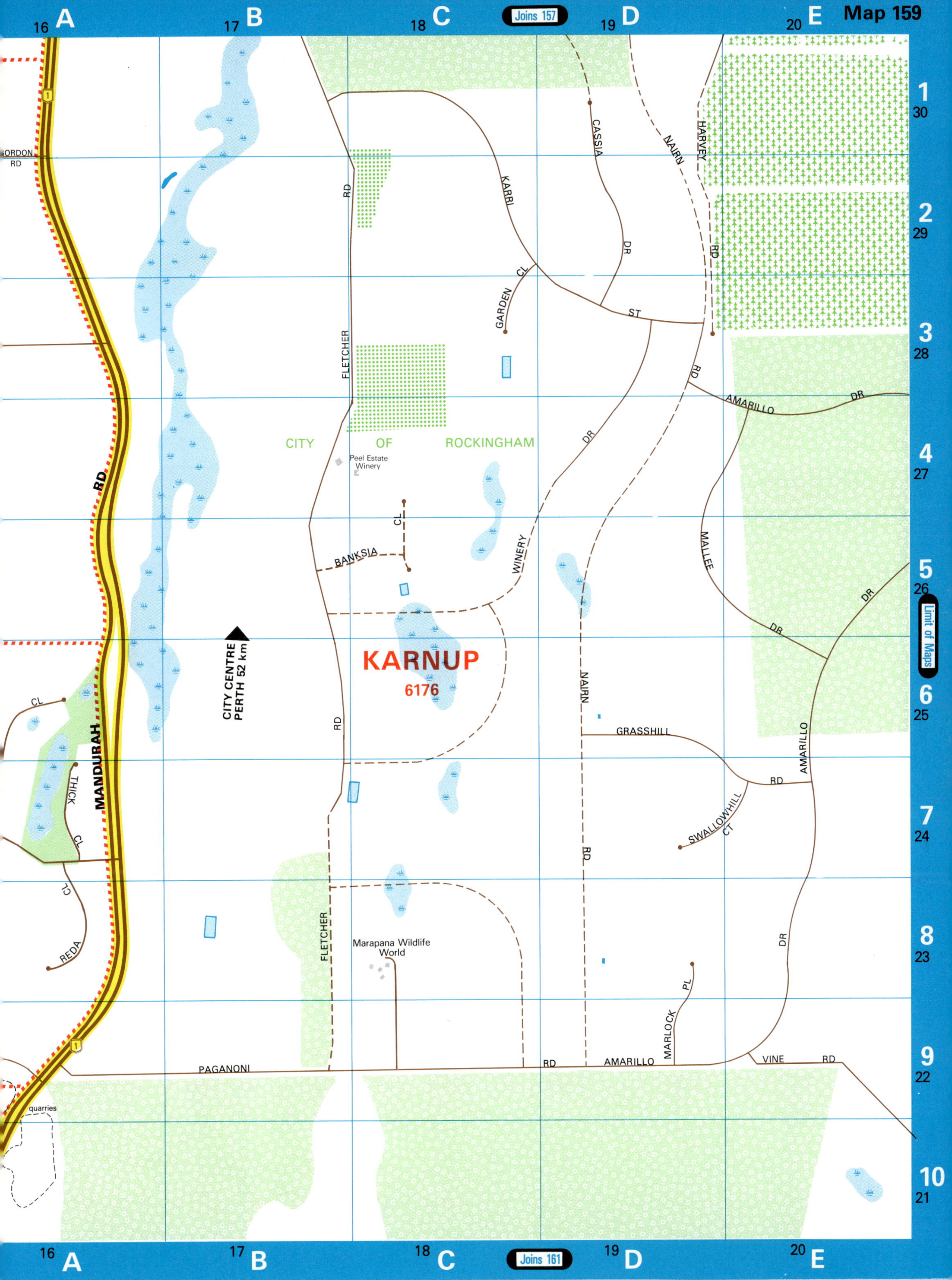

Joins 157
Joins 161
16 A
17 B
18 C
19 D
20 E
1 30
2 29
3 28
4 27
5 26
6 25
7 24
8 23
9 22
10 21
Limit of Maps
KARNUP
6176
CITY OF ROCKINGHAM
Peel Estate Winery
Marapana Wildlife World
CITY CENTRE PERTH 52 km
MANDURAH RD
GORDON RD
FLETCHER RD
KARRI
CASSIA DR
NAIRN
HARVEY RD
GARDEN CL
ST
AMARILLO DR
MALLEE DR
DR
WINERY DR
BANKSIA
CL
NAIRN RD
GRASSHILL RD
SWALLOWHILL CT
AMARILLO DR
MARLOCK PL
PAGANONI RD
AMARILLO
VINE RD
THICK CL
CL
REDA CL
quarries

POLICE STATION .... Pol
HOSPITAL ....
POST OFFICE ....
PUBLIC TELEPHONE ....
TRAFFIC FLOW ....
TRAFFIC LIGHTS ....

FOR COMPREHENSIVE LEGEND, SEE PAGE 3

Map 160

SINGLETON 6175

MADORA 6210

SAN REMO 6210

MEADOW SPRINGS 6210

INDIAN OCEAN

CITY CENTRE PERTH 57 km

CITY OF ROCKINGHAM / CITY OF MANDURAH

Joins 158 (top) / Joins 163 (bottom)

SCALE 1:20 000 — 0, 500 m, 1 km, 2 km

PRIMARY RECTANGLE PEEL BG 33

Streets and features (Singleton): Indiana Pde, Murdoch Dr, Brownrigg St, Bentley St, Bannon St, McVeigh St, Singleton Beach Rd, Emerald Ct, Jade Ct, Mandurah Rd, Whitehead St, Fane Ct, Royce St, Reilly St, Singleton Sporting Complex, Robin Ct, Coffey St, Murdoch Dr, Fanning Wy, Dutton Wy, Cavender Wy, Baudin Wy, FS, Finch Ct, Bight Rd, Reefs Rd, Penson St, Foreshore Rd, Treasure Rd, Treasure Heath, Prosser Wy, Wenn St, Glew St, Laird Wy, Manders St, Damon St, Penson Pl.

Streets and features (Madora): dog beach, Swiftshire Rd, Chilena Pl, Ariel Pl, Avoca Pl, Diana Pl, Thetis St, Gambia Pl, Diadem Pl, Barden Rd, Nereus Pl, Hyacinth Pl, Pagoda Pl, Cornwallis Dr, Lochinvar Pl, Anglore Pl, Bengal St, Caspar Pl, Lanciera Pl, Beach Rd, McLennan Park, Assam St, Madora Dr, Madora Bay Tavern, Success Rd, Melia Wy, tennis, Orelia St, Albion Rd, Wanstead Ct, Lotus St, Sabina Pde, Gilmore Ct, Protector Ct, Atwick Ct, Tranby St, Caro Ln, Challenger Wy, Hooghly St.

Streets and features (San Remo): Karinga Rd, Karinga Res, Orestes St, Hera Ct, Jannali Wy.

Fremantle Rd, Mandurah Rd, quarry, quarries.

Map 161

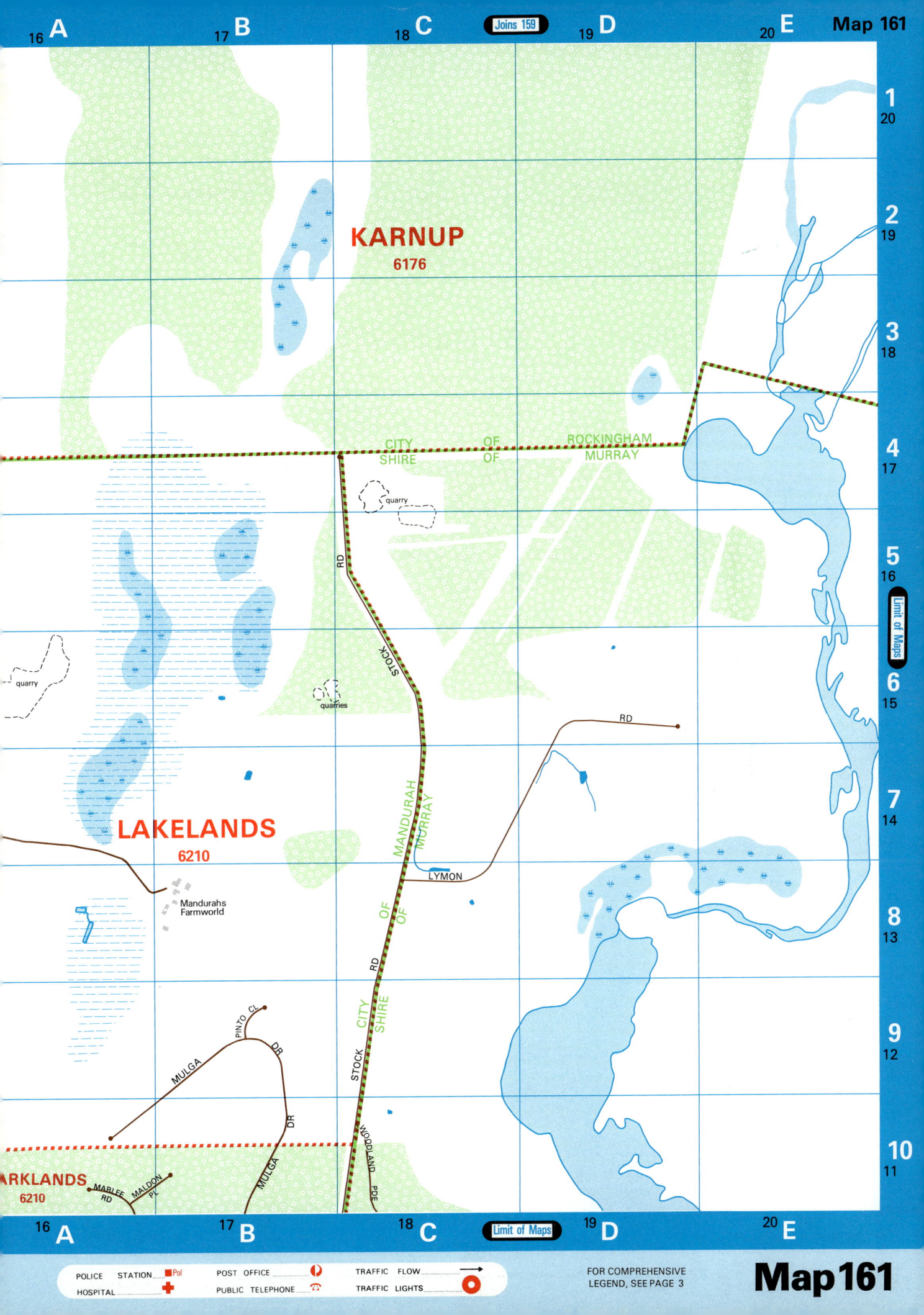

KARNUP 6176

LAKELANDS 6210

PARKLANDS 6210

Mandurahs Farmworld

CITY OF ROCKINGHAM / SHIRE OF MURRAY

Stock Rd / Mandurah Rd

Lymon Rd

Mulga Dr, Pinto Cl, Mablee Rd, Maldon Pl, Woodland Pde

quarry, quarries

Joins 159

Limit of Maps

Legend:
- POLICE STATION — Pol
- HOSPITAL — +
- POST OFFICE
- PUBLIC TELEPHONE
- TRAFFIC FLOW →
- TRAFFIC LIGHTS

FOR COMPREHENSIVE LEGEND, SEE PAGE 3

PRIMARY RECTANGLE
MURRAY BG 32

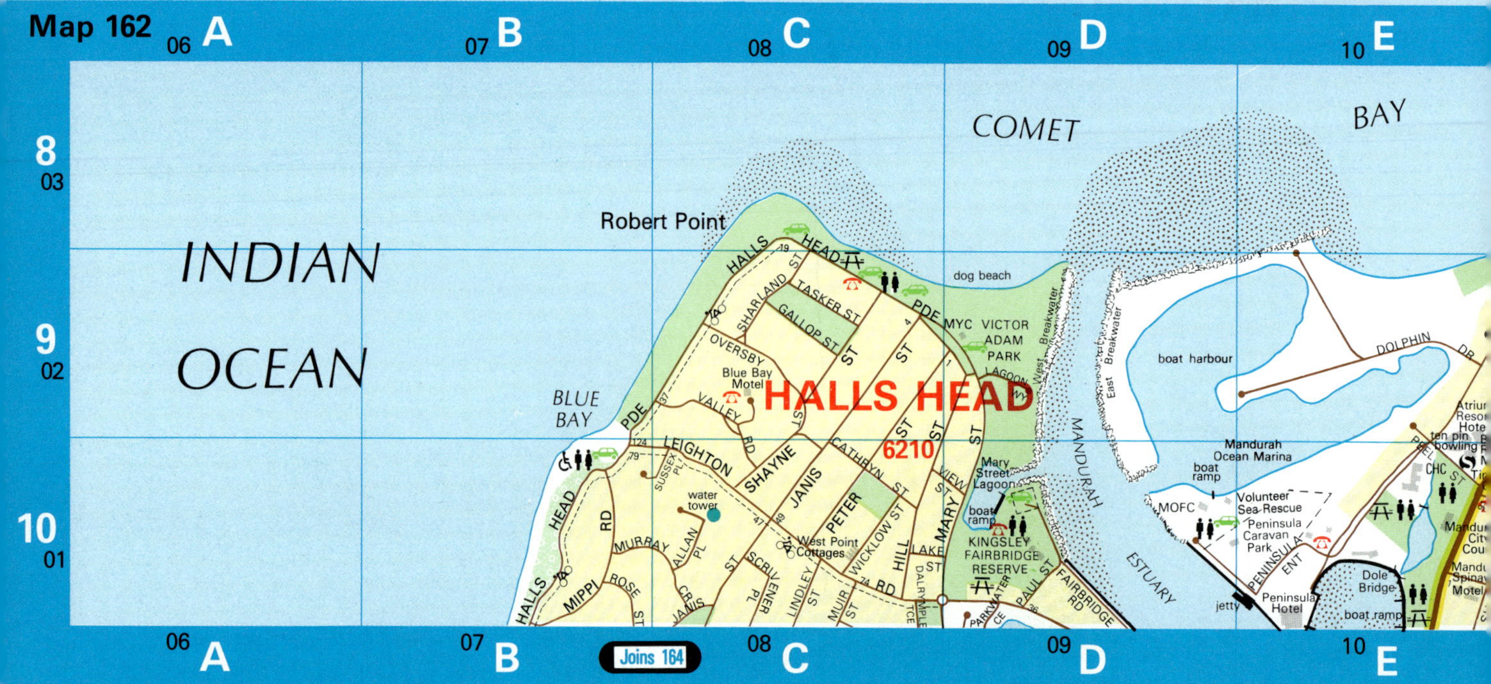

Map 162 & 162A

0 500 m 1 km 1·5 km
SCALE 1:20 000

PRIMARY RECTANGLE
PEEL BG 33

POLICE STATION Pol
HOSPITAL
POST OFFICE
PUBLIC TELEPHONE
TRAFFIC FLOW
TRAFFIC LIGHTS

FOR COMPREHENSIVE LEGEND, SEE PAGE 3

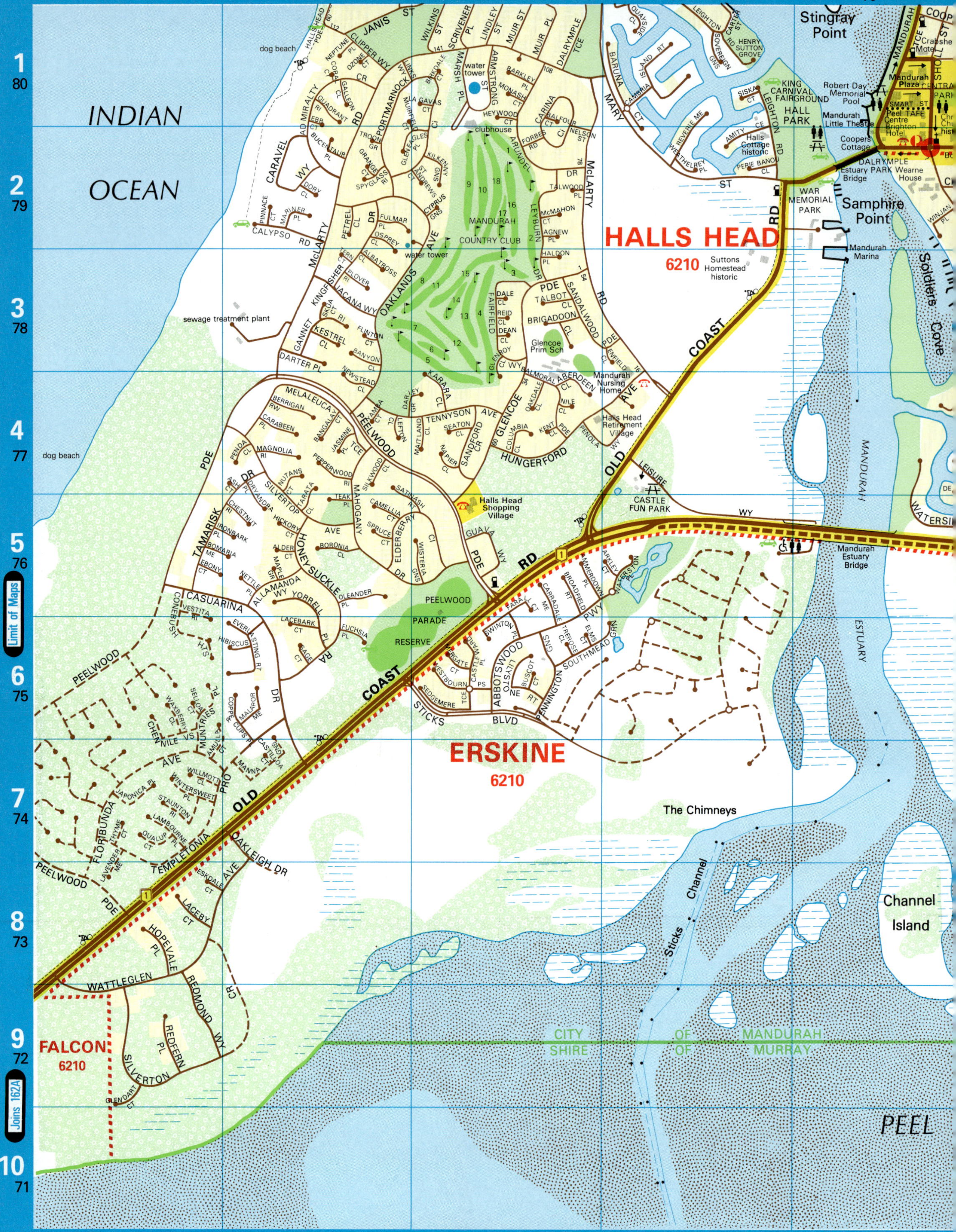

0 500 m 1 km 2 km

SCALE 1:20 000

PRIMARY RECTANGLE
BG 32

POLICE STATION Pol · POST OFFICE · TRAFFIC FLOW · HOSPITAL · PUBLIC TELEPHONE · TRAFFIC LIGHTS

FOR COMPREHENSIVE LEGEND, SEE PAGE 3

Map 166

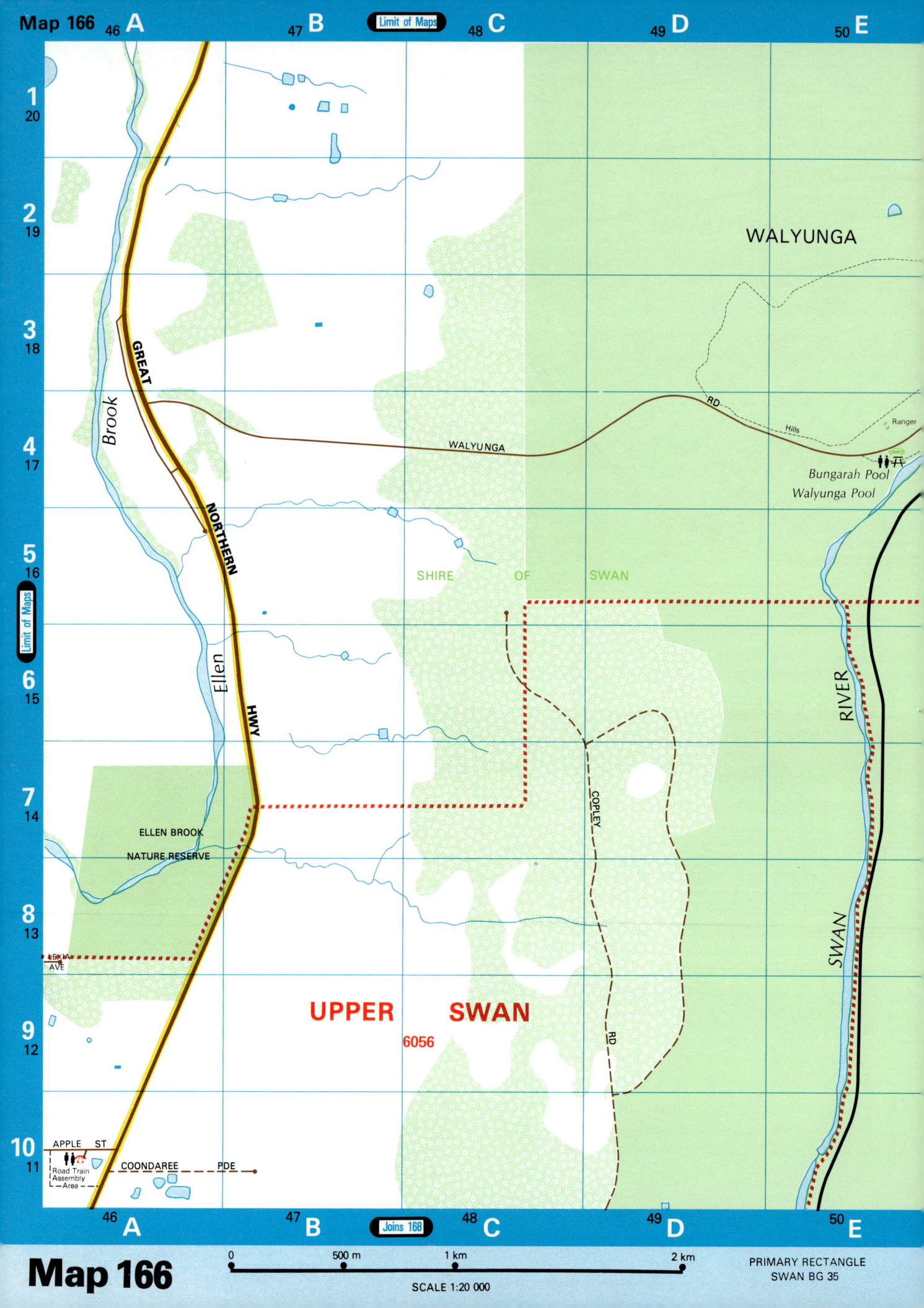

WALYUNGA

WALYUNGA RD

Bungarah Pool
Walyunga Pool

SHIRE OF SWAN

Ellen Brook

GREAT NORTHERN HWY

ELLEN BROOK NATURE RESERVE

COPLEY RD

SWAN RIVER

LEXIA AVE

UPPER SWAN
6056

APPLE ST
Road Train Assembly Area
COONDAREE PDE

SCALE 1:20 000
0 — 500 m — 1 km — 2 km

PRIMARY RECTANGLE
SWAN BG 35

Map 167

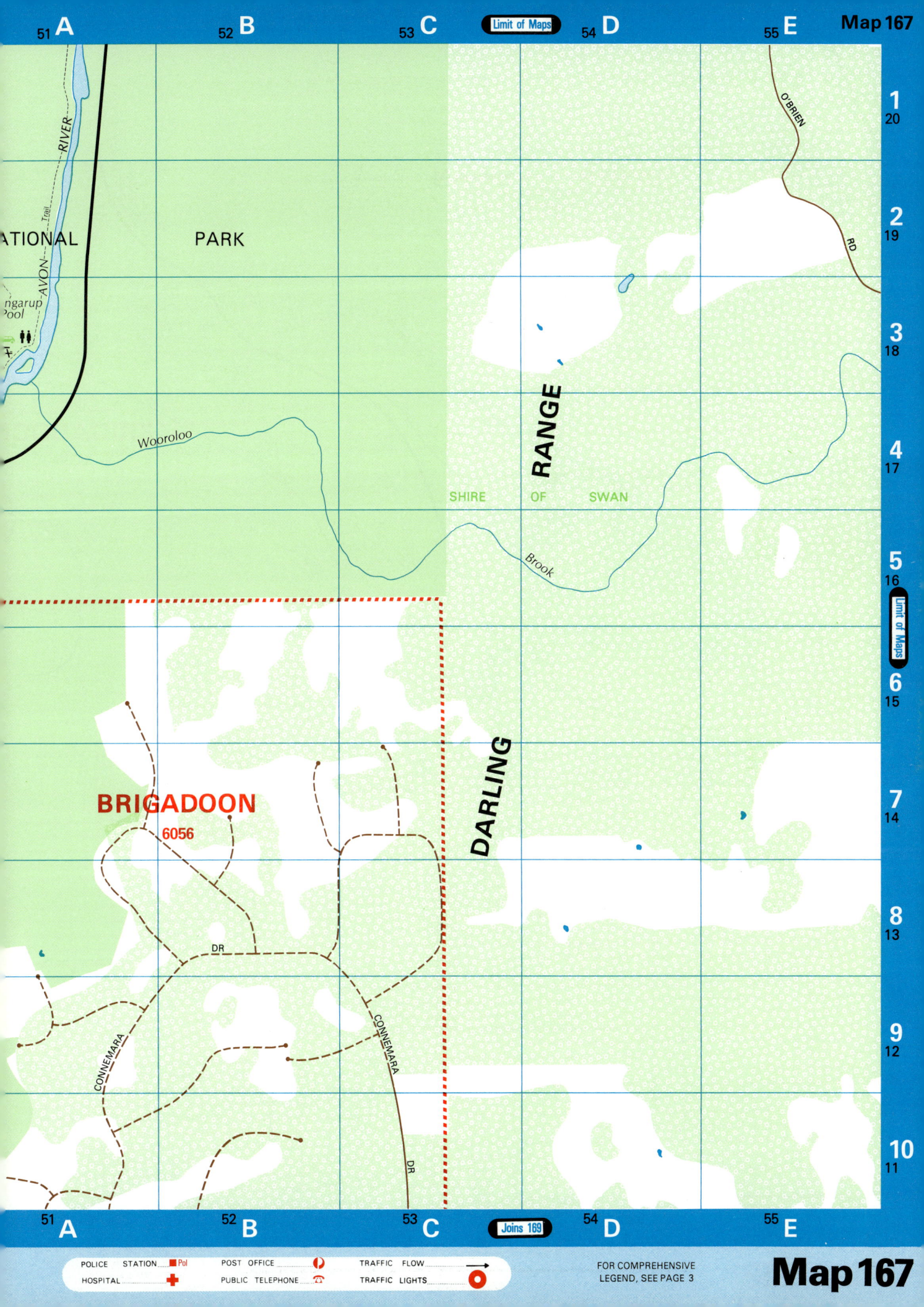

NATIONAL PARK

AVON RIVER

Wooroloo

SHIRE OF SWAN

DARLING RANGE

Brook

BRIGADOON 6056

CONNEMARA DR

CONNEMARA DR

O'BRIEN RD

Limit of Maps

Joins 169

POLICE STATION — Pol
HOSPITAL — +
POST OFFICE
PUBLIC TELEPHONE
TRAFFIC FLOW →
TRAFFIC LIGHTS

FOR COMPREHENSIVE LEGEND, SEE PAGE 3

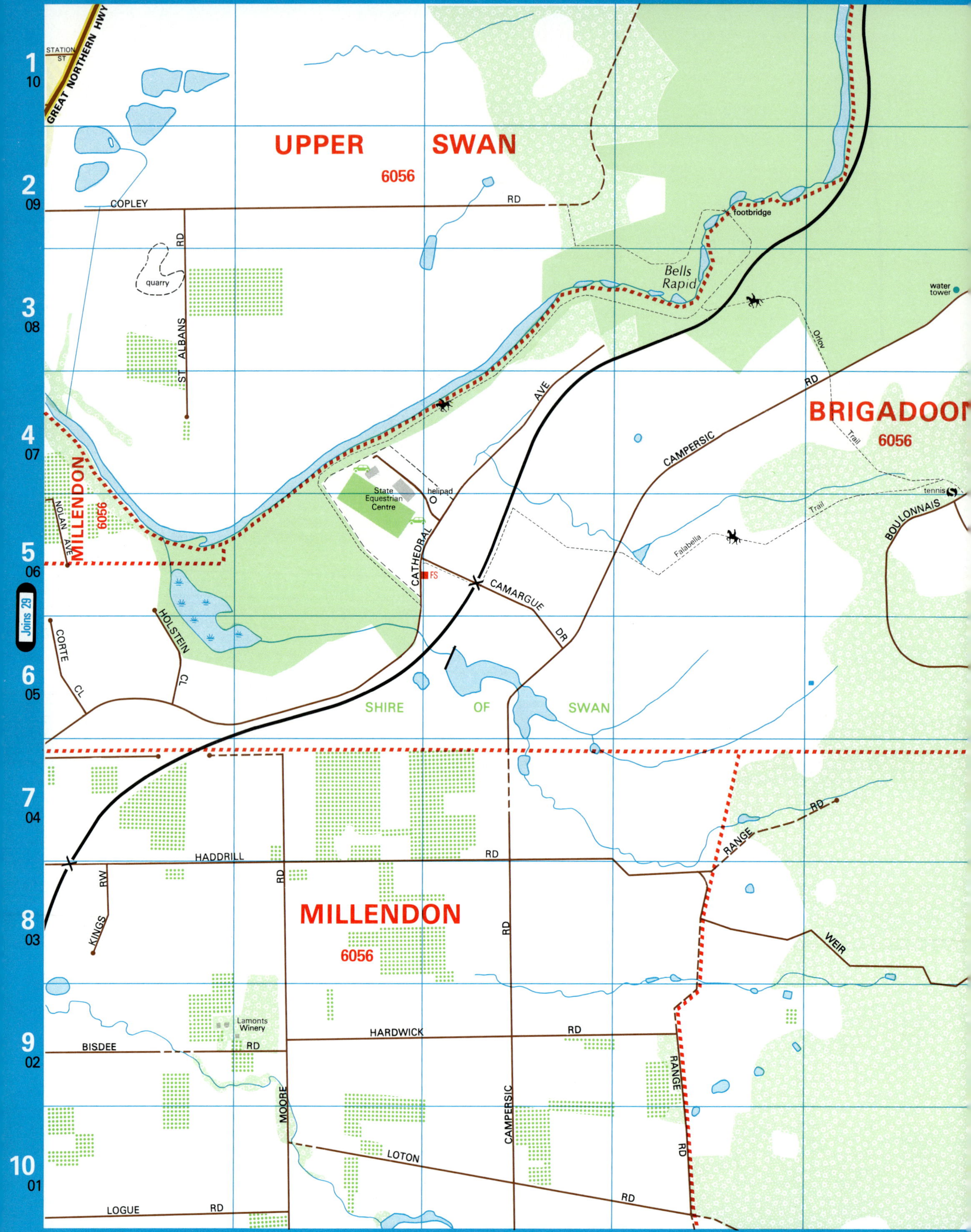

UPPER SWAN
6056
BRIGADOON
6056
MILLENDON
6056
MILLENDON
6056
SHIRE OF SWAN
GREAT NORTHERN HWY
STATION ST
COPLEY RD
ST ALBANS RD
quarry
footbridge
Bells Rapid
water tower
Orlov
Trail
tennis
BOULONNAIS
Falabella
Trail
CAMPERSIC RD
AVE
CATHEDRAL
State Equestrian Centre
helipad
FS
CAMARGUE DR
NOLAN AVE
HOLSTEIN CL
CORTE CL
HADDRILL RD
KINGS RW
RD
RANGE RD
WEIR
CAMPERSIC RD
Lamonts Winery
BISDEE RD
HARDWICK RD
MOORE
RANGE RD
LOTON RD
LOGUE RD
1 10
2 09
3 08
4 07
5 06
6 05
7 04
8 03
9 02
10 01
Joins 29

0 500 m 1 km 2 km

SCALE 1:20 000

PRIMARY RECTANGLE
SWAN BG 35

Map 169

TO FIND A STREET

ABBREVIATIONS

Al	Alley
Ar	Arcade
Ave	Avenue
Blvd	Boulevard
Bk	Break
By	Bypass
Ch	Chase
Ci	Circle
Cc	Circuit
Cs	Circus
Cl	Close
Cnr	Corner
Ct	Court
Ce	Cove
Cy	Courtyard
Cr	Crescent
Cst	Crest
Cro	Cross
Dl	Dale
Dip	Dip
Dr	Drive
Ed	Edge
El	Elbow
Ent	Entrance
Es	Esplanade
Fo	Follow
Fmn	Formation
Fwy	Freeway
Fry	Fairway
Gp	Gap
Gns	Gardens
Gl	Glade
Glen	Glen
Grn	Green
Gr	Grove
Hts	Heights
Hwy	Highway
Int	Interchange
Hl	Hill
La	Lane
Lkt	Lookout
Lp	Loop
Ml	Mall
Me	Mews
Mr	Meander
Pa	Plaza
Pde	Parade
Pwy	Parkway
Ps	Pass
Pt	Path
Pl	Place
Pro	Promenade
Qs	Quays
Ra	Ramble
Rt	Retreat
Rge	Ridge
Ri	Rise
Rd	Road
Rty	Rotary
Rw	Row
Sp	Spur
Sq	Square
St	Street
Tce	Terrace
Tp	Top
Tr	Tor
Tk	Track
Trl	Trail
Tn	Turn
Vl	Vale
Vw	View
Vs	Vista
Wk	Walk
Wy	Way
Yd	Yard

The following pages contain an alphabetical list of the street names in the MAP SECTION of this publication.

The STREET NAME appears in heavy type, the designation of STREET, ROAD, AVENUE, etc., appears immediately below in the abbreviated form, as shown in the ABBREVIATIONS listing.

To the right of the abbreviation is the SUBURB. Following this is the MAP NUMBER AND ALPHANUMERIC GRID REFERENCE.

EXAMPLE

To locate KEANE ST, WEMBLEY.

(i) Look up the *street* and *suburb* in the INDEX TO STREET NAMES.
(ii) Take note of the *map number* and *alphanumeric grid reference*.

map number → **59** **D** **9** ← alphanumeric grid reference

(iii) Turn to MAP NUMBER 59. Look up from the letter D and across from the number 9. Keane St will appear in the rectangle formed by this reference.

KEADY
St Belmont............ 74 E 3
KEAL
St Balcatta............ 46 A 5
KEANE
Ct Noranda............ 47 C 4
Rd Forrestdale........ 104 D 10
St Wembley............ 59 D 9
St Mt Helena......... 55 B 5
St Mt Helena......... 55 B 5
KEANEY
Pl Bentley............. 83 B 5
Pl City Beach........ 58 D 5
KEANS
Ave Sorrento............ 30 B 5

State Large Scale Series Reference → PRIMARY RECTANGLE PERTH BG 34 — **Map 59**

THE STREET DIRECTORY AS AN INDEX TO THE STATE LARGE SCALE SERIES

The grid referencing system used in this publication conforms to the 1:1 000 sheet lines of the State Large Scale Mapping Series (SLSMS). The black numbers located in the margins refer to the the eastings and northings within this system (eastings in the top and bottom margins, northings in the side margin). By quoting the Primary Rectangle reference, located at the foot of the map, and then the eastings and northings, the 1:1 000 map sheet of any grid square can be identified.

EXAMPLE:
KEANE ST., WEMBLEY:
  alphanumeric grid reference 59 D 9
  SLSMS reference   59 19 52
would appear on 1:1 000 sheet 19·52 of the PERTH BG 34 Primary Rectangle. The number of this sheet would be quoted as—
  PERTH 1000 BG 34 19·52

Page 170

INDEX TO STREET NAMES

A

AARON
Ct Parmelia......... 131 C 7
AARONS
Cl Mirrabooka......... 33 B10
ABALONE
Cr Waikiki............ 145 B 3
Pl Burns............... 18 D 3
ABBA
Pl Merriwa............. 11 C 8
ABBESS
Pl Kingsley............ 24 D 9
ABBETT
St Scarborough........ 44 E10
ABBEY
Gns Mt Claremont....... 71 A 4
Rd Armadale.......... 116 D 5
St Morley.............. 48 C 8
St Warwick............ 31 E 6
ABBOT
Wy Wilson.............. 84 A 6
ABBOTSFORD
St Leederville........ 60 C10
ABBOTSWOOD
Pwy Erskine........... 164 C 6
ABBOTT
Ct Leeming............ 93 A 8
Wy Dianella........... 61 C 2
Wy Swan View.......... 51 B 7
ABDALE
Ct Westfield......... 106 B10
Rd Chidlow............ 42 A 5
Rd Chidlow............ 41 E 5
St Gwelup............. 45 C 5
ABEL
Ct Beldon............. 23 D 4
ABELIA
Ct Duncraig........... 31 A 7
ABERCAIRN
Wy Lynwood............ 94 C 3
ABERCORN
Rd Forrestfield....... 86 C 1
ABERCROMBIE
Rd Hope Valley....... 121 E10
Rd Postans........... 130 E 3
ABERDARE
Rd Nedlands........... 71 D 5
Rd Shenton Park....... 72 A 5
Rd Shenton Park....... 71 D 5
Wy Warwick............ 31 E 7
ABERDEEN
Cl Halls Head........ 164 C 4
St Northbridge........ 1C A 1
St Northbridge........ 1C E 1
St Northbridge........ 72 E 1
St Perth City......... 73 E 1
St Perth City......... 60 E10
St West Perth........ 60 D10
Wy Kinross............ 18 E 1
ABERFELDY
Cr Duncraig........... 31 B 5
ABERFOYLE
Pl Hamersley.......... 32 A 8
ABERLE
St Hamilton Hill...... 91 B10
ABERNETHY
Gr Armadale.......... 116 A 4
Rd Belmont............ 74 C 2
Rd Byford............ 135 B 2
Rd Cloverdale......... 75 A 6
Rd Kewdale............ 75 C 9
Rd Oakford........... 133 B 2

Rd Oakford........... 134 D 1
Rd Oakford........... 133 D 2
ABINGDON
Pl Westfield......... 106 C10
St Swan View.......... 51 C 7
St Morley............. 48 D 9
ABINGER
Rd Lynwood............ 94 C 2
St Morley............. 47 D 6
ABITIBI
Tn Joondalup.......... 19 C 2
ABJORNSON
St Manning............ 83 B 4
ABNEY
Pl Trigg.............. 44 C 8
St Beldon............. 23 C 4
ABOYNE
Pl Armadale.......... 116 B 3
Rd Gooseberry H...... 77 D 2
ABRAHAM
Pl Murdoch............ 92 B 7
ABRAMS
St Balcatta........... 45 D 3
ABROLHOS
Cl Shelley............ 93 C 1
ABRUS
Ct Ferndale........... 94 C 1
ABSOLON
St Mundijong......... 143 B10
St Palmyra............ 91 C 4
Wy Hillarys........... 30 B 1
ACACIA
Cl Armadale.......... 116 B 7
Ct Beechboro.......... 48 C 4
Pl Lynwood............ 94 C 2
Rd Maida Vale........ 77 A 1
Wy Duncraig........... 30 D 6
Wy Yangebup......... 102 A 9
ACADIA
Gns Craigie........... 23 E 4
ACALYPHA
Vw Yangebup......... 111 E 1
ACANTHUS
Rd Willetton.......... 93 C 2
ACAPULCO
Rd Safety Bay....... 137 B10
ACARA
Ct Heathridge......... 19 D10
ACER
Ct Forrestfield....... 76 B 8
Glen Duncraig......... 31 B 9
ACFOLD
Pl Swan View.......... 51 B 8
ACHERON
Rd San Remo......... 163 C 2
ACHESON
Cr Woodvale........... 24 A 6
ACHIEVEMENT
Wy Wangara............ 25 B 6
ACHILLES
Pl Greenfields...... 163 D10
Rt Iluka.............. 18 E 6
ACKLAND
Wy Cottesloe.......... 70 D10
ACKMAR
Wy Swan View.......... 51 C 7
ACKWORTH
Cr Warwick............ 31 D 6
Rd Banjup............ 104 A10
ACOL
Pl Beckenham.......... 85 D 5
ACORN
Me Kiara.............. 48 E 6

ACOURT
Rd Banjup............ 104 A 6
Rd Jandakot.......... 103 E 4
ACTINOTUS
Rd Walliston.......... 88 A 2
ACTION
Pl Wangara............ 25 B 7
Wy Malaga............. 33 C 9
ACTON
Ave Bentley........... 84 C 4
Ave Kewdale........... 74 E 7
Ave Rivervale......... 74 B 3
Ri Kingsley........... 24 B 9
ACUTE
Ct Rockingham....... 137 B 6
ADA
Ct Hamilton Hill..... 101 C 3
St Riverton........... 83 E10
St Sth Fremantle...... 90 C 8
St Subiaco............ 71 E 3
St Waterman........... 30 C10
ADAIA
Dr Alexander Hts..... 33 B 5
ADAIR
Ave Kelmscott....... 117 A 2
Pde Coolbinia......... 60 E 5
Rd Mundaring.......... 68 C 2
ADALIA
St Kallaroo........... 23 C 7
ADAMS
Cst Ocean Reef....... 19 A10
Ct Westfield......... 106 C 9
Dr Welshpool.......... 84 C 1
Rd Caversham.......... 50 A 5
Rd Dalkeith........... 81 B 1
Rd Mariginiup......... 17 B 7
Rd Red Hill........... 37 C10
St Bateman............ 92 D 4
St Mundijong......... 142 E 7
St O'Connor........... 91 D 7
St Thornlie........... 95 C 3
ADAMSON
Cl Kingsley........... 31 B 2
Rd Brentwood.......... 92 D 3
Rd Parmelia.......... 131 C 6
St Mundijong......... 143 B10
ADANA
St Mandurah......... 165 B 2
ADARE
Ct Waterford.......... 83 D 6
Pl Coodanup......... 165 C 3
Wy Kingsley........... 31 C 1
ADDERLEY
St Mt Claremont...... 71 A 6
ADDINGHAM
Ct Craigie............ 23 E 6
ADDINGTON
St Morley............. 47 E 7
Wy Marangaroo........ 32 B 6
ADDISON
St South Perth....... 73 B 9
Wy Warwick............ 31 D 8
ADDLESTONE
Rd Embleton........... 48 B10
ADDLEWELL
Glen Kiara............ 48 D 6
ADELA
Pl Spearwood........ 101 A 6
Pl Warwick............ 31 D 8
ADELAIDE
Ci Craigie............ 23 E 4
Cr Helena Valley..... 65 B 7
St Fremantle.......... 1D C 5
St Fremantle.......... 90 C 5
St High Wycombe...... 64 B 6
St Sth Guildford..... 63 E 5

Tce East Perth........ 1C B 4
Tce East Perth........ 73 B 4
Tce Perth City........ 1C A 3
Tce Perth City........ 73 B 4
ADELIA
St Bayswater.......... 62 A 6
ADELINA
Ct Westfield......... 106 B 8
St Wilson............. 84 B 6
ADELMA
Pl Dalkeith........... 81 D 3
Rd Dalkeith........... 81 C 1
Rd Dalkeith........... 81 C 3
ADELONG
Ci Merriwa............ 10 B 8
ADELPHI
St Bayswater.......... 62 A 4
St Bayswater.......... 61 E 4
ADEN
Ct Munster........... 101 B 9
Pl Balcatta........... 45 E 4
ADENANDRA
Wy Greenwood......... 31 D 3
ADENIA
Rd Ferndale........... 84 B10
Rd Riverton........... 94 A 1
Rd Riverton........... 84 A10
ADENMORE
Wy Kingsley........... 31 C 2
ADER
Ct Marangaroo........ 32 D 5
ADERYN
Pl Willetton.......... 93 D 4
ADEY
Ct Leeming.......... 102 E 1
ADIE
Ct Bentley............ 83 E 4
ADINA
Rd City Beach........ 58 D 9
Wy Rockingham...... 137 D 6
ADISHAM
St Maddington........ 96 B 5
ADMELLA
Ri Currambine......... 19 A 3
ADMIRAL
Gr Heathridge......... 23 D 1
Gr Heathridge......... 19 D10
Rd Bedfordale....... 127 C 2
Rd Byford........... 127 D10
ADMIRALTY
Cr Halls Head....... 164 B 2
ADONIS
Rd Silver Sands..... 163 A 5
St Mundijong........ 142 E 8
ADORA
St Alexander Hts.... 33 A 5
ADORI
Pl City Beach......... 58 D 5
ADRIA
Rd Alexander Hts.... 32 E 6
ADRIAN
St Palmyra............ 91 B 3
St Welshpool.......... 84 C 2
ADRIATIC
Me Currambine......... 19 A 3
ADRINA
Ct South Lake....... 102 B 7
ADROIT
Ct Rockingham....... 137 B 5
St Riverton........... 94 A 1
ADUR
St Dianella........... 47 A 8
AERIAL
Pl Morley............. 48 D 7

AEROLITE
Wy Beldon............. 23 D 4
AFFLECK
Rd Perth Airport..... 75 D 1
Rd Perth Airport..... 63 D10
AFON
Ave Shoalwater...... 136 D 8
AFRIC
St Middle Swan....... 50 D 5
Wy Kallaroo........... 23 B 7
AFRICA
Ave Swanbourne....... 70 D 8
AGAR
Rd Lesmurdie.......... 87 D 4
AGATE
Ct Maida Vale......... 76 D 2
AGATHEA
Ct Dianella........... 47 B 6
AGATI
Pl Forrestfield....... 76 B 9
AGATON
St Hamersley.......... 31 C 9
AGER
St Dianella........... 61 C 1
AGETT
Rd Claremont.......... 71 B10
Rd Malaga............. 47 C 3
AGINCOURT
Dr Forrestfield....... 86 D 2
Dr Willetton.......... 93 B 6
AGNES
Cl Lesmurdie.......... 87 C 1
Ct Iluka.............. 18 E 6
St Beaconsfield...... 90 D 8
AGNEW
Pl Armadale.......... 116 C 4
Pl Halls Head....... 164 C 2
AGONIS
Pl Forrestfield....... 76 B 6
Pl Wanneroo.......... 24 D 1
AGOSTINO
Rd Kelmscott........ 107 C10
AHERN
St Hamilton Hill..... 101 B 2
AHERNE
Ct Bull Creek........ 93 A 4
AHOY
Rd Spearwood........ 100 E 6
AIDRIE
Ct Duncraig........... 31 A 8
AIKEN
St Myaree............. 91 E 2
AILBY
St Gosnells........... 95 E 8
AILEEN
St Mandurah......... 163 A 8
AILSA
Ct Alexander Hts.... 33 B 5
St Wembley Dns...... 59 A 5
AILSWORTH
Ct Thornlie........... 95 B 7
AINGER
Rd Quinns Rocks..... 10 B 1
AINSBURY
Pde Clarkson.......... 14 C 2
AINSLEY
Ct Westfield......... 106 B 9
AINSLIE
Ct Kardinya........... 91 E 7
Rd Nth Fremantle..... 80 D10
AINSTEY
Cl Armadale.......... 116 A 4

For detailed information regarding the street referencing system used in this book, turn to page 170.

171

A

		Map	Ref.
AINSWORTH			
Lp	Booragoon	92	B 1
AINTREE			
St	Hamersley	31	D10
AIRDRIE			
Cnr	Kinross	19	A 2
AIRLIE			
Pl	Coogee	100	E 8
St	Claremont	80	E 1
St	Kallaroo	23	C 5
AITKEN			
Dr	Winthrop	92	A 4
Pl	Noranda	47	D 5
Rd	Armadale	116	E 6
Wy	Kewdale	75	C 8
AJAX			
Pl	Beldon	23	D 4
Pl	San Remo	163	C 1
AKEBIA			
Wy	Forrestfield	76	C 8
AKITA			
Ct	Merriwa	11	C 9
ALABASTER			
Dr	Jandakot	112	D 2
Tce	Hillarys	23	A 9
ALACRITY			
Pl	Henderson	111	A10
ALAMEIN			
Cr	Swanbourne	70	D 8
ALAN			
Ct	Beldon	23	D 4
St	Balcatta	46	B 4
ALANDALE			
Rd	Greenmount	51	B10
ALANYA			
Cl	Cannington	84	D 6
ALARIC			
Ct	Lynwood	94	B 4
ALATA			
Ct	Parkerville	53	C 7
Pl	Duncraig	31	B 8
ALBA			
Ct	Mirrabooka	47	B 2
Ri	Ocean Reef	18	E 8
ALBACORE			
Dr	Sorrento	30	C 3
St	Golden Bay	158	D 9
ALBAN			
Rd	Bickley	89	B 3
ALBANY			
Ct	Beldon	23	D 4
Hwy	Armadale	117	A 8
Hwy	Armadale	116	E 2
Hwy	Beckenham	85	B 9
Hwy	Bedfordale	117	B 8
Hwy	Bedfordale	128	C 3
Hwy	Cannington	84	D 6
Hwy	E Victoria Pk	74	A 9
Hwy	Gosnells	96	B 8
Hwy	Gosnells	106	D 6
Hwy	Kelmscott	106	D 6
Hwy	Kenwick	95	D 2
Hwy	Maddington	96	A 4
Hwy	Maddington	95	E 3
Hwy	Victoria Park	73	D 6
Rd	Bedfordale	128	E 2
ALBATROSS			
Cl	Halls Head	164	B 3
Cr	Maida Vale	76	D 1
Ct	Heathridge	23	C 1
Ct	Yangebup	102	A10
Dr	Two Rocks	2	D 1
Pl	Rockingham	137	B 9
Ps	Willetton	93	C 4
ALBEMARLE			
St	Doubleview	59	A 2
St	Scarborough	58	E 2
Wy	High Wycombe	64	C10
ALBERMARLE			
Cl	Coodanup	165	C 3

		Map	Ref.
ALBERT			
Ct	Wanneroo	25	B 3
Rd	Lesmurdie	87	C 6
Rd	Middle Swan	50	E 2
Rd	Middle Swan	36	E10
St	Balcatta	46	A 8
St	Bellevue	51	A10
St	Claremont	71	A10
St	Mosman Park	80	D 6
St	North Perth	60	D 7
St	Osborne Park	46	A10
St	Osborne Park	60	B 2
St	South Perth	73	A 8
ALBION			
Ave	Munster	111	B 3
Pl	Carine	45	A 1
Rd	Madora	160	C 8
St	Cottesloe	80	D 2
St	Craigie	23	C 6
St	E Cannington	85	B 7
ALBIZIA			
Cl	Forrestfield	76	C10
ALBOURNE			
Pl	Balga	46	B 2
Wy	Balga	46	B 2
ALBRECHT			
Pl	Thornlie	95	C 3
ALBURY			
Cl	Iluka	18	E 5
ALBYNE			
Pl	Hamersley	31	D 9
ALCESTER			
Rd	East Fremantle	90	E 2
ALCESTIS			
Ct	Iluka	18	D 5
ALCISTON			
Wy	Huntingdale	95	C10
ALCOCK			
St	Maddington	96	B 3
ALCONBURY			
Rd	Kingsley	24	D10
ALDAM			
Cr	Shelley	83	C10
ALDAY			
St	St James	84	A 2
ALDER			
Ct	Ballajura	33	C 5
Ct	Halls Head	164	B 5
Me	Iluka	18	D 4
Pl	Morley	48	C 5
Pl	Thornlie	95	B10
Wy	Duncraig	31	B 6
Wy	Forrestfield	76	D10
ALDERBURY			
St	Floreat	59	B10
St	Floreat	71	C 1
ALDERCRESS			
Ri	Connolly	19	A 7
ALDERHAUS			
Dr	Kingsley	31	C 3
ALDERHURST			
Cr	Bayswater	48	C10
ALDERLEY			
Pl	Coodanup	165	D 3
Sq	Wilson	84	C 6
ALDERSEA			
Ci	Clarkson	14	C 1
Rd	Dianella	47	A10
ALDERSYDE			
Rd	Bickley	78	C10
Rd	Bickley	88	D 2
Rd	Piesse Brook	78	B 7
ALDGATE			
St	Mandurah	165	B 1
ALDINGTON			
St	Maddington	96	A 4
ALDIS			
St	Greenwood	31	D 5

		Map	Ref.
ALDOUS			
Pl	Booragoon	92	B 2
ALDRIDGE			
Rd	Booragoon	92	C 3
Rd	Brentwood	92	D 2
Ri	Clarkson	14	D 3
ALDWICK			
Pl	Balga	46	C 2
ALDWORTH			
Cr	Gosnells	95	E 7
ALDWYCH			
St	Bayswater	61	E 5
ALEPPO			
Dr	Kardinya	92	A 9
ALERI			
Ri	Currambine	19	A 6
ALEXANDER			
Cl	Lesmurdie	87	E 3
Ct	Wellard	140	B 2
Dr	Alexander Hts	33	B 5
Dr	Dianella	47	B10
Dr	Koondoola	33	C 9
Dr	Landsdale	33	B 2
Dr	Landsdale	26	B 8
Dr	Menora	61	A 5
Dr	Mirrabooka	47	C 4
Dr	Yokine	61	B 2
Pl	Dalkeith	81	C 1
Rd	Ardross	82	B 9
Rd	Belmont	74	D 3
Rd	Byford	126	C10
Rd	Dalkeith	81	C 3
Rd	Padbury	23	D 8
Rd	Rivervale	74	C 5
St	Balcatta	46	A 5
St	Wembley	59	E 9
ALEXANDRA			
Ave	Claremont	70	E10
Pl	Bentley	84	C 4
Rd	East Fremantle	90	E 2
Rd	Hovea	53	A 7
St	Rockingham	137	B 3
St	South Perth	73	A 8
ALEXANDRIA			
Vw	Mindarie	14	A 5
ALEXIS			
Pl	Duncraig	30	E 3
ALFA			
Pl	Balcatta	45	D 4
ALFONSO			
St	North Perth	60	E 9
ALFORD			
Rd	Jarrahdale	152	E 8
Ri	Leeming	92	E 9
St	Balcatta	46	B 7
ALFRED			
Cl	Safety Bay	145	A 1
Pl	Ocean Reef	19	A 9
Rd	Claremont	71	A 6
Rd	Mt Claremont	71	A 6
Rd	Nth Fremantle	80	C10
Rd	Swanbourne	70	D 6
Rd	Swanbourne	70	E 6
St	Belmont	74	D 2
St	Mt Helena	55	A 1
St	Spearwood	101	C 4
ALFREDA			
Ave	Morley	48	B 8
Ave	Noranda	48	B 5
ALFRETON			
Wy	Duncraig	31	A 4
ALGA			
St	Scarborough	44	D 9
ALICE			
Ave	Sth Fremantle	90	C10
Dr	Mullaloo	23	B 1
Rd	Cardup	135	B 7
Rd	Lesmurdie	87	C 8
Rd	Mt Helena	55	A 4
Rd	Mt Helena	54	E 1
Rd	Mt Helena	40	E 7

		Map	Ref.
Rd	Mt Helena	40	E10
Rd	Roleystone	108	A 8
St	Bassendean	62	D 2
St	Bellevue	51	A10
St	Doubleview	45	A 9
ALICIA			
Gns	Ballajura	33	C 4
St	Kallaroo	23	B 7
ALIDADE			
Wy	Beldon	23	C 4
ALIFFE			
St	Embleton	48	A10
ALISON			
Rd	Attadale	81	C 9
St	Mt Helena	55	B 2
St	Mt Helena	41	B10
ALISTAIR			
Rd	Bibra Lake	102	D 2
St	Huntingdale	95	D 8
ALLAMANDA			
Dr	South Lake	102	C 6
Gns	Mirrabooka	47	B 1
Wy	Forrestfield	76	C 9
Wy	Halls Head	164	B 5
ALLAMBIE			
Dr	Craigie	23	D 6
Dr	Stoneville	54	B 7
ALLAN			
Pl	Darlington	66	A 2
Pl	Halls Head	162	C10
ALLARA			
Pl	Currambine	19	A 6
ALLARD			
Pl	Leeming	93	C 9
ALLAWAH			
Ct	Armadale	116	C 6
ALLEN			
Cl	Rockingham	136	E 6
Ct	Bentley	83	E 3
Ct	Queens Park	85	A 3
Rd	Armadale	105	D10
Rd	Forrestdale	115	C 2
Rd	Forrestdale	115	C 2
Rd	Westfield	106	A 7
St	East Fremantle	90	E 1
St	South Perth	73	A10
ALLENBY			
Rd	Dalkeith	81	C 3
ALLENSWOOD			
Rd	Greenwood	31	D 4
ALLEN-WILLIAMS			
Pde	Winthrop	92	C 5
ALLERTON			
Wy	Booragoon	92	C 2
ALLESTREE			
Rd	Darlington	66	B 4
ALLIN			
Pl	Parmelia	131	A 7
ALLINGA			
Cr	Craigie	23	D 4
ALLINSON			
Dr	Girrawheen	32	B 8
ALLIS			
Hts	Yangebup	111	E 1
ALLISON			
Cl	Willetton	93	D 4
ALLMAN			
Rd	Parkerville	53	D 7
ALLNUTT			
St	Mandurah	163	A10
ALLOA			
St	Maddington	96	A 2
St	Maddington	95	E 3
ALLORA			
St	Mandurah	165	A 2
ALLOTT			
Pl	Marangaroo	32	D 6
ALLOWAY			
Pl	Armadale	116	B 2

		Map	Ref.
ALLOY			
Wy	E Rockingham	137	E 1
ALLPIKE			
Rd	Darlington	66	B 6
St	Guildford	49	E10
ALL SAINTS			
Wy	Churchlands	59	C 5
ALLSPICE			
Vs	Mirrabooka	47	B 1
Vs	Mirrabooka	33	B10
ALLUM			
Dr	Serpentine	155	B 2
Grn	Merriwa	11	C 9
ALMA			
Pl	Beldon	23	E 3
Rd	Mt Lawley	61	A 8
Rd	North Perth	61	A 8
Rd	North Perth	60	D 7
St	Fremantle	1D	C 6
St	Fremantle	90	C 6
St	Maylands	61	E 6
ALMADINE			
Dr	Carine	30	E10
ALMERIA			
Pde	Upper Swan	29	E 1
Pl	Waikiki	145	C 6
ALMOND			
Ave	Shoalwater	136	D 9
Dr	Rowethorpe	144	
Pl	Shoalwater	136	D 9
St	Guildford	49	E10
Wy	Forrestfield	86	D 1
Wy	Forrestfield	76	D10
ALMONDBURY			
Rd	Ardross	82	B10
Rd	Mt Lawley	61	C 8
St	Bayswater	62	B 6
ALMONDTREE			
La	Maida Vale	65	A 9
ALMURTA			
St	Nollamara	46	D 5
Wy	Nollamara	46	D 5
ALNESS			
Ct	Duncraig	31	A 7
St	Applecross	82	C 6
St	Ardross	82	C 6
ALOCASIA			
Cl	South Lake	102	D 5
ALOLA			
Ct	Alexander Hts	33	A 4
St	Kelmscott	107	A 7
ALONSO			
St	Coolbellup	101	D 2
ALPERTON			
Ct	Kingsley	24	A 9
ALPHA			
Cl	Iluka	18	E 6
ALPIN			
Ct	Coolbellup	102	A 1
ALPINE			
La	Ballajura	33	C 6
Rd	Kalamunda	77	C 9
ALPORT			
Cl	Carine	30	E 9
ALPS			
St	Mt Helena	55	B 6
ALROY			
St	Warwick	31	E 7
ALSACE			
St	Carine	45	A 1
ALSOP			
Pl	Kardinya	91	E 6
Wk	Carine	31	A 9
ALSTON			
Ave	Como	82	E 2
ALTAIR			
Cl	Alexander Hts	33	A 5
St	Dianella	61	B 1
Wy	Beldon	23	D 4

172

For detailed information regarding the street referencing system used in this book, turn to page 170.

A

		Map	Ref.
ALTA LAGUNA			
Cr	Ballajura	33	D 8
ALTHORNE			
Wy	Girrawheen	32	B 8
ALTO			
Cl	Iluka	18	E 4
ALTON			
Ct	Rossmoyne	93	A 2
St	Kenwick	85	D 9
ALTONA			
St	Bibra Lake	101	D 4
St	West Perth	72	C 2
ALTONE			
Rd	Beechboro	49	A 4
Rd	Kiara	49	A 7
Rd	Lockridge	49	A 7
ALTURA			
Ri	Dianella	47	B 5
ALUMINA			
Rd	E Rockingham	137	D 2
ALVAH			
St	St James	84	A 3
ALVAN			
St	Mt Lawley	61	B 8
St	Subiaco	72	A 1
ALVASTON			
Dr	Carine	31	A10
ALVER			
Rd	Doubleview	59	B 2
ALVIS			
Pl	North Beach	44	D 3
ALYCON			
Pl	Kallaroo	23	B 5
ALYTH			
Rd	Floreat	59	B 8
ALYXIA			
Pl	Duncraig	31	B 7
Pl	Ferndale	84	C10
AMADEUS			
Gns	Joondalup	19	C 2
AMANDA			
Dr	Westfield	106	B 7
AMARILLO			
Dr	Karnup	159	E 4
Dr	Karnup	159	E 4
AMAROO			
Ct	Armadale	116	B 4
Pl	Duncraig	30	D 8
Rd	Parkerville	39	B 7
St	Lesmurdie	87	B 2
AMAZON			
Dr	Beechboro	48	D 3
Dr	Greenfields	165	C 1
Dr	Greenfields	163	C10
AMBASSADOR			
Ct	Thornlie	95	B 8
AMBER			
Cl	Warnbro	145	D 6
Ct	Maida Vale	64	D10
Gr	Ballajura	33	C 6
Gr	Edgewater	24	B 3
Pl	Carine	45	B 1
Wy	Thornlie	95	B 9
AMBERGATE			
Cl	Canning Vale	94	A10
St	Karrinyup	44	E 2
AMBERLEY			
Wy	Balga	46	B 3
Wy	Hamilton Hill	101	A 3
AMBERTON			
Ave	Girrawheen	32	C 7
La	Girrawheen	32	D 7
AMBLESIDE			
Ave	Mt Hawthorn	60	B 6
Cl	Balga	32	C10
AMBON			
St	Kensington	73	D 9

		Map	Ref.
AMBRIDGE			
St	Hamersley	31	D 9
AMBROSE			
St	Innaloo	45	B 9
St	Rockingham	137	C 4
AMCER			
Ri	Stratton	51	B 3
AMEER			
Wy	Craigie	23	E 4
AMELIA			
St	Balcatta	46	A 5
St	Balcatta	45	D 5
St	Nollamara	46	C 5
AMERY			
St	Como	83	A 3
AMETHYST			
Cr	Armadale	116	E 6
Wy	Carine	45	A 1
AMHERST			
Ave	Darlington	66	A 5
Rd	Canning Vale	94	D 3
Rd	Canning Vale	104	E 1
Rd	Midland	50	A 9
Rd	Swan View	51	C 9
St	Fremantle	90	D 5
St	South Perth	72	E 8
St	White Gum Vly	90	D 6
AMIENS			
Cr	Millendon	29	C 7
AMINYA			
Ave	Wanneroo	20	E 9
Rd	Bickley	88	C 4
AMITY			
Blvd	Coogee	100	E 9
Ce	Halls Head	164	D 2
Cl	Sorrento	30	B 4
AMMERDOWN			
Pl	Erskine	164	C 5
AMORIA			
Ct	Mullaloo	23	B 3
AMPHION			
Pl	Leeming	93	B 8
AMSTEL			
Ct	Yanchep	4	E 2
AMSTEY			
St	Riverton	93	E 1
St	Riverton	83	E10
AMULLA			
Ct	Halls Head	164	A 7
AMUR			
Cl	Beechboro	48	E 2
Pl	Bateman	92	D 3
AMY			
Ct	Munster	101	B10
Lp	Craigie	23	E 4
St	Byford	135	D 1
St	Perth City	61	A10
ANABAR			
Wy	Beechboro	48	D 3
ANACONDA			
Dr	Gosnells	105	E 2
Dr	Gosnells	95	E10
Pl	Sorrento	30	B 4
ANADARA			
Pl	Mullaloo	23	B 3
ANCHOR			
Cl	Ballajura	33	D 8
Pl	Safety Bay	137	B10
ANCHORAGE			
Dr	Mindarie	10	B 2
Dr	Mindarie	14	B 3
ANCHORS			
Wy	Yanchep	4	C 5
ANCILLA			
St	Mullaloo	23	B 3
ANCONA			
Pl	Warnbro	145	C 8
ANDADO			
Pl	Lynwood	94	D 3

		Map	Ref.
ANDANTE			
St	Falcon	162A	D10
ANDELL			
Pl	Redcliffe	63	A10
ANDERSON			
Ct	Sth Guildford	63	B 4
Pl	Kelmscott	117	B 1
Rd	Forrestfield	86	D 1
Rd	Forrestfield	76	D10
Rd	Henderson	111	B 6
Rd	Nowergup	13	E 5
Rd	Peel Estate	133	A 7
St	Glendalough	60	B 4
Wy	Thornlie	95	B 4
ANDERTON			
Rt	Murdoch	92	C 6
ANDES			
Cl	Waikiki	145	C 2
ANDREA			
Dr	Henley Brook	28	D 9
Wy	Queens Park	85	A 2
ANDREAS			
Rd	Roleystone	108	A 6
Rd	Roleystone	107	E 6
ANDRENE			
Ct	Leeming	92	E10
ANDREW			
Rd	Waikiki	145	B 4
St	Kalamunda	77	C 8
St	Mandurah	163	A 9
St	Scarborough	44	D 9
ANDREWS			
Ave	E Rockingham	129	C10
Ct	Padbury	23	C10
Pl	Cottesloe	70	D10
Rd	East Fremantle	90	D 2
Rd	Wilson	84	A 6
Wy	Herne Hill	36	E 4
Wy	Kardinya	91	E 7
ANDROMEDA			
St	Rockingham	137	A 8
ANDROS			
Pl	Safety Bay	145	B 1
Rd	Safety Bay	145	B 1
ANEC			
Ct	South Lake	102	C 8
St	Waikiki	145	D 2
ANEMBO			
Cl	Duncraig	30	D 7
Pl	Kelmscott	106	E 6
Rd	Carmel	88	E 7
ANEMONE			
Wy	Mullaloo	23	B 5
ANERLEY			
St	Hamersley	45	D 1
ANGALORE			
Rd	Madora	160	D 7
ANGAS			
Pl	Thornlie	95	A 4
ANGEL			
Cl	Hillarys	30	B 1
ANGELA			
Wy	Maddington	96	B 4
ANGELICO			
St	Woodlands	59	B 3
ANGELINA			
Ct	Kingsley	31	B 1
ANGELO			
Pl	Armadale	116	C 7
St	Armadale	116	C 7
St	South Perth	73	B 9
St	South Perth	72	E 8
ANGLE			
Pl	Mullaloo	23	C 3
ANGLER			
Ct	Wilson	84	A 8
Wy	Sorrento	30	D 3

		Map	Ref.
ANGLESEA			
Cr	Belhus	29	C 3
St	E Victoria Pk	74	B10
ANGLESEY			
Dr	Kardinya	91	D 9
ANGLESY			
Ci	Port Kennedy	156	C 4
ANGORRA			
Rd	Armadale	116	E 4
ANGOVE			
Dr	Hillarys	30	A 2
La	Bicton	81	A10
St	North Perth	60	E 7
ANGUS			
Ave	Spearwood	101	B 6
Ct	Duncraig	31	A 5
ANGWIN			
St	East Fremantle	90	D 2
ANHAM			
St	Armadale	116	C 6
ANITA			
Pl	Lesmurdie	87	B 4
ANITRA			
Ct	Coogee	100	E 9
Ct	Sorrento	30	C 4
ANKETELL			
Rd	Mt Helena	40	D 9
Rd	Oakford	124	A 9
Rd	Oakford	123	E 9
Rd	Stoneville	40	C 9
Rd	Wandi	123	B 9
St	Kensington	73	D 9
ANN			
St	Darlington	66	B 4
Wy	Rossmoyne	93	B 2
ANNA			
Pl	Wanneroo	21	A 8
ANNAN			
Ct	Hamersley	32	A 9
ANNATO			
Pl	Forrestfield	86	E 1
St	Greenwood	31	D 4
ANNE			
Ave	Walliston	87	E 1
Pl	Scarborough	58	D 1
Rd	Hovea	52	E 9
ANNEAN			
Lp	Cooloongup	137	C10
ANNEAR			
St	Beckenham	85	C 5
ANNETTS			
Rd	Walliston	88	A 5
ANNIE			
St	Hamilton Hill	90	E 9
St	Welshpool	74	D10
ANNISON			
Rd	Morley	47	E 8
ANNOIS			
Rd	Bibra Lake	102	D 5
ANONA			
Pl	Riverton	83	E10
ANSCOMBE			
Lp	Leeming	93	A 9
ANSON			
Ct	Hillarys	23	A 8
ANSTEY			
Rd	Bassendean	63	B 2
Rd	Forrestdale	115	B 3
Rd	Forrestdale	114	E 5
Rd	Secret Harbour	158	E 3
St	Claremont	80	E 1
St	Mundijong	143	A 8
St	South Perth	73	A10
ANSTIE			
Wy	Bull Creek	93	B 7
ANSTRUTHER			
Rd	Mandurah	165	B 1
Rd	Mandurah	163	B10

		Map	Ref.
ANTEO			
Ct	Lynwood	94	B 2
ANTHEA			
St	Hazelmere	64	A 1
ANTHILL			
Rd	Roleystone	108	B 6
ANTHONY			
Pl	Sawyers Valley	55	A 9
St	Lesmurdie	87	D 1
St	South Perth	73	B 8
Wy	Tuart Hill	46	C 9
ANTIBES			
Ct	Mindarie	14	B 3
ANTIGONUS			
St	Coolbellup	91	E10
ANTIGUA			
St	Safety Bay	137	C10
ANTILA			
Pl	Rockingham	137	B 7
ANTILL			
St	Willagee	91	D 5
ANTON			
St	Armadale	116	C 8
ANTONIO			
St	Coolbellup	101	D 2
ANTONY			
St	Palmyra	91	A 2
ANTRIM			
Ct	Woodvale	24	C 6
St	Leederville	60	C 9
ANVIL			
Cl	Sth Guildford	63	C 4
Wy	Chidlow	43	C 4
Wy	Welshpool	84	D 1
Wy	Welshpool	74	E10
ANZAC			
Rd	Mt Hawthorn	60	B 6
St	Bayswater	62	C 6
Tce	Bassendean	49	A10
Tce	Bayswater	48	D10
APALIE			
Trl	Edgewater	24	B 3
APARA			
Ct	South Lake	102	D 6
Pl	Koongamia	65	C 1
Wy	Nollamara	46	C 9
APEX			
Cl	Leeming	93	C 8
APLEY			
St	Maddington	96	B 6
APOLLO			
Pl	Duncraig	30	E 3
Wy	Carlisle	74	B 7
APPERLEY			
St	Kenwick	95	C 1
APPIAN			
Wy	Hamersley	32	A10
APPLE			
St	Upper Swan	166	A10
APPLE BLOSSOM			
Dr	Mirrabooka	47	B 1
Dr	Mirrabooka	33	B10
APPLEBY			
St	Balcatta	46	A 4
APPLEDORE			
St	Beckenham	85	C 7
APPLETON			
St	Carlisle	74	D 8
APPLETREE			
Pl	Woodvale	24	B 7
APPROACH			
Rd	Boya	65	D 5
APRICOT			
St	Forrestfield	76	C 6
APRIL			
Rd	Dianella	46	E 9

For detailed information regarding the street referencing system used in this book, turn to page 170.

A

		Map	Ref.
APSLEY			
Rd	Willetton	93	C 3
APUS			
Cl	Rockingham	137	B 7
AQUANITA			
Pl	Wanneroo	21	A 9
AQUARIUS			
Cl	Falcon	162A	D 1
AQUILA			
Cl	Rockingham	137	B 7
Ri	Kingsley	31	B 2
AQUITANIA			
Cl	Port Kennedy	156	D 4
ARA			
Ce	Wandi	123	C 7
ARABELLA			
Rt	Currambine	19	A 3
ARABIAN			
Ct	Armadale	106	A 10
ARAGON			
Wy	Wilson	84	B 6
ARALIA			
Pl	Dianella	47	B 6
Wy	Forrestfield	76	D 10
ARALUEN			
St	Morley	48	C 3
ARANDA			
Pl	Leederville	60	C 7
ARAWA			
Pl	Craigie	23	D 6
ARBERY			
Ave	Sorrento	30	C 6
ARBON			
Pl	Lynwood	94	C 2
Wy	Lockridge	49	A 6
ARBOR			
Ct	Duncraig	30	E 6
Gr	Leeming	102	E 2
ARBORDALE			
St	Floreat	59	B 10
ARBOUR			
Pl	Westfield	106	C 9
ARBUCKLE			
Pl	Gwelup	45	C 7
ARBUTHNOT			
St	Kelmscott	107	A 10
ARC			
Pl	Beldon	23	C 2
ARCADIA			
Dr	Shoalwater	144	C 1
Dr	Shoalwater	136	C 10
Pl	Dianella	47	B 5
Pl	Shoalwater	136	C 7
ARCAMAN			
Pl	South Lake	102	C 8
ARCHDEACON			
St	E Victoria Pk	84	A 1
St	Nedlands	71	E 10
ARCHER			
Ave	Cullacabardee	34	B 3
St	Carlisle	74	B 8
St	Midland	50	B 9
St	Wanneroo	24	E 5
ARCHIBALD			
Pl	Lesmurdie	87	C 2
Rd	Balcatta	46	B 8
St	Willagee	92	A 5
St	Willagee	91	D 5
ARCHIDAMUS			
Rd	Coolbellup	91	E 10
ARCOT			
Ct	Meadow Sprgs	163	D 5
ARCTIC			
Cl	Waikiki	145	C 4
ARDAGH			
St	Morley	48	B 7

		Map	Ref.
ARDEN			
Ct	Hillarys	23	B 10
St	East Perth	73	C 3
ARDESSIE			
St	Ardross	82	C 9
ARDGAY			
Pl	Duncraig	31	A 7
ARDILL			
Cl	Noranda	48	A 4
ARDISIA			
Ct	Forrestfield	76	D 10
ARDLEIGH			
Cr	Hamersley	31	E 9
Cr	Hamersley	31	E 10
ARDMAIR			
Cl	Armadale	116	A 2
ARDMORE			
Ct	Meadow Sprgs	163	C 3
ARDROSS			
Cr	Coolbinia	60	E 4
Cr	Menora	60	E 5
St	Applecross	82	C 9
St	Ardross	82	D 8
St	Armadale	116	B 3
Wy	Noranda	47	C 4
ARDROSSAN			
Lp	Kingsley	24	C 9
ARDTALLA			
Ct	Duncraig	30	E 8
ARGO			
Ct	Craigie	23	D 6
ARGONAUT			
Ave	Waikiki	145	D 4
ARGOSY			
Pl	Morley	48	D 7
St	Falcon	162A	C 1
ARGUS			
Cl	Craigie	23	D 5
Ct	Greenfields	163	D 9
ARGYLE			
Cl	Edgewater	19	E 9
Ct	Thornlie	95	A 7
Pl	Carine	45	A 1
Pl	Yangebup	112	B 1
St	Bentley	84	A 5
St	Herne Hill	36	D 5
St	Leederville	60	C 9
ARGYLL			
Cl	Westfield	106	C 6
Pl	Duncraig	31	C 8
ARIEL			
Ct	Alexander Hts	33	A 5
Pl	Coolbellup	101	D 2
Pl	Madora	160	D 6
ARIES			
Cl	Greenfields	163	E 10
Ct	Rockingham	137	A 7
Ct	Shelley	83	D 10
ARILIA			
St	Balcatta	46	A 4
ARISTEA			
Pl	Roleystone	108	A 9
ARISTOS			
Wy	Marangaroo	32	D 6
ARISTRIDE			
Ave	Kallaroo	23	A 7
ARITI			
Ave	Wanneroo	20	C 10
ARKABA			
Me	Ocean Reef	19	A 8
ARKANA			
Rd	Balga	46	B 4
Wy	Balcatta	46	B 4
ARKANSAS			
Wy	Greenfields	165	C 2
ARKLEY			
Ct	Erskine	164	D 5

		Map	Ref.
ARKWELL			
Ave	Rockingham	137	A 7
St	Willagee	91	D 4
Wy	Marmion	30	C 7
ARKWRIGHT			
Rd	Hillman	138	A 4
Rd	Rockingham	137	E 4
ARLINGTON			
Ave	South Perth	73	B 8
Dr	Willetton	93	E 7
Lp	Coogee	100	E 8
ARLUNYA			
Ave	Belmont	74	D 3
Ave	Cloverdale	74	E 4
ARMADA			
Cl	Port Kennedy	156	D 4
St	Bayswater	62	A 4
ARMADALE			
Cr	Coolbinia	60	D 4
Pl	Greenfields	163	D 9
Rd	Armadale	116	A 5
Rd	Forrestdale	115	A 5
Rd	Kewdale	74	C 6
Rd	Rivervale	74	B 3
ARMAGH			
St	Victoria Park	73	D 7
ARMATA			
Wk	Mirrabooka	33	A 10
ARMITAGE			
Rd	Kelmscott	106	E 10
ARMITT			
St	Kewdale	74	E 8
ARMOUR			
Wy	Lesmurdie	87	E 3
ARMSTRONG			
Rd	Applecross	82	D 5
Rd	Hope Valley	121	C 8
Rd	Jarrahdale	152	D 6
Rd	Kelmscott	107	B 10
Rd	Wilson	84	A 7
Sq	Duncraig	30	E 5
St	Halls Head	164	C 1
Wy	Noranda	48	A 6
ARMYTAGE			
Wy	Hillarys	23	C 10
ARNE			
Ct	Ocean Reef	18	E 8
ARNEL			
St	Kelmscott	106	E 7
ARNEY			
Ct	Yanchep	4	C 5
Pl	Melville	91	E 1
ARNISDALE			
Rd	Duncraig	31	B 6
ARNO			
Cr	Attadale	81	D 8
ARNOLD			
Cr	North Lake	92	A 10
Pl	Balga	32	A 8
Rd	Serpentine	155	A 5
St	Mandurah	165	C 2
ARNOS			
Wy	Girrawheen	32	C 7
ARNOTT			
St	North Beach	44	D 4
St	Trigg	44	D 4
ARRAN			
Ct	Warwick	31	C 8
ARRAS			
St	Nedlands	71	E 6
ARRETON			
Cl	Willetton	94	A 4
Cl	Willetton	93	E 4
ARRIGO			
St	Wangara	24	E 6
ARROCHAR			
Ct	Hamersley	32	A 9
ARROL			
St	Carine	45	A 1

		Map	Ref.
ARROWROCK			
Rt	Greenfields	165	E 2
ARROWSMITH			
Ri	Marangaroo	32	C 4
ARTANE			
Ct	Waterford	83	C 7
ARTARMON			
Ri	Kallaroo	23	A 6
ARTELLO BAY			
Rd	Midvale	51	A 8
ARTHUR			
Ct	Carine	31	C 10
Rd	Gooseberry H	77	C 1
Rd	Hamilton Hill	101	B 1
Rd	Lesmurdie	87	C 5
Rd	Safety Bay	144	E 1
Rd	Wattle Grove	86	A 3
St	Cannington	85	A 8
St	Caversham	49	D 4
St	Inglewood	61	D 5
St	Kewdale	74	E 7
St	Mosman Park	80	E 7
St	Shenton Park	72	A 4
St	West Perth	60	D 10
St	West Swan	35	D 10
ARTHUR HEAD			
	Fremantle	1D	B 5
ARUMA			
Wy	City Beach	58	D 4
ARUN			
Pl	Nollamara	46	E 4
ARUNDALE			
Cr	Wembley Dns	59	A 3
ARUNDEL			
Ct	Maida Vale	76	D 4
Dr	Halls Head	164	C 2
Dr	Wellard	140	B 1
St	Bayswater	62	A 5
St	Fremantle	1D	C 6
St	Fremantle	90	C 6
St	Kensington	73	C 9
ARUNDLE			
Ave	Greenmount	65	C 1
Ave	Greenmount	51	C 10
ARVIDA			
St	Malaga	47	C 1
ARVIDSON			
Ct	Leeming	93	B 8
ASCARI			
La	Joondalup	19	D 7
ASCHAM			
Wy	North Lake	102	A 1
ASCHE			
Wy	Two Rocks	2	C 2
ASCOT			
Dr	Redcliffe	63	A 10
Pl	Ascot	62	D 8
Tce	Ascot	62	D 8
ASH			
Ct	Armadale	116	D 4
Ct	Halls Head	164	B 4
Gr	Duncraig	31	B 8
Pl	Greenwood	31	C 4
Rd	Beechina	57	D 2
Rd	Carmel	88	C 5
Rd	Chidlow	57	A 2
Rd	Chidlow	56	D 2
St	Maddington	96	C 4
Wy	Morley	48	A 8
ASHBOURNE			
Wy	Hamilton Hill	101	B 3
ASHBURN			
Vs	Currambine	19	B 5
ASHBURTON			
Ct	Mandurah	165	A 4
Dr	Gosnells	106	A 2
Dr	Gosnells	105	E 2
Dr	Heathridge	19	B 10
St	Bentley	84	A 5
St	E Victoria Pk	73	E 10
Tce	Fremantle	90	D 6

		Map	Ref.
ASHBY			
Cl	High Wycombe	76	B 5
Ct	Leeming	93	A 10
St	Morley	48	A 9
St	Mt Hawthorn	60	B 6
St	Wanneroo	21	C 10
Tce	Viveash	50	B 5
ASHCROFT			
Wy	Balga	32	D 9
ASHER			
Rd	Paulls Valley	67	A 10
Rd	Paulls Valley	78	E 3
ASHFIELD			
Pde	Ashfield	62	E 6
Pde	Bayswater	62	E 6
St	Dianella	47	C 10
ASHFORD			
Ave	Rockingham	137	C 6
Ct	Marangaroo	32	A 5
St	Maddington	96	B 5
ASHINGTON			
St	Dianella	47	B 9
ASHLAR			
Ct	Hillarys	23	B 10
ASHLEY			
Ave	Kewdale	74	D 7
Ave	Quinns Rocks	10	E 9
Dr.	Kelmscott	107	A 7
Rd	Hope Valley	122	A 4
Rd	Hope Valley	121	E 5
Rd	Wanneroo	20	B 2
ASHMORE			
Wy	Sorrento	30	B 3
Wy	Sorrento	30	C 3
ASHNESS			
Cl	Balga	46	C 1
ASHOVER			
Gr	Carine	31	A 9
ASHSTEAD			
St	Morley	48	B 6
St	Sawyers Valley	68	E 1
ASHTON			
Ave	Claremont	71	B 7
Rd	Leeming	93	A 8
Ri	Woodvale	24	B 5
ASHURST			
Dr	Lesmurdie	87	A 1
Dr	Lesmurdie	77	B 10
Pl	Huntingdale	95	D 9
ASHWOOD			
Cl	Ballajura	33	C 5
Ct	Craigie	23	E 5
ASHWORTH			
St	Cloverdale	75	A 2
ASPEN			
Cl	Canning Vale	94	A 10
Cl	Greenwood	31	C 2
Cl	Cooloongup	137	E 8
Ct	Forrestfield	76	C 10
Gr	Ballajura	33	D 5
Pl	Stoneville	54	A 4
ASPENDALE			
Pl	Hillarys	30	A 1
ASQUITH			
Ct	Greenwood	31	B 3
St	Mt Claremont	70	B 7
St	Munster	111	B 1
St	Munster	101	B 10
St	Victoria Park	73	D 6
ASSAI			
Gl	Warnbro	145	E 9
ASSAM			
St	Madora	160	C 7
ASTEN			
Rd	City Beach	58	D 6
ASTER			
Ave	Willetton	93	D 3
Ct	Thornlie	95	A 9
ASTERIA			
St	Silver Sands	163	A 8

174

For detailed information regarding the street referencing system used in this book, turn to page 170.

B

		Map	Ref.
ASTEROID			
Wy	Carlisle	74	C 8
ASTINAL			
Dr	Gosnells	96	A 10
Dr	Gosnells	95	E 10
ASTLEY			
Pl	Kingsley	31	D 1
St	Gosnells	96	C 9
ASTON			
Ct	Carine	30	E 10
St	Joondalup	19	D 7
Wy	Gosnells	96	A 8
ASTRA			
Ct	Ocean Reef	18	E 7
ASTRAL			
Ave	Carlisle	74	C 8
ASTROLOMA			
Pl	Koongamia	65	B 1
ASWAN			
Vw	Joondalup	19	D 3
ATALA			
Pl	Marangaroo	32	D 6
ATALANTA			
Dr	Two Rocks	3	B 10
Ri	Ocean Reef	18	E 8
ATHEL			
Ct	Leeming	103	A 1
Rd	Woodlands	59	B 2
ATHELSTAN			
St	Cottesloe	80	D 1
ATHENA			
Ct	Cooloongup	137	D 8
Pl	Roleystone	108	B 9
ATHENIAN			
Cl	Padbury	30	E 1
ATHENS			
Cl	Dianella	47	A 6
ATHERTON			
Pl	Greenfields	165	C 2
ATHLONE			
Rd	Floreat	59	B 9
ATKIN			
Pl	Ocean Reef	23	A 1
ATKINS			
Rd	Applecross	82	D 5
Rd	Mundaring	68	C 7
St	Jarrahdale	152	C 7
Wy	Eden Hill	48	E 9
ATKINSON			
Ct	Stratton	51	B 4
Rd	Medina	130	D 5
ATLANTA			
Dr	Two Rocks	3	B 10
ATLANTIC			
Wy	Waikiki	145	C 4
ATLAS			
Ct	Welshpool	85	A 1
ATMA			
Cl	Iluka	19	A 6
ATOLL			
Ct	Mullaloo	23	A 4
ATTFIELD			
St	Fremantle	1D	C 6
St	Fremantle	90	C 6
St	Guildford	63	E 1
St	Guildford	49	E 10
St	Maddington	96	A 5
St	Maddington	95	D 3
St	Sth Fremantle	90	C 7
ATTRA			
Pl	Balga	32	E 10
St	Balcatta	45	E 4
ATTUNGA			
Rd	Roleystone	108	A 8
Rd	Roleystone	107	E 8
ATTWELL			
St	Landsdale	25	D 9

		Map	Ref.
ATTWOOD			
Pl	Clarkson	14	C 3
Wy	Rockingham	137	B 4
ATWELL			
Ct	Kardinya	92	A 7
Rd	Mundijong	150	C 6
Rd	Munster	111	A 1
St	Belmont	74	D 1
ATWICK			
Ct	Madora	160	D 8
Pl	Coogee	100	E 10
Wy	Craigie	23	E 7
AUBOROUGH			
St	Doubleview	59	A 1
St	Doubleview	45	A 10
AUBREY			
Ct	Wanneroo	20	C 7
AUCKLAND			
St	North Perth	60	D 5
AUDAX			
Ct	Merriwa	14	C 1
AUDEN			
Ct	Spearwood	101	C 8
AUDREY			
St	Mahogany Crk	53	C 10
AUGHTON			
St	Bayswater	62	C 5
AUGUST			
Ct	Bull Creek	93	A 7
AUGUSTA			
Ct	Connolly	19	B 6
Gr	Yanchep	4	E 2
Me	Meadow Sprgs	163	C 6
St	Willetton	93	C 2
AUGUSTUS			
Wy	Marangaroo	32	C 6
AUKS			
Ri	Ballajura	33	E 6
AULBERRY			
Pde	Leeming	92	E 9
AULD			
Ct	Waikiki	145	D 2
AUMERLE			
Wy	Spearwood	101	C 5
AURELIAN			
St	Palmyra	91	B 3
AURIC			
Pl	Maddington	96	B 5
AURIGA			
Cl	Rockingham	137	A 7
AURIOL			
Ct	Carine	30	E 9
AURORA			
Gr	Ocean Reef	18	E 7
Gr	Willetton	93	C 7
AURUM			
St	Ascot	62	D 9
AUSSAT			
Dr	Eden Hill	48	D 8
Dr	Kiara	48	D 8
Dr	Morley	48	D 8
AUSTEN			
St	Munster	101	B 9
AUSTIN			
Ave	Kenwick	95	E 3
Cl	Mt Helena	55	H 3
Ct	Cooloongup	137	D 10
Pl	Winthrop	92	B 4
St	Shenton Park	72	A 4
Wy	Padbury	23	D 8
AUSTRALIA II			
Dr	Crawley	72	A 10
AUSTRALIND			
St	Swanbourne	70	E 9
AUSTRALIS			
Ave	Mirrabooka	47	A 2
AUTHUR			
St	West Swan	49	D 1

		Map	Ref.
AUTUMN			
Cr	Thornlie	95	B 10
Ct	Duncraig	31	B 7
AVALON			
Cl	Woodvale	24	B 3
Pde	Falcon	162A	A 4
AVARD			
Pl	Armadale	116	B 7
AVARNA			
St	Belmont	74	D 1
AVEBURY			
Ct	Maddington	96	C 3
AVELEY			
Rd	Belhus	29	C 3
St	Willetton	93	C 2
AVENELL			
Rd	Bayswater	62	B 4
AVERY			
Ave	Dianella	61	B 1
Ave	Dianella	47	B 10
Ct	Booragoon	92	C 3
St	Neerabup	16	A 2
AVIEMORE			
Cl	Hamersley	32	A 9
Lp	Kingsley	24	C 10
AVIGNON			
Rt	Port Kennedy	145	D 10
Wy	Beechboro	48	C 4
AVILA			
Pl	Kenwick	86	A 10
Wy	Alexander Hts	33	A 5
AVION			
Wy	Claremont	71	A 9
AVOCA			
Cl	Willetton	93	E 5
Pl	Madora	160	C 6
Pl	Merriwa	11	C 9
AVOCADO			
Dr	Dianella	47	B 6
AVOCET			
Ct	Kingsley	31	C 1
Gr	Ballajura	33	E 6
Pl	Coodanup	165	E 9
Pl	Yangebup	102	A 9
Rd	Stirling	45	D 5
St	Langford	95	A 2
St	Wungong	116	C 10
AVOLA			
Ce	Merriwa	10	B 9
AVON			
Cr	Viveash	50	B 6
Ct	Thornlie	95	D 5
Pl	Warwick	31	D 7
AVONDALE			
Ct	Mindarie	10	B 2
Rd	Maddington	96	C 6
AVONIA			
Rd	Kalamunda	77	D 10
AVONLEE			
Rd	Armadale	116	C 8
AVONMORE			
Tce	Cottesloe	80	C 5
AVRO			
Pl	Hamersley	46	A 1
AWHINA			
Pl	Kallaroo	23	C 5
AWL			
Ct	Mirrabooka	47	A 1
AXBRIDGE			
St	Karrinyup	44	E 4
AXEWOOD			
Pl	Beechboro	48	C 3
AXFORD			
Ave	Midvale	51	A 9
St	Como	83	B 1
AXMINSTER			
St	Warnbro	145	D 7

		Map	Ref.
AXON			
Ave	Victoria Park	74	A 7
Ave	Victoria Park	73	E 7
St	Subiaco	72	B 1
St	Subiaco	72	B 2
AYLESFORD			
Dr	Marangaroo	32	B 4
Wy	Thornlie	95	B 3
AYLWIN			
Ct	Carine	45	C 1
AYR			
Ce	Mindarie	14	B 3
St	Floreat	59	C 7
AYRES			
Ct	Clarkson	14	C 2
Ct	Lynwood	94	A 5
Rd	Stoneville	54	B 4
AYTON			
Rd	Kelmscott	106	E 10
Wy	Duncraig	30	E 5
AZALEA			
Pl	Ballajura	33	C 5
St	Maddington	96	C 5
AZARA			
Pl	Lynwood	94	B 1
AZEEZA			
Ct	Darlington	66	B 2
AZELIA			
Rd	Spearwood	100	E 4
St	Alexander Hts	33	A 5
AZTEC			
Dr	Jandakot	103	C 3

B

		Map	Ref.
BAAL			
St	Cullacabardee	34	A 3
St	Palmyra	91	B 3
BABEL			
Rd	Welshpool	84	D 1
BABINGTON			
Cr	Bayswater	48	C 10
BACCELLO			
Wy	Armadale	116	C 3
BACCHANTE			
Ci	Ocean Reef	18	E 6
BACCHUS			
Me	Karrinyup	44	E 2
BACK			
Cl	Bull Creek	93	A 6
BACKHOUSE			
Rd	Kingsley	31	C 2
BACKSHALL			
Pl	Wanneroo	24	D 4
BACON			
Pl	Beechboro	49	A 5
St	Wilson	84	C 8
BADBURY			
Rd	Armadale	116	D 3
BADEN			
Rd	Bickley	88	C 5
Rd	Carmel	88	C 5
St	Joondanna	60	B 3
St	Osborne Park	60	B 3
BADER			
Wy	Stirling	45	D 7
BADGERUP			
Rd	Wangara	25	B 7
Rd	Wanneroo	25	D 4
Rd	Wanneroo	21	D 10
BADHAM			
Cl	Beaconsfield	90	E 8
BADJA			
Wy	Merriwa	11	C 9
BADRICK			
St	Warwick	31	D 8

		Map	Ref.
BAGDEN			
Pl	Morley	48	B 6
BAGE			
Ct	Hillarys	23	C 10
BAGLEY			
Rd	Warwick	31	D 6
BAGODA			
St	Queens Park	85	B 2
BAGOT			
Ct	Leeming	93	A 10
Pl	Hillarys	30	B 2
Rd	Subiaco	72	A 2
BAGSHOT			
Pl	Morley	47	E 8
BAHAMA			
Cl	Sorrento	30	B 4
Pl	Safety Bay	145	B 1
BAHEN			
Rd	Hacketts Gully	79	A 9
Rd	Hacketts Gully	78	D 7
BAIKAL			
Me	Joondalup	19	D 1
BAILE			
Rd	Canning Vale	94	B 8
BAILEY			
Ci	Rossmoyne	93	B 3
Lkt	Mosman Park	80	C 7
Pl	Beechboro	49	A 5
Rd	Carabooda	8	C 5
Rd	Glen Forrest	67	A 3
Rd	Glen Forrest	53	A 10
Rd	Lesmurdie	87	B 3
St	Hamilton Hill	101	A 2
St	Trigg	44	C 4
BAILEYS			
Rt	Morley	48	C 7
BAILLIE			
Ave	E Victoria Pk	84	A 1
BAINBRIDGE			
Ci	Iluka	18	E 5
BAINTON			
Rd	Leeming	103	B 1
Rd	Leeming	93	B 10
Rd	Thornlie	95	C 3
BAIRD			
Ave	Nedlands	71	D 8
Pl	Samson	91	D 8
BAJADA			
Rd	Stirling	45	D 8
BAKER			
Ave	Perth City	61	A 10
Ct	Alexander Hts	33	B 4
Ct	Langford	94	E 1
Ct	Langford	84	E 10
Ct	North Lake	102	C 1
Ct	Waikiki	145	E 1
Me	Leda	139	C 3
Rd	Perth Airport	63	B 7
St	Fremantle	90	D 7
BALA			
Wy	Joondalup	19	D 2
BALAKA			
Gns	Warnbro	145	E 8
Wy	Queens Park	84	E 3
BALANDA			
Pl	Armadale	116	B 6
BALANNUP			
Rd	Forrestdale	105	A 8
BALANUS			
Wy	Heathridge	23	D 1
Wy	Heathridge	19	D 10
BALBIRI			
Cl	Wilson	84	C 7
BALBOA			
Ct	Sorrento	30	C 4
Rw	Willetton	93	D 6

For detailed information regarding the street referencing system used in this book, turn to page 170.

B

	Map	Ref.
BALCATTA		
Rd Balcatta	46	A 2
Rd Balcatta	45	B 2
Rd Gwelup	45	C 2
BALCOMBE		
St Balga	46	B 4
Wy Balga	46	B 3
BALDIVIS		
Rd Baldivis	147	A 4
Rd Baldivis	147	B 8
Rd Baldivis	139	B 9
Rd Leda	139	C 4
Rd Wellard	139	D 4
BALDOCK		
Rd Mt Helena	41	B 7
St Bentley	84	B 5
BALDWIN		
Ave Mt Pleasant	82	D 7
Rd Serpentine	155	A 2
St Como	83	A 4
St Kewdale	75	D 8
BALEEN		
Ct Waikiki	145	B 4
BALER		
Ct Mullaloo	23	B 5
BALFERN		
Ct Hamersley	31	C 9
Wy Hamersley	31	C 9
Wy Spearwood	101	A 4
BALFOUR		
Ct Halls Head	164	C 1
Rd Swan View	51	B 7
St Cottesloe	70	D 9
St Huntingdale	105	C 2
St Huntingdale	95	D 10
St Southern River	105	A 5
BALGA		
Ave Balga	46	C 1
Pl Gooseberry H	77	C 1
Pl Koongamia	65	B 1
St Wembley Dns	58	E 3
Wy Mullaloo	23	A 5
BALGONIE		
Ave Girrawheen	32	B 6
BALGOR		
Ct Kelmscott	117	B 1
BALHAM		
Pl Kingsley	31	B 2
BALIN		
La Clarkson	14	E 10
BALISTA		
St Riverton	94	A 1
BALL		
Ct Huntingdale	105	D 1
Rd Mundaring	68	C 2
St Queens Park	85	A 2
BALLAN		
Ct Morley	48	D 6
BALLANTINE		
Rd Warwick	31	D 6
BALLANTRAE		
Ct Kingsley	24	C 9
BALLANTYNE		
Rd Kewdale	74	E 9
BALLARAT		
St Morley	47	E 8
BALLARD		
Ct Cooloongup	137	D 10
Me Jandakot	112	E 2
Pl Maddington	96	D 4
BALLART		
Wy Dianella	47	B 6
BALLEROY		
Pl Port Kennedy	145	D 10
BALLIDON		
Cr Carine	31	A 10
BALLINA		
Cl Merriwa	10	B 9
Wy Armadale	116	B 5

	Map	Ref.
BALLOCH		
St Kingsley	24	C 9
BALLOT		
Rd Chidlow	42	C 4
Wy Balcatta	45	D 4
BALLYBUNION		
Cr Connolly	19	B 8
BALMAIN		
Rd Greenmount	51	B 10
Wy Heathridge	23	D 1
Wy Heathridge	19	D 10
BALMORAL		
Pde Halls Head	164	C 4
Rd Gooseberry H	77	D 2
Rd Jarrahdale	153	B 8
St E Victoria Pk	84	A 1
St E Victoria Pk	74	A 10
Wy Kallaroo	23	B 7
BALNEY		
Pl Balga	46	C 2
St Balga	46	C 1
BALODIS		
Pl Winthrop	92	B 6
BALOO		
Cr Falcon	162A	A 4
Gr Kingsley	31	D 2
Pl Koongamia	65	B 2
BALRANALD		
St Mandurah	165	B 4
BALTIC		
Me Waikiki	145	C 3
BALTIMORE		
Pde Merriwa	10	B 8
Pde Merriwa	11	C 8
Pl Willetton	93	D 7
BALTUSROL		
Ri Connolly	19	B 8
BALUK		
St Wanneroo	20	C 8
BALWARRA		
Ave Dianella	46	E 9
Wy Quinns Rocks	10	A 10
BALWYN		
Ct Cooloongup	137	C 9
BAMBIL		
Pl Lynwood	94	C 3
BAMBOORE		
Cr Wanneroo	20	D 8
BAMBRA		
Pl Iluka	18	E 6
BAMBROOK		
St Sawyers Valley	55	D 8
BAMFORD		
Pl Balcatta	46	A 6
BAMLETT		
St Kelmscott	116	E 2
BAMPTON		
Wy Warnbro	145	D 7
BAMSHILL		
Pl Thornlie	95	B 8
BANACH		
St Maddington	96	B 6
BANCROFT		
Rd Greenfields	165	D 2
BAND		
St Lathlain	74	B 6
BANDALONG		
Wy High Wycombe	64	C 9
BANDERA		
Cl Warnbro	145	E 8
BANDERRA		
St Wanneroo	20	D 9
BANDICOOT		
Pl Wungong	116	D 9
BANFF		
Ct Duncraig	31	A 7
BANFIELD		
Gr Clarkson	14	C 1

	Map	Ref.
BANGALAY		
Ct Halls Head	164	B 4
Wy Dianella	47	B 6
BANGALLA		
Pl Balcatta	46	A 4
BANGALOW		
Pl South Lake	102	E 4
BANGOR		
Pl Beldon	23	D 3
Pl Dudley Park	165	C 5
BANINGAN		
Ave Jandakot	112	D 3
BANJINE		
Rd Koongamia	65	B 2
BANJUNA		
St Falcon	162A	A 4
BANK		
St E Victoria Pk	74	B 9
St Guildford	49	D 10
St Welshpool	84	C 1
BANKEN		
Ct Forrestdale	115	C 4
BANKEND		
Duncraig	30	E 7
BANKFIELD		
Rt Ocean Reef	18	E 6
BANKHURST		
Wy Greenwood	31	D 5
BANKS		
Ave Beechina	43	E 7
Ave Hillarys	23	B 8
Pl Willetton	93	D 7
BANKSIA		
Ci Thornlie	95	B 3
Cl Karnup	159	C 5
Ct Jandakot	103	A 5
Dl Marmion	30	D 9
Es Canning Vale	104	B 1
Gr Stoneville	40	C 7
Pl Yangebup	101	E 9
Rd Morley	48	C 4
Rd Walliston	88	A 1
Rd Walliston	87	E 1
Rd Wellard	140	C 4
Rd Wellard	132	D 10
Rd Welshpool	85	C 2
Rd Westfield	106	C 7
St Joondanna	60	C 3
St Mandurah	163	B 10
St Tuart Hill	60	C 2
St Tuart Hill	46	C 10
Tce Kensington	73	C 8
Tce South Perth	73	C 8
BANNER		
Pl Lesmurdie	87	E 3
Pl Swan View	51	C 8
BANNERMAN		
Ct Marangaroo	32	C 6
BANNICK		
Ct Canning Vale	94	C 7
BANNISTER		
Rd Canning Vale	94	A 7
Rd Canning Vale	93	D 9
Rd Padbury	23	D 2
St Fremantle	1D	B 5
St Fremantle	90	B 5
BANNON		
St Singleton	160	D 2
BANOOL		
Cr City Beach	58	E 9
BANOU		
Ct Ocean Reef	18	E 8
BANSTEAD		
Wy Morley	48	B 8
BANTOCK		
St Joondanna	60	D 4
BANTRY		
Rd Floreat	59	A 8

	Map	Ref.
BANYALLA		
Ct South Lake	102	E 6
BANYAN		
Cl Marangaroo	32	E 4
BANYANDAH		
Blvd Wanneroo	20	B 5
BANYARD		
Ave Kelmscott	106	C 8
BANYON		
Cl Halls Head	164	B 3
BARALDA		
Ct Rockingham	137	C 8
BARAMBA		
Rd City Beach	58	D 6
BARBADOS		
Cl Safety Bay	145	C 1
BARBARA		
Rd Roleystone	108	A 5
St Falcon	162A	D 10
BARBARICH		
Dr Gidgegannup	39	B 5
BARBARY		
Rd High Wycombe	64	B 9
BARBEL		
Cl E Cannington	85	D 4
BARBER		
Pl Riverton	93	E 1
St Kalamunda	77	D 6
BARBERRY		
Ct Dianella	47	B 5
BARBET		
Hts Ballajura	33	E 6
BARBETTE		
Rd Willetton	93	D 6
BARBICAN		
St E Riverton	83	E 9
St W Shelley	83	D 9
BARBIGAL		
Pl Lesmurdie	77	C 10
Rd Roleystone	108	A 8
Rd Roleystone	107	E 8
BARBLETT		
Wy Kardinya	91	E 7
BARBROOK		
Wy Warnbro	145	D 8
BARCLAY		
Ave Padbury	23	D 10
Ave Padbury	30	E 1
Rd Karrinyup	92	A 9
BARCOMBE		
Wy Gosnells	106	B 1
Wy Leeming	103	A 1
BARCOO		
Ave Nedlands	71	C 9
BARCROFT		
Me Jandakot	112	A 7
BARD		
Pl Balga	32	C 10
BARDEN		
St Madora	160	D 6
BARDFIELD		
Wy Gosnells	106	C 2
BARDIA		
Cr Swanbourne	70	D 8
BARDOC		
Ct Hillman	137	E 6
Wy Greenfields	163	E 7
BARDOLPH		
Rd Spearwood	101	C 6
BARDON		
Pl Maylands	61	D 8
BARDSLEY		
Ave Girrawheen	32	C 6
BARDWELL		
St Thornlie	95	D 1
BARELLAN		
Ct Armadale	116	C 8

	Map	Ref.
BARENCO		
Pl Willetton	94	A 3
BARETTA		
Rd Wangara	24	E 7
BARFIELD		
Pl Hilton	91	A 9
Rd Banjup	122	E 2
Rd Banjup	112	E 10
BARFORD		
St Maddington	96	B 3
BARGATE		
Wy Kingsley	24	D 10
BARGE		
Ct Armadale	116	C 9
Rd Bedfordale	127	C 8
BARHAM		
Rd Glen Forrest	66	D 7
Wy Currambine	19	A 2
BARI		
Pl Mindarie	14	B 3
BARING		
St Mosman Park	80	D 6
BARKALA		
Wy Stoneville	40	B 8
BARKER		
Ave Balcatta	46	B 6
Ave Como	83	A 2
Ct Parmelia	131	B 8
Dr Duncraig	30	E 4
Pl Bicton	81	A 9
Pl Karrinyup	45	A 4
Rd Sth Guildford	63	D 4
Rd Subiaco	72	A 1
Rd Wellard	132	C 10
St Bedford	61	D 1
St Belmont	74	C 1
St Belmont	62	C 10
St Nth Fremantle	90	C 1
BARKLEY		
Pl Halls Head	164	C 1
BARLEE		
Cl Greenfields	165	D 1
Cl Thornlie	94	E 6
Cr Cooloongup	137	E 10
Cr Waikiki	145	E 1
Cr Waikiki	137	E 1
Pl Edgewater	20	A 9
St Mt Lawley	61	B 9
St Mundaring	68	A 3
Wy Beechboro	49	B 5
BARLETTA		
Pl Mindarie	14	B 3
BARLOW		
Ct Lockridge	49	A 7
Ct Maddington	96	D 3
Pl Carine	30	E 9
St Sawyers Valley	55	A 10
Wy Balga	32	C 10
BARMING		
St Gosnells	96	A 9
BARMOND		
Rd Cannington	84	D 5
BARNARD		
Pl Noranda	47	D 5
St Alfred Cove	82	B 10
BARNATO		
St Hamersley	45	D 1
St Hamersley	31	D 10
BARNDIE		
Wy Wanneroo	20	E 8
BARNES		
Ct Craigie	23	E 6
Rd Roleystone	107	D 8
St Innaloo	45	C 8
St Rockingham	137	A 9
Wy Mandurah	165	C 1
Wy Morley	48	D 8
BARNET		
Pl Kingsley	31	B 2
Pl North Perth	60	D 7
St North Perth	60	D 8

B

BARNETT
Ct Morley .... 62 A 1
St Fremantle .... 1D C 4
St Fremantle .... 90 C 4
BARNEY
Ct Parmelia .... 131 A 9
St Glendalough ...... 60 B 5
BARNFIELD
Rd Claremont........... 70 E 9
BARNSBURY
Rd Warwick .... 31 D 8
BARNSLEY
Rd Mt Claremont...... 70 E 4
St Queens Park ...... 85 A 3
BARNSTON
Wy Langford .... 94 E 2
BARON
Wy Gosnells .... 95 E 9
Wy Jandakot .... 103 C 3
BARONE
Rd Craigie .... 23 D 4
BARONET
Rd Lesmurdie .... 87 E 3
BARON-HAY
Ct Kensington .... 83 D 1
Ct Kensington .... 73 D 10
BAROOLA
Pl Ocean Reef .... 19 A 8
BAROSSA
Hts Ocean Reef .... 19 A 7
BAROY
St Falcon .... 162A C 2
BARQUE
Me Waikiki .... 145 C 4
Pl Kallaroo .... 23 B 7
BARR
Ct Thornlie .... 95 B 8
St Dianella .... 47 C 10
BARRA
Cl Leeming .... 103 A 1
Pl Wanneroo .... 20 C 10
BARRACK
Sq Perth City .... 1C E 4
Sq Perth City .... 72 E 4
St Perth City .... 1C A 3
St Perth City .... 73 D 1
BARRACUDA
Ct Sorrento .... 30 C 4
Dr Willetton .... 93 C 7
BARRADINE
Wy Craigie .... 23 C 5
BARRALLIER
Ci Mirrabooka .... 33 A 9
Wy Padbury .... 23 D 8
BARRAMUNDI
St Golden Bay .... 158 D 9
BARRANDUNA
Dr Armadale .... 116 E 5
BARRANJOEY
Wy Sorrento .... 30 C 4
BARRATT
Pl Oakford .... 124 A 4
St North Beach .... 44 C 3
BARRE
Pl Duncraig .... 30 E 4
BARRETT
Rd Mahogany Crk ..... 67 B 1
St Herne Hill .... 36 C 5
St Southern River ... 105 A 4
St Spearwood .... 101 B 8
St Wembley .... 60 A 9
BARRETT-LENNARD
Pde Winthrop .... 92 A 2
BARRICADE
Ct Willetton .... 93 D 5
BARRICK
Rd Calista .... 130 E 7

BARRIDALE
Dr Kingsley .... 31 C 1
Dr Kingsley .... 31 C 2
Dr Kingsley .... 24 C 10
BARRIER
Grn Ocean Reef......... 18 E 6
BARRINE
Gns South Lake....... 102 C 7
BARRINGTON
St Bibra Lake......... 101 D 9
St Leederville.......... 60 C 9
St Spearwood........ 101 B 9
BARRISDALE
Rd Ardross .... 82 C 10
BARRON
Ct Rockingham...... 137 A 7
Pde Joondalup........... 19 D 7
Rd Kalamunda......... 77 B 5
Wy Orelia .... 131 B 5
BARROW
Cr Shelley .... 93 C 1
BARROWS
Wy Balga .... 32 B 9
BARRUL
Pl Thornlie.............. 94 E 6
BARRY
Rd Dianella .... 47 A 9
St Mandurah.......... 163 A 8
BARSDEN
St Cottesloe............ 80 D 3
BARSON
Ct Thornlie............. 95 B 5
BARTER
Pl Warnbro .... 145 C 6
Rd Naval Base ...... 121 A 8
BARTIZAN
Pl Willetton............ 93 E 5
BARTLETT
Cr Karrinyup .... 45 B 6
Pl Parmelia .... 131 A 8
St Willagee .... 91 C 5
BARTLING
Cr Bateman .... 92 D 4
BARTON
Pde Bassendean........ 63 B 3
Wy Merriwa .... 11 D 10
BARTRAM
Rd Banjup .... 113 D 5
Rd Forrestdale........ 114 A 5
Rd Jandakot .... 112 E 5
BARUNA
Ct Halls Head .... 164 D 1
BARUNGA
Wy Craigie .... 23 C 5
BARUSSELA
Ave Greenmount........ 51 B 10
BARWELL
Rd Medina .... 130 E 5
St Silver Sands ..... 163 B 6
BARWON
Rd Craigie .... 23 D 5
St Lesmurdie .... 87 D 3
BARWON HEADS
Tce Connolly............. 19 A 8
BARYNA
St Armadale .... 116 B 7
BASALT
Pl Carine .... 44 E 1
BASCOMBE
Ri Hillarys .... 23 B 10
BASILDON
Rd Lesmurdie .... 87 A 4
Wy Lynwood .... 94 C 4
BASINGHALL
St E Victoria Pk ..... 74 A 9
St E Victoria Pk ..... 83 E 1
St E Victoria Pk ..... 73 E 10

BASKERVILLE
Rd Mundijong......... 143 A 6
BASLE
Ce Mindarie .... 10 B 2
BASLOW
Ct Carine .... 31 A 9
BASS
Cl E Cannington ..... 85 D 4
Ct Waikiki .... 145 C 5
Rd Bull Creek.......... 92 E 6
BASSENDEAN
Pde Bassendean........ 63 B 4
Rd Bayswater .... 62 C 4
BASSETT
Pl Lesmurdie .... 87 D 1
Rd Middle Swan....... 50 C 4
St Willagee .... 91 C 4
BASSINGHAM
Rd Balcatta .... 46 A 5
Rd Balcatta .... 45 E 5
BASTION
Ct Willetton............ 93 D 5
BATAVIA
Ct Port Kennedy .. 156 D 4
Pl Kallaroo .... 23 C 7
Wy Salter Point........ 83 A 8
BATEMAN
Rd Brentwood .... 92 E 2
Rd Mt Pleasant .... 92 E 1
Rd Mt Pleasant .... 82 E 9
St Byford .... 135 C 3
St Fremantle .... 90 D 5
St Mosman Park.... 81 A 7
BATES
Pl Lockridge............ 49 B 7
Pl Woodvale .... 24 B 5
Rd Innaloo .... 45 C 9
Wy Warnbro .... 145 C 9
BATESON
Hts Clarkson .... 14 D 3
BATH
Rd Embleton .... 48 B 10
Rd Morley................ 48 B 9
St Wembley .... 60 A 7
St Wembley .... 59 E 7
BATHURST
Ct Willetton............ 93 E 6
Pl Port Kennedy .. 156 D 6
St Dianella .... 61 B 1
BATON ROUGE
Gp Mindarie .... 14 B 4
BATT
Ct Noranda .... 48 B 6
BATTEN
Rd E Cannington ..... 85 B 5
St Coolbellup .... 91 D 10
BATTERSBY
Rd Anketell .... 132 B 1
Rd Anketell .... 123 B 10
BATTERSEA
Rd Canning Vale... 104 A 5
Wy Morley................ 48 D 9
BATTERY
Rd Parkerville .... 53 D 6
BATTRASS
Pl Innaloo .... 45 C 9
St Innaloo .... 45 C 9
BATTYE
Rd Kardinya .... 91 E 7
BAUDIN
Pl Coogee .... 100 E 9
Wy Singleton .... 160 D 3
BAUER
Pl Cannington .... 84 D 6
St Cannington .... 84 D 6
BAUERA
Gl South Lake....... 102 D 5

BAUHINIA
Rd Forrestfield......... 76 C 10
Ri Dianella .... 46 E 6
BAVICH
Rd Armadale .... 116 D 5
BAWDAN
St Willagee .... 91 D 4
BAXENDALE
Wy Westfield .... 106 B 9
BAXTER
Cl Huntingdale ..... 105 D 2
Pl Dianella .... 47 A 8
Pl Morley .... 48 C 4
Wy Padbury .... 23 D 8
BAY
Ct Armadale .... 106 A 10
Rd Claremont........... 81 B 1
Rd Claremont........... 71 B 10
Rd Nedlands .... 71 B 10
St Kwinana Beach 129 E 8
BAYHAM
Pl Huntingdale .... 95 D 9
BAYLEY
Cl Gosnells .... 95 E 10
St Dianella .... 61 B 1
St Midland .... 50 A 8
BAYLISS
Rd Kardinya .... 91 E 7
BAYLY
St Nth Fremantle... 90 B 1
BAY MEADOW
Hts Connolly............. 19 A 6
BAYOU
Ct Heathridge .... 23 C 1
BAYPORT
Cc Mindarie .... 14 B 5
BAYSHORE
Pl Safety Bay .... 145 B 1
BAYSWATER
St Bedford .... 61 E 2
BAY VIEW
Cl Mosman Park ... 80 E 6
St Bayswater .... 62 A 3
St Rockingham...... 136 E 5
Tce Claremont........... 71 A 10
Tce Mosman Park.... 80 E 4
Tce Peppermint Gr... 80 E 4
BAYVIEW
Vs Ballajura .... 33 C 6
BAZAAR
Tce Scarborough ...... 44 D 10
BEACH
Rd Balga .... 32 D 9
Rd Carine .... 31 A 9
Rd Coogee .... 100 E 8
Rd Hamersley .... 31 D 9
Rd Malaga .... 33 C 10
Rd Malaga .... 47 D 1
Rd Mirrabooka .... 33 A 9
Rd Waterman .... 30 C 9
St Bicton .... 81 B 8
St Cottesloe .... 80 C 5
St Fremantle .... 1D C 4
St Fremantle .... 90 C 4
St Kwinana Beach 130 A 7
BEACHAM
Cr Medina .... 130 D 5
Pl Medina .... 130 D 5
St Coodanup .... 165 C 6
BEACHPORT
Rt Clarkson .... 14 E 10
BEACHTON
St North Beach ...... 44 C 2
BEACHWAY
Safety Bay .... 145 B 2

BEACON
Cl E Cannington ..... 85 C 4
Rd Parkerville .... 53 A 1
Rd Parkerville .... 53 C 4

BEACONSFIELD
Ave Midvale............... 50 E 9
St St James .... 84 B 2
BEADELL
Ct Marangaroo .... 32 C 6
BEADMAN
Ct Medina .... 130 E 6
BEAGLE
Cl Mosman Park.... 80 E 7
Pl Belmont.............. 74 D 1
Pl Port Kennedy ... 156 C 5
Pl Thornlie .... 94 E 6
St Mosman Park.... 80 E 7
BEALE
Pl Willetton .... 93 D 2
BEALES
Pl Roleystone .... 107 E 9
BEAM
Ct Morley................. 48 C 7
Rd Mandurah .... 163 A 9
Rd Ocean Reef .... 23 A 1
BEAMAN
St Dianella .... 47 A 7
BEAMISH
Ave Brentwood .... 92 E 2
Ave Mt Pleasant .... 92 E 1
Cl Currambine .... 19 B 5
Ct Meadow Sprgs. 163 C 6
BEARD
St Beaconsfield ...... 90 D 8
St Naval Base....... 121 A 9
BEARING
Pde Mullaloo .... 23 C 4
BEASLEY
Rd Leeming .... 93 B 9
BEATON
St Wilson .... 84 A 7
BEATRICE
Ave Shelley .... 83 C 10
Rd Dalkeith .... 81 C 3
St Doubleview .... 45 B 10
St Innaloo .... 45 B 10
BEATTY
Ave E Victoria Pk ..... 74 A 8
BEAUFORT
St Bedford .... 61 E 3
St Embleton .... 62 A 2
St Highgate .... 61 B 10
St Inglewood .... 61 D 5
St Mt Lawley .... 61 C 7
St Perth City .... 1C A 2
St Perth City .... 73 A 2
St Perth City .... 61 B 10
BEAUFORTIA
St Forrestfield......... 76 D 9
BEAUMARKS
Ct Mindarie .... 14 B 6
BEAUMONT
Wy Greenwood .... 31 E 4
BEAVER
Pl Noranda .... 47 D 4
St Tuart Hill............. 46 C 10
BEAVIS
Ct Noranda .... 48 B 5
Dr Sth Guildford ...... 63 E 3
BEAZLEY
Ave Curtin Uni 135
Ri Armadale .... 116 E 9
BEBICH
Dr Wanneroo .... 25 B 3
BEBINGTON
Ct Wilson .... 84 D 7
BECHER LAKES
Blvd Port Kennedy ... 156 D 2
BECK
Pl Warwick .... 31 D 8
BECKENHAM
St Beckenham .... 85 B 9

For detailed information regarding the street referencing system used in this book, turn to page 170.

177

B

		Map	Ref.
BECKET			
Ct	Westfield	106	B 9
BECKETT			
Cl	Munster	111	B 1
BECKFORD			
Cl	E Cannington	85	D 4
BECKINGTON			
Wy	Karrinyup	44	E 2
BECKLER			
Ct	Padbury	23	D 10
BECKLEY			
Ci	Leeming	92	E 8
BECKWORTH			
Ave	Kiara	48	E 7
BECTON			
Ct	Kingsley	24	B 9
BEDALE			
St	Dianella	61	D 1
St	Dianella	47	D 10
St	Swan View	51	D 8
BEDARRA			
Ct	Merriwa	11	D 5
BEDBROOK			
Pl	Shenton Park	71	D 3
BEDDI			
Rd	Duncraig	30	D 7
BEDELIA			
Wy	Hamersley	31	C 9
BEDFORD			
Ave	Subiaco	72	B 2
Cr	Forrestfield	76	A 3
Cr	Forrestfield	75	E 3
Rd	Ardross	82	D 10
St	Bayswater	48	C 10
St	Bentley	84	C 4
St	East Fremantle	90	E 3
St	Mt Helena	54	E 1
St	Nedlands	71	C 8
St	North Perth	60	E 5
BEDFORDALE HILL			
Rd	Armadale	116	A 4
BEDIVERE			
Pl	Carine	45	C 1
BEDWELL			
Cr	Booragoon	92	D 1
BEE			
St	Karrinyup	45	A 5
BEEBIN			
Pl	Yangebup	112	A 1
BEECH			
Cl	Riverton	83	E 9
Ct	South Lake	102	C 6
Rd	Kingsley	31	C 3
BEECHAM			
Rd	Mt Claremont	71	A 5
BEECHBORO			
Ct	Morley	48	C 8
Rd N	Bayswater	48	C 10
Rd N	Beechboro	48	C 3
Rd N	Malaga	48	C 3
Rd N	Morley	48	C 7
Rd N	Whiteman	34	B 2
Rd N	Whiteman	27	B 10
Rd S	Bayswater	62	B 4
BEECHCROFT			
Pl	Westfield	106	A 9
BEECHES			
Me	Brigadoon	169	A 2
BEECHWOOD			
Gr	Hillarys	23	A 9
BEECROFT			
Me	Merriwa	11	D 9
BEELARA			
Wy	Wanneroo	20	D 10
BEELEY			
St	Balga	46	C 4

		Map	Ref.
BEELIAR			
Dr	Munster	111	A 1
Dr	Yangebup	112	B 1
BEENAN			
Cl	Karawara	83	C 5
BEENONG			
Rd	Darlington	66	A 4
St	Wanneroo	20	D 10
BEENUP			
Pl	Lesmurdie	77	C 10
BEENYUP			
Rd	Banjup	123	C 2
Rd	Banjup	113	C 7
Rd	Byford	135	D 2
Rd	Jandakot	113	A 4
BEERMULLAH			
Wy	Waikiki	145	C 1
BEESLEY			
Ct	Jandakot	112	E 2
St	E Victoria Pk	84	A 2
BEESTON			
Cr	Marangaroo	32	D 6
BEETE			
Pl	Beechboro	49	B 3
St	Welshpool	75	A 9
BEGA			
Pl	Munster	101	B 9
Pl	Safety Bay	145	A 1
St	Greenmount	51	E 10
St	Kelmscott	106	E 6
BEGONIA			
Cl	Lynwood	94	C 1
Cl	Yangebup	101	D 10
St	Duncraig	30	E 6
Wy	Forrestfield	76	D 9
BEHAN			
St	Bentley	84	B 5
BEHN			
Ce	Woodvale	24	A 6
BELAIR			
Pl	Cooloongup	137	E 8
BEL-AIR			
Pl	Connolly	19	C 8
BELAIRE			
Tce	Kelmscott	106	E 7
BELARIUS			
St	Coolbellup	101	E 2
BELFAST			
St	Morley	48	A 7
BELFORD			
Rd	City Beach	58	D 6
BELGRADE			
Rd	Wanneroo	20	E 8
BELGRAVE			
St	Maylands	61	E 6
BELGRAVIA			
St	Belmont	74	C 1
St	Belmont	62	C 10
St	Cloverdale	75	A 5
BELHAM			
St	Bayswater	62	A 3
Wy	Balcatta	45	E 4
BELHUS			
Dr	Trigg	44	C 4
BELINDA			
Ave	Cloverdale	74	E 5
BELIZE			
Ct	Mindarie	14	B 3
BELKA			
Ct	Balga	46	B 2
BELL			
Cr	Wattle Grove	75	E 10
Ct	Armadale	116	C 9
Ct	Heathridge	23	E 2
Ct	Morley	48	D 8
St	Canning Vale	94	C 1
St	Kewdale	74	E 9
St	Rockingham	136	D 5
St	Thornlie	95	B 7

		Map	Ref.
BELLA			
Ct	Gosnells	106	A 1
BELLAIRS			
Rd	Kardinya	92	A 9
BELLAMY			
St	O'Connor	91	D 7
BELLANA			
Ct	Currambine	19	A 6
BELLANGER			
Dr	Beldon	23	E 3
BELLARA			
Rd	City Beach	58	E 7
BELLBIRD			
Ave	Huntingdale	105	C 1
Ct	High Wycombe	64	B 9
La	Ballajura	34	A 7
Pl	Armadale	116	A 4
BELLEVIEW			
Cr	Dianella	47	B 5
BELLEVUE			
Ave	Dalkeith	81	D 2
Rd	Bellevue	51	A 10
St	Bayswater	62	C 7
Tce	Fremantle	90	C 5
Tce	Swanbourne	70	E 8
Tce	West Perth	1C	D 3
Tce	West Perth	72	D 3
BELLEW			
Wy	Noranda	47	E 5
BELLIDA			
Pl	Ferndale	84	C 10
BELLIER			
Pl	Hamilton Hill	101	B 3
BELLINGER			
Pl	Jandakot	112	E 3
BELLINGHAM			
Pl	Padbury	30	E 2
BELLION			
Dr	Hamilton Hill	100	D 1
BELLIS			
Pl	Belmont	62	D 9
BELLONA			
Pl	Willetton	93	D 6
BELLOWS			
St	Welshpool	74	D 10
BELLPORT			
Ri	Mindarie	14	B 3
BELMAURICE			
St	Dianella	47	A 9
BELMONT			
Ave	Belmont	74	C 3
Ave	Cloverdale	74	E 6
Ave	Kewdale	75	A 8
Rd	Kenwick	95	E 1
Rd	Kenwick	85	E 9
St	Sth Fremantle	90	C 8
BELMORE			
Gns	Ocean Reef	18	E 6
BELPER			
Ct	Carine	31	A 10
BELROSE			
Cr	Cooloongup	137	D 10
Ent	Kallaroo	23	A 8
BELSTEAD			
Ave	Noranda	48	B 5
BELTANA			
Rd	Craigie	23	C 6
BELTON			
Pl	Balcatta	46	A 7
BELVEDAIRE			
Wy	Lynwood	94	C 2
BELVEDERE			
Rd	Hamersley	31	D 9
BELVIDERE			
St	Belmont	74	E 1
St	Redcliffe	62	E 10
BELVOIR			
Pl	Ballajura	34	A 7

		Map	Ref.
BELVON			
Ct	Heathridge	23	E 2
BELYEA			
St	Gosnells	96	A 10
BEMURRAH			
Cl	Wilson	84	B 8
BEN			
Cl	Craigie	23	D 6
Pl	Willetton	93	D 6
St	Redcliffe	63	A 7
St	Redcliffe	62	E 6
BENAN			
St	Kallaroo	23	B 6
BENARA			
Rd	Beechboro	48	D 5
Rd	Caversham	49	C 5
Rd	Morley	48	C 5
Rd	Noranda	48	A 5
Rd	Noranda	47	D 5
BENBULLEN			
Blvd	Kingsley	31	D 2
Rd	Kalamunda	77	E 8
BENDIGO			
Ct	Willetton	93	E 3
Wy	City Beach	58	D 5
BENDIX			
Wy	Girrawheen	32	C 9
BENDSTEN			
Pl	Balcatta	45	D 2
BENEDICK			
Rd	Coolbellup	101	E 2
BENELLI			
Pl	Alexander Hts	32	E 6
BENGAL			
St	Madora	160	C 7
BEN HALL			
Ri	Gnangara	25	D 5
BENJAFIELD			
Wy	Hamersley	45	D 1
Wy	Hamersley	31	D 10
BENJAMIN			
St	Armadale	116	C 6
Wy	Rockingham	137	A 5
BENMUNI			
Rd	Wanneroo	25	C 2
Rd	Wanneroo	21	C 10
BENNELONG			
Pl	Leederville	60	C 7
BENNESS			
Grn	Winthrop	92	A 5
BENNETT			
Ave	Hamilton Hill	100	D 2
Ct	Leeming	93	B 9
Rd	Quinns Rocks	10	B 1
St	Caversham	49	B 5
St	East Perth	1C	B 4
St	East Perth	73	B 4
BENNETTS			
Pl	Sorrento	30	B 3
BENNEWITH			
St	Hilton	91	C 8
BENNINGFIELD			
Rd	Bull Creek	93	A 7
BENNION			
St	Trigg	44	C 5
BENOA			
Ct	Merriwa	10	B 9
BENOWA			
Dr	Glen Forrest	66	E 3
BENPORATH			
St	Victoria Park	73	E 6
BENT			
St	Cannington	85	A 7
St	City Beach	58	D 5
St	Safety Bay	144	E 1
BENTLEY			
Cl	Mt Claremont	71	B 5
Pl	Hovea	52	E 9

		Map	Ref.
St	Hamersley	31	C 10
St	Singleton	160	D 1
St	Stoneville	54	B 4
BENTON			
Wy	Safety Bay	136	E 10
Wy	Warwick	31	E 6
BENTWOOD			
Ave	Woodlands	59	B 3
BENWEE			
Rd	Floreat	59	A 9
BENZIE			
Wy	Lynwood	94	A 3
BEONADDY			
Rd	Eglinton	7	D 2
BEOR			
Wy	Herne Hill	36	D 4
BEPTON			
Wy	Balga	46	D 2
BEQUIA			
Pl	Safety Bay	137	A 10
BERALA			
Ct	Westfield	106	B 10
BERBERIS			
Wy	Forrestfield	76	C 8
BEREHAVEN			
Ave	Thornlie	95	B 6
Ave	Thornlie	95	C 4
BERENICE			
Me	Currambine	19	A 2
BERESFORD			
Gns	Swan View	51	C 9
Pl	Leeming	93	A 8
BERGALL			
Ct	Ferndale	84	D 8
BERKELEY			
Ave	Nollamara	46	B 5
Cr	Floreat	59	C 9
Ct	Nollamara	46	B 5
St	Heathridge	19	B 9
BERKLEY			
Rd	Alexander Hts	32	E 4
Rd	Marangaroo	32	C 4
BERKSHIRE			
Dr	Beldon	23	D 4
Pl	Kardinya	92	A 6
Rd	Forrestfield	76	C 8
BERLE			
Wy	High Wycombe	64	D 9
BERMONDSEY			
St	Leederville	60	C 10
BERMUDA			
Dr	Ballajura	33	C 7
Rd	Safety Bay	145	B 2
BERN			
Rd	Ferndale	84	B 10
BERNARD			
Rd N	Carabooda	8	A 1
Rd S	Carabooda	8	B 3
St	Claremont	71	B 9
St	Kelmscott	107	A 10
St	Leederville	60	C 9
St	Mt Helena	55	B 1
BERNARD MANNING			
Dr	Duncraig	30	D 3
BERNBOROUGH			
Pl	Wanneroo	21	B 9
Wy	Byford	126	A 4
BERNDT			
Gr	Winthrop	92	C 4
BERNEDALE			
Wy	Duncraig	31	A 7
BERNERA			
Dr	Willetton	93	C 6
BERNICE			
Wy	Thornlie	95	C 3
BERNIER			
Rd	Shelley	83	C 10

For detailed information regarding the street referencing system used in this book, turn to page 170.

B

		Map	Ref.
BERNLEY			
Dr	Viveash	50	B 5
BERRETT			
Pl	Parmelia	131	A 6
BERRIGAN			
Dr	Jandakot	102	E 7
Dr	South Lake	102	C 8
Rw	Halls Head	164	B 4
St	Nollamara	46	D 7
BERRIMA			
Ct	Glen Forrest	66	D 4
Rd	Roleystone	107	E 8
BERRIMAN			
Dr	Wangara	24	E 7
BERRIO			
Wy	Iluka	18	E 5
BERRY			
Ct	Bassendean	63	A 3
Ct	Maddington	96	C 6
Dr	Maida Vale	77	A 2
St	Hamilton Hill	101	B 2
St	Safety Bay	144	E 1
BERRYMAN			
St	Mt Hawthorn	60	B 5
BERSICA			
Ct	Kardinya	92	A 7
BERSON			
Ct	Munster	101	C 9
BERSTED			
St	Balga	46	B 1
BERSWICK			
Gr	Leeming	103	A 1
BERT			
St	Gosnells	96	B 10
BERTAL			
Wy	Balcatta	45	E 3
BERTIE			
St	Guildford	49	D 10
BERTOLA			
Pl	Willetton	93	B 6
BERTRAM			
Rd	Casuarina	131	D 9
Rd	Caversham	49	E 4
Rd	Parmelia	131	C 10
St	Coodanup	165	E 8
St	Darlington	66	B 3
St	Dianella	47	B 7
St	Maddington	96	C 5
St	Northbridge	60	E 10
BERWICK			
Cl	Kingsley	24	C 10
St	E Victoria Pk	84	A 1
St	E Victoria Pk	74	A 10
St	Jarrahdale	152	D 6
St	St James	84	A 2
St	Victoria Park	73	D 7
BERWYN			
Rd	Girrawheen	32	C 6
BERYL			
Ave	Millendon	29	E 9
Ave	Shelley	83	D 9
St	Balcatta	46	A 6
Wy	Lynwood	94	A 2
BESSANT			
Ct	Westfield	106	B 10
BESSELL			
Ave	Como	83	B 1
Ave	Nedlands	81	E 1
BEST			
Ct	High Wycombe	64	C 10
St	Bassendean	63	A 4
BETTENAY			
Rd	Roleystone	108	C 8
BETTI			
Rd	Kalamunda	77	C 9
BETTINI			
Rd	Newburn	75	E 2
BETTLES			
St	Marmion	30	C 7

		Map	Ref.
BETTY			
St	Chidlow	56	E 2
St	Chidlow	42	E 10
St	Nedlands	71	C 10
BETULA			
St	Riverton	93	E 1
BEVAN			
Pl	Willetton	93	B 7
Rd	Roleystone	108	C 10
BEVERIDGE			
St	Bentley	84	A 5
St	Bentley	83	E 5
BEVERLEY			
Cr	Quinns Rocks	10	E 1
Pl	Cloverdale	74	E 4
Rd	Cloverdale	74	E 4
St	Coolbinia	60	E 3
St	Morley	48	B 7
Tce	Sth Guildford	63	B 5
BEVIS			
Ct	Bibra Lake	102	B 6
Ct	Byford	126	E 9
BEXLEY			
Cl	Swan View	51	C 9
Rd	Yanchep	4	D 1
St	Gosnells	106	C 3
Wy	Girrawheen	32	C 8
BIALA			
St	Kelmscott	107	A 7
BIARRITZ			
Wy	Connolly	19	C 7
BIBANUP			
Ct	Hillman	137	D 6
BIBBY			
Ct	Wanneroo	25	C 5
BIBRA			
Dr	Bibra Lake	102	B 5
Dr	North Lake	102	C 1
Dr	North Lake	92	C 10
Rd	Bibra Lake	102	A 2
BICHENO			
Wy	Willetton	93	E 5
BICKFORD			
Pl	Hamilton Hill	101	B 3
Wy	Bibra Lake	102	A 8
Wy	Bibra Lake	101	E 8
BICKLEY			
Cr	Manning	83	A 4
Ct	Hilton	91	A 9
Rd	Beckenham	85	B 8
Rd	Cannington	85	A 8
Rd	Kenwick	86	A 9
Rd	Kenwick	85	E 8
Rd	Maddington	86	B 10
St	Como	83	A 4
St	Naval Base	121	B 8
St W	Como	82	E 5
BICKNER			
Wy	Parmelia	131	A 5
BICKNOR			
St	Marangaroo	32	A 4
BIDDENDEN			
St	Thornlie	95	B 5
BIDDY			
Pl	Waikiki	145	E 1
BIDEFORD			
St	Warnbro	145	D 8
BIGHT REEFS			
Rd	Singleton	160	D 3
BIGNEL			
Pl	Redcliffe	63	A 10
BIGNELL			
Pl	Herne Hill	36	D 4
BIGOLA			
Ct	Kallaroo	23	A 7
BILBY			
Pl	Gosnells	105	E 1
Rd	Girrawheen	32	E 7

		Map	Ref.
BILGOMAN			
Rd	Glen Forrest	66	C 1
Rd	Glen Forrest	52	C 1
BILINGA			
Rd	Balga	46	C 4
BILKURRA			
Wy	Armadale	116	E 5
BILLABONG			
Ce	Wilson	84	A 9
Wy	Kelmscott	116	E 1
BILLARA			
St	Maida Vale	76	E 2
BILLEROY			
Rd	Roleystone	108	B 8
BILLING			
Pl	Armadale	116	E 9
BILLINGS			
Wy	Winthrop	92	B 4
BILOXIE			
Pl	Warnbro	145	D 6
BIMBLE			
Cl	South Lake	102	C 5
BINBROOK			
Pl	Darlington	66	B 4
BINBURRA			
Wy	Armadale	116	E 5
BINDAREE			
Tce	Kingsley	31	E 2
BINDARING			
Pde	Claremont	80	E 1
BINDEN			
Pl	Hamersley	31	D 10
BINDER			
St	Mt Helena	54	E 5
BINDOO			
Ri	Woodvale	24	C 6
BINGARRA			
Cl	Port Kennedy	156	D 4
BINGFIELD			
Rd E	Medina	130	D 3
Rd W	Medina	130	D 4
BINGHAM			
St	Newburn	76	A 1
St	Newburn	75	E 2
BINLEY			
Pl	Maddington	95	E 5
BINNACLE			
Rd	Ocean Reef	23	B 1
BINNEY			
Ri	South Lake	102	C 8
BINSHAW			
Ave	Byford	126	B 10
BINSTEAD			
Ct	Koondoola	33	A 8
BINYA			
Ct	Kalamunda	77	D 9
BIRBECK			
Wy	Spearwood	101	A 5
BIRCH			
Pl	Greenwood	31	D 5
Pl	Stoneville	54	A 4
Rd	Padbury	30	D 2
St	Attadale	81	D 8
St	Maddington	96	B 4
BIRCHFIELD			
Ave	Woodvale	24	B 6
BIRCHINGTON			
St	Beckenham	85	C 6
BIRCHLEY			
Cr	Balga	32	B 10
Rd	Coodanup	165	D 5
Rd	Yangebup	111	D 2
Sq	Balga	32	B 10
BIRCHWOOD			
Ave	Woodlands	59	C 3

		Map	Ref.
BIRD			
Rd	Kalamunda	77	B 7
Rd	Peel Estate	141	C 7
St	Cottesloe	80	D 2
St	Mosman Park	81	A 7
Wk	Willetton	93	C 4
BIRDIE			
Ct	Cooloongup	138	A 9
BIRDLAND			
Ct	Edgewater	24	B 2
La	Ballajura	33	C 5
BIRDUP			
Cl	Kelmscott	106	E 6
BIRDWOOD			
Ave	Como	73	B 10
Cs	Bicton	91	A 1
Cs	Bicton	81	A 10
Cs E	Bicton	91	A 1
Cs E	Bicton	81	A 10
Cs W	Bicton	91	A 1
Cs W	Bicton	81	A 10
Pde	Dalkeith	81	D 3
Rd	Melville	91	D 1
St	Innaloo	45	B 8
BIRKBECK			
Ave	Cottesloe	70	D 10
BIRKDALE			
Ct	Cooloongup	137	E 8
Ct	Halls Head	164	C 1
Pl	Currambine	19	B 4
St	Floreat	71	D 1
St	Floreat	59	D 10
BIRKENHEAD			
Rge	Mindarie	10	B 2
BIRKETT			
St	Bedford	61	D 2
St	Dianella	61	C 1
BIRKSGATE			
Rd	Nth Fremantle	90	A 4
BIRNAM			
Ct	Yanchep	4	E 1
Rd	Canning Vale	94	C 10
Rd	Canning Vale	104	D 1
BIRREL			
Pl	Gosnells	106	A 1
BIRRELL			
St	Mt Hawthorn	60	B 4
BIRT			
Ct	High Wycombe	76	B 2
BIRTWISTLE			
Pl	Roleystone	107	D 9
BISCAY			
Cl	Ocean Reef	18	E 8
Rd	Sorrento	30	C 5
BISCAYNE			
St	Safety Bay	145	B 1
BISDEE			
Rd	Millendon	168	A 9
Rd	Millendon	29	E 9
BISHOP			
Cl	Armadale	116	A 4
Rd	Balcatta	46	B 6
Rd	Dalkeith	81	B 2
Rd	Middle Swan	50	D 3
Rd	Mundijong	143	A 2
Rd	Mundijong	142	B 2
St	Jolimont	71	E 1
St	Jolimont	59	E 10
St	Morley	47	E 10
BISHOP HALE			
Wy	Churchlands	59	C 4
BISHOP RILEY			
Wy	Churchlands	59	C 4
BISHOPS			
Cl	Quinns Rocks	10	B 10
Rw	East Perth	1C	B 3
Rw	East Perth	73	B 3

		Map	Ref.
BISHOPSGATE			
St	Carlisle	74	B 7
St	Lathlain	74	A 7
St	Welshpool	74	C 10
BITTERN			
Ct	Stirling	45	D 5
BITTON			
St	Hamilton Hill	101	B 1
BLACKADDER			
Rd	Swan View	51	B 6
BLACKALL			
Dr	Greenwood	31	C 4
Dr	Greenwood	31	D 4
BLACKBOY			
Ct	Thornlie	95	A 9
Gr	Wandi	123	A 7
Rd	Greenmount	51	B 9
Ri	Parmelia	131	B 1
Wy	Beechboro	48	C 4
Wy	Morley	48	C 4
BLACKBURN			
St	Bellevue	51	A 9
St	Maddington	95	E 4
BLACKBURNE			
Dr	Kelmscott	106	E 6
BLACKBUTT			
Ct	Morley	48	D 5
Dr	Greenwood	31	C 5
Me	Ballajura	33	C 5
Rd	Woodlands	59	C 2
Wy	Canning Vale	104	E 1
Wy	Forrestfield	86	E 1
Wy	Forrestfield	76	E 10
BLACKDOUNE			
Wy	Balga	46	B 2
BLACKDOWN			
Wy	Karrinyup	44	E 4
BLACKETT			
Ct	Roleystone	107	E 8
BLACKFORD			
St	Mt Hawthorn	60	B 4
BLACKHAM			
Wy	Balga	46	C 2
BLACKLOCK			
Rd	Belmont	74	D 2
BLACKMAN			
Rd	Mt Pleasant	82	D 10
BLACKMORE			
Ave	Girrawheen	32	B 7
BLACKSMITH			
Ct	Bibra Lake	102	C 5
Dr	Leda	139	C 3
BLACKTHORN			
Rd	Eden Hill	48	D 9
Rd	Greenwood	31	E 3
BLACKTHORNE			
Cr	South Lake	102	B 6
BLACKWALL REACH			
Pde	Bicton	81	A 9
BLACKWATTLE			
Pde	Padbury	31	A 3
BLACKWOOD			
Ave	Hamilton Hill	101	A 2
Dr	Armadale	117	A 4
Pde	Mandurah	165	A 4
St	Gosnells	105	E 2
BLADON			
Wy	Swan View	51	D 7
BLAIKIE			
St	Myaree	92	A 2
BLAIN			
Ct	Leeming	93	B 9
BLAIR			
Ct	Waikiki	145	C 2
Ct	Kinross	19	C 2
Pl	Mt Helena	55	C 5
Rd	Oakford	124	D 4
Rd	Yokine	60	E 1
St	Karrinyup	44	E 5

For detailed information regarding the street referencing system used in this book, turn to page 170.

179

B

	Map	Ref.
BLAIR ATHOL		
St E Victoria Pk......	74	B 10
BLAIZE		
Cl Leeming............	93	D 9
BLAKE		
Ct Padbury............	23	E 9
St Bedfordale........	127	C 2
St North Perth.......	60	E 6
BLAKELEY		
St Mandurah.........	163	B 10
BLAKERS		
Rge Winthrop.........	92	B 4
BLAKEY		
Ri Winthrop..........	92	A 3
St Waikiki............	145	C 6
BLAMEY		
Pl Como...............	83	C 2
Pl O'Connor.........	91	C 6
BLAMIRE		
Rd Kalamunda.......	77	D 8
BLANCHARD		
Rd Swan View........	51	B 6
BLANCHE		
Pl Ballajura..........	33	D 4
St Gosnells...........	96	A 8
St Gosnells...........	95	E 8
BLANCOA		
Rd Ferndale..........	84	C 10
St High Wycombe..	64	C 9
BLAND		
Cr Redcliffe..........	75	A 1
Pl Beechboro........	49	B 5
St Como...............	83	C 2
St Kensington.......	73	C 10
BLANDFIELD		
Wy Lynwood...........	94	B 4
BLANTYRE		
Wy Westfield..........	116	B 1
BLAVEN		
Wy Ardross............	82	C 9
BLAXLAND		
Ave Two Rocks.......	2	D 4
Wy Padbury............	23	D 8
BLAY		
Pl Calista.............	130	E 8
Rd Calista.............	130	E 8
BLEAN		
St Gosnells...........	95	E 8
BLECHYNDEN		
St St James..........	84	A 2
BLEE		
Ct Rockingham.....	137	B 5
BLEINHEIM		
Pl Ocean Reef......	18	E 9
BLENCOWE		
St Leederville.......	60	B 10
BLENHEIM		
Pl Swan View.......	51	D 7
Tce Mt Claremont...	71	A 4
BLENNY		
Cl Cannington......	84	D 5
BLIGH		
Pl Thornlie..........	95	A 4
BLIGHT		
Ct Kingsley..........	31	B 3
St Maddington.....	96	B 6
BLINCO		
St Fremantle........	90	D 4
BLISSETT		
Wy Hamersley........	32	A 10
BLOCK		
Pl Ocean Reef......	18	E 10
BLOCKLEY		
Wy Bassendean.....	48	D 10
BLOMFIELD		
Ct Kewdale..........	74	E 6

	Map	Ref.
BLONDELL		
Dr Munster...........	101	B 9
BLOODWOOD		
Ci South Lake......	102	D 5
Dr Marangaroo.....	32	D 4
BLOOM		
Ct Huntingdale.....	95	E 10
BLOUNT		
Cl Winthrop.........	92	B 5
Ct Duncraig.........	31	A 8
BLUE		
Gr Alexander Hts...	33	B 4
BLUEBAY		
Hl Ballajura..........	33	C 8
BLUEBELL		
Ct Thornlie..........	95	B 10
Wy Bibra Lake.......	102	C 5
BLUEBUSH		
Ri Thornlie..........	95	A 9
BLUE FIN		
Dr Golden Bay......	158	D 9
BLUE GUM		
Pl Midvale...........	51	B 8
BLUEGUM		
Cl Armadale........	116	D 4
Cl Woodvale........	24	D 8
Pl Ballajura.........	33	C 4
Rd Beechboro.......	48	C 3
Rd Morley............	48	C 5
Rd Thornlie.........	95	B 10
BLUEJAY		
Cl Woodvale........	24	D 8
Gns Ballajura.........	33	D 5
BLUE MOUNTAIN		
Dr Joondalup.......	19	C 2
BLUERISE		
Ce Falcon............	162A	D 4
BLUEWATER		
Ri Mullaloo.........	23	A 3
BLUE WREN		
Pl Stoneville........	40	B 7
BLUFF		
Cl Mindarie.........	10	B 2
BLUNDELL		
St West Swan......	35	D 9
BLUNT		
Pl Spearwood.....	101	C 4
BLYTHE		
Ave Yokine.............	60	D 1
Cl Iluka..............	18	E 5
Pl Armadale........	116	D 5
Pl Willetton.........	93	E 5
Rw Kardinya.........	92	A 8
BLYTHESWOOD		
Ave Byford.............	135	D 1
Rd Byford.............	126	D 10
BLYTHEWOOD		
Wy Heathridge......	23	E 2
BLYTHWOOD		
St Mandurah.......	165	A 4
BOAB		
Pl Beechboro......	48	C 3
BOABAB		
Ct Alexander Hts..	32	E 5
BOAG		
Pl Morley............	47	E 10
Rd Morley............	47	E 10
BOARD		
Ave Redcliffe.........	75	A 1
BOAS		
Ave Joondalup.......	19	E 6
BOBTAIL		
Cl Wungong........	116	B 9
BOCACCIO		
Ct Sorrento.........	30	C 3
BODEMAN		
Rd Wandi............	123	C 6

	Map	Ref.
BODENSEE		
Gr Joondalup.......	19	C 1
BODICOAT		
Dr Wungong........	116	C 9
BODMIN		
Ave City Beach......	70	D 2
BODRUM		
Ct Mindarie.........	10	B 2
BOEING		
Wy Jandakot.........	103	B 7
BOHEMIA		
Gr Armadale........	116	B 2
Pl Noranda..........	47	C 4
St Spearwood......	101	C 4
Wy Lynwood..........	94	A 3
BOLARO		
Pl Hillman...........	137	E 5
BOLAS		
Ct Myaree...........	92	A 1
BOLD		
Pl Lynwood..........	94	C 2
BOLDERWOOD		
Dr South Lake......	102	D 6
BOLD PARK		
Dr City Beach.......	59	A 9
BOLGER		
Pl Booragoon......	92	C 2
BOLINGBROKE		
St Spearwood......	101	B 4
BOLIVAR		
Ct Safety Bay.......	137	B 10
BOLIVER		
Pl Langford.........	95	A 1
BOLLARD		
Me Parmelia..........	131	B 10
BOLOKA		
Ri Kingsley..........	31	D 2
BOLT		
Ct Lesmurdie.......	77	B 10
Pl Bull Creek........	93	A 6
St Beaconsfield....	90	E 9
BOLTON		
Ave Victoria Park.....	73	E 4
Pl Fremantle........	90	D 6
St East Fremantle..	90	D 1
Wy Orelia..............	131	A 5
BOLUS		
Ct Woodvale.......	24	B 7
BOLWARRA		
Hts South Lake.....	102	D 6
BOMARIA		
Cl South Lake......	102	C 6
Me Halls Head.......	164	A 5
BOMBALA		
Cl Merriwa..........	11	D 8
BOMBARD		
St Ardross...........	82	C 7
St Mt Pleasant.....	82	D 7
BONA		
Cl Willetton.........	93	E 5
BONA VISTA		
Rd Greenmount....	51	E 10
BONCHESTER		
Ct Duncraig.........	30	E 7
BOND		
St Midland..........	50	C 8
St Mosman Park...	80	D 4
BONDI		
Cr Warnbro.........	145	E 6
St Mt Hawthorn...	60	B 4
BONDINI		
Wy Bibra Lake.......	102	B 5
BONE		
St St James.........	84	A 3
BONEWOOD		
Ct Beckenham.....	85	B 10

	Map	Ref.
BONFIELD		
Wy Midvale...........	51	A 7
BONGIOVANNI		
Ct Lesmurdie.......	87	C 5
BONHAM		
Ct Leeming.........	102	E 1
BONITO		
Pl Golden Bay......	158	D 9
Wy Sorrento..........	30	D 3
BONN		
Ct Armadale........	116	A 4
BONNER		
Dr Malaga...........	33	C 10
BONNEVILLE		
Wy Joondalup.......	19	C 2
BONNEY		
St Huntingdale....	95	C 9
BONNIE DOON		
Gns Connolly.........	19	A 6
BONNIEVALE		
St Glendalough...	60	B 5
BONNYDOON		
Ct Cooloongup....	137	E 7
BONSALL		
Pl Carine............	31	A 9
BOOK		
St Perth City........	1C	B 2
St Perth City........	73	B 2
BOOKER		
St Attadale..........	81	D 8
St Dianella..........	47	A 8
BOOKHAM		
St Morley............	61	E 1
BOOLARDY		
Rd Golden Bay.....	158	E 8
BOOLIGAL		
St Lesmurdie.......	87	D 3
BOOMERANG		
Rd Peel Estate......	141	B 1
Rd Peel Estate......	133	C 10
Rd Peel Estate......	140	D 2
BOON		
Ct Marmion.........	30	D 8
Ct Rockingham...	137	A 7
St Willagee..........	91	C 5
BOONA		
Ct Karawara........	83	C 5
Ct Maida Vale.....	76	E 4
BOONDI		
Pl Kelmscott.......	107	A 9
BOONGALA		
Cl Karawara.........	83	C 4
BOONOOLOO		
Ct Kalamunda.....	77	D 6
Rd Kalamunda.....	77	C 7
BOORABILLA		
Wy Greenmount....	51	D 9
BOORAL		
St Lesmurdie.......	87	D 3
BOORALIE		
Wy Maida Vale.....	76	E 4
BOOTH		
Ct Samson..........	91	C 8
Pl Balcatta..........	45	D 3
Pl Bellevue.........	65	A 2
BOOTIE		
Pl Hillarys..........	23	E 2
BORDEN		
Rd Marangaroo....	32	A 6
St Maddington....	96	B 4
BOREAS		
Ct Duncraig.........	31	A 3
BOREE		
Rd Kalamunda.....	77	C 8
BOREHAM		
St Cottesloe........	80	D 1

	Map	Ref.
BORELL		
Pl Kardinya.........	91	E 9
BORN		
Rd Casuarina.......	132	C 9
BORNEO		
Ave Swanbourne.....	70	D 7
BORONIA		
Ave Nedlands........	71	D 8
Cl Halls Head......	164	B 5
Cl Westfield........	106	C 8
Cr City Beach......	58	D 8
Ct Greenwood.....	31	C 5
Ct Morley............	48	D 5
Ct Thornlie.........	95	A 9
Rd Banjup...........	113	E 7
Rd Walliston........	88	A 2
St Innaloo..........	45	B 10
Trl Canning Vale..	104	B 1
Trl Canning Vale..	94	B 10
BORTOLO		
Dr Greenfields.....	163	D 9
BOSBERRY		
Rt Mirrabooka.....	47	B 1
BOSCASTLE		
Ave City Beach......	70	D 2
BOSCOMBE		
Ave City Beach......	58	C 10
Ave City Beach......	70	D 1
BOSKOOP		
Pl Mirrabooka.....	47	B 2
BOSSEA		
Cl Ferndale.........	94	C 1
St Marangaroo....	32	D 4
BOSSUT		
Ct Merriwa..........	11	E 9
BOSTOCK		
Rd Nedlands........	71	C 10
St White Gum Vly..	90	E 6
BOSTON		
Ct Woodvale.......	24	C 7
St Balcatta..........	46	A 5
Wy Booragoon......	92	C 1
Wy Booragoon......	82	C 10
BOSWELL		
Pl Spearwood.....	101	B 8
BOSWORTH		
Pl Leeming.........	93	D 8
St Hamersley......	31	E 10
BOTANY		
La Merriwa..........	11	D 8
BOTHE		
Ct Armadale........	116	A 4
BOTTEGA		
Pl Lesmurdie.......	87	D 2
BOTTLEBRUSH		
Dr Greenwood.....	31	C 5
Dr Kiara..............	48	D 7
Dr Morley............	48	D 5
Dr Rowethorpe....	144	
Dr Thornlie.........	95	B 9
BOTTRILL		
St Hamilton Hill...	100	E 1
BOUCHER		
St Kewdale..........	74	D 7
BOUD		
Ave Perth Airport...	63	B 9
BOUGAINVILLEA		
Ave Forrestfield.....	76	B 8
Ct Marangaroo....	32	D 4
BOULDER		
Ave Redcliffe.........	63	A 8
Ave Redcliffe.........	62	A 7
Rd Malaga...........	48	A 3
St Bentley...........	84	B 3
St E Victoria Pk....	74	A 8
BOULONNAIS		
Dr Brigadoon.......	169	B 6
Dr Brigadoon.......	168	E 5

180   **For detailed information regarding the street referencing system used in this book, turn to page 170.**

B

	Map	Ref.
BOULTER		
St Willagee	91	D 5
BOULTON		
St Dianella	61	B 1
St Mandurah	164	E 3
BOUNDARY		
Rd Kenwick	86	A 7
Rd Kenwick	85	E 8
Rd Mandurah	165	A 2
Rd Mosman Park	80	D 7
Rd Shoalwater	136	C 7
Rd St James	84	A 3
Rd Wattle Grove	86	B 5
BOUNTY		
Ct Port Kennedy	156	D 4
Pl Ocean Reef	23	B 1
BOURBON		
St Hamilton Hill	101	B 4
BOURKE		
St Kensington	73	C 10
St Leederville	60	C 8
St North Perth	60	D 8
St Yokine	60	E 2
BOURNAN		
Hts Parmelia	131	B 9
BOURNE		
St Morley	48	A 9
BOURNEMOUTH		
Cr Wembley Dns	58	E 3
Pde Trigg	44	C 7
BOURNVILLE		
St Wembley	60	A 9
St Wembley	59	D 9
BOUVARDIA		
Wy Greenwood	31	D 3
BOUVERIE		
Pl Leederville	60	C 7
BOVELL		
Gns Leeming	93	D 9
BOW		
Pl Mullaloo	23	A 3
St Wilson	84	B 8
BOWDEN		
Pl Armadale	116	C 8
St Bayswater	61	E 5
St Maylands	61	E 5
BOWEN		
Pl Stoneville	54	B 4
Pl Willetton	94	A 3
St O'Connor	91	D 7
BOWER		
Gr Two Rocks	2	D 2
Pl Noranda	47	C 5
St Doubleview	59	A 2
St Scarborough	58	E 2
St Thornlie	95	A 3
BOWES		
Ct Kingsley	24	D 10
BOWKETT		
St Redcliffe	75	A 1
BOWLER		
Pl Bull Creek	92	E 4
BOWLES		
Ct Murdoch	92	C 7
BOWLING		
Pl Melville	91	D 2
BOWMAN		
Ct Winthrop	92	A 6
St Shenton Park	71	D 4
St South Perth	72	D 7
BOWOOD		
Rt Kiara	48	E 6
BOWRA		
Ave Woodlands	59	C 1
Ct Leeming	93	C 8
BOWSTRING		
Pl Joondalup	19	D 4
BOWTELL		
Rd Lesmurdie	87	B 5

	Map	Ref.
BOWYER		
Cl Willetton	93	B 7
Pl Byford	135	E 2
BOXHILL		
St Morley	47	D 6
BOXLEY		
Gr Marangaroo	32	A 5
Pl Langford	94	E 2
BOXWORTH		
Ct Huntingdale	95	C 9
BOYA		
Cr Boya	65	D 4
Wy Balcatta	45	D 3
BOYAMYNE		
Rd Parkerville	39	B 10
BOYARE		
Ave Mirrabooka	46	E 1
BOYCE		
Rd Balcatta	46	B 8
BOYD		
Cr Hamilton Hill	100	D 1
Ct Padbury	23	D 10
St Palmyra	91	B 1
BOYLE		
La Orange Grove	96	D 1
Pl Morley	47	E 7
Rd Welshpool	75	B 10
BOYLEN		
Ri Winthrop	92	C 6
BRABANT		
Wy Hamersley	31	D 9
BRABHAM		
St Gosnells	95	D 7
BRABOURNE		
St Maddington	96	A 4
BRACADALE		
Ave Duncraig	31	A 5
BRACEBY		
Cl Willetton	93	E 5
BRACEWELL		
Ct Yangebup	112	A 1
Ct Yangebup	102	A 10
BRACKEN		
Ct Duncraig	31	A 8
Rd Pickering Bk	89	D 9
Rd Thornlie	95	B 9
Wy Bibra Lake	102	B 6
BRACKLEY		
Rd Armadale	116	D 4
BRACKNELL		
St Yanchep	4	D 2
BRACKS		
St Nth Fremantle	90	C 1
St Nth Fremantle	80	C 10
BRADBOURNE		
Dr Carine	30	D 10
BRADBURY		
Pl Alexander Hts	32	E 6
Rd Hamilton Hill	91	B 10
St Rockingham	137	C 8
Wy Samson	91	D 8
BRADDOCK		
Rd Wellard	140	C 3
St Kelmscott	116	C 1
BRADEN		
Wy Marmion	30	C 8
BRADFORD		
St Cannington	84	E 8
St Coolbinia	60	E 3
St Kewdale	75	B 7
St Menora	61	A 5
BRADLEY		
Ct Samson	91	D 8
Rd Southern River	105	D 4
St Yokine	46	C 9
Wy High Wycombe	64	A 10
Wy Lockridge	49	A 7

	Map	Ref.
BRADSHAW		
Cr Manning	83	B 6
Rd Byford	135	E 1
St Eden Hill	49	A 9
BRADWELL		
Ct Carine	45	A 2
BRADY		
Gl Winthrop	92	B 5
Rd Jarrahdale	152	E 7
Rd Lesmurdie	87	B 5
St Glendalough	60	B 5
St Wangara	25	A 5
BRAE		
Ct Cooloongup	137	E 7
Rd Claremont	71	A 10
Rd High Wycombe	76	B 3
BRAEMAR		
St Rockingham	137	D 7
BRAEMORE		
St Armadale	116	C 3
BRAESIDE		
Rd Mt Lawley	61	B 6
BRAEWOOD		
Ct Nollamara	46	C 6
BRAGOR		
Pl Ardross	82	C 10
BRAHE		
Pl Padbury	30	D 1
BRAIBRISE		
Rd Wilson	84	B 6
BRAID		
St Perth City	1C	B 1
St Perth City	73	B 1
BRAITHWAITE		
Rd Lockridge	49	A 7
BRALICH		
St Warnbro	145	C 10
BRALLOS		
Ps Karrakatta	71	C 5
BRAMALL		
St East Perth	61	C 10
BRAMBLE		
Pl Edgewater	24	A 1
Wy Ballajura	33	C 5
BRAMFIELD		
Rd Maddington	96	B 3
BRAMLING		
St Maddington	96	B 5
BRAMPTON		
Pl Meadow Sprgs	163	C 6
Wy Lynwood	94	D 3
BRAMSHAW		
Me Meadow Sprgs	163	D 5
BRAMSTON		
St Spearwood	101	A 8
BRAMWELL		
Rd Noranda	47	C 5
BRANCH		
Cs Success	112	D 5
Cs Yangebup	112	C 3
BRANCHFIELD		
Wy Falcon	162A	D 4
BRAND		
Dr Curtin Uni	135	
Pl Morley	47	E 7
Rd High Wycombe	76	C 4
St Cloverdale	75	A 2
BRANDIS		
Ct High Wycombe	76	D 1
BRANDON		
Me Parmelia	131	C 7
St Kensington	73	C 8
St South Perth	73	C 8
Wy Lynwood	84	D 10
BRANDWOOD		
Gns Leeming	102	E 2

	Map	Ref.
BRANKSOME		
Gns City Beach	70	C 1
Gns City Beach	58	D 10
BRANSBY		
St Embleton	48	A 10
BRANSON		
Ct Caversham	49	B 6
BRANT		
Rd Kelmscott	116	C 1
BRANTON		
Ct Duncraig	31	B 5
BRASSEY		
St Swanbourne	70	E 8
BRAUNTON		
St Bicton	81	A 9
BRAXAN		
St Glen Forrest	66	D 2
BRAY		
Ct Bateman	92	D 5
La Kingsley	24	D 10
Pl Beechboro	49	A 4
St Gosnells	96	A 5
St Kelmscott	106	D 9
BRAYBROOK		
Pl Craigie	23	E 5
BRAYDON		
Rd Attadale	81	D 10
BRAZIER		
Rd Mt Helena	55	D 5
Rd Yanchep	4	C 5
Ri Padbury	30	D 2
BREADEN		
Dr Cooloongup	137	C 10
BREADSALL		
Cl Carine	30	E 10
BREAKER		
Cl Silver Sands	163	B 5
BREAKSEA		
Pl Merriwa	11	D 9
BREARLEY		
Ave Redcliffe	63	A 8
Me Hillarys	23	A 10
BRECHIN		
Ct Duncraig	31	C 8
Rt Armadale	116	B 1
BRECKNOCK		
Wy Girrawheen	32	D 8
BRECON		
Pl Wanneroo	20	E 9
BREDE		
Pl Balga	46	B 1
BREDGAR		
Wy Marangaroo	32	B 6
BREDHURST		
Rd Marangaroo	32	A 4
BREEN		
Pl Bateman	92	E 5
Pl Padbury	30	D 1
BREEZE		
Ct Gosnells	106	B 2
Ct Sorrento	30	D 4
BREMEN		
Wy Iluka	18	E 5
BREMER		
Pl Thornlie	95	D 7
BRENCHLEY		
St Beckenham	85	C 9
BRENDA		
Rd Maida Vale	76	D 2
BRENDON		
Pl Cannington	84	E 5
Wy Karrinyup	44	E 5
BRENNAN		
St Fremantle	1D	C 6
St Fremantle	90	C 6
Wy Belmont	74	C 1

	Map	Ref.
BRENT		
Cl Kingsley	31	B 2
BRENTFORD		
Ave Viveash	50	B 4
BRENTHAM		
St Leederville	60	C 7
St Mt Hawthorn	60	C 6
BRENTWOOD		
Ave Brentwood	93	A 3
Rd Kenwick	86	A 8
Rd Kenwick	85	E 9
Rd Wattle Grove	86	B 5
BRESNAHAN		
Pl Marangaroo	32	C 5
BRETAGNE		
Pl Port Kennedy	156	D 1
BRETBY		
Cl Carine	31	A 9
BRETT		
Pl Gosnells	106	C 2
BRETTON		
Ct Swan View	51	B 7
BREWER		
Pl Mirrabooka	47	A 5
Rd Forrestfield	76	D 6
Rd Maida Vale	76	D 4
St Perth City	1C	B 1
St Perth City	73	B 1
BRIALD		
Pl Dianella	47	A 6
BRIAN		
Ave Morley	48	B 7
Ave Mt Pleasant	92	E 1
Ave Yokine	46	D 9
St Armadale	116	E 5
BRIAR		
Ct Kingsley	31	C 2
Ct Leeming	103	A 2
Pl Ferndale	84	E 9
BRIBIE		
Pl Warnbro	145	D 5
BRICE		
Cl Leeming	93	C 9
BRICKNELL		
Rd Attadale	81	E 9
BRIDAL		
Cr Kenwick	95	D 1
BRIDGE		
Me Waikiki	145	C 4
Rd Canning Vale	105	A 1
Rd Canning Vale	95	A 10
St Guildford	49	C 10
St Queens Park	84	E 3
St Sth Guildford	63	C 2
St Wilson	84	A 8
BRIDGEDALE		
Cl Beldon	23	D 2
BRIDGES		
Rd Melville	91	C 1
BRIDGET		
Pl Shelley	83	C 10
BRIDGEWATER		
Cr Karrinyup	45	A 5
Ct Waikiki	145	C 2
Dr Kallaroo	23	B 6
Dr Kallaroo	23	C 5
BRIDGEWAY		
Ave Ferndale	84	E 8
BRIDGWOOD		
Rd Lesmurdie	87	D 1
BRIDLE		
Dr Maida Vale	64	E 9
BRIDSON		
Ct Hamilton Hill	101	A 3
St Bassendean	63	A 3
BRIE BRIE		
Cr Kalamunda	77	A 5
BRIENZ		
Dr Joondalup	19	D 2

For detailed information regarding the street referencing system used in this book, turn to page 170.

B

		Map	Ref.
BRIGADE			
Rd	Armadale	115	D 5
BRIGADOON			
Cl	Halls Head	164	C 3
Pl	Cooloongup	137	E 7
BRIGALOW			
Wy	Armadale	116	B 5
Wy	Lesmurdie	87	D 3
BRIGETA			
Rd	Paulls Valley	79	A 1
BRIGGS			
Ct	Hilton	91	A 9
Pl	Armadale	116	C 9
Rd	Byford	135	B 1
Rd	Byford	126	B 10
St	Bassendean	63	B 2
St	Kewdale	74	D 8
St	Mosman Park	80	E 8
St	South Lake	102	D 8
St	Welshpool	74	C 10
BRIGHT			
Rd	Calista	130	E 8
St	Kensington	73	C 9
BRIGHTON			
Cl	Warnbro	145	E 5
Ct	Hillarys	23	A 10
Pl	Greenfields	163	E 9
Rd	Rivervale	74	A 3
Rd	Scarborough	44	D 10
St	Cottesloe	70	D 10
St	Leederville	60	C 9
BRIGID			
Cl	Lesmurdie	87	D 2
BRIGNELL			
Gns	Parmelia	131	B 7
BRILL			
St	Kenwick	95	D 1
BRILLEE			
St	Carine	45	A 1
BRILLIANT			
Ri	Stratton	51	B 3
BRINAWARR			
Cl	Currambine	19	B 5
BRINCKLEY			
Cr	Koondoola	33	A 9
BRINDAL			
Cl	Bicton	81	A 9
BRINDLE			
Rd	Parkerville	53	D 3
St	Coolbellup	91	C 10
BRINDLEY			
St	Belmont	74	D 4
St	Wilson	84	C 6
BRINE			
Pl	Wembley Dns	59	A 4
Rd	Kalamunda	77	B 5
BRINKLEY			
St	Cannington	84	D 5
St	Martin	107	D 3
BRINTON			
Cl	E Cannington	85	D 4
BRISBANE			
Dr	Padbury	23	E 10
Pl	Perth City	61	A 10
St	Morley	47	E 8
St	Perth City	61	A 10
Tce	Perth City	61	A 10
BRISTOL			
Ave	Bicton	91	B 1
Ave	Bicton	81	B 10
Rd	Roleystone	118	D 2
St	Warnbro	145	D 6
Wy	Forrestfield	86	C 2
BRISTON			
Pl	North Beach	44	D 2
BRITANNIA			
Ave	Yangebup	111	C 3
Pl	Port Kennedy	156	C 4
Rd	Mt Hawthorn	60	C 7
Wy	Craigie	23	E 7

		Map	Ref.
BRITNALL			
Pl	Leeming	93	A 10
BRITTAIN			
St	Como	83	B 2
BRITTON			
Pl	Wandi	123	B 3
BRIX			
St	Wembley Dns	59	A 4
BRIXEY			
Ct	Armadale	116	C 9
BRIXHAM			
Wy	Warnbro	145	C 7
BRIXTON			
Rd	Bentley	84	A 1
St	Beckenham	85	C 7
St	Cottesloe	80	D 3
St	Kenwick	85	D 9
BROAD			
St	Kensington	73	C 10
BROADBEACH			
Blvd	Hillarys	23	A 9
BROADBENT			
Lp	Leeming	102	E 1
BROADFIELD			
Rt	Erskine	164	C 5
BROADHURST			
Cr	Bateman	92	D 7
BROADLEY			
Pl	Gosnells	106	C 1
BROADMEADOWS			
St	Bibra Lake	101	D 5
BROADMOOR			
Ave	Dianella	47	B 5
Grn	Currambine	19	C 4
Me	Meadow Sprgs	163	D 2
BROADWATER			
Gns	South Lake	102	C 7
BROADWAY			
	Bassendean	63	A 1
	Bassendean	62	E 1
	Crawley	71	E 9
	Embleton	48	B 10
	Nedlands	82	A 1
	Nedlands	71	E 9
Rd	Bickley	88	C 3
Rt	Ocean Reef	19	A 7
BROCK			
St	Orange Grove	86	C 8
BROCKLEY			
Pl	Kingsley	24	B 9
BROCKMAN			
Ave	Bull Creek	93	B 4
Ave	Dalkeith	81	D 2
Ct	Duncraig	30	E 8
Pl	Sth Fremantle	90	D 10
Rd	Midland	50	C 9
Rt	Bentley	84	C 5
St	Falcon	162A	E 10
St	Henley Brook	29	B 9
BROCKMILL			
Ave	Beechboro	49	A 5
BROCKWAY			
Rd	Claremont	71	C 6
Rd	Karrakatta	71	C 5
Rd	Martin	108	A 4
Rd	Mt Claremont	71	C 6
Rd	Shenton Park	71	C 2
BROCKWELL			
Ct	Hillarys	23	A 9
Pl	Oakford	124	A 5
BRODIA			
Pl	Two Rocks	2	C 2
BRODIE			
Ct	Midvale	51	A 7
BRODIE-HALL			
Dr	Bentley	83	D 2
BRODRICK			
St	Karrinyup	45	A 3

		Map	Ref.
BROLGA			
Ct	High Wycombe	76	D 1
Gr	Armadale	116	B 3
Pl	Gosnells	106	A 4
Pro	Willetton	93	C 4
Wy	Stirling	45	D 6
BROME			
St	Gosnells	96	A 8
BROMFIELD			
Dr	Kelmscott	117	B 2
Dr	Kelmscott	107	B 10
BROMLEY			
Pl	Kingsley	24	A 9
Rd	Herne Hill	37	B 7
Rd	Hilton	91	C 9
St	Beckenham	85	B 9
St	Embleton	62	A 2
BROMPTON			
Pl	Alexander Hts	33	B 5
Rd	City Beach	58	D 5
Rd	Wembley Dns	58	D 5
BRONDON			
St	Balcatta	46	B 3
BRONTE			
Cl	Kallaroo	23	A 7
Ct	Munster	101	B 10
St	East Perth	1C	B 2
St	East Perth	73	B 3
BRONZE WING			
Pl	Mundaring	68	C 1
BRONZEWING			
Ct	Wungong	116	C 10
BROOK			
Pl	Gosnells	96	A 7
Pl	Kelmscott	107	A 9
Rd	Darlington	66	A 4
Rd	Glen Forrest	66	C 4
Rd	Jarrahdale	152	D 6
Rd	Kenwick	86	A 5
Rd	Kenwick	85	E 7
Rd	Wattle Grove	86	A 5
St	Bassendean	63	B 1
St	East Perth	1C	B 2
St	East Perth	73	B 2
St	Kingsley	24	D 10
St	Middle Swan	50	E 3
BROOKDALE			
Dr	Armadale	116	B 7
St	Floreat	71	C 1
St	Floreat	59	C 9
St	Floreat	59	C 10
BROOKE			
Gns	Bateman	92	E 3
BROOKES			
Wy	Calista	130	E 7
BROOKING			
Rd	Coodanup	165	C 7
Rd	Mahogany Crk	67	C 1
Rd	Mahogany Crk	53	C 9
Rd	Parkerville	53	C 6
BROOKLAND			
Cr	Marangaroo	32	B 4
BROOKLANDS			
Dr	Henley Brook	28	C 10
BROOKLEA			
Pl	Ferndale	84	E 9
BROOKMAN			
Ave	Langford	94	E 1
St	Perth City	61	A 10
BROOKMOUNT			
Ra	Padbury	30	E 2
BROOKS			
Ct	Bibra Lake	102	D 2
Dr	Bayswater	62	A 6
Pl	Wandi	123	C 4
Ps	Clarkson	14	D 2
Rd	Roleystone	108	B 5
St	Kalamunda	77	D 7
BROOKSBY			
St	Melville	91	D 2

		Map	Ref.
BROOKSIDE			
Ave	Kelmscott	106	D 6
Ave	South Perth	73	B 7
La	Parkerville	53	C 6
BROOKTON			
Hwy	Karragullen	109	C 6
Hwy	Karragullen	108	E 4
Hwy	Kelmscott	107	B 10
Hwy	Kelmscott	116	E 1
Hwy	Kelmscott	106	E 10
Hwy	Roleystone	108	A 9
Hwy	Roleystone	107	D 10
BROOKVALE			
Ri	Kallaroo	23	A 8
BROOKWOOD			
Ct	Beckenham	85	A 10
BROOME			
Pl	Warnbro	145	E 5
St	Cottesloe	80	C 4
St	Cottesloe	70	C 10
St	Forrestdale	115	A 6
St	Highgate	61	B 9
St	Nedlands	71	C 8
St	South Perth	73	B 9
St	South Perth	73	C 8
BROOMHALL			
Wy	Noranda	47	C 6
BROPHY			
St	Kardinya	92	A 8
BRORA			
Gr	Greenmount	65	C 1
BROSNAN			
St	Dianella	61	D 1
BROUGHTON			
St	Balcatta	46	A 4
Wy	Orelia	131	B 5
Wy	Rockingham	137	A 7
BROULA			
Rd	Kalamunda	77	D 8
BROUN			
Ave	Bedford	61	E 3
Ave	Embleton	62	A 1
Ave	Embleton	48	A 10
Ave	Embleton	48	B 10
Cr	Bedford	61	E 3
Rd	Coodanup	165	C 6
Wy	Bassendean	63	A 5
BROWN			
Ave	Naval Base	121	B 8
Cr	Armadale	116	B 2
Pl	Beechboro	49	B 4
Rd	Attadale	81	C 8
Rd	Bicton	81	C 8
St	Byford	126	D 10
St	Claremont	71	B 9
St	East Perth	1C	B 2
St	East Perth	73	B 2
St	Middle Swan	50	E 3
Wy	Karrinyup	45	B 5
BROWNE			
Ave	Dalkeith	81	E 2
St	Subiaco	72	A 3
BROWNELL			
Cr	Medina	130	E 4
Pl	Medina	130	E 5
BROWNFIELD			
Dr	Swan View	51	D 8
BROWNING			
Rd	Armadale	116	D 10
St	Yokine	61	A 2
Wy	Gooseberry H	77	D 5
Wy	Munster	101	C 9
BROWNLEY			
Ct	Roleystone	108	C 7
BROWNRIGG			
St	Singleton	160	D 2
BROXBURN			
Pl	Duncraig	31	B 5
BRUCE			
Cl	Como	83	B 3
Ct	Leeming	93	B 8

		Map	Ref.
Ct	Wellard	132	B 10
Rd	Maida Vale	76	C 5
Rd	Morley	48	B 9
Rd	Wattle Grove	86	B 5
St	Como	83	B 4
St	Hillarys	30	C 2
St	Leederville	60	C 8
St	Nedlands	81	E 1
St	Nedlands	71	E 10
BRUE			
Ct	Sorrento	30	B 4
BRUMBY			
Ct	High Wycombe	76	D 1
Pl	Armadale	116	B 5
BRUNEL			
Pl	Morley	48	D 7
St	Stirling	45	E 9
BRUNING			
Rd	Manning	83	B 5
BRUNONIA			
Rty	Halls Head	164	A 7
BRUNS			
St	Kelmscott	116	C 1
BRUNSWICK			
Rd	Thornlie	94	E 6
BRUNY			
Pl	Shelley	93	C 2
BRUSH			
Ct	Canning Vale	104	A 1
BRUSHFIELD			
Wy	Gwelup	45	C 6
BRUTON			
St	Balcatta	45	E 4
BRYAH			
Ct	Yangebup	112	A 1
BRYAN			
Pl	Balcatta	45	D 4
Wy	Cottesloe	80	C 1
BRYANT			
Ave	Mosman Park	80	E 6
BRYDEN			
Pl	Gosnells	106	A 1
Rd	Carmel	88	D 7
BRYNE			
Pl	Leeming	93	A 8
BUBARA			
Wy	Ferndale	84	D 9
BUCAT			
St	Hamilton Hill	101	B 1
BUCENTAUR			
Pl	Halls Head	164	B 2
BUCHAN			
Cl	Spearwood	101	B 8
Pl	Hillarys	23	B 9
BUCHANAN			
Ave	Greenwood	31	B 5
Rd	Roleystone	107	B 7
Ri	Coogee	100	E 10
Wy	Padbury	30	C 1
BUCKHAVEN			
Ct	Kingsley	24	C 10
BUCKIE			
Ct	Warwick	31	C 7
BUCKINGHAM			
Cr	Kardinya	91	E 9
Dr	Wangara	24	E 6
Rd	Kelmscott	107	A 10
Rd	Swan View	51	B 9
BUCKLAND			
Ave	Mosman Park	80	D 6
Rd	Jarrahdale	152	D 4
BUCKLE			
Ct	Waikiki	145	B 3
St	Balcatta	45	E 5
BUCKLEY			
St	Jandakot	102	D 9
BUCKNELL			
Pl	Swan View	51	B 9
Rd	Bibra Lake	102	D 3

182 For detailed information regarding the street referencing system used in this book, turn to page 170.

C

		Map	Ref.
BUCKTHORN			
Ct	Duncraig	31	B 7
Wy	Duncraig	31	B 7
BUDDEN			
Wy	Medina	130	D 5
BUGATTI			
Wy	Balcatta	45	D 4
BUGENDORE			
St	Maida Vale	76	E 1
St	Maida Vale	76	E 2
BUGLE			
St	Parkerville	54	A 8
BUKTENICA			
Ct	Spearwood	101	B 6
BUKU			
St	Greenwood	31	D 3
BULBEY			
St	Bellevue	64	D 1
BULBUL			
Ct	Armadale	116	B 3
BULIDA			
Ct	Kelmscott	106	E 6
BULIMBA			
Rd	Nedlands	71	C 10
BULKIRRA			
Pl	Helena Valley	65	C 6
BULLA			
Pl	Hillarys	30	B 1
St	Lesmurdie	87	D 3
BULLARA			
Ra	Jarrahdale	152	A 5
Rd	Craigie	23	D 5
BULLARRA			
Rd	Greenmount	51	B 10
BULL CREEK			
Dr	Bull Creek	92	E 5
Rd	Rossmoyne	93	A 3
BULLECOURT			
St	Middle Swan	50	D 5
BULLER			
St	Inglewood	61	C 4
BULLFINCH			
St	Huntingdale	95	B 10
St	Huntingdale	105	C 1
St	Spearwood	101	C 5
Wy	Ballajura	34	A 8
Wy	Ballajura	33	E 8
BULLOCKBUSH			
Rd	Kelmscott	107	A 8
BULONG			
Ave	Redcliffe	63	A 7
BULRUSH			
Dr	Bibra Lake	102	C 5
BULWER			
Ave	Perth City	61	A 10
St	Perth City	61	A 9
St	Perth City	1C	B 1
St	Perth City	73	B 1
BUNBURY			
Pl	Rockingham	137	B 5
Pl	Winthrop	92	A 5
BUNDA			
Pl	Waikiki	145	D 2
BUNDALLA			
Ct	Kelmscott	116	D 1
BUNDERRA			
Cl	Karawara	83	C 4
BUNDEY			
Cl	Merriwa	11	C 9
BUNDY			
Cl	South Lake	102	D 6
BUNGANA			
Ave	Perth Airport	63	B 6
BUNGAREE			
Rd	Wilson	84	A 6
BUNINYONG			
Rd	Greenmount	51	B 9

		Map	Ref.
BUNNEY			
Pl	Byford	135	E 2
Rd	Kelmscott	116	D 1
BUNNING			
Ct	Hamersley	31	D 9
Pl	Kardinya	91	E 7
Rd	Gidgegannup	41	B 2
Rd	Mt Helena	55	A 2
Rd	Mt Helena	41	B 10
St	Bentley	84	A 5
BUNTER			
Ct	Leeming	93	D 8
BUNTHORNE			
Ct	Duncraig	30	D 3
BUNTINE			
Rd	Wembley Dns	59	A 4
Rd	Wembley Dns	59	A 5
Wy	Girrawheen	32	B 7
BUNYA			
St	Dianella	47	C 5
St	Noranda	47	C 5
BUNYAN			
Cl	Spearwood	101	C 8
BUOY			
St	Ocean Reef	23	A 1
BURBANK			
Ct	Padbury	30	E 1
BURBRIDGE			
Ave	Koondoola	32	E 7
BURCH			
St	South Perth	73	A 10
BURCHELL			
Wy	Kewdale	75	A 7
BURDEKIN			
Wy	Merriwa	11	C 10
BURDETT			
Pl	Padbury	30	D 2
Rt	Murdoch	92	B 7
BURDHAM			
Wy	Balga	46	D 2
BURES			
Ct	Girrawheen	32	B 9
BURFORD			
Pl	Nth Fremantle	80	C 9
St	Balga	32	A 10
St	Eden Hill	48	E 9
BURGANDY			
Ct	Thornlie	95	C 8
BURGAY			
Ct	Osborne Park	59	D 2
BURGES			
St	Noranda	48	B 5
BURGESS			
Cr	Belhus	29	C 6
Rd	Red Hill	169	D 6
St	Hamersley	31	D 10
St	Leederville	60	D 8
St	Midland	50	B 8
BURGLAND			
Dr	Girrawheen	32	B 8
BURGUNDY			
Cr	Spearwood	101	B 4
La	Ellenbrook	29	B 1
BURHAM			
Ct	Marangaroo	32	A 5
Rd	Kenwick	95	C 1
BURI			
Ce	Warnbro	145	E 9
BURKE			
Dr	Alfred Cove	81	E 9
Dr	Attadale	81	C 7
Pl	Orelia	131	B 6
Pl	Padbury	30	D 1
Rd	Canning Vale	94	D 2
St	Mt Helena	55	A 1
BURKINSHAW			
Dr	Glen Forrest	66	D 5
Rd	Glen Forrest	66	D 3

		Map	Ref.
BURLEY			
St	Mandurah	163	B 10
BURLEY GRIFFIN			
Me	Joondalup	19	D 2
BURLINGTON			
St	Naval Base	121	B 7
St	St James	84	B 2
BURLINSON			
Cr	Koondoola	33	A 8
BURLOS			
Ct	Joondalup	19	D 3
BURMA			
Rd	Baldivis	148	A 4
Rd	Lesmurdie	87	C 1
Rd	Lesmurdie	77	C 10
BURNA			
St	Falcon	162A	A 4
BURNBY			
Cro	Leeming	92	E 10
BURNDALE			
Rd	Armadale	116	E 9
BURNETT			
Ave	Leeming	93	A 10
Dr	Clarkson	14	C 3
Rd	Manning	83	B 5
St	Embleton	62	A 2
Wy	Naval Base	121	A 3
BURNEY			
Ct	Kardinya	92	A 7
BURNHAM			
Wy	Girrawheen	32	C 8
Wy	Shelley	93	C 1
BURNISTON			
St	Scarborough	44	E 10
BURNLEY			
St	Thornlie	95	C 8
BURNS			
Ave	Yokine	60	E 2
Rd	Armadale	126	D 1
Rd	Armadale	116	D 10
Rd	Kalamunda	77	D 4
St	Cloverdale	75	A 6
St	Nth Fremantle	90	C 1
BURNS BEACH			
Rd	Burns	18	E 3
Rd	Joondalup	19	C 2
Rd	Wanneroo	16	A 10
Rd	Wanneroo	15	E 10
BURNSIDE			
Ct	Kingsley	31	C 1
St	Bayswater	62	A 5
Wy	Waikiki	145	C 2
BURNTOAK			
Wy	Kingsley	24	B 10
BURRA			
Ct	Clarkson	14	D 1
St	Mundaring	68	C 1
BURRAGAH			
Wy	Duncraig	30	D 8
BURRAN			
Ct	Armadale	116	C 5
Ct	Maida Vale	77	A 3
BURRELL			
St	Byford	126	E 10
BURRENDAH			
Blvd	Willetton	93	C 5
BURREN GATE			
	Willetton	93	C 4
BURRIDGE			
Wy	Hamilton Hill	101	C 1
BURRINJUCK			
Rd	Gooseberry H.	77	D 1
BURROUGHS			
Rd	Karrinyup	45	A 5
BURROWA			
St	Armadale	116	B 6

		Map	Ref.
BURROWS			
Pl	Parmelia	131	A 8
Pl	Winthrop	92	A 4
BURSARIA			
Cr	Ferndale	94	B 1
Cr	Ferndale	84	B 10
BURSLEM			
Dr	Maddington	95	D 4
Dr	Thornlie	95	D 7
BURSWOOD			
Rd	Victoria Park	73	E 5
BURT			
St	Cottesloe	80	D 2
St	Fremantle	1D	C 3
St	Fremantle	90	C 3
St	Kalamunda	77	D 7
St	Mt Lawley	61	A 7
St	North Perth	61	A 7
St	Quinns Rocks	10	A 1
Wy	East Perth	1C	B 4
Wy	East Perth	73	B 4
BURTENSHAW			
Cl	Leeming	93	D 8
Wy	Calista	130	E 8
BURTON			
Pl	Greenmount	51	D 10
Pl	Parmelia	131	C 8
Rd	Greenmount	65	D 1
Rd	Greenmount	51	E 10
Rt	Stratton	51	A 4
St	Cannington	84	C 5
BURTONIA			
Cl	Duncraig	30	E 6
Wy	Forrestfield	76	B 8
BURWASH			
Pl	Maddington	96	A 5
Pl	Nollamara	46	E 5
BURWOOD			
Rd	Balcatta	46	B 8
St	Nedlands	71	E 5
BURY			
St	Northbridge	1C	E 1
St	Northbridge	72	E 1
BUSCOE			
Pl	Currambine	19	A 2
BUSCOT			
Ct	Erskine	164	C 6
BUSH			
Cl	Beckenham	85	D 5
Rd	Canning Mills	98	E 8
St	St James	84	A 2
BUSHBY			
St	Midland	50	E 7
St	Midvale	50	E 8
BUSHELL			
Pl	Ardross	82	D 8
BUSHEY			
Rd	Wembley Dns	58	E 3
BUSHINN			
Me	Padbury	30	E 2
BUSHLAND			
Rt	Neerabup	15	E 6
BUSHLANDS			
Rd	Hovea	52	B 1
BUSHMEAD			
Rd	Hazelmere	50	A 10
Rd	Hazelmere	64	B 1
BUSHY			
Gr	Canning Vale	94	D 9
Rd	Spearwood	101	A 5
BUSSELL			
Pl	Beechboro	49	B 5
Rd	Wembley Dns	58	E 3
BUSYCON			
Pl	Heathridge	23	E 1
BUTCHER			
Rd	Byford	126	D 7
Rd	High Wycombe	76	B 2
Rd	Roleystone	117	E 1

		Map	Ref.
St	Kwinana Beach	130	B 5
St	Mundijong	143	A 8
BUTLER			
Ave	Swanbourne	70	E 7
St	Langford	94	E 1
St	Willagee	92	A 5
St	Willagee	91	D 5
Wy	Mosman Park	80	E 4
BUTSON			
Pl	Redcliffe	62	E 10
Rd	Leeming	93	A 9
St	Hilton	91	B 9
BUTT			
La	Maylands	62	B 10
Pl	Orelia	131	A 4
Pl	Orelia	130	E 4
BUTTEL			
Tp	Winthrop	92	C 5
BUTTERCUP			
Ri	Duncraig	30	D 4
BUTTERICK			
Pl	Girrawheen	32	A 7
BUTTERWORTH			
Ave	Koondoola	33	A 8
BUTTLER			
Pl	Joondanna	60	C 2
BUTTON			
St	Munster	111	B 4
BUVELOT			
Pl	Woodvale	24	B 4
BUXTON			
Rd	Wembley Dns	58	E 5
St	Mt Hawthorn	60	B 6
BUZZA			
St	St James	84	A 3
BYASS			
Ri	Leeming	93	C 8
BYBLIS			
Pl	Koongamia	65	B 1
BYERS			
Rd	Midland	50	B 5
BYFIELD			
Rd	Parkerville	53	C 5
BYFLEET			
St	Morley	48	A 8
BYFORD			
Dr	Byford	135	D 1
BYGUM			
La	Martin	96	D 3
BYLAND			
St	Doubleview	59	A 1
BYRNE			
Cl	Padbury	23	E 9
BYRO			
Rd	Golden Bay	158	D 8
BYRON			
Ct	Kallaroo	23	B 7
Rd	Armadale	126	D 1
Rd	Armadale	116	D 10
Rd	Kalamunda	77	D 4
Rd	Yokine	61	A 2
St	Leederville	60	D 7
BYWATER			
Wy	Wilson	84	B 9
BYWOOD			
Wy	Lynwood	94	D 2
BYWORTH			
Pl	Balga	46	C 2

C

CABALLO
Ct Safety Bay 137 B 10

C

		Map	Ref.
CABARITA			
La	Kingsley	31	D 2
Rd	Armadale	116	B 5
Rd	Kalamunda	77	C 10
CABELL			
St	Yokine	46	C 9
CABERNET			
Ct	Armadale	116	E 4
CABLE			
Ce	Mosman Park	80	C 8
Cl	Armadale	116	B 3
Pl	Morley	48	C 7
St	The Lakes	57	E 2
CABRA			
Pl	Waterford	83	D 6
CABRAMATTA			
St	Bayswater	62	E 6
CABRINI			
Rd	Marangaroo	32	A 5
CACHUCA			
Ct	Duncraig	30	D 3
CADBURY			
St	Warnbro	145	D 8
CADD			
St	Balcatta	45	E 4
St	Hilton	91	A 8
CADDEN			
St	E Victoria Pk	83	E 2
CADDY			
Ave	Leederville	60	B 9
Ci	Cooloongup	138	A 9
Ci	Cooloongup	137	E 9
CADE			
Pl	Greenwood	31	D 4
St	Hamilton Hill	101	B 2
St	Mt Helena	41	B 6
CADIZ			
Ct	Sorrento	30	C 4
Pl	Coogee	101	A 9
Pl	Warnbro	145	E 7
CADMUS			
St	Balcatta	46	A 4
CADOGAN			
St	Kingsley	31	C 2
CADOR			
Ct	Carine	31	C 9
CAEN			
Ri	Mindarie	14	B 4
CAESAR			
Ct	Munster	101	B 9
St	Beaconsfield	90	E 8
CAESIA			
Pl	Mirrabooka	32	E 9
CAFFERY			
Pl	Hamilton Hill	101	C 3
CAFFRA			
Cl	Warnbro	145	E 9
CAFFRUM			
Grn	Mirrabooka	47	B 2
CAGNEY			
Wy	Lesmurdie	87	D 2
CAHILL			
Ct	Wilson	84	B 7
CAHOW			
Gr	Ballajura	33	E 8
CAIN			
Pl	Leeming	93	C 8
St	North Beach	44	C 2
CAIRD			
Pl	Lynwood	94	B 4
CAIRN			
Ave	Duncraig	31	B 6
Rd	Sawyers Valley	55	C 9
Rd	Southern River	105	B 8
CAIRNHILL			
St	Greenmount	65	D 1
CAITHNESS			
Rd	Floreat	59	B 8

		Map	Ref.
CAITUP			
Pl	Hillarys	30	C 2
CAKORA			
La	Merriwa	11	D 10
CALABAR			
Ct	Merriwa	11	C 9
CALABRESE			
Ave	Wanneroo	24	D 4
CALADENIA			
Rd	Walliston	88	A 2
St	Greenwood	31	C 4
Wy	Koongamia	65	B 2
CALAIS			
Rd	Scarborough	58	E 3
Rd	Wembley Dns	58	E 4
Wy	Sorrento	30	C 4
CALBOURNE			
Wy	Kingsley	24	D 10
CALDECOTT			
St	Thornlie	95	B 4
CALDER			
Rt	Merriwa	11	C 9
Wy	Bateman	92	D 7
CALDERA			
Cl	Leeming	102	E 1
Cl	Mindarie	10	A 2
CALDWELL			
Pl	Carine	30	E 10
St	Hamilton Hill	91	A 9
CALE			
Pl	Spearwood	101	A 5
St	Como	82	E 3
CALEB			
Pl	Hamersley	31	D 10
CALECTASIA			
St	Greenwood	31	C 5
CALEDONIA			
Ave	Currambine	19	A 3
CALEDONIAN			
Ave	Maylands	62	A 8
Ave	Maylands	61	E 7
CALEEN			
Ct	Wilson	84	C 7
CALEY			
Ct	Mirrabooka	47	A 1
Pl	Two Rocks	2	E 3
Rd	Padbury	23	D 8
CALGARY			
Pl	Kingsley	24	C 9
St	Ardross	82	C 9
CALIBAN			
Wy	Coolbellup	101	D 2
CALICO			
Ct	Mirrabooka	47	B 1
CALISO			
Ct	Warnbro	145	E 9
CALISTA			
Ave	Calista	130	E 6
CALLAGHAN			
Wy	Noranda	47	C 5
CALLAN			
Pl	Waterford	83	D 6
Rd	Floreat	59	A 8
St	Hovea	52	E 8
CALLAWA			
St	Golden Bay	158	D 7
CALLAWAY			
Cr	Kardinya	91	E 8
St	Bull Creek	93	B 6
St	Wangara	25	C 8
CALLEY			
Dr	Leeming	92	E 9
CALLIANDRA			
Pl	Roleystone	108	B 9
Wy	Forrestfield	76	C 9
CALLICOMA			
Ct	South Lake	102	D 6

		Map	Ref.
CALLINGTON			
Ave	City Beach	70	D 1
CALLION			
Ri	Padbury	30	E 1
CALLISON			
Wy	Koondoola	32	E 7
CALLISTEMON			
St	Greenwood	31	C 6
CALLUNA			
Wy	Forrestfield	76	C 7
CALM			
Ct	Safety Bay	145	B 1
CALNE			
Pl	Maddington	96	C 2
CALNON			
St	Bassendean	63	B 2
CALOPHYLLA			
Ct	Wanneroo	24	D 1
CALPIN			
Cr	Attadale	81	D 8
CALTHORPE			
Pl	Kingsley	31	D 3
CALUME			
St	Hillman	138	A 5
St	Hillman	137	E 5
CALVER			
Pl	City Beach	58	D 5
CALVERT			
Pl	Greenfields	163	C 10
Wy	Girrawheen	32	C 7
CALWAY			
Ri	Kiara	48	E 6
CALYPSO			
Rd	Halls Head	164	B 2
Rt	Ocean Reef	18	E 8
St	Safety Bay	145	B 2
CALYTRIX			
Rd	Roleystone	108	B 9
CAM			
Ct	Merriwa	11	C 9
CAMARGUE			
Dr	Brigadoon	168	C 5
CAMARINO			
Dr	Woodvale	24	A 6
CAMBELL			
Rd	Armadale	116	C 9
CAMBERLEY			
St	Thornlie	95	C 4
CAMBERWARRA			
Dr	Craigie	23	C 6
Dr	Craigie	23	C 7
CAMBERWELL			
Rd	Balga	46	B 1
St	Beckenham	85	B 8
St	E Victoria Pk	84	A 1
CAMBEY			
Me	Parmelia	131	A 10
Wy	Brentwood	92	D 3
CAMBOON			
Rd	Malaga	47	D 3
Rd	Morley	47	D 7
Rd	Noranda	47	D 5
CAMBORNE			
Ave	City Beach	70	D 2
Wy	Thornlie	95	B 5
CAMBRIA			
St	Kallaroo	23	C 5
CAMBRIA ISLAND			
Rt	Halls Head	164	D 1
CAMBRIAN			
Ml	Alexander Hts	33	A 4
Pl	Willetton	93	D 3
CAMBRIDGE			
Cr	Cooloongup	137	C 9
Dr	Greenfields	165	E 2
Me	Kingsley	31	B 1
Rd	Forrestfield	86	D 1
St	Floreat	59	C 10

		Map	Ref.
St	Leederville	60	B 10
St	Maylands	61	D 7
St	Wembley	60	A 10
St	Wembley	59	E 10
CAMBUS			
Ct	Riverton	93	E 1
CAMDEN			
Gl	Mindarie	14	B 6
Pl	Thornlie	95	D 6
St	Belmont	74	C 2
St	Dianella	47	D 9
St	Wembley Dns	59	A 5
CAMELIA			
Ave	Mt Claremont	71	B 5
Ct	Ferndale	84	D 8
Ct	Greenwood	31	D 6
Ct	North Perth	60	E 8
CAMELLIA			
Ct	Halls Head	164	B 5
CAMELOT			
Ct	Thornlie	95	C 8
Pl	Westfield	106	D 6
St	Carine	45	C 1
St	Carine	31	C 10
CAMER			
Ct	Huntingdale	95	D 9
CAMERON			
Cl	Lesmurdie	87	D 1
Ct	Willetton	94	A 1
Ct	Willetton	93	E 1
Grn	Floreat	71	C 1
Rd	Gidgegannup	40	A 6
Rd	Gidgegannup	39	D 6
Rd	Gidgegannup	40	D 6
St	Embleton	62	B 1
St	Karrinyup	45	A 4
St	Langford	94	E 3
St	Quinns Rocks	10	A 1
St	Thornlie	94	E 4
Wy	Kardinya	92	A 9
CAMFIELD			
Lp	Parmelia	131	B 7
Pl	Beechboro	49	B 4
Pl	Beldon	23	D 3
Rd	Greenmount	66	A 1
Rd	Greenmount	52	A 1
Rd	Greenmount	65	E 1
Rd	Greenmount	51	E 10
CAMILLO			
St	Coolbellup	91	D 10
CAMIRA			
Pl	Gooseberry H	77	D 2
Wy	Iluka	18	E 6
CAMM			
Ave	Bull Creek	93	A 4
Pl	Beechboro	49	A 3
Pl	Hillarys	30	A 2
Pl	Waikiki	137	E 10
CAMMARAY			
Ct	Thornlie	95	B 8
CAMMILLO			
Rd	Kelmscott	106	C 9
Rd	Westfield	106	B 6
CAMP			
Ct	Leeming	93	B 8
CAMPBELL			
Ave	Kensington	73	B 10
Ct	Noranda	48	A 6
Dr	Hillarys	30	B 1
Rd	Canning Vale	104	C 4
St	Belmont	74	C 3
St	E Cannington	85	B 5
St	Kensington	73	B 10
St	Rivervale	74	B 5
St	Rivervale	74	C 4
St	Subiaco	72	A 3
St	West Perth	1C	D 1
St	West Perth	72	D 1
Wy	Parkerville	53	D 4
Wy	Rockingham	137	A 9

		Map	Ref.
CAMPERSIC			
Rd	Brigadoon	169	A 3
Rd	Brigadoon	168	D 4
Rd	Herne Hill	37	C 4
Rd	Middle Swan	37	C 10
Rd	Millendon	168	C 10
CAMPHOR			
Cl	South Lake	102	D 6
CAMPION			
Ave	Balcatta	46	B 7
Cl	Spearwood	101	B 8
Cr	Attadale	81	B 7
St	Duncraig	31	B 7
CAMPSBOURNE			
St	Balcatta	46	A 3
St	Balcatta	45	E 3
CAMPSIE			
St	Nedlands	71	E 5
St	North Perth	60	D 8
CAMSELL			
Wy	Ferndale	84	D 8
CANADA			
St	Dianella	47	C 9
CANADICE			
Ct	Joondalup	19	D 3
CANARA			
Rd	Balga	46	C 4
CANARY			
Pl	Kardinya	92	A 9
CANAVAN			
Cr	Manning	83	B 4
CANBERRA			
Cl	Port Kennedy	156	D 4
CANDELO			
Lp	Greenfields	163	E 7
CANDIDA			
Cl	Currambine	19	A 5
CANDIRU			
Ct	Sorrento	30	D 3
CANDISH			
Ct	Booragoon	92	C 2
Gr	Armadale	115	E 5
CANDLEBARK			
Pl	South Lake	102	C 6
CANDLER			
Wy	Two Rocks	2	C 2
CANDLEWOOD			
Blvd	Joondalup	19	D 3
CANDY			
St	Morley	47	E 9
CANE			
Ct	Beechboro	48	C 3
Ct	Gosnells	106	A 3
Pl	Heathridge	19	B 9
CANHAM			
Wy	Greenwood	32	A 3
Wy	Greenwood	31	E 3
Wy	Orelia	131	A 5
CANIS			
Ct	Kingsley	31	B 2
CANN			
Pl	Marmion	30	D 6
Rd	Attadale	81	C 8
CANNA			
Pl	Wanneroo	20	E 6
Wy	Ardross	82	C 10
CANNES			
Pl	Warnbro	145	E 6
CANNI			
Pl	Willetton	94	A 3
CANNING			
Ave	Mt Pleasant	92	D 1
Hwy	Alfred Cove	81	E 10
Hwy	Applecross	82	B 9
Hwy	Como	83	A 4
Hwy	East Fremantle	90	D 2
Hwy	Melville	81	C 10
Hwy	Palmyra	91	A 1
Hwy	South Perth	73	B 10

184   **For detailed information regarding the street referencing system used in this book, turn to page 170.**

C

		Map	Ref.
Hwy	Victoria Park	73	C 7
Pde	Como	83	A 6
Rd	Canning Mills	98	E 7
Rd	Carmel	88	A 6
Rd	Kalamunda	77	D 7
Rd	Karragullen	109	A 2
Rd	Pickering Bk	98	E 1
Rd	Walliston	87	E 1
St	Balcatta	46	A 5

CANNING BEACH
| Rd | Applecross | 82 | D 4 |

CANNING DAM
| Rd | Bedfordale | 128 | E 5 |
| Rd | Karragullen | 119 | B 10 |

CANNING MILLS
Rd	Canning Mills	98	C 10
Rd	Kelmscott	107	A 9
Rd	Martin	108	A 2
Rd	Martin	107	C 4
Rd	Roleystone	107	B 6
Rd E	Canning Mills	98	E 8

CANNING PARK
| Ave | Maddington | 96 | A 3 |

CANNING RIVER
| Gns | Wilson | 84 | B 9 |

CANNON
Ct	Alexander Hts	33	B 5
Ct	Leeming	93	B 10
St	Bayswater	48	D 10

CANNS
| Rd | Armadale | 117 | A 4 |
| Rd | Bedfordale | 117 | D 9 |

CANNY
| Rd | St James | 84 | A 2 |

CANON
| Pl | Lynwood | 94 | B 2 |

CANT
| Ct | Hillarys | 30 | B 1 |

CANTARA
| Ri | Ocean Reef | 19 | A 8 |

CANTER
| Ct | Orange Grove | 86 | D 7 |

CANTERBURY
Ci	Currambine	19	B 5
Ct	Nollamara	46	C 6
Dr	Willetton	94	A 3
Me	Port Kennedy	156	D 1
Tce	E Victoria Pk	74	A 10
Tce	E Victoria Pk	83	E 1
Tce	E Victoria Pk	73	E 10
Tce	Meadow Sprgs	163	C 6

CANTLE
| St | East Perth | 61 | C 10 |

CANTLEBURY
| Rd | Bayswater | 62 | B 4 |

CANTONMENT
| St | Fremantle | 1D | B 5 |
| St | Fremantle | 90 | B 5 |

CANTRAY
| Ave | Applecross | 82 | B 9 |

CANTUA
| Ct | Greenwood | 31 | D 3 |
| Wy | Forrestfield | 86 | E 1 |

CANTWELL
| Cr | Forrestfield | 76 | A 9 |
| Cr | Forrestfield | 75 | E 9 |

CANUNGRA
| Rd | City Beach | 58 | E 9 |

CANVALE
| Rd | Canning Vale | 94 | C 8 |

CAPE
Ct	Sorrento	30	C 5
St	Osborne Park	60	A 1
St	Tuart Hill	60	B 1
St	Yokine	60	D 1

CAPEL
| Me | Merriwa | 11 | C 10 |
| Pl | Morley | 48 | C 6 |

CAPERTON
| Ct | Ferndale | 84 | D 8 |

		Map	Ref.
CAPILANO			
Ave	Yanchep	4	E 2
CAPILL			
Cnr	Leeming	93	D 9
CAPITAL			
Dr	Malaga	33	C 9
CAPLE			
St	Willagee	91	E 4
CAPORN			
St	Crawley	72	A 9
St	Mosman Park	81	A 7
St	Wanneroo	21	A 4
St	Wanneroo	20	D 4
CAPPER			
Pl	Kardinya	92	A 9
CAPRELLA			
St	Heathridge	23	E 1
CAPRI			
Pl	Dianella	47	B 6
Pl	Safety Bay	145	B 1
CAPRICE			
Pl	Heathridge	19	C 9
Pl	Willetton	93	D 2
St	Swan View	51	C 4
CAPSTONE			
Wy	Marangaroo	32	C 5
CAPTAIN			
Ct	Heathridge	23	C 2
CAPTIVITY			
Wy	Iluka	18	E 5
CAPULET			
St	Coolbellup	102	A 1
St	Coolbellup	101	E 1
CARA			
Rd	Greenmount	51	B 10
CARABEEN			
Pl	Halls Head	164	B 4
Rd	Maddington	96	B 4
CARABOODA			
Rd	Carabooda	9	A 5
Rd	Carabooda	8	E 5
CARACAS			
Cl	Safety Bay	137	B 9
CARAMA			
St	Wanneroo	20	D 9
CARATTI			
Rd	Henderson	111	D 9
CARAVEL			
Wy	Halls Head	164	B 2
CARAWATHA			
Ave	Armadale	116	E 3
Rd	Parkerville	53	C 6
CARBERRY			
Sq	Clarkson	14	D 2
CARBINE			
St	Ascot	62	D 9
CARBON			
Ct	Osborne Park	59	D 1
CARBRIDGE			
Wy	Duncraig	31	A 6
CARCOO			
Ct	Beckenham	85	B 7
CARCOOLA			
Ct	Nollamara	46	C 5
St	Nollamara	46	C 5
CARDEW			
St	Melville	91	D 2
CARDIFF			
St	E Victoria Pk	74	A 8
CARDIGAN			
Cl	Coodanup	165	C 3
St	Hamilton Hill	100	E 1
Tce	Jolimont	71	E 1
CARDIN			
Ri	Greenfields	163	E 10
CARDINAL			
Cr	Leeming	93	B 8

		Map	Ref.
CARDINGTON			
Wy	Huntingdale	95	D 9
CARDOC			
St	Lynwood	94	C 3
CARDUP SIDING			
Rd	Cardup	135	B 6
Rd	Cardup	134	E 6
CARDWELL			
Ave	Noranda	48	A 5
CAREENING			
Wy	Coogee	100	E 10
CAREW			
Pl	Chidlow	42	C 10
Pl	Greenwood	31	D 5
CAREY			
Ct	Kingsley	31	B 3
Pl	Cooloongup	137	C 10
Pl	Gosnells	106	B 2
St	Kensington	73	C 9
St	Willagee	91	E 4
CARFAX			
Pl	Two Rocks	2	C 2
CARGILL			
St	Victoria Park	73	D 7
CARIBBEAN			
Dr	Safety Bay	145	B 1
CARIDEAN			
St	Heathridge	19	D 10
St	Heathridge	23	E 1
CARINA			
Ci	Halls Head	164	C 1
Cl	Rockingham	137	A 7
CARINDA			
Pl	Alexander Hts	33	A 5
CARINYA			
Pl	City Beach	58	D 5
CARINYAH			
Rd	Canning Mills	99	C 5
Rd	Pickering Bk	99	B 2
Rd	Pickering Bk	109	D 2
Rd	Pickering Bk	99	D 10
CARISBROOKE			
St	Maddington	96	B 4
CARISSA			
Wy	Forrestfield	76	B 9
CARLETON			
Cr	Forrestfield	86	D 1
CARLISLE			
Rd	Kalamunda	78	A 8
St	Shoalwater	144	C 1
St	Shoalwater	136	C 10
CARLOW			
Ci	Waterford	83	C 6
CARLSON			
Pl	Banjup	113	D 3
Pl	Booragoon	92	D 1
CARLTON			
Pl	Swan View	51	C 6
St	Leederville	60	C 9
CARLUKE			
Pl	Warwick	31	C 3
CARLYLE			
Cr	Duncraig	31	A 6
CARMAN			
Wy	Bassendean	48	E 10
CARMEL			
Rd	Carmel	88	A 6
Rd E	Carmel	88	C 7
CARMEN			
Ct	Joondalup	19	C 3
CARMICK			
Wy	Ferndale	84	D 9
CARMIGNANI			
Rd	Gnangara	25	D 1
Rd	Gnangara	21	D 10
CARMIL			
Pl	Alexander Hts	33	A 5

		Map	Ref.
CARMODY			
Ce	Gosnells	106	A 2
Rd	Waikiki	145	D 1
St	Hamilton Hill	101	C 1
Wy	Bull Creek	93	A 5
CARNABY			
Pl	Alexander Hts	33	B 3
CARNAC			
Cl	Riverton	94	B 1
Ct	Gosnells	96	A 10
St	Fremantle	90	C 7
CARNARVON			
Cr	Coolbinia	60	E 4
Ri	Ocean Reef	19	A 9
St	E Victoria Pk	74	A 8
CARNATION			
Pl	Yangebup	101	D 10
CARNEGIE			
Lp	Cooloongup	137	D 10
Rd	Bassendean	63	B 3
Wy	Padbury	23	D 9
CARNEY			
Rd	Welshpool	85	D 3
CARNOUSTIE			
Ct	Yanchep	4	E 2
Gns	Meadow Sprgs	163	D 5
CARNWRATH			
Wy	Duncraig	31	A 7
CAROB			
Pl	Greenwood	31	E 3
CAROB TREE			
Pl	Lesmurdie	87	D 4
CAROLE			
Rd	Maddington	95	E 2
CAROLINE			
Grn	Marangaroo	32	C 5
St	Armadale	116	E 3
Wy	Madora	160	D 8
CAROLYN			
Pl	Forrestfield	76	A 6
CARON			
Pl	Mandurah	165	A 4
CARONIA			
Grn	Iluka	18	E 3
CAROSA			
Rd	Wanneroo	20	C 3
CAROUSEL			
Rd	Cannington	84	E 6
CARPENE			
Pl	Kalamunda	77	E 10
CARPENTER			
Rt	Leda	139	C 3
CARPUL			
Pl	Waikiki	145	D 2
CARR			
Cr	Warwick	31	D 7
Pl	Leederville	60	D 9
Pl	Myaree	91	E 3
St	Hilton	91	A 8
St	South Perth	73	A 9
St	West Perth	60	D 9
CARRADALE			
Gl	Hillarys	23	A 10
Me	Erskine	164	C 5
CARRADINE			
Rd	Armadale	117	A 4
Rd	Bedfordale	117	C 6
CARRAMAR			
Dr	Kalamunda	77	A 4
Rd	Neerabup	15	E 8
St	Joondanna	60	D 3
CARRICK			
Rd	Armadale	116	E 7
St	Woodlands	59	B 2
Wy	Waterford	83	C 6
CARRIGG			
Cr	Kelmscott	116	E 2
CARRINGAL			
Pl	Armadale	116	C 3

		Map	Ref.
CARRINGTON			
St	Fremantle	91	A 5
St	Hamilton Hill	101	A 2
St	Hilton	91	A 5
St	Inglewood	61	D 6
St	Mt Lawley	61	C 6
St	Nedlands	71	C 8
St	North Perth	60	D 5
St	O'Connor	91	A 5
St	Palmyra	91	A 4
CARRIPAN			
Rd	Landsdale	32	C 1
CARROLL			
Dr	Bicton	81	B 6
St	Applecross	82	B 8
St	Ardross	82	B 8
St	Dalkeith	81	D 4
CARRON			
Rd	Applecross	82	D 4
Ri	Hillarys	30	B 1
CARROO			
Hts	Ocean Reef	18	E 8
CARSON			
Ave	Gosnells	96	B 9
Ct	Gosnells	106	A 3
Pl	Heathridge	19	C 9
Rd	Malaga	47	C 1
St	E Victoria Pk	84	A 1
St	Stoneville	54	C 2
CARSTAIRS			
Ct	Beechboro	49	A 3
Rd	Darlington	66	B 3
CARTER			
St	Halls Head	164	D 1
St	Hamilton Hill	101	A 1
St	Hamilton Hill	91	A 10
St	Maddington	96	C 4
CARTERTON			
Pl	Padbury	30	E 1
CARTHAGE			
Rd	Falcon	162A	B 3
Vs	Currambine	19	A 3
CARTMELL			
Wy	Balga	32	B 8
CARTWRIGHT			
Rd	Balga	32	B 9
CARUSO			
Ct	Kenwick	95	E 2
CARVEL			
Pl	Ocean Reef	23	B 2
CARVIE			
St	Hillman	137	D 6
CARWOOD			
Cr	Henley Brook	36	A 4
CARY			
Grn	Bateman	92	E 4
St	Munster	101	C 9
CARYOTA			
Ct	Warnbro	145	E 2
CASCADE			
Ave	Dianella	46	E 9
Cl	Safety Bay	136	E 10
Cl	Woodvale	24	C 7
Hts	Ballajura	33	D 7
CASELLA			
Pl	Wandi	123	B 7
CASEY			
Ct	Kingsley	24	D 10
St	Cloverdale	75	A 2
CASHEL			
Wy	Waterford	83	C 6
CASILDA			
Pl	Cooloongup	137	C 9
Rd	Duncraig	30	E 3
St	Falcon	162A	D 9
CASINO			
Rd	Glen Forrest	66	E 3
St	Welshpool	85	B 1
St	Welshpool	75	B 10

For detailed information regarding the street referencing system used in this book, turn to page 170.

185

C

		Map	Ref.
CASMA			
Ct	Ferndale	84	D 9
Gr	Ballajura	33	C 5
CASPAR			
Pl	Madora	160	D 7
Rd	Madora	160	D 7
CASPIAN			
Me	Waikiki	145	C 4
Ri	Greenfields	163	D 9
Wy	Brigadoon	169	A 5
CASSARD			
Ct	Ferndale	84	D 8
CASSERLEY			
Ave	Girrawheen	32	C 8
Rd	Rockingham	136	E 9
Wy	Orelia	131	C 9
CASSERLY			
Dr	Leeming	102	E 1
Dr	Leeming	92	E 10
CASSIA			
Dr	Karnup	157	C 10
Dr	Karnup	159	D 1
Pl	Thornlie	95	A 9
St	Greenwood	31	C 4
Wy	Morley	48	D 6
CASSIDY			
Pl	Murdoch	92	C 7
Rd	Thornlie	95	B 5
CASSILDA			
Wy	Two Rocks	2	C 2
CASSILIS			
Ct	Greenfields	163	E 10
CASSINIA			
Rd	Duncraig	30	E 6
CASSIO			
Pl	Hamilton Hill	101	B 3
CASSOTI			
Rd	Karragullen	109	B 7
CASSOWARY			
Dr	Ballajura	34	A 9
Dr	Ballajura	33	D 9
Rd	High Wycombe	64	C 10
CASTAWAY			
Ct	Sorrento	30	C 4
CASTELLA			
Dr	Dudley Park	165	C 5
Wy	Mullaloo	23	A 3
CASTELLON			
Cr	Coogee	100	E 9
CASTILE			
St	Wembley Dns	59	A 5
CASTILLO			
Ri	Mirrabooka	47	B 1
CASTILLOA			
Ct	Halls Head	164	B 7
CASTLE			
Ct	Forrestfield	86	D 1
Ct	Kallaroo	23	B 8
Ct	Thornlie	95	C 7
Pl	Armadale	116	D 5
Rd	Serpentine	155	B 1
Rd	Woodlands	59	B 2
St	North Beach	44	C 1
Wy	Lathlain	74	A 4
CASTLECOVE			
Wy	Yanchep	4	E 2
CASTLECRAG			
Dr	Kallaroo	23	A 8
CASTLEFERN			
Wy	Duncraig	31	A 5
CASTLEGATE			
Wy	Woodvale	24	B 4
CASTLEMAIN			
Hts	Leeming	93	C 9
CASTLEREAGH			
Ci	Port Kennedy	156	D 2
Cl	Willetton	93	C 6
CASTLE ROCK			
Tn	Joondalup	19	C 3

		Map	Ref.
CASTLEROSE			
Ri	Kelmscott	106	E 6
CASTLEROY			
Pl	Connolly	19	A 6
CASTLETON			
St	Balcatta	46	A 6
CASTLEWARD			
Pl	Erskine	164	C 6
CASUARINA			
Ct	Canning Vale	94	C 10
Dr	Halls Head	164	A 5
Pl	Henley Brook	36	A 4
Rd	Casuarina	132	D 9
Rd	Maida Vale	77	A 1
Rd	Sawyers Valley	55	E 9
Wy	Morley	48	C 5
Wy	Wanneroo	21	C 9
CASULA			
Ave	Coodanup	165	D 4
CASWELL			
Ct	Marangaroo	32	D 6
CATALANO			
Rd	Canning Vale	94	A 6
Rd	Canning Vale	93	E 8
CATALINA			
St	Safety Bay	145	B 2
CATALPA			
Cr	South Lake	102	C 5
CATAMBRO			
Wy	Waikiki	145	C 1
CATANIA			
Ct	Mindarie	14	B 3
CATENARY			
Ct	Mullaloo	23	C 4
CATESBY			
St	City Beach	58	D 7
CATHEDRAL			
Ave	Brigadoon	168	C 5
Ave	Millendon	29	E 7
Ave	Perth City	1C	A 3
Ave	Perth City	73	A 3
CATHERINE			
Cl	Woodvale	24	B 7
Pl	Lesmurdie	87	C 2
St	Bedford	61	D 3
St	Bentley	84	C 2
St	Byford	135	D 1
St	Morley	61	E 1
St	Safety Bay	136	D 10
St	Subiaco	72	B 1
CATHRYN			
Pl	Willetton	94	A 3
St	Halls Head	162	C 10
CATLIN			
Ct	Gosnells	95	E 9
CATO			
Pl	Lockridge	49	B 7
St	Glendalough	60	A 5
CATRINE			
Ct	Kingsley	24	C 9
CAULFIELD			
Cl	Willetton	93	E 3
CAUSEWAY			
	East Perth	73	C 5
CAVALAIRE			
Me	Port Kennedy	156	D 1
CAVALIER			
Ct	Thornlie	95	C 7
CAVAN			
St	Bicton	81	B 9
CAVE			
Pl	Bull Creek	93	B 6
CAVELL			
Pl	Huntingdale	95	D 9
CAVELLA			
Ct	Willetton	93	E 2
CAVENDER			
St	Singleton	160	D 3

		Map	Ref.
CAVENDISH			
Ce	Mt Claremont	71	A 4
St	Highgate	61	A 9
Wy	Lynwood	94	B 3
CAVERSHAM			
Ave	Caversham	50	A 6
Ave	Caversham	49	D 5
St	Perth City	1C	B 1
St	Perth City	73	B 1
CAWARRA			
Cr	Craigie	23	D 5
CAWSTON			
Rd	Attadale	81	C 7
CAXTON			
Rd	Claremont	71	B 10
CAYLEY			
St	Glendalough	60	A 4
Wy	Midvale	51	A 6
CAYUGA			
Pl	Joondalup	19	C 1
CECELIA			
Rd	Caversham	50	A 5
CECIL			
Ave	Cannington	84	E 6
Pl	Hamersley	31	E 9
Rd	Gnangara	26	D 7
Rd	Pinjar	17	A 3
St	Glen Forrest	66	D 3
CEDAR			
Ct	Mirrabooka	33	B 10
Ct	Spearwood	101	A 4
Pl	Beechboro	48	E 3
Pl	Mullaloo	23	A 4
Pl	Woodlands	59	C 3
St	Bayswater	48	C 10
Wy	Forrestfield	76	B 10
Wy	Maddington	96	C 5
CEDERDALE			
Wy	Safety Bay	137	A 9
CEDRIC			
St	Balcatta	45	E 5
St	Innaloo	45	D 9
St	Stirling	45	E 6
CEDUNA			
Cl	Currambine	19	A 4
CEDUS			
Pl	Menora	61	A 3
CELEBRATION			
St	Beckenham	85	C 6
CELESTINE			
St	Wanneroo	20	D 10
CELIA			
Pl	Coogee	100	E 10
Pl	Duncraig	30	D 3
CELINA			
Cr	Kingsley	31	C 3
CELOSIA			
Wy	Ferndale	94	B 1
CELTIC			
Pl	Kallaroo	23	B 6
CELTIS			
Pl	Lynwood	94	B 2
CEMY			
Pl	Kewdale	74	C 7
CENTAUR			
Gns	Heathridge	19	C 9
St	Kallaroo	23	B 5
St	Riverton	93	C 1
CENTAURUS			
St	Rockingham	137	A 7
CENTENARY			
Ave	Wilson	84	A 7
Ave	Wilson	83	E 6
Dr	Rowethorpe	144	
CENTENNIAL			
Gns	Hillarys	30	A 1
Gns	Hillarys	23	A 10

		Map	Ref.
CENTRAL			
Ave	Ardross	82	D 9
Ave	Beaconsfield	91	A 8
Ave	Hazelmere	64	B 2
Ave	Inglewood	61	C 6
Ave	Maylands	61	D 8
Ave	Menora	61	B 4
Ave	Mt Lawley	61	B 5
Ave	Mt Pleasant	82	D 9
Ave	Redcliffe	63	A 7
Ave	Redcliffe	62	E 7
Ave	Swanbourne	70	E 8
Rd	Kalamunda	77	D 7
Rd	Rossmoyne	93	A 1
Tce	Beckenham	85	B 7
CENTRE			
Rd	Kelmscott	106	D 5
Rd	Westfield	106	C 5
St	Queens Park	84	E 3
St	Shenton Park	71	E 4
CEPHALOTUS			
Rd	Walliston	88	A 2
CERBERUS			
Ave	Lynwood	94	B 2
CERES			
Pl	Coolbellup	101	E 2
CERI			
Cl	Port Kennedy	156	D 4
CERUTTY			
St	Huntingdale	95	D 10
CERVANTES			
Lp	Yangebup	112	A 1
Lp	Yangebup	102	A 10
Pl	Sorrento	30	B 4
CESTRUM			
Ri	South Lake	102	C 5
CETUS			
Ce	Kingsley	31	B 2
Ct	Rockingham	137	B 7
CHACO			
Wy	Willetton	93	E 2
CHAD			
St	Greenfields	165	D 1
Wy	Joondalup	19	D 2
CHADD			
Pl	Wembley Dns	59	A 4
CHADLINGTON			
Dr	Padbury	31	A 2
CHADSTONE			
Rd	Craigie	23	D 7
Rd	Craigie	23	E 6
CHADWELL			
St	Kenwick	95	D 1
CHADWICK			
Pde	Wungong	116	B 9
St	Hilton	91	B 7
CHADWIN			
Pl	Padbury	23	E 10
CHAFFERS			
St	Morley	48	C 6
CHAILEY			
Pl	Balga	46	C 1
CHALCOMBE			
Wy	Warwick	31	D 7
CHALE			
St	Gosnells	96	A 9
CHALFONT			
Wy	Swan View	51	B 7
CHALICE			
Ri	Mirrabooka	47	B 1
CHALK HILL			
Rd	Medina	130	C 5
CHALKLEY			
Pl	Bayswater	62	C 1
CHALLENGE			
Blvd	Wangara	25	B 7
Pl	Balcatta	46	A 2

		Map	Ref.
CHALLENGER			
Ave	Kwinana Twn	C 131	A 8
Ave	Manning	83	B 7
Ave	Morley	48	D 6
Ave	Parmelia	131	A 8
Dr	Thornlie	95	C 8
Pde	City Beach	70	D 8
Pde	City Beach	58	C 10
Pde	Iluka	18	D 5
Pl	Melville	91	D 3
Rd	Madora	160	D 7
Ri	Coogee	110	E 1
CHALLIS			
Rd	Armadale	116	C 3
CHALMERS			
Ave	Waikiki	145	C 3
Ct	Mindarie	10	B 2
Pl	Leeming	93	A 8
St	Fremantle	90	D 5
CHALWELL			
St	Rockingham	136	D 5
CHAMBERLAIN			
Ci	Bateman	92	E 4
Pl	Heathridge	19	C 9
Rd	Rivervale	74	B 4
St	Cottesloe	80	D 1
St	Gosnells	106	A 3
St	Gosnells	105	D 2
St	North Perth	60	D 7
St	O'Connor	91	C 7
Wy	Armadale	116	A 3
CHAMBERS			
Wy	Noranda	47	E 5
CHAMBON			
Ce	Coodanup	165	D 4
CHAMPION			
Dr	Armadale	106	A 10
Dr	Armadale	116	B 1
Rd	Lesmurdie	87	B 5
CHAMPIONS			
Ct	Connolly	19	C 8
CHAMPLIN			
Wy	Ferndale	84	C 9
CHANCELLOR			
St	Claremont	71	B 7
CHANCERY			
Cr	Bull Creek	93	B 7
Cr	Willetton	93	B 7
Ct	Forrestfield	86	D 2
Ct	Port Kennedy	156	D 1
Ct	Thornlie	95	B 8
La	Alexander Hts	33	B 5
La	Willetton	93	B 6
CHANDILLA			
St	Gosnells	106	A 4
St	Gosnells	105	E 3
CHANDLER			
Av E	Floreat	59	C 9
Av W	Floreat	59	B 9
Cl	Wellard	140	B 1
Pl	Floreat	59	C 9
Rd	Sorrento	30	C 4
CHANDOS			
Pl	Swan View	51	C 7
Wy	Greenwood	31	D 4
CHANGTON			
Wy	Balga	46	D 4
CHANNAR			
Ri	Duncraig	31	A 3
CHANNEL			
Dr	Heathridge	19	C 10
CHANNON			
St	Bentley	84	D 4
St	Cannington	84	D 4
CHANTILLY			
Tce	Meadow Sprgs	163	C 2
Wy	Connolly	19	B 8
CHANTRY			
Pl	Kiara	48	E 6
CHAPARRAL			
Cr	Willetton	93	D 7

For detailed information regarding the street referencing system used in this book, turn to page 170.

C

		Map	Ref.
CHAPEL			
Ct	Kingsley	24	D 9
CHAPLIN			
Ct	Hillarys	23	A 9
CHAPMAN			
Rd	Bentley	84	C 5
Rd	Calista	130	E 8
Rd	Cannington	84	C 6
Rd	St James	84	B 3
St	Bassendean	63	A 3
St	Bassendean	62	E 3
St	East Perth	61	B 10
St	Swan View	51	C 5
CHAPPEL			
St	Dianella	61	C 2
CHARACIN			
Ct	Sorrento	30	C 3
CHARDONNAY			
Gr	Armadale	116	E 4
CHARENTE			
Cl	Port Kennedy	156	D 1
CHARF			
Ct	Riverton	93	E 1
CHARING			
Cr	Marangaroo	32	A 6
CHARLBURY			
Wy	Eden Hill	48	E 8
CHARLES			
Ct	Woodvale	24	B 7
La	Mt Claremont	71	A 5
Rd	Mahogany Crk	67	C 2
St	Bentley	84	C 2
St	Byford	126	D 10
St	Cottesloe	80	D 1
St	E Rockingham	129	D 9
St	E Rockingham	129	E 10
St	Karrinyup	45	B 5
St	Kelmscott	106	E 8
St	Maida Vale	76	E 1
St	Maylands	61	E 6
St	Midland	50	C 7
St	North Perth	60	E 7
St	Shenton Park	71	D 5
St	South Perth	72	E 8
St	Sth Fremantle	90	C 8
St	West Perth	60	E 10
CHARLESON			
St	Myaree	92	A 1
CHARLES RILEY			
Rd	North Beach	44	D 3
Rd	Trigg	44	D 4
CHARLESWORTH			
St	Gosnells	106	C 2
CHARLOTTE			
Ce	Joondalup	19	C 3
CHARLTON			
Ct	Kingsley	31	B 2
Pl	Thornlie	95	D 3
Rd	Kewdale	74	D 6
CHARLWOOD			
Wy	Morley	47	D 7
CHARNLEY			
Cl	Gosnells	106	A 2
CHARNWOOD			
Ave	Two Rocks	2	C 2
Pl	Two Rocks	2	C 2
St	Morley	48	A 9
CHARON			
Pl	Craigie	23	E 7
Rd	Falcon	162A	B 3
CHARONIA			
Rd	Mullaloo	23	A 4
CHARRINGTON			
Ct	Leeming	102	E 1
CHARSLEY			
Cr	Marmion	30	C 8
St	Willagee	92	A 4
St	Willagee	91	E 4

		Map	Ref.
CHARTHOUSE			
Rd	Safety Bay	145	B 1
Rd	Waikiki	145	C 3
CHARTWELL			
Pl	Leeming	103	B 1
Wy	Swan View	51	D 7
CHASE			
Ct	Langford	94	E 2
Ct	Woodvale	24	B 8
Wy	Balcatta	46	B 4
CHASLEY			
Ct	Westfield	116	B 1
CHAT			
Pl	Yangebup	102	A 8
CHATAWAY			
Rd	Girrawheen	32	E 8
CHATEAU			
Pl	Belhus	29	B 2
CHATFIELD			
Rd	Serpentine	155	B 6
CHATHAM			
Rd	Midland	50	A 9
St	Inglewood	61	C 4
CHATSWORTH			
Rd	Highgate	61	A 9
Tce	Claremont	71	A 3
CHATTON			
St	Dianella	47	B 9
CHAUCER			
Cl	Spearwood	101	B 9
St	Yokine	61	A 2
Wy	Kalamunda	77	D 5
CHAUNCEY			
Ct	Kingsley	31	C 1
Pl	Beechboro	49	B 4
CHAUNCY			
St	East Fremantle	80	E 10
CHEAM			
Pl	Morley	47	D 6
CHEDDAR			
Pl	Karrinyup	44	E 5
CHEDWORTH			
Wy	Eden Hill	48	E 8
CHELLASTON			
Cr	Carine	30	E 9
CHELLS			
Ct	Thornlie	95	D 5
CHELMER			
Wy	Willetton	93	E 3
CHELMORTON			
Lp	Carine	44	E 1
Lp	Carine	30	E 10
CHELMSFORD			
Ave	Port Kennedy	156	D 1
Rd	Mt Lawley	61	A 8
Rd	North Perth	61	A 8
CHELSEA			
Ct	Dianella	47	D 8
Ct	Kingsley	24	B 9
St	Perth City	1C	B 1
St	Perth City	73	B 1
CHELSFIELD			
St	Gosnells	96	A 8
CHELSFORD			
Rd	Warwick	31	D 7
CHELTENHAM			
St	West Swan	35	B 10
St	Yanchep	4	E 2
CHENARD			
St	Carine	45	A 1
CHENEY			
Ct	Swan View	51	B 8
Vl	Clarkson	14	C 2
CHENILE			
Me	Mirrabooka	47	A 2
CHENIN			
La	Ellenbrook	29	D 1

		Map	Ref.
CHENNILE			
Vs	Halls Head	164	A 6
CHEPSTOW			
Dr	Mandurah	163	A 10
CHERITON			
St	Perth City	1C	B 1
St	Perth City	73	B 1
CHERITONS			
Pl	Armadale	116	C 4
CHEROKEE			
Rd	Jandakot	103	C 2
CHERRY			
Ct	Morley	48	C 9
Gr	Maida Vale	64	E 8
Rd	Woodlands	59	C 2
Wy	Westfield	106	B 7
CHERRY HILLS			
Cr	Connolly	19	C 6
Rt	Meadow Sprgs	163	C 5
CHERRYWOOD			
Ave	Dianella	47	B 4
CHERTLEY			
St	Morley	48	A 9
CHERTSEY			
St	Mt Lawley	61	C 9
CHERUB			
Cl	Ballajura	33	D 6
Vs	Currambine	19	A 4
CHERWELL			
Ave	Beechboro	48	C 3
CHESAPEAKE			
Ct	Iluka	19	A 6
CHESHAM			
Wy	Hamilton Hill	100	E 2
CHESNEY			
St	Morley	48	B 6
CHESSELL			
Dr	Duncraig	30	E 8
Rd	Curtin Uni	135	
CHESSINGTON			
Gns	Mt Claremont	71	A 5
Wy	Kingsley	31	B 2
CHESSON			
Pl	Riverton	93	C 1
St	Alfred Cove	82	A 10
St	Dianella	46	E 8
CHESTER			
Ave	Dianella	47	B 10
Ave	Two Rocks	2	D 2
Ct	Forrestfield	86	C 1
Ct	Orelia	131	B 6
Pl	Beechboro	49	B 4
Rd	Claremont	71	B 10
St	Sth Fremantle	90	D 8
St	Subiaco	72	B 3
Wy	Rockingham	137	A 8
CHESTERFIELD			
Rd	E Rockingham	138	A 1
Rd	Mirrabooka	46	E 3
CHESTERS			
Wy	Winthrop	92	B 4
CHESTERTON			
Dr	Thornlie	95	B 8
Rd	Bassendean	48	D 10
Rd	Bassendean	62	E 1
St	Spearwood	101	C 9
CHESTNUT			
Gr	Mirrabooka	47	B 1
Pl	Beechboro	48	C 4
Pl	South Lake	102	C 6
Ri	Jarrahdale	152	C 10
Ri	Halls Head	164	B 4
CHETWYND			
Wy	Booragoon	92	C 3
CHEVALIER			
Wy	Thornlie	95	A 5
CHEVENING			
Pl	Beckenham	85	C 8

		Map	Ref.
CHEVIN			
Rd	Roleystone	108	B 4
Rd	Roleystone	107	C 4
CHEVIOT			
Pl	Dianella	47	D 7
St	Dianella	47	C 7
CHEYNE			
Cl	Thornlie	95	A 6
Wk	Applecross	82	B 8
CHIBA			
Rt	Merriwa	10	B 9
CHICA			
Ct	Karawara	83	D 4
CHICH			
Pl	Cannington	84	E 5
CHICHESTER			
Dr	Woodvale	24	B 5
Wy	Nollamara	46	D 5
CHICORY			
Pl	Thornlie	95	A 8
CHICQUITA			
Pl	Wanneroo	21	A 9
CHIDDINGTON			
St	Beckenham	85	C 9
CHIDLEY			
Pl	Rockingham	137	A 7
Pl	Yanchep	4	E 1
Rd	City Beach	58	D 6
Wy	Mosman Park	81	A 7
CHIDLOW			
St	Mt Helena	55	C 4
CHIDZEY			
Dr	Armadale	116	A 4
Dr	Armadale	115	E 4
CHIFLEY			
Pl	Huntingdale	95	C 10
CHIGWELL			
Pl	Carine	31	C 9
CHILCOTT			
Pl	Calista	130	E 7
St	Calista	130	E 7
CHILENA			
Pl	Madora	160	D 6
CHILGROVE			
Wy	Balga	46	C 2
CHILHAM			
Cl	Marangaroo	32	A 6
Pl	Gosnells	96	A 8
CHILKO			
Ct	Joondalup	19	D 3
CHILTON			
St	Willagee	91	E 4
CHILVER			
St	Kewdale	75	C 5
CHINE			
Ct	Ocean Reef	23	A 1
Pl	Hamersley	31	E 9
St	Mosman Park	81	A 6
CHINN			
Rd	Karrakatta	71	C 5
Rd	Shenton Park	71	C 4
CHINTA			
St	Wanneroo	20	C 10
CHIPALA			
Ct	Ballajura	33	C 4
Ct	Edgewater	24	B 3
Rd	Balga	46	C 4
CHIPLA			
Wy	Lynwood	94	B 3
CHIPPER			
Cl	Bedfordale	128	A 5
Cl	Leeming	93	C 10
St	Mundaring	68	B 1
St	Mundaring	54	B 10
Vw	Parmelia	131	C 7
CHIPPING			
Rd	City Beach	58	D 4
Rd	City Beach	58	D 6

		Map	Ref.
CHIRAZ			
St	Greenmount	65	B 1
CHIRETON			
Pl	Beechboro	49	B 4
CHISHAM			
Ave	Kwinana Twn C	131	A 7
Ave	Parmelia	131	A 7
CHISHOLM			
Cr	Wattle Grove	85	E 1
Cr	Wattle Grove	75	E 10
Wy	Balga	32	B 10
CHISLEHURST			
Rd	Lesmurdie	87	B 2
CHISWICK			
Pl	Kingsley	24	C 10
St	Riverton	93	E 1
St	Wembley Dns	58	E 5
CHITON			
Pl	Heathridge	19	D 10
CHITTAWARRA			
Ct	Glen Forrest	66	C 1
Ct	Glen Forrest	52	C 1
CHITTY			
Rd	Pinjar	17	A 1
CHIVALRY			
Wy	Thornlie	95	C 7
CHIVERS			
Ct	Samson	91	C 7
CHIVERTON			
Pl	Beldon	23	E 3
CHOBHAM			
Wy	Morley	47	D 6
CHOKOLICH			
St	Wangara	24	E 6
CHONJU			
Rd	Karrakatta	71	C 5
CHOSELEY			
Pl	Langford	94	E 2
CHOULES			
Pl	Myaree	92	A 2
CHRISP			
Pl	Yanchep	4	C 5
CHRISTCHURCH			
Tce	Currambine	19	C 5
CHRISTENSEN			
St	Kardinya	92	A 7
CHRISTIAN			
Ct	Bayswater	62	B 3
CHRISTIE			
Ct	Wanneroo	20	C 10
Ct	Yangebup	101	E 10
CHRISTINA			
Ct	Craigie	23	E 6
Pde	Nth Fremantle	80	C 9
Pl	Lesmurdie	87	E 4
St	Hazelmere	50	A 10
St	Hazelmere	64	B 1
CHRISTINE			
Cr	Spearwood	100	E 7
CHRISTISON			
Wy	Rockingham	137	A 6
CHRISTMAS			
Ave	Heathridge	19	B 9
Ave	Orelia	131	A 5
CHRISTMAS TREE			
Ave	Rowethorpe	144	
CHRISTOPHER			
Cl	Willetton	93	E 5
CHRISTOWE			
Dr	Swan View	51	C 7
CHRYSOSTOM			
St	North Beach	44	C 4
St	Trigg	44	C 4
CHUDITCH			
Cl	Wungong	116	C 9
CHUDLEIGH			
St	Fremantle	90	E 4

C

		Map	Ref.
CHUNG WAH			
La	Northbridge	1C	E 1
CHURCH			
Ave	Armadale	116	D 7
La	Claremont	71	A 9
La	Como	83	A 6
Rd	Maddington	95	E 3
Rw	Perth City	72	D 2
Rw	West Perth	1C	D 2
St	Kelmscott	106	E 9
St	Perth City	60	E 10
St	Wanneroo	20	C 8
CHURCHDOWN			
St	Thornlie	95	C 5
CHURCHER			
Rd	Baldivis	157	E 7
CHURCHILL			
Ave	Mandurah	165	A 2
Ave	Shoalwater	136	C 8
Ave	Subiaco	72	B 1
Dr	Swan View	51	C 7
Pl	Shoalwater	136	C 8
CHURCHILL EAST			
Ave	Munster	111	C 3
CHURCHILL WEST			
Ave	Munster	111	B 3
CHURCHLANDS			
Ave	Churchlands	59	B 5
CHURCHMAN BROOK			
Rd	Bedfordale	118	A 6
Rd	Bedfordale	117	D 6
CHURM			
St	Hamilton Hill	91	B 10
CHURNSIDE			
Ct	Yanchep	3	E 10
CHURT			
Pl	Morley	47	E 3
CHURTON			
Cr	Warwick	31	D 8
CHUSAN			
Ct	Warnbro	145	E 9
Grn	Iluka	18	D 4
CICADA			
Ct	Huntingdale	95	C 10
CIMBOR			
Wy	Parmelia	131	B 8
CIMBROOK			
Wy	Duncraig	31	B 7
CINGALEE			
Pl	Craigie	23	D 7
CINNABAR			
Pl	Carine	30	E 10
CINQUE PORTS			
Pl	Connolly	19	A 8
CIRCE			
Ci N	Dalkeith	81	C 2
Ci S	Dalkeith	81	C 2
CIRO			
Rd	Kelmscott	106	E 6
CIRRUS			
Ct	Willetton	93	E 2
CITRON			
Ct	Armadale	116	A 5
St	Perth City	1C	E 1
St	Perth City	72	E 1
CITRUS			
Gr	High Wycombe	64	C 10
St	Upper Swan	29	E 1
CIVIC			
Dr	Wanneroo	20	D 8
Pl	Stirling	45	D 8
CLABON			
St	Girrawheen	32	B 7
CLAIRE			
Ce	Joondalup	19	D 2
St	Forrestfield	86	D 2

		Map	Ref.
CLAISEBROOK			
Rd	East Perth	1C	B 2
Rd	East Perth	73	B 2
Rd	Perth City	1C	B 1
Rd	Perth City	73	B 1
CLAMP			
Ct	Bibra Lake	102	D 3
CLANCY			
Wy	Thornlie	95	C 4
CLANDON			
Wy	Morley	48	B 8
CLANMEL			
Rd	Floreat	59	B 9
CLAPHAM			
St	Beckenham	85	B 9
CLAPTON			
Ct	Kingsley	24	A 10
CLARA			
Rd	Hamilton Hill	101	B 1
Rd	Hamilton Hill	91	B 10
St	Byford	135	D 1
St	Gosnells	96	C 9
St	Gosnells	96	C 10
CLARE			
Ct	Winthrop	92	C 5
Rd	Hovea	53	A 10
St	Sorrento	30	C 6
CLARECASTLE			
Rt	Mindarie	14	A 4
CLAREDON			
Ct	Alexander Hts	32	E 6
CLAREMONT			
Cr	Claremont	71	A 9
Cr	Swanbourne	71	A 9
CLARENCE			
Rd	Armadale	116	D 4
Rd	Naval Base	121	A 3
Rd	Westfield	106	C 4
St	Mt Lawley	61	B 9
St	South Perth	72	E 8
St	Tuart Hill	60	B 1
St	Tuart Hill	46	B 10
Wy	Westfield	106	C 4
CLARENCE BEACH			
Rd	Henderson	110	E 6
Rd	Munster	110	E 6
CLARENDON			
Ct	Thornlie	95	B 8
St	Cottesloe	80	D 1
CLAREVILLE			
Cr	Kallaroo	23	A 6
Cr	Kallaroo	23	A 7
CLARICE			
Ave	Yokine	46	D 9
St	Langford	95	A 1
St	Mandurah	165	C 1
CLARINDA			
Ave	Orelia	131	B 5
CLARK			
Ct	Bibra Lake	101	D 5
Pl	Karrinyup	45	A 4
Pl	Orelia	131	A 4
Pl	Orelia	130	E 5
Rd	Gidgegannup	42	C 3
St	Crawley	71	E 8
St	Nedlands	71	E 8
Wy	Orelia	131	A 5
CLARKE			
Cr	Joondalup	19	D 7
Rd	Morley	48	B 9
St	E Cannington	85	A 5
St	O'Connor	91	A 6
Wy	Bassendean	63	A 3
Wy	Bateman	92	D 7
CLARKSIDE			
Ct	Wanneroo	20	C 7
CLARKSON			
Ave	Wanneroo	20	A 1
Ave	Wanneroo	16	B 10
Rd	Maylands	74	A 2

		Map	Ref.
CLASSEN			
Pl	Mirrabooka	33	A 10
CLASSON			
Gns	Leeming	103	A 1
CLAUDE			
St	Rivervale	74	A 3
CLAUGHTON			
Wy	Bassendean	63	A 4
CLAUNELLE			
Rd	Armadale	116	C 3
CLAUSE			
St	Willagee	91	D 4
CLAVERING			
Rd	Bayswater	62	B 3
CLAVERTON			
St	North Perth	60	E 8
CLAY			
Pl	Padbury	23	D 10
St	Eden Hill	49	B 8
St	Thornlie	95	B 7
CLAYBUSH			
Ct	Woodvale	24	C 7
CLAYDEN			
Ct	Swan C Homes	144	
Rd	Newburn	75	E 3
CLAYDON			
St	Willetton	93	D 7
CLAYGATE			
Rd	Hamilton Hill	100	E 3
Wy	Kingsley	31	C 3
CLAYMORE			
St	E Rockingham	129	E 9
CLAYTON			
Cl	Heathridge	23	E 2
Ct	Ferndale	84	C 9
Rd	Ferndale	84	C 10
Rd	Helena Valley	65	D 6
St	Bellevue	65	A 1
St	Bellevue	50	D 10
St	East Fremantle	91	A 1
St	East Fremantle	81	A 10
CLEARVIEW			
Ave	Yokine	46	D 10
CLEARWATER			
Pl	Hillarys	22	E 9
CLEAT			
Pl	Ocean Reef	23	A 1
CLEAVE			
Ct	Padbury	30	E 2
CLEAVER			
St	Chidlow	42	D 5
St	West Perth	60	D 9
Tce	Belmont	74	C 2
Tce	Rivervale	74	B 3
CLELAND			
Cl	Clarkson	11	D 10
St	Mt Claremont	71	A 6
CLEMATIS			
Rd	Woodlands	59	C 2
CLEMENT			
Dr	Karrinyup	45	A 2
St	Bedford	61	C 3
St	Swanbourne	70	D 9
CLEMENTI			
Rd	Mandogalup	122	C 9
CLEMENTS			
Ct	Edgewater	20	A 9
Gr	Armadale	116	C 4
Rd	Jandakot	103	A 3
Rd	Booragoon	92	B 1
Rd	Booragoon	82	B 10
CLEMROS			
Wy	Leeming	93	C 10
CLENHAM			
Wy	Westfield	106	C 10
CLENNETT			
Cl	Cooloongup	137	C 9

		Map	Ref.
CLEOPATRA			
St	Palmyra	91	B 2
CLERE			
Ri	Woodvale	24	B 4
CLERMONT			
Wy	Iluka	18	D 5
CLEVE			
Wy	Gosnells	95	E 8
CLEVEDON			
Pl	Kallaroo	23	C 7
Wy	Karrinyup	44	E 4
CLEVELAND			
Ct	Meadow Sprgs	163	C 3
St	Dianella	61	B 1
CLEWS			
St	Kardinya	91	E 7
CLIANTHUS			
Rd	Walliston	88	A 2
Wy	Koongamia	65	C 2
CLIEVEDEN			
St	North Perth	60	E 8
CLIFF			
Pl	Gosnells	96	C 9
Rd	Claremont	70	E 10
St	Fremantle	1D	B 5
St	Fremantle	90	B 5
St	Kensington	73	C 9
St	Marmion	30	C 8
St	Sorrento	30	C 7
St	West Perth	1C	D 3
St	West Perth	72	D 3
Wy	Claremont	70	E 10
CLIFFE			
St	South Perth	73	C 9
CLIFFORD			
St	Maddington	86	B 9
Vl	Hillarys	30	C 1
Wy	Bull Creek	92	E 4
Wy	Noranda	47	C 6
CLIFFSIDE			
La	Canning Vale	94	B 9
Ri	Ballajura	33	C 4
Trl	Edgewater	20	A 10
CLIFFTOP			
Ct	Edgewater	24	B 1
CLIFTON			
Cr	Mt Lawley	61	B 7
Ct	Kardinya	91	E 7
Gns	Kallaroo	23	B 2
Rd	Canning Vale	104	A 3
Rd	Canning Vale	103	E 1
Rd	Leeming	93	D 10
Rd	Parkerville	53	D 7
St	Byford	135	D 1
St	Chidlow	56	D 1
St	Kelmscott	106	E 7
St	Maddington	96	A 4
St	Nedlands	71	E 8
St	Rockingham	137	C 7
St	Scarborough	44	D 10
CLIMPING			
St	Balga	46	C 1
CLINKER			
Rd	Ocean Reef	23	B 2
CLINT			
Wy	Calista	130	D 7
CLINTON			
Ave	St James	84	A 3
St	Kingsley	31	D 3
CLIO			
St	Falcon	162A	D 10
CLIPPER			
Ct	Edgewater	20	A 10
Dr	Ballajura	33	D 7
Dr	Port Kennedy	156	D 4
Pl	Yanchep	4	C 3
Wy	Halls Head	164	B 1
CLIVE			
Rd	Cottesloe	70	E 10
Rd	Mt Lawley	61	B 8
St	Bicton	81	B 8

		Map	Ref.
St	Mt Pleasant	82	D 7
St	West Perth	72	C 1
St	West Perth	1C	D 1
CLIVERTON			
Ct	Marmion	30	C 9
CLOATES			
St	Innaloo	59	C 1
CLOISTER			
Ave	Como	83	A 7
Ave	Manning	83	B 7
CLONTARF			
Rd	Hamilton Hill	90	E 10
St	Sorrento	30	C 6
CLOTILDE			
St	East Perth	1C	B 2
St	East Perth	73	B 2
St	Mt Lawley	61	C 9
CLOVELLY			
Cr	Lynwood	84	D 10
Ct	Maida Vale	76	D 4
Rd	City Beach	58	D 6
Wy	Warnbro	145	D 7
CLOVER			
Pl	Bibra Lake	102	C 5
Sq	Girrawheen	32	B 6
CLOVERTREE			
St	Maddington	96	C 5
CLOWES			
Ct	Thornlie	95	D 4
CLUBB			
Ave	Daglish	71	D 3
Ct	Winthrop	92	A 5
St	Karrinyup	45	A 7
CLUBHOUSE			
La	Gnangara	25	E 2
CLUELOW			
Ri	Leeming	93	C 9
CLUNE			
Ave	Leederville	60	B 8
Pl	Coogee	100	E 8
St	Bayswater	62	C 3
CLYBUCCA			
Pl	Armadale	116	C 4
CLYDE			
Ave	Baldivis	146	D 8
Ave	Malaga	48	A 3
Pl	Mandurah	162	E 9
Pl	Westfield	106	C 6
Rd	Menora	61	A 5
CLYDESDALE			
St	Alfred Cove	82	A 10
St	Armadale	115	E 1
St	Como	83	A 6
St	Victoria Park	73	C 7
CLYO			
Wy	Kallaroo	23	B 6
CLYTIE			
Rd	Silver Sands	163	B 7
COACHMAN			
Ct	Leda	139	B 2
COACHWOOD			
Gns	Ballajura	33	C 4
Wy	Maddington	96	C 5
COAL			
Pl	Merriwa	11	C 10
COAST			
Rd	Beechboro	48	D 1
Rd	West Swan	50	A 1
Rd	West Swan	49	D 1
COATELAN			
Dr	Stirling	45	E 9
COATES			
St	Hamilton Hill	91	B 10
COBALT			
Pl	Koondoola	32	E 9
Pl	Riverton	94	B 1
Wy	Maddington	96	B 1
COBAR			
St	Armadale	116	B 4

188   **For detailed information regarding the street referencing system used in this book, turn to page 170.**

Map Ref.

COBB
Pl Gosnells 106 A 2
St Doubleview 59 A 2
St Scarborough 58 D 2
COBBLE
Ct Bibra Lake 102 C 5
COBBLER
Pl Mirrabooka 47 A 5
COBBLERS
Rd Falcon 162A B 4
Rd Falcon 162A D 10
COBBY
La Baldivis 147 C 1
La Baldivis 139 D 10
COBDEN
St Bayswater 62 C 5
COBHAM
Ave Nollamara 46 D 7
Pl Marangaroo 32 A 3
Wy Westfield 106 B 8
COBINE
Ri Parmelia 131 A 9
St Spearwood 101 C 6
Wy Greenwood 31 E 6
COBRADAH
Cl Lesmurdie 87 B 5
Wy Kingsley 31 D 3
COBURG
St Forrestfield 76 D 10
COCHRAM
Ct Mt Claremont 71 A 4
COCKATOO
Ct High Wycombe 64 B 10
Dr Mundaring 68 C 1
Pl Wungong 116 B 9
COCKBURN
Rd Coogee 100 E 9
Rd Hamilton Hill 100 D 2
Rd Henderson 121 A 1
Rd Henderson 110 E 8
Rd Munster 110 E 3
Rd Spearwood 100 E 7
COCKLE
Pl Mullaloo 23 B 4
COCKLESHELL
Gr Padbury 30 E 2
COCKMAN
Cro Stratton 51 A 4
Rd Greenwood 31 E 4
Wy Orelia 131 A 4
COCKPIT
Wy Ocean Reef 23 A 2
COCKRAM
Pl Beechboro 49 A 5
Rd Kelmscott 106 D 6
Rd Martin 96 E 9
Rd Orange Grove 97 B 6
St Cannington 84 E 7
St Mundijong 142 E 8
COCOS
Ct Warnbro 145 E 9
Dr Bibra Lake 102 A 7
Dr Bibra Lake 101 E 7
Gr Kiara 48 D 7
Pl Marangaroo 32 D 4
St Maddington 96 B 5
COD
Wy Burns 18 D 3
CODY
St Wilson 84 A 6
Wy Clarkson 14 D 3
COFFEY
Pl Koondoola 33 A 9
Rd Banjup 113 C 9
Rd Belmont 62 D 10
Rd Serpentine 154 D 8
St Singleton 160 D 3
COGHLAN
Rd Subiaco 72 B 2

Map Ref.

COGLAN
Cl Murdoch 92 D 6
COHEN
Pl Beechboro 49 B 5
COHN
Pl Hillarys 30 B 2
St Carlisle 74 C 10
St Kewdale 74 D 8
COHUNA
Dr Armadale 116 C 6
COIPASA
Pl Joondalup 19 C 3
COLAC
Pl Kalamunda 77 B 6
Wy Duncraig 30 E 3
COLAHAN
Wy Ferndale 84 E 9
COLBERT
Rd Willetton 93 B 7
COLBY
Wy Thornlie 95 B 3
COLDLAKE
Ct Joondalup 19 D 3
COLDSTREAM
Cc Merriwa 11 C 9
St Leederville 60 C 9
COLDWELL
Rd Kenwick 85 E 5
Rd Wattle Grove 86 A 4
COLDWELLS
St Bicton 81 B 9
COLE
Gr Parmelia 131 B 9
Pl Dianella 47 A 7
St Kewdale 75 A 8
St Midland 50 D 6
St Mundaring 69 B 1
COLEBATCH
Cr Joondalup 19 E 4
Hl Kardinya 91 E 8
COLEBY
St Balcatta 46 A 5
COLEMAN
Cr Melville 91 C 3
Pl Beckenham 85 B 9
Rd Calista 130 E 8
Wy Karrinyup 45 A 7
COLERAINE
St Subiaco 71 E 3
COLERIDGE
Pl North Lake 102 A 1
COLES
Pl Padbury 30 E 1
Pl Yanchep 4 C 4
COLEVILLE
Cr Spearwood 101 B 5
COLGRAIN
Wy Duncraig 31 A 8
COLGRAVE
Wy Duncraig 31 B 5
COLIBAN
Gr Joondalup 19 C 2
COLIBRI
Ct Willetton 93 C 6
COLIN
Gr West Perth 72 C 2
Gr West Perth 1C D 2
Pl Wembley Dns 58 E 3
Pl West Perth 60 D 10
Rd Scarborough 58 E 2
Rd Wembley Dns 58 E 4
St Dalkeith 81 D 1
St West Perth 72 C 2
St West Perth 1C D 1
COLKIRK
Wy Willetton 93 D 2
COLL
Pl Warwick 31 C 7

Map Ref.

COLLAROY
Ct Kallaroo 23 A 6
COLLEEN
St Gosnells 106 C 1
St Gosnells 96 C 10
COLLEGE
Ct Karrinyup 44 D 5
Ct Serpentine 151 B 10
Rd Claremont 71 B 8
Rd Gooseberry H 77 C 4
St Inglewood 61 C 4
COLLERAN
Wy Booragoon 92 C 1
COLLETT
Wy Leeming 93 A 8
COLLICK
St Hilton 91 B 9
COLLIE
St Fremantle 1D B 6
St Fremantle 90 B 6
COLLIER
Ave Balcatta 46 B 7
Ps Joondalup 19 D 7
Rd Bassendean 62 D 2
Rd Embleton 62 A 1
Rd Morley 48 A 10
St Applecross 82 B 8
St Ardross 82 B 8
St Silver Sands 163 B 6
St Wembley 60 A 7
St Wembley 59 E 7
COLLINGWOOD
Rd Bedfordale 127 D 2
St Dianella 47 C 7
St Osborne Park 60 A 2
St Osborne Park 59 E 1
Wy Dianella 47 C 7
COLLINS
Ct High Wycombe 64 B 10
Ct Morley 48 D 8
Pde Mullaloo 23 A 4
Rd Kalamunda 77 E 8
Rd Roleystone 118 A 1
Rd Willetton 94 A 5
Rd Willetton 93 E 5
St Kensington 73 C 9
St South Perth 73 C 9
St Yokine 60 D 2
COLLINSON
St Beaconsfield 90 E 9
St Dianella 46 E 8
Wy Leeming 93 A 9
COLLIS
Rd Wattleup 112 A 10
COLLISON
Pl Marangaroo 32 C 5
COLLOVA
Wy Wattleup 121 C 2
COLLYER
St Belmont 62 E 10
COLMAN
St Mandurah 165 A 1
COLMAR
St Ferndale 84 C 10
COLNE
Wy Girrawheen 32 C 9
COLO
Ct Greenwood 31 B 4
COLOMBARD
La Ellenbrook 29 C 1
COLOMBO
St Victoria Park 73 D 6
St Victoria Park 73 D 7
COLONIAL
Ci Gnangara 26 A 5
Ci Gnangara 25 E 5
Dr Bibra Lake 102 C 3
Me Edgewater 24 A 1
COLONY
Ct Thornlie 95 C 8

Map Ref.

COLORADO
Pl Beechboro 48 E 4
COLPOYS
Pl Coogee 101 A 10
COLRAY
Ave Osborne Park 60 A 3
COLREAVY
Pl Padbury 23 E 10
COLSON
Cl Hillarys 30 B 1
COLSTOUN
Rd Ashfield 62 E 4
COLUMBA
Pl Peppermint Gr 80 D 4
COLUMBIA
Cl Halls Head 164 C 4
Cl Rockingham 137 B 7
Wy Beechboro 48 D 4
COLUMBUS
Ct Port Kennedy 156 C 4
COLVILLE
St Waikiki 145 D 2
COLWYN
Rd Bayswater 62 D 5
Rd Mt Helena 54 E 3
COMA
Pl Beldon 23 D 3
COMBE
Pl Sorrento 30 C 3
COMBELLACK
Wy High Wycombe 76 C 1
COMBWICH
Ct Karrinyup 44 E 2
COMER
St Como 82 E 1
COMET
Ct Alexander Hts 32 E 6
St Beckenham 85 D 6
St Mandurah 165 A 3
COMIC COURT
Cc Byford 125 E 7
COMINO
St Cloverdale 75 A 2
COMMERCE
Ave Armadale 116 D 7
Ci Malaga 33 C 9
COMMERCIAL
Rd Forrestdale 114 D 8
Rd Shenton Park 71 E 5
St Sth Fremantle 90 C 9
COMMONWEALTH
Ave North Perth 60 D 7
COMMUNITY
Dr Westfield 106 C 7
COMO
Pl Joondalup 19 D 2
COMPASS
Ci Yanchep 4 C 5
Pl Ballajura 33 D 7
Pl Waikiki 145 B 3
Rd Jandakot 103 C 3
COMPTON
Cl Munster 101 B 10
Pl Kewdale 74 E 8
Rd Gosnells 105 E 1
St Balga 46 D 2
Wy Morley 48 A 9
COMRIE
Rd Canning Vale 104 C 1
Rd Canning Vale 94 C 10
St Floreat 59 C 8
COMSTOCK
Wy Woodvale 24 B 7
CONCORD
Pl Connolly 19 C 8
Rd Dianella 47 C 10
CONCORDIA
Wy Rockingham 137 D 7

Map Ref.

CONCRAIGE
Wy Willetton 93 E 4
CONDER
Pl Woodvale 24 C 5
CONDOR
Ci Willetton 93 C 4
Pl Armadale 116 B 4
St Innaloo 45 D 10
CONE
Pl Menora 61 A 5
CONEBUSH
Hts Halls Head 164 A 6
CONELLAN
Tce Parmelia 131 A 10
CONEY
Dr Wattle Grove 75 E 10
CONGDON
St Claremont 70 E 10
St Nth Fremantle 80 C 10
Wy Booragoon 92 B 3
CONGHA
Ct Hillman 137 E 6
CONGO
Pl Beechboro 48 E 4
CONGRESSIONAL
Cr Connolly 19 C 6
CONICAL
Ri Woodvale 24 B 5
CONIDAE
Dr Heathridge 23 E 1
Dr Heathridge 23 E 2
CONIFER
Cl Ballajura 33 C 5
Rd Karragullen 109 B 7
St Maddington 96 C 4
CONIGRAVE
Rd Yangebup 111 E 1
Rd Yangebup 101 E 10
CONISTON
Wy Balga 32 C 9
Wy Ferndale 84 C 10
CONLAN
Ave Wanneroo 20 D 8
CONLON
St Waterford 83 E 6
CONNAUGHT
St Forrestfield 86 C 1
St Leederville 60 C 9
CONNAUGHTON
St Kewdale 74 E 7
CONNELL
Ave Kelmscott 106 E 6
Ave Martin 106 E 1
Ave Martin 96 E 10
St Belmont 74 D 2
Wy Girrawheen 32 D 7
CONNELLY
Wy Booragoon 92 B 2
CONNEMARA
Dr Brigadoon 167 A 9
Dr Brigadoon 169 B 1
Dr Thornlie 95 C 5
CONNOLLY
Dr Alkimos 8 A 6
Dr Butler 11 A 2
Dr Clarkson 15 A 8
Dr Clarkson 14 D 2
Dr Currambine 19 B 4
Dr Eglinton 7 C 3
Dr Kinross 19 A 1
Dr Merriwa 11 C 7
Dr Tamala Park 15 A 8
St Wembley 60 B 9
CONNOR
Rd Forrestfield 77 A 10
Rd Lesmurdie 77 B 10
Rd Lesmurdie 87 C 1
CONOCHIE
Cr Manning 83 B 6

For detailed information regarding the street referencing system used in this book, turn to page 170.

C

		Map	Ref.
CONON			
Rd	Applecross	82	B 7
CONQUEST			
Ct	Thornlie	95	C 8
CONRAD			
Ct	Spearwood	101	B 9
CONRADI			
Pl	Stoneville	54	C 4
CONROY			
Pl	Bull Creek	92	E 4
Pl	Hillarys	30	B 1
St	Maylands	61	D 8
CONSERVATION			
Cl	Munster	110	E 1
CONSTANCE			
St	Bayswater	62	D 5
St	Darlington	66	B 6
St	Nollamara	46	C 8
St	Yokine	46	C 9
CONSTANTINE			
Ct	Thornlie	95	B 4
Wy	Marangaroo	32	C 4
CONSTELLATION			
Dr	Ocean Reef	18	E 8
CONSTITUTION			
St	East Perth	73	C 3
CONSULATE			
Ct	Thornlie	95	B 8
CONTEST			
Cl	Kallaroo	23	B 7
CONTI			
Rd	Wanneroo	20	C 3
CONTO			
Ave	Dianella	47	C 9
CONTOUR			
Dr	Mullaloo	23	B 2
Dr	Mullaloo	23	C 3
Rd	Roleystone	107	D 9
CONTROL			
Cl	Mullaloo	23	C 2
CONVINE			
Rd	Karragullen	109	A 9
CONWAY			
Ct	Beaconsfield	90	E 8
Gr	Heathridge	19	C 9
Lp	Waikiki	145	D 2
Rd	Hope Valley	121	B 8
Rd	Kwinana Beach	121	B 9
COOBA			
Pl	Duncraig	30	E 6
COODANUP			
Dr	Coodanup	165	C 5
COODE			
St	Bayswater	62	A 3
St	Bedford	61	D 1
St	Como	83	A 2
St	Dianella	47	C 9
St	Fremantle	91	A 4
St	Maylands	61	D 6
St	Mt Lawley	61	C 8
St	South Perth	73	A 10
COOGAN			
Cl	Yangebup	102	A 10
COOGEE			
Rd	Ardross	82	C 8
Rd	Mariginiup	16	E 2
Rd	Mt Pleasant	82	D 8
Rd	Munster	111	B 5
St	Mt Hawthorn	60	C 6
COOGLY			
Rd	Mundijong	151	A 6
COOINDA			
Cl	Quinns Rocks	10	A 10
COOK			
Ave	Hillarys	30	A 1
Ave	Hillarys	23	A 10
Ct	Port Kennedy	156	D 5
Pl	Lesmurdie	87	E 1
St	Bull Creek	92	E 6

		Map	Ref.
St	Canning Vale	94	B 5
St	Crawley	72	A 9
St	Darlington	66	C 6
St	Mt Helena	55	A 3
St	Silver Sands	163	B 6
St	Thornlie	95	C 8
St	West Perth	72	C 1
COOKE			
Cl	Kiara	48	E 7
St	Hilton	91	C 9
COOKES			
Wy	Chidlow	42	B 7
COOKHAM			
Rd	Lathlain	74	A 5
COOLABAH			
Dr	Armadale	116	E 4
Wy	Forrestfield	76	E 10
COOLANGATTA			
Rd	Darlington	66	A 4
Rt	Hillarys	30	A 1
COOLAWANYAH			
St	Golden Bay	158	D 7
COOLBELLUP			
Ave	Coolbellup	91	D 10
Ave	Coolbellup	101	E 1
COOLBINIA			
Pl	Queens Park	85	B 3
COOLGA			
Rd	Koongamia	65	B 2
COOLGARDIE			
Ave	East Fremantle	90	E 1
Ave	Redcliffe	63	A 7
Ave	Redcliffe	62	E 7
St	Bentley	84	B 4
St	Mundaring	68	A 4
St	Subiaco	72	A 3
St	West Perth	1C	D 1
St	West Perth	72	C 1
Tce	Perth City	1C	B 1
Tce	Perth City	73	B 1
COOLHAM			
Wy	Balga	46	D 2
COOLIBAH			
Ave	Mandurah	165	B 4
Ct	Ballajura	33	C 3
Dr	Greenwood	31	C 5
Pl	Duncraig	30	E 6
Wy	Bibra Lake	102	A 8
Wy	Bibra Lake	101	E 8
COOLIDGE			
St	Como	83	A 4
COOLINGA			
Rd	Lesmurdie	87	B 5
COOLOON			
St	Queens Park	85	B 3
COOMA			
St	Wanneroo	20	E 10
COOMBE			
Ave	Armadale	116	D 8
Pl	Kingsley	31	C 2
St	Bayswater	62	A 6
COOMBS			
Pl	Bateman	92	D 4
Pl	Mandurah	165	C 1
St	Rockingham	136	E 6
COOMEL			
Cl	Hillman	137	E 6
COOMOORA			
Rd	Ardross	82	C 10
Rd	Mt Pleasant	82	D 10
COOMS			
Ps	Winthrop	92	D 4
COONADOO			
Ct	Jandakot	103	C 8
COONDAREE			
Pde	Upper Swan	166	A 10
COONEWARRA			
Wy	Quinns Rocks	10	A 10

		Map	Ref.
COONGAN			
Ave	Greenmount	65	B 1
Ct	Heathridge	19	B 9
COONONG			
Pl	Armadale	116	B 5
COOPER			
Ave	Kenwick	95	D 1
Ct	Leda	139	C 2
Rd	Jandakot	112	D 1
Rd	Jandakot	102	D 10
Rd	Morley	47	D 7
Rge	Winthrop	92	B 5
St	Crawley	71	E 8
St	Landsdale	25	B 10
St	Mandurah	164	E 1
St	Midland	50	D 7
St	Mullaloo	23	A 4
St	Nedlands	71	E 8
COOPS			
Ave	Thornlie	95	B 4
COORA			
Pl	Nollamara	46	D 7
COORANGA			
Rd	Falcon	162A	C 2
COORONG			
Pl	Kallaroo	23	B 5
COOTAMUNDRA			
Wy	Maida Vale	76	E 3
COOTHALLIE			
Rd	Chidlow	57	A 2
Rd	Chidlow	56	D 2
COPE			
Pl	Kelmscott	117	B 1
St	Hamersley	32	A 10
St	Midland	50	D 8
COPELAND			
Dr	Redcliffe	75	A 1
Gns	Ocean Reef	19	A 6
COPLEY			
Rd	Upper Swan	168	A 2
Rd	Upper Swan	166	D 7
Rd	Upper Swan	29	E 2
St	Bayswater	62	A 4
COPPER			
Cl	Carine	30	E 10
COPPERCUPS			
Pl	Halls Head	164	B 6
Rt	Mirrabooka	47	B 2
COPPERFIELD			
Rd	Greenfields	163	E 9
COPPERHEAD			
Ave	Padbury	30	E 1
COPPERWAITE			
Rd	Kardinya	92	A 7
COPPIN			
La	Parkerville	53	E 9
Rd	Mahogany Crk	67	D 3
Rd	Mundaring	67	E 2
Rd	Parkerville	53	E 8
COPPING			
Rd	Mundaring	53	E 10
COQUINA			
Cl	Heathridge	23	D 1
CORAL			
Ct	Halls Head	164	B 1
Pl	Ballajura	33	D 7
Rd	Kalamunda	77	D 9
Rd	Safety Bay	145	B 1
St	Craigie	23	C 7
St	Martin	96	C 7
St	Scarborough	44	C 8
St	Sth Fremantle	90	C 7
Wy	Kalamunda	77	D 9
CORALBERRY			
Cr	Dianella	46	E 5
CORALGUM			
Ct	Morley	48	D 5
CORALIE			
Ct	Armadale	116	D 7

		Map	Ref.
CORAN			
Gns	Warnbro	145	D 6
Pl	Westfield	106	B 8
CORANDER			
Gns	Carine	45	A 2
CORBEL			
St	Shelley	83	D 9
CORBETT			
St	Dianella	47	B 9
St	Gosnells	106	B 2
St	Scarborough	58	E 2
Wy	Booragoon	92	C 3
CORBOY			
St	Wembley	59	E 10
CORBUSIER			
Pl	Balcatta	45	E 2
CORBY			
La	Carine	31	A 9
CORCORAN			
St	Duncraig	30	D 7
CORD			
St	Joondalup	19	D 6
CORDELIA			
Ave	Coolbellup	102	A 1
Ave	Coolbellup	101	D 2
Pl	Alexander Hts	33	A 5
Rd	Armadale	116	B 7
CORDEROY			
Wy	Noranda	48	A 5
CORDOVA			
Ct	Craigie	23	E 6
CORDROY			
Wy	Hamersley	45	D 1
Wy	Hamersley	31	D 10
CORDY			
Pl	Beckenham	85	B 10
COREEN			
Wy	Kalamunda	77	E 6
CORELLA			
Ct	Ballajura	34	A 7
Pl	Cooloongup	137	D 9
St	Lesmurdie	87	D 3
St	Stirling	45	D 6
CORFIELD			
St	Gosnells	106	A 1
St	Gosnells	96	A 10
St	Gosnells	106	B 2
St	Gosnells	95	E 8
CORFU			
Ct	Sorrento	30	C 4
St	Falcon	162A	B 2
CORIMA			
Pl	Craigie	23	D 5
CORIN			
Wy	Wattleup	121	D 7
CORINNA			
St	Falcon	162A	D 10
CORINTH			
La	Gnangara	25	E 4
CORINTHIAN			
Rd E	Riverton	84	A 10
Rd E	Riverton	83	D 10
Rd W	Rossmoyne	83	B 10
Rd W	Shelley	83	C 10
CORIO			
Ct	Currambine	19	A 3
CORK			
Pl	Warnbro	145	E 8
Rd	Floreat	59	A 8
CORKHILL			
St	Nth Fremantle	80	D 10
CORMACK			
Rd	Alfred Cove	92	A 1
CORMORANT			
Cro	Willetton	93	C 5
Ct	Heathridge	23	C 1
Ct	Southern River	105	A 7
Gns	Ballajura	33	E 8
Pl	Coodanup	165	E 9

		Map	Ref.
Rd	Two Rocks	2	D 1
Wy	Yangebup	102	A 10
CORN			
Wy	Bibra Lake	102	C 4
CORNCRAKE			
Ct	Southern River	105	C 9
CORNELIAN			
Cr	Carine	30	E 10
St	Scarborough	58	E 2
CORNELL			
Rd	Cannington	84	E 7
St	Yokine	46	D 10
CORNFIELD			
Pl	Hillarys	30	A 2
CORNHILL			
Cr	Alexander Hts	33	B 5
CORNISH			
Ave	Woodvale	24	C 6
Cr	Manning	83	A 7
Pl	Mirrabooka	47	B 1
St	Armadale	116	D 7
CORNWALL			
Cl	Morley	48	D 8
St	Dianella	47	A 9
St	Lathlain	74	A 4
St	Swanbourne	70	E 7
CORNWALLIS			
Rd	Madora	160	C 3
CORONA			
Cl	Rockingham	137	B 7
Cr	Cannington	84	C 6
Ct	Heathridge	23	D 1
Wy	Belhus	29	B 3
CORONATA			
Dr	Warnbro	145	E 8
Wy	Mirrabooka	46	E 1
CORONATION			
St	Doubleview	59	B 2
St	North Perth	60	D 7
St	Woodlands	59	B 1
CORONET			
Ct	Thornlie	95	C 6
CORONILLA			
Wy	Forrestfield	76	E 7
CORREA			
Pl	Willetton	93	C 2
Wy	Mirrabooka	47	A 1
CORRIE			
Ct	Kingsley	24	C 9
CORRIEDALE			
Pl	Thornlie	95	B 2
CORRIGAN			
Ri	Wungong	126	E 3
Wy	Greenwood	32	A 3
Wy	Greenwood	31	E 3
CORRIGIN			
Hts	Parmelia	131	A 9
CORRING			
Wy	Parmelia	131	A 9
CORRINGLE			
Gr	South Lake	102	C 3
CORRINGTON			
Ci	Nollamara	46	E 6
CORRY			
St	E Cannington	85	D 4
CORRY LYNN			
Rd	Claremont	71	A 10
CORSAIR			
Ct	Heathridge	19	C 9
Dr	Willetton	93	D 6
Pl	Padbury	30	E 1
Rd	Port Kennedy	156	C 5
CORSER			
St	Kewdale	74	D 4
CORT			
Wy	Rockingham	137	E 4
CORTE			
Cl	Brigadoon	168	A 6

190   **For detailed information regarding the street referencing system used in this book, turn to page 170.**

C

Name	Type	Suburb	Map	Ref.
CORTIS	Wy	Langford	95	A 2
CORVETTE	Cl	Waikiki	145	C 4
CORVUS	Pl	Rockingham	137	B 7
CORWIN	Ri	Iluka	18	E 3
COSGROVE	Ct	Armadale	115	E 3
	St	Balcatta	46	B 4
COSMELIA	Wy	Lynwood	94	B 2
COSMO	Pl	Midland	50	B 7
COSMOS	St	E Cannington	85	D 4
COSSACK	Ct	Kingsley	31	C 2
COSSINGTON	Ct	Dianella	47	A 7
COSSOM	Pl	Bayswater	62	C 4
COSSON	Wy	High Wycombe	64	A 10
COSTA BRAVA	Pl	Safety Bay	145	C 1
COSTA RICA	Pl	Safety Bay	137	C 10
COSTELLO	St	Maddington	96	B 5
COSTON	Pl	Morley	48	B 8
COTHERSTONE	Rd	Kalamunda	77	C 8
COTHILL	Ct	Eden Hill	49	A 8
COTRELL	Rd	Carmel	88	D 7
COTTAGE	Dr	Rowethorpe	144	
	La	Roleystone	107	E 6
COTTERELL	El	Merriwa	11	D 10
COTTINGLEY	Pl	Swan View	51	D 7
COTTON	Cr	Bull Creek	93	B 6
	Pl	Hillarys	23	C 10
	Pl	Waikiki	145	E 1
COTTONWOOD	Cr	Dianella	46	E 6
COTTRILL	St	Myaree	91	E 1
COULSEN	Cl	Noranda	47	D 4
COULSON	St	Wilson	84	B 6
	Wy	Canning Vale	94	D 5
COULSTON	Rd	Boya	65	C 2
	Rd	Darlington	66	A 4
	Rd	Darlington	65	E 4
	Wy	Gosnells	106	B 1
COULTAN	Rd	Noranda	47	D 6
COUNCIL	Ave	Rockingham	137	C 7
	Pl	East Fremantle	90	D 2
	Rd	Mundaring	68	A 2
COUNSEL	Rd	Coolbellup	101	D 1
COUNTRY CLUB	Blvd	Connolly	19	B 8
COURAGEOUS	Pl	Ocean Reef	18	E 8
COURT	Pl	Subiaco	60	B 10
	St	Gosnells	95	D 7
	St	Highgate	61	B 10
COURTHOPE	St	Kensington	73	D 8
COURTLEA	Cl	Ferndale	84	D 9
COURTNEY	Pl	Wattle Grove	85	E 4
COUSENS	St	Jarrahdale	152	E 8
COUSINS	Cl	Kalamunda	77	E 10
	Pl	Stoneville	54	C 4
	St	Karrinyup	44	D 7
COVE	Ct	Beldon	23	C 2
	Ct	Mandurah	164	E 4
COVENTRY	Ct	Kingsley	24	B 9
	Pde	Nth Fremantle	80	C 8
	Pl	Greenfields	163	D 9
	Rd	Roleystone	107	C 7
	Rd	Shoalwater	136	C 8
COVERLEY	St	Alfred Cove	82	A 10
COVICH	Ave	Hamilton Hill	90	E 9
COWALLA	Gns	Beldon	23	E 2
COWAN	Cl	Kingsley	31	D 1
	Gns	Bellevue	50	E 9
	Pl	Safety Bay	137	A 10
	St	Alfred Cove	82	A 10
	St	Armadale	116	B 4
	St	Maddington	96	A 5
COWCHER	Pl	Medina	130	D 4
	Wy	E Medina	130	D 4
	Wy	W Medina	130	D 4
COWELL	Pl	Calista	130	E 7
COWEN	St	Mundijong	143	B 10
COWIE	Pl	Dianella	47	A 8
	Pl	Leeming	93	D 8
COWLE	St	Landsdale	25	C 9
	St	West Perth	60	E 9
COWLEY	St	Yokine	46	C 9
COWLING	St	Attadale	81	C 9
	Wy	Parmelia	131	B 7
COWLISHAW	Ri	Parmelia	131	B 8
COWPER	Rd	Sorrento	30	C 6
	St	Lynwood	94	C 3
COWRA	Ct	Armadale	116	C 9
	St	Forrestfield	86	C 1
COWRIE	Cr	Mt Pleasant	82	E 10
	Ct	Waikiki	145	C 3
	Pl	Mullaloo	23	B 3
COX	Cr	Quinns Rocks	10	A 10
	Ct	Middle Swan	50	E 4
	Ct	Craigie	23	E 6
	St	Mandurah	163	B 10
	St	Maylands	61	E 6
	St	Willagee	91	D 5
COYLE	Rd	Beldon	23	E 3
	Rd	Peel Estate	133	A 10
	Rd	Peel Estate	132	E 10
CRABBE	Pl	Karrinyup	44	E 7
CRABTREE	St	Alexander Hts	32	E 4
	Wy	Medina	130	E 4
CRADDON	Rd	Oakford	124	B 5
CRADLE	Cl	Alexander Hts	33	B 4
CRAGHILL	Wy	Oakford	124	D 5
CRAGO	Rd	Leeming	92	E 9
CRAIG	Me	Safety Bay	137	A 10
	Pl	Winthrop	92	C 5
	St	Ascot	62	B 10
	St	Mundaring	68	B 1
	St	Nth Fremantle	80	C 9
	St	Victoria Park	73	E 5
	St	Wembley Dns	59	A 5
	Wy	Jarrahdale	152	E 7
CRAIGIE	Cr	Manning	83	A 7
	Dr	Beldon	23	D 4
	Pl	Armadale	116	A 3
	Pl	Armadale	115	E 3
CRAIL	St	Floreat	59	C 8
CRAIN	Ct	Beechboro	49	A 2
CRAKE	Ct	High Wycombe	64	B 10
	Pl	Yangebup	102	B 8
CRAMPTON	El	Murdoch	92	C 7
CRANA	Pl	Karawara	83	C 4
CRANBROOK	St	Coolbinia	60	D 3
CRANDON	St	Fremantle	1D	C 6
	St	Fremantle	90	C 6
	St	Gosnells	96	A 9
	St	Gosnells	95	E 8
CRANE	Cl	Ocean Reef	19	A 10
	Ct	High Wycombe	76	B 1
	Glen	Ballajura	33	E 8
	St	Hamersley	31	D 10
	St	Henderson	111	A 6
CRANFORD	Ave	Brentwood	92	E 2
CRANLEIGH	St	Morley	47	E 7
	St	West Swan	36	A 10
	St	West Swan	35	C 10
	St	Whiteman	35	A 9
CRANLEY	Pl	Lynwood	94	D 3
CRANWELL	Rd	Balcatta	46	A 5
	St	Thornlie	95	C 5
CRANWOOD	Blvd	Viveash	50	B 6
	Cr	Viveash	50	B 4
CRATER	Pl	Rockingham	137	A 8
CRATHIE	Ct	Kingsley	24	C 9
CRAVEN	Rd	Mundaring	67	D 1
	Rd	Mundaring	53	D 10
	St	Bedford	61	D 3
CRAWFORD	Ct	Safety Bay	145	A 1
	Rd	Dianella	61	D 2
	Rd	Inglewood	61	D 5
	Rd	Maylands	61	D 5
	Rd	Orelia	131	B 5
	St	Cannington	85	A 8
	St	E Cannington	85	B 6
	St	Mandurah	163	C 10
CRAWLEY	Ave	Crawley	72	A 7
	Gr	Heathridge	23	E 3
	Rd	Armadale	116	D 3
CRAWSHAW	Cr	Manning	83	A 4
CRAYDEN	Rd	Kalamunda	77	D 9
CREANEY	Dr	Kingsley	31	B 1
	Dr	Kingsley	24	B 10
CREATON	St	E Victoria Pk	83	E 2
	St	St James	84	A 3
CREEK EDGE	Cl	Swan View	51	A 5
CREEK VIEW	Cl	Rossmoyne	93	A 3
CREER	Ct	Noranda	47	E 4
CREERY	Rd	Mandurah	164	E 2
CRELLIN	Wy	Cloverdale	75	A 2
CREMORNE	Ct	Kallaroo	23	A 7
CREON	Wy	Silver Sands	163	B 7
CRESCENT	Rd	Kalamunda	77	E 6
CRESSALL	Rd	Balcatta	45	E 3
CRESSBROOK	Wy	Carine	30	D 9
CRESSIDA	Wy	Westfield	106	A 9
CRESSWELL	Rd	Dianella	61	A 1
	Rd	Dianella	46	E 9
CREST	Ave	Mt Pleasant	82	E 10
	Cl	Ballajura	33	D 6
	Ct	Edgewater	24	A 1
	Ct	Thornlie	95	C 7
	Pl	Safety Bay	136	D 10
CRESTIA	Ct	Bibra Lake	102	C 5
CRESTVIEW	Cr	Kalamunda	77	C 7
	La	Ballajura	33	C 5
CRESWICK	Grn	Kiara	48	E 6
CRETE	Cr	Swanbourne	70	D 8
CREW	Ct	Ocean Reef	23	B 2
CREWE	St	Bicton	81	B 8
CRIBB	Ct	Redcliffe	63	A 9
CRICKLEWOOD	Wy	Carine	45	B 2
CRIDDLE	Pl	Jandakot	112	E 3
CRIEFF	St	Floreat	59	C 7
CRIMEA	St	Embleton	48	A 10
	St	Morley	48	A 6
	St	Noranda	48	A 5
CRINGLE	St	Ocean Reef	23	A 1
CRIPPS	Ct	Duncraig	31	A 3
CRISAFULLI	Ave	Wanneroo	20	C 9
CRISP	Pl	Karrinyup	45	A 3
CRITERIUM	Pl	Middle Swan	50	E 4
CROASDALE	Rd	Roleystone	107	D 9
CROCKER	Dr	Malaga	47	C 2
	Dr	Malaga	33	C 10
	Pl	Karrinyup	45	A 2
	Rd	Innaloo	45	C 8
	St	Rockingham	137	C 4
	Wy	Innaloo	45	C 8
CROCUS	Rd	Kalamunda	77	E 5
	Wy	Ferndale	84	C 9
CROESUS	St	Morley	48	C 7
CROFT	Ave	Dianella	47	D 10
	St	Gosnells	96	B 10
CROFTER	Ct	Leda	139	B 2
CROFTON	Pl	Lynwood	94	C 1
	Ri	Mindarie	14	B 3
CROKE	La	Fremantle	1D	B 6
	St	Fremantle	1D	B 6
	St	Fremantle	90	B 6
CROMARTY	Rd	Floreat	59	B 7
CROMER	Gns	Parmelia	131	B 9
	Gr	Kallaroo	23	B 8
	Pl	Lynwood	84	D 10
	Rd	Brentwood	92	D 2
	Wy	North Beach	44	D 2
CROMFORD	Wy	Carine	30	E 10
CROMPTON	Rd	Rockingham	138	A 1
	Rd	Rockingham	137	E 4
CROMWELL	Rd	Alexander Hts	33	B 5
	Rd	Sawyers Valley	55	A 8
CRONIN	Pl	Armadale	116	C 3
CRONULLA	Pl	Hillarys	30	A 1
CROSBIE	Cr	Middle Swan	50	D 4
	Rd	Midland	50	B 7
CROSBY	Pl	Beckenham	85	C 10
	St	Floreat	59	D 9
CROSS	Rd	Bedfordale	127	D 2
	Rd	Spearwood	100	E 6
	St	Bayswater	62	B 5
	St	Queens Park	84	E 2
	St	Shenton Park	72	A 4
	St	Swanbourne	70	D 9
CROSSANDRA	Wy	Greenwood	31	D 2
CROSSFORD	St	Thornlie	95	D 6
CROSSLAND	Ct	Peppermint Gr	80	D 3
	Pl	Hillarys	30	A 2
	Wy	Kardinya	92	A 6
CROSSWAY		Swan View	51	A 5
CROWCOMBE	Wy	Karrinyup	44	E 4

191

D

		Map	Ref.
CROWEA			
St	Greenwood	31	D 4
Wy	Ferndale	94	C 1
Wy	Ferndale	84	C 10
CROWHURST			
Wy	Morley	47	E 7
CROWLEY			
Pl	Dianella	47	A 7
CROWLIN			
Gns	Armadale	116	B 2
CROWN			
Ct	Carine	31	C 10
Ct	Thornlie	95	C 7
St	Rivervale	74	C 4
CROWTHER			
El	Ocean Reef	23	A 1
El	Ocean Reef	19	A 10
Rd	Wanneroo	20	B 5
St	Bayswater	62	B 6
CROXDALE			
Cr	High Wycombe	76	C 1
CROXTON			
Pl	North Beach	44	D 3
Pl	Stirling	45	D 7
Rd	Piesse Brook	78	A 7
CROYDEN			
Rd	Roleystone	108	A 10
Rd	Roleystone	118	D 1
CROYDON			
Ave	Currambine	19	A 5
Ave	Yokine	46	D 10
St	Bellevue	65	B 1
St	Dianella	47	D 10
St	Nedlands	71	E 5
CRUCIS			
Cl	Mirrabooka	46	E 1
CRUFTS			
Wy	Canning Vale	104	A 4
CRUISE			
Ct	Heathridge	23	D 1
Rd	Safety Bay	137	A 10
Rd	Safety Bay	145	B 1
CRUMP			
La	Forrestfield	76	E 5
CRUSADER			
Dr	Thornlie	95	C 8
St	Falcon	162A	B 3
CRUSE			
Rd	Belhus	29	C 4
CRYSTAL			
Cl	Edgewater	24	A 1
Ct	Armadale	116	E 6
Pl	Wattle Grove	86	E 5
CRYSTAL BROOK			
Rd	Lesmurdie	87	A 5
Rd	Wattle Grove	86	C 5
St	Dianella	47	C 8
CRYSTALUNA			
Dr	Golden Bay	158	D 9
CRYSTALVIEW			
Ce	Ballajura	33	D 7
CUBBINE			
Cl	Hillman	137	D 7
CUBLEY			
Pl	Carine	30	D 9
CUDAL			
Pl	Armadale	116	B 6
CUE			
Ct	Gosnells	95	E 10
Pl	Swan View	51	C 5
CUFF			
St	Hamersley	31	D 9
CULFORD			
Ct	Westfield	106	B 10
CULHAM			
Ct	Thornlie	94	E 7
Gns	Heathridge	23	E 2
CULL			
Ct	Armadale	116	B 6

		Map	Ref.
CULLEN			
Ct	Westfield	106	C 8
St	Bayswater	62	C 3
St	Shenton Park	72	A 4
CULLIGAN			
Rd	Thornlie	95	C 5
CULLODEN			
Rd	Duncraig	31	A 6
CULLOTON			
Cr	Balga	32	B 9
CULROSS			
Ave	Thornlie	95	C 5
Pl	Armadale	116	B 2
CULROY			
Gr	Kinross	19	A 1
CULVER			
St	Hamilton Hill	90	D 9
CULWALLA			
Cl	Kallaroo	23	C 6
CULWORTH			
Pl	Bassendean	48	E 10
Rd	Bassendean	48	D 10
CUMBERLAND			
Dr	Hillarys	23	A 9
Rd	Forrestfield	86	D 1
Wy	Bassendean	49	A 10
Wy	Beldon	23	D 2
Wy	Waikiki	145	C 2
CUMBOR			
Wy	Samson	91	C 8
CUMBRAE			
Ct	Dianella	47	A 7
CUMMING			
Rd	Oakford	132	D 4
CUMMINGS			
Wy	Duncraig	31	A 5
CUMMINS			
St	Willagee	91	E 5
CUMNOCK			
Pl	Duncraig	31	A 7
CUMULUS			
Pl	Willetton	93	E 2
CUNNINGHAM			
Lp	Mirrabooka	33	A 10
Pl	Padbury	30	C 1
St	Applecross	82	B 8
St	Ardross	82	B 9
Tce	Daglish	71	D 3
CUNNINGTON			
Wy	Queens Park	85	A 5
CUNNOLD			
Cl	Pickering Bk	99	B 1
St	Pickering Bk	99	B 1
St	Pickering Bk	89	C 10
CUPAR			
Cl	Beldon	23	D 3
Pl	Greenwood	31	C 7
CUPELLO			
Dr	Swan View	51	D 5
CURALO			
Me	South Lake	102	E 6
CURAN			
St	Coolbellup	101	D 1
CURBAR			
St	Balcatta	46	A 6
CURBUR			
Rd	Duncraig	31	A 5
CUREDALE			
St	Beaconsfield	90	E 7
CURL			
Ct	Kallaroo	23	A 6
CURLEW			
Ct	Ballajura	33	E 8
Ct	Westfield	106	C 10
Rd	Dalkeith	81	D 5
St	Mandurah	165	A 3
Wy	Yangebup	102	B 10

		Map	Ref.
CURLEWIS			
St	Huntingdale	95	D 10
CURLINGTON			
Cr	Balga	46	D 3
CURO			
St	Jarrahdale	152	E 8
CURRAJONG			
Cr	Craigie	23	D 5
Rd	Duncraig	30	E 6
CURRAN			
Ct	Joondalup	19	C 2
Ct	Kalamunda	77	B 6
Pl	Leeming	92	E 8
CURRAWONG			
Cr	Walliston	87	E 1
Dr	Gooseberry H	77	C 4
Wy	Thornlie	95	A 3
CURRELL			
Ct	Parmelia	131	B 8
CURRIE			
Gr	Mirrabooka	33	A 10
Pl	Bibra Lake	102	D 2
Pl	Kardinya	91	E 7
St	Jolimont	71	E 2
St	Waikiki	145	C 5
St	Warnbro	145	D 9
CURRONG			
Wy	Nollamara	46	D 6
CURRUTHERS			
Rd	Mt Pleasant	92	E 1
CURTIN			
Ave	Cottesloe	80	D 3
Ave	Cottesloe	70	D 10
Ave	Mosman Park	80	C 7
CURTIS			
Pl	Melville	91	D 1
Rd	Melville	91	D 2
Rd	Melville	81	D 10
St	Lesmurdie	87	D 1
St	Mt Lawley	61	B 9
Wy	Girrawheen	32	D 7
CURVE			
Rd	Swan View	51	D 7
CURVEN			
Rd	Hamilton Hill	101	C 1
Rd	Hamilton Hill	91	C 10
CURZON			
Ct	Willetton	93	E 7
CUSACK			
Rd	Malaga	47	D 3
Wy	Kardinya	91	D 7
CUSTANCE			
St	Lathlain	74	B 5
CUTANA			
Pl	Kelmscott	106	E 6
CUTHBERT			
St	Shenton Park	71	E 5
CUTHBERTSON			
Dr	Cooloongup	138	A 9
Dr	Cooloongup	137	E 8
CUTLASS			
Pl	Safety Bay	137	B 10
St	Jandakot	103	C 3
CUTLER			
Rd	Carabooda	9	B 6
Rd	Jandakot	103	A 9
CUTTER			
Cr	Beldon	23	D 3
Rd	Waikiki	145	C 3
CUTTLE			
Ct	Mullaloo	23	B 3
CUTTLER			
Ave	Beechboro	49	A 4
CUTTS			
St	Hamilton Hill	101	C 1
CUVIER			
Pl	Yangebup	112	B 1
CYCAS			
Ct	Marangaroo	32	D 4

		Map	Ref.
CYCLAMEN			
Ct	Wanneroo	24	D 2
CYGNET			
Cl	Ballajura	34	A 8
Cr	Dalkeith	81	D 2
Ct	High Wycombe	64	D 10
Ct	Yangebup	102	A 9
Pl	Forrestdale	115	A 6
Pl	Lynwood	94	C 2
St	Dianella	47	C 8
St	Kallaroo	23	C 7
CYGNI			
St	Mandurah	165	B 2
CYGNUS			
Cl	Churchlands	59	C 7
St	Rockingham	137	A 8
CYMOSA			
Pl	Mirrabooka	33	A 10
CYPRESS			
Ct	Greenwood	31	C 5
Ct	Morley	48	C 4
Ct	Thornlie	95	A 8
Me	Warnbro	145	D 6
Rd	Forrestfield	86	B 1
Rd	Forrestfield	76	B 10
St	Willetton	93	B 3
CYPRESS POINT			
Rt	Connolly	19	C 6
CYPRIAN			
Pl	Oakford	124	A 3
CYPRUS			
Ct	Coogee	100	E 10
Gns	Halls Head	164	C 2
CYRIL			
Rd	High Wycombe	64	C 10
St	Bassendean	62	E 3

D

		Map	Ref.
DACE			
Ct	Sorrento	30	C 4
DACELO			
Cl	Churchlands	59	C 7
DACRE			
Ct	Hamilton Hill	100	E 2
St	Balcatta	45	E 4
DADGER			
St	Mandurah	165	A 3
DADLEY			
St	Hamilton Hill	101	A 2
DAFFODIL			
Ct	Spearwood	101	A 9
DAGENHAM			
Cr	Midvale	51	A 7
DAGLISH			
Rt	Joondalup	19	E 7
St	Wembley	60	A 9
DAGMAR			
Wy	Swan View	51	C 7
DAGNALL			
Ct	Greenwood	31	E 4
DAHLIA			
St	E Cannington	85	D 4
DAIN			
Ct	Leeming	93	B 9
DAINE			
Ct	Swan View	51	B 7
DAINES			
St	Two Rocks	2	C 2
DAINTREE			
Cl	Jandakot	112	E 2
Ct	Merriwa	11	C 9
DAIRY			
Ct	Bibra Lake	102	D 3
DAIS			
St	Dianella	47	B 5

		Map	Ref.
DAISY			
Rd	Cardup	135	C 7
DAKAR			
Ce	Mindarie	10	B 2
DAKIN			
Gl	Winthrop	92	A 4
St	Daglish	71	D 2
DALBY			
Ct	Willetton	94	A 3
Rd	Hovea	53	B 9
St	Falcon	162A	B 4
St	Warwick	31	D 6
DALE			
Cl	Halls Head	164	C 3
Ct	Two Rocks	2	D 3
Dr	Gooseberry H	77	B 3
Pl	Booragoon	92	B 2
Pl	Darlington	66	C 7
Pl	Orange Grove	86	D 9
Rd	Armadale	116	C 5
Rd	Middle Swan	36	C 10
Rd	Pickering Bk	109	C 2
Rd	Pickering Bk	99	E 10
Sq	Ballajura	33	D 5
St	Kelmscott	116	E 1
St	Sth Fremantle	90	D 7
DALEVIEW			
Cl	Glen Forrest	66	D 1
Cl	Glen Forrest	52	D 1
DALEY			
St	Greenwood	32	A 4
St	Yokine	60	D 2
DALGETY			
Rd	Middle Swan	36	E 9
Rd	Red Hill	37	C 9
St	Cottesloe	80	D 2
St	East Fremantle	90	E 3
DALISON			
Ave	Wattleup	122	A 1
Ave	Wattleup	121	C 1
DALKEITH			
Rd	Nedlands	71	D 10
DALLAS			
Cr	Wanneroo	20	C 7
DALLEN			
St	Southern River	105	E 7
DALLEY			
St	Byford	126	E 9
DALLINGTON			
Cr	Balga	46	C 1
DALLWIN			
St	Dianella	47	A 9
DALMAIN			
St	Kingsley	31	B 2
DALMATIA			
Pl	Como	83	A 4
DALMENY			
St	Perth City	1C	B 1
St	Perth City	73	B 1
D'ALONZO			
Pl	Balcatta	46	A 6
DALRAY			
Ct	Byford	126	B 4
DALRY			
Rd	Darlington	66	A 3
DALRYMPLE			
Pl	Alexander Hts	33	A 3
Tce	Halls Head	164	C 1
Tce	Halls Head	162	C 10
DALSTON			
Cr	Kardinya	92	A 7
DALTON			
Cr	Kingsley	31	C 1
Cr	Kingsley	24	C 10
Pl	Wilson	84	B 6
DALVIK			
Ave	Merriwa	10	B 8
Ave	Merriwa	11	B 8

D

		Map	Ref.
DALWOOD			
Ct	Hamersley	31	E 9
Rd	Swan View	51	B 7
DALY			
Ct	Leeming	93	A 8
Pl	Padbury	23	D 5
St	Ascot	62	C 10
St	Belmont	62	C 10
St	Belmont	74	D 1
St	Cloverdale	74	E 3
St	Sth Fremantle	90	D 8
DALZIELL			
St	Maddington	96	A 4
DAMASCUS			
Dr	Greenmount	51	C 9
DAMEPATTIE			
Dr	Two Rocks	3	B 9
Dr	Two Rocks	2	C 1
Dr	Willetton	93	D 6
DAMERHAM			
Rd	Armadale	116	D 3
DAMIAN			
Rd	Jandabup	21	E 8
DAMON			
St	Singleton	160	D 4
DAMOUR			
Cr	Swanbourne	70	D 8
DAMPIER			
Ave	City Beach	58	D 7
Ave	Falcon	162A	E 10
Ave	Kallaroo	23	B 6
Ave	Mullaloo	23	A 3
Ct	Thornlie	95	C 8
Dr	Golden Bay	158	D 7
Lp	Mirrabooka	33	A 10
Rd	Welshpool	85	C 1
Rd	Welshpool	75	C 10
St	City Beach	58	E 7
DAMPIERA			
Ct	Forrestfield	77	A 6
Wy	Ferndale	94	C 1
Wy	Ferndale	84	C 10
DAMSON			
Gr	Armadale	116	C 4
Wy	Greenwood	31	D 4
DANAHER			
Me	Clarkson	14	D 2
DANBURY			
Cr	Girrawheen	32	B 7
DANBY			
St	Doubleview	59	A 1
DANCE			
Dr	Middle Swan	50	D 3
DANCY			
Wy	Armadale	115	E 4
DANDALOO			
Cr	Wanneroo	20	D 10
Rd	City Beach	58	E 9
DANDENONG			
Rd	Attadale	81	D 10
Rt	Alexander Hts	33	A 4
DANE			
Pl	Spearwood	101	A 4
Pl	Willetton	94	A 2
St	E Victoria Pk	74	A 10
DANEHILL			
Pl	Balga	46	B 1
Wy	Balga	46	B 1
DANGAN			
St	Perth City	61	A 10
DANIA			
Cl	Craigie	23	E 6
DANIEL			
St	Attadale	81	D 8
DANN			
Pl	Marmion	30	C 8
St	Willagee	91	C 5
DANOHILL			
St	Huntingdale	95	D 8

		Map	Ref.
DANTE			
Cl	Wembley Dns	59	A 5
Ct	Bentley	84	D 3
Pl	Greenfields	163	D 9
DANUBE			
Ave	Beechboro	48	D 5
DANVERS			
Cl	Marangaroo	32	D 5
DANZIL			
St	Willagee	91	C 5
DAPHNE			
St	North Perth	60	E 7
DARA			
Ct	Wanneroo	20	E 10
DARBY			
Pl	Redcliffe	63	A 6
St	Bayswater	62	A 7
St	Maylands	62	A 7
DARCH			
St	Mullaloo	23	A 5
St	Yokine	60	D 1
DARDANUS			
Wy	Heathridge	19	D 9
DARGIN			
Pl	Greenwood	31	E 4
Pl	Orelia	131	A 6
St	Mt Helena	55	A 3
Wy	Rockingham	137	A 8
DARIAN			
Dr	Willetton	93	C 7
DARILE			
St	Hillman	138	A 6
DARING			
Pl	Wilson	84	A 8
DARKAN			
St	Mundaring	68	C 1
St	Mundaring	68	C 2
St	Mundaring	54	C 10
DARKIN			
Ct	Warwick	31	E 5
DARKINS			
Rt	Parmelia	131	A 10
DARLEY			
Ci	Bull Creek	93	A 6
Gr	Halls Head	164	B 4
St	South Perth	72	E 7
DARLING			
Cl	Beechboro	48	E 3
Ct	Maddington	96	C 4
Ct	Padbury	30	D 1
St	Hilton	91	A 7
St	South Perth	73	C 8
Vs	Parmelia	131	B 10
Wy	Greenfields	165	C 1
DARLINGTON			
Rd	Darlington	52	A 1
Rd	Darlington	66	A 2
Rd	Darlington	66	B 4
DARLOT			
Cr	South Perth	73	B 7
Ct	Waikiki	145	D 2
DARNELL			
Ave	Mt Pleasant	92	D 1
DARNLEY			
Ave	Greenwood	31	B 5
DARRA			
Pl	Coodanup	165	C 4
DARROCH			
St	Hamilton Hill	91	A 9
DARROWBY			
Pl	Sawyers Valley	69	A 1
DART			
Ct	Warwick	31	D 7
DARTER			
Ct	Sorrento	30	C 4
Pl	Halls Head	164	B 3
DARTFORD			
Cr	Marangaroo	32	B 6
St	Bull Creek	93	A 7

		Map	Ref.
DARTMOUTH			
Ave	City Beach	70	D 1
DARTNALL			
Rd	Parkerville	53	C 8
DARVEL			
Cl	Kinross	19	A 2
DARVELL			
Rd	Willetton	93	C 3
DARWIN			
Cr	Beechboro	48	D 4
Pl	Warnbro	145	E 7
DARWINIA			
Pl	Greenwood	31	C 6
DATUM			
Pl	Mullaloo	23	C 4
DATURA			
Ct	Lynwood	94	B 2
DAUNTLESS			
Wy	Duncraig	30	D 3
DAUPHIN			
Pl	Willetton	93	E 2
DAUPHINE			
Pl	Joondalup	19	C 2
DAVA			
St	Duncraig	31	A 7
DAVALLIA			
Rd	Duncraig	31	B 8
DAVENA			
St	Dianella	47	A 9
DAVENPORT			
Rd	Booragoon	92	C 1
St	Karrinyup	45	A 5
DAVENTRY			
Dr	Alexander Hts	32	E 5
DAVESIA			
Me	Ferndale	84	D 10
DAVEY			
Rd	Mundijong	143	A 7
Rd	Pickering Bk	99	B 1
St	Mandurah	165	A 1
DAVID			
Cl	Osborne Park	60	A 1
Cr	Hillarys	23	C 10
Pl	Calista	130	E 8
Pl	Mandurah	165	A 3
Rd	Waikiki	145	B 4
St	Ardross	82	D 8
St	Kelmscott	106	E 8
St	Kensington	73	C 10
St	Maida Vale	76	D 1
St	Maida Vale	64	D 10
St	Mt Pleasant	82	D 8
St	Mullaloo	23	A 5
St	Yokine	46	C 1
DAVIDSON			
Pl	Noranda	47	D 5
Rd	Attadale	81	C 9
Tce	Joondalup	19	E 6
DAVIE			
Ct	Willetton	93	D 3
DAVIES			
Cr	Gooseberry H	77	C 5
Cr	Kardinya	92	A 8
Ct	Gosnells	106	C 2
La	Bentley	84	C 3
Rd	Claremont	71	A 8
Rd	Dalkeith	81	D 1
St	Beaconsfield	90	E 7
St	E Cannington	85	A 5
DAVILAK			
Ave	Hamilton Hill	100	E 1
Cr	Manning	83	A 5
St	Como	83	A 5
DAVIS			
Ct	Morley	48	C 5
Ct	Woodlands	59	C 2
Pl	Hamersley	45	D 1
Pl	Heathridge	19	B 10
Rd	Attadale	81	C 9
Rd	Helena Valley	65	B 3

		Map	Ref.
Rd	Kelmscott	106	D 9
St	Ascot	62	E 8
DAVISON			
St	Kenwick	95	E 1
St	Maddington	96	A 2
St	Maddington	95	E 2
DAVIT			
Pl	Ocean Reef	23	B 1
DAVON			
St	Hamilton Hill	91	B 10
DAVY			
St	Alfred Cove	82	A 10
St	Booragoon	92	C 1
St	Wembley Dns	58	E 3
DAWE			
Ct	Gosnells	96	A 8
DAWES			
Ct	Padbury	23	E 10
Ct	Two Rocks	2	E 3
DAWKINS			
Ct	Leda	130	E 10
DAWLISH			
Wy	Warnbro	145	D 7
DAWN			
Pl	Beldon	23	E 3
Rd	Walliston	87	E 1
DAWS			
Pl	Swan View	51	C 5
DAWSON			
Ave	Forrestfield	76	B 8
Cl	Noranda	47	E 4
Pl	Lynwood	94	B 4
Rd	Brentwood	92	D 2
Rd	Perth Airport	75	C 6
St	Armadale	116	B 7
St	Beldon	23	D 4
Wy	Parmelia	131	C 6
DAXTER			
St	Thornlie	95	A 6
DAY			
Pl	Heathridge	23	E 2
Rd	E Rockingham	138	A 3
Rd	Hillman	138	A 5
Rd	Mandurah	163	A 9
Rd	Rockingham	138	A 4
St	Kardinya	91	D 9
DAYANA			
Cl	Midvale	51	A 9
DAYLESFORD			
Rd	Bassendean	63	C 2
DAYLIGHT			
Cl	Beldon	23	E 3
DAYRELL			
Rd	Nowergup	12	B 8
DEAGUE			
Ct	North Perth	60	E 7
DEAKIN			
Ct	Kelmscott	106	E 7
St	Bassendean	63	A 3
St	Swanbourne	70	E 9
DEAL			
Cl	Warnbro	145	D 6
St	Marangaroo	32	B 6
DEALY			
Cl	Cannington	84	D 4
DEAN			
Ct	Halls Head	164	B 4
Ct	Woodvale	24	B 3
Gr	Woodvale	24	B 5
Pl	Lockridge	49	A 5
Rd	Bateman	92	D 5
Rd	North Lake	102	D 1
St	Claremont	71	A 10
St	Karrinyup	45	B 5
St	Kelmscott	106	E 9
St	Mt Helena	55	B 7
DEANE			
St	Cottesloe	80	C 4
DEANERY			
Me	Churchlands	59	C 4

		Map	Ref.
DEANMORE			
Rd	Karrinyup	44	E 8
Rd	Scarborough	44	E 10
DEANNA			
Ct	Cooloongup	137	E 9
DEARLE			
St	Hamilton Hill	101	C 1
DEASEY			
Pl	Noranda	47	C 5
DEAUVILLE			
Pl	Connolly	19	C 8
DEB			
St	Falcon	162	B 2
DEBDEN			
Pl	Carine	31	C 10
DEBENHAM			
St	Thornlie	95	B 4
Wy	Hillarys	23	B 9
DE BERNALES			
Wk	Cottesloe	80	C 2
DE BURGH			
Rd	Caversham	50	A 5
Rd	Caversham	49	E 5
DECIDUOUS			
Ri	Yangebup	111	E 1
DECIMA			
St	Innaloo	45	B 8
DECORA			
Ct	Wanneroo	24	D 2
DECOURCEY			
Wy	Marangaroo	32	C 4
DEE			
Rd	Applecross	82	B 5
DEELEY			
St	Maylands	61	D 8
DEEPDENE			
Cl	Heathridge	23	E 2
Rd	Wattleup	121	D 2
DEEPWATER			
Cc	Merriwa	11	C 10
DEERHOUND			
Hts	Currambine	19	A 5
DEERING			
St	Balga	46	C 4
St	Beaconsfield	90	E 9
DEERNESS			
Wy	Armadale	116	D 8
DEE WHY			
Gr	Kallaroo	23	A 8
DEFOE			
Ct	Kingsley	24	D 10
DE GREY			
Cl	Cooloongup	137	D 10
Cl	Mandurah	164	E 4
Cl	Heathridge	19	B 7
St	Innaloo	45	C 10
DEGREY			
Cl	Gosnells	105	E 2
DEIGHTON			
Wy	Merriwa	11	C 8
DE LAETER			
Wy	Bentley	83	D 1
DELAFIELD			
Wy	Balcatta	45	E 4
DELAGE			
St	Joondalup	19	D 6
Wy	Balcatta	45	E 4
DELAMBRE			
Ri	Sorrento	29	B 4
DELAMERE			
Ave	Iluka	18	E 3
Ave	South Perth	73	C 7
Wy	Westfield	106	B 8
DELANY			
Me	Clarkson	14	C 3
DELAWARE			
Pl	Kallaroo	23	C 6

For detailed information regarding the street referencing system used in this book, turn to page 170.

D

		Map	Ref.
DELAWNEY			
St	Balcatta	46	A 3
St	Balcatta	45	E 3
DELBRIDGE			
Dr	Kenwick	86	A 9
DELCOMYN			
Pl	Craigie	23	D 6
DELHI			
St	West Perth	1C	D 1
St	West Perth	72	D 1
DELICH			
Rd	Carabooda	8	B 1
DELL			
Rd	Sth Guildford	63	E 4
Wy	Wanneroo	24	E 1
DELLA			
Rd	Malaga	48	B 1
Rd	Noranda	48	B 5
Rd	Woodvale	24	D 8
DELLAMARTA			
Rd	Wangara	24	E 6
DELLAR			
Rd	Maddington	96	C 3
DELLAVANZO			
St	Maddington	96	A 5
St	Maddington	95	E 5
DELLER			
St	Bibra Lake	101	D 3
DELLWOOD			
La	Ballajura	33	C 6
DELMONT			
Pl	Greenfields	163	D 7
DELMORE			
Gl	Kiara	48	E 6
DELPHI			
Ct	Rossmoyne	83	B 10
Pl	Coogee	101	A 9
DELPHINE			
Ave	Dianella	61	B 2
DELPHINUS			
Pl	Rockingham	137	B 8
DELRAY			
Cl	Warnbro	145	D 6
DELTA			
Ct	Byford	126	A 5
Ct	Ocean Reef	23	B 1
DELTOID			
Pl	Heathridge	19	D 10
DELVES			
Pl	Noranda	48	A 4
DELWOOD			
Ct	Port Kennedy	156	E 2
Pl	Willetton	93	D 7
DEMASSON			
Ri	Leeming	102	E 1
DEMPSEY			
Pl	Kenwick	95	E 1
St	Cloverdale	75	A 7
DEMPSTER			
Pl	Mariginiup	17	A 6
Rd	Karrinyup	44	E 2
Rd	Shoalwater	136	C 9
Rd	Sorrento	30	C 5
DENBY			
Ct	Carine	30	E 9
St	Balga	32	D 10
St	Wilson	84	C 3
DENE			
Ct	Gosnells	105	E 1
St	Mt Lawley	61	B 6
DENFORD			
St	Kenwick	95	E 1
St	Kenwick	85	E 10
DENHAM			
St	Mandurah	165	B 3
St	Spearwood	101	B 6
Wy	Thornlie	95	D 6

		Map	Ref.
DENHOLME			
Pl	Stoneville	54	B 5
DENIC			
Ri	Leeming	93	C 9
DENIEN			
St	Willagee	91	E 4
DENIS			
St	Subiaco	72	A 2
DENISE			
Cl	Shelley	93	B 1
DENISON			
Ct	Merriwa	11	D 9
DENMARK			
Wy	Warwick	31	D 6
DENNELL			
Ct	Marangaroo	32	D 6
DENNING			
Ct	Armadale	116	A 3
DENNINUP			
Wy	Malaga	33	D 10
DENNIS			
St	Quinns Rocks	10	A 1
St	Stirling	45	D 7
DENNISON			
Dr	Ocean Reef	18	E 9
St	Inglewood	61	D 4
DENNY			
Ave	Kelmscott	106	D 8
Wy	Alfred Cove	92	A 1
Wy	Lynwood	94	E 2
DENSTON			
Wy	Girrawheen	32	C 8
DENT			
Ct	Orelia	131	A 5
DENTON			
St	Wembley	60	A 10
DERBAL			
St	Medina	130	D 5
DERBI			
Rd	Alexander Hts	33	A 5
DERBY			
Cl	Warnbro	145	D 6
Rd	Shenton Park	71	E 4
Rd	Subiaco	71	E 3
Rd	Swanbourne	70	E 8
St	West Perth	60	E 9
DEREK			
Rd	Coodanup	165	C 7
DERICOTE			
Wy	Greenwood	31	D 6
DERINTON			
Wy	Hamilton Hill	101	A 3
DERISLEIGH			
St	Cannington	84	E 4
DERMER			
Rd	Hamilton Hill	90	E 9
DE ROUEN			
Ri	Sorrento	30	C 4
DERRIL			
Ave	Dianella	46	E 9
DERRINGTON			
Cr	Balga	32	A 8
DERRITON			
St	Ferndale	84	C 9
DERRY			
Ave	Armadale	116	E 4
DERWENT			
Cr	Jandakot	112	D 3
Mr	Joondalup	19	D 2
Pl	Lynwood	94	C 3
Pl	Rockingham	137	B 6
DESBY			
Pl	Leeming	92	E 10
DESCHAMP			
Rd	Morley	48	A 6
DESFORD			
Cl	Shelley	83	B 10

		Map	Ref.
DESTIN			
Cl	Warnbro	145	E 6
DETLING			
Ct	Westfield	116	B 1
DEVENISH			
Rd	Lockridge	49	B 7
St	E Victoria Pk	84	A 2
St	E Victoria Pk	83	E 1
St	E Victoria Pk	73	E 10
Wy	Leeming	93	C 9
DEVERELL			
Wy	Bentley	84	A 5
DEVEREUX			
St	Armadale	116	C 6
DEVINE			
St	Maddington	96	C 6
DEVITT			
Gr	Parmelia	131	B 9
DEVLIN			
St	Darlington	66	B 2
DEVLING			
Pl	Morley	47	D 8
DEVON			
Ct	Warwick	31	D 8
Pl	Mahogany Crk	53	C 10
Rd	Bassendean	63	B 2
Rd	Swanbourne	70	E 9
St	Midland	50	A 9
DEVONSHIRE			
St	Morley	48	C 6
Tce	Armadale	116	C 7
DEVONWAY			
	Lynwood	94	D 1
DEW			
Cl	Ballajura	33	C 5
St	Forrestdale	115	A 6
DEWAR			
Ct	Mandurah	165	B 3
Pl	Balga	32	E 10
St	Armadale	116	B 5
St	Falcon	162A	A 1
St	Morley	48	A 10
St	Morley	61	E 1
DEWEY			
St	Shelley	83	E 9
DEWIS			
Pl	Bull Creek	93	B 6
DEXTER			
Ct	Willetton	93	E 2
DEYOUNG			
Rd	Craigie	23	E 7
DIABLO			
Wy	Connolly	19	A 7
DIADEM			
Pl	Madora	160	C 6
DIAMANTINA			
Wy	Henderson	111	A 8
Wy	Rockingham	137	B 6
DIAMOND			
Dr	Ocean Reef	23	A 1
Pl	Kardinya	91	D 7
St	Beckenham	85	C 5
DIANA			
Cr	Lockridge	49	A 6
Pl	Madora	160	D 6
St	Innaloo	45	B 9
DIANE			
Pl	Henley Brook	28	C 10
DIANELLA			
Dr	Dianella	47	A 7
Rd	Walliston	87	E 2
DIANNE			
Cl	Rossmoyne	93	B 2
St	Hamilton Hill	101	A 1
DIBB			
St	Balcatta	46	B 7
DIBBLE			
St	Mt Helena	55	A 4

		Map	Ref.
DICKENS			
Wk	Carine	31	A 10
DICKENSON			
Wy	Booragoon	92	B 2
DICKSON			
Dr	Middle Swan	50	D 4
DIDCOT			
St	Warwick	31	D 7
DIEMEN			
Ct	Heathridge	23	C 1
DIGBY			
St	Gosnells	96	A 10
St	Gosnells	106	B 1
DILALI			
Rd	City Beach	58	E 7
DILGA			
Ct	Currambine	19	A 5
DILKARA			
Pl	Kalamunda	77	B 6
Wy	City Beach	58	D 4
DILKERA			
Pl	Currambine	19	A 4
DILLENIA			
Wy	Greenwood	31	E 3
DILLON			
Gl	Joondalup	19	C 2
Pl	Gosnells	106	A 1
Ri	Yangebup	112	A 1
DIMBOOLA			
Pl	Currambine	19	A 4
DIMITRIOS			
Ct	Wanneroo	24	E 1
DIMOND			
Ct	Leeming	103	B 1
DIMSDALE			
Pl	Iluka	18	E 6
DINGHY			
Pl	Ocean Reef	22	E 1
DINROY			
St	Duncraig	31	B 6
DINSDALE			
Pl	Hamersley	31	E 10
DION			
Pl	Coolbellup	101	E 1
DIONNE			
Pl	Gosnells	106	A 1
DIOR			
Pl	Greenfields	163	D 10
DIOSMA			
Wy	Forrestfield	76	C 8
DIRECTION			
Pl	Morley	48	D 7
DIRK			
Pl	Willetton	93	E 7
DIRK HARTOG			
Rd	Bull Creek	92	E 6
DISANTHUS			
Pl	Dianella	47	B 6
DISCOVERY			
Cr	Port Kennedy	156	D 4
Dr	Morley	48	D 7
Dr	Thornlie	95	C 8
DISNEY			
Rd	Parmelia	131	C 7
St	Brentwood	92	D 2
DIVINEY			
Ct	Lynwood	94	A 2
DIVISION			
Rd	Mandurah	165	A 2
St	Welshpool	84	D 1
St	Welshpool	74	E 10
DIXEY			
Ct	Leeming	92	E 10
DIXIE			
Rd	Kelmscott	116	D 1
Rd	Kelmscott	106	D 10

		Map	Ref.
DIXON			
Ave	Kewdale	74	E 6
Me	Leda	130	E 10
Pl	Kardinya	92	A 5
Pl	Woodvale	24	A 5
Pwy	Woodvale	24	C 5
Rd	Bibra Lake	102	B 1
Rd	E Rockingham	138	A 4
Rd	Kalamunda	77	D 6
Rd	Rockingham	137	B 4
St	Beaconsfield	90	E 8
St	Beaconsfield	90	E 9
St	Embleton	62	B 2
St	Kardinya	92	A 5
DMIETRIEFF			
Rd	Bedfordale	128	A 2
DOBBINS			
St	Wangara	25	A 6
DOBELL			
St	Huntingdale	95	D 10
DOBIE			
St	Bull Creek	93	A 6
DOBRA			
Rd	Yangebup	101	C 9
Rd	Yangebup	101	C 10
DOBSON			
Ct	Safety Bay	137	A 10
Pl	Hillarys	30	C 1
DOCKER			
Cl	Merriwa	11	D 10
DOCKRELL			
Ri	Marangaroo	32	C 6
DOCONING			
Rd	Beechina	57	D 1
Rd	Beechina	43	E 7
DODD			
Pl	Warnbro	145	D 9
Rd	Bickley	88	E 3
Rd	Noranda	47	C 9
St	Hamilton Hill	91	B 10
St	Wembley	60	A 6
DODDS			
Pl	Beechboro	49	A 3
Pl	Innaloo	45	C 9
DODINGTON			
Pl	Parkerville	53	D 4
DODONAEA			
Ct	Duncraig	31	A 7
DODONIA			
Gns	City Beach	58	D 7
DOEPEL			
St	Nth Fremantle	90	C 2
DOGHILL			
Rd	Baldivis	148	A 7
Rd	Baldivis	147	D 8
Rd	Baldivis	147	E 1
DOHERTY			
Hts	Parmelia	131	C 8
Rd	Coolbellup	92	A 10
St	Embleton	62	B 2
DOIG			
Pl	Beaconsfield	90	E 8
DOLAN			
St	Willagee	91	D 4
Wy	Lockridge	49	A 6
DOLEY			
Rd	Byford	135	A 4
Rd	Byford	126	A 10
DOLIUM			
Ct	Heathridge	23	D 1
DOLLIER			
St	Banjup	103	B 3
DOLLIS			
Wy	Kingsley	24	C 9
Wy	Westfield	106	B 9
DOLOMITE			
Ct	Churchlands	59	B 5
Rd	Carine	30	E 10

194

Map Ref.

DOLPHIN
Dr Mandurah 162 E 9
Rd Safety Bay 145 A 1
Wy Beldon 23 C 2
DOLTON
Pl Warnbro 145 D 8
DOMAIN
Ct Greenmount 51 B 10
DOME
Pl Victoria Park 73 E 4
DON
Cl Beechboro 48 E 3
Pl Hamersley 46 A 1
DONAHUE
Cl Noranda 47 E 4
DONALD
Ct Armadale 116 B 6
Dr Safety Bay 145 A 1
Rd Maida Vale 76 E 1
Sq Bayswater 62 B 7
St Willetton 93 C 3
Wy Bayswater 62 B 7
DONALDSON
St Queens Park 85 A 3
DONAR
St Innaloo 59 B 1
DONATA
Ct Willetton 93 D 4
DONATTI
Rd Innaloo 45 C 8
DONAVON
Ri Murdoch 92 B 7
DONCASTER
Gns Port Kennedy 156 D 2
DONEGAL
Cl Alexander Hts 33 A 4
Rd Floreat 59 A 8
DONERAILE
Ct Waterford 83 D 6
DONEY
St Alfred Cove 82 A 10
DONGALA
Wy Ferndale 84 C 9
DONGARA
St Innaloo 45 C 10
DONNA
St Morley 48 A 9
St Rossmoyne 93 A 2
DONNE
Ct Spearwood 101 C 8
DONNELLY
Gns Mandurah 165 A 4
St Bentley 84 A 5
DONNES
St Bull Creek 92 E 6
DONNINGTON
Rd Balcatta 46 A 5
DONOVAN
St Osborne Park 60 B 4
DOOLETTE
St Spearwood 101 C 5
DOOLEY
St Naval Base 121 B 7
DOOMBEN
Ct Willetton 93 D 3
DOON
Wy Hamersley 31 E 9
DOONAN
Rd Nedlands 71 C 10
DOONDA
St Mandurah 163 B 9
DOONGALLA
Rd Attadale 81 C 7
DOONSIDE
Pl Morley 48 D 6
DOORIGO
Rd Armadale 116 B 5

Map Ref.

DORA
Pl Woodvale 24 B 5
St Queens Park 84 E 4
DORADEEN
Cl Hillman 137 E 6
DORADEL
Ave Kelmscott 116 E 1
DORADO
Ct Rockingham 137 B 7
St Golden Bay 158 D 9
DORADO BEACH
Cr Connolly 19 B 6
DORAL
Ct Meadow Sprgs. 163 C 2
Pl Connolly 19 C 8
DORAM
Ct Swan View 51 C 5
DORAN
Pl Willetton 93 D 2
DORANDAL
Ct Alexander Hts 32 E 6
DORCAS
Wy Coolbellup 101 D 1
Wy Coolbellup 91 D 10
DORCHESTER
Ave Warwick 31 C 7
Ct Mullaloo 23 A 3
Rd Forrestfield 86 C 2
DOREEN
St Mandurah 165 B 4
DORIC
St Scarborough 58 E 2
St Shelley 83 C 10
DORIGO
Pl Gosnells 95 E 7
DORIOT
Wy Carine 45 A 1
DORIS
St North Perth 60 D 5
DORKING
Pl Morley 48 B 9
Rd City Beach 58 D 6
DORMANS
Rd Morley 47 C 6
DORNIE
Pl Ardross 82 C 9
DORNOCH
Ct Duncraig 31 B 5
DOROTHY
Ave Falcon 162A E 10
St Ashfield 62 E 5
St Fremantle 90 D 3
St Gosnells 106 A 1
St Gosnells 96 B 10
DORRE
Ct Shelley 93 C 1
DORRINGTON
Rd Kalamunda 77 B 5
DORSET
Pl Thornlie 95 B 2
St Kallaroo 23 B 7
DORSETSHIRE
Me Iluka 18 E 4
DORWARD
Ct Kardinya 92 A 9
DORY
Cl Halls Head 164 B 2
Pl Willetton 93 E 6
Rd Beldon 23 C 3
DORYANTHES
Pl Wanneroo 20 E 6
DOSINIA
Pl Heathridge 23 D 1
DOTTEREL
Pl Kingsley 31 C 1
Trl Ballajura 33 D 6
Wy Yangebup 102 A 8

Map Ref.

DOUGALL
St Cardup 135 D 3
DOUGLAS
Ave Kensington 73 C 10
Ave South Perth 73 B 8
Ave Subiaco 72 A 2
Ave Yokine 46 D 9
Ct Duncraig 31 A 6
Rd Canning Mills 98 B 4
Rd Canning Mills 97 E 4
Rd Chidlow 56 B 2
Rd Henley Brook 36 B 4
Rd Martin 107 E 2
Rd Martin 97 E 9
Rd West Swan 36 B 4
St Fremantle 90 C 7
St West Perth 60 D 10
DOUNE
Pl Willetton 93 D 4
DOUNLEY
St Balga 46 D 2
DOURO
Ct Kingsley 31 C 2
Pl West Perth 72 C 1
Rd Sth Fremantle 90 C 9
DOUST
St Cannington 84 D 5
St Hilton 91 C 7
DOVE
Ct High Wycombe 64 B 10
Ct Mundaring 68 C 1
La Armadale 116 B 4
Me Joondalup 19 C 3
St Stirling 45 E 6
St Thornlie 95 A 4
DOVER
Cr Wembley Dns 58 E 4
Ct Marangaroo 32 A 5
Ct Mosman Park 80 D 5
Pde Port Kennedy 156 D 2
Pl Yangebup 101 E 10
Rd Scarborough 58 D 2
St Greenfields 163 E 9
St Mt Hawthorn 60 C 5
DOVERIDGE
Dr Duncraig 31 A 3
DOVERLEA
St Lynwood 94 D 1
DOWD
St Welshpool 75 A 10
St Welshpool 85 B 1
St Welshpool 85 C 1
DOWDEN
St Shoalwater 136 D 9
DOWEL
Ct Ocean Reef 23 B 2
DOWELL
Cl Bedfordale 127 D 3
Pl Bibra Lake 102 D 3
St Sawyers Valley 69 A 1
DOWER
Ct Armadale 116 D 3
St Mandurah 165 B 1
St Mandurah 163 B 10
DOWIE
St Mt Helena 55 C 7
DOWLEY
Ct Queens Park 85 A 3
DOWLING
Pl Orelia 131 B 5
St Rockingham 137 C 5
DOWNER
Wy Bull Creek 93 A 4
DOWNEY
Dr Manning 83 B 6
Dr Mosman Park 81 A 8
DOWNHILL
Wy Langford 95 A 2
DOWNING
Cr Wanneroo 20 C 7
St Carlisle 74 C 10

Map Ref.

DOWNSBOROUGH
Ave Kewdale 74 E 8
DOWNY
Grn Mirrabooka 47 A 1
DOWSE
Ct Coogee 100 E 8
DOWSON
Wy Midland 50 C 8
DOYLE
Ct Greenwood 31 C 4
St Morley 48 C 9
St Mosman Park 80 D 5
St Noranda 47 E 4
DRABBLE
Rd City Beach 58 D 3
Rd Scarborough 58 D 2
DRACENA
St Greenwood 31 C 5
DRACONIS
St Heathridge 23 E 1
DRAKE
St Bayswater 62 A 3
St Embleton 62 A 3
St Morley 47 D 10
St Morley 61 E 1
St Osborne Park 60 A 3
St Osborne Park 59 E 3
Wy Morley 61 E 2
DRAKES
Wk Sorrento 30 B 6
DRAKESWOOD
Rd Warwick 31 E 6
DRAMMEN
El Merriwa 11 C 9
DRAPER
Ct Currambine 19 A 2
Rd Mahogany Crk 67 C 1
Rd Wattle Grove 85 E 1
Rd Wattle Grove 75 E 10
St Floreat 71 C 1
DRAY
Ct Belmont 62 E 10
DRAYCOTT
St Karrinyup 44 E 5
DRAYTON
Ct Westfield 106 C 10
St Bassendean 48 D 10
Wy North Beach 44 D 2
DRAYTON GREEN
Wy Kingsley 24 B 10
DREGHORN
Rd Darlington 66 B 6
DRESDEN
Gr Iluka 18 D 4
DRESS
Ci Warnbro 145 E 6
DRESSLER
Wy Girrawheen 32 B 8
DREVON
Pl Marangaroo 32 D 5
DREW
Rd Ardross 82 C 9
St Stirling 45 E 6
St Wembley 60 A 7
DREYER
Ct Yanchep 4 C 4
Rd Roleystone 108 A 8
Wy Bull Creek 93 A 5
DREYFUS
Pl Dianella 47 C 9
DRIFFIELD
St Hamersley 31 D 9
DRIFTWOOD
Rd Silver Sands 163 B 5
Ri Quinns Rocks 10 A 10
DRILBY
Wy Gosnells 96 A 8

Map Ref.

DRINAN
Pl Hillarys 30 B 1
DRISCOLL
Dr Canning Vale 104 C 6
Wy Morley 48 A 7
Wy Morley 47 E 7
DRIVER
Rd Landsdale 32 D 1
Rd Landsdale 25 D 10
Wy Bull Creek 93 B 5
DROGHEDA
Wy Waterford 83 D 6
DROMANA
Pl Craigie 23 C 5
DROSERA
Ct Forrestfield 76 C 10
DRUMFERN
St Ardross 82 C 9
DRUMMER
Wy Heathridge 23 B 1
Wy Heathridge 19 B 10
DRUMMOND
Cr Duncraig 30 E 5
Ct Kelmscott 107 A 10
St Bedford 61 D 2
St Leederville 60 C 9
St Redcliffe 62 E 9
DRUMORE
El Stratton 51 A 3
DRURY
Ct Marmion 30 D 8
St Willagee 91 D 4
DRYANDRA
Cr Greenmount 65 E 1
Ct Greenwood 31 C 4
Dr Mirrabooka 47 A 1
Dr Mirrabooka 33 A 10
Pl Halls Head 164 B 4
Wy Armadale 116 A 6
Wy Thornlie 95 A 8
DRYDEN
St Munster 101 B 9
St Yokine 61 A 2
DRYNAN
St Bayswater 62 B 2
DRYSDALE
Rd Craigie 23 D 7
St Eden Hill 49 A 9
St Gosnells 105 E 3
St Innaloo 45 C 10
St Shelley 93 C 1
DUART
Rd Trigg 44 D 4
DUBLIN
Cl Warnbro 145 E 6
DUBOVE
Rd Spearwood 101 C 4
DUCHART
Wy Coogee 100 E 9
DUCHESS
Pl Duncraig 30 D 3
DUCKETT
Dr Manning 83 A 7
DUCKPOND
Rd Peel Estate 140 D 5
DUCKWORTH
Dr Perth Airport 63 B 8
DUDLEY
Rd Kenwick 95 C 1
Rd Kenwick 85 C 10
St Midland 50 C 7
St Rivervale 74 C 4
DUFF
Pl Booragoon 92 C 3
Rd Ferndale 94 B 1
Rd Riverton 84 B 10
DUFFIELD
Ave Hamilton Hill 90 E 9
Gr Carine 30 E 9

For detailed information regarding the street referencing system used in this book, turn to page 170.

E

		Map	Ref.
DUFFY			
Rd	Carine	45	B 1
Rd	Carine	31	C 10
St	Bayswater	62	C 2
Tce	Woodvale	24	D 7
DUGDALE			
St	Warwick	31	D 8
DUGGAN			
Ct	Balga	32	A 8
Ct	Kardinya	92	A 9
DUKE			
St	Bentley	84	C 5
St	East Fremantle	90	D 3
St	Inglewood	61	D 4
St	Karrinyup	44	E 8
St	Scarborough	44	E 10
St	Subiaco	72	A 3
Wy	Lesmurdie	87	B 3
DUKETON			
Wy	Kenwick	85	E 10
DULCIFY			
Ct	Brigadoon	169	B 3
DULVERSON			
Pl	South Lake	102	D 7
DULWICH			
Pl	Kingsley	31	B 2
St	Beckenham	85	C 8
St	West Swan	35	B 10
DUMAS			
Cl	Winthrop	92	A 4
Rd	Curtin Uni	135	
DU MAURIER			
Rd	North Lake	92	A 10
DUMBARTON			
Cr	Menora	60	E 5
Rd	Canning Vale	104	C 1
DUMFRIES			
Pl	Floreat	59	C 7
Rd	Floreat	59	B 7
DUMOND			
St	Bentley	84	A 4
DUMONT			
Ct	Kingsley	31	C 2
DUMSDAY			
Dr	Forrestdale	114	E 6
DUNBAR			
Cl	Kingsley	24	C 10
Ct	Meadow Sprgs	163	C 5
St	Claremont	71	B 10
DUNBLANE			
Rd	Floreat	59	C 8
DUNCAN			
Cl	Lynwood	94	A 5
Pl	Mahogany Crk	53	C 10
Rd	Coodanup	165	C 7
St	Victoria Park	74	A 7
St	Victoria Park	73	E 7
DUNCANNON			
Ri	Mindarie	14	A 3
DUNCRAIG			
Ct	Cooloongup	137	E 7
Rd	Applecross	82	C 5
Rd	Duncraig	30	D 6
DUNCTON			
Ct	Leeming	93	A 10
DUNDALK			
St	Floreat	59	B 9
DUNDAS			
Ct	Waikiki	145	D 2
Pl	Greenfields	165	C 1
Rd	Forrestfield	76	A 7
Rd	Forrestfield	75	E 7
Rd	High Wycombe	76	A 1
Rd	High Wycombe	64	A 10
Rd	Inglewood	61	C 3
DUNDEBAR			
Rd	Wanneroo	21	A 7
Rd	Wanneroo	20	D 8

		Map	Ref.
DUNDEE			
Cl	Warnbro	145	E 6
Ct	Duncraig	31	A 6
St	Leeming	93	C 10
Wy	Westfield	106	C 6
DUNDULA			
Ct	Currambine	19	A 5
DUNEDIN			
St	Mt Hawthorn	60	D 4
DUNELT			
Pl	Marangaroo	32	D 6
DUNFEE			
Pl	Hamersley	45	D 1
DUNFORD			
St	Willagee	91	E 5
DUNGARVAN			
Cl	Waterford	83	C 6
DUNHAM			
Wy	Heathridge	19	B 9
DUNHOLME			
Pl	Huntingdale	95	D 9
Pl	Osborne Park	46	A 10
St	Osborne Park	46	A 10
DUNK			
Pl	Coogee	100	E 8
DUNKELD			
Glen	Kinross	18	E 1
St	Floreat	59	B 7
DUNKLEY			
Ave	Applecross	82	A 9
Pl	Bayswater	62	A 3
DUNLOP			
Ri	Kinross	19	A 1
DUNMORE			
Cc	Merriwa	10	B 9
DUNNELL			
St	Maddington	96	B 5
DUNOON			
St	Kingsley	24	C 9
DUNRAVEN			
Dr	Yangebup	112	A 1
Dr	Yangebup	102	B 10
DUNROSSIL			
Pl	Scarborough	58	E 3
St	Scarborough	58	E 3
DUNSCORE			
Wy	Kinross	19	A 2
DUNSTAN			
Pl	Murdoch	92	C 7
DUNSTER			
Rd	Innaloo	45	C 8
St	Karrinyup	44	E 4
DUNSTONE			
Rd	Bayswater	62	D 6
DUNTON			
Pl	Redcliffe	62	E 10
DUNVEGAN			
Rd	Applecross	82	D 4
DUPAIN			
Ct	Dianella	47	A 7
DUPONT			
Ave	City Beach	58	D 7
DURA			
Rd	Parkerville	53	C 6
DURACK			
Cl	Bateman	92	D 3
Cr	Gosnells	106	A 2
Pl	Koondoola	33	A 8
St	Coodanup	165	C 6
Wy	Padbury	23	D 9
DURAL			
Wy	Armadale	116	B 5
DURANT			
Wy	Brentwood	92	E 3
DURBAN			
Cr	Kingsley	31	C 3
Cr	Warnbro	145	E 7

		Map	Ref.
St	Belmont	74	D 1
St	Belmont	62	E 10
DURDHAM			
Cr	Bicton	81	A 9
DURFORD			
St	Balga	46	D 2
DURHAM			
Cl	Greenfields	163	D 8
Pl	Bull Creek	93	B 5
Rd	Bayswater	62	C 4
St	Lathlain	74	A 4
Wy	Balga	46	D 3
Wy	Forrestfield	86	C 1
DURI			
St	Armadale	116	C 9
DURNSFORD			
Wy	Westfield	106	B 8
DURRANT			
Ave	Parmelia	131	C 5
Wy	High Wycombe	76	B 1
DURRAS			
Pl	Mandurah	165	B 4
Pl	South Lake	102	C 7
DURRINGTON			
Gl	Clarkson	14	D 3
DURSTON			
Rd	Wembley Dns	58	E 6
DUSKY			
La	Mirrabooka	47	B 2
DUSTING			
Rd	Balcatta	46	C 7
DUTTON			
Cl	Lynwood	94	D 3
Cl	Merriwa	11	C 9
Cr	Hamersley	45	D 1
Cr	Hamersley	31	D 10
Rd	Armadale	116	A 3
Wy	Singleton	160	D 3
DUVAL			
Ct	Marangaroo	32	D 6
Rd	Darlington	66	A 1
DUVERNEY			
Cr	Coodanup	165	D 3
DUX			
Ct	Duncraig	31	A 7
DUXBURY			
Pl	Willetton	93	E 1
DVORETSKY			
Cl	Golden Bay	159	A 7
DWYER			
Cr	Gosnells	106	A 2
Gns	Joondalup	19	E 5
St	Karrinyup	45	A 3
DYER			
Rd	Bassendean	62	E 2
St	Kelmscott	106	E 9
St	West Perth	1C	D 1
St	West Perth	72	D 1
DYMCHURCH			
Ct	Marangaroo	32	B 3
DYMOND			
Pl	Leda	130	E 9
DYSART			
Ct	Kingsley	24	C 9
DYSON			
Ct	Leeming	93	C 8
Ct	Westfield	106	B 10
St	Kensington	73	C 8
St	South Perth	73	C 8

E

		Map	Ref.
EACHAM			
Ct	South Lake	102	C 8
EACOTT			
St	Mandurah	163	B 9

		Map	Ref.
EADE			
Ct	Greenwood	31	D 4
EAGAR			
Cnr	Leeming	92	E 10
EAGLE			
Ct	High Wycombe	64	A 10
Ct	Huntingdale	105	D 1
Dr	Jandakot	103	C 4
Me	Cooloongup	137	E 9
Ri	Yangebup	102	A 9
St	Craigie	23	D 7
St	Mundaring	68	D 1
St	Mundaring	54	D 10
Vw	Armadale	116	A 3
EAGLEHAWK			
Gr	Wungong	116	C 10
EAGLEMONT			
Dr	Swan View	51	C 5
EAGLES			
Wk	Willetton	93	C 4
EALING			
Me	Kingsley	24	A 9
EALY			
St	Mt Helena	55	A 5
EARL			
Ct	Calista	130	E 9
Ct	Merriwa	11	C 9
St	Bentley	83	E 5
St	Perth City	61	A 10
EARLS			
Ct	Mt Claremont	71	A 5
Ct	Safety Bay	145	A 1
Ct	Thornlie	95	C 5
Pl	Balga	32	E 9
EARLSFERRY			
Grn	Kinross	19	A 2
EARLSTON			
Pl	Booragoon	92	C 3
Wy	Booragoon	92	C 3
EARN			
Pl	Hamersley	32	A 9
EARNLEY			
Wy	Balga	46	C 2
EARNSHAW			
Lp	Leeming	92	E 10
EARTHAM			
Pl	Balga	46	B 2
EASELEY			
Rd	Hamilton Hill	101	A 4
EASON			
Rd	Sawyers Valley	54	E 9
EAST			
Pde	East Perth	73	C 2
Pde	East Perth	61	C 10
Pde	Mt Lawley	61	C 9
Rd	Pickering Bk	99	B 2
Rd	Shoalwater	136	C 9
Rd	Wanneroo	24	E 3
St	East Fremantle	90	D 3
St	Fremantle	90	D 4
St	Guildford	63	E 1
St	Guildford	49	E 10
St	Maylands	61	E 8
St	Mt Hawthorn	60	B 6
Tce	Kalamunda	77	C 6
EASTBOURNE			
Cr	Nollamara	46	D 5
St	Lynwood	94	D 2
St	Mosman Park	80	D 6
EAST CHURCHILL			
Ave	Yangebup	111	C 3
EASTDENE			
Ci	Nollamara	46	D 4
EASTFIELD			
Ct	Ferndale	84	E 9
EASTLAND			
St	Dianella	46	E 8
EASTLEIGH			
Pl	Mt Helena	55	C 3

		Map	Ref.
EAST LORNE			
St	Floreat	59	C 8
EASTON			
Ct	Boya	65	C 5
St	East Fremantle	90	E 1
St	East Fremantle	80	E 10
EASTWOOD			
Wy	Hamersley	45	E 1
Wy	Martin	96	C 7
EATON			
Ct	Woodvale	24	B 6
Pl	Noranda	47	C 4
St	Morley	47	E 8
EATTS			
Rd	Roleystone	108	B 7
EBB			
Ct	Halls Head	164	B 1
EBBS			
Ct	Murdoch	92	C 7
EBERT			
St	Coolbellup	91	D 10
EBONY			
Cr	Warnbro	145	D 6
Ct	Halls Head	164	A 5
EBRO			
Wy	Willetton	93	D 4
EBSWORTH			
St	Mt Lawley	61	C 9
EBURY			
Pl	Hamersley	31	E 9
ECCLES			
Pl	Hamersley	31	E 9
ECCLESBORNE			
St	Mosman Park	80	D 5
ECCLESTONE			
St	Warnbro	145	C 6
ECHIDNA			
Ct	Wungong	116	B 9
ECHO			
Rd	Kalamunda	77	D 5
ECKERSLEY			
Hts	Winthrop	92	A 5
ECKFORD			
Wy	Duncraig	31	A 8
ECKO			
Rd	Kelmscott	116	E 1
ECLIPSE			
Cr	Kallaroo	23	B 6
Wy	Beckenham	85	D 5
ECTON			
St	Gosnells	106	C 2
EDALE			
Wy	Balga	46	D 4
EDDIE BARRON			
Dr	Midland	50	D 6
EDDINGTON			
Rd	Warwick	31	D 7
EDDY			
Cl	Leda	130	E 10
St	Coodanup	165	D 5
EDDYSTONE			
Ave	Beldon	23	D 3
Ave	Craigie	23	D 7
Ave	Heathridge	23	E 2
Ave	Joondalup	19	E 10
EDELINE			
St	Spearwood	101	B 6
EDEN			
Cl	Winthrop	92	C 5
Me	Kinross	19	A 2
St	Innaloo	45	C 7
St	Mandurah	165	A 2
St	West Perth	60	E 9
EDGAR			
Ct	Beaconsfield	90	E 7
Wy	Mt Pleasant	92	D 1

E

		Map	Ref.
EDGE			
Ct	Thornlie	95	C 9
Pl	Dianella	47	D 8
EDGECUMBE			
St	Como	83	A 6
EDGEFIELD			
Wy	North Beach	44	D 3
EDGEHILL			
St	Scarborough	44	D 9
EDGEL			
Ct	Kingsley	31	C 3
EDGEROI			
Wy	Armadale	116	C 6
EDGEVIEW			
Me	Ballajura	33	D 5
EDGEWARE			
Pl	Kingsley	31	B 1
St	Lynwood	84	D 10
EDGEWATER			
Dr	Edgewater	20	A 9
Dr	Edgewater	24	B 2
Rd	Safety Bay	145	B 2
Rd	Salter Point	83	A 8
EDGINGTON			
Cr	Koondoola	32	E 7
EDGLEY			
Pl	Thornlie	95	D 3
EDINA			
Ct	Two Rocks	3	B 10
EDINBORO			
Pl	Joondanna	60	C 3
St	Mt Hawthorn	60	C 4
EDINBRIDGE			
Rd	Kenwick	95	C 1
EDINBURGH			
Ave	Kinross	18	E 1
Cl	Falcon	162A	B 4
Rd	Forrestfield	86	C 1
St	South Perth	73	A 8
EDINGER			
Cnr	Leeming	102	E 1
EDISON			
St	Dianella	47	B 7
Wy	Dianella	47	B 7
EDITH			
Cl	Kingsley	24	D 10
Rd	Safety Bay	144	E 1
St	Darlington	66	C 7
St	Mosman Park	80	D 6
St	Perth City	61	A 10
EDLASTON			
Rd	Carine	30	E 9
EDMISTON			
Wy	Winthrop	92	B 6
EDMONDSON			
Cr	Karrinyup	45	A 6
St	Beaconsfield	90	E 9
EDMONTON			
Pl	Kingsley	31	B 1
EDMUND			
St	Beaconsfield	90	D 7
St	White Gum Vly	90	D 6
Tce	Kelmscott	106	E 8
Wy	Calista	130	E 9
EDNA			
Rd	Dalkeith	81	D 2
St	Tuart Hill	46	C 10
Wy	Duncraig	30	E 4
EDNAH			
St	Como	82	E 2
St	Wembley Dns	59	A 5
EDNEY			
Rd	High Wycombe	76	C 1
Rd	High Wycombe	64	D 10
EDSELL			
Dr	Armadale	116	A 4
EDWARD			
Cr	Byford	135	D 1
Rd	Lesmurdie	87	D 7

		Map	Ref.
St	Beckenham	85	D 4
St	Bedford	61	D 1
St	Bellevue	64	E 1
St	Bellevue	50	E 10
St	Cottesloe	80	E 1
St	E Rockingham	129	D 9
St	Kenwick	85	D 5
St	Mariginiup	20	D 3
St	Nedlands	71	D 9
St	North Beach	44	C 3
St	Osborne Park	60	B 2
St	Osborne Park	46	B 10
St	Perth City	1C	A 1
St	Perth City	73	B 1
St	Queens Park	84	E 3
St	Sorrento	30	D 6
St	West Swan	36	A 7
EDWARDS			
Cr	Redcliffe	62	E 10
Ent	Stratton	51	B 4
Grn	Floreat	71	C 1
Pde	Mosman Park	80	D 7
Rd	High Wycombe	64	C 10
St	Booragoon	92	B 3
St	Leda	130	E 10
EDWIN			
St	Kingsley	31	C 2
EDWYNA			
St	Mosman Park	80	D 5
EGAN			
Pl	Midland	50	E 6
Rd	Mt Helena	55	B 4
St	Armadale	116	B 7
St	Midland	50	E 6
EGERTON			
St	Beckenham	85	C 6
EGEUS			
Wy	Coolbellup	91	E 10
EGHAM			
Pl	Morley	47	E 7
Rd	Lathlain	74	A 5
Rd	Victoria Park	73	E 5
EGINA			
St	Mt Hawthorn	60	B 6
EGLINTON			
Cr	Hamersley	31	D 10
EGMONT			
Ct	Currambine	19	B 5
Rd	Henderson	111	A 5
EGRET			
Hts	Kingsley	25	A 10
Hts	Kingsley	31	E 1
Me	Coolongup	137	E 9
Pl	Yangebup	102	B 8
St	Stirling	45	D 6
EIDER			
Pl	Wilson	84	A 8
EIGHTH			
Ave	Bassendean	49	B 10
Ave	Inglewood	61	C 5
Ave	Kensington	73	C 9
Ave	Maylands	61	D 7
Rd	Armadale	116	A 6
EIGHTY			
Rd	Baldivis	147	A 3
Rd	Baldivis	157	D 2
Rd	Baldivis	146	E 6
Rd	Karnup	157	D 10
EILDON			
Ct	Joondalup	19	C 2
Ct	South Lake	102	D 6
Pl	Falcon	162A	B 4
EILEEN			
Ave	Whitby	143	B 6
St	Bassendean	63	A 3
St	Cottesloe	80	C 1
St	Gosnells	106	A 5
EISENHOWER			
Dr	Yanchep	3	D 10
ELA			
St	Leeming	93	A 8

		Map	Ref.
ELABANA			
Cr	Dianella	47	A 9
ELAND			
Pl	Marangaroo	32	E 6
ELANORA			
Dr	Cooloongup	138	A 8
Dr	Cooloongup	137	E 8
Pl	Greenfields	163	D 9
Rd	Armadale	116	C 3
St	Joondanna	60	D 4
Wy	Yanchep	4	D 1
Wy	Yanchep	3	D 10
ELATA			
Ct	Thornlie	95	A 9
Gr	Mirrabooka	47	A 1
Me	Warnbro	145	E 8
ELBE			
Ct	Beechboro	48	D 2
Ct	Riverton	83	E 10
ELBUET			
Wy	Parmelia	131	E 2
ELBURY			
Ct	Kingsley	31	C 1
ELCAR			
La	Joondalup	19	D 7
ELCHO			
Wy	Yanchep	3	D 10
ELDER			
Pde	Bassendean	63	A 4
Pl	Fremantle	90	B 4
Pl	Fremantle	1D	B 5
Pl	Padbury	23	D 9
St	Perth City	1C	D 2
St	Perth City	72	D 2
Wy	Bellevue	65	A 1
ELDERBERRY			
Ci	Halls Head	164	B 5
Dr	Lynwood	94	B 3
Dr	South Lake	102	C 7
ELDERFIELD			
Rd	Manning	83	C 6
ELDERSLIE			
Wy	Duncraig	31	A 5
ELDON			
Cl	Merriwa	11	C 9
St	Dianella	61	C 1
St	Shoalwater	136	D 8
ELDORA			
Cr	Falcon	162A	D 10
EL DORADO			
St	Osborne Park	46	B 10
St	Tuart Hill	46	C 10
ELDWICK			
Lp	Swan View	51	C 7
ELEANOR			
Ct	Craigie	23	E 7
St	Como	83	B 3
ELECTRA			
St	Bateman	92	D 4
St	Craigie	23	E 7
ELEGANT			
Dr	Greenfields	163	D 10
ELETTRA			
Cl	Morley	48	D 6
ELEVENTH			
Ave	Inglewood	61	D 5
Rd	Armadale	115	E 8
Rd	Wungong	116	A 9
Rd	Wungong	126	B 1
ELFA			
Ct	Alexander Hts	32	E 5
ELFIN			
Gr	Warnbro	145	E 8
ELFREDA			
Ave	Sorrento	30	D 5
St	Chidlow	56	A 5
ELGEE			
Rd	Bellevue	50	D 9

		Map	Ref.
ELGIN			
Ct	Duncraig	31	A 7
Rd	Canning Vale	104	C 2
ELGON HILL			
	Willetton	93	C 3
ELIA			
Ct	Swan View	51	B 6
ELIAS			
Ct	Greenwood	31	C 5
ELIMATTA			
Wy	City Beach	58	D 8
ELINOR			
Pl	Coolbellup	101	E 2
ELIOT			
Cl	Parmelia	131	A 9
Rd	Armadale	126	D 1
ELIZA			
Ct	Hamilton Hill	101	C 3
ELIZABETH			
Ave	Mundaring	68	A 4
Pl	Karragullen	109	A 2
Rd	Wanneroo	20	E 8
St	Bayswater	62	A 7
St	Beckenham	85	C 5
St	Cloverdale	74	D 4
St	Cottesloe	70	D 10
St	E Cannington	85	C 4
St	Kalamunda	77	D 5
St	Kewdale	74	D 5
St	Mandurah	165	B 1
St	Maylands	61	E 9
St	Nedlands	71	D 9
St	North Perth	60	E 6
St	Osborne Park	46	A 10
St	Shoalwater	136	C 8
St	South Perth	73	B 9
St	White Gum Vly	90	E 7
ELK			
Ct	Connolly	19	A 7
ELKHORN			
St	E Cannington	85	D 3
ELKINGTON			
Me	Clarkson	14	E 2
ELL			
Pl	Cooloongup	137	C 10
ELLA			
Pl	Duncraig	30	D 3
ELLAM			
St	Victoria Park	73	C 7
St	Welshpool	84	B 2
ELLARA			
Ct	Alexander Hts	33	B 4
ELLARD			
Ave	Belmont	74	E 1
ELLEKER			
Cl	Greenfields	163	E 9
ELLEMENT			
Pde	Coogee	100	E 8
ELLEN			
St	Fremantle	90	C 4
St	Fremantle	1D	C 5
St	Kelmscott	116	E 2
St	Subiaco	72	B 1
ELLENBRAE			
Pl	Marangaroo	32	C 4
ELLEN BROOK			
Dr	Ellenbrook	29	C 2
Dr	Upper Swan	29	D 2
ELLENDALE			
Ct	Armadale	116	A 4
Dr	Heathridge	24	A 2
Dr	Heathridge	23	E 3
St	Golden Bay	158	D 8
ELLERBY			
St	Glendalough	60	A 6
Wy	Koondoola	32	E 5
ELLERSDALE			
Ave	Warwick	31	D 7

		Map	Ref.
ELLERSLIE			
Ct	Greenfields	163	D 9
ELLERY			
Ct	Jandakot	112	E 2
ELLESMERE			
Ct	Cooloongup	137	E 8
Hts	Hillarys	23	A 9
Pl	Jandakot	112	E 2
Rd	Lynwood	94	D 2
Rd	Mt Lawley	61	C 9
Rd	Swan View	51	B 7
St	Mt Hawthorn	60	C 4
St	North Perth	60	D 4
ELLICE			
St	Embleton	48	A 10
ELLINGHAM			
St	North Beach	44	D 2
ELLIOT			
Pl	Thornlie	95	A 5
Rd	Wanneroo	20	E 10
ELLIOTT			
Cr	Scarborough	44	D 7
Pl	Willetton	93	E 7
Rd	Chidlow	56	A 3
Rd	Claremont	71	A 8
Rd	Karrinyup	44	D 7
Rd	Mt Helena	55	C 5
Rd	Trigg	44	C 5
St	Midvale	51	A 9
ELLIS			
Ct	High Wycombe	64	D 9
Ct	Medina	130	E 4
Gr	Woodvale	24	B 5
Rd	Kelmscott	117	A 2
St	Mandurah	163	B 10
St	Wilson	84	A 6
ELLISON			
Dr	Langford	95	A 1
Dr	Padbury	30	D 2
Dr	Willagee	91	E 5
ELLON			
Pl	Duncraig	31	C 8
ELM			
Cl	Westfield	106	C 9
Ct	Ballajura	33	C 5
Ct	Dianella	47	B 9
St	Hamersley	31	E 10
ELMA			
St	Coolbinia	60	E 4
St	North Perth	60	D 4
ELMHURST			
Wy	Greenwood	31	E 4
ELMORE			
Pl	Orelia	131	A 5
St	Mt Helena	55	B 3
Wy	Mandurah	165	B 4
ELMS			
Ct	Erskine	164	C 6
Ct	Winthrop	92	C 6
ELMSFIELD			
Rd	Midvale	51	A 9
St	Belmont	74	D 1
St	Belmont	62	D 10
ELMSLIE			
St	Orelia	130	E 3
ELMTON			
Ct	Duncraig	31	A 3
Wy	Carine	31	A 9
ELMWOOD			
Ave	Woodlands	59	B 4
Cr	Lesmurdie	77	D 10
Ct	Marangaroo	32	C 4
ELONA			
Cl	Willetton	93	E 5
ELOUERA			
Rd	Westfield	106	B 8
Wy	City Beach	58	D 8
ELOURE			
Pl	Willetton	93	D 3

For detailed information regarding the street referencing system used in this book, turn to page 170.

197

E

		Map	Ref.
ELPHIN			
Cl	Kingsley	24	C 9
St	Floreat	59	A 9
ELPHINSTONE			
Rt	Iluka	18	D 3
ELSE			
Wy	Clarkson	14	C 2
ELSEGOOD			
St	Dianella	61	C 2
ELSFIELD			
Wy	Bassendean	62	E 1
Wy	Bassendean	48	E 10
ELSHAW			
St	Queens Park	85	A 2
ELSIE			
St	Gosnells	106	C 1
St	Waterman	30	C 9
ELSKIE			
Ri	Joondalup	19	C 2
ELSON			
Rd	Piesse Brook	78	B 5
ELSTAR			
Cl	Alexander Hts	33	A 6
ELSTEAD			
Wy	Balga	46	E 2
Wy	Morley	48	B 9
ELSTREE			
Ave	Coolbinia	60	E 4
Ave	Menora	61	A 5
Ct	Lynwood	94	D 1
ELSWICK			
St	Safety Bay	137	A 10
ELTHAM			
Pl	Kingsley	24	B 10
St	Wembley Dns	59	A 5
ELTON			
Pl	Stirling	45	D 8
St	Maddington	96	A 4
ELVEDEN			
St	Doubleview	59	A 1
ELVEN			
St	North Perth	60	D 8
ELVINA			
Ri	Clarkson	14	E 10
ELVINGTON			
Wy	Thornlie	95	B 6
ELVIRA			
St	Palmyra	91	B 2
ELVIRE			
St	Midland	50	B 7
St	Waterman	30	C 10
ELWARD			
Pl	Balga	32	B 10
Wy	Balga	46	B 1
Wy	Balga	32	B 10
ELWOOD			
Ct	Craigie	23	E 5
ELWORTHY			
Pl	Karrinyup	45	A 5
ELY			
St	Hamilton Hill	101	B 2
ELYSEE			
Ct	Port Kennedy	145	D 10
EMANDER			
Dr	Dianella	47	C 8
EMANUEL			
Ct	Marangaroo	32	C 5
Ct	Wattle Grove	86	D 5
EMBA			
Pl	Spearwood	101	A 4
Pl	Two Rocks	2	C 2
EMBASSY			
Ct	Thornlie	95	B 8
EMBDEN			
St	Welshpool	75	B 10

		Map	Ref.
EMBERSON			
Rd	Morley	48	B 6
Rd	Noranda	48	B 6
EMBLEM			
Ct	Alexander Hts	32	E 5
EMBLETON			
Ave	Embleton	62	B 1
Ave	Embleton	48	B 10
EMBLEY			
Ct	Merriwa	11	C 10
EMDEN			
Cl	Iluka	18	E 4
EMERALD			
Ave	Mt Pleasant	82	E 9
Ct	Maida Vale	76	D 1
Ct	Singleton	160	E 2
Ct	Singleton	158	E 10
Pl	Armadale	116	E 7
Rd	Maddington	96	B 1
Tce	West Perth	1C	D 2
Tce	West Perth	72	E 2
Wy	Carine	44	E 1
Wy	Edgewater	24	A 1
EMERY			
Ct	Leeming	92	E 10
EMILE			
Ct	North Lake	102	A 1
EMILIA			
Dr	Currambine	19	A 3
St	Coolbellup	91	D 10
EMILY			
St	St James	84	B 2
EMMA			
Ct	Iluka	18	E 5
Pl	Nth Fremantle	90	A 5
EMMERSON			
St	North Perth	60	D 8
St	Stoneville	54	C 4
EMMS			
Ct	High Wycombe	76	B 1
EMPEN			
Ct	Leeming	93	A 9
Wy	Hillarys	30	B 1
EMPEROR			
Ave	Beldon	23	C 4
Cl	Armadale	115	E 4
EMPIRE			
Ave	Churchlands	59	B 6
Ave	City Beach	58	D 6
Ave	Wembley Dns	59	A 6
Rd	Carmel	88	C 7
Wy	Thornlie	95	D 7
EMPIRE ROSE			
Ct	Byford	125	D 5
EMPRESS			
Ct	Ocean Reef	19	A 9
EMSWORTH			
Wy	Balga	46	D 2
EMU			
Cl	Ballajura	34	A 8
Ct	High Wycombe	64	D 10
Pl	Yangebup	102	B 10
Rd	Wungong	116	B 9
St	Thornlie	95	A 3
ENARD			
Pl	Ardross	82	C 8
ENDEAVOUR			
Ave	Bull Creek	92	E 6
Ct	Thornlie	95	C 4
Dr	Malaga	33	C 9
Dr	Port Kennedy	156	D 5
Rd	Hillarys	23	B 8
Rd	Morley	48	A 10
ENDGATE			
Ct	Lynwood	94	B 4
ENDORA			
Me	Stratton	51	A 3
ENEABBA			
Pl	Armadale	116	C 4

		Map	Ref.
ENFIELD			
Cl	Halls Head	164	D 3
Rd	Hamersley	31	D 9
St	Lathlain	74	A 5
ENGADINE			
Pl	Duncraig	30	D 8
ENGLAND			
St	Hamilton Hill	101	C 2
ENGLER			
St	Booragoon	92	C 3
ENID			
Rd	Kalamunda	77	D 10
ENNIS			
Ave	Cooloongup	137	E 8
Ave	Port Kennedy	157	A 2
Ave	Rockingham	137	D 3
Ave	Waikiki	145	E 4
Ave	Warnbro	146	A 10
Ave	Warnbro	145	E 6
Ct	Orelia	131	C 5
Ct	Waterford	83	C 6
Pl	Ascot	62	D 8
ENRICK			
El	Marangaroo	32	D 5
ENSAY			
Pl	Dudley Park	165	C 5
ENSIGN			
Dr	Swan View	51	B 8
Wy	Beldon	23	C 2
ENTERPRISE			
Ave	Two Rocks	2	B 2
Dr	Malaga	33	C 9
ENTRANCE			
Rd	Spearwood	100	E 6
ENVALL			
Ri	Marangaroo	32	C 5
Wy	Leeming	92	E 9
ENZO			
St	Willetton	93	E 5
EONE			
St	Falcon	162A	B 2
EPPALOCK			
Gr	South Lake	102	C 7
EPPING			
Gr	Kallaroo	23	A 7
Me	Willetton	93	E 2
EPSOM			
Ave	Forrestfield	76	A 9
Ave	Newburn	75	D 6
Ave	Redcliffe	75	A 1
Ave	Redcliffe	62	D 8
ERCEG			
Rd	Yangebup	101	C 10
EREBUS			
Ct	Alexander Hts	33	A 3
ERIC			
St	Como	82	E 1
St	Cottesloe	80	D 1
St	Hazelmere	50	B 10
St	Midland	50	D 6
ERICA			
Ave	Mt Claremont	71	B 6
Ct	Greenwood	31	D 4
Ct	Stoneville	54	A 4
St	Coodanup	165	C 4
St	Kelmscott	106	D 9
ERIE			
Wy	Joondalup	19	D 2
ERINA			
La	Merriwa	11	E 9
ERINDALE			
Rd	Balcatta	45	D 3
Rd	Gwelup	45	D 4
Rd	Hamersley	31	E 10
Rd	Warwick	31	E 7
ERINDOON			
Wy	Waikiki	145	C 1

		Map	Ref.
ERITH			
Cl	Kingsley	31	B 1
Ct	Glendalough	60	A 6
St	Kenwick	95	E 1
ERLISTOUN			
St	Golden Bay	158	D 8
ERNEST			
St	Safety Bay	145	A 1
ERODIUM			
Pl	Lynwood	94	B 1
EROS			
Pl	San Remo	163	C 1
ERPINGHAM			
Rd	Hamilton Hill	101	B 3
ERRINA			
Pl	Willetton	93	D 4
Rd	Alexander Hts	32	E 5
ERRINBEE			
St	Riverton	83	D 10
ERSKINE			
Ct	Woodvale	24	B 5
Pl	City Beach	58	D 6
ESCALLONIA			
St	Dianella	47	B 5
ESCALUS			
St	Coolbellup	101	E 2
ESCOT			
Rd	Innaloo	45	B 9
ESHER			
Pl	Morley	48	B 7
ESK			
Cl	Craigie	23	D 6
Rd	City Beach	58	D 6
ESKDALE			
Ct	Erskine	164	A 8
St	Roleystone	107	E 7
ESLA			
Pl	Carine	45	B 1
ESPERANCE			
St	E Victoria Pk	73	E 10
ESPERANTO			
Wy	Balga	46	D 3
ESPLANADE			
(see also The Esplanade)			
	Dalkeith	81	E 2
	Nedlands	81	E 1
	Rockingham	136	D 4
	South Perth	72	E 6
ESPRIT			
Pwy	Greenfields	163	E 10
ESSEX			
Ct	Quinns Rocks	10	B 9
La	Fremantle	1D	C 5
St	Bayswater	62	A 4
St	Bayswater	61	E 5
St	Forrestfield	86	C 1
St	Fremantle	1D	B 6
St	Fremantle	90	B 6
St	Wembley	59	E 9
ESSINGTON			
St	Huntingdale	95	C 9
ESTA			
Pl	Duncraig	30	E 3
ESTELLE			
Pl	Parkerville	39	C 10
ESTEVAN			
Wy	Ferndale	84	D 10
ESTHER			
Pl	Gosnells	96	B 8
St	Belmont	74	D 2
St	Eden Hill	49	A 9
St	Rivervale	74	C 4
ESTON			
Pl	Willetton	94	A 3
ESTREL			
Rd	Wanneroo	25	C 3

		Map	Ref.
ESTUARY			
Pl	Ballajura	33	C 6
Wy	Heathridge	23	C 1
Wy	Heathridge	19	D 10
ETCHELL			
Ct	Ocean Reef	23	A 2
ETCHINGHAM			
Rd	Balga	46	B 2
ETHAN			
Ct	Riverton	84	A 10
ETHEL			
St	Guildford	63	C 1
St	Guildford	49	C 10
St	North Perth	61	A 9
St	Waterman	30	C 9
ETHELWYN			
St	Hilton	91	B 7
ETHERINGTON			
Ave	Spearwood	101	B 7
ETNA			
Ct	Alexander Hts	33	A 3
Pl	Rossmoyne	83	B 10
ETON			
St	Joondanna	60	D 4
St	North Perth	60	D 5
ETWALL			
Pl	Carine	30	E 10
ETWELL			
St	E Victoria Pk	84	A 2
St	E Victoria Pk	83	E 1
EUCALYPT			
Ct	Duncraig	31	B 8
EUCALYPTUS			
Blvd	Canning Vale	94	B 10
Blvd	Canning Vale	104	C 1
Wy	Maida Vale	77	A 3
EUCLA			
St	Mt Hawthorn	60	B 4
EUCLID			
Cl	Beldon	23	C 4
EUCUMBENE			
Cr	Joondalup	19	D 2
Gns	South Lake	102	E 6
EUDANDA			
Pl	Cannington	84	D 5
EUDORIA			
St	Gosnells	96	A 9
St	Gosnells	106	B 1
EUGENE			
Ct	Morley	48	C 6
Pl	Karragullen	108	C 5
EUREKA			
Pl	Armadale	115	E 4
Rd	Wilson	84	A 7
EURO			
Ct	Currambine	19	B 6
Pl	Gosnells	105	E 1
EUROPA			
Ct	Kallaroo	23	B 6
Ct	Port Kennedy	156	D 4
EUSTON			
Pl	Alexander Hts	33	B 4
Pl	Wembley Dns	59	A 3
St	Wembley Dns	58	E 3
EVA			
St	Maddington	96	B 1
EVANDALE			
Rd	Landsdale	32	D 3
Rd	Marangaroo	32	D 3
St	Floreat	59	C 10
St	Mandurah	165	B 4
EVANS			
Pl	Bayswater	62	A 3
Pl	Padbury	23	E 7
Pl	Two Rocks	2	D 3
St	Mt Helena	55	B 5
St	Shenton Park	71	D 4
St	Warnbro	145	C 4

198 For detailed information regarding the street referencing system used in this book, turn to page 170.

F

		Map	Ref.
Wy	Byford	126	C 10
Wy	Byford	126	D 10

EVAS
Pl Wattleup .... 121 D 3
EVE
Ct Booragoon ...... 92 B 1
EVELINE
Rd Middle Swan .... 50 C 5
EVELYN
Ct Wanneroo .... 25 B 3
Rd Claremont .... 71 B 10
St Gosnells .... 96 B 10
St Whitby .... 143 B 7
EVENING PEAL
Ct Byford .... 126 A 6
EVENLODE
Rt Padbury .... 30 E 1
EVERARD
Cl Jandakot .... 112 E 2
Cl Woodvale .... 24 B 4
EVEREST
Pl Alexander Hts .... 33 B 3
EVERETT
St Crawley .... 72 A 10
EVERETTE
Wy Hope Valley ..... 121 D 7
EVERGREEN
Ct Leeming .... 102 E 2
Gns Neerabup .... 16 B 5
Ra Ballajura .... 33 C 4
EVERINGHAM
St Carine .... 45 A 1
St Carine .... 31 A 10
EVERITT
Pl High Wycombe .. 76 A 2
EVERLASTING
Gns Mirrabooka ..... 47 B 2
Rt Halls Head ..... 164 B 6
EVERSHED
St Myaree .... 92 A 2
EVERSLEY
St Balcatta .... 46 A 4
EVERTON
St Floreat .... 59 D 9
EVES
Pl Cannington ...... 84 D 4
EWART
Gr Midland .... 50 E 7
St Midland .... 50 E 7
St Midvale .... 50 E 8
EWELL
Ct Marangaroo ..... 32 A 5
St Morley .... 61 E 1
EWEN
St Doubleview ..... 59 A 1
St Scarborough .... 44 D 10
St Scarborough .... 58 E 1
St Woodlands ...... 59 B 1
EWERS
Pl Booragoon .... 92 B 3
EWING
Ave Bull Creek .... 93 A 4
Dr Hillarys .... 30 A 2
St Bentley .... 84 C 3
St Welshpool .... 84 D 2
EXBURY
Ct Thornlie .... 95 B 6
Rd Armadale .... 116 D 3
EXCALIBUR
Ci Westfield .... 106 D 7
Wy Carine .... 31 C 9
EXCELSIOR
Rt Hillarys .... 23 A 8
St Shenton Park ... 71 E 4
EXCELSUM
Tce Mirrabooka .... 47 A 1
EXCHANGE
Wy Malaga .... 33 C 9

EXCHEQUER
Ave Greenfields .... 163 E 9
EXE
Ct Beechboro .... 48 D 4
EXELDIA
Pl Belmont .... 74 E 3
EXETER
Pl Greenfields .... 163 E 9
Pl Iluka .... 18 E 6
St Warnbro .... 145 D 7
EXFORD
Wy Karrinyup .... 45 A 4
EXHIBITION
Dr Malaga .... 33 C 10
Wy Cooloongup .... 137 C 9
EXLEY
Cl Kardinya .... 92 B 6
EXMOOR
Ct Hillarys .... 23 B 10
EXMOUTH
Pl Thornlie .... 95 D 6
EXODON
Pl Heathridge ...... 19 D 10
EXON
Ct Westfield ...... 106 A 9
EXPEDITION
Dr Thornlie .... 95 B 8
EXPLORER
Dr Thornlie .... 95 D 6
EXTENSION
Rd Bassendean .... 63 B 1
EXTON
Pl Spearwood .... 101 C 4
EYNESFORD
St Gosnells .... 96 A 8
EYRE
Cl Bull Creek .... 92 E 7
Ct Mt Claremont ... 71 A 4
Ct Two Rocks .... 2 D 4
Pl Padbury .... 30 D 1
St Rivervale .... 74 C 3
St Waikiki .... 145 D 2

F

FABIAN
Cl Willetton .... 93 C 5
FACEY
Ct Huntingdale ... 105 D 2
Rd Gnangara .... 26 B 2
FAGAN
St Chidlow .... 56 A 8
St Yokine .... 46 D 9
FAGENCE
Wy Thornlie .... 95 A 6
FAGIN
Wy Forrestfield ..... 86 D 1
FAIRBAIRN
Gns Bellevue .... 50 E 9
Rd Coogee .... 100 E 10
Rd Munster .... 101 A 10
St Fremantle .... 1D A 1
St Fremantle .... 90 C 5
St Mosman Park .. 80 E 8
FAIRBRIDGE
Rd Halls Head .... 162 D 10
FAIRBROTHER
St Belmont .... 74 D 2
FAIRFAX
Rd Swan View ..... 51 C 7
FAIRFIELD
Dr Ballajura .... 33 D 4
Gns Canning Vale .... 94 A 9
Gr Heathridge ...... 23 E 2
St Mt Hawthorn ... 60 C 5
St Mt Hawthorn ... 60 C 6
Wy Halls Head .... 164 C 3

FAIRFORD
St Bassendean .... 62 D 2
FAIRHAVEN
Tce Hillarys .... 22 E 9
FAIRISLE
Pl Warwick .... 31 C 7
FAIRLANE
Dr Carine .... 45 A 1
FAIRLAWN
Gns Heathridge ...... 24 A 2
Gns Heathridge ...... 23 E 2
FAIRLIE
Pl Coodanup ..... 165 C 3
Rd Canning Vale .. 104 B 2
FAIRLIGHT
Ri Kallaroo .... 23 A 7
St Mosman Park ... 80 D 5
FAIRMILE
St Warnbro .... 145 D 7
FAIRS
St Embleton .... 62 A 2
FAIRSET
St Thornlie .... 95 B 4
FAIRVIEW
Gns Waterford .... 83 C 7
Pl Dianella .... 47 B 5
St Coogee .... 100 E 8
FAIRWAY
Crawley .... 71 E 9
Ci Connolly .... 19 A 7
Cr Meadow Sprgs 163 C 4
East Yokine .... 60 E 1
East Yokine .... 46 E 10
Pl Cooloongup .... 138 A 8
Vw Casuarina ...... 132 C 5
West Yokine .... 60 E 1
West Yokine .... 46 E 10
FAITH
St Thornlie .... 95 A 5
FALCON
Ave Churchlands ..... 59 C 7
Cl Ballajura .... 33 E 7
Ct High Wycombe 64 B 10
Ct Willetton .... 93 C 4
Pl Jandakot .... 103 B 8
St Rockingham .. 137 A 9
FALCONER
St Willetton .... 93 C 7
FALKIRK
Ave Maylands .... 61 E 7
Ct Kinross .... 19 A 2
FALLBROOK
Ave Woodvale .... 24 D 8
FALLON
Pl Armadale .... 116 A 2
Pl Armadale .... 115 E 2
FALLOW
Cr Spearwood .... 101 A 8
FALLS
Rd Hovea .... 53 A 5
Rd Hovea .... 52 E 5
Rd Lesmurdie .... 87 A 2
Rd Lesmurdie .... 87 C 1
Rd Serpentine .... 155 B 4
FALMOUTH
Ave City Beach ..... 70 C 1
FALSTAFF
Cl Greenfields .... 165 E 2
Cr Spearwood .... 101 C 5
FALTER
Ct Marangaroo ..... 32 D 6
FANCOTE
Ave Munster .... 111 E 4
St Kelmscott ..... 106 D 8
FANE
St Singleton .... 160 E 2
FANNING
Wy Singleton .... 160 D 3

FANSTONE
Ave Munster .... 111 C 4
FANTAIL
Dr Bibra Lake .... 102 B 6
Wy Huntingdale ... 105 C 1
FANTOME
Rd Craigie .... 23 E 7
FARADAY
St Mt Hawthorn ... 60 D 6
St Westfield ...... 106 B 10
FARALL
Ct Erskine .... 164 C 5
FARDON
Tr Winthrop .... 92 B 5
FARGO
Wy Welshpool .... 85 D 2
FARINA
Dr Yokine .... 60 D 3
Rd Jarrahdale .... 153 C 4
FARLEIGH
Dr Willetton .... 93 D 6
FARLEY
Wy Bayswater .... 48 D 10
FARM
St Hamersley ...... 31 E 9
FARMAN
Pl Hamersley ...... 46 A 1
FARMER
Ave Wungong ..... 116 B 10
St Noranda .... 47 C 6
St North Perth ..... 60 E 7
Wy Parmelia .... 131 C 7
FARMERS
Grn Beechboro ...... 48 D 5
FARMFIELD
Wy Morley .... 48 D 8
FARMHOUSE
Dr Bibra Lake .... 102 C 5
FARMVIEW
Dr Bellevue .... 65 A 2
Pl Bibra Lake .... 102 D 2
FARNABY
La Beckenham ..... 85 D 5
FARNE
Cl Warwick .... 31 C 8
FARNELL
Wy Alexander Hts .. 32 E 6
FARNESIAN
Ci Mirrabooka ...... 47 A 2
FARNHAM
Pl Gosnells .... 106 B 2
St Bentley .... 84 A 5
St Bentley .... 83 E 5
Wy Morley .... 48 A 6
FARNLEY
St Mt Lawley .... 61 C 9
Wy Duncraig .... 30 D 4
FARO
Vs Mindarie .... 14 B 4
FARR
Ave North Perth ..... 60 D 8
FARRALL
Rd Midvale .... 51 A 8
Rd Stratton .... 51 A 3
FARRANT
St Gooseberry H .. 77 C 2
FARRAWA
Cl Cannington ..... 84 D 6
FARRELL
Pl Noranda .... 47 D 4
Ri Bull Creek .... 93 A 5
St Hilton .... 91 A 4
Wy Padbury .... 30 D 1
FARREN
Hts Clarkson .... 14 D 1
FARRER
Pl Thornlie .... 95 A 5

FARRIER
Rd Mirrabooka ..... 47 A 5
FARRIN
Ct Willetton .... 93 E 3
St Attadale .... 81 D 8
FARRINGDON
Pl Alexander Hts .. 33 B 6
Wy Huntingdale ..... 95 D 9
FARRINGTON
Rd Leeming .... 92 D 10
Rd North Lake ..... 92 A 10
St Kardinya .... 92 A 9
St Warnbro .... 145 C 7
FARRIS
Pl Innaloo .... 45 B 8
St Innaloo .... 45 B 9
St Rockingham .. 137 A 9
FARROW
Wy Bibra Lake .... 102 C 4
FASHODA
Pl Bayswater .... 62 A 6
FASOLO
Cl Lesmurdie .... 87 E 4
FATHOM
Ct Heathridge ..... 19 C 10
FAULKNER
Ave Belmont .... 74 C 3
St Wembley Dns .. 59 A 5
Wy Eden Hill .... 49 A 8
FAULL
Cl Leeming .... 93 C 9
FAUNTLEROY
Ave Perth Airport .... 63 B 7
Ave Redcliffe .... 63 B 7
St Guildford .... 49 E 10
FAVELL
Wy Balga .... 32 B 9
FAVENC
Wy Padbury .... 23 E 10
FAVERSHAM
St Beckenham ..... 85 C 7
Wy Heathridge .... 23 E 2
FAWCETT
Rd Munster .... 111 A 2
Wy Warwick .... 31 D 7
FAWDON
St Safety Bay .... 136 E 10
FAWELL
St Midland .... 50 D 6
FAWK
Cnr Ballajura .... 34 A 7
FAWKNER
Gns Hillarys .... 30 B 3
Rd Two Rocks .... 2 D 3
FAWLER
Gl Padbury .... 30 E 2
FAWLEY
Rt Mindarie .... 14 C 6
FAY
St Nth Fremantle .. 80 C 10
FAYE
Cr Gooseberry H .. 77 B 4
FEAST
Rd Serpentine .... 151 A 9
FEATHERTOP
Ri Alexander Hts .. 33 C 5
FEDDERS
St Morley .... 48 A 7
FEDERAL
Cl Gosnells .... 105 E 1
St Cottesloe .... 70 C 9
St Osborne Park .. 46 B 10
St Subiaco .... 71 E 3
St Tuart Hill .... 46 B 10
FEDERATION
St Mt Hawthorn ... 60 B 5
St Mt Hawthorn ... 60 B 6

For detailed information regarding the street referencing system used in this book, turn to page 170.

199

F

		Map	Ref.
FEENEY			
St	Nth Fremantle	90	D 1
FEILMAN			
Dr	Leda	138	D 1
FELDMAN			
Cr	Parkerville	53	D 5
FELDTS			
Rd	Martin	98	A 10
Rd	Martin	97	E 10
FELGATE			
Ct	Westfield	106	B 8
Pl	Warwick	31	C 9
FELICIA			
Ct	Dianella	47	B 5
Pl	Westfield	106	B 8
FELL			
Pl	Wembley Dns	59	A 5
FELLBRIDGE			
Wy	Langford	94	E 1
FELPHAM			
St	Balga	46	D 3
FELSPAR			
St	Welshpool	85	D 3
FELSTEAD			
Cr	Hamersley	31	D 10
FELTHAM			
Wy	Kingsley	31	B 1
FELTON			
El	Mindarie	14	C 5
Pl	Mandurah	165	A 4
Rd	City Beach	58	D 7
St	Balcatta	45	E 5
FENCHURCH			
St	Alexander Hts	33	B 3
FENDAM			
St	Waikiki	145	C 6
St	Warnbro	145	C 6
FENELLIA			
Cr	Craigie	23	D 5
FENIAN			
Cl	Iluka	18	D 4
FENIMORE			
Ave	Munster	101	B 9
FENN			
Ct	Ferndale	94	C 1
FENNAGER			
Wy	Calista	130	D 7
FENNELL			
Ct	Stoneville	54	C 4
FENNESSY			
Grn	Murdoch	92	D 6
FENTON			
Pl	Myaree	91	E 1
St	Kewdale	75	B 9
St	Mundaring	68	B 1
Wy	Hamilton Hill	101	B 4
Wy	Hillarys	30	C 1
FENWICK			
St	Balga	32	B 10
FERDINAND			
Cr	Coolbellup	101	D 2
FEREDY			
St	Embleton	62	A 2
FERGUSON			
Rd	Glen Forrest	66	C 3
Rd	Greenmount	66	A 1
Rd	Greenmount	52	A 1
Rd	Karragullen	108	D 4
St	Alfred Cove	82	A 10
St	Bellevue	50	D 9
St	Falcon	162A	A 3
St	Kewdale	75	C 8
St	Maylands	62	A 7
St	Maylands	61	E 6
St	Middle Swan	50	E 3
St	Midland	50	D 7
St	Midvale	50	D 8
Wy	Wattle Grove	75	E 10

		Map	Ref.
FERGUSSON			
Cl	West Swan	36	A 6
Cl	West Swan	35	E 5
FERMANER			
St	Karrinyup	45	A 5
FERMOY			
Cl	Waterford	83	C 6
FERN			
Cl	Warnbro	145	D 6
Gr	Ballajura	33	C 3
Pl	Wilson	84	C 6
Pl	Woodvale	24	C 6
Rd	Paulls Valley	78	C 5
Rd	Wilson	84	B 8
St	Swanbourne	70	E 8
FERNAN			
Rd	High Wycombe	64	B 9
FERNANDO			
Pl	Safety Bay	137	B 9
FERNCROFT			
Wy	Kingsley	31	C 2
FERNDALE			
Cr	Ferndale	84	B 10
Cr	Ferndale	94	C 1
Cr	Ferndale	84	C 9
St	Floreat	71	B 1
St	Floreat	59	B 10
FERNDENE			
Me	Hillarys	23	B 9
FERNDOWN			
Ct	Currambine	19	B 4
Gr	Meadow Sprgs.	163	D 1
FERN HILL			
Pl	Hovea	52	E 6
FERNHURST			
Cr	Balga	46	D 2
FERNIE			
Gns	Winthrop	92	A 6
FERNLEA			
St	Warwick	31	D 8
FERN LEAF			
Ct	Leeming	103	B 2
FERNTREE			
Cl	Thornlie	95	B 10
Wy	Beechboro	48	C 4
Wy	Coodanup	165	D 5
FERNWOOD			
Sq	Padbury	31	A 2
FERRAR			
St	Menora	61	A 6
St	Mt Lawley	61	A 6
FERRARA			
Wy	Girrawheen	32	D 7
FERRARI			
Rd	Roleystone	119	A 2
FERRER			
Pl	Woodlands	59	B 3
FERRES			
St	White Gum Vly	90	E 7
FERRIER			
Dr	Peron	136	C 5
St	Swan View	51	B 8
FERRIS			
Grn	Parmelia	131	B 8
Wy	Spearwood	101	A 5
FERRY			
St	South Perth	72	E 6
FIDLER			
Ct	Parmelia	131	A 9
FIELD			
Ave	Redcliffe	75	A 1
St	Beaconsfield	90	E 7
St	Kingsley	31	C 3
St	Morley	48	A 5
St	Mt Lawley	61	B 8
Wy	Ferndale	84	D 10
FIELDER			
Ct	Kardinya	92	A 6

		Map	Ref.
FIELDGATE			
Sq	Balga	32	B 9
FIFE			
Ct	Willetton	93	D 3
Gns	Ocean Reef	19	A 10
St	Forrestfield	76	C 10
FIFTH			
Ave	Bassendean	49	B 10
Ave	Beaconsfield	90	E 7
Ave	Kensington	73	D 8
Ave	Mandurah	165	B 3
Ave	Mt Lawley	61	C 6
Ave	Rossmoyne	93	B 1
Ave	Rossmoyne	83	B 10
Ave	Shoalwater	136	C 7
Rd	Armadale	116	C 6
St	Bicton	81	C 10
FIFTY			
Rd	Baldivis	146	E 2
FIG			
Ct	Edgewater	24	B 2
FIGTREE			
Pl	Beechboro	48	C 3
FILBERT			
St	Greenwood	31	B 5
FILBURN			
St	Scarborough	44	D 9
FILIP			
Wy	West Swan	35	E 9
FILKINS			
St	Bassendean	48	D 10
FILLMORE			
Wy	Gosnells	106	A 1
FILMER			
Pl	Leeming	102	E 1
FIMISTON			
Pl	Balcatta	46	A 6
FIN			
Ct	Beldon	23	C 4
Pl	Willetton	93	E 6
FINCH			
Cl	Langford	95	A 2
Ct	High Wycombe	76	B 1
Ct	Kingsley	24	D 9
Pl	Bull Creek	93	B 6
Pl	Yangebup	102	B 10
Ri	Ballajura	33	D 7
Wy	Mt Claremont	71	A 5
FINCHAVEN			
St	Kensington	73	C 10
FINCHLEY			
Cr	Balga	46	D 1
Cr	Balga	32	D 10
Ri	Mt Claremont	71	A 5
St	Lynwood	94	D 3
FINDEN			
St	Two Rocks	2	C 3
FINDLAY			
Rd	Leeming	93	A 10
FINDON			
Cr	Balga	46	C 3
FINEY			
St	Cottesloe	80	D 2
FINGALL			
Wy	Willetton	94	A 4
FINKE			
Ct	Mirrabooka	33	A 9
FINLAY			
Ct	Lesmurdie	87	C 2
Ct	Rivervale	74	C 5
Pl	Wangara	24	E 5
FINLAYSON			
St	Subiaco	72	B 3
FINN			
Ct	Singleton	160	D 3
Hl	Winthrop	92	C 6
Wy	Tuart Hill	46	C 9
FINNAN			
St	Cloverdale	75	A 2

		Map	Ref.
FINNEGAN			
Wy	Landsdale	25	D 8
FINNERTY			
St	Fremantle	1D	C 3
St	Fremantle	90	C 3
St	Karrinyup	45	B 5
FINNEY			
Cr	Marmion	30	D 8
St	Willagee	91	E 5
FINNISS			
Cro	Hillarys	30	B 1
Ct	Mirrabooka	33	A 9
FINSTOCK			
Me	Padbury	31	A 2
FINTRY			
Cl	Kinross	18	E 2
FINULA			
Pl	Lynwood	94	A 5
FIONA			
St	Morley	47	D 8
FIONN			
Ct	Ardross	82	C 9
St	Hamersley	31	E 9
FIR			
Ct	Beechboro	48	C 4
Ct	Westfield	106	B 10
FIRBY			
St	Cloverdale	75	A 3
FIRCROFT			
Wy	Hamersley	31	E 10
FIREBALL			
Wy	Ocean Reef	23	A 1
FIREBUSH			
Ct	Heathridge	19	C 10
FIREFALLS			
Cl	Huntingdale	95	B 10
FIREFLY			
Pl	Iluka	18	E 4
FIRESTONE			
Ct	Yanchep	3	E 10
Pl	Meadow Sprgs.	163	D 5
FIRETAIL			
Ct	Armadale	116	B 4
Ct	Kingsley	31	C 1
Pl	Kenwick	95	E 2
FIRETHORN			
Rt	Mirrabooka	33	A 10
FIREWOOD			
Rd	Mundaring	69	D 6
Rd	Mundaring	68	D 9
FIRLE			
St	Maddington	96	B 4
FIRNS			
Rd	Serpentine	155	E 8
FIRSBY			
St	Osborne Park	46	A 10
FIRST			
Ave	Applecross	82	D 5
Ave	Bassendean	63	A 1
Ave	Bassendean	49	A 10
Ave	Bickley	88	C 4
Ave	Burns	18	D 3
Ave	Claremont	71	C 8
Ave	Kensington	73	C 8
Ave	Kwinana Beach	129	D 8
Ave	Mandurah	165	B 2
Ave	Midland	50	A 8
Ave	Mt Lawley	61	B 7
Ave	Rossmoyne	93	A 2
Ave	Shoalwater	136	C 7
St	Bicton	81	B 9
St	Redcliffe	63	A 10
FIRTH			
Ct	Duncraig	31	B 6
FIRWOOD			
Tr	Woodvale	24	D 8
FISCHER			
Rd	Darlington	66	B 2

		Map	Ref.
FISHER			
Pl	Armadale	116	E 4
Pl	Bull Creek	92	E 5
St	Ashfield	62	E 3
St	Belmont	74	D 2
St	Cloverdale	75	A 5
St	Forrestdale	114	E 6
St	Rockingham	136	E 5
St	White Gum Vly	90	E 6
FISK			
Pl	Morley	48	D 7
FITCH			
Ri	Willetton	93	C 7
St	Singleton	158	D 10
FITZGERALD			
Ct	Kingsley	31	B 3
Rd	Morley	48	A 8
St	North Perth	61	A 7
St	Northbridge	1C	E 1
St	Northbridge	72	E 1
St	West Perth	60	E 9
FITZPATRICK			
St	Bentley	84	A 5
Wy	Noranda	48	A 5
Wy	Padbury	23	E 9
FITZROY			
Cl	Coodanup	165	A 4
Cl	Cooloongup	137	D 10
Ct	Gosnells	105	E 2
Pl	Balga	46	B 1
Pl	Heathridge	19	B 9
Rd	Rivervale	74	B 3
St	Dianella	47	D 9
St	Queens Park	85	A 5
St	West Perth	60	E 10
FITZWATER			
Wy	Spearwood	101	C 5
FLAMBOROUGH			
St	Doubleview	59	A 1
St	Doubleview	45	A 10
FLAME			
Cl	Mirrabooka	47	A 1
Ct	Thornlie	95	A 5
St	Falcon	162A	C 2
FLAMETREE			
Pl	Beechboro	48	C 4
FLAMINGO			
Tr	Ballajura	33	D 5
Wy	Willetton	93	C 4
FLANDERS			
Ct	Swan View	51	C 9
Pl	Alexander Hts	32	E 6
FLANDRIN			
St	Carine	45	A 1
FLANNAGAN			
Rd	Applecross	82	D 4
FLANNAN			
Pl	Warwick	31	C 7
FLAVIA			
St	Falcon	162A	C 3
FLAX			
St	Maddington	96	C 5
FLECKER			
Ct	Winthrop	92	A 5
FLEET			
St	Fremantle	1D	B 5
St	Fremantle	90	B 5
St	Leederville	60	D 8
Wy	Beldon	23	C 3
FLEETWING			
Hts	Ocean Reef	18	E 8
FLEETWOOD			
Cc	Woodvale	24	B 3
Rd	Lynwood	94	D 1
Rd	Lynwood	84	D 10
FLEMING			
Cl	Morley	48	D 8
FLEMMING			
Ct	Forrestdale	115	A 6

200   For detailed information regarding the street referencing system used in this book, turn to page 170.

F

		Map	Ref.
FLETA			
Ct	Duncraig	30	D 4
FLETCHER			
Rd	Karnup	159	B 3
Rd	Karnup	159	B 8
Rd	Karnup	157	B10
Rd	Lesmurdie	87	D 1
St	Applecross	82	C 7
St	Cannington	84	D 6
St	East Fremantle	90	E 3
St	Rockingham	136	D 5
St	Yokine	46	D 9
Wy	Mandurah	165	C 1
Wy	Mandurah	163	C10
FLETCHING			
St	Balga	46	C 1
FLEUR			
Rd	Greenmount	51	C 9
FLIGHT			
St	Falcon	162A	B 3
FLINDELL			
St	O'Connor	91	C 6
FLINDERS			
Ave	Hillarys	30	A 1
Ave	Hillarys	23	B10
Ave	Hillarys	30	C 1
Ave	Hillarys	22	E10
Cr	Bull Creek	92	E 7
Ct	Thornlie	95	C 9
La	Rockingham	137	C 4
St	Bayswater	62	C 2
St	Falcon	162A	E 5
St	Mt Hawthorn	60	C 5
St	Mt Hawthorn	60	C 6
St	Nollamara	46	D 5
St	Yokine	60	D 2
St	Yokine	46	D 9
FLINDS			
Pl	Lynwood	94	D 3
FLINN			
Ave	Kelmscott	116	D 2
FLINT			
Ct	Leeming	93	B 8
Rd	Glen Forrest	66	E 1
Rd	Glen Forrest	52	E 1
St	Victoria Park	73	E 6
FLINTON			
Ct	Halls Head	164	C 1
FLOOD			
St	Subiaco	72	A 1
FLORA			
Ave	Bayswater	48	D10
Ct	Jandakot	103	A 6
Gns	Alexander Hts	33	A 5
Rd	Hovea	52	D 7
St	Midland	50	C 6
Tce	Lesmurdie	87	D 4
Tce	North Beach	44	C 1
Tce	Waterman	30	C10
FLORENCE			
Rd	Nedlands	71	D10
Rd	Cottesloe	70	D10
St	Rockingham	136	E 5
St	West Perth	60	D 9
Wy	Dianella	47	A 6
FLOREY			
Pl	Huntingdale	105	D 1
FLORIAN			
Pl	Duncraig	31	A 4
FLORIBUNDA			
Ave	Halls Head	164	A 7
Ave	Sorrento	30	D 6
Gns	Mirrabooka	47	B 2
FLORIDA			
Rd	Safety Bay	137	B 9
FLORIZEL			
St	Coolbellup	91	E10
FLOTILLA			
Dr	Heathridge	23	C 1
Dr	Heathridge	19	C10
FLOYD			
St	Trigg	44	C 5
FLUELLEN			
Wy	Hamilton Hill	101	C 3
FLYNN			
Dr	Neerabup	16	D 3
Dr	Neerabup	15	D 4
Rd	The Lakes	57	D 7
St	Churchlands	59	D 8
St	Wembley	59	D 8
FOAM			
Pl	Ocean Reef	23	B 1
FOGERTHORPE			
Cr	Maylands	61	E 9
FOLEY			
Ct	Leeming	92	E 9
Pl	Balcatta	45	E 4
Pl	Rockingham	137	B 9
St	Balcatta	46	A 2
FOLLY			
Rd	Baldivis	147	B 5
FONTAINE			
St	Balcatta	45	E 4
FONTANA			
Ce	Joondalup	19	D 1
Ct	Greenfields	163	D10
FONTANO			
Rd	Wattle Grove	86	E 5
FONTLEY			
Rd	Kingsley	31	C 3
FONTS			
Pl	Embleton	48	C10
FORBES			
Ct	Merriwa	11	C 8
La	Perth City	1C	A 1
La	Perth City	73	A 1
Rd	Applecross	82	D 5
Rd	Halls Head	164	C 2
Rd	Perth City	1C	A 1
Rd	Perth City	73	A 1
Rd	Perth City	61	A10
St	Ascot	62	E 8
FORD			
Rd	Lesmurdie	87	A 4
St	Ascot	62	D 8
St	Bentley	84	B 4
St	Marmion	30	D 8
St	Midland	50	A 8
FORDE			
Pl	Armadale	116	E 5
FORDER			
St	Noranda	47	D 6
FORDHAM			
Ct	Ballajura	34	A 7
Dr	Swan View	51	C 9
FORDRED			
Pl	Parmelia	131	A 8
FORE			
St	Perth City	61	A10
FOREMAN			
St	Kenwick	85	E 9
FORESHORE			
Dr	Singleton	160	C 4
Ent	Wilson	84	B 9
FOREST			
Ave	Jarrahdale	153	A 8
Cr	Thornlie	95	B 9
Ct	Armadale	116	D 6
Gr	Casuarina	132	C 4
Rd	Henley Brook	36	B 3
Wk	Kardinya	92	B 7
FOREST HILL			
Dr	Kingsley	24	B 9
FOREST LAKES			
Dr	Thornlie	95	A 9
FORESTVILLE			
Ct	Kallaroo	23	A 6
Me	Hillarys	23	A 9
FORFAR			
Glen	Kinross	19	A 2
FORGE			
Dr	Chidlow	43	B 7
St	Welshpool	74	D10
FORMAN			
Ct	Queens Park	85	A 4
FORMBY			
Ct	Currambine	19	C 4
Wy	Bull Creek	92	E 4
FORRES			
Pl	Greenwood	31	C 6
FORREST			
Ave	East Perth	1C	B 3
Ave	East Perth	73	B 3
Ave	Mundaring	68	A 5
Ct	Kiara	48	E 7
Dr	Kings Park	72	B 7
Gr	Two Rocks	2	D 3
Pl	Perth City	1C	A 2
Pl	Perth City	73	A 2
Pl	Perth City	1C	A 2
Rd	Armadale	116	B 8
Rd	Armadale	116	C 7
Rd	Armadale	115	D 9
Rd	Banjup	113	B 1
Rd	Bibra Lake	102	A 4
Rd	Bibra Lake	101	D 3
Rd	Forrestdale	114	B 4
Rd	Forrestdale	115	B 7
Rd	Hamilton Hill	101	A 1
Rd	Jandakot	113	A 1
Rd	Jandakot	102	D 9
Rd	Jandakot	112	E 1
Rd	Padbury	23	C 9
Rd	Pickering Bk	89	B 7
Rd	Swan View	51	D 8
Rd	Yangebup	102	C 9
St	Cottesloe	80	C 2
St	Cottesloe	80	D 2
St	Fremantle	91	A 4
St	Fremantle	90	D 4
St	Mandurah	165	A 1
St	Mandurah	163	A10
St	Mt Lawley	61	A 8
St	North Beach	44	C 3
St	North Perth	61	A 8
St	Palmyra	91	A 4
St	Peppermint Gr	80	E 2
St	Sawyers Valley	54	D 9
St	South Perth	73	A10
St	Subiaco	72	A 1
Wk	Subiaco	72	A 1
FORRESTER			
Rd	Safety Bay	144	D 1
Rd	Safety Bay	136	D10
FORSTER			
Ave	Lathlain	74	A 7
Pl	Munster	101	C10
Wy	Noranda	48	B 6
FORSYTH			
Cl	Mosman Park	80	D 7
St	O'Connor	91	B 5
FORT			
St	Morley	61	E 2
FORTESCUE			
Ct	Mandurah	164	E 4
Lp	Heathridge	19	B10
St	East Fremantle	90	E 3
FORTESQUE			
Rd	Cooloongup	137	E10
FORTINI			
Ct	Hamilton Hill	101	A 1
FORTIS			
Pl	Carine	31	A 9
FORTUNE			
St	Balcatta	46	A 7
St	Shenton Park	71	E 4
St	South Perth	73	A10
St	Warwick	31	D 7
FORTUNELLA			
Gr	Armadale	116	A 5
FORTVIEW			
Rd	Mt Claremont	70	E 5
FORTY			
Rd	Port Kennedy	156	E 3
Rd	Secret Harbour	159	A 2
FORWARD			
Ct	High Wycombe	76	C 2
St	Mandurah	163	A10
St	Manning	83	B 4
St	Welshpool	84	B 1
FOSBERY			
Ct	Wanneroo	20	C 8
FOSS			
St	Bicton	91	B 1
St	Bicton	81	B10
St	Palmyra	91	B 1
FOSTER			
Ct	Calista	130	E 9
Rd	Coodanup	165	C 4
Rd	Kelmscott	106	D10
St	Safety Bay	137	A10
Wy	Jarrahdale	152	E 7
FOSTON			
Dr	Duncraig	31	A 4
St	Carine	45	C 1
FOTHERGILL			
St	Fremantle	1D	C 5
St	Fremantle	90	C 5
FOTI			
Rd	Pickering Bk	89	A10
FOULKES			
Pl	Mandurah	165	A 2
FOUNDERS			
La	Hillarys	30	A 1
FOUNDRY			
St	Maylands	61	E 7
FOUNTAIN			
Ct	Safety Bay	136	E10
Wy	Huntingdale	105	D 1
Wy	Huntingdale	95	D10
FOUNTAINS			
Ct	Armadale	116	E 5
FOURTH			
Av E	Maylands	61	D 8
Ave	Applecross	82	D 5
Ave	Bassendean	63	A 1
Ave	Bassendean	49	A10
Ave	Burns	18	D 3
Ave	Kensington	73	C 8
Ave	Mandurah	165	B 3
Ave	Mt Lawley	61	C 6
Ave	Rossmoyne	93	B 2
Ave	Shoalwater	136	C 7
Rd	Armadale	116	H 7
FOWLER			
Pl	Armadale	116	B 3
Rw	Leeming	92	E 9
FOX			
Cl	Waikiki	137	E10
Ct	Leeming	93	A 8
Grn	Floreat	71	C 1
St	Spearwood	101	C 6
FOXALL			
Pl	South Lake	102	C 6
FOXCROFT			
Ct	Kardinya	91	C 6
FOXGLOVE			
Gns	Mirrabooka	33	A10
FOXLEY			
Pl	Martin	107	C 2
FOXON			
Rd	Bibra Lake	102	D 3
FOXTON			
Dr	Oakford	124	A 4
St	Maddington	96	B 3
FOXWOOD			
Wy	Langford	94	E 1
FOYLE			
Ct	Bayswater	62	B 3
FRAGRANT			
Gns	Mirrabooka	47	B 1
Gns	Mirrabooka	33	B10
FRAME			
Ct	Leederville	60	D 9
FRAMFIELD			
Wy	Balga	46	C 2
FRAN			
Ct	Merriwa	14	C 1
FRANCAIS			
Rd	Carmel	88	E 7
Rd	Pickering Bk	88	E 9
FRANCE			
St	Mandurah	165	B 1
St	Mandurah	163	B10
FRANCES			
St	Midland	50	B 7
St	Mt Lawley	61	A 6
Tce	Mosman Park	80	E 4
FRANCIS			
Ave	Karrinyup	45	A 6
Rd	Applecross	82	A 9
Rd	Carmel	87	D 6
Rd	Kalamunda	77	C 9
St	Bayswater	62	A 4
St	Martin	96	C 7
St	Middle Swan	50	D 5
St	Northbridge	1C	E 1
St	Northbridge	72	E 1
St	Perth City	73	A 1
St	Subiaco	72	B 2
St	Waikiki	145	B 4
FRANCISCO			
Cr	Bull Creek	93	A 6
Pl	Lathlain	74	B 5
St	Belmont	74	C 3
St	Rivervale	74	B 4
St	Sth Fremantle	90	C 7
FRANGIPANI			
Lp	Marangaroo	32	D 4
FRANKLAND			
Ave	Banjup	112	D10
Ave	Banjup	122	E 2
Ct	Gosnells	106	A 3
FRANKLIN			
La	Joondalup	19	D 6
Rd	Wanneroo	21	B 9
St	Cannington	85	A 7
St	Leederville	60	D 7
St	Swanbourne	70	E 9
FRANKLYN			
Pl	Willetton	93	E 3
FRANT			
Wy	Balga	46	D 3
FRAPE			
Ave	Yokine	60	D 1
FRASER			
Ave	West Perth	1C	D 4
Ave	West Perth	72	D 4
Dr	Greenmount	51	C10
La	South Perth	72	E 6
Rd	Applecross	82	B 5
Rd	Banjup	113	C 1
Rd	Banjup	103	E 8
Rd	Canning Vale	104	A 5
Rd	Quinns Rocks	10	E10
Rd N	Canning Vale	104	C 2
Rd N	Canning Vale	94	D10
St	Bicton	91	A 1
St	East Fremantle	90	E 1
St	Rockingham	136	D 4
St	Swanbourne	70	E 9
Wy	Padbury	23	E 8
FRASER PARK			
Rd	E Victoria Pk	84	A 1
FRAWLEY			
Gns	Murdoch	92	B 6
Ra	Clarkson	14	D 2
FRAYNE			
Pl	Wandi	123	E 7

G

		Map	Ref.
FRECKLETON			
Ct	Wandi	123	D 6
FRED BURTON			
Wy	City Beach	58	D 9
FREDERIC			
St	Gosnells	96	A 8
St	Helena Valley	65	B 3
St	Midland	50	B 7
St	Naval Base	121	B 7
FREDERICK			
Rd	Hamilton Hill	101	B 1
Rd	Hamilton Hill	91	B 10
St	Belmont	74	D 1
St	Shoalwater	136	D 7
St	Wanneroo	20	C 8
FREEDMAN			
Rd	Menora	61	A 4
Wy	Winthrop	92	A 5
FREEHOLD			
Pl	Padbury	30	E 2
FREELAND			
Sq	Eden Hill	48	D 8
Wy	Eden Hill	48	D 8
FREEMAN			
Dr	Rossmoyne	93	A 3
Rd	Forrestdale	124	C 2
St	Melville	91	D 3
Wy	Marmion	30	D 7
FREESIA			
Wy	Willetton	93	C 2
FREETH			
Ct	Brentwood	92	E 2
Pl	Mariginiup	16	E 7
Rd	Spearwood	101	C 4
FREMANTLE			
Rd	Gosnells	96	A 7
Rd	Gosnells	95	E 8
Rd	Madora	160	D 9
Rd	Mandurah	165	C 2
Rd	Mandurah	163	C 10
Rd	Meadow Sprgs	163	C 3
FREMANTLE ROCKINGHAM			
Hwy	Henderson	111	A 7
Hwy	Medina	130	C 6
Hwy	Munster	111	A 2
FREMONT			
Pl	Leeming	103	B 1
FRENCH			
Rd	Melville	91	C 1
St	Ashfield	62	E 4
St	Joondanna	60	C 4
St	Tuart Hill	60	C 1
St	Tuart Hill	46	C 10
FRENSHAM			
Pl	Martin	107	C 1
Pl	Martin	97	C 10
FRESHWATER			
Cl	Claremont	71	B 10
Pde	Claremont	71	A 10
Rt	Hillarys	22	E 10
FRIAR			
Pl	Dianella	61	C 2
Rd	Armadale	116	D 5
FRIAR JOHN			
Wy	Coolbellup	101	E 1
FRIARY			
Cl	Kingsley	31	C 2
FRICKER			
Rd	Perth Airport	75	D 1
FRIDAY			
Cnr	Swan View	51	B 5
FRIGATE			
Cl	Waikiki	145	C 5
Cr	Yanchep	4	C 3
FRIMLEY			
Pl	Morley	48	A 8
Wy	Morley	48	A 8
Wy	Morley	47	E 8

		Map	Ref.
FRINTON			
Ave	City Beach	70	D 1
Pl	Greenwood	31	E 5
St	Bayswater	62	B 7
FRITH			
St	Chidlow	41	D 7
FRITHVILLE			
Rd	Balcatta	46	A 5
FROBISHER			
Ave	Munster	111	B 4
Ave	Sorrento	30	C 6
St	Osborne Park	60	A 3
FROME			
Pl	Lynwood	94	C 2
St	Karrinyup	45	A 5
Wy	Cooloongup	137	C 10
FROST			
Cl	Munster	101	B 10
St	Swan View	51	C 6
FRUIN			
Ct	Warnbro	145	D 8
FRY			
Pl	Woodlands	59	C 3
St	Balcatta	45	E 4
St	Mt Pleasant	92	E 1
FRYE			
Ct	Kelmscott	116	D 1
FRYS			
La	Armadale	116	D 5
FUCHSIA			
Cl	Dianella	46	E 5
Pl	Halls Head	164	B 6
FULFORD			
St	Scarborough	59	A 1
St	Scarborough	45	A 10
FULHAM			
Pl	Duncraig	30	D 4
St	Cloverdale	74	E 5
St	Kewdale	74	D 5
FULLER			
Cl	Leeming	92	E 9
FULLWOOD			
Wk	Woodvale	24	C 5
FULMAN			
Wy	Lynwood	94	D 2
FULMAR			
Me	Ballajura	33	D 6
Pl	Halls Head	164	B 2
St	Stirling	45	D 5
St	Thornlie	95	A 6
Wy	Armadale	116	A 3
FULTON			
Cl	Currambine	19	B 4
Cl	Willetton	93	E 2
St	Hamilton Hill	91	B 10
FULWELL			
Ct	Yanchep	4	E 1
FUNNEL			
St	Queens Park	85	A 2
FURL			
Ct	Midland	50	E 6
Ct	Ocean Reef	23	B 2
FURLEY			
Rd	Southern River	104	E 4
FURNACE			
Rd	Welshpool	85	A 2
FURNESS			
Wy	Koondoola	32	E 7
FURNISS			
Rd	Landsdale	25	C 10
FURNISSDALE			
Rd	Furnissdale	165	E 8
FUSCHIA			
Ct	Thornlie	94	E 6
FUSSEL			
Grn	Stratton	51	A 4

		Map	Ref.
FYFE			
Ci	Bull Creek	92	E 4
Ci	Bull Creek	92	E 5
Ct	Trigg	44	D 8
St	Helena Valley	65	D 6
FYNE			
Ct	Duncraig	31	A 6
FYSH			
Pl	Huntingdale	95	D 10

G

		Map	Ref.
GABELL			
Wy	Koondoola	33	A 8
GABO			
Rd	Greenmount	51	C 10
GABRIEL			
Pl	Kewdale	74	D 6
St	Cloverdale	74	E 6
GABYON			
Ct	Hillman	137	D 7
GADD			
St	Jandakot	112	D 4
GADSDON			
St	Cottesloe	80	C 1
GAEBLER			
Rd	Banjup	112	E 10
GAEL			
Pl	Kallaroo	23	B 6
GAGE			
St	Two Rocks	2	C 3
GAINSBOROUGH			
Wy	Mullaloo	23	A 3
GAIRDNER			
Dr	Kardinya	91	D 7
Dr	Nedlands	71	E 5
GAIRLOCH			
Pl	Joondalup	19	C 2
St	Applecross	82	C 5
St	Mt Pleasant	82	D 7
GALAHAD			
Pl	Westfield	106	C 8
Wy	Carine	31	C 10
GALANT			
Cl	Kallaroo	23	B 7
GALATEA			
Gr	Two Rocks	3	C 10
Rd	Falcon	162A	C 2
GALAXY			
Ct	Alexander Hts	33	A 4
St	Beckenham	85	D 7
Wy	Carlisle	74	C 7
GALE			
Ct	Calista	130	E 7
St	Langford	94	E 1
GALEN			
Ct	Mirrabooka	33	A 10
Ri	Woodvale	24	B 6
GALENA			
Ct	High Wycombe	76	D 1
Pl	Carine	44	E 1
Wy	Ferndale	94	C 1
GALERU			
Pl	Wanneroo	20	E 8
GALIAN			
Wy	Spearwood	101	B 7
GALILEE			
Gr	Joondalup	19	D 2
Pl	Jandakot	112	E 2
GALINA			
Ce	Padbury	30	E 2
GALLAGHER			
St	Eden Hill	49	A 8

		Map	Ref.
GALLANT			
Ct	Midvale	51	A 7
Ct	Thornlie	95	C 7
Wy	Lynwood	94	D 3
GALLEON			
Cl	Halls Head	164	B 1
Ct	Safety Bay	137	A 10
Pl	Yanchep	4	C 4
Rd	Beldon	23	C 2
GALLEY			
Cl	Port Kennedy	156	D 4
Pl	Ocean Reef	23	A 2
GALLIERS			
Ave	Armadale	116	D 3
GALLIN			
Ct	Leeming	93	C 8
GALLIPOLI			
Dr	Greenmount	51	B 9
St	Lathlain	74	A 6
GALLOP			
Cl	Heathridge	23	E 2
Pl	Midvale	51	A 6
Rd	Dalkeith	81	D 1
St	Halls Head	162	C 9
St	Hilton	91	A 6
St	West Perth	60	E 9
GALLOWAY			
St	Attadale	81	D 9
GALONG			
Pl	Armadale	116	B 5
GALPINI			
Pl	Mirrabooka	47	A 2
GALSTON			
Pl	Duncraig	31	A 7
GALSWORTHY			
Pl	Spearwood	101	C 8
GALVIN			
Ct	Leeming	93	B 8
Rd	Whitby	143	B 7
GALWAY			
Cl	Nollamara	46	E 7
Ct	Mindarie	14	C 5
Gr	Waterford	83	D 7
GALWEY			
St	Leederville	60	D 7
GAMA			
Ct	Lynwood	94	B 1
GAMAGE			
Wy	Lockridge	49	A 7
GAMBA			
Pl	Booragoon	92	D 1
GAMBIA			
Ct	Beechboro	48	E 4
Pl	Madora	160	D 6
Wy	Beldon	23	E 3
GAMBIE			
Cl	Murdoch	92	C 6
GAMBLE			
Pl	Orelia	131	B 5
St	Warnbro	145	C 8
Wy	Karrinyup	44	E 7
GAMBLEN			
Wy	Winthrop	92	B 4
GAMBLIN			
Wy	Parmelia	131	B 8
GAMESON			
Wy	Girrawheen	32	C 8
GAMOL			
Pl	Mandurah	163	D 6
GANFIELD			
Wy	Balga	32	E 10
GANGES			
Pl	Beechboro	48	E 3
GANNAWAY			
St	Wilson	84	B 6
GANNET			
Ct	Armadale	116	A 4
Ct	High Wycombe	76	C 1

		Map	Ref.
Ri	Halls Head	164	B 3
St	Stirling	45	D 6
Trl	Ballajura	33	E 7
GANNETT			
St	Bateman	92	D 3
GANTON			
Ri	Meadow Sprgs	163	D 5
GARDEN			
Cl	Karnup	159	C 3
Gr	Ballajura	33	C 4
Gr	Edgewater	24	B 1
Me	Kardinya	92	B 5
Pl	Spearwood	101	A 8
Rd	Hope Valley	121	C 8
Rd	Spearwood	101	A 9
St	Cannington	85	A 8
St	South Perth	73	A 8
St	Swanbourne	70	E 8
St	Thornlie	94	E 8
GARDENIA			
St	Thornlie	95	B 8
Tce	Dianella	46	E 6
GARDEN ISLAND			
Hwy	Cooloongup	138	A 6
Hwy	Cooloongup	137	E 7
Hwy	Shoalwater	136	D 8
GARDEN PARK			
Dr	Wanneroo	20	E 4
GARDINER			
Ave	Munster	111	B 5
Rd	Karragullen	109	B 10
Rd	Roleystone	119	A 1
St	Belmont	74	E 1
St	Belmont	62	E 10
St	East Perth	61	C 10
GARDINIA			
Pl	Mullaloo	23	B 5
GARDNER			
St	Como	82	E 5
GARFIELD			
Wy	Greenwood	31	D 5
GARIVER			
St	Leeming	93	B 9
GARLAND			
Ct	Kardinya	92	B 6
Rd	Dalkeith	81	C 1
Rd	Roleystone	108	A 9
St	Victoria Park	73	C 7
Wy	Trigg	44	D 9
GARLING			
St	Kardinya	91	E 5
St	O'Connor	91	C 5
St	Willagee	92	A 5
St	Willagee	91	E 5
GARNET			
St	Armadale	116	E 5
Wy	Maddington	96	B 1
GARNETT			
Pl	Balga	46	D 1
GARNKIRK			
Rd	Greenwood	31	B 5
GARNSWORTHY			
Gr	Stratton	51	B 4
Pl	Bassendean	63	B 2
GARRATT			
Ct	Westfield	106	B 9
Rd	Bayswater	62	A 6
GARRETT			
Cnr	Parmelia	131	B 7
GARRICK			
Wy	Balga	46	E 1
Wy	Currambine	19	A 2
GARRIGAN			
Pl	Clarkson	14	C 2
GARRONG			
Cl	Edgewater	24	B 3
GARROW			
Ct	Kingsley	24	C 9
GARRY			
St	Coolbellup	91	C 10

202

For detailed information regarding the street referencing system used in this book, turn to page 170.

G

		Map	Ref.
GARSON			
Ct	Noranda	47	D 5
GARTON			
Pl	Duncraig	31	A 6
GARTRELL			
St	Midland	50	D 7
GARVEY			
Pl	Gosnells	106	A 3
St	Cloverdale	75	A 3
St	Waterford	83	E 5
GARY			
Rd	Maddington	96	A 2
GASCOYNE			
Ave	Woodvale	24	B 6
Dr	Gosnells	106	A 3
St	E Victoria Pk	73	E 10
St	Nollamara	46	C 8
Wy	Cooloongup	137	E 9
Wy	Waikiki	145	E 1
GASKELL			
Rd	Whiteman	28	A 7
GASKIN			
Rd	Kenwick	86	A 9
Rd	Kenwick	85	E 10
GATESHEAD			
Ave	Mindarie	10	A 2
GATLING			
Wy	Willetton	93	C 7
GATTON			
Wy	Embleton	62	B 1
GAULL			
Pl	Embleton	62	B 1
GAUNT			
Rd	Spearwood	101	A 4
St	Eden Hill	49	B 8
GAVARNIE			
Wy	Coodanup	165	D 3
GAVIN			
Ct	Lynwood	94	A 2
Wy	Kingsley	31	D 1
GAVOUR			
Rd	Wattle Grove	86	D 5
GAWLER			
Ct	Merriwa	11	C 10
Ct	Willetton	93	E 3
Pl	Mirrabooka	33	A 9
Wy	Calista	130	D 7
GAY			
St	Dianella	46	E 7
St	Huntingdale	105	C 2
GAYFORD			
Wy	Girrawheen	32	B 7
GAYHURST			
Rd	Kenwick	95	D 1
GAYSWOOD			
Wy	Morley	48	C 8
GAYTON			
Pl	North Beach	44	D 2
Rd	City Beach	58	E 7
GAZA			
Ct	Greenmount	51	C 9
GAZANIA			
Gr	Yangebup	101	D 10
GAZE			
Ct	Armadale	116	C 3
Ct	Thornlie	95	B 6
GAZELLE			
Pl	Marangaroo	32	E 6
GEAR			
Ct	Middle Swan	50	D 4
GEARY			
St	Mundaring	54	C 9
GECKO			
Rd	Wungong	116	C 10
GEDDES			
Cl	Duncraig	31	A 8
St	Balcatta	46	A 2
St	Victoria Park	73	D 7

		Map	Ref.
GEDLING			
Cl	Lynwood	94	A 4
GEEBUNG			
St	Maddington	96	C 4
GEELONG			
Cl	Beldon	23	D 4
Ct	Bibra Lake	101	D 5
GELLIBRAND			
Rd	Orelia	131	B 6
GEM			
Ce	Craigie	23	E 4
Ct	High Wycombe	76	D 1
GEMINI			
Ri	Ocean Reef	23	B 2
Wy	Carlisle	74	C 7
GEMMA			
Rd	Henderson	121	A 1
GEMMELL			
Pl	Bull Creek	92	E 5
Wy	Hillarys	30	B 1
GEMSARNA			
Cr	Kelmscott	107	B 10
GENEFF			
St	Innaloo	45	C 9
GENESTA			
Cr	Dalkeith	81	C 2
Pl	Two Rocks	2	C 1
GENIE			
Ct	Cooloongup	137	D 8
GENOA			
Cl	Ballajura	33	D 8
Ct	Kingsley	31	C 2
GENTLE			
Rd	Medina	130	C 8
GEOGRAPHE			
Wy	Thornlie	94	E 6
GEORDIE			
Ct	Coogee	100	E 10
Ri	Sorrento	30	C 5
GEORGE			
Ave	Claremont	71	B 10
Rd	Lesmurdie	87	A 4
Rd	Middle Swan	36	D 9
Rd	Roleystone	108	B 7
St	Alfred Cove	82	A 10
St	Belmont	74	E 1
St	Byford	126	C 10
St	Byford	135	D 1
St	Cottesloe	80	D 4
St	East Fremantle	90	D 3
St	Gosnells	95	E 8
St	Jarrahdale	152	E 8
St	Kelmscott	106	E 8
St	Kensington	73	D 10
St	Mandurah	165	A 1
St	Maylands	61	E 7
St	Midland	50	C 7
St	Mt Helena	55	B 5
St	North Beach	44	C 2
St	Queens Park	84	E 4
St	Rockingham	136	E 5
St	Stirling	45	E 9
St	West Perth	1C	D 2
St	West Perth	72	D 2
St	West Swan	36	B 7
Wy	Cannington	84	D 6
GEORGEFF			
St	Henley Brook	36	A 1
St	Henley Brook	35	E 1
St	Henley Brook	28	E 10
GEORGES			
Cl	Kallaroo	23	B 7
GEORGETOWN			
Dr	Safety Bay	137	B 10
GEORGETTE			
Wy	Rockingham	137	D 7
GEORGIAN			
Ri	Willetton	93	C 5
GEORGINA			
St	Bayswater	62	B 6

		Map	Ref.
GEORGJEMMA			
Pl	Carabooda	8	B 1
GERAL			
Ct	Leeming	102	E 1
GERALD			
St	Armadale	116	C 7
St	Como	83	A 3
St	Gosnells	96	C 9
St	Mt Lawley	61	B 9
St	Spearwood	101	B 6
GERALDINE			
St	Bassendean	62	E 3
St	Cottesloe	80	C 1
GERALDTON			
Gr	Rockingham	137	B 5
GERARD			
St	E Cannington	85	A 5
St	E Victoria Pk	74	B 10
GERBER			
Ct	Willetton	94	A 3
GERDA			
Ct	Greenwood	31	D 6
GERMAIN			
Wy	Lockridge	49	A 5
GEROSA			
Pl	Alexander Hts	33	A 6
GERRING			
St	Rivervale	74	B 5
GERTRUDE			
Ave	Westfield	106	C 5
GERTY			
St	Southern River	105	D 8
GETTING			
St	Lathlain	74	B 6
GEYER			
Pl	Bull Creek	92	E 5
GHOST GUM			
Rd	Willetton	93	D 4
GIBB			
Cr	Balga	46	D 4
Rd	Waikiki	145	D 1
GIBBERD			
Rd	Balcatta	45	D 3
GIBBON			
St	Mosman Park	80	D 6
GIBBONS			
Ave	Guildford	49	E 10
GIBBS			
Rd	Banjup	113	A 8
Rd	Forrestdale	114	A 7
Rd	Nowergup	12	A 7
Rd	Nowergup	8	D 10
Rd	Nowergup	11	E 1
St	E Cannington	85	A 5
St	E Cannington	85	A 4
St	Mullaloo	23	A 5
St	Rivervale	74	D 4
GIBLA			
St	Mandurah	163	B 8
GIBLETT			
St	Serpentine	154	E 3
GIBNEY			
Ave	Glendalough	60	B 4
St	Cottesloe	80	C 5
Vs	Leederville	60	B 8
GIBSON			
Ave	Padbury	30	D 2
Ave	Padbury	23	E 9
Ct	Morley	48	C 6
St	Ardross	82	D 7
St	Hilton	91	A 8
St	Mandurah	165	A 1
St	Mt Pleasant	82	D 7
Wy	Beechboro	49	A 2
GIDDENS			
Ct	North Lake	102	A 1
GIDGEE			
Pl	Duncraig	30	D 6

		Map	Ref.
GIDGI			
Wy	Waikiki	145	E 1
Wy	Waikiki	137	E 10
GIFFORD			
Ct	Currambine	19	C 5
Gns	City Beach	58	E 6
Ri	Meadow Sprgs	163	D 6
Wy	Dianella	47	A 10
GILBA			
Cl	Hillman	137	D 6
GILBERT			
Rd	Duncraig	30	D 3
Rd	Lesmurdie	87	B 5
St	Bayswater	62	A 7
GILBERTSON			
Rd	Kardinya	92	A 9
GILBEY			
Ct	Westfield	106	B 9
GILCHRIST			
Ave	Bibra Lake	102	D 2
Rd	Lesmurdie	87	B 7
St	Kenwick	86	A 10
GILCOE			
Pl	Roleystone	107	E 10
GILD			
St	Cloverdale	74	E 5
St	Cloverdale	74	E 6
GILDERCLIFFE			
St	Scarborough	45	A 9
GILES			
Ave	Padbury	23	D 10
Pl	Mirrabooka	33	A 9
Pl	Waikiki	137	E 10
St	Bull Creek	92	E 7
St	Lesmurdie	87	C 4
St	North Beach	44	C 4
GILFELLON			
Rd	Stoneville	54	C 4
GILL			
La	Mundaring	54	A 10
St	Booragoon	92	B 2
St	East Fremantle	90	E 1
St	Morley	47	D 7
St	Mosman Park	80	D 4
St	Mundaring	68	A 1
St	North Perth	60	D 5
St	Parkerville	54	A 8
St	Parkerville	53	E 7
GILLAM			
Dr	Kelmscott	116	C 1
Pl	Dianella	47	A 9
Wy	Beechboro	49	A 3
GILLARK			
St	Mandurah	165	A 3
GILLEN			
Ct	Padbury	23	D 9
Pl	Waikiki	145	E 1
GILLESPIE			
Cl	Willetton	93	C 7
GILLETT			
Dr	Kardinya	91	E 8
GILLON			
Rd	Noranda	48	B 6
St	Karawara	83	C 5
GILMERTON			
Wy	Greenwood	31	B 5
GILMORE			
Ave	Calista	130	E 8
Ave	Leda	138	E 1
Ave	Medina	130	E 5
Pl	Forrestfield	86	D 2
St	Kingsley	31	B 2
St	Madora	160	C 8
GILMOUR			
Rd	Roleystone	108	C 6
GILROY			
St	Cloverdale	74	E 3
Wy	Lesmurdie	87	C 3
GILWELL			
Ave	Kelmscott	106	D 8

		Map	Ref.
GIMBER			
St	Melville	91	C 2
GIMLET			
Ct	Forrestfield	76	D 8
Pl	Thornlie	95	A 8
St	Coodanup	165	D 6
GIPPS			
Ct	Hillarys	30	B 1
GIPSY			
Ct	Beldon	23	E 3
GIRALT			
Rd	Marangaroo	32	B 5
GIRO			
Cl	Middle Swan	50	E 3
GIRRAWEEN			
St	Armadale	116	A 6
GIRRAWHEEN			
Ave	Girrawheen	32	C 8
Dr	Gooseberry H	77	B 2
GIRTON			
Pl	Bentley	84	A 4
St	West Swan	35	B 9
GIRVAN			
Pl	Darlington	66	B 2
GITTOS			
Ct	Noranda	47	D 4
GLADE			
Ct	Warwick	31	E 7
GLADMAN			
Wy	Karrinyup	44	E 7
GLADSTONE			
Ave	South Perth	73	B 5
Ave	Swan View	51	B 8
Rd	Armadale	116	D 4
Rd	Kalamunda	78	A 9
Rd	Leeming	93	A 9
Rd	Rivervale	74	A 4
Rd	Serpentine	151	A 10
Rd	Walliston	88	B 1
Rd	Walliston	78	A 10
St	Perth City	1C	B 1
St	Perth City	73	B 1
St	St James	84	B 3
GLADYS			
Rd	Lesmurdie	87	B 5
St	Darlington	66	B 6
GLAMIS			
Pl	Floreat	59	B 8
GLAMORGAN			
St	E Cannington	85	D 4
GLANTON			
Wy	Dianella	47	A 7
GLANVILLE			
St	Mosman Park	80	D 6
GLASNEVIN			
Ct	Waterford	83	C 7
GLASSFORD			
Rd	Kewdale	75	A 7
GLASTONBURY			
Rd	Armadale	116	D 5
GLAUERT			
Rd	Coodanup	165	C 7
GLEBE			
Rd	Darlington	66	B 5
Rd	Roleystone	107	E 8
St	North Perth	60	E 8
GLEDDEN			
St	Morley	47	D 7
GLEDDON			
Rd	Bull Creek	93	A 4
Wy	Hillarys	30	C 2
GLEDHILL			
Wy	Leeming	92	E 8
Wy	Wilson	84	C 7
GLEED			
Ct	Gosnells	95	E 10

G

		Map	Ref.
GLEN			
Ct	Ferndale	84	C 9
Ct	Thornlie	95	C 9
Pl	Wanneroo	24	E 1
Rd	Darlington	66	A 5
Rd	Darlington	66	A 7
Rd	Lesmurdie	87	C 1
St	Leederville	60	B 10
St	Rockingham	137	D 6
GLENARBER			
Wy	Willetton	93	E 6
GLEN AVON			
St	Lesmurdie	87	D 4
GLENBANK			
Cr	Kallaroo	23	C 5
GLENBAR			
Rd	Duncraig	30	E 8
GLENBAWN			
Dr	South Lake	102	C 7
GLENBROOK			
Dr	Ballajura	33	C 4
Rd	Thornlie	95	D 5
GLENBURN			
Rd	Glen Forrest	67	A 5
Rd	Glen Forrest	66	C 5
Rd	Mahogany Crk	67	A 5
GLENCAIRN			
Wy	Lynwood	94	C 3
GLENCOE			
Lp	Kinross	19	A 5
Pde	Halls Head	164	C 4
Pl	Cooloongup	137	E 7
Pl	Lynwood	94	C 2
Rd	Ardross	82	C 9
GLENDALE			
Ave	Hamersley	31	D 9
Cr	Jandakot	103	A 5
Me	Ballajura	33	C 5
GLENDART			
Ct	Erskine	164	A 9
GLENDOWER			
St	Parkerville	53	D 7
St	Perth City	61	A 9
Wy	Spearwood	101	B 3
GLENEAGLES			
Cl	Connolly	19	C 8
Lp	Cooloongup	137	E 9
Pl	Halls Head	164	B 2
Wy	Hamersley	32	A 10
GLENELG			
Ave	Doubleview	59	A 3
Ave	Wembley Dns	59	A 5
Cl	Warnbro	145	E 7
Ct	Meadow Sprgs	163	D 1
Pl	Connolly	19	B 8
St	Applecross	82	C 6
St	Mt Hawthorn	60	B 6
St	Mt Pleasant	82	D 7
GLENFERN			
Ct	Hillarys	30	A 1
GLENFERRIE			
Rd	Welshpool	85	D 2
GLENFIELD			
Pl	Kelmscott	116	E 1
Rd	Kingsley	31	C 1
GLENFINNAN			
Ct	Hamersley	32	A 8
GLENGARIFF			
Dr	Floreat	59	A 9
GLENGARRY			
Dr	Duncraig	31	A 3
St	Lynwood	94	C 3
GLENHURST			
Ct	Westfield	106	B 8
GLENISLA			
Rd	Bickley	88	D 4
Rd	Carmel	88	D 8
GLENISTER			
Rd	Hamilton Hill	101	A 3

		Map	Ref.
GLENKERRY			
Rd	Willetton	93	E 3
GLENLEA			
Dr	Helena Valley	65	B 3
GLENMERE			
Rd	Warwick	31	D 8
GLENMONT			
Gns	Ballajura	33	D 5
GLENMOOR			
Ri	Dianella	47	B 4
GLENMOY			
Ave	Willetton	93	E 4
GLENN			
Ave	Mosman Park	80	E 7
Pl	Duncraig	30	E 5
Pl	Victoria Park	73	E 4
GLENNON			
Vw	Clarkson	14	D 2
Wy	Rossmoyne	93	B 3
GLENORCHY			
Cr	Hamersley	32	A 9
GLENORN			
Ct	Yangebup	111	E 1
GLENROTHES			
Cr	Yanchep	4	D 2
GLENROWAN			
Pl	Willetton	93	E 6
GLENROY			
Ave	Golden Bay	158	D 8
Cl	Halls Head	164	C 4
Ct	Hovea	52	D 7
Gns	Port Kennedy	156	D 2
GLENROYD			
St	Mt Lawley	61	B 7
GLENSHEE			
Lp	Kingsley	31	C 1
Lp	Kingsley	24	C 10
GLENSIDE			
Cr	Craigie	23	E 4
GLENSTAR			
Ri	Edgewater	19	E 9
GLENTEN			
Wy	Ferndale	84	D 9
GLENTIES			
Rd	Floreat	59	A 8
GLENTWORTH			
Ave	Tuart Hill	46	C 10
GLENUNGA			
Wy	Craigie	23	D 7
GLENVIEW			
Pl	Helena Valley	65	B 4
GLENWAY			
Ri	Helena Valley	65	B 3
Lp	Cooloongup	137	E 8
GLENWOOD			
Ave	Glen Forrest	66	C 3
Ave	Helena Valley	65	B 4
Pl	Helena Valley	65	B 4
Wy	Balcatta	46	A 4
Wy	Balcatta	45	E 4
GLESNA			
Pl	Riverton	93	D 1
GLEW			
St	Singleton	160	D 4
GLICK			
Rd	Coolbinia	61	A 4
GLIDDON			
Rd	Hovea	53	B 5
GLINIS			
Ct	Ferndale	84	C 10
GLOAMING			
Wy	Byford	125	C 3
GLOMAR			
Ri	Sorrento	30	B 4
GLORIANA			
Vw	Ocean Reef	18	E 8

		Map	Ref.
GLOSSOP			
St	Wangara	25	A 6
GLOSTER			
St	Subiaco	72	A 3
St	Subiaco	71	E 3
GLOUCESTER			
Ave	Shoalwater	136	C 8
Cr	Shoalwater	136	C 10
Ct	Willetton	93	E 6
Rd	Kalamunda	77	E 10
St	Mandurah	165	A 3
St	Swanbourne	70	E 7
St	Victoria Park	73	D 7
GLOVER			
Pl	Dianella	47	C 7
Pl	Huntingdale	95	D 9
Pl	Dianella	47	C 7
St	Landsdale	25	D 9
GLOVES			
Pl	Beechboro	49	A 4
GLUCLUB			
St	Riverton	84	A 10
GLYDE			
Cl	Winthrop	92	B 4
Rd	Lesmurdie	87	D 1
St	Bayswater	62	B 5
St	East Fremantle	90	C 4
St	East Perth	1C	B 2
St	East Perth	73	B 2
St	Mosman Park	80	D 5
St	Mt Hawthorn	60	C 5
St	South Perth	72	E 9
GLYNDEBOURNE			
Ave	Thornlie	95	D 6
GLYNDEN			
Wy	Helena Valley	65	B 3
GNANGARA			
Dr	Waikiki	145	D 3
Rd	Cullacabardee	26	D 7
Rd	Henley Brook	28	D 7
Rd	Landsdale	26	A 7
Rd	Landsdale	25	B 9
Rd	Whiteman	27	B 7
GNOBAR			
Wy	Mullaloo	23	A 5
GOBBA			
Ct	Bayswater	62	D 7
GODBOLD			
Cl	Shelley	83	C 10
GODDARD			
St	Lathlain	74	A 7
St	Rockingham	137	C 5
Wy	Bull Creek	93	A 5
Wy	Langford	95	A 1
GODECKE			
Ri	Carine	30	E 9
GODEL			
Rd	Nowergup	12	A 1
Rd	Nowergup	9	A 10
GODERICH			
St	East Perth	1C	B 3
St	East Perth	73	B 3
St	Perth City	1C	B 3
St	Perth City	73	B 3
GODFREY			
Pl	Kingsley	24	D 9
St	Queens Park	85	A 3
St	Walliston	88	A 1
GODIN			
Ct	Churchlands	59	B 5
GODNEY			
Ct	Kiara	48	E 7
GODSTONE			
St	Morley	48	A 7
GODWIN			
Ave	Manning	83	B 5
St	Lesmurdie	87	C 4
GODWIT			
Rt	Bedfordale	128	A 6

		Map	Ref.
GOFFE			
St	Spearwood	101	B 5
GOGO			
Rd	Golden Bay	158	D 8
GOLD			
St	Sth Fremantle	90	C 7
GOLDBURY			
St	Duncraig	30	D 4
GOLDEN			
Cr	High Wycombe	76	B 1
GOLDERS			
Wy	Girrawheen	32	E 9
GOLDERS GREEN			
La	Kingsley	24	B 9
GOLDFINCH			
Ave	Churchlands	59	C 6
Gr	Ballajura	33	E 6
Pl	Armadale	116	A 4
GOLDING			
St	Dianella	47	A 7
St	West Perth	60	D 10
GOLDMEAD			
St	Bayswater	62	A 7
GOLDNEY			
Ct	Leda	130	E 10
GOLDSBOROUGH			
St	Fremantle	1D	C 4
St	Fremantle	90	C 4
GOLDSMITH			
Dr	Leda	139	C 1
Rd	Claremont	81	C 1
Rd	Dalkeith	81	C 1
Rd	Spearwood	101	B 6
GOLDSWORTHY			
Rd	Claremont	71	B 10
GOLF			
Pl	Cooloongup	137	E 9
Rd	Lynwood	94	A 2
St	Ascot	62	B 9
GOLF VIEW			
St	Yokine	46	D 10
GOLFVIEW			
Pl	Gnangara	25	D 3
GOLINE			
Ct	Hillman	137	E 5
GOLLAN			
Pl	Coodanup	165	C 4
GONERIL			
Wy	Coolbellup	101	D 1
GONZALO			
Pl	Coolbellup	101	D 3
GOODALL			
St	Cloverdale	75	A 2
St	Gosnells	106	B 1
St	Gosnells	96	B 10
St	Lesmurdie	87	C 3
GOODCHILD			
Pl	Bellevue	65	A 2
GOODMAN			
Rt	Parmelia	131	C 7
GOODWIN			
Wy	Leeming	103	B 1
Wy	Willetton	93	B 10
GOODWOOD			
Pde	Rivervale	73	E 1
GOOLEMA			
Pl	Wanneroo	20	E 7
GOOLLELAL			
Dr	Kingsley	24	D 10
Dr	Kingsley	31	E 1
GOOMARL			
St	Mandurah	165	A 2
GOONANG			
Rd	City Beach	58	E 7
GOONGARRIE			
Dr	Cooloongup	137	D 10
Dr	Waikiki	145	C 1
St	Bayswater	62	D 5

		Map	Ref.
GOORAY			
St	Glen Forrest	66	E 2
GOOSEBERRY HILL			
Rd	Gooseberry H	77	A 2
Rd	Maida Vale	76	E 2
GORDIN			
Wy	Byford	135	C 3
GORDON			
Ave	Quinns Rocks	10	A 1
Pl	Huntingdale	95	D 10
Rd	Greenfields	163	D 6
Rd	Hamilton Hill	90	E 10
Rd	Mandurah	163	B 6
Rd	Munster	111	E 5
Rd	Secret Harbour	159	A 1
Rd	Serpentine	155	B 3
Rd E	Osborne Park	60	A 2
Rd W	Dianella	47	B 6
Rd W	Osborne Park	60	A 2
St	Bayswater	62	A 7
St	Cottesloe	80	E 1
St	East Fremantle	80	E 10
St	Maida Vale	76	E 1
St	Nedlands	71	D 8
St	West Perth	1C	D 1
St	West Perth	72	D 1
Wy	Swan C Homes	144	
GORE			
Pl	Hillarys	23	C 9
GORHAM			
Wy	Spearwood	101	A 4
GORMAN			
Pl	Calista	130	E 8
St	Greenwood	32	A 5
GORRY			
Rd	Chidlow	56	E 7
GOSCH			
St	Hamilton Hill	91	B 10
GOSFORTH			
Ct	Safety Bay	136	E 10
GOSHAWK			
Gns	Ballajura	34	A 7
Pl	Huntingdale	105	C 1
GOSLIN			
St	Sawyers Valley	54	E 9
GOSNELLS			
Rd E	Martin	96	D 4
Rd E	Orange Grove	96	E 3
Rd W	Martin	96	C 6
GOSS			
Ave	Manning	83	B 4
GOSSAGE			
Rd	Peel Estate	134	B 9
Rd	Peel Estate	133	C 9
GOSSAMER			
Ave	Mirrabooka	33	A 10
GOSSE			
Rd	Padbury	23	C 8
GOSTELOW			
Rd	Glen Forrest	66	C 1
GOTHA			
Wy	Forrestfield	86	C 1
GOUDHURST			
Pl	Gosnells	96	B 9
GOUGH			
Pl	Booragoon	92	D 1
Pl	Noranda	47	C 4
Pl	Samson	91	D 9
GOULBURN			
Pl	Merriwa	11	D 10
GOULD			
Pl	Marangaroo	32	C 4
Pl	Parmelia	131	A 9
St	Osborne Park	59	E 4
GOVAN			
Rd	Canning Vale	104	A 2
Rd	Canning Vale	103	E 1
Rd	Canning Vale	93	E 10

204   **For detailed information regarding the street referencing system used in this book, turn to page 170.**

G

		Map	Ref.
GOVERNMENT			
Rd	Nedlands	71	C 7
Rd	Wooroloo	43	E 2
GOVERNOR			
Rd	E Rockingham	137	C 1
GOVERNORS			
Ave	Perth City	1C	A 4
Ave	Perth City	73	A 4
GOWER			
Ct	Willetton	93	E 7
St	Spearwood	101	C 5
GOWTHER			
St	Leeming	93	A 8
GOYDER			
El	Merriwa	11	C 8
Pl	Bateman	92	D 7
GRACE			
Rd	Kalamunda	77	C 9
St	Ferndale	84	D 8
St	Scarborough	44	D 10
GRACECHURCH			
Cr	Leeming	93	B 8
GRADE			
Rd	Kelmscott	107	A 9
GRADIENT			
Wy	Beldon	23	C 4
Wy	Beldon	23	D 3
GRADY			
Cl	Leeming	92	E 10
Ct	Waikiki	137	E 10
GRAELOU			
Rd	Lesmurdie	87	A 4
GRAFHAM			
Rd	Wungong	116	B 8
GRAFTON			
Dr	Mandurah	165	B 5
Rd	Bayswater	62	A 6
St	Craigie	23	D 5
GRAHAM			
Cr	Redcliffe	75	A 1
Cr	Swan C Homes	144	
Ct	Cottesloe	80	D 3
Rd	Gooseberry H	77	C 1
Rd	Gooseberry H	65	C 10
Rd	Menora	60	E 5
Rd	Quinns Rocks	10	E 10
St	Spearwood	101	B 4
GRAHAME			
St	Mt Helena	55	B 4
St	Mt Helena	55	B 5
GRAINGER			
Dr	Mt Claremont	71	B 5
Wy	Thornlie	95	A 6
GRAMPIANS			
Ave	Yanchep	3	E 10
Hts	Mirrabooka	47	A 1
GRANADILLA			
St	Duncraig	31	A 8
GRANBY			
Cr	Nedlands	71	C 10
St	Lesmurdie	87	C 4
GRANCEY			
Ave	Mundaring	54	A 10
GRAND			
Blvd	Joondalup	19	D 4
Pde	Redcliffe	75	A 1
GRAND BANK			
Ed	Mindarie	14	B 3
GRANDE			
Wy	Beechboro	48	E 4
GRANDIS			
Dr	Thornlie	94	E 8
GRANDPRE			
Cr	Hamilton Hill	101	B 3
GRAND PROMENADE			
	Bedford	61	E 4
	Dianella	47	B 9
	Dianella	61	C 2
	Doubleview	59	A 1

		Map	Ref.
	Doubleview	45	A 9
	Karrinyup	45	A 7
GRANDSTAND			
Rd	Ascot	62	B 8
Rd	Ascot	62	C 10
GRANGE			
Cr	Gooseberry H	65	A 10
Ct	Eden Hill	48	E 8
Ct	Halls Head	164	B 2
Ct	Kingsley	24	C 9
Ct	Yanchep	4	E 2
Dr	Cooloongup	137	D 9
St	Claremont	70	E 10
GRANGER			
Wy	Noranda	48	B 5
GRANITE			
Ct	Maddington	96	D 3
Pl	Welshpool	85	D 3
Rd	Parkerville	53	D 5
GRANSMOOR			
Wy	Willetton	93	D 3
GRANT			
Pl	Banjup	113	D 5
Pl	Bentley	84	C 4
St	Claremont	70	E 10
St	Cottesloe	70	C 10
St	Cottesloe	70	E 10
St	Duncraig	30	E 5
St	Embleton	62	A 1
St	Innaloo	45	B 10
St	Orange Grove	96	D 1
St	Perth City	61	A 10
St	Woodlands	59	B 1
GRANTALA			
Pl	Ocean Reef	19	A 7
GRANTHAM			
Pl	Carlisle	74	C 8
St	Floreat	59	C 8
St	Wembley	60	A 8
St	Wembley	59	E 8
GRANTON			
Wy	Kingsley	24	C 9
GRANVILLE			
Gr	Noranda	48	B 5
Wy	Willetton	93	E 2
GRAPHIC			
Ct	Beldon	23	C 2
GRASBY			
Gr	Winthrop	92	B 5
St	Floreat	71	C 1
GRASMERE			
Ave	City Beach	58	D 7
Pl	Westfield	106	B 10
Wy	Westfield	106	B 10
GRASSBIRD			
Lp	Yangebup	102	A 7
GRASSHILL			
Rd	Karnup	159	D 6
GRATWICK			
Tce	Murdoch	92	B 7
Wy	Koondoola	33	A 8
GRAVE			
Ps	Bateman	92	D 4
GRAVENEY			
Wy	Maddington	96	B 4
GRAVITY			
St	Beckenham	85	D 7
GRAY			
Ave	Yokine	60	E 2
Cl	Kiara	48	D 8
Ct	Hamilton Hill	101	B 1
Ct	Mundaring	67	D 1
Dr	Midvale	50	E 7
Rd	Armadale	115	E 5
Rd	Gooseberry H	77	A 3
Rd	Mandurah	165	B 1
Rd	Mandurah	163	B 10
St	Shenton Park	71	E 4
GRAYLANDS			
Rd	Claremont	71	B 7

		Map	Ref.
GRAYSON			
Ct	Wilson	84	A 8
GREALIS			
St	Armadale	116	C 7
GREAT EASTERN			
Hwy	Ascot	62	C 10
Hwy	Bellevue	51	A 9
Hwy	Belmont	74	C 1
Hwy	Belmont	62	C 10
Hwy	Chidlow	56	B 7
Hwy	Chidlow	57	C 7
Hwy	Glen Forrest	53	A 10
Hwy	Glen Forrest	52	C 10
Hwy	Glen Forrest	66	D 1
Hwy	Greenmount	65	B 1
Hwy	Greenmount	51	D 10
Hwy	Guildford	49	E 9
Hwy	Mahogany Crk	53	C 10
Hwy	Midland	50	A 9
Hwy	Mundaring	54	A 10
Hwy	Mundaring	68	C 1
Hwy	Redcliffe	63	A 7
Hwy	Rivervale	74	A 4
Hwy	Sawyers Valley	69	A 1
Hwy	Sawyers Valley	55	B 10
Hwy	Sth Guildford	63	C 4
Hwy	The Lakes	57	E 1
Hwy	Victoria Park	73	D 5
GREAT EASTERN HWY			
By	Hazelmere	64	B 4
By	Sth Guildford	63	B 5
GREAT NORTHERN			
Hwy	Herne Hill	36	D 6
Hwy	Middle Swan	50	D 3
Hwy	Middle Swan	36	D 8
Hwy	Midland	50	C 7
Hwy	Millendon	29	D 8
Hwy	Upper Swan	168	A 1
Hwy	Upper Swan	166	A 3
Hwy	Upper Swan	29	E 2
GREAT SOUTHERN			
Hwy	The Lakes	57	E 4
GREBE			
Ct	High Wycombe	76	D 1
Ct	Kingsley	24	E 9
Ct	Warnbro	156	C 1
Gns	Yangebup	102	A 10
St	Stirling	45	D 7
GRECIAN			
Cl	Currambine	19	A 4
GREEN			
Ave	Balcatta	46	B 7
Cl	Connolly	19	C 8
Cl	Kardinya	92	B 8
Rd	Hillarys	23	B 1
St	Joondanna	60	B 4
St	Kewdale	74	E 8
Wk	Leeming	93	D 9
GREENACRE			
St	Dianella	47	A 7
GREEN CROFT			
Gns	Leeming	102	E 2
GREENCROFT			
Gns	Warnbro	145	D 6
GREENDALE			
Pl	Kelmscott	107	A 9
GREENE			
St	Rockingham	137	A 6
GREENER			
Wy	Kelmscott	106	E 6
GREENFIELD			
St	Cannington	84	E 7
GREENFIELDS			
Ci	Wanneroo	24	E 1
Ci	Wanneroo	20	E 10
GREENFORD			
Ri	Kingsley	24	B 9
GREENGAGE			
Ct	Armadale	116	C 4
GREENGATE			
Ct	Beldon	23	D 2

		Map	Ref.
GREENHAM			
Pl	Bibra Lake	102	D 3
St	Cottesloe	70	E 10
GREENHAVEN			
Gl	Neerabup	16	A 5
GREENHILL			
Ct	Kallaroo	23	C 6
GREENHOLM			
Ct	Kingsley	31	C 1
GREENHOOD			
Ct	Gosnells	105	E 2
GREENLAW			
St	Duncraig	31	A 7
GREENLEA			
Ct	Warnbro	145	D 6
Ri	Leeming	102	E 2
GREENLEES			
Wy	Carabooda	8	D 7
GREENMOUNT			
Hts	Hillarys	23	B 10
GREENOAK			
Pl	Woodvale	24	C 9
GREENOAKS			
Gns	Ballajura	33	C 6
GREENOCK			
Ave	Como	82	E 3
Gns	Kinross	18	E 1
GREENOUGH			
Wy	Gosnells	106	A 3
GREENPARK			
Rd	Alexander Hts	33	B 4
GREENSHIELDS			
Wy	Redcliffe	62	E 8
GREENSIDE			
St	Dianella	47	B 8
GREENSLADE			
St	Hamilton Hill	91	B 10
GREEN VALE			
Hts	Leeming	103	A 1
GREENVILLE			
St	Swanbourne	70	E 8
GREENWAY			
Ave	Thornlie	95	A 4
Pl	Kingsley	31	B 1
St	Perth City	61	B 10
GREENWELL			
St	Scarborough	44	D 8
GREENWICH			
Ct	Kingsley	24	B 10
Pl	Dianella	47	C 8
GREENWOOD			
Ct	Westfield	106	C 9
Pl	Lynwood	94	D 2
Rt	Alexander Hts	33	A 4
GREGONA			
Pl	Kalamunda	77	E 10
GREGORY			
Ave	Padbury	23	D 9
Ct	Noranda	47	E 4
Ct	Two Rocks	2	E 4
St	Belmont	74	E 1
St	Wembley	60	A 9
Wy	Coolbellup	102	A 1
GREGSON			
St	Rockingham	137	A 6
GREIG			
Ct	Marmion	30	D 7
St	Willagee	91	E 5
GRENADA			
Pl	Safety Bay	145	B 1
GRENADIER			
Dr	Thornlie	95	C 6
GRENFELL			
Ave	Duncraig	31	B 6
Wy	Leeming	93	B 8
GRENVILLE			
Ave	Sorrento	30	B 5
Pl	Safety Bay	145	B 2

		Map	Ref.
Rd	Gooseberry H	77	B 2
Rd	Stoneville	54	B 5
St	Tuart Hill	60	C 1
GRESHAM			
St	Victoria Park	74	A 7
St	Victoria Park	73	E 8
GRETA			
Ct	Cooloongup	137	D 10
Pl	Thornlie	94	E 6
GRETEL			
Ct	Two Rocks	2	B 1
Dr	Falcon	162A	D 9
Wy	Willetton	93	D 6
GRETHAM			
Rd	Balga	46	B 3
GRETNA			
Ct	Kinross	18	E 2
GREVILLE			
Wy	Girrawheen	32	A 7
GREVILLEA			
Ave	Roleystone	108	B 9
Cr	Swan View	51	D 9
Ct	Wanneroo	20	E 5
Pl	Canning Vale	104	C 1
Pl	Heathridge	19	C 10
Rd	Walliston	87	E 2
Wy	Heathridge	19	C 10
GREY			
Ct	Yanchep	4	C 3
Rd	Padbury	30	D 1
Rd	Padbury	23	D 10
St	Bayswater	62	D 1
St	Bayswater	48	D 10
St	Cannington	85	A 7
St	Fremantle	90	C 7
GREYGUM			
Cr	Quinns Rocks	10	A 10
GREYHOUND			
Dr	Merriwa	10	B 10
GREY-SMITH			
Gns	Woodvale	24	B 4
GRIBBLE			
Ave	Armadale	116	B 6
Rd	Bull Creek	92	E 5
Rd	Gwelup	45	C 3
GRID			
Ct	Beldon	23	D 2
GRIEVE			
Cl	Winthrop	92	B 4
GRIFFELL			
Wy	Duncraig	30	E 8
GRIFFIN			
Cr	Manning	83	B 6
St	Booragoon	92	C 1
GRIFFITH			
Wy	Thornlie	95	C 4
GRIFFITHS			
Pl	Hilton	91	B 8
Rd	Wanneroo	20	E 7
St	Kelmscott	107	A 8
St	Rivervale	74	A 4
GRIFFON			
Wy	Alexander Hts	32	E 5
GRIGG			
Pl	Hilton	91	B 9
Rd	Mt Helena	55	B 1
GRIGGS			
Wy	Rockingham	136	D 5
GRIGO			
Cl	Safety Bay	145	A 1
GRIMREY			
Rd	Lockridge	49	B 6
GRIMSAY			
Rd	Ardross	82	A 8
GRIMSEL			
Ct	Coodanup	165	D 3
GRINDLEFORD			
Dr	Balcatta	46	A 8

For detailed information regarding the street referencing system used in this book, turn to page 170.

H

		Map	Ref.
GRINSTEAD			
Wy	Balga	46	B 1
GRISKER			
Rd	Wanneroo	25	C 2
GRIVER			
St	Cottesloe	70	D 10
GROAT			
St	North Beach	44	D 2
GROGAN			
Cl	Lockridge	49	B 6
Rd	Newburn	76	A 2
Rd	Newburn	75	D 1
Rd	Perth Airport	75	D 1
GROOM			
Me	Leda	139	C 2
GROSE			
St	Cannington	84	E 7
Wy	Noranda	47	D 4
GROSSE			
Rd	Applecross	82	C 5
GROSVENOR			
Rd	Bayswater	62	A 6
Rd	Bayswater	61	E 6
Rd	Mt Lawley	61	B 8
Rd	North Perth	61	A 8
St	Beaconsfield	90	E 8
GROVE			
Ct	Greenwood	31	B 3
Hl	Mt Claremont	71	A 4
Rd	Kenwick	85	E 4
Rd	Lesmurdie	87	B 2
Rd	Lesmurdie	87	E 3
Rd	Walliston	88	A 2
St	Shoalwater	136	E 1
GROVEDALE			
Rd	Floreat	71	C 1
Rd	Floreat	59	C 10
GROVE END			
Rge	Mt Claremont	71	A 5
GROVELANDS			
Dr	Westfield	106	B 9
Wy	Westfield	106	B 10
GROVENOR			
Pl	Alexander Hts	33	B 6
GROVER			
Ct	Leeming	103	A 1
Pl	Hillarys	30	C 1
Wy	Medina	130	D 5
GROVES			
Ave	Alfred Cove	81	E 10
GROWSE			
Pl	Noranda	47	D 4
GROYDER			
Wy	Padbury	30	D 1
GRUNDY			
Wy	Thornlie	95	A 6
GUARDIAN			
Ct	Iluka	18	E 5
GUARNARD			
Rd	Golden Bay	158	E 9
GUAVA			
Ct	Forrestfield	86	D 1
Wy	Halls Head	164	C 5
GUELFI			
Rd	Balcatta	46	A 5
Rd	Balcatta	45	E 5
GUGERI			
Rd	Herne Hill	37	A 6
Rd	Middle Swan	37	A 10
St	Claremont	71	B 9
St	Mundaring	68	A 1
GUILDFORD			
Rd	Ashfield	62	D 4
Rd	Bassendean	63	A 1
Rd	Bayswater	62	A 7
Rd	Maylands	62	A 7
Rd	Maylands	61	D 8
Rd	Mt Lawley	61	C 8

		Map	Ref.
GUINEVERE			
Wy	Carine	31	C 10
GUINIVERE			
Wy	Westfield	106	C 7
GULL			
Ave	Two Rocks	2	C 1
Ct	Yangebup	102	B 9
Rd	Peel Estate	150	B 9
Rd	Peel Estate	149	E 8
Rd	Serpentine	150	C 10
Rd	Serpentine	154	D 1
St	Marmion	30	C 7
St	Wungong	126	C 3
Wy	Yangebup	102	B 9
GULLAN			
Cl	Noranda	47	D 4
GULLANE			
Ct	Currambine	19	B 4
GULSON			
Ct	Waikiki	145	E 1
GUM			
Ct	Yangebup	101	E 9
GUMBLOSSOM			
Wy	Quinns Rocks	10	A 10
GUMMERY			
St	Bedford	61	D 1
GUMMOW			
St	Hamilton Hill	101	C 2
Wy	Girrawheen	32	C 6
GUMNUT			
Cl	Maida Vale	77	A 3
Cl	Swan View	51	B 7
Cr	Safety Bay	137	A 10
GUNBAR			
Wy	Kalamunda	77	C 7
GUNBOWER			
Rd	Ardross	82	D 10
Rd	Mt Pleasant	82	D 10
GUNBY			
St	Maddington	96	A 4
GUNDILL			
St	Booragoon	92	B 1
GUNEE			
Rd	City Beach	58	E 7
GUNGURRU			
Ct	Swan View	51	D 9
GUNIDA			
St	Mullaloo	23	A 4
GUNJIN			
Rd	Hacketts Gully	89	C 1
Rd	Hacketts Gully	79	C 9
GUNN			
Ct	Thornlie	95	B 7
St	Floreat	71	C 1
GUNNAMATTA			
Pl	Kelmscott	116	C 1
GUNSAN			
Rt	Mindarie	14	C 6
GUNTER			
Gr	Beldon	23	C 4
GUPPY			
Rd	Kalamunda	77	E 9
GURIAN			
Gns	Kingsley	31	D 2
GURNARD			
Ct	Sorrento	30	C 3
Rd	Ferndale	84	D 9
GURNERS			
La	Byford	126	A 8
La	Byford	125	E 8
GURNEY			
Rd	Spearwood	101	B 5
GURON			
Rd	Duncraig	30	E 5
GUTHRIE			
St	Cannington	85	A 7
St	Osborne Park	60	A 2
St	Osborne Park	59	E 1

		Map	Ref.
GUTTERIDGE			
Rd	Banjup	113	B 2
GUY			
Ct	Beechboro	49	B 2
Pl	Melville	91	D 1
GWALIA			
Pl	Bibra Lake	102	C 5
Pl	Gosnells	95	E 10
GWEDUE			
Ct	Mullaloo	23	B 3
GWELUP			
St	Karrinyup	45	A 6
GWENDOLINE			
Dr	Beldon	23	D 2
GWENNETH			
Tce	South Lake	102	C 8
GWENYFRED			
Rd	Kensington	73	D 8
GWYNNE			
Pl	Roleystone	108	B 4
GYMEA			
Ct	Armadale	116	A 7
GYMPIE			
Wy	Willetton	93	C 2
GYPSUM			
Ct	Koondoola	32	E 9
GYPSY			
Ri	Swan View	51	A 6

H

		Map	Ref.
HABGOOD			
St	East Fremantle	80	E 10
HACKBRIDGE			
Wy	Bayswater	62	C 1
HACKETT			
Dr	Crawley	72	A 10
Ps	Winthrop	92	A 4
Rd	Dalkeith	81	C 1
St	Bellevue	51	A 10
St	Mandurah	163	A 10
HACKETTIANA			
Ave	South Lake	102	B 6
HACKING			
Pl	Padbury	23	E 9
HACKNEY			
Wy	Yanchep	4	C 4
HADDEN			
Rd	Bicton	81	B 10
HADDINGTON			
St	Beldon	23	D 3
HADDRILL			
Rd	Millendon	168	A 7
Rd	Millendon	29	E 8
St	Bayswater	62	A 4
HADLEIGH			
Wy	Girrawheen	32	B 9
HADLEY			
Gns	Kardinya	91	E 8
Pl	Karrinyup	45	A 6
Pl	Noranda	47	E 4
St	Shoalwater	136	D 9
HADLOW			
Ct	Leeming	93	A 9
Pl	Marangaroo	32	A 5
Pl	Thornlie	95	C 5
HAFFNER			
Ct	Maddington	96	B 3
HAGAN			
Ct	Bull Creek	93	A 7
HAGART			
Wy	Lockridge	49	A 5
HAGUE			
Ct	Ocean Reef	19	A 9

		Map	Ref.
HAIG			
Rd	Attadale	81	D 9
Rd	Dalkeith	81	D 3
St	Ashfield	62	D 4
St	Tuart Hill	46	C 10
HAIGH			
Rd	Canning Vale	105	A 1
Rd	Canning Vale	94	E 9
HAILSHAM			
Rd	Nollamara	46	D 5
HAILWOOD			
Ct	Kingsley	31	B 1
HAIMLEE			
St	Kelmscott	106	E 9
HAINE			
St	Gosnells	95	E 8
HAINES			
Rd	Baldivis	148	A 1
HAINING			
Ave	Cottesloe	80	D 1
HAINSWORTH			
Ave	Girrawheen	32	D 8
La	Girrawheen	32	D 8
HAITI			
Pl	Safety Bay	145	C 1
HAKATA			
Pl	Merriwa	11	C 9
HAKEA			
Cl	Ballajura	33	C 5
Ct	Forrestfield	76	D 10
Ct	Morley	48	C 5
Ct	Thornlie	95	A 8
Pa	Canning Vale	94	C 10
Pl	Sorrento	30	D 5
Rd	Nowergup	9	D 10
Rd	Westfield	106	C 7
Rd	Woodlands	59	C 1
HALCYON			
Pl	Ocean Reef	18	E 8
Wy	Churchlands	59	C 5
HALDANE			
St	Mt Claremont	70	E 5
HALDON			
Pl	Halls Head	164	C 3
HALE			
Gr	Woodvale	24	B 5
Rd	City Beach	58	D 4
Rd	Forrestdale	105	A 10
Rd	Forrestdale	114	D 2
Rd	Forrestfield	86	B 1
Rd	Forrestfield	76	C 10
Rd	Wattle Grove	86	A 3
Rd	Wattle Grove	85	E 3
Rd	Wembley Dns	59	A 4
Rd	Wembley Dns	58	E 4
Rd	Woodlands	59	A 4
St	Beaconsfield	90	D 8
St	East Perth	73	C 4
St	North Beach	44	C 1
St	North Beach	30	C 10
HALESWORTH			
Rd	Jolimont	71	D 1
HALEY			
Ave	Leederville	60	C 8
HALF MOON			
Cr	Merriwa	11	D 8
HALGANIA			
Wy	Duncraig	31	B 8
HALIDON			
St	Kingsley	24	C 10
St	Kingsley	31	D 1
HALIFAX			
Cst	Mindarie	14	B 3
Pl	Mundaring	68	C 1
HALKIN			
Pl	Hamilton Hill	101	A 3
Rd	Girrawheen	32	B 7
HALL			
Ave	Maylands	74	B 1
Pl	Kardinya	92	A 7

		Map	Ref.
Rd	Neerabup	15	A 2
Rd	Quinns Rocks	10	E 1
Rd	Roleystone	108	A 8
Rd	Roleystone	107	E 8
Rd	Serpentine	154	E 2
Rd	Serpentine	154	E 8
Rd	Serpentine	150	E 10
St	Karrinyup	45	A 5
St	Mandurah	163	A 10
HALLAM			
Cl	Booragoon	92	B 1
HALLAND			
Wy	Balga	46	D 3
HALLATT			
Gns	Upper Swan	29	E 3
HALLEENDALE			
Rd	Walliston	88	A 3
HALLETT			
Rd	Parkerville	53	C 9
HALLEY			
Rd	Balcatta	46	A 2
St	Innaloo	45	B 7
HALLIDAY			
St	Bayswater	62	C 6
St	Morley	61	E 1
HALLIN			
Ct	Ardross	82	C 8
HALLS HEAD			
Pde	Halls Head	164	B 1
Pde	Halls Head	162	C 9
HALMSTAD			
Pl	Mindarie	10	B 1
HALSE			
Cr	Melville	91	C 2
Pl	Karrinyup	44	E 3
HALSEY			
Cl	Cannington	84	D 6
HALSTEAD			
St	Hamilton Hill	101	C 1
HALTON			
St	Balcatta	46	A 5
HALVORSON			
Rd	Morley	48	A 8
Rd	Morley	47	E 8
HALWEST			
Wy	Alexander Hts	33	A 4
HAM			
Cl	Beldon	23	D 2
Pl	Morley	47	E 6
HAMBLEDON			
Cr	Armadale	116	D 3
HAMELIN			
Pl	Hillarys	23	B 10
HAMER			
Ave	Wembley Dns	58	E 4
Pde	Inglewood	61	C 5
Pde	Mt Lawley	61	B 5
HAMERSLEY			
Ave	Morley	48	C 8
Ct	Cooloongup	137	C 9
Pl	Morley	48	B 8
Rd	Caversham	50	A 7
Rd	Caversham	49	D 7
Rd	Sorrento	30	B 5
Rd	Subiaco	72	A 3
Rd	Subiaco	71	E 2
St	Cottesloe	80	C 1
St	Cottesloe	70	C 10
St	Kelmscott	117	B 1
St	Kelmscott	107	B 10
St	Midland	50	D 7
St	North Beach	44	C 3
Wy	Kardinya	92	A 7
HAMES			
St	Hamilton Hill	101	B 1
HAMILTON			
Ct	Gosnells	96	B 10
Ct	Yanchep	4	E 1
Gns	Mt Claremont	71	B 5
Pl	Safety Bay	145	B 2

		Map	Ref.
Rd	Hamilton Hill	**101**	A 4
Rd	High Wycombe	**64**	B 9
Rd	Munster	**111**	A 1
Rd	Munster	**101**	A10
Rd	Spearwood	**101**	A 5
St	Bassendean	**63**	A 3
St	Bayswater	**62**	B 5
St	Cannington	**84**	D 5
St	East Fremantle	**90**	E 2
St	Osborne Park	**60**	A 1
St	Osborne Park	**46**	A 9
St	Queens Park	**84**	E 3
St	Subiaco	**72**	C 1
St	Subiaco	**60**	C10
Tce	Greenmount	**51**	C10
Wy	Silver Sands	**163**	C 4
HAMLET			
Cl	Beldon	**23**	E 3
Ct	Bibra Lake	**102**	C 5
HAMLYN			
Glen	Kiara	**48**	D 6
HAMMAD			
St	Palmyra	**91**	B 2
HAMMOND			
Rd	Claremont	**71**	B 9
Rd	Jandakot	**112**	D 2
Rd	Success	**112**	D 6
Rd	Yangebup	**112**	D 1
Rd	Yangebup	**102**	D10
St	West Perth	**60**	E 9
HAMPDEN			
Cl	Dianella	**47**	B 5
Rd	Crawley	**71**	E 7
Rd	Nedlands	**71**	E 7
St	Rivervale	**74**	B 2
St	South Perth	**73**	B 9
HAMPSHIRE			
Dr	Iluka	**18**	E 5
Gns	Parmelia	**131**	B 7
St	E Victoria Pk	**84**	A 1
St	E Victoria Pk	**74**	A10
St	E Victoria Pk	**83**	E 1
HAMPSTEAD			
Ct	Kingsley	**24**	B10
HAMPTON			
Ct	Thornlie	**95**	B 8
Rd	Fremantle	**1D**	C 5
Rd	Fremantle	**90**	C 6
Rd	Sth Fremantle	**90**	D 8
Sq E	Morley	**48**	C 9
Sq W	Morley	**48**	C 9
St	Greenfields	**163**	C 7
St	Karrinyup	**45**	A 4
St	Kewdale	**74**	E 7
St	Victoria Park	**73**	E 6
Tce	Joondalup	**19**	E 4
HANCOCK			
Pl	Kardinya	**91**	E 6
Pl	Waikiki	**145**	D 2
St	Doubleview	**59**	A 1
St	Doubleview	**45**	A10
St	Mandurah	**163**	A10
St	Nollamara	**46**	D 6
HANDA			
St	Armadale	**116**	B 3
HANDCOCK			
Wy	Kingsley	**31**	C 1
HANDLEY			
Cl	Leeming	**92**	E10
HANLEY			
Pl	Hillarys	**30**	C 3
St	Stoneville	**54**	B 4
HANLIN			
Rd	Forrestdale	**115**	B 6
St	Mosman Park	**80**	E 8
Wy	Samson	**91**	C 9
HANLON			
St	Hamilton Hill	**91**	A10
HANN			
Ct	Gosnells	**106**	A 3
Pl	Padbury	**23**	D10
St	Leederville	**60**	C 9
HANNABY			
St	Dianella	**46**	E 8
HANNAFORD			
Ave	Clarkson	**14**	E10
HANNAH			
Ct	Duncraig	**31**	A 5
Pl	Leeming	**93**	C 8
HANNAN			
Pl	Huntingdale	**105**	D 1
Pl	Huntingdale	**95**	D10
HANNANS			
St	Morley	**48**	C 7
HANNIBAL			
St	Palmyra	**91**	A 2
HANOVER			
Pl	North Perth	**60**	E 7
Pl	Waterford	**83**	D 6
St	Forrestfield	**76**	C10
HANRAHAN			
Lp	Kardinya	**91**	D 8
HANRETTY			
St	Warnbro	**145**	C 6
HANSA			
Pl	Marangaroo	**32**	E 6
HANSEN			
Ave	Rockingham	**137**	C 7
Rd	Armadale	**115**	E 3
St	Coolbellup	**91**	C10
HANSON			
St	Maddington	**86**	B10
Wy	Mandurah	**165**	B 4
HANTKE			
Pl	Welshpool	**84**	D 2
HANWELL			
Ct	Kingsley	**31**	B 2
Wy	Bassendean	**62**	D 1
HANWORTH			
St	Balcatta	**46**	A 5
HANZELL			
Rd	Darlington	**66**	A 2
HAPPINESS			
La	Mundaring	**54**	B10
HARBER			
Dr	Armadale	**116**	C10
HARBINGER			
Pl	Iluka	**18**	E 3
HARBOR			
Rd	Kwinana Beach	**129**	E 7
HARBORD			
Ave	Coodanup	**165**	C 4
Ct	Kallaroo	**23**	A 7
HARBORNE			
St	Glendalough	**60**	A 5
St	Wembley	**60**	A 9
HARBOUR			
Ct	Safety Bay	**145**	A 2
Rd	Kalamunda	**77**	B 6
Rd	Sth Fremantle	**90**	C 9
HARBOUR TOWN			
Hts	Connolly	**19**	C 6
HARCOURT			
Dr	Hillarys	**30**	C 2
Pl	Bellevue	**65**	B 2
Pl	Bull Creek	**93**	A 5
St	Bassendean	**63**	A 2
St	Bassendean	**63**	B 2
St	Inglewood	**61**	D 5
HARCUS			
Rt	Merriwa	**11**	C 9
HARDAKER			
St	Eden Hill	**49**	A 9
HARDEY			
Rd	Ascot	**62**	C 9
Rd	Belmont	**62**	D10
Rd	Belmont	**74**	E 1
Rd	Cloverdale	**75**	A 3
Rd	Glen Forrest	**67**	A 6
Rd	Glen Forrest	**66**	D 1
Rd	Glen Forrest	**52**	D 1
Rd	Glen Forrest	**66**	E 4
Rd	Kewdale	**75**	E 9
Rd	Maylands	**74**	B 1
Rd	Maylands	**62**	B10
Rd	Serpentine	**154**	E 5
Rd	Wattle Grove	**86**	A 1
Rd	Wattle Grove	**75**	E10
St	Bull Creek	**93**	A 6
St	Hamilton Hill	**100**	E 1
St	Hamilton Hill	**90**	E10
HARDINGE			
Rd	Canning Mills	**88**	A 9
Rd	Canning Mills	**87**	B 9
Rd	Orange Grove	**86**	E 9
HARDWICK			
Rd	Millendon	**168**	B 9
St	Morley	**48**	B 7
HARDWOOD			
Rt	Merriwa	**10**	B 8
HARDY			
Ct	Two Rocks	**2**	C 2
Rd	Ashfield	**62**	E 5
Rd	Bayswater	**62**	D 6
Rd	Nedlands	**72**	A 7
Rd	Nedlands	**71**	E 7
St	North Perth	**60**	D 7
St	South Perth	**72**	E 7
HARES			
St	Wilson	**84**	B 6
HAREWOOD			
Pl	Marangaroo	**32**	D 5
St	Forrestfield	**86**	C 1
HARFLEUR			
Pl	Hamilton Hill	**101**	B 4
HARFOOT			
St	Willagee	**91**	D 4
HARFORD			
Ave	Viveash	**50**	B 5
Wy	Girrawheen	**32**	C 8
HARGRAVE			
Dr	Thornlie	**95**	A 4
Pl	Parmelia	**131**	C 7
St	Stirling	**45**	E 6
HARGREAVES			
Rd	Coolbellup	**101**	D 1
Rd	Coolbellup	**91**	D10
Rd	Rockingham	**138**	A 4
St	Ascot	**62**	C10
St	Belmont	**62**	C10
HARKINS			
St	Balga	**46**	C 3
HARLEM			
Pl	Greenfields	**163**	D 8
HARLEY			
Cl	Safety Bay	**137**	A10
Pl	Kingsley	**31**	C 2
St	Belmont	**74**	D 2
St	Highgate	**61**	A 9
Tce	Mosman Park	**80**	D 7
Wy	Medina	**130**	E 5
HARLOCK			
Cl	Murdoch	**92**	B 7
HARLOND			
Ave	Malaga	**47**	D 1
HARLOW			
Ct	Westfield	**106**	B 9
Pl	Calista	**130**	E 7
Rd	Calista	**130**	E 7
HARMAN			
Ct	Ashfield	**62**	E 4
Rd	Sorrento	**30**	C 4
St	Belmont	**74**	E 3
St	Leda	**130**	D10
HARNESS			
St	Kingsley	**24**	C10
HAROLD			
Rd	Maida Vale	**76**	D 3
Rd	Swan View	**51**	B 7
St	Ascot	**62**	B 9
St	Bellevue	**51**	A10
St	Darlington	**66**	C 6
St	Dianella	**61**	B 2
St	Glen Forrest	**66**	D 3
St	Gosnells	**106**	C 1
St	Mt Lawley	**61**	B 9
HARP			
Ct	Mullaloo	**23**	B 3
HARPENDEN			
St	Huntingdale	**95**	C10
St	Southern River	**105**	B 2
HARPER			
Ct	Mandurah	**165**	C 3
Pl	Winthrop	**92**	B 5
Rd	Banjup	**113**	C 4
St	Caversham	**49**	C 7
St	Midland	**50**	B 8
St	Victoria Park	**73**	E 6
Tce	South Perth	**72**	E 7
HARRAS			
Ct	Marangaroo	**32**	D 6
HARRAY			
St	Hamersley	**32**	A 8
HARRIER			
Cl	Huntingdale	**105**	C 1
Ct	High Wycombe	**76**	B 1
Pl	Stirling	**45**	E 7
Pl	Yangebup	**102**	A10
Wy	Beldon	**23**	E 3
HARRINGTON			
Cr	Leeming	**93**	C 8
HARRIOTT			
St	Willagee	**91**	E 5
HARRIS			
Pl	Jarrahdale	**152**	D 7
Rd	Bicton	**91**	B 1
Rd	Bicton	**81**	B10
Rd	Caversham	**50**	C 3
Rd	Hope Valley	**122**	A 8
Rd	Malaga	**47**	C 3
Rd	Palmyra	**91**	B 1
St	Beckenham	**95**	B 1
St	Beckenham	**85**	B10
St	Carlisle	**74**	C 8
St	Mariginiup	**20**	D 3
St	Welshpool	**74**	D 9
Wy	Balga	**46**	E 3
HARRISON			
Rd	Armadale	**116**	E 7
Rd	Forrestfield	**76**	B 6
St	Balcatta	**46**	B 7
St	Nollamara	**46**	C 7
St	Rockingham	**136**	D 5
St	Willagee	**92**	A 4
St	Willagee	**91**	E 4
Wy	Calista	**130**	E 8
HARROD			
St	Willagee	**91**	E 4
HARROGATE			
St	Leederville	**60**	C10
HARROLYN			
Ave	Riverton	**83**	E 9
HARROW			
Pl	Lynwood	**94**	C 3
St	Cullacabardee	**34**	B 8
St	Kewdale	**74**	D 8
St	Maylands	**61**	E 6
St	Mt Hawthorn	**60**	D 6
St	West Swan	**36**	A 8
St	West Swan	**35**	B 9
St	West Swan	**35**	D 8
HARROWSHILL			
Rd	Morley	**48**	D 9
HARROW WEALD			
Wy	Kingsley	**24**	B 8
HARRY			
St	Gosnells	**106**	B 2
Wy	Willetton	**93**	C 3
HART			
Ct	Wanneroo	**20**	C 7
Pde	Naval Base	**121**	A 3
Rd	Serpentine	**155**	B 5
St	Lesmurdie	**77**	B10
St	Roleystone	**108**	B 6
HARTFIELD			
Cr	Leeming	**93**	A 9
Rd	Forrestfield	**86**	B 1
Rd	Forrestfield	**86**	D 2
St	Queens Park	**85**	A 3
Wy	Balga	**46**	C 4
HARTFORD			
Gr	Iluka	**18**	E 5
HARTINGTON			
Wy	Carine	**30**	E 9
HARTLAND			
Pl	Yanchep	**4**	D 4
Wy	Warnbro	**145**	D 7
HARTLEAP			
La	Beldon	**23**	E 3
HARTLEY			
Ct	Greenwood	**31**	D 4
St	Coolbellup	**91**	C10
St	Gosnells	**96**	B 8
Wy	Balga	**32**	B 9
HARTMAN			
Dr	Wangara	**25**	B 8
HARTOG			
Gr	Mirrabooka	**33**	A 9
St	Innaloo	**59**	C 1
HARTREE			
Ct	Leeming	**93**	C 9
HARTUNG			
La	Mundaring	**54**	B10
St	Mundaring	**54**	A10
Wy	Bull Creek	**93**	A 4
HARTWELL			
St	Coolbinia	**60**	E 3
HARVARD			
Pl	Greenfields	**163**	D 9
Wy	Canning Vale	**94**	C 7
HARVEL			
Cl	Glen Forrest	**66**	D 2
HARVEST			
Lp	Edgewater	**24**	A 1
Rd	Morley	**48**	B 9
Rd	Nth Fremantle	**90**	C 1
Rd	Nth Fremantle	**80**	D10
Tce	Scarborough	**44**	D10
Tce	West Perth	**1C**	D 2
Tce	West Perth	**72**	D 2
HARVEY			
Cl	Gosnells	**105**	E 2
Cr	Kardinya	**91**	D 6
Rd	Karnup	**159**	D 1
Rd	Karnup	**157**	D10
Rd	Shenton Park	**71**	D 5
St	Mosman Park	**80**	D 5
St	Victoria Park	**73**	E 6
HARWOOD			
Ct	Trigg	**44**	D 7
Pl	West Perth	**60**	E10
Ri	Leeming	**93**	C 9
St	Hilton	**91**	B 7
HASCOMBE			
Wy	Morley	**48**	B 9
HASELMERE			
Cs	Rockingham	**137**	C 7
HASKELL			
Gns	Clarkson	**14**	D 2
HASLEMERE			
Dr	Armadale	**116**	E 2
Wy	Morley	**48**	B 9
HASLER			
Rd	Osborne Park	**60**	A 4
Rd	Osborne Park	**59**	D 3
HASPER			
Pl	Marmion	**30**	C 8
HASSELL			
Cr	Bull Creek	**92**	E 7
Ct	Bull Creek	**92**	E 7
HASSETT			
Rd	Roleystone	**108**	B 6
St	Cloverdale	**75**	A 2

For detailed information regarding the street referencing system used in this book, turn to page 170.

H

		Map	Ref.
HASTINGS			
Ct	Jandakot	112	E 8
St	Scarborough	58	D 2
St	Scarborough	44	D 10
St	Wanneroo	20	C 8
HATCH			
Ct	Forrestdale	104	E 8
Ct	High Wycombe	64	B 7
Pl	Bibra Lake	102	B 7
HATCHER			
Wy	Lynwood	94	A 4
HATFIELD			
Wy	Booragoon	92	B 2
Wy	Girrawheen	32	D 7
HATHERLEY			
Pde	Winthrop	92	B 5
HATTON			
Ct	Bassendean	63	A 3
Gr	Carine	31	A 9
Rd	Westfield	106	B 9
HAVEL			
Pl	Beechboro	48	D 3
HAVELOCK			
St	West Perth	1C	D 2
St	West Perth	72	D 2
St	West Perth	60	D 10
HAVEN			
Ct	Silver Sands	163	B 5
Pl	Thornlie	95	B 9
Pl	Willetton	93	D 2
HAVENVALE			
Cr	Dianella	47	C 8
HAVERFORD			
St	Alexander Hts	32	E 5
HAVERING			
Ct	Kingsley	31	B 2
HAWDON			
Me	Hillarys	30	C 1
St	Stoneville	54	B 4
HAWFORD			
Wy	Willetton	93	D 4
HAWICK			
Ct	Warwick	31	C 3
HAWK			
Cl	Ballajura	33	E 8
Ct	High Wycombe	64	B 10
Gr	Willetton	93	C 4
Pl	Craigie	23	E 6
Wy	Byford	135	D 1
Wy	Byford	126	D 10
HAWKE			
Ps	Bateman	92	D 5
St	Stoneville	54	B 4
HAWKER			
Ave	Warwick	31	C 7
Ave	Warwick	31	C 8
Cl	Kardinya	92	A 6
St	Safety Bay	144	E 1
St	Safety Bay	136	E 10
St	Shoalwater	136	E 1
HAWKES			
St	Coolbellup	91	D 10
HAWKESBURY			
Dr	Willetton	94	A 4
HAWKEVALE			
Rd	High Wycombe	64	D 9
HAWKINS			
Ave	Sorrento	30	C 5
Rd	Roleystone	108	A 5
Rd N	Jandabup	21	E 5
Rd S	Jandabup	21	D 8
Rd S	Wanneroo	21	D 9
St	Embleton	48	A 10
St	Mt Pleasant	82	D 8
St	Rockingham	137	D 6
HAWKSBURN			
Rd	Rivervale	74	A 3
HAWKSBURY			
Gr	Port Kennedy	156	D 1

		Map	Ref.
HAWKSHEAD			
Wy	Balga	32	C 10
HAWKSTONE			
Rd	Roleystone	108	B 10
St	Cottesloe	70	D 10
HAWKVALLEY			
Cr	Maida Vale	64	E 9
HAWLEY			
Pl	Marangaroo	32	A 6
HAWTER			
Rd	Glen Forrest	66	C 3
HAWTHORN			
St	Mt Hawthorn	60	C 6
HAWTHORNE			
Cr	Swan C Homes	144	
Pl	Victoria Park	73	E 5
HAWTIN			
Rd	Forrestfield	76	D 8
Rd	Maida Vale	76	E 4
HAY			
Ct	Greenwood	31	B 5
Rd	Redcliffe	63	A 6
St	East Perth	1C	B 3
St	East Perth	73	C 4
St	Jolimont	71	D 1
St	Perth City	73	A 3
St	Perth City	1C	E 2
St	Perth City	72	E 2
St	Subiaco	72	B 1
St	West Perth	72	D 1
St	West Perth	1C	D 2
HAYBURN			
St	Scarborough	58	E 1
HAYDEN			
Cl	Noranda	47	C 6
Ct	Myaree	92	A 3
St	Mt Helena	41	B 4
Wy	Langford	95	A 1
HAYDN BUNTON			
Dr	Subiaco	72	B 1
HAYES			
Ave	Dianella	46	E 8
Ave	Yokine	60	E 1
Ave	Yokine	46	E 10
Ct	Thornlie	95	B 7
Rd	Leeming	93	B 9
Rd	Pickering Bk	99	C 3
Tce	Mosman Park	80	D 7
HAYFIELD			
Wy	Duncraig	31	A 4
HAYLE			
Ct	Willetton	94	A 2
HAYLEY			
St	Maddington	96	A 2
HAYMAN			
Ct	Coogee	100	E 9
Rd	Bentley	83	E 2
Rd	Como	83	C 1
HAYMARKET			
Pl	Alexander Hts	33	B 4
HAYNES			
Ct	Armadale	116	C 6
Ct	Kardinya	91	D 8
Rd	Sorrento	30	C 5
St	Kalamunda	77	D 6
St	North Perth	60	D 6
St	Wembley Dns	59	A 4
HAYSOM			
St	Trigg	44	C 5
HAYWARD			
Pde	Coogee	100	E 9
Rd	Martin	96	D 6
St	Bayswater	62	A 6
St	Myaree	91	E 2
Wy	Myaree	91	E 2
HAYWOOD			
Trl	Leeming	93	D 8
HAZE			
Rd	Falcon	162A	C 1

		Map	Ref.
HAZEL			
Ave	Quinns Rocks	10	E 9
Ave	Woodlands	59	B 1
St	Como	83	A 1
St	Como	73	A 10
HAZELBURY			
St	Greenwood	31	E 4
HAZELHURST			
St	Kewdale	75	B 7
HAZELMERE			
Cr	Hazelmere	64	A 1
Cs	Hazelmere	64	A 2
HAZELTINE			
Ct	Yanchep	4	E 2
HAZELWOOD			
Lp	Carine	30	D 9
Ra	Ballajura	33	C 6
HAZEN			
Ce	Joondalup	19	C 1
HAZLETT			
Cl	South Lake	102	C 6
Pl	Waikiki	145	D 2
HEAD			
St	Melville	91	D 2
HEADINGLY			
Rd	Kalamunda	77	D 6
HEADLAND			
Rd	Hamilton Hill	91	B 10
Ri	Ballajura	33	C 8
HEADLEY			
Pl	Bayswater	62	D 1
HEAL			
Rd	Morley	48	C 6
St	Hamilton Hill	101	B 2
HEALD			
Pl	Medina	130	E 4
HEALEY			
Pl	Gooseberry H	77	C 3
Pl	Noranda	48	B 6
HEALY			
Rd	Hamilton Hill	91	A 10
Rd	Hamilton Hill	101	B 1
Rd	Hamilton Hill	90	E 10
HEARD			
Wy	Glendalough	60	A 6
HEARDER			
Ave	Hope Valley	121	C 8
HEARLE			
St	Armadale	116	B 2
HEARN			
Ct	Hillarys	23	B 10
HEATH			
Pl	Thornlie	95	A 8
Rd	Kalamunda	77	B 6
Rd	Roleystone	108	C 6
Ri	Carine	31	A 9
St	Singleton	160	D 4
HEATHCROFT			
Rd	Balga	32	D 10
HEATHER			
Pl	Dianella	46	E 4
Rd	Lesmurdie	87	E 1
Rd	Roleystone	108	A 7
St	Martin	96	C 7
HEATHERLEA			
Pwy	Leeming	103	A 1
HEATON			
Rd	Yokine	46	C 9
Wy	Safety Bay	136	E 10
HEBBARD			
St	Samson	91	C 9
HEBBLE			
Lp	Banjup	113	E 4
HEBE			
Rd	Banjup	104	B 9
HECTOR			
St	Osborne Park	60	B 2
St	Tuart Hill	60	C 2

		Map	Ref.
St	Yokine	60	E 2
St W	Osborne Park	60	A 1
St W	Osborne Park	59	E 1
St W	Osborne Park	45	E 10
HEDGEROWS			
Gns	Padbury	30	E 2
HEDGES			
Pl	Kewdale	74	E 8
Rd	Hovea	52	E 8
HEDLAND			
St	E Victoria Pk	73	E 10
HEDLEY			
Pl	Bentley	84	B 5
St	Bentley	84	B 5
HEFRON			
Gl	Wungong	126	E 2
St	Mt Helena	55	B 4
St	Rockingham	137	C 8
Wy	Parmelia	131	C 6
HEHIR			
St	Belmont	74	C 1
HEIDELBERG			
Rd	Bickley	88	C 3
HELBY			
Cl	Merriwa	11	C 9
HELEN			
Cr	Byford	135	D 1
Cr	Byford	126	D 10
St	Applecross	82	B 8
St	Bellevue	50	E 10
St	Hamilton Hill	91	B 10
St	Inglewood	61	C 4
HELENA			
Cr	Thornlie	95	D 5
Pl	Hamilton Hill	101	B 3
Rd	Cooloongup	137	D 9
St	Guildford	63	D 1
St	Midland	50	B 8
St	Mundaring	54	C 10
Tce	Mundaring	68	D 1
Tce	Sawyers Valley	68	E 1
Tce	Sawyers Valley	54	E 10
HELENA VALLEY			
Rd	Helena Valley	65	A 4
Rd	Helena Valley	66	A 9
Rd	Helena Valley	64	D 3
Rd	Helena Valley	65	E 7
Rd	Paulls Valley	78	C 1
Rd	Piesse Brook	78	A 1
HELLAM			
Gr	Booragoon	92	B 2
HELLENIC			
Rd	Roleystone	108	A 6
HELM			
St	Maddington	96	B 5
St	Mt Pleasant	82	D 6
HELMSLEY			
St	Scarborough	58	E 1
HELPMAN			
Ct	Huntingdale	95	D 10
Wy	Padbury	30	D 1
HELSALL			
Ct	Sorrento	30	B 4
Ct	Willetton	93	D 6
HELSTON			
Ave	City Beach	70	D 1
Ct	Midland	50	D 6
HEMELEERS			
St	Gosnells	106	C 1
HEMINGWAY			
Dr	Westfield	106	C 7
HEMMINGS			
Ci	Clarkson	11	E 10
HEMSEY			
St	Balga	46	B 1
HENBURY			
Ct	Connolly	19	A 7
HENDERSON			
Ave	Redcliffe	63	B 8
Dr	Armadale	115	E 4

		Map	Ref.
Dr	Kallaroo	23	A 7
Pl	High Wycombe	64	D 9
Rd	Munster	111	E 7
Rd	Stoneville	54	B 5
St	Fremantle	1D	C 5
St	Fremantle	90	C 5
HENDON			
Pl	Wilson	84	B 8
Wy	Hamersley	32	A 10
Wy	Hamersley	31	E 10
Wy	Kelmscott	116	C 2
HENDRA			
St	Cloverdale	74	E 4
HENDY			
Grn	Murdoch	92	B 6
Rd	Hope Valley	121	D 8
HENKIN			
St	Bellevue	51	A 10
St	Bellevue	64	E 1
HENLEY			
Pl	Attadale	81	C 9
Rd	Ardross	82	D 10
St	Como	82	E 4
St	Henley Brook	29	B 10
St	Henley Brook	28	C 9
St	Henley Brook	28	E 10
St	Manning	83	B 4
HENN			
Cl	Winthrop	92	A 6
HENNESSY			
Ave	Orelia	131	B 5
Pl	Mandurah	165	C 1
Wy	Rockingham	136	E 9
HENNIKER			
Wy	Koondoola	33	A 8
HENNING			
Cr	Manning	83	B 6
HENRIETTA			
Ave	Armadale	116	E 2
St	Bayswater	62	A 2
St	Kewdale	74	D 6
HENRY			
St	Cottesloe	80	D 1
St	E Cannington	85	A 6
St	East Perth	1C	B 2
St	East Perth	73	B 2
St	Fremantle	1D	B 5
St	Fremantle	90	B 5
St	Henley Brook	29	B 7
St	Midland	50	D 7
St	Naval Base	121	B 7
St	Rockingham	137	D 7
St	Shenton Park	72	A 3
HENRY BULL			
Dr	Bull Creek	93	A 7
HENSHAW			
La	Claremont	71	A 7
HENSMAN			
Rd	Shenton Park	72	A 4
Rd	Subiaco	72	A 3
St	Chidlow	56	D 1
St	Kensington	73	B 10
St	South Perth	73	B 10
St	South Perth	72	E 9
HENSON			
St	Mandurah	163	A 8
St	Silver Sands	163	A 8
HENTON			
Pl	Heathridge	23	E 2
HENTY			
Ct	Mirrabooka	47	A 1
Ct	Two Rocks	2	E 3
Lp	Woodvale	24	B 7
HENVILLE			
St	Fremantle	90	D 9
HEPBURN			
Ave	Alexander Hts	32	E 3
Ave	Ballajura	33	C 3
Ave	Duncraig	30	E 3
Ave	Greenwood	31	D 3
Ave	Marangaroo	32	A 3

H

		Map	Ref.
Ave	Sorrento	30	B 3
Wy	Balga	32	D 10
Wy	Booragoon	92	D 1

HEPPELL
| Gns | Clarkson | 14 | C 2 |

HEPPINGSTONE
| St | South Perth | 73 | C 7 |

HEPWORTH
| Rd | Trigg | 44 | C 6 |
| Wy | Noranda | 47 | D 6 |

HERA
Ave	Riverton	83	D 10
Cl	Cooloongup	137	D 8
Ct	San Remo	160	C 10

HERACLES
| Ave | Riverton | 83 | D 10 |

HERALD
Ave	Willetton	93	D 2
Cl	Kalamunda	77	D 9
Ri	Greenfields	163	E 10

HERBERT
Ct	Wungong	116	B 9
Rd	Karragullen	109	B 7
Rd	Shenton Park	71	E 5
St	Chidlow	56	D 2
St	Doubleview	45	A 10
St	Maddington	95	E 4
St	Nth Fremantle	80	C 10

HERCULES
| St | Rockingham | 137 | A 9 |

HERDSMAN
Ct	Jandakot	112	E 3
Pde	Glendalough	60	A 6
Pde	Wembley	59	D 8

HEREFORD
| Pl | Spearwood | 101 | C 4 |

HERITAGE
Ct	Willetton	93	E 5
La	Mt Claremont	71	B 5
Tce	Gnangara	26	B 4

HERLIHY
| Wy | Warnbro | 145 | C 9 |

HERMES
| Rd | Gooseberry H | 77 | B 2 |
| St | Riverton | 83 | D 10 |

HERMIONE
| Wy | Coolbellup | 91 | E 10 |

HERMITAGE
Dr	Ellenbrook	29	C 2
Pl	Hillarys	23	A 9
St	Dudley Park	165	C 5

HERMITE
| Ri | Sorrento | 30 | C 3 |

HERNDON
| Cl | Cannington | 84 | D 5 |

HERNE
| St | Herne Hill | 36 | C 7 |

HERON
Cl	Ballajura	33	E 6
Cl	Chidlow	42	C 8
Cl	Edgewater	19	E 9
Ct	High Wycombe	64	A 10
Ct	Westfield	106	B 10
Pl	Churchlands	59	D 7
Pl	Lynwood	94	A 4
Pl	Maddington	95	D 4
Pl	Rockingham	137	B 9
St	Mandurah	165	A 4
Wy	Yangebup	102	A 9

HERRESHOFF
| Ra | Ocean Reef | 19 | A 9 |

HERRIARD
| Rd | Armadale | 116 | D 2 |

HERRING
| Ct | Sorrento | 30 | C 3 |

HERSCHELL
| Blvd | Ocean Reef | 18 | E 7 |
| Wy | Coogee | 100 | E 10 |

HERSEY
| Pl | Beckenham | 85 | A 9 |

HERTFORD
Cl	Bull Creek	93	B 5
Pl	E Victoria Pk	83	E 1
Pl	Iluka	18	E 4
St	E Victoria Pk	83	D 1

HERTHA
| Pl | Innaloo | 45 | C 8 |
| St | Innaloo | 45 | C 9 |

HERTZ
| Wy | Morley | 48 | C 7 |

HESFORD
| Ave | Mt Pleasant | 92 | E 1 |

HESKEITH
| Ave | Armadale | 116 | A 2 |
| Ave | Armadale | 115 | E 3 |

HESKETH
| Rd | Greenmount | 51 | C 9 |

HESLOP
| Rd | Lesmurdie | 87 | D 1 |

HESPERIA
| Ave | City Beach | 58 | D 8 |

HESS
| Ct | Marangaroo | 32 | E 6 |

HESSEL
| Ct | Greenwood | 31 | D 5 |

HESTER
Ave	Merriwa	14	C 1
Ave	Merriwa	11	D 10
Ave	Nowergup	12	A 9
St	Bayswater	62	A 4
St	Langford	95	A 2
Wy	Greenwood	31	E 4

HESTIA
| Pl | San Remo | 163 | C 1 |
| Wy | San Remo | 163 | C 2 |

HESTON
| Cl | Leeming | 92 | E 9 |

HETHERINGTON
Cl	Jarrahdale	152	A 4
Dr	Bull Creek	93	B 7
St	Nth Fremantle	80	C 10

HEWETT
| Wy | Balga | 32 | B 9 |

HEWISON
Rd	Medina	130	E 4
Rd	Pickering Bk	98	E 1
Rd	Pickering Bk	88	E 10
St	Leeming	93	A 8

HEWITT
Cl	Noranda	48	A 4
Wy	Booragoon	92	D 1
Wy	Booragoon	82	D 10

HEWSON
| Pl | Maida Vale | 76 | E 4 |

HEWTON
| St | Morley | 47 | E 9 |

HEYLMORE
| Pl | Medina | 130 | E 6 |
| Rd | Medina | 130 | E 6 |

HEYSEN
| Cst | Woodvale | 24 | C 5 |

HEYSHOTT
| Rd | Balga | 46 | C 1 |

HEYTESBURY
| Rd | Subiaco | 72 | A 3 |
| Rd | Subiaco | 71 | E 3 |

HEYWOOD
| Ct | Halls Head | 164 | C 1 |

HIBBERTIA
| Cr | Ferndale | 94 | B 1 |
| Ct | Forrestfield | 76 | E 7 |

HIBERNIA
| Ri | Sorrento | 30 | B 4 |

HIBISCUS
Cl	Marangaroo	32	D 5
Ct	Churchlands	59	C 5
Dr	Forrestfield	76	E 7
Me	Canning Vale	104	C 1

HICKEY
Ave	Daglish	71	E 2
Cl	Noranda	48	B 5
St	Ardross	82	B 9

HICKMAN
| Rd | Silver Sands | 163 | B 5 |

HICKORY
Ct	Halls Head	164	B 5
Dr	Thornlie	95	A 9
Rd	Quinns Rocks	10	A 10
St	Sth Fremantle	90	C 10

HICKS
Rd	Kelmscott	117	A 1
Rd	Kelmscott	107	B 10
St	Forrestfield	76	B 9
St	Gosnells	96	B 9
St	Gosnells	106	C 1
St	Karrinyup	45	B 6
St	Leeming	93	C 9
St	Mundijong	143	A 10
Wy	Hillarys	23	B 8

HICKSON
| Ave | Armadale | 116 | C 4 |

HIDDEN VALLEY
Rd	Parkerville	53	A 1
Rd	Parkerville	39	B 7
Rt	Clarkson	14	E 1
Rt	Clarkson	11	E 10

HIGGINS
| Pl | Armadale | 116 | E 4 |
| Wy | Bayswater | 62 | C 6 |

HIGGINSON
| Rd | Mt Helena | 54 | D 2 |
| Rd | Stoneville | 54 | C 2 |

HIGGS
| St | Noranda | 47 | C 4 |

HIGH
Rd	Ferndale	94	B 1
Rd	Lynwood	94	C 2
Rd	Riverton	94	A 1
Rd	Riverton	93	C 1
Rd	Roleystone	107	D 9
Rd	Wanneroo	21	A 9
Rd	Wanneroo	20	E 9
St	Fremantle	1D	B 5
St	Fremantle	1D	C 5
St	Fremantle	90	C 5
St	Midland	50	A 9
St	Sorrento	30	C 7
St	South Perth	73	B 9

HIGHAM
Ct	Leeming	93	A 8
Rd	Marangaroo	32	B 5
Rd	Nth Fremantle	80	D 10

HIGHAM HILL
| | Swan View | 51 | A 5 |

HIGHBRIDGE
| Wy | Karrinyup | 45 | A 2 |

HIGHBURY
| Cr | Beckenham | 85 | A 9 |
| St | Floreat | 59 | D 9 |

HIGHCLERE
| Blvd | Marangaroo | 32 | C 6 |

HIGHCLIFFE
| Ri | Currambine | 19 | B 5 |

HIGHFIELD
| Ri | Hillarys | 23 | A 9 |

HIGHLANDS
| Rd | Joondanna | 60 | D 4 |
| Rd | North Perth | 60 | D 4 |

HIGHMAN
| St | Sth Guildford | 63 | D 3 |

HIGH PEAK
| Pl | Lesmurdie | 87 | A 2 |

HIGHROYD
| St | Menora | 61 | A 6 |

HIGH TOR
| | Woodvale | 24 | B 8 |

HIGH VIEW
| Rd | Greenmount | 51 | E 10 |

HIGHVIEW
Ri	Ballajura	33	C 4
St	Alexander Hts	33	A 4
Tce	Wilson	84	A 8

HILARION
| Rd | Duncraig | 30 | E 4 |

HILBERT
| Rd | Armadale | 115 | E 9 |
| Rd | Forrestdale | 125 | E 1 |

HILDA
Rd	Waikiki	145	B 5
St	Coolbinia	60	D 4
St	North Perth	60	D 4
St	Shenton Park	71	E 5

HILL
Ct	Thornlie	95	B 9
Pl	Attadale	81	C 10
Rd	Hope Valley	122	A 8
Rd	Parkerville	53	C 9
Rd	Roleystone	107	D 5
St	Bayswater	62	B 5
St	East Perth	1C	B 3
St	East Perth	73	B 3
St	Gooseberry H	77	D 2
St	Guildford	63	C 1
St	Halls Head	162	C 10
St	Innaloo	45	C 8
St	Kelmscott	117	A 1
St	Menora	61	A 6
St	Perth City	1C	B 4
St	Perth City	73	B 4
St	South Perth	73	A 9
Tce	Mosman Park	80	E 4

HILLARY
| St | Willagee | 91 | E 4 |

HILLCREST
Dr	Darlington	66	B 5
Rd	Alexander Hts	33	A 5
Rd	Alexander Hts	32	E 5
Rd	Kewdale	74	D 9
Rd	Mundaring	54	B 9
St	Coogee	100	E 8

HILLEGINE
| Ct | Gosnells | 96 | A 7 |
| Ct | Gosnells | 95 | E 7 |

HILLIER
| Cr | Hamilton Hill | 101 | C 1 |
| Pl | Hamersley | 46 | A 1 |

HILLINGDON
| Cl | Kingsley | 31 | B 1 |

HILLMAN
Ct	Westfield	106	C 9
St	Rockingham	137	B 2
St	Sth Guildford	63	C 3

HILLOCK
| Ci | Leeming | 93 | C 8 |

HILLSBOROUGH
| Dr | Nollamara | 46 | C 5 |
| Dr | Nollamara | 46 | C 7 |

HILLSDEN
| Rd | Darlington | 66 | A 4 |

HILLSIDE
Ave	Claremont	70	E 10
Cl	Edgewater	24	B 1
Cr	Gooseberry H	77	B 3
Gr	Maylands	62	A 9
Gr	Ballajura	33	D 5
Rd	Armadale	116	E 7
Rd	East Fremantle	90	D 2

HILLTOP
Cl	Mahogany Crk	53	D 10
Dr	Rowethorpe	144	
Pl	Edgewater	24	A 1
Pl	Kelmscott	117	B 1
Ri	Willetton	93	D 7

HILL VIEW
Pl	Bentley	84	A 5
Rd	Mt Lawley	61	B 7
Tce	Bentley	84	A 5
Tce	St James	84	A 3

HILLVIEW
Ct	Gosnells	96	A 7
Pl	Thornlie	95	B 10
Ri	Cooloongup	137	E 8
St	Kalamunda	77	E 7

HILLWAY
	Nedlands	81	E 1
	Nedlands	71	E 10
	Swan View	51	E 8

HILLWOOD
| Ave | Warwick | 31 | D 6 |

HILO
| Pl | Warnbro | 145 | E 8 |

HILORY
| St | Coolbellup | 101 | D 1 |
| St | Coolbellup | 91 | D 10 |

HILTON
Cr	Maddington	96	B 4
Gr	Redcliffe	63	A 6
Pl	Duncraig	30	D 4
Rd	Roleystone	108	A 7

HINDERWELL
| St | Scarborough | 44 | E 10 |

HINDLE
| Ct | Leeming | 93 | A 9 |

HINDMARSH
Ave	Yokine	60	E 1
Ave	Yokine	46	E 10
Cl	Edgewater	20	A 8

HINDOO
| El | Stratton | 51 | B 3 |

HINDS
| Ct | Waikiki | 137 | E 10 |

HINES
| Rd | Hilton | 91 | B 7 |
| Rd | O'Connor | 91 | B 6 |

HINKLER
| Rd | Kalamunda | 78 | A 9 |
| St | Kenwick | 86 | A 10 |

HINSLEY
| Pl | Noranda | 47 | D 5 |

HIRD
| Rd | Jandakot | 112 | D 3 |

HISCOX
| Pl | Redcliffe | 63 | A 10 |

HISLOP
| Rd | Attadale | 81 | E 10 |

HIS MAJESTYS
| La | Perth City | 1C | E 2 |

HISPANO
| Pl | Carine | 31 | A 10 |

HITCHCOCK
| Pl | Wattleup | 121 | C 3 |
| St | St James | 84 | A 3 |

HITEK
| Ct | Merriwa | 14 | C 1 |

HOAD
| Ct | Kardinya | 91 | D 9 |

HOBART
Pl	Willetton	93	D 2
St	Bayswater	61	E 4
St	Mt Hawthorn	60	D 6
St	North Perth	60	D 6

HOBBS
Ave	Como	83	B 1
Ave	Dalkeith	81	E 2
Dr	Armadale	116	D 9
Rd	Gooseberry H	77	B 3

HOBIE
| Pl | Ocean Reef | 23 | A 2 |

HOBLEY
Pl	Eden Hill	49	A 8
St	Mandurah	163	A 10
Wy	Spearwood	101	C 7

HOBSONS
| Ave | Munster | 111 | B 3 |
| Ct | Iluka | 18 | E 4 |

HOBY
| Rd | Noranda | 48 | A 6 |

For detailed information regarding the street referencing system used in this book, turn to page 170.

H

		Map	Ref.
HOCKIN			
St	Willagee	91	C 5
HOCKING			
Pde	Sorrento	30	B 5
Rd	Kingsley	24	E10
HODDER			
Wy	Karrinyup	45	A 3
HODDLE			
Ct	Langford	94	E 4
HODGE			
Ct	Marmion	30	D 8
St	Willagee	91	C 4
HODGES			
Dr	Connolly	19	B 9
Dr	Joondalup	19	D 8
Dr	Ocean Reef	19	A 9
Pl	Innaloo	45	B 8
St	Innaloo	45	B 9
St	Middle Swan	50	D 5
St	Shoalwater	136	D 8
Wy	Canning Vale	93	E 8
HODGSON			
Pl	Kardinya	92	A 8
St	Mundaring	68	B 1
St	Tuart Hill	60	B 2
Wy	Kewdale	75	A 7
HOE			
Ct	Langford	94	E 3
HOGARTH			
St	Cannington	85	A 7
Wy	Bateman	92	D 6
HOGG			
Rd	Naval Base	121	A 4
St	Redcliffe	63	A10
HOKESFERN			
St	Morley	47	D 6
HOKIN			
St	Waikiki	145	C 6
HOKING			
Pl	Coogee	100	E 9
HOLBECK			
St	Doubleview	45	B 9
HOLBORN			
Cl	Kingsley	31	B 1
HOLBROOK			
Gns	Carine	30	E 9
Rd	Glen Forrest	66	C 7
HOLCOMBE			
Rd	Warnbro	145	D 9
HOLDEN			
Ct	Noranda	47	C 4
Dr	Noranda	48	A 5
Dr	Noranda	47	E 5
Rd	Kenwick	86	A 6
Rd	Roleystone	108	A 7
St	Carlisle	74	C 5
HOLDER			
St	St James	84	A 4
Wy	Malaga	47	D 1
HOLDHURST			
Wy	Morley	48	B 7
HOLDING			
St	Middle Swan	50	E 4
HOLDSWORTH			
St	Fremantle	1D	C 5
St	Fremantle	90	C 5
HOLFORD			
Wy	Wilson	84	A 6
HOLILOND			
Wy	Morley	47	E 7
HOLLAND			
Cl	Winthrop	92	B 5
Pl	Wilson	84	A 8
St	Fremantle	91	A 4
St	Fremantle	90	D 4
St	Gosnells	96	B 9
St	Palmyra	91	A 4
St	Wembley	59	E 9
Wy	Kingsley	31	D 1

		Map	Ref.
HOLLETON			
Tce	Padbury	30	E 1
HOLLETT			
Rd	Morley	48	B 7
Rd	Stoneville	54	A 3
HOLLEY			
Pl	Marangaroo	32	D 6
HOLLING			
St	Maddington	96	B 6
HOLLINGSWORTH			
Ave	Koondoola	33	A 8
Wy	Leeming	93	D 9
HOLLIS			
Rd	Wilson	84	B 8
St	Samson	91	C 9
HOLLISTER			
Wy	Noranda	47	C 5
HOLLITT			
St	Noranda	47	D 4
HOLLY			
Me	Ballajura	33	C 3
Pl	Willetton	93	D 3
Wy E	Kalamunda	77	C 8
Wy W	Kalamunda	77	C 8
HOLLYBUSH			
Ct	Forrestfield	76	C 7
Wy	Westfield	106	B10
HOLLYOAK			
Pl	Thornlie	95	A 9
HOLM			
St	Maylands	61	E 6
HOLMAN			
St	Alfred Cove	81	E10
St	Melville	81	D10
HOLMES			
Cl	Wandi	123	E 3
Pl	Hilton	91	B 8
Rd	Forrestfield	77	A 6
Rd	Forrestfield	76	D10
Rd	Maida Vale	77	A 5
Rd	Munster	112	A 6
Rd	Munster	111	D 7
Rd	Oakford	124	E 5
St	Shelley	83	D 9
St	Southern River	105	B 3
HOLMESDALE			
Pl	Darlington	65	E 3
Rd	Midland	50	A 9
HOLMESFIELD			
Cr	Carine	31	A10
HOLMFIRTH			
St	Coolbinia	60	E 4
St	Menora	61	A 5
HOLMWOOD			
Wy	Embleton	48	B10
HOLPIN			
Pl	Glen Forrest	66	E 3
HOLROYD			
Rd	Pickering Bk	89	D10
HOLSTEIN			
Cl	Brigadoon	168	A 6
HOLTEN			
Ct	Cooloongup	137	C 8
HOLTON			
Cl	Cannington	84	E 5
HOLWELL			
Gns	Clarkson	14	E10
HOLYHEAD			
Grn	Mindarie	14	C 6
HOLYROOD			
St	Leederville	60	C10
HOMER			
St	Dianella	61	B 2
HOMESTEAD			
Ave	Bibra Lake	102	C 5
Dr	Leda	139	B 1
Gns	Edgewater	24	A 2
Pl	Beechboro	48	D 4
Rd	Gosnells	96	A 7

		Map	Ref.
Rd	Gosnells	95	E 7
Rd	Mahogany Crk	67	C 1
Rd	Mahogany Crk	53	C10
HOMEWOOD			
St	Cloverdale	74	E 5
HONEY			
Pl	Beckenham	85	A 9
Rd	Forrestfield	86	E 2
St	Mariginiup	21	A 3
St	Mt Helena	55	B 4
HONEYBUSH			
Dr	Joondalup	19	E10
HONEYDEW			
Cl	Maida Vale	64	E 8
HONEYEATER			
Gl	Huntingdale	105	D 1
Rt	Wungong	116	B 9
HONEYSETT			
Ct	Hamilton Hill	101	C 3
HONEYSUCKLE			
Cl	Ballajura	33	C 5
Gr	Neerabup	16	B 6
Pl	Thornlie	95	B10
Ra	Halls Head	164	B 5
HONEYTREE			
Pl	Falcon	162A	C 4
HONEYWELL			
Blvd	Mirrabooka	47	A 1
Blvd	Mirrabooka	33	A10
HONIARA			
Wy	Mindarie	14	B 4
HONISTER			
Cl	Balga	32	C10
HONOR			
Ave	Hope Valley	121	C 8
HONOUR			
Ave	Bicton	81	B 7
HOOD			
Pl	Gosnells	106	A 1
Pl	Port Kennedy	156	C 6
St	Forrestfield	86	D 2
St	Hamilton Hill	101	A 1
St	Hamilton Hill	91	A10
St	Wembley	72	A 1
St	Wembley	60	A10
Tce	Sorrento	30	C 5
HOOGHLY			
St	Madora	160	C 9
HOOK			
Rd	Karrakatta	71	C 5
HOOKWAY			
Cr	Roleystone	108	B 6
HOOKWOOD			
St	Morley	47	D 6
HOOLEY			
Rd	Midland	50	D 8
Rd	Midvale	50	E 8
St	Swanbourne	70	D 8
HOOSON			
Wy	Wilson	84	A 7
HOPE			
Ave	Manning	83	B 7
Ave	Redcliffe	75	B 1
Ave	Salter Point	83	B 7
Cr	Lesmurdie	77	D10
Pl	Waikiki	145	D 1
Rd	Ardross	82	C 8
Rd	Bibra Lake	102	B 1
Rd	Canning Vale	104	A 3
Rd	Jandakot	103	A 3
Rd	Palmyra	91	C 1
St	Beechboro	49	A 3
St	Hilton	91	A 6
St	Mosman Park	80	E 5
St	North Beach	44	C 1
St	Perth City	61	A10
St	Waterman	30	C10
St	White Gum Vly	90	E 6

		Map	Ref.
HOPETOUN			
Rd	Canning Vale	104	B 4
Rd	South Perth	73	A 8
Tce	Shenton Park	71	D 5
HOPEVALE			
Pl	Erskine	164	A 8
HOPE VALLEY			
Rd	Hope Valley	122	B 9
Rd	Hope Valley	121	D 7
Rd	Mandogalup	123	A 9
Rd	Mandogalup	122	C 9
Rd	Naval Base	121	B 5
Rd	Wandi	123	C 7
HOPEWELL			
St	Canning Vale	94	C 5
HOPGOOD			
St	Melville	91	D 1
HOPKINS			
Pl	Waikiki	145	D 2
Rd	Nowergup	13	A 5
Rd	Nowergup	12	D 2
Rd	Nowergup	9	D 8
Wy	Spearwood	101	C 8
HOPKINSON			
Rd	Byford	125	D 7
Rd	Cardup	142	D 2
Rd	Cardup	134	D 9
Wy	Wilson	84	A 6
HOPMAN			
Ri	Clarkson	14	E10
HOPSON			
Cl	Booragoon	92	C 2
HOPTON			
St	Karrinyup	44	E 2
HORACE			
Rd	Lesmurdie	87	C 7
St	Bellevue	51	A10
St	Mt Helena	55	A 7
HORATIO			
St	East Perth	73	C 3
HORDERN			
St	Victoria Park	73	D 6
HORGAN			
St	Mosman Park	80	D 6
HORIZON			
Pl	Edgewater	24	B 1
Rge	Canning Vale	94	B10
Rt	Ballajura	33	C 3
HORLEY			
St	Bayswater	62	C 1
HORNER			
Wy	Herne Hill	36	E 4
HORNET			
Ri	Willetton	93	C 7
St	Hamersley	45	E 1
St	Hamersley	31	E10
HORNPIPE			
Ct	Yanchep	4	C 5
HORNSBY			
Ct	Kallaroo	23	A 6
St	Melville	91	C 3
HORNSEY			
Rd	Floreat	59	C10
Wy	Balga	46	E 1
HORRIE MILLER			
Dr	Perth Airport	75	C 6
HORROCKS			
Rd	Booragoon	92	A 1
Rd	Booragoon	82	A10
HORSESHOE			
La	Beechina	57	D 2
HORSHAM			
Wy	Nollamara	46	D 4
HORSLAY			
Wy	Noranda	48	A 5
HORSLEY			
St	Swan View	51	B 7

		Map	Ref.
HORTON			
Cr	Marangaroo	32	C 6
Pl	Leeming	92	E 9
HORWOOD			
Rd	Swan View	51	C 8
HOSKEN			
Rd	Gosnells	96	A 8
HOSKIN			
St	Cloverdale	75	A 4
HOSKINS			
Rd	Landsdale	25	C 9
St	Hamilton Hill	91	A10
HOSPITAL			
Ave	Nedlands	72	A 6
HOSSACK			
Ave	Lynwood	94	A 3
HOTCHIN			
St	Dalkeith	81	D 1
Wy	Kardinya	91	E 7
HOTCHKIN			
Pl	Kewdale	74	D 8
HOTCHKISS			
Dr	Balcatta	45	D 4
HOTHAM			
Ct	Alexander Hts	33	A 4
St	Bayswater	61	E 5
HOTSPUR			
Rd	Spearwood	101	A 4
HOUGH			
Rd	Attadale	81	C 8
HOUGHTON			
Wy	Winthrop	92	B 5
HOUSTON			
Ave	Dianella	61	B 1
Ave	Dianella	47	B10
St	Mt Helena	55	D 6
St	Rockingham	137	A 5
HOUTMANS			
St	Shelley	93	B 2
HOVE			
Ct	Forrestfield	86	D 2
Ct	Lynwood	84	D10
Ct	Nollamara	46	D 5
Pl	Warnbro	145	E 7
HOVEA			
Ave	Sorrento	30	D 6
Cr	City Beach	58	D 7
Cr	Walliston	88	A 2
Ct	Casuarina	132	D 5
Ct	Mahogany Crk	67	C 2
Ct	Morley	48	D 4
Pl	Coodanup	165	C 4
Pl	Maddington	96	C 3
HOVIA			
Tce	Kensington	73	C 8
Tce	South Perth	73	C 8
HOWARD			
Pde	Salter Point	83	B 8
Pl	Kelmscott	117	B 1
St	Bedfordale	127	C 2
St	Fremantle	1D	C 6
St	Fremantle	90	C 6
St	Perth City	1C	E 3
St	Perth City	72	E 3
HOWARTH			
St	Melville	91	D 2
HOWE			
St	Bedfordale	127	C 2
St	Osborne Park	60	A 3
St	Osborne Park	59	E 1
St	Yangebup	111	C 2
HOWELL			
St	Marmion	30	D 7
St	Willagee	91	E 4
HOWES			
Cr	Dianella	47	A 9
HOWICK			
Ct	Coogee	100	E 8
St	Lathlain	74	A 6
St	Victoria Park	73	E 5

210

For detailed information regarding the street referencing system used in this book, turn to page 170.

	Map	Ref.
HOWIE		
St Woodlands	59	B 1
HOWITT		
Rd Padbury	30	D 1
HOWLAND		
Rd Sorrento	30	B 3
HOWLETT		
Pl Leeming	92	E 10
St North Perth	60	E 7
HOWSON		
St Hilton	91	B 9
Wy Bibra Lake	101	C 7
HOWTREE		
Pl Floreat	59	C 9
HOXTON		
Ri Carine	31	A 10
HOYA		
Ct Thornlie	95	A 10
HOYLAKE		
Ct Connolly	19	C 8
HOYLE		
Rd Hope Valley	121	C 8
Rd Medina	130	E 4
HOYTON		
Pl Parmelia	131	C 6
HUBBARD		
Dr Padbury	23	D 9
Pl Safety Bay	145	A 1
Wy Medina	130	D 5
HUBBLE		
St East Fremantle	90	D 3
HUBE		
Ct Huntingdale	95	E 10
HUBERT		
Rd Maylands	62	A 8
St Belmont	74	D 2
St Darlington	66	C 6
St E Victoria Pk	74	A 9
St E Victoria Pk	84	B 1
St Guildford	63	D 1
St Guildford	49	D 10
HUCKLE		
St Balcatta	46	B 8
St Tuart Hill	46	B 9
HUDLESTON		
Rd Mt Claremont	70	E 4
HUDMAN		
Rd Boya	65	E 5
HUDSON		
Ave Girrawheen	32	B 7
Ct Beechboro	48	E 2
Ct Spearwood	101	C 7
St Bayswater	62	A 2
St Glen Forrest	66	D 2
HUGGINS		
Rd Thornlie	95	C 3
HUGH		
Ct Como	83	A 1
Pl Munster	101	B 9
St Guildford	49	D 10
St Waterman	30	C 10
HUGHENDEN		
Dr Thornlie	95	B 5
HUGHES		
Ct Padbury	23	D 10
Ct Safety Bay	137	A 10
Rd Armadale	116	E 6
St Canning Vale	94	D 7
St Hilton	91	A 7
HUGO		
St Stirling	45	D 8
HULA		
Ce Joondalup	19	D 2
HULBERT		
St Sth Fremantle	90	D 10
HULL		
Ct Waikiki	145	C 4
Gr Woodvale	24	C 6

	Map	Ref.
St Dianella	46	E 8
Wy Beechboro	49	A 4
HULLEY		
Pl High Wycombe	64	B 8
Rd High Wycombe	64	B 8
HUMBERT		
St Woodlands	59	B 4
HUME		
Ct Midland	50	E 7
Ct Parmelia	131	C 5
Pl Padbury	30	C 1
Rd High Wycombe	64	B 9
Rd Thornlie	95	B 6
HUMMERSTON		
Rd Kalamunda	77	E 7
Rd Paulls Valley	78	C 5
Rd Piesse Brook	78	A 7
St Mt Helena	55	C 7
HUMMINGBIRD		
Gns Ballajura	33	E 6
HUMPHREY		
Rd Mundaring	68	B 2
HUMPHRY		
St St James	84	A 4
HUNGERFORD		
Ave Halls Head	164	C 4
HUNNICUTT		
Cl Yangebup	112	A 1
HUNSTON		
St Balcatta	46	B 8
HUNT		
La Kingsley	31	B 1
Pl Maylands	62	A 9
Pl Parmelia	131	B 7
St Malaga	47	C 1
St Thornlie	95	C 4
HUNTER		
Dr Lesmurdie	87	E 3
St North Perth	60	E 6
Wy Padbury	23	D 8
HUNTINGDALE		
Cr Connolly	19	C 9
Rd Huntingdale	95	C 10
Rd Huntingdale	105	D 1
HUNTINGDON		
St E Victoria Pk	83	E 2
HUNTINGTON		
Rd Coogee	100	E 8
HUNTLEY		
St Gooseberry H	77	D 4
HUNTLY		
Ct Duncraig	31	A 4
HUNTRISS		
Rd Doubleview	45	B 10
Rd Karrinyup	45	B 7
Rd Woodlands	59	B 2
HUNTSMAN		
Pl Coodanup	165	D 4
HUNTSVILLE		
Ct Wanneroo	20	C 7
HUON		
El Merriwa	11	C 9
Rd Willetton	93	E 2
HURFORD		
St Hamilton Hill	100	E 1
St Hamilton Hill	90	E 10
HURLEY		
St Canning Vale	94	A 5
Wy Bull Creek	93	B 6
Wy Hillarys	23	C 10
HURLINGHAM		
Rd South Perth	73	B 7
HURLSTON		
Wy Koondoola	33	A 8
HURON		
Ct Leeming	103	A 1
Me Joondalup	19	C 2
HURRELL		
Wy Rockingham	137	D 4

	Map	Ref.
HURREY		
Pl Beechboro	49	A 2
HURST		
Pl Safety Bay	145	A 1
Rd Henderson	111	C 7
St Attadale	81	E 9
Tr Clarkson	14	C 1
HURSTFORD		
Cl Peppermint Gr	80	E 2
HUSTLER		
St Dianella	47	A 8
HUTCHINGS		
Wy Kardinya	92	A 7
HUTCHISON		
St Rivervale	74	D 4
HUTT		
Ct Two Rocks	2	D 3
Rd Morley	48	A 9
St Mt Lawley	61	B 8
HUTTON		
Cst Woodvale	24	B 3
Ct Rockingham	137	A 6
Pl Woodvale	24	A 5
St Osborne Park	60	A 1
St Osborne Park	46	B 10
St Osborne Park	59	E 2
HUXLEY		
Ct Westfield	106	B 9
Pl Spearwood	101	B 8
HYACINTH		
Cl Heathridge	19	C 10
Pl Madora	160	D 7
HYAM		
St Hamilton Hill	101	B 1
HYBANTHUS		
Rd Ferndale	94	C 1
HYBRID		
Ct Banjup	104	B 9
HYDE		
Ct Hillarys	23	A 10
St Midland	50	D 8
St Mt Lawley	61	A 8
HYDRA		
Cl Rockingham	137	A 8
Pl Kingsley	31	C 2
HYDRANGEA		
Pl Alexander Hts	32	E 5
HYEM		
Rd Herne Hill	36	D 2
HYLAND		
Cr Clarkson	14	D 1
St Bassendean	63	B 3
Wy Wilson	84	B 7
HYMUS		
St Rockingham	136	D 4
HYNE		
Ct Leeming	93	C 9
Rd Sth Guildford	63	C 3
HYNES		
Rd Dalkeith	81	C 2
Wy Hamilton Hill	101	B 2
HYTHE		
Pl Kenwick	95	C 1
Rd Marangaroo	32	B 5
Wy Wembley Dns	58	E 3

I

	Map	Ref.
IANDRA		
Lp Willetton	93	D 7
IBBOT		
Ct Langford	94	E 3
IBIS		
Cl Ballajura	33	E 8
Ct Gosnells	106	A 3
Ct Kingsley	24	E 10
Ct Westfield	106	C 10

	Map	Ref.
Ct Yangebup	102	B 10
Pl High Wycombe	76	A 2
Pl Willetton	93	B 4
St Stirling	45	E 7
IBIZA		
Ct Mindarie	14	A 3
IBSEN		
Ct Spearwood	101	B 9
IDA		
St Balcatta	46	B 5
St Bassendean	62	E 1
St Bassendean	48	E 10
St Eden Hill	48	E 9
IDAHO		
Pl Craigie	23	C 7
IDEN		
Pl Huntingdale	95	D 9
IDYLL		
Ct Heathridge	19	C 9
IGRAN		
Cr Gosnells	95	E 7
IKARA		
Pl Armadale	116	A 6
Rd City Beach	58	E 9
ILBERY		
St Beechina	57	D 1
St Beechina	43	D 10
St Quinns Rocks	10	A 1
ILDA		
Rd Canning Vale	94	C 7
ILEX		
Wy Forrestfield	76	C 7
ILFORD		
Pl Thornlie	95	C 3
ILINA		
Ct Willetton	93	D 6
ILKESTON		
Pl Mirrabooka	46	E 4
ILLABROOK		
St Mandurah	165	B 4
ILLAWARRA		
Cr N Ballajura	33	C 4
Cr S Ballajura	33	C 9
Me Edgewater	19	E 10
Rd Karragullen	109	B 2
Rd Karragullen	109	C 3
ILLAWONG		
Wy Kingsley	31	D 3
ILLINGBRIDGE		
St Morley	48	B 7
ILLOWRA		
Wy Duncraig	30	D 7
ILLYARRIE		
Pl Willetton	93	D 4
St Greenwood	31	C 6
ILMA		
St Gosnells	106	C 1
ILUKA		
Ave Mullaloo	23	A 5
ILUMBA		
Rd Nollamara	46	D 6
Wy Nollamara	46	D 6
IMANDRA		
Cc Jandakot	112	E 3
IMBER		
Pl Langford	94	E 2
IMELDA		
St Woodlands	59	B 4
IMJIM		
Rd Karrakatta	71	C 5
IMPERIAL		
Ct Armadale	115	E 4
Ct Ocean Reef	18	E 9
Ct Thornlie	95	D 8
INAJA		
Me Warnbro	145	E 8
INCA		
Pl Willetton	93	D 6

	Map	Ref.
INCANA		
Ct Kelmscott	106	E 6
Pl Morley	48	C 5
INCE		
Ct Parmelia	131	A 6
Rd Attadale	81	E 10
IND		
St Lesmurdie	87	E 3
INDIA		
St Inglewood	61	C 3
INDIANA		
Pde Singleton	160	D 1
Pde Singleton	160	D 2
INDIGO		
Cl Mirrabooka	33	A 10
Ct Riverton	94	B 1
Pl South Lake	102	C 6
INDLE		
St Willagee	91	E 5
INDOOROOPILLY		
Pl Connolly	19	C 6
INDUS		
Cl Rockingham	137	B 8
Ct Alexander Hts	32	E 5
Ct Beechboro	48	C 5
ING		
Pl Noranda	47	C 4
INGHAM		
Ct Willetton	93	C 7
INGLESIDE		
Me Coodanup	165	D 4
INGLIS		
Ct Kingsley	31	D 1
Ct Medina	130	E 6
Pl Willetton	93	E 3
INGRAM		
Rd Baldivis	147	A 2
St Hamilton Hill	101	B 1
INGVARSON		
Wy Bibra Lake	102	C 2
INKPEN		
Wy Orelia	131	A 4
INLET		
Gr Mullaloo	23	A 3
Tr Ballajura	33	C 3
INMAN		
Ct Merriwa	11	C 8
INNAMINCKA		
Rd Greenmount	51	B 10
Rd Greenmount	51	C 10
INNES		
Pl Girrawheen	32	B 7
INNESTON		
Ri Greenfields	163	D 9
INSTONE		
St Hilton	91	B 9
INSTOW		
Pl Warnbro	145	D 8
INTERIM		
Rd Spearwood	101	C 6
INTREPID		
Ct Two Rocks	2	C 1
INVERARAY		
Cr Hamersley	32	A 8
INVERELL		
Pl Greenfields	165	C 1
INVERIE		
Cl Applecross	82	D 4
INVERLEITH		
St Sth Fremantle	90	C 4
INVERNESS		
Ci Westfield	106	C 6
Cr Menora	60	E 5
Dr Meadow Sprgs	163	C 4
Ed Connolly	19	C 6
St Malaga	47	C 1
INVESTIGATOR		
Dr Waikiki	145	C 3

For detailed information regarding the street referencing system used in this book, turn to page 170.

211

J

		Map	Ref.
INVICTA			
Pl	Gwelup	45	C 5
INWOOD			
Pl	Currambine	19	B 6
Pl	Murdoch	92	B 7
IOLANTHE			
Dr	Duncraig	30	D 5
St	Bassendean	62	E 2
St	Bassendean	48	E 10
St	Eden Hill	48	E 9
St	Swanbourne	70	D 7
IONA			
Pl	Greenwood	31	B 5
Rd	Canning Vale	104	A 3
IONE			
Pl	Craigie	23	D 7
IONESCO			
St	Spearwood	101	C 9
IONIC			
Pl	Shelley	93	C 1
St	Rossmoyne	93	B 1
St	Shelley	93	C 1
IPSWICH			
Cr	Girrawheen	32	E 7
Ri	Greenfields	163	C 9
IRELAND			
Ct	Koondoola	33	A 9
Wy	Bassendean	48	E 10
IRENE			
Pl	Beldon	23	D 3
St	Nth Fremantle	80	C 10
St	Perth City	61	A 10
IRIAN			
Rd	Riverton	94	A 1
IRIS			
Ave	Dalkeith	81	D 3
Pl	Maddington	96	D 3
Pl	Yangebup	101	D 10
IRON			
Rd	Parkerville	54	A 5
IRON BARK			
Rw	Willetton	93	D 5
IRONBARK			
Pl	Halls Head	164	A 5
Pl	Maddington	96	C 5
Rd	Morley	48	D 4
IRONCAP			
Pl	Armadale	116	B 5
IRONWOOD			
Ave	Heathridge	19	C 10
Wy	Thornlie	94	E 7
IROQUOIS			
Gns	Joondalup	19	D 2
IRRAWADDY			
Dr	Greenfields	165	D 1
Pl	Beechboro	48	E 4
IRVERNA			
Pl	Girrawheen	32	B 7
IRVINE			
Ce	Mindarie	14	B 5
Ct	Cooloongup	137	E 7
Dr	Malaga	47	D 1
St	Bayswater	62	C 3
St	Peppermint Gr	80	D 3
IRVING			
Ave	Falcon	162A	E 10
IRWIN			
Cl	Gosnells	105	E 2
Pl	Maida Vale	76	E 3
Pl	Padbury	23	E 9
Rd	Embleton	62	B 1
Rd	Embleton	48	B 10
Rd	Wangara	25	A 6
St	Bellevue	64	C 1
St	Bellevue	50	E 10
St	East Fremantle	91	A 3
St	Henley Brook	36	B 2
St	Leeming	93	A 8
St	Perth City	1C	A 3
St	Perth City	73	A 3

		Map	Ref.
IRYMPLE			
Rd	Karragullen	108	E 6
Rd	Mt Helena	41	A 9
Rd	Roleystone	108	C 6
ISA			
St	Willetton	93	C 2
ISAAC			
St	Melville	91	D 2
Wy	Calista	130	E 8
ISAACS			
Ct	Huntingdale	95	D 10
Rd	Pickering Bk	99	A 1
Rd	Pickering Bk	89	A 10
ISABELLA			
Cr	Manning	83	A 7
Ct	Currambine	19	B 3
Ct	Stirling	46	A 6
ISDELL			
Pl	Gosnells	106	A 1
Pl	Heathridge	19	A 9
ISEO			
Pl	Joondalup	19	D 3
ISHAM			
Cl	Carine	31	A 10
ISLAND			
Pl	Heathridge	23	D 1
Rt	Ballajura	33	D 8
St	Sth Fremantle	90	D 10
ISLINGTON			
St	Lynwood	94	B 3
ISLIP			
Ct	Bateman	92	D 6
Pl	Woodlands	59	C 2
St	Rockingham	137	D 4
ISMA			
Ct	Mundijong	143	A 6
ISMAIL			
St	Wangara	25	A 6
ISOBEL			
St	Bentley	84	C 3
ISTED			
Ave	Hamilton Hill	101	B 2
ITAR			
Ct	Marangaroo	32	E 6
ITEA			
Ct	High Wycombe	64	D 10
Pl	Mindarie	14	B 4
Pl	South Lake	102	D 4
IVANAC			
Pl	Morley	48	D 9
IVANHOE			
Cr	Falcon	162A	A 4
Pl	Gosnells	105	E 1
St	Bassendean	63	A 1
St	Bassendean	49	A 10
St	Eden Hill	49	A 9
St	Golden Bay	158	D 7
St	Morley	48	C 7
Wy	Westfield	106	D 6
IVERMEY			
Rd	Hamilton Hill	101	A 1
Rd	Hamilton Hill	91	A 10
IVERS			
Ct	Langford	95	B 1
IVES			
Cl	Samson	91	C 8
Pl	Armadale	116	C 5
St	Hamilton Hill	101	A 1
St	Hamilton Hill	101	A 2
IVESTON			
Rd	Lynwood	94	C 2
IVO			
Pl	Joondalup	19	D 2
IVORY			
Ce	Warnbro	145	E 9
Ct	Kingsley	31	D 3
St	Noranda	47	D 4

		Map	Ref.
IVY			
Cl	Ballajura	33	C 6
Pl	Mirrabooka	33	B 10
St	Thornlie	95	B 10
St	Redcliffe	63	B 5
St	West Perth	60	E 9
IVYTHORNE			
Pde	Kiara	48	D 7

J

		Map	Ref.
JABE			
Pl	Willetton	93	E 4
JABIRU			
Cl	Huntingdale	95	C 10
Ct	High Wycombe	76	A 1
Ri	Ballajura	33	D 6
JACANA			
Pde	Ballajura	33	E 7
Pl	Gosnells	105	E 3
Wy	Halls Head	164	B 3
JACARANDA			
Ave	Jarrahdale	153	A 8
Ave	Mt Claremont	71	B 6
Ave	Rowethorpe	144	
Ct	Roleystone	108	A 3
Dr	Ballajura	33	C 4
Dr	Wanneroo	24	D 2
Pl	Maddington	96	C 4
JACCARD			
Wy	Lynwood	94	C 1
JACK			
Rd	Wattle Grove	86	E 4
JACKADDER			
Wy	Woodlands	59	C 3
JACKMAN			
St	Willagee	91	E 4
JACKSON			
Ave	Curtin Uni	135	
Ave	Karrinyup	44	E 7
Ave	Winthrop	92	B 4
Rd	Karawara	83	C 4
Rd	Peel Estate	141	B 2
Rd	Peel Estate	140	E 3
Rd	Walliston	78	A 10
St	Bassendean	62	D 2
St	Nth Fremantle	90	C 1
JACOBINA			
Wy	Forrestfield	76	C 9
JACOBSEN			
Wy	Thornlie	95	D 4
JACOBY			
St	Mahogany Crk	67	C 2
St	Mundaring	68	A 1
St	Mundaring	67	D 1
JACQUELINE			
Dr	Thornlie	95	C 3
St	Bayswater	62	D 6
JACQUES			
Pl	Orelia	131	B 5
JADA			
Ct	Kingsley	31	C 2
JADE			
Ct	Dianella	47	B 8
Ct	High Wycombe	76	B 2
Ct	Singleton	160	E 3
Gr	Edgewater	24	A 2
Pl	Wembley Dns	59	A 4
St	Armadale	116	E 7
St	Maddington	96	B 1
JAEGER			
Sq	Ballajura	34	A 7
Sq	Ballajura	33	E 7
JAFFA			
Cl	Armadale	116	A 7
JAGGS			
St	Wattleup	112	A 10
Wy	Kardinya	91	D 6

		Map	Ref.
JAGOE			
Ct	Marmion	30	D 7
St	Willagee	91	D 5
JAKOB			
Pl	Hamilton Hill	101	B 1
JAKOBSONS			
Wy	Morley	47	D 10
JAMAICAN			
Rd	Safety Bay	145	C 1
JAMBANIS			
Rd	Wanneroo	25	C 1
JAMES			
Ave	Hazelmere	64	A 1
Rd	Kalamunda	77	C 9
Rd	Kardinya	91	E 7
Rd	Middle Swan	50	E 2
Rd	Swanbourne	70	E 8
St	Armadale	116	C 7
St	Bassendean	63	A 2
St	Bayswater	62	B 3
St	Bellevue	50	E 9
St	Bull Creek	93	A 6
St	Cannington	85	A 8
St	E Rockingham	129	D 9
St	East Perth	1C	A 2
St	Fremantle	1D	C 3
St	Fremantle	90	C 3
St	Gosnells	106	B 1
St	Guildford	49	C 10
St	Mariginiup	20	D 3
St	North Beach	44	C 8
St	Northbridge	1C	E 1
St	Northbridge	72	E 1
St	Perth City	1C	A 2
St	Perth City	73	A 2
St	Shenton Park	71	E 5
St	Swan View	51	C 6
JAMESON			
St	Cannington	85	A 6
St	Mosman Park	80	E 7
St	South Perth	73	B 8
St	Swanbourne	70	D 8
JAMESTOWN			
Tce	Greenfields	165	E 2
JAMIESON			
Ri	Byford	126	E 9
JAMY			
Pl	Hamilton Hill	101	C 3
JANA			
Ct	Beechboro	48	D 3
Rd	Thornlie	95	C 3
JANDA			
Ct	Armadale	116	B 4
JANDAKOT			
Rd	Banjup	104	A 10
Rd	Banjup	103	D 9
Rd	Jandakot	102	E 6
JANDU			
St	Wanneroo	20	C 9
JANE			
Rd	Applecross	82	D 6
St	Darlington	66	B 6
JANECZEK			
Rd	Mundaring	68	C 5
JANET			
Rd	Safety Bay	144	E 1
St	Hazelmere	50	A 10
St	Rossmoyne	93	A 2
St	West Perth	60	E 9
JANGA			
Ct	Wanneroo	24	D 1
JANICE			
Ave	Falcon	162A	E 9
JANIS			
St	Halls Head	164	B 1
St	Halls Head	162	C 10
JANNALI			
Wy	Armadale	116	B 7
Wy	San Remo	160	C 10
JANSON			
Rd	Hamilton Hill	100	E 3

		Map	Ref.
JANTER			
Cl	Willetton	93	D 7
JANTHINA			
Cr	Heathridge	23	D 1
JAPONICA			
Hts	Mirrabooka	33	B 10
Pl	Halls Head	164	A 7
JARABA			
Ave	Gooseberry H	77	C 4
JARDINE			
Ct	Thornlie	95	B 7
Pl	Padbury	30	C 1
St	Stirling	45	D 4
JARMAN			
Ave	Manning	83	A 6
Cl	Kardinya	92	B 6
JARRAD			
St	Cottesloe	80	C 3
JARRAH			
Cl	Baldivis	157	E 5
Cl	Wandi	123	B 8
Cl	Westfield	106	C 8
Ct	Beechboro	48	C 3
Ct	High Wycombe	64	A 10
Ct	Yangebup	102	A 9
Gr	Gosnells	105	E 2
Pl	Woodvale	24	C 6
Rd	E Victoria Pk	83	D 1
Rd	Mundaring	54	C 8
Rd	Roleystone	108	A 7
Rd	Roleystone	108	A 8
Rd	St James	84	A 3
Rd	Stoneville	54	C 7
St	Coodanup	165	D 6
JARRAHDALE			
Rd	Jarrahdale	152	B 2
Rd	Jarrahdale	153	C 5
Rd	Jarrahdale	151	D 1
Rd	Jarrahdale	152	D 6
JARRAHGLEN			
Ri	Jarrahdale	152	A 5
JARRET			
St	Woodlands	59	B 3
JARRIL			
Pl	Koongamia	65	B 1
JARROT			
Pl	Dianella	47	C 9
JARVIS			
Ct	Swan View	51	C 5
Rd	Baldivis	157	B 7
St	O'Connor	91	C 7
JASMIN			
Ct	Maida Vale	77	A 2
Wy	Maida Vale	77	A 2
JASMINE			
Cl	Edgewater	24	A 2
Ct	Thornlie	95	A 10
Lp	Willetton	93	C 7
Me	Ballajura	33	C 4
Pl	Halls Head	164	B 4
JASON			
Ct	Kelmscott	106	E 6
Ct	Thornlie	95	A 6
Pl	Padbury	23	D 9
Pl	Stoneville	54	B 7
Rd	Balcatta	46	B 7
St	Melville	91	D 2
St	Wooroloo	43	D 1
St	Yokine	46	B 4
JASPER			
Cl	Balcatta	45	E 5
Pl	Armadale	116	E 7
Wy	Edgewater	20	A 10
JAUGLE			
Pl	Waikiki	145	C 1
JAVA			
Pl	Waikiki	145	C 3
JAVANICA			
Ct	Warnbro	145	E 9
JAVEZ			
Dr	Quinns Rocks	10	A 1

For detailed information regarding the street referencing system used in this book, turn to page 170.

Map Ref.

JAVON
Ct Alexander Hts 32 E 6
JAY
Ct Huntingdale 105 C 1
Gr Ballajura 33 D 6
Pl Quinns Rocks 10 B 9
St Cloverdale 75 A 3
JEAN
St Hamilton Hill 90 E 9
St Hilton 91 A 10
JEANES
Rd Karrinyup 44 E 7
JEANHULLEY
Rd High Wycombe 64 C 10
JEAVONS
Pl South Lake 102 E 6
JECKS
Pl Orelia 131 A 4
Pl Stratton 51 A 3
St Rockingham 137 B 4
JEDDA
Rd Balcatta 46 B 7
JEDDAH
Ct Mindarie 14 B 5
JEDDO
Ct Langford 94 E 2
JEFFERIES
Wy Leeming 93 A 9
JEFFERS
Ct Orelia 131 B 6
Wy Greenwood 31 E 5
JEFFERSON
Dr Marangaroo 32 D 6
JEFFERY
Rd Dianella 47 C 10
St Hilton 91 A 9
JEFFREY
St Kewdale 74 E 8
JELLICOE
Rd Glen Forrest 66 C 6
JEMERSON
St Willagee 91 E 5
JENARK
Wy Kewdale 74 E 7
Wy Midvale 51 A 8
JENEVER
Pl Bentley 84 B 4
JENKIN
St Sth Fremantle 90 C 8
JENKINS
Ave Nedlands 71 C 9
Pl Wembley Dns 58 E 5
JENKINSON
St Gosnells 95 E 9
JENNIFER
Pl Alexander Hts 33 A 5
Rd Morley 47 D 8
Wy Rossmoyne 83 B 10
JENNINGS
Ct Langford 95 A 2
Rd High Wycombe 64 B 10
Wy Lockridge 49 A 7
JENOLAN
Wy Merriwa 11 C 10
JENSEN
Ct Leeming 92 E 9
JENVEY
St Morley 48 D 7
JEROME
Ave Sorrento 30 D 6
Pl Willetton 93 E 2
JERRAT
Dr East Fremantle 80 E 9
JERSEY
St Jolimont 71 E 2
St Jolimont 59 E 10
St Wembley 59 E 8

JERVIS
Wy Sorrento 30 C 5
JERVOIS
St Dianella 47 C 7
St Yangebup 111 C 4
JERVOISE BAY
Ce Munster 110 D 3
JESMOND
Pl Dianella 47 B 9
St Safety Bay 136 E 10
JESSAMINE
St Dianella 47 B 6
JESSEL
Ct Balga 46 E 4
Pl Duncraig 31 A 8
JESSICA
Ct Munster 101 B 9
JESSIE
Rd Gooseberry H 77 C 1
St Byford 126 D 10
St Cannington 84 E 7
JESSUP
Me Joondalup 19 D 2
JET
St Kelmscott 107 A 7
JETTY
Pl Heathridge 19 C 10
Rd Claremont 71 A 10
JEWEL
Ct Langford 94 E 4
JEWELL
Pde Nth Fremantle 90 C 1
St East Perth 73 C 2
JIB
Cl Waikiki 145 B 3
Ct Ocean Reef 23 A 2
Pl Ballajura 33 D 8
JILLARA
Ct Lesmurdie 87 B 2
Wy Lesmurdie 87 B 1
JILLIAN
St Riverton 83 E 10
JILLMAN
Wy Ferndale 84 C 9
JIMBELL
St Mosman Park 80 E 6
JIMBIRI
Wy Wanneroo 20 E 8
JIMMONS
Wy Thornlie 95 B 3
JINDA
Rd Koongamia 65 B 2
JINDABYNE
Hts South Lake 102 E 7
JINDARRA
Cl Cooloongup 137 D 9
JINDINGA
Wy Wanneroo 20 D 9
JOEL
Tce East Perth 61 C 10
Tce Mt Lawley 61 C 10
JOFFRE
Rd Trigg 44 C 6
JOHANNAH
St Nth Fremantle 90 D 1
JOHANSON
Pro Murdoch 92 C 6
JOHN
Cr Byford 135 D 1
Cr Byford 126 D 10
Pl Mullaloo 23 A 5
St Armadale 116 D 7
St Bayswater 62 B 3
St Bentley 84 C 3
St Claremont 71 B 9
St Coodanup 165 E 9
St Cottesloe 80 C 2
St Darlington 66 B 4
St E Rockingham 129 D 9
St Gooseberry H 77 D 1
St Henley Brook 28 E 8
St Inglewood 61 D 6
St Middle Swan 50 E 3
St Midland 50 C 6
St Mt Lawley 61 C 7
St Northbridge 1C E 1
St Northbridge 72 E 1
St Nth Fremantle 90 D 1
St Nth Fremantle 80 D 10
St Shenton Park 71 D 5
St Welshpool 84 D 2
JOHN FARRANT
Dr Gooseberry H 77 A 1
Dr Gooseberry H 65 B 10
JOHNMOORE
Ct Glen Forrest 66 D 1
JOHNS
Ct Osborne Park 46 A 9
JOHNSMITH
St Embleton 48 A 10
St Morley 48 A 10
St Morley 47 E 10
JOHNSON
Ave Guildford 63 D 1
Cl Winthrop 92 A 5
Cr Mullaloo 23 A 4
Pde Mosman Park 80 E 5
Pl Wattle Grove 86 C 5
Rd Casuarina 131 E 8
Rd Jarrahdale 153 C 1
Rd Maylands 74 A 1
Rd Maylands 62 A 10
Rd The Spectacles 131 D 3
Rd The Spectacles 122 D 10
Rd Wellard 139 D 2
Rd Wellard 131 E 10
St Guildford 63 C 1
St Guildford 49 C 10
St Redcliffe 62 E 10
St Wembley 60 A 7
JOHNSTON
Rd Canning Vale 103 E 1
Rd Canning Vale 93 E 10
Rd Jandakot 103 D 5
Rd Parkerville 53 D 6
St Mt Helena 55 B 6
St Peppermint Gr 80 D 4
Wy Padbury 23 E 9
JOHNS WOOD
Blvd Mt Claremont 71 A 4
Dr Kingsley 24 B 9
JOHN XXIII
Ave Mt Claremont 71 B 4
JOINER
Pl Parmelia 131 B 8
St Melville 91 E 3
JOLIMONT
Tce Jolimont 59 E 10
JOLLEY
Gr Winthrop 92 C 6
Rd Wellard 140 D 1
JOLSTRA
Cr Joondalup 19 D 2
JOMAR
Ct Gosnells 95 E 7
JONATHAN
St Bellevue 50 E 10
JONES
Cl Winthrop 92 B 4
Ct Serpentine 155 B 1
Pl Waikiki 145 C 6
St Balcatta 46 A 5
St Kalamunda 77 A 4
St O'Connor 91 B 6
St Stirling 46 A 6
St Stirling 45 E 8
JON SANDERS
Dr Glendalough 60 A 6
Dr Glendalough 59 E 5
Dr Osborne Park 59 D 3

JOOLEEN
Wy Thornlie 94 E 5
JOONDALUP
Dr Edgewater 24 A 2
Dr Edgewater 23 E 1
Dr Joondalup 19 E 3
Pl Wanneroo 20 C 7
JOONDANNA
Dr Joondanna 60 B 4
JOPE
Pl Duncraig 30 E 8
JORDAN
St Cloverdale 75 A 3
St Two Rocks 2 B 2
JORDON
Rd Chidlow 42 C 3
JOSBURY
Cl Coodanup 165 C 3
JOSCELYN
Pl Glen Forrest 66 C 2
St Glen Forrest 66 C 3
JOSE
Ct Samson 91 D 8
JOSEFA
Cl Iluka 18 D 5
JOSEPH
Rd Gidgegannup 40 E 4
Rd Safety Bay 144 E 1
Rd Safety Bay 136 E 10
St Leederville 60 B 9
St Maylands 61 E 8
JOSEPHINE
Cr Kalamunda 77 B 7
Wy Alexander Hts 33 A 5
JOSEPHSON
St Fremantle 1D C 5
St Fremantle 90 C 5
JOSIP
Pl Osborne Park 60 A 1
JOSLIN
Pl Duncraig 30 D 4
St Hilton 91 B 8
JOVAN
Pl Greenfields 163 D 9
JOY
Cl Willetton 93 E 2
St Dianella 46 E 7
JOYCE
Ave Hamilton Hill 91 B 10
Ct Hillarys 23 B 10
Pl Bateman 92 E 5
Rd Gnangara 26 A 1
St Dalkeith 81 D 2
St Lesmurdie 87 B 4
St Scarborough 44 D 9
JOYNER
Wy Armadale 116 B 6
JUAN
St Thornlie 95 B 5
JUANIA
Pl Warnbro 145 E 9
JUBAEA
Gns Mt Claremont 71 B 5
JUBILEE
Ave Eden Hill 48 E 8
Ave Jandakot 112 D 2
Cr City Beach 58 C 10
Dr Waikiki 145 C 2
Pl Eden Hill 48 E 8
Rd Forrestfield 86 D 1
St Beckenham 85 C 6
St South Perth 73 B 8
JUCARA
Me Warnbro 145 E 9
JUDD
St South Perth 72 D 7
JUDGE
Ave Claremont 71 B 7

JUDGES
Gns Leda 130 E 9
JUDI
Ct Greenmount 51 C 10
JUDITH
Rd Wattle Grove 86 E 4
JUETT
Vl Winthrop 92 B 4
JUGAN
St Glendalough 60 B 5
JUKES
Wy Glendalough 60 A 6
JULIA
Pl Willetton 94 A 3
St Waikiki 145 B 4
JULIET
Rd Coolbellup 102 A 1
JULL
Ct Kardinya 91 E 8
St Armadale 116 D 6
JUNE
Rd Gooseberry H 77 B 1
Rd Safety Bay 144 E 1
Rd Safety Bay 136 E 9
JUNEE
Pl Armadale 116 C 4
JUNIPER
Ct Thornlie 95 A 8
Pl Ballajura 33 C 5
Wy Duncraig 31 B 8
Wy Forrestfield 76 B 9
Wy Willetton 93 C 2
JUNO
Ct Kallaroo 23 B 7
Pl Coolbellup 101 D 2
JUPITER
Cl Greenfields 163 D 9
St Carlisle 74 B 9
JUPP
Ct Westfield 106 B 8
St Hamersley 31 E 10
JURA
Ct Duncraig 31 A 6
Rd Canning Vale 104 A 3
JURIEN
Cl Warnbro 145 E 7
Wy Thornlie 95 D 6
JURRELL
St Mandurah 163 C 10
JURY
Cl Ocean Reef 19 B 10
JUSTIN
Dr Sorrento 30 D 5
St Lesmurdie 87 B 2
JUSTINIAN
St Palmyra 91 C 3
JUTLAND
Pde Dalkeith 81 C 4
Ri Ocean Reef 18 E 9
JUXON
Pl Hamilton Hill 101 B 3

K

KABA
Ct Ocean Reef 19 B 10
KABBARLI
St Falcon 162A B 3
KADGO
Pl Waikiki 145 D 2
KADI
Ct Marangaroo 32 D 6
KADINA
Rd Gooseberry H 77 D 2
St Craigie 23 D 6
St North Perth 60 D 7

For detailed information regarding the street referencing system used in this book, turn to page 170.

K

		Map	Ref.
KADUKA			
Wy	Lynwood	94	D 3
KAGE			
Pl	Mindarie	10	A 1
KAIBER			
Ave	Yanchep	4	C 4
KALAMATTA			
Wy	Gooseberry H	77	C 2
KALAMUNDA			
Rd	Gooseberry H	77	A 3
Rd	High Wycombe	64	B 7
Rd	Kalamunda	77	C 5
Rd	Maida Vale	64	D 10
Rd	Maida Vale	76	E 1
Rd	Sth Guildford	64	A 6
Rd	Sth Guildford	63	D 3
KALANG			
Pl	Stoneville	54	A 7
KALANGEDY			
Dr	Riverton	93	D 1
KALARA			
Rd	Koongamia	65	B 2
Wy	Koongamia	65	B 2
KALARI			
Dr	City Beach	58	D 9
KALBARRI			
St	Lesmurdie	87	D 3
KALEE			
Ct	Huntingdale	105	D 1
KALGAN			
Cl	Heathridge	24	A 3
Rd	Welshpool	84	D 2
KALGOORLIE			
St	Ascot	62	D 9
St	Mosman Park	80	E 4
St	Mt Hawthorn	60	C 6
KALINDA			
Dr	City Beach	58	E 7
KALIX			
El	Merriwa	10	B 8
KALLANG			
Rd	Coodanup	165	C 7
KALLAROO			
Pl	Mullaloo	23	C 5
KALLATINA			
Wy	Iluka	18	D 5
KALMIA			
Rd	Bibra Lake	102	A 8
Wy	Forrestfield	76	C 3
KALOOMBA			
St	Armadale	116	E 5
KALYAN			
Cl	Greenfields	163	E 7
KALYBA			
Pl	Duncraig	31	A 3
KALYUNG			
Ct	Queens Park	85	B 3
KAMARA			
Ct	Wanneroo	24	D 1
KAMBALDA			
Rd	Mundaring	68	B 2
Wy	Kewdale	74	D 7
KANANGRA			
Cr	Greenwood	31	B 4
KANDA			
Pl	Mindarie	14	B 5
KANE			
Pl	Balga	46	B 1
St	Kingsley	31	D 3
KANELLA			
Rd	Shelley	83	C 10
KANGAROO			
Cl	Wungong	116	B 6
KANIMBLA			
Pl	Iluka	18	D 5
Rd	Bicton	91	B 1
Rd	Nedlands	71	E 7
Wy	Morley	47	D 7

		Map	Ref.
KANOWNA			
Av E	Redcliffe	63	A 8
Av W	Redcliffe	62	E 7
KANTO			
Ct	Marangaroo	32	D 6
KANYA			
Pl	Coodanup	165	C 4
KAOLUNGA			
Wy	Lesmurdie	87	D 1
KAPALUA			
Wy	Connolly	19	C 8
KAPARA			
Wy	Currambine	19	A 5
KAPOK			
Ct	Alexander Hts	32	E 4
Ct	High Wycombe	76	A 1
Ct	Lynwood	94	B 2
KAPYONG			
Rd	Karrakatta	71	C 5
Rd	Swanbourne	70	D 8
KARA			
Ct	Armadale	115	E 4
KARABIL			
Rd	Nollamara	46	D 7
Wy	Nollamara	46	D 6
KARALUNDIE			
Wy	Mullaloo	23	A 5
KARAMARRA			
Pl	Kingsley	31	D 2
KARANGA			
St	Falcon	162A	D 10
KARARA			
Cl	Halls Head	164	C 4
KARBRO			
Dr	Cardup	135	A 9
KARDINYA			
Rd	Kardinya	92	A 6
KAREELA			
Ct	Duncraig	30	D 8
Rd	Riverton	83	E 10
KAREL			
Ave	Bull Creek	93	B 3
Ave	Jandakot	103	A 2
Ave	Leeming	103	A 1
Ave	Leeming	93	A 10
Ave	Rossmoyne	93	B 3
Ct	Alexander Hts	33	A 3
KARELLA			
St	Nedlands	71	D 7
KARGOTICH			
Rd	Forrestdale	125	B 2
Rd	Forrestdale	115	B 10
Rd	Mundijong	142	B 9
Rd	Oakford	125	B 4
Rd	Oakford	134	A 2
Rd	Peel Estate	150	B 6
Rd	Peel Estate	134	B 9
KARI			
Ct	Westfield	106	B 7
KARIMBA			
St	Wanneroo	20	B 7
KARINGA			
Rd	San Remo	163	C 1
Rd	San Remo	160	C 10
KARIONG			
Ci	Duncraig	30	D 8
KARL			
Pl	Mundaring	54	A 10
KARLA			
Pl	City Beach	58	D 3
KARNUP			
Rd	Peel Estate	154	A 3
Rd	Serpentine	154	C 3
KARO			
Pl	Duncraig	31	A 8
KAROBORUP			
Rd	Carabooda	8	D 10
Rd N	Carabooda	8	C 6

		Map	Ref.
KAROO			
St	South Perth	72	E 9
KAROONDA			
Rd	Booragoon	92	C 2
St	Armadale	116	C 8
KARRALIKA			
Ave	Lesmurdie	77	D 10
Cr	Martin	106	E 2
KARRAWA			
Gns	Port Kennedy	156	D 4
KARRI			
Ave	Canning Vale	104	B 1
Ct	Gooseberry H	77	D 1
Ct	Woodvale	24	C 6
Ct	Yangebup	102	A 10
Ct	Yangebup	101	E 10
Pl	Thornlie	95	B 10
Ri	Parmelia	131	B 10
St	Karnup	159	C 2
Wy	Ferndale	94	C 1
Wy	Ferndale	84	C 10
KARRINYUP			
Rd	Balcatta	46	A 8
Rd	Innaloo	45	B 7
Rd	Karrinyup	45	A 6
Rd	Stirling	45	D 7
Rd	Trigg	44	D 5
KARU			
Rd	Kalamunda	77	D 8
KARUAH			
Wy	Greenwood	31	C 3
KARUNJIE			
Rd	Golden Bay	158	D 9
KASARINA			
Rd	Riverton	93	D 1
KASBA			
Gr	Joondalup	19	D 2
KATANNING			
St	Bayswater	62	D 5
KATE			
St	E Victoria Pk	74	A 9
KATEENA			
Rd	City Beach	58	E 7
KATHARINE			
Pl	Helena Valley	65	B 4
St	Bellevue	65	A 2
St	Helena Valley	65	B 3
KATHLEEN			
Ave	Maylands	61	E 8
Cl	Maida Vale	76	D 2
Rd	Lesmurdie	87	D 4
St	Bassendean	63	A 3
St	Cottesloe	70	D 10
St	Trigg	44	C 5
St	Yokine	46	C 9
KATHRYN			
Cr	Dalkeith	81	C 1
KATISHA			
St	Duncraig	30	D 3
KATOORA			
Pl	Ocean Reef	19	A 6
KATRINA			
Tce	Kelmscott	107	A 7
KATRINE			
Cr	Joondalup	19	C 3
St	Floreat	59	B 7
Wy	Hamersley	31	E 9
KATTA			
Pl	Gooseberry H	77	B 2
KAUFMAN			
Ave	Ocean Reef	23	A 1
KAURI			
Pl	Duncraig	31	B 8
KAVANAGH			
St	Leederville	60	B 9
St	Mt Pleasant	82	D 6
St	Wembley	60	B 9
KAWINA			
Rd	Bickley	88	B 2

		Map	Ref.
KAY			
Pl	Midland	50	D 6
St	Scarborough	58	D 1
KAYLE			
St	North Perth	60	E 8
KAZAN			
Cl	Joondalup	19	D 1
KEADY			
Ri	Clarkson	14	D 2
St	Belmont	74	E 3
KEAL			
St	Balcatta	46	A 5
KEALL			
Ps	Winthrop	92	A 5
KEANE			
Cl	Winthrop	92	B 5
Ct	Noranda	47	C 4
Rd	Forrestdale	115	A 4
Rd	Forrestdale	114	D 1
Rd	Forrestdale	104	D 10
St	Cloverdale	75	C 5
St	Kewdale	74	E 7
St	Lesmurdie	87	D 2
St	Midland	50	C 8
St	Peppermint Gr	80	D 3
St	Wanneroo	20	C 8
St	Wembley	59	D 9
St E	Mt Helena	55	B 5
St W	Mt Helena	55	A 5
KEANEY			
Pl	City Beach	58	D 5
Pl	Waterford	83	E 5
KEANS			
Ave	Sorrento	30	B 5
KEARNEY			
Me	Marangaroo	32	C 4
KEARNS			
Cr	Ardross	82	C 8
KEARSLEY			
Ri	Murdoch	92	C 6
KEATES			
Rd	Armadale	126	D 1
Rd	Armadale	116	D 10
KEATLEY			
Cr	Woodvale	24	B 7
Ct	Mirrabooka	47	B 1
KEATS			
Pl	Spearwood	101	B 7
Rd	Gooseberry H	77	D 4
St	Silver Sands	163	B 5
KEAYS			
Rd	Kelmscott	107	C 10
KEBBLE			
Cl	Hillarys	23	B 9
KEBROYD			
Wy	Kallaroo	23	B 6
KEDRON			
Pl	Greenfields	163	D 10
KEEBLE			
Wy	Balga	46	D 1
KEEDES			
Ct	Parmelia	131	A 8
KEEGAN			
St	O'Connor	91	C 7
KEEL			
Ce	Waikiki	145	C 5
Pl	Ocean Reef	23	B 2
KEELEY			
Wy	Girrawheen	32	A 6
KEEMORE			
Dr	Balga	46	D 1
Wy	Balga	46	E 1
KEENAN			
Rd	Chidlow	41	D 6
St	Gosnells	95	E 7
St	Hamilton Hill	91	B 10
St	Wungong	126	C 4
Wy	Winthrop	92	A 4

		Map	Ref.
KEENE			
Pl	Waikiki	145	D 2
KEIGHTLEY			
Rd C	Shenton Park	72	A 4
Rd E	Shenton Park	72	A 4
Rd W	Shenton Park	72	A 4
Rd W	Shenton Park	71	E 4
KEIR			
Cl	Leeming	92	E 10
KEIRA			
St	Kelmscott	116	C 2
KEIRNAN			
St	Mundijong	142	E 5
St	Whitby	143	C 7
KEITH			
Rd	Rossmoyne	93	B 3
KELBY			
Cl	Morley	47	D 7
KELL			
Pl	Lesmurdie	87	A 3
Pl	Wembley Dns	59	A 3
KELLAM			
Wy	Medina	130	D 6
KELLAR			
Pl	Bellevue	65	A 2
Wy	Thornlie	95	A 5
KELLERMAN			
Wy	Gosnells	106	A 2
KELLETT			
Cl	Gwelup	45	C 7
KELLOW			
Pl	Fremantle	90	D 6
KELLY			
Cl	Parmelia	131	B 6
Ct	Willetton	93	B 7
Pl	Beckenham	85	B 7
Pl	Noranda	48	A 4
Pl	Willetton	93	E 6
Rd	Girrawheen	32	B 8
St	Cloverdale	75	A 3
St	Silver Sands	163	B 6
KELLYHILL			
Vw	Carine	44	E 2
KELSALL			
Cr	Manning	83	A 5
KELSEY			
Gr	Mirrabooka	33	B 10
KELSO			
Ct	Duncraig	31	A 7
Pl	Greenfields	165	D 2
KELTON			
Wy	Thornlie	95	C 5
KELTY			
Pl	Wilson	84	B 7
KELVEDON			
Wy	Huntingdale	95	D 9
KELVIN			
Rd	Duncraig	31	B 7
Rd	Maddington	96	A 2
Rd	Maddington	86	B 10
Rd	Orange Grove	86	C 9
Rd	Wattle Grove	86	E 6
St	Maylands	62	A 8
KEMBLA			
St	Kelmscott	116	D 2
Wy	Willetton	93	D 2
KEMI			
Ct	Joondalup	19	D 2
KEMMISH			
Ave	Parmelia	131	B 8
Cr	Melville	91	D 2
KEMP			
Ave	Quinns Rocks	10	E 10
Pl	Embleton	48	A 10
Pl	Rivervale	74	B 3
Rd	Mt Pleasant	82	D 9
Rd	Yangebup	112	C 1
Rd	Yangebup	102	C 10
St	Wanneroo	24	E 5

K

		Map	Ref.
KEMPENFELDT			
Ave	Sorrento	30	C 5
KEN			
St	Wembley Dns	58	E 5
KENDAL			
Ct	Westfield	106	B 9
Wy	Greenwood	31	E 4
KENDREW			
Cr	Joondalup	19	E 7
Ct	Willetton	94	A 4
KENHELM			
St	Balcatta	46	A 2
KENILWORTH			
St	Bayswater	62	A 6
St	Bayswater	61	E 6
St	Maylands	62	A 6
St	Maylands	61	E 6
KENMARE			
Ave	Thornlie	95	C 6
KENMORE			
Cr	Floreat	59	C 8
Rd	Mahogany Crk	67	B 2
Rd	Mahogany Crk	53	B 10
KENMURE			
Ave	Ashfield	62	E 5
Ave	Bayswater	62	D 6
KENNA			
Rd	Newburn	75	E 4
KENNARD			
St	Kensington	73	D 9
KENNEDY			
Cl	Bull Creek	92	E 7
Rd	Morley	61	D 1
Rd	Morley	47	D 10
St	Alfred Cove	81	E 10
St	Inglewood	61	D 6
St	Maylands	61	D 6
St	Melville	91	D 1
Wy	Padbury	23	C 9
KENNEDYA			
Dr	Joondalup	19	C 4
Rd	Walliston	88	A 2
KENNERLY			
St	Cloverdale	75	A 4
KENNETH			
Rd	High Wycombe	64	C 8
KENNETT			
St	Maddington	96	B 3
KENNINGTON			
Rd	Morley	48	A 7
KENNON			
Ct	Spearwood	101	A 4
St	Willetton	93	C 6
KENNY			
Dr	Duncraig	30	D 5
St	Bassendean	63	A 2
St	Mosman Park	80	C 6
KENRICK			
St	Balcatta	45	D 5
KENSAL GREEN			
Wy	Kingsley	24	B 9
KENSINGTON			
Ave	Dianella	47	D 9
Ct	Cooloongup	137	C 8
St	Bellevue	51	A 10
St	East Perth	1C	B 2
St	East Perth	73	B 2
KENSITT			
St	Stoneville	54	B 5
KENT			
Cl	Halls Head	164	C 4
Rd	Maida Vale	76	D 5
Rd	Marangaroo	32	A 5
St	Bentley	83	B 5
St	Bicton	81	B 8
St	Cannington	84	D 4
St	E Rockingham	129	D 9
St	E Victoria Pk	83	D 1
St	E Victoria Pk	73	E 10
St	Kensington	83	D 2

		Map	Ref.
St	Rockingham	137	A 4
St	Spearwood	101	A 5
St	Viveash	50	B 5
St	Wilson	84	C 7
Wy	Malaga	33	C 10
KENTIA			
Cl	Warnbro	145	E 8
Lp	Wanneroo	24	D 2
KENTISH			
Rd	Serpentine	154	E 10
KENTMERE			
Pl	Balga	32	C 9
KENTON			
Ct	Kingsley	31	B 1
St	Lynwood	94	D 1
Wy	Calista	130	E 6
Wy	Rockingham	137	D 6
KENWICK			
Rd	Kenwick	86	A 10
Rd	Kenwick	85	D 10
Rd	Maddington	86	B 10
Wy	Balga	32	C 10
KEPERRA			
Pl	Yanchep	3	E 10
KEPLER			
Cl	Mullaloo	23	C 3
KEPPEL			
Pl	Coogee	100	E 9
KEPPELL			
Me	Rockingham	137	A 9
Rd	Marmion	30	D 7
St	Willagee	91	D 5
KERIOR			
St	Mullaloo	23	A 5
KEROSENE			
La	Baldivis	138	E 9
KERR			
Pl	Hillarys	30	C 2
Pl	Yanchep	4	C 5
St	Leederville	60	C 10
KERRISON			
Pde	Armadale	116	A 3
KERRY			
Pl	Hamilton Hill	101	A 1
St	Dianella	47	B 10
St	Hamilton Hill	101	A 1
KERSEY			
Wy	Carine	30	E 9
KERSHAW			
Ave	Lesmurdie	87	B 4
Gns	Leeming	92	E 9
St	Byford	135	C 3
St	Subiaco	72	B 4
KERSWELL			
Wy	Warnbro	145	D 8
KERUN			
Ct	Armadale	116	D 3
Rd	Chidlow	42	B 6
KERWIN			
Wy	Lockridge	49	A 6
KESLAKE			
Wy	Lynwood	94	B 4
KESSACK			
St	Lathlain	74	A 6
KESSELL			
La	Beldon	23	E 5
KESTAL			
Pl	Kewdale	74	D 6
KESTON			
St	Gosnells	96	B 10
KESTRAL			
Ct	High Wycombe	76	B 1
KESTREL			
Ci	Wungong	116	B 9
Cl	Halls Head	164	B 3
Me	Edgewater	20	A 10
Pde	Ballajura	33	A 3
St	Karrinyup	44	E 3

		Map	Ref.
Wy	Thornlie	95	A 6
Wy	Yangebup	102	A 8
KETCH			
Ce	Ballajura	33	C 8
Cl	Ocean Reef	23	A 1
Pl	Waikiki	145	C 4
KETTERING			
Wy	Huntingdale	95	C 9
KEVIN			
Rd	Kelmscott	117	A 1
St	Stoneville	54	D 4
KEW			
Cl	Kingsley	24	C 10
St	Cloverdale	75	A 6
St	Kewdale	74	E 8
St	Welshpool	74	D 10
KEWDALE			
Rd	Kewdale	75	C 8
Rd	Welshpool	85	A 2
Rd	Welshpool	75	A 10
KEXBY			
St	Balcatta	45	E 5
KEY			
Pl	Noranda	47	C 5
KEYES			
St	Lathlain	74	B 6
KEYMER			
St	Ascot	62	D 9
St	Belmont	62	D 9
St	Belmont	74	E 1
St	Cloverdale	75	A 2
St	Forrestfield	76	A 10
St	Newburn	75	D 8
KEYS			
Ct	Leeming	93	A 9
KEY WEST			
Dr	Mullaloo	23	A 3
KIAH			
Ct	Kingsley	31	D 1
KIAMA			
Ct	Greenwood	31	B 4
Rd	Armadale	116	B 5
KIANDRA			
Pde	Ballajura	33	E 8
Rd	Kelmscott	106	E 6
Wy	High Wycombe	64	B 10
KIDBROKE			
Pl	Westfield	106	C 10
KIDBROOKE			
Wy	Kingsley	31	B 1
KIDD			
Ct	Middle Swan	50	E 4
Rd	Kenwick	95	D 2
KIDDIE			
St	Dianella	46	E 8
KIDMAN			
Ave	Sth Guildford	63	C 2
Ct	Thornlie	95	A 2
KIDSON			
St	Kardinya	92	A 7
KIDSTON			
Ct	Clarkson	14	E 10
KIELMAN			
Rd	Willetton	93	E 2
KIEREN			
Ct	Middle Swan	50	E 4
KIERNAN			
Pl	Kallaroo	23	B 7
KIESEY			
St	Spearwood	100	E 8
KIEV			
Ct	Lesmurdie	87	E 4
KILARNEY			
Hts	Kallaroo	22	E 8
KILBRIDE			
Cl	Waterford	83	C 6

		Map	Ref.
KILBURN			
La	Kelmscott	116	C 2
Rd	Parkerville	53	D 4
Ri	Kingsley	24	B 9
KILCAIRN			
Pl	Greenwood	31	B 4
KILDARE			
Pl	Beldon	23	D 4
Rd	Floreat	59	B 9
KILIMA			
Cl	Stoneville	54	B 6
KILKENNY			
Ci	Waterford	83	C 7
Gns	Halls Head	164	C 2
Pl	Marangaroo	32	C 5
Rd	Floreat	59	B 8
KILLALOE			
Pl	Waterford	83	D 6
KILLAMARSH			
Pl	Carine	30	E 9
KILLARA			
Dr	Willetton	94	A 3
Dr	Willetton	93	E 3
Pl	Gooseberry H	65	A 9
Wy	Craigie	23	E 4
KILLARNEY			
Cl	Connolly	19	B 8
Pl	Cooloongup	137	C 7
Rt	Meadow Sprgs	163	C 6
St	Mt Hawthorn	60	C 5
KILLILAN			
Rd	Applecross	82	D 5
KILLIN			
Pl	Duncraig	31	C 8
KILMESTON			
Ct	Maddington	96	C 3
KILMORY			
Gr	Kinross	19	A 2
KILMURRAY			
Wy	Balga	32	E 9
KILN			
Rd	Carabooda	8	E 9
Rd	Cardup	135	D 7
St	Ballajura	3	D 9
St	Malaga	33	D 9
KILPA			
Ct	City Beach	58	D 4
KILRENNY			
Cr	Greenwood	31	B 5
KILRUSH			
Pl	Waterford	83	C 7
KILSYTH			
Wy	Hamersley	32	A 9
KILTER			
Pl	Rivervale	74	C 5
KILVER			
Me	Kiara	48	D 6
KIM			
Cl	Willetton	93	E 5
KIMBARA			
Pl	Nollamara	46	C 5
St	Nollamara	46	C 5
KIMBARLEE			
Wy	Lesmurdie	87	B 1
KIMBER			
Pl	Mt Helena	55	B 4
St	Innaloo	45	C 10
KIMBERLEY			
Rd	Hillarys	30	B 2
St	Belmont	62	D 10
St	Leederville	60	C 10
Wy	Lynwood	94	C 4
KIMBLE			
Ct	Carine	30	D 9
KIN BAY			
El	Mindarie	14	B 4
KINBRACE			
Wy	Lynwood	94	D 2

		Map	Ref.
KINCAID			
Rd	Greenfields	165	D 2
KINCARDINE			
Cr	Floreat	59	C 8
KINCRAIG			
Cl	Westfield	106	C 6
Wy	Duncraig	30	E 7
KINDRA			
Wy	Nollamara	46	C 6
KING			
Cl	Winthrop	92	B 4
Me	Cooloongup	137	D 9
Pl	Padbury	23	C 10
Rd	Beechboro	48	D 3
Rd	Kalamunda	78	A 9
Rd	Oakford	133	A 5
Rd	Peel Estate	141	B 4
Rd	Peel Estate	133	B 10
Rd	Sth Guildford	64	A 7
St	Bayswater	62	B 2
St	Claremont	71	D 1
St	Coogee	100	E 8
St	East Fremantle	90	D 3
St	Gosnells	96	A 5
St	Gosnells	95	E 5
St	Kensington	73	C 9
St	Perth City	1C	E 2
St	Perth City	72	E 2
St	Shenton Park	71	E 1
KING ALBERT			
Rd	Trigg	44	C 6
KINGALLON			
Ct	Rockingham	137	C 7
KINGDON			
St	Mandurah	163	B 9
KING EDWARD			
Dr	Heathridge	19	B 9
Rd	Osborne Park	59	D 1
Rd	Osborne Park	45	E 10
St	South Perth	72	E 2
KINGFISHER			
Ave	Ballajura	34	A 6
Ave	Ballajura	33	E 7
Dr	Halls Head	164	B 3
Lp	High Wycombe	76	B 1
Lp	Willetton	93	C 4
Pl	Stirling	45	E 6
Pl	Yangebup	102	A 10
Vw	Wungong	116	C 10
Wy	Kingsley	24	E 10
KING GEORGE			
St	Innaloo	45	B 10
St	Shoalwater	136	C 8
St	Victoria Park	73	D 8
KINGHAM			
Pl	Armadale	115	E 4
KINGHORN			
Pl	Redcliffe	62	E 10
KINGIA			
Ct	Forrestfield	76	C 10
KINGS			
Ct	Carine	31	C 10
Rd	Subiaco	72	C 2
Rw	Millendon	168	A 8
Rw	Mt Claremont	71	A 5
KINGSALL			
Rd	Attadale	81	D 9
KINGSBRIDGE			
Rd	Warnbro	145	D 7
KINGSBURY			
Dr	Jarrahdale	153	A 8
KINGSCOTE			
Pl	Greenfields	163	E 9
St	Kewdale	75	D 8
KINGSDOWN			
Rd	Maddington	96	B 4
KINGSFIELD			
Ave	Swan View	51	C 6
KINGSFOLD			
St	Balga	46	B 1

For detailed information regarding the street referencing system used in this book, turn to page 170.

K

		Map	Ref.
KINGSFORD			
Ct	Port Kennedy	156	D 1
Dr	Willetton	93	C 7
Wy	Huntingdale	95	C 10
KINGSLAND			
Ave	City Beach	58	D 8
KINGSLEY			
Cl	Spearwood	101	C 8
Dr	Kingsley	31	B 1
Dr	Kingsley	24	B 10
Dr	Sth Guildford	63	C 3
Tce	Kelmscott	107	A 7
KINGS LYNN			
Ri	Mindarie	14	B 4
KINGS MILL			
Rd	Pickering Bk	99	D 1
KINGSMILL			
Gns	Winthrop	92	A 4
St	Claremont	70	E 9
KINGS PARK			
Ave	Crawley	72	B 7
Rd	West Perth	72	C 2
Rd	West Perth	1C	D 2
KINGSTON			
Ave	West Perth	60	D 9
Cl	Heathridge	23	E 2
Pl	Kardinya	92	A 2
Pl	Midland	50	D 6
Rd	Mt Helena	41	A 8
St	Embleton	48	B 10
St	Nedlands	71	E 6
Wy	Safety Bay	145	C 1
KINGSTON HEATH			
Blvd	Meadow Sprgs	163	D 2
Ct	Connolly	19	C 8
KINGSWAY			
	Landsdale	32	B 1
	Nedlands	71	E 10
KINGSWOOD			
St	Mt Helena	55	C 4
KING WILLIAM			
St	Bayswater	62	B 5
St	Bayswater	62	C 6
St	Sth Fremantle	90	C 8
KINKUNA			
Wy	City Beach	58	D 4
KINLEY			
Pl	Balga	32	B 10
Rd	Banjup	123	B 2
KINLOCH			
Pl	Duncraig	31	B 6
KINLOCK			
Ave	Ferndale	84	D 9
KINNANE			
Pl	Attadale	81	C 8
KINNINMONT			
Ave	Nedlands	71	D 8
KINROSS			
Cl	Kingsley	24	C 9
Cr	Floreat	59	C 2
Dr	Kinross	19	A 1
Rd	Applecross	82	C 6
KINSALE			
Dr	Mindarie	10	A 2
Dr	Mindarie	14	A 3
KINSELLA			
St	Joondanna	60	B 3
KINTAIL			
Rd	Applecross	82	C 5
KINTORE			
Pl	Padbury	23	E 10
Rd	Mundaring	53	D 9
Rd	Parkerville	53	D 6
KINTYRE			
Cr	Floreat	59	C 8
Pl	Kingsley	24	B 9
KIORA			
La	Merriwa	11	D 10

		Map	Ref.
KIPLING			
St	Munster	101	C 9
KIRBY			
Pl	Marangaroo	32	A 4
St	Willagee	91	D 4
Wy	Samson	91	C 8
KIRIP			
Ct	Glen Forrest	66	E 3
KIRK			
Cl	Westfield	106	C 6
Rd	Kardinya	92	A 6
KIRKBY			
St	Trigg	44	C 4
KIRKCALDY			
Gr	Darlington	66	B 3
KIRKCOLM			
Wy	Warwick	31	C 8
KIRKDALE			
Rd	Kalamunda	77	D 8
KIRKE			
Ce	Merriwa	10	B 8
St	Balcatta	46	A 2
St	Eden Hill	49	A 8
KIRKHAM HILL			
Tce	Maylands	61	E 9
KIRKLAND			
Pl	Melville	91	D 2
Wy	Parmelia	131	B 6
KIRKPATRICK			
Cr	Noranda	47	D 5
KIRKSTALL			
St	East Perth	1C	B 2
St	East Perth	73	B 2
Wy	Sawyers Valley	55	A 10
KIRKSTONE			
Pl	Balga	32	C 10
KIRKUS			
Rd	Medina	130	E 5
KIRKWALL			
Cl	Warnbro	145	C 8
KIRKWOOD			
Rd	Swanbourne	70	D 9
KIRN			
Cl	Willetton	94	A 4
KIRO			
St	Carabooda	8	C 8
KIRRA			
Ct	Hillarys	22	E 10
KIRRIBILLI			
Ct	Kallaroo	23	A 6
KIRTON			
Ct	Redcliffe	63	A 9
KIRWAN			
St	Floreat	71	C 1
Wy	Winthrop	92	A 3
KIRWIN			
Pl	Willetton	93	E 3
KISHORN			
Rd	Applecross	82	D 5
Rd	Mt Pleasant	82	E 6
KISSANE			
Ct	Willetton	94	A 2
KITCHENER			
Ave	Bayswater	62	A 6
Ave	Victoria Park	74	A 7
Ave	Victoria Park	73	E 6
Rd	Alfred Cove	92	A 1
Rd	Alfred Cove	91	E 1
Rd	Bassendean	63	A 5
Rd	Booragoon	92	B 1
Rd	Melville	91	D 1
St	Mandurah	165	A 2
St	Nedlands	71	E 5
St	North Beach	44	C 3
St	Trigg	44	C 4
St	Tuart Hill	60	C 1
Wy	Victoria Park	73	E 5

		Map	Ref.
KITE			
Ct	High Wycombe	64	A 10
Ct	Huntingdale	105	D 1
Me	Ballajura	33	E 6
Pl	Waikiki	145	B 3
KITSON			
Pl	Maddington	95	E 3
St	Rockingham	137	C 8
KITTYHAWK			
Pde	Ballajura	33	D 6
KITTYS GORGE			
Tk	Jarrahdale	152	C 10
KIWA			
Pl	Cooloongup	137	E 8
KIWI			
Cl	Ballajura	33	E 8
KLEIN			
Ct	Winthrop	92	A 4
St	Karrinyup	45	A 7
KLEINIG			
Rd	Perth Airport	75	D 6
KLEM			
Ave	Redcliffe	75	A 2
Ave	Salter Point	83	B 8
Rd	Ardross	82	D 8
KLENK			
Rd	Attadale	81	C 8
KNAPHILL			
Hts	Mirrabooka	47	B 1
KNEBWORTH			
Ave	Perth City	61	A 10
KNIGHT			
Ave	Yokine	46	D 9
Pl	Calista	130	E 9
Rd	Gnangara	26	B 3
St	Langford	95	A 1
St	Wembley Dns	58	F 4
KNIGHTSBRIDGE			
Cr	Mullaloo	23	A 2
Wy	Thornlie	95	C 8
KNOLL			
Pl	Kiara	48	E 6
KNOLLWOOD			
Ct	Ballajura	33	C 4
KNOT			
Ri	Ballajura	34	A 8
Wy	Yangebup	102	A 10
KNOTT			
Ct	Westfield	106	A 9
KNOWLE			
Wy	Warnbro	145	D 7
KNOWLES			
St	Balcatta	45	E 4
KNOX			
Cr	Melville	91	C 2
KNUCKEY			
Ct	Roleystone	107	E 10
Dr	Roleystone	107	E 10
KNUTSFORD			
Ave	Kewdale	74	D 5
Ave	Rivervale	74	B 3
St	Fremantle	1D	C 5
St	Fremantle	90	D 5
St	North Perth	60	E 6
St	Swanbourne	70	E 9
KOALA			
St	Doubleview	59	A 2
KOBELKE			
St	Dianella	61	B 1
St	Dianella	47	B 10
KOCHIA			
Ct	Heathridge	19	C 10
KOEL			
Ct	High Wycombe	64	A 10
Wy	Thornlie	95	A 4
KOEPPE			
Rd	Claremont	71	B 10

		Map	Ref.
KOLAN			
Cl	Mandurah	165	B 4
El	Merriwa	11	C 8
KOMAN			
Wy	Girrawheen	32	C 7
KONDA			
Cl	Warnbro	145	E 8
KONDIL			
Pl	City Beach	58	E 9
KOOJAN			
Ave	Sth Guildford	63	C 4
KOOKABURRA			
Ave	Cullacabardee	34	A 3
Cl	Ballajura	33	E 7
Cr	High Wycombe	76	A 1
Cr	High Wycombe	64	D 10
Ct	Armadale	116	B 3
Pl	Darlington	66	A 5
St	Stirling	45	E 6
Tce	Ballajura	33	D 6
Wy	Gosnells	106	A 4
KOOKERBROOK			
St	Mandurah	165	A 2
KOOLAMA			
Pl	Kallaroo	23	C 5
KOOLAN			
Dr	Shelley	93	C 1
KOOLGOO			
Wy	Koongamia	65	B 2
KOOLINDA			
St	Falcon	162A	B 3
KOOLJACK			
St	Mandurah	165	B 3
KOOLUNDA			
Ct	Karawara	83	C 5
KOOLYANGA			
Rd	Mullaloo	23	A 2
KOOLYN			
Gr	Kingsley	31	D 1
KOOMBANA			
Wy	Kallaroo	23	B 7
KOONDOOLA			
Ave	Koondoola	32	E 8
KOORALBYN			
Wy	Connolly	19	C 6
KOORANA			
Rd	Mullaloo	23	B 4
KOORDA			
St	Coolbinia	60	E 4
KOORINGAL			
Ct	Kingsley	31	E 3
KOOROODA			
Rd	Nollamara	46	D 5
KOOTINGAL			
St	Armadale	116	C 5
KOOYONG			
Rd	Kewdale	74	C 6
Rd	Rivervale	74	A 3
KOOYONGA			
St	Yanchep	3	E 10
KOPAI			
Cr	Waikiki	145	C 1
KORARA			
Cl	Ocean Reef	18	E 6
KORBEL			
Cl	Greenfields	163	E 9
KORBOSKY			
Rd	Lockridge	49	A 8
KOREL			
Gns	Swanbourne	70	D 9
Pl	Coogee	101	A 10
Pl	Sorrento	30	C 4
KORELLA			
St	Mullaloo	23	A 4
KORONG			
Rd	Golden Bay	158	E 8

		Map	Ref.
KOTAS			
Cl	Wanneroo	24	E 1
KOTT			
Pl	Lesmurdie	87	C 4
Tce	Claremont	71	A 8
KRASNOSTEIN			
Hl	Winthrop	92	A 5
KRISTIANSEN			
Ct	Greenwood	31	D 4
KRUGER			
Pl	Booragoon	92	C 1
KRUGGER			
Pl	Leeming	93	A 10
KRUI			
Cl	Merriwa	11	C 10
KRUSE			
Pl	Mirrabooka	32	E 9
KULINDI			
Cr	Wanneroo	20	B 5
KULLAROO			
Ct	Hillman	137	E 6
KUNDILLI			
Wy	Wanneroo	20	D 10
KUNDYL			
Ct	Kelmscott	117	B 2
KURAMUN			
Pl	Parkerville	39	B 10
KURANDA			
Pl	Greenmount	66	A 1
KURDA			
Pl	Balga	46	C 5
Rd	Balga	46	B 5
KURDAL			
Rd	Coodanup	165	C 8
KURNALL			
Rd	Welshpool	85	B 1
Rd	Welshpool	75	C 10
KURRAJONG			
Dr	Thornlie	95	A 9
Pl	Greenwood	31	C 5
Pl	Safety Bay	137	A 9
Rd	Safety Bay	137	A 9
St	Roleystone	108	B 8
Wy	Westfield	106	B 7
KURRAWA			
St	Hillman	137	E 6
KUTCHARO			
Cr	Joondalup	19	C 2
KWEDA			
Wy	Nollamara	46	D 8
KWINANA			
Fwy	Bull Creek	92	E 5
Fwy	Como	82	E 2
Fwy	Jandakot	102	E 3
Fwy	Leeming	92	E 5
Fwy	Salter Point	83	A 9
Fwy	South Lake	102	E 7
Fwy	South Perth	72	D 7
KWINANA BEACH			
Rd	Kwinana Beach	129	D 8
KYABRAM			
Rd	Armadale	116	C 3
KYARA			
Ct	Clarkson	14	D 1
KYARRA			
Pl	Innaloo	45	C 9
St	Innaloo	45	C 9
KYBRA			
Ct	Iluka	18	E 3
Ct	Morley	48	D 7
Me	Rockingham	137	B 5
St	Falcon	162A	B 4
KYEEMA			
Ch	Carine	44	E 2
KYLE			
Ave	Curtin Uni	135	
Ct	Hamersley	32	A 9

216 For detailed information regarding the street referencing system used in this book, turn to page 170.

L

		Map	Ref.
Ct	Joondalup	19	E 5
Pl	Swan View	51	E 9

KYLENA
| Gl | Ocean Reef | 18 | E 7 |

KYLIE
Rd	Kelmscott	107	B 6
Rd	Roleystone	107	C 6
St	Wembley Dns	59	A 5
Wy	Kingsley	24	D 10

KYME
| Ct | Gosnells | 106 | D 2 |

KYOGLE
| Pl | Armadale | 116 | B 6 |

KYREAN
| St | Falcon | 162A | A 4 |

L

LABOUCHERE
| Rd | Como | 83 | A 1 |
| Rd | South Perth | 72 | E 8 |

LABYRINTH
| St | Waikiki | 145 | D 2 |
| Wy | South Lake | 102 | C 8 |

LACEBARK
| Cl | South Lake | 102 | C 6 |
| Ct | Halls Head | 164 | B 6 |

LACEBY
| Ct | Erskine | 164 | A 8 |

LACE LEAF
| Wy | South Lake | 102 | C 6 |

LACEPEDE
| Dr | Sorrento | 30 | B 4 |

LACEY
Ct	Parmelia	131	B 6
Rd	Eglinton	7	D 1
Rd	Mundaring	54	A 8
Rd	Parkerville	54	A 6
St	Beckenham	85	B 6
St	E Cannington	85	B 6
St	Perth City	1C	B 1
St	Perth City	73	B 1
St	Sawyers Valley	54	D 10

LACHLAN
Rd	Thornlie	95	B 6
Rd	Willetton	94	A 2
Wy	Bibra Lake	102	C 8

LACONIA
| Ct | Riverton | 83 | D 10 |

LACROSSE
| Ri | Sorrento | 30 | C 3 |

LADNER
| St | O'Connor | 91 | D 7 |

LADY EVELYN
| Rt | Joondalup | 19 | C 4 |

LADYWELL
| St | Beckenham | 85 | B 10 |

LAFFEY
| Ct | Willetton | 93 | D 2 |

LAGA
| Ct | Stirling | 45 | D 7 |

LA GAVAS
| Ct | Halls Head | 164 | C 1 |

LAGO
| Pl | Joondalup | 19 | D 8 |

LAGONDA
| Dr | Gwelup | 45 | C 5 |
| Pl | Marangaroo | 32 | D 6 |

LAGOON
Dr	Yanchep	4	C 5
Hts	Ballajura	33	D 7
Pl	Beldon	23	C 2
Wy	Halls Head	162	D 9

LA GRANGE
Gns	Currambine	19	C 5
Pl	Meadow Sprgs	163	C 5
Rd	Stoneville	40	A 8

		Map	Ref.
Rd	Stoneville	39	E 9
St	Innaloo	59	C 1
St	Innaloo	45	C 10

LAGUNA
| Ri | Mullaloo | 23 | A 3 |
| St | Safety Bay | 145 | B 1 |

LAIDLAW
| St | Hilton | 91 | B 9 |

LAIDLEY
| Wy | Greenfields | 163 | E 8 |

LAIRD
| Ct | Greenwood | 31 | B 4 |
| St | Singleton | 160 | D 4 |

LAKE
Ave	Shenton Park	71	E 3
Rd	Armadale	116	A 1
Rd	Armadale	106	A 10
Rd	Armadale	115	D 5
Rd	Forrestdale	114	C 6
Rd	Forrestdale	115	E 1
Rd	Kelmscott	106	D 4
Rd	Neerabup	12	B 8
Rd	Westfield	106	C 6
St	Cannington	85	A 6
St	Halls Head	162	C 10
St	Mariginiup	20	D 1
St	Northbridge	1C	E 1
St	Northbridge	72	E 1
St	Perth City	61	A 10
St	Rockingham	136	D 6
Tce	Wilson	84	D 4

LAKE CARINE
| Gns | Carine | 31 | C 10 |

LAKE EDGE
| La | South Lake | 102 | D 6 |

LAKEFARM
| Rt | Ballajura | 33 | E 5 |

LAKEHILL
| Gns | Edgewater | 20 | A 10 |

LAKELANDS
| Dr | Gnangara | 26 | A 3 |
| Dr | Gnangara | 25 | D 5 |

LAKEMBA
| Wy | Waikiki | 145 | D 1 |

LAKE MONGER
| Dr | Leederville | 60 | B 8 |
| Dr | Wembley | 60 | A 8 |

LAKERISE
| Me | Edgewater | 20 | A 10 |

LAKES
Rd	Greenfields	165	E 2
Rd	Greenfields	163	E 10
Rd	Hazelmere	64	B 3
Wy	Jandakot	102	E 4

LAKESEND
| Rd | Thornlie | 95 | B 9 |

LAKESHORE
| Cl | Ballajura | 33 | C 7 |

LAKESIDE
Dr	Joondalup	20	A 8
Dr	Joondalup	19	E 4
Dr	Joondalup	19	E 9
Dr	Thornlie	95	B 10
Rd	Churchlands	59	C 6

LAKEVALLEY
| Dr | Edgewater | 20 | A 9 |
| Dr | Edgewater | 19 | E 9 |

LAKE VIEW
Dr	Gidgegannup	40	A 4
Dr	Gidgegannup	39	E 4
Rd	Chidlow	42	C 10
St	E Victoria Pk	74	A 9
Tce	Westfield	106	C 5

LAKEVIEW
Dr	Edgewater	24	B 1
Pl	Bibra Lake	102	D 2
St	Mariginiup	21	B 1

LAKE VISTA
| | Edgewater | 20 | A 10 |

		Map	Ref.
LAKEWAY			
Dr	Kingsley	31	E 1
Dr	Kingsley	24	E 10
St	Claremont	71	A 7

LAKEY
| St | Southern River | 104 | E 5 |

LALINA
| Wy | Wanneroo | 20 | E 9 |

LALOR
Ct	Coodanup	165	B 4
Ct	Rockingham	137	B 9
Pl	Kalamunda	77	E 9
Rd	Kenwick	86	A 5
Rd	Kenwick	95	E 1
Rd	Kenwick	85	E 10
St	Scarborough	44	D 9

LAMARCK
| Pl | Heathridge | 23 | D 1 |

LAMB
Ave	Bentley	84	C 4
Pl	Munster	101	C 10
St	Bassendean	63	B 1
St	South Perth	73	C 7

LAMBASA
| Pl | Mindarie | 10 | A 2 |
| Pl | Waikiki | 145 | D 1 |

LAMBERT
La	Wungong	126	C 3
Pl	Alfred Cove	81	E 10
St	Alfred Cove	81	E 10
St	Huntingdale	105	D 2

LAMBERTIA
| St | Greenwood | 31 | C 6 |
| Wy | Ferndale | 84 | C 10 |

LAMBETH
| Pl | Kingsley | 31 | B 1 |

LAMBOURNE
| Pl | Halls Head | 164 | A 7 |
| Rt | Mirrabooka | 33 | B 9 |

LAMOND
Cl	Kinross	19	A 2
St	Alfred Cove	91	E 1
St	Melville	91	E 1

LAMONT
| St | Midland | 50 | D 6 |

LAMPARD
| St | Hamersley | 31 | D 10 |

LAMPE
| Ct | Woodvale | 24 | B 4 |

LAMPERD
| Me | Murdoch | 92 | C 7 |

LANA
| Ct | Rossmoyne | 93 | B 1 |

LANAGAN
| Ri | South Lake | 102 | C 6 |

LANARK
Me	Duncraig	31	A 8
St	Coolbinia	60	E 4
St	Menora	60	E 5

LANCASTER
Pl	Maddington	96	D 3
Rd	Wangara	24	D 8
St	Dianella	61	B 2
St	Spearwood	101	B 4

LANCE
Ct	Thornlie	95	D 7
Pl	Kewdale	74	D 7
St	Mt Helena	55	C 7

LANCEFIELD
| Rd | Morley | 48 | C 6 |

LANCELOT
| Cl | Westfield | 106 | D 7 |
| St | Carine | 45 | C 1 |

LANCER
| Ct | Alexander Hts | 32 | E 5 |

LANCETT
| Ct | Sorrento | 30 | C 4 |

LANCHESTER
| Wy | Stirling | 45 | E 8 |

		Map	Ref.
LANCIER			
Pl	Madora	160	D 7
Pl	Rockingham	137	D 7

LANCING
| Rd | Westfield | 106 | B 9 |
| Wy | Balga | 46 | C 1 |

LANDA
| Ct | Clarkson | 14 | D 1 |

LANDELLS
| Ri | Hillarys | 30 | C 1 |

LANDER
| St | Southern River | 105 | B 5 |

LANDERS
| Rd | Lesmurdie | 87 | D 3 |

LANDGREN
| Rd | Casuarina | 132 | A 7 |

LANDON
| Wy | Mt Claremont | 71 | A 6 |
| Wy | Swanbourne | 71 | A 6 |

LANDOR
Gns	Bellevue	50	D 9
Gns	Woodvale	24	B 6
Rd	Gooseberry H	77	C 2

LANDRA
| Gns | City Beach | 58 | E 7 |

LANDRAIL
| Rd | Stirling | 45 | E 7 |

LANDSBOROUGH
| Wy | Padbury | 30 | D 1 |

LANDSDALE
| Rd | Landsdale | 32 | D 2 |

LANE
Ce	Kallaroo	23	A 8
Rd	Kalamunda	77	E 9
St	Cottesloe	80	E 1
St	Perth City	61	A 10

LANEA
| Ct | Belmont | 74 | E 2 |

LANG
Ct	Huntingdale	95	D 9
Rd	Mundijong	142	E 4
St	Brentwood	92	B 3
St	Jarrahdale	152	D 6
St	Kelmscott	117	C 1

LANGDALE
| St | Wembley Dns | 58 | E 5 |

LANGFORD
| Ave | Langford | 95 | A 2 |
| Ave | Langford | 94 | E 2 |

LANGHAM
| Gns | Wilson | 84 | C 6 |
| St | Nedlands | 71 | D 8 |

LANGHOLM
| Pl | Duncraig | 31 | A 7 |

LANGLER
| St | E Victoria Pk | 84 | A 1 |

LANGLEY
Cr	Innaloo	45	C 8
Me	Iluka	18	E 6
Pl	Innaloo	45	C 8
Rd	Bayswater	62	A 3
St	Rockingham	136	E 6
Wy	Booragoon	92	C 2
Wy	Innaloo	45	C 8

LANGRIDGE
| Cr | Orelia | 131 | A 4 |

LANGSFORD
| St | Claremont | 71 | B 9 |

LANGTON
| St | Stirling | 45 | E 6 |

LANGWORTH
| Rd | Balcatta | 46 | A 5 |

LANHAM
| Ct | Koondoola | 33 | A 1 |

LANIGAN
| Cl | Wembley | 60 | A 9 |

LANIUS
| St | Beechboro | 49 | B 5 |

		Map	Ref.
LANRICK			
Pl	Girrawheen	32	B 7

LANSBY
| Ct | Riverton | 83 | E 10 |

LANSDOWNE
Rd	Gooseberry H	77	C 3
Rd	Kensington	73	D 8
St	Jolimont	71	E 1
Tn	Merriwa	11	D 10

LANSING
| St | Queens Park | 84 | E 3 |

LANSKIE
| Ct | Joondalup | 19 | C 3 |

LANTANA
Ave	Mt Claremont	71	B 5
Cr	Dianella	46	E 4
Wy	Westfield	106	C 7

LANTERN
| Ct | Safety Bay | 137 | B 10 |

LANYON
| St | Mandurah | 165 | B 1 |

LAPAGE
| St | Belmont | 74 | C 1 |
| St | Belmont | 62 | C 10 |

LAPOINYA
| Pl | Stoneville | 40 | D 8 |

LAPSLEY
| Rd | Claremont | 71 | A 8 |

LAPWING
| Ct | Iluka | 18 | D 5 |

LARA
| Ct | Cooloongup | 137 | D 10 |

LARCH
| Ct | Woodvale | 24 | C 7 |
| Pl | Forrestfield | 76 | C 10 |

LARISSA
| Rd | Willetton | 93 | E 4 |

LARIX
| Wy | Forrestfield | 76 | C 9 |

LARK
| Ct | Yangebup | 102 | A 10 |
| Me | Ballajura | 33 | D 6 |

LARKIN
| Ct | Medina | 130 | E 6 |

LARKSPUR
Cro	Yangebup	101	E 9
La	Ballajura	33	E 8
Pl	Heathridge	19	C 10
Pl	Thornlie	95	A 8

LARMER
| Pl | Bull Creek | 93 | A 4 |

LARNE
| Pl | Mindarie | 14 | B 3 |
| St | Mt Hawthorn | 60 | C 5 |

LA ROCHELLE
| Ra | Port Kennedy | 156 | E 1 |
| Ra | Port Kennedy | 145 | E 10 |

LARSEN
| Rd | Byford | 126 | B 9 |

LARSSON
| Wk | Clarkson | 14 | C 1 |

LARUNDEL
| Rd | City Beach | 58 | D 9 |

LARWOOD
| Cr | High Wycombe | 64 | D 7 |

LA SALLE
| Ave | Middle Swan | 50 | C 3 |

LASCELLES
| Pde | Gooseberry H | 77 | C 1 |
| Pde | Gooseberry H | 65 | C 10 |

LASER
| Pl | Ocean Reef | 23 | A 1 |

LA SEYNE
| Cr | Warnbro | 145 | C 3 |

LASHAM
| St | Viveash | 50 | B 5 |

L

		Map	Ref.
LATANIA			
Gr	Warnbro	145	E 8
LATERAL			
Lp	Beldon	23	D 2
LATERITIA			
Ct	Kelmscott	106	E 6
LATHAM			
Rd	Ferndale	84	D 9
St	Alfred Cove	91	E 1
St	Alfred Cove	81	E 10
St	Ashfield	62	E 5
LATHLAIN			
Pl	Lathlain	74	A 6
LATHWELL			
St	Armadale	116	D 2
LATIMER			
Wy	Langford	95	B 2
LATROBE			
Me	Jandakot	112	E 3
St	Yokine	60	E 2
LAUFFER			
Wy	Mahogany Crk	67	B 7
LAUGHLAN			
St	Morley	48	B 7
LAUGHTON			
Wy	Leeming	93	B 8
LAUNCESTON			
Ave	City Beach	70	D 2
LAUNDERS			
Ct	Jandakot	102	E 10
LAURA			
Ri	Marangaroo	32	C 4
LAUREL			
Cl	Riverton	83	E 10
Ct	Mullaloo	23	A 5
Ct	Thornlie	95	A 9
Rd	Woodlands	59	C 2
St	Forrestfield	76	D 10
St	Mullaloo	23	A 5
LAURENA			
Pl	Maida Vale	76	E 2
LAURENCE			
Rd	Innaloo	45	B 7
Rd	Walliston	88	A 1
Rd	Walliston	78	A 10
LAURI			
Ct	Lynwood	94	C 4
LAURIE			
St	Cloverdale	74	D 5
St	Kewdale	74	D 5
LAURINA			
Pl	Morley	48	D 5
LAVALLE			
Ri	South Lake	102	D 5
LAVAN			
St	Bassendean	62	D 3
LAVANT			
Wy	Balga	46	B 2
LAVENDER			
Ct	Dianella	46	E 5
Ct	Thornlie	95	A 7
Me	Halls Head	164	A 8
LAVERY			
Dr	Casuarina	132	C 8
LAVINIA			
Cr	Coolbellup	101	E 2
Ct	Kallaroo	23	B 7
Pl	Mariginiup	17	C 9
LAW			
Cr	Armadale	116	D 8
Ct	Winthrop	92	A 6
St	Embleton	48	A 10
LAWLER			
Gr	Winthrop	92	A 3
St	North Perth	60	D 4
St	South Perth	73	B 8
St	Subiaco	72	A 2
St	Subiaco	71	E 2

		Map	Ref.
LAWLEY			
Cr	Mt Lawley	61	B 7
Ct	Joondalup	19	D 5
Pl	Mt Lawley	61	B 7
Rd	Lesmurdie	77	C 10
St	North Beach	44	C 1
St	Tuart Hill	60	B 1
St	West Perth	60	E 9
St	Yokine	60	D 1
LAWLOR			
Rd	Attadale	81	C 9
LAWNBROOK			
Rd E	Bickley	88	C 4
Rd W	Walliston	88	A 2
Rd W	Walliston	87	E 2
LAWRENCE			
Ave	West Perth	1C	D 1
Ave	West Perth	72	D 1
Cl	Darlington	66	B 7
St	Bayswater	62	A 4
St	Bedford	61	D 1
St	Como	83	B 3
St	Gosnells	95	D 7
Wy	Byford	135	B 5
Wy	Samson	91	D 9
LAWRIE			
Ct	Clarkson	14	D 2
LAWSON			
Pl	Munster	101	B 9
Rd	Henley Brook	36	A 3
Rd	Henley Brook	35	E 3
Rd	Hillman	138	B 5
St	Bentley	84	A 5
Wy	Darlington	66	A 2
Wy	Padbury	23	E 8
LAYBURN			
Pl	Ferndale	84	C 10
LAYMAN			
St	Booragoon	92	D 1
St	Booragoon	82	D 10
LAYTHORNE			
St	Nollamara	46	E 6
LEA			
Cl	Rossmoyne	93	B 1
Pl	Sorrento	30	D 4
Rd	Koondoola	33	A 9
LEACH			
Ave	Riverton	93	E 1
Ave	Riverton	83	E 10
Cr	Rockingham	137	B 6
Hwy	Bateman	92	D 3
Hwy	Bentley	84	D 3
Hwy	Bull Creek	93	A 3
Hwy	Cloverdale	75	A 7
Hwy	Kewdale	75	A 8
Hwy	Palmyra	91	B 4
Hwy	Rossmoyne	93	B 2
Hwy	Shelley	93	C 1
Hwy	Shelley	83	D 10
Hwy	Welshpool	74	D 10
Hwy	Willagee	91	E 3
Hwy	Wilson	84	B 7
Hwy	Winthrop	92	A 3
Pl	Gnangara	26	A 7
Rd	Wanneroo	20	D 8
St	Marmion	30	C 8
LEACON			
Pl	Maddington	96	B 6
LEAFY			
Pl	Edgewater	24	A 1
LEAHY			
Ct	Leeming	93	B 10
LEAKE			
Pl	Belhus	29	C 5
St	Ascot	62	D 9
St	Bayswater	62	B 5
St	Belmont	62	D 9
St	Belmont	74	E 1
St	Forrestdale	115	A 9
St	Fremantle	1D	B 5
St	Fremantle	90	B 5
St	North Perth	60	E 8
St	Peppermint Gr	80	E 3

		Map	Ref.
LEALT			
Pl	Ardross	82	C 10
LEANDER			
St	Beldon	23	E 3
St	Falcon	162A	C 1
LEANE			
St	South Perth	73	B 8
LEANNE			
Cl	Woodvale	24	B 8
LEAR			
Pl	Coolbellup	101	D 1
LEAROYD			
St	Mt Lawley	61	A 6
LEARY			
Pl	Ferndale	84	C 9
LEASE			
Rd	Peron	136	C 5
LEASHAM			
Ct	Medina	130	E 6
Wy	Medina	130	E 6
LEASIDE			
Wy	Greenwood	31	D 5
Wy	Spearwood	101	A 5
LEATH			
Rd	Naval Base	121	A 9
LEATHERWOOD			
Ri	South Lake	102	D 5
Wy	Huntingdale	105	B 1
Wy	Huntingdale	95	B 10
LEAVIS			
Pl	Spearwood	101	B 9
LEAWOOD			
Cr	Boya	65	C 4
LEBEO			
Ct	Heathridge	19	D 9
LECKY			
Ct	Girrawheen	32	D 9
LEDA			
Ct	Merriwa	14	C 1
St	Hamilton Hill	100	E 1
LEDAN			
Pl	Helena Valley	64	E 6
LEDBROOKE			
St	Bicton	81	B 7
LEDBURY			
St	Balga	32	B 9
LEDGAR			
Rd	Balcatta	45	D 3
LEDGARD			
St	Rockingham	137	A 6
LEDGE			
Pl	Sorrento	30	D 4
LEDGER			
Rd	Gooseberry H	77	C 3
St	Warnbro	145	C 9
LEE			
Ave	Hilton	91	B 8
Ct	Kingsley	24	A 10
Dr	Perth Airport	63	B 9
Pl	Bicton	81	A 9
Pl	Noranda	47	E 4
Rd	Naval Base	121	B 8
Rd	Sawyers Valley	54	E 10
St	Ascot	62	B 9
St	Forrestfield	86	D 2
St	Morley	47	B 9
Wy	Thornlie	95	B 3
LEECE			
Pl	Booragoon	92	C 3
St	Coolbellup	101	D 1
LEEDER			
St	Glendalough	60	A 5
St	Safety Bay	136	D 9
LEEDS			
St	Dianella	47	C 10
St	Dianella	61	D 1

		Map	Ref.
LEEMING			
Rd	Jandakot	103	C 1
Rd	Leeming	103	B 1
Rd	North Lake	102	D 1
LEE-STEERE			
Dr	Mariginiup	16	E 7
LEEUWIN			
Pde	Rockingham	137	B 6
LEEVES			
Ct	Quinns Rocks	10	B 10
LEEWARD			
Cl	Safety Bay	137	B 9
LEEWAY			
Ct	Osborne Park	59	E 1
Ct	Osborne Park	45	E 10
Dr	Ocean Reef	19	B 10
LE FANU			
Pl	Mt Claremont	70	E 3
LEFROY			
Ave	Bellevue	50	D 9
Ave	Herne Hill	36	C 6
Rd	Beaconsfield	90	D 8
Rd	Bull Creek	93	B 5
Rd	Hilton	91	A 8
Rd	Kelmscott	116	E 1
Rd	Sth Fremantle	90	D 8
Rd	Yanchep	4	C 5
St	Mandurah	163	A 9
St	Serpentine	154	E 1
St	Trigg	44	C 5
St	Woodlands	59	B 4
LEGANA			
Ave	Kingsley	31	D 2
LEGEND			
Cr	Greenfields	165	E 2
Pl	Cooloongup	137	D 8
LEGG			
St	Bull Creek	93	A 7
LEGGE			
Pl	Beckenham	85	C 7
LEGGETT			
St	Balcatta	46	A 5
LEGHORN			
Rd	Newburn	75	E 1
Rd	Newburn	63	E 10
Rd	Orelia	131	C 5
St	Rockingham	137	B 6
LE GRAND			
Gns	Marangaroo	32	C 5
LEHMANN			
Ct	Kingsley	31	D 1
LEHMANS			
Me	Gwelup	45	C 6
LEICESTER			
Sq	Alexander Hts	33	B 4
St	Leederville	60	C 8
LEICHARDT			
St	St James	84	B 2
LEICHHARDT			
Ave	Padbury	30	D 1
Dr	Two Rocks	2	D 3
St	Bull Creek	92	E 7
LEIDEN			
Pl	Forrestfield	86	C 1
LEIGH			
Cl	Willetton	93	E 4
Ct	Marangaroo	32	B 5
Pl	Girrawheen	32	D 9
St	Mandurah	165	A 3
St	Victoria Park	73	E 5
LEIGHTON			
Rd	Halls Head	162	C 10
Rd	Halls Head	164	D 1
LEILA			
St	Cannington	84	E 6
LEINSTER			
Pl	Waterford	83	D 6

		Map	Ref.
LEIPOLD			
Rd	Peel Estate	142	A 4
Rd	Peel Estate	141	C 4
LEISURE			
Wy	Halls Head	164	D 4
Wy	Safety Bay	145	B 2
LEITH			
Ct	Greenwood	31	B 7
Pl	Ferndale	84	D 9
Pl	High Wycombe	64	D 9
Pl	Morley	47	C 6
St	Chidlow	42	C 4
LEITHDALE			
Rd	Darlington	66	B 5
LEMANA			
Ct	Nollamara	46	C 5
Rd	Nollamara	46	C 6
LEMMEY			
Rd	Sawyers Valley	54	D 10
LEMNOS			
St	Shenton Park	71	C 3
LEMON			
Ct	High Wycombe	76	C 1
Gr	Armadale	116	A 5
St	Wilson	84	A 6
LEMONGRASS			
Gr	Woodvale	24	D 8
Tce	Ballajura	33	C 4
LEMONTREE			
Gr	Maida Vale	65	A 9
LENA			
Cr	Beechboro	48	E 3
Ct	Greenfields	165	D 1
St	Beckenham	85	B 7
St	Tuart Hill	46	C 9
St	Tuart Hill	46	C 10
LENHAM			
Wy	Marangaroo	32	A 4
LENHAY			
Ct	Willetton	93	D 7
LENNA			
Ct	Karawara	83	C 4
LENNARD			
Gns	Bellevue	50	D 9
St	Dianella	47	C 9
St	Dianella	61	B 1
St	Herne Hill	37	B 6
St	Herne Hill	36	C 6
St	Marmion	30	C 8
LENNON			
St	Morley	47	E 9
LENNOX			
Pl	Hamersley	31	E 10
Rd	Thornlie	95	C 5
Wy	Kinross	19	A 2
LENNOXTOWN			
Rd	Duncraig	31	A 6
LENORE			
Rd	Wanneroo	25	A 5
Rd	Wanneroo	21	A 10
St	Roleystone	108	B 7
LENORI			
Rd	Gooseberry H	77	B 3
LENSHAM			
Pl	Armadale	116	D 8
LENSWOOD			
Rt	Clarkson	14	E 10
LENTARA			
Cr	City Beach	58	D 8
Pl	Forrestdale	125	D 2
LENTONA			
Rd	Alfred Cove	81	E 10
LENTZ			
Wy	Swan C Homes	144	
LENZO			
Ct	Gnangara	26	B 3

L

		Map	Ref.
LEO			
Pl	Mullaloo	23	A 4
Pl	Rockingham	137	B 8
Pl	Spearwood	101	C 4
LEON			
Rd	Dalkeith	81	C 2
LEONARD			
Pl	Bull Creek	92	E 5
St	Victoria Park	73	D 8
Wy	Spearwood	101	C 7
Wy	Yanchep	4	C 5
LEONE			
St	Thornlie	95	A 7
LEONORA			
St	Como	82	E 4
LEONTES			
Wy	Coolbellup	91	E10
LEOPOLD			
Ct	Woodvale	24	A 5
St	Nedlands	71	C10
LEPAS			
St	Heathridge	23	D 1
LEROUX			
Rt	Padbury	31	A 2
LESCHEN			
Wy	Darlington	66	A 2
LESCHENAULTIA			
Pl	Chidlow	42	B 8
St	Greenwood	31	D 5
St	Roleystone	108	A 9
Wy	Forrestfield	76	E 7
LESINA			
Wy	Clarkson	14	D 3
LESLIE			
Pl	Balcatta	46	B 8
Rd	Middle Swan	50	C 4
Rd	Nth Fremantle	80	C 9
Rd	Wandi	123	D 7
St	Cannington	84	D 6
St	Mandurah	164	E 2
St	Mt Lawley	61	C 9
St	Mundaring	54	B 9
St	Serpentine	154	E 4
St	Southern River	105	D 4
LESMURDIE			
Rd	Lesmurdie	87	C 3
Rd	Lesmurdie	77	D10
Rd E	Walliston	78	A10
Rd E	Walliston	77	E10
LE SOUEF			
Dr	Kardinya	91	D 7
LESSAR			
Pl	Lynwood	94	A 4
LESSER			
St	Leederville	60	C10
LESSING			
Pl	South Lake	102	B 7
LESTER			
Dr	Thornlie	95	B 3
LESUEUR			
Ri	Sorrento	30	C 3
LETCHFORD			
St	Samson	91	C 9
LETCHWORTH CENTRE			
Ave	Salter Point	83	B 8
LETHBRIDGE			
Ct	Ashfield	62	E 4
LETITIA			
Rd	Nth Fremantle	80	C10
LETIZIA			
Ct	Yangebup	112	A 1
LETON			
Cl	Halls Head	164	B 4
LETSOM			
Wy	Langford	94	E 1
LEUCOSIA			
Ct	Heathridge	23	E 1

		Map	Ref.
LEUMEAH			
St	Armadale	116	C 3
LEURA			
Ave	Claremont	71	B 9
St	Nedlands	71	E 7
LEVANDER			
Pl	Wilson	84	B 8
LEVANT			
Pl	Kingsley	31	C 3
LEVEANDER			
Pl	Wilson	84	B 8
LEVEN			
Pl	Armadale	116	B 3
Ri	Kinross	19	A 2
LEVER			
St	Marmion	30	C 8
St	Willagee	91	D 4
LEVERBURGH			
St	Ardross	82	C10
LEVEY			
Ri	Winthrop	92	A 4
LEVIATHAN			
Wy	Padbury	30	E 1
Wy	Padbury	23	E10
LEVIEN			
Pl	Winthrop	92	C 5
LEVINE			
Ct	Thornlie	95	C 3
LEVINGTON			
Gns	Parmelia	131	C 8
LEWES			
Rd	Nollamara	46	D 5
LEWIN			
Ct	Gosnells	96	A10
Ct	Gosnells	106	B 1
Wy	Scarborough	58	D 2
LEWINGTON			
Gns	Bibra Lake	102	B 5
St	Beaconsfield	90	E 7
St	Rockingham	137	B 4
LEWIS			
Ave	Curtin Uni	135	
Cl	Bull Creek	93	A 6
Cl	Noranda	48	B 6
Ct	Armadale	116	C 9
Ct	Padbury	23	D10
Ct	Samson	91	D 9
Rd	Forrestfield	86	D 2
Rd	Forrestfield	76	E10
Rd	Kalamunda	77	E 9
Rd	Martin	96	C 6
Rd	Perth Airport	75	C 5
Rd	Serpentine	155	B 2
Rd	Wattle Grove	86	D 3
St	Mandurah	163	C 1
LEWIS JONES			
Cro	Stratton	51	A 3
LEXCEN			
Cr	Ocean Reef	19	A10
LEXIA			
Ave	Upper Swan	166	A 8
LEXINGTON			
Rt	Iluka	18	E 5
LEY			
St	Como	83	A 6
LEYBOURNE			
St	Thornlie	95	B 5
LEYBURN			
Dr	Halls Head	164	C 2
LEYLAND			
St	St James	84	A 3
LEYMAR			
Wy	Willetton	94	A 3
Wy	Willetton	93	E 3
LEYS			
Rd	Wungong	126	E 2
LEYTON			
Ct	Kingsley	24	B10

		Map	Ref.
LIATA			
Ct	Thornlie	95	A 8
LIBERTON			
Pl	Coodanup	165	C 3
Rd	Chidlow	42	E 8
Rd	Wooroloo	43	A 3
LIBRARY			
La	Mundaring	68	B 1
LICHENDALE			
St	Floreat	59	B10
LICHFIELD			
St	Victoria Park	74	A 8
St	Victoria Park	73	E 7
LIDDELL			
Hts	Leeming	92	E 8
St	Girrawheen	32	A 7
LIDDELOW			
Rd	Banjup	123	D 2
Rd	Banjup	113	D 4
Rd	Wandi	123	D 5
St	Kenwick	95	D 2
LIEGE			
St	Cannington	84	E 8
St	Woodlands	59	C 3
LIFFORD			
Rd	Floreat	59	A 8
Wy	Bellevue	65	A 2
LIFU			
Ct	Cooloongup	137	D10
LIGHT			
St	Dianella	47	B 7
St	Dianella	47	D 9
St	Shoalwater	136	D 8
LIGHTBODY			
Rd	Peel Estate	141	D 9
Rd	Peel Estate	149	E 1
LIGHTHOUSE			
Cl	Ballajura	33	C 8
Cl	Coogee	100	D10
Lp	Mindarie	10	B 2
LIKELY			
Pl	Stratton	51	A 4
LILAC			
Gns	Edgewater	24	B 2
Pl	Dianella	47	B 7
Pl	Huntingdale	95	D 8
LILACDALE			
Rd	Innaloo	45	C 7
LILBURNE			
Rd	Duncraig	30	E 3
LILIAN			
Ave	Applecross	82	A 9
Ave	Armadale	116	D 2
Ave	Kelmscott	116	D 2
Gr	Redcliffe	63	A 6
Rd	Maida Vale	76	E 3
LILIKA			
Rd	City Beach	58	E 8
St	Armadale	116	A 6
LILLA			
St	Peppermint Gr	80	E 4
Wy	Lesmurdie	87	D 4
LILLIAN			
Ct	Beldon	23	D 4
St	Cottesloe	80	D 4
LILLIE			
St	Kalamunda	77	C 8
LILLY			
Ct	Spearwood	101	C 7
St	Sth Fremantle	90	D 7
LILYDALE			
Rd	Chidlow	42	C 4
Rd	Chidlow	56	D 1
Rd	Gidgegannup	42	D 2
LILYSTONE			
Rt	Erskine	164	C 6
LIMA			
Cl	Warnbro	145	E 6

		Map	Ref.
LIMB			
Wy	Kardinya	91	E 6
LIME			
Cl	Quinns Rocks	10	B10
Ct	Armadale	115	E 4
St	East Perth	1C	B 2
St	East Perth	73	B 2
St	Nth Fremantle	80	C 9
LIMEKILNS			
Grn	Padbury	30	E 2
LIMER			
Pl	Parmelia	131	B 9
LIMERICK			
Pl	Waterford	83	C 6
LIMOSA			
Gl	Warnbro	145	E 8
LIMPET			
Ct	Mullaloo	23	B 3
LINA			
Cl	Craigie	23	E 4
LINCOLN			
La	Joondalup	19	D 8
Rd	Forrestfield	86	D 2
Rd	Morley	47	D 7
St	Highgate	61	A10
LIND			
Ct	Langford	95	A 1
Ct	Quinns Rocks	10	B10
LINDEMAN			
Hts	Merriwa	11	E10
LINDEN			
Cl	Beckenham	85	B 8
Ct	Kingsley	31	D 1
Gns	Floreat	59	C 9
St	Dianella	47	B 7
Wy	Forrestfield	76	B10
LINDFIELD			
Rt	Kallaroo	23	A 8
St	Balga	46	B 4
LINDHOLM			
Rt	Mindarie	14	B 5
LINDISFARNE			
Wy	Balcatta	46	A 4
LINDLEY			
Ave	Kelmscott	116	D 1
Rd	Halls Head	164	C 1
St	Embleton	62	A 1
St	Halls Head	162	C10
LINDSAY			
Dr	Morley	48	B 6
Pl	Bicton	81	A 6
Pl	Glen Forrest	66	D 4
Rd	Wangara	25	A 7
St	Kalamunda	77	D 5
St	Perth City	1C	A 1
St	Perth City	73	A 1
St	Rockingham	137	D 1
Wy	Padbury	30	D 1
Wy	Padbury	23	D10
LINDWAY			
St	Balga	32	A 9
LINDY			
Wy	Westfield	106	B 8
LINEAR			
Ave	Mullaloo	23	B 3
LINESMANS			
La	Jandakot	103	A 3
LING			
Pl	High Wycombe	64	D 9
LINGFIELD			
Wy	Morley	48	B 9
LINHAM			
Ct	Kenwick	95	C 1
LINK			
Rd	Naval Base	121	B 7
Vw	Cooloongup	138	A 9
Wy	Mullaloo	23	C 3

		Map	Ref.
LINKS			
Ct	Claremont	71	A 6
Ct	Mt Claremont	71	A 7
Rd	Ardross	82	C10
Wy	Halls Head	164	B 1
LINKWATER			
St	Shelley	83	E 8
LINTHORN			
Cr	Greenmount	51	D10
LINTHORNE			
Wy	Balga	32	E10
LINTON			
Ct	Marangaroo	32	A 4
Pl	Morley	48	C 9
Rd	Attadale	81	C 9
St	Byford	126	E 1
St	Byford	135	E 1
St N	Byford	126	D10
LINTOTT			
Wy	Spearwood	101	B 7
LINVILLE			
Ave	Cooloongup	137	D10
St	Falcon	162A	B 4
LINX			
Ct	Alexander Hts	32	E 6
LION			
St	Carlisle	74	B 8
St	Mt Helena	55	C 5
St	Sawyers Valley	55	D 7
LIONEL			
Ct	Duncraig	30	E 8
Rd	Darlington	66	B 1
Rd	Darlington	52	B 1
St	Byford	126	D10
St	Naval Base	121	B 6
LIPSCOMBE			
Ct	Medina	130	E 5
LIQUIDAMBAR			
Hts	Mirrabooka	47	A 2
LISA			
Ct	Karrinyup	45	A 6
Pl	Mt Pleasant	82	D10
LISBON			
Ct	Lynwood	94	A 3
Pl	Warnbro	145	E 5
Wy	Armadale	116	A 5
LISERON			
Wy	Ferndale	84	C 8
LISFORD			
Ave	Two Rocks	2	C 2
Ave	Two Rocks	3	D10
LISLE			
St	Mt Claremont	71	A 6
St	Swanbourne	71	A 6
LISMORE			
Ct	Duncraig	31	B 5
LISSADELL			
St	Floreat	71	C 1
St	Floreat	59	C10
LISSIMAN			
St	Gosnells	96	B 7
LISTER			
Cl	Mosman Park	80	D 7
St	Swan View	51	B 8
LISTON			
Pl	Greenfields	165	C 2
LITHGOW			
Dr	Clarkson	14	C 2
LITHIA			
Rd	E Rockingham	137	E 1
LITIC			
Cl	Bull Creek	93	A 5
LITTLE			
La	Kingsley	31	C 2
Pl	Cardup	135	A10
St	Bayswater	62	B 4
St	Karrinyup	45	B 7
LITTLEDALE			
St	Scarborough	44	E 9

For detailed information regarding the street referencing system used in this book, turn to page 170.

219

L

	Map	Ref.
LITTLEFIELD		
Rd High Wycombe	76	C 2
LITTLE GIBRALTAR		
Rd Karrakatta	71	C 5
LITTLEHAM		
Lp Quinns Rocks	10	B 10
LITTLE HIGH		
St Fremantle	1D	B 5
LITTLE HOWARD		
St Fremantle	1D	C 6
St Fremantle	90	C 6
LITTLE JOHN		
Rd Armadale	116	C 4
LITTLE LAKE		
Ri South Lake	102	D 6
LITTLELYS		
Rd Karragullen	108	E 1
LITTLE MARINE		
Pde Cottesloe	70	C 10
LITTLEMORE		
Rd Orelia	131	A 4
Wy Eden Hill	48	D 9
LITTLE PARRY		
St Perth City	1C	A 1
St Perth City	73	A 1
LITTLE RUSSELL		
St North Perth	61	A 6
LITTLETON		
St Falcon	162A	D 10
LITTLE WALCOTT		
St North Perth	60	E 6
LITTON		
Cl Stirling	45	E 10
LITTORINA		
Ave Heathridge	23	D 1
LIVERPOOL		
Pl Alexander Hts	33	B 5
St Shoalwater	136	C 7
LIVESEY		
St Mundijong	142	E 6
LIVINGSTON		
Dr Canning Vale	104	A 1
Dr Canning Vale	94	A 10
Dr Canning Vale	103	E 1
LIVINGSTONE		
Rd Rockingham	137	B 7
Rd Serpentine	150	C 8
St Beaconsfield	90	D 8
Wy Padbury	23	E 8
LIVONIA		
Pl Mullaloo	23	B 4
Pl Two Rocks	3	B 10
LIWARA		
Pl Greenwood	31	B 6
LLANGI		
Wy Stoneville	40	C 9
LLOYD		
Rd Baldivis	148	A 1
Rd Baldivis	140	A 10
St Cannington	84	D 5
St Midland	50	D 9
St Sth Fremantle	90	D 9
LOARING		
Rd Bickley	88	D 2
St Mandurah	163	A 9
LOBELIA		
Dr Greenmount	65	E 1
St Greenwood	31	D 4
St Mt Claremont	71	B 6
St Roleystone	108	B 8
LOCH		
St Claremont	71	C 9
St North Perth	60	D 5
Vw Craigie	23	E 3
LOCHEE		
St Mosman Park	80	D 5
Wy Bull Creek	93	A 7

	Map	Ref.
LOCHINVAR		
St Madora	160	D 7
LOCHSIDE		
Gr South Lake	102	C 7
LOCKE		
Cr East Fremantle	80	E 10
St Mt Pleasant	82	D 7
Vw Bedfordale	117	A 5
LOCKEPORT		
Ent Mindarie	14	C 6
LOCKETT		
Cst Winthrop	92	C 5
St Coolbellup	101	C 1
St Coolbellup	91	C 10
LOCKEVILLE		
Cl Beldon	23	D 2
LOCKHART		
Pl Gosnells	106	D 1
Rd Kelmscott	116	C 1
St Como	83	A 3
St Como	83	A 6
LOCKIEL		
Wy Armadale	116	B 1
LOCKSLEY		
Ave Armadale	116	C 6
LOCKWOOD		
Rd Beechina	57	C 2
Rd Beechina	43	D 10
Rd Bickley	89	C 4
Rd Hacketts Gully	79	D 9
St Yokine	60	D 2
St Yokine	46	D 10
LOCKYER		
Ct Duncraig	31	A 9
Ri Roleystone	107	E 9
LOCOCK		
St Redcliffe	62	E 7
LODER		
Wy Sth Guildford	63	B 4
LODESWORTH		
Rd Balga	46	B 3
LODWICK		
St Willagee	91	D 4
LOEP		
Ct Parmelia	131	A 8
LOFOTEN		
Wy Ferndale	84	D 8
LOFTIA		
Vw Clarkson	11	D 10
LOFTIE		
Gns Bellevue	50	D 9
LOFTIES		
St Forrestdale	114	E 6
LOFTUS		
St Leederville	60	D 10
St Nedlands	71	C 8
LOFTY		
Ct Woodvale	24	B 5
LOGAN		
Cl Armadale	115	E 5
Ct Padbury	30	C 1
Rd Leeming	93	A 10
Wy Noranda	47	C 6
LOGGER		
Rd Karragullen	109	C 6
LOGPINE		
Cr Westfield	106	C 8
LOGUE		
Ct Balga	32	B 8
Ct Heathridge	19	B 9
Rd Millendon	168	A 10
LOIRE		
Ce Greenfields	163	D 10
LOLA		
Pl Mandurah	163	A 9
LOMA		
St Cottesloe	80	D 2

	Map	Ref.
LOMATIA		
Wy Forrestfield	76	C 7
LOMBARD		
St Leeming	93	B 8
LOMBARDY		
St Woodlands	59	B 4
LOMOND		
Rd Greenwood	31	B 4
LONCAR		
Ri Gwelup	45	C 6
LONDON		
St Joondanna	60	D 4
St Mt Hawthorn	60	D 5
Wy Bateman	92	E 7
LONE PINE		
Wy Greenmount	51	B 9
LONG		
St Hilton	91	A 9
LONG BEACH		
Pro Mindarie	14	B 6
LONGFELLOW		
Rd Gooseberry H	77	D 4
LONGFIELD		
Rd Maddington	96	A 4
LONGFORD		
Pl Karrinyup	45	A 2
LONGHURST		
Wy Queens Park	84	E 2
LONG ISLAND		
Ps Connolly	19	B 7
LONGREACH		
Pde Coogee	101	A 10
LONG REEF		
Pl Hillarys	23	A 10
LONGROYD		
St Mt Lawley	61	A 7
LONGSON		
St Hamilton Hill	91	C 10
LONGSTAFF		
Gns Dianella	47	A 7
LONNIE		
St Daglish	71	D 3
LONSDALE		
St Yokine	60	E 2
LOOKOUT		
Rd Kalamunda	77	A 8
LOORANAH		
St Armadale	116	E 4
LORD		
St Bassendean	49	B 10
St Beechboro	49	B 3
St Bentley	84	A 5
St Eden Hill	49	B 9
St Highgate	61	B 10
St Lockridge	49	B 6
St Mt Lawley	61	C 9
St Perth City	73	B 2
St Perth City	1C	B 3
St West Swan	49	C 2
St West Swan	35	C 10
St Whiteman	35	C 4
St Whiteman	28	C 9
LORD FURY		
Ct Byford	126	A 7
LORD MASELLE		
Pl Mariginiup	17	E 7
LORENZO		
St Thornlie	95	B 4
LORETS		
Grn Mirrabooka	33	B 10
LORETTO		
St Subiaco	72	A 2
LORI		
Rd Kelmscott	117	B 1
LORIAN		
Rd Gnangara	26	A 3

	Map	Ref.
LORIENT		
Cl Warnbro	145	C 6
LORIKEET		
Ct Stirling	45	E 7
Hts Ballajura	33	D 6
Lp High Wycombe	76	B 1
Wy Gosnells	106	A 3
Wy Gosnells	105	E 3
LORILET		
Ct Ballajura	34	A 8
LORIMER		
Rd Munster	112	A 7
Rd Wattleup	112	A 9
Rd Yangebup	112	A 3
LORIS		
Wy Kardinya	92	A 7
LORNE		
Pl Mandurah	165	B 4
Rd Duncraig	31	A 8
LORRAINE		
Pl Hamilton Hill	101	B 1
St Carine	45	A 1
LORRIKEET		
Gr Wungong	116	B 10
LORRIMAR		
Pl Murdoch	92	C 7
LOTHIAN		
Rd Canning Vale	94	A 10
Rd Canning Vale	103	E 1
St Floreat	59	C 8
LOTON		
Ave Bellevue	50	D 9
Ave Midland	50	D 9
Rd Claremont	81	C 1
Rd Millendon	168	B 10
St Woodlands	59	B 4
LOTUS		
Cl Coogee	100	E 9
Cl Craigie	23	E 6
St Madora	160	D 8
LOUDEN		
St Balga	32	A 10
LOUGHTON		
Cl Hazelmere	64	A 2
Wy Balga	32	C 9
LOUISA		
St Sth Fremantle	90	C 8
LOUISE		
Pl Gnangara	25	E 4
St Nedlands	71	D 10
St Rockingham	137	C 6
LOUKES		
St Fremantle	90	D 4
LOURDES		
St Lesmurdie	87	D 1
LOURENS		
Dl Winthrop	92	A 4
LOUTH		
Rd Floreat	59	B 9
LOVATT		
Ct Leeming	93	C 10
LOVE		
St Cloverdale	75	A 3
St Myaree	91	E 2
LOVEGROVE		
Cl Mt Claremont	71	B 5
Ct Byford	135	D 1
Wy Morley	47	D 9
LOVEKIN		
Dr Kings Park	72	B 6
LOVELL		
Wy Bayswater	48	D 10
LOVETT		
Pl Noranda	48	B 6
Pl Queens Park	85	A 4
St Scarborough	44	A 8
LOWAN		
Pl Karawara	83	D 4
St Thornlie	95	A 4

	Map	Ref.
LOWANA		
Pl Iluka	19	A 4
LOWANNA		
Wy Armadale	116	B 4
Wy City Beach	58	D 8
LOWANNAA		
Rd Martin	106	E 2
LOWDEN		
Ct Lynwood	94	C 4
Rd Greenfields	163	D 10
LOWE		
St Karrinyup	44	D 7
LOWEN		
Pl Stirling	46	A 6
LOWER PARK		
Rd Maddington	96	A 2
LOWES		
St Cloverdale	74	E 4
Wy Padbury	23	E 9
LOWLANDS		
Rd Mundijong	150	B 7
Rd Peel Estate	150	B 7
Rd Peel Estate	149	E 6
LOWRIE		
Gr Leeming	93	A 8
LOWRY		
St Shelley	83	E 8
LOWTH		
Rd Beckenham	85	C 8
LOWTHER		
Tce Nollamara	46	E 8
LOXHAM		
Pl Greenwood	31	E 5
LOXLEIGH		
Wy Kiara	48	E 7
LOXTON		
St Mandurah	165	A 2
LOXWOOD		
Rd Balga	46	E 3
LOYOLA		
Wy Attadale	81	D 9
LUBA		
Rd Innaloo	45	C 9
LUBBERDINA		
Ct Gosnells	95	E 7
LUCAS		
Rd Swan View	51	B 7
St Willagee	91	C 1
LUCCA		
Ct Coogee	101	A 9
St Churchlands	59	B 5
LUCCOMBE		
Wy Karrinyup	45	A 2
LUCERNE		
Gns Edgewater	20	A 9
LUCICH		
St Kelmscott	106	E 8
LUCINE		
Ct Heathridge	19	D 10
LUCIUS		
Rd Hamilton Hill	100	E 2
LUCKEN		
Pl Bibra Lake	102	D 3
LUCKHURST		
Dr Mandurah	165	C 1
Dr Mandurah	163	C 10
LUCKNOW		
Pl West Perth	72	C 1
LUCRAFT		
Gns Winthrop	92	B 5
LUCY		
St Gosnells	96	C 10
LUDERMAN		
Rd Noranda	47	C 4
LUDFORD		
St Balcatta	46	A 4

220

For detailed information regarding the street referencing system used in this book, turn to page 170.

M

		Map	Ref.
LUDGATE			
Wy	Gwelup	45	C 4
LUDLANDS			
St	Morley	48	A 8
LUDLOW			
Pl	Lynwood	94	D 1
Wy	Warnbro	145	C 8
LUDWIG			
Pl	Duncraig	31	A 4
LUFF			
Cr	Attadale	81	D 8
LUFFE			
Ct	Swan View	51	B 9
LUFFINGHAM			
St	Melville	91	C 2
LUGG			
Ce	Winthrop	92	C 5
Pl	Casuarina	132	A 8
LUGGER			
Pl	Yanchep	4	C 3
LUISINI			
Rd	Wangara	25	B 8
LUISTA			
Ct	Yanchep	4	E 2
LUITA			
St	Wembley Dns	58	E 5
LUKE			
Ct	Thornlie	95	A 7
LUKIN			
Ave	Darlington	66	B 6
Dr	Butler	11	B 7
Pl	Bull Creek	92	B 4
Rd	Hillarys	30	B 3
Wy	Bassendean	63	A 1
Wy	Bassendean	49	A 10
LUKS			
Ce	Winthrop	92	C 5
LULWORTH			
Pl	Marangaroo	32	C 6
LUMEAH			
Ct	Darlington	65	E 3
LUMSDEN			
Rd	Karnup	157	B 8
Rd	Wangara	24	E 6
LUNAR			
Ct	Mullaloo	23	C 4
Wy	Beckenham	85	C 6
LUNDY			
Ce	Kiara	48	D 6
LUNE			
Cl	Beechboro	48	D 3
LUPIN			
Cl	Thornlie	95	A 8
Ct	Wanneroo	24	E 1
LUPINO			
St	Mundijong	143	C 10
LUPTON			
Wy	Lockridge	49	A 6
LURGAN			
Pl	Merriwa	11	C 10
LURNEA			
Pl	Karawara	83	C 4
LUSCOMBE			
St	Kewdale	74	D 6
Wy	Coogee	100	E 10
LUSHINGTON			
Dr	Padbury	30	C 1
LUSITANIA			
Ct	Port Kennedy	156	D 4
LUTEY			
Ave	Daglish	71	E 2
LUTH			
Ave	Daglish	71	D 3
LUTON			
Cl	Ballajura	34	A 8
LUTZ			
Ct	Gosnells	96	A 9

		Map	Ref.
LUYER			
Ave	Beckenham	85	D 4
Ave	E Cannington	85	C 3
LYAL			
Ct	Thornlie	95	B 7
LYALL			
St	Ascot	62	E 8
St	Redcliffe	62	E 8
St	Shenton Park	71	E 5
St	South Perth	72	D 7
LYDD			
Cl	Marangaroo	32	A 4
St	Gosnells	95	E 9
LYDDEN			
St	Maddington	96	B 6
LYDIA			
Ct	Greenwood	31	C 5
Pl	Greenfields	163	D 9
LYELL			
Gr	Woodvale	24	B 4
LYELTA			
St	Falcon	162A	E 9
LYGNERN			
Cr	Kallaroo	23	B 6
LYGON			
Ct	North Lake	102	A 2
LYMBURNER			
Dr	Hillarys	30	B 2
LYMINGE			
St	Gosnells	95	E 8
LYMON			
Rd	Lakelands	161	C 8
LYN			
Cl	Riverton	83	E 9
LYNAS			
Wy	Quinns Rocks	10	B 10
LYNCH			
Pl	Hilton	91	B 9
LYNDA			
Cr	Cooloongup	137	D 9
St	Falcon	162A	C 2
LYNDALE			
Ave	Lynwood	94	B 3
St	Gwelup	45	C 5
LYNDHURST			
Cr	Ferndale	84	C 9
Rd	Kalamunda	77	D 9
St	Dianella	47	C 8
LYNDOCH			
Cr	Greenwood	31	D 5
LYNDON			
Ct	Heathridge	19	B 9
St	Nollamara	46	C 8
LYNE			
St	Gosnells	95	E 9
LYNEHAM			
Pl	Bassendean	62	D 1
LYNESS			
Pl	Ferndale	84	D 9
LYNMOUTH			
Rd	Dianella	47	A 9
LYNN			
St	Hilton	91	A 9
St	Trigg	44	C 4
LYNSTEAD			
St	Beckenham	85	C 7
LYNTON			
Ct	Yanchep	4	D 5
Rd	Willetton	93	E 3
St	Doubleview	59	A 1
St	Doubleview	45	A 10
St	Mt Hawthorn	60	B 6
St	Swanbourne	70	C 4
LYNWOOD			
Ave	Lynwood	94	D 1
LYNX			
Pl	Rockingham	137	B 8

		Map	Ref.
LYON			
Pl	Hovea	52	E 10
Rd	Banjup	123	A 1
Rd	Banjup	113	A 9
Rd	Wandi	123	A 8
LYONIA			
Ct	Forrestfield	76	D 9
LYONS			
Cl	Noranda	48	B 4
Ct	Cooloongup	137	D 10
Ct	Heathridge	19	B 9
St	Beckenham	85	C 9
St	Cottesloe	70	D 10
St	Rivervale	74	C 4
LYRE			
St	Stirling	45	E 6
LYREBIRD			
Lp	Armadale	116	B 3
Sq	Ballajura	33	E 6
Wy	Thornlie	95	A 3
LYSANDER			
Dr	Heathridge	19	C 9
LYSONS			
Wy	Bateman	92	D 5
LYSTER			
Rd	Jarrahdale	153	A 5
LYTHAM			
Ct	Meadow Sprgs	163	D 6
Me	Connolly	19	C 8
LYTHE			
Pl	Willetton	93	E 4

M

		Map	Ref.
MABEL			
Rd	Carmel	87	D 7
Rd	Lesmurdie	87	C 8
St	Kensington	73	C 10
St	North Perth	60	E 6
MABENA			
Pl	Ocean Reef	18	E 7
MABERLY			
Cr	Rossmoyne	93	A 3
MABLEY			
Ct	Greenwood	31	D 5
MACADAM			
Pl	Balcatta	45	E 2
MACALISTER			
Gns	Mirrabooka	33	A 10
MACAO			
Rd	High Wycombe	64	B 9
MACARTHUR			
Ave	Padbury	23	E 7
Ct	Willetton	94	A 4
St	Cottesloe	80	C 5
St	Morley	48	A 7
MACAU			
Pl	Warnbro	145	E 5
MACAULAY			
Ave	Duncraig	31	B 4
MACAW			
Gns	Ballajura	33	D 5
MACBEAN			
Pl	Duncraig	31	A 6
MACCABEAN			
Ave	Dianella	46	E 9
MACDONALD			
Ave	Padbury	23	D 9
Rd	Applecross	82	C 5
MACDOUGALL			
Ri	Duncraig	31	A 6
MACEDON			
Pl	Craigie	23	C 7
MACEDONIA			
Pl	North Perth	60	E 7
St	Naval Base	121	B 8

		Map	Ref.
MACEWAN			
St	Leederville	60	C 10
MACEY			
St	East Perth	73	C 2
MACFARLANE			
Ri	Duncraig	31	A 5
MACGREGOR			
Dr	Padbury	23	D 10
MACHIE			
St	Wangara	24	E 7
MACHIN			
Pl	Beckenham	85	A 10
MACINTOSH			
Ri	Duncraig	30	E 5
MACK			
Pl	High Wycombe	76	B 2
MACKAY			
Cr	Gosnells	96	A 10
Pl	Cooloongup	137	E 9
St	Kewdale	75	B 7
Wy	Hillarys	23	C 10
MACKAYA			
Ct	South Lake	102	D 5
MACKENZIE			
Pl	Beechboro	48	E 2
Rd	Applecross	82	C 6
MACKEREL			
Ct	Sorrento	30	C 4
MACKIE			
Rd	Roleystone	107	E 9
St	Victoria Park	73	D 8
MACKINLAY			
Pl	Winthrop	92	B 5
MACLAGGAN			
Tn	Coodanup	165	C 3
MACLAGLAN			
St	Jandakot	102	D 10
MACLEAN			
Wy	Greenfields	163	E 8
MACLEAY			
Dr	Padbury	23	E 10
MACLENNAN			
Rd	Applecross	82	C 5
MACLEOD			
Rd	Applecross	82	C 7
MACMILLAN			
Ri	Duncraig	31	A 5
MACMORRIS			
Wy	Spearwood	101	B 4
MACNAB			
Ri	Duncraig	31	A 6
MACQUARIE			
Ave	Padbury	23	D 8
Wy	Willetton	94	A 5
MACRAE			
Rd	Applecross	82	C 5
MACROBERTSON			
Dr	Perth Airport	63	B 8
MADANA			
Pl	Craigie	23	C 7
MADDEN			
Wy	Brentwood	92	E 2
Wy	Parmelia	131	C 6
MADDERSON			
Rd	High Wycombe	76	C 2
MADDINGTON			
Rd	Maddington	96	B 2
Rd	Maddington	95	E 4
Rd	Orange Grove	96	C 2
Rd	Orange Grove	86	D 10
MADDOCK			
St	Mundaring	68	B 1
MADDOX			
Cr	Melville	91	C 3
Pl	Parmelia	131	B 6

		Map	Ref.
MADEIRA			
Ave	Beechboro	48	E 4
Pl	Safety Bay	137	B 10
Rd	Lynwood	94	A 2
MADELEINE			
Ct	North Lake	102	A 2
Ct	Two Rocks	2	B 1
MADELEY			
St	Landsdale	25	E 9
MADER			
Cr	Armadale	116	E 2
Rd	Mundijong	143	A 7
MADERA			
Pl	Lesmurdie	87	B 2
MADEW			
St	Roleystone	107	E 7
MADISON			
Cl	Middle Swan	50	E 4
Cl	Cooloongup	137	E 7
St	Canning Vale	94	D 6
MADORA BEACH			
Rd	Madora	160	C 7
MADRONA			
Cr	Greenwood	31	C 4
MAGAZINE			
Ct	Munster	110	E 2
MAGELLAN			
Cl	Waikiki	145	C 4
MAGENTA			
Cl	Thornlie	95	A 7
Cl	Waikiki	145	E 2
Pl	Riverton	94	A 1
Ri	Clarkson	14	D 1
Ri	Clarkson	11	D 10
MAGENUP			
Dr	Wandi	123	B 6
MAGILL			
Pl	Coodanup	165	C 4
MAGNA			
Ce	Mirrabooka	33	B 10
MAGNET			
Rd	Lynwood	94	C 6
MAGNOLIA			
Cl	Ballajura	33	C 6
Gns	Yangebup	101	D 10
Me	Edgewater	24	A 2
Ri	Halls Head	164	B 4
St	North Perth	60	E 7
Wy	Forrestfield	76	C 9
MAGOG			
Ct	Greenfields	165	D 2
MAGPIE			
Ct	High Wycombe	76	C 1
Ct	Yangebup	102	A 9
Pl	Gosnells	105	E 3
Pl	Wungong	116	B 9
Ri	Ballajura	34	A 8
MAGRO			
Pl	Morley	48	C 7
MAGUIRE			
Ave	Beechboro	49	A 4
Rd	Helena Valley	65	C 6
MAHARA			
Rd	Kelmscott	106	E 5
MAHDI			
St	Bayswater	62	A 6
MAHLBERG			
Ave	Woodlands	59	B 1
MAHOGANY			
Ct	Woodvale	24	C 5
Dr	Halls Head	164	B 4
Rd	Morley	48	C 5
St	Maddington	96	C 5
MAHONIA			
Ct	Duncraig	30	E 6
Wy	Forrestfield	76	C 9
MAIDA VALE			
Rd	High Wycombe	76	B 2
Rd	Maida Vale	76	D 2

M

		Map	Ref.
MAIDOS			
St	Ashfield	62	D 4
MAIDSTONE			
Wy	Morley	48	C 9
MAIKAI			
Pl	Kewdale	74	D 9
MAIN			
St	Balcatta	46	B 8
St	Osborne Park	60	B 3
MAINSAIL			
Cr	Waikiki	145	B 3
Dr	Ocean Reef	22	E 1
Dr	Ocean Reef	18	E 10
MAINSTONE			
Pl	Hamilton Hill	91	A 10
MAIR			
Pl	Mullaloo	23	A 5
MAIS			
Ct	Bateman	92	D 4
MAISIE			
Cr	Wembley Dns	59	A 4
St	Millendon	29	D 8
MAITLAND			
Cl	Cooloongup	137	E 9
Cl	Halls Head	164	C 4
Pl	Thornlie	95	B 8
Rd	Balga	46	B 1
Rd	Balga	32	B 10
Ri	Woodvale	24	A 5
MAJELLA			
Rd	Balga	46	D 4
MAJESTIC			
Cl	Applecross	82	B 4
Cl	Port Kennedy	156	C 4
Ct	Thornlie	95	D 8
Pde	Dianella	47	A 6
Pl	Connolly	19	A 6
MAKIN			
Ct	Byford	126	D 9
MALABAR			
Cr	Craigie	23	C 6
Rd	Sawyers Valley	55	B 9
Wy	Bibra Lake	101	D 4
MALABOR			
Me	Halls Head	164	B 6
MALACARI			
Ct	Hamilton Hill	91	B 10
MALACCA			
Wy	Mindarie	14	C 6
MALAGA			
Dr	Malaga	47	E 1
Dr	Noranda	48	A 4
Dr	Noranda	47	E 4
MALAK			
Ct	Wanneroo	20	E 10
MALARKEY			
Rd	Byford	135	A 1
Rd	Byford	126	A 10
MALAWI			
Ct	Joondalup	19	C 2
MALAYA			
Rd	Swanbourne	70	D 8
MALBA			
Cr	Dianella	46	E 9
MALBELING			
Cl	Hillman	137	E 5
MALCOLM			
Ct	Noranda	47	C 4
Rd	Maddington	95	E 2
St	Fremantle	90	D 3
St	North Beach	44	C 1
St	Spearwood	101	C 4
St	West Perth	72	D 2
St	West Perth	1C	D 3
MALDEN			
Rd	Kingsley	31	B 2
MALDON			
Pl	Parklands	161	A 10
Wy	Mt Pleasant	92	D 1

		Map	Ref.
MALE			
Ct	Winthrop	92	A 4
MALEY			
Ct	Ashfield	62	E 4
St	Ashfield	62	E 4
St	Bull Creek	93	B 6
MALIBU			
Rd	Safety Bay	145	A 2
Rd	Safety Bay	137	C 10
MALINDI			
St	Willetton	93	C 3
MALLAIG			
Pl	Warwick	31	C 7
MALLAND			
St	Myaree	92	A 2
MALLARD			
Ave	Bibra Lake	102	C 3
Ri	Kingsley	24	E 10
St	Thornlie	95	A 6
Wy	Cannington	84	D 5
MALLEE			
Ct	Thornlie	94	E 9
Dr	Karnup	159	D 5
Pl	Armadale	116	D 4
Pl	Morley	48	D 5
Wy	Forrestfield	76	C 8
MALLION			
St	Embleton	62	A 2
MALLOW			
Wy	Forrestfield	76	D 10
MALONE			
Ct	Thornlie	95	B 4
Me	Clarkson	14	C 1
Rd	Swan View	51	D 8
St	Willagee	91	C 5
MALONEY			
Wy	City Beach	58	D 4
MALOY			
Ct	Hamilton Hill	101	C 3
MALSBURY			
St	Bicton	81	B 9
MALTARA			
Pl	Iluka	18	E 5
MALTARRA			
Pl	Nollamara	46	D 4
St	Nollamara	46	D 4
MALTON			
Ct	Dianella	47	C 9
Pl	City Beach	58	E 6
MALU			
Cl	Ballajura	33	C 5
Ct	Greenwood	31	D 4
Ct	Westfield	106	C 8
MALUMBA			
Cr	Lesmurdie	77	B 10
MALVERN			
Rd	Rivervale	74	A 3
Ri	Greenfields	163	E 9
St	West Swan	35	E 9
MALVOLIO			
Rd	Coolbellup	101	E 2
MAMILLIUS			
St	Coolbellup	101	E 1
MAMO			
Pl	Greenwood	31	C 5
MANAKOORA			
Ri	Sorrento	30	B 3
MANAPOURI			
Mr	Joondalup	19	C 1
MANBARI			
Cr	Wanneroo	20	C 8
MANBERRY			
Wy	Yangebup	112	A 1
Wy	Yangebup	102	A 10
Wy	Yangebup	111	E 1
MANBY			
St	Gosnells	95	E 8

		Map	Ref.
MANCHESTER			
St	Victoria Park	73	E 9
MANDAL			
Cl	Mindarie	14	B 5
MANDALA			
Cr	Bateman	92	D 4
MANDALAY			
Pl	Craigie	23	D 7
MANDARA			
Ct	Duncraig	31	B 8
MANDARIN			
Ct	Craigie	23	E 4
Rd	Maddington	96	A 1
Wy	Armadale	116	A 5
MANDERS			
Wy	Singleton	160	D 4
MANDEVILLA			
St	Forrestfield	76	C 7
MANDFIELD			
Wy	Parmelia	131	B 7
MANDOGALUP			
Rd	Mandogalup	122	B 4
MANDOO			
Rd	Shoalwater	136	D 9
MANDOON			
Cl	Darlington	65	E 4
MANDORA			
Wy	Riverton	93	D 1
MANDURAH			
By	Mandurah	165	A 5
Rd	Baldivis	146	C 4
Rd	Baldivis	146	C 9
Rd	Baldivis	138	D 7
Rd	E Rockingham	138	B 1
Rd	E Rockingham	130	B 9
Rd	Karnup	159	A 7
Rd	Karnup	157	B 5
Rd	Karnup	160	E 4
Rd	Kwinana Beach	130	B 7
Rd	Leda	138	C 5
Tce	Mandurah	163	A 9
Tce	Mandurah	164	E 1
MANGANO			
Pl	Wanneroo	24	D 4
MANGINI			
St	Morley	47	E 9
MANGLES			
St	Warnbro	145	C 8
MANGO			
Pl	Dianella	46	E 5
MANGOWINE			
Cl	Heathridge	23	E 2
MANIANA			
Pl	Queens Park	85	B 3
Rd N	Queens Park	85	B 3
Rd S	Queens Park	85	A 3
MANILA			
Pl	Warnbro	145	C 8
MANILDRA			
Dr	Mandurah	165	B 4
MANITO			
Ct	Joondalup	19	C 1
MANITOBA			
Pl	Jandakot	112	E 3
MANJIRI			
Dr	Glen Forrest	66	D 4
MANLEY			
St	Cannington	84	D 5
MANLY			
Cr	Warnbro	145	E 7
Pl	Yanchep	3	E 10
Vl	Kallaroo	23	A 8
MANN			
Ct	Winthrop	92	A 5
Pl	Roleystone	107	E 9
St	Cottesloe	80	E 1
St	Cottesloe	70	E 10
St	Mundaring	54	B 10

		Map	Ref.
Wy	Bassendean	62	E 1
Wy	Bassendean	48	E 10
MANNA			
Cl	Mirrabooka	47	B 2
Ct	South Lake	102	E 3
Gns	Halls Head	164	B 7
MANNAW			
Pl	Hillman	137	E 7
MANNERS			
Pl	Bull Creek	92	E 4
St	E Victoria Pk	83	E 2
MANNING			
Ave	Gosnells	106	D 1
Ave	Martin	106	D 1
Rd	Como	83	A 6
Rd	Manning	83	B 5
Rd	Waterford	83	D 5
Rd	Wilson	84	A 6
Ri	Woodvale	24	B 5
St	Fremantle	90	E 1
St	Mosman Park	80	E 7
St	Scarborough	44	D 9
Tce	South Perth	73	B 7
MANNION			
Wy	Kardinya	91	E 9
MANNITE			
Pl	Stirling	45	E 7
MANNOCK			
Rd	Bentley	84	B 5
MANOFF			
Rd	Balcatta	46	C 8
MANOLAS			
Wy	Girrawheen	32	A 8
MANOOKA			
Wy	Kalamunda	77	D 9
MANOR			
Ct	Westfield	106	B 9
Gns	Coodanup	165	D 5
MANSARD			
Rd	Willetton	94	A 3
Rd	Willetton	93	E 3
MANSEL			
Pl	Duncraig	31	A 8
MANSELL			
St	Morley	47	E 9
MANSON			
St	Swan View	51	B 8
MANSTON			
Rd	Thornlie	95	B 5
MANTON			
Ct	Hamersley	31	E 9
MANTUA			
Cr	Churchlands	59	B 6
MANUEL			
Cr	Redcliffe	62	E 9
MANUKA			
Pl	Duncraig	30	E 6
MANUS			
Pl	Lynwood	94	A 4
MANXMAN			
Ct	Padbury	30	E 1
MANXTON			
Wy	Lynwood	94	C 2
MANYA			
Cl	Greenfields	165	D 2
MANYARRA			
Tn	Joondalup	19	C 2
MAPLE			
Gr	Halls Head	164	B 5
Me	Duncraig	31	B 8
Pl	Maddington	96	C 4
St	Greenwood	31	C 4
St	Lathlain	74	A 4
Vs	Parmelia	131	C 7
MAPLE HILL			
Ct	Woodvale	24	B 7
MAPLETON			
Pl	Duncraig	31	A 3
St	Stirling	45	E 10

		Map	Ref.
MAPLIN			
Pl	Rossmoyne	93	A 1
MAPSTONE			
Gns	Murdoch	92	B 2
MAQUIRE			
Rd	Hillarys	30	C 2
Wy	Bull Creek	93	B 5
MARADU			
Cr	Wanneroo	20	D 9
MARANDA			
Gr	Ocean Reef	19	A 7
MARANEL			
St	Falcon	162A	D 10
MARANGAROO			
Dr	Ballajura	33	C 6
Dr	Girrawheen	32	A 3
Dr	Koondoola	32	E 6
MARANON			
Cr	Beechboro	48	E 3
MARAPANA			
Rd	City Beach	58	D 4
MARAROA			
Ct	Padbury	30	E 1
MARBAN			
Wy	Wattleup	121	D 2
MARCH			
St	Gwelup	45	C 5
St	Spearwood	101	B 4
MARCHAMLEY			
Pl	Carlisle	74	C 8
St	Carlisle	74	B 6
MARCHANT			
Dr	Bibra Lake	102	D 3
Rd	Samson	91	C 4
Wy	Morley	62	A 1
MARCHESI			
St	Kewdale	75	B 3
MARCHETTI			
Rd	Pickering Bk	89	A 9
MARCON			
St	Two Rocks	2	C 3
MARCONI			
St	Morley	48	C 8
MARCUS			
Ave	Booragoon	92	B 2
MARDA			
Wy	Nollamara	46	D 3
MARDAN			
Ct	Silver Sands	163	C 3
MARDELLA			
St	Coolbinia	60	E 4
MARDEN			
Pl	Roleystone	108	B 7
Rd	Thornlie	95	C 3
St	Marangaroo	32	A 4
MARDI			
Ct	Armadale	116	C 8
MARDIE			
St	Beaconsfield	90	D 7
MARDOLF			
St	Lesmurdie	87	B 2
MAREE			
Cl	Byford	126	D 9
Pl	Gnangara	26	A 4
St	Hamersley	32	A 10
St	Hamersley	31	E 10
MARGARET			
Pl	Heathridge	19	B 9
Rd	Hovea	52	E 8
St	Ashfield	62	E 4
St	Cottesloe	70	C 10
St	Gosnells	105	E 1
St	Maylands	62	A 8
St	Midland	50	C 6
St	Southern River	105	E 4
St	Waterman	30	C 10
St	Wilson	84	B 8
Tce	Walliston	87	E 1

222   **For detailed information regarding the street referencing system used in this book, turn to page 170.**

M

		Map	Ref.
MARGATE			
Pl	Marangaroo	32	B 3
MARGERY			
Cl	Beldon	23	D 3
Rd	High Wycombe	64	B 9
MARGINATA			
Pl	Wanneroo	24	D 1
MARIA			
Pl	Mandurah	165	B 3
St	Mandurah	165	A 3
MARIAN			
Ave	Armadale	116	C 6
St	Innaloo	45	B 10
St	Leederville	60	D 7
MARIA			
Cl	Maddington	96	D 3
MARIANNE			
Wy	Alexander Hts	33	A 5
MARIANO			
Ct	Rockingham	137	D 6
MARIE			
Wy	Kalamunda	77	B 7
MARIGINIUP			
Rd	Mariginiup	21	A 3
MARIGOLD			
Gr	Ballajura	33	C 5
Pl	Waikiki	145	C 2
Pl	Yangebup	101	E 10
MARILLANA			
Dr	Golden Bay	158	D 8
MARIMBA			
Cr	City Beach	58	E 9
MARIMONT			
St	Hilton	91	B 7
MARIN			
Vw	Mindarie	14	B 3
MARINA			
Blvd	Ocean Reef	23	B 1
MARINE			
Pde	Cottesloe	80	C 4
Pde	Cottesloe	70	C 10
Pde	Swanbourne	70	C 9
Tce	Fremantle	1D	B 6
Tce	Fremantle	90	C 6
Tce	Marmion	30	C 7
Tce	Sorrento	30	C 7
Tce	Sth Fremantle	90	C 9
MARINER			
Pl	Cooloongup	137	D 8
Pl	Halls Head	164	B 2
MARINERS			
Ce	Ballajura	33	C 8
MARINO			
Pl	Waterford	83	C 6
MARIO			
Ct	Lesmurdie	87	D 4
Wy	Craigie	23	E 6
MARION			
Ct	Beldon	23	E 3
Rd	Maddington	96	A 1
St	Eden Hill	49	A 9
St	Midland	50	C 9
Wy	Gooseberry H	77	C 2
MARITA			
Rd	Nedlands	71	C 10
MARITANA			
Rd	Kallaroo	23	B 7
Rd	Malaga	48	A 3
St	Morley	48	C 8
MARITIME			
Ave	Kardinya	92	A 9
Rd	Silver Sands	163	B 5
Tce	Coogee	110	E 1
MARJORIE			
Ave	Riverton	83	E 3
Ave	Shelley	83	E 9
Pde	Rockingham	137	B 5
St	Mullaloo	23	A 5

		Map	Ref.
MARK			
Pl	Spearwood	101	C 4
Pl	Thornlie	95	B 7
MARKALING			
Cl	Hillman	137	E 6
MARKER			
Rd	Ocean Reef	23	A 1
Rd	Ocean Reef	19	A 10
MARKET			
St	Fremantle	1D	B 5
St	Fremantle	90	B 5
St	Guildford	63	C 1
St	Guildford	49	C 10
St	Kensington	73	C 9
St	Rockingham	137	C 6
St	West Perth	1C	D 1
St	West Perth	72	D 1
MARKHAM			
Pl	Bentley	84	C 4
Rd	High Wycombe	64	C 9
Wy	Balga	32	D 10
Wy	High Wycombe	64	C 9
Wy	Swan View	51	C 8
Wy	Swan View	51	C 9
MARKS			
Pl	Morley	48	C 6
Pl	Rockingham	137	B 5
MARLANDY			
Ct	Woodvale	24	B 6
MARLBORO			
Rd	Swan View	51	C 8
MARLBOROUGH			
Cl	Greenfields	163	E 10
St	East Perth	61	B 10
St	Maylands	61	E 6
St	Mosman Park	80	E 7
MARLEE			
Ct	Langford	94	E 1
Rd	Parklands	161	A 10
MARLENE			
Wy	Bibra Lake	102	C 2
MARLEY			
Wy	Warnbro	145	D 8
MARLIN			
Ct	Dalkeith	81	B 2
Pl	Beldon	23	C 4
Wy	Golden Bay	158	E 9
MARLOCK			
Ct	Forrestfield	76	C 10
Ct	Mirrabooka	32	E 10
Ct	Morley	48	D 5
Dr	Greenwood	31	D 4
Pl	Karnup	159	D 9
Pl	Woodlands	59	B 2
Rd	Woodlands	59	B 2
MARLOO			
Rd	Balga	46	C 5
Rd	Greenmount	51	C 10
MARLOW			
St	Wembley	59	D 9
Wy	Thornlie	95	B 5
MARLOWE			
Pl	Munster	101	B 10
MARMALADE			
Wy	Maddington	96	A 1
MARMION			
Ave	Beldon	23	C 3
Ave	Burns	18	E 1
Ave	Butler	10	E 3
Ave	Clarkson	14	C 5
Ave	Craigie	23	C 6
Ave	Currambine	19	A 3
Ave	Eglinton	7	B 4
Ave	Heathridge	19	A 9
Ave	Heathridge	23	B 1
Ave	Karrinyup	44	D 4
Ave	Marmion	30	D 7
Ave	North Beach	44	E 2
Ave	Padbury	30	C 1
Ave	Padbury	23	C 8
Ave	Sorrento	30	D 3

		Map	Ref.
Ave	Trigg	44	C 6
Ave	Waterman	30	D 9
St	Booragoon	92	C 1
St	Cottesloe	80	D 2
St	Cottesloe	70	D 10
St	Dianella	47	C 9
St	East Fremantle	90	D 3
St	Fremantle	90	D 3
St	Kelmscott	106	E 10
St	Melville	91	C 3
St	Myaree	92	A 2
St	Myaree	91	E 2
St	North Perth	61	A 7
St	Palmyra	91	B 3
MARMOT			
Wy	Ferndale	84	D 8
MARNIE			
Rd	Darlington	66	B 2
Rd	Glen Forrest	66	D 2
MAROOG			
Wy	Nollamara	46	D 7
MAROONA			
Pl	Greenfields	163	E 7
MAROONAH			
Rd	Golden Bay	158	E 8
MAROUBRA			
Vs	Hillarys	22	E 10
MARQUIS			
Ct	Gosnells	95	E 9
St	Bentley	84	A 4
St	Bentley	83	E 5
St	Mt Helena	55	B 5
MARR			
St	Myaree	92	A 1
MARRABOOR			
Pl	Jandakot	112	E 3
MARRADONG			
St	Coolbinia	60	E 3
MARRAWA			
Wy	Queens Park	85	B 3
MARRI			
Cr	Lesmurdie	87	A 5
Ct	Morley	48	D 5
Ct	Parklands	163	E 5
Rd	Duncraig	30	D 6
Rd	Mahogany Crk	67	B 1
St	Wembley Dns	58	E 3
MARRIAMUP			
St	Cannington	84	D 4
MARRIOT			
St	Cannington	85	A 7
Wy	Morley	48	A 7
Wy	Morley	47	E 7
MARRIOTT			
Rd	Boya	65	C 4
Rd	Jandakot	103	C 2
MARRI PARK			
Dr	Casuarina	132	C 4
MARROW			
Cl	Yangebup	101	E 10
MARRYAT			
Ct	Hamilton Hill	101	A 2
MARS			
St	Carlisle	74	B 7
St	Welshpool	74	D 10
MARSDEN			
St	Scarborough	44	D 8
Wy	Padbury	23	E 7
MARSENGO			
Rd	Bateman	92	D 6
MARSH			
Ave	Manning	83	B 7
Ct	Jarrahdale	152	A 4
Ct	Swan View	51	A 7
Pl	Halls Head	164	C 1
Rd	Armadale	116	E 7
Wy	Bull Creek	93	B 6

		Map	Ref.
MARSHALL			
Rd	Beechboro	48	E 1
Rd	High Wycombe	64	A 10
Rd	Malaga	48	B 1
Rd	Malaga	47	D 1
Rd	Myaree	92	A 3
Rd	West Swan	49	B 1
St	Mosman Park	81	A 7
Wy	Samson	91	C 8
MARSHWOOD			
Pl	Sawyers Valley	55	B 8
MARTELL			
St	Sawyers Valley	54	E 9
St	Warnbro	145	C 7
MARTELLI			
Pl	Stirling	45	D 5
MARTHA			
St	Beaconsfield	90	D 8
St	Guildford	49	E 9
St	Sth Fremantle	90	D 8
MARTIN			
Ave	Nedlands	71	D 8
Ave	Rivervale	74	B 3
Ct	Balga	46	E 3
Pl	Bibra Lake	102	E 3
Pl	Canning Vale	94	B 6
Pl	Greenwood	31	E 5
Rd	Mundaring	68	A 4
Rd	Mundaring	67	E 7
Rd	Perth Airport	63	B 8
Rd	Rockingham	137	B 7
Rd	Sorrento	30	C 6
St	Kelmscott	106	E 8
MARTINDALE			
Ave	Thornlie	95	C 4
MARTINUP			
Ct	Heathridge	23	E 2
MARTOCK			
Wy	Karrinyup	44	E 3
MARTON			
Rd	Balcatta	46	A 4
MARTYN			
Rd	Mandurah	163	B 8
MARU			
Wy	Lesmurdie	87	D 3
MARVELL			
Ave	Munster	101	B 10
Ave	Spearwood	101	B 8
MARWOOD			
Wy	Willetton	93	E 5
MARY			
Cr	Eden Hill	49	A 8
Dr	Lesmurdie	87	B 5
St	Bentley	84	C 3
St	Byford	135	D 1
St	Claremont	71	B 9
St	Como	82	E 3
St	Halls Head	164	D 1
St	Halls Head	162	D 10
St	Hazelmere	64	A 2
St	Highgate	61	A 9
St	Maylands	62	A 9
St	Maylands	61	E 9
St	Quinns Rocks	10	E 9
St	Wangara	24	E 5
St	Wannero	25	A 5
St	Waterman	30	C 9
MARYBROOK			
Rd	Heathridge	23	E 2
MARYLEBONE			
Ct	Alexander Hts	33	B 5
MASCOT			
Ct	Hillarys	23	A 10
MASEFIELD			
Ave	North Lake	102	A 1
MASLIN			
Cr	Darlington	66	A 3
MASON			
Ct	Serpentine	151	B 10
Ct	South Lake	102	B 6
Me	Leda	139	B 1

		Map	Ref.
Pl	Mirrabooka	47	A 4
Rd	Forrestdale	114	B 1
Rd	Kalamunda	77	D 1
Rd	Kwinana Beach	130	A 2
Rd	Kwinana Beach	129	D 2
St	Armadale	116	D 4
St	Cannington	84	D 7
St	Chidlow	42	D 10
Wy	Padbury	23	D 9
MASONMILL			
Rd	Carmel	88	A 8
MASSEY			
Pl	Morley	47	D 9
St	Rossmoyne	93	B 3
Wy	Rossmoyne	93	B 2
MAST			
Ct	Waikiki	145	D 3
Pl	Ocean Reef	23	A 1
MASTERS			
Rd	Byford	126	A 8
Rd	Byford	125	E 5
St	Kenwick	86	A 10
MASTICO			
Cl	Iluka	18	E 3
MASULI			
Wy	Armadale	116	C 9
MATAITAI			
Lp	Cooloongup	137	D 8
MATAPAU			
St	Karrakatta	71	C 5
MATFIELD			
St	Marangaroo	32	B 4
Wy	Gosnells	95	E 7
MATHER			
Dr	Neerabup	16	B 3
Rd	Beaconsfield	90	E 9
Rd	Hamilton Hill	90	E 9
MATHESON			
Rd	Applecross	82	B 8
MATHEW			
St	Falcon	162A	E 10
MATHEWS			
Pl	Belmont	62	D 10
MATHIESON			
Rd	Ascot	62	D 9
Rd	Chidlow	56	B 4
MATHIS			
Wy	Carine	45	B 1
MATHOURA			
St	Midland	50	D 7
MATILDA			
Ct	Cooloongup	137	E 7
Me	Craigie	23	E 4
St	Huntingdale	95	D 9
MATIPO			
Cl	Duncraig	31	B 8
MATISON			
St	Southern River	105	C 7
MATISSE			
Wy	Kingsley	24	D 10
MATLOCK			
St	Mandurah	165	B 4
St	Mt Hawthorn	60	C 5
St	Mt Hawthorn	60	C 6
MATSEN			
Cl	Booragoon	92	B 2
MATSON			
St	Medina	130	E 4
MATTHEW			
Ave	Leeming	93	A 8
Wy	Thornlie	95	B 7
MATTHEWS			
Cl	Noranda	48	A 4
Wy	Stoneville	54	B 6
MATTINGLEY			
Hts	Murdoch	92	C 6
MATTISON			
Wy	Greenwood	32	A 5

For detailed information regarding the street referencing system used in this book, turn to page 170.

223

M

		Map	Ref.
MATZ			
Ct	Hamilton Hill	101	C 3
MAUD			
Rd	Maida Vale	76	E 5
MAUDE			
Pl	Lesmurdie	87	C 2
St	E Victoria Pk	74	B 10
MAULDON			
Me	Winthrop	92	A 4
MAUNA			
Ct	Yanchep	4	E 1
MAURICE			
St	Embleton	62	A 2
MAWI			
Ce	Marangaroo	32	D 6
MAWSON			
Cr	Hillarys	23	B 10
Ct	Morley	48	C 6
MAXINE			
Ct	Lesmurdie	87	A 2
MAXWELL			
Ave	Noranda	48	A 5
Rd	Caversham	50	A 5
St	Beaconsfield	90	D 8
St	Serpentine	154	E 3
MAXWORTHY			
Pl	Hamilton Hill	101	B 3
MAY			
Ave	Subiaco	72	B 1
Cl	Armadale	116	C 5
Cl	Mosman Park	80	E 7
Ct	Leeming	92	E 4
Ct	Nollamara	46	D 8
Dr	Kings Park	72	A 5
Dr	Nollamara	46	D 8
Rd	Eden Hill	48	E 9
St	Bayswater	62	A 4
St	Bedford	61	E 3
St	Bellevue	51	A 10
St	East Fremantle	90	E 3
St	Gosnells	96	B 10
St	Rockingham	137	A 5
St	Scarborough	44	D 9
MAYBACH			
Wy	Dianella	47	B 6
MAYBOLE			
Ct	Greenwood	31	C 2
MAYBUD			
Rd	Duncraig	30	E 4
MAYCOCK			
Pl	Orelia	131	B 6
MAYDWELL			
Wy	Calista	130	E 7
MAYER			
Cl	Noranda	48	A 4
MAYFAIR			
Ct	Cooloongup	137	C 9
Pl	Willetton	93	E 2
St	Mt Claremont	70	E 6
St	Nollamara	46	C 7
St	West Perth	72	C 1
St	West Perth	1C	D 1
MAYFIELD			
Rd	Safety Bay	144	E 1
St	Balga	46	C 4
MAYFLOWER			
Cl	Port Kennedy	156	D 6
Cr	Craigie	23	C 7
MAYHEW			
Rd	Darlington	66	A 2
MAYHILL			
Pl	Craigie	23	D 7
MAY HOLMAN			
Dr	Bassendean	62	D 2
MAYNARD			
Wy	Karrinyup	45	A 3
MAYNE			
Cl	Kardinya	92	B 6
Pl	Merriwa	10	B 8

		Map	Ref.
MAYO			
Ct	Lynwood	94	B 2
MAYOR			
Rd	Munster	111	A 1
MAZZINI			
St	E Victoria Pk	83	E 2
MCALINDEN			
Cl	Noranda	48	B 5
MCALISTER			
Pl	Thornlie	95	A 3
MCALLISTER			
Wy	Beechboro	49	A 4
MCATEE			
Ct	Fremantle	90	D 7
MCBAIN			
Ct	Langford	95	A 2
MCBETH			
Wy	Kardinya	92	A 9
MCCABE			
Pl	Nth Fremantle	80	C 8
St	Mosman Park	80	D 8
St	Nth Fremantle	80	D 8
MCCAFFREY			
Rd	Mariginiup	17	C 9
MCCALL			
Pl	Wanneroo	25	B 4
MCCALLUM			
Ave	Daglish	71	E 2
Cr	Ardross	82	B 9
La	Victoria Park	73	D 6
Rd	Mundaring	69	A 7
Rd	Mundaring	68	D 6
MCCANN			
Me	Rockingham	137	A 7
MCCARTER			
Rd	Booragoon	92	B 2
MCCARTHY			
Pl	Noranda	48	A 6
St	Armadale	116	B 7
St	Perth City	61	B 10
MCCARTNEY			
Cr	Lathlain	74	A 6
MCCASKILL			
Wy	Noranda	48	A 5
MCCAW			
Me	Yangebup	112	A 1
MCCLEERY			
St	Beaconsfield	90	D 7
MCCLELLAND			
St	Ferndale	84	D 9
MCCLEMANS			
Rd	Mt Claremont	70	E 4
MCCLINTOCK			
Gns	Alexander Hts	33	B 4
MCCLURE			
St	Safety Bay	136	D 10
MCCOMB			
Rd	Perth Airport	63	B 7
Rd	Redcliffe	63	B 7
MCCOOMBE			
Ave	Samson	91	D 9
MCCORKILL			
Rd	Pickering Bk	89	B 10
MCCORMACK			
Pl	Maida Vale	76	E 3
St	Armadale	116	D 4
MCCORMICK			
St	Warnbro	145	D 9
MCCOURT			
St	Leederville	60	B 10
MCCOY			
St	Booragoon	92	A 3
St	Melville	91	E 3
St	Myaree	92	A 3
St	Myaree	91	E 3
MCCUBBIN			
Blvd	Woodvale	24	B 5

		Map	Ref.
MCCULUM			
St	Stirling	45	E 9
MCDERMOTT			
St	Welshpool	74	E 9
MCDONAGH			
Pl	Lockridge	49	B 6
MCDONALD			
Cr	Bassendean	62	D 2
Rd	Baldivis	146	E 1
St	Como	83	A 2
St	Como	73	B 10
St	Herne Hill	36	D 3
St	Joondanna	60	C 2
St	Osborne Park	60	B 2
St	Yokine	60	D 2
St W	Osborne Park	60	A 2
MCDOWELL			
Cr	Kingsley	31	C 2
St	Kewdale	75	D 8
St	Welshpool	85	C 2
St	Welshpool	75	D 10
MCEWAN			
Cr	Mosman Park	80	D 4
MCFARLANE			
Ci	Mirrabooka	47	A 1
Cl	Willetton	93	E 3
MCGANN			
St	Bayswater	62	A 7
MCGILL			
St	Kewdale	74	E 8
MCGILLIVRAY			
Gns	Winthrop	92	B 3
Rd	Mt Claremont	71	B 2
MCGILVRAY			
Ave	Morley	47	E 7
Ave	Noranda	47	E 6
MCGLEW			
Rd	Glen Forrest	52	D 1
Rd	Glen Forrest	66	D 2
St	Eden Hill	49	A 9
MCGLINN			
Wy	Cloverdale	75	A 3
MCGOLDRICK			
Pl	Parmelia	131	A 10
MCGOWAN			
Ce	Bateman	92	D 3
MCGRATH			
Ave	Swan C Homes	144	
Pl	Armadale	115	E 4
Pl	Noranda	47	E 4
MCGREGOR			
Rd	Palmyra	91	B 4
St	Embleton	62	A 2
MCGUINESS			
Dr	Leeming	93	C 8
MCGURK			
Ct	Byford	126	D 9
MCINESS			
Ct	Greenwood	31	C 1
MCINTOSH			
St	Queens Park	85	A 3
MCINTYRE			
Wy	Kenwick	95	D 2
MCKANNA			
Gns	Parmelia	131	B 6
MCKAY			
Ct	Bibra Lake	102	D 3
Dr	Serpentine	155	C 1
St	Bentley	83	E 5
St	Waterford	83	E 5
MCKEAN			
Wy	Parmelia	131	B 6
MCKEE			
Cl	Bateman	92	D 7
Pl	Kingsley	31	D 1
MCKENZIE			
Gr	Kelmscott	106	E 4
Rd	Samson	91	C 9
Rd	Shoalwater	136	C 9

		Map	Ref.
St	Wembley	60	A 9
Wy	Embleton	62	A 1
Wy	Embleton	48	A 10
MCKEON			
St	Redcliffe	62	E 10
MCKEOWN			
Ct	Armadale	116	C 5
MCKERRACHER			
St	Mandurah	165	A 3
MCKIE			
Pl	Noranda	47	D 6
MCKIMMIE			
Rd	Palmyra	91	B 3
St	Embleton	62	A 2
MCKINLAY			
Ave	Padbury	30	D 1
MCKINNON			
St	Jandakot	102	D 10
MCKIRDY			
Wy	Marmion	30	D 7
MCKIVETT			
Cr	Leeming	102	E 1
MCKLEERY			
Rd	Kardinya	92	A 9
MCKNIGHT			
St	Melville	91	E 2
MCLACHLAN			
Wy	Belmont	62	D 10
MCLAREN			
Ave	Hope Valley	121	C 7
Ave	Yangebup	111	E 2
St	Sth Fremantle	90	C 9
MCLARTY			
Ave	Joondalup	19	D 4
Rd	Halls Head	164	B 3
Rd	Halls Head	164	C 2
Rd	Shoalwater	136	C 10
St	Cloverdale	75	A 4
Wy	High Wycombe	76	B 1
Wy	High Wycombe	64	B 10
MCLAUGHLAN			
Rd	Postans	131	B 2
Rd	Postans	122	B 10
MCLEAN			
Rd	Canning Vale	94	D 8
St	Dianella	47	C 10
St	Melville	91	C 2
St	Rockingham	137	A 6
MCLEISH			
Pl	Thornlie	95	B 7
MCLENNAN			
Dr	Nowergup	9	A 10
Dr	Nowergup	8	E 10
MCLEOD			
Rd	Wattleup	111	E 10
St	Lockridge	49	A 7
MCLERNON			
Pl	South Lake	102	E 7
MCLINTOCK			
Wy	Karrinyup	44	E 7
MCLURE			
Cl	Parmelia	131	A 9
MCMAHON			
Ct	Halls Head	164	C 2
St	Rockingham	137	A 6
St	Thornlie	95	A 6
Wy	Kardinya	91	E 6
Wy	Samson	91	D 9
MCMANUS			
St	Wilson	84	A 7
MCMASTER			
St	Victoria Park	73	D 8
MCMILLAN			
St	Victoria Park	73	E 8
MCNABB			
Lp	Como	83	B 3
Pl	Lesmurdie	87	D 4

		Map	Ref.
MCNAMARA			
Dr	Thornlie	95	A 7
Wy	Cottesloe	80	E 1
Wy	Cottesloe	70	E 10
MCNEECE			
Pl	O'Connor	91	C 6
MCNEIL			
St	Peppermint Gr	80	E 2
MCNEILL			
Rd	Armadale	115	E 1
MCNESS			
Ct	Noranda	47	C 5
Dr	Karragullen	119	B 2
Dr	Roleystone	119	A 4
Dr	Roleystone	118	D 1
Dr	Roleystone	108	D 10
St	Kalamunda	77	D 8
MCNICHOLL			
St	Rockingham	137	B 5
MCPHARLIN			
Ave	Quinns Rocks	10	A 1
MCPHERSON			
Ave	Noranda	48	B 6
St	Menora	60	E 6
MCRAE			
Ct	Padbury	23	C 8
Rd	Kalamunda	77	D 8
MCVEIGH			
St	Singleton	160	D 2
MCVICAR			
Pl	Mt Helena	55	B 5
MCWHAE			
Pl	Bull Creek	93	A 5
Rd	Hillarys	30	C 1
MEAD			
Ave	Naval Base	121	A 3
Ce	Ocean Reef	19	A 10
Cl	Woodvale	24	B 7
Gr	Floreat	71	D 1
Rd	E Rockingham	138	B 4
St	Byford	135	B 2
St	Kalamunda	77	D 6
St	Mundijong	143	B 10
St	Warnbro	145	C 6
MEADOW			
Cl	Kardinya	92	B 8
Ct	Cooloongup	137	E 7
Gr	Leeming	103	A 1
La	Parkerville	53	D 4
Me	Lynwood	94	B 3
Pl	Quinns Rocks	10	B 9
Pl	Wanneroo	24	E 1
St	Guildford	63	D 1
St	Guildford	49	D 10
MEADOWBANK			
Gns	Hillarys	23	A 10
Tce	South Lake	102	D 6
MEADOWBROOK			
Blvd	Dianella	47	A 5
Dr	Lynwood	94	B 3
Pro	Currambine	19	B 5
MEADOW SPRINGS			
Dr	Meadow Sprgs	163	C 3
MEADOWVALE			
Ave	South Perth	73	B 7
MEADOWVIEW			
Dr	Ballajura	33	D 6
Dr	Ballajura	33	E 6
Me	Canning Vale	94	B 9
MEAGHER			
Dr	Floreat	71	B 1
Wy	Beechboro	49	A 4
MEAKERS			
Wy	Girrawheen	32	D 8
MEANDER			
Wy	Maddington	96	C 5
MEARES			
Ave	Kwinana Twn C	131	A 9
St	Guildford	49	C 10

224   **For detailed information regarding the street referencing system used in this book, turn to page 170.**

M

		Map	Ref.
MEARS			
Pl	Spearwood	101	B 7
MEDA			
Cl	Beechboro	48	D 3
Ct	Gosnells	106	A 3
Pl	Heathridge	19	B 10
MEDBURY			
Rd	Balga	46	C 4
MEDFORD			
Ct	Meadow Sprgs	163	C 2
Ct	Woodvale	24	B 3
MEDHURST			
Cr	Nollamara	46	E 5
MEDINA			
Ave	Medina	130	E 4
MEDINAH			
Me	Connolly	19	C 6
MEDLAR			
Gr	South Lake	102	D 5
MEDULLA			
Rd	Jarrahdale	152	A 3
MEECH			
Wy	Clarkson	14	C 2
MEECHAM			
Wy	Karrinyup	45	A 4
MEECHIN			
Wy	Beechboro	49	A 2
MEEHAN			
Cl	Mirrabooka	33	A 10
MEEK			
Ct	Gosnells	106	A 1
MEELAH			
Rd	City Beach	58	D 9
Wy	Koongamia	65	B 1
MEENAAR			
Cr	Coolbinia	60	E 3
MEERE			
La	Clarkson	14	E 10
MEGA			
St	Wanneroo	20	C 9
MEGALONG			
St	Nedlands	72	A 7
MEGAN			
Wy	Westfield	106	B 8
MEGGS			
Cl	Padbury	23	E 8
MEGIDDO			
Wy	Duncraig	31	A 8
MEHARRY			
Rd	Hillarys	30	C 2
Rd	Leeming	93	A 10
MEIERS			
St	Nth Fremantle	90	B 2
MEKONG			
Pl	Beechboro	48	E 2
Wy	Greenfields	165	C 2
MELAK			
Cl	Coogee	101	A 9
MELALEUCA			
Cl	Casuarina	132	C 8
Ct	Canning Vale	104	A 2
Ct	Morley	48	D 4
Dr	Greenwood	31	C 4
Rd	Lesmurdie	87	A 4
Tce	Halls Head	164	B 4
MELANDA			
St	Kelmscott	106	E 7
MELBA			
Pl	Balga	46	E 3
Pl	Thornlie	95	E 4
MELBOURNE			
Cl	Port Kennedy	156	D 6
St	St James	84	B 3
Wy	Morley	47	E 8
MELDON			
Wy	Dianella	47	B 10

		Map	Ref.
MELDRETH			
Ct	Willetton	93	D 4
MELDRUM			
Wy	Koondoola	33	A 7
MELENE			
Rd	Duncraig	30	E 5
MELIA			
St	Duncraig	30	D 6
MELIADOR			
Wy	Midvale	51	A 9
MELINGA			
Ct	Karawara	83	D 5
MELISSA			
St	Duncraig	30	D 3
MELITA			
St	Falcon	162A	C 1
MELL			
Rd	Spearwood	101	A 7
MELLAR			
Ct	Midland	50	D 8
MELLER			
Rd	Bibra Lake	102	C 6
MELLIODORA			
Ci	Mirrabooka	32	E 10
MELLOR			
Ct	Karrinyup	44	E 2
Ct	Leeming	93	C 9
MELLOWS			
Pl	Padbury	30	E 7
MELO			
Ct	Heathridge	23	D 1
MELODY			
St	Kelmscott	106	E 7
MELOWAY			
Dr	Maida Vale	76	E 1
MELROSE			
Cr	Menora	61	A 5
Cst	Kinross	19	A 1
St	Leederville	60	C 8
St	Rossmoyne	93	B 2
MELSON			
Wy	Booragoon	92	B 1
Wy	Booragoon	82	B 10
MELTON			
Ct	Yanchep	4	E 1
MELUN			
St	Spearwood	101	B 5
MELVIEW			
Ct	Melville	91	D 1
MELVILLE			
Ct	Helena Valley	65	C 4
Pde	Como	82	E 1
Pde	South Perth	72	D 6
Pde	South Perth	72	D 7
Pl	South Perth	72	D 6
St	Claremont	71	B 8
St	Cottesloe	70	E 10
MELVILLE BEACH			
Rd	Applecross	82	B 8
MELVIN			
Ave	Thornlie	95	C 4
MELVISTA			
Ave	Nedlands	71	C 10
MEMORIAL			
Ave	Carlisle	74	B 8
Ave	Chidlow	56	D 2
Ave	Millendon	29	D 7
Dr	Mosman Park	80	E 5
MENAI			
Rt	Greenwood	31	B 3
MENAS			
Pl	Coolbellup	101	E 2
MENCHETTI			
Rd	Neerabup	15	B 1
MENDIP			
Me	Willetton	93	C 6

		Map	Ref.
MENDS			
St	South Perth	72	E 7
Wy	Waikiki	145	E 1
MENGLER			
Ave	Claremont	71	B 6
Ave	Mt Claremont	71	B 6
MENLI			
Pl	Orelia	131	A 4
MENNER			
Ct	Scarborough	44	D 8
MENSA			
Cl	Rockingham	137	B 8
MENTONE			
Rd	Balga	46	B 1
MENZ			
St	Embleton	62	B 1
MENZIES			
Grn	Duncraig	31	A 6
Pl	Thornlie	94	E 4
St	North Perth	60	E 7
St	Rivervale	74	C 4
MEPHAN			
St	Maylands	62	A 8
St	Maylands	61	E 8
MERANDA			
Ct	Hillarys	23	A 9
MERCATO			
Ct	Kewdale	74	D 6
MERCEDES			
Ave	Falcon	162A	C 2
MERCER			
Ct	Leda	130	E 9
La	Joondalup	19	D 6
Pl	Noranda	47	C 5
Pl	Thornlie	95	B 7
Rd	Riverton	94	A 1
Wy	Balga	32	D 9
MERCURY			
Pl	Morley	48	D 6
St	Carlisle	74	B 9
St	Kewdale	74	D 7
MERCY			
Me	Queens Park	85	A 4
Pl	Wembley	60	A 9
MEREBEIN			
Rd	Mt Helena	41	A 9
MEREDITH			
Wy	Dianella	47	A 9
Wy	Koondoola	33	A 9
MERENDA			
Rd	Balcatta	45	E 5
MEREWORTH			
Rd	Thornlie	95	B 5
Wy	Girrawheen	32	A 6
Wy	Marangaroo	32	A 6
MERGATE			
Ct	Erskine	164	C 6
MERIAN			
Cl	Bentley	84	D 3
MERIDIAN			
Dr	Mullaloo	23	B 3
Me	Waikiki	145	C 3
MERILEE			
Tce	Kelmscott	107	A 8
MERILUP			
Ct	Hillman	137	E 5
MERINDAH			
Mr	Falcon	162A	D 1
MERINGA			
Ct	Currambine	19	A 5
MERINO			
Ct	Thornlie	95	B 2
MERION			
Ct	Yanchep	4	E 2
Pl	Connolly	19	B 6
MERIVALE			
Wy	Greenwood	31	D 4

		Map	Ref.
MERIWA			
St	Nedlands	71	E 7
MERLE			
St	Mandurah	163	A 8
MERLEY			
Cr	City Beach	58	E 6
Wy	Lynwood	94	C 2
MERLIN			
Cl	Westfield	106	C 8
Dr	Carine	31	A 10
St	Falcon	162A	E 9
St	Rockingham	137	D 7
MERMAID			
Wy	Heathridge	23	B 1
Wy	Heathridge	19	C 10
MEROPE			
Cl	Rockingham	137	B 8
MERRICK			
Ct	Bayswater	62	A 5
Wy	Duncraig	31	B 6
MERRIFIELD			
Ave	Kelmscott	106	D 8
Ci	Leeming	93	D 9
Pl	Mullaloo	23	A 6
MERRIL			
Pl	Ferndale	84	D 9
MERRIVALE			
Rd	Pickering Bk	99	C 2
Rd	Pickering Bk	89	C 10
MERRYFUL			
Rd	Mandurah	163	C 8
MERSEY			
Pl	Beechboro	48	D 4
Rd	Shoalwater	144	C 1
Rd	Shoalwater	136	C 10
MERSTON			
St	Nollamara	46	C 8
MERTON			
Pl	Kingsley	24	B 10
Rd	Roleystone	107	E 7
St	Victoria Park	74	A 8
St	Victoria Park	73	E 8
Wy	Morley	48	B 7
MERTZ			
Ct	Hillarys	23	C 9
MERUKA			
Rt	Hillarys	23	A 10
MERYLL			
Pl	Duncraig	30	E 4
MESSENGER			
St	Kelmscott	116	D 1
MESSINES			
Ct	Greenmount	51	B 9
METCALFE			
Rd	Ferndale	84	D 10
Rd	Lynwood	94	B 3
METEOR			
St	Beckenham	85	D 7
METHUEN			
Wy	Duncraig	31	C 8
METTAM			
St	Trigg	44	C 5
METTERS			
St	Subiaco	72	A 1
METZ			
Wy	Wembley Dns	59	B 5
MEULLER			
Wy	Thornlie	95	A 5
MEUSE			
St	Cannington	84	E 7
MEWS			
Rd	Fremantle	1D	B 6
Rd	Fremantle	90	B 6
Rd	Sth Fremantle	90	C 5
MEYER			
Cl	Kelmscott	106	E 6
Ct	Woodvale	24	B 7

		Map	Ref.
MEYRICK			
Ct	Currambine	19	B 6
Wy	Langford	94	E 3
MIAMBA			
Ct	Karawara	83	C 5
MICA			
Ct	Carine	45	A 1
MICHAEL			
Cr	Boya	65	C 4
Ct	High Wycombe	64	D 9
Ct	Shelley	93	B 1
Rd	Roleystone	108	A 9
Rd	Roleystone	107	E 9
Rd	Waikiki	145	B 4
St	Beaconsfield	90	E 4
St	Cardup	135	D 3
St	Yokine	46	D 9
MICHEL			
Cr	Gosnells	105	E 1
MICHELLE			
Pl	Hamilton Hill	91	A 10
St	Wilson	84	B 8
MICHIGAN			
Ct	Edgewater	20	A 9
Hts	Jandakot	112	E 2
MICKLEHAM			
Rd	Morley	48	C 9
MICKLETON			
Tce	Bassendean	48	E 10
MICROMETER			
Pl	Mullaloo	23	B 2
MIDAS			
Rd	Malaga	47	D 2
MIDDLE			
Ce	Kallaroo	23	A 6
MIDDLE SWAN			
Rd	Caversham	50	A 2
Rd	Middle Swan	50	C 2
MIDDLETON			
St	Cloverdale	75	A 3
St	Newburn	75	D 7
Wy	Bull Creek	93	A 6
MIDGLEY			
St	Lathlain	74	A 5
MIDHURST			
St	Westfield	106	B 10
MIDLAND			
Rd	Hazelmere	64	D 4
Rd	Maida Vale	76	E 1
Rd	Maida Vale	64	E 10
Rt	Mindarie	14	C 5
MIDVALE			
Pl	Midvale	50	D 8
MIDWAY			
St	Riverton	84	A 10
MIFFLIN			
Pl	Leeming	93	A 8
MIGNON			
Ct	Armadale	116	B 6
MIGNONETTE			
St	North Perth	60	E 7
MIGO			
Pl	Rockingham	137	B 9
MIGUEL			
Rd	Bibra Lake	101	E 8
Rd	Yangebup	101	E 9
MIKADO			
Ct	Duncraig	30	D 3
MILBOURNE			
St	Beaconsfield	90	D 9
MILDENHALL			
St	Huntingdale	95	C 9
MILDMAY			
St	Balga	46	E 1
MILDURA			
Pl	Rockingham	137	B 5
Rd	Craigie	23	C 4
Rd	Mt Helena	41	A 10

For detailed information regarding the street referencing system used in this book, turn to page 170.

225

M

		Map	Ref.
MILES			
Pl	Wandi	123	C 6
Rd	Kewdale	75	A 9
St	Karrinyup	45	A 7
MILETI			
Rd	Lesmurdie	87	E 1
MILETO			
St	Dianella	61	C 1
MILEURA			
St	Golden Bay	158	D 8
MILFORD			
Cl	Gooseberry H	77	C 1
Cl	Leeming	93	A 8
Pl	Nollamara	46	D 8
St	E Victoria Pk	84	B 1
Wy	Nollamara	46	C 7
MILGAR			
St	Mandurah	163	B 8
MILGUN			
Dr	Yangebup	112	A 1
Dr	Yangebup	102	A 10
MILICICH			
Ce	Gwelup	45	C 7
MILINA			
Ct	Wanneroo	20	E 10
St	Hillman	137	D 7
MILITARY			
Rd	Bellevue	50	D 10
Rd	Hazelmere	64	D 2
MILL			
Pl	Armadale	116	C 9
Pl	Mandurah	164	E 3
St	Perth City	1C	E 3
St	Perth City	72	E 3
St	Wungong	126	C 4
MILLAN			
Pl	Hamilton Hill	101	A 2
MILLAR			
Pl	Willetton	94	A 3
Rd	Baldivis	139	A 6
Rd	Baldivis	138	D 6
Rd	North Beach	44	C 1
Rd	Wellard	140	A 4
Rd	Wellard	139	E 3
St	Beechboro	49	A 4
MILLARS			
Rd	Jarrahdale	152	E 5
MILLBANK			
Ct	Alexander Hts	33	B 4
MILLBRACE			
Gl	Byford	135	D 3
MILLBROOK			
Cl	Jarrahdale	152	A 4
Gr	Beldon	23	D 3
MILLCREST			
St	Doubleview	59	A 1
St	Scarborough	58	E 1
MILLEARA			
Rd	Martin	106	E 2
MILLEN			
St	Kelmscott	116	E 2
MILLENDEN			
St	East Fremantle	91	A 2
MILLER			
Ave	Redcliffe	62	E 9
Pl	Booragoon	92	C 1
Rd	Perth Airport	63	B 9
St	Bellevue	51	A 10
St	E Victoria Pk	74	A 8
St	Maddington	96	B 5
MILLERICK			
Wy	Noranda	47	D 5
MILLET			
St	Joondanna	60	D 3
MILLFARM			
Cl	Padbury	30	E 2
MILLGATE			
Rd	Balga	32	B 10

		Map	Ref.
MILLGROVE			
Ave	Cooloongup	137	C 10
MILLHOUSE			
Rd	Belhus	29	B 3
MILLIGAN			
Ave	Kiara	48	D 5
Rd	Parkerville	53	E 7
Rd	Stoneville	54	A 7
St	Northbridge	1C	E 1
St	Northbridge	72	E 1
St	Perth City	1C	E 2
St	Perth City	72	E 2
MILLIMUMUL			
Wy	Mullaloo	23	A 5
MILLINGTON			
Ave	Daglish	71	E 3
St	Ardross	82	B 8
MILLMAN			
Wy	Armadale	116	C 7
MILL POINT			
Cl	South Perth	72	D 5
Rd	South Perth	73	A 8
Rd	South Perth	72	D 6
MILLPORT			
Dr	Warwick	31	C 8
MILLS			
Ave	Bayswater	62	A 5
Ct	Beechboro	48	C 3
Rd	Darlington	66	C 7
Rd	Glen Forrest	66	C 7
Rd E	Martin	107	A 1
Rd E	Martin	96	D 10
Rd W	Martin	96	B 7
St	Cannington	84	D 4
St	Coogee	100	E 8
St	Queens Park	84	E 1
St	Spearwood	100	E 8
St	Welshpool	84	E 2
MILLSON			
Rd	Maida Vale	76	E 3
MILLSTREAM			
Cl	Jandakot	112	E 2
Ri	Hillarys	23	B 10
MILLUNA			
St	Falcon	162A	D 10
MILMOE			
La	Maylands	61	E 9
MILNE			
Ct	Ocean Reef	19	A 9
Dr	Armadale	116	A 1
Gr	Parmelia	131	C 8
St	Bayswater	62	B 6
St	Bicton	81	B 8
St	Lesmurdie	87	D 1
MILNER			
Rd	High Wycombe	76	B 3
St	Quinns Rocks	10	A 9
MILROY			
St	Willagee	91	D 5
MILSON			
Ct	Kallaroo	23	B 8
St	South Perth	73	B 9
MILSTEAD			
Wy	Marangaroo	32	A 5
MILTON			
Ave	Balcatta	46	B 6
Ct	Beldon	23	D 3
Pl	Munster	101	C 10
Pl	Orelia	131	A 5
St	Glendalough	60	B 4
St	Mt Hawthorn	60	B 4
St	Yokine	60	E 2
MILVERTON			
Ave	Karrinyup	44	E 4
MIMBALUP			
Cl	Hillman	137	E 5
MIMOSA			
Ave	Mt Claremont	71	B 6
Ct	Kelmscott	116	C 1
Ct	Marangaroo	32	E 4
St	Forrestfield	76	C 7

		Map	Ref.
MIMY			
Ct	Gosnells	96	A 7
Ct	Gosnells	95	E 7
MINA			
Ct	Duncraig	30	E 3
MINCHIN			
Cr	Middle Swan	50	D 4
Ct	Padbury	23	C 10
Pl	Bull Creek	93	A 5
MINCHINSON			
St	Shoalwater	136	D 9
MINDA			
Pl	Wanneroo	20	E 10
MINDARIE			
Dr	Quinns Rocks	10	A 10
MINDEN			
Ri	Sorrento	30	C 4
MINDEROO			
Cr	Golden Bay	158	E 8
MINER			
Cl	Thornlie	95	B 5
MINERVA			
St	Noranda	47	D 4
Wy	Carine	31	A 10
MINIBAH			
St	Wembley Dns	58	E 3
MINIGWAL			
Lp	Waikiki	145	D 1
MINILYA			
Ave	Hilton	91	A 7
Ct	Gosnells	105	E 3
St	Heathridge	19	B 9
St	Innaloo	45	C 10
MINIM			
Cl	Mosman Park	80	E 8
MINKARA			
Ct	Iluka	18	E 5
MINNEOLA			
Rd	Armadale	116	A 4
MINNERVA			
Pl	Currambine	19	A 4
MINNIE			
Ct	Marangaroo	32	C 4
MINNIPA			
Ci	Currambine	19	A 4
MINORA			
Pl	Rivervale	74	A 3
Rd	Dalkeith	81	C 3
MINOS			
Pl	San Remo	163	C 1
MINSTER			
Pl	Marangaroo	32	B 4
MINSTREL			
Wy	Ocean Reef	18	E 7
MINT			
St	E Victoria Pk	74	A 9
MINTARO			
Pl	Iluka	18	E 4
MINTERN			
Ct	Thornlie	95	C 3
MINTO			
Ct	Jandakot	112	E 3
MIPIA			
Ct	South Lake	102	C 7
MIPPI			
Rd	Halls Head	162	B 10
MIRADOR			
Rd	Morley	47	D 8
MIRA MAR			
St	Doubleview	59	A 2
MIRANDA			
Cr	Cooloongup	101	D 2
Me	Marangaroo	32	D 5
Rd	Darlington	66	C 5
Wy	Gosnells	106	A 1
MIRBELIA			
Ct	Greenwood	31	C 4

		Map	Ref.
MIRFIELD			
St	Roleystone	107	E 7
MIRO			
St	Wattleup	121	C 3
MIRRABOOKA			
Ave	Balga	46	E 4
Ave	Balga	32	E 10
Ave	Girrawheen	32	E 8
Ave	Marangaroo	32	E 3
Ave	Nollamara	46	E 5
MIRREEN			
Ct	Karawara	83	C 5
MIRRELIA			
Wy	Ferndale	94	B 1
MIRRIA			
Wy	Armadale	116	E 4
MIRROR			
Pl	Ocean Reef	23	A 2
MISSION			
Pl	Cooloongup	137	E 7
MISSION HILLS			
Pl	Connolly	19	A 8
MISSISSIPPI			
Dr	Greenfields	165	C 1
MISSOURI			
Ct	Beechboro	48	E 3
MISTLETOE			
Dr	Huntingdale	105	D 1
Dr	Huntingdale	95	C 10
MISTRAL			
Pl	Willetton	93	D 6
St	Falcon	162A	D 10
MISTY			
Rd	Parkerville	53	D 4
MITCHAM			
St	Wembley Dns	59	A 5
MITCHELL			
Cl	Parmelia	131	C 8
Cr	Middle Swan	50	E 3
Ct	Beechboro	48	E 3
Fwy	Balcatta	45	D 1
Fwy	Edgewater	23	E 1
Fwy	Glendalough	60	A 5
Fwy	Joondalup	19	C 3
Fwy	Leederville	60	B 7
Fwy	Neerabup	15	B 5
Fwy	Neerabup	14	E 1
Fwy	Nowergup	11	C 3
Fwy	Osborne Park	60	A 3
Fwy	Stirling	45	D 8
Fwy	West Perth	60	D 10
Fwy	Woodvale	24	A 5
Pl	Padbury	23	E 9
Pl	Two Rocks	2	D 4
Rd	Bickley	88	C 1
Rd	Bickley	78	C 10
Rd	Darlington	66	A 1
Rd	Walliston	88	A 2
St	Ardross	82	C 7
St	Bentley	84	C 5
St	Karrinyup	45	A 4
St	Mt Lawley	61	C 9
St	Wungong	126	D 3
St N	Ardross	82	C 8
St N	Mt Pleasant	82	D 7
St S	Ardross	82	C 8
St S	Mt Pleasant	82	C 7
MITFORD			
Gr	Port Kennedy	156	D 2
St	Swanbourne	70	E 8
MITRA			
Ct	Mullaloo	23	B 3
MITRE			
Ct	Mirrabooka	32	E 9
MITTON			
Pl	Sawyers Valley	55	A 9
MIZZEN			
Ct	Waikiki	145	D 1
Pl	Ocean Reef	23	B 2
MOAT			
St	Mandurah	163	B 8

		Map	Ref.
MOCKERIDGE			
Cc	Middle Swan	50	E 4
MODENA			
Pl	Balga	46	D 1
MODILLION			
Av N	Shelley	83	D 9
Av S	Riverton	93	D 1
Av S	Riverton	83	D 10
MOENNICH			
Ct	Coolbellup	102	A 2
Ct	Coolbellup	101	E 2
MOFFAT			
Pl	Warwick	31	C 8
MOFFETT			
Rd	Carmel	87	D 6
MOFFLIN			
Ave	Claremont	71	B 7
Ave	Darlington	66	B 5
St	Samson	91	C 8
MOGO			
St	Armadale	116	B 7
MOINGUP			
St	Lesmurdie	87	D 4
MOIR			
Pl	Midvale	50	E 8
Rd	Kardinya	91	E 6
St	Perth City	61	A 10
MOIRA			
Ave	Forrestfield	86	D 1
MOLDAVIA			
St	Tuart Hill	46	B 9
MOLINE			
Ct	Churchlands	59	C 4
MOLLERIN			
Pl	South Lake	102	C 6
MOLLISON			
Gns	Gwelup	45	C 7
MOLLOY			
St	Dianella	46	B 9
MOLLYHAWK			
Pl	Two Rocks	2	D 1
MOLO			
Ct	Wilson	84	B 6
MOLONG			
St	Armadale	116	E 5
MONA			
Ave	Beckenham	85	B 8
MONACO			
Ave	North Lake	102	A 10
Ave	North Lake	92	A 10
Pl	Dianella	47	A 6
Pl	Warnbro	145	C 1
MONAGHAN			
Ct	Hamilton Hill	101	B 3
MONANG			
Pl	Mandurah	163	B 8
MONARCH			
Ct	Thornlie	95	C 7
Ct	Wanneroo	20	C 7
MONASH			
Ave	Como	83	B 1
Ave	Nedlands	72	A 6
Ave	Nedlands	71	E 6
Ct	Halls Head	164	C 1
MONCLAIR			
Ct	Meadow Sprgs	163	C 6
MONCRIEFF			
Rd	Langford	95	A 1
MONESS			
Pl	Shelley	83	D 8
St	Shelley	83	D 8
MONEY			
Pl	Melville	91	D 2
Rd	Attadale	81	D 10
Rd	Melville	91	D 1
Rd	Melville	81	D 10
St	Perth City	1C	A 1
St	Perth City	73	A 1

M

MONGER
St Perth City .... 1C A 1
St Perth City .... 73 A 1
MONK
Ave Kensington .... 73 B 10
Gl Ocean Reef .... 19 A 9
Pl Noranda .... 47 C 6
St Kensington .... 73 B 10
MONKHOUSE
Wy Hillarys .... 23 C 9
MONKTON
Wy Warnbro .... 145 D 8
MONMOUTH
St Mt Lawley .... 61 A 7
St North Perth .... 61 A 7
MONOTA
Ave Shelley .... 83 D 9
MONS
Rd Hovea .... 53 A 9
St Ashfield .... 62 E 4
MONSON
Ct Leeming .... 102 E 1
MONSOON
Cl Waikiki .... 145 C 3
MONSTERA
Ct Alexander Hts .... 32 E 5
MONTAGUE
Wy Coolbellup .... 101 E 1
Wy Kallaroo .... 23 A 8
MONTCLAIRE
Ave Woodvale .... 24 B 6
MONTEBELLO
Ri Yangebup .... 101 E 10
MONTEGO
Cl Safety Bay .... 145 B 1
MONTEREY
Cr Warnbro .... 145 D 6
Ct Kardinya .... 92 A 8
Ct Nollamara .... 46 B 5
Dr Woodvale .... 24 B 4
St Nollamara .... 46 B 5
MONTES
Sq Riverton .... 83 E 10
MONTESSORI
Pl Kingsley .... 31 D 1
MONTFORT
Pl Morley .... 48 B 6
MONTGOMERY
Ave Mt Claremont ..... 71 A 8
St Hilton .... 91 A 8
Wy Malaga .... 47 C 1
MONTREAL
Rd Midland .... 50 A 9
Rd E Midland .... 50 E 9
Rt Meadow Sprgs 163 D 5
St Craigie .... 23 E 7
St Fremantle .... 90 E 5
St White Gum Vly .. 90 E 6
MONTROSE
Ave Darlington .... 66 A 4
Ave Girrawheen .... 32 D 8
Ci Westfield .... 106 C 7
St Lynwood .... 84 D 10
St Nollamara .... 46 C 6
Wk Mindarie .... 14 B 4
Wy Nollamara .... 46 C 6
MONUMENT
Dr Beldon .... 23 C 2
St Mosman Park ..... 80 D 6
MONYASH
Rd Carine .... 45 B 1
Rd Carine .... 31 B 10
MOOJEBING
St Bayswater .... 62 D 5
MOOLA
Ct Mahogany Crk ... 67 B 7
MOOLANDA
Blvd Kingsley .... 31 D 1
Blvd Kingsley .... 24 D 9

MOOLTUNYA
Ct Kingsley .... 31 D 2
MOOLYEEN
Rd Brentwood .... 92 D 2
Rd Mt Pleasant .... 92 D 1
MOONDARRA
Ci South Lake .... 102 D 7
Wy Joondalup .... 19 D 3
MOONDINE
Dr Wembley .... 59 E 7
MOONDYNE
Trl Gnangara .... 25 D 6
MOONEY
Pl O'Connor .... 91 B 6
St Bayswater .... 62 C 3
MOONGLOW
Ri Maida Vale .... 65 A 9
MOONIE
St Willetton .... 93 D 2
MOONSTONE
Pl Gosnells .... 105 E 1
MOORBY
Pl Balcatta .... 46 B 6
MOORE
Ave Bellevue .... 50 E 9
Ct Cooloongup .... 137 E 9
Dr Currambine .... 19 A 4
Dr Iluka .... 18 E 5
Dr Joondalup .... 19 C 4
Gns Kardinya .... 91 C 4
Pl Willetton .... 93 E 3
Rd Herne Hill .... 37 B 4
Rd Millendon .... 168 B 10
St Bayswater .... 62 A 6
St Dianella .... 61 C 1
St East Perth .... 1C B 2
St East Perth .... 73 B 2
St Forrestdale .... 114 E 6
St Kenwick .... 95 C 1
St Perth City .... 1C A 2
St Perth City .... 73 A 2
St Wungong .... 126 D 2
MOORGATE
St E. Victoria Pk .... 74 A 10
St E. Victoria Pk .... 73 E 9
MOORHEAD
Wy Koondoola .... 32 E 8
MOORHEN
Dr Yangebup .... 102 A 10
MOORHOUSE
St Willagee .... 92 A 3
St Willagee .... 91 E 3
MOORING
Cr Ocean Reef .... 23 B 1
Cr Ocean Reef .... 19 B 10
MOORLAND
St Doubleview .... 45 A 9
St Scarborough ..... 44 E 9
MOORO
Dr Mt Claremont .... 71 B 5
St Kingsley .... 24 E 9
MOORPARK
Ave Yanchep .... 4 E 1
MOORT
Pl Stoneville .... 54 A 3
MOOSE
Cl Beechboro .... 48 D 3
MOPSA
Wy Coolbellup .... 91 E 10
MORAGO
Cr Cloverdale .... 74 E 5
MORAN
Ct Wanneroo .... 25 B 4
Rd Kalamunda .... 77 B 5
St Beaconsfield ..... 90 D 9
St Embleton .... 62 B 1
MORANG
Ct Craigie .... 23 E 5

MORAY
Ave Floreat .... 59 C 7
Rd Glen Forrest ..... 66 E 3
MORDEN
St Wembley Dns .... 59 A 5
MORE
Cr Bull Creek .... 93 A 7
Ct Hamersley .... 31 E 9
MOREE
Cl Iluka .... 19 A 6
MOREING
Rd Attadale .... 81 C 10
St Ascot .... 62 D 8
St Redcliffe .... 62 D 8
MORESBY
Gr Rockingham ..... 137 B 5
St Kensington .... 73 C 10
MORETON
Cr Warnbro .... 145 D 6
MORETTI
Rt Leda .... 130 E 10
MORFITT
St Mandurah .... 163 B 9
MORGAN
Pl Bibra Lake .... 102 C 3
Pl Hillarys .... 30 C 1
Rd Armadale .... 116 B 2
Rd Redcliffe .... 75 A 1
St Cannington .... 85 A 7
St Rockingham ..... 137 C 4
St Shenton Park .... 71 D 4
Wy Girrawheen .... 32 D 7
MORGANS
St Tuart Hill .... 60 B 1
MORIALTA
Pl Iluka .... 18 D 5
MORIARTY
Rd Welshpool .... 84 D 1
MORILLA
Rd Mundaring .... 68 C 1
MORINE
Ct Hillman .... 137 E 5
MORLEY
Dr Balcatta .... 46 B 8
Dr Dianella .... 47 A 8
Dr Dianella .... 46 B 8
Dr Morley .... 48 A 8
Dr Morley .... 47 D 8
Dr Morley .... 46 B 8
Dr E Eden Hill .... 49 A 8
Dr E Morley .... 48 C 8
St Maddington ...... 96 A 4
St Naval Base .... 121 B 8
MORNING CLOUD
Vl Willetton .... 93 D 6
MORNINGTON
St Armadale .... 116 C 8
MORPHETT
Cr Bateman .... 92 D 5
MORRELL
Ct Greenwood .... 31 C 5
Rd Glen Forrest ..... 66 E 4
Wy Armadale .... 116 C 9
Wy Lesmurdie .... 87 E 2
MORRIETT
St Attadale .... 81 D 7
MORRIS
Ct Gosnells .... 106 B 1
Dr Forrestfield ...... 76 D 10
Pl Innaloo .... 45 B 9
Rd Innaloo .... 45 B 9
St Hilton .... 91 A 9
MORRISH
Pl Como .... 83 C 2
MORRISON
Dr Kelmscott .... 117 B 1
Rd Forrestfield ...... 86 B 1
Rd Midland .... 50 E 8
Rd Midvale .... 51 A 7
Rd Swan View .... 51 C 7

St Como .... 83 B 3
St Maylands .... 61 E 7
St Redcliffe .... 62 E 8
Wy Willetton .... 93 C 3
MORRISTON
St North Perth .... 60 D 9
MORRIT
Wy Parmelia .... 131 C 7
MORRITT
St Greenwood .... 32 A 5
MORROW
Me Kardinya .... 91 D 8
MORSE
Pl Morley .... 48 C 7
Rd Bibra Lake .... 101 D 8
MORT
St Rivervale .... 74 B 5
MORTIMER
Rd Wellard .... 132 C 9
Rd Wellard .... 131 E 9
St Wattleup .... 112 A 10
MORTIMER NEW
Rd Herne Hill .... 37 B 7
MORTLAKE
Pl Kingsley .... 31 B 1
MORTLOCK
St Hamilton Hill .... 101 A 1
MORTON
Gr Clarkson .... 11 E 10
Rd Carmel .... 88 D 7
Rd Hamilton Hill .... 101 B 2
MORUNDAH
Pl Kelmscott .... 106 E 1
MORVEN
Ct Greenwood .... 31 B 4
MORWELL
Ct Hillarys .... 23 B 10
MOSAIC
St E Shelley .... 83 E 8
St W Shelley .... 83 D 8
MOSELEY
Hl Kardinya .... 91 D 8
MOSEY
Ct Bull Creek .... 93 A 6
St Landsdale .... 25 C 9
MOSMAN
Ct Kallaroo .... 23 B 7
Tce Mosman Park .... 80 E 4
MOSS
Cl Leeming .... 93 B 8
Ct Kingsley .... 31 D 1
St East Fremantle .. 90 E 3
St Huntingdale ...... 95 D 8
Vl Floreat .... 71 C 1
MOSSPAUL
Cl Duncraig .... 30 E 7
MOSTYN
Pl Warnbro .... 145 C 7
MOTH
Ct Ocean Reef .... 23 A 1
MOTIVATION
Dr Wangara .... 25 B 8
MOTRIL
Ave Coogee .... 101 A 9
MOTT
Cl Mosman Park ... 80 D 7
Ct Hillarys .... 30 A 2
Pl Bull Creek .... 92 E 4
MOTTEE
Rd Bateman .... 92 D 5
MOTTERAM
Ave Claremont .... 71 B 8
MOTTLECAH
Wy Mirrabooka .... 32 E 10
MOTTLEY
St Attadale .... 81 E 8
MOTTRAM
Wy Morley .... 48 D 9

MOUAT
St Fremantle .... 1D B 5
St Fremantle .... 90 B 5
MOULDEN
Ave Yokine .... 60 D 1
Ave Yokine .... 46 D 10
MOULTON
St Calista .... 130 E 6
St Coodanup .... 165 D 6
MOUNSEY
Rd Kwinana Beach 130 B 5
St Kardinya .... 92 A 8
MOUNT
St Bellevue .... 51 A 10
St Claremont .... 71 A 9
St Greenmount ..... 66 A 1
St Kelmscott .... 107 B 9
St Perth City .... 1C D 3
St Perth City .... 72 D 3
St West Perth .... 1C D 3
St West Perth .... 72 D 3
Tce Kalamunda .... 77 B 6
MOUNTAIN
Tce Northbridge ...... 1C E 1
Tce Northbridge ...... 72 E 1
MOUNTAIN VIEW
Kelmscott .... 106 D 7
MOUNT HAVEN
St Kalamunda .... 77 D 9
MOUNTJOY
Rd Nedlands .... 71 D 10
St Middle Swan ..... 50 D 3
MOUNTS BAY
Rd Crawley .... 72 A 4
Rd Perth City .... 72 E 3
Rd West Perth ...... 1C D 4
Rd West Perth ...... 72 D 4
MOUNT VIEW
Tce Mt Pleasant ...... 82 E 9
MOUSEHOLE
Cr Yanchep .... 4 C 5
MOXAM
Pl Lynwood .... 94 B 4
MOYLAN
Rd Wattleup .... 121 D 3
Rd Wattleup .... 111 D 10
MOYLE
Cl Leeming .... 93 A 8
Pl Hillarys .... 30 C 2
MOYSEY
Cl Parmelia .... 131 B 7
MRS TRIVETT
Pl Fremantle .... 1D B 5
MT HENRY
Rd Como .... 83 A 7
Rd Manning .... 83 A 8
Rd Salter Point ..... 83 A 8
MT PROSPECT
Cr Maylands .... 61 E 8
MUDALLA
Pl Wanneroo .... 20 E 8
Wy Koongamia .... 65 B 2
MUDGE
St Myaree .... 92 A 1
MUDGEE
Ct South Lake .... 102 D 5
MUDLARK
Cr Ballajura .... 34 A 8
Cr Ballajura .... 33 E 8
Wy Yangebup .... 102 B 8
MUELLER
Ct Padbury .... 23 E 10
Pl Hovea .... 53 A 6
MUIR
Cl Waikiki .... 137 E 10
Ct Banjup .... 113 D 6
Pl Booragoon .... 92 C 3
Pl Halls Head .... 164 C 1
St Halls Head .... 164 C 1

For detailed information regarding the street referencing system used in this book, turn to page 170.

227

N

		Map	Ref.
St	Halls Head	162	C 10
St	Innaloo	45	C 8

MUIRDICK
| St | Innaloo | 45 | C 8 |

MUIRFIELD
| Ct | Halls Head | 164 | B 1 |
| Wy | Joondalup | 19 | D 3 |

MUIRHEAD
| Wy | Kingsley | 24 | C 9 |

MUIRON
| Pl | Merriwa | 11 | D 9 |

MULBERRY
| La | Mirrabooka | 47 | A 1 |

MULBERRY FARM
| La | White Gum Vly | 90 | E 6 |

MULBERRYTREE
| Cl | Swan View | 51 | D 9 |

MULGA
Dr	Lakelands	161	B 9
Dr	Parklands	161	B 10
Pl	Duncraig	30	D 6
Pl	Thornlie	95	A 10

MULGOA
| Ct | Duncraig | 30 | D 9 |

MULL
| Ct | Hamersley | 32 | A 10 |
| Gr | Ocean Reef | 19 | A 10 |

MULLALOO
| Dr | Mullaloo | 23 | B 5 |

MULLER
| St | North Beach | 44 | C 4 |

MULLEWA
| Cr | Coolbinia | 60 | D 3 |

MULLIGAN
Dr	Greenwood	32	A 5
Dr	Greenwood	31	E 5
Wy	Orelia	131	B 5

MULLINGAR
| Cl | Waterford | 83 | D 6 |

MULLINGS
| Wy | Myaree | 91 | E 1 |

MULLION
| St | Mullaloo | 23 | A 4 |

MULLOWAY
| Ct | Burns | 18 | D 3 |
| Ct | Sorrento | 30 | C 3 |

MULUMBA
| Pl | Stoneville | 54 | C 3 |

MUMFORD
| Pl | Balcatta | 45 | E 2 |

MUNDANUP
| Cl | Kelmscott | 107 | A 6 |

MUNDARING WEIR
Rd	Bickley	78	C 9
Rd	Hacketts Gully	79	A 5
Rd	Kalamunda	78	A 8
Rd	Kalamunda	77	E 7
Rd	Mundaring	68	C 3
Rd	Piesse Brook	78	C 8

MUNDAY
| Wy | Medina | 130 | D 5 |

MUNDEN
| Pl | Westfield | 106 | C 10 |

MUNDEREE
| Pl | Wanneroo | 20 | C 10 |

MUNDFORD
| St | North Beach | 44 | D 2 |

MUNDI
| Pl | Wanneroo | 20 | C 10 |

MUNDIJONG
Rd	Baldivis	140	A 8
Rd	Baldivis	139	C 8
Rd	Mundijong	142	D 9
Rd	Peel Estate	142	A 4
Rd	Peel Estate	141	D 8
Rd	Peel Estate	140	E 7

		Map	Ref.

MUNJA
St	Golden Bay	158	D 7
Wy	Nollamara	46	D 7
Wy	Queens Park	85	A 4

MUNNS
| Pl | Kardinya | 91 | E 7 |

MUNRO
Ct	Noranda	47	E 4
Rd	Applecross	82	C 6
St	East Fremantle	80	E 10
St	Jarrahdale	152	E 7
St	Mundijong	143	A 9

MUNSEY
| St | Ardross | 82 | B 9 |

MUNSIE
| Ave | Daglish | 71 | E 2 |

MUNT
| St | Bayswater | 62 | C 3 |

MUNTRIES
| Pl | Halls Head | 164 | A 6 |

MUNYARD
| Wy | Morley | 48 | A 6 |

MURCHISON
Rd	Cooloongup	137	D 10
Rd	Waikiki	145	E 1
St	Coolbinia	60	E 3
St	Shenton Park	71	E 5
Tce	Perth City	1C	B 1
Tce	Perth City	73	B 1
Wy	Gosnells	106	A 2
Wy	Gosnells	105	E 2
Wy	Mandurah	165	A 5

MURDOCH
Ct	Lynwood	94	A 2
Dr	Bateman	92	D 5
Dr	Greenfields	165	D 1
Dr	Greenfields	163	D 10
Dr	Murdoch	92	D 9
Dr	Singleton	160	D 1
Dr	Singleton	160	D 3
Rd	Thornlie	95	A 7
Wy	Banjup	113	D 3

MUREX
| Ct | Mullaloo | 23 | B 3 |

MURIEL
Ave	Innaloo	45	C 10
Ave	Woodlands	59	C 1
Cl	Iluka	18	E 6
Pl	Leederville	60	C 8
Rd	Jandakot	102	E 9
St	Bayswater	62	C 4
St	Gosnells	96	C 10
St	Midland	50	C 6

MUROS
| Cl | Warnbro | 145 | C 8 |
| Pl | Midvale | 51 | A 8 |

MURPHY
| St | O'Connor | 91 | B 6 |
| Wy | Warnbro | 145 | C 9 |

MURRAY
Ave	Mosman Park	80	D 5
Cr	Halls Head	162	B 10
Ct	Beechboro	48	E 4
Dr	High Wycombe	64	C 8
Dr	Hillarys	30	B 1
Pl	Duncraig	31	A 5
Rd	Armadale	116	D 4
Rd	Bicton	81	B 10
Rd	Henley Brook	35	E 4
Rd	Palmyra	91	B 1
Rd	Welshpool	85	B 2
St	Bayswater	62	A 5
St	Como	83	B 4
St	Como	73	B 10
St	Dalkeith	81	D 2
St	Perth City	72	D 1
St	Perth City	1C	E 2
St	West Perth	1C	D 1
St	West Perth	72	D 1
Wy	Karrinyup	45	B 2

MUSCA
| Cl | Rockingham | 137 | A 9 |

		Map	Ref.

MUSEUM
| St | Perth City | 1C | A 1 |
| St | Perth City | 73 | A 1 |

MUSGRAVE
| Ct | Willetton | 93 | E 7 |

MUSGROVE
| Cr | Boya | 65 | D 4 |

MUSK
| Ct | High Wycombe | 64 | A 10 |

MUSKETEER
| Ave | Jandakot | 103 | B 4 |

MUSKOKA
| Ave | Wanneroo | 20 | C 7 |

MUSSEL
| Pl | Mullaloo | 23 | B 4 |

MUSSON
| Rd | Henderson | 121 | C 1 |

MUSTANG
| Rd | Armadale | 105 | E 10 |

MUSWELL
| St | Balga | 32 | B 9 |

MUTTON
| Rd | Kelmscott | 106 | D 7 |

MYALL
| Pl | Dianella | 47 | B 8 |
| Rd | Banjup | 113 | B 3 |

MYAREE
| Wy | Duncraig | 30 | D 5 |

MYEE
| Ct | Currambine | 19 | A 4 |

MYERA
| St | Swanbourne | 71 | A 7 |

MYERICK
| St | Mandurah | 163 | B 9 |

MYERS
St	Crawley	72	A 9
St	Crawley	71	E 9
St	Tuart Hill	60	B 1

MYIMBAR
| Wy | Nollamara | 46 | C 7 |

MYINDEE
| Wy | Nollamara | 46 | C 7 |

MYLES
| Rd | Swan View | 51 | B 7 |
| St | E Rockingham | 129 | D 9 |

MYNAS
| Gr | Ballajura | 33 | E 7 |

MYOLA
| Rd | Kenwick | 86 | A 10 |
| Rd | Maddington | 96 | A 1 |

MYRA
| Pl | Shelley | 83 | C 10 |

MYRNA
| Wy | Lynwood | 94 | A 2 |

MYRTLE
Ave	Sorrento	30	D 6
Ct	Morley	48	D 5
Ct	Thornlie	94	E 9
St	Perth City	61	A 9
St	Walliston	87	E 2
St	Willetton	93	C 2

N

NABAWA
| St | Riverton | 94 | A 1 |

NABBERU
| Lp | Cooloongup | 137 | E 9 |

NADELL
| Ct | Mt Helena | 55 | A 5 |

NADINE
| Pl | Woodvale | 24 | B 6 |

NAGAMBIE
| Cl | South Lake | 102 | E 7 |

		Map	Ref.

NAGEL
| Pl | Dianella | 61 | B 1 |

NAILSWORTH
| St | Cottesloe | 80 | D 1 |

NAIRN
Ct	Woodvale	24	B 4
Rd	Applecross	82	B 6
Rd	Bickley	88	C 4
Rd	Coodanup	165	E 8
Rd	Karnup	159	D 1
Rd	Karnup	159	D 6
Rd	Thornlie	95	B 6
St	Fremantle	1D	B 5
St	Fremantle	90	B 5

NAIVASHA
| Tn | Joondalup | 19 | D 2 |

NALDER
| Wy | Clarkson | 14 | C 2 |

NALLAN
| Pl | Yangebup | 101 | E 10 |

NALPA
| Wy | Duncraig | 30 | D 5 |

NALYA
| Ct | Coodanup | 165 | C 4 |
| Pl | Swan View | 51 | E 8 |

NAMATJIRA
| Pl | Leederville | 60 | C 7 |
| Wy | Kenwick | 86 | A 10 |

NAMOI
| Pl | Armadale | 116 | A 6 |
| Tn | Merriwa | 11 | C 8 |

NAMUR
| St | North Perth | 60 | E 6 |

NANCE
| St | Kewdale | 74 | E 9 |

NANCY
| Wy | Coogee | 100 | E 10 |

NANDA
| Cl | Kingsley | 31 | D 2 |

NANDI
| Ct | Waikiki | 145 | D 1 |

NANDINA
| Ave | Mt Claremont | 71 | B 6 |
| Cl | Ballajura | 33 | C 6 |

NANDUS
| Ct | Heathridge | 23 | E 1 |

NANGA
| Rd | Golden Bay | 158 | D 8 |

NANGANA
| Wy | Kalamunda | 77 | A 4 |

NANGAR
| St | Yokine | 60 | D 3 |

NANGETTY
| St | Innaloo | 45 | C 10 |

NANGKITA
| Rd | Kalamunda | 77 | D 10 |
| Wy | Kalamunda | 77 | D 10 |

NANHOB
| St | Bayswater | 62 | B 5 |
| St | Mt Lawley | 61 | B 7 |

NANIKA
| Cr | Joondalup | 19 | C 3 |

NANKIVELL
| Wy | Koondoola | 32 | E 8 |

NANNATEE
| Wy | Wanneroo | 24 | D 1 |
| Wy | Wanneroo | 20 | D 10 |

NANNINE
| Ave | White Gum Vly | 90 | E 7 |

NANOVICH
| Ave | Girrawheen | 32 | B 8 |

NANSON
| St | Wembley | 59 | E 9 |
| Wy | Nollamara | 46 | C 8 |

NANTELLIS
| Rd | Martin | 96 | C 7 |

NANVEN
| Pl | Rivervale | 74 | C 5 |

		Map	Ref.

NAPA
| Cl | Warnbro | 145 | D 7 |

NAPEAN
| Pl | Armadale | 116 | C 4 |

NAPIER
Cl	Halls Head	164	C 4
Me	Yangebup	112	A 1
Me	Yangebup	102	A 10
Pl	Wungong	116	B 8
Rd	Marangaroo	32	A 3
Rd	Morley	47	E 7
Rd	Nth Fremantle	90	C 7
St	Cottesloe	80	C 1
St	Cottesloe	80	D 1
St	Forrestdale	115	A 7
St	Nedlands	71	C 8

NAPOLEON
| St | Cottesloe | 80 | D 3 |
| Wy | Craigie | 23 | E 6 |

NARANGA
| Pl | Stoneville | 40 | B 8 |

NARCISSUS
| Ave | Lynwood | 94 | B 4 |

NARDIE
| Pl | Hillman | 137 | E 6 |

NARDINA
| Cr | Dalkeith | 81 | D 3 |

NARDOO
| Wy | Maddington | 96 | B 5 |

NAREE
| Rd | Wilson | 84 | C 7 |

NARLA
Pl	Koongamia	65	B 1
Pl	Queens Park	85	B 3
Rd	Swanbourne	70	E 7
Rt	Stoneville	54	A 4
Wy	Nollamara	46	D 7

NAROOMA
| St | Armadale | 116 | B 5 |

NARRABEEN
| Pl | Kallaroo | 23 | A 6 |

NARRAN
| Cl | Edgewater | 20 | A 10 |
| Pl | Swan View | 51 | E 9 |

NARRIK
| Ct | Kelmscott | 117 | B 2 |

NARRUNG
| Wy | Nollamara | 46 | D 7 |

NARRYER
| Hts | Marangaroo | 32 | C 5 |

NARVAL
| Wy | Ferndale | 84 | C 9 |

NARWOOD
| Pl | Midvale | 51 | A 7 |

NASEBY
| Pl | Carine | 30 | D 9 |

NASH
Pl	Beechboro	49	A 3
St	Daglish	71	D 3
St	Hillarys	23	B 9
St	Kelmscott	107	A 8
St	Perth City	1C	A 2
St	Perth City	73	A 2

NASMYTH
| Rd | Rockingham | 137 | E 3 |

NASURA
| Gr | Armadale | 117 | A 3 |

NATALIE
| Ct | Alexander Hts | 33 | A 5 |
| Wy | Balcatta | 46 | A 3 |

NATASHA
| Wy | Westfield | 106 | C 6 |

NATHAM
| Rd | South Lake | 102 | C 6 |
| Sq | Swan View | 51 | C 6 |

NATHANIEL
| Wy | Orelia | 131 | A 5 |

NATICA
| Pl | Mullaloo | 23 | B 4 |

N

		Map	Ref.
NATIONAL PARK			
Rd	Swan View	51	D 6
NATTAI			
Ct	Armadale	116	B 6
NAUNTON			
Cr	Eden Hill	48	D 9
Wy	Eden Hill	48	D 9
NAUTICAL			
Ct	Yanchep	4	C 5
Gr	Beldon	23	C 3
NAUTILUS			
Cl	Port Kennedy	156	D 4
Cr	Scarborough	44	D 8
Pl	Scarborough	44	D 8
Wy	Kallaroo	23	B 6
NAVAL			
Pde	Ocean Reef	18	E 9
NAVARRE			
Rw	Greenfields	163	E 8
NAVEL			
Cl	Armadale	115	E 4
NAYLOR			
Pl	Lesmurdie	87	E 3
St	Hamilton Hill	90	D 10
NEALE			
Pl	Cooloongup	137	C 10
NEALIE			
Cl	Mirrabooka	47	A 1
NEAP			
La	Mullaloo	23	C 3
NEARWATER			
Wy	Shelley	83	D 8
NEAVE			
Cl	Leeming	92	E 8
St	Pickering Bk	99	B 1
NEAVES			
Rd	Mariginiup	17	A 5
Rd	Pinjar	16	E 5
NEBO			
Cl	Willetton	93	C 6
NEEDWELL			
Rd	Bibra Lake	102	D 3
NEERABUP			
Rd	Clarkson	14	D 5
NEESHAM			
St	Booragoon	92	C 1
NEIL			
St	Osborne Park	60	A 3
St	Rossmoyne	93	A 2
NEILSON			
Ave	Armadale	116	B 8
Cr	Darlington	66	B 4
NEKAYA			
Wy	Duncraig	30	D 3
NELLIGAN			
Ave	Girrawheen	32	B 7
St	Dianella	47	A 8
NELSON			
Ave	East Perth	73	C 4
Cr	East Perth	73	C 4
Cr	Lesmurdie	87	A 2
Pl	Beldon	23	D 4
Rd	Darlington	66	C 7
St	Bedfordale	127	C 2
St	Bedfordale	117	C 10
St	Halls Head	164	C 2
St	Inglewood	61	D 5
St	Sth Fremantle	90	C 7
NEMESIA			
Ct	Heathridge	19	B 10
NENAGH			
Gr	Waterford	83	D 7
NENE			
Cl	Beechboro	48	D 3
NEON			
Cl	Lynwood	94	A 4
St	Heathridge	19	D 10

		Map	Ref.
NEPEAN			
Pl	Willetton	94	A 4
NEPETA			
Cl	Thornlie	95	A 8
NEPTUNE			
Gns	Beldon	23	D 3
Pl	Halls Head	164	B 1
Pl	Waikiki	145	B 3
St	Mt Helena	55	C 4
St	Mt Helena	41	D 10
St	Scarborough	44	D 8
NERANG			
Ct	Armadale	116	B 5
El	Merriwa	11	C 9
NEREUS			
Pl	Currambine	19	A 3
Pl	Madora	160	D 6
NERIDA			
Pl	Sorrento	30	B 4
Wy	Lynwood	94	A 2
NERINE			
St	Falcon	162A	D 9
NERITA			
Pl	Heathridge	19	D 10
NERITE			
Pl	Mullaloo	23	B 3
NERRENA			
Ct	Greenfields	165	E 2
NERRIMA			
Ct	Cooloongup	137	D 9
St	Falcon	162A	C 2
NESS			
Ce	Joondalup	19	D 4
Rd	Applecross	82	B 7
NESTOR			
Wy	Silver Sands	163	A 8
NESTOR BRAE			
La	Kalamunda	77	D 6
NETHERBY			
Rd	Duncraig	31	B 5
NETHERCOTT			
St	Huntingdale	95	C 9
NETHERWOOD			
Ct	High Wycombe	64	D 10
NETLEY			
Pl	Armadale	116	D 5
Rd	Maida Vale	77	A 2
St	Morley	48	A 7
NETTLE			
Pl	Halls Head	164	B 5
Tce	Mirrabooka	47	C 1
Wy	South Lake	102	D 5
NETTLETON			
Rd	Byford	135	D 3
Rd	Jarrahdale	153	A 4
Rd	Jarrahdale	152	D 5
Wy	Safety Bay	145	A 1
NEUMAN			
Rd	Red Hill	37	C 8
NEUMANN			
Gr	Winthrop	92	C 4
NEVILLE			
Dr	Wanneroo	20	C 6
Rd	Dalkeith	81	C 2
St	Bayswater	62	B 7
NEVIN			
St	Wangara	25	A 5
NEVIS			
Pl	Safety Bay	145	C 1
NEVORIA			
Pl	Padbury	30	E 1
Pl	Padbury	23	E 10
NEWARK			
Pl	Connolly	19	A 6
NEWBERY			
Rd	Wembley Dns	58	E 3

		Map	Ref.
NEWBOLD			
Ct	Gosnells	106	B 2
Rd	Casuarina	132	C 3
St	Hilton	91	A 6
NEW BOND			
St	Midland	50	C 7
NEWBOROUGH			
Pl	Huntingdale	95	D 10
St	Doubleview	45	A 7
St	Scarborough	44	E 7
NEWBRIDGE			
Pl	Shelley	83	E 8
NEWBURN			
Rd	High Wycombe	76	B 1
Rd	High Wycombe	64	B 10
Rd	Kewdale	75	D 8
Rd	Newburn	75	D 7
NEWBURY			
St	Balga	32	A 10
NEWBY			
Pl	Sorrento	30	B 3
NEWCAP			
Pl	Merriwa	14	C 1
NEWCASTLE			
St	Leederville	60	D 9
St	Northbridge	1C	A 1
St	Northbridge	73	A 1
St	Northbridge	60	E 10
St	Perth City	73	A 1
St	Perth City	1C	A 1
St	West Perth	60	D 9
NEWCOMBE			
Wy	Padbury	30	D 2
NEWCOMEN			
Rd	Stirling	45	E 9
NEW COURT			
Dl	Mt Claremont	71	A 4
NEW CROSS			
Rd	Kingsley	24	B 10
NEWELL			
Ce	Joondalup	19	C 2
Pl	Cooloongup	137	C 10
Wy	Noranda	47	D 5
NEWENDEN			
St	Maddington	96	A 5
St	Maddington	95	E 5
NEW ENGLAND			
Dr	Hillarys	23	B 10
NEWEY			
St	Rivervale	74	A 4
NEWGATE			
St	Alexander Hts	33	B 6
NEWHAM			
Wy	Kingsley	31	B 2
NEWHAVEN			
Hts	Ballajura	33	D 6
Pl	Canning Vale	94	A 9
Pl	Kingsley	24	C 10
Wy	Nollamara	46	D 5
NEWICK			
St	Balga	46	C 1
NEWINGTON			
Pl	Kingsley	24	B 10
St	Morley	48	C 8
NEWLIN			
Me	Clarkson	14	D 1
NEWLYN			
Pl	Yanchep	4	D 4
Rd	Willetton	94	A 2
St	Belmont	74	C 3
Wy	Coodanup	165	D 3
NEWMAN			
Ct	Cooloongup	137	C 9
Pl	Kenwick	85	E 10
Rd	Darlington	66	B 3
Rd	Yanchep	4	C 3
St	Fremantle	1D	C 5

		Map	Ref.
NEWMARKET			
Cl	Currambine	19	B 4
St	Hamilton Hill	90	D 10
NEWNHAM			
St	Leederville	60	B 9
NEWPORT			
Dr	Dudley Park	165	C 5
Gns	Hillarys	23	B 10
Wy	Balga	46	D 1
Wy	Balga	32	D 10
Wy	Lynwood	94	D 2
NEWQUAY			
Cl	Yanchep	4	D 5
NEWRIC			
Rd	Glen Forrest	66	E 5
NEWRY			
Cl	Waterford	83	D 6
St	Floreat	59	C 10
NEWSAM			
Cl	Lynwood	94	B 4
NEWSTEAD			
Cl	Halls Head	164	B 4
Cr	Parmelia	131	A 8
NEWTON			
Ct	Armadale	116	D 5
Rd	Perth Airport	63	C 6
St	Bayswater	62	C 6
St	Mt Helena	55	C 3
St	Spearwood	101	B 8
NEWTOWN			
Gr	Beldon	23	D 2
NIAGARA			
Pl	Greenfields	165	D 2
Pl	Morley	48	D 6
NICHOL			
St	Mundaring	68	B 1
St	Mundaring	54	B 10
NICHOLAS			
Ave	Quinns Rocks	10	E 9
Cr	Hilton	91	B 8
Rd	Wanneroo	25	A 2
St	Gosnells	96	A 9
St	Rossmoyne	93	B 2
NICHOLAY			
Ct	Bull Creek	93	B 7
NICHOLL			
St	Daglish	71	D 3
St	Glen Forrest	66	C 1
NICHOLLI			
Ct	Ballajura	33	C 6
Ct	Gosnells	106	A 1
St	Duncraig	31	A 7
NICHOLLS			
Cr	Bull Creek	93	B 5
Pl	Padbury	23	C 10
NICHOLSON			
Cr	Lesmurdie	77	D 10
Ct	Canning Vale	94	C 9
Lp	Bateman	92	D 5
Pl	Ballajura	33	C 4
Rd	Canning Vale	104	B 7
Rd	Canning Vale	94	C 9
Rd	Cannington	85	A 8
Rd	Ferndale	84	E 10
Rd	Forrestdale	114	C 4
Rd	Forrestdale	114	C 9
Rd	Lynwood	94	D 4
Rd	Lynwood	84	E 10
Rd	Oakford	133	D 3
Rd	Oakford	124	D 6
Rd	Subiaco	72	A 3
Rd	Subiaco	71	E 3
Rd	Leederville	60	C 10
NICKS			
La	Northbridge	1C	E 1
NICOL			
Cl	Kardinya	91	E 6
Cl	Lynwood	94	A 4
NICOLAS			
Dr	Casuarina	132	A 9

		Map	Ref.
NIDA			
St	Huntingdale	95	D 10
NIELDS			
St	Ferndale	84	E 9
NIGEL			
Ct	Leeming	93	B 8
NIGER			
Pl	Beechboro	48	D 4
NIGHTINGALE			
Hts	Ballajura	34	A 8
Rd	Swanbourne	70	D 7
NIGHTJAR			
St	Stirling	45	D 6
NILA			
St	Wembley Dns	59	B 5
NILE			
Cl	Halls Head	164	C 4
Ct	Padbury	23	E 8
Pl	Beechboro	48	E 4
St	East Perth	73	C 3
NILSEN			
Rge	Clarkson	14	C 1
NIMBIN			
Rd	Gooseberry H	77	D 3
NIMBUS			
Cl	Willetton	93	E 2
NIMON			
Pl	Stirling	45	D 7
NIMROD			
Pl	Hillarys	23	C 10
St	Hamersley	31	D 10
NINA			
Ct	Ocean Reef	19	A 7
Gr	Beldon	23	D 4
NINDA			
Pl	Shoalwater	136	D 9
Rd	Shoalwater	136	D 9
St	Coodanup	165	D 8
NINEHAM			
Ave	Spearwood	101	C 6
NINGALOO			
Wy	Thornlie	95	D 7
NINNIS			
Pl N	Hillarys	23	C 10
Pl S	Hillarys	23	C 10
NINTH			
Ave	Inglewood	61	C 5
Ave	Maylands	61	D 6
Rd	Wungong	116	B 9
Rd	Wungong	126	C 1
NIOKA			
St	Balcatta	46	A 5
NIPSIC			
Ct	Iluka	18	E 4
NIRIBI			
Rd	City Beach	58	C 7
NISBET			
Rd	Applecross	82	C 4
St	Ascot	62	D 8
NISSEN			
Pl	Swan View	51	C 5
NITA			
Pl	Riverton	93	D 1
NOACK			
Rd	Millendon	29	E 4
NOBLE			
Ct	Dianella	47	A 6
St	Kewdale	75	A 8
St	Willetton	93	D 3
NODDING			
Gns	Mirrabooka	46	E 1
NODE			
Ct	Mullaloo	23	A 3
NOEL			
Ct	Wanneroo	20	C 5
Rd	Gooseberry H	77	C 4
St	Helena Valley	65	B 3
St	Hilton	91	B 7

For detailed information regarding the street referencing system used in this book, turn to page 170.

O

		Map	Ref.
NOETIA			
Ct	Heathridge	23	D 1
NOLA			
Ave	Scarborough	58	D 2
Pl	Maddington	96	B 3
NOLAN			
Ave	Millendon	168	A 5
Ave	Millendon	29	E 5
Pl	Bayswater	62	A 6
Pl	Beldon	23	D 4
Wy	Bateman	92	D 5
NOLIN			
Ct	Jandakot	112	E 2
NOLLAMARA			
Ave	Nollamara	46	C 7
NOLT			
Ct	Leeming	93	A 8
NOLYANG			
Cr	Wanneroo	20	D 8
NOME			
Pl	Warnbro	145	E 6
NOOKAWARRA			
Pl	Kelmscott	107	B 10
NOOKIE			
St	Mandurah	165	A 2
NOONAMEENA			
Pl	Darlington	65	E 3
NOONAN			
Ct	Willetton	94	A 4
Dr	Wanneroo	20	D 9
Rd	Cooloongup	137	D 2
NOONGAH			
Pl	Nollamara	46	C 7
St	Nollamara	46	C 7
NOONGAR			
Wy	Riverton	94	A 1
Wy	Riverton	84	A 10
NORA			
Ct	Safety Bay	145	A 1
NORANDA			
Ave	Morley	47	C 6
Pl	Noranda	47	D 6
NORBERT			
St	East Perth	1C	B 2
St	East Perth	73	B 2
NORBERTINE			
Cl	Queens Park	85	A 4
NORBURY			
Cr	City Beach	58	E 6
Wy	Greenwood	31	E 6
Wy	Langford	94	E 3
NORCO			
Wy	Bayswater	62	A 7
NORCOTT			
Vs	Marangaroo	32	D 5
NORDMANN			
Wy	Mirrabooka	47	B 1
NOREATT			
Pl	Leeming	93	C 10
NOREENA			
Ave	Golden Bay	158	D 8
NORFOLK			
Ct	Bateman	92	D 7
La	Ballajura	33	C 4
La	Fremantle	1D	C 6
Ri	Mt Claremont	71	B 1
Ri	Mt Claremont	71	B 1
St	Forrestfield	86	C 2
St	Fremantle	1D	C 6
St	Fremantle	90	C 6
St	North Perth	61	A 8
St	South Perth	73	A 9
NORHAM			
St	North Perth	60	E 8
NORKETT			
Rd	Mandogalup	122	D 6
NORLAND			
Wy	Spearwood	101	A 4

		Map	Ref.
NORLIN			
St	Kewdale	75	C 7
NORLING			
Rd	High Wycombe	76	C 1
Rd	High Wycombe	64	C 10
NORLUP			
Pl	Heathridge	23	E 2
NORMA			
Pl	Mandurah	165	A 4
Rd	Alfred Cove	82	A 10
Rd	Myaree	92	A 3
St	Walliston	88	A 1
St	Walliston	87	E 1
NORMAN			
Pl	Innaloo	45	C 7
Rd	Cardup	143	B 1
Rd	Cardup	135	C 10
Rd	Roleystone	108	A 9
St	Bellevue	51	A 10
St	Fremantle	90	D 7
St	Gosnells	106	C 1
St	Innaloo	45	B 7
St	Karrinyup	45	B 7
St	Welshpool	84	B 2
St	Wembley Dns	58	E 5
NORMANBY			
Rd	Inglewood	61	C 3
Rd	Inglewood	61	C 4
NORMANDY			
Gns	Port Kennedy	156	D 1
NORRIE			
Ct	Koondoola	32	E 7
NORRING			
St	Cooloongup	145	C 1
St	Cooloongup	137	C 10
NORRIS			
Pl	Bull Creek	92	E 4
St	Cloverdale	75	A 4
NORSEMAN			
St	E Victoria Pk	74	A 9
NORTH			
Cr	Byford	126	D 10
Rd	Bassendean	63	B 1
Rd	Bassendean	63	B 3
Rd	Bedfordale	127	D 8
Rd	Shoalwater	136	C 8
Rd	Beckenham	85	B 6
St	Cottesloe	70	C 9
St	Midland	50	C 7
St	Mt Lawley	61	B 6
St	Swanbourne	70	C 9
NORTHAMPTON			
St	E Victoria Pk	83	E 2
NORTH BANFF			
Rd	Floreat	59	C 7
NORTH BEACH			
Dr	Osborne Park	46	B 9
Dr	Tuart Hill	46	B 9
Rd	Gwelup	45	C 4
Rd	Karrinyup	45	A 2
Rd	North Beach	44	C 2
NORTHCOTE			
St	Chidlow	56	D 1
NORTHECUT			
Ri	Parmelia	131	C 7
NORTHEND			
Cl	Swan View	51	A 5
NORTHEY			
St	Ascot	62	B 10
NORTHGATE			
St	Karrinyup	45	A 6
NORTH LAKE			
Rd	Alfred Cove	82	A 10
Rd	Bibra Lake	102	A 3
Rd	Kardinya	91	E 8
Rd	Myaree	92	A 3
Rd	North Lake	102	A 1
Rd	North Lake	92	A 10
Rd	Winthrop	92	A 4
NORTHMOLE			
Dr	Nth Fremantle	90	A 3

		Map	Ref.
NORTHMOOR			
Rd	Eden Hill	48	E 9
NORTHMORE			
Cr	Winthrop	92	A 4
St	Daglish	71	D 2
NORTHOLT			
St	Lesmurdie	87	B 4
NORTH QUAY			
Rd	Nth Fremantle	1D	B 3
Rd	Nth Fremantle	90	B 4
NORTHRIDGE			
Dr	Ballajura	33	C 4
NORTH RUSHY			
Rd	Mundaring	69	D 8
NORTHSHORE			
Ave	Kallaroo	23	A 7
Dr	Kallaroo	22	E 8
NORTHSTEAD			
St	Karrinyup	44	E 7
St	Scarborough	44	E 10
NORTHUMBERLAND			
Ave	Alexander Hts	33	B 5
Rd	Forrestfield	86	C 1
NORTHWARD			
Rd	Roleystone	108	A 7
NORTHWOOD			
Dr	Mirrabooka	47	A 2
Dr	Mirrabooka	47	A 5
St	Leederville	60	B 10
Wy	Kallaroo	23	B 7
NORTON			
Ave	Coodanup	165	D 4
Ave	Coodanup	165	D 6
Dr	Dianella	61	B 1
Dr	Dianella	47	B 10
Rd	High Wycombe	76	B 1
Rge	Winthrop	92	C 4
St	South Perth	73	B 10
NORVILLS			
Cr	Kiara	48	E 7
NORWESTER			
Gns	Iluka	18	E 6
NORWICH			
Cl	Greenfields	163	E 9
NORWOOD			
Rd	Maida Vale	76	E 4
Rd	Rivervale	74	A 3
NOTLEY			
Ct	Samson	91	D 9
Ct	Wanneroo	20	C 6
NOTT			
Pl	Bull Creek	93	A 4
Pl	Yanchep	4	C 5
NOTTINGHAM			
St	E Victoria Pk	83	E 1
NOTTING HILL			
Dr	Roleystone	107	E 9
NOTTS			
Ct	Meadow Sprgs	163	D 5
NOUMEA			
Pl	Waikiki	145	D 1
NOVA			
Ct	Cooloongup	137	D 9
Ct	Marangaroo	32	D 6
NOWERGUP			
Rd	Nowergup	12	A 4
Rd	Nowergup	11	E 4
NOWRA			
Pl	Kelmscott	107	A 6
NOWRANIE			
Pl	Hillman	137	E 6
NOYES			
St	Munster	101	C 10
NUGENT			
St	Balcatta	46	B 2
NULLAGINE			
Wy	Gosnells	106	A 2

		Map	Ref.
NUMBAT			
Ct	Wungong	116	B 9
NUMULGI			
St	Armadale	116	B 6
NUNDAH			
Ct	Glen Forrest	66	D 4
NUNN			
Cl	Bateman	92	D 7
St	Hamilton Hill	100	E 1
NUNWEEK			
St	Booragoon	92	C 2
NURDI			
Wy	Riverton	93	C 1
NURRARI			
Cl	Waikiki	145	D 1
NURSTEAD			
Ave	Bassendean	63	B 1
NUTANS			
Ct	Halls Head	164	B 4
NUTBUSH			
Ave	Falcon	162A	C 4
NUTCHER			
Wy	Parmelia	131	B 7
NUTFIELD			
St	Bayswater	62	D 1
NUTLEY			
St	Balga	46	C 4
St	Maddington	96	B 3
NUTWOOD			
Ct	Marangaroo	32	E 5
NUYTSIA			
Ave	Sorrento	30	D 6
Pl	Greenwood	31	C 6
NYAANIA			
Ct	Glen Forrest	66	C 1
Ct	Glen Forrest	52	C 1
NYAMUP			
Wy	Bentley	84	B 5
NYANDI			
Ct	Thornlie	94	E 6
NYANG			
Ct	Yangebup	102	A 10
NYARA			
Cr	Craigie	23	D 5
NYE			
Wy	Orelia	131	A 4
NYM			
Pl	Spearwood	101	C 5
NYRAN			
Pl	Armadale	116	A 6
NYUNDA			
Dr	Wanneroo	24	D 1
Dr	Wanneroo	20	D 10
NYYERBUP			
Ci	Munster	110	D 1

O

		Map	Ref.
OAK			
Ave	Mandurah	165	B 3
Ct	Ballajura	33	C 4
Ct	Forrestfield	76	D 9
Gns	Edgewater	24	A 3
St	Cannington	84	E 8
Wy	Jarrahdale	152	D 7
OAKAJEE			
Ct	Gosnells	95	E 10
OAKAPPLE			
Dr	Duncraig	30	D 4
OAKDALE			
Cl	Halls Head	164	C 4
Cl	Safety Bay	137	A 10
St	Floreat	59	B 10
OAKES			
Rd	Cloverdale	75	A 5

		Map	Ref.
OAKFIELD			
Pl	Kelmscott	106	C 9
OAKHAM			
Pl	Balcatta	46	A 4
OAKLAND			
Ave	Cloverdale	74	E 5
Cl	Woodvale	24	B 6
Hts	Leeming	92	E 8
OAKLAND HILLS			
Blvd	Currambine	19	A 5
OAKLANDS			
Ave	Halls Head	164	B 3
OAKLEAF			
Ci	Mirrabooka	47	A 1
OAKLEIGH			
Dr	Erskine	164	B 7
Rd	Darlington	66	B 6
OAKLEY			
Ct	Kenwick	86	A 10
Pl	Medina	130	E 6
Rd N	Medina	130	D 6
Rd S	Medina	130	D 6
OAKMONT			
Ave	Meadow Sprgs	163	C 4
Tn	Connolly	19	C 8
OAKNEY			
Ave	Nollamara	46	E 7
OAKOVER			
Rd	Middle Swan	36	E 8
St	East Fremantle	91	A 3
Wy	Gosnells	106	A 2
Wy	Heathridge	19	A 7
OAK TREE			
Ct	Langford	95	A 1
OAKWOOD			
Ave	Woodlands	59	C 3
Cl	Beechboro	48	C 3
Ct	Currambine	19	B 5
OATLEY			
Pl	Duncraig	30	D 8
OATS			
Ct	Midland	50	E 6
St	Carlisle	74	C 9
St	E Victoria Pk	84	B 1
St	E Victoria Pk	74	B 10
St	Kewdale	74	C 9
OBAN			
Ct	Duncraig	31	A 6
Pl	Warnbro	145	E 7
Rd	City Beach	58	D 6
O'BEIRNE			
St	Claremont	71	A 9
OBERON			
Cl	Dianella	47	B 5
Ct	Waikiki	145	C 4
Gr	Armadale	117	A 7
Pl	Greenfields	163	E 9
Pl	Yanchep	3	E 10
OBERTHUR			
Cr	Bull Creek	93	B 6
OBION			
Cl	Willetton	93	D 3
OBORNE			
Cl	Leeming	93	C 10
O'BRIEN			
Pl	Westfield	106	C 7
Rd	Gidgegannup	39	B 1
Rd	Gidgegannup	167	E 1
OCEAN			
Ct	City Beach	58	D 6
Dr	Quinns Rocks	10	E 1
Dr	Quinns Rocks	10	E 9
Dr	Sth Fremantle	90	C 10
Pde	Burns	18	D 3
Pl	Waikiki	145	B 4
Rd	Spearwood	100	E 7
Rd	Sth Fremantle	90	C 10
Rd	Kwinana Beach	130	E 4
OCEAN FALLS			
Blvd	Mindarie	14	B 5

Map Ref.

OCEANIC
Ct Port Kennedy 156 D 5
Dr City Beach 58 D 10
Dr Floreat 59 A 9
OCEAN REEF
Rd Edgewater 24 A 3
Rd Heathridge 23 D 2
Rd Iluka 18 D 5
Rd Ocean Reef 23 A 2
OCEAN SHORES
Ed Connolly 19 A 7
OCEANSIDE
Pro Mullaloo 22 E 4
OCEAN VIEW
Pde Gooseberry H 65 C 9
Pde Gooseberry H 77 D 1
Rd Edgewater 24 A 1
OCHILTREE
Wy Kardinya 92 A 7
OCKHAM
St Lynwood 94 D 3
OCKLEY
Sq Embleton 48 B 10
O'CONNELL
St Hamilton Hill 101 C 2
Wy High Wycombe 64 B 9
O'CONNOR
Rd Mahogany Crk 67 C 4
Rd Stratton 51 B 4
Rd Swan View 51 C 4
Wy Wangara 24 E 5
OCTANS
Ct Rockingham 137 B 9
O'DEA
St Carlisle 74 B 7
ODELL
Ct Carine 31 A 9
O'DELL
St Thornlie 95 B 3
ODER
Ct Beechboro 48 D 2
ODERN
Cr Swanbourne 70 C 8
ODERNA
St Falcon 162A D 10
ODESSA
Pl Beldon 23 D 3
ODIN
Dr Balcatta 45 D 4
Dr Stirling 45 D 6
Rd Innaloo 59 C 1
Rd Innaloo 45 C 10
ODO
St North Beach 44 C 2
O'DONOUGH
Pl Beechboro 49 A 3
OFFHAM
Wy Balga 46 B 3
OFFICE
Rd E Rockingham 130 A 8
OFFLEY
St Hamilton Hill 101 A 4
OFFORD
St Armadale 116 C 8
OGILVIE
Rd Applecross 82 D 5
Rd Mt Pleasant 82 D 7
O'GRADY
Wy Girrawheen 32 C 6
OGRAM
Pl Beechboro 49 A 3
O'HARA
Ct Greenwood 32 A 5
St Beaconsfield 91 A 9
St Rockingham 137 C 7
OHIO
Ct Greenfields 165 D 1

Map Ref.

O'KANE
Ct Munster 110 D 3
OKEHAMPTON
Rd Warnbro 145 D 7
OKELY
Rd Carine 45 A 1
Rd Carine 31 A 10
OKEWOOD
Pl Morley 48 C 9
Wy Morley 48 C 9
OLBAH
Pl Armadale 116 B 6
OLCOTE
St Doubleview 59 A 2
OLD ALBANY
Rd Bedfordale 118 C 6
Rd Roleystone 118 B 2
OLD BALCATTA
Rd Gwelup 45 C 2
OLD BRICKWORKS
Rd Byford 135 E 3
OLD COACH
Pl Roleystone 107 D 10
OLD COAST
Rd Falcon 162 C 4
Rd Halls Head 164 B 6
OLD COLLIER
Rd Morley 47 E 10
OLD FARM
La Stoneville 54 B 3
OLDFIELD
Rd Girrawheen 32 A 6
OLDHAM
Cr Hilton 91 B 9
Pl Leeming 93 A 10
St Hillarys 30 B 2
Wy Yanchep 4 C 4
OLDING
St Melville 91 D 3
Wy Melville 91 D 3
OLD LAKE
Gr Wilson 84 A 9
OLD NORTHAM
Rd Chidlow 43 A 9
Rd Chidlow 56 C 5
Rd Wooroloo 43 D 7
OLD PERTH
Rd Bassendean 63 A 1
OLD PINJARRA
Rd Greenfields 165 E 3
OLDRIDGE
St Hamilton Hill 101 A 4
OLD SAWYERS
Rd Sawyers Valley 55 A 10
Rd Sawyers Valley 69 B 1
OLD STATION
Rd Karragullen 109 A 1
OLD TOODYAY
Rd Red Hill 37 C 10
OLD YANCHEP
Rd Carabooda 9 C 5
Rd Carabooda 8 D 1
Rd Nowergup 13 B 1
Rd Yanchep 5 E 5
OLD YORK
Rd Greenmount 51 D 10
OLEANDER
Dr Peron 136 C 5
Pl Halls Head 164 B 5
St Maddington 96 C 6
Wy Kallaroo 23 B 7
O'LEARY
Rd Padbury 30 D 2
OLEASTER
Wy Greenwood 31 C 4
OLEBURY
St Nollamara 46 C 8

Map Ref.

OLENEK
Pl Beechboro 48 D 2
OLFE
St Bayswater 62 B 5
OLGA
Ct Iluka 18 E 5
Pl Daglish 71 E 2
Rd Maddington 95 E 5
OLGIATA
Cl Meadow Sprgs 163 D 6
OLINDA
Ave City Beach 58 E 6
Ct Greenfields 163 D 9
Ct Spearwood 101 B 5
OLIPHANT
St Kenwick 86 A 10
OLIVA
Cl Alexander Hts 33 A 5
OLIVE
Ce Mullaloo 23 B 3
Gr Beechboro 48 C 4
Rd Falcon 162A C 2
Rd Millendon 36 D 1
Rd Millendon 29 D 10
St Guildford 63 D 1
St Guildford 49 D 10
St Myaree 92 A 1
St North Perth 60 E 8
St South Perth 73 A 8
St Subiaco 72 B 2
OLIVER
Ct Kardinya 91 E 9
Ct Middle Swan 50 E 4
Pl St James 84 B 4
St Bellevue 64 D 1
St Dianella 47 A 8
St Hillarys 30 C 1
St Mt Helena 54 E 7
St Scarborough 58 D 2
OLLIS
St Greenwood 31 E 4
St Safety Bay 136 E 10
Wy Parmelia 131 C 5
OLMAR
Pl Westfield 106 C 9
OLNEY
Ct Balga 32 B 8
Pl Huntingdale 95 C 9
OLSEN
Ct Leeming 93 C 9
Ct Woodvale 24 C 5
OLYMPIC
Pl Ardross 82 D 8
Wy Connolly 19 C 8
OLYMPUS
Ri Greenfields 163 C 10
OMAHA
Cl Gosnells 105 E 1
O'MALLEY
St Osborne Park 59 D 2
O'MARA
Pl Belmont 62 D 10
OMBERSLEY
Wy Coodanup 165 D 3
O'MEAGHER
Rd Karragullen 109 B 2
OMEO
Pl Karragullen 108 D 6
OMMANNEY
St Hamilton Hill 90 E 10
ONDINE
Pl Greenwood 31 E 5
O'NEILE
Pde Redcliffe 62 E 9
ONSLOW
Cl Gooseberry H 77 B 3
Pl Joondalup 19 D 7
Rd Shenton Park 72 A 4
Rd Shenton Park 71 D 4
St Chidlow 56 E 2

Map Ref.

St Fremantle 90 E 4
St South Perth 72 E 9
ONTARIO
Cr Joondalup 19 C 2
Rd Dianella 47 C 9
ONYX
Ct Carine 45 A 1
Ct High Wycombe 64 A 10
Rd Armadale 116 E 6
OORAMA
Ct Ocean Reef 18 E 7
OPAL
Ct Maida Vale 64 D 10
Dr Edgewater 24 A 1
Pl Riverton 83 E 9
Wy Armadale 116 E 7
OPHELIA
Gr Armadale 117 A 4
OPHEUS
Ri Merriwa 11 D 9
OPHIR
Ct Hamilton Hill 101 C 3
OPORTO
Ri Coogee 101 A 10
OPPERMAN
Pl Middle Swan 50 E 4
ORANA
Cr Brentwood 93 A 2
Cr City Beach 58 E 9
Pl Byford 126 D 9
Pl Helena Valley 65 C 3
St Lesmurdie 87 C 3
Wy Helena Valley 65 C 3
Wy Roleystone 108 A 8
ORANGE
Ave Perth City 61 A 10
Ave Upper Swan 29 E 1
Gr Armadale 115 E 4
Gr Currambine 19 A 4
La Darlington 66 A 5
Pl Beechboro 48 E 3
Rd Darlington 66 A 4
ORANGEDALE
Rd Lesmurdie 87 D 4
ORANGE VALLEY
Rd Kalamunda 77 C 9
Rd Kalamunda 77 D 9
ORANIA
Me Warnbro 145 E 9
ORARA
Me Merriwa 10 B 8
ORBELL
Rd Hillarys 30 C 2
Wy Bull Creek 92 E 5
ORBERRY
Pl Thornlie 95 A 6
ORBISON
Pl Willetton 94 A 2
ORBIT
St Beckenham 85 D 7
ORCHARD
Ave Armadale 116 D 6
Ave Midvale 51 A 8
Rd Maddington 86 B 10
Rd South Lake 102 B 6
St Upper Swan 29 E 1
ORCHID
Ct Clarkson 14 D 1
Ct High Wycombe 76 A 1
Ct Thornlie 105 A 1
Dr Roleystone 108 B 7
Dr Roleystone 108 B 8
Rd Neerabup 13 C 9
Rd Nowergup 13 B 4
St Joondanna 60 D 2
ORD
Cl Mandurah 165 D 1
Rd Heathridge 19 C 9
St Fremantle 90 C 4
St Fremantle 1D C 5

Map Ref.

St Nedlands 71 C 8
St West Perth 72 C 2
St West Perth 1C D 2
OREGON
Pl Cooloongup 138 A 7
O'REILLY
Cl Beaconsfield 90 E 7
ORELIA
Ave Orelia 131 A 4
St Madora 160 D 8
ORESTES
St San Remo 163 C 1
St San Remo 160 C 10
ORIANA
Ri Iluka 18 D 3
St Belmont 74 D 1
ORIENT
Cl Iluka 18 E 4
St Sth Fremantle 90 C 9
ORIOLE
St Stirling 45 E 8
Wy Thornlie 95 A 3
ORION
Ct Craigie 23 D 6
Rd Silver Sands 163 B 6
St Rockingham 137 B 9
Wy Marangaroo 32 D 5
ORISSA
Pl Two Rocks 2 C 2
ORIZABA
Pl Rockingham 137 D 7
ORKNEY
Rd Greenwood 31 C 5
ORLANDO
St Kelmscott 106 E 9
ORLEANS
Dr Port Kennedy 156 D 1
Dr Port Kennedy 145 D 10
St Spearwood 101 B 5
ORLESTONE
St Gosnells 95 E 8
ORME
Ct Westfield 106 C 9
ORMEAU
Pl Greenfields 163 D 9
ORMISTON
Gns Clarkson 14 E 10
ORMOND
Cl Swan View 51 C 5
Ct Woodvale 24 C 7
Pl Warnbro 145 E 7
Rd Attadale 81 D 8
Vw Mirrabooka 33 B 10
ORMSBY
Tce Mandurah 162 E 9
Tce San Remo 163 C 1
Tce Silver Sands 163 A 7
ORNUM
Pl Innaloo 45 B 7
ORONSAY
Rd Greenwood 31 C 7
O'ROURKE
Cl Murdoch 92 D 7
OROYA
Cl Morley 48 C 8
ORPINGTON
St Cloverdale 75 A 3
ORR
Pl Stirling 45 D 6
St Maddington 95 E 4
ORREL
Ave Floreat 59 C 9
ORRIN
Ct Duncraig 31 A 7
ORROCK
Ct Leeming 93 D 9

For detailed information regarding the street referencing system used in this book, turn to page 170.

P

		Map	Ref.
ORRONG			
Pl	Kewdale	74	D 9
Rd	Carlisle	74	B 6
Rd	Lathlain	74	A 4
Rd	Rivervale	74	A 4
Rd	Rivervale	73	E 3
Rd	Welshpool	84	E 1
Rd	Welshpool	74	E 10
ORSETT			
Wy	Gosnells	106	C 2
ORSOVA			
St	Tuart Hill	46	B 9
ORTON			
Rd	Byford	135	E 5
Rd	Casuarina	131	E 5
Rd	Oakford	133	A 5
Rd	Oakford	134	A 5
Rd	Oakford	132	D 5
Rd	Oakford	134	D 5
ORUNGAL			
Pl	Iluka	18	E 4
ORVILLE			
Pl	Hamersley	31	D 9
ORWELL			
Cr	Woodvale	24	A 6
Ct	Munster	101	C 10
OSBORN			
St	Waikiki	145	C 5
OSBORNE			
Pde	Claremont	80	E 1
Pl	Stirling	45	D 7
Rd	Dianella	46	E 6
Rd	East Fremantle	90	E 2
St	Joondanna	60	D 3
St	Mt Helena	54	D 4
St	Stoneville	54	D 4
St	Tuart Hill	60	D 2
OSBOURN			
Pl	Kewdale	74	E 8
OSCAR			
St	Armadale	116	B 8
OSLO			
La	Willetton	93	C 7
Pl	Warnbro	145	D 7
OSMASTON			
Rd	Carine	31	A 10
Rd	Carine	30	E 9
OSMOND			
Cl	Marangaroo	32	C 5
St	Kenwick	95	D 3
OSPREY			
Ci	Ballajura	33	D 6
Cl	Halls Head	164	B 2
Cl	Stirling	45	D 6
Dr	Yangebup	102	A 9
Gr	Edgewater	20	A 10
Rd	Two Rocks	2	D 1
Wy	Thornlie	95	A 6
OSPRINGE			
St	Gosnells	95	E 8
OSTEN			
Pl	Langford	94	E 3
OSTEND			
Pl	Warnbro	145	E 5
Rd	Scarborough	58	E 1
OSTLE			
St	Mullaloo	23	A 5
O'SULLIVAN			
Dr	Westfield	106	B 8
Pl	Mariginiup	16	E 8
OSWALD			
St	Coolbellup	101	D 1
St	Innaloo	59	D 1
St	Innaloo	45	D 10
St	Victoria Park	73	D 6
OSWELL			
St	Cloverdale	74	E 3
OSWIN			
Ct	Lynwood	94	B 4

		Map	Ref.
OTAGO			
Cl	Meadow Sprgs.	163	D 1
Ct	Currambine	19	C 5
Me	Mirrabooka	47	B 2
OTFORD			
Pl	Merriwa	11	D 8
OTHELA			
Pwy	Leeming	103	A 1
OTISCO			
Cr	Joondalup	19	C 3
OTLEY			
Pl	Gosnells	106	B 1
St	Dianella	47	A 8
OTRAM			
Wy	Churchlands	59	B 5
OTTAWA			
Cr	Beechboro	48	D 3
Wy	Wanneroo	20	C 6
OTTAWAY			
St	Kelmscott	106	D 10
OTTER			
Ct	Willetton	93	D 7
Me	Merriwa	14	C 1
OTTERDEN			
St	Gosnells	95	E 8
OTWAY			
Cr	High Wycombe	64	B 9
Pl	Bedfordale	127	E 5
Pl	Craigie	23	C 8
Pl	Shoalwater	136	D 8
St	Swanbourne	70	E 9
OUGDEN			
Wy	Medina	130	E 3
OUTLOOK			
Cl	Helena Valley	65	C 3
Dr	Edgewater	24	A 1
Dr	Edgewater	20	A 10
OUTRAM			
Pl	Hamilton Hill	91	A 10
St	West Perth	72	C 2
OUTRIDGE			
Rd	Baldivis	157	C 2
OUTTON			
Wy	Singleton	160	D 3
OUTTRIM			
Rd	Glen Forrest	66	C 2
OVENS			
Pl	Rockingham	137	B 6
Rd	Thornlie	95	B 8
St	Padbury	30	E 1
St	Padbury	23	E 10
OVER			
Ave	Lesmurdie	87	B 4
OVERSBY			
St	Halls Head	162	C 9
OVERTON			
Gns	Cottesloe	80	C 2
OWEN			
Pl	Hamersley	31	C 10
Pl	Hamilton Hill	101	C 3
Rd	Darlington	66	A 5
Rd	Hamilton Hill	101	A 3
Rd	Kelmscott	116	C 2
Rd	Parkerville	53	C 5
Rd	Safety Bay	144	E 1
St	Falcon	162A	E 10
St	Mandurah	165	C 1
OWENS			
Ct	Belmont	74	E 2
OWGAN			
Pl	Bull Creek	93	B 7
OWL			
Ce	Ballajura	33	D 5
Ct	Gosnells	106	A 4
OWSTON			
St	Mosman Park	80	E 7
OWTRAM			
Rd	Armadale	116	D 4

		Map	Ref.
OXCLIFFE			
Rd	Doubleview	59	A 2
OXFORD			
Cl	Leederville	60	C 10
Cl	Mandurah	165	B 5
Ct	Maida Vale	76	D 3
Ct	Mt Claremont	71	A 5
St	Kensington	73	C 10
St	Leederville	60	C 7
St	Maylands	61	D 5
St	Mt Hawthorn	60	C 6
OXLEIGH			
Dr	Malaga	33	D 10
OXLEY			
Ave	Padbury	23	C 8
Pl	Greenmount	66	A 2
Pl	Greenmount	65	E 2
Pl	Rockingham	137	B 6
Rd	Banjup	113	E 10
Rd	Forrestdale	114	A 10
Rd	Forrestdale	115	A 10
Rd	Greenmount	66	A 1
Rd	Greenmount	65	E 2
Rd	Hovea	53	A 7
Rd	Hovea	52	E 8
OXTED			
Pl	Morley	48	A 7
Pl	Morley	47	E 7
OYSTER			
Ct	Craigie	23	D 7
OZARK			
Gns	Joondalup	19	D 3
Pl	Warnbro	145	E 7
OZONE			
Ct	Halls Head	164	B 1
Pde	Cottesloe	70	C 10
Pde	Trigg	44	D 8
Rd	Marmion	30	C 8
Tce	Kalamunda	77	A 9

P

		Map	Ref.
PACE			
Rd	Medina	130	E 5
PACIFIC			
Ave	Swanbourne	70	D 7
Ct	Waikiki	145	C 4
Wy	Beldon	23	C 2
PACKARD			
St	Joondalup	19	D 7
PACKER			
St	Beckenham	85	A 9
St	Mt Helena	55	C 4
PACKET			
Pl	Yanchep	4	C 4
PACKHAM			
Rd	Hamilton Hill	101	B 2
PADBURY			
Ave	Millendon	37	A 1
Ave	Millendon	36	C 1
Ave	Red Hill	37	D 2
Ci	Sorrento	30	B 5
Ct	Eden Hill	48	E 8
Pl	Eden Hill	48	E 9
Rd	Darlington	66	A 2
Rd	Darlington	65	E 2
Tce	Midland	50	C 9
Wy	Eden Hill	48	E 9
PADDINGTON			
St	Bayswater	62	D 5
St	North Perth	60	E 5
PADDY TROY			
Ml	Fremantle	90	C 5
PADSTOW			
St	Karrinyup	44	E 3
PAGANONI			
Rd	Karnup	159	B 9
PAGDEN			
Pl	Lynwood	94	B 4

		Map	Ref.
PAGE			
Ave	Bentley	84	A 4
Dr	Mullaloo	23	A 4
Rd	Kelmscott	106	D 7
St	Attadale	81	C 7
PAGEANT			
Lp	Heathridge	19	C 9
PAGES			
Wy	Martin	96	E 10
PAGET			
St	Hilton	91	B 9
PAGHAN			
Rd	Balcatta	46	B 5
PAGNELL			
Ct	Hamilton Hill	100	E 3
Wy	Swan View	51	D 8
PAGODA			
Gns	Mirrabooka	33	B 10
Pl	Madora	160	C 7
PAINE			
Ct	Karrinyup	45	A 6
Rd	Morley	48	B 7
PAISLEY			
Ct	Warwick	31	C 7
PAITT			
St	Willagee	91	D 5
PAKENHAM			
St	Fremantle	1D	B 5
St	Fremantle	90	B 5
St	Mt Lawley	61	C 9
PALAMINO			
Wy	Armadale	115	D 2
PALAMUNA			
Ct	Hillman	137	E 6
PALANA			
Rd	City Beach	58	D 9
PALARI			
Rd	Ocean Reef	23	B 1
PALERMO			
Ct	Merriwa	14	C 1
Ct	Merriwa	11	C 10
PALGRAVE			
El	Marangaroo	32	C 4
PALIN			
Ct	Langford	95	A 1
St	Palmyra	91	B 1
PALISADE			
La	Willetton	93	E 5
PALLARUP			
Lp	Waikiki	145	E 1
PALLAS			
Pl	Willetton	93	E 6
Wy	San Remo	163	C 1
PALLENS			
Gr	Mirrabooka	46	E 1
PALLINUP			
Pl	Gosnells	105	E 2
Pl	Mandurah	165	A 4
PALLITT			
St	St James	83	E 3
PALL MALL			
	Bayswater	62	C 7
PALM			
Cst	Ballajura	33	D 8
Ct	Beechboro	48	C 3
Ct	Thornlie	95	B 10
Dr	Warnbro	145	D 5
Me	Edgewater	24	B 2
Pl	Wilson	84	C 6
Rd	Roleystone	108	C 10
Tce	Forrestfield	86	E 1
PALMA			
Pl	Coogee	101	A 10
PALMATEER			
Dr	Bickley	88	C 5
Dr	Carmel	88	C 6
Dr	Walliston	88	B 2

		Map	Ref.
PALMER			
Cr	High Wycombe	76	A 1
Pl	Embleton	62	B 1
St	Attadale	81	D 8
St	Warnbro	145	C 5
Wy	Mandurah	163	C 9
PALMEROSE			
Ct	North Lake	92	A 10
PALMERSTON			
St	Bassendean	63	A 2
St	Mosman Park	80	E 7
St	Northbridge	1C	E 1
St	Northbridge	72	E 1
St	Perth City	60	E 10
St	St James	84	B 4
PALM SPRINGS			
Blvd	Warnbro	145	E 9
PALOMA			
Lp	Marangaroo	32	D 5
PALOS			
Ct	Sorrento	30	D 4
PALTARA			
Wy	Wanneroo	20	E 10
PALTARRA			
Rd	Nollamara	46	C 5
PALTRIDGE			
Ave	Carlisle	74	B 6
PALUMA			
Ct	Greenfields	163	D 9
Ct	Warnbro	145	E 8
PAMBULA			
Ct	South Lake	102	D 8
PAMMENT			
St	Nth Fremantle	80	E 4
PAMPUS			
Ct	Mirrabooka	47	B 1
PAN			
Cl	Morley	48	D 6
PANACHE			
Gns	Joondalup	19	C 3
PANAMA			
Pl	Safety Bay	137	B 10
PANAMUNA			
Dr	Falcon	162A	A 3
Dr	Willetton	93	D 5
PANAX			
Ct	South Lake	102	C 6
PANDANUS			
Me	Canning Vale	104	B 1
PANDORA			
Dr	City Beach	58	E 9
Wy	Currambine	19	B 3
Wy	Waikiki	145	D 1
PANGBOURNE			
St	Wembley	59	E 9
PANJADA			
Pl	Heathridge	19	B 10
PANNELL			
Rd	Bateman	92	D 4
Wy	Girrawheen	32	E 8
PANORAMA			
Dr	Kelmscott	106	E 6
Gns	Ballajura	33	D 6
Hts	Canning Vale	94	B 10
Pl	Neerabup	16	A 4
PANORAMIC			
Tce	Forrestfield	77	A 8
Tce	Kalamunda	77	A 8
PANSY			
St	North Perth	60	E 5
PANTON			
Cr	Karrinyup	45	B 2
Ct	Middle Swan	50	C 6
Rd	Greenfields	163	C 6
PAPE			
Pl	Shoalwater	136	D 8

232 For detailed information regarding the street referencing system used in this book, turn to page 170.

P

		Map	Ref.
PAPERBARK			
Dr	Willetton	93	D 5
Wy	Morley	48	C 5
PAPERCAP			
St	Gosnells	106	B 1
PAPPAS			
St	Wangara	25	A 7
PAPUANA			
Pl	Marangaroo	32	D 5
PAR			
Ct	Cooloongup	138	A 8
PARADISE			
Qs	Ballajura	33	C 8
PARAGON			
Hts	Currambine	19	A 3
PARAGUAY			
Ave	Greenfields	165	D 1
PARAKA			
Wy	Forrestdale	114	E 5
PARAKEELA			
Gr	Maddington	96	D 3
PARAKEET			
Wy	Coogee	100	E 9
PARALLEL			
Rd	Karrakatta	71	C 5
PARAMATTA			
Rd	Doubleview	59	A 2
Rd	Doubleview	45	B 10
PARAMOUNT			
Dr	Wangara	25	B 6
PARANA			
Cr	Beechboro	48	E 4
PARANT			
Pl	Carine	45	B 1
PARARA			
Me	Iluka	18	E 5
PARDEE			
El	Greenfields	165	D 2
PARDOO			
Pl	Golden Bay	158	D 7
Ri	Yangebup	102	A 10
PARER			
Cl	Thornlie	94	E 4
PARHAM			
Rd	Quinns Rocks	10	A 1
PARIAN			
Pl	Rossmoyne	93	B 1
PARILLA			
Ct	Greenfields	163	D 10
PARIN			
Rd	Marangaroo	32	A 4
PARINGA			
Me	Currambine	19	A 5
Pl	Gosnells	95	E 10
St	Morley	48	C 6
PARIS			
Pl	Coolbellup	101	E 1
Wy	Karrinyup	45	B 4
PARK			
Ave	Crawley	72	A 7
Ce	Kardinya	92	B 8
Cl	Greenwood	31	C 4
Dr	Cooloongup	137	C 9
La	Alexander Hts	33	A 4
La	Bassendean	63	A 1
La	Canning Vale	94	A 9
La	Claremont	71	A 10
La	Kardinya	92	B 8
La	Willetton	93	E 2
Pl	Bibra Lake	101	D 6
Rd	Byford	135	C 2
Rd	Byford	126	D 10
Rd	Crawley	72	A 7
Rd	Crawley	71	E 7
Rd	Hovea	66	D 1
Rd	Hovea	52	D 8
Rd	Kenwick	85	C 1
Rd	Kenwick	95	E 1
Rd	Mandurah	165	B 1

		Map	Ref.
Rd	Mandurah	163	B 8
Rd	Mandurah	163	B 10
Rd	Midvale	51	A 8
Rd	Mt Lawley	61	B 8
Rd	Mt Pleasant	82	E 8
Rd	Nedlands	71	E 7
St	Bedford	61	D 4
St	Como	83	A 4
St	Cullacabardee	34	A 1
St	Cullacabardee	33	E 1
St	Henley Brook	36	A 1
St	Henley Brook	35	D 1
St	Subiaco	72	B 2
St	Trigg	44	D 8
St	Tuart Hill	46	B 10
St	Whiteman	35	B 1
Wy	Casuarina	132	C 5
Wy	Innaloo	45	A 7
PARK BEACH			
Cl	Shelley	83	E 8
PARKE			
Rd	Gooseberry H	77	C 5
PARKER			
Ave	Kelmscott	116	E 1
Ave	Sorrento	30	B 6
Pl	Bentley	83	D 2
Pl	Winthrop	92	C 5
Rd	Claremont	81	B 1
Rd	Parkerville	53	C 7
St	Bassendean	63	A 2
St	East Fremantle	80	E 10
St	Northbridge	1C	B 1
St	Northbridge	72	E 1
St	South Perth	72	E 7
PARKES			
St	Yangebup	102	B 7
PARKFIELD			
Pl	Craigie	23	E 6
Rd	Kelmscott	106	C 10
PARKHILL			
Wy	Wilson	84	A 6
PARKHURST			
Ri	Padbury	30	E 2
PARKIN			
Ct	Eden Hill	48	E 8
Rd	Roleystone	108	B 6
St	Rockingham	136	D 5
PARKINSON			
Ct	Hillarys	23	B 9
Pl	Hillarys	23	C 9
St	Noranda	47	D 5
PARKLAND			
Cl	Edgewater	24	B 1
Dr	Warnbro	145	D 6
Lp	Cooloongup	138	A 7
Rd	Osborne Park	60	A 4
Rd	Osborne Park	59	E 4
Rd	Stoneville	54	A 3
Trl	Canning Vale	94	A 10
PARKLANDS			
Sq	Riverton	93	D 1
PARKSIDE			
Ave	Mt Pleasant	92	E 1
Ave	Mt Pleasant	82	E 10
Dr	Thornlie	95	D 5
Gns	Ballajura	33	C 5
Ra	Woodvale	24	D 9
PARKSTONE			
Gr	Meadow Sprgs	163	C 6
Rt	Currambine	19	B 5
PARK VIEW			
Grn	Churchlands	59	C 4
PARKVIEW			
Dr	Ballajura	33	C 6
Pde	Redcliffe	63	A 10
Rd	Mandurah	165	B 2
Ri	Willetton	93	B 6
PARKVISTA			
Ave	Ballajura	33	C 6
Ct	Lynwood	94	C 4
Gr	Carine	31	C 10

		Map	Ref.
PARKWATER			
Ce	Halls Head	162	D 10
PARKWAY			
	Crawley	72	A 9
	Swan View	51	E 7
	Warwick	31	D 8
Gns	Parmelia	131	B 10
Rd	Bibra Lake	102	C 2
Rd	Thornlie	95	B 9
Trl	Ballajura	33	D 5
PARKWOOD			
Gns	Coodanup	165	D 4
PARLIAMENT			
Pl	West Perth	1C	D 2
Pl	West Perth	72	D 2
PARMELIA			
Ave	Parmelia	131	B 9
Gr	Salter Point	83	A 8
St	Sth Fremantle	90	C 9
Wy	Bassendean	62	E 1
Wy	Craigie	23	E 6
Wy	Madora	160	C 7
PARNELL			
Ave	Marmion	30	D 8
Ave	Sorrento	30	C 5
Pde	Bassendean	63	B 3
Rd	Hamilton Hill	91	A 10
PARR			
Cl	Padbury	23	D 9
PARRAMATTA			
La	Willetton	94	A 4
PARRI			
Rd	Wangara	25	A 8
PARROT			
Ct	Gosnells	106	A 4
Ct	High Wycombe	64	B 10
PARROTT			
Wy	Spearwood	101	B 6
PARRY			
Ave	Bateman	92	D 5
Ave	Bull Creek	93	A 5
St	Claremont	70	E 10
St	East Fremantle	90	E 1
St	Fremantle	1D	C 4
St	Fremantle	90	C 4
St	Perth City	1C	A 1
St	Perth City	73	A 1
PARSONS			
Ave	Manning	83	B 7
Ave	Parmelia	131	B 7
Ct	Leeming	93	A 10
Rd	Mundijong	150	E 6
St	Embleton	62	A 1
Wy	Innaloo	45	B 8
PARTLET			
Rd	Duncraig	30	E 3
PARTLON			
Ri	Leeming	102	E 1
PARTRIDGE			
St	Henley Brook	35	C 2
St	Orelia	130	E 4
Wy	Thornlie	95	A 4
PARWICH			
Ri	Carine	30	D 10
PASCAL			
Ri	Merriwa	11	E 10
PASCO			
Ct	Woodvale	24	B 4
PASCOE			
Rt	Merriwa	11	C 9
St	Bellevue	50	E 10
St	Karrinyup	44	E 4
St	Kelmscott	116	E 1
PASKIN			
St	Balcatta	46	A 4
PASS			
Cr	Beaconsfield	90	E 8
Rd	High Wycombe	64	D 10
PASSERINE			
Cl	Edgewater	24	B 2

		Map	Ref.
PASSEY			
Pl	Kardinya	91	E 9
PASSIFLORA			
Dr	Forrestfield	76	D 9
PASSMORE			
Ave	Nth Fremantle	80	D 10
St	Rossmoyne	93	B 2
St	Southern River	105	C 9
PAT			
St	Lynwood	94	B 4
PATCHEM			
Wy	Balga	46	B 3
PATCHETT			
St	Cloverdale	75	A 4
PATERSON			
Ct	Munster	101	B 10
Gns	Winthrop	92	B 4
Pl	Padbury	23	E 9
Rd	Armadale	117	A 4
Rd	Greenfields	165	A 1
Rd	Henley Brook	36	A 2
Rd	Henley Brook	35	E 2
Rd	Kelmscott	117	A 2
Rd	Kewdale	74	D 7
St	Bayswater	62	A 4
St	Como	83	A 6
St	Mundijong	143	A 8
PATFIELD			
Pl	Kelmscott	106	C 10
St	Myaree	91	E 2
PATHFINDER			
Rd	Padbury	30	E 1
Rd	Padbury	23	E 10
PATON			
Cl	Winthrop	92	A 4
Me	Quinns Rocks	10	B 10
Pl	Samson	91	C 8
PATONGA			
Rd	City Beach	58	D 9
PATRICIA			
Rd	Kalamunda	77	C 9
St	Caversham	49	C 3
St	E Victoria Pk	84	A 1
PATRICK			
Ct	Girrawheen	32	C 7
Vs	Parmelia	131	A 9
Wy	Huntingdale	95	D 10
PATTERSON			
Dr	Middle Swan	50	E 4
Pl	Myaree	92	A 2
Pl	Myaree	91	E 2
Rd	Beechina	43	D 9
Rd	Bickley	89	B 3
Rd	E Rockingham	137	D 2
Rd	Kwinana Beach	130	A 8
Rd	Pickering Bk	89	C 7
Rd	Rockingham	137	B 4
PATTIE			
St	Cannington	84	E 6
PATTON			
Rd	Mundaring	68	B 2
PATULA			
Pl	Menora	61	A 4
PAUL			
St	Halls Head	162	D 10
Wy	Orelia	131	A 4
PAULETT			
Wy	Belmont	62	D 10
PAULIK			
Wy	Hamilton Hill	101	A 3
PAULINA			
Wy	Coolbellup	91	D 10
PAULINE			
Ave	Kalamunda	77	E 9
PAULL			
Me	Bull Creek	93	A 5
St	Furnissdale	165	E 6
PAULLS VALLEY			
Rd	Helena Valley	78	D 3
Rd	Paulls Valley	78	E 4

		Map	Ref.
PAUSIN			
Cr	Bibra Lake	102	D 2
PAVETA			
Ct	Greenwood	31	D 4
PAVETTA			
Cr	Forrestfield	76	B 6
PAVLOVICH			
Ct	Wattleup	112	A 10
PAVO			
Cl	Rockingham	137	B 9
PAVONIA			
Hts	South Lake	102	B 2
PAWLETT			
Wy	Karrinyup	44	E 3
PAYNE			
Cl	Leeming	93	B 9
Hl	Ocean Reef	23	A 1
Hl	Ocean Reef	19	A 10
St	Shoalwater	136	D 9
PEACH			
St	North Perth	60	E 8
PEACHEY			
Ave	Kewdale	74	E 7
PEACOCK			
Cl	Armadale	116	A 3
Grn	Ballajura	33	E 7
St	Cloverdale	75	A 4
PEAK			
Ct	Leeming	93	D 8
Vw	Ballajura	33	D 6
Vw	Canning Vale	104	B 1
PEAKE			
Pl	Mandurah	165	B 3
Wy	Medina	130	D 5
PEARCE			
Rge	Winthrop	92	C 5
St	Quinns Rocks	10	E 1
St	Sawyers Valley	69	A 1
PEARL			
Ct	Maida Vale	64	D 10
Pde	Scarborough	44	D 8
Rd	Cloverdale	75	A 4
St	Sorrento	30	C 3
PEARSALL			
Gns	Mullaloo	23	A 5
PEARSE			
Rd	Success	112	A 8
Rd	Wattleup	122	A 2
Rd	Wattleup	112	A 10
St	Cottesloe	80	C 3
St	Nth Fremantle	90	C 1
PEARSON			
Cr	Bull Creek	93	B 6
Pl	Jandakot	113	A 3
Pl	Floreat	59	D 6
St	Ashfield	62	E 5
St	Bayswater	62	D 4
St	Churchlands	59	C 6
St	Kelmscott	116	D 2
St	Osborne Park	59	D 3
St	Woodlands	59	C 4
Wy	Osborne Park	59	D 3
PEASHOLM			
St	City Beach	58	D 3
St	Scarborough	58	D 3
PEBBLE BEACH			
Ed	Connolly	19	A 4
PEBBLEWOOD			
Rd	Woodvale	24	D 8
PECAN			
Ct	South Lake	102	B 6
Ri	Mirrabooka	47	A 2
PECHEY			
Rd	Swan View	51	D 7
PECKHAM			
Cr	Kingsley	24	C 10
St	Beckenham	85	B 9
PECOS			
Ct	Dudley Park	165	C 5
Pl	Beechboro	48	D 3

For detailed information regarding the street referencing system used in this book, turn to page 170.

P

		Map	Ref.
PECTEN			
Cl	Heathridge	23	D 1
PEDDER			
Pl	Joondalup	19	D 3
Wy	Parmelia	131	C 6
PEDDIE			
Pl	Balga	32	D 10
PEDERICK			
Rd	Neerabup	16	D 1
PEDERSEN			
St	Cloverdale	75	A 4
PEDLER			
Pl	Balga	32	D 9
PEEBLES			
Rd	Floreat	59	C 8
PEEL			
Ct	Armadale	116	C 4
Ct	Kwinana Twn C	131	A 7
Me	Mindarie	10	B 2
Pde	Coodanup	165	C 8
Rd	Coogee	111	A 5
Rd	O'Connor	91	C 6
St	Guildford	49	E 10
St	Jolimont	71	E 1
St	Mandurah	163	A 10
St	Mandurah	162	E 9
PEELWOOD			
Pde	Halls Head	164	A 8
Pde	Halls Head	164	B 4
PEERLESS			
Pl	Noranda	48	B 5
PEET			
Cr	Trigg	44	C 7
Ct	Noranda	47	D 6
Rd	Kalamunda	77	C 8
Rd	Roleystone	107	E 8
PEGASUS			
Ri	Ocean Reef	18	E 8
St	Rockingham	137	B 8
PEGG			
Ct	Wattle Grove	75	E 10
PEGGS			
Pl	Leeming	103	A 1
PEGLER			
St	Willagee	91	E 4
PEGLEY			
Dr	Lynwood	94	B 3
PEGUS			
St	Thornlie	95	C 3
PEIRSE			
Wy	Marmion	30	C 8
PELHAM			
St	Armadale	116	C 8
Wy	Girrawheen	32	D 9
PELICAN			
Ct	Churchlands	59	C 7
Ct	Heathridge	19	C 10
Ct	Two Rocks	2	D 1
Ct	Waikiki	145	C 2
Lp	High Wycombe	76	C 1
Pde	Ballajura	34	A 8
Pde	Ballajura	33	E 8
Pl	Mandurah	165	A 3
Pl	Wilson	84	B 7
Ra	Yangebup	102	A 8
PELLEW			
Gns	Willetton	93	C 7
PELLY			
Ce	Joondalup	19	C 3
PELSART			
Pl	Heathridge	19	C 10
PEMBROKE			
Ct	Warnbro	145	C 7
St	Bicton	81	B 9
PEMBURY			
Cr	Ferndale	84	B 9
Rd	Thornlie	95	B 5
PENANG			
Lp	Warnbro	145	E 7

		Map	Ref.
PENDA			
Cl	Halls Head	164	B 4
PENDEEN			
St	Cloverdale	75	A 6
PENDER			
Ct	Thornlie	95	D 6
PENDINE			
St	Carine	45	B 1
PENDOCK			
Pl	Willetton	93	D 4
PENDRAGON			
Ct	Westfield	106	C 7
PENDULA			
Gns	Mirrabooka	47	A 1
PENELOPE			
Pl	Innaloo	45	C 7
PENGILLY			
Rd	Orelia	131	A 4
Rd	Orelia	130	E 4
PENGUIN			
Cl	Heathridge	23	C 1
Rd	Safety Bay	144	D 1
Rd	Safety Bay	136	D 10
Rd	Shoalwater	144	C 1
St	Dianella	47	C 7
PENHURST			
Ct	Thornlie	95	B 6
PENINSULA			
Ave	Heathridge	23	C 1
Ent	Mandurah	162	E 10
Pl	Safety Bay	136	E 10
Rd	Maylands	62	A 9
Rd	Maylands	74	B 1
Rd	Maylands	61	D 8
Rd	Wilson	84	C 8
Tr	Ballajura	33	D 7
PENION			
Cl	Heathridge	19	D 10
PENISTONE			
St	Greenwood	31	E 6
PENJAN			
Pl	Kelmscott	106	E 6
PENLEA			
Hts	Kiara	48	E 7
PENMAR			
Ct	Woodvale	24	B 6
PENN			
Pl	Koondoola	33	A 8
Pl	Koongamia	65	B 2
St	Maddington	96	A 5
PENNANT			
Pl	Woodvale	24	A 7
St	North Perth	60	D 7
PENNELL			
Rd	Claremont	71	B 10
St	Chidlow	56	C 2
PENNINA			
Wy	Meadow Sprgs	163	D 5
PENNINE			
Wy	Hamersley	31	C 9
PENNINGTON			
Gns	Erskine	164	C 6
St	Kensington	73	C 9
PENNO			
Ct	Leeming	93	C 8
PENNY			
La	Woodvale	24	B 7
Pl	Kelmscott	107	A 9
PENOLA			
Ct	Clarkson	11	E 10
Wy	Halls Head	164	C 4
PENRITH			
Ct	Meadow Sprgs	163	D 5
Ct	Willetton	94	A 4
Pl	Balga	46	B 1
St	Mandurah	165	A 3
PENROSE			
Ct	Maddington	96	C 3

		Map	Ref.
PENRYN			
Ave	City Beach	70	D 1
Ct	Kewdale	74	E 7
St	Kewdale	74	E 7
PENSHURST			
St	Marangaroo	32	B 6
PENSON			
Pl	Singleton	160	D 4
St	Singleton	160	D 3
PENTECOST			
Ave	Beechboro	48	D 2
PENTLAND			
Ave	Duncraig	31	B 5
Cr	Dudley Park	165	C 4
PENZANCE			
St	Bassendean	62	E 1
St	Bassendean	48	E 10
PEOPLES			
Ave	Gooseberry H	77	C 2
PEPIN			
Ct	Joondalup	19	D 2
PEPLER			
Ave	Salter Point	83	B 8
PEPPER			
Cl	Ballajura	33	C 6
St	Falcon	162A	A 4
St	South Perth	73	B 8
PEPPERING			
Wy	Balga	46	B 2
PEPPERMINT			
Cr	Ballajura	33	C 5
Dr	Greenwood	31	C 5
Dr	Thornlie	95	B 10
Pl	Morley	48	D 6
PEPPERWOOD			
Gr	Woodvale	24	D 8
Ri	Halls Head	164	B 4
PEPYS			
Ct	Spearwood	101	B 8
PERA			
Me	Beldon	23	C 4
PERCH			
Ct	Sorrento	30	C 3
PERCY			
Rd	Bayswater	62	B 7
St	Gosnells	96	C 10
PERDITA			
Wy	Coolbellup	91	D 10
PEREGRINE			
Dr	Kingsley	31	C 2
Ri	Ballajura	33	E 6
PERGODA			
Pl	Edgewater	24	A 3
PERICLES			
Ct	Rockingham	137	D 7
PERIDA			
Wy	Greenfields	163	E 9
PERIE BANOU			
Cl	Halls Head	164	D 2
PERILYA			
Rd	Craigie	23	D 5
PERINA			
Pl	Wilson	84	B 6
Wy	City Beach	58	D 4
PERIVALE			
Cl	Kingsley	31	B 2
PERIWINKLE			
Rd	Mullaloo	23	B 3
Wy	Lynwood	94	B 7
PERKINS			
Rd	Melville	91	C 1
PERMAN			
Pl	Kewdale	74	D 6
PERON			
Cl	Cooloongup	137	C 9
PERREN			
Pl	E Cannington	85	C 4

		Map	Ref.
PERRETT			
Rd	Whitby	143	C 1
PERRIAM			
Cl	Parmelia	131	B 8
PERRIN			
Cr	Clarkson	14	D 1
Wy	High Wycombe	76	B 1
PERRONA			
Gns	Mullaloo	23	B 3
PERRY			
Cl	Bateman	92	D 4
La	Jolimont	59	D 10
La	Subiaco	71	E 2
Pl	Quinns Rocks	10	A 9
Rd	Martin	96	E 10
PERRY LAKES			
Dr	Floreat	71	A 1
Dr	Floreat	59	A 10
PERSEUS			
Ct	Rockingham	137	B 9
Rd	Silver Sands	163	B 8
PERSIMMON			
Pl	Kalamunda	77	B 4
St	North Perth	60	E 8
PERTH			
St	Bedford	61	E 3
St	Cottesloe	80	D 1
PERUVALE			
St	Carine	45	C 1
PESCATORE			
Pl	Golden Bay	158	E 9
PETALITE			
Pl	Armadale	116	E 7
PETER			
Rd	High Wycombe	64	B 9
St	Attadale	81	D 4
St	Halls Head	162	C 10
St	Kelmscott	106	E 8
St	Shoalwater	136	D 9
Wy	Rossmoyne	93	A 2
PETERBOROUGH			
Cr	Iluka	18	E 3
Cr	Morley	48	D 9
PETERKIN			
Me	Stratton	51	B 4
PETERS			
Pl	Morley	47	D 9
Wy	Bibra Lake	102	D 3
Wy	Oakford	124	D 5
PETHER			
Rd	Manning	83	B 5
PETHERBRIDGE			
St	Lathlain	74	B 6
PETILIA			
Ct	High Wycombe	76	C 1
PETINA			
Ct	Silver Sands	163	B 4
PETRA			
St	Bicton	91	A 1
St	Bicton	81	A 10
St	East Fremantle	91	A 2
St	East Fremantle	81	A 10
St	Palmyra	91	A 2
PETRANA			
Pl	Henley Brook	28	C 9
PETRE			
Gr	Clarkson	14	D 2
PETREL			
Cl	Armadale	116	B 4
Cl	Beldon	23	C 4
Cl	Halls Head	164	B 2
Cl	Wilson	84	B 7
Ct	Huntingdale	105	C 1
Pl	Ballajura	34	A 7
Wy	Two Rocks	2	D 1
PETRY			
St	Langford	94	D 2

		Map	Ref.
PETTERSON			
Ave	Kardinya	91	D 8
Ave	Samson	91	D 9
PETTIT			
Pl	Lesmurdie	87	C 5
St	Naval Base	121	A 3
PETUNIA			
St	Kalamunda	77	E 10
PEVERETT			
La	Oakford	124	E 9
PHAR LAP			
Dr	Byford	126	B 3
PHEASANT			
Cl	Armadale	116	B 3
Wy	Ballajura	34	A 7
PHEE			
Pl	Greenwood	31	E 5
PHIEL			
Ct	Kenwick	95	D 1
PHILANTE			
St	Falcon	162A	D 10
PHILIP			
Rd	Dalkeith	81	B 1
St	East Fremantle	81	A 10
St	Shoalwater	136	C 8
PHILLIMORE			
St	Fremantle	1D	B 5
St	Fremantle	90	B 5
PHILLIP			
Cl	Mullaloo	23	A 3
Ct	Padbury	23	D 10
Gr	Kalamunda	77	D 9
St	Maddington	95	E 5
Wy	Osborne Park	46	A 9
PHILLIPS			
Ct	Kiara	48	D 7
Gr	Innaloo	45	B 10
Pl	Greenfields	163	D 9
Pl	Karrinyup	45	A 7
Pl	Wanneroo	25	C 5
Rd	Mahogany Crk	67	D 2
Rd	Mundaring	68	A 1
Rd	Mundaring	67	D 2
Rd	Newburn	75	D 4
Rd	Wattleup	121	E 1
Rd	Wattleup	111	E 10
St	Dianella	47	C 6
Wy	Dianella	47	C 6
PHILLIPS-FOX			
Tce	Woodvale	24	B 4
PHILMORE			
Cr	Kardinya	91	D 9
PHILP			
Ave	Como	83	A 5
Cl	Huntingdale	95	E 10
PHIPPS			
St	Bicton	81	A 9
PHOEBE			
St	Southern River	105	C 7
PHOENIX			
Pro	Iluka	18	E 4
Rd	Bibra Lake	102	A 4
Rd	Bibra Lake	101	D 4
Rd	Spearwood	101	D 4
St	Dianella	47	B 7
PHYLLIS			
St	Nth Fremantle	80	D 10
PHYLMA			
St	Armadale	116	C 3
PIAGGIO			
Pl	Bayswater	62	A 6
PICARD			
Ct	Merriwa	11	D 10
PICARO			
Pl	Kewdale	74	E 9
PICASSO			
Ct	Kingsley	24	D 10
PICCADILLY			
Wy	Dianella	47	A 6

234

For detailed information regarding the street referencing system used in this book, turn to page 170.

P

		Map	Ref.
PICEA			
Pl	Forrestfield	76	D 9
PICKERING			
Wy	Booragoon	92	C 1
PICKERING BROOK			
Rd	Pickering Bk	99	A 1
Rd	Pickering Bk	89	C 10
Rd	Pickering Bk	99	E 1
Rd	Pickering Bk	88	E 10
PICKETT			
St	Bayswater	62	C 2
St	Swan View	51	C 6
PICTON			
Ct	Mindarie	14	C 5
Me	Riverton	84	A 10
Tce	Alexander Hts	33	A 3
PICTOR			
Ct	Rockingham	137	B 9
PIEDMONT			
Ct	Nollamara	46	C 7
St	Nollamara	46	C 7
PIER			
St	East Fremantle	80	E 10
St	Perth City	1C	A 2
St	Perth City	73	A 3
St	Perth City	1C	A 3
St	Perth City	73	A 3
St	Perth City	1C	B 1
PIERCEY			
Ct	Redcliffe	63	A 9
PIERCY			
Ct	Kardinya	92	A 7
St	Guildford	49	E 10
Wy	Kardinya	92	A 7
PIERRE			
Pl	Padbury	23	C 9
PIESSE			
Pl	Armadale	116	A 4
PIGEON			
Ct	Langford	95	A 1
PIGGOTT			
St	Armadale	116	C 8
PIKE			
Ct	Parmelia	131	A 9
La	Clarkson	14	D 1
Rd	Baldivis	146	C 7
St	Karrinyup	45	A 5
PILBARA			
St	Welshpool	75	A 10
St	Welshpool	84	E 1
PILBARRA			
St	White Gum Vly	90	D 7
PILGRIM			
St	South Perth	73	A 10
Wy	Hamilton Hill	101	A 3
PILKINGTON			
Cs	Beechboro	49	A 3
PILLAPAI			
Ct	Kingsley	31	E 2
PILLARGO			
Pl	Stirling	45	E 7
PILLING			
Pl	Hilton	91	A 9
PILSLEY			
Pl	Carine	31	A 10
PIMELIA			
Ct	Greenwood	31	C 6
Ct	Swan View	51	D 8
Gr	Thornlie	95	A 9
PIMLOTT			
St	Dianella	47	A 8
PINAFORE			
Ct	Duncraig	30	E 3
PINASTER			
Pl	Mosman Park	80	D 7
St	Menora	61	A 4
PINDARA			
Pl	Lesmurdie	87	B 3

		Map	Ref.
PINDARI			
Ct	Kelmscott	116	D 1
Pl	Hillarys	23	B 9
Pl	Peppermint Gr	80	E 2
Rd	City Beach	58	E 8
Rd	Lesmurdie	77	B 10
PINE			
Ave	Swan C Homes	144	
Ct	Forrestfield	76	C 9
Ct	Meadow Sprgs	163	C 5
Ct	Westfield	106	C 9
Gns	Ballajura	33	D 4
Gns	Woodvale	24	D 9
Gr	Kardinya	92	B 7
Gr	Martin	96	D 7
St	Henley Brook	28	C 7
St	Menora	61	A 4
Tce	Boya	65	D 4
Tce	Darlington	66	A 4
PINEBROOK			
Gns	Forrestfield	76	C 10
Rd	Cardup	135	C 6
PINECREST			
Gns	Dianella	47	B 4
PINEDALE			
Gns	Ballajura	33	C 4
St	E Victoria Pk	84	A 2
St	E Victoria Pk	83	E 2
Wy	Safety Bay	137	A 9
PINE GAP			
	Swan View	51	A 6
PINEGROVE			
Me	Currambine	19	B 6
Vs	Meadow Sprgs	163	D 2
PINEHURST			
Gns	Meadow Sprgs	163	D 6
PINELAKE			
Trl	Mariginiup	17	A 8
PINE TREE			
La	Mt Claremont	71	B 5
PINETREE			
Cl	Alexander Hts	32	E 5
Cl	Armadale	116	C 5
PINETREE GULLY			
Rd	Willetton	93	C 7
PINE VALLEY			
Ps	Connolly	19	B 5
PINEWOOD			
Ave	Kardinya	92	A 8
Ave	Woodlands	59	C 4
Grn	Mirrabooka	33	A 10
Pl	Beechboro	48	C 3
Wk	Canning Vale	94	A 9
PINGRUP			
Rd	Waikiki	145	E 1
PINJAR			
Ct	Waikiki	145	C 1
Rd	Mariginiup	16	D 9
Rd	Neerabup	13	D 9
Rd	Neerabup	16	E 1
Rd	Nowergup	13	C 3
Rd	Pinjar	16	E 5
Rd	Wanneroo	20	C 5
PINJARRA			
Rd	Mandurah	165	A 2
PINMORE			
Me	Iluka	19	A 5
PINNACE			
Ct	Halls Head	164	B 2
PINNAROO			
Dr	Padbury	30	E 1
Dr	Padbury	23	E 10
PINNELLI			
Rd	Wanneroo	20	C 9
PINNER			
Ct	Kingsley	31	B 2
Pl	Lynwood	94	D 1
PINNOCK			
Cl	Kardinya	92	A 6

		Map	Ref.
PINOT			
Tce	Ellenbrook	29	D 1
PINTA			
Ct	Iluka	18	E 4
PINTAIL			
Pde	Ballajura	33	E 7
PINTO			
Cl	Lakelands	161	B 9
PINXTON			
Ct	Carine	31	A 10
PIONEER			
Ct	Samson	91	D 9
Ct	Wembley	60	A 9
Dr	Edgewater	24	A 1
Dr	Thornlie	95	C 8
Dr	Yangebup	102	B 10
Pl	Gosnells	96	A 7
PIPER			
Ct	Greenwood	31	B 5
Pl	Bateman	92	D 7
St	Quinns Rocks	10	A 10
PIPERS			
Pl	Kalamunda	77	B 8
PIPIDINNY			
Rd	Eglinton	7	B 1
Rd	Eglinton	7	D 1
PIPIT			
Cl	Huntingdale	105	D 1
Pl	Stirling	45	E 7
PIRIA			
Cl	Iluka	18	E 5
PIRIANDA			
Cl	Clarkson	14	E 10
PIRIE			
St	Willetton	93	D 2
PIRRA			
Ct	Craigie	23	C 8
Ct	Two Rocks	2	C 2
PIRRETT			
Ct	Leeming	102	E 1
PISTOL			
St	Spearwood	101	C 6
PITCHFORD			
Ave	Maddington	96	B 6
Gl	Clarkson	14	D 2
PITINO			
Ct	Osborne Park	45	D 10
PITMAN			
St	Myaree	91	E 2
PITONGA			
Wy	Greenwood	31	B 3
PITT			
Ct	Morley	48	C 5
Rd	Martin	96	E 4
St	Dianella	47	B 9
St	Kensington	73	C 10
St	Midland	50	A 9
St	St James	84	B 4
Wy	Booragoon	92	B 2
PITTA			
Pl	Thornlie	94	E 6
PITTERSEN			
Rd	Greenmount	65	D 1
PITTS			
La	White Gum Vly	90	E 6
PITTWATER			
Cl	Kallaroo	23	A 7
PIVER			
Cnr	Ocean Reef	19	A 10
PLACID			
Ct	Joondalup	19	D 2
Ct	South Lake	102	C 7
PLACINA			
Pl	Willetton	93	C 7
PLAIN			
St	East Perth	1C	B 4
St	East Perth	73	B 4

		Map	Ref.
PLANE			
Ct	Beldon	23	D 2
PLANET			
Ct	Beckenham	85	D 7
St	Carlisle	74	B 7
St	Mandurah	165	B 3
St	Welshpool	74	C 10
PLANKTON			
Pl	Heathridge	23	C 1
Pl	Heathridge	19	C 10
PLANT			
St	Ascot	62	B 9
PLANTAGENET			
Cr	Hamilton Hill	101	B 2
PLANTATION			
Dr	Swan C Homes	144	
St	Menora	61	A 4
PLATT			
Cl	Mosman Park	80	D 7
Ct	Booragoon	92	C 1
PLATTE			
Ct	Gosnells	106	C 3
Wy	Beechboro	48	D 3
PLAYDEN			
Wy	Balga	46	D 3
PLAYFIELD			
St	E Victoria Pk	84	A 3
PLAYLE			
St	Myaree	92	A 2
PLEASANT			
Pl	Shelley	93	C 10
PLEASANT GROVE			
Ci	Falcon	162A	C 4
PLEVNA			
Ct	Lynwood	94	B 4
PLOUGHSHARE			
Pl	South Lake	102	D 5
PLOVER			
Dr	Willetton	93	D 7
Dr	Yangebup	102	A 9
Dr	Yangebup	101	E 9
Pl	Ballajura	34	A 2
Rd	High Wycombe	76	C 2
Ri	Halls Head	164	B 3
Wy	Kingsley	24	E 9
Wy	Stirling	45	D 5
PLUM			
Ct	Thornlie	95	B 9
PLUME			
Ct	Lesmurdie	87	E 3
PLUMMER			
St	E Victoria Pk	83	E 2
PLUMRIDGE			
Wy	South Lake	102	C 7
PLYMOUTH			
Ce	Ocean Reef	18	E 8
St	Midland	50	A 9
POAD			
St	Armadale	116	A 3
St	Armadale	115	E 2
POETS			
La	Kalamunda	77	D 5
POIMENA			
Me	Kingsley	31	E 3
POINCAIRE			
St	Balcatta	46	A 5
St	Balcatta	45	E 5
POINCIANA			
Pl	Wanneroo	24	D 2
POINS			
Pl	Spearwood	101	C 5
POINSETTIA			
Gr	South Lake	102	D 5
Wy	Dianella	46	E 5
POINT			
Pl	Fremantle	1D	C 5
St	Fremantle	1D	C 4
St	Fremantle	90	C 5

		Map	Ref.
POINTER			
Wy	Girrawheen	32	B 6
POINT PERON			
Rd	Peron	136	B 4
POINT WALTER			
Rd	Bicton	91	B 1
Rd	Bicton	81	B 10
POISON LEASE			
Rd	Mundaring	69	D 3
POLA			
St	Dianella	47	B 10
St	Dianella	61	C 1
POLGLASS			
Wy	Ardross	82	C 9
POLLARD			
Ct	Yangebup	112	A 1
Pl	Booragoon	92	B 2
St	Glendalough	60	A 5
Wy	Warnbro	145	C 9
POLLETTI			
Rd	Jandakot	112	E 1
Rd	Jandakot	102	E 10
POLLITT			
Cl	Armadale	116	D 9
POLLOCK			
Ct	Kingsley	24	D 10
St	Bentley	84	B 4
POLO			
Cl	Willetton	93	E 4
POLYANTHA			
Gns	Mirrabooka	33	B 10
POLYGON			
Pl	Greenmount	51	C 10
POMADERRIS			
Pl	South Lake	102	D 6
POMELO			
Wy	Armadale	115	E 4
POMEROY			
Pl	Carine	45	C 2
Rd	Lesmurdie	87	D 5
Rd	Walliston	88	A 4
POMFRET			
Rd	Spearwood	101	B 5
POMPANO			
Ct	Heathridge	19	E 10
POND			
Ave	Perth Airport	63	B 8
Pl	South Lake	102	D 6
PONTIAC			
Ave	Cloverdale	74	E 5
PONY			
Wy	Oakford	124	C 6
POOLE			
Ave	Crawley	72	A 7
Pl	Bateman	92	E 5
Pl	Mosman Park	80	D 7
St	Naval Base	121	A 1
St	Welshpool	85	A 1
POOLYA			
Rd	City Beach	58	D 3
POORE			
Gr	Coogee	100	E 9
POPE			
Me	North Lake	102	A 1
St	Two Rocks	2	B 1
POPLAR			
Cl	Edgewater	24	A 2
Ct	Forrestfield	76	B 10
Pl	Thornlie	95	B 10
Pl	Warnbro	145	D 6
St	Willetton	93	B 3
PORLOCK			
Wy	Karrinyup	44	E 5
PORONGURUP			
Dr	Clarkson	14	D 1
Dr	Clarkson	11	D 10

For detailed information regarding the street referencing system used in this book, turn to page 170.

235

Q

		Map	Ref.
PORPOISE			
Ct	Coogee	100	E 9
Gr	Waikiki	145	C 2
PORT			
Cl	Leeming	103	A 1
Pl	Yanchep	4	C 5
Rd	Herne Hill	37	B 8
PORT BEACH			
Rd	Nth Fremantle	90	A 4
Rd	Nth Fremantle	1D	B 3
Rd	Nth Fremantle	80	B 10
PORTCULLIS			
Dr	Willetton	93	E 6
PORTEOUS			
Rd	Sorrento	30	C 5
PORTER			
Gns	Leda	130	D 10
St	Beaconsfield	90	E 8
St	Gwelup	45	C 4
PORT KEMBLA			
Dr	Bibra Lake	101	D 5
PORT KENNEDY			
Dr	Port Kennedy	156	E 6
PORTLAND			
Pl	Safety Bay	145	B 2
Rt	Iluka	18	E 3
St	Nedlands	71	E 8
PORTMARNOCK			
Cc	Connolly	19	C 7
Ci	Halls Head	164	B 2
PORT PIRIE			
St	Bibra Lake	101	D 5
PORTREE			
Wy	Ardross	82	C 9
Wy	Duncraig	31	A 6
PORT ROYAL			
Dr	Safety Bay	137	B 10
PORTRUSH			
Me	Meadow Sprgs	163	D 5
PORTSEA			
Ct	Meadow Sprgs	163	C 5
Pl	Connolly	19	B 8
Pl	Cooloongup	137	E 7
PORTSIDE			
Gr	Ballajura	33	D 8
PORTSMOUTH			
Pl	Waikiki	145	C 3
PORTULACA			
St	Willetton	93	C 2
POSEIDON			
Rd	Heathridge	23	C 2
Rd	Heathridge	19	C 10
Wy	Lynwood	94	E 8
POSSNER			
Wy	Henderson	111	A 7
POSSUM			
Ct	High Wycombe	64	B 10
Pl	Kelmscott	107	A 9
Wy	Stoneville	54	B 4
POSTANS			
Rd	Hope Valley	121	E 9
Rd	Postans	130	E 3
Rd	Wattleup	121	E 3
POSTLING			
St	Kenwick	95	E 1
POTOROO			
Pl	Wungong	116	B 9
POTTER			
Ave	Salter Point	83	B 7
Ct	Spearwood	101	C 7
Pl	Bateman	92	D 7
POTTS			
St	Melville	91	D 3
POUND			
Cl	Byford	126	D 9
Pl	Roleystone	107	D 9
POVEY			
Pl	Parmelia	131	A 8

		Map	Ref.
POW			
St	West Swan	50	A 1
POWELL			
Cr	Wungong	116	B 9
Ct	Orelia	131	B 5
Rd	Baldivis	147	E 10
Rd	Coogee	100	E 8
St	Cloverdale	75	A 3
St	Joondanna	60	B 3
POWER			
Ave	Wattleup	121	E 1
Ave	Wattleup	111	E 10
Pl	Attadale	81	D 9
St	Embleton	62	B 2
POWIS			
Ct	Greenwood	31	D 4
Ct	Langford	94	E 2
St	Glendalough	60	A 6
Wy	Warnbro	145	C 9
POYNINGS			
St	Balga	46	C 3
POYNTER			
Dr	Duncraig	30	E 7
POYNTON			
Ave	Midland	50	B 8
POZIERES			
Rd	Swanbourne	70	D 7
PRAIRIE DUNES			
Pl	Connolly	19	B 6
PRASE			
Pl	Carine	45	A 1
PRATT			
Ct	Maddington	95	E 3
St	Cloverdale	75	A 2
PRECISION			
Ave	Mullaloo	23	B 3
PREEDY			
Ct	Bateman	92	D 5
PREEN			
St	Booragoon	92	B 1
PREFECT			
Pl	Duncraig	31	A 7
PREISS			
Wy	Mirrabooka	32	E 10
PRENDIVILLE			
Ave	Ocean Reef	19	A 8
Wy	Langford	94	D 3
PRENDWICK			
Wy	Willetton	93	E 4
PRENTICE			
Pl	South Lake	102	C 8
PRESCOTT			
Ct	Lynwood	94	A 3
Dr	Gosnells	96	A 10
Dr	Gosnells	95	E 10
Dr	Murdoch	92	B 7
PRESIDENT			
St	Kewdale	74	E 8
St	Welshpool	74	D 10
PRESTON			
Ct	Two Rocks	2	D 3
Rd	Parmelia	131	C 6
St	Como	82	E 1
St	Mandurah	163	A 10
Wy	Balga	46	D 2
PRESTON POINT			
Rd	Attadale	81	C 10
Rd	Bicton	81	B 10
Rd	East Fremantle	90	D 2
Rd	East Fremantle	80	E 10
PRESTWICK			
Cl	Meadow Sprgs	163	C 5
Me	Connolly	19	C 9
PRIAM			
Rd	Silver Sands	163	A 7
PRICE			
Ct	Wungong	116	B 8
St	Fremantle	90	C 7

		Map	Ref.
St	Wembley	72	A 1
St	Wembley	71	E 1
PRICHARD			
Rd	Greenmount	65	C 1
PRIDER			
Ct	Kardinya	91	E 8
PRIDMORE			
Glen	Clarkson	14	D 3
PRIES			
Pl	Kelmscott	106	D 7
PRIES PARK			
Rd	Kelmscott	106	E 5
PRIEST			
Rd	Landsdale	25	E 8
PRIESTLEY			
St	Embleton	62	A 1
St	Embleton	48	A 10
PRIMARY			
Rd	Yanchep	4	C 4
PRIMROSE			
Hts	Joondalup	19	D 3
St	Perth City	61	A 9
PRINCE			
St	Gosnells	95	D 8
St	Queens Park	85	A 4
PRINCE ALBERT			
Ct	Mt Claremont	71	A 4
PRINCEP			
Pl	Warnbro	145	E 8
PRINCE REGENT			
Dr	Heathridge	19	B 9
PRINCES			
St	Cottesloe	80	C 4
PRINCESS			
Rd	Balga	46	C 3
Rd	Balga	32	C 10
Rd	Crawley	72	A 10
Rd	Doubleview	59	B 2
Rd	Doubleview	45	B 10
Rd	Mt Helena	55	A 4
Rd	Nedlands	71	C 10
St	East Perth	73	C 2
St	Huntingdale	95	D 9
Wy	Balga	46	C 2
PRINCETON			
Ct	Thornlie	95	C 6
St	Kelmscott	106	E 7
PRINCEVILLE			
Tr	Connolly	19	C 7
PRINDIVILLE			
Dr	Wangara	24	E 7
PRINSEP			
Rd	Attadale	81	C 10
Rd	Jandakot	103	A 5
Rd	Jandakot	102	E 10
Rd	Melville	91	C 1
PRINTER			
St	Dianella	47	C 9
PRION			
Pl	Stirling	45	E 8
St	Thornlie	95	A 6
PRIORY			
Rd	Maida Vale	76	E 2
Wy	Greenfields	165	E 2
PRISCILLA			
Ave	Beldon	23	D 3
PRISK			
St	Karrinyup	45	A 6
PRISKE			
Wy	Rivervale	74	C 5
PRISM			
Pl	Beldon	23	C 4
PRITCHARD			
Cl	Lesmurdie	87	D 2
St	Kewdale	74	D 9
St	O'Connor	91	C 7
PROBERT			
Rd	Thornlie	95	B 3

		Map	Ref.
PROCLAMATION			
St	Subiaco	72	B 2
PROCTOR			
St	Samson	91	C 8
PROGRESS			
Dr	Bibra Lake	102	A 4
Dr	Chidlow	57	B 1
Dr	North Lake	102	A 1
Dr	North Lake	92	A 10
St	Morley	47	E 10
Wy	Belmont	74	D 4
Wy	Cloverdale	74	D 4
PROMONTORY			
Pde	Ballajura	33	C 8
PROSPECT			
Cr	Kalamunda	77	A 8
Gr	Heathridge	24	A 3
Pl	Claremont	70	E 10
Pl	West Perth	60	E 10
Rd	Armadale	116	D 6
St	Claremont	70	E 10
PROSPECTOR			
Gns	Edgewater	24	A 1
PROSPERITY			
Rd	Mt Helena	40	D 10
Rd	Stoneville	40	D 10
PROSPERO			
Cr	Coolbellup	101	D 2
PROSSER			
Wy	Myaree	92	A 2
Wy	Singleton	160	D 4
PROTEA			
Ct	Stoneville	54	B 3
Pl	Canning Vale	103	E 1
St	Greenwood	31	C 6
PROTECTOR			
Ct	Madora	160	C 8
PROUT			
Rd	Armadale	116	D 8
PROVIDENCE			
Tce	Iluka	18	E 5
PROWSE			
St	Bassendean	63	B 1
St	Beaconsfield	91	A 8
St	West Perth	72	C 1
St	West Perth	1C	D 1
PRUDEN			
Rd	Whitby	143	D 9
PRUDHOE			
Ct	Merriwa	11	D 10
PRUINOSA			
Me	Alexander Hts	32	E 5
PRUITI			
Cr	Lesmurdie	87	C 4
PUCAS			
Ct	Beechboro	49	A 3
PUDNEY			
Pl	Orelia	131	A 6
PUDSEY			
St	Balcatta	45	E 5
PUFFIN			
Cl	Rockingham	137	B 9
PUG			
Rd	Baldivis	139	C 5
PUGLIA			
Pl	Koondoola	33	A 8
PULLAN			
Pl	Greenwood	31	C 5
PULLMAN			
Pl	Willetton	93	C 6
PULO			
Pl	Brentwood	92	E 3
Rd	Brentwood	92	E 3
PUNARI			
Pl	Lynwood	94	C 4
PUNCHEON			
St	Langford	94	E 1

		Map	Ref.
PUNT			
Rd	Rivervale	73	E 3
PUNTIE			
Cr	Maylands	61	E 2
PURCELL			
Gr	Kardinya	91	D 9
PURDIE			
Ave	Ardross	82	D 8
PURDOM			
Rd	Wembley Dns	59	A 4
Rd	Wembley Dns	58	E 4
PURDY			
Pl	Canning Vale	94	A 6
PURITAN			
Cl	Ocean Reef	18	E 8
PURKISS			
St	Cannington	84	D 5
PURLEY			
Cr	Lynwood	94	D 1
St	Bayswater	48	C 10
PURSER			
Ce	Murdoch	92	C 7
PURSLOWE			
St	Glendalough	60	B 5
St	Mt Hawthorn	60	B 5
PURSUIT			
Cl	Middle Swan	50	E 4
PURTON			
Pl	Bellevue	51	A 10
PURUS			
Cl	Beechboro	48	D 4
PURVES			
Wy	Armadale	116	A 7
PURVIS			
St	Hamilton Hill	101	C 2
PUSEY			
St	Bentley	84	B 5
PUTTENHAM			
St	Morley	47	E 7
PYA			
Pl	Joondalup	19	C 2
PYCOMBE			
Wy	Balga	46	C 3
PYE			
Pl	Safety Bay	136	D 10
PYMBLE			
Ct	Kallaroo	23	A 7
PYRMONT			
Pl	Greenmount	51	B 10
PYRTON			
Pl	Duncraig	30	E 8
PYRUS			
St	Duncraig	30	E 6
Wy	Forrestfield	76	C 8
PYTCHLEY			
St	Thornlie	95	B 6

Q

		Map	Ref.
QUADEA			
Rd	Nollamara	46	C 5
Wy	Nollamara	46	D 5
QUADRANT			
Ri	Halls Head	164	B 1
QUAIL			
Ct	High Wycombe	64	B 10
Ct	Wungong	116	C 10
Gr	Ballajura	34	A 9
Gr	Ballajura	33	E 8
Pl	Langford	95	A 1
Ri	Willetton	93	C 4
St	Mt Helena	41	D 7
St	Stirling	45	E 8
QUALUP			
Ct	Halls Head	164	A 7

236

R

		Map	Ref.
QUAMBY			
Ct	Silver Sands	163	B 4
Pl	Rockingham	137	B 9
QUAND			
Me	Edgewater	19	E 10
QUANDONG			
Pl	Armadale	116	C 3
QUARIMOR			
Rd	Bibra Lake	101	D 6
QUARKUM			
St	Wanneroo	20	E 8
QUARNDON			
Cl	Carine	30	E 10
QUARRAM			
Wy	Gosnells	96	A 10
QUARRY			
Ct	Glen Forrest	66	D 3
Ra	Edgewater	24	B 1
Ra	Edgewater	20	B 10
Rd	Hamilton Hill	100	E 2
Rd	Martin	96	E 6
St	Fremantle	1D	C 4
St	Fremantle	90	C 4
Wy	Greenfields	163	D 7
QUAY			
Ct	Sorrento	30	B 4
QUAYSIDE			
Cl	Halls Head	164	D 1
QUEBEC			
Rd	Midland	50	B 9
QUEEN			
St	Bayswater	62	B 7
St	Bentley	84	B 4
St	Claremont	71	B 10
St	Fremantle	1D	C 5
St	Fremantle	90	C 5
St	Gosnells	96	A 9
St	Maylands	62	A 8
St	Perth City	1C	E 2
St	Perth City	72	E 2
St	South Perth	72	D 6
QUEENS			
Cr	Mt Lawley	61	B 8
Gr	Mt Claremont	71	A 4
Rd	Ardross	82	D 9
Rd	Mt Pleasant	82	E 9
Rd	Sth Guildford	63	D 3
QUEENSCLIFF			
Ct	Kallaroo	23	A 8
QUEENSCLIFFE			
Rd	Doubleview	59	A 2
Ri	Greenfields	163	E 8
QUEENSLEA			
Dr	Claremont	71	A 10
QUEENS PARK			
Rd	Wilson	84	C 7
QUEENSVILLE			
Ave	Lynwood	94	D 3
QUEENSWAY			
Rd	Landsdale	26	A 9
QUEEN VICTORIA			
St	Fremantle	1D	C 4
St	Fremantle	90	C 4
St	Nth Fremantle	90	C 1
QUELEA			
Pl	Ballajura	33	E 8
QUENINGTON			
Ct	Maida Vale	76	D 4
QUERRIN			
Ave	Willetton	93	E 1
QUESNEL			
Pl	Joondalup	19	D 1
QUICKLY			
Cr	Hamilton Hill	101	C 3
QUILLEN			
Vw	Joondalup	19	D 3
QUILTER			
Dr	Duncraig	31	A 8

		Map	Ref.
QUIN			
Pl	Innaloo	45	B 8
St	Rockingham	137	A 5
St	Swan View	51	C 6
QUINAULT			
Lp	Joondalup	19	D 4
QUINCE			
Wy	Coolbellup	91	E 10
QUINDALUP			
Ct	Hillman	137	E 6
QUINLAN			
St	Coolbellup	91	C 10
QUINN			
Ave	Bentley	84	C 4
Ct	Noranda	47	D 4
St	Willagee	91	E 3
QUINNS			
Rd	Merriwa	11	E 10
Rd	Neerabup	12	A 10
Rd	Quinns Rocks	10	A 1
QUIRK			
Dl	Winthrop	92	A 5
QUOKKA			
El	Wungong	116	C 9
QUOLL			
Pa	Wungong	116	C 10
QUONDONG			
St	Nollamara	46	C 4
QUORN			
Cl	Mandurah	165	B 4
St	Wembley Dns	59	A 5

R

		Map	Ref.
RAASAY			
Pl	Warwick	31	C 8
RABONE			
Wy	Boya	65	D 5
RABY			
Ct	Cooloongup	137	C 10
RACE			
St	Willagee	91	D 5
RACHAL			
Pl	Greenfields	163	E 10
RACHEL			
Ct	Glen Forrest	66	E 4
RACONTEUR			
Dr	Ascot	62	C 9
RADBORN			
St	Greenmount	51	D 10
RADBOURN			
St	Marmion	30	D 9
RADDEN			
Gr	Winthrop	92	B 4
RADFORD			
Pl	Bellevue	65	B 2
Pl	Safety Bay	136	D 10
RADIAN			
Rd	Beldon	23	D 2
RADIATA			
St	Coodanup	165	D 6
St	Maddington	96	C 4
RADIUM			
St	Bentley	84	D 3
St N	Welshpool	84	D 3
RADNEY			
St	Willagee	91	E 4
RADNOR			
St	Leeming	93	B 9
Wy	Coolbellup	92	A 10
RADSTOCK			
Pl	Merriwa	11	D 9
St	Karrinyup	45	A 4
RAE			
Pl	Hillarys	30	B 1
Pl	Leeming	93	B 8

		Map	Ref.
Rd	Cooloongup	137	C 9
Rd	Safety Bay	137	A 9
Rd	Safety Bay	136	D 9
St	Leederville	60	D 7
RAEBURN			
Rd	Roleystone	108	A 5
RAESIDE			
Cr	Cooloongup	137	C 10
RAFF			
Pl	Leeming	93	C 8
Pl	Padbury	30	D 2
RAFFAELE			
Pl	Murdoch	92	C 7
RAFFERTY			
Cl	Mandurah	163	C 8
Rd	Mandurah	163	C 8
RAGAMUFFIN			
Tce	Willetton	93	D 5
RAGEN			
Al	Leederville	60	C 8
RAGLAN			
Cl	Falcon	162A	B 4
Rd	Mt Lawley	61	A 8
Rd	North Perth	61	A 8
RAIBLE			
Gr	Marangaroo	32	C 5
RAIL			
St	Balga	46	C 3
RAILS			
Cr	Wungong	126	D 2
RAILTON			
Pl	Dianella	47	B 9
Pl	Dudley Park	165	C 5
RAILWAY			
Ave	Armadale	116	D 2
Ave	Kelmscott	106	D 10
Ave	Middle Swan	50	D 4
Ave	Westfield	106	D 5
Cr	Herne Hill	36	D 6
Cr	Millendon	29	E 7
Pde	Bassendean	63	A 1
Pde	Bayswater	62	A 5
Pde	Bayswater	62	B 4
Pde	Beckenham	85	B 8
Pde	Bibra Lake	101	D 6
Pde	E Cannington	85	A 6
Pde	Glen Forrest	66	D 2
Pde	Herne Hill	36	D 7
Pde	Herne Hill	36	E 1
Pde	Leederville	60	B 10
Pde	Maylands	61	E 6
Pde	Middle Swan	36	D 9
Pde	Midland	50	C 2
Pde	Millendon	36	E 1
Pde	Millendon	29	E 7
Pde	Mt Lawley	61	C 8
Pde	Queens Park	85	A 5
Pde	Upper Swan	29	E 1
Pde	Welshpool	84	D 2
Rd	Gooseberry H	77	C 3
Rd	Kalamunda	77	D 6
Rd	Karrakatta	71	C 6
Rd	Shenton Park	71	D 4
Rd	Subiaco	72	A 1
Rd	Subiaco	71	E 3
St	Cottesloe	80	D 2
St	Cottesloe	70	D 10
St	West Perth	1C	D 1
St	West Perth	72	D 1
St	West Perth	60	D 10
Tce	Mundaring	68	C 1
Tce	Rockingham	137	A 4
Tce	Sawyers Valley	69	A 1
Tce	Sawyers Valley	55	B 10
Tce	Sawyers Valley	54	D 10
RAIN			
Pl	Bayswater	62	A 6
RAINBIRD			
Rd	Gosnells	105	E 1
RAINBOW			
Ct	Gosnells	95	E 10
Vw	Ocean Reef	18	E 9

		Map	Ref.
RAINE			
Tce	Winthrop	92	B 4
RAINER			
Me	Willetton	94	A 3
St	Karrinyup	44	D 7
RAINIE			
Pl	Parmelia	131	B 8
RAIN LOVER			
Ct	Byford	126	A 8
RAINSFORD			
Wy	Parkerville	53	D 5
RAINSWORTH			
Gns	Heathridge	23	E 2
RAINTREE			
Ri	Marangaroo	32	D 4
RAITHBY			
Pl	Martin	97	D 9
RAKE			
Ct	Ocean Reef	19	A 10
RAKOA			
Pl	Cooloongup	137	D 8
St	Falcon	162A	C 1
RALEIGH			
Rd	Bayswater	62	B 4
Rd	Sorrento	30	B 6
St	Belmont	74	E 1
St	Carlisle	74	B 8
RALPHS			
St	Armadale	116	B 3
RALSTON			
Pl	Dianella	47	B 5
Rd	Kardinya	92	A 7
St	Hamilton Hill	101	C 1
RAMBLER			
Grn	Ocean Reef	18	E 6
RAMBURES			
Wy	Hamilton Hill	101	B 3
RAMBUTAN			
Pl	South Lake	102	C 5
RAMM			
Pl	Armadale	116	B 2
RAMOSE			
Cl	Heathridge	19	D 10
RAMPART			
Wy	Willetton	93	D 5
RAMSAY			
Cl	Noranda	48	A 5
Gr	Woodvale	24	C 6
St	Karrinyup	45	B 5
RAMSDALE			
Lp	Leeming	92	E 10
St	Doubleview	59	A 2
St	Scarborough	59	A 2
RAMSDEN			
Ave	E Victoria Pk	84	A 2
Wy	Morley	48	A 6
Wy	Morley	47	E 6
RAMSEY			
Ct	Cannington	84	E 5
RAMSGATE			
Rt	Mindarie	14	B 5
RAMSHAW			
St	Scarborough	44	D 8
RANA			
Ct	Willetton	93	D 4
RANCE			
St	Stirling	46	A 6
RANCEBY			
Ave	Coodanup	165	C 3
RANCH			
Rd	Mariginiup	16	D 9
RAND			
Ave	Waikiki	145	C 4
St	Maddington	95	E 5
RANDALL			
St	Dianella	61	C 1
Wy	Langford	95	A 1

		Map	Ref.
RANDELL			
Cr	Ocean Reef	23	A 1
Cr	Ocean Reef	19	A 10
La	Perth City	60	E 9
Pl	Perth City	60	E 9
Rd	Mundijong	150	C 1
St	Mandurah	165	A 1
St	Mandurah	163	A 10
St	Perth City	60	E 9
RANDERSON			
Pl	Dianella	47	D 8
RANELAGH			
Cr	South Perth	73	B 7
RANFORD			
Lp	Kardinya	92	A 6
Rd	Canning Vale	94	A 10
Rd	Canning Vale	104	B 1
Rd	Canning Vale	93	C 8
Rd	Forrestdale	105	A 7
Rd	Forrestdale	115	C 2
St	Kelmscott	117	A 1
Wy	Hillarys	30	B 2
RANGE			
Ct	High Wycombe	64	D 9
Ct	Mullaloo	23	C 4
Rd	Herne Hill	37	D 2
Rd	Millendon	37	D 1
Rd	Millendon	168	D 7
Rt	Parmelia	131	B 10
RANGER			
Rd	Yokine	60	E 1
Trl	Edgewater	24	A 1
RANGE VIEW			
Rd	High Wycombe	64	C 10
Wy	Thornlie	95	C 4
RANGEVIEW			
Ct	Maddington	96	C 4
Dr	Bellevue	65	A 1
Pl	Canning Vale	104	A 1
Rd	Alexander Hts	33	A 4
Rd	Landsdale	33	A 3
RANKIN			
Rd	Shenton Park	71	E 3
Wy	Booragoon	92	C 1
RANLEIGH			
Wy	Greenwood	31	E 5
RANMERE			
Wy	Langford	95	A 1
RANMORE			
Wy	Morley	47	D 6
RANNOCH			
Ci	Hamersley	32	A 9
Ci	Hamersley	31	E 9
Ri	Joondalup	19	C 2
St	Floreat	59	C 8
RAPANIA			
Ri	Yangebup	111	E 1
RAPHAEL			
St	Subiaco	72	A 2
RAPIDS			
Rd	Peel Estate	154	A 4
Rd	Peel Estate	150	A 9
RAPKIN			
St	Langford	94	E 3
RASON			
Cl	Cooloongup	137	E 9
Pde	Bellevue	50	E 10
RATCLIFFE			
Rd	Booragoon	92	D 1
RATHAY			
St	Kensington	73	D 9
St	Victoria Park	73	D 9
RATHBONE			
Rd	Riverton	93	E 1
RATHMINES			
Pl	Coodanup	165	D 4
RATTAN			
Ce	Warnbro	145	E 8
RAVEN			
St	High Wycombe	76	B 2

For detailed information regarding the street referencing system used in this book, turn to page 170.

R

	Map	Ref.
RAVENDALE		
Dr Dudley Park	165	B 5
RAVEN HILL		
Rd Thornlie	95	C 4
RAVENSCAR		
St Doubleview	45	B 9
RAVENSCROFT		
Wy Westfield	106	C 9
RAVENSDEN		
St Thornlie	95	B 6
RAVENSLEA		
Dr Lynwood	94	B 4
RAVENSWOOD		
Ct Nollamara	46	C 5
Dr Nollamara	46	C 6
Rd High Wycombe	76	C 4
Rd Maida Vale	76	D 4
RAWLINS		
St Glendalough	60	A 6
St Rockingham	137	A 6
RAWLINSON		
Dr Marangaroo	32	C 5
St O'Connor	91	D 6
RAWSON		
St Subiaco	72	A 3
RAY		
Cl Byford	126	E 10
Ct Gosnells	96	A 10
Ct Sorrento	30	C 4
Rd Kewdale	74	C 6
Rd Swan View	51	B 8
St Rockingham	137	A 5
St South Perth	72	E 7
RAYMENT		
St Lathlain	74	B 6
RAYMOND		
Ave Bayswater	62	B 2
Pl Waikiki	145	B 4
Rd Walliston	88	A 1
St Mt Pleasant	82	D 8
St Yokine	46	D 10
RAYNE		
St Maddington	96	B 4
REA		
St South Perth	72	E 10
REACH		
Pl Huntingdale	95	D 9
REACHER		
Pl Ocean Reef	19	A 10
READ		
Ave Mosman Park	80	E 7
Pl Bull Creek	93	B 7
Pl Dianella	47	A 7
St Cooloongup	137	C 9
St Dianella	47	A 7
St E Victoria Pk	74	B 10
St Rockingham	137	B 6
St Waikiki	145	C 2
READER		
Pl Caversham	49	B 5
READSHAW		
Rd Duncraig	30	D 4
REARDON		
Ct Leeming	93	A 10
REBECCA		
Ct Beldon	23	D 4
Pl South Lake	102	C 7
REBELL		
Pl Mosman Park	80	D 7
RECREATION		
Dr Shoalwater	136	D 7
Rd Byford	135	B 4
Rd Hamilton Hill	100	E 2
Rd Kalamunda	77	C 7
REDA		
Cl Golden Bay	159	A 8
REDBANK		
Ri Clarkson	14	E 10

	Map	Ref.
REDBUD		
Trl Edgewater	24	B 2
REDCLIFFE		
Ave Balga	46	D 1
Ave Balga	32	D 10
Ave Marangaroo	32	D 4
Rd Cardup	135	B 7
Rd Redcliffe	63	A 7
St E Cannington	85	A 6
REDCOURT		
Rd Attadale	81	D 10
REDDINGTON		
Wy Brentwood	92	E 2
REDDY		
Ave Mundaring	68	B 2
Ct Balga	46	E 4
REDE		
St Gosnells	96	A 9
St Gosnells	95	E 9
REDEMPTORA		
Rd Henderson	111	A 7
REDFERN		
Cl Hillarys	23	A 9
Cl Thornlie	95	B 9
Pl Erskine	164	A 9
Rd Parkerville	53	D 8
St North Perth	60	E 6
St Subiaco	72	A 2
St Subiaco	71	E 3
REDFIN		
Cr Beldon	23	C 3
REDFOX		
Cr Huntingdale	105	C 1
Cr Huntingdale	95	C 10
REDGUM		
Ave Bellevue	65	A 2
Ct Kewdale	74	E 6
Ct Thornlie	95	B 9
Dr Ballajura	33	C 5
La Swan View	51	B 6
St Greenwood	31	C 6
Wy Morley	48	D 6
REDHEART		
Dr Thornlie	95	A 9
REDHILL		
Pl Greenfields	163	E 8
Rd Red Hill	37	D 8
RED JACKET		
Pl Iluka	19	A 5
Pl Iluka	18	E 5
REDLANDS		
St Bayswater	62	C 1
St Bayswater	48	C 10
REDMOND		
Rd Hamilton Hill	101	C 1
Rd Hamilton Hill	91	C 10
St Salter Point	83	B 8
Wy Erskine	164	A 9
REDOUBT		
Rd Willetton	93	E 5
REDROSS		
Ct Armadale	116	B 4
REDRUTH		
Ct Yanchep	4	D 5
REDTINGLE		
Rd Westfield	106	B 8
REDUNCA		
Wy Mirrabooka	46	E 1
RED WATTLE		
Pl Churchlands	59	C 6
REDWOOD		
Cr Melville	91	C 2
Ct Alexander Hts	32	E 4
Ct Beechboro	48	C 3
La Willetton	93	C 4
REED		
Cl Thornlie	95	A 9
Rd Attadale	81	D 10
Rd Jarrahdale	152	B 2
Ri Roleystone	107	E 9

	Map	Ref.
REEDS		
Rd Carmel	88	B 6
REEF		
Ct Sorrento	30	D 5
Pl Safety Bay	145	A 2
REEN		
St Kewdale	74	E 9
St St James	84	A 4
REES		
Dr Quinns Rocks	10	A 10
St O'Connor	91	C 7
REEVE		
St Swanbourne	70	D 8
REEVES		
Ct Balga	46	E 3
Ct Kelmscott	106	E 7
Pl Swan View	51	B 8
REFLECTION		
Cl Edgewater	20	B 10
Gns Ballajura	33	C 7
Me Safety Bay	136	E 10
REGAL		
Cl Dianella	47	A 6
Dr Thornlie	95	C 7
REGAN		
Pl Armadale	116	B 2
St Coolbellup	101	D 1
St Rockingham	137	B 4
REGATTA		
Dr Edgewater	20	A 10
REGDEL		
Rd Lesmurdie	87	B 2
REGEHR		
St Warnbro	145	C 6
REGELIA		
Ct Ferndale	84	C 10
REGENCY		
Dr Thornlie	95	C 6
REGENT		
Ave Mt Pleasant	92	E 2
Dr Alexander Hts	33	B 6
Gr Morley	48	C 7
St Leederville	60	C 9
St E Mt Lawley	61	E 7
St W Mt Lawley	61	B 7
Wy Mt Pleasant	92	E 2
REGENTS		
Me Mt Claremont	71	A 4
REGGIO		
Rd Kewdale	75	C 8
REGINA		
Ct Greenfields	163	C 9
Ct Hamilton Hill	101	A 4
Rd Westfield	106	C 10
REGINALD		
St Cottesloe	80	D 4
St Queens Park	85	B 4
REGIS		
Ct Dianella	47	B 5
Ct Mullaloo	23	A 2
REGNANS		
Cl Mirrabooka	32	E 10
REIBE		
Ave Kewdale	74	E 7
REID		
Cl Halls Head	164	C 3
Ct Kingsley	31	D 1
Hwy Balcatta	45	D 1
Hwy Balga	46	C 2
Hwy Beechboro	48	E 1
Hwy Carine	44	E 1
Hwy Malaga	48	A 3
Hwy Malaga	47	D 3
Hwy Mirrabooka	47	A 3
Hwy West Swan	49	C 2
Pro Joondalup	19	E 6
Rd Lesmurdie	87	C 5
Rd Perth Airport	75	C 1
St Bassendean	63	A 4

	Map	Ref.
St Bassendean	62	E 4
St Kardinya	91	E 7
REIGATE		
St Gosnells	106	C 2
REILLY		
Ct Leeming	93	A 9
Rd Forrestdale	104	E 9
Rd Whitby	143	C 5
St Orelia	131	B 5
St Singleton	160	D 2
Wy Greenwood	31	E 4
REINHOLD		
Pl Carabooda	8	C 8
RELIANCE		
Cl Ocean Reef	18	E 9
Ct Waikiki	145	C 2
REMAN		
Rd Bayswater	62	A 3
REMEMBRANCE		
Gr Greenmount	51	C 10
RENDELL		
Wy Koondoola	33	B 9
RENE		
Rd Dalkeith	81	D 2
RENEGADE		
Wy Kingsley	31	D 3
RENISON		
Dr Greenfields	163	C 10
RENMARK		
St Balcatta	46	B 8
RENNIE		
Cr N Hilton	91	B 8
Cr S Hilton	91	B 8
RENNINGTON		
St Dianella	47	B 9
RENNISON		
St Beckenham	85	B 9
RENOU		
St E Cannington	85	A 6
St Padbury	30	D 2
St Queens Park	85	A 5
Wy Bateman	92	D 7
RENOWN		
Ave Claremont	70	E 10
Wy Sorrento	30	B 5
RENSHAW		
Blvd Clarkson	14	C 2
Pl Morley	47	E 8
RENTNEY		
Wy Willetton	93	E 3
RENTON		
St Melville	91	D 3
RENVILLE		
Wy Lynwood	94	C 2
RENWICK		
St South Perth	73	B 10
REPATRIATION		
Rd Pickering Bk	89	A 8
REPTON		
St West Swan	35	C 9
REQUA		
Cr Warnbro	145	D 8
RESERVE		
Cl Greenwood	31	B 3
Dr Mandurah	163	C 9
Rd Pickering Bk	98	E 1
Rd Spearwood	101	B 7
St Bicton	81	B 8
St Claremont	71	B 9
St Scarborough	44	C 9
St Shoalwater	136	C 7
St Wembley	59	D 9
RESERVOIR		
Cl Mosman Park	80	D 7
Rd Orange Grove	96	E 3
Rd Orange Grove	86	D 10
Rd Chidlow	56	C 2
St Chidlow	42	C 10

	Map	Ref.
RESOLUTE		
Wy Ocean Reef	18	E 8
RESOLUTION		
Dr Ascot	62	C 9
Dr Waikiki	145	C 2
RESTON		
Ct Duncraig	31	A 7
St Balcatta	46	A 5
RETREAT		
Me Canning Vale	94	A 10
RETUSA		
Ct Ferndale	84	B 10
REUBEN		
St Beaconsfield	90	D 7
REVELEY		
Ct Samson	91	C 8
St Waikiki	145	C 5
REVERIE		
Me Halls Head	164	D 2
REVESBY		
Pl Coodanup	165	C 4
St Maddington	96	B 4
REWELL		
Ct Parmelia	131	C 8
REX		
St Gosnells	106	C 1
REYNOLDA		
Grn Hillarys	23	A 10
REYNOLDS		
Ave Greenfields	163	D 10
Cl Swan View	51	C 6
Dr Swan View	51	C 6
Rd Applecross	82	D 6
Rd Forrestfield	86	A 1
Rd Forrestfield	76	A 10
Rd Mt Pleasant	92	D 1
Rd Mt Pleasant	82	D 10
St East Fremantle	90	D 2
RHAGODIA		
Ct Heathridge	19	C 10
RHEINGOLD		
Pl Mirrabooka	47	B 2
RHEOLA		
St West Perth	72	C 2
RHINE		
Cr Beechboro	48	E 3
Wy Swan View	51	C 8
RHODES		
Cl Mindarie	14	B 6
Cr Calista	130	E 5
Pl Jarrahdale	152	D 6
Pl Maida Vale	76	D 4
Pl Mosman Park	80	E 6
Ri Coogee	101	A 9
St Morley	47	E 6
RHONDA		
Ave Willetton	93	B 3
RHONE		
Pl Beechboro	48	C 4
RHUS		
Ct Yangebup	112	A 1
RHYDER		
Ct Murdoch	92	C 7
RHYL		
Cl Warnbro	145	E 7
Pl Langford	94	E 1
RIANA		
Pl Silver Sands	163	B 4
RIBBLE		
Pl Beechboro	48	D 3
RIBER		
Ct Carine	31	C 10
RICA		
Cl Duncraig	30	E 8
RICE		
Pl Armadale	116	D 8
Rd Oakford	125	A 10

238

For detailed information regarding the street referencing system used in this book, turn to page 170.

Map Ref.

RICH
St Gooseberry H.... 77 C 4
RICHARD
Cl Waikiki 145 C 4
Pl Armadale 116 D 6
Pl Orelia 131 A 4
St Maylands 62 A 9
RICHARDS
Cr Craigie 23 E 4
Pl Noranda 47 D 4
Rd High Wycombe 64 C 9
RICHARDSON
Ar Winthrop 92 B 5
Ave Claremont 80 E 1
Ave Claremont 70 E 10
Ct Woodvale 24 A 5
Rd Coogee 110 E 1
Rd Hovea 53 A 4
Rd Middle Swan 50 C 5
Rd Parkerville 53 D 5
Rd Stoneville 54 A 5
St Kwinana Beach 130 B 6
St Mundijong 142 E 7
St Serpentine 154 E 2
St Serpentine 154 E 4
St Serpentine 150 E 10
St South Perth 72 D 8
St West Perth 72 C 1
Tce Daglish 71 E 2
RICHES
Wy Bull Creek 93 A 4
RICHMOND
Ave Shoalwater 136 D 7
Pl Kingsley 24 B 9
St Cannington 84 D 7
St Leederville 60 C 8
St North Perth 60 D 8
RICKARD
Rd Glen Forrest 67 A 2
RICKETTS
Ct Rockingham 137 A 8
Wy Greenwood 31 E 4
RICKMAN
Pl Marangaroo 32 D 5
St Balcatta 46 A 4
RIDGE
Cl Edgewater 24 B 1
Rd Glen Forrest 66 D 5
St South Perth 72 E 9
St Wembley Dns 58 E 5
RIDGEHAVEN
Ct Canning Vale 94 B 10
Ra Ballajura 33 D 5
RIDGE HILL
Rd Gooseberry H 65 A 10
Rd Helena Valley 65 C 7
Rd Maida Vale 65 A 10
Rd Maida Vale 76 E 1
RIDGETOP
Trl Ballajura 33 D 5
RIDGEWAY
Rd Bellevue 50 E 10
RIDGEWOOD
Wy Ferndale 84 D 9
RIDGWAY
Pl Mahogany Crk 53 D 10
RIDING
Wy Bull Creek 93 B 7
RIDLEY
Ct Leeming 92 E 8
Ct Medina 130 D 4
Rd Wattle Grove 86 E 4
Wy S Medina 130 D 4
Wy W Medina 130 D 4
RIG
Ct Ocean Reef 23 B 2
RIGA
Cr Willetton 93 D 3
RIGBY
Ave Spearwood 101 A 7
St Willagee 91 D 4

RIGDEN
St Armadale 116 C 8
RIGEL
St Mandurah 165 B 2
RIGGS
Pl Parmelia 131 B 7
Wy Hamilton Hill 90 E 10
RIGOLL
Ct Mundijong 143 A 6
RILEY
Pl Leda 130 E 9
Rd Claremont 81 B 1
Rd Dalkeith 81 C 1
Rd Kardinya 91 D 7
Rd Mt Helena 55 A 6
Rd Mt Helena 54 D 6
Rd Parkerville 53 C 6
Rd Riverton 94 A 1
Rd Riverton 84 A 10
Rd Stoneville 54 A 6
St Tuart Hill 60 B 1
RIMMER
Rd Landsdale 25 C 9
RIMU
Pl Duncraig 31 B 8
RINALDI
Cr Karrinyup 44 D 7
RINALDO
Cr Coolbellup 101 E 2
Pl Coolbellup 101 E 2
RINGAROOMA
Wy Willetton 93 E 6
RINGMER
Wy Balga 46 C 4
RINGTAIL
Pl Wungong 116 C 10
RINGWOOD
Rd Armadale 116 D 4
RINSEY
Pl Kewdale 74 C 7
RINTEL
Ct Koondoola 33 B 8
RINTOUL
Lp Booragoon 92 B 1
RIO
Ct Beechboro 48 E 4
St Bayswater 62 C 3
RIO GRANDE
Ave Greenfields 165 D 2
RIO MARINA
Wy Mindarie 14 C 6
RIPLEY
Pl Embleton 48 B 10
Wy Duncraig 31 A 4
RIPPLE
Wy Bateman 92 D 4
RIPPLEWOOD
Ave Thornlie 95 D 6
RISBY
St Gosnells 95 E 8
RISELEY
Rd Naval Base 121 A 9
St Applecross 82 C 7
St Ardross 82 C 8
St Booragoon 92 C 2
RISLEY
Wy Carine 45 B 1
Wy Carine 31 B 10
RITCHIE
Wy Cloverdale 75 A 4
RITSON
Wy Lynwood 94 B 4
RIVE
Pl Thornlie 95 A 7
RIVER
Ave Maddington 96 A 6
Ave Maddington 95 E 6
Ct Greenfields 165 C 1

Rd Bayswater 62 D 6
Rd Cannington 84 E 8
Rd Herne Hill 36 C 2
Rd Kelmscott 106 E 9
St Bassendean 49 B 10
Wy Salter Point 83 B 9
RIVER BANK
Dr Gosnells 96 A 7
RIVERBED
Ps Wilson 84 A 9
RIVERBY
Cl Shelley 83 D 9
RIVER FIG
Pl Alexander Hts 32 E 4
RIVER GUM
Dr Rowethorpe 144
RIVERGUM
Pl Morley 48 D 5
RIVERS
St Bibra Lake 101 D 8
RIVERSDALE
Gns Currambine 19 C 5
Rd Rivervale 74 A 3
Rd Rivervale 73 E 3
Rd Welshpool 85 D 3
RIVERSEA
Vw Mosman Park 80 D 8
RIVERSIDE
Dr East Perth 73 B 4
Dr Furnissdale 165 D 7
Dr Mosman Park 81 A 7
Dr Perth City 1C A 4
Dr Perth City 73 A 4
Dr Sth Guildford 63 C 3
Dr West Perth 1C D 4
Dr West Perth 72 D 4
La Armadale 115 E 5
Rd East Fremantle 90 D 1
Rd East Fremantle 80 D 10
RIVERSLEA
Ave Maylands 61 D 8
RIVERTON
Dr E Riverton 84 A 9
Dr E Riverton 83 E 9
Dr E Shelley 84 A 8
Dr N Shelley 83 B 10
Dr W Rossmoyne 93 A 2
RIVER VIEW
Ave Sth Guildford 63 C 4
St South Perth 72 E 8
Tce Mt Pleasant 82 E 10
RIVERVIEW
Ct Dalkeith 81 B 2
Pl Mosman Park 81 A 6
Rd E Victoria Pk 83 E 2
Ri Wilson 84 B 9
St Coodanup 165 D 6
RIVERWAY
Applecross 82 D 5
RIVETT
Pl Marmion 30 D 9
Wy Brentwood 92 E 2
RIVIERA
Ct Connolly 19 C 9
ROACH
Pl Orelia 131 B 6
Rd Kalamunda 78 A 7
ROAMER
St Heathridge 19 C 9
ROANOKE
Gr Connolly 19 A 7
ROBANN
Wy Morley 47 D 8
ROBB
Rd Hamilton Hill 100 D 3
Rd Spearwood 100 D 4
ROBBINS
Pl Shelley 93 B 2
Pl Winthrop 92 A 4
Rt Leda 130 E 9

ROBE
Ct Heathridge 19 B 9
Pl Armadale 116 C 4
ROBERT
Pl Calista 130 E 8
Rd Kalamunda 77 C 7
Rd Quinns Rocks 10 E 10
St Bellevue 50 E 9
St Como 82 E 4
St Como 82 E 5
St Dalkeith 81 C 2
ROBERTA
St Daglish 71 E 2
ROBERTO
St Willetton 93 C 3
ROBERTS
Pl Greenmount 51 C 10
Rd Attadale 81 C 8
Rd Henley Brook 28 E 9
Rd Kelmscott 107 A 10
Rd Kelmscott 116 E 1
Rd Lathlain 74 B 7
Rd Rivervale 74 B 6
Rd Subiaco 72 B 1
St Bayswater 62 B 6
St Joondanna 60 B 2
St Osborne Park 60 A 2
St W Osborne Park 60 A 2
ROBERTSBRIDGE
Rd Nollamara 46 D 5
ROBERTSON
Pl Bibra Lake 102 D 3
Rd Byford 135 C 5
Rd Cardup 135 B 9
Rd Gooseberry H 77 B 2
Rd Kardinya 91 E 6
Rd Whitby 143 A 7
St Hazelmere 64 A 1
St Perth City 1C B 1
St Perth City 73 B 1
ROBIN
Ave Sorrento 30 B 6
Ce Ballajura 33 D 5
Ct Armadale 116 D 5
Ct High Wycombe 64 B 10
Ct Singleton 160 D 3
Gns Stirling 45 E 7
Rd Roleystone 108 A 7
St Menora 61 A 6
ROBINA
Rd Gosnells 106 B 2
ROBIN HOOD
Ave Armadale 116 C 6
ROBINS
Rd Kalamunda 77 C 9
Ri Stratton 51 B 3
ROBINSON
Ave Belmont 74 C 3
Ave Cloverdale 74 E 5
Ave Perth City 61 A 10
Ave Quinns Rocks 10 E 9
Ct Greenmount 65 E 1
Pl Rockingham 137 B 7
Rd Bellevue 50 E 10
Rd Eden Hill 48 E 9
Rd Greenmount 65 E 1
Rd Herne Hill 37 A 2
Rd Mahogany Crk 67 D 1
Rd Mahogany Crk 53 D 10
Rd Morley 48 A 9
Rd Rockingham 137 B 7
Rd Roleystone 107 D 5
Rd Wandi 123 E 5
St Forrestdale 114 E 6
St Fremantle 91 A 4
St Inglewood 61 C 5
St Mt Lawley 61 B 6
St Mundijong 143 B 10
St Nedlands 71 C 8
St Subiaco 72 B 2
Tce Daglish 72 A 1
Tce Daglish 71 E 1

ROBINSWOOD
Fo Jarrahdale 152 B 6
ROB ROY
Me Iluka 18 D 4
St Swanbourne 70 E 9
ROBSON
Wy Murdoch 92 C 7
ROBUSTA
Rd Kalamunda 77 E 4
ROBYN
St Morley 47 D 7
ROCHDALE
Rd Mt Claremont 71 A 6
Rd Mt Claremont 70 E 4
ROCHE
Ct Bull Creek 93 B 6
Rd Duncraig 30 E 6
ROCHELE
Ct Woodvale 24 A 6
ROCHESTER
Ave Beckenham 85 C 9
Ci Balga 32 A 10
Ci Balga 46 B 1
Wy Dianella 47 A 10
Wy Meadow Sprgs 163 C 3
ROCHFORD
Wy Girrawheen 32 D 8
ROCK
Cr Karragullen 109 B 6
ROCKBANK
Pl Kiara 48 D 7
ROCKE
St Coolbellup 91 D 10
ROCKETT
Vl Padbury 30 E 2
Wy Bull Creek 93 B 5
ROCKFORD
St Mandurah 163 A 10
ROCKINGHAM
Rd E Rockingham 129 D 9
Rd Hamilton Hill 101 A 2
Rd Henderson 111 C 9
Rd Kwinana Beach 130 B 4
Rd Kwinana Beach 121 B 10
Rd Kwinana Beach 129 E 8
Rd Munster 111 B 1
Rd Naval Base 121 B 7
Rd Rockingham 137 A 3
Rd Spearwood 101 B 7
Rd Wattleup 121 C 2
ROCKLEA
Pl Silver Sands 163 B 4
ROCKLIFF
Ave Karrinyup 44 E 7
ROCKTON
Rd Nedlands 71 C 10
ROCK VIEW
Pl Kelmscott 107 B 9
RODD
Pl Hamilton Hill 101 C 3
RODDA
St Morley 48 A 8
St Morley 47 E 8
RODEN
Pl Duncraig 31 A 8
RODERICK
Cl Gosnells 106 A 3
Ct Heathridge 19 B 10
RODGERS
Cl Forrestfield 76 D 10
Ct Roleystone 108 D 9
Pl Bull Creek 93 A 6
St Greenwood 31 E 6
RODING
Ct Girrawheen 32 C 9
RODINGA
Cl Rossmoyne 93 B 2
RODONDO
Pl Shelley 93 C 1

For detailed information regarding the street referencing system used in this book, turn to page 170.

R

		Map	Ref.
ROE			
Cl	Bull Creek	92	E 7
Ct	Padbury	23	C 8
Hwy	Beckenham	85	C 10
Hwy	Bellevue	64	D 2
Hwy	Bibra Lake	102	A 2
Hwy	Bibra Lake	101	E 3
Hwy	Forrestfield	76	A 8
Hwy	Hamilton Hill	101	A 2
Hwy	Hazelmere	64	D 4
Hwy	High Wycombe	76	D 3
Hwy	High Wycombe	64	D 10
Hwy	Langford	94	E 4
Hwy	Leeming	93	D 9
Hwy	Lynwood	94	A 5
Hwy	Middle Swan	50	D 2
Hwy	Midvale	50	E 9
Hwy	Wattle Grove	85	E 2
Hwy	Wexcombe	50	E 6
Pl	Beechboro	49	A 3
St	Northbridge	1C	E 1
St	Northbridge	72	E 1
St	Perth City	1C	A 2
St	Rockingham	137	B 2
ROEBOURNE			
Pl	Redcliffe	62	E 7
ROEBUCK			
Dr	Salter Point	83	A 7
St	Innaloo	59	C 1
ROEDEAN			
St	West Swan	35	B 10
ROGATE			
St	Balga	46	D 1
ROGER			
St	Midland	50	D 6
ROGERS			
La	Armadale	116	D 3
St	Rockingham	137	D 4
Wy	Landsdale	25	C 9
ROGERSON			
Rd	Mt Pleasant	92	D 1
Rd	Mt Pleasant	82	D 10
ROKEBURY			
Wy	Morley	48	C 9
ROKEBY			
Rd	Shenton Park	72	A 3
Rd	Subiaco	72	A 3
ROKEFORD			
Wy	Morley	47	E 6
ROKEWOOD			
Wy	Karragullen	109	A 1
ROLAND			
Rd	Gidgegannup	39	B 3
Rd	Parkerville	53	C 4
Rd	Parkerville	39	C 9
ROLLA			
Gr	Waikiki	145	C 2
ROLLAND			
Ct	Leeming	93	A 10
ROLLESTON			
Dl	Alexander Hts	33	A 4
ROLLINGS			
Cr	Kwinana Beach	130	B 5
ROLLINSON			
Rd	Hamilton Hill	100	D 1
ROMA			
Pl	Lesmurdie	87	D 1
St	Munster	110	E 1
ROMAN			
Rd	Whitby	143	A 8
ROMARO			
Ct	Koondoola	33	A 9
ROME			
Rd	Melville	91	E 3
Rd	Melville	81	E 10
Rd	Wanneroo	21	A 8
Wy	Dianella	47	A 6
ROMEO			
Rd	Carabooda	8	B 10
Rd	Coolbellup	101	E 1

		Map	Ref.
ROMFORD			
Pl	Kingsley	31	B 1
ROMNEY			
St	Beckenham	85	C 6
Wy	Lynwood	94	C 2
ROMSEY			
Gr	Kiara	48	E 7
RONA			
St	North Beach	44	C 4
RONALD			
St	Balcatta	46	B 7
RONAN			
Pl	Willetton	93	D 3
Rd	Roleystone	107	C 6
RON CHAMBERLAIN			
Dr	Duncraig	30	D 7
RONEZ			
El	Merriwa	10	B 9
RONLYN			
Rd	Furnissdale	165	E 7
RONNEBY			
Rd	Lesmurdie	77	C 10
RONSARD			
Pl	Yangebup	101	E 10
ROOKE			
Wy	Clarkson	14	C 2
ROOKWOOD			
St	Henley Brook	36	A 1
St	Henley Brook	29	A 10
St	Menora	61	A 6
St	Mt Lawley	61	B 8
St	Mt Pleasant	82	D 7
ROOSEVELT			
St	Redcliffe	63	A 10
ROOTES			
Rd	Lesmurdie	87	C 5
ROOTH			
Rd	Lesmurdie	87	C 4
ROPELE			
Dr	Lynwood	94	A 4
ROPER			
St	O'Connor	91	C 7
RORIE			
Pl	Willetton	94	A 2
ROSALIE			
St	Shenton Park	72	A 4
ROSALIND			
Ct	Rossmoyne	93	B 2
Wy	Coolbellup	101	E 2
ROSANNA			
St	Yanchep	4	E 1
ROSCOMMON			
Rd	Floreat	59	A 9
ROSCORLA			
Ave	Yokine	60	E 1
Ave	Yokine	46	E 10
ROSCREA			
Cl	Waterford	83	C 7
ROSE			
Ave	Bayswater	62	B 4
Ave	South Perth	73	A 8
Ct	Lesmurdie	87	C 4
Pl	Morley	48	C 5
Pl	Wilson	84	C 6
Rd	Cardup	135	D 7
Rd	Mundijong	143	C 10
St	Halls Head	162	B 10
St	Sth Fremantle	90	C 8
St	Upper Swan	29	D 2
ROSEA			
Cl	Maida Vale	77	A 2
Ct	Thornlie	94	E 7
ROSEATE			
Cl	Ballajura	33	E 6
ROSEBANK			
Gns	Alexander Hts	33	A 5
ROSEBERRY			
Ave	South Perth	73	B 8

		Map	Ref.
ROSEBERY			
St	Bayswater	61	E 5
St	Bedford	61	C 2
St	Bedford	61	D 4
St	Jolimont	71	E 1
ROSEBURY			
Ave	Alexander Hts	33	B 5
ROSEDALE			
Rd	Chidlow	56	C 1
Rd	Chidlow	42	C 10
Rd	Chidlow	41	E 6
Rd	Gidgegannup	42	A 8
St	Floreat	71	C 1
St	Floreat	59	C 10
ROSEDENE			
Wy	Greenwood	31	E 5
ROSEHEATH			
Blvd	Kiara	48	D 6
ROSEHILL			
Cr	Willetton	94	A 1
ROSEKELLY			
Rd	Gosnells	106	B 1
ROSELLA			
Ci	Ballajura	34	A 7
Ci	Ballajura	33	E 7
Ct	Kingsley	31	C 1
Gp	Wungong	116	B 9
Pl	Gosnells	106	A 4
St	Lesmurdie	87	D 4
St	Stirling	45	E 6
ROSEMARY			
Ct	Huntingdale	95	D 10
ROSEMONT			
Pl	Leeming	103	A 1
ROSEMOUNT			
Tce	Lesmurdie	87	B 4
ROSENDO			
St	Cottesloe	80	C 4
ROSETTA			
Ri	Gnangara	25	E 5
St	Bassendean	63	B 2
ROSETTE			
Cl	Craigie	23	C 7
ROSEVILLE			
Cl	Kallaroo	23	A 7
ROSEWOOD			
Ave	Woodlands	59	B 3
Cr	Dianella	46	E 5
Pl	Thornlie	105	B 1
St	Rockingham	136	E 6
ROSHER			
Pl	Bayswater	62	A 7
Rd	Maylands	62	A 7
Rd	Lockridge	49	A 7
ROSKHILL			
Pl	Applecross	82	D 4
ROSMEAD			
Ave	Beechboro	48	D 4
ROSMUNDE			
Ct	Leederville	60	B 9
ROSNAY			
Ct	Yanchep	4	D 1
ROSNEATH			
Tce	Kinross	18	E 1
ROSS			
Ave	Sorrento	30	B 6
Ct	Safety Bay	145	A 1
Ct	Spearwood	101	C 6
Dr	Perth Airport	63	B 8
Pl	Thornlie	95	C 3
Rd	Kardinya	91	E 8
St	Cloverdale	74	D 5
St	Jandabup	21	D 9
St	Kewdale	74	D 5
ROSSER			
St	Cottesloe	80	D 3
ROSSETTI			
Ct	North Lake	102	A 1

		Map	Ref.
ROSSITER			
Hts	Hillarys	30	B 1
Wy	Winthrop	92	C 5
ROSSLARE			
Pro	Mindarie	14	A 4
ROSSLYN			
St	Leederville	60	B 10
ROSSMOOR			
Ct	Woodvale	24	B 3
ROSSMOYNE			
Dr	Rossmoyne	93	A 1
Dr	Rossmoyne	83	B 10
ROSTELLAN			
Pl	Willetton	94	A 3
ROSTRATA			
Ave	Willetton	94	A 5
Ave	Willetton	93	E 3
ROTARY			
Ave	Gosnells	96	B 9
ROTHBURY			
Rd	Embleton	62	A 2
ROTHER			
Pl	Nollamara	46	E 5
ROTHERFIELD			
Rd	Balga	46	B 3
ROTHESAY			
Hts	Mindarie	10	B 2
Hts	Mindarie	14	B 3
St	Forrestfield	86	C 1
ROTHSAY			
Cr	Menora	61	A 4
ROTHSCHILD			
Pl	Midvale	51	A 8
ROTHWALD			
Pl	Hillarys	23	B 10
ROTHWELL			
Ct	Wattleup	121	C 2
ROTOHINE			
Cr	Falcon	162A	C 10
Pl	Cooloongup	137	D 8
ROTORUA			
Gr	Joondalup	19	D 3
ROUEN			
Cst	Mindarie	10	B 2
ROUNTREE			
Rd	Brentwood	92	D 2
Wy	Marmion	30	C 8
ROUSE			
Rd	Greenfields	163	D 7
ROUS HEAD			
Rd	Nth Fremantle	90	A 4
ROUSSET			
Rd	Mariginiup	21	B 2
Rd	Mariginiup	17	C 10
ROWALLAN			
St	Osborne Park	60	A 3
ROWAN			
Pl	Mullaloo	23	A 4
Pl	Woodlands	59	B 1
ROWE			
Ave	Rivervale	74	A 3
Ct	Balga	46	E 4
Ct	Samson	91	C 9
Pl	Midland	50	E 7
Pl	Noranda	47	C 5
Rd	Peel Estate	150	A 10
Rd	Peel Estate	149	C 10
St	Malaga	47	D 1
St	Midland	50	E 6
ROWENA			
St	Falcon	162A	D 10
ROWLAND			
Pl	Gosnells	106	A 2
Pl	Hamilton Hill	100	E 1
St	Subiaco	72	A 2

		Map	Ref.
ROWLANDS			
Ct	Padbury	23	D 9
St	Kewdale	74	D 8
St	Maylands	61	E 7
ROWLEY			
Pl	Bull Creek	93	A 4
Pl	Mariginiup	21	A 2
Rd	Banjup	123	A 3
Rd	Banjup	122	E 3
Rd	Byford	125	E 3
Rd	Forrestdale	125	A 2
Rd	Forrestdale	124	B 3
Rd	Wungong	126	A 3
St	Kelmscott	117	B 1
ROWNEY			
Cl	Bateman	92	D 7
ROWSLEY			
Wy	Carine	31	A 9
ROXBY			
La	Willetton	93	C 1
ROXTON			
St	Viveash	50	B 4
ROXWELL			
Wy	Girrawheen	32	C 8
ROY			
Rd	Coodanup	165	C 7
St	Mt Lawley	61	B 9
St	Welshpool	84	C 2
ROYAL			
Rd	Safety Bay	136	D 5
St	East Perth	1C	B 2
St	East Perth	73	B 2
St	Kenwick	95	C 2
St	Tuart Hill	46	B 10
St	Yokine	46	D 10
ROYAL MELBOURNE			
Ave	Connolly	19	C 8
ROYALOAK			
Glen	Padbury	30	E 2
ROYAL PALM			
Dr	Warnbro	145	E 9
ROYCE			
Ct	Joondalup	19	D 8
Gr	Booragoon	92	B 2
Rd	Greenfields	163	E 9
St	Singleton	160	D 2
ROYDHOUSE			
St	Wembley	60	A 10
ROYDON			
Wy	Girrawheen	32	D 8
ROYER			
Ct	Ashfield	62	E 4
ROYSON			
Pl	Dianella	47	C 9
ROYSTON			
Pl	Mt Helena	55	B 5
RUAN			
Ct	Kewdale	74	C 6
RUBY			
Ave	Langford	84	E 10
Ct	Armadale	116	E 8
Ct	Maida Vale	76	D 1
St	Bellevue	51	B 10
St	North Perth	60	E 6
RUDALL			
Ct	Clarkson	14	E 1
Ct	Gosnells	106	A 2
St	Serpentine	155	A 4
Wy	Padbury	30	D 2
RUDDER			
Ct	Heathridge	23	D 1
RUDDERHAM			
Dr	Nth Fremantle	90	A 4
RUDDICK			
Pl	Hamilton Hill	101	A 3
RUDGE			
Pl	Lockridge	49	B 7
St	Noranda	47	C 5
St	Willagee	91	D 4

240

For detailed information regarding the street referencing system used in this book, turn to page 170.

S

	Map	Ref.
RUDKIN		
Pl Koondoola	32	E 7
RUDLOC		
Rd Morley	61	E 1
Rd Morley	47	E 10
RUDWICK		
St Mosman Park	80	E 6
RUDYARD		
Ct Willetton	93	E 3
RUFFIAN		
Lp Willetton	93	D 6
RUFOUS		
Pl Stirling	45	E 6
RUGBY		
St Bassendean	62	D 1
St Bassendean	48	D 10
St West Swan	35	C 10
RUISLIP		
St Leederville	60	B 9
RULE		
St Nth Fremantle	80	C 9
RUMBLE		
St Embleton	48	B 10
RUMMER		
Wy Bateman	92	D 4
RUNDAL		
St Bayswater	48	D 10
RUNDLE		
St Kelmscott	106	E 10
RUNYON		
Rd Midvale	51	A 9
RUPARA		
Me Currambine	19	A 6
RUPERT		
St Armadale	116	C 5
St Cannington	84	D 7
St Kenwick	95	C 1
St Kenwick	95	D 3
St Maylands	62	A 7
St Subiaco	72	A 3
RUSE		
Ct Padbury	23	E 8
St Osborne Park	59	E 2
RUSHAM		
Pl Morley	48	A 6
RUSHBROOK		
Wy Thornlie	95	B 6
RUSHBY		
Wy Samson	91	D 8
RUSHTON		
Ct Kardinya	91	D 6
Rd Martin	97	A 5
Rd Martin	96	E 6
St Victoria Park	73	E 6
Tce Armadale	116	C 3
RUSHY		
Rd Mundaring	69	E 10
RUSSELIA		
Wy Roleystone	108	A 9
RUSSELL		
Ave North Perth	61	A 6
Rd Greenmount	51	C 10
Rd Landsdale	25	B 10
Rd Maida Vale	76	D 1
Rd Munster	111	A 5
Rd Success	112	B 8
St E Cannington	85	B 4
St Fremantle	1D	C 6
St Fremantle	90	C 7
St Morley	62	A 1
St Morley	47	D 9
St Morley	61	E 2
RUSSLEY		
Gr Yanchep	4	E 1
RUSTHALL		
Wy Huntingdale	105	D 1
RUSTIC		
Cl Ballajura	33	C 4
Gns Neerabup	16	A 5

	Map	Ref.
RUTH		
Ct Duncraig	30	D 3
St Como	83	B 2
St Perth City	61	A 10
RUTHERFORD		
Rd Dianella	47	A 9
RUTHIN		
Wy Wanneroo	20	E 10
RUTHVEN		
Pl Duncraig	31	C 8
RUTLAND		
Ave Carlisle	74	B 9
Ave Lathlain	74	A 7
Ave Lathlain	73	E 5
Ave Welshpool	84	C 1
RYAN		
Ave Dianella	47	C 10
Ct Bull Creek	93	A 6
Ct Midland	50	E 6
St Rockingham	137	A 6
Wy Lesmurdie	87	E 2
RYANS		
Ct Redcliffe	63	A 9
RYCE		
Ct Eden Hill	48	D 8
RYDAL		
Ct Cooloongup	137	D 10
Pl Carine	30	E 10
RYDE		
Cl Warnbro	145	E 7
St Gosnells	95	E 9
RYE		
Gr Wanneroo	24	E 1
Pl Nollamara	46	D 6
RYECROFT		
Rd Darlington	66	B 5
Rd Glen Forrest	66	C 5
RYELANE		
St Maddington	96	A 2
RYLAND		
Rd Kelmscott	116	D 1
Rd Kelmscott	106	D 10
RYLSTON		
St Scarborough	58	E 2
RYNDLE		
St Doubleview	59	A 1
RYRIE		
Ave Como	83	B 2

S

	Map	Ref.
SABINA		
Dr Madora	160	C 8
St Menora	61	A 4
St Woodlands	59	B 3
SABOT		
Pl Ocean Reef	23	A 1
SACKVILLE		
Tce Doubleview	45	A 8
Tce Scarborough	44	D 8
SACRAMENTO		
Ave Beechboro	48	E 2
SADDLEBACK		
Ci Maida Vale	64	E 9
Gr Canning Vale	94	D 5
SADDLEHILL		
Ra Ballajura	33	C 5
SADDLER		
Pl Mirrabooka	47	A 4
SADKO		
Cl Willetton	93	C 7
SADLER		
Dr Maida Vale	64	E 8
SADLIER		
Ct Stoneville	54	C 6
St Dalkeith	81	E 3
St Subiaco	71	E 3

	Map	Ref.
SADOC		
St Woodlands	59	B 3
SAFARI		
Pl Carabooda	8	D 4
SAFETY BAY		
Rd Rockingham	136	D 5
Rd Safety Bay	145	A 2
Rd Safety Bay	144	D 1
Rd Shoalwater	136	D 9
Rd Waikiki	146	A 5
Rd Waikiki	145	C 5
SAFFRON		
Ct Kelmscott	106	D 10
Ct Riverton	94	B 1
SAGA		
Ct Cooloongup	137	D 8
Pl Willetton	93	D 6
SAGE		
Ct Halls Head	164	D 5
Rd Thornlie	95	B 4
St Embleton	48	A 10
SAGGERS		
Cr Beckenham	85	D 5
Dr Swan C Homes	144	
SAIL		
Ct Waikiki	145	C 3
Gr Ballajura	33	D 6
Tce Heathridge	23	C 1
SAILFISH		
Cl Beldon	23	C 3
SAINSBURY		
Rd O'Connor	91	B 5
Names prefixed with the abbreviation 'St' (Saint) are listed alphabetically, ie. St Albans follows Stakehill.		
SAINT		
Ps Winthrop	92	C 6
SAINT CLOUD		
Gns Connolly	19	B 8
SALACIA		
Ct Alexander Hts	33	A 5
Me Willetton	93	D 6
SALADIN		
St Swanbourne	70	E 9
SALAMANDER		
Pl Dianella	47	B 6
St Dianella	47	B 6
SALAR		
Pl Dianella	47	B 6
SALATA		
Pl Duncraig	30	E 4
SALCOMBE		
Wy Warnbro	145	D 8
SALCOTT		
Rd Girrawheen	32	D 9
SALEHAM		
St Lathlain	74	A 6
SALEN		
Ct Ardross	82	C 10
SALFORD		
St Victoria Park	73	E 8
SALINAS		
Ct Woodvale	24	B 3
SALISBURY		
Ave South Perth	73	B 8
Rd Beechboro	48	D 4
Rd Midvale	50	D 4
Rd Rivervale	74	B 2
Rd Swan View	51	C 8
St Bayswater	61	E 5
St Bedford	61	C 3
St Cottesloe	70	E 9
St Leederville	60	D 6
St St James	84	B 2
St Subiaco	72	B 5
SALIX		
Wy Forrestfield	76	C 9

	Map	Ref.
SALKILLD		
La Rockingham	136	E 5
SALMAR		
Wy Balga	46	D 4
SALMOND		
Wy Bull Creek	93	A 4
SALMON GUM		
Gr Beechboro	48	C 3
Ri Willetton	93	D 5
SALMSON		
St Balcatta	45	D 4
SALPIETRO		
St Bibra Lake	101	C 8
SALTASH		
Ave City Beach	70	D 2
SALTER		
Pl Parmelia	131	C 8
Rd Kelmscott	117	A 2
Rd Kelmscott	116	E 2
SALTER POINT		
Pde Salter Point	83	B 9
SALVADO		
Ave East Fremantle	90	E 1
Rd Floreat	59	B 10
Rd Wembley	60	A 10
Rd Wembley	59	E 10
St Cottesloe	80	E 4
SALVADOR		
Cl Safety Bay	145	B 1
SALVATOR		
St Noranda	47	D 4
SALVIA		
Ct Ferndale	84	B 10
Ct Yangebup	101	D 10
SALWAY		
Pl Spearwood	101	B 5
SALWEEN		
Pl Beechboro	48	E 3
Pl Greenfields	165	C 2
SAMBELL		
Cl Churchlands	59	C 4
SAMICHON		
Rd Karrakatta	71	C 5
SAMOS		
Pl Mindarie	14	B 5
SAMPSON		
Cl Kalamunda	77	E 9
Cl Midland	50	D 6
Rd Kalamunda	77	D 10
Rd Lesmurdie	77	D 10
St Maddington	95	E 4
SAMS		
Pl Spearwood	101	B 7
SAMSON		
Ct Duncraig	30	E 8
Ct Henley Brook	36	A 3
Pl Helena Valley	65	A 4
St Helena Valley	65	B 5
St Hilton	91	A 7
St Mosman Park	80	E 7
St Sawyers Valley	55	D 9
St White Gum Vly	90	D 7
SAMSUN		
Vs Mindarie	10	B 2
SAMUAL		
Ct North Lake	102	A 2
SAMUEL		
St Mt Helena	55	B 3
St Rockingham	136	E 5
SAN		
Pl Mullaloo	23	B 5
SAN ANTONIO		
Gns Iluka	18	D 6
SANDALFORD		
Dr Beldon	23	E 3
SANDALWOOD		
Ave Woodlands	59	C 4
Cl Beechboro	48	C 3
Cl Falcon	162A	B 4

	Map	Ref.
Dr Greenwood	31	D 4
Pde Halls Head	164	C 3
St Maddington	96	C 5
SANDAY		
Pl Warwick	31	C 8
SANDELAND		
Ave Coodanup	165	C 4
SANDER		
Ct Bentley	84	C 5
SANDERLING		
Ct Two Rocks	2	D 1
Dr Thornlie	95	A 6
Gr Ballajura	33	E 7
St Stirling	45	E 6
SANDERS		
Ce Sorrento	30	D 3
Lp Kardinya	91	E 6
SANDERSON		
Rd Bull Creek	93	A 5
Rd Lesmurdie	87	C 4
St Embleton	62	B 2
St Kalamunda	77	D 7
SANDFORD		
Cr Halls Head	164	C 4
Gr Parmelia	131	B 8
SANDGATE		
St South Perth	73	B 10
Wy Marangaroo	32	A 7
SANDHURST		
Cl Brigadoon	169	C 2
Rd Dianella	61	B 1
SANDLEFORD		
Wy Morley	48	C 8
SAN DOMINGO		
Cl Safety Bay	145	B 1
SANDON		
El Merriwa	11	C 9
Rd Thornlie	95	B 5
SANDOVER		
Cr Winthrop	92	A 6
Dr Karrinyup	45	A 2
Rd Darlington	65	E 5
SANDOW		
Grn Clarkson	14	C 2
SANDOWN		
Rd Willetton	93	D 3
SANDPIPER		
Cl Ballajura	33	E 6
Lp Yangebup	102	A 10
Pl Coodanup	165	E 5
Rd Stirling	45	D 7
St Sorrento	30	D 5
St Two Rocks	2	D 1
SANDRA		
Pl Welshpool	74	D 9
St Falcon	162A	A 3
Wy Rossmoyne	93	A 2
SANDRIDGE		
St Gosnells	96	A 9
SANDRINGHAM		
St Trigg	44	D 4
SANDS		
Ct Huntingdale	95	D 10
SANDSNAIL		
Pl Mullaloo	23	B 3
SANDSTONE		
Pl Marmion	30	D 9
SANFORD		
Ct Heathridge	19	B 9
St Gosnells	106	A 2
Vw Alexander Hts	33	A 3
SAN JACINTA		
Rd Armadale	115	E 4
SAN JOSE		
Ct Safety Bay	137	C 10
SAN MARINO		
Pl Hillarys	23	A 8

For detailed information regarding the street referencing system used in this book, turn to page 170.

S

		Map	Ref.
SAN MIGUEL			
Dr	Currambine	19	A 3
Dr	Leeming	102	E 1
Rd	Hope Valley	121	C 7
SAN PABLO			
Me	Iluka	18	D 3
SAN ROSA			
Rd	Wanneroo	24	D 1
SANTA			
Wy	Wanneroo	20	E 9
SANTIAGO			
Pl	Safety Bay	145	B 1
Pwy	Ocean Reef	19	A 7
SAPLING			
Wy	Wanneroo	24	E 1
Wy	Westfield	106	C 8
SAPPER			
Wy	Karrakatta	71	C 5
SAPPHIRE			
Ct	Armadale	116	E 8
Ct	Maida Vale	76	D 1
SAPPHO			
Pl	Two Rocks	3	B 10
SAPPLETON			
Rt	Merriwa	14	C 1
SARACEN			
Wy	Marangaroo	32	D 5
SARAH			
St	Maylands	62	A 8
SARATOGA			
Ci	Coodanup	165	D 5
Gr	Iluka	18	E 4
SARICH			
Ct	Osborne Park	45	D 10
Wy	Bentley	83	D 2
SARK			
Pl	Warnbro	145	E 6
SARRE			
Pl	Marangaroo	32	A 3
St	Gosnells	106	B 1
SARTORIAL			
Pl	Greenfields	163	E 10
SASKATCHEWAN			
Wy	Greenfields	165	D 1
SASOON			
Pl	Armadale	116	C 3
SASSE			
Ave	Mt Hawthorn	60	B 6
SASSOON			
Pl	North Lake	102	A 1
SATELLITE			
Pl	Carlisle	74	B 6
Rt	Kiara	48	E 7
SATINASH			
Rt	Halls Head	164	B 4
SATINOVER			
Wy	Wandi	123	B 4
SATURN			
St	Beckenham	85	C 8
SAUNDERS			
St	Como	83	A 3
St	Como	82	E 3
St	East Perth	1C	B 2
St	East Perth	73	B 2
St	Henley Brook	28	E 9
St	Mosman Park	81	A 6
St	North Beach	44	C 3
St	Safety Bay	144	D 1
St	Safety Bay	136	D 10
St	Swanbourne	70	E 8
Wy	Karragullen	109	A 1
SAUREL			
Wy	Ferndale	84	D 9
SAVAGE			
Rd	Kelmscott	107	B 10
SAVARIS			
Ct	Beldon	23	D 3

		Map	Ref.
SAVERY			
Wy	Rockingham	138	A 4
Wy	Rockingham	137	E 4
SAVOIR			
Ct	Craigie	23	E 5
SAVONA			
Gr	Mindarie	14	C 6
SAVOY			
Pl	Duncraig	30	E 3
SAW			
Ave	Kings Park	72	A 4
Ave	Rockingham	136	D 5
Ct	Booragoon	92	B 1
Dr	Darlington	65	E 3
Rd	Armadale	116	E 6
Rd	Kardinya	91	E 7
SAWLE			
Rd	Hamilton Hill	101	B 2
SAWLEY			
Ct	Carine	30	E 9
SAWYER			
Rd	Calista	130	E 8
SAWYERS			
Rd	Mt Helena	55	B 6
Rd	Sawyers Valley	69	A 1
Rd	Sawyers Valley	55	A 10
SAXBY			
Ct	Balcatta	46	B 6
SAXON			
Ct	Langford	94	E 3
Pl	Bateman	92	E 4
SAYCE			
Sq	Winthrop	92	A 3
SAYER			
Cr	Gosnells	106	A 4
Rd	Hope Valley	122	A 3
St	Midland	50	C 9
St	Swanbourne	70	D 8
SCADDAN			
St	Bassendean	62	E 1
St	Duncraig	31	B 7
St	Wembley	60	E 7
St	Wembley	59	E 8
SCAFFELL			
Gns	Carine	30	D 10
SCALBY			
St	Doubleview	59	A 1
St	Scarborough	58	E 1
SCALES			
Wy	Spearwood	101	B 6
SCALLOP			
Cl	Heathridge	23	B 1
SCALLOWAY			
Cc	Mindarie	14	B 6
SCANDRETT			
Wy	Bateman	92	D 6
SCANLON			
Wy	Lockridge	49	B 7
SCAPHELLA			
Ave	Mullaloo	23	B 4
SCARBOROUGH BEACH			
Rd	Doubleview	45	A 10
Rd	Innaloo	59	B 1
Rd	Mt Hawthorn	60	C 5
Rd	North Perth	60	D 6
Rd	Osborne Park	60	A 4
Rd	Osborne Park	59	D 4
Rd	Scarborough	44	E 10
SCARCLIFFE			
Wy	Carine	30	D 10
SCARP			
Cl	Edgewater	24	B 1
Rd	Jarrahdale	153	A 10
Tce	Willetton	93	E 6
SCARP VIEW			
	Swan View	51	B 5
SCARSDALE			
Ave	Coodanup	165	C 4

		Map	Ref.
SCENIC			
Cr	South Perth	73	C 7
Dr	City Beach	58	E 10
Dr	Falcon	162A	D 1
Dr	Kewdale	74	D 7
Dr	Maida Vale	77	A 2
Dr	Wanneroo	24	C 1
Dr	Wanneroo	20	C 6
SCEPTRE			
Ct	Two Rocks	3	B 10
SCHACHT			
Ct	Myaree	92	A 1
SCHIPP			
Rd	Piesse Brook	78	A 5
SCHMITT			
Rd	Kalamunda	77	E 8
SCHNAPPER			
Ct	Burns	18	D 3
SCHOCH			
Rd	Parkerville	54	A 4
SCHOFIELD			
Rd	Wattle Grove	86	D 3
St	Eden Hill	49	A 9
St	Hamilton Hill	91	C 10
SCHOOL			
Rd	Dalkeith	81	C 2
Rd	Karragullen	109	B 2
St	Kalamunda	77	D 6
SCHOONER			
Pl	Waikiki	145	C 5
Pl	Yanchep	4	C 3
SCHRUTH			
St N	Kelmscott	116	D 1
St N	Kelmscott	106	D 10
St S	Armadale	116	D 3
SCHUNKE			
Cl	Lesmurdie	87	B 6
SCIANO			
Ave	Jandakot	112	E 2
SCIRON			
Ct	High Wycombe	76	C 1
SCOFIELD			
Pl	Banjup	113	D 6
SCOLE			
Pl	Huntingdale	95	D 9
SCOLLEY			
Rd	Medina	130	E 4
SCOTIA			
Pl	Armadale	116	C 5
Pl	Morley	48	D 6
SCOTT			
Ct	Woodlands	59	C 2
Pl	Hillarys	23	C 10
Rd	Gidgegannup	39	A 2
Rd	Kelmscott	107	B 10
Rd	Kelmscott	117	C 1
Rd	Mundijong	142	C 5
Rd	Safety Bay	136	D 9
Rd	Wanneroo	20	E 8
St	Beaconsfield	90	D 9
St	Boya	65	C 2
St	Claremont	71	D 6
St	Cloverdale	75	A 6
St	Greenmount	65	C 1
St	Guildford	63	D 1
St	Guildford	49	D 10
St	Helena Valley	65	C 3
St	Kewdale	74	E 7
St	Leederville	60	B 7
St	Mandurah	163	B 10
St	South Perth	72	D 6
St	Sth Fremantle	90	C 9
St	Willetton	93	D 3
SCOULER			
Wy	Bateman	92	E 5
SCRIBBLY GUM			
Sq	Willetton	93	C 4
SCRIVENER			
Pl	Halls Head	164	C 1
Pl	Halls Head	162	C 10
Rd	Serpentine	155	B 7

		Map	Ref.
SCRIVNER			
Rd	Herne Hill	37	C 7
SCROOP			
Wy	Spearwood	101	A 4
SCUD			
St	Falcon	162A	B 4
SCULPTOR			
Cl	Rockingham	137	B 9
SCUTTI			
Pl	Koondoola	33	A 9
SCYLLA			
Ct	Willetton	94	A 4
SCYTHE			
St	Willetton	93	E 7
SEABIRD			
Pl	Craigie	23	C 7
SEABORNE			
St	Mahogany Crk	53	D 9
St	Parkerville	53	D 6
SEABREEZE			
St	Safety Bay	145	B 2
SEABROOK			
Gr	Clarkson	14	C 2
Pl	Jandakot	112	E 2
St	Dianella	47	C 7
St	Mt Hawthorn	60	C 7
Wy	Dianella	47	C 7
Wy	Medina	130	D 6
SEABROOKE			
Ave	Rockingham	137	A 9
SEACOM			
Ct	Morley	48	C 6
SEACREST			
Dr	Sorrento	30	C 4
St	Safety Bay	145	B 2
SEAFLOWER			
Cr	Craigie	23	C 8
SEAFORTH			
Ave	Gosnells	106	D 2
Lp	Kallaroo	23	A 8
Rd	Balcatta	46	B 8
Rd	Shoalwater	136	C 10
SEAGATE			
St	Safety Bay	145	A 1
St	Safety Bay	137	B 10
Tn	Kinross	18	E 1
SEAGULL			
Cl	Ballajura	33	E 8
Wy	Yangebup	102	A 9
SEAHAM			
Wy	Mindarie	10	A 2
SEAHAVEN			
St	Safety Bay	145	B 2
SEAHORSE			
Ri	Ballajura	33	D 8
SEALE			
Cl	Duncraig	31	A 8
St	Beckenham	85	C 9
SEALEY			
Rd	Glen Forrest	66	C 4
SEAMET			
Ri	Merriwa	14	C 1
SEAPEAK			
Rd	Ocean Reef	23	B 1
SEARLE			
Rd	Ardross	82	B 10
St	Middle Swan	50	D 3
SEARS			
Pl	Kingsley	31	C 1
SEASIDE			
Gns	Mullaloo	23	A 3
SEASPRAY			
Cst	Ballajura	33	D 8
SEATON			
Cl	Halls Head	164	C 4
Pl	Girrawheen	32	B 8
SEA VIEW			
St	Beaconsfield	90	D 7

		Map	Ref.
SEAVIEW			
Pl	Quinns Rocks	10	A 1
St	Cottesloe	70	E 10
Tce	Kalamunda	77	C 7
Tce	Munster	110	E 1
SEAWARD			
Lp	Sorrento	30	B 4
SEAWAY			
Me	Iluka	18	E 5
SEAWIND			
Dr	Silver Sands	163	B 4
SEBAGO			
Ct	Joondalup	19	D 2
SEBASTIAN			
Cr	Coolbellup	101	D 2
SECOND			
Ave	Bassendean	63	A 1
Ave	Bassendean	49	A 10
Ave	Bickley	88	C 4
Ave	Burns	18	D 2
Ave	Claremont	71	B 6
Ave	Eden Hill	49	A 9
Ave	Kensington	73	C 5
Ave	Kwinana Beach	129	E 8
Ave	Mandurah	165	B 2
Ave	Midland	50	A 8
Ave	Mt Claremont	71	C 6
Ave	Mt Lawley	61	C 7
Ave	Rossmoyne	93	C 2
Ave	Rossmoyne	83	B 10
Ave	Shoalwater	136	C 7
St	Redcliffe	63	A 8
SECTOR			
Pl	Mullaloo	23	C 3
SEDDON			
St	Subiaco	72	A 1
SEDGE			
Pl	Duncraig	31	B 7
SEDGEFORD			
Rd	North Beach	44	D 2
SEDGEMERE			
Tce	Erskine	164	C 6
SEDGES			
Gr	Canning Vale	104	C 1
SEDGMAN			
Me	Murdoch	92	B 7
SEDWICK			
St	Attadale	81	E 8
SEFTON			
Ave	Viveash	50	B 5
Ct	Silver Sands	163	C 4
Rd	Roleystone	108	C 6
SEGRAVE			
St	Gwelup	45	B 7
SEINE			
Cl	Beechboro	48	C 4
SEKEM			
St	North Perth	60	E 8
SELBY			
Ct	Mindarie	14	B 5
St	Armadale	116	C 8
St	Daglish	71	D 3
St	Floreat	71	C 1
St	Floreat	59	D 10
St	Shenton Park	71	D 2
St	Thornlie	95	B 4
St N	Osborne Park	59	D 4
SELDEN			
St	North Perth	60	D 4
SELENE			
Wy	San Remo	163	C 1
SELHAN			
Pl	Balga	46	B 3
SELHURST			
Wy	Balga	46	C 2
SELINA			
St	Innaloo	45	B 10

242

For detailed information regarding the street referencing system used in this book, turn to page 170.

S

		Map	Ref.
SELKIRK			
Rd	Armadale	116	D 7
Rd	Mundaring	68	C 3
Rd	Serpentine	151	C 10
St	North Perth	60	E 5
SELLARS			
Wy	Bull Creek	93	B 5
SELLEN			
Ct	Leeming	93	D 9
SELLENGER			
Ave	Samson	91	C 9
Ct	City Beach	58	D 4
SELLNER			
Pl	Willetton	93	E 3
SELLOA			
Ct	Halls Head	164	A 6
Pl	Mirrabooka	33	B 9
SELSDON			
Ct	Westfield	106	B 9
Rd	Westfield	106	B 9
SELSEY			
Wy	Balga	46	D 1
SELSFIELD			
Pl	Balga	46	C 2
SELSTED			
Pl	Glendalough	60	A 5
SELTRUST			
Pl	Ocean Reef	18	E 8
SELWAY			
Pl	Brentwood	92	E 3
Rd	Brentwood	92	E 3
SELWYN			
Ct	Girrawheen	32	C 9
Ri	Greenfields	163	D 10
SEMILLON			
La	Ellenbrook	29	D 2
SEMINOLE			
Ave	Meadow Sprgs	163	C 6
Cl	Connolly	19	C 8
Gns	Armadale	116	A 5
Gns	Armadale	115	E 5
SEMPLE			
Rd	Jandakot	102	E 7
Rd	South Lake	102	D 9
SENATE			
St	Claremont	71	B 8
SENECA			
Gns	Joondalup	19	C 3
SENEGAL			
Gr	Warnbro	145	E 9
SENIOR			
Ct	Mundijong	142	E 8
SENTINEL			
Gns	Leeming	103	A 1
SENTRON			
Pl	Merriwa	14	C 1
SENTRY			
Cl	Woodvale	24	B 6
Wy	Mirrabooka	33	B 10
SEPIA			
Ct	Rockingham	137	B 8
SEPPELT			
Pl	Marangaroo	32	C 6
SEQUOIA			
Rd	Duncraig	31	A 8
SERENA			
Gr	Armadale	116	E 3
St	Falcon	162A	B 3
SERENOA			
Ct	Warnbro	145	E 8
SERGEANT			
Rd	Melville	91	C 9
SERLES			
St	Armadale	116	D 3
SERPA			
Rd	Nowergup	9	D 9

		Map	Ref.
SERPENTINE			
Gns	Clarkson	14	D 1
Gns	Clarkson	11	D 10
Ri	Jandakot	112	D 2
SERRATA			
Pl	Ferndale	84	C 10
Wy	Mirrabooka	47	B 1
SERVETUS			
St	Swanbourne	70	E 8
SERVICE			
St	Mandurah	165	B 1
St	Mandurah	163	B 10
SESA			
Cl	Iluka	18	D 3
SETTLER			
Pl	Greenmount	51	B 9
Wy	Edgewater	24	A 1
SETTLERS			
Ct	Bibra Lake	102	C 5
Ct	Gwelup	45	B 4
Rd	Bedfordale	117	B 8
Wy	Gosnells	96	A 7
SEVENOAKS			
St	Beckenham	85	B 8
St	Bentley	84	C 2
St	Cannington	85	A 6
SEVENTH			
Ave	Bassendean	49	B 10
Ave	Inglewood	61	C 5
Ave	Kensington	73	D 9
Ave	Maylands	61	D 7
Rd	Armadale	116	B 6
SEVERN			
Ct	Beechboro	48	D 4
SEVILLE			
Cl	Hillarys	23	A 10
Ct	Mindarie	10	A 2
Dr	Armadale	116	A 4
SEVINGTON			
St	Maddington	96	A 5
SEWELL			
Ct	Leeming	93	A 10
Ct	Noranda	48	B 5
Pl	Hillarys	30	B 1
St	East Fremantle	90	D 3
SEXTANT			
Ave	Waikiki	145	C 3
SEXTON			
Ct	Kardinya	92	B 8
Rd	Inglewood	61	C 3
St	Mt Helena	55	A 6
St	Sawyers Valley	54	E 9
SEXTY			
St	Armadale	116	C 6
SEYMOUR			
Ave	Dianella	46	E 9
Ave	Floreat	59	C 9
St	Willetton	94	A 2
Rd	Kalamunda	77	E 9
SHACKLETON			
Ave	Hillarys	23	B 9
St	Bassendean	63	A 3
SHACKLOCK			
Cr	Winthrop	92	B 5
SHADBOLT			
St	Booragoon	92	D 2
SHADWELL			
Ct	Caversham	49	B 5
Wy	Morley	48	C 6
SHADY			
Gr	Ballajura	33	D 4
Gr	Yangebup	111	E 1
SHADYGLEN			
Me	Edgewater	20	A 10
SHADYTREE			
La	Maida Vale	64	E 10
SHAFTESBURY			
Ave	Alexander Hts	33	B 3
Ave	Bayswater	62	A 5

		Map	Ref.
Ave	Bedford	61	D 2
St	South Perth	73	B 9
SHAFTO			
La	Perth City	1C	E 2
SHAKESPEARE			
Ave	Balcatta	46	B 5
Ave	Yokine	61	B 2
Ave	Yokine	60	E 2
Rd	Kalamunda	77	D 5
St	Leederville	60	D 7
St	Mt Hawthorn	60	D 4
SHALA			
La	Joondalup	19	D 3
SHALFORD			
St	Bayswater	62	C 1
Wy	Girrawheen	32	C 7
SHALLCROSS			
St	Yangebup	111	C 1
St	Yangebup	101	C 10
SHALLOW			
Cl	Waikiki	145	C 3
St	Spearwood	101	B 4
SHALVEY			
Cl	Duncraig	30	D 8
SHAMROCK			
Ct	Two Rocks	2	B 1
Wy	Huntingdale	95	D 10
SHAND			
St	Dianella	47	A 8
SHANKS			
Ct	Armadale	116	C 8
SHANLEY			
Rd	Mundijong	151	B 2
SHANN			
Gr	Kardinya	91	E 8
St	Floreat	71	C 1
SHANNON			
Cl	Woodvale	24	B 7
Cr	Beechboro	48	C 3
Rd	Dianella	47	A 6
Rd	Mandurah	163	A 9
Ri	Mt Claremont	71	A 5
St	Floreat	59	B 9
SHANTO			
Ct	Dudley Park	165	C 5
SHAPCOTT			
St	Ardross	82	B 9
SHARBA			
Cl	Willetton	93	E 4
SHARDLOW			
Lp	Carine	31	A 9
SHARK			
Ct	Sorrento	30	C 3
SHARLAND			
St	Halls Head	162	C 9
SHARMAN			
St	Medina	130	E 6
SHARON			
Ave	Swanbourne	70	D 7
Dr	Carine	45	B 2
SHARPE			
Cl	Waikiki	145	E 1
Wy	High Wycombe	64	A 10
SHARYN			
Rd	Walliston	87	E 1
SHASHTA			
Dr	Greenfields	165	C 1
SHASTA			
Gr	Lesmurdie	87	A 4
Rd	Lesmurdie	87	A 4
SHAW			
Cl	Brentwood	92	E 2
Me	Leda	130	E 9
Pl	Innaloo	45	C 9
Pl	Kewdale	74	D 7
Rd	Dianella	61	B 1
Rd	Dianella	47	B 10
Rd	Innaloo	45	C 9
Rd	Kelmscott	117	A 2

		Map	Ref.
Rd	Wanneroo	20	C 8
St	Safety Bay	136	D 9
St	Silver Sands	163	B 6
SHAWFIELD			
St	Westfield	106	C 10
SHAWFORD			
Pl	Innaloo	45	D 10
SHAWOOD			
Pl	Willetton	93	E 3
SHAYNE			
St	Halls Head	162	C 10
SHEA			
Gr	Leeming	93	A 9
SHEAHAN			
Wy	Marmion	30	D 8
SHEARER			
Ct	Leda	139	C 1
St	Myaree	92	A 2
SHEARMAN			
St	Attadale	81	D 9
SHEARN			
Cr	Doubleview	59	A 1
Cr	Doubleview	59	A 2
SHEARWATER			
Dr	Stirling	45	E 7
Pl	Coodanup	165	E 9
Tce	Ballajura	33	E 8
Tce	Two Rocks	2	D 1
Wy	Gosnells	105	E 1
SHEEDY			
St	Sth Fremantle	90	C 8
SHEEN			
Ct	Kingsley	31	B 1
Pl	Embleton	48	C 10
SHEFFIELD			
Cl	Greenfields	163	D 8
Pl	Hillarys	23	A 10
Rd	Wattle Grove	86	A 4
Rd	Wattle Grove	85	E 3
Rd	Welshpool	75	C 10
Rd	Welshpool	85	D 1
SHEILA			
St	Mosman Park	80	E 6
SHELBRED			
Wy	Balga	46	B 3
SHELBURN			
Rd	Thornlie	95	D 5
SHELDRAKE			
St	Stirling	45	D 6
Wy	Willetton	93	D 3
SHELDWICH			
St	Thornlie	95	B 5
SHELL			
Cl	Cooloongup	137	E 10
Ct	Beldon	23	C 2
SHELLEY			
Pl	Kallaroo	23	B 7
Rd	Kalamunda	77	D 5
St	Byford	135	D 1
St	Shelley	83	D 9
Wy	Munster	101	B 10
SHELLY			
Ce	Greenfields	165	E 2
SHELSHAW			
St	Melville	91	C 3
SHELTON			
Lp	Leeming	93	C 8
St	Waikiki	145	C 5
SHELVOCK			
Cr	Koondoola	32	E 7
SHEMELS			
Ct	Leeming	102	E 1
SHENTON			
Ave	Currambine	19	A 6
Ave	Guildford	63	C 1
Ave	Iluka	18	E 6
Ave	Joondalup	19	D 5
Pl	Claremont	71	A 8
Rd	Claremont	71	B 8

		Map	Ref.
Rd	Swanbourne	70	E 9
Rd	Wanneroo	25	B 2
St	Northbridge	1C	E 1
St	Northbridge	72	E 1
Tce	Parmelia	131	C 8
SHEOAK			
Cl	Baldivis	157	E 6
Cl	Beechboro	48	C 4
Ct	Banjup	113	C 9
Ct	Forrestfield	76	D 9
Hts	Parmelia	131	B 10
Pl	Armadale	116	D 4
Rd	Maddington	96	C 5
St	Greenwood	31	C 6
SHEPHERD			
Ct	Forrestdale	104	E 7
St	Glen Forrest	66	E 3
St	Hilton	91	A 8
SHEPHERDS BUSH			
Dr	Kingsley	31	B 1
Dr	Kingsley	24	C 10
SHEPPARD			
Wy	Marmion	30	C 8
SHEPPERTON			
Rd	E Victoria Pk	84	B 1
Rd	E Victoria Pk	74	B 10
Rd	Victoria Park	74	A 8
Rd	Victoria Park	73	E 6
SHEPWAY			
Pl	Marangaroo	32	B 5
SHERBORNE			
Rd	Gooseberry H	77	B 3
SHERBOURNE			
Wy	Armadale	116	D 5
SHERE			
Pl	Morley	47	C 6
St	Kenwick	95	E 1
St	Kenwick	85	E 10
SHERIDAN			
Cr	Willetton	93	D 7
Ct	Munster	101	B 9
Pl	Kingsley	31	D 2
Wy	Port Kennedy	156	D 2
SHERIFF			
Pl	Armadale	116	C 5
SHERINGHAM			
Rt	Currambine	19	B 5
SHERINGTON			
Rd	Greenwood	31	E 4
Rd	Mundaring	68	B 5
SHERLOCK			
Ct	Gosnells	106	A 5
SHERMAN			
Ct	Kingsley	31	D 1
St	Canning Vale	94	B 5
SHERWIN			
Pl	Wandi	123	B 6
SHERWOOD			
Ct	Armadale	116	C 5
Ct	Perth City	1C	E 3
Ct	Perth City	72	E 3
Pl	Alexander Hts	33	A 5
Rd	Dalkeith	81	C 1
St	Maylands	62	A 7
St	Maylands	61	E 7
SHETLAND			
Pl	Greenfields	163	E 9
Rd	Westfield	106	A 10
Ri	Kinross	19	A 2
SHIEL			
Wy	Hamersley	31	E 9
SHIELD			
Rd	Lesmurdie	87	E 3
SHIELDS			
Cr	Booragoon	92	A 1
SHIER			
St	Wilson	84	A 6
SHILLINGTON			
Wy	Thornlie	95	A 5
Wy	Wanneroo	25	B 4

For detailed information regarding the street referencing system used in this book, turn to page 170.

S

		Map	Ref.
SHIMMINGS			
Pl	Gwelup	45	C 6
SHINGLE			
Gr	Edgewater	24	A 1
SHINJI			
Ct	Joondalup	19	D 1
SHINNERS			
Grn	Clarkson	14	D 2
SHIPBOURNE			
Wy	Huntingdale	105	D 1
Wy	Huntingdale	95	E 10
SHIPLEY			
Pl	Balga	46	B 3
SHIPTON			
Pl	Willetton	93	E 2
SHIPWRIGHT			
Ave	Leda	139	C 3
SHIRAZ			
La	Ellenbrook	29	B 1
SHIRLEY			
Ave	Mt Pleasant	92	E 1
Rd	Walliston	87	E 1
SHIRLOCK			
St	Two Rocks	2	C 2
SHOAL			
Ct	Munster	110	E 1
Ri	Ballajura	33	C 7
SHOALHAVEN			
Ri	Jandakot	112	E 2
SHOALWATER			
Rd	Shoalwater	136	C 9
SHOEMAKER			
Vw	Padbury	30	E 2
SHOLL			
Ave	North Beach	44	C 3
Pl	Greenwood	31	E 6
St	Mandurah	164	E 1
St	Mandurah	162	E 10
SHORAN			
Ct	Ocean Reef	23	B 1
SHORE			
Pl	Mullaloo	23	A 3
SHOREBIRD			
Pde	Woodvale	24	C 8
SHOREVIEW			
Tce	Ballajura	33	D 8
SHORNE			
Pl	Marangaroo	32	B 5
SHORT			
Cl	Caversham	49	C 5
St	Bayswater	62	B 5
St	Cannington	84	E 8
St	Fremantle	1D	B 5
St	Fremantle	90	B 5
St	Joondanna	60	B 3
St	Kenwick	86	A 9
St	Mandurah	163	C 9
St	Mt Helena	54	D 1
St	North Beach	44	C 3
St	Perth City	1C	A 2
St	Perth City	73	A 2
St	Safety Bay	145	B 2
St	Sth Guildford	63	D 4
SHORTLAND			
Wy	Girrawheen	32	A 6
SHOWELL			
St	Hamilton Hill	90	E 10
SHREEVE			
Rd	Canning Vale	105	A 1
Rd	Canning Vale	94	E 10
SHRIKE			
Cl	Bedfordale	117	E 5
Ct	Westfield	106	B 10
Gns	Ballajura	33	E 7
SHUFFREY			
St	Fremantle	1D	C 4
St	Fremantle	90	C 4
SICILIA			
Pl	Balcatta	46	A 7

		Map	Ref.
SICKLEMORE			
Rd	Parmelia	131	C 7
St	Brentwood	92	D 2
SIDCUP			
Wy	Kelmscott	106	D 10
SIDDELEY			
Pl	Noranda	47	C 5
SIDDONS			
Wy	Booragoon	92	D 2
SIERRA			
Ch	Leeming	102	E 1
SIEVEWRIGHT			
St	Silver Sands	163	B 6
SIFORD			
Wy	Jarrahdale	152	E 7
SILAS			
St	East Fremantle	90	E 3
SILBERT			
Ci	Winthrop	92	A 4
SILICA			
Rd	Carine	44	E 1
Rd	Carine	30	E 10
SILICON			
Rd	Canning Vale	104	A 3
Rd	Canning Vale	103	E 4
SILKEBORG			
Cr	Joondalup	19	D 3
SILKPOD			
Gns	South Lake	102	D 6
Hts	Mirrabooka	47	B 2
SILKWOOD			
Cl	Halls Head	164	B 4
Wy	Beechboro	48	C 4
SILKY OAK			
La	Willetton	93	D 4
SILKYOAK			
Pl	Morley	48	D 6
SILL			
St	Bentley	83	E 6
SILLMON			
Wy	Duncraig	30	E 4
SILVAN			
Ct	Greenfields	163	D 10
SILVER			
Gr	Warnbro	145	E 8
Pl	Carine	44	E 1
Pl	Morley	48	E 4
Rd	Lesmurdie	87	C 1
St	Sth Fremantle	90	C 7
SILVERADO			
Ave	Yanchep	3	D 10
SILVERDALE			
Rd	Lesmurdie	87	C 5
SILVERHILL			
Lp	Armadale	115	E 4
SILVERMALLEE			
Cl	Westfield	106	C 8
SILVERSMITH			
St	Leda	139	B 1
SILVERTON			
Cr	Erskine	164	A 9
SILVERTOP			
Ave	Halls Head	164	B 4
Cl	Warnbro	145	D 6
Tce	Willetton	93	D 4
SILVERWOOD			
St	Embleton	48	A 10
SILVESTRO			
Ct	Lesmurdie	87	E 4
SIMCOE			
Ct	Joondalup	19	D 3
SIME			
Rd	Mt Helena	56	A 6
SIMEON			
Cl	Forrestfield	77	A 5

		Map	Ref.
SIMMONDS			
Pde	Winthrop	92	B 3
St	Morley	47	E 6
SIMMONS			
Lp	Parmelia	131	A 9
St	Beechina	57	D 1
St	Beechina	43	D 10
SIMMS			
Rd	Hamilton Hill	91	B 10
SIMNIA			
Pl	Mullaloo	23	B 3
SIMON			
Ct	Bibra Lake	102	D 3
Pl	City Beach	58	D 6
SIMONS			
Ct	Langford	94	E 2
Dr	Roleystone	108	C 7
St	Coolbellup	101	D 1
St	Coolbellup	91	D 10
Wy	Langford	94	E 1
SIMPER			
Cr	White Gum Vly	90	E 7
Rd	Yangebup	101	D 10
St	Wembley	59	E 9
SIMPSON			
Ave	Rockingham	137	B 7
Dr	Padbury	23	B 9
Rd	Karragullen	109	A 1
St	Applecross	82	C 7
St	Ardross	82	C 7
St	Quinns Rocks	10	A 1
St	West Perth	60	D 10
SINAGRA			
St	Wanneroo	20	D 8
SINCLAIR			
Cr	Winthrop	92	C 4
Pl	Morley	48	C 6
St	Armadale	116	D 3
St	Rivervale	74	C 4
SINGAPORE			
Ave	Swanbourne	70	D 7
SINGLETON			
Pl	Mosman Park	80	D 6
SINGLETON BEACH			
Rd	Singleton	160	D 2
SINIAN			
Cr	Willetton	93	D 7
SION			
Cl	Waterford	83	C 7
SIR CHARLES COURT			
Dr	Swanbourne	70	D 7
SIRDAR			
Pl	Gooseberry H	77	B 3
SIREN			
Rd	Heathridge	23	C 1
SIRIUS			
Pl	Iluka	18	D 4
Pl	Port Kennedy	156	D 5
SISELY			
Rd	Gooseberry H	77	D 1
SISKA			
Cl	Willetton	93	D 6
Ct	Halls Head	164	D 1
SITKA			
Pl	Cannington	84	D 6
SITTANA			
Pl	Beechboro	48	E 2
SITTELLA			
Pa	Wungong	116	B 10
Rt	Chidlow	42	B 8
St	Stirling	45	E 7
SITWELL			
Cl	Spearwood	101	C 8
SIXTH			
Ave	Applecross	82	C 5
Ave	Inglewood	61	C 5
Ave	Kensington	73	D 9
Ave	Maylands	61	D 7
Ave	Shelley	93	C 1

		Map	Ref.
Ave	Shelley	83	C 10
Rd	Armadale	116	C 7
SIXTY EIGHT			
Rd	Baldivis	157	C 3
SKATE			
Ct	Sorrento	30	C 4
SKEAHAN			
St	Spearwood	101	C 5
SKEIT			
Rd	Landsdale	32	C 3
Rd	Marangaroo	32	C 3
SKELWITH			
Cl	Balga	46	C 1
SKERNE			
Ri	Padbury	31	A 2
SKEW			
Rd	Bayswater	62	B 3
SKIDDAW			
Pl	Balga	46	C 1
SKIFF			
Ct	Waikiki	145	C 4
Wy	Heathridge	23	C 1
SKINNER			
St	Fremantle	1D	C 3
St	Fremantle	90	C 3
SKIPPER			
Pl	Ballajura	33	D 8
SKIPPERS			
Rw	Bayswater	62	C 7
SKIPTON			
Wy	City Beach	58	D 5
SKOKIE			
Ct	Currambine	19	B 5
SKOTTOWE			
Pwy	Parmelia	131	A 10
SKUA			
Ct	Halls Head	164	B 3
Gr	Armadale	116	B 4
St	Stirling	45	E 7
SKYE			
Cl	Warnbro	145	E 6
Cl	Westfield	106	C 6
Ct	Greenwood	31	B 5
SKYLARK			
Rt	Ballajura	34	A 7
Rt	Ballajura	33	E 7
Vw	Armadale	116	A 3
SKYLINE			
Ri	Ballajura	33	D 5
SKYTOWN			
Pl	Queens Park	85	A 4
Pl	Queens Park	84	E 4
SLAB GULLY			
Rd	Roleystone	108	A 8
Rd	Roleystone	107	E 8
SLADDEN			
St	Jarrahdale	152	E 7
SLADE			
St	Bayswater	62	C 5
St	Greenfields	163	C 7
SLALOM			
Dr	Wembley Dns	58	E 4
SLATER			
Ct	Kardinya	92	B 6
SLEAT			
Rd	Applecross	82	D 6
Rd	Mt Pleasant	82	D 7
SLEE			
Ave	Kelmscott	106	D 9
SLEEMAN			
Cl	O'Connor	91	D 6
SLEIGHT			
St	St James	84	A 4
SLINDON			
St	Nollamara	46	D 6
SLIP			
St	Fremantle	1D	B 5
St	Fremantle	90	B 5

		Map	Ref.
SLOAN			
Ct	Leeming	92	E 8
Ct	Thornlie	95	A 6
Dr	Leda	130	E 9
St	Rockingham	136	D 5
SLOOP			
Ct	Waikiki	145	C 4
Pl	Heathridge	23	D 1
Ri	Ballajura	33	D 8
SMALES			
Rd	Quinns Rocks	10	B 1
SMALL			
St	Beechboro	49	A 3
SMALLMAN			
Cr	Greenwood	32	A 4
SMART			
Ct	Dianella	47	A 8
St	Mandurah	164	E 1
SMEATON			
Rd	Parkerville	53	E 7
SMEED			
St	Noranda	47	D 5
SMILAX			
Ct	High Wycombe	64	D 10
SMITH			
Cl	Armadale	116	C 9
Cr	High Wycombe	64	B 10
Ct	Yanchep	4	C 3
St	Beechboro	49	A 3
St	Claremont	71	B 9
St	Dianella	47	D 9
St	East Perth	61	D 10
St	Furnissdale	165	E 7
St	Glen Forrest	66	D 4
St	Highgate	61	B 10
St	Hilton	91	A 8
St	Karrinyup	45	A 6
St	Morley	47	D 9
St	Mosman Park	80	E 5
St	Serpentine	155	A 3
SMITHERSON			
St	Noranda	47	D 4
SMITHS			
Ave	Redcliffe	62	E 9
SMOKEWOOD			
Pl	Leeming	103	A 2
SMOOTHSTONE			
Ct	Joondalup	19	D 3
SMULLEN			
Pl	Balcatta	46	A 6
SMULLIN			
St	Hamilton Hill	101	A 1
SMYTH			
Rd	Nedlands	71	D 7
Rd	Shenton Park	71	D 5
SMYTHE			
St	Rockingham	137	A 4
SNARE			
Pl	Hamilton Hill	101	B 3
SNEDDON			
Pl	Balga	32	B 8
SNELL			
St	Maylands	62	A 8
SNIPE			
Ct	High Wycombe	64	B 10
SNOOK			
Cr	Hilton	91	B 9
Pl	Armadale	116	A 4
Rd	Perth Airport	63	B 7
SNOW			
St	Wilson	84	B 6
SNOWBALL			
Rd	Kalamunda	77	B 5
SNOWBERRY			
Rt	Mirrabooka	47	A 2
SNOWBIRD			
Gns	Joondalup	19	C 3
SNOWDROP			
Rt	Mirrabooka	47	B 1

Map Ref.

SNOWY
- Cl Alexander Hts 33 B 4

SOALL
- Ct Booragoon 92 B 1

SOAMES
- Pl Bentley 84 B 4

SOBOTKA
- Pl Winthrop 92 C 5

SOCHA
- Ct Greenfields 163 E 9

SOGAN
- Ri Yangebup 111 E 1

SOLANDER
- Rd Hillarys 23 B 9

SOLANDRA
- Wy Forrestfield 76 B 9

SOLAR
- St Beckenham 85 C 7
- Wy Carlisle 74 C 8

SOLAS
- Rd Morley 48 D 8

SOLDIERS
- Rd Byford 135 C 5
- Rd Cardup 143 B 2
- Rd Cardup 135 B10
- Rd Roleystone 118 A 3
- Rd Roleystone 117 E 1
- Rd Roleystone 107 E10

SOLDIERS COVE
- Tce Mandurah 164 E 3

SOLENT
- Rd Armadale 116 D 2

SOLEY
- Pl Ferndale 84 D 9

SOLLY
- Ct Bull Creek 93 B 5

SOLLYA
- Ct Roleystone 108 B 9
- Pl Ferndale 84 C10

SOLO
- Ct Cooloongup 137 C 9
- Ct Two Rocks 3 B10

SOLOMON
- Rd Banjup 113 A 1
- Rd Banjup 103 B10
- St Beaconsfield 90 D 7
- St Fremantle 90 D 6
- St Mosman Park 80 D 6
- St Palmyra 91 B 2

SOLQUEST
- Wy Cooloongup 137 D 8

SOLUS
- Ce Woodvale 24 B 5

SOMERS
- St Belmont 74 E 1

SOMERSBY
- Rd Iluka 18 D 3
- Rd Welshpool 75 A10

SOMERSET
- Cr Mosman Park 80 D 7
- Pl Safety Bay 145 B 2
- Ri Kardinya 92 A 6
- St E Victoria Pk 84 B 1
- St E Victoria Pk 74 B10
- St Forrestfield 86 C 2
- St Viveash 50 B 4

SOMERTON
- Rd Bassendean 62 D 1
- Rd Bassendean 62 E 1
- Rd Bayswater 48 D10
- Rd Karrinyup 45 A 5

SOMERVILLE
- Blvd Winthrop 92 B 5
- St East Perth 1C B 1
- St Perth City 73 B 1

SOMME
- Ri Port Kennedy 156 E 1

SONEGO
- Ave Kelmscott 116 D 1

Map Ref.

SONIA
- St Scarborough 58 E 2

SOPHIA
- St Bellevue 51 A10

SOPHY
- Ct Duncraig 30 D 3

SORATA
- El Iluka 19 A 4
- El Iluka 18 E 4

SORAYA
- Pl Cooloongup 137 D 9

SORBONNE
- Cr Canning Vale 94 D 7

SORELL
- Gns Joondalup 19 C 2

SORENSEN
- Rd High Wycombe 76 A 1
- Rd High Wycombe 64 B10

SORREL
- Ct Forrestfield 76 B10

SORRENTO
- St North Beach 44 C 2

SOTTOGRANDE
- Vw Connolly 19 B 6

SOUTER
- Wy Noranda 48 B 4

SOUTH
- Cr Byford 135 D 1
- Rd Pickering Bk 99 C 3
- Rd Shoalwater 136 C10
- St Beaconsfield 90 D 7
- St Hilton 91 B 7
- St Kardinya 92 A 8
- St Kardinya 91 E 8
- St Leeming 93 B 7
- St Murdoch 92 D 7
- St Samson 91 D 7
- St Sth Fremantle 90 C 7
- Tce Como 73 A10
- Tce Fremantle 1D C 6
- Tce Fremantle 90 C 6
- Tce Sth Fremantle 90 C 8

SOUTH BANFF
- Rd Floreat 59 D 8

SOUTHBOURNE
- St Scarborough 44 D 9

SOUTHDOWN
- Pl Thornlie 95 B 3

SOUTHEND
- Rd Hamilton Hill 100 E 2

SOUTHERN
- Tce Connolly 19 C 7

SOUTHERN CROSS
- Ci Ocean Reef 18 E 8
- Ci Ocean Reef 18 E 9

SOUTHERN RIVER
- Rd Gosnells 106 A 1
- Rd Gosnells 105 D 3
- Rd Southern River 105 A 8

SOUTHGATE
- Ct Kingsley 31 B 1
- Rd Langford 94 E 2

SOUTH LAKE
- Dr South Lake 102 C 7

SOUTHMEAD
- Grn Erskine 164 C 6

SOUTH PERTH
- Es South Perth 72 D 5

SOUTHPOINTE
- Cr Ballajura 33 C 8

SOUTHPORT
- St Leederville 60 C10

SOUTHSEA
- Rd Quinns Rocks 10 B 9

SOUTH VIEW
- Rd Mt Lawley 61 B 6

SOUTHWARK
- Wy Morley 48 A 7

Map Ref.

SOUTHWELL
- Cr Hamilton Hill 101 C 2

SOUTH WESTERN
- Hwy Armadale 116 D 9
- Hwy Byford 135 C 4
- Hwy Byford 126 D 8
- Hwy Cardup 135 C 7
- Hwy Mundijong 151 C 5
- Hwy Serpentine 155 B 4
- Hwy Serpentine 151 C 8
- Hwy Whitby 143 D 5
- Hwy Wungong 126 D 2

SOVEREIGN
- Ave Port Kennedy 156 D 1
- Ave Willetton 93 C 7
- Dr Thornlie 95 C 7
- Dr Two Rocks 2 B 1
- Dr Two Rocks 3 B10
- Gns Halls Head 164 D 1
- Pl Forrestfield 86 D 2

SOWDEN
- Dr Samson 91 C 8

SPAGNOLO
- Pl Beckenham 85 C 7

SPAR
- Pl Ocean Reef 23 A 2

SPARGO
- St Myaree 92 A 2

SPARKES
- Ct Girrawheen 32 C 8

SPARKMAN
- Rd Mundijong 142 C 7

SPARKS
- Rd Henderson 111 A 7

SPARROW
- Cl Ballajura 33 D 6
- Ct High Wycombe 64 B10
- Wy Spearwood 101 C 7

SPEARGRASS
- Cl Alexander Hts 32 E 5

SPEARWOOD
- Ave Bibra Lake 101 D 6
- Ave Spearwood 101 A 6

SPEIGHT
- Ri Gwelup 45 C 7

SPELHURST
- Tce Thornlie 95 D 5

SPENCE
- Ct Leeming 93 B 8
- Rd Pinjar 16 E 1
- St Trigg 44 C 6

SPENCER
- Ave Yokine 60 E 1
- Ct Redcliffe 62 E 9
- Pl Serpentine 154 E 3
- Rd Kelmscott 116 D 1
- Rd Langford 95 A 1
- Rd Langford 84 E10
- Rd Thornlie 95 C 6
- St Bayswater 62 C 2
- St Jandakot 102 D 9

SPERRY
- Ct Ferndale 84 C 9

SPEY
- Pl Ferndale 84 B 9
- Rd Applecross 82 B 6

SPICER
- Ct Craigie 23 E 6
- Pl Bellevue 65 A 2

SPIERS
- Pl Middle Swan 50 D 4
- Rd Quinns Rocks 10 A 1

SPIGL
- Wy Bateman 92 D 6

SPINAWAY
- Cr Brentwood 93 A 3
- Pde Falcon 162A B 2
- Pde Falcon 162A C10
- St Craigie 23 C 7

Map Ref.

SPINIFEX
- Pl Canning Vale 95 A10

SPINNAKER
- Cl Waikiki 145 B 3
- Cst Ballajura 33 D 8
- Dr Ocean Reef 23 A 2

SPINNER
- La Leda 139 B 3

SPINOZA
- St Mt Lawley 61 A 6

SPIRULA
- Wy Heathridge 23 D 1

SPOONBILL
- Gr Kingsley 32 A 1
- Gr Kingsley 31 E 1
- Rd Stirling 45 E 7

SPORING
- Wy Hillarys 23 B 9

SPOTTED GUM
- Wy Willetton 93 D 4

SPRIGG
- Pl Booragoon 92 C 1

SPRING
- Ave Midland 50 C 6
- Cl Greenwood 32 A 6
- Ct Ballajura 33 C 3
- Rd Kalamunda 77 E 6
- Rd Parkerville 53 D 6
- Rd Roleystone 108 A 6
- Rd Roleystone 107 E 6
- Rd Thornlie 95 B 3
- St Perth City 1C E 3
- St Perth City 72 E 3

SPRINGDALE
- Rd Canning Mills 108 D 1
- Rd Canning Mills 98 E10
- Rd Kalamunda 77 E 9
- Rd Roleystone 108 D 3

SPRINGFIELD
- Cl Warnbro 145 D 6
- Ct Kallaroo 23 B 7
- Rd Bedfordale 128 A 3
- St Willetton 93 C 5

SPRINGFIELDS
- Cl Banjup 123 E 1
- Cl Banjup 113 E10

SPRINGHAM
- Ct Merriwa 14 C 1

SPRINGHILL
- Pl Two Rocks 2 C 3

SPRING PARK
- Rd Midland 50 B 8
- Trl Ballajura 33 C 4

SPRINGPARK
- Tr Neerabup 16 B 7

SPRINGSIDE
- Ave Mt Pleasant 92 E 1
- Ave Mt Pleasant 82 E10
- Cr Glen Forrest 66 D 2

SPRINGVALE
- Dr Warwick 31 D 8

SPRINGWOOD
- Wy Woodvale 24 C 7

SPRINT
- Cl Middle Swan 50 D 4

SPRITE
- Pl Waikiki 145 C 3

SPROXTON
- Wy Embleton 62 B 1

SPRUCE
- Ct Halls Head 164 B 5
- Rd Morley 48 B 7
- St Greenwood 31 D 5

SPUR
- Ct Ocean Reef 23 B 1

SPYGLASS
- Ci Canning Vale 94 B10
- Ct Safety Bay 137 B10
- Gr Connolly 19 B 8

Map Ref.

- Hl Ballajura 33 D 7
- Ri Halls Head 164 B 2

SQUATTER
- Ct Edgewater 24 A 2

SQUIRE
- Ave Heathridge 23 B 1

SQUIRES
- Gns Stratton 51 B 4

STACEY
- Rd Carmel 88 D 7
- St Willagee 91 E 4

STACK
- St Fremantle 90 D 5

STADIA
- Ct Beldon 23 C 4

STAFF
- Ct Beldon 23 D 2

STAFFORD
- Ct Leeming 93 B10
- Rd Kenwick 95 D 1
- St Midland 50 C 8
- St Victoria Park 73 C 7
- Wy Wanneroo 25 B 3

STAGG
- Ct Kardinya 92 B 6

STAINER
- Ave Rockingham 137 A 9
- St Willagee 91 E 4

STAINES
- St Lathlain 74 A 6

STAINTON
- Pl Leeming 92 E 9

STAKEHILL
- Rd Baldivis 157 B 8
- Rd Port Kennedy 157 A 8

ST ALBANS
- Ave Highgate 61 B 9
- Rd Baldivis 147 D 4
- Rd Baldivis 139 E 9
- Rd Nollamara 46 D 7
- Rd Upper Swan 168 A 4

STALKER
- Rd Gosnells 96 A10

STALLWOOD
- Gns Leeming 93 A 8

STAMFORD
- St Leederville 60 C 9
- Wy Wattleup 121 C 3

STAMMERS
- Pl Myaree 91 E 1

STAMOS
- Ct Samson 91 D 9

STAMPEL
- Gns Kardinya 91 E 9

STANBURY
- Cr Morley 48 A10
- Pl Kardinya 92 A 9
- Wy Booragoon 92 C 3

STANCLIFFE
- St Menora 61 B 5
- St Mt Lawley 61 B 5

STANDEN
- Ct Kalamunda 77 E 7

STANDING
- Rd Lesmurdie 77 B10

STANDISH
- Wy Woodvale 24 B 6

ST ANDREWS
- Ct Halls Head 164 C 2
- Dr Yanchep 4 E 1
- Lp Cooloongup 138 A 9
- Lp Cooloongup 137 E 9
- Wy Duncraig 31 B 6

STANFORD
- Rd Kallaroo 23 B 5
- St Maddington 96 C 6
- Wy Malaga 47 C 1

For detailed information regarding the street referencing system used in this book, turn to page 170.

S

		Map	Ref.
STANHOPE			
Gns	Midvale	51	A 8
Rd	Kalamunda	78	A 9
Rd	Kalamunda	77	E 8
Rd	Walliston	88	A 1
St	Cottesloe	80	D 2
STANILAND			
St	Orange Grove	96	D 1
STANLEY			
Gr	Winthrop	92	C 6
Pl	Padbury	23	E 8
Rd	Byford	126	D 9
St	Bellevue	64	D 1
St	Belmont	74	E 1
St	Belmont	62	E 10
St	Dianella	47	B 7
St	Glen Forrest	66	C 2
St	Maida Vale	76	D 1
St	Mt Lawley	61	C 9
St	Nedlands	71	D 10
St	Scarborough	58	D 1
St	Scarborough	44	D 10
STANMORE			
Ct	Lynwood	84	D 10
St	Shenton Park	72	A 4
STANNARD			
St	Bentley	84	A 4
St	St James	84	A 4
ST ANNE			
Pl	Stirling	45	D 5
ST ANNES			
Rt	Connolly	19	C 8
Tce	Meadow Sprgs	163	C 5
STANSMORE			
Tce	Woodvale	24	A 5
STANSTED			
Cr	Marangaroo	32	B 5
ST ANTHONY			
Dr	Stirling	45	D 5
STANTON			
Cr	Greenwood	32	A 6
Rd	Redcliffe	62	E 10
St	Safety Bay	136	D 10
STANYFORD			
Pl	Hamilton Hill	101	C 3
Wy	Medina	130	D 6
STAPLEFORD			
Pl	Swan View	51	D 8
STAPLEHURST			
St	Kenwick	85	D 10
STAPLES			
St	Nth Fremantle	80	C 10
STAPPLETON			
Rt	Merriwa	11	C 10
STAR			
St	Carlisle	74	B 7
St	Mandurah	165	A 3
St	Welshpool	74	D 10
STARBOARD			
Ct	Waikiki	145	C 3
STARCAP			
Pl	Quinns Rocks	10	B 10
STARICK			
Wy	Gosnells	95	E 10
STARLIGHT			
Gr	Gnangara	25	D 6
STARLING			
St	Hamilton Hill	100	E 1
STARRS			
Rd	Quinns Rocks	10	A 1
STATE			
St	Victoria Park	73	E 9
STATHAM			
St	Glen Forrest	52	D 1
St	Glen Forrest	66	D 2
STATION			
St	Bayswater	62	B 5
St	Cannington	85	A 8
St	Cottesloe	80	D 2

		Map	Ref.
St	E Cannington	85	B 6
St	E Cannington	85	C 4
St	Gosnells	96	C 8
St	Guildford	49	E 10
St	Martin	96	C 8
St	Upper Swan	168	A 1
St	Upper Swan	29	E 1
St	Wembley	60	A 10
STATON			
Rd	East Fremantle	90	E 2
STAUNTON			
Gr	Mirrabooka	33	B 10
Pl	Halls Head	164	A 7
STAVELEY			
Pl	Innaloo	45	D 10
STAWELL			
La	Willetton	93	C 7
Wy	Padbury	23	E 8
STAY			
Ct	Ocean Reef	23	A 1
ST BARBARA			
Tce	Mosman Park	80	D 8
ST BARNABAS			
Pl	Mosman Park	80	D 6
ST BRIGIDS			
Tce	Doubleview	45	A 10
Tce	Scarborough	45	A 10
Tce	Scarborough	58	E 1
ST CLAIR			
Ci	Edgewater	20	A 9
Ci	Edgewater	19	E 9
Pl	Cooloongup	137	E 8
St	Yanchep	4	E 2
ST CLOUD			
Gns	Connolly	19	B 8
ST COLUMBAS			
Ave	Wembley	60	A 9
ST DAVIDS			
Ri	Churchlands	59	C 5
STEAD			
St	Maddington	96	B 5
STEAMER			
Ct	Heathridge	23	C 1
STEBBING			
Rd	Maddington	96	A 1
Wy	Girrawheen	32	E 8
STEDHAM			
Wy	Balga	46	B 1
STEDMAN PARKWAY			
	Leeming	92	E 10
STEEDMAN			
Lp	Mirrabooka	46	E 1
Lp	Mirrabooka	32	E 10
STEEL			
Ct	Sth Guildford	63	C 4
Rd	Gnangara	26	B 3
St	Willagee	91	C 4
STEELE			
Rd	Sorrento	30	C 5
St	Eden Hill	49	A 9
STEEN			
Ct	Clarkson	14	C 1
STEERFORTH			
Dr	Coodanup	165	C 3
STEFANELLI			
Cl	Wandi	123	D 4
STEFFANONI			
Pl	Kardinya	91	E 6
STEINBECK			
Pl	Spearwood	101	B 8
STEINER			
Ave	Jandakot	112	E 4
STELLA			
Pl	Alexander Hts	33	A 4
STELLAR			
Ct	Beckenham	85	C 7
STELLFOX			
Cl	Murdoch	92	B 7

		Map	Ref.
STEM			
Pl	Ocean Reef	19	A 10
ST EMILIES			
Rd	Kalamunda	77	C 5
STENNESS			
Pl	Duncraig	31	A 5
STENNETT			
St	Gosnells	106	A 2
STENT			
St	Beechboro	49	A 3
STENTON			
Cnr	Leeming	93	D 9
STEPHANIE			
St	Dalkeith	81	C 1
STEPHANO			
Wy	Coolbellup	101	D 2
STEPHEN			
St	E Cannington	85	B 4
St	Guildford	49	C 10
St	Orange Grove	96	E 1
St	Queens Park	85	A 4
STEPHENS			
St	Ocean Reef	19	A 9
STEPHENSON			
Ave	City Beach	71	A 3
Ave	Osborne Park	59	C 4
Ave	Osborne Park	45	D 10
Ave	Wembley Dns	59	A 7
Gns	Winthrop	92	A 5
Rd	Gosnells	106	B 2
St	Sawyers Valley	69	A 1
STEPMOON			
St	Falcon	162A	B 4
STEPNEY			
Rd	Armadale	116	D 8
STERLING			
Cl	Craigie	23	E 7
STERN			
Cl	Waikiki	145	C 3
STEVE			
St	Kelmscott	106	E 8
STEVEN			
St	Claremont	71	B 9
St	Morley	47	D 8
St	Wanneroo	21	A 7
STEVENAGE			
St	Huntingdale	95	C 3
St	Yanchep	4	D 3
STEVENS			
Pl	Kardinya	91	E 8
Rd	Bedfordale	128	A 4
Rd	High Wycombe	64	C 8
St	Daglish	71	D 2
St	Fremantle	1D	C 6
St	Fremantle	90	D 6
St	Hilton	91	A 6
St	Mundaring	54	A 9
St	Sawyers Valley	54	D 9
St	White Gum Vly	90	E 6
STEVENSON			
Ce	Warnbro	145	C 8
Pl	Byford	135	E 1
Pl	Byford	126	E 10
St	Mandurah	165	A 2
Wy	Spearwood	101	B 8
Wy	Willetton	93	E 3
STEVINGTON			
St	Kelmscott	106	E 10
STEWARD			
Wy	Orelia	131	A 4
STEWART			
Ct	Kallaroo	23	A 7
Gr	Armadale	117	A 3
Rd	High Wycombe	76	C 2
St	Mandurah	163	A 9
St	Scarborough	58	D 1
Wy	Kardinya	91	E 6
Wy	Noranda	47	E 6
STEWARTBY			
Cr	Viveash	50	B 5

		Map	Ref.
STEYNING			
Wy	Balga	46	C 3
ST FRANCIS			
Blvd	Merriwa	11	D 8
ST GEORGE			
Gr	Morley	48	D 7
ST GEORGES			
Ave	Westfield	106	C 5
Ct	Connolly	19	A 6
Tce	Perth City	1C	A 3
Tce	Perth City	1C	E 2
Tce	Perth City	72	E 3
ST HELIER			
Dr	Sorrento	30	B 4
STICKS			
Blvd	Erskine	164	C 6
STILEMAN			
Hts	Kardinya	91	E 8
STILES			
Ave	Rivervale	74	A 4
Ct	Como	83	A 1
Ct	Padbury	30	E 1
STILLWATER			
Gns	South Lake	102	D 6
Wy	Edgewater	24	A 1
Wy	Edgewater	20	A 10
STINTON			
St	Mandurah	163	B 9
STIRK			
Pl	Alfred Cove	82	A 10
Rd	Alfred Cove	92	A 1
St	Kalamunda	77	D 6
STIRLING			
Cl	Port Kennedy	156	C 5
Cl	Swan View	51	D 8
Cr	Hazelmere	50	B 10
Cr	Hazelmere	64	C 2
Cr	High Wycombe	64	B 7
Ct	Noranda	47	E 6
Gr	Mandurah	163	C 10
Hwy	Claremont	71	B 9
Hwy	Cottesloe	80	C 2
Hwy	Mosman Park	80	D 5
Hwy	Nedlands	71	D 8
Hwy	Nth Fremantle	90	C 1
Hwy	Nth Fremantle	80	C 10
Rd	Claremont	71	A 9
Rd	Forrestdale	115	B 9
Rd	Greenmount	51	D 10
St	Fremantle	1D	C 4
St	Fremantle	90	C 4
St	Guildford	49	D 10
St	Highgate	61	B 10
St	Perth City	1C	A 2
St	Perth City	73	A 2
St	Perth City	61	B 10
St	South Perth	72	D 6
St	Southern River	105	D 8
STIRLING WATERS			
Ave	Stirling	45	D 5
ST IVES			
Ce	Warnbro	145	C 8
Dr	Yanchep	4	D 5
Lp	Kallaroo	23	A 7
ST JAMES			
Pl	Greenfields	163	E 10
ST JOHN			
Rd	Wattle Grove	86	A 1
Rd	Wattle Grove	85	E 2
ST JOHNS			
Ct	Kingsley	31	A 1
ST JOSEPH			
Cl	Stirling	45	D 5
ST KILDA			
Rd	Balga	46	B 1
Rd	Kewdale	74	D 6
Rd	Rivervale	74	B 3
ST LAURENT			
Cl	Greenfields	163	E 9
Me	Port Kennedy	145	D 10

		Map	Ref.
ST LAWRENCE			
Dr	Beechboro	48	C 3
ST LEONARDS			
Ave	Leederville	60	B 10
St	Mosman Park	80	D 5
ST LUCIA			
Cl	Safety Bay	145	C 1
ST MALO			
Ce	Warnbro	145	C 6
Ct	Mindarie	14	B 4
ST MARKS			
Dr	Hillarys	23	B 9
ST MICHAEL			
Tce	Mt Pleasant	82	D 10
ST MICHAELS			
Ave	Connolly	19	C 9
Ct	Cooloongup	137	E 9
STOATE			
Pl	Mirrabooka	32	E 10
STOCK			
Rd	Attadale	81	C 10
Rd	Bibra Lake	101	C 8
Rd	Coolbellup	101	C 1
Rd	Herne Hill	37	A 5
Rd	Lakelands	161	C 9
Rd	Melville	91	C 2
Rd	O'Connor	91	C 5
Rd	Samson	91	C 9
Rd	Yangebup	111	C 9
Rd	Yangebup	101	C 9
STOCKDALE			
Ave	Sorrento	30	C 6
Cr	Wembley Dns	59	A 8
Rd	Kewdale	74	E 6
Rd	O'Connor	91	B 7
STOCKER			
Cl	Craigie	23	E 5
Rd	Roleystone	107	C 10
Rd	Roleystone	117	D 1
STOCKMAN			
Wy	Cannington	84	D 4
STOCKWELL			
Wy	Kingsley	24	B 9
STODDART			
Wy	Bateman	92	D 4
STOKE			
Ct	Girrawheen	32	E 7
Pl	Morley	48	C 9
Ri	Kingsley	24	B 10
St	Mt Pleasant	82	D 7
STOKES			
Rt	Clarkson	14	D 1
St	Rockingham	136	E 6
St	White Gum Vly	91	A 7
STONE			
Cr	Darlington	66	A 3
Ct	Bibra Lake	102	D 2
Ct	Kardinya	92	A 9
Rd	Claremont	81	C 1
Rd	Dalkeith	81	C 1
Rd	Lesmurdie	87	C 1
St	Bayswater	62	B 7
St	Chidlow	43	A 9
St	Chidlow	42	C 9
St	Maylands	62	A 8
St	Mosman Park	80	E 8
St	Nth Fremantle	80	C 9
St	South Perth	72	D 6
St	Wungong	126	D 1
STONECREEK			
Cl	Thornlie	95	B 9
STONEGATE			
Rd	Roleystone	107	E 7
STONEHAM			
Rd	Attadale	81	C 7
St	Ascot	62	C 10
St	Joondanna	60	C 3
St	Tuart Hill	60	C 1
STONEHOUSE			
Cr	Bentley	84	A 5

246

For detailed information regarding the street referencing system used in this book, turn to page 170.

Map Ref.

STONELEIGH
Rd Mt Helena 54 D 7
STONEMAN
St Karrinyup 45 B 6
STONER
Ct Mandurah 165 C 1
Pl Innaloo 45 C 9
St Innaloo 45 C 9
St Rockingham 137 A 6
STONESFIELD
Ct Padbury 30 E 2
STONEVILLE
Rd Gidgegannup 40 B 2
Rd Mundaring 54 B10
Rd Stoneville 54 B 4
Rd Stoneville 40 B 9
STONEY
Rd Gnangara 26 A 1
Rd Gnangara 25 E 1
STONEYKIRK
Lp Kingsley 24 C10
STOREY
Pl Yangebup 111 D 1
Rd Thornlie 95 A 5
STORMBIRD
Vs Iluka 18 E 4
STORMON
Ri Winthrop 92 C 6
STORMONT
Pl Willetton 93 E 5
STORRINGTON
Cr Balga 46 C 3
STORRS
Pl Winthrop 92 B 4
STORTHES
St Mt Lawley 61 B 7
STOTT
Cl Armadale 116 C 3
Pl Bull Creek 93 A 5
Rd Welshpool 85 C 1
Wy Duncraig 30 E 7
STOW
Ct Wembley Dns 59 A 4
ST PATRICK
Cl Stirling 45 D 5
ST PATRICKS
Rd Sorrento 30 C 7
ST PETERS
Pl Inglewood 61 C 4
Rd East Fremantle 90 D 2
ST PIERRE
Me Currambine 19 B 4
ST QUENTIN
Ave Claremont 71 A 9
STRADBROKE
Gns Merriwa 11 D10
STRAIN
St Bicton 81 B 8
STRAITSMEN
Vw Iluka 18 E 3
STRANG
Ct Hamilton Hill 90 D 9
St Hamilton Hill 90 D 9
STRATFORD
Ct Greenfields 163 C10
Pl Bentley 84 A 5
Pl Kingsley 24 B10
St East Fremantle 91 A 1
STRATHALLAN
Ave Yanchep 3 D10
Ave Yanchep 4 E 1
STRATHAVEN
Cr Greenwood 31 B 5
STRATHCONA
St West Perth 60 D10
STRATHEARN
Rd Forrestfield 86 C 1

STRATHIG
Cl Kingsley 24 C10
STRATHLEVEN
Me Iluka 19 A 4
Me Iluka 18 E 4
STRATHYRE
Dr Duncraig 31 C 8
STRATTON
Blvd Stratton 51 B 4
St Hamilton Hill 101 A 1
STRATUS
Pl Willetton 93 E 2
STRAUGHAIR
St Hamilton Hill 91 B10
STRAWBERRY
Dr Armadale 116 A 5
Dr Armadale 115 E 4
STREATHAM
St Beckenham 85 B 8
STREATLEY
Rd Lathlain 74 A 4
STREETON
Pro Woodvale 24 C 4
STREICH
Ave Armadale 116 D 5
Ave Kelmscott 116 D 1
Ave Kelmscott 106 D10
STRELITZIA
Ave Forrestfield 76 C 9
STRELLEY
Rd Golden Bay 158 E 8
STRETCH
Rd Mt Helena 54 E 4
STRETTLE
Rd Glen Forrest 66 E 1
Rd Mahogany Crk 67 B 1
STRETTON
Pl Balcatta 45 D 2
Wy Kenwick 95 E 1
Wy Kenwick 85 E10
STRICKLAND
Ct Coogee 101 A 9
Rd Ardross 82 D10
St Mt Claremont 71 A 6
St South Perth 73 A10
STRINGY BARK
Ra Willetton 93 D 5
STRINGYBARK
Dr Forrestfield 76 D 9
STRODE
Ave Hamilton Hill 101 A 2
STROMA
St Armadale 116 B 2
STROMBUS
Wy Heathridge 23 D 1
STROME
Rd Applecross 82 D 4
STROUGHTON
Rd Balga 46 D 3
STRUAN
Ct Kingsley 31 B 1
STRUTT
Wy Noranda 47 E 5
ST TROPEZ
Ct Port Kennedy 156 D 1
STUART
Cr Lesmurdie 87 C 6
Ct Bateman 92 E 3
Dr Henderson 111 A 7
Pl Rockingham 137 B 6
Pl Two Rocks 2 D 3
Pl Willetton 93 E 3
St Greenmount 51 B10
St Inglewood 61 D 5
St Koongamia 65 B 1
St Maylands 61 E 5
St Mosman Park 80 D 4
St Perth City 60 E10

STUBBERFIELD
St Innaloo 45 C 7
STUBBINS
Pl Carine 45 B 2
STUBBS
Pl Booragoon 92 B 2
St Balcatta 46 B 4
Tce Claremont 71 B 7
Tce Daglish 72 A 1
Tce Daglish 71 E 3
Tce Karrakatta 71 C 6
Tce Shenton Park 71 D 5
STUDLEY
Rd Attadale 81 D 8
STUDZOR
St Warnbro 145 C 9
STURRY
Pl Marangaroo 32 A 4
STURT
Cl Gosnells 105 E 2
Pl Padbury 30 D 1
St Bull Creek 92 E 7
STURTRIDGE
Rd Lockridge 49 A 6
ST VINCENT
Pl Ocean Reef 19 A 9
St Bedfordale 127 D 2
ST VINCENTS
Ave Wembley 60 A 9
STYLE
Ct Bibra Lake 102 C 5
STYLIS
Ce Mindarie 14 C 6
STYNE
Rd City Beach 58 D 6
SUBIACO
Rd Subiaco 72 B 1
Rd Subiaco 60 B10
SUBLIME
Gl Neerabup 15 E 5
SUCCESS
Cr Salter Point 83 A 8
Dr Rockingham 137 B 5
Rd Bassendean 49 A10
St Beldon 23 C 4
St Madora 160 C 7
St Madora 160 D 7
SUDBURY
Ct Leeming 93 C 8
Pl Mirrabooka 47 A 4
Wy City Beach 58 D 5
SUDLOW
Rd Bibra Lake 101 E 5
St Embleton 62 A 1
SUE ELLEN
Pl Balcatta 46 B 8
SUELEX
St Willetton 93 D 3
SUFFOLK
Bk Brigadoon 169 A 6
St Fremantle 1D C 6
St Fremantle 90 C 6
SUGARBIRD LADY
Rd Perth Airport 75 D 1
Rd Perth Airport 63 D10
SUGARS
Ct Redcliffe 63 A10
SUGARWOOD
Dr Thornlie 94 E 7
SUIZA
Pl Carine 31 A10
SULINA
Ct Duncraig 30 E 5
Pl Kallaroo 23 B 6
SULLIVAN
Rd Duncraig 30 D 3
St Beckenham 85 C 8
St Jandakot 102 D10
Wy Kardinya 92 A 6

SULMAN
Ave Salter Point 83 B 8
Rd Wembley Dns 59 A 3
Rd Wembley Dns 58 E 4
SULPHUR
Ce Stratton 51 A 2
Rd Orelia 131 A 6
SULTAN
Wy Nth Fremantle 90 A 3
SULTANA
Rd E Forrestfield 76 C 5
Rd E Maida Vale 76 C 5
Rd W High Wycombe 76 B 3
SUMMER
Pl Thornlie 95 C 2
SUMMERFIELD
Pl Gooseberry H 65 B10
Pl Gooseberry H 65 C 3
Rd Serpentine 151 A10
Rd Serpentine 155 B 1
Rd Serpentine 150 D 7
Rd Serpentine 150 E 9
SUMMERHAYES
Dr Karrinyup 45 A 4
SUMMERHILL
Ct Warnbro 145 D 6
SUMMERLAKES
Pde Ballajura 33 C 7
SUMMERLEA
Ave Meadow Sprgs 163 C 5
SUMMERS
St East Perth 73 C 1
St Perth City 1C B 1
St Perth City 73 B 1
SUMMERTON
Rd Medina 130 D 6
SUMMIT
Ct Dianella 47 B 5
Gr Swan View 51 C 6
Rd Mundaring 54 B 8
SUMMONS
Wy Warnbro 145 C 8
SUMPTON
St Hilton 91 B 8
SUMREAL
Cl Swan View 51 C 6
SUMTER
Cl Iluka 18 E 4
SUN
Pl Greenfields 165 C 2
SUNART
Cl Hamersley 32 A 8
Cl Hamersley 31 E 9
SUNBIRD
Pl Ocean Reef 23 B 2
SUNBURY
Rd Victoria Park 74 A 7
Rd Victoria Park 73 E 6
SUNDERCOMBE
St Osborne Park 59 E 2
SUNDERLAND
Cl Greenfields 163 E 9
Pl Noranda 47 D 6
SUNDEW
Ct Parkerville 53 C 7
Pl Thornlie 95 B10
Rd Gooseberry H 77 B 3
Ri Joondalup 19 E 9
SUNNINGDALE
Ch Meadow Sprgs 163 C 5
Ci Cooloongup 137 E 6
Rd Yanchep 4 E 1
St Morley 47 E 7
SUNNING HILL
Rd Stoneville 54 B 6
SUNNYSIDE
Rd Floreat 59 C10
SUNRISE
Hts Maida Vale 65 A10

SUNSET
Cr Kalamunda 77 B 7
Ct Spearwood 101 C 8
Dr Ballajura 33 C 8
Gr Canning Vale 94 A10
Pl Sorrento 30 D 4
Tce Kelmscott 107 A 7
Wy Stoneville 40 A 9
SUNSET HILL
Rd Swan View 51 E 8
SUNSHINE
Pl Bibra Lake 102 C 5
SUNVEST
Pl Merriwa 14 C 1
SUPERIOR
Ri Edgewater 20 A 9
SURBITON
Rd East Fremantle 90 D 2
SURF
Dr Secret Harbour 158 E 1
SURREY
Ct Viveash 50 B 4
Rd Kewdale 74 C 6
Rd Rivervale 74 A 4
Rd Wilson 84 A 9
St Bassendean 63 B 1
St Dianella 61 C 1
St Dianella 47 C10
SUSAN
Rd Landsdale 25 A 9
St Kensington 73 D 8
St Maylands 62 A 8
SUSANNAH
Wy Gidgegannup 40 A 6
SUSO
St Woodlands 59 B 4
SUSSEX
Pl Currambine 19 B 4
Pl Halls Head 162 C10
Rd Forrestfield 86 C 1
Rd Forrestfield 76 C10
St E Victoria Pk 74 A 9
St E Victoria Pk 83 D 1
St E Victoria Pk 73 E10
St Maylands 61 E 5
St Nollamara 46 D 7
St Spearwood 101 A 5
SUTCLIFFE
Cl Armadale 116 A 4
Rd Mundaring 68 D 2
St Dalkeith 81 D 1
St Thornlie 95 A 5
SUTHERLAND
Ave Dianella 47 A 9
Cl N Guildford 49 D10
Cl S Guildford 49 D10
Cr Winthrop 92 C 6
Dr Thornlie 95 B 7
Pde Parmelia 131 B 8
St Balga 46 D 4
St Bayswater 62 C 6
St West Perth 1C D 1
St West Perth 72 D 1
St West Perth 60 D10
Wy Cloverdale 75 B 3
SUTTON
Ct Belmont 62 E10
Rd High Wycombe 64 C10
Rd Naval Base 121 A 5
St Cannington 85 A 6
St Mandurah 163 A10
St Mandurah 164 E 1
SUVA
Gl Merriwa 10 B 9
Pl Cooloongup 145 D 1
Pl Cooloongup 137 D10
SVILICICH
Rd Herne Hill 36 C 7
SWAGGY
Ct Edgewater 24 A 1

For detailed information regarding the street referencing system used in this book, turn to page 170.

T

		Map	Ref.
SWAIN			
Cl	Booragoon	92	B 1
SWAINSON			
Pl	Dianella	47	B 5
SWALLOW			
Ct	Ballajura	33	E 6
Ct	Churchlands	59	C 7
Dr	Yangebup	102	A 9
Gr	Waikiki	145	C 2
Lp	High Wycombe	76	B 1
SWALLOW HILL			
Ct	Karnup	159	D 7
SWAMP			
Rd	Forrestdale	114	C 7
SWAN			
Ave	Midvale	50	E 7
Cl	Mandurah	165	A 4
Ct	Yangebup	102	A 8
Rd	Attadale	81	C 10
Rd	High Wycombe	64	C 10
Rd	Mahogany Crk	67	C 1
Rd	Mahogany Crk	53	C 10
Rd	Middle Swan	50	E 1
Rd	Middle Swan	50	E 3
Rd	Middle Swan	36	E 10
Rd	Swan View	51	D 8
St	Guildford	49	C 10
St	Guildford	49	E 10
St	Henley Brook	29	C 8
St	Mosman Park	80	D 4
St	Nth Fremantle	90	B 2
St	Nth Fremantle	90	C 1
St	Osborne Park	46	B 9
St	South Perth	73	C 1
St	Sth Guildford	50	A 10
St	Tuart Hill	46	C 9
St	Yokine	46	D 9
SWANAGE			
Ave	City Beach	58	C 10
SWAN BANK			
Rd	Maylands	74	A 1
Rd	Maylands	62	A 10
SWANBOURNE			
St	Fremantle	90	D 5
SWANLEY			
St	Gosnells	106	B 2
St	Marangaroo	32	B 6
SWANSEA			
St	E Victoria Pk	74	A 8
St	Swanbourne	70	D 8
St E	E Victoria Pk	84	B 1
St E	E Victoria Pk	74	B 10
SWANSON			
Rd	Willetton	93	E 2
Wy	Ocean Reef	23	A 1
SWANSTON			
St	Yokine	60	E 2
SWAN VIEW			
Rd	Greenmount	51	D 10
Rd	Swan View	51	D 9
Tce	Maylands	62	A 9
SWANVIEW			
Tce	South Perth	73	C 7
SWEENEY			
Wy	Padbury	23	C 8
SWEENY			
St	Kardinya	92	A 7
SWEETING			
St	Guildford	49	E 10
St	Woodlands	59	B 4
SWEETMAN			
St	Ardross	82	C 8
St	Hilton	91	A 7
SWIFT			
Ct	High Wycombe	64	B 10
Pl	Willetton	93	D 3
SWIFTS			
Ct	Rockingham	136	E 8
St	Greenwood	32	A 4
SWIFTSHIRE			
Rd	Madora	160	C 6

		Map	Ref.
SWINCER			
Wy	Koondoola	33	A 6
SWINGLER			
Wy	Gosnells	106	A 1
Wy	Gosnells	105	E 2
SWINSTONE			
St	Rockingham	137	A 7
SWINTON			
Pl	Erskine	164	C 6
SYCAMORE			
Cl	Rockingham	137	D 5
Dr	Duncraig	31	B 8
Ri	Dianella	47	A 7
SYDENHAM			
Rd	Doubleview	59	B 2
St	Beckenham	85	C 9
St	Cloverdale	75	C 2
St	Cloverdale	74	E 3
St	Dianella	47	C 8
St	Kewdale	74	C 6
St	Redcliffe	75	A 2
SYDNEY			
Rd	Gnangara	26	A 4
Rd	Gnangara	25	E 8
Rd	Gnangara	21	E 10
St	Cottesloe	80	C 6
St	Gnangara	26	C 7
St	North Perth	60	D 5
St	Queens Park	84	E 3
St	Sth Fremantle	90	C 8
SYGNA			
Ct	Iluka	18	E 3
SYKES			
Ave	Innaloo	45	C 9
Pl	Hamilton Hill	101	B 2
SYLVAN			
Cr	Leeming	103	A 2
Gns	Carine	31	A 9
SYLVANA			
Wy	Willetton	93	E 3
SYLVIA			
Pl	Duncraig	30	E 8
St	Balcatta	46	B 7
St	Nollamara	46	C 7
Wy	Eden Hill	48	E 9
SYMES			
Cl	Armadale	116	B 3
SYMMS			
Ct	High Wycombe	76	C 1
SYMON			
Cl	Bull Creek	93	A 7
SYMONS			
Ct	Padbury	30	D 2
SYNGE			
Pl	Waterford	83	C 6
SYNNOT			
Vw	Marangaroo	32	C 5
SYREE			
Ct	Marmion	30	C 7
SYRINX			
Pl	Mullaloo	23	B 3
SYROS			
Ct	Mindarie	14	B 4

T

		Map	Ref.
TAAFFE			
Rd	Swan View	51	E 4
TABARD			
St	Greenwood	31	E 5
TABLO			
Ct	South Lake	102	D 6
TACK			
Pl	Ocean Reef	19	A 10
TACOMA			
Lp	Dudley Park	165	B 5

		Map	Ref.
TAFT			
Rd	Warwick	31	D 6
TAGON			
La	Merriwa	11	D 8
TAGUS			
Ct	Beechboro	48	E 3
Ct	Currambine	19	A 2
TAHARA			
Vl	Ocean Reef	18	E 8
TAHOE			
Cl	Thornlie	95	A 8
Ri	Edgewater	20	A 9
TAILOR			
Rd	Burns	18	D 3
TAIN			
St	Applecross	82	C 6
St	Ardross	82	C 7
TAIT			
Ct	Noranda	48	B 4
Pl	Coolbellup	102	A 2
St	Armadale	116	C 5
TAKARI			
Cr	City Beach	58	E 9
TAKURA			
Cl	Greenfields	163	E 10
TALBINGO			
Tn	Joondalup	19	D 1
TALBOT			
Ave	Como	83	A 4
Cl	Halls Head	164	C 3
Dr	Kingsley	31	D 1
Dr	Kingsley	24	D 10
Dr	Swan C Homes	144	B 4
Rd	Hazelmere	64	B 4
Rd	Hazelmere	64	D 6
Rd	Southern River	105	B 9
Rd	Sth Guildford	64	A 4
Rd	Sth Guildford	63	E 3
Rd	Stratton	51	B 2
Rd	Swan View	51	C 5
Rd	Woodlands	59	C 2
Wy	Woodlands	59	C 2
TALDRA			
Wy	Greenfields	163	E 7
TALGA			
Cl	Wilson	84	B 6
TALGARTH			
Wy	City Beach	58	D 5
TALIA			
Pl	Mandurah	165	B 4
TALLAGANDRA			
Ct	Serpentine	154	E 8
TALLAS			
Rd	Silver Sands	163	A 7
TALLERACK			
Wy	Forrestfield	76	B 8
TALLERING			
Hts	Woodvale	24	B 5
TALLIS			
Cl	Hillarys	23	B 3
TALLKARRI			
Cl	Westfield	106	C 8
TALLOW			
Pl	South Lake	102	D 5
Ra	Edgewater	24	B 2
TALL TREE VIEW			
	Swan View	51	B 6
TALMA			
Pl	Gwelup	45	C 5
TALUS			
Dr	Armadale	116	D 9
TALWIN			
Ct	Westfield	106	C 9
TALWOOD			
Pl	Halls Head	164	C 7
TAMALA			
Rd	City Beach	58	E 8

		Map	Ref.
TAMALEE			
Pl	Hillman	137	E 5
TAMAR			
Cl	Currambine	19	A 2
Cl	Wilson	84	B 8
Pl	Palmyra	91	B 3
St	East Perth	73	C 1
St	Palmyra	91	B 3
TAMARIND			
Cr	Westfield	106	C 9
TAMARINE			
Wy	Swan View	51	C 5
TAMARISK			
Ave	Wanneroo	24	D 2
Ct	Dianella	46	E 4
Dr	Halls Head	164	A 5
Wy	Woodlands	59	B 2
TAMBAR			
Pl	Currambine	19	A 5
TAMBLYN			
Cl	Woodvale	24	B 8
Pl	Karrinyup	44	D 7
Pl	Stoneville	54	B 6
TAMBULAM			
Wy	Armadale	116	C 3
TAMBULAN			
Rd	Maida Vale	77	A 3
TAMBY			
Ct	Southern River	105	C 8
TAME			
Ct	Dianella	47	A 9
TAMMA			
Ct	Heathridge	19	B 10
TAMMERLANE			
Hts	Iluka	18	E 5
TAMPICO			
Ct	Safety Bay	137	B 10
TAMWORTH			
Wy	Kardinya	92	A 6
TANA			
Ct	Leeming	103	A 2
Ct	Waikiki	145	D 1
TANAGER			
Trl	Ballajura	33	D 5
TANAH			
Cl	Kingsley	31	D 2
TANAMI			
Ct	Karrinyup	44	E 2
TANBY			
Pl	Cooloongup	137	D 10
TANDARRA			
Pl	Wembley Dns	58	C 5
TANDINA			
Wy	Kingsley	31	D 2
TANDOU			
Cl	South Lake	102	C 8
Ct	Edgewater	20	A 9
TANDY			
Ct	Duncraig	31	B 8
St	Salter Point	83	B 8
St	West Perth	60	D 10
TANGADEE			
Rd	Golden Bay	158	D 7
TANGAROA			
Cl	Cooloongup	137	D 8
TANGELO			
Ct	Armadale	116	A 4
TANGENT			
Pl	Mullaloo	23	B 2
TANGERINE			
Cl	Armadale	115	E 5
TANGLEWOOD			
Pl	Currambine	19	A 2
TANGMERE			
Wy	Balga	46	C 1

		Map	Ref.
TANGNEY			
Cr	Kardinya	91	D 8
Cr	Samson	91	D 8
Ct	Kardinya	91	D 8
TANKERTON			
Wy	Coodanup	165	C 3
TANNADICE			
Cl	Kingsley	24	C 10
TANNAH			
Wy	Mt Helena	40	D 9
TANNER			
Ce	Clarkson	14	C 2
Ct	Leda	139	C 2
Pl	Kardinya	92	A 7
Pl	Morley	48	C 6
Rd	Carmel	87	E 7
St	Middle Swan	50	D 4
TANNING			
Wy	Woodvale	24	C 7
TANSEY			
Wy	Falcon	162A	B 4
TANSON			
Rd	Parmelia	131	B 5
St	Attadale	81	D 8
TANSOR			
Pl	Willetton	93	E 4
TANTINI			
Cl	Lynwood	94	C 3
TANUNDA			
Rd	Spearwood	100	E 7
TAPLIN			
Rd	Perth Airport	63	B 8
TAPLOW			
Ct	Westfield	106	C 10
TAPPER			
La	Claremont	71	B 7
Rd	Banjup	113	B 4
St	White Gum Vly	90	E 6
TAPPING			
St	Mariginiup	20	D 2
Wy	Quinns Rocks	10	A 10
TARA			
Ct	Woodvale	24	B 7
St	Morley	61	D 1
Vs	Leederville	60	B 8
Wy	Kelmscott	106	E 6
TARATA			
Cl	Halls Head	164	B 5
Ct	Duncraig	31	B 8
Wy	Forrestfield	76	B 9
TARAW			
Cl	Warnbro	145	E 9
TARBENIAN			
Wy	Brigadoon	169	A 4
TARBET			
Ct	Hamersley	32	A 9
TARCOOLA			
Rt	Ocean Reef	19	A 7
TAREE			
Ct	Greenwood	31	C 3
Pl	Roleystone	108	A 7
St	Bentley	84	A 4
St	Glen Forrest	66	E 3
St	St James	84	A 4
TAREENA			
St	Nedlands	71	E 7
TARIS			
Pl	Karrinyup	45	A 6
TARLING			
Pl	Maddington	96	D 1
TARLTON			
Rd	Perth Airport	63	B 7
TARNDALE			
Wy	South Lake	102	C 7
TARO			
Pl	Kingsley	31	D 2
TAROLINTA			
Gns	Ocean Reef	18	E 7

248

For detailed information regarding the street referencing system used in this book, turn to page 170.

T

		Map	Ref.
TARONGA			
Dr	Kelmscott	106	E 6
Pl	Carabooda	8	A 2
TARONGO			
Wy	City Beach	58	D 3
TAROONA			
Ct	Iluka	18	E 4
TARRA			
Cl	Clarkson	14	E 2
TARRAGON			
Pl	Thornlie	94	E 8
TARRAJI			
Tce	Marangaroo	32	C 4
TARRANT			
Pl	Padbury	30	D 2
Wy	Bateman	92	D 7
TARRAWAN			
Rd	Armadale	116	B 5
TARRUP			
St	Chidlow	42	C 4
TARU			
Ct	Willetton	93	B 6
TARUN			
Ct	Cannington	84	D 4
TARUP			
Pl	Hillman	137	E 5
TARWARRI			
Cl	Hillman	137	E 6
TARWHINE			
Pl	Golden Bay	158	D 9
TASCA			
Pl	Duncraig	31	B 7
TASKER			
Rd	Kwinana Beach	130	C 6
Rd	Medina	130	C 6
St	Halls Head	162	C 9
TASMAN			
Ct	Mirrabooka	33	A 9
Ct	Thornlie	95	C 1
Pl	Shelley	93	C 1
Pl	Waikiki	145	C 3
Rd	Beldon	23	C 2
St	Glendalough	60	B 5
St	Mt Hawthorn	60	B 5
TASSELL			
Pl	Stoneville	54	C 4
St	Embleton	62	A 1
TATE			
Pl	Kardinya	92	A 7
Rd	High Wycombe	64	A 9
St	Leederville	60	B 10
St	South Perth	73	B 9
St	Welshpool	84	C 2
TATHRA			
Wy	Clarkson	14	D 1
TATLOCK			
Wy	Stratton	51	B 4
TATTLER			
Pl	Huntingdale	105	D 1
Pl	Yangebup	102	A 8
TAUNTON			
Wy	Karrinyup	45	A 5
TAUPO			
Gl	Joondalup	19	D 2
TAURA			
Cl	Marangaroo	32	D 5
TAURANGA			
Rt	Mindarie	14	C 6
TAURUS			
Ct	Rockingham	137	B 9
TAVISTOCK			
Cr	Lynwood	94	D 1
TAWNY			
Wy	Thornlie	95	A 4
TAWORRI			
Wy	City Beach	58	D 9
TAWSON			
Pl	Leeming	92	E 10

		Map	Ref.
TAXAL			
Cl	Carine	30	E 9
TAY			
Ct	Cooloongup	137	E 10
Ct	Gosnells	106	B 1
Gl	Joondalup	19	D 3
Pl	Hamersley	32	A 10
Pl	North Perth	60	D 7
TAYLOR			
Cl	Leda	130	E 9
Cr	Midland	50	D 6
Rd	Forrestdale	124	A 2
Rd	Forrestdale	114	A 8
Rd	Kalamunda	77	A 4
Rd	Mundijong	142	E 4
Rd	Nedlands	71	C 10
St	Hilton	91	A 7
St	Victoria Park	73	C 6
Wy	Hillarys	23	C 9
TAYWOOD			
Dr	Wanneroo	20	C 6
TEAGUE			
Cl	Bull Creek	93	B 6
Cl	Waikiki	145	E 2
St	Victoria Park	74	A 7
St	Victoria Park	73	E 6
TEAGUER			
St	Wilson	84	A 6
TEAK			
Ct	Woodvale	24	C 6
Pl	Halls Head	164	B 5
Wy	Maddington	96	C 6
TEAKDALE			
Cl	Safety Bay	137	A 10
TEAKLE			
Rd	Osborne Park	59	E 3
TEAKWOOD			
Ave	Woodlands	59	B 4
TEAL			
Ct	High Wycombe	64	C 10
Ct	Yangebup	102	A 8
Me	Ballajura	33	E 8
Me	Willetton	93	C 4
St	Falcon	162A	D 9
TEALE			
Ct	Gwelup	45	C 5
TEANO			
Pl	Marangaroo	32	C 5
TEAR			
St	Chidlow	57	A 2
TEBB			
Me	Clarkson	14	D 1
TECOMA			
St	Duncraig	31	B 8
Wy	Dianella	46	E 5
TEDDINGTON			
Rd	Victoria Park	73	E 6
TEDRAKE			
St	Willagee	91	E 5
TEE			
Ave	Mundaring	54	B 10
TEECE			
Pl	Hamilton Hill	101	C 3
TEELE			
St	Beckenham	85	B 9
TEES			
Ct	Beechboro	48	C 3
Ct	Mindarie	14	A 3
TEE TREA			
Wy	Thornlie	95	A 9
TEETREE			
Ct	Beechboro	48	C 5
TEHANI			
Cl	Cooloongup	137	D 8
TEIGH			
St	Gosnells	96	A 8

		Map	Ref.
TELEPHONE			
La	Baldivis	140	A 4
La	Baldivis	148	C 1
La	Baldivis	139	E 3
TELEVISION			
Rd	Bickley	88	B 4
TELFORD			
Cr	Stirling	45	E 9
St	Marmion	30	D 9
TELITA			
Ct	Coodanup	165	C 4
TELLA			
St	Gooseberry H	77	C 1
TELLEN			
St	Mullaloo	23	B 4
TELOPIA			
Dr	Duncraig	31	A 8
TELSTAR			
Dr	Morley	48	C 6
Pl	Heathridge	19	D 9
TEMBY			
Ave	Kalamunda	77	B 6
Ct	Kardinya	91	D 8
Pl	Swan View	51	C 6
St	Beckenham	85	B 7
TEMPANY			
Wy	Koondoola	33	A 7
TEMPEST			
Pl	Waikiki	145	B 3
TEMPLAR			
Ct	Iluka	18	E 4
TEMPLE			
St	Victoria Park	73	E 8
TEMPLEMAN			
Pl	Midland	50	C 8
TEMPLEMORE			
Dr	Heathridge	23	E 2
Gns	Waterford	83	D 6
TEMPLETON			
Cr	Girrawheen	32	A 7
TEMPLETONIA			
Ave	Sorrento	30	D 6
Cr	City Beach	58	D 8
Pro	Halls Head	164	A 4
Rt	Canning Vale	104	C 1
TEN ACRE			
Wy	Stoneville	54	B 3
TENARDI			
Ct	Greenwood	31	C 6
TENBY			
Cl	Merriwa	11	C 9
TENCH			
Pl	Mirrabooka	32	E 9
TENDRING			
Wy	Girrawheen	32	D 9
TENELLA			
Me	Warnbro	145	E 9
TENERIFFE			
Pl	Mirrabooka	47	B 1
Pl	Mirrabooka	33	B 10
TENET			
Ct	Merriwa	11	C 10
TENGGARA			
Ave	Two Rocks	3	B 10
TENNANT			
St	Welshpool	84	B 2
TENNESSEE			
Ct	Greenfields	165	C 1
TENNIVALE			
Pl	North Perth	60	D 7
TENNYSON			
Ave	Halls Head	164	C 4
Rd	Gooseberry H	77	D 4
St	Bellevue	51	A 10
St	Leederville	60	D 7
TEN SELDAM			
Ci	Winthrop	92	C 5

		Map	Ref.
TENTERDEN			
Wy	Gosnells	106	C 1
TENTH			
Ave	Inglewood	61	C 4
Ave	Maylands	61	D 6
Rd	Armadale	115	E 7
TERANCA			
Rd	Greenfields	165	E 2
TERENCE			
St	Gosnells	96	A 8
TERESA			
Ct	Kelmscott	117	B 1
TERKA			
Ct	Dudley Park	165	C 5
TERN			
Ct	Halls Head	164	B 3
Ct	Thornlie	95	A 6
Lp	Yangebup	102	A 10
TERRACE			
Rd	East Perth	1C	B 4
Rd	East Perth	73	B 4
Rd	Guildford	49	D 10
Rd	Perth City	1C	A 4
Rd	Perth City	73	A 4
TERREX			
Ri	Merriwa	14	C 1
TERRIER			
Pl	Southern River	105	B 9
TERRIGAL			
Pl	Maida Vale	77	A 3
Wy	Armadale	116	B 6
TERRY			
Cr	Mandurah	163	C 9
Rd	Karrakatta	71	C 5
Rd	Leeming	93	B 10
Rd	Quinns Rocks	10	E 10
Vl	Willetton	93	C 6
TESLIN			
Rd	Mt Claremont	70	E 4
TESSA			
Ct	Duncraig	30	D 4
TETLOW			
Pl	Bibra Lake	102	D 3
TETO			
Pl	Spearwood	101	C 5
TETWORTH			
Cr	Nollamara	46	E 5
TEUTONIA			
Ct	High Wycombe	76	D 1
TEVIOT			
Pl	Beechboro	48	D 3
TEW			
Gr	Padbury	30	E 2
TEWSON			
Rd	Westfield	106	B 9
THACKERAY			
St	Spearwood	101	B 8
THAKE			
Ct	Koondoola	33	A 9
THAMES			
Ct	Beechboro	48	E 2
THATCHED			
Ct	Bibra Lake	102	E 2
THATCHER			
Rd	Byford	135	B 1
Rd	Byford	126	B 10
THAXTED			
Pl	Swan View	51	C 6
THEA			
Wk	Willetton	93	D 6
THEAKSTON			
Grn	Leeming	92	E 8
THE ARCADE			
	Doubleview	45	A 10
THE AVENUE			
	Alexander Hts	33	A 5
	Crawley	72	A 10
	Leederville	60	C 9

		Map	Ref.
	Midland	50	C 8
	Nedlands	81	E 1
	Warnbro	145	E 6
THEBA			
Ct	Heathridge	23	E 1
THE BEACON			
	Swan View	51	D 8
THE BOULEVARD			
	City Beach	58	D 7
	Floreat	59	A 8
	Gooseberry H	77	B 2
	Wembley	59	D 9
	Wembley	59	D 10
THE BOULEVARDE			
	Mt Hawthorn	60	C 6
THE BROADWATER			
	Ballajura	33	D 8
THE BULWARK			
	Willetton	93	C 3
THE CEDARS			
	Woodvale	24	A 7
THE CEDUS			
	Claremont	71	A 8
THE CITADEL			
	Forrestfield	76	C 8
THE CLOSE			
	Swan View	51	A 5
THE COOMBE			
	Mosman Park	81	A 6
THE CORKSCREW			
	Gooseberry H	77	B 2
THE COURT			
	Redcliffe	62	E 8
	Woodvale	24	B 8
THE COVE			
	Ballajura	33	C 7
	Canning Vale	94	A 10
	Mullaloo	23	A 3
	Munster	110	E 1
THE CRESCENT			
	Helena Valley	65	C 5
	Maddington	96	A 4
	Midland	50	D 8
	Redcliffe	62	E 9
THE CREST			
	Canning Vale	94	B 10
	Woodvale	24	B 7
	Woodvale	24	B 8
THE CROWSNEST			
	Willetton	93	C 4
THE CURLEW			
	Willetton	93	C 4
THE DOVECOTE			
	Willetton	93	C 4
THE ELBOW			
	Swan View	51	A 7
THE ESCARPMENT			
	Willetton	93	B 5
THE ESPLANADE			
(see also Esplanade)			
	Ballajura	33	D 8
	Mt Pleasant	92	E 1
	Mt Pleasant	82	E 6
	Mt Pleasant	82	E 6
	Peppermint Gr	80	E 3
	Perth City	1C	E 3
	Perth City	72	E 3
	Redcliffe	62	E 7
	Scarborough	58	C 1
	Scarborough	44	C 9
	South Perth	72	E 6
	Trigg	44	C 5
THE EYRIE			
	Willetton	93	C 4
THE GABLES			
	Ballajura	33	C 6
THE GAP			
	Ocean Reef	18	E 8

For detailed information regarding the street referencing system used in this book, turn to page 170.

T

		Map	Ref.
THE GETAWAY			
	Gooseberry H	77	B 4
THE GLEN			
	Kingsley	24	E 9
THE GRANGE			
	Mullaloo	23	A 3
THE GROVE			
	Armadale	116	D 8
	Ballajura	33	C 5
	Churchlands	59	C 5
	Wembley	60	A 9
	Woodvale	24	D 7
THE HAVEN			
	Ballajura	33	C 7
	Woodvale	24	A 8
THE HEIGHTS			
	Ballajura	33	C 8
	Canning Vale	94	B 10
THE HORSESHOE			
	Wandi	123	B 5
THE LAKES			
	Ballajura	33	D 8
	Connolly	19	A 9
THE LANE			
	Churchlands	59	C 5
	Gooseberry H	77	C 3
THE LANTERNS			
	Carine	44	E 1
THELMA			
St	Como	83	B 2
St	Como	82	E 2
St	Mosman Park	80	D 6
St	West Perth	1C	D 1
St	West Perth	72	D 1
THE LODGE			
	Mt Claremont	71	A 4
	Mullaloo	23	A 3
THE LOOP			
	Edgewater	24	B 1
THE MALL			
	Alexander Hts	33	B 4
THE MARLOWS			
	Mt Claremont	71	A 4
THE MEAD			
	Kiara	48	E 6
THE MEWS			
	Kardinya	92	A 6
	Kingsley	24	B 9
THE NARROW			
Rd	Wilson	84	B 7
THE OAKS			
	Brigadoon	169	A 4
THE OUTLOOK			
	Coogee	110	E 1
THE PARAPET			
	Willetton	93	C 5
THE PINNACLE			
	Willetton	93	C 5
THE PINNACLES			
	Edgewater	20	A 10
THE PLAZA			
	Sorrento	30	B 6
THE PROMENADE			
	Mt Pleasant	82	D 8
THE QUARRY			
	Swan View	51	A 6
THE QUARTERDECK			
	Ballajura	33	C 8
	Willetton	93	C 5
THERA			
St	Falcon	162A	B 3
THE RAMBLE			
	Booragoon	92	B 1
	Booragoon	82	B 10
	Canning Vale	94	B 10
	Parmelia	131	B 10
	Woodvale	24	B 8

		Map	Ref.
THE RETREAT			
	Forrestfield	76	D 8
THE RETURN			
	Woodvale	24	B 8
THE RIDGE			
	Woodvale	24	B 7
	Yangebup	101	E 10
THE RIDGEWAY			
	Swan View	51	B 5
THE RISE			
	Ballajura	33	C 6
	Woodvale	24	B 8
THE ROPE			
Wk	Mosman Park	80	D 6
THE ROSE			
	Padbury	30	E 2
THESEUS			
Wy	Coolbellup	101	E 1
Wy	Coolbellup	91	E 10
THE SPIT			
Pl	Kallaroo	23	A 6
THE STRAND			
	Applecross	82	C 4
	Bayswater	62	A 4
	Bayswater	61	E 4
	Bedford	61	D 2
	Dianella	47	A 7
	Dianella	47	B 9
	Dianella	61	C 1
	Maddington	95	E 4
THE SUMMIT			
	Yangebup	102	A 9
THE TAFFRAIL			
	Willetton	93	C 5
THE TERN			
	Willetton	93	C 5
THE TERRACE			
	Fremantle	1D	C 5
	Fremantle	90	C 5
THETIS			
Pl	Cooloongup	137	D 8
St	Madora	160	D 6
THE TOR			
	Willetton	93	B 5
THE VALE			
	Willetton	94	A 2
	Willetton	93	E 2
THE VISTA			
	Canning Vale	94	B 10
	Gooseberry H	77	C 5
THEYDON			
Gr	Two Rocks	2	D 2
THICK			
Cl	Golden Bay	159	A 7
THIMBLE			
Ct	Ocean Reef	23	B 2
THIRD			
Av E	Maylands	61	D 8
Ave	Applecross	82	D 5
Avc	Bassendean	63	A 1
Ave	Bassendean	49	A 10
Ave	Burns	18	D 3
Ave	Kelmscott	106	D 9
Ave	Kensington	73	C 8
Ave	Kwinana Beach	129	E 8
Ave	Mandurah	165	B 3
Ave	Midland	50	A 8
Ave	Mt Lawley	61	C 6
Ave	Rossmoyne	93	B 2
Ave	Shoalwater	136	C 7
Ave	Westfield	116	B 1
Ave	Westfield	106	C 10
Rd	Armadale	116	D 6
St	Bicton	81	B 10
THIRLMERE			
Rd	Mt Lawley	61	C 9
THIRROUL			
Gr	Kingsley	31	E 3

		Map	Ref.
THISTLE			
Ct	Dianella	46	E 5
St	Welshpool	75	B 10
THOMAS			
Ct	Kingsley	31	C 1
Rd	Anketell	132	C 2
Rd	Byford	126	A 8
Rd	Casuarina	131	E 4
Rd	Glen Forrest	66	E 2
Rd	Kwinana Beach	130	A 3
Rd	Mahogany Crk	67	B 3
Rd	Medina	130	C 3
Rd	Oakford	133	A 1
Rd	Oakford	124	C 9
Rd	Oakford	125	C 9
Rd	Orelia	131	B 3
Rd	Parkerville	53	E 9
Rd	Parmelia	131	C 4
St	Armadale	116	D 7
St	Chidlow	56	C 2
St	E Cannington	85	A 5
St	Gidgegannup	55	D 4
St	Gosnells	106	A 5
St	Mosman Park	80	D 4
St	Nedlands	71	E 10
St	Safety Bay	136	D 9
St	South Lake	102	D 9
St	South Perth	73	B 8
St	Sth Fremantle	90	D 10
St	Subiaco	72	B 3
Wy	Kardinya	92	A 7
Wy	Karrinyup	45	A 7
THOMASIA			
St	Huntingdale	105	B 1
St	Huntingdale	95	B 10
THOMPSON			
Dr	Wanneroo	20	C 5
Pl	Kewdale	74	E 8
Rd	Bassendean	63	B 1
Rd	Nth Fremantle	80	C 9
Rd	Roleystone	118	A 1
St	Ascot	62	D 8
St	North Perth	60	D 8
Wy	Bull Creek	93	B 6
THOMSON			
Pl	Jandakot	112	D 2
Rd	Claremont	71	B 10
St	Mandurah	165	C 1
St	Mandurah	163	C 10
THONGSBRIDGE			
Ct	Menora	61	A 6
THOR			
Ct	Ocean Reef	18	E 8
St	Innaloo	59	C 1
St	Innaloo	45	C 10
THORBURN			
Ave	Beechboro	49	A 3
THORLEY			
Rd	Pickering Bk	89	D 9
St	Perth City	1C	B 1
St	Perth City	73	B 1
Wy	Lockridge	49	B 6
THORMAN			
Pl	Booragoon	82	D 10
THORN			
St	Melville	91	D 2
Wy	Canning Vale	94	B 6
THORNBER			
Pl	Noranda	47	D 5
THORNBILL			
Pl	Mahogany Crk	67	C 3
Wy	Churchlands	59	C 6
THORNBOROUGH			
Rd	Greenfields	163	D 7
THORNBURY			
Cl	Mundaring	54	A 10
THORNE			
Pl	Wellard	132	C 10
Pl	Yangebup	111	C 1
Rd	Hacketts Gully	78	E 7
St	Herne Hill	36	D 4

		Map	Ref.
THORNETT			
St	Hilton	91	B 7
THORNEY			
Wy	Balga	46	D 3
THORNHILL			
Wy	Greenwood	31	C 7
THORNLIE			
Ave	Thornlie	95	C 3
THORNTON			
Pl	Gooseberry H	77	C 4
St	Morley	47	E 9
THORNWICK			
Cr	Chidlow	43	A 10
Cr	Chidlow	42	E 10
THOROGOOD			
St	Victoria Park	73	E 5
THORPE			
Pl	Carine	31	A 10
Pl	Roleystone	108	C 7
St	Morley	47	D 9
St	Rockingham	136	E 5
Wy	Kwinana Beach	130	A 6
THORSAGER			
St	Coolbellup	91	C 10
THORSON			
Wy	Lockridge	49	B 6
THRALL			
St	Innaloo	45	B 10
THREADLEAF			
Wy	Mirrabooka	47	B 1
THREDBO			
Pl	Merriwa	11	C 10
THREE KANGAROOS			
Wy	Byford	126	D 8
THROSBY			
St	Shelley	83	D 9
Wy	Padbury	23	E 10
THROSSELL			
Lp	Waikiki	145	E 2
Pl	Clarkson	14	D 1
Rd	Greenmount	51	E 10
Rd	Swan View	51	E 8
St	Como	83	B 2
St	Dalkeith	81	D 3
St	Perth City	61	A 9
St	Sawyers Valley	54	E 10
THRUM			
Cl	Leeming	103	A 1
Wy	Kardinya	91	E 6
THURBURN			
Rt	Marangaroo	32	C 6
THURLES			
Ave	Floreat	59	B 8
Ct	Waterford	83	D 6
THURLOE			
St	Bicton	81	B 9
THURLOW			
Ave	Yokine	60	E 1
Ave	Yokine	46	E 10
THURSLEY			
Wy	Gosnells	106	C 1
Wy	Gosnells	96	C 10
Wy	Morley	47	C 6
THURSO			
Rd	Myaree	91	E 3
THURSTON			
St	Mt Lawley	61	B 6
THYME			
Cl	Thornlie	94	E 8
Ct	Halls Head	164	A 7
Ct	Mirrabooka	46	E 2
TIA			
Ave	High Wycombe	76	C 1
Ave	High Wycombe	64	C 10
Pl	Willetton	93	E 4
TIAN			
Cl	Willetton	94	A 3
TIANA			
Ce	Casuarina	132	D 5

		Map	Ref.
TIBER			
Ave	Beechboro	48	E 3
TIBRADDEN			
Wy	Redcliffe	63	A 7
TIBSHELF			
Pl	Carine	30	E 10
TICEHURST			
Wy	Balga	46	D 1
TICHBORNE			
St	Jandakot	102	D 10
TICKLIE			
Rd	Armadale	116	A 3
TICKNER			
Pl	Mandurah	165	C 3
TIDE			
Pl	Beldon	23	C 2
TIDEFALL			
St	Safety Bay	145	B 1
TIETKINS			
Wy	Padbury	23	E 10
TIFERA			
Ci	Kallaroo	23	B 6
TIFWAY			
Pl	Carabooda	8	E 7
TIGHE			
St	Cloverdale	75	A 6
St	Jolimont	71	E 1
St	Jolimont	59	E 10
TIGRIS			
Wy	Beechboro	48	D 3
TIJOU			
Cl	Coogee	100	E 8
TIJUANA			
Rd	Armadale	116	C 9
TILBY			
St	Cloverdale	75	A 2
TILFORD			
Pl	Morley	48	A 9
TILL			
St	Cloverdale	75	A 3
St	Herne Hill	36	E 4
TILLBROOK			
St	Glen Forrest	66	D 3
TILLER			
Rd	Ocean Reef	23	A 2
TILLI			
Pl	Welshpool	84	D 3
TILLIA			
Ct	Forrestfield	76	A 10
TILLINGA			
St	Armadale	116	A 6
St	Balcatta	46	B 5
TILLINGDON			
Wy	Morley	47	E 6
TILLMAN			
Pl	Kelmscott	106	D 10
Pl	Wilson	84	B 8
TILNEY			
St	Booragoon	92	B 1
TILSTON			
Cl	Willetton	93	E 4
TILTON			
Tce	City Beach	58	D 6
TIMARU			
Cl	Port Kennedy	156	D 4
TIMBARRA			
St	Armadale	116	D 6
TIMBERCREST			
Rd	Thornlie	95	B 9
TIMBERLANE			
Cr	Beechboro	48	C 3
Dr	Woodvale	24	B 8
TIMBER RIDGE			
Rt	Leeming	102	E 2
TIMBERTOP			
	Woodvale	24	B 8
Cst	Parmelia	131	B 10

250

For detailed information regarding the street referencing system used in this book, turn to page 170.

T

		Map	Ref.
TIMBRELL			
Wy	Leeming	93	C 9
TIMES			
Ci	Greenfields	165	E 2
TIMEWELL			
Pl	Dianella	47	A 8
St	Dianella	47	A 8
TIMIDON			
Pl	Duncraig	30	E 4
TIMMS			
Pl	Morley	47	E 8
TIMO			
Ct	Ferndale	84	D 9
TIMOR			
St	Duncraig	31	B 7
TINAROO			
Ct	South Lake	102	C 7
TINDAL			
Ave	Yangebup	111	E 8
Ave	Yangebup	101	E10
Wy	Clarkson	14	D 2
TINDALE			
Rd	Lesmurdie	87	B 3
St	Mandurah	163	B 8
TINGA			
Pl	Kelmscott	116	C 1
TINGLE			
Cl	Maida Vale	77	A 2
Ct	Greenwood	31	C 4
TINSEL			
Pl	Mirrabooka	33	A10
TINTAGEL			
Ct	City Beach	58	D10
TINTAL			
Pl	Kardinya	92	A 7
Wy	Bateman	92	D 7
TINTO			
Rd	Welshpool	75	D10
TIPPERARY			
Ri	Padbury	31	A 2
TIPPETT			
Ct	Willetton	93	E 6
TIPPING			
Rd	Kewdale	75	C 7
TIPUANA			
Pl	Edgewater	24	B 3
Pl	Thornlie	95	A 9
TIREE			
St	Armadale	116	B 2
TITICACA			
Me	Joondalup	19	D 1
TITUS			
Rd	Lockridge	49	A 6
TIVELLA			
Ct	Willetton	93	E 3
TIVERTON			
St	Lynwood	84	D10
St	Perth City	73	A 1
TOBAGO			
Pl	Safety Bay	145	C 1
TOBIN			
Ct	Thornlie	95	D 6
Hl	Clarkson	14	C 2
St	Mt Helena	55	C 3
Wy	Cooloongup	137	C10
TOBOL			
Ce	Coodanup	165	D 4
TOCOMA			
Ct	Meadow Sprgs	163	C 4
TODD			
Ave	Como	83	B 1
Ave	Peron	136	B 5
Ct	Morley	48	D 8
Ct	Huntingdale	105	E 1
St	Bellevue	50	E 9
St	Spearwood	101	B 7
TODEA			
Ct	Duncraig	31	A 8

		Map	Ref.
TOKAY			
La	Ellenbrook	29	B 1
TOLBURY			
La	Kiara	48	E 7
TOLEDO			
Cl	Cannington	84	E 5
TOLLEY			
Ct	Hamilton Hill	90	E10
TOLLINGTON PARK			
Rd	Kelmscott	116	D 1
Rd	Kelmscott	106	D10
TOLSON			
St	Balga	32	B10
TOLWORTH			
Wy	Embleton	62	B 1
TOMAGO			
Lp	Merriwa	10	B 8
TOMAH			
Rd	Armadale	116	B 5
Rd	Wattle Grove	85	E 1
Rd	Welshpool	75	D10
TOMATIN			
Ct	Duncraig	30	E 7
TOMISLAV			
Pl	Wattleup	121	D 2
TOMLIN			
St	West Swan	50	A 2
TOMLINSON			
Pl	Armadale	116	C 3
Rd	Hovea	53	B10
St	Welshpool	84	C 1
TOM MILLAR			
Cl	Kalamunda	77	C 7
TOMS			
Ct	Bayswater	62	A 6
TONBRIDGE			
Wy	Morley	48	A 7
Wy	Thornlie	95	C 5
TONE			
Ct	Gosnells	106	A 3
Pl	Karrinyup	44	E 2
TONKIN			
Hwy	Bayswater	62	C 3
Hwy	Maddington	86	C 9
Hwy	Maddington	96	D 2
Hwy	Malaga	48	B 3
Hwy	Martin	96	D 6
Hwy	Morley	48	B 9
Hwy	Newburn	75	C 6
Hwy	Orange Grove	86	C 9
Hwy	Orange Grove	96	D 2
Hwy	Perth Airport	75	B 1
Hwy	Redcliffe	63	A 9
Hwy	Wattle Grove	76	A10
Hwy	Wattle Grove	86	B 6
Pl	Girrawheen	32	D 8
Rd	Hilton	91	C 8
St	Mundijong	142	E 6
St	Serpentine	154	E 4
TONRITA			
Pl	Wanneroo	20	C 8
TONTAVE			
Rd	Balga	46	B 4
TOODYAY			
Rd	Gidgegannup	40	A 1
Rd	Gidgegannup	39	D 2
Rd	Gidgegannup	38	E 4
Rd	Middle Swan	51	A 2
Rd	Red Hill	37	C10
Rd	Viveash	50	D 4
TOONA			
Gns	Edgewater	24	B 3
TOONGABBIE			
Ct	Kingsley	31	E 2
Wy	Armadale	116	C 4
TOORA			
Pl	Cooloongup	137	D10
TOORAK			
Rd	Armadale	116	B 4
Rd	Rivervale	74	B 3

		Map	Ref.
TOORIE			
Ct	Currambine	19	A 4
TOOTING			
St	Beckenham	85	C 6
TOOVEY			
Ct	Padbury	31	A 2
TOOWONG			
St	Bayswater	62	A 5
St	Bayswater	61	E 4
TOPAZ			
Ct	Armadale	117	A 6
Ct	High Wycombe	76	D 2
Gns	Edgewater	24	A 1
Pl	Carine	45	A 1
TOPEKA			
Pl	Wanneroo	20	D 9
TOPMAST			
Pl	Ocean Reef	22	E 1
TOR			
Pl	City Beach	58	D10
TORBAY			
Me	Warnbro	145	E 7
TORCROSS			
St	Warnbro	145	D 8
TORENIA			
Wy	Yangebup	101	E10
TOREOPANGO			
Ave	Two Rocks	2	D 1
TORGOYLE			
Rd	Wattleup	111	D 8
TORNADO			
Rd	Ocean Reef	19	A10
TORONTO			
Pl	Wanneroo	20	C 6
TORQUATA			
Dr	Mirrabooka	46	E 1
Dr	Mirrabooka	32	E 9
TORQUIL			
Rd	Coolbellup	91	E 9
TORRENS			
Cl	Mullaloo	23	B 3
Ct	Cottesloe	70	C10
Lp	Waikiki	145	D 1
Pl	Greenfields	165	D 1
St	Cottesloe	80	C 1
St	Cottesloe	70	C10
St	Swan View	51	C 9
TORRES			
Pl	Willetton	93	E 7
TORRIDON			
Ave	Lynwood	94	B 3
St	Ardross	82	D10
TORWOOD			
Cl	Maddington	96	D 4
Dr	Gooseberry H	77	D 1
Gr	Edgewater	24	B 2
TOSCANA			
Dr	Merriwa	14	C 1
TOTNES			
Gr	Yanchep	4	D 5
TOTTENHAM			
St	Chidlow	56	D 1
TOUCAN			
Wy	Ballajura	33	E 7
TOULON			
Ci	Mindarie	14	B 4
Ct	Port Kennedy	145	D10
Gr	Coogee	101	A 9
TOULOUSE			
Wy	Port Kennedy	156	D 1
TOUR			
Pl	Middle Swan	50	E 4
TOWARDA			
Wy	Wanneroo	20	C 9
TOWER			
Rd	Roleystone	107	C 5
St	Leederville	60	C 9

		Map	Ref.
TOWERHILL			
Ct	Greenmount	65	E 2
Rd	Alexander Hts	33	B 6
TOWERS			
St	Kewdale	74	E 7
TOWIE			
St	Cloverdale	75	A 5
TOWNCENTRE			
Dr	Thornlie	95	A 7
TOWNING			
St	Embleton	62	B 1
TOWNLEY			
St	Armadale	116	C 8
TOWNSEND			
Dl	Mt Claremont	71	A 5
Rd	Jandabup	21	C 2
Rd	Rockingham	137	A 7
St	Armadale	116	C 8
St	Malaga	33	D 9
TOWNSHEND			
Ave	Balcatta	46	C 8
Rd	Subiaco	72	B 2
Wy	Kardinya	91	E 8
TOWNSING			
Dr	Curtin Uni	135	
Rd	Kardinya	91	E 8
TOWNSON			
Pl	Leeming	92	E 9
TOWTON			
St	Redcliffe	62	E 9
Wy	Langford	95	A 2
TRACY			
Tn	Woodvale	24	B 7
TRADE WINDS			
Dr	Safety Bay	145	B 1
TRAFALGAR			
Ct	Lesmurdie	87	B 2
Gns	Marangaroo	32	C 5
Rd	East Perth	73	C 2
Rd	Lesmurdie	87	A 3
TRAFFORD			
Ct	Craigie	23	D 6
St	Beaconsfield	90	D 7
TRAIL RIDGE			
	Canning Vale	94	D 9
TRAILRIDGE			
Tn	Leeming	103	A 2
TRAILWOOD			
Dr	Woodvale	24	A 8
TRAINE			
Ct	Heathridge	19	B 9
TRALEE			
Rd	Floreat	59	B 8
Wy	Waterford	83	D 6
TRANBY			
Ct	Beldon	23	E 2
St	Madora	160	C 9
Wy	Rowethorpe	144	
TRANGIE			
Wy	Westfield	106	B10
TRANMERE			
Pl	Craigie	23	E 4
TRANMORE			
Wy	City Beach	58	D 5
TRANQUIL			
Dr	Neerabup	16	A 5
Dr	Neerabup	15	E 7
Rd	Kelmscott	107	A10
TRANSIT			
Rd	Jarrahdale	151	C 3
Wy	Mullaloo	23	C 4
TRANSOM			
Wy	Ocean Reef	23	A 1
Wy	Ocean Reef	19	A10
TRAPEZE			
Ct	Ocean Reef	23	B 2
TRAPPERS			
Dr	Woodvale	24	B 6

		Map	Ref.
TRASK			
Dl	Clarkson	14	D 2
TRATTON			
St	Balga	46	D 3
TRAVANCORE			
St	Maylands	61	E 8
TRAVERS			
Gns	Kelmscott	117	A 1
St	Spearwood	101	B 5
Wy	Swan View	51	C 8
TRAVERSE			
Rd	Mullaloo	23	C 4
TRAYLEN			
Rd	Bayswater	62	A 7
Rd	Kalamunda	77	C 7
Rd	Mt Helena	54	D 4
Rd	Stoneville	54	C 4
TREASURE			
Pl	Singleton	160	D 4
Rd	Queens Park	84	E 3
Rd	Singleton	160	D 4
Rd	Welshpool	85	A 2
Rd	Welshpool	75	B10
TREAVE			
St	Cloverdale	74	E 6
TREBY			
Pl	Leeming	92	E 8
St	Armadale	116	E 8
TREDALE			
Ave	Armadale	116	E 8
TREEBY			
Rd	Anketell	132	A 2
Rd	Anketell	123	A 5
St	Coolbellup	91	D10
TREE HAVEN			
Vs	Leeming	102	E 1
TREEN			
St	Balga	32	A 9
TREE TOP			
Ave	Edgewater	24	A 1
Ave	Edgewater	20	A10
TREETOP			
Ci	Canning Vale	104	B 1
Ci	Canning Vale	94	B10
TREFFONE			
St	Redcliffe	63	A 9
TREGENNA			
Pl	Gooseberry H	77	D 2
TRELION			
Pl	Rivervale	74	C 6
TRELLIS			
Pl	Spearwood	101	A 8
TREMANDRA			
Wy	Lynwood	94	B 3
TREMLETT			
St	Thornlie	95	B 4
TREMONT			
Pl	Craigie	23	D 7
TRENT			
Ct	Koondoola	33	B 8
St	Gosnells	96	A10
St	Viveash	50	B 5
TRENTON			
Wy	Duncraig	31	B 7
TREPHINA			
Me	Clarkson	14	E10
TREROSE			
Cl	Erskine	164	C 6
TRESCO			
Pl	Bentley	84	A 4
TRESIDDER			
Rd	Lockridge	49	B 6
TRESISE			
St	Carine	45	C 1
St	Carine	31	C 9
TRESTRAIL			
Ave	Roleystone	108	B 6

For detailed information regarding the street referencing system used in this book, turn to page 170.

251

U

	Map Ref.
TREVALLY	
Pl Golden Bay	158 D 9
Wy Sorrento	30 C 3
TREVALLYN	
Gns South Lake	102 C 7
TREVITHICK	
Cl Stirling	45 E 10
TREVOR	
Ct Roleystone	108 A 9
TRIAN	
Rd Carabooda	8 C 7
TRIBUTE	
St E Riverton	83 E 9
St W Shelley	83 D 10
TRICHET	
Rd Wanneroo	21 B 9
TRICIA	
Ct Shelley	83 D 9
TRICOURT	
Gr Riverton	93 E 1
TRIDENT	
Tce Willetton	93 D 7
Wy Mirrabooka	33 B 10
TRIESTE	
Ct Mindarie	14 B 6
TRIFUND	
Ct Merriwa	10 B 10
TRIGG	
Pl North Lake	92 A 10
Pl Trigg	44 C 6
TRILLER	
Pl Huntingdale	105 C 1
St Stirling	45 D 6
TRIMBLE	
Rd Gidgegannup	41 A 3
TRINIDAD	
St Safety Bay	145 B 1
TRINITY	
Ave East Perth	73 C 4
Ct Safety Bay	137 A 9
Wy Kingsley	24 B 9
TRINK	
St Cloverdale	75 A 5
TRINNICK	
Pl Booragoon	92 D 2
TRIPOD	
Pl Mullaloo	23 B 3
TRIPOLI	
Pl Currambine	19 A 3
TRISTANIA	
Ri Duncraig	31 B 8
TRISTRAM	
Gns Parmelia	131 A 9
TRITON	
Ave Waikiki	145 C 5
Cr Bedfordale	117 A 6
Ct Riverton	84 A 10
Pl Mullaloo	23 B 4
TRITONIA	
Wy Thornlie	94 E 7
TRIUMPH	
Ave Wangara	25 B 7
TROCHIDAE	
Wy Heathridge	23 E 1
TROODE	
St Munster	101 A 10
St West Perth	60 D 10
TROON	
Ce Connolly	19 B 8
Ct St James	84 B 4
Ct Yanchep	4 E 2
Gr Halls Head	164 B 2
Pl Westfield	106 C 6
TROPICAL	
Gns Ballajura	33 C 7
TROPICANA	
Wy Safety Bay	145 A 2

	Map Ref.
TROSS	
Gr Willetton	93 C 7
TROTMAN	
Cr Yanchep	4 C 3
TROTT	
Rd Lesmurdie	87 E 2
TROTTER	
Rd Walliston	88 B 1
TROUBRIDGE	
Rt Ocean Reef	18 E 7
TROUT	
Ct Sorrento	30 C 3
TROY	
Ave Marmion	30 C 8
Pl San Remo	163 C 1
St Applecross	82 B 8
St Bassendean	62 E 1
St Bassendean	48 E 10
Tce Daglish	71 E 2
TROYTOWN	
Wy Melville	91 E 1
TRUARN	
St Mandurah	163 C 10
TRUGANINA	
Rd Malaga	48 A 2
Rd Malaga	47 C 3
TRUMPER	
Rd Manning	83 C 6
TRURO	
Ct Yanchep	4 C 5
Pl City Beach	58 D 10
TRUSCAN	
Cl Cooloongup	137 C 9
TRUSLEY	
Wy Karrinyup	44 E 2
TRUSLOVE	
Wy Duncraig	30 E 8
TRUSMORE	
Cr Craigie	23 E 5
TRUSTING	
La White Gum Vly	90 E 6
TRUSTY	
Gr Stratton	51 A 3
TRYAL	
Rt Currambine	19 A 2
TSAVO	
St Mundaring	54 C 10
TUAM	
Cl Waterford	83 D 6
St Victoria Park	73 E 9
TUART	
Ave Mandurah	165 B 2
Ct Thornlie	95 A 10
Dr Baldivis	157 D 5
Pl Morley	48 B 4
Pl Yangebup	102 A 9
Rd Greenwood	31 C 6
Rd Lesmurdie	87 D 3
Rd Oakford	132 D 2
Rd Oakford	123 D 10
Rge Parmelia	131 B 10
St Applecross	82 B 5
St Hamilton Hill	91 A 10
St Yokine	60 D 1
TUART TRAIL	
Edgewater	24 B 2
TUBLIA	
Ct Karawara	83 C 4
TUCK	
St Armadale	116 D 5
TUCKER	
St Medina	130 D 5
TUCKETT	
St Carlisle	74 B 10
TUCKEY	
St Mandurah	165 A 1

	Map Ref.
TUCKFIELD	
St Fremantle	1 D 3
St Fremantle	90 C 3
Wy Nollamara	46 D 6
TUCUMA	
Ct Warnbro	145 E 8
TUDOR	
Av N Shelley	83 E 8
Av S Riverton	83 E 10
Rd Armadale	116 D 6
TUFFIN	
Rd Glen Forrest	66 C 1
TUG	
Ce Merriwa	14 C 1
Ce Merriwa	11 C 10
TULARE	
Tn Joondalup	19 D 2
TULIP	
Pl Dianella	46 E 5
TULIPWOOD	
Pl South Lake	102 D 4
TULL	
Ct High Wycombe	64 D 10
TULLAMORE	
Ave Thornlie	95 D 5
Cl Waterford	83 C 7
TULLEY	
Ct Rockingham	137 B 9
TULLOCH	
Cl Brigadoon	169 B 2
Ct Jandabup	21 B 8
Wy Byford	126 A 1
TULLOW	
Rd Floreat	59 A 9
TULLY	
Ct Bull Creek	93 A 6
Ct Ocean Reef	19 A 6
TULSA	
Ct Mindarie	14 A 3
TULSE	
Ri Kingsley	24 B 9
TUMBA	
Ct Joondalup	19 D 2
TUMMELL	
Ct Armadale	116 B 3
TUMUT	
Pl Merriwa	11 C 8
Rd City Beach	58 D 10
TUNDER	
St Wanneroo	20 E 8
TUNIS	
Pl Coogee	101 A 10
TUNNEL	
Rd Swan View	51 D 6
TUNNEY	
Rd Peel Estate	132 E 6
TUNNICLIFFE	
St Parmelia	131 A 9
TUPELO	
Ct Greenwood	31 D 4
TUPPER	
Pl Bateman	92 E 6
TURANA	
Pl Rockingham	137 A 9
TURF	
Ct Greenmount	51 B 9
TURFAN	
Wy Munster	101 B 9
TURLEY	
Ct Langford	94 E 2
Wy Langford	94 E 2
TURNATT	
Wy Wanneroo	20 E 8
TURNBERRY	
Cl Meadow Sprgs	163 C 5
Pl Connolly	19 C 8

	Map Ref.
TURNBULL	
Rd Neerabup	16 B 3
Wy Trigg	44 D 4
TURNER	
Ave Bentley	83 D 2
Cl Duncraig	30 E 8
Gr Lesmurdie	87 C 5
Pl Kelmscott	106 D 6
Rd Byford	135 B 4
Rd Carmel	88 C 7
Rd Kelmscott	107 A 5
St Highgate	61 B 10
St Maddington	96 C 4
St Serpentine	155 A 4
St Warnbro	145 C 7
TURNSTONE	
Dr Two Rocks	2 D 1
Rd Stirling	45 D 6
TURO	
Cl Willetton	93 E 1
TURON	
St Morley	48 C 7
TURPIN	
Pl Parmelia	131 A 8
TURRAMURRA	
Wy Greenwood	31 B 3
TURRET	
Rd Willetton	93 D 6
TURRIFF	
Rd Floreat	59 C 8
TURSTIN	
Glen Kiara	48 E 6
TURTON	
St Guildford	49 E 10
St Nth Fremantle	90 D 1
St Nth Fremantle	80 D 10
TURVEY	
La Mundaring	54 B 10
TUSCAN	
Pl Rossmoyne	93 B 1
St Rossmoyne	93 B 1
Wy Gnangara	26 A 5
TUSCANY	
Wy Churchlands	59 A 6
TUSCARORA	
Rt Connolly	19 A 6
TUXEN	
Pl Bull Creek	93 A 5
Pl Hillarys	30 B 2
TWAIN	
Cl Munster	101 B 10
TWEED	
Cl Warnbro	145 E 6
Cl Westfield	106 C 6
Cr Coolbinia	60 E 4
TWEEDDALE	
Rd Applecross	82 C 5
TWELFTH	
Rd Forrestdale	115 D 7
TWICKENHAM	
Dr Kingsley	31 A 1
Dr Kingsley	24 A 9
Dr Kingsley	24 A 10
Rd Victoria Park	73 E 6
TWILIGHT	
Me Merriwa	11 D 9
TWIN	
Vw Swan View	51 C 5
TWIN BRANCH	
Ri Leeming	103 A 2
TWINING	
Pl Mirrabooka	33 A 10
TWOMEY	
Pl Willetton	93 E 3
TWO ROCKS	
Rd Two Rocks	2 D 4
Rd Yanchep	3 A 7
Rd Yanchep	4 C 1

	Map Ref.
TWYFORD	
Ct Duncraig	31 A 4
Pl Innaloo	45 D 10
TYBALT	
Pl Coolbellup	101 E 1
TYDEMAN	
Rd Nth Fremantle	90 B 1
TYERS	
Rd Roleystone	108 A 6
Rd Roleystone	107 E 6
Wy Kardinya	92 B 6
TYLER	
St Joondanna	60 B 3
St Tuart Hill	60 B 1
St Tuart Hill	46 B 9
St Tuart Hill	46 B 10
TYNDALL	
Vs Alexander Hts	33 B 4
TYNE	
Ct Safety Bay	136 E 10
St Dianella	47 A 10
TYNEMOUTH	
Cl Merriwa	11 C 10
TYNESIDE	
Gr Currambine	19 C 5
Rt Meadow Sprgs	163 D 1
TYRANT	
Cl Willetton	93 D 7
TYRE	
Ave Riverton	84 A 10
TYRELL	
St Nedlands	71 E 10
TYRRELL	
Ct Edgewater	20 A 9
TYSON	
Pl Quinns Rocks	10 A 10

U

	Map Ref.
UDALL	
Pl Gwelup	45 C 5
UFTON	
St Gwelup	45 C 5
ULCOMBE	
St Kenwick	95 E 1
St Marangaroo	32 B 6
ULLAPOOL	
Rd Applecross	82 D 6
Rd Mt Pleasant	82 D 7
ULLSWATER	
Gl Joondalup	19 D 1
Pl Balga	32 C 10
ULLYOTT	
St Kelmscott	116 D 1
ULM	
Ct Thornlie	95 A 7
St Osborne Park	60 A 3
ULRIC	
Ct Duncraig	30 E 8
ULRICH	
St Wembley Dns	59 B 5
ULSTER	
Rd Floreat	59 B 9
UMINA	
Pl Armadale	116 B 7
St High Wycombe	64 C 9
UNDERDALE	
Pl Coodanup	165 C 4
UNDERWOOD	
Ave Floreat	71 B 1
Ave Floreat	71 C 1
Gr Kardinya	91 E 6
UNGAROO	
Rd Balga	46 C 4
UNICORN	
Pl Craigie	23 E 7

252

For detailed information regarding the street referencing system used in this book, turn to page 170.

V

		Map	Ref.
UNION			
Rd	Carmel	88	D 8
St	Bayswater	62	A 3
St	North Perth	60	E 6
St	Subiaco	72	A 3
UNNARO			
St	Hillman	137	D 6
UNWIN			
Ave	Wembley Dns	59	A 4
Cr	Salter Point	83	B 9
UPHAM			
St	Jolimont	59	E 10
St	Wembley	60	A 10
UPLANDS			
Gns	Willetton	93	C 7
UPNOR			
St	Wilson	84	A 8
UPPSLA			
Pl	Canning Vale	94	C 8
UPSON			
Ct	Leeming	93	C 8
UPTON			
Pl	Langford	94	E 1
Rd	High Wycombe	64	A 10
St	St James	84	A 2
URALLA			
Wy	Martin	97	E 10
URANA			
Rd	Armadale	116	C 4
URAWA			
Rd	Duncraig	30	D 5
St	Dianella	47	B 7
URBAHNS			
Cr	Bateman	92	D 7
Wy	Hillarys	30	B 2
URCH			
Rd	Kalamunda	77	C 7
Rd	Roleystone	107	D 7
URCHIN			
Me	Waikiki	145	B 3
UREN			
St	Morley	48	A 9
URILLA			
Me	Currambine	19	A 5
URINGA			
Wy	Wanneroo	20	E 10
URLICH			
Cl	Leeming	102	E 1
URQUHART			
Pl	Kewdale	74	E 8
URSA			
Pl	Kingsley	31	B 2
URWICK			
Ct	North Lake	92	A 10
USHER			
Pl	Wattleup	121	C 3
UTAH			
Gr	Joondalup	19	D 3
UTINGA			
Pl	Lynwood	94	C 4
UTLEY			
Rd	Peel Estate	154	A 9

V

		Map	Ref.
VAAL			
Gr	Joondalup	19	D 3
VAGG			
St	Bull Creek	93	A 6
VAHLAND			
Ave	Riverton	93	E 1
Ave	Riverton	83	E 10
Ave	Willetton	93	E 3
VAL			
St	Rockingham	137	A 4

		Map	Ref.
VALANCE			
Wy	Gwelup	45	C 5
VALCAN			
Rd	Orange Grove	86	D 7
Rd	Wattle Grove	86	D 6
VALE			
Rd	Hazelmere	64	B 4
Rd	High Wycombe	64	B 6
St	Fremantle	90	D 3
St	Malaga	33	D 9
St	Mt Lawley	61	A 7
VALENCIA			
Ave	Churchlands	59	B 6
Ct	Alexander Hts	33	A 5
Gr	Armadale	117	A 4
Rd	Carmel	88	D 7
Wy	Maddington	86	B 10
VALENTINE			
Ave	Dianella	47	C 9
Dr	Greenfields	165	E 1
Dr	Greenfields	163	E 10
Rd	Kelmscott	116	D 1
Rd	Perth Airport	63	B 6
St	Kewdale	75	B 7
VALENTINO			
Cl	Greenfields	163	E 9
VALENTO			
Rd	Pickering Bk	89	A 6
VALERIAN			
Wy	Thornlie	94	E 7
VALERIE			
St	Dianella	61	C 1
VALEST			
Pl	Darlington	65	E 3
VALIANT			
Cl	Lesmurdie	87	E 3
VALKYRIE			
Pl	Gosnells	95	E 10
Pl	Two Rocks	3	B 10
VALLACK			
Gr	Mirrabooka	32	E 10
VALLE			
Ct	Wandi	123	C 6
VALLEY			
Cl	Canning Vale	104	A 1
Rd	Halls Head	162	C 9
Rd	Kalamunda	77	E 7
Rd	Wembley Dns	58	E 5
VALLEY BROOK			
Rd	Caversham	49	B 6
VALLEY VIEW			
Rd	Mundaring	54	B 9
Rd	Roleystone	108	A 7
VALLEYVIEW			
Trl	Canning Vale	94	B 10
VALMAE			
Rd	Riverton	93	C 1
VALONIA			
Rd	Langford	94	E 3
VANCE			
Cl	Kingsley	24	D 10
Pl	Bull Creek	93	B 7
St	Mandurah	165	A 3
St	Thornlie	95	B 4
VANDA			
Pl	Maddington	96	B 5
VANDEN			
Wy	Joondalup	19	D 6
VANDERLIN			
Rt	Merriwa	11	D 10
VANESSA			
Rd	Falcon	162A	D 9
Wy	Swan View	51	C 5
VANGUARD			
Ct	Port Kennedy	156	C 4
VANSTON			
Ct	Westfield	106	B 10
VARCOE			
Rd	Koondoola	32	E 7

		Map	Ref.
VARINA			
Ct	Alexander Hts	33	A 5
VARLEY			
Cr	Cooloongup	137	C 10
St	Lesmurdie	87	C 5
St	Riverton	93	E 1
VARNA			
Ce	Mindarie	14	B 5
Pl	Coolbellup	92	A 10
VARRIS			
Wy	Orelia	131	A 4
VARUNA			
Wy	Waikiki	145	C 3
VASSE			
Ct	Yangebup	101	E 10
VASTO			
Pl	Balcatta	46	A 3
VAUCLUSE			
Ave	Claremont	71	B 9
Pl	Kallaroo	23	A 6
VAUGHAN			
Pl	Hamilton Hill	101	C 1
St	Dianella	61	B 1
VAUGHEY			
Rd	Quinns Rocks	10	A 10
VAUX			
St	Rockingham	136	D 5
VEER			
Ct	Ocean Reef	19	B 10
VEGA			
St	Falcon	162A	E 10
St	Wembley Dns	59	A 5
VEITCH			
St	Bayswater	62	B 5
VELA			
Ct	Rockingham	137	B 8
VELDT			
Me	Mirrabooka	33	B 10
VELIGER			
Ct	Heathridge	19	D 10
VELLGROVE			
Ave	Lynwood	94	C 4
VELSHEDA			
Grn	Ocean Reef	18	E 7
VENICE			
Ct	Dianella	47	A 6
VENN			
St	North Perth	61	A 7
St	Peppermint Gr	80	D 4
VENOSA			
Ct	Heathridge	23	D 1
VENTNOR			
Ave	Mt Pleasant	82	D 9
Ave	West Perth	72	C 2
St	Scarborough	58	D 2
VENTURA			
Ct	Willetton	94	A 2
VENTURE			
Ri	Ballajura	33	D 5
VENTURER			
Ct	Thornlie	95	C 9
VENTURI			
Dr	Ocean Reef	23	A 2
Dr	Ocean Reef	19	A 10
VENUS			
Ct	Greenfields	163	E 10
St	Bateman	92	D 3
Wy	Hillarys	23	B 9
VERA			
Rd	Darlington	66	A 6
Rd	Darlington	65	E 7
St	Cottesloe	80	D 2
St	Gosnells	96	D 10
St	Morley	47	E 9
VERA VIEW			
Pde	Cottesloe	70	C 9
VERBENA			
Cr	Dianella	46	E 4
Pl	Greenmount	65	E 1
Pl	Willetton	93	C 2

		Map	Ref.
VERCO			
Ct	Booragoon	92	B 1
VERDELHO			
Dr	Ellenbrook	29	C 1
VERDON			
Pl	Riverton	94	A 1
VERDUN			
St	Belmont	74	D 2
St	Nedlands	71	E 6
VERESDALE			
Rt	Coodanup	165	D 3
VERMONT			
Ave	Meadow Sprgs	163	C 4
St	Nollamara	46	C 6
VERNA			
Rd	Jandakot	102	E 8
St	Gosnells	106	A 4
St	Gosnells	96	C 10
St	Gosnells	105	E 5
VERNAL			
Vi	Greenmount	51	B 10
VERNALLAN			
Wy	Lesmurdie	77	C 10
VERNON			
Ave	Mundaring	68	A 6
Pl	Padbury	30	D 2
Pl	Spearwood	101	C 5
St	Noranda	47	D 4
St	Trigg	44	D 4
VERNS			
Ce	Woodvale	24	B 4
VERONA			
Cr	Falcon	162A	D 9
VERONICA			
St	Riverton	83	E 10
VEROS			
Pl	Marangaroo	32	D 5
VERRILL			
Wy	Armadale	116	D 8
VERSTEEG			
Gr	Martin	98	A 9
Gr	Martin	97	E 9
VERTICORDIA			
Pl	Greenwood	31	C 6
Rd	Walliston	87	E 2
VERTON			
Dr	Shelley	83	E 8
VERVAIN			
Wy	Riverton	84	A 9
VESTA			
Cr	Shelley	83	D 10
VESTAL			
Cl	Iluka	19	A 5
VESTEY			
Ct	Duncraig	31	A 8
VESTITA			
Ri	Halls Head	164	A 5
VIA VISTA			
Dr	Mariginiup	17	E 6
VICKERS			
St	Hamersley	46	A 1
St	Stirling	45	E 1
VICKERY			
St	Rockingham	136	D 5
VICTA			
Rd	Jandakot	103	C 3
VICTOR			
Rd	Darlington	66	A 6
Rd	Darlington	65	E 7
St	Highgate	61	B 10
St	Hilton	91	B 7
St	Newburn	75	C 7
VICTORIA			
Ave	Claremont	71	A 10
Ave	Claremont	81	B 1
Ave	Dalkeith	81	C 3
Ave	Perth City	1C	A 4
Ave	Perth City	73	A 4

		Map	Ref.
Ci	Greenfields	163	E 8
Ct	Craigie	23	E 6
Ct	Thornlie	95	B 8
Pde	Midvale	50	E 9
Rd	Balga	46	B 2
Rd	Beechboro	48	D 2
Rd	Hovea	53	A 5
Rd	Hovea	52	E 5
Rd	Kenwick	86	A 9
Rd	Malaga	48	A 2
Rd	Malaga	47	C 2
Rd	Wattle Grove	86	C 7
Rd	West Swan	50	A 2
Rd	West Swan	49	C 2
Sq	Perth City	1C	A 3
Sq	Perth City	73	A 3
St	Dianella	47	D 10
St	Guildford	49	C 10
St	Midland	50	B 8
St	Mosman Park	80	D 6
St	Redcliffe	62	E 5
St	Rockingham	137	B 3
St	South Perth	73	A 8
St	St James	84	B 3
St	West Perth	60	E 9
St N	Redcliffe	62	E 8
Wy	Osborne Park	46	A 10
VICTORIA QUAY			
Rd	Fremantle	90	B 4
Rd	Fremantle	1D	B 5
VICTORSEN			
Pde	Clarkson	14	D 3
VICTORY			
Pl	Lesmurdie	87	A 2
VIDICOMBE			
Ri	Leeming	102	E 1
VIDLER			
St	Cloverdale	75	A 4
VIETNAM			
Ave	Swanbourne	70	D 8
VIEW			
Ave	Langford	94	E 1
Ct	Edgewater	24	E 1
Rd	Mt Pleasant	82	E 6
Rd	Safety Bay	145	B 3
St	Dianella	47	D 8
St	Halls Head	162	D 10
St	Kelmscott	107	D 8
St	Kensington	73	C 9
St	Maylands	61	D 8
St	North Perth	60	E 8
St	Peppermint Gr	80	E 3
St	Subiaco	72	A 3
St	Yangebup	111	C 2
Tce	Bicton	81	B 10
Tce	Darlington	65	E 4
Tce	East Fremantle	81	A 10
Tce	East Fremantle	80	E 10
Tce	Quinns Rocks	10	A 9
Wy	Kalamunda	77	B 7
VIEWCREST			
Ri	Coogee	100	E 8
Wy	Sorrento	30	C 5
VIEWPOINTE			
Ce	Ballajura	33	D 8
VIEWWAY			
	Nedlands	71	E 10
	Swan View	51	E 7
VIGILANT			
Tce	Ocean Reef	18	E 7
VIGNA			
Pl	Ferndale	84	C 9
VIGORS			
Ave	Bull Creek	93	A 6
Ct	Duncraig	30	E 8
VIKING			
Rd	Dalkeith	81	C 2
Rd	Waikiki	145	B 5
VILAMOUR			
Cl	Currambine	19	B 6
VILBERIE			
Wy	Kiara	48	E 7

For detailed information regarding the street referencing system used in this book, turn to page 170.

W

		Map	Ref.
VILLA			
Ct	Kallaroo	23	A 8
VILLAGE			
Pl	Mosman Park	80	D 6
Wk	Ocean Reef	18	E 10
VILLANOVA			
St	Wanneroo	24	D 4
VILLAWOOD			
Dr	Coodanup	165	D 4
VILLIERS			
St	Bassendean	63	A 5
St	Bassendean	62	E 4
St	Yokine	46	D 9
Wy	Lynwood	94	C 4
VINCA			
Wy	Forrestfield	76	B 8
VINCENT			
Ave	Balga	46	B 5
Rd	Dianella	61	B 2
Rd	Wanneroo	20	D 5
St	Bassendean	62	E 4
St	Leederville	60	D 9
St	Mt Lawley	61	A 9
St	Nedlands	71	C 10
St	North Perth	60	D 9
St W	Leederville	60	B 8
VINE			
Ct	Greenwood	31	D 4
Ct	Kenwick	95	E 1
Rd	Karnup	159	E 9
St	Herne Hill	36	C 7
St	North Perth	60	E 8
VINES			
Ave	Ellenbrook	29	B 1
Ct	Leeming	93	C 1
VINEYARD			
Rw	Swan View	51	D 5
VINNICOMBE			
Dr	Canning Vale	94	A 6
VINTAGE			
La	Gnangara	26	A 4
VINTEN			
Ri	Leeming	92	E 8
VIOLA			
Ct	Lynwood	94	B 1
VIOLET			
Ave	Shelley	83	C 10
Gr	Shenton Park	71	E 5
St	Middle Swan	50	C 6
St	Mosman Park	80	D 5
St	West Perth	60	E 9
VIRGIL			
Ave	Yokine	61	B 2
Ave	Yokine	60	E 2
VIRGILIA			
St	Duncraig	30	E 6
Tce	South Lake	102	E 5
Wy	Forrestfield	76	B 10
VIRGINIA			
Ave	Maddington	96	B 6
VIRGO			
Cl	Greenfields	163	E 10
VISCOUNT			
Ct	Thornlie	95	C 7
Rd	Morley	47	D 8
VISSER			
St	Coolbellup	101	D 1
VISTA			
Ave	Rockingham	136	D 5
Cl	Balcatta	45	E 5
Cl	Edgewater	24	B 2
Ct	Morley	48	D 6
Dr	Parkerville	53	E 4
Gr	Armadale	117	A 3
Pde	Ballajura	33	C 5
Pl	Safety Bay	145	A 1
St	Kensington	73	C 9
VISTULA			
Ave	Beechboro	48	E 3
Tce	Kelmscott	106	E 7

		Map	Ref.
VIVEASH			
Rd	Middle Swan	50	D 4
Rd	Midland	50	C 9
Rd	Stratton	51	D 3
Rd	Swan View	51	D 5
VIVIAN			
St	Rivervale	74	A 3
St	Rivervale	73	E 3
Wy	Boya	65	D 5
VIX			
St	Dalkeith	81	D 1
VLAMING			
Ri	Coogee	100	E 10
VLAMINGH			
Pde	Mosman Park	80	C 8
VODICE			
St	Wattleup	121	C 2
VOLANTE			
El	Ocean Reef	18	E 6
VOLGA			
Ct	Beechboro	48	E 4
Pl	Greenfields	165	D 2
VOLICH			
Pl	Swan View	51	C 7
VOLOS			
Ce	Mindarie	14	C 5
VOLTA			
Wy	Wilson	84	A 6
VOLTAIRE			
Vs	Merriwa	11	D 9
VOLUNTEER			
Pl	Ocean Reef	18	E 8
VOLUTE			
Pl	Mullaloo	23	B 5
VOYAGE			
Rd	Heathridge	23	C 1
VOYAGER			
Ct	Cooloongup	137	D 8
Dr	Thornlie	95	C 8
VULCAN			
Rd	Canning Vale	94	A 6
Ri	Iluka	18	E 4

W

		Map	Ref.
WADDELL			
Ct	Middle Swan	50	E 4
Rd	Bicton	81	C 10
Rd	Palmyra	91	C 1
St	Kewdale	74	D 6
WADDINGHAM			
Wy	Medina	130	E 5
WADDINGTON			
Cr	Koondoola	33	A 8
WADE			
Cl	Duncraig	30	E 7
Ct	Girrawheen	32	C 7
Ct	Leeming	93	C 8
Sq	Stratton	51	A 4
St	Embleton	62	A 1
St	Embleton	48	B 10
St	Gosnells	96	B 10
St	Joondanna	60	B 2
St	Mariginiup	20	E 3
St	Perth City	61	A 10
St	Silver Sands	163	B 5
WADHURST			
St	Balga	46	D 3
WAGOORA			
Pl	Koongamia	65	B 2
Wy	Koongamia	65	B 2
WAGTAIL			
Ri	Ballajura	33	E 8
WAHROONGA			
Rd	Kelmscott	116	E 2
Wy	Greenwood	31	B 3
Wy	Greenwood	31	B 4

		Map	Ref.
WAIDUP			
St	Wanneroo	20	E 9
WAIGEN			
Pl	South Lake	102	D 8
WAIKIKI			
Rd	Safety Bay	145	A 1
Rd	Safety Bay	137	A 10
WAIMEA			
Rd	Safety Bay	144	D 1
Rd	Safety Bay	136	D 9
WAINWRIGHT			
Cl	Willetton	93	C 7
WAITARA			
Cr	Greenwood	31	B 4
WAITE			
Ct	Lynwood	94	A 2
Pl	City Beach	58	D 6
WAKATIPU			
Wy	Joondalup	19	D 3
WAKE			
Ct	Redcliffe	63	A 9
St	Dianella	47	C 10
WAKEFIELD			
Pde	Currambine	19	A 6
Rd	High Wycombe	64	C 10
St	Carlisle	74	B 8
WAKEHURST			
Pl	Kelmscott	106	D 10
WAKELAN			
Ce	Dianella	47	A 7
WAKELEY			
Pl	Duncraig	30	D 9
WAKELIN			
Cl	Woodvale	24	B 4
WAKELY			
Cs	Jandakot	103	A 3
WALANNA			
Dr	Karawara	83	D 5
WALBA			
Pl	Coogee	101	A 9
Wy	Swanbourne	70	C 9
WALBECK			
Rd	Kalamunda	77	B 7
WALCHA			
St	Mullaloo	23	A 4
Wy	Armadale	116	A 6
WALCOTT			
St	Coolbinia	60	D 4
St	Menora	61	A 6
St	Mt Lawley	61	B 8
WALDECK			
Rd	Caversham	49	C 5
St	Mosman Park	80	C 6
WALDEMAR			
St	Gwelup	45	C 5
WALDEN			
Pl	Morley	47	E 8
WALDERTON			
Ave	Balga	46	C 3
WALDING			
Rd	Carabooda	7	E 1
WALDON			
St	Wilson	84	B 6
WALDORF			
St	Carine	45	C 2
WALDRON			
Blvd	Greenfields	163	D 10
WALES			
Ct	Clarkson	14	C 1
St	Forrestfield	86	C 1
WALGA			
Ct	Yokine	60	D 2
WALGEN			
Ct	Wanneroo	20	D 10
WALGREEN			
Cr	Calista	130	E 7
Pl	Calista	130	E 6

		Map	Ref.
WALJERIN			
Rd	Gooseberry H	77	D 2
WALKER			
Ave	Rockingham	136	D 5
Ave	West Perth	72	C 2
Cr	High Wycombe	76	B 1
Cr	High Wycombe	64	B 10
Ct	Kardinya	92	A 8
Pl	Gosnells	106	A 2
Rd	Serpentine	154	C 6
Rd N	Serpentine	150	C 10
St	Mt Helena	55	B 4
St	Mundaring	54	B 9
St	Sawyers Valley	54	C 10
St	Sth Fremantle	90	C 10
St	Wembley	60	A 6
St	Yanchep	4	C 3
WALKINGTON			
Wy	Eden Hill	48	E 8
WALL			
St	Maylands	62	A 10
WALLABA			
Wy	Lesmurdie	87	B 5
WALLABY			
Pl	Wungong	116	B 10
Wy	Chidlow	41	D 5
WALLACE			
Ct	Duncraig	31	A 5
St	Belmont	62	D 10
WALLANGARRA			
Ct	Kingsley	31	E 3
Dr	Bedfordale	128	A 4
Dr	Bedfordale	127	E 3
WALLAWA			
St	Wanneroo	20	B 5
WALLER			
Pl	Innaloo	45	C 9
St	Armadale	116	A 1
St	Lathlain	74	A 6
St	Rockingham	137	A 5
WALLEROO			
Pl	Rockingham	137	B 5
WALLIABUP			
Wy	Bibra Lake	102	C 5
WALLINGTON			
Rd	Balga	32	B 10
WALLIS			
Ct	Greenmount	51	E 9
La	Lesmurdie	87	E 4
WALLSEND			
St	Safety Bay	136	E 9
WALLWORK			
Cl	Hilton	91	A 9
WALMSLEY			
Dr	Noranda	48	A 5
WALNEY			
Ave	Dianella	46	E 9
Wy	Dianella	46	E 9
WALNUT			
Rd	Bickley	89	A 2
Rd	Bickley	88	D 3
Rd	Pickering Bk	89	C 6
WALPOLE			
Pl	Clarkson	14	D 1
Pl	Clarkson	11	D 10
St	Bentley	84	A 4
St	St James	84	A 4
St	Swanbourne	70	D 9
WALSH			
Ave	Redcliffe	75	A 2
Pl	Booragoon	92	C 2
WALTER			
Cl	Bateman	92	D 4
Cr	Embleton	48	A 9
Pl	Nth Fremantle	80	C 10
Rd E	Bassendean	49	A 9
Rd E	Bayswater	48	D 9
Rd W	Bedford	61	D 2
Rd W	Dianella	61	C 2
Rd W	Inglewood	61	C 4
Rd W	Morley	48	A 9

		Map	Ref.
Rd W	Morley	47	D 10
St	Claremont	71	B 9
St	Coodanup	165	E 9
St	East Fremantle	90	E 1
St	Gosnells	96	A 10
Wy	Hamersley	31	C 10
WALTER PADBURY			
Blvd	Padbury	30	E 3
WALTERS			
Dr	Osborne Park	60	A 4
Dr	Osborne Park	59	E 3
Rd	Byford	126	D 5
St	South Perth	73	A 10
WALTHAM			
Ct	Armadale	116	D 2
Ct	Bateman	92	D 2
Rd	Armadale	116	D 2
St	Mullaloo	23	A 4
Wy	Morley	48	B 8
WALTON			
Cr	Mundijong	143	A 6
Pl	Quinns Rocks	10	A 1
St	Bayswater	62	B 6
St	Queens Park	84	E 3
WALYUNGA			
Blvd	Clarkson	14	D 1
Rd	Upper Swan	166	C 4
St	Lesmurdie	87	D 4
WAMBA			
Rd	Coodanup	165	C 8
WAMPUM			
Pl	Heathridge	23	D 1
WANAPING			
Rd	Kenwick	85	D 10
WANBROW			
Wy	Duncraig	30	E 4
WANDANA			
Cl	Iluka	18	E 5
WANDARRA			
Cl	Karawara	83	C 4
WANDARRIE			
Ave	Yokine	60	E 1
WANDEARA			
Cr	Mundaring	68	D 1
WANDEARAH			
Wy	Kingsley	31	D 1
WANDI			
Dr	Wandi	123	C 4
WANDILLA			
Me	Iluka	18	D 5
WANDINA			
Pl	Duncraig	30	D 5
WANDOO			
Dr	Baldivis	157	E 4
Rd	Duncraig	30	E 6
Rd	Forrestfield	76	E 10
Rd	Morley	48	C 4
St	Kelmscott	116	E 1
WANDU			
Rd	Greenmount	51	E 9
WANGALLA			
Pl	Koongamia	65	B 1
Rd	Koongamia	65	B 1
WANGOOLA			
Tce	Armadale	116	E 5
WANILL			
Pl	Wanneroo	20	C 8
WANJEEP			
St	Coodanup	165	C 7
St	Coodanup	165	D 4
WANJINA			
Cr	Wanneroo	20	E 10
WANLISS			
St	Jarrahdale	152	E 7
St	Rockingham	137	A 4
WANN			
Ct	Upper Swan	29	E 2
WANNDINA			
Ave	Dianella	47	B 7

W

		Map	Ref.
WANNEROO			
Rd	Balga	32	A 8
Rd	Balga	46	B 2
Rd	Carabooda	8	B 4
Rd	Girrawheen	32	A 7
Rd	Joondanna	60	D 2
Wy	Landsdale	32	A 2
Rd	Marangaroo	32	A 4
Rd	Neerabup	16	A10
Rd	Neerabup	15	B 2
Rd	Nollamara	46	C 7
Rd	Nowergup	12	A 7
Rd	Nowergup	11	D 2
Rd	Tuart Hill	60	D 1
Rd	Wangara	24	E 8
Rd	Wanneroo	20	B 3
Rd	Wanneroo	24	D 4
Rd	Yanchep	5	E 8
WANNYNE			
St	Mandurah	163	B 8
WANSTEAD			
Ct	Madora	160	C 8
St	Gwelup	45	B 5
WANUI			
St	Falcon	162A	C 1
WAPENGO			
Cl	South Lake	102	E 7
WARAKER			
Rd	Hillarys	30	C 3
Wy	Leeming	93	A 9
WARATAH			
Ave	Dalkeith	81	C 2
Blvd	Canning Vale	104	A 1
Blvd	Canning Vale	94	A10
Ct	Hillarys	30	A 1
Ct	Maddington	96	C 4
Dr	Westfield	106	B 7
Pl	Dalkeith	81	B 2
Rd	Morley	48	C 5
WARBLER			
Cl	Edgewater	24	B 1
Ct	High Wycombe	76	C 1
WARBROOK			
Pl	Coodanup	165	C 3
WARBURTON			
Ave	Padbury	30	D 1
WARBY			
La	Clarkson	14	E10
WARD			
Ave	Greenmount	51	E10
Cr	Kelmscott	106	D 8
Ct	Langford	95	A 1
Pl	Embleton	62	A 2
Rd	E Rockingham	129	D10
St	Mandurah	163	B10
St	Samson	91	C 9
WARDALL			
Pl	Morley	48	C 5
WARDE			
St	Midland	50	D 7
WARDELL			
Lp	Dudley Park	165	C 5
WARDEN			
St	Claremont	71	B 8
WARDIE			
St	Sth Fremantle	90	C 8
WARDLE			
Pl	Hamilton Hill	90	E 9
Rd	Hamilton Hill	90	E 9
WARDLOW			
Wy	Balga	32	B10
WARDONG			
Pl	Wanneroo	20	C 9
Rd	Balga	46	C 5
WARE			
St	Embleton	62	B 2
St	Rockingham	137	A 6
WAREANA			
St	Menora	61	A 3

		Map	Ref.
WARFIELD			
Pl	Martin	97	D10
WARILDA			
Ct	Currambine	19	A 5
WARING			
Wy	Kardinya	91	E 6
WARLINGHAM			
Dr	Lesmurdie	87	C 2
WARMAN			
Ct	Leeming	92	E 9
St	Neerabup	16	A 3
WARNBRO BEACH			
Rd	Safety Bay	145	B 3
Rd	Waikiki	145	B 4
WARNBRO SOUND			
Ave	Port Kennedy	156	E 1
Ave	Warnbro	145	D 6
WARNER			
Dr	Padbury	23	E 9
La	Rockingham	137	A 8
Pl	Greenwood	32	A 4
Rd	High Wycombe	64	C 9
Rd	Parmelia	131	B 7
WARNES			
St	Maylands	61	E 7
WARNHAM			
Rd	Cottesloe	80	C 2
WAROONGA			
Rd	Nedlands	71	C10
WARRAGOON			
Cr	Attadale	81	E 9
WARRAJAH			
St	Stirling	45	D 7
WARRALONG			
Cr	Coolbinia	60	E 3
WARRAMUNGA			
Pl	Rockingham	137	B 5
WARRANDYTE			
Dr	Craigie	23	E 4
Dr	Craigie	23	E 5
WARREEN			
Pl	City Beach	58	D 5
WARREGO			
St	Kensington	73	C10
WARREN			
Ave	Bayswater	62	A 3
Pl	Mandurah	165	A 4
Rd	Maida Vale	76	D 1
Rd	Yokine	60	E 1
St	Gosnells	96	A10
St	Hilton	91	A 9
Wy	Mullaloo	23	A 5
WARRI			
Rd	City Beach	58	D 3
WARRIDA			
Wy	Maddington	96	C 3
WARRIE			
St	Golden Bay	158	E 7
WARRIGAL			
Wy	Chidlow	43	A 3
Wy	Greenwood	31	C 4
WARRINA			
Pl	Armadale	116	C 4
WARRINGAH			
Cl	Kallaroo	23	A 6
WARRINGTON			
Rd	Byford	135	B 4
Rd	Lesmurdie	87	B 3
WARRIOR			
Hts	Padbury	31	A 2
WARRUGA			
Wy	Wanneroo	20	B 5
WARSAW			
Pl	Joondanna	60	E 1
WARTON			
Rd	Banjup	114	A 2
Rd	Banjup	104	B10
Rd	Banjup	113	E 3

		Map	Ref.
Rd	Canning Vale	105	A 2
Rd	Canning Vale	104	D 6
Rd	Thornlie	95	C 9
St	Cottesloe	80	C 5
WARUP			
St	Mandurah	163	B 9
WARWICK			
Pl	Girrawheen	32	B 6
Pl	Willetton	93	E 3
Rd	Duncraig	31	A 6
Rd	Marmion	30	E 6
Rd	Sorrento	30	D 6
Rd	Warwick	32	A 6
Rd	Warwick	31	E 6
St	Claremont	71	B10
St	Leederville	60	B 9
St	St James	84	A 3
WASDALE			
Ct	Balga	32	D10
WASHER			
St	E Victoria Pk	84	A 2
WASHINGTON			
St	Victoria Park	73	D 7
WASLEY			
St	Mt Lawley	61	A 9
St	North Perth	61	A 9
WATER			
St	Redcliffe	63	A 6
WATERBURY			
St	Dianella	47	B 8
WATEREDGE			
Rd	Thornlie	95	B 8
WATERFALL			
Ce	Greenfields	165	E 2
Rd	Forrestfield	86	E 2
WATERFORD			
Ave	Waterford	83	D 6
Dr	Gidgegannup	40	A 5
Dr	Gidgegannup	39	E 6
Dr	Hillarys	30	B 1
Dr	Hillarys	30	C 2
St	Inglewood	61	D 5
WATERHALL			
Rd	Sth Guildford	64	A 2
Rd	Sth Guildford	64	A 4
Rd	Sth Guildford	63	E 5
WATERLOO			
Cr	East Perth	73	C 3
Cr	Lesmurdie	87	A 2
Rd	Alexander Hts	33	B 3
Rd	Cooloongup	137	E 8
St	Joondanna	60	B 3
St	Tuart Hill	60	B 1
St	Tuart Hill	46	B10
WATERSBY			
Cr	Shelley	83	D 8
WATERSIDE			
Dr	Mandurah	164	E 5
Pl	South Lake	102	C 7
Rt	Wilson	84	B 9
WATERSTON			
Gns	Hillarys	23	A 9
Pl	Erskine	164	D 5
WATERSUN			
Dr	Silver Sands	163	B 4
WATERTON			
Wy	Cooloongup	137	C 9
WATERVIEW			
Pde	Redcliffe	62	E 7
WATERVILLE			
Rt	Meadow Sprgs	163	C 6
Tr	Connolly	19	B 8
WATERWAY			
Cr	Armadale	116	A 3
Ct	Churchlands	59	D 7
WATERWHEEL			
Rd	Bedfordale	127	C 1
Rd	Bedfordale	117	D10
WATERWORKS			
Rd	Forrestdale	115	C 6

		Map	Ref.
WATFORD			
Pl	Kelmscott	106	D 9
WATKINS			
Pl	Dalkeith	81	C 1
Rd	Dalkeith	81	B 1
Rd	Mundijong	143	A 9
St	Eden Hill	49	B 8
St	Fremantle	90	D 6
St	Hilton	91	A 6
St	White Gum Vly	90	D 6
WATKINSON			
Ct	Armadale	116	A 4
WATLING			
Ave	Lynwood	94	C 1
WATSON			
Ave	Coodanup	165	D 6
Hl	Winthrop	92	A 4
Pl	Maylands	61	E 9
Pl	Ocean Reef	19	A10
Rd	Mundaring	69	E 6
Rd	Mundaring	69	E10
Rd	Yangebup	111	C 2
St	Bassendean	63	A 3
St	Gosnells	96	A 9
WATSONIA			
Rd	Gooseberry H	77	A 1
Rd	Gooseberry H	77	A 3
Rd	Gooseberry H	65	A10
St	Maddington	96	C 5
WATT			
Rd	Noranda	48	A 5
St	Hillarys	30	B 1
St	Stirling	45	E 9
St	Swanbourne	70	D 8
WATTEN			
Pl	Duncraig	31	A 7
WATTERTON			
Pl	Hamilton Hill	101	B 3
WATTLE			
Av E	Nowergup	13	B 8
Av W	Neerabup	12	A 9
Ave	Dalkeith	81	C 3
Ave	Gooseberry H	77	B 3
Ave	Mandurah	165	B 3
Ave	Rowethorpe	144	
Cl	Westfield	106	C 9
Ct	Baldivis	157	E 4
Ct	Bibra Lake	102	B 5
Ct	Mahogany Crk	67	D 1
Dr	Morley	48	D 5
Me	Wanneroo	24	E 1
Pl	Balcatta	46	C 8
Pl	Canning Vale	104	A 1
Rd	Serpentine	154	C 7
St	South Perth	73	A 9
St	Tuart Hill	60	C 1
St	Tuart Hill	46	C10
Wy	Huntingdale	95	D 8
WATTLEBIRD			
Pl	Wungong	116	C10
WATTLEGLEN			
Ave	Erskine	164	A 9
WATTLEUP			
Rd	Wattleup	122	A 2
Rd	Wattleup	121	D 2
WATTON			
Ct	Swan View	51	C 8
WATTS			
Pl	Bentley	83	D 2
Pl	Leeming	93	A 9
Rd	Shoalwater	136	C10
Rd	Shoalwater	144	D 1
Rd	Wilson	84	A 9
WAUGH			
Ct	North Lake	92	A10
St	Mt Pleasant	82	E 8
St	North Perth	60	E 6
WAUHOP			
Rd	East Fremantle	80	E 9
WAVEL			
Ave	Riverton	93	D 1
Ave	Riverton	83	D10

		Map	Ref.
WAVELEA			
St	Safety Bay	145	B 2
WAVELL			
Rd	Dalkeith	81	D 3
WAVERLEY			
Pl	Dianella	47	B 9
Rd	Coolbellup	92	A10
Rd	Coolbellup	101	E 1
Rd	Coolbellup	91	E10
Rt	Mt Claremont	71	A 4
St	Dianella	47	B10
St	Shenton Park	71	E 4
St	South Perth	73	A 9
Wy	Lynwood	94	C 4
WAVERTON			
Ct	Kallaroo	23	A 6
WAVERTREE			
Pl	Leederville	60	C 7
WAWANNA			
Pl	Huntingdale	95	D 9
WAXBERRY			
Cl	Halls Head	164	A 6
WAXHAM			
Pl	North Beach	44	D 2
WAY			
Rd	South Perth	73	C 7
WAYEELA			
Pl	City Beach	58	D 5
WAYFARER			
Rd	Heathridge	19	C 9
WAYLEN			
Rd	Greenmount	66	A 1
Rd	Greenmount	52	A 1
Rd	Shenton Park	71	D 4
St	Guildford	49	D10
WAYMAN			
St	Mt Pleasant	92	D 1
WEABER			
Ct	Marangaroo	32	C 6
WEAPONESS			
Rd	Scarborough	58	E 1
Rd	Wembley Dns	58	E 3
WEARNE			
Wy	Yangebup	112	A 3
WEATHERBURN			
Wy	Kardinya	91	D 6
WEATHERILL			
Wy	Noranda	47	D 5
WEATHERLEY			
Dr	Two Rocks	2	C 1
Pl	Halls Head	164	D 2
WEAVELL			
St	Hamilton Hill	91	A10
WEAVER			
Ct	Kardinya	92	A 6
Ct	Noranda	47	E 5
La	Leda	139	B 1
WEBB			
Pl	Hillarys	23	C10
Rd	Mundijong	142	E 5
St	Cottesloe	80	D 3
St	Gosnells	96	A 9
St	Rossmoyne	93	B 3
WEBBER			
La	Baldivis	139	E10
Pl	Dianella	47	A 7
St	Willagee	91	C 5
WEBSTER			
Rd	Forrestfield	76	D 9
St	Nedlands	71	D10
WEDDALL			
Rd	Lockridge	49	A 6
WEDGE			
Ct	Cooloongup	137	E 8
Ct	Merriwa	10	B 9
Pl	Bentley	84	D 4
Rd	Yangebup	112	A 3
WEDGETAIL			
Ct	Wungong	116	B 9

For detailed information regarding the street referencing system used in this book, turn to page 170.

W

		Map	Ref.
WEDGEWOOD			
Dr	Edgewater	24	A 2
WEEBILL			
St	Stirling	45	D 7
WEEBO			
St	Golden Bay	158	D 7
WEEKS			
Pl	Beechboro	49	B 3
Wy	Bull Creek	93	B 7
WEELARA			
Rd	City Beach	58	D 3
WEEMA			
Ct	Swan View	51	B 8
WEEROO			
Pl	Stirling	45	E 7
WEIR			
Cr	Beckenham	85	C 7
Pl	Bateman	92	D 5
Pl	Morley	48	C 5
Rd	Malaga	33	D 10
Rd	Millendon	168	E 8
WELBOURN			
Rd	Swan View	51	D 8
WELBOURNE			
Hts	Parmelia	131	C 7
WELBURN			
St	Nollamara	46	E 8
WELBY			
Pl	Myaree	92	A 1
WELCH			
Rd	Roleystone	108	B 7
Wy	Warnbro	145	C 8
WELD			
Ave	Perth City	1C	A 1
Ave	Perth City	73	A 1
Ct	Morley	48	A 9
Pl	Woodvale	24	B 5
Rd	Palmyra	91	B 1
Rd	Swan View	51	B 8
Sq W	Morley	48	A 9
St	Forrestdale	114	E 6
St	Nedlands	71	C 8
St	Rockingham	137	C 2
WELDON			
Wy	City Beach	58	D 5
WELDWOOD			
Rd	Ocean Reef	23	B 2
WELL			
Pl	Bibra Lake	102	C 5
WELLA			
Ct	Coolbellup	101	D 3
WELLAND			
Wy	Beechboro	48	C 3
WELLARD			
Gr	Woodvale	24	C 5
Rd	E Rockingham	130	B 8
Rd	Leda	131	A 10
Rd	Leda	139	C 1
Rd	Leda	130	C 8
St	Bibra Lake	101	D 9
St	Serpentine	154	E 3
WELLATON			
St	Midland	50	E 7
St	Midvale	50	E 8
WELLER			
Rd	Hovea	53	B 10
WELLESLEY			
Wy	Samson	91	C 2
WELLINGTON			
Ct	Alexander Hts	33	B 6
Pde	Yokine	60	E 2
Pl	West Perth	1C	D 1
Pl	West Perth	72	D 1
Rd	Dianella	47	C 7
Rd	Morley	47	E 9
St	East Perth	1C	B 3
St	East Perth	73	A 2
St	Mosman Park	81	A 6
St	Mosman Park	80	D 6
St	Perth City	73	A 2

		Map	Ref.
St	Perth City	1C	E 2
St	Queens Park	85	A 5
St	West Perth	1C	D 1
St	West Perth	72	D 1
WELLMAN			
St	Guildford	63	D 1
St	Guildford	49	D 10
St	Perth City	61	A 10
WELLS			
Ct	Noranda	48	B 5
Pl	Bull Creek	92	E 5
Pl	Calista	130	E 9
Pl	Padbury	23	D 9
Rd	Kwinana Beach	129	D 8
Rd	Yangebup	111	C 3
St	Bellevue	64	D 1
St	Bellevue	50	D 10
St	Mariginiup	20	D 3
WELLSTEAD			
Wy	Coodanup	165	C 2
WELSH			
Ct	Leeming	103	A 1
Pl	Landsdale	25	D 9
WELSHPOOL			
Rd	Carmel	88	A 7
Rd	Carmel	87	D 6
Rd	E Cannington	85	C 3
Rd	Lesmurdie	87	A 5
Rd	Queens Park	85	C 3
Rd	Wattle Grove	86	A 4
Rd	Welshpool	84	C 1
WELTON			
St	Balcatta	46	A 5
WELWYN			
Ave	Manning	83	B 8
Ave	Salter Point	83	B 7
Ave	Yanchep	4	D 3
WENDEN			
Pl	Willetton	94	A 2
WENDLEBURY			
Wy	Eden Hill	48	D 9
WENDLING			
Rd	North Beach	44	D 7
WENDO			
Ct	Hillman	137	D 6
WENDOUREE			
Rd	Wilson	84	A 6
WENDOWIE			
Pl	Serpentine	154	E 3
WENDRON			
St	Cloverdale	75	A 6
WENLOCK			
Rd	Wattleup	121	D 2
WENN			
Rd	Singleton	160	D 4
WENTLETRAP			
Wy	Mullaloo	23	B 3
WENTWORTH			
Gr	Morley	48	D 7
Pde	Jandakot	113	A 4
Pde	Jandakot	112	E 2
St	Cottesloe	80	D 1
St	Yanchep	4	E 2
Wy	Padbury	23	D 8
WERNDLEY			
St	Armadale	116	B 7
WERONA			
Ct	Willetton	93	C 6
WERRIBEE			
Cr	Willetton	93	E 2
WESBANK			
Vs	Ocean Reef	18	E 7
WESCAP			
Ri	Merriwa	11	C 10
WESCO			
Rd	Nowergup	13	A 3
Rd	Nowergup	12	B 4

		Map	Ref.
WESLEY			
St	Balcatta	46	B 8
St	Sth Fremantle	90	D 8
WESSEX			
St	Carine	45	B 1
St	Carine	31	C 10
WEST			
Ct	Bull Creek	93	A 7
Pde	East Perth	61	C 10
Pde	Hazelmere	64	A 1
Pde	Mt Lawley	61	C 9
Pde	Sth Guildford	64	A 1
Pde	Sth Guildford	63	D 2
Rd	Bassendean	63	B 3
St	West Perth	72	C 1
Tce	Kalamunda	77	A 6
Tce	Maida Vale	77	A 4
WESTALL			
Tce	Leeming	92	E 9
WESTBORNE			
Rd	Roleystone	108	A 7
WESTBOROUGH			
St	Scarborough	44	C 10
WESTBOURN			
Ps	Erskine	164	C 6
WESTBOURNE			
Wy	Lynwood	94	D 1
WESTBROOK			
St	Calista	130	D 7
Wy	Girrawheen	32	D 8
WESTBURY			
Cr	Bicton	91	A 1
Cr	Bicton	81	A 10
Rd	South Perth	73	C 8
WESTCHESTER			
Rd	Malaga	47	C 1
Rd	Malaga	33	C 10
WEST CHURCHILL			
Ave	Munster	111	B 3
WEST COAST			
Dr	Marmion	30	C 8
Dr	North Beach	44	C 2
Dr	Sorrento	30	B 4
Dr	Trigg	44	C 6
Dr	Waterman	30	C 10
Hwy	City Beach	58	C 7
Hwy	City Beach	70	D 1
Hwy	Scarborough	44	C 8
Hwy	Scarborough	58	D 2
Hwy	Sorrento	30	B 5
Hwy	Swanbourne	70	D 5
Hwy	Trigg	44	C 4
Hwy	Waterman	30	C 10
Tce	Trigg	44	C 7
WESTCOTT			
Rd	Medina	130	D 6
Rd	Serpentine	154	B 10
WESTER			
Cl	Currambine	19	A 4
WESTERHAM			
Wy	Huntingdale	95	D 9
WESTERLY			
Cr	Heathridge	19	D 9
Wy	Cooloongup	137	C 9
WESTERN			
Ave	High Wycombe	64	B 9
Ave	Yokine	46	D 9
La	Welshpool	84	D 2
Pl	High Wycombe	64	B 9
WESTFIELD			
Rd	Armadale	116	A 2
Rd	Kelmscott	106	C 8
Rd	Westfield	106	B 10
St	Maddington	96	A 3
St	Maddington	96	B 4
WESTGATE			
Ct	Leeming	102	E 1
Wy	Marangaroo	32	A 3
WESTHAM			
Ct	Kingsley	24	A 9

		Map	Ref.
WESTHAVEN			
Dr	Woodvale	24	A 7
WESTLAKE			
Rd	Morley	48	A 7
Rd	Morley	47	E 7
St	Wilson	84	A 7
WESTLAKES			
Blvd	Ballajura	33	C 7
WESTLAND			
Pl	Waterford	83	D 6
WEST LORNE			
St	Floreat	59	B 8
WESTMINSTER			
Ct	Armadale	116	E 5
Ct	Willetton	93	E 5
Gr	Port Kennedy	156	D 2
Pl	Alexander Hts	33	B 6
Rd	Leeming	93	A 9
St	E Victoria Pk	74	A 10
St	E Victoria Pk	83	E 2
WESTMORLAND			
Dr	Leeming	93	B 8
St	E Victoria Pk	83	E 2
WESTON			
Ave	South Perth	73	B 7
Dr	Swan View	51	D 6
Rd	Pickering Bk	89	A 7
Rd	Pickering Bk	88	E 10
St	Carlisle	74	B 7
St	Maddington	96	A 3
St	Naval Base	121	A 8
Tce	Kelmscott	107	A 8
Wy	Kardinya	91	E 9
WESTONS			
Rd	Pickering Bk	99	D 5
WESTRA			
Gr	Ocean Reef	18	E 6
WESTRALIA			
Gns	Rockingham	137	B 6
St	East Perth	61	C 10
WESTRAY			
Ct	Warnbro	145	C 9
WEST SWAN			
Rd	Belhus	29	C 6
Rd	Caversham	49	D 9
Rd	Henley Brook	36	B 3
Rd	Henley Brook	29	B 10
Rd	West Swan	36	A 8
Rd	West Swan	49	C 1
WEST VIEW			
Blvd	Mullaloo	23	A 3
WESTVIEW			
Cl	Armadale	117	A 3
Pl	Greenmount	65	E 1
St	Karrinyup	44	E 7
St	Scarborough	58	E 1
St	Scarborough	44	E 10
WESTWARD			
St	Willetton	93	C 6
WESTWELL			
St	Beckenham	85	B 9
WESTWIND			
Hts	Iluka	18	E 3
WETHERED			
St	Leeming	93	B 8
WETHERELL			
Rd	Belhus	28	C 6
WEXFORD			
Ct	Waterford	83	C 6
WEYDALE			
St	Doubleview	59	A 2
WHALEBACK			
Ave	Lynwood	94	C 4
Hts	Alexander Hts	33	B 3
WHARF			
St	Cannington	84	E 6
St	Queens Park	85	A 4
St	Wilson	84	D 7
WHARFING			
La	Beaconsfield	90	D 8

		Map	Ref.
WHARTON			
Rd	Wattle Grove	75	E 10
WHATLEY			
Cr	Bayswater	62	A 5
Cr	Bayswater	62	B 5
Cr	Maylands	61	E 6
Cr	Mt Lawley	61	C 8
WHEALMARY			
Ct	Padbury	31	A 2
WHEARE			
Ct	Winthrop	92	C 5
WHEATCROFT			
Rd	Darlington	66	A 2
St	Scarborough	44	D 9
WHEATLEY			
Ct	Greenwood	31	C 6
Dr	Bull Creek	93	A 7
Pl	Kewdale	74	D 7
Pl	Morley	48	B 8
St	Gosnells	96	B 8
St	Kewdale	74	D 7
WHEATSTONE			
Dr	Kiara	48	D 7
Dr	Morley	48	C 7
WHEELER			
Rd	Hamilton Hill	101	A 1
Rd	Karrinyup	44	E 7
St	Belmont	74	C 2
St	Morley	47	E 9
WHEELWRIGHT			
Gns	Leda	139	C 3
Rd	Lesmurdie	87	C 3
WHELAN			
Rd	Kardinya	91	E 7
WHELK			
Pl	Mullaloo	23	B 3
WHEYLAND			
St	Willagee	91	E 5
WHILEY			
Ct	Rockingham	137	A 9
Rd	Marmion	30	C 9
WHIMBREL			
St	Stirling	45	D 7
WHIPPLE			
St	Balcatta	45	D 2
WHISTLEPIPE			
Ct	Forrestfield	76	E 8
WHISTLER			
Cl	Edgewater	24	B 2
Grn	Wungong	116	C 10
WHISTON			
Cr	Clarkson	14	C 2
WHITBURN			
Rd	Kingsley	24	C 10
WHITBY			
Ct	Bentley	84	B 5
El	Mindarie	14	C 6
St	Mundijong	143	A 8
WHITCOMBE			
Wy	Alexander Hts	33	A 4
WHITE			
Pl	Subiaco	60	C 10
Rd	Kalamunda	77	D 7
Rd	Orange Grove	86	D 7
Rd	Quinns Rocks	10	A 1
St	Bayswater	62	C 3
St	Mt Helena	55	B 4
St	Nth Fremantle	80	C 10
St	Osborne Park	46	A 10
WHITECAP			
Ct	Edgewater	24	A 1
WHITECHAPEL			
La	Kingsley	24	B 10
WHITECHURCH			
Me	Port Kennedy	156	E 2
WHITEGUM			
Ct	Marangaroo	32	D 4
WHITEHALL			
Rd	Hazelmere	64	A 2

256   **For detailed information regarding the street referencing system used in this book, turn to page 170.**

W

		Map	Ref.
WHITEHAVEN			
Cr	Balga	32	C 10
WHITEHEAD			
St	Singleton	160	D 2
WHITEHOUSE			
Dr	Koondoola	32	E 9
WHITELEY			
Rd	Wungong	116	A 10
WHITELY			
St	Hamersley	45	E 1
WHITEMAN			
Rd	Hazelmere	64	C 1
Rd	Midland	50	C 10
St	Thornlie	95	A 6
WHITEPEAK			
Pl	Padbury	30	E 2
WHITESIDE			
St	Cloverdale	75	A 4
WHITEWOOD			
St	Greenwood	31	C 5
WHITFELD			
St	Floreat	71	D 1
Tce	Winthrop	92	B 4
WHITFIELD			
Dr	Two Rocks	2	D 3
Rd	Bassendean	63	A 4
St	Rockingham	137	C 7
WHITFORDS			
Ave	Hillarys	30	A 2
Ave	Hillarys	23	A 8
Ave	Kingsley	24	A 8
Ave	Padbury	23	D 8
WHITHAM			
Rd	Perth Airport	75	C 4
WHITING			
Ct	Sorrento	30	C 4
WHITLAM			
St	Chidlow	41	D 8
St	Mt Helena	55	B 1
St	Mt Helena	41	B 10
WHITLEY			
Cr	Karrinyup	44	D 7
Ct	Meadow Sprgs	163	D 6
WHITLOCK			
Cr	South Lake	102	C 6
WHITMORE			
Pl	Coolbellup	101	E 2
WHITNELL			
Gns	Murdoch	92	D 7
WHITNEY			
Cr	Mt Claremont	71	A 4
Pl	Alexander Hts	33	A 4
WHITSUNDAY			
Ave	Merriwa	11	D 10
WHITTAKER			
Cr	Armadale	116	A 2
Cr	Bull Creek	93	A 7
St	Bayswater	62	A 5
WHITTINGTON			
Ave	Carine	30	D 9
St	Kelmscott	117	A 2
WHITTLE			
Ct	Bicton	91	A 1
Pl	Stirling	45	E 9
WHITTLESFORD			
St	E Victoria Pk	84	A 2
WHITTOCK			
St	Embleton	62	B 1
WHITTOME			
St	Middle Swan	50	D 4
WHITTON			
Ct	Kingsley	31	B 2
St	Hamilton Hill	100	E 1
WHITWORTH			
Ave	Girrawheen	32	C 8
Pl	Noranda	47	C 5
WHOLLEY			
St	Bayswater	62	A 7

		Map	Ref.
WHYALLA			
St	Willetton	93	C 2
WHYATT			
Pl	Parmelia	131	C 8
WICCA			
St	Kewdale	74	D 5
St	Rivervale	74	C 4
WICHMANN			
Rd	Attadale	81	C 8
WICKENS			
St	Beckenham	85	C 6
WICKHAM			
Pl	Ascot	62	E 7
Pl	East Perth	1C	B 3
Pl	East Perth	73	B 3
Pl	East Perth	1C	B 3
St	East Perth	73	B 3
WICKLING			
Dr	Beckenham	85	B 7
WICKLOW			
St	Halls Head	162	C 10
St	Thornlie	95	C 5
WICKS			
St	Bassendean	62	D 3
St	Eden Hill	48	D 9
WIDDICOMBE			
Pl	Myaree	91	E 2
St	Myaree	91	E 2
WIDGEE			
Rd	Caversham	49	B 4
Rd	Noranda	48	A 4
Rd	Noranda	47	C 4
WIDGEON			
Cl	Stirling	45	D 7
WIGGINS			
Cl	Greenwood	32	A 6
Rd	Orelia	131	B 5
WILBER			
St	Rossmoyne	93	B 2
WILBERFORCE			
St	Mt Hawthorn	60	D 6
St	North Beach	44	C 3
WILBY			
Pl	Bentley	84	B 4
Pl	Thornlie	94	E 6
St	North Beach	44	D 5
WILCANNIA			
Cr	Currambine	19	A 4
Wy	Armadale	116	C 4
WILCOCK			
Ave	Balcatta	46	B 7
WILD			
Cl	Bull Creek	93	B 7
Rd	Hillarys	23	C 9
St	Beckenham	85	B 9
WILDE			
St	Embleton	62	A 1
WILDFLOWER			
Dr	Neerabup	16	A 6
WILDING			
St	Doubleview	45	A 9
St	Karrinyup	45	A 7
WILDON			
St	Bellevue	50	D 10
WILDWOOD			
Hts	Leeming	103	A 1
WILEY			
Pl	Cannington	84	E 4
WILFORD			
Rd	Baldivis	139	E 9
WILFRED			
Ct	Thornlie	95	A 3
Rd	Canning Vale	104	A 2
Rd	Canning Vale	103	A 3
St	Thornlie	94	B 3
WILGA			
Ct	Banjup	113	D 9
St	Maddington	96	C 4

		Map	Ref.
WILGERUP			
Pl	Hillman	137	E 6
WILKES			
St	Hamilton Hill	101	B 1
WILKIE			
Ave	Yanchep	4	B 4
St	Sth Guildford	63	C 2
St	Stirling	46	A 6
St	Stirling	45	E 6
WILKINS			
Rd	Kalamunda	77	E 10
Rd	Mt Helena	55	D 6
St	Bellevue	64	E 1
St	Bellevue	50	E 10
St	Halls Head	164	C 1
WILKINSON			
Ct	Wellard	132	D 10
Gns	Winthrop	92	B 6
Rd	Baldivis	148	C 5
Rd	Baldivis	140	D 9
Rd	Baldivis	147	E 10
St	Fremantle	91	A 4
St	Gosnells	106	B 2
WILLANDRA			
Pl	Hillarys	23	B 9
WILLARA			
Rd	Gooseberry H	77	C 4
WILLARING			
Dr	Beckenham	85	A 9
WILLCOCK			
Ave	Daglish	71	E 2
St	Ardross	82	C 8
St	Ferndale	84	D 9
Wy	Joondalup	19	D 7
WILLCOX			
St	Chidlow	56	C 1
WILLERI			
Dr	Canning Vale	94	A 6
Dr	Willetton	94	A 3
WILLESDEN			
Ave	Kingsley	31	B 3
WILLIAM			
Rd	Coodanup	165	E 9
Rd	Mt Helena	55	A 1
Rd	Mt Helena	41	A 10
St	Armadale	116	D 7
St	Ascot	62	B 10
St	Beckenham	85	B 7
St	Byford	126	D 10
St	Cottesloe	70	E 10
St	E Cannington	85	D 4
St	Fremantle	1D	C 5
St	Fremantle	90	C 5
St	Glen Forrest	66	D 3
St	Herne Hill	37	A 3
St	Highgate	61	A 9
St	Midland	50	B 8
St	Mt Lawley	61	A 8
St	Northbridge	1C	A 1
St	Perth City	61	A 10
St	Perth City	1C	E 3
St	Perth City	72	E 3
St	Rockingham	136	E 5
St	Shenton Park	72	A 3
St	Wattle Grove	85	E 3
WILLIAMBURY			
Dr	Yangebup	112	A 1
Dr	Yangebup	111	E 1
Dr	Yangebup	101	E 10
WILLIAMS			
Ct	Melville	91	D 2
Pl	Ocean Reef	23	A 1
Rd	Armadale	116	A 5
Rd	Coolbellup	91	C 10
Rd	Coolbellup	101	D 1
Rd	Dianella	46	E 8
Rd	Kelmscott	116	C 2
Rd	Melville	91	D 1
Rd	Melville	81	D 10
Rd	Nedlands	71	E 8
Rd	Nollamara	46	E 8
St	Gooseberry H	77	C 2
St	Kalamunda	77	D 5

		Map	Ref.
WILLIAMSON			
Ave	Belmont	74	D 1
Ave	Cloverdale	74	E 3
La	Stratton	51	B 4
Rd	Kardinya	92	A 8
St	Bayswater	62	B 7
Wy	Trigg	44	D 3
WILLIAMSTOWN			
Rd	Doubleview	59	A 3
Rd	Woodlands	59	B 3
WILLIS			
Rd	Hamilton Hill	90	E 9
St	E Victoria Pk	84	A 1
St	E Victoria Pk	74	A 10
St	Mosman Park	80	D 4
St	Warnbro	145	C 7
WILLITON			
Rd	Karrinyup	44	E 3
WILLMOTT			
Cl	Halls Head	164	A 7
Dr	Cooloongup	137	C 10
Dr	Waikiki	145	D 1
WILLOUGHBY			
Rd	Lesmurdie	87	B 4
Rt	Clarkson	14	D 1
Wy	Swan View	51	C 5
WILLOW			
Ct	Cooloongup	137	C 9
Pl	Beechboro	48	C 4
Rd	Warwick	31	D 8
Rd	Woodlands	59	C 3
Wy	Maddington	96	C 5
Wy	Maida Vale	77	A 3
Wy	Woodlands	59	C 2
WILLOWCREEK			
Me	Woodvale	24	D 9
WILLOWMEAD			
Wy	Westfield	106	C 9
WILLOWS			
Rd	Forrestdale	115	C 10
WILLS			
Cl	Bull Creek	92	E 7
Ct	Cooloongup	137	E 10
Ct	Mirrabooka	33	A 10
Pl	Oakford	124	B 5
Pl	Padbury	23	D 10
St	Bayswater	62	A 7
WILLSHIRE			
Wy	Yangebup	101	E 10
WILMINGTON			
Cr	Balga	46	C 2
WILMORE			
Cl	Woodvale	24	C 7
Grn	Mirrabooka	33	B 10
WILMOT			
Ct	Jandakot	112	E 2
WILNA			
Pl	Helena Valley	65	B 3
WILPON			
St	Beckenham	85	B 9
WILSLEY			
St	Gosnells	96	A 9
WILSMORE			
Gr	Kardinya	91	E 8
St	Daglish	71	D 2
WILSON			
Cr	Wembley Dns	59	A 3
La	Bateman	92	E 3
Pl	Belmont	62	D 9
Pl	Gooseberry H	77	D 1
Pl	Two Rocks	2	D 3
Rd	Chidlow	56	B 3
Rd	Hovea	53	A 3
Rd	Middle Swan	37	A 10
Rd	Padbury	23	D 8
St	Bassendean	63	A 2
St	Cannington	85	A 1
St	Claremont	80	E 1
St	High Wycombe	64	B 8
St	Wungong	126	C 3

		Map	Ref.
WILTON			
Pl	Scarborough	44	D 8
WILTS			
Pl	Leeming	93	B 8
WILUNA			
Ave	White Gum Vly	90	E 7
Ct	Gosnells	95	E 7
St	Coolbinia	60	D 3
WILURA			
Rd	Mundaring	53	E 10
WIMBA			
Pl	Coodanup	165	C 4
WIMBLEDON			
Dr	Kingsley	31	B 2
St	Beckenham	85	A 9
WIMMERA			
Pl	Huntingdale	95	E 10
WIMPOLE			
Ct	Alexander Hts	33	B 4
WINCANTON			
Rd	Karrinyup	44	E 5
WINCH			
Pl	Ocean Reef	19	A 10
WINCHELSEA			
Rd	Nollamara	46	D 4
WINCHESTER			
Rd	Armadale	116	D 2
Rd	Bibra Lake	101	D 8
Wy	Leeming	93	B 8
WINDALE			
Pl	Cooloongup	137	D 10
WINDARRA			
Dr	City Beach	58	D 9
Hts	Marangaroo	32	C 6
Wy	Armadale	116	C 5
WINDELL			
St	Innaloo	45	C 10
WINDELYA			
Rd	Kardinya	92	B 9
WINDEMERE			
Cr	Nollamara	46	D 8
WINDERA			
Cl	Mandurah	165	B 3
WINDERMERE			
Ci	Joondalup	19	D 1
Wy	Greenfields	165	D 1
WINDFIELD			
Rd	Melville	91	D 3
WINDICH			
Ct	Padbury	23	C 9
Pl	Leederville	60	C 8
Rd	Bull Creek	92	E 6
WINDLASS			
Ave	Ocean Reef	23	B 1
Ave	Ocean Reef	19	B 10
WINDMILL			
Dr	Bibra Lake	102	C 4
WINDOO			
Pl	Koongamia	65	B 1
Rd	Parkerville	53	C 6
WINDSOR			
Ave	Dianella	46	E 9
Ave	Roleystone	108	B 9
Ct	Balcatta	46	A 3
Dr	Gosnells	95	D 7
Pl	Kallaroo	23	C 7
Rd	Wangara	25	A 9
St	Claremont	70	E 9
St	East Fremantle	90	E 2
St	East Perth	61	B 10
Wy	Falcon	162A	B 4
WINDWARD			
Cl	Safety Bay	137	A 10
Lp	Ocean Reef	23	A 2
WINDY RIDGE			
La	Kalamunda	77	A 8
WINEBERRY			
Lp	South Lake	102	D 5

For detailed information regarding the street referencing system used in this book, turn to page 170.

257

W

		Map	Ref.
WINERY			
Dr	Karnup	159	C 5
WINFIELD			
Pl	Greenfields	163	E 10
St	Hamilton Hill	100	E 2
St	Lynwood	94	D 1
WINGALA			
Gr	Kallaroo	23	B 8
WINGATE			
Ave	Hazelmere	64	B 1
WINGFIELD			
Ave	Crawley	72	A 7
WINGHAM			
St	Marangaroo	32	A 6
WINGROVE			
Rd	Langford	94	E 3
WINIFRED			
Rd	Bayswater	62	B 4
Rd	Forrestfield	76	A 10
St	Mosman Park	80	D 5
WINJAN			
Pl	Mandurah	164	E 2
WINJANA			
Rd	Lesmurdie	87	C 3
WINMARLEY			
St	Floreat	59	D 9
WINNACOTT			
St	Willagee	91	D 4
WINNIPEG			
Ct	Greenfields	163	D 10
WINNUNGA			
Pl	Armadale	116	B 6
WINSFORD			
St	Karrinyup	44	E 2
WINSHAM			
Rd	Karrinyup	44	E 3
WINSHIP			
Ave	Wanneroo	20	C 7
WINSOR			
Rd	Kalamunda	77	C 8
WINSPORT			
Ct	Merriwa	11	C 10
WINSTANLEY			
Rd	Roleystone	108	B 7
WINSTER			
Cl	Duncraig	31	A 4
Ct	Innaloo	45	D 10
WINSTON			
Cr	Viveash	50	B 5
Rd	Lesmurdie	87	B 2
WINTERBOURNE			
Gl	Maddington	96	C 2
WINTERFOLD			
Rd	Coolbellup	91	D 9
Rd	Hilton	91	B 10
WINTERSWEET			
Pl	Halls Head	164	A 7
Ra	Mirrabooka	47	A 2
WINTERTON			
Wy	Girrawheen	32	D 7
WINTHROP			
Ave	Crawley	72	A 7
Ave	Nedlands	72	A 6
Dr	Winthrop	92	B 5
WINTON			
Rd	Joondalup	19	D 6
St	Kewdale	75	C 8
WINYA			
Wy	Falcon	162A	D 1
WIRIA			
Ct	Wanneroo	20	D 10
WIRILDA			
Cr	Greenwood	31	C 3
Wy	Lynwood	94	B 2
WIRIN			
Rd	Forrestdale	114	E 6
St	Willetton	93	D 4

		Map	Ref.
WIRREGA			
Rd	Jandabup	21	E 5
WIRTH			
Cl	Bull Creek	93	B 5
WISBECH			
St	Bayswater	62	B 6
WISBOROUGH			
Cr	Balga	46	D 1
WISDOM			
Pl	Winthrop	92	C 5
WISE			
Pl	Joondalup	19	D 5
WISHART			
St	Gwelup	45	C 6
WISHAW			
Gr	Leeming	93	D 9
WISTERIA			
Ct	Forrestfield	76	C 7
Gns	Halls Head	164	C 5
Pde	Edgewater	24	A 3
Pl	Thornlie	95	A 8
Wy	Ferndale	94	C 1
WITCOMB			
Pl	South Perth	73	A 7
WITHERS			
Cl	Murdoch	92	B 6
Gr	Woodvale	24	C 5
WITHNELL			
St	Dianella	46	E 7
St	E Victoria Pk	74	B 10
WITLEY			
St	Bayswater	48	C 10
WITNEY			
Pl	Leeming	92	E 8
WITTENBERG			
Dr	Canning Vale	94	C 8
WITTENOOM			
Pl	Duncraig	30	E 8
Rd	High Wycombe	76	A 3
Rd	High Wycombe	64	A 9
St	East Perth	1C	B 1
St	East Perth	73	B 2
WITTERING			
Cr	Balga	46	D 2
WITTON			
Ct	Willetton	93	E 3
WOBURN			
Wy	Kelmscott	106	C 10
WODGINA			
Pl	Kingsley	31	C 2
WODJIL			
St	Heathridge	19	C 10
WOKING			
St	Morley	48	B 8
WOLFE			
Rd	Banjup	123	E 1
Rd	Oakford	124	B 5
WOLLASTON			
Ave	Armadale	116	A 6
Ave	Armadale	115	D 8
Rd	Mt Claremont	70	F 3
WOLLONG			
Pl	Nollamara	46	C 6
WOLSELEY			
Rd	Morley	47	D 7
WOLSELY			
Rd	East Fremantle	90	E 1
WOLYA			
Pl	Balga	46	C 4
Wy	Balga	46	C 4
WOMBAT			
Rd	High Wycombe	76	B 1
WONAMBI			
Wy	Wanneroo	20	C 10
Wy	Wanneroo	24	D 1
WONGA			
Rd	Morley	48	A 6
Rd	Morley	47	E 6

		Map	Ref.
WONGAN			
Ave	Hilton	91	A 6
WONYILL			
St	Wanneroo	24	D 1
St	Wanneroo	20	D 10
WOOD			
Ct	Kardinya	91	E 8
Ct	Leda	138	D 1
Ct	Lesmurdie	87	E 3
Pl	Thornlie	95	B 9
Rge	Edgewater	20	B 10
St	Bassendean	62	D 3
St	Fremantle	90	D 4
St	Inglewood	61	C 3
St	Swanbourne	70	D 8
St	White Gum Vly	90	D 6
WOODALL			
Ct	High Wycombe	64	D 10
Ra	Booragoon	92	B 3
St	Dianella	61	C 1
WOODBINE			
Rd	Pickering Bk	99	E 2
Tce	Mirrabooka	33	B 10
WOODBRIDGE			
Cl	Swan View	51	A 6
Dr	Cooloongup	137	E 7
Dr	Greenmount	51	D 9
Me	Beldon	23	E 2
WOODCHESTER			
Pl	Nollamara	46	D 8
Rd	Nollamara	46	D 8
WOODFORD			
Ct	Koondoola	33	A 8
Rd	Lynwood	94	D 2
WOODFORD WELLS			
Wy	Kingsley	24	B 10
WOODHALL			
St	Stirling	46	A 6
St	Stirling	45	E 6
WOODHAMS			
St	Willagee	91	E 4
WOODHOUSE			
Rd	East Fremantle	80	E 10
Rd	Maylands	61	E 9
Wy	Noranda	47	E 5
WOODLAND			
Dl	Canning Vale	94	A 10
Gr	Maida Vale	64	E 10
Lp	Edgewater	24	A 1
Pde	Lakelands	161	C 10
Pl	Casuarina	132	C 3
St	Jarrahdale	152	E 8
WOODLANDS			
Gr	Wanneroo	24	E 1
Rd	Golden Bay	158	D 7
St	Menora	61	A 6
St	Woodlands	59	B 4
WOODLARK			
Pl	Willetton	93	B 7
WOODLEA			
Cst	Leeming	102	E 1
WOODLEY			
Cr	Melville	91	C 3
Wy	Parmelia	131	A 6
WOODLOES			
St	Cannington	84	E 8
WOODLUPINE			
Ct	Forrestfield	76	B 10
Ri	Woodvale	24	D 9
WOODMAN			
Pl	Beechboro	48	C 3
WOODMAN POINT			
Vw	Munster	110	A 9
WOODMAR			
Me	Dianella	47	B 5
WOODMORE			
Rd	Langford	94	E 3
WOODPECKER			
Ave	Willetton	93	C 4

		Map	Ref.
WOODPINE			
Ct	Ballajura	33	D 5
WOODROFFE			
Pl	Alexander Hts	33	A 4
WOODROW			
Ave	Dianella	61	B 1
Ave	Yokine	61	A 1
Pl	Dianella	61	B 1
St	Queens Park	85	A 4
WOODROYD			
St	Mt Lawley	61	A 7
WOODS			
Cl	Winthrop	92	C 5
Ct	Kingsley	31	C 1
Rd	Perth Airport	63	B 8
WOODSIDE			
St	Doubleview	45	B 9
WOODSOME			
St	Mt Lawley	61	A 6
WOODSPRING			
Gr	Ballajura	33	C 4
Trl	Canning Vale	94	B 9
WOODSTOCK			
St	Mt Hawthorn	60	C 5
WOODTHORPE			
Dr	Willetton	94	A 5
Dr	Willetton	93	E 6
WOODVALE			
Dr	Woodvale	24	C 7
WOODVIEW			
Ct	Edgewater	24	B 1
WOODVILLE			
Hts	Hillarys	23	A 10
St	North Perth	60	E 7
WOODWARD			
Ave	Caversham	49	D 6
Ci	Marangaroo	32	C 6
WOOLCOCK			
Ct	Ashfield	62	E 4
WOOLCOOT			
Rd	Wellard	140	A 3
Rd	Wellard	132	A 10
WOOLEEN			
St	Golden Bay	158	D 8
WOOLERONG			
Wk	Marangaroo	32	D 5
WOOLF			
Ct	North Lake	102	A 1
WOOLGAR			
Wy	Lockridge	49	A 6
WOOLLCOTT			
Ave	Henley Brook	35	D 4
Ave	West Swan	36	A 5
Ave	Whiteman	35	A 4
WOOLLEY			
St	Willetton	93	D 3
WOOLLYBRUSH			
Pl	Bibra Lake	102	B 6
WOOLNOUGH			
Hts	Kardinya	91	D 7
St	Daglish	71	D 2
WOOLOOMOOLOO			
Rd	Greenmount	51	C 10
WOOLOWRA			
Rd	Greenmount	51	C 10
WOOLTANA			
St	Como	83	A 5
WOOLWICH			
Cl	Kallaroo	23	B 7
St	Leederville	60	B 9
WOONAN			
Ct	Karawara	83	C 4
St	Wanneroo	20	B 5
WOONGAN			
St	Southern River	105	E 5
WOONONA			
Pl	Kallaroo	23	C 6

		Map	Ref.
WOORAMEL			
Cr	Gosnells	106	A 3
Cr	Gosnells	105	E 3
St	Heathridge	19	B 9
Wy	Cooloongup	137	E 9
Wy	Nollamara	46	C 8
WOOTLIFF			
Wy	Swan C Homes	144	
WORDSWORTH			
Ave	Gooseberry H	77	D 4
Ave	Yokine	61	B 2
Ave	Yokine	60	E 2
St	Dianella	61	B 2
WORLANNA			
Dr	Currambine	19	A 5
WORLEY			
St	Willagee	91	E 4
WORLINGTON			
Pl	Meadow Sprgs	163	D 5
WORNER			
Cr	Karrinyup	45	B 7
WORONGA			
Pl	Duncraig	30	D 8
WORRALDA			
St	Maida Vale	76	E 2
WORRALL			
Ct	Orelia	131	A 6
WORTEL			
Ct	Wilson	84	B 8
WORTH			
Pde	Ascot	62	E 8
WORTHING			
St	Balga	46	C 3
WORTHINGTON			
Rd	Booragoon	92	C 2
WORTLEY			
Rd	Greenmount	65	B 1
WOTAN			
St	Innaloo	59	C 1
WOTTON			
St	Bayswater	62	C 1
St	Embleton	48	C 10
WRAY			
Ave	Fremantle	1D	C 6
Ave	Fremantle	90	C 6
Cl	Bateman	92	E 4
WREFORD			
Ct	Gosnells	96	B 9
WREN			
Cl	Willetton	93	C 4
Ct	High Wycombe	64	B 10
Ct	Thornlie	95	A 10
Me	Ballajura	33	E 8
Pl	Yangebup	102	A 8
St	Dianella	47	C 8
St	Mt Pleasant	82	D 6
WREXHAM			
St	Bicton	81	B 9
WRIGHT			
Ave	Swanbourne	70	E 4
Cr	Bayswater	62	D 7
Pl	Kelmscott	106	E 6
Pl	Padbury	23	D 10
Rd	Forrestdale	114	B 3
Rd	Forrestdale	104	C 9
Rd	Henderson	111	A 6
Rd	Mundijong	143	A 10
Rd	Mundijong	150	E 4
Rd	Munster	111	A 5
St	Bayswater	62	C 2
St	Cloverdale	74	E 4
St	East Perth	61	B 10
St	Highgate	61	B 10
St	Kewdale	74	D 7
St	White Gum Vly	90	D 7
WRIGLEY			
St	Dianella	47	C 7
WROTHAM			
Pl	Marangaroo	32	B 3

Y

		Map	Ref.
WROXTON			
St	Midland	50	D 7
WROY			
St	Beechboro	49	A 3
WUNGONG			
Cl	Wungong	126	E 4
Rd	Armadale	116	D 10
Rd	Wungong	126	C 2
WUNGONG SOUTH			
Rd	Byford	126	B 6
Rd	Wungong	126	B 3
WYALONG			
Pl	South Lake	102	D 5
WYATT			
Rd	Bayswater	62	D 6
Rd	Wanneroo	25	A 2
WYCHCROSS			
St	Balga	46	C 4
WYCOMBE			
Rd	High Wycombe	76	C 1
Rd	High Wycombe	64	C 10
WYEE			
Pl	Armadale	116	A 6
Pl	Gooseberry H	77	D 1
WYEREE			
Rd	Mandurah	163	B 9
WYGONDA			
Rd	Roleystone	108	A 7
Rd	Roleystone	107	E 7
WYKES			
Ct	Wanneroo	20	C 7
WYLDE			
Rd	Morley	47	D 6
WYLIE			
Ce	Winthrop	92	B 5
Pl	Karrinyup	45	B 6
Pl	Leederville	60	C 7
WYLOO			
Pl	Armadale	116	C 5
WYMAN			
Ct	Girrawheen	32	C 9
WYMOND			
Rd	Roleystone	118	A 2
Rd	Roleystone	117	E 1
WYNDHAM			
St	St James	84	B 2
Wy	Yokine	46	D 9
WYNNE			
St	Hazelmere	64	A 1
St	Hazelmere	50	A 10
WYNNUM			
Pl	Yanchep	4	E 2
WYNYARD			
St	Belmont	74	C 2
St	Yokine	60	D 2
Wy	Thornlie	95	B 4
Wy	Willetton	93	D 7
WYOLA			
St	Cooloongup	137	C 10
WYONG			
Pl	Armadale	116	E 5
Rd	Bentley	84	B 5
WYSS			
La	North Lake	102	A 1
WYTHBURN			
Ave	Balga	46	C 1
Ave	Balga	32	C 10
WYTON			
Pl	Gosnells	96	A 8
WYUNA			
Cr	Lesmurdie	87	C 4

		Map	Ref.
WYVILLE			
Ct	Huntingdale	95	D 9

Y

		Map	Ref.
YACHT			
Ct	Heathridge	23	C 1
YAGOONA			
St	Duncraig	31	B 7
YALATA			
Me	Iluka	18	E 3
YALE			
Rd	Thornlie	95	A 4
Rd	Thornlie	94	E 6
YALGOO			
Ave	White Gum Vly	91	A 6
YALGUN			
Rd	City Beach	58	E 8
YALKE			
St	Gidgegannup	42	A 9
St	Gidgegannup	41	E 9
YALLAMBEE			
Cr	Wanneroo	20	C 9
Pl	City Beach	58	D 5
Pl	Karawara	83	C 5
Wy	Queens Park	84	E 3
YALLAN			
St	Mandurah	163	B 8
YALLUP			
Pl	Cannington	84	D 5
YALTARA			
Rd	City Beach	58	D 4
YAMATO			
Cl	Iluka	18	E 3
YAMBA			
Ct	Halls Head	164	B 4
YAMPI			
Ct	Huntingdale	105	D 1
Wy	Willetton	93	D 2
YANAGIN			
Cr	City Beach	58	E 8
YANCHEP BEACH			
Rd	Yanchep	5	B 4
Rd	Yanchep	4	C 3
YANDINA			
Cl	Duncraig	30	D 8
YANGALA			
Cl	Ocean Reef	19	A 8
YANGEBUP			
Rd	Jandakot	112	D 1
Rd	Yangebup	102	A 10
Rd	Yangebup	111	C 1
Rd	Yangebup	101	D 10
YANGET			
St	Mandurah	163	B 8
YANMAR			
Pl	Mandurah	163	B 8
YANNA			
Pl	Wanneroo	20	E 8
YANREY			
St	Golden Bay	158	D 8
YARALLA			
Pl	Karawara	83	D 5
YARDARM			
Ct	Ocean Reef	23	A 2
YARDOO			
Ct	Wanneroo	20	C 9
YARDY			
Ct	Merriwa	10	B 8

		Map	Ref.
YARINGA			
St	Golden Bay	158	D 8
Wy	City Beach	58	D 9
YARLE			
Ct	Cooloongup	137	C 9
YARNAL			
Pl	Ferndale	84	D 9
YARRA			
Cl	Cooloongup	137	E 9
Cl	Willetton	94	A 3
YARRAM			
Rd	Balcatta	46	B 7
YARRAWARRAH			
Me	Duncraig	30	D 9
YARRICK			
St	O'Connor	91	C 7
YARRIMUP			
Cl	Duncraig	30	E 8
YARRUK			
St	Yokine	60	D 2
YASS			
Ct	Yanchep	3	E 10
Wy	Merriwa	11	C 9
YATALA			
Me	Iluka	18	E 4
YATE			
Ct	Morley	48	D 5
Pl	Forrestfield	76	D 9
YATES			
Ct	North Lake	92	A 10
YAWL			
Ct	Ballajura	33	D 8
Ct	Ocean Reef	23	A 1
YEAMAN			
Ct	Koondoola	33	B 8
YEARLING			
Pl	Huntingdale	95	D 9
YEATES			
La	Stratton	51	B 4
Rd	Kwinana Beach	130	B 5
YEEDA			
Rd	Golden Bay	158	D 8
St	Riverton	93	D 1
YEEDONG			
Rd	Falcon	162A	B 4
YELDON			
Tr	Winthrop	92	B 6
YELLAND			
Wy	Bassendean	62	D 2
YELLOWSTONE			
Pl	Greenfields	165	D 1
Wy	Joondalup	19	C 1
YELTA			
Cl	Iluka	18	E 4
YELVERTON			
Rd	Mahogany Crk	67	C 3
YENISEY			
Cr	Beechboro	48	D 4
YENNERDIN			
Rd	Parkerville	53	C 6
YEO			
Ct	Cooloongup	137	C 9
Ct	Koondoola	33	A 7
YEOVIL			
Cr	Bicton	91	A 1
Cr	Bicton	81	A 10
Wy	Karrinyup	44	E 3
YERA			
Pl	Wanneroo	20	E 8
YEULBA			
St	Falcon	162A	D 10

		Map	Ref.
YEW			
Ct	Mirrabooka	47	A 2
Pl	Lynwood	94	B 2
YILGARN			
St	Mundaring	68	B 2
St	Shenton Park	71	E 5
St	White Gum Vly	90	D 7
YIRRIGAN			
Dr	Dianella	47	A 5
Dr	Mirrabooka	46	E 4
YOLANDE			
Pl	City Beach	58	D 6
YOMBA			
St	Kewdale	74	E 8
YONGA			
St	Wanneroo	20	C 8
YORICH			
Ct	Willetton	93	D 4
YORK			
Ave	Bentley	84	B 5
Rd	Furnissdale	165	E 7
Rd	Greenwood	32	A 6
St	Bedford	61	E 4
St	Forrestfield	86	D 1
St	Hilton	91	A 9
St	Inglewood	61	D 5
St	North Perth	61	A 7
St	South Perth	72	E 8
St	Subiaco	72	B 1
St	Tuart Hill	60	B 1
St	Tuart Hill	46	B 10
St	Viveash	50	B 5
Tce	Mosman Park	80	E 5
YORKSHIRE			
Ri	Iluka	18	E 3
YORNA			
Rd	Balga	46	B 4
Rd	Kalamunda	77	B 8
YORRELL			
Pl	Halls Head	164	B 5
YORSTON			
Pl	Hamilton Hill	101	C 2
YOULE-DEAN			
Rd	West Swan	35	C 6
YOUNG			
La	Lynwood	94	A 5
Pl	Hamilton Hill	101	B 1
Pl	Hamilton Hill	91	B 10
Pl	Padbury	23	D 10
Rd	Baldivis	147	C 5
Rd	Baldivis	147	D 9
St	Bayswater	61	E 3
St	Gosnells	106	A 3
St	Melville	91	D 1
YOUNGS			
Pl	Parmelia	131	A 6
YPRES			
Rd	Westfield	106	B 7
YUIN			
St	Golden Bay	158	D 7
YUKON			
Cl	Greenfields	165	D 2
Cl	Willetton	93	C 7
Pl	Beechboro	48	E 3
YULAN			
Cl	Greenwood	31	C 3
Ct	Huntingdale	95	D 8
YULE			
Ave	Middle Swan	50	C 2
Rd	Bickley	89	C 3
Rd	Heathridge	19	D 10
St	City Beach	58	D 6
St	Maddington	96	B 3
St	Mandurah	165	A 4

		Map	Ref.
YULEMA			
St	Mullaloo	23	A 4
YUNA			
Ri	Ocean Reef	18	E 7
St	Falcon	162A	B 2
YURRAH			
Pl	Kelmscott	106	E 6

Z

		Map	Ref.
ZAMBESI			
Dr	Greenfields	165	D 1
ZAMIA			
Pl	Parmelia	131	B 10
Pl	Greenwood	31	C 5
Pl	Parkerville	53	C 7
Rd	Gooseberry H	77	B 2
St	Mt Claremont	71	B 6
ZANNI			
St	Canning Vale	93	E 7
ZANTE			
Rd	Newburn	75	E 2
ZANTHUS			
Ct	Roleystone	107	E 10
ZAVIA			
St	Falcon	162A	C 3
ZEBINA			
St	East Perth	61	C 10
ZEIL			
Ct	Alexander Hts	33	A 4
ZELKOVA			
Dr	Lynwood	94	B 2
ZENITH			
St	Shelley	83	E 8
ZENOBIA			
St	Palmyra	91	B 3
Tce	Westfield	106	C 4
ZEST			
Ct	Mariginiup	17	E 7
ZETA			
Cr	O'Connor	91	B 6
ZIATAS			
Rd	Pinjar	17	A 2
ZIERA			
Pl	Lynwood	94	B 2
ZIG ZAG			
Rd	Baldivis	139	B 10
Rd	Baldivis	147	D 1
ZIG ZAG SCENIC			
Dr	Gooseberry H	65	C 9
ZINNIA			
Pl	Morley	48	C 5
Wy	Willetton	93	C 2
ZIRCON			
Ct	Carine	30	E 10
ZIRCONIA			
Dr	E Rockingham	137	D 1
ZODIAC			
Ct	Greenfields	163	E 10
ZOLLNER			
Cl	Connolly	19	A 6
ZUVELA			
Ct	Murdoch	92	C 7

FACILITIES GUIDE CONTENTS

Airports and Airline Offices 261
Ambulance 261
Aquatic Centres (see Beaches and Swimming Centres) 261
Art Galleries 283
Beaches and Swimming Centres 261
Blood Donor Clinics 261
Boat Ramps 261
Bowling:
    Lawn 261
    Ten Pin 262
Bus Transfer Stations and Coach Departure Points:
    Bus - Transperth 262
    Coach - Day Tours 262
    Coach - Interstate 262
Caravan Parks 262
Cemeteries and Crematoria 262
Child Care Centres 262
Child Health Centres 264
Churches and Places of Worship 265
Cinemas 295
Colleges of TAFE 269
Community and Recreation Centres 269
Consulates and Legations 269
Croquet Clubs 269
Drive-in Cinemas 295
Education Institutions:
    Administration 269
    Colleges of TAFE 269
    Off Site Pre-Primary Centres 270
    Schools 270
    Special Schools 276
    Universities 276
Ferry Terminals 276
Fire Services:
    Volunteer Fire Stations 276
    W.A. Bush Fires Board Fire Stations 276
    W.A. Fire Brigades Board Permanent 276
Golf Courses:
    Private 276
    Public 276
Government Departments:
    Commonwealth 276
    Local 278
    State 278
Homes for Children 280
Hospitals:
    Casualty or Emergency 280
    Private 280
    Public 280
Hostels, Y.H.A. 296
Hotels, Taverns and Wine Bars 280
Leisure Centres 286
Libraries 282
Localities, Postcodes and Postal Districts 282
Motels 283
Museums and Art Galleries 283
Nursing, Rest Homes, Hostels and Retirement Communities 284
Off Road Vehicle Areas 286
Ovals, Parks, Reserves and Leisure Centres 286
Police Stations - Traffic and Licensing Centres 290
Postal Districts, Postcodes and Localities 282
Post Offices (Official) 291

Pre-Primary Centres - Off Site 270
Psychiatric Services:
    Clinics 291
    Extended Care Units 291
    Hospitals 292
    Other Facilities 292
Public Transport (see Bus - Transperth) 262
Racing Tracks:
    BMX 292
    Car and Motorcycle 292
    Dog 292
    Horse 292
    Trotting 292
Railway Stations:
    Country Passenger Stations 292
    Freight Terminals 292
    Perth - Armadale Line 292
    Perth - Fremantle Line 292
    Perth - Midland Line 292
Recreation Centres 269
Religious Establishments 265
Reserves 286
Retirement Communities and Homes 284
Rowing Clubs 295
Rubbish Tips and Baling Plants 292
Schools (see Education Institutions) 270
Sea Rescue Group (Volunteer) 292
Shire Council Offices (see Government, Local) 278
Shopping Centres (Major) 292
Skating Rinks:
    Ice 293
    Roller 293
Sporting Venues (Major):
    Athletics 293
    Baseball 293
    Basketball 293
    Cricket 294
    Cycling 294
    Football 294
    Hockey 294
    Netball 294
    Soccer 294
    Squash 294
    Swimming 294
    Tennis 294
    Water Polo 294
Squash Centres 294
State Emergency Service 294
Suburbs (see Localities, Postcodes and Postal Districts) 282
Swimming Centres 261
Taverns 280
Tennis Clubs and Public Courts:
    Public Courts 294
    Tennis Clubs 294
Theatres, Cinemas and Drive-in Cinemas 295
Universities 276
Water Skiing Areas 295
Weighbridges (Public) 295
Wine Bars 280
Wineries 295
Yachting, Rowing and Angling Clubs 295
Y.H.A. Hostels 296

FACILITIES GUIDE

AIRPORTS & AIRLINE OFFICES

	Map	Ref.
AIR NEW ZEALAND, 11th Floor, National Bank of Australia Building, 50 St Georges Tce, Perth	1C	A 3
ANSETT AIRLINES OF AUSTRALIA, International House, 26 St Georges Tce, Perth	1C	A 3
ANSETT WA, International House, 26 St Georges Tce, Perth	1C	A 3
AUSTRALIAN AIRLINES, CML Building, 55 St Georges Tce, Perth	1C	A 3
BRITISH AIRWAYS, 140 St Georges Tce, Perth	1C	E 3
CATHAY PACIFIC AIRWAYS, Elder House, 111 St Georges Tce, Perth	1C	E 3
GARUDA INDONESIAN AIRWAYS, National Mutual Centre, 111 St Georges Tce, Perth	1C	E 3
JANDAKOT AIRPORT Light aircraft and charters, Hope Rd, Jandakot	103	C 5
JAPAN AIRLINES, 5 Mill St, Perth	1C	E 3
MALAYSIAN AIRLINE SYSTEM, Allendale Sq, 77 St Georges Tce, Perth	1C	E 3
PERTH AIRPORT - DOMESTIC TERMINAL Brearly Ave	63	C 8
PERTH AIRPORT - INTERNATIONAL TERMINAL Horrie Miller Dr	63	D 10
QANTAS AIRWAYS, Allendale Sq, 77 St Georges Tce, Perth	1C	E 3
QANTAS AIRWAYS, TRAVEL CENTRE, Central Park, 55 William St, Perth	1C	E 3
ROTTNEST AIRBUS, Fauntleroy Ave, Perth Airport	63	B 7
ROYAL BRUNEI AIRLINES, Hay St, Perth	1C	E 2
SINGAPORE AIRLINES, Commercial Union Building, 179 St Georges Tce, Perth	1C	E 3
SKYWEST AIRLINES PTY LTD, 234 Great Eastern Hwy, Ascot	62	D 9
SOUTH AFRICAN AIRWAYS (SAA), Exchange House, 68 St Georges Tce, Perth	1C	E 3
THAI INTERNATIONAL AIRWAYS, 5 Mill St, Perth	1C	A 3

AMBULANCE

Emergency Tel. 000

Non Emergency Tel. 277 8899

ST JOHN AMBULANCE

	Map	Ref.
ARMADALE, Streich Ave	116	D 8
CENTRAL, 2 Glyde St, East Perth	1C	B 2
COCKBURN, View St, Yangebup	111	C 2
FREMANTLE, Parry St	1D	C 4
GOSNELLS, 138 Wheatley St	96	C 10
KALAMUNDA, Railway Rd	77	D 6
KENSINGTON, George St	73	D 9
KEWDALE, Cnr Kewdale & Abernethy Sts	75	B 8
MANDURAH, Cnr Ranceby St & Pinjarra Rd	165	C 2
MELVILLE, Marcus Ave, Booragoon	92	B 2
MIDLAND, Lot 84 Great Northern Hwy	50	C 5
MORLEY, 63 Collier Rd	48	A 10
MUNDARING, 75 Jacoby St	68	B 1
OSBORNE PARK, 162 Edward St	46	B 10
QUEEN ELIZABETH II MEDICAL CENTRE, Cnr Hospital Ave & Aberdare Rd, Nedlands	72	A 5
RIVERTON, Lot 50 High Rd	94	A 1
ROCKINGHAM, Kent St	137	A 4
SERPENTINE, Richardson St	154	E 3
ST JOHN AMBULANCE AUSTRALIA W.A., AMBULANCE SERVICE H.Q., 209 Great Eastern Hwy, Belmont	62	C 10
WANNEROO, 3 Frederick St	20	D 9
WARWICK, Cnr Wanneroo Rd & Marangaroo Dr	32	A 5
YANCHEP - TWO ROCKS, Lot 201 Welwyn Ave, Yanchep	4	D 3

BEACHES & SWIMMING CENTRES

	Map	Ref.
AQUA MOTION WANNEROO	20	D 8
ARMADALE AQUATIC CENTRE	116	C 2
BALGA AQUATIC CENTRE	46	C 1
BART CLAYDEN AQUATIC CENTRE	74	D 4
BATHERS BEACH	1D	B 6
BAYSWATER AQUATIC CENTRE	48	B 10
BEATTY PARK OLYMPIC POOL	60	D 9
BENNION BEACH	44	B 5
BICTON POOL	81	A 9
BILGOMAN OLYMPIC POOL	66	A 1
BOLD PARK SWIMMING POOL	59	A 8
BRIGHTON BEACH	44	C 10
BURNS BEACH	18	C 3
CANNING AQUATIC CENTRE	84	B 5
CHALLENGER BEACH	121	A 4
CITY BEACH	58	C 9
CLAREMONT AQUATIC CENTRE	71	A 8
COMO BEACH	82	E 1
COOGEE BEACH	100	D 8
COTTESLOE BEACH	80	C 2
FLOREAT BEACH	58	C 8
FREMANTLE AQUATIC CENTRE	1D	C 4
HAMERSLEY POOL	44	C 3
INGLEWOOD AQUATIC CENTRE	61	B 2
KALAMUNDA AQUATIC CENTRE	77	D 8
KELMSCOTT AQUATIC CENTRE	106	E 9
KWINANA AQUATIC CENTRE	131	A 7
KWINANA BEACH	129	D 8
LEIGHTON BEACH	80	C 9
LENNARD POOL	30	B 9
MANDURAH AQUATIC REC. CENTRE	165	B 2
MARMION BEACH	30	B 7
MAYLANDS WATERLAND	74	B 2
MELVILLE AQUATIC CENTRE	92	B 2
METTAMS POOL	44	C 4
MULLALOO BEACH	22	E 5
NATIONAL PARK POOL	52	C 7
NORTH BEACH	44	C 2
NORTH COTTESLOE BEACH	80	C 1
PALM BEACH	136	E 4
PORT BEACH	90	B 1
ROBERT DAY MEMORIAL POOL	164	E 1
ROCKINGHAM AQUATIC CENTRE	137	C 6
ROCKINGHAM BEACH	137	A 4
SCARBOROUGH BEACH	44	C 10
SHOALWATER BAY BEACH	136	C 7
SOMERSET POOL	74	B 10
SORRENTO BEACH	30	B 6
SOUTH BEACH	90	C 10
SOUTH TRIGG	44	C 7
SUPERDROME	71	B 2
SWAN AQUATIC CENTRE	50	E 6
SWANBOURNE BEACH	70	C 9
THORNLIE AQUATIC CENTRE	95	C 5
TRIGG BEACH	44	C 6
WANNEROO WATER WORLD	24	A 8
WARNBRO BEACH	145	B 3
WATERMANS BEACH	30	C 9
WEST MIDLAND POOL	50	A 8
WESTERN AUSTRALIAN SPORTS CENTRE	71	B 2
WHITFORD BEACH	22	E 8
YANCHEP BEACH	4	B 5

BLOOD DONOR CLINICS

	Map	Ref.
FREMANTLE CENTRE, 17 Hampton Rd, Fremantle	1D	C 6
PERTH CENTRAL CITY, 43 King St, Perth	1C	E 2
PERTH CENTRE, 290 Wellington St, Perth	1C	A 2

BOAT RAMPS

	Map	Ref.
BASSENDEAN, Pickering Park, off Bassendean Pde (unsealed)	62	B 3
BAYSWATER, between River and Constance Sts	62	E 7
BELMONT, off Abernethy Rd (unsealed)	74	B 1
COODANUP, off Norton Ave	165	D 6
CRAWLEY, Matilda Bay	72	A 9
CRAWLEY, off Hackett Dr	72	A 10
DUDLEY PARK, off Waterside Dr	165	A 5
EAST FREMANTLE, Riverside Rd	80	D 10
FALCON, off Avalon Pde	162A	A 4
FALCON, off Dampier Ave	162A	E 10
FALCON, off Spinaway Pde	162A	B 2
FURNISSDALE, off the end of Furnissdale Rd	165	E 8
GNANGARA LAKE, Alexander Dr	26	B 7
GUILDFORD, Swan St (unsealed)	49	B 10
HALLS HEAD, Lagoon Boat Harbour, Mary St	162	D 10
HILLARYS BOAT HARBOUR, West Coast Hwy	30	A 4
KWINANA BEACH, Kwinana Beach Rd	129	D 8
MANDURAH, off Mandurah Tce	162	E 10
MANDURAH, off Peninsula Ent	162	D 10
MANNING, Cloister Ave, (unsealed)	82	E 7
MAYLANDS, Clarkson Rd	74	A 2
MT PLEASANT, Deepwater Point	82	E 8
MUNSTER, off Cockburn Rd	110	D 4
NAVAL BASE, off Sutton Rd	121	A 4
OCEAN REEF BOAT HARBOUR, Marina Blvd	18	E 10
PALM BEACH, Esplanade (2 ramps)	136	D 4
PEPPERMINT GROVE, Johnston St	80	E 4
POINT WALTER, Point Walter Reserve (2 ramps)	81	C 6
QUINNS ROCKS, Robert Rd	10	E 10
RIVERVALE, Goodwood Pde	73	E 2
ROCKINGHAM MARINA, Point Peron Rd	136	B 3
SAFETY BAY, Safety Bay Rd	144	E 1
SAFETY BAY, Safety Bay Rd	144	E 2
SOUTH PERTH, Coode St	73	A 7
TRIGG, The Esplande	44	C 5
TWO ROCKS MARINA, Pope St	2	B 2

BOWLING

LAWN

	Map	Ref.
AIR FORCE ASSOCIATION, Benningfield Rd, Bullcreek	93	A 3
ARMADALE, Gwynne Park (off Forrest Rd)	116	C 8
BASSENDEAN, 10 Whitfield St	63	A 1
BAYSWATER, Murray St	62	A 5
BEDFORD, Cnr Grand Promenade & Catherine St	61	D 3
BELLEVUE RSL, Purton Place, Bellevue	51	A 10
BELMONT PARK, Great Eastern Hwy, Ascot	62	C 10
BLIND BOWLING CLUB, 2 Plain St, East Perth	1C	B 4
BYFORD, South Western Hwy	135	D 1
CANNINGTON, Cnr George St & Chapman Rd	84	D 7
CARLISLE - LATHLAIN, Cnr Roberts Rd & Bishopsgate St, Carlisle	74	B 7
CITY BEACH, Kalinda Dr	58	E 7
CIVIC CENTRE, Hensman St, South Perth	73	A 10
CLAREMONT, Bay View Tce	71	A 10
CLOVERDALE, Cnr Abernethy Rd & Keane St, Belmont	75	A 6
COCKBURN, Rockingham Rd, Spearwood	101	B 5
COTTESLOE - PEPPERMINT GROVE, 3 Leake St, Peppermint Grove	80	E 2
DALKEITH - NEDLANDS, Jutland Pde, Dalkeith	81	C 4
DEAF, Cnr Mends St & Labouchere Rd, South Perth	72	E 7
DOUBLEVIEW, Shearn Cr	59	A 1
DUDLEY PARK, Gillark St, Mandurah	165	A 3
EAST FREMANTLE, Fletcher St	90	E 3
FLOREAT PARK, Howtree Pl, Floreat	59	C 9
FORREST PARK, Harold St, Mt Lawley	61	B 9
FORRESTFIELD, Cnr Hartfield & Morrison Rds, Forrestfield	86	C 1
FREMANTLE, Ellen St	1D	C 4
GLEN FORREST, McGlew Rd	66	D 2
GOSNELLS, Cnr Albany Hwy & Dorothy St	96	C 9
HILTON PARK, Shepherd St, Hilton	91	A 8

	Map	Ref.
HOLLYWOOD - SUBIACO, Cnr Smyth Rd & Verdun St, Nedlands	71	D 6
INNALOO, Cnr Langley Cr & Birdwood St	45	C 8
KALAMUNDA, Kalamunda Rd	77	D 6
KITCHENER PARK, Roberts Rd, Subiaco	60	B10
KWINANA BOWLING CLUB, Brownell Cr, Medina	130	E 5
LEEDERVILLE, Cambridge St	60	C10
LEEMING, Bainton Rd	103	B 1
MANDURAH, Allnutt St	163	B10
MANNING MEMORIAL, Challenger Ave, Manning	83	C 7
MAYLANDS, Clarkson Rd	74	B 1
MELVILLE, Canning Hwy, Alfred Cove	82	A 9
MIDLAND JUNCTION, Morrison Rd, Midland	50	C 7
MILLS PARK, Brixton St, Beckenham	85	C 8
MORLEY, Garson Ct, Noranda	47	E 6
MORRISON PARK, Morrison Rd, Swan View	51	A 7
MOSMAN PARK, Bay View Tce	80	E 5
MT LAWLEY, Cnr Queens Cr & Storthes St	61	B 7
MT PLEASANT, Bedford Rd, Ardross	82	D 9
MUNDARING, Coolgardie St.	68	B 2
NOLLAMARA, Lemana Rd	46	C 6
NORTH BEACH, Kitchener St, North Beach	44	D 3
NORTH FREMANTLE, 40 Stirling Hwy	80	C10
NORTH PERTH, Woodville Reserve, Farmer St	60	E 7
OSBORNE PARK, Park St, Tuart Hill	46	B 9
PERTH AND TATTERSALLS, 2 Plain St, East Perth	1C	B 4
PICKERING BROOK, Weston Rd	88	E10
QUINNS ROCKS, Tapping Wy	10	B10
RIVERTON ROSSMOYNE, Tuscan St, Rossmoyne	93	B 1
ROCKINGHAM, Kent St	137	A 4
ROLEYSTONE, Wygonda Rd	108	A 8
ROYAL PARK, Cnr Charles & Vincent Sts, North Perth	60	E 9
SAFETY BAY, Gloucester Cr.	136	C10
SCARBOROUGH, 75 Deanmore Rd	44	E 8
SORRENTO, Percy Doyle Res., Warwick Rd, Duncraig	30	E 7
SOUTH PERTH, Cnr Mends St & Labouchere Rd	72	E 7
SPORTSMENS ASSOCIATION, Stancliffe St, Mt Lawley	61	B 5
SWANBOURNE, Off Odern Cr	70	D 8
SWAN, James St, Guildford	49	E10
THORNLIE, Thornlie Ave	95	C 4
VICTORIA PARK, Kent St, East Victoria Park	73	E 9
WA YUGOSLAV, Jones St, Balcatta	46	A 7
WANNEROO, Crisafulli Ave	20	D 9
WAR VETERANS, RSL War Veterans Home, Alexander Dr, Mt Lawley	61	A 5
WARNBRO, Okehampton Rd	145	D 6
WEMBLEY, Gregory St	60	A 7
WILLETTON, Burrendah Blvd	93	D 5
YANCHEP, Yanchep Beach Rd	4	D 3
YOKINE, Wordsworth Ave	60	E 2

	Map	Ref.
TEN PIN		
CANNINGTON LANES, Cnr Burton St & Chapman Rd, Cannington	84	C 5
FAIRLANES CITY, 175 Adelaide Tce, East Perth	1C	B 4
FAIRLANES CRAIGIE BOWL, 9 Perilya Rd, Craigie	23	D 5
FAIRLANES MIRRABOOKA BOWL, 9 Chesterfield Dr, Mirrabooka	46	E 4
KELMSCOTT BOWL, 265 Railway Ave, Kelmscott	116	D 3
MELVILLE SUPERBOWL, Cnr Leach Hwy & Stock Rd, Melville	91	C 3
MORLEY BOWL, Cnr Walter Rd & Coode St, Morley	47	D10
NORTH PERTH INDOOR SPORTS CENTRE, 464 Fitzgerald St, North Perth	61	A 7
OSBORNE PARK SUPERBOWL, Cnr Scarborough Beach Rd & Sundercombe St, Osborne Park	59	E 2
PELICAN BOWL, 96 Mandurah Tce, Mandurah	162	E10
ROCKINGHAM LANES, Patterson Rd, Rockingham	137	A 5

BUS TRANSFER STATIONS & COACH DEPARTURE POINTS

BUS - TRANSPERTH

	Map	Ref.
ARMADALE (Armadale Interchange), Streich Ave	116	D 7
CANNINGTON,(Cannington Interchange), Sevenoaks St	85	A 6
INNALOO, Odin Rd	59	C 1
KALAMUNDA, Mead St	77	D 7
KARRINYUP, (Karrinyup Shopping Centre), Karrinyup Rd	45	A 6
KELMSCOTT, (Kelmscott Interchange), Railway Ave	106	D 8
KWINANA, Rockingham Rd	130	B 3
MIDLAND, (Midland Interchange), Victoria St	50	B 8
MIRRABOOKA, Ilkeston Pl	46	E 4
MORLEY, Bishop St	47	E10
PERTH CITY BUS JUNCTION, Mounts Bay Rd	1C	E 3
ROCKINGHAM, Simpson Ave	137	C 7
WARWICK, Beach Rd	31	C 8
WELLINGTON ST BUS STATION, Wellington St, Perth	1C	E 2
WILLETTON (Southlands Shopping Centre), Burrendah Blvd	93	C 5

COACH - DAY TOURS

	Map	Ref.
All Coaches, Wellington St, Perth (Outside Wellington St Bus Station)	1C	E 2

COACH - INTERSTATE

	Map	Ref.
BUS AUSTRALIA, Wellington St, Perth (Under Horseshoe Bridge)	1C	E 2
GREYHOUND, East Perth Rail Terminal	61	C10
PIONEER EXPRESS, East Perth Rail Terminal	61	C10
TRANSCONTINENTAL COACH LINES, East Perth Rail Terminal	61	C10

CARAVAN PARKS

	Map	Ref.
ARMADALE TOURIST VILLAGE, South Western Hwy, Armadale	116	D10
BANKSIA TOURIST VILLAGE, Lot 198 Midland Rd, Hazelmere	64	E 7
BELVEDERE, 153 Mandurah Tce, Mandurah	163	A 9
BURNS BEACH, 275 Burns Beach Rd, Burns	18	D 3
CARAVAN VILLAGE, 2462 Albany Hwy, Gosnells	106	D 2
CARENIUP, 467 Nth Beach Rd, Gwelup	45	B 2
CARINE GARDENS, 234 Balcatta Rd, Balcatta	45	C 1
CAVERSHAM, 746 Benara Rd, Caversham	49	C 5
CEE & SEE, Cnr Governer St & Rockingham Rd, East Rockingham	137	C 1
CENTRAL, 34 Central Ave, Redcliffe	62	E 7
CHEROKEE VILLAGE, Cnr Hocking & Wanneroo Rds, Kingsley	24	E 9
COOGEE BEACH, Cockburn Rd, Coogee	100	E 8
ESTUARY, 25 Olive Rd, Falcon	162A	D 2
FORRESTFIELD, Hawtin Rd, Forrestfield	76	D 9
FREMANTLE VILLAGE & CHALET CENTRE, Cnr Rollinson & Cockburn Rds, Hamilton Hill	100	D 1
GUILDFORD, Lot 4 West Swan Rd, West Swan	36	A 7
JANDAKOT, Lot 11 Hammond Rd, Jandakot	112	D 2
KELMSCOTT, 80 River Rd, Kelmscott	106	E10
KENLORN, 229 Treasure Rd, Queens Park	85	A 2
KINGSWAY, Cnr Wanneroo Rd & Kingsway, Landsdale	32	A 2
LAKE VIEW TERRACE, Cnr Lake Rd & Lake View Tce, Westfield	106	C 5
LAKELANDS, Cnr Sydney Rd & Lakelands Dr, Gnangara	26	A 3
LAKESIDE, Cnr Fifty Rd & Mandurah Rd, Baldivis	146	D 1
LUCKY, 20 Henson St, Mandurah	163	A 8
MIAMI, Lot 2 Old Coast Rd, Falcon	162A	D 2
MIDLAND, 2 Toodyay Rd, Middle Swan	50	C 5
MUNDARING, Great Eastern Hwy, Mundaring	53	D10
OCEAN REEF CARAVAN VILLAGE, 30 Mangano Pl, Wanneroo	24	D 5
ORANGE GROVE, 19 Kelvin Rd, Orange Grove	86	D 6
PALM BEACH, Cnr Fisher & Lake Sts, Rockingham	136	E 6
PENINSULA, Ormsby Tce, Mandurah	162	E10
PERTH TOURIST, 319 Hale Rd, Forrestfield	86	B 1
QUINNS ROCKS, Lot 211 Ocean Dr, Quinns Rocks	10	A 2
ROCKINGHAM HOLIDAY VILLAGE, 51 Dixon Rd, East Rockingham	138	B 3
SERPENTINE FALLS, 2622 South Western Hwy, Serpentine	155	B 4
SORRENTO BEACH, 7 West Coast Hwy, Sorrento	30	B 5
SPRINGVALE, Maida Vale Rd, High Wycombe	76	C 2

	Map	Ref.
STARHAVEN, 14-18 Pearl Pde, Scarborough	44	D 8
TIMBERTOP, Peel St, Mandurah	162	E10
WANNEROO, Lot 32 Wanneroo Rd, Wanneroo	24	D 2
WOODMAN POINT, Cockburn Rd, Munster	110	E 2
W.A. WATER SKI PARK, Lot 101 St Albans Rd, Baldivis	139	E 6

CEMETERIES & CREMATORIA

	Map	Ref.
EAST PERTH (Old), East Perth	73	C 3
EAST ROCKINGHAM, East Rockingham	130	B 9
FREMANTLE, Palmyra	91	B 5
GUILDFORD, South Guildford	63	D 5
JARRAHDALE, Jarrahdale	152	D 7
KARRAKATTA, Railway Rd Entrance	71	C 6
KARRAKATTA, Smyth Rd Entrance	71	D 6
KENWICK, Kenwick	95	D 2
MANDURAH, Mandurah	165	B 3
MIDLAND, Swan View	51	B 6
MUNDARING, Mundaring	68	C 1
PINNAROO VALLEY MEMORIAL PARK, Padbury	24	A 9
SERPENTINE, Serpentine	155	B 3

CHILD CARE CENTRES

	Map	Ref.
ABC CHILD CARE CENTRE, 13 Suffolk St, Fremantle	1D	C 6
AUNTIE JANET'S CHILD CARE CENTRE, 84 East St, Maylands	61	E 7
AUNTY JOAN'S CHILD CARE CENTRE, 10 Palmerston St, Bentley	84	B 3
AUSSIE KIDS CHILD CARE CENTRE, 52 Salvado Rd, Wembley	60	A10
BABUSHKA CHILD CARE CENTRE, 36 Marri Cr, Lesmurdie	87	B 5
BALCATTA CHILD CARE CENTRE, 344 Albert St, Balcatta	46	A 7
BALGA CAMPUS CHILD CARE, 18 Loxwood Rd, Balga	46	E 2
BALGA SALVATION ARMY NEIGHBOURHOOD CENTRE, 17 Lavant Wy, Balga	46	C 2
BALLAJURA CHILD CARE CENTRE, 118 Illawarra Cr, Ballajura	33	D 7
BASSENDEAN CHILD CARE CENTRE, 30 Whitfield St, Bassendean	63	A 1
BEAUFORT CHILD CARE CENTRE, 286 Beaufort St, Perth	61	A10
BEECHBORO FAMILY CENTRE, Amazon Dr, Beechboro	48	D 3
BELMONT CHILDRENS DAY CARE CENTRE, Cnr Epsom Ave & Sydenham St, Belmont	75	A 1
BELVIDERE CHILD CARE CENTRE, 150 Keymer St, Belmont	74	E 1
BENTLEY CHILD CARE CENTRE, 7 Queen St, Bentley	84	C 3
BIRRA-LI CHILD CARE CENTRE, 1 Stacey St, Willagee	91	E 5
BLUE GUM CHILD CARE CENTRE, 33 Moolyeen Rd, Brentwood	92	D 2

Name	Map Ref.
BOOGURLARRI COMMUNITY HOUSE, 25-27 Brookman Ave, Langford	94 E 1
BOORAGOON OCCASIONAL CHILD CARE CENTRE, 525 Marmion St, Booragoon	92 B 1
BRENTWOOD CHRISTIAN CHILD CARE, 44 Moolyeen Rd, Brentwood	92 D 2
BRIGHTON NURSERY AND CHILD CARE CENTRE, 6A Lichfield St, Victoria Park	73 E 8
BROCKMAN HOUSE CHILD CARE CENTRE, 27 Hull Wy, Beechboro	49 A 4
BULLCREEK CHILD CARE CENTRE, 37 Chancery Cr, Willetton	93 B 7
BUZY KIDZ CARE CENTRE, 9 Pacific Way, Beldon	23 C 3
CANNING COLLEGE CHILD CARE CENTRE, Marquis St, Bentley	83 E 5
CAREY'S PLACE ONE PARENT CENTRE, 193 Canning Hwy, East Fremantle	90 E 2
CARINE CHILD CARE CENTRE, 34 Kersey Wy, Carine	31 A 9
CARINE COLLEGE OF TAFE CHILD CARE CENTRE, Almadine Dr, Carine	30 E10
CAROUSEL OCCASIONAL CHILD CARE CENTRE, Carousel Shopping Centre, Albany Hwy, Cannington	84 E 7
CARRINGTON CHILD CARE CENTRE, 70 Carrington Street, Palmyra	91 A 3
CATHERINE McAULEY DAY CARE CENTRE, Station St, Wembley	60 A 9
CATHERINE'S DAY CARE CENTRE, 1 Mansell St, Morley	47 D 9
CHIDLOW PLAY GROUP, Cnr Northam Rd & Northcote St, Chidlow	56 D 1
CHILD GUIDANCE CLINIC CRECHE, 3 Selby St, Shenton Park	71 D 4
CHILDREN'S PROTECTION SOCIETY, 286 Beaufort St, Perth	61 A10
CITY OF BAYSWATER NEIGHBOURHOOD CENTRE, 42 Rudloc Rd, MORLEY	47 E10
CITY OF GOSNELLS MOTIVATED MUMS CHILD CARE, Kenwick Rd, Kenwick	85 E10
CITYPLACE CHILD CARE CENTRE, Cnr City Station Complex, Cnr Wellington & Barrack Sts, Perth	1C A 2
CLAREMONT DAY NURSERY, 2 Alfred Rd, Claremont	71 C 6
COMMUNICARE OCCASIONAL CARE CENTRE, 28 Cecil Ave, Cannington	84 E 6
COMO PLAY SCHOOL CHILD CARE CENTRE, 47 Birdwood Ave, Como	73 C10
COOLABAROO NEIGHBOURHOOD CENTRE, Parkside Dr, Thornlie	95 D 5
COOLBELLUP DAY CARE CENTRE, 219-221 Torquil Rd, Coolbellup	91 E 9
COTTESLOE DAY CARE CENTRE, 80 Railway St, Cottesloe	70 D10
CUBBY HOUSE CHILD CARE INNALOO, 20 Muriel Ave, Innaloo	45 C10
CURTIN UNIVERSITY - BARNEY'S PLACE, Curtin University, Brand Dr, Bentley	83 E 5
CURTIN UNIVERSITY - DI'S PLACE, Curtin University, Chessell Rd, Bentley	83 E 4
DAISY HOUSE OCCASIONAL CARE CENTRE, 1 Wade Ct, Girrawheen	32 C 7
DIANNE'S HOMESTEAD, 483 Fitzgerald St, North Perth	61 A 7
DINKY DI CHILD CARE CENTRE, 12 Barnes St, Innaloo	45 B 8
DUNCRAIG CHILD CARE CENTRE, 40 Warwick Rd, Duncraig	30 E 6
ENDEAVOUR CHILD CARE CENTRE, 21 Endeavour Rd, Hillarys	23 B 9
ESME FLETCHER DAY NURSERY, Cnr Parry & High Sts, Fremantle	90 C 5
FARNHAM HOUSE DAY CARE CENTRE, 1 Strathcona St, West Perth	60 D10
FLORENCE HUMMERSTON OCCASIONAL CHILD CARE CENTRE, 3 The Esplanade, Perth	1C A 3
FORRESTFIELD CHILD CARE CENTRE, 12 Anderson Rd, Forrestfield	76 D10
FRANK KONECNY FAMILY CENTRE, Cnr Parmelia Ave & Skottowe Pwy, Parmelia	131 B10
FRED NOTLEY DAY NURSERY, 32 Collick St, Hilton	91 C 8
FREMANTLE CHILD CARE CENTRE, 114 Attfield St, Fremantle	90 C 8
FREMANTLE CHILDRENS SERVICES CENTRE, 15 Quarry St, Fremantle	1D C 4
FROG HOLLOW CHILD CARE CENTRE, 14 Orchard Ave, Armadale	116 D 6
G KORSUNSKI-CARMEL SCHOOL & CHILD CARE CENTRE, Cresswell Rd, Dianella	61 A 1
GIRRAWHEEN CHILD CARE CENTRE, 68 Hudson Ave, Girrawheen	32 C 7
GLENDALOUGH NEIGHBOURHOOD CENTRE, 29 Jugan St, Glendalough	60 B 5
GURLONGGA NJININJ CHILDRENS CENTRE, 52 Newcastle St, East Perth	1C A 1
GWYNNE PARK DAY CARE CENTRE, 101 Forrest Rd, Armadale	116 C 7
HAPPY KIDS, Cnr Kingfisher Ave & Jacana Ave, Ballajura	33 E 7
HARMONY CHILD LEARNING CENTRE, Cnr Sackville St & Hancock St, Doubleview	45 A 8
HEATHRIDGE CHILD CARE CENTRE, 91 Prince Regent Dr, Heathridge	19 B 9
HIGH WYCOMBE FAMILY CENTRE, 104 Edney Rd, High Wycombe	76 C 1
HUMPTY DUMPTY DAY CARE CENTRE, 46 Subiaco Rd, Subiaco	60 C10
HUNTINGDALE CHILD CARE CENTRE, 11 Lilac Pl, Huntingdale	95 D 8
ITALIAN AUSTRALIAN CHILD MINDING CENTRE, 21 Barnett St, North Perth	60 D 8
JACK AND JILL CHILD CARE CENTRE, 4 Aldgate St, Mandurah	165 B 1
JENNIFER LOCKWOOD CHILD CARE CENTRE, 386 Lord St, Perth	61 B10
KALAMUNDA DAY CARE CENTRE, Cnr Banksia and Godfrey Sts, Walliston	88 A 1
KARRINYUP CHILD CARE CENTRE, 22 Davenport St, Karrinyup	45 A 5
KELMSCOTT SENIOR HIGH SCHOOL OCCASIONAL CARE CENTRE, Cnr Third Ave & Camillo Rd, Kelmscott	106 D 9
KENWICK CHILD CARE CENTRE, 7 Stafford Rd, Kenwick	95 D 1
KIDZ KLUB CHILD CARE CENTRE, 192 Yale Rd, Thornlie	95 A 6
KINDER INNE CHILD CARE, 378 Roberts Rd, Subiaco	72 B 1
KINDY-CARE KINDERGARTEN, 135 Kingsley Dr, Kingsley	31 B 1
KINGSLEY FAMILY CENTRE, 48 Peregrine Dr, Kingsley	31 C 2
KOONDOOLA NEIGHBOURHOOD CENTRE, 4 Tempany Wy, Koondoola	33 A 7
KULUNGAH MYAH FAMILY CENTRE, Le Souef Dr, Kardinya	91 E 6
KWINANA CHILD CARE CENTRE, Peel Ct, Kwinana Town Centre	131 A 7
LADY GOWRIE CHILD CENTRE, 3 Yaralla Pl, Karawara	83 D 5
LADY GOWRIE CHILD CENTRE, (Brownlie Tower) 32 Dumond St, Bentley	84 A 4
LANGFORD CHILD HOME CARE CENTRE, 21 Southgate Rd, Langford	94 E 2
LEEMING FAMILY CENTRE, Cnr Farrington & Aulberry Pde, Leeming	92 E10
LEONARD STREET DAY CARE CENTRE, 67a Leonard St, Victoria Park	73 D 8
LESMURDIE DAY CARE CENTRE, 140 Lesmurdie Rd, Lesmurdie	77 D10
MANDURAH CHILD CARE CENTRE, Library Rd, Mandurah	165 C 2
MANDURAH OCCASIONAL CHILD CARE CENTRE, Tuart Ave, Mandurah	165 B 2
MANDURAH PLAYGROUND CENTRE, Pinjarra Rd, (behind Mandurah District Library)	165 C 3
MANDY'S DAY CARE CENTRE, 320 Shepperton Rd, E.Victoria Park	74 B10
MARANGAROO FAMILY CENTRE, 46 Highclere Blvd, Marangaroo	32 C 5
MARISTELLA KINDERGARTEN, 60 Attfield St, Fremantle	90 C 6
MARITA ROAD DAY CARE CENTRE, 13 Marita Rd, Nedlands	71 C 9
MARJORIE MANN LAWLEY DAY CARE CENTRE, 30 Clifton Cr, Mt Lawley	61 B 7
MELVILLE DAY CARE CENTRE, 39 Rome St, Melville	91 E 1
MIDLAND CHILD CARE CENTRE, 6 The Avenue, Midland	50 C 8
MIDLAND COLLEGE OF TAFE CHILD CARE CENTRE, Midland College of TAFE, Lloyd St, Midland	50 D 5
MIDLAND - GUILDFORD CHILD CARE CENTRE, 35 Amherst Rd, Midland	50 A 9
MIDVALE CHILD CARE CENTRE, 22-26 Hooley Rd, Midvale	50 E 8
MINDERS CHILD CARE CENTRE, 77 Marina Blvd, Ocean Reef	23 B 1
MIRRABOOKA MULTICULTURAL DAY CARE CENTRE, 28 Chesterfield Rd, Mirrabooka	46 E 4
MOOLANDA CHILD CARE CENTRE, Moolanda Blvd, Kingsley Pl, Mirrabooka	24 D10
MORLEY DAY CARE, 2 Mansell St, Morley	47 D 9
MOSMAN PARK CHILD CARE, 46 Glyde St, Mosman Park	80 D 5
MOTHER GOOSE DAY CARE CENTRE, 38 Monmouth St, Mt Lawley	61 A 7
MOUNT HELENA PLAY GROUP, Chidlow St, Mt Helena	55 C 5
MOUNT LAWLEY NEIGHBOURHOOD CENTRE, 715 Beaufort St, Mt Lawley	61 B 7
MUNDARING CHILD CARE SERVICE, 2 Brooking Rd, Mahogany Creek	53 C10
MURDOCH UNIVERSITY CHILD CARE CENTRE, South St, Murdoch	92 C 8
NEDLANDS DAY CARE CENTRE, 79 Williams Rd, Nedlands	71 E 7
NGAL-A BLUEBIRD CHILD CARE CENTRE, 1 Baron-Hay Court, Kensington	73 D10
NGAL-A CYGNET CHILD CARE CENTRE, Baron-Hay Court, Kensington	73 D10
NORANDA COMMUNITY & FAMILY CENTRE, Cnr Garson Ct & Forder St, Noranda	47 D 6
NORTH BEACH CHILD CARE CENTRE, 78 Edgefield Wy, North Beach	44 D 3
NORTH BEACH PLAYSCHOOL, 107 Lynn St, Trigg	44 D 4
OSBORNE CHILD CARE CENTRE, 170 Hamilton St, Osborne Park	46 A 9
PADBURY CHILD CARE CENTRE, Giles Ave, Padbury	23 D10
PERTH TECHNICAL COLLEGE CHILD CARE CENTRE, 25 Aberdeen St, Perth	1C A 1
PETER PAN CHILD CARE CENTRE, 126 Alexander Rd, Rivervale	74 C 5
POINT RESOLUTION OCCASIONAL CARE CENTRE, 53 Jutland Pde, Dalkeith	81 C 4
RED ROBIN DAY CARE CENTRE, 42 Frederic St, Midland	50 C 7
RIVERDALE CHILD CARE CENTRE, 57 River Rd, Kelmscott	106 E 9
ROCKINGHAM MULTIFUNCTIONAL CENTRE, Cnr Council Ave & Sepia Ct	137 B 8

Name	Map Ref.
ROCKINGHAM OCCASIONAL CHILD CARE CENTRE, Cnr Council Ave & Sepia Ct, Rockingham	137 B 8
ROLEYSTONE FAMILY CENTRE, 19 Wygonda Rd, Roleystone	107 E 7
ROSTRATA FAMILY CARE, Prendwick Wy, Willetton	93 E 4
ROYAL PERTH HOSPITAL CHILD MINDING CENTRE, Wellington St, Perth	1C A 3
SALISBURY CHILD CARE CENTRE, 127 Salisbury St, Bedford	61 D 4
SALVATION ARMY BALGA DAY CARE CENTRE, 14-18 Lavant Wy, Balga	46 C 2
SILVERWOOD DAY NURSERY, 27 Silverwood St, Embleton	48 A 10
SMALL WORLD, 35 Tenth Ave, Inglewood	61 C 4
SMILEYS CHILD CARE CENTRE, 170 Samson St, Hilton	91 A 7
SOUTH BENTLEY COMMUNITY OCCASIONAL CARE CENTRE, Cnr Hillview Place & Hillview Tce, Bentley	84 A 5
SOUTH LAKE OTTEY FAMILY CENTRE, 2 South Lake Dr, South Lake	102 C 7
SOUTH PERTH DAY CARE CENTRE, 113a Angelo & Cnr Sandgate St, South Perth	73 B 9
SPEECH & HEARING CENTRE FOR DEAF CHILDREN, Dodd St, Wembley	60 A 6
ST HILDA'S AFTER SCHOOL CARE PROGRAMME, Bay View Tce, Mosman Park	80 E 4
ST JAMES DAY NURSERY, 56 Victoria St, St James	84 B 3
SUBICARE, 295 Bagot Rd, Subiaco	72 A 2
SUDBURY COMMUNITY HOUSE CHILD CARE, 30 Chesterfield Rd, Mirrabooka	47 A 3
SUNSHINE CHILD CARE CENTRE, 139 Safety Bay Rd, Shoalwater	136 D 9
SUPERDROME DAY CARE, Perth Superdrome, Stephenson Ave, Mount Claremont	71 A 2
SWAN CHILD CARE CENTRE, 36 Diana Cr, Lockridge	49 A 6
SWAN VIEW FAMILY CENTRE, Marlboro Rd, Swan View	51 C 8
SWANBOURNE SERVICES CHILD CARE CENTRE, Sayer St, Swanbourne	70 D 8
THE CHILDRENS HOSPITAL CHILD CARE CENTRE, Cnr Roberts Rd & Thomas St, Subiaco	72 C 1
THE INTERNATIONAL CHILD CARE CENTRE, Doig Pl, Beaconsfield	90 E 8
THE LITTLE KIDS PLACE, 245 South Tce, Sth Fremantle	90 C 7
THE UNIVERSITY CHILD CARE CLUB (UNICARE), 24 Parkway, Crawley	72 A 10
THORNLIE CHILD CARE CENTRE, 13 Merino Ct, Thornlie	95 B 2
TIMBERTOPS FAMILY CENTRE, Chichester Dr, Woodvale	24 B 5
TODDLERS DAY CARE CENTRE, 62 Carnarvon St, East Victoria Park	74 A 8
TOM THUMB DAY CARE CENTRE, 7 Hobart St, North Perth	60 D 6
TOMATO LAKE CHILD CARE CENTRE, 23 Paterson Rd, Kewdale	74 D 7
TREASURE ISLAND CHILD CARE CENTRE, 30 Cecil Ave, Cannington	84 E 6
UNICARE, 24 Parkway, Nedlands	72 A 9
VICTORIA PARK COMMUNITY CHILD CARE CENTRE, 1-5 Sussex St, East Victoria Park	74 A 9
VIRGINIA AVE DAY CARE CENTRE, 7 Virginia Ave, Maddington	96 B 6
WACAE CHURCHLANDS CAMPUS CHILD CARE CENTRE, Pearson St	59 C 6
WACAE NEDLANDS CHILD CARE CENTRE, 57 Leura St, Nedlands	71 E 7
WAIKIKI PLAY SCHOOL, 1 Norring St, Cooloongup	137 C 10
WAROOGA CHILD CARE CENTRE, 47 Riley Rd, Riverton	94 A 1
WARWICK CHILD CARE CENTRE, Lot 164 Beach Rd, Warwick	31 D 9
WATC CHILD CARE CENTRE (Ascot), Grandstand St, Ascot	62 C 9
WATC CHILD CARE CENTRE (Belmont), Goodwood Pde, Rivervale	73 D 1
WEMBLEY NURSERY AND CHILD CARE CENTRE, 19 Herdsman Pde, Wembley	59 E 7
WEST PERTH CHILD CARE & NURSERY SCHOOL, 38 Cleaver St, West Perth	60 D 9
WESTERLY FAMILY CENTRE, Westerly Wy, Cooloongup	137 D 9
WHITFORD FAMILY CENTRE, 21 Endeavour Rd, Hillarys	23 B 9
WHITFORD OCCASIONAL CARE CENTRE, 21 Endeavour Rd, Hillarys	23 B 9
WILLETTON CHILD CARE CENTRE, Burrendah Blvd, Willetton	93 C 5
WIND IN THE WILLOWS, 28-30 Wilson St, Bassendean	63 A 2
WIRRA BIRRA CHILD CARE CENTRE, Corfield St, Gosnells	95 E 9
WOODLANDS CHILD CARE, 40 Liege St, Osborne Park	59 C 2
WOODVALE CHILD CARE CENTRE, 177-179 Timberlane Dr, Woodvale	24 C 5

CHILD HEALTH CENTRES

Name	Map Ref.
ALEXANDER PARK, Melrose Cr, Menora	61 A 5
ALFRED COVE, Lambert Pl	81 E 10
ARDROSS, 778 Canning Hwy, Applecross	82 C 7
ARMADALE, 412 Streich Ave South	116 D 7
ARMADALE, Community Health & Development Centre, Armadale - Kelmscott Hospital, Albany Hwy	116 E 2
BALCATTA, Jones St, (Rear of Amelia Heights Shopping Centre)	46 A 4
BALGA, 6 Penrith Pl	46 C 1
BALLAJURA, Lot 114 Illawarra Cr	33 D 6
BASSENDEAN, 1 James St	63 A 1
BATEMAN, Parry Ave	92 D 5
BAYSWATER, 23 King William St	62 B 5
BECKENHAM, 27 Birchington St	85 C 6
BEECHBORO, 106 Amazon Dr	48 D 3
BELMONT, Cnr Epsom Ave & Sydenham St, Redcliffe	75 A 1
BENTLEY SOUTH, Cnr Hill View Tce & Walpole St, Bentley	84 A 5
BENTLEY, Chapman Rd	84 B 4
BICTON, Westbury Cr	91 A 1
BLACKMORE (Girrawheen), Innis Pl, Girrawheen	32 B 7
BRENTWOOD, Moolyeen Rd	92 D 2
BULL CREEK, Francisco Cr	93 A 6
BYFORD, Park Rd	135 D 1
CARINE, Cnr Davillia & Beach Rds, Duncraig	31 B 8
CARLISLE, Oats St	74 B 10
CHIDLOW, Cnr Northcote St & Old Northam Rd	56 D 1
CHURCHLANDS COLLEGE, Cromarty Rd, Churchlands	59 B 6
CITY BEACH, Boronia Cr	58 D 8
CLAREMONT, 328 Stirling Hwy	71 A 9
CLOVERDALE, Daly St	74 E 3
COMO, Cnr Alston Ave & Labouchere Rd	83 A 2
COOLBELLUP, Cordelia Ave	101 E 1
COTTESLOE, 81 Forrest St	80 D 2
CRAIGIE, 14 Camberwarra Dr	23 C 7
DIANELLA, 236 The Strand	61 D 1
DOUBLEVIEW, Cnr Hancock St & Scarborough Beach Rd	45 A 10
DUNCRAIG, 59 Marri Rd	30 E 5
EAST FREMANTLE, 80 Canning Hwy	90 D 2
EDEN HILL, Ivanhoe St	49 A 8
EMBLETON, McKenzie Wy	62 A 1
FERNDALE, Bursaria Cr	84 B 10
FORRESTDALE, Weld St	114 E 6
FORRESTFIELD, 35 Edinburgh Rd	86 D 1
FORSTER PARK, Cnr Keane St & Abernethy Rd, Cloverdale	75 A 6
FREMANTLE, Cnr High & Parry Sts	1D C 5
GIRRAWHEEN, 29 Hainsworth Ave	32 D 9
GLEN FORREST, Lot 15 Marnie Rd	66 D 2
GOOSEBERRY HILL, 4 Ledger Rd	77 D 3
GOSNELLS, 2289 Albany Hwy	96 C 9
GREENWOOD, 5 Calectasia St	31 D 10
GUILDFORD, Cnr Meadow & Helena Sts	63 D 1
HAMERSLEY, 7 Glendale Ave	31 D 10
HAMILTON HILL, 52 Redmond Rd	101 C 1
HAMILTON HILL, Cnr Hurford & Starling Sts	100 E 1
HAMPTON, Hampton Sq W, Morley	48 C 8
HEATHRIDGE, 16 Sail Tce	23 C 2
HIGH WYCOMBE, Cnr Edney & Wycombe Rds	76 C 1
HIGHGATE, Cnr Curtis & Harold Sts, Mt Lawley	61 B 9
HILLMAN, Unnaro St	137 E 6
HILTON PARK, Cnr Paget St & Rennie Cr, Hilton	91 B 8
HOLLYWOOD, Cnr Monash Ave & Smyth Rd, Nedlands	71 D 6
HUNTINGDALE PARK, Lot 163-164 Baron Wy, Gosnells	95 E 9
INGLEWOOD, Cnr Beaufort St & Tenth Ave	61 D 5
INNALOO, Cnr Morris & Escot Rds	45 B 9
KALAMUNDA, 19A Mead St	77 D 7
KALLAROO, Batavia Pl	23 C 7
KARAWARA, 3 Yaralla Pl	83 D 5
KARDINYA, Ochiltree Wy	92 A 7
KARRINYUP, Cnr Klein St & Edmondson Cr	45 A 7
KELMSCOTT SOUTH, Grasmere Wy, Westfield	106 B 10
KELMSCOTT, 2821 Albany Hwy	106 D 8
KENSINGTON, 14 Collins St	73 C 9
KENWICK, Royal St	95 C 1
KINGSLEY, Moolanda Blvd	24 D 10
KOONDOOLA, Burbridge Ave	32 E 7
KOONGAMIA, Mudalla Way	65 B 2
KWINANA, Peel Ct	131 C 7
LANGFORD, Cnr Brookman & Langford Ave	94 E 2
LATHLAIN, Cnr Lathlain Pl & Howick St	74 B 6
LEEDERVILLE, Loftus Community Centre, Cnr Loftus & Vincent Sts	60 D 8
LEEMING, Cnr Meharry Rd & Burnett Ave	93 A 10
LESMURDIE, Sanderson Rd	87 C 4
LOCKRIDGE, 32 Weddall Rd	49 A 6
LYNWOOD, Cnr Kenton & Edgeware Sts	84 D 10
LYNWOOD, Hosack Ave	94 B 3
MADDINGTON, 7 Olga Rd	95 E 4
MANDURAH, Cnr Peel St & Ormsby Tce	162 E 10
MANNING, Bradshaw Cr	83 B 6
MAYLANDS, Cnr Ninth Ave & Guildford Rd	61 E 7
MIDDLE SWAN, Whittome St	50 D 3
MIDLAND, 12 The Avenue	50 C 8
MORLEY, 6 Wellington Rd	47 E 9
MOSMAN PARK, Bay View Tce	80 E 5
MT CLAREMONT, 25 Strickland St	71 A 5
MT HAWTHORN WEST, The Boulevarde, Mt Hawthorn	60 C 5
MULLALOO, 27 Koorana Wy	23 B 4
MUNDARING, 12 Craig St	68 B 1
NEDLANDS, Melvista Ave	81 E 1
NOLLAMARA, 5 Carcoola St (Opposite Apara Wy)	46 C 6
NORANDA, Cnr Garson Ct & Benara Rd	47 E 5
NORTH BEACH, 28 Castle St	44 C 1
NORTH COTTESLOE, 328 Marmion St, Cottesloe	70 D 10
NORTH PERTH, Haynes St	60 D 6
NORTH PERTH, View St	60 E 8
NORTH WEST SCARBOROUGH, Cnr Deanmore Rd & Blair St, Karrinyup	44 E 7
OSBORNE PARK, 149-151 Main St	60 B 1
PADBURY, Cnr Alexander & Caley Rds	23 D 8
QUEENS PARK, Cnr Godfrey & Barnsley Sts	85 A 3
RIVERTON, Cnr Barbican St & Tudor Ave	83 E 9
RIVERVALE, 18 Gt Eastern Hwy	74 A 3
ROCKINGHAM PARK, Centaurus St, Rockingham	137 B 7
ROCKINGHAM, Smythe St	137 B 4
ROLEYSTONE, 44 Jarrah Rd	108 A 7
ROSSMOYNE, Third Ave	93 B 1

	Map	Ref.
SAFETY BAY, Safety Bay Rd	136	D 10
SCARBOROUGH, Deanmore Square, Harvest Tce	44	D 10
SHENTON PARK, 334 Onslow Rd	71	D 4
SORRENTO, 108 High St	30	D 7
SOUTH LAKE, South Lake Dr	102	C 7
SOUTH PERTH, Hensman St	73	A 9
SPEARWOOD, 27 March St	101	B 5
SUBIACO, 138 Hamersley Rd	72	A 2
SWAN VIEW, 80 Salisbury Rd	51	C 8
SWANBOURNE, 15A Otway St	70	E 9
THORNLIE, Thornlie Ave	95	C 5
TRIGG, 107 Lynn St, Trigg	44	D 3
TUART HILL, Cnr Cape & Darch Sts, Yokine	60	D 1
TWO ROCKS, Cnr Carfax Pl & Bower Gr	2	D 2
VICTORIA PARK, 4-6 Temple St	73	E 8
VICTORIA PARK, Cnr Kent St & Gloucester St	73	E 9
WANNEROO, Civic Dr	20	D 8
WARNBRO, Currie St	145	C 5
WATTLEUP, Marban Wy	121	D 2
WEMBLEY DOWNS, 130 Weaponess Rd	58	E 3
WEMBLEY, Joan Waters Community Centre, 40 Alexander St	59	E 9
WEST PERTH, 16 Rheola St	72	C 2
WILLAGEE, 36 Worley St	91	E 4
WILLETTON, Lot 102 Burrendah Blvd	93	C 5
WOODLANDS, Cnr Ewen & Bowra Sts	59	C 1
WOODVALE, Chichester Dr	24	B 5
YANGEBUP, Swallow Dr	102	A 9
YOKINE, Blythe Ave	60	E 1
YOKINE, Flinders St	46	D 9

CHURCHES & PLACES OF WORSHIP

ANGLICAN

	Map	Ref.
APPLECROSS, St George, Cnr Kintail & Maclennan Rds	82	C 5
ARDROSS, St David, Cnr Simpson & Bombard Sts	82	C 8
ARMADALE, St Matthew, Cnr Jull St & Prospect Rd	116	E 6
BALGA, Good Shepherd, Cnr Climping St & Balga Ave	46	C 1
BASSENDEAN, St Mark the Evangelist, 4 Wilson St	63	A 2
BAYSWATER, St Augustine, Cnr Roberts & Murray Sts	62	B 5
BEACONSFIELD, St Paul The Apostle, 164 Hampton Rd	90	D 7
BELLEVUE, Good Shepherd, 45 Clayton St	64	E 1
BICTON, St Christopher, Cnr Waddell Rd & Brown St	81	C 8
BULL CREEK, All Saints College, Ewing Ave	93	B 4
BYFORD, St Aidan, Cnr Clifton & Mary Sts	135	D 1
CANNINGTON, St Michael & All Angels, 46 George St	84	D 6
CHIDLOW, All Hallows, Cnr Tottenham St & Old Northam Rd	56	D 1
CITY BEACH, St Christopher, Cnr Templetonia Cr & Tamala Rd	58	E 8
CLAREMONT, Christ Church, Cnr Stirling Hwy & Queenslea Dr	71	A 10
CLOVERDALE, All Saints, Belgravia St	74	E 4
COMO, St Augustine, Cnr Park & Cale Sts	83	A 4
COTTESLOE, St Philip, Cnr Napier & Marmion Sts	80	D 2
DALKEITH, St Lawrence, Cnr Viking & Alexander Rds	81	C 3
DARLINGTON, St Cuthbert, Cnr Darlington & Hillsden Rds	66	A 4
DIANELLA, All Saints, 420 Grand Promenade	47	B 9
DUNCRAIG, St Nicholas, Cnr Poynter Dr & Beach Rd	31	A 9
EAST VICTORIA PARK, Holy Trinity, Cnr Whittlesford & Washer Sts	84	A 2
FLOREAT, St Nicholas, 47 Berkeley Cr	59	C 9
FORRESTFIELD, St Stephen, 7 Salix Wy, near Cnr Strelitzia Ave	76	C 9
FREMANTLE, St John the Evangelist, St Johns Sq, Adelaide St	1D	C 5
GLEN FORREST, St Andrew, McGlew Rd	66	D 2
GOSNELLS, All Saints, Cnr Dorothy & Hicks Sts	96	B 9
GRAYLANDS, St Michael & All Angels, 71 First Ave, Claremont	71	B 6
GREENWOOD, St John the Evangelist, Calectasia St (near Cnr Coolibah Dr)	31	D 5
GUILDFORD, St Matthew, Stirling Sq	49	D 10
HAMERSLEY, Holy Cross, Cnr Aintree St & Glendale Ave	31	D 10
HIGH WYCOMBE, (meets at Community Hall), Cnr Western Ave & Cyril Rd	64	C 10
HIGHGATE, St Alban, Cnr Beaufort St & St Alban's Ave	61	B 9
HILTON, St Edward, 12 Holmes Pl	91	C 8
INGLEWOOD, St Francis, Cnr Wood & Robinson Sts	61	D 4
JARRAHDALE, St Paul, Atkins St	152	E 7
KALAMUNDA, St Barnabas, Cnr Railway & Spring Rds	77	D 6
KALLAROO, Resurrection, Cnr Dampier & Aristride Aves	23	B 6
KARRINYUP, St Francis of Assisi, Burroughs Rd (opposite Shopping Centre)	45	A 5
KELMSCOTT, St Mary in the Valley, River Rd	106	E 9
KENSINGTON, St Martin, 54 Dyson St	73	C 8
LESMURDIE, St Swithun, 193 Lesmurdie Rd	87	D 1
LOCKRIDGE, Resurrection, Arbon Wy	49	A 6
LYNWOOD, St Augustine, Cnr Tavistock Cr & Kenton St	94	D 1
MADDINGTON, St Luke, Cnr Westfield & Sheoak St	96	C 5
MANDURAH, Christs Church, Cnr Sholl St & Pinjarra Rd	164	E 2
MANNING, St Peter, Cnr Welwyn Ave & Griffin Cr	83	B 7
MAYLANDS, St Luke, Cnr Rowlands & George Sts	61	E 7
MELVILLE, Holy Cross, Cnr McLean St & Coleman Cr	91	D 2
MIDDLE SWAN, St Mary, Yule Ave	50	C 2
MIDLAND, Ascension, Spring Park Rd	50	B 8
MOSMAN PARK, All Saints, 31 Jameson St	80	E 7
MOSMAN PARK, St Luke, 18 Monument St	80	D 4
MT HAWTHORN, St Peter, 96 Flinders St	60	C 5
MT HELENA, St Mark, Cnr Keane St West & Ealy St	55	A 5
MT LAWLEY, Perth College Chapel, Lawley Cr	61	C 8
MT LAWLEY, St Patrick, Cnr Beaufort St & First Ave	61	C 7
MT PLEASANT, St Michael, Cnr The Promenade & Gunbower Rd	82	D 10
MUNDARING, Epiphany, Mann St	54	A 10
NEDLANDS, St Andrew, Cnr Stirling Hwy & Napier St	71	C 9
NEDLANDS, St Margaret, Cnr Tyrell & Elizabeth Sts	71	E 9
NOLLAMARA, St Paul, Cnr Nollamara Ave & Poinsettia Wy, Dianella	46	E 5
NORANDA, St Martin, 77 Bramwell Rd	47	D 5
NORTH BEACH, St Michael & All Angels, Cnr George & James Sts	44	C 1
NORTH PERTH, St Hilda, Cnr View & Glebe Sts	60	E 8
OSBORNE PARK, All Saints, Cnr Hutton & Albert Sts	46	A 10
PADBURY, St Luke, Alexander Rd (Near corner of Forrest Ave)	23	D 9
PALMYRA, St Peter & St Mark, 2 Hammad St	91	A 2
PARKERVILLE, St Michael & All Angels, Parkerville Childrens Home	53	C 4
PARMELIA, All Saints, Cnr Chisham Ave & Bickner Wy	131	A 7
PERTH, St Georges Cathedral, 38 St Georges Tce	1C	A 3
RIVERVALE, St Barnabas, 239 Orrong Rd	74	C 6
ROCKINGHAM, St Nicholas, Council Ave	137	C 8
ROLEYSTONE, St Christopher, Hall Rd	107	E 8
SAFETY BAY, St George, Cnr Thomas St, Rae & Scott Rds	136	D 9
SCARBOROUGH, St Columba, 150 Northstead St	44	E 9
SERPENTINE, St Stephen, Cnr South West Hwy & Falls Rd	155	B 3
SHELLEY, St Andrew, Bernier Rd	83	C 10
SHENTON PARK, St Matthew, Cnr Hensman & Keightley Rds	72	A 4
SOUTH PERTH, St Mary the Virgin, Cnr Karoo & Ridge Sts	72	E 9
SUBIACO, St Andrew, 259 Barker Rd	72	A 2
SWANBOURNE, St Oswald, Cnr Shenton Rd & Derby St	70	E 9
THORNLIE, St Andrew, Cnr Thornlie Ave & Camberley St	95	C 4
UPPER SWAN, All Saints, Henry St	29	B 7
VICTORIA PARK, St Peter, 15 Leonard St	73	E 7
WANNEROO, St Peter, Cnr Leach Rd & Crisafulli Ave	20	D 8
WEMBLEY DOWNS, St Paul the Apostle, 57 Brompton Rd	58	D 3
WEMBLEY, St Edmund, 54 Pangbourne St	59	E 9
WEST PERTH, St Mary, 42 Colin St	1C	D 2
WESTFIELD, Harold King Community Centre, Grovelands Dr	106	B 9
WILLAGEE, St Thomas of Canterbury, 79 Archibald St	91	E 5
WILLETTON, Willetton High School, Pinetree Gully Rd	93	C 6
YANCHEP, St James, Lagoon Dr	4	D 4
YOKINE, Holy Family, 166 Lawley St	60	D 1

APOSTOLIC

	Map	Ref.
BAYSWATER, 7 Slade St	62	B 5
DIANELLA, Cnr Hannaby & Eastland Sts	46	E 8
GOSNELLS, (meets at Eddie Mills Senior Citizen Centre) Cnr Dorothy & Astley Sts	96	C 8
MELVILLE, (meets at Melville Civic Centre) Almondbury Rd, Ardross	82	C 10
MIDLAND, (meets at Callisthenics Centre) Gray Dr, Midvale	50	E 7

ASSEMBLIES OF GOD

	Map	Ref.
ARMADALE, Cnr Forrest & Sixth Rds	116	C 7
BELMONT, 240 Epsom Ave	75	A 1
CLAREMONT, (meets at Claremont Town Hall), 327 Stirling Hwy	71	A 9
DUNCRAIG, (meets at Duncraig High School), Readshaw Rd	30	D 4
FREMANTLE, 233 South Tce	90	C 8
GIRRAWHEEN, 77 Girrawheen Ave	32	C 7
GOSNELLS, (meets at Victory Fellowship Hall) 39-41 Dorothy St, Gosnells	96	B 10
HEATHRIDGE, (meets at Community Centre), Sail Tce, Heathridge	23	C 1
HIGH WYCOMBE, (meets at High Wycombe Family Centre), Edney Rd, High Wycombe	76	C 1
KWINANA, Cnr Westcott Rd & Sharman St, Medina	130	D 5
MANDURAH, (meets at Lesser Hall, Aquatic Recreation Centre), Pinjarra Rd, Mandurah	165	B 2
MORLEY, 334 Walter Rd	48	A 9
MT LAWLEY, Cnr Chelmsford Rd & Hyde St	61	A 9
MUNDARING, (meets at Mundaring Shire Hall), Cnr Nichol & Jacoby Sts, Mundaring	68	B 1
NOLLAMARA, 114 Nollamara Ave	46	D 6
NORTH BEACH, (meets at Hockey Club), Wendling Rd, North Beach	44	D 2
NORTHBRIDGE, 68-70 Aberdeen St	1C	A 1
PADBURY, (meets at Padbury High School), Giles Ave, Padbury	23	D 10
PALMYRA, (meets at Palmyra Recreation Centre), Cnr Canning Hwy, & Murray Rd, Palmyra	91	C 1
QUINNS ROCKS, (meets at Gumblossom Hall), Gumblossom Park	10	B 10
ROCKINGHAM, Cnr Dixon Rd & Nasmyth St	137	E 4
SAFETY BAY, (meets at McLarty Hall), McLarty Rd, Shoalwater	136	C 10
VICTORIA PARK, (meets at Presidential Suite), 896 Albany Hwy	74	A 10

265

	Map	Ref.
WANNEROO, (meets at Wanneroo Senior High School), Quarkum St	20	E 9
WILLETTON, (meets at Bill Cole Centre) Cnr High & Riley Rds	94	A 1
YANCHEP,(meets at High School Library), Lagoon Dr	4	D 4
YANGEBUP, (meets at Community Hall) Cnr Swallow & Moorhen St	102	A 9

BAHA'I FAITH

SOUTH PERTH, 27 Lawler St	73	B 8

BAPTIST

ATTADALE, 47 Davis Rd	81	D 10
BALLAJURA,(meets at Illawarra Primary Sch), Illawarra Cr	33	C 5
BAYSWATER,(Romanian) 451 Guildford Rd	62	B 6
BEDFORD, Cnr Rosebery & Park Sts	61	D 4
BEECHBORO, (meets at East Beechboro Primary Sch), Brockmill Ave	49	A 4
BELLEVUE, 37 Gt Eastern Hwy	51	A 9
BENTLEY, Cnr Chapman & Pusey Sts	84	B 4
BYFORD, South Western Hwy	126	D 9
CARLISLE, 100 Star St	74	C 8
CLAREMONT, 322 Stirling Hwy	71	A 9
COMO, 111 Robert St	82	E 4
COOLBELLUP, Cnr Waverley & Doherty Rds	92	A 10
CRAIGIE, Camberwarra Dr	23	D 7
DALKEITH, 123 Waratah Ave	81	C 2
EAST FREMANTLE, Cnr Canning Hwy & Fortescue St	90	E 2
EAST VICTORIA PARK, (Ukranian) 86 Hubert St	74	A 10
GIRRAWHEEN, Cnr Hainsworth Ave & Salcott Rd	32	D 9
GOSNELLS, Cnr Albany Hwy & Verna St	96	C 10
KELMSCOTT, 29 Third Ave	106	D 9
KINGSLEY, Cnr Duffy Tce & Woodvale Dr, Woodvale	24	D 6
LAKE JOONDALUP, Kennedya Dr, Joondalup	19	D 5
LEEDERVILLE (Spanish), 156 Tower St	60	C 9
LEEMING, (meets at Leeming Heights Community Hall), Westall Tce	92	E 9
LESMURDIE, Brady Rd	87	C 5
MAIDA VALE, Edney Rd, High Wycombe	64	D 10
MANDURAH, Cnr Pinjarra Rd & Rio Grande Ave, Greenfields	165	D 2
MAYLANDS, Cnr Coode St & Seventh Ave	61	D 7
MELVILLE, Cnr Sergeant Rd & Hornsby St	91	C 3
MORLEY, 55 Vera St	47	E 9
MOSMAN PARK, Cnr Fairlight & Eastbourne Sts	80	D 5
MT HAWTHORN, Cnr Hobart & Edinboro Sts	60	C 5
MT PLEASANT, Cnr Rogerson Rd & Darnell Ave	92	D 1
NORTH BEACH, Cnr Groat & Sorrento Sts	44	D 2
PERTH, Cnr Stirling & James Sts	1C	A 2
RIVERTON, Modillion Ave North	83	D 9
ROCKINGHAM, Lot 2 Gnangara Dr, Waikiki	145	D 3
SCARBOROUGH, Cnr Brighton Rd & Westview St	44	E 10
SOUTH PERTH, Lawler St	73	B 8
THE LAKES, (meets at South Lake Primary Sch), Mason Ct, South Lake	102	C 6
THORNLIE, Wynyard Wy	95	B 4
VICTORIA PARK, (Slavic) 60 Armagh St	73	D 7
WATTLE GROVE, Welshpool Rd	85	E 3
WEMBLEY DOWNS, 20 Brix St	59	A 4
YOKINE, Cnr Flinders St & Frape Ave	60	D 1

BAPTIST INDEPENDENT

ARMADALE, (Calvary), Seventh Rd	116	C 6
BEECHBORO, (meets at Caversham Memorial Hall), West Swan Rd	49	D 5
BULL CREEK, Cnr Granville Wy & Vahland Ave	93	E 2
GREENWOOD, (meets at Greenwood High Sch), Coolibah Dr	31	B 5
LOCKRIDGE, (meets at Pre-School Centre), Cnr Diana Cr & Titus Rd	49	A 6
MIDVALE, (meets at Midvale Hall), Wellaton St	50	E 8
MT HELENA, Cnr Keane St East & Chidlow St	55	C 5
NOLLAMARA, Cnr Hillsborough & Ravenswood Drvs	46	C 1
PADBURY, (meets at Padbury Hall), Cnr Alexander & Caley Rds	23	D 8

BEECHBORO LOCKRIDGE FAMILY CARE

CAVERSHAM Lot 74 Lord St	49	B 5

BRETHREN

ARMADALE, Outram Rd	116	D 5
BALCATTA, 38 Collier Ave	46	B 6
BALGA, 31 Fieldgate Sq	32	B 9
BEDFORD, 261 Coode St	61	D 1
CARRAMAR,(meets at Carramar Community Centre), Redgum Wy, Morley	48	D 6
COTTESLOE, Cnr Edward & Gordon Sts	80	E 1
DUNCRAIG, (meets at Recreation Centre), Cnr Warwick Rd & Marmion Ave	30	D 7
HAMILTON HILL, Cnr Redmond Rd & Carmody St	101	E 1
LYNWOOD, 32-34 Latham Rd, Ferndale	84	D 9
NORTH COASTAL, (meets at Ocean Ridge Community Centre), Sail Tce, Heathridge	23	C 1
NORTH PERTH, 117 Angove St	60	E 7
SAWYERS VALLEY, Cnr Ashstead St & Helena Tce	68	E 1
SWAN, (meets at Midland Christian School), Midland	50	B 9
VICTORIA PARK, Cnr Berwick & Rathay Sts, Kensington	73	E 9
WEMBLEY DOWNS, 9 Quorn St	59	A 5
WILSON, Cnr Bungaree & Andrew Rds	84	A 6
WUNGONG-ARMADALE,(meets at Armadale High School), South West Hwy, Armadale	116	D 7

BUDDHIST

NOLLAMARA, (Society of Western Australia) 18-20 Nanson Wy	46	C 8
PERTH CITY,(Vietnamese), Chanh Giac, Money St	1C	A 1

CHRISTADELPHIAN

OSBORNE PARK, Cnr Hector & Edward Sts	60	B 2
THORNLIE, Cnr Yale and Murdoch Rds	94	E 6
VICTORIA PARK, 62 Canning Hwy	73	D 7
YOKINE, 82 Spencer Ave	61	A 1

CHRISTIAN AND MISSIONARY ALLIANCE

CANNING VALE, Southern Districts Alliance, Lot 40 Warton Rd	105	B 1

CHRISTIAN SCIENCE

EMBLETON, Cnr Collier Rd & Embleton Ave	62	B 1
FREMANTLE, Cnr East St & Canning Hwy	90	D 3
MIDLAND, Cnr The Crescent & Keane St	50	C 8
PERTH, 264 St Georges Tce	1C	D 2

CHRIST, CHURCH OF (Non Denom.)

CITY BEACH, Tumut Rd	58	D 10
EMBLETON, Cnr Broun Ave & Parsons St	62	A 1
GREENMOUNT, 513 Great Eastern Hwy	65	C 1
RIVERTON, 62 Riley Rd	94	A 1

CHRIST, CHURCHES OF

ALEXANDER HEIGHTS, (meets at Alinjarra Primary School), Adaia Dr	33	B 5
APPLECROSS, Cnr Riseley & Wilcock Sts, Ardross	82	C 8
BALGA, Cnr Heyshott Rd & Climping St	46	C 1
BASSENDEAN, 4 Ivanhoe St	63	A 1
BULL CREEK, 55 Agincourt Dr, Willetton	93	B 5
COTTESLOE, 4 Irvine St, Peppermint Grove	80	D 3
DALKEITH ROAD, Cnr Dalkeith Rd & Edward St, Nedlands	71	D 9
DIANELLA, 1 Waverley St	47	B 9
EASTERN HILLS, 373 Chidlow St, Mt Helena	55	C 5
FOOTHILLS, 287 Hawtin Rd, Forrestfield	76	E 7
FREMANTLE, 217 High St	1D	C 5
HAMILTON HILL, 19 Winterfold Rd	91	B 10
INGLEWOOD, 146 Sixth Ave	61	C 6
JOONDALUP, (meets at Edith Cowan University), Joondalup Dr	19	F 8
KALAMUNDA, Cnr Canning & Fletcher Rds, Lesmurdie	87	E 1
KELMSCOTT/ARMADALE, Cnr Lake & Centre Rds, Westfield	106	C 5
KINGSLEY, 58 New Cross Rd	24	C 10
KWINANA, Cnr Heald Pl & Matson St, Medina	130	E 4
MANDURAH, Lot 25 Teranca Rd, Greenfields	165	E 2
MANNING, Cnr Cloister Ave & Cornish Cr	83	B 7
MAYLANDS, 47 Eighth Ave	61	E 7
MIDLAND, 22 Viveash Rd	50	C 8
MT HELENA, 373 Chidlow St	55	C 5
MURDOCH, (meets at Murdoch University), South St	92	C 7
NOLLAMARA, Cnr Carcoola St & Apara Wy	46	D 6
NORANDA, 198 Crimea St	48	A 6
PERTH, 142 Beaufort St	1C	A 1
RIVERVALE, Cnr Kooyong & Alexander Rds	74	C 6
ROCKINGHAM, Cnr Rae Rd & Federick St, Safety Bay	136	D 9
SCARBOROUGH, Cnr Karrinyup & Huntriss Rds, Gwelup	45	B 7
SOUTH PERTH, Cnr Murray St & McNabb Lp, Como	83	B 3
SOUTHERN HILLS, 5 Champion Dr, Armadale	116	C 3
SUBIACO, Cnr Bagot Rd & Rowland St	72	A 2
THORNLIE, Cnr Spencer & Sandon Rds	95	C 5
WARNBRO,(meets at Warnbro Prim. School), Fairmile St	145	D 7
WARWICK, Cnr Dugdale St & Ellersdale Rds	31	D 8
WEMBLEY DOWNS, Cnr Bournemouth & Arundle Crs	59	A 3
WEMBLEY, 63 Nanson St	59	E 9
WHITFORD, Scaphella Ave, Mullaloo	23	B 4

CONGREGATIONAL

ARMADALE, (FIEC), 150 Forrest Rd	116	B 8
BECKENHAM, (FIEC), Cnr Saturn & Streatham Sts	85	C 8
KELMSCOTT, (FIEC), Rundle St	106	E 10
ROLEYSTONE, Croyden Rd	108	A 10

FELLOWSHIP OF INDEPENDENT EVANGELICAL (FIEC)

ARMADALE, Congregational, 150 Forrest Rd	116	B 8
ASHFIELD, Christian Fellowship, (Cyril Jackson Recreation Centre), Fisher St	62	E 3
BECKENHAM, Conregational, Cnr Saturn & Streatham Sts	85	C 8
BELMONT, Christian Fellowship, Cnr Keane St & Belmont Ave	74	E 6
GLEN FORREST, Christian Fellowship, (meets at Glen Forrest Hall), Cnr Marnie Rd & Statham St	66	D 2
KELMSCOTT, Congregational, Rundle St	106	E 10

FORRESTFIELD BIBLE F'SHIP

FORRESTFIELD, 45 Berkshire Rd	76	D 8

FOURSQUARE GOSPEL

BEECHBORO, Lot 74 Lord St	49	B 5
KALAMUNDA, (meets at Agricultural Hall), Canning Rd	77	D 7
KALLAROO, (meets at Kallaroo Community Hall), Dampier Ave	23	B 6
KOONDOOLA, (meets at Koondoola Community Hall), Burbridge Ave	32	E 7
MORLEY, Cnr Morley Dr & Timms Pl	47	E 8
OCEAN REEF, (meets at Ocean Reef Senior High School), Cnr Hodges St & Venturi Rd	19	A 10
VICTORIA PARK, 67 Armagh St	73	D 7

	Map Ref.
FREE REFORMED	
ARMADALE, Fifth Rd	116 C 6
BEDFORDALE, Wandoo St, Kelmscott	116 E 1
BYFORD, Cnr Mead St & Soldiers Rd	135 C 2
KELMSCOTT, Lake Rd	106 A 9

FREE SERBIAN ORTHODOX

EAST PERTH, 38 Marlborough St .... 61 C 10

GRACE BIBLE CHURCH

MADDINGTON, (meets at Maddington Senior High Sch), Dellar Rd .... 96 C 3

GREEK ORTHODOX

DIANELLA, Church of St Nektarious, Dianella Dr .... 47 A 7
FORRESTFIELD, Monastry of St John of the Mountain, Holmes Rd .... 76 E 9
NORTHBRIDGE, Cnr Parker & Francis Sts .... 1C E 1
WEST PERTH, Cnr Charles & Carr Sts .... 60 E 10

HINDU TEMPLE

CANNING VALE, Lot 41 Warton Rd .... 105 A 1

JEHOVAHS WITNESSES

ARMADALE, Williams Rd .... 116 B 4
BECKENHAM, 33-35 Ladywell St .... 85 C 10
BELDON, Coyle Rd .... 24 A 3
CLOVERDALE, Orrong Rd ...... 74 C 8
DIANELLA, 44 Chelsea Ct ...... 47 D 8
DOUBLEVIEW, 224 Woodside St .... 45 B 9
EMBLETON, 5-7 Irwin St .... 62 B 1
GREENFIELDS, (Kingdom Hall), off Pinjarra Rd .... 165 E 3
GREENMOUNT, Wooloomooloo Rd .... 51 C 9
JOONDANNA, Baden St .... 60 C 3
KARAWARA, Kent St .... 83 D 5
MT HELENA, Evans St .... 55 B 4
MT LAWLEY, John St .... 61 C 7
NOLLAMARA, 411 Flinders St .... 46 D 5
NORTH BEACH, Cnr Charles Riley Rd & Edgefield Wy .... 44 D 3
ROCKINGHAM, Wanliss St .... 137 B 4
SPEARWOOD, Caffery Pl ..... 101 C 3
SUBIACO, 15 Catherine St ..... 72 B 1
WATTLE GROVE, (Assembly Hall), Cnr Welshpool Rd & Bruce Rds ... 86 A 4
WHITE GUM VALLEY, Lot 1 Edmund St .... 90 D 6

JEWISH

MENORA, Perth Hebrew Congregation, Cnr Plantation St & Freedman Rd .... 61 A 4
MT LAWLEY, Temple David Progressive Congregation, 34 Clifton Cr .... 61 B 7

KINGS CITY

PERTH, 381 Murray St .... 1C E 2

LATTER DAY SAINTS - THE CHURCH OF JESUS CHRIST OF

ARMADALE, Carawatha Ave .116 E 3
ATTADALE, Cnr Preston Pt & Prinsep Rds .... 81 C 10

	Map Ref.
BALLAJURA, Cnr Knot Ri & Pelican Pde	34 A 8
CLOVERDALE, Cnr Hardey Rd & Sydenham St	74 E 2
COMO, Cnr Labouchere Rd & Eric St	83 A 1
DOUBLEVIEW, 71 Princess Rd	59 B 1
GREENMOUNT, Cnr Wooloomooloo & Gabo Rds	51 C 10
HEATHRIDGE, 123 Caridean St	19 D 10
ROCKINGHAM, 38 Casserly Rd	137 A 9
THORNLIE, 215 Yale Rd	94 E 6
WARWICK, 44 Hawker Ave	31 C 8
YOKINE, 163 Wordsworth Ave	61 B 2

LATTER DAY SAINTS, RE-ORG.

FREMANTLE, 198 High St ..... 90 D 4
WOODLANDS, Cnr Lombardy St & Elmswood Ave .... 59 B 4

LIBERAL CATHOLIC

PERTH, (St John the Divine), Lacey & Brewer Sts .... 1C B 1

LUTHERAN

BELMONT, (Latvian) 60 Cleaver Tce .... 74 C 2
DUNCRAIG, Cnr Glengary Dr & Hepburn Ave .... 31 A 3
LYNWOOD, (Immanuel) Lot 7 Nicol Rd .... 94 A 4
MANDURAH, (meets at Anglican Church) Pinjarra Rd .... 164 E 2
MORLEY, (Bethlehem) Cnr Robinson Rd & Weld St ..... 48 A 9
MT LAWLEY, (Hungarian) Cnr Beaufort St & First Ave .. 61 C 7
PERTH, (St John) 16 Aberdeen St .... 1C A 1
ROCKINGHAM, Cnr Parkin & Florence Sts .... 136 E 5

MACEDONIAN ORTHODOX

NORTH PERTH, 69 Angove St .... 60 E 7
NORTH PERTH, Macedonia Pl .... 60 E 7

MISSIONS TO SEAMEN

FREMANTLE, Flying Angel Club, 76 Queen Victoria St ... 1D C 3

MOSLEM

PERTH, Cnr William & Robinson Sts .... 61 A 10
RIVERVALE, 7 Malvern Rd .... 74 A 3

NAZARENE, CHURCH OF

NOLLAMARA, Cnr Hayes Ave & Morley Dr .... 46 E 8

NEW APOSTOLIC

KOONDOOLA, Cnr Koondoola & Burbidge Aves .... 32 E 8
RIVERVALE, 179 Armadale Rd .... 74 C 5

NEW CHURCH IN AUSTRALIA

EAST PERTH, 176 Adelaide Tce .... 1C B 4

NORTHSIDE CHRISTIAN

WANGARA, Lot 1 Unit 5 Dellamarta Rd .... 24 E 6

	Map Ref.
PEOPLES CHRISTIAN	
PERTH, (meeting place) 816 Hay St	1C E 2

POLISH CATHOLIC

MAYLANDS, Eighth Ave .... 61 E 7

POTTERS HOUSE, THE

ARMADALE, Cnr Forrest Rd & Railway Ave .... 116 D 6
FREMANTLE, 2/22 Bannister St .... 1D B 5
MANDURAH, (meets at Mewburn Centre), Scholl St .... 164 E 1
MIDLAND, 8 Stafford St .... 50 C 8
ROCKINGHAM, (meets at The Westerly Family Centre), Cnr Willmont Dr & Westerly Wy, Cooloongup .... 137 D 9
SCARBOROUGH, 62 Scarborough Beach Rd ...... 44 D 10
VICTORIA PARK, (meets at Police & Citizens Youth Club), Cnr Rathay & Anketell Sts, Kensington ...... 73 D 10
WHITFORDS, (meets at Whitfords Community Centre), Caley Rd, Padbury .... 23 D 8

PRESBYTERIAN

BALGA, (meets Community Hall), Princess Rd .... 46 C 1
BASSENDEAN, 14 Broadway .... 63 A 1
BICTON, Cnr Harris Rd & View Tce .... 81 B 10
CHINESE, (meets at Scots Fremantle), Cnr Parry St & South Tce, Fremantle .... 1D C 6
FREMANTLE, Scots, Cnr Parry St & South Tce ...... 1D C 6
GUILDFORD, (meets at Primary Sch), Helena St .... 63 C 1
JOONDALUP, (meets at Ocean Reef Senior High School), Venturi Dr, Ocean Reef .... 19 A 10
KARDINYA LAKES, (meets at Kardinya Primary School), Ochiltree Wy .... 92 A 7
KOREAN, (meets at Bicton), Cnr Harris Rd & View Tce, Bicton .... 81 B 10
LEEDERVILLE, Cnr Kimberley & Ruislip Sts ..... 60 C 9
PADBURY, (meets at St Marks Anglican Sch), St Marks Dr, Hillarys .... 23 B 8
PEPPERMINT GROVE, Cnr Keane & Venn Sts .... 80 D 3

QUAKERS, SOCIETY OF FRIENDS

MT LAWLEY, 35 Clifton Cr ...... 61 B 7

REFORMED

GOSNELLS, 55 Mills Rd .... 96 C 8
VICTORIA PARK, 5 Colombo St .... 73 D 6
WILLETON, Cnr Portcullis Dr & Gloucester Ct .... 93 E 6

RHEMA FAMILY CHURCH

VICTORIA PARK, 1 Thorogood St .... 73 E 5

ROMAN CATHOLIC

ARDROSS, St Benedict, Alness St .... 82 C 7
ARMADALE, St Francis Xavier, Cnr Sth Western Hwy & Thomas St .... 116 E 7

	Map Ref.
ASHFIELD, St Mark, 33 Haig St	62 E 4
ATTADALE, St Joseph Pignatelli, Cnr Davidson & Money Rds	81 D 9
BALCATTA, St Lawrence, 392 Albert St	46 B 6
BALGA, St Gerard, Changton Wy	46 D 4
BALLAJURA, (meets at Catholic Primary School), Cnr Pelican Pde & Cassowary Dr	33 E 8
BASSENDEAN, St Joseph, Hamilton St	63 A 1
BATEMAN, Mass Centre Corpus Christi College, Murdoch Dr	92 D 5
BAYSWATER, St Columba, Cnr Roberts & Almondbury Sts	62 B 6
BEACONSFIELD, Christ the King, Cnr Lefroy Rd & Livingstone St	90 D 8
BEDFORD, St Peters, Wood St, Inglewood	61 D 3
BELMONT, St Anne, Hehir St	74 C 1
BENTLEY, Santa Clara, Cnr Coolgardie & Pollock Sts	84 B 4
BRENTWOOD, Regine Caeli, Cnr Bateman & Adamson Rds	92 E 3
CARLISLE, Church of the Holy Name, Solar Wy	74 C 8
CHIDLOW, (Our Lady of Good Counsel), Cnr Wilcox & Old Northam Rds	56 D 1
CITY BEACH, The Holy Spirit, Bent St	58 D 5
CLAREMONT, St Thomas, Cnr College Rd & Melville St	71 B 8
CLOVERDALE, Notre Dame, Daly St	74 E 3
COMO, Holy Family, Thelma St	83 A 2
COMO, St Pius, Ley St	83 A 6
COOLBELLUP, Friar John Wy	101 E 1
COTTESLOE, Star Of The Sea, Cnr Stirling Hwy & McNeil St	80 E 2
CRAIGIE, Our Lady of the Missions, Camberwarra Dr	23 C 6
CRAWLEY, St Thomas Moore Chapel, Stirling Hwy	72 A 7
DALKEITH, Carmelite Monastery, Adelma Rd	81 D 1
DALKEITH, St Josephs Chapel (Sunset Hos.), Jutland Pde	81 D 3
DARLINGTON, Hillsden Rd	66 A 3
DIANELLA, Our Ladys Assumption, 354 Grand Promenade	47 B 10
EAST CANNINGTON, St Francis, Redcliffe St	85 B 6
EAST FREMANTLE, The Immaculate Conception, Canning Hwy	90 E 2
EAST PERTH, St Francis Xavier, Windsor St	61 B 10
EAST VICTORIA PARK, Our Lady Help of Christians, Camberwell St	84 A 1
EMBLETON, Holy Trinity, Burnett St	62 A 2
FLOREAT, St Cecilia, Grantham St	59 C 8
FREMANTLE, St Patrick, Adelaide St	1D C 4
GIRRAWHEEN, Our Lady of Mercy, Patrick Ct	32 C 7
GLENDALOUGH, St Bernadette, Jugan St	60 A 5
GOSNELLS, Our Lady Of the Most Blessed Sacrament, Cnr Isdell Pl & Corfield St	106 A 1
GREENMOUNT, Cnr Bullarra & Innamincka Rds	51 B 9

	Map Ref.
GREENWOOD, All Saints, Cnr Liwara Pl & Orkney Rd	31 B 6
GUILDFORD, St Mary, Cnr James & Attfield Sts	49 E10
GWELUP, St Theresa, North Beach Rd	45 C 5
HAMILTON HILL, Holy Cross, Dianne St	101 A 1
HERNE HILL, Gt Northern Hwy	36 D 4
HIGHGATE, Sacred Heart, Mary St	61 B 9
HILTON, Our Lady of Mt Carmel, Cnr Collick & Laidlaw Sts	91 B 9
INGLEWOOD, All Hallows, Central Ave	61 C 6
INNALOO, St Dominic, Beatrice St	45 B10
JARRAHDALE, Aitkins St	152 E 7
JOONDANNA, St Denis, Cnr Roberts & Osborne Sts	60 D 2
KALAMUNDA, Holy Family, Burt St	77 D 7
KARRAGULLEN, Canning Rd	109 A 2
KARRINYUP, Our Lady of Good Counsel, Miles St	45 A 6
KELMSCOTT, The Good Shepherd, Streich Ave	106 D 9
KENSINGTON, Holy Cross, Broad St	73 C10
KENWICK, Sacred Heart, Discovery Dr	95 B 8
LANGFORD, St Judes, Prendiville Wy	94 E 2
LEEDERVILLE, St Mary, Franklin St	60 D 7
LESMURDIE, (Monastery) Lesmurdie Rd	87 D 1
LOCKRIDGE, Mass Centre, Arbon Wy	49 A 6
MADDINGTON, Alcock St	96 B 2
MAIDA VALE, Lilian Rd	76 E 3
MANDURAH, Creery Rd	165 A 2
MAYLANDS, Queen of Martyrs, Seventh Ave West	61 D 7
MEDINA, St Vincent, Pace Rd	130 E 5
MENORA, St Paul, Rookwood St	61 A 6
MIDLAND, St Brigid, Cnr Gt Northern Hwy & Morrison Rd	50 C 7
MORLEY, The Infant Jesus, Smith St	47 D 9
MOSMAN PARK, Corpus Christi, Palmerston St	80 E 5
MUNDARING, Sacred Heart, 18 Coolgardie St	68 B 2
MYAREE, Corpus Christi,(meets at Mel Maria Prim Sch), Evershed St	92 A 2
NAVAL BASE, McLaren Ave	121 C 7
NEDLANDS, Holy Rosary, Thomas St	71 E 9
NOLLAMARA, Our Lady of Lourdes, Flinders St	46 D 8
NORTH BEACH, Our Lady of Grace, Kitchener St	44 C 3
NORTH FREMANTLE, St Anne, Alfred Rd	80 C10
NORTH PERTH, Monastery, Vincent St	60 E 9
NORTHBRIDGE, St Brigids, Fitzgerald St	60 E10
OCEAN REEF, Mass Centre, Prendiville College, Prendiville Ave,	19 A 8
PALMYRA, Our Lady of Fatima, 8 Foss St	91 B 1
PERTH, All Saints Chapel, Allendale Sq, 77 St Georges Tce	1C E 3
PERTH, St Marys Cathedral, Victoria Sq	1C A 3
PICKERING BROOK, Merrivale Rd	89 C10
QUEENS PARK, St Joseph, Railway Parade	84 E 4

	Map Ref.
REDCLIFFE, St Maria Goretti, Morrison St	63 A 9
RIVERTON, Our Lady Queen of the Apostles, Tribute St East	83 E 9
RIVERVALE, St Augustine, Gladstone Rd	74 A 4
ROCKINGHAM, Our Lady Of Lourdes, 1 Townsend St	137 A 7
ROSSMOYNE, Pallotine Mission Centre, Fifth Ave	93 B 1
SCARBOROUGH, Immaculate Heart, Cnr Deanmore & Scarborough Beach Rds	44 E 9
SERPENTINE, St Kevin, Richardson St	154 E 3
SHENTON PARK, St Aloysius, Henry St	72 A 4
SOUTH PERTH, St Columba, Forrest St	73 A 8
SPEARWOOD, St Jerome, Edeline St	101 B 6
SUBIACO, St Catherine, Bedford Ave	72 B 2
SUBIACO, St Josephs, Salvado Rd	60 B10
SWANBOURNE, St Mel, Fraser St	70 E 9
THORNLIE, Sacred Heart, Discovery Dr	95 B 8
TUART HILL, St Kieran, Tyler St	60 B 1
VICTORIA PARK, St Joachim, Shepperton Rd	73 E 7
WANNEROO, St Anthonys, Wanneroo Rd	20 D 7
WATERFORD, Clontarf, 295 Manning Rd, Waterford	83 E 6
WEMBLEY, Our Lady of Victories, Marlow St	59 E10
WILLAGEE, Our Lady Queen of Peace, Milroy St	91 D 4
WILLETTON, St John & Paul, 23 Pinetree Gully Rd	93 C 7
WILSON, Fern Rd	84 B 8
WOODLANDS, Angelico St	59 B 3

RUSSIAN ORTHODOX

	Map Ref.
BAYSWATER, 161 Whatley Cr	62 A 5

SALVATION ARMY

	Map Ref.
ARMADALE, Williams Rd	116 B 4
BALGA, Cnr Princess Rd & Lavant Way	46 C 2
BENTLEY, Dumond St	84 A 5
FLOREAT, Brookdale St	59 C10
GOSNELLS, Goodall St	106 B 1
HEATHRIDGE, Christmas Ave	19 C 9
KWINANA, Cnr Medina Ave & Hoyle Rd	130 E 4
MANDURAH, (meets at CWA Hall), Cooper St	165 A 1
MORLEY, 565 Walter Rd	48 D 9
MT HAWTHORN, Matlock St	60 C 5
PERTH (Fortress), 333 William St, Northbridge	1C A 1
RIVERVALE, Francisco St	74 B 4
ROCKINGHAM, Cnr Read St & Willmot Dr	137 C10
SOUTHWELL, 57 Erpingham Rd, Hamilton Hill	101 C 3
SUBIACO, Rowlands St	72 A 2
SWAN VIEW, 371 Morrison Rd	51 C 7
WILLAGEE, Ellison St	91 E 5

SCIENTOLOGY, CHURCH OF

	Map Ref.
PERTH, 39-41 King St	1C E 2

SEEKERS CENTRE

	Map Ref.
SUBIACO, 44 Barker Rd	72 C 1

SERBIAN ORTHODOX

	Map Ref.
HIGHGATE, 31 Smith St	61 B10

SEVENTH DAY ADVENTIST

	Map Ref.
ARMADALE, Cnr Wungong & Ninth Rd, Wungong	126 C 1
BELMONT, Cnr Fulham St & Paterson Rd, Kewdale	74 D 7
BICKLEY, Cnr Broadway & Heidelberg Rds	88 C 3
CARMEL, Carmel College, Glenisla Rd	88 C 6
COTTESLOE, 97 Napier St	80 D 2
FREMANTLE, 10 Cleopatra St, Palmyra	91 A 2
GOSNELLS, 95 Wheatley St	96 C 9
MAIDA VALE, 345 Kalamunda Rd	64 D10
MANDURAH, Cnr Wyeree & Anstruther Rds	163 B 9
MIDLAND, 10 Brockman Rd	50 D 9
MORLEY, 156 Benara Rd, Noranda	48 A 5
MOUNT LAWLEY, 52 Walcott St	61 B 8
NORTH BEACH, Cnr Wendling Rd & Waxham Pl	44 D 2
OSBORNE PARK, 127 Edward St	60 B 1
PERTH, 50 Havelock St, West Perth	1C D 2
QUEENS PARK, 140-142 Wharf St, Cannington	84 E 6
ROCKINGHAM, 21 Wanliss St	137 B 4
ROSSMOYNE, Sherwin Lodge, Cnr Webb St & Bull Creek Rd	93 B 3
SPANISH SPEAKING, 48 Havelock St, West Perth	1C D 2
VICTORIA PARK, Cnr Horden & Geddes Sts	73 D 6
WANNEROO, Wanneroo Recreation Centre, Scenic Dr	20 C 8
WILLETTON, Willetton High School, Pinetree Gully Rd	93 C 6

SEVENTH DAY ADVENTIST REFORM MOVEMENT

	Map Ref.
GUILDFORD, 6 James St	49 E10

SHILOH FAITH

	Map Ref.
BALGA, 8 Balga Ave	46 C 1

SPIRITUALISM

	Map Ref.
BASSENDEAN, (meets at Town Council) Old Perth Rd	63 A 1
HIGHGATE, 388 Stirling St	61 B 9
MAYLANDS, 123 Caledonian Ave	61 E 7
MELVILLE, Community Hall, Cnr Winnacott & Archibald Sts, Willagee	91 D 5

SPIRITUALIST

	Map Ref.
BECKENHAM, (Community Hall) Cnr Lacey St & Railway Pde	85 B 7
SUBIACO, (meets at Friendly Soc. Hall) Cnr Townshend Rd & Churchill Ave	72 B 1

UKRANIAN CATHOLIC

	Map Ref.
MAYLANDS, Cnr Sherwood & Ferguson Sts	62 A 7

UKRANIAN ORTHODOX

	Map Ref.
MAYLANDS, 2 Ferguson St	62 A 7

UNITED PENTECOSTAL

	Map Ref.
DOUBLEVIEW, Cnr Hancock & Moorland Sts	45 A 9

UNITING CHURCH IN AUSTRALIA

	Map Ref.
APPLECROSS, Cnr Kishorn & Mackenzie Rds	82 D 6
ARMADALE - KELMSCOTT, Lowanna Wy	116 C 4
BALLAJURA, (Primary School) Illawarra Cr	33 C 5
BASSENDEAN, Cnr Old Perth Rd & Hamilton St	63 A 1
BAYSWATER, 13 Murray St	62 B 5
BEDFORD, Cnr Shaftesbury Ave & Craven St	61 D 2
BEECHBORO, (meets at East Beechboro Primary School) Brockmill Ave	49 A 4
BELDON, Cnr Pacific Wy & Cutter Cr	23 C 3
BELMONT, 44 Somers St	74 E 2
BENTLEY, Rowethorpe, Hillview Tce	83 E 4
BYFORD, Clifton St	135 D 1
CANNINGTON, Woodloes St	84 E 9
CARINE, (meets at Senior High School) Everingham St	31 A10
CARLISLE, Cnr Archer & Star Sts	74 B 7
CLAREMONT, (St Aidans), Cnr Princess & Chester Rds	71 B10
COMO, 90 McDonald St	83 A 2
COOLBELLUP, Cnr Mamillius St & Waverley Rd	101 E 1
DARLINGTON, Cnr Allestree & Darlington Rds	66 B 4
DIANELLA, The Strand (near Golding St)	47 B 8
DUNCRAIG, (meets at St Stephen's School), Doveridge Dr	31 A 3
DUNCRAIG, Cnr Manuka Pl & Wandoo Rd	30 E 6
DUNCRAIG, (meets at St Stephen's School), Doveridge Dr	31 A 3
EAST VICTORIA PARK, St Davids, 16 Mint St	74 A 9
FLOREAT, All Saints, Cnr Turriff & Peebles Rds	59 C 8
FLOREAT, Forum Church, Cnr Berkeley Cr & Brookdale St	59 C 8
FORRESTFIELD, 57-59 Hale Rd	76 D10
FREMANTLE, Cnr Market & Cantonment Sts	1D B 5
GIRRAWHEEN, Cnr Salcott Rd & Hainsworth Ave	32 D 8
GLEN FORREST, McGlew Rd	66 D 2
GOSNELLS, Cnr Bert & Hicks Sts	96 B 9
GRAYLANDS, Cnr Graylands Rd & First Ave, Claremont	71 B 6
GREENWOOD, Marlock Dr	31 D 5
GUILDFORD, 91 James St	49 D10
INNALOO, Cnr Grant & King George Sts	45 B10
JOONDANNA, Cnr Green & Banksia Sts	60 C 2
KALAMUNDA, Cnr Heath Rd & Brooks St	77 D 6
KARDINYA, Le Souef Dr	91 E 6
KENSINGTON, Cnr Collins & Oxford Sts	73 C 9
LEEMING, (meets at Leeming Primary Sch) Meharry Rd	93 A10
MANDURAH, Pinjarra Rd	165 A 2

268

	Map	Ref.
MANNING, Cnr Goodwin Ave & Crawshaw Cr	83	B 4
MAYLANDS-MT LAWLEY, 165 Railway Pde, (near Central Ave)	61	D 7
MEDINA, Cnr Medina Ave & Atkinson Rd	130	E 5
MELVILLE, 64 Kitchener Rd	91	D 1
MIDLAND, (meets at Courthouse), Helena St	50	B 8
MORLEY, Lincoln Rd	47	E 7
MOSMAN PARK, 2 Willis St	80	D 4
MT HAWTHORN, 115 Kalgoorlie St	60	C 5
MT PLEASANT, Cnr Reynolds & Coomoora Rds	82	D 10
MUNDARING, Cnr Stoneville Rd & Hartung St	54	B 10
MUNDIJONG, Paterson St	143	A 8
NEDLANDS, Aldersgate, Cnr Princess Rd & Bruce St	71	E 10
NEDLANDS, St Pauls, 40 Kingsway	71	E 9
NORTH PERTH, 129 Raglan Rd	61	A 8
OSBORNE PARK, Federal St, between Main & Edward Sts	46	B 10
PALMYRA, Cnr Canning Hwy & Carrington St	91	A 1
PERTH, (St Andrews), Cnr St Georges Tce & Pier St	1C	A 3
PERTH, (Trinity Church), 72 St Georges Tce	1C	E 3
PERTH, (Wesley Church), Cnr William St & Hay St	1C	E 2
QUEENS PARK, Stockman Wy, Cannington	84	E 4
RIVERVALE, Cnr Great Eastern Hwy & Gladstone Rd	74	A 3
ROCKINGHAM, Erindoon Way, Waikiki	145	C 1
SCARBOROUGH, Cnr Moorland & Northstead Sts	44	E 9
SHENTON PARK, Cnr Derby & Onslow Rds	71	E 4
SOUTH PERTH, Cnr Angelo & Sandgate Sts	73	B 9
SPEARWOOD, 330 Rockingham Rd	101	B 6
SUBIACO, 223 Bagot Rd	72	A 2
SWAN VIEW, Cnr Watton Ct & Salisbury Rd	51	C 8
SWANBOURNE, Cnr Watt & Walpole Sts	70	D 8
WANNEROO, (meets at Anglican Church) Cnr Leach Rd & Crisafulli Ave	20	D 8
WATERMAN, Euroka Village, Flora Tce	30	C 10
WEMBLEY DOWNS, Cnr Calais Rd & Minibah St	58	E 3
WEMBLEY, 35 Pangbourne St	59	E 9
WEST PERTH, Ross Memorial, Cnr Hay & Colin Sts	1C	D 1
WILLETTON, Herald Ave	93	D 2
YOKINE, Cnr Golf View & Lockwood Sts	46	D 10

WESTMINSTER PRESBYTERIAN

	Map	Ref.
BEECHBORO (Convenant), Cnr Cherwell St & Amazon Dr	48	D 3
BULL CREEK, 32 Bull Creek Dr	92	E 4
KELMSCOTT, (meets at Kelmscott Hall) River Rd	106	E 9
KINGSLEY, Cnr Moolanda Blvd & Calthorpe Pl	31	D 3
MAIDA VALE, 4 Maida Vale Rd	76	D 2
MANDURAH, (meets at Glencoe Primary Sch), Balmoral Pde, Halls Head	164	C 3
WESTMINSTER THEOLOGICAL COLLEGE, 35 Fairway West, Yokine	46	E 10

COMMUNITY & RECREATION CENTRES

	Map	Ref.
ALMA VENVILLE, Eighth Ave, Maylands	61	E 7
ARMADALE, Townley St	116	C 8
BALCATTA, Balcatta Snr High School, Poincaire St	45	E 5
BALGA, Princess Rd	32	C 10
BECKENHAM, Streatham St	85	C 8
BELMONT, Elizabeth St, Cloverdale	74	D 4
BLUE GUM, Moolyeen Rd, Brentwood	92	D 2
CARRAMAR, Redgum Wy, Morley	48	C 6
CLEM KENTISH, Wellard St, Serpentine	155	A 3
CYRIL JACKSON, Fisher St, Bassendean	62	E 3
DIANELLA, Light St	47	B 7
FALLS FARM, Cagney Wy, Lesmurdie	87	D 2
FLOREAT PARK, Howtree Pl, Floreat	59	C 9
GIRRAWHEEN, Salcott Rd	32	D 9
GOOSEBERRY HILL, Ledger Rd	77	D 3
GREENWOOD, Ranleigh Wy	31	E 5
HAMERSLEY, Centre Cl	31	D 10
HAROLD KING, Grovelands Dr, Westfield	106	B 9
HERB GRAHAM SPORTS COMPLEX, Chesterfield Rd, Mirrabooka	47	A 3
INNALOO, Morris Pl	45	C 9
JOAN WATTERS, Alexander St, Wembley	59	E 9
KALLAROO, Dampier Ave	23	B 6
KANYANA, McCoombe Ave, Samson	91	D 9
KARRINYUP, Davenport St	45	A 5
KENWICK, 17 Royal St	95	C 1
KWINANA, Gilmore Ave	131	A 7
LANGFORD, Langford Ave	94	E 2
LEEDERVILLE - WEMBLEY, Oxford St, Leederville	60	C 9
LEEMING, Farrington Rd	92	E 10
LES HANSMAN, 246 Walter Rd West, Morley	47	E 10
LOFTUS RECREATION CENTRE, Cnr Loftus & Richmond Sts, Leederville	60	D 8
MADDINGTON, Cnr Yule & Alcock Sts	96	B 3
MANDOGALUP, Hope Valley Rd	122	D 9
MIDVALE, Gray Dr	50	E 7
MT HAWTHORN, Cnr The Boulevard & Scarborough Beach Rd	60	C 5
MULBERRY FARM CONVENTION - RECREATION CENTRE, Hamersley Rd, Caversham	49	E 7
MUNDIJONG, Paterson St	143	A 9
NOLLAMARA, Lemana Rd	46	C 5
NORTH BEACH, 17 Kitchener St	44	D 3
OCEAN RIDGE, Sail Tce, Heathridge	23	C 1
OUTREACH, Ramsden Ave, E.Victoria Park	84	A 2
PALMYRA, Murray Rd	91	C 1
RICHARD RUSHTON, Baron Wy, Gosnells	95	E 9
SHENTON PARK, 240 Onslow Rd	71	E 4
SORRENTO-DUNCRAIG, 40 Warwick Rd, Duncraig	30	D 7
SWAN VIEW, Salisbury Rd	51	C 8
THORNLIE, Glenbrook Rd	95	D 5
TWO ROCKS, Lisford Ave	2	C 2
VICTORIA PARK, Cnr Kent & Gloucester Sts	73	E 9
WANNEROO, Scenic Dr	20	B 8
WARNBRO, Okehampton Rd	145	D 6
WARWICK LEISURE CENTRE, Cnr Warwick & Wanneroo Rds	32	A 6
WARWICK, Dorchester Ave	31	D 8
WHALEBACK, Basildon Wy, Lynwood	94	C 4
WHITFORD, MacDonald Ave, Padbury	23	D 10
YOKINE, McDonald St	60	D 2

CONSULATES & LEGATIONS

	Map	Ref.
AUSTRIA - Hon. Consul for, 21 Howard St, Perth	1C	E 3
BELGIAN - Hon. Consul for, 16 St Georges Tce, Perth	1C	A 3
BRITAIN - Consul General of, 95 St Georges Tce, Perth	1C	E 3
CANADA - Hon. Consul for, 111 St Georges Tce, Perth	1C	E 3
CHILE - Hon. Consul for, 33 Grant St, Cottesloe	70	D 10
DENMARK - Hon. Consul for, 19 Phillimore St, Fremantle	1D	B 5
FINLAND - Hon. Consul for, 1/85 Macleod Rd, Applecross	82	C 7
FRANCE - Hon. Consul for, 146 Mounts Bay Rd, Perth	1C	D 3
FRENCH GOVERNMENT COMMERCIAL OFFICE, 231 Adelaide Tce, Perth	1C	B 4
GERMANY (FEDERAL REPUBLIC OF) - Hon. Consul for, 16 St Georges Tce, Perth	1C	A 3
GREECE Consul for, 16 St Georges Tce, Perth	1C	A 3
HONDURAS - Hon. Consul for, 44 Troy Tce, Daglish	71	E 2
INDONESIA - Hon. Consul for, 85 Forrest St, Cottesloe	80	D 2
IRELAND - Hon. Consul General for, 10 Lilika Rd, City Beach	58	E 8
ITALY - Consul of, 31 Labouchere Rd, South Perth	72	E 7
JAPAN - Consul General of, Forrest Centre, 221 St Georges Tce, Perth	1C	E 2
MALAYSIA - Consul of, Airways House, 195 Adelaide Tce, East Perth	1C	B 4
MALTA - Hon. Consul for, Bassendean Medical Centre, 1 Old Perth Rd, Bassendean	63	A 1
MEXICO - Hon. Consul for, 3/8 Victoria Ave, Perth	1C	A 4
NEPAL, Hon. Consul General for, 16 Robinson St, Nedlands	71	C 8
NETHERLANDS - Hon. Consul for, The Mill Point Centre, 83 Mill Point Rd, South Perth	72	D 6
NEW ZEALAND - Consul of, 16 St Georges Tce, Perth	1C	A 3
NORWAY - Hon. Consul for, 11 Cliff St, Fremantle	1D	B 5
PAKISTAN - Hon. Consul for, 26 Carnarvon Cr, Coolbinia	60	E 4
PORTUGAL - Hon Consul for, 242 South Tce, Fremantle	90	C 7
SEYCHELLES - Hon. Consul General for, 271 Canning Rd, Lesmurdie	87	E 2
SPAIN - Hon. Consul for, 181 Adelaide Tce, East Perth	1C	B 4
SRI LANKA - Hon Consul for, 66 Mill Point Rd, South Perth	72	D 6
SWEDEN - Hon. Consul for, 23 Walters Dr, Osborne Park	59	E 3
SWITZERLAND - Hon. Consul for, 5 Marie Wy, Kalamunda	77	B 7
THAILAND - Hon. Consul General for, 135 Victoria Ave, Dalkeith	81	B 2
USA Consul General of, 16 St Georges Tce, Perth	1C	A 3
YUGOSLAVIA - Consul of, 24 Colin St, West Perth	72	C 2

CROQUET CLUBS

	Map	Ref.
BASSENDEAN, Hamilton St	63	A 2
BAYSWATER, Murray St	62	A 5
COMO, Comer St	82	E 1
EAST FREMANTLE, Allen St	90	E 3
FLOREAT PARK, Howtree Pl, Floreat	59	C 9
FREMANTLE, Ellen St	90	C 4
GOSNELLS, Dorothy St	96	C 9
HALLS HEAD, Old Coast Rd, Erskine	164	C 6
LEEDERVILLE, Holyrood St	60	C 10
MIDLAND, Morrison Rd	50	C 7
NEDLANDS, Bruce St	81	E 1
NORTH PERTH, Namur St	60	E 7
VICTORIA PARK, Rushton Rd	73	E 6

EDUCATION INSTITUTIONS

ADMINISTRATION

	Map	Ref.
ANGLICAN SCHOOLS COMMISSION, Blackboy Wy, Beechboro	48	C 4
CATHOLIC EDUCATION OFFICE OF WA, 50 Ruislip St, Leederville	60	B 9
DISTANCE EDUCATION CENTRE, Parliament Pl, West Perth	1C	D 2
MINISTRY OF EDUCATION HEAD OFFICE, 151 Royal St, East Perth	1C	B 2
WA OFFICE OF HIGHER EDUCATION, 30 Richardson St, West Perth	72	C 1

COLLEGES OF TAFE

	Map	Ref.
APPLECROSS TAFE CENTRE, 37 Ardessie St, Ardross	82	C 9
BALGA CAMPUS, 18 Loxwood Rd, Balga	46	E 2
BENTLEY CAMPUS, Hayman Rd, Bentley	83	E 2
CARINE CAMPUS, Cnr Marmion Ave & Almadine Dr, Carine	44	E 1
CARLISLE CAMPUS, Cnr Oats & Bank St, East Victoria Park	74	B 10
CENTRAL METROPOLITAN COLLEGE OF TAFE (Directorate), 25 Aberdeen St, Perth	1C	A 1
CHURCHLANDS TAFE CENTRE, Senior High School, Lucca St, Churchlands	59	B 5
CLAREMONT SCHOOL OF ART, 7 Princess Rd, Claremont	71	B 10
FREMANTLE CAMPUS - FLEET ST ANNEXE, Fleet St, Fremantle	1D	B 5

269

	Map Ref.
FREMANTLE CAMPUS - SOUTH TCE ANNEXE, South Tce, Fremantle	1D C 6
FREMANTLE CAMPUS, Grosvenor St, Beaconsfield	90 E 8
JOONDALUP CAMPUS, (within Shire Office), Boas Ave, Joondalup	19 E 6
LEEDERVILLE CAMPUS, Richmond St, Leederville	60 D 8
MIDLANDS REGIONAL COLLEGE, Lloyd St, Middle Swan	50 D 5
MT LAWLEY CAMPUS - HEALTH SCIENCE ANNEXE, 107 Charles St, West Perth	60 E 10
MT LAWLEY CAMPUS, Harold St, Mt Lawley	61 B 9
NORTH METROPOLITAN COLLEGE (Directorate), 18 Loxwood Rd, Balga	46 E 2
PEEL (MANDURAH) TAFE CENTRE, Cnr Smart St Mall & Mandurah Tce, Mandurah	164 E 1
PERTH CAMPUS - ST BRIGID'S ANNEXE, Cnr Aberdeen & Fitzgerald Sts, Perth	1C E 1
PERTH CAMPUS, 25 Aberdeen St, Perth	1C A 1
ROCKINGHAM CAMPUS, Simpson Ave, Rockingham	137 D 5
ROSSMOYNE TAFE CENTRE, Senior High School, Keith Rd, Rossmoyne	93 B 3
SCARBOROUGH TAFE CENTRE, Senior High School, Newborough St, Doubleview	45 A 7
SOUTH EAST METROPOLITAN COLLEGE (Directorate), Hayman Rd, Bentley	83 E 2
SOUTH METROPOLITAN COLLEGE OF TAFE (Directorate), Grosvenor St, Beaconsfield	90 E 8
SUBIACO TAFE CENTRE, Perth Modern School, Roberts Rd, Subiaco	72 C 1
TAFE CENTRAL OFFICE, 151 Royal St, East Perth	1C B 2
TAFE EXTERNAL STUDIES COLLEGE, Prospect Pl, West Perth	60 E 10
THORNLIE CAMPUS, Burslem Dr, Thornlie	95 D 6
VICTORIA PARK TAFE CENTRE, Kent St Senior High School, Cnr Lansdowne Rd & Rathay St, Kensington	73 E 9
WEMBLEY CAMPUS, 133 Salvado Rd, Wembley	59 E 10
WOODSOME ST TAFE CENTRE, Woodsome St, Mt Lawley	61 B 5

OFF SITE PRE-PRIMARY CENTRES

	Map Ref.
APPLECROSS, Cnr Tain St & Canning Hwy	82 C 7
ARMADALE, 44 William St	116 D 7
ATTADALE, Davis Rd	81 C 9
BALCATTA, 8 Jedda Rd	46 B 7
BASSENDEAN, 9 Hamilton St	63 A 1
BATEMAN, Parry Ave	92 D 5
BEACONSFIELD, 66 Jenkin St	90 D 8
BECKENHAM, 27 Birchington St	85 C 6
BLACKMORE, Innes Pl, Girrawheen	32 B 7
BOORAGOON, Kennedy St, Alfred Cove	81 E 10
BUNGAREE, Centaurus St, Rockingham	137 B 7
CALISTA, Maydwell Wy	130 E 7
CARAWATHA, Troytown Wy, Melville	91 E 1
CARINE, Alvaston Dr	31 A 9
CHURCHLANDS, Brookdale St, Floreat	59 C 8
CITY BEACH, Boronia Cr	58 D 8
COOLBINIA, Holmfirth St, Menora	61 A 5
DAVALLIA, Beach Rd, Carine	31 B 8
DEANMORE, Cnr Blair St & Deanmore Rd, Karrinyup	44 E 7
EAST MAYLANDS, 9 Richards St, Maylands	62 A 9
EDEN HILL, Ivanhoe St	49 A 8
EMBLETON, McKenzie Wy	62 A 1
FLOREAT PARK, Birkdale St, Floreat	59 D 9
GOSNELLS, Rear 2317 Albany Hwy	96 C 9
GRAYLANDS, Adderley St, Mount Claremont	71 A 4
GUILDFORD, Cnr Helena & Meadow Sts	63 D 1
HAINSWORTH, 29 Hainsworth Ave, Girrawheen	32 D 9
HAMPTON PARK, Hampton Sq W, Morley	48 C 8
HIGHGATE, 4 Broome St	61 B 10
HILLCREST, 2 Hudson St, Bayswater	62 B 3
HILTON, Rennie Cr South	91 B 8
INGLEWOOD, 186 Grand Pro, Bedford	61 D 3
KAPINARA, 15 Bendigo Wy, City Beach	58 D 5
KARRINYUP, Blackdown Wy	44 E 4
KENSINGTON, Vista St	73 C 9
KINLOCK, 50 Bursaria Cr, Ferndale	84 B 10
KOONGAMIA, Mudalla Wy	65 B 2
KOORILLA, Cordelia Ave, Coolbellup	101 E 2
KYILLA, 13 Haynes St, North Perth	60 D 6
LANGFORD, Lot 180 Imber Pl	94 E 3
LATHLAIN, 2 Planet St, Carlisle	74 B 7
LESMURDIE, Sanderson Rd	87 C 5
LOCKRIDGE, Barlow Ct	49 A 7
LOCKRIDGE, Diana Cr	49 A 6
LYNWOOD, Cnr Kenton & Edgeware Sts	84 D 10
MAIDA VALE, Casuarina Rd	77 A 1
MARMION, 108 High St, Sorrento	30 C 7
MIDLAND, William St	50 B 8
MIDVALE, Cnr Ewart St & Morrison Rd	50 E 7
MORLEY, 15 Brand Pl	47 E 7
MOSMAN PARK, Solomon St	80 D 5
MOUNT HAWTHORN, 202 Scarborough Beach Rd	60 C 5
MOUNT HELENA, Chidlow St	55 C 4
MOUNT PLEASANT, 22 Darnell Ave	92 D 1
MUNDARING, 81 Jacoby St	68 B 1
MUNDIJONG, Paterson St	143 A 8
NEERIGEN BROOK, Gwynne Park Reserve, Forrest Rd, Armadale	116 C 7
NEWBOROUGH, Cnr Jackson & Wilding Sts, Doubleview	45 A 7
NOLLAMARA, 13 Carcoola St	46 C 6
NORTH BALGA, Penrith Pl, Balga	46 C 1
NORTH FREMANTLE, 2 Thompson Rd	80 C 9
NORTH INNALOO, Morris Rd, Innaloo	45 B 9
NORTH PARMELIA, Warner Rd, Parmelia	131 C 7
PALMYRA, Cnr McKimmie Rd & Zenobia St	91 B 3
RICHMOND, 72 Osborne Rd, East Fremantle	90 E 1
ROLEYSTONE, 12 Jarrah Rd	108 A 7
SAFETY BAY, 14 Watts Rd	136 D 10
SCARBOROUGH, 6 Bazaar Tce	44 D 10
SOUTH TERRACE, 32 Attfield St, Fremantle	1D C 6
SUBIACO, 138 Hamersley Rd	72 A 2
SUTHERLAND, Chatton St, Dianella	47 B 9
THORNLIE, 39 Coops Ave	95 B 4
TUART HILL, Cnr Cape & Stoneham Sts	60 C 1
WARRIAPENDI, Cnr Finchley Cr & Balga Ave, Balga	46 D 1
WATTLEUP, Marban Wy	121 D 2
WEMBLEY DOWNS, 15 Euston St	59 A 3
WEST MORLEY, Tara St, Morley	61 D 1
WESTMINISTER, 25 Edale Wy, Balga	46 D 3
WILLAGEE, Cnr Worley & Howell Sts	91 E 4
WILLETTON, 6 Kingfisher Lp	93 C 3
WILSON, 4 Hares St	84 B 6
WIRRABIRRA, Otterden St, Gosnells	95 E 8
WOODLANDS, 16 Tamarisk Wy	59 B 2
YANCHEP, Bower Gr, Two Rocks	2 D 2

SCHOOLS

	Map Ref.
ABORIGINAL COMMUNITY COLLEGE, 139 Sydney Rd, Gnangara	26 A 6
ACTON AVENUE PRE-SCHOOL CENTRE, 415 Acton Ave, Kewdale	74 E 7
ALINJARRA PRIMARY SCHOOL, Northumberland Ave, Alexander Hts	33 B 5
ALL SAINTS' COLLEGE, Ewing Ave, Bull Creek	93 B 4
ALLENSWOOD PRIMARY SCHOOL, Merivale Wy, Greenwood	31 D 5
AMELIA HEIGHTS PRE-SCHOOL, 14 Marton Rd, Balcatta	46 A 4
ANGLICAN COMM. SCHOOL OF ST MARK, St Marks Dr, Hillarys	23 B 8
ANZAC TERRACE PRIMARY SCHOOL, Anzac Tce, Bassendean	48 E 10
APPLECROSS PRIMARY SCHOOL, Kintail Rd, Applecross	82 C 5
APPLECROSS SENIOR HIGH SCHOOL, Links Rd, Ardross	82 C 9
AQUINAS COLLEGE, Mount Henry Rd, Salter Point	83 A 8
ARANMORE CATHOLIC COLLEGE, 49 Franklin St, Leederville	60 D 7
ARANMORE CATHOLIC PRIMARY SCHOOL, 20 Brentham St, Leederville	60 C 7
ARDROSS PRIMARY SCHOOL, Links Rd, Ardross	82 C 9
ARMADALE EDUCATION SUPPORT CTR, 169 South Western Hwy, Armadale	116 D 8
ARMADALE JOHN CALVIN PRIMARY SCHOOL, Dale Rd, Armadale	116 C 5
ARMADALE PRIMARY SCHOOL, 1 Carradine Rd, Bedfordale	117 A 5
ARMADALE SENIOR HIGH SCHOOL, 169 South Western Hwy, Armadale	116 D 8
ASHBURTON DRIVE PRIMARY SCHOOL, Nullagine Wy, Gosnells	106 A 2
ASHFIELD PRIMARY SCHOOL, Margaret St, Ashfield	62 E 4
ASSUMPTION CATHOLIC PRIM SCHOOL, Gordon Rd, Mandurah	163 C 6
ATTADALE PRE-SCHOOL, Point Walter Rd, Bicton	91 B 1
ATTADALE PRIMARY SCHOOL, Wichmann Rd, Attadale	81 D 9
BALCATTA PRIMARY SCHOOL, Main St, Balcatta	46 B 7
BALCATTA SENIOR HIGH SCHOOL, Poincaire St, Balcatta	45 E 5
BALDIVIS PRIMARY SCHOOL, Fifty Rd, Baldivis	147 A 1
BALGA ABORIGINAL PRE-SCHOOL, 25 Edale Wy, Balga	46 D 3
BALGA JUNIOR PRIMARY SCHOOL, Walderton Ave, Balga	46 D 2
BALGA PRIMARY SCHOOL, Fernhurst Cr, Balga	46 D 2
BALGA SENIOR HIGH SCHOOL, Markham Wy, Balga	32 D 10
BALLAJURA CATHOLIC PRIMARY SCHOOL, Cassowary Dr, Ballajura	33 E 8
BALLAJURA PRIMARY SCHOOL, Illawarra Cr, Ballajura	33 D 6
BAMBARA PRIMARY SCHOOL, Gosse Rd, Padbury	23 D 8
BANKSIA MONTESSORI SCHOOL, 53 Wordsworth Ave, Yokine	61 A 2
BANKSIA PARK PRIMARY SCHOOL, Hicks St, Leeming	93 C 9
BASSENDEAN PRIMARY SCHOOL, Cnr West Rd & Harcourt St, Bassendean	63 B 2
BATEMAN PRIMARY SCHOOL, Bartling Cr, Bateman	92 D 4
BAYSWATER CHILDRENS CENTRE, 13 Roberts St, Bayswater	62 A 5
BAYSWATER PRIMARY SCHOOL, Murray St, Bayswater	62 B 5
BEACONSFIELD PRIMARY SCHOOL, Hale St, Beaconsfield	90 D 8
BEAUFORT COLLEGE, 381 Beaufort St, Perth	61 B 10
BEAUMARIS PRIMARY SCHOOL, Santiago Pwy, Ocean Reef	19 A 7
BECKENHAM PRIMARY SCHOOL, Railway Pde, Beckenham	85 B 8
BEECHBORO CHRISTIAN SCHOOL, Surrey Rd, Rivervale	74 A 3
BEECHBORO PRIMARY SCHOOL, King Rd, Beechboro	48 D 3
BEEHIVE MONTESSORI SCHOOL, Curtin Ave, Cottesloe	80 C 7
BELDON EDUCATION SUPPORT CENTRE, Pacific Wy, Beldon	23 C 3
BELDON PRIMARY SCHOOL, Pacific Wy, Beldon	23 C 3
BELLEVUE PRIMARY SCHOOL, Clayton St, Bellevue	50 E 10

270

	Map Ref.
BELMAY PRIMARY SCHOOL, 410 Sydenham St, Cloverdale	75 A 2
BELMONT ABORIGINAL PRE-SCHOOL, 7 Casey St, Cloverdale	75 A 2
BELMONT PRIMARY SCHOOL, Great Eastern Hwy, Belmont	62 C 10
BELMONT SENIOR HIGH SCHOOL, Fisher St, Belmont	74 D 3
BENTLEY ABORIGINAL PRE-SCHOOL, 22 Coolgardie St, Bentley	84 B 4
BENTLEY JUNIOR PRIMARY SCHOOL, Hedley St, Bentley	84 B 5
BENTLEY PRE-SCHOOL, 6 John St, Bentley	84 C 3
BENTLEY PRIMARY SCHOOL, Hedley St, Bentley	84 B 5
BIBLE BAPTIST CHRISTIAN ACADEMY, Lot 374 Chidlow St, Mount Helena	55 C 4
BIBRA LAKE PRIMARY SCHOOL, Annois Rd, Bibra Lake	102 C 4
BICTON PRIMARY SCHOOL, View Tce, Bicton	81 B 10
BIRRALEE PRIMARY SCHOOL, Odin Rd, Innaloo	45 C 8
BLACKMORE PRIMARY SCHOOL, Allinson Dr, Girrawheen	32 B 7
BLUE GUM MONTESSORI CHILDREN CENTRE, 2 Homestead Ave, Bibra Lake	102 D 2
BOORAGOON PRIMARY SCHOOL, Clements Rd, Booragoon	92 B 1
BOORDAAK SCHOOL, Fremantle Hosp G Block, Alma St, Fremantle	1D C 6
BOYARE PRIMARY SCHOOL, Cnr Threadleaf Wy & Appleblossom Dr, Mirrabooka	47 B 1
BRAMFIELD PARK PRIMARY SCHOOL, Yule St, Maddington	96 B 3
BRENTWOOD PRIMARY SCHOOL, Moolyeen Rd, Brentwood	92 D 2
BRIDGEWATER PRE-SCHOOL, Cnr McLean & Luffingham Sts, Melville	91 C 2
BROOKMAN PRE-PRIMARY, Brookman Ave, Langford	94 E 1
BROOKMAN PRIMARY SCHOOL, Brookman Ave, Langford	94 E 1
BUCKLAND HILL SCHOOL, McCabe St, Mosman Park	80 D 7
BULL CREEK PRIMARY SCHOOL, Hardy St, Bull Creek	93 A 6
BUNGAREE PRIMARY SCHOOL, Centaurus St, Rockingham	137 B 8
BURBRIDGE PRE-SCHOOL, Lot 205 Burbridge Ave, Koondoola	32 E 7
BURBRIDGE SCHOOL, Burbridge Ave, Koondoola	33 A 7
BURRENDAH E.C.E. CENTRE, Castlereagh Cl, Willetton	93 C 6
BURRENDAH PRIMARY SCHOOL, Pinetree Gully Rd, Willetton	93 C 6
BYFORD PRE-SCHOOL, Park Rd, Byford	135 D 1
BYFORD PRIMARY SCHOOL, Clifton St, Byford	135 D 1

	Map Ref.
CALISTA PRIMARY SCHOOL, Chilcott St, Calista	130 E 7
CAMBERWARRA PRIMARY SCHOOL, Currajong Cr, Craigie	23 D 5
CAMBOON PRIMARY SCHOOL, Forder St, Noranda	47 D 6
CANNING SENIOR COLLEGE, Marquis St, Bentley	83 E 5
CANNINGTON PRIMARY SCHOOL, Wharf St, Cannington	84 E 6
CANNINGTON SENIOR HIGH SCHOOL, 301 Sevenoaks St, Cannington	85 A 6
CARAWATHA LANGUAGE DEVELOP CTR, Cnr Archibald St & North Lake Rd, Willagee	91 E 5
CARAWATHA PRIMARY SCHOOL, Cnr Archibald St & North Lake Rd, Willagee	91 E 5
CARINE PRIMARY SCHOOL, Osmaston Rd, Carine	30 E 10
CARINE SENIOR HIGH SCHOOL, Everingham St, Carine	31 A 10
CARLISLE LANGUAGE DEVELOP CTR, 271 Orrong Rd, Carlisle	74 C 7
CARLISLE PRIMARY SCHOOL, 271 Orrong Rd, Carlisle	74 C 7
CARMEL COLLEGE, Glenisla Rd, Carmel	88 C 6
CARMEL SCHOOL, Cressell Rd, Dianella	61 A 1
CARSON STREET SCHOOL, Carson St, East Victoria Park	84 A 1
CASTLEREAGH SCHOOL, Castlereagh Cl, Willetton	93 C 6
CAVERSHAM PRIMARY SCHOOL, Coast Rd, West Swan	49 E 1
CECIL ANDREWS SENIOR HIGH SCHOOL, Seville Dr, Armadale	116 B 4
CHALLIS E.C.E. CENTRE, Williams Rd, Armadale	116 B 4
CHALLIS PRIMARY SCHOOL, Williams Rd, Armadale	116 B 4
CHALLIS S.P.E.R. CENTRE, Williams Rd, Armadale	116 B 4
CHARTHOUSE PRIMARY SCHOOL, Rand Ave, Waikiki	145 C 3
CHIDLEY EDUCATIONAL CENTRE, Owston St, Mosman Park	81 A 7
CHIDLOW PRIMARY SCHOOL, Lilydale Rd, Chidlow	42 D 10
CHILD STUDY CENTRE, Fairway, Nedlands (Inset Map 120, University of W.A.)	120 A 9
CHISHOLM CATHOLIC COLLEGE, Bedford Campus, 1104 Beaufort St, Bedford	61 E 3
CHISHOLM CATHOLIC COLLEGE, Senior Campus, 103 Wood St, Inglewood	61 C 3
CHRIST CHURCH GRAMMAR SCHOOL, Queenslea Dr, Claremont	71 A 10
CHRIST THE KING SCHOOL, 59 Lefroy Rd, Beaconsfield	90 D 8
CHRISTIAN BROTHERS COLLEGE, 51 Ellen St, Fremantle	1D C 4

	Map Ref.
CHRYSALIS MONTESSORI SCHOOL, Charles Veryard Pavillion, Bourke St, North Perth	60 C 7
CHURCHLANDS PRIMARY SCHOOL, Cromarty Rd, Floreat	59 C 7
CHURCHLANDS SENIOR HIGH SCHOOL, Lucca St, Churchlands	59 B 5
CITY BEACH PRIMARY SCHOOL, Marapana Rd, City Beach	58 E 9
CITY BEACH SENIOR HIGH SCHOOL, Kalinda Dr, City Beach	58 E 9
CLAREMONT PRE-SCHOOL, Bernard St, Claremont	71 B 9
CLAREMONT PRIMARY SCHOOL, Bay View Tce, Claremont	71 A 10
CLIFTON HILLS PRIMARY SCHOOL, Connell Ave, Kelmscott	106 E 7
CLONTARF ABORIGINAL COLLEGE, 295 Manning Rd, Waterford	83 E 6
CLOVERDALE ED. SUPPORT CENTRE, Fisher St, Cloverdale	74 E 4
CLOVERDALE PRIMARY SCHOOL, Fisher St, Cloverdale	74 E 4
COLLEGE PARK KINDERGARTEN, Princess Rd, Nedlands	71 C 10
COLLIER PRIMARY SCHOOL, Hobbs Ave, Como	83 B 1
COMO PRE-SCHOOL, Alston Ave, Como	83 A 2
COMO PRIMARY SCHOOL, Thelma St, Como	83 A 2
COMO SENIOR HIGH SCHOOL, Bruce St, Como	83 B 3
CONNOLLY PRIMARY SCHOOL, Fairway Ci, Connolly	19 C 7
CONON ROAD KINDERGARTEN, Cnr Conon Rd & Canning Hwy, Applecross	82 B 7
COODANUP HIGH SCHOOL, Wanjeep St, Coodanup	165 C 4
COOGEE PRIMARY SCHOOL, Mayor Rd, Munster	110 E 1
COOINDA KINDERGARTEN, Margaret St, Wilson	84 B 8
COOLABAROO NEIGHBOURHOOD CENTRE, Parkside Dr, Thornlie	95 D 5
COOLBELLUP PRIMARY SCHOOL, Cnr Ebert St & Hilory St, Coolbellup	91 D 10
COOLBELLUP S.P.E.R. CENTRE, Cnr Ebert & Hilory Sts, Coolbellup	91 D 10
COOLBINIA PRIMARY SCHOOL, Bradford St, Coolbinia	60 E 4
COOLOONGUP PRIMARY SCHOOL, Westerly Wy, Cooloongup	137 D 9
CORPUS CHRISTI COLLEGE, Murdoch Dr, Bateman	92 D 5
COTTESLOE PRIMARY SCHOOL, 530 Stirling Hwy, Cottesloe	80 D 3
COTTESLOE SCH. IMPAIRED HEARING, Johnston St, Peppermint Grove	80 D 4
CRAIGIE PRE-SCHOOL, 14 Camberwarra Dr, Craigie	23 C 7

	Map Ref.
CRAIGIE PRIMARY SCHOOL, Spinaway St, Craigie	23 D 6
CRAIGIE SENIOR HIGH SCHOOL, Arawa Pl, Craigie	23 D 6
CREANEY EDUCATION SUPPORT CENTRE, Creaney Dr, Kingsley	24 B 9
CREANEY PRIMARY SCHOOL, Creaney Dr, Kingsley	24 B 9
CULUNGA CATHOLIC ABORIGINAL SCHOOL, 104 Harrow St, West Swan	35 E 8
CYGNET MONTESSORI SCHOOL, 5 Parkland Rd, Osborne Park	59 E 5
CYRIL JACKSON EDUCATION SUPP. CTR, Reid St, Bassendean	62 E 3
CYRIL JACKSON SENIOR HIGH SCHOOL, Reid St, Bassendean	62 E 3
DALE CHRISTIAN SCHOOL, 150 Forrest Rd, Armadale	116 B 8
DALKEITH PRE-SCHOOL, 167 Victoria Ave, Dalkeith	81 C 3
DALKEITH PRIMARY SCHOOL, Circe Ci, Dalkeith	81 C 2
DALMAIN PRIMARY SCHOOL, Dalmain St, Kingsley	31 B 2
DARLINGTON PRE-SCHOOL, Glen Rd, Darlington	66 A 5
DARLINGTON PRIMARY SCHOOL, Glen Rd, Darlington	66 A 5
DAVALLIA PRIMARY SCHOOL, Juniper Wy, Duncraig	31 B 8
DAWSON PARK PRIMARY SCHOOL, Bougainvillea Ave, Forrestfield	76 B 8
DEANMORE PRIMARY SCHOOL, Deanmore Rd, Karrinyup	44 E 7
DIANELLA HEIGHTS PRIMARY SCHOOL, Beaman St, Dianella	47 A 7
DIANELLA PRIMARY SCHOOL, Cleveland St, Dianella	61 B 1
DISTANCE EDUCATION CENTRE, Cnr Havelock St & Parliament Pl, West Perth	1C D 2
DOUBLEVIEW PRIMARY SCHOOL, St Brigids Tce, Doubleview	45 A 10
DRYANDRA PRIMRY SCHOOL, Dryandra Dr, Mirrabooka	47 A 1
DUDLEY PARK PRIMARY SCHOOL, Gillark St, Mandurah	165 B 3
DUNCRAIG PRIMARY SCHOOL, Roche Rd, Duncraig	30 E 6
DUNCRAIG SENIOR HIGH SCHOOL, Readshaw Rd, Duncraig	30 D 4
DURHAM ROAD SCHOOL, Durham Rd, Bayswater	62 C 4
EAST BEECHBORO PRIMARY SCHOOL, Brockmill Ave, Beechboro	49 A 4
EAST BELMAY PRE-SCHOOL, Board Ave, Redcliffe	75 A 1
EAST CLAREMONT PRIMARY SCHOOL, Cnr Bay & Princess Rds, Claremont	71 B 10
EAST FREMANTLE PRE-SCHOOL, 8 Forrest St, Fremantle	90 D 4
EAST FREMANTLE PRIMARY SCHOOL, 8 Forrest St, Fremantle	90 D 4

School	Map Ref.
EAST GREENWOOD PRIMARY SCHOOL, Mulligan Dr, Greenwood	32 A 5
EAST HAMERSLEY PRIMARY SCHOOL, Cnr Earn Pl & Doon Wy, Hamersley	32 A 9
EAST HAMILTON HILL PRIMARY SCHOOL, Bradbury Rd, Hamilton Hill	91 C 10
EAST KENWICK PRIMARY SCHOOL, Kenwick Rd, Kenwick	85 E 10
EAST MADDINGTON PRIMARY SCHOOL, Cnr Pitchford Ave & Westfield St, Maddington	96 C 5
EAST MAYLANDS PRIMARY SCHOOL, Kelvin St, Maylands	62 A 8
EAST VICTORIA PARK ED. SUPP. CTR, Beatty Ave, East Vic Park	74 A 8
EAST VICTORIA PARK PRIMARY SCHOOL, Beatty Ave, East Vic Park	74 A 8
EAST WAIKIKI PRIMARY SCHOOL, Willmott Dr, Waikiki	137 D 10
EAST WANNEROO PRIMARY SCHOOL, High Rd, Wanneroo	20 E 9
EASTERN HILLS SENIOR HIGH SCHOOL, Keane St East, Mount Helena	55 C 4
EDDYSTONE PRIMARY SCHOOL, Littorina Ave, Heathridge	23 E 1
EDEN HILL PRIMARY SCHOOL, Ivanhoe St, Eden Hill	49 A 9
EDGEWATER PRIMARY SCHOOL, Tree Top Ave, Edgewater	24 A 1
EDNEY PRIMARY SCHOOL, Newburn Rd, High Wycombe	76 C 1
EDWARDS MATRICULATION COLLEGE, Cnr Ladner & South Sts, O'Connor	91 D 7
EL SHADDAI CHRISTIAN SCHOOL, Cnr Sharman St & Oakley Rd Nth, Medina	130 E 6
EMBLETON PRIMARY SCHOOL, Collier Rd, Embleton	62 A 1
EMMANUEL CHRISTIAN SCHOOL, 3 Salcott Rd, Girrawheen	32 D 9
EMMAUS CHRISTIAN SCHOOL, Admiral Rd, Bedfordale	127 C 3
ETHEL COOPER PRE SCHOOL, 34 Ingram St, Hamilton Hill	101 B 1
FALLS ROAD PRIMARY SCHOOL, 50 Falls Rd, Lesmurdie	87 C 1
FERNDALE PRIMARY SCHOOL, Karri Wy, Ferndale	94 C 1
FLOREAT PARK PRIMARY SCHOOL, Chandler Ave, Floreat	59 C 9
FOOTHILLS SCHOOL, 18 Victoria St, Guildford	49 C 10
FOREST CRESCENT PRIMARY SCHOOL, Forest Cr, Thornlie	95 A 10
FORRESTDALE PRE-SCHOOL, 3 Weld St, Forrestdale	114 E 6
FORRESTDALE PRIMARY SCHOOL, Broome St, Forrestdale	115 A 7
FORRESTFIELD CHRISTIAN SCHOOL, 336 Hawtin Rd, Forrestfield	76 D 8
FORRESTFIELD E.C.E. CENTRE, Sussex Rd, Forrestfield	76 C 10
FORRESTFIELD PRE-SCHOOL, 35 Edinburgh Rd, Forrestfield	86 D 1
FORRESTFIELD PRIMARY SCHOOL, Sussex Rd, Forrestfield	76 C 10
FORRESTFIELD SENIOR HIGH SCHOOL, Berkshire Rd, Forrestfield	76 C 7
FREDERICK IRWIN ANGLICAN COMMUNITY SCHOOL, Gordon Rd, Meadow Springs	163 D 6
GIBBS STREET PRIMARY SCHOOL, Gibbs St, East Cannington	85 B 4
GIRRAWHEEN PRIMARY SCHOOL, Arnos Wy, Girrawheen	32 C 7
GIRRAWHEEN SENIOR HIGH SCHOOL, Calvert Wy, Girrawheen	32 C 7
GLADYS NEWTON SCHOOL, Balga Ave, Balga	46 D 1
GLEN FORREST PRIMARY SCHOOL, Burkinshaw Rd, Glen Forrest	66 D 4
GLENCOE PRIMARY SCHOOL, Balmoral Pde, Halls Head	164 C 3
GLENDALE PRE-SCHOOL, 9 Glendale Ave, Hamersley	31 D 10
GLENDALE PRIMARY SCHOOL, Glendale Ave, Hamersley	31 D 10
GLENGARRY PRIMARY SCHOOL, Cnr Glengarry & Doveridge Dr, Duncraig	31 A 5
GOOD SHEPHERD PRIMARY SCHOOL, Cnr Marmion & Arbuthnot Sts, Kelmscott	106 E 10
GOOLLELAL PRIMARY SCHOOL, Cadogan St, Kingsley	31 D 2
GOOSEBERRY HILL PRIMARY SCHOOL, Ledger Rd, Gooseberry Hill	77 D 3
GOSNELLS PRIMARY SCHOOL, Hicks St, Gosnells	96 C 10
GOSNELLS SENIOR HIGH SCHOOL, Southern River Rd, Gosnells	105 E 1
GOVERNOR STIRLING SENIOR HIGH, Ford St, Midland	50 A 8
GRAYLANDS PRIMARY SCHOOL, 103 Alfred Rd, Mt Claremont	71 B 6
GREENFIELDS PRIMARY SCHOOL, Zambesi Dr, Greenfields	163 D 1
GREENMOUNT PRIMARY SCHOOL, Innamincka Rd, Greenmount	51 C 10
GREENWOOD PRE-SCHOOL, 5 Calectasia Ave, Greenwood	31 D 6
GREENWOOD PRIMARY SCHOOL, Peppermint Dr, Greenwood	31 C 5
GREENWOOD SENIOR HIGH SCHOOL, Coolibah Dr, Greenwood	31 B 5
GROVELANDS E.C.E. CENTRE, Grovelands Dr, Westfield	106 B 9
GROVELANDS PRIMARY SCHOOL, Grovelands Dr, Westfield	106 B 9
GUILDFORD GRAMMAR PREPARATORY SCHOOL, Great Eastern Hwy, Midland	50 A 8
GUILDFORD GRAMMAR SCHOOL, 11 Terrace Rd, Guildford	49 E 9
GUILDFORD MONTESSORI SCHOOL, 34 Swan St, Guildford	49 E 10
GUILDFORD PRIMARY SCHOOL, Cnr Helena & Johnson Sts, Guildford	63 C 1
GUMNUT MONTESSORI SCHOOL, 75 Graylands Rd, Claremont	71 B 6
GWELUP PLAY CENTRE, North Beach Rd, Gwelup	45 C 5
GWYNNE PARK PRIMARY SCHOOL, Tijuana Rd, Armadale	116 B 8
HAINSWORTH PRIMARY SCHOOL, Harford Wy, Girrawheen	32 D 8
HALE SCHOOL, Hale Rd, Wembley Downs	59 A 4
HALIDON PRIMARY SCHOOL, Halidon St, Kingsley	24 D 10
HAMILTON SENIOR HIGH SCHOOL, Purvis St, Hamilton Hill	101 C 2
HAMPTON PARK PRIMARY SCHOOL, Hamersley Pl, Morley	48 B 8
HAMPTON SENIOR HIGH SCHOOL, Morley Dr East, Morley	48 C 8
HARMAN STREET PRE-SCHOOL, 23 Harman St, Cloverdale	74 E 3
HAWKER PARK PRIMARY SCHOOL, Hawker Ave, Warwick	31 C 8
HAZEL ORME PRE-SCHOOL, 96 Sampson St, White Gum Valley	90 E 6
HEARING ASSESSMENT CENTRE, 53 Curtin Ave, Cottesloe	80 C 5
HEATHRIDGE PRIMARY SCHOOL, Channel Dr, Heathridge	19 D 10
HELENA COLLEGE, Bilgoman Rd, Glen Forrest	66 C 2
HELENA SCHOOL, Ryecroft Rd, Darlington	66 B 5
HELENA VALLEY PRIMARY SCHOOL, Ridge Hill Rd, Helena Valley	65 C 6
HENSMAN STREET PRE-SCHOOL, Hensman St, South Perth	73 A 9
HERNE HILL PRIMARY SCHOOL, Argyle St, Herne Hill	36 E 5
HIGH WYCOMBE CATHOLIC PRIMARY SCHOOL, Lot 1311, Wittenoom Rd, High Wycombe	64 B 8
HIGH WYCOMBE PRIMARY SCHOOL, Newburn Rd, High Wycombe	64 B 9
HIGHGATE PRIMARY SCHOOL, Lincoln St, Highgate	61 A 10
HILLARYS PRE-SCHOOL, Shackleton Ave, Hillarys	23 B 10
HILLCREST PRIMARY SCHOOL, 2 Bay View St, Bayswater	62 A 3
HILLMAN PRIMARY SCHOOL, Unnaro St, Hillman	137 E 6
HILTON PRIMARY SCHOOL, Rennie Cr North, Hilton	91 B 8
HOLLYWOOD PRE-SCHOOL, Cnr Smyth Rd & Monash Ave, Nedlands	71 D 6
HOLLYWOOD PRIMARY SCHOOL, Monash Ave, Nedlands	71 D 6
HOLLYWOOD SENIOR HIGH SCHOOL, Smyth Rd, Nedlands	71 D 5
HOLY NAME SCHOOL, 65 Lion St, Carlisle	74 C 7
HOLY ROSARY SCHOOL, 35 Williamstown Rd, Doubleview	59 B 3
HOLY SPIRIT SCHOOL, Brompton Rd, City Beach	58 D 5
HOPE VALLEY PRIMARY SCHOOL, McLaren Ave, Hope Valley	121 C 7
HUNTINGDALE PRIMARY SCHOOL, Matilda St, Huntingdale	95 D 10
ILLAWARRA PRIMARY SCHOOL, Illawarra Cr, Ballajura	33 C 5
INFANT JESUS SCHOOL, 1 Russell St, Morley	47 D 9
INGLEWOOD PRIMARY SCHOOL, 34 Normanby St, Inglewood	61 D 4
IONA PRESENTATION COLLEGE, 33 Palmerston St, Mosman Park	80 E 5
IONA PRIMARY SCHOOL, Buckland Ave, Mosman Park	80 D 6
JANDAKOT PRIMARY SCHOOL, Beenyup Rd, Jandakot	102 D 10
JARRAHDALE PRIMARY SCHOOL, Wanliss St, Jarrahdale	152 E 8
JESS THOMAS PRE-SCHOOL, 29 March St, Spearwood	101 B 5
JOHN CALVIN SENIOR HIGH SCHOOL, 18 Robin Hood Ave, Armadale	116 C 6
JOHN CURTIN SENIOR HIGH SCHOOL, Ellen St, Fremantle	90 D 4
JOHN FORREST SENIOR HIGH SCHOOL, Drake St, Morley	61 E 2
JOHN SEPTIMUS ROE ANGLICAN COMMUNITY SCHOOL, Cnr Boyare & Mirrabooka Aves	46 E 1
JOHN WOLLASTON COMMUNITY SCHOOL, Cnr Lake & Centre Rds, Westfield	106 C 6
JOHN XXIII COLLEGE, John XXIII Ave, Mount Claremont	71 B 4
JOLIMONT PRIMARY SCHOOL, 657 Hay St, Jolimont	71 E 1
J.P. McKENZIE PLAY CENTRE, Cnr George & Hubble Sts, East Fremantle	90 D 3
KADEE ABORIGINAL PRE-SCHOOL, 54 Lawrence St, Bayswater	62 A 4
KALAMUNDA CHRISTIAN SCHOOL, Halleendale Rd, Walliston	87 E 3
KALAMUNDA EDUCATION SUPPORT CTR, Heath Rd, Kalamunda	77 C 6
KALAMUNDA PRE-SCHOOL, Lot 411 Spring Rd, Kalamunda	77 D 6
KALAMUNDA PRIMARY SCHOOL, Heath Rd, Kalamunda	77 C 6
KALAMUNDA SENIOR HIGH SCHOOL, Canning Rd, Kalamunda	77 D 8
KALLAROO PRE-SCHOOL, 23 Batavia Pl, Kallaroo	23 C 7
KAPINARA PRIMARY SCHOOL, Catesby St, City Beach	58 D 6
KARDINYA PRIMARY SCHOOL, Ochiltree Wy, Kardinya	92 A 7
KARRAGULLEN PRIMARY SCHOOL, 188 School Rd, Karragullen	109 A 2
KARRINYUP PRIMARY SCHOOL, Hampton St, Karrinyup	45 A 4

Name	Map Ref.
KELMSCOTT JOHN CALVIN SCHOOL, Lake Rd, Kelmscott	106 A 9
KELMSCOTT PRE-SCHOOL, 55 River Rd, Kelmscott	106 E 9
KELMSCOTT PRIMARY SCHOOL, River Rd, Kelmscott	106 E 9
KELMSCOTT SENIOR HIGH SCHOOL FARM, Cammillo Rd, Kelmscott	106 D 10
KELMSCOTT SENIOR HIGH SCHOOL, Cnr Third Ave & Cammillo Rd, Kelmscott	106 D 9
KENSINGTON PRIMARY SCHOOL, 73 Banksia Tce, Kensington	73 C 9
KENT STREET SENIOR HIGH SCHOOL, Kent St, Kensington	73 E 9
KENWICK SCHOOL, Moore St, Kenwick	95 C 1
KERRY STREET COMMUNITY SCHOOL, 20 Forrest Rd, Hamilton Hill	101 A 1
KEWDALE JUNIOR PRIMARY SCHOOL, Cnr Acton Ave & Keane St, Kewdale	74 E 7
KEWDALE PRIMARY SCHOOL, Cnr Belmont Ave & Kew St, Kewdale	75 A 7
KEWDALE SENIOR HIGH SCHOOL, President St, Kewdale	74 D 8
KIDS CENTRE, 58 Chester St, South Fremantle	90 D 9
KIDS OPEN LEARNING SCHOOL, 76 Seventh Ave, Maylands	61 D 7
KIM BEAZLEY SCHOOL, Cnr Stevens St & Yalgoo Ave, White Gum Valley	90 E 6
KINDAIMANNA PRE-SCHOOL, Grasmere Wy, Kelmscott	106 B 10
KINDY-CARE, 135 Kingsley Dr, Kingsley	31 B 1
KINGSLEY PRIMARY SCHOOL, Lathwell St, Armadale	116 D 2
KINGSWAY CHRISTIAN COLLEGE, 157 Kingsway, Landsdale	32 C 1
KINLOCK PRIMARY SCHOOL, Latham Rd, Ferndale	84 D 9
KOLBE CATHOLIC COLLEGE, Cnr Simpson Ave & Dowling St, Rockingham	137 D 5
KOONAWARRA PRIMARY SCHOOL, Goss Ave, Manning	83 B 4
KOONDOOLA PRIMARY SCHOOL, Burbridge Ave, Koondoola	33 A 7
KOONGAMIA PRIMARY SCHOOL, Meelah Rd, Koongamia	65 B 1
KOORILLA EDUCATION SUPPORT CTR, Benedick Rd, Coolbellup	101 E 2
KOORILLA PRIMARY SCHOOL, Benedick Rd, Coolbellup	101 E 2
KULLARK ABORIGINAL PRE-SCHOOL, (meets at Uniting Church), Cnr Grant & King George Sts, Innaloo	45 B 10
KULUNGA ABORIGINAL PRE-SCHOOL, Rennie Cr South, Hilton	91 B 8
KWINANA SENIOR HIGH SCHOOL, Gilmore Ave, Medina	131 A 6
KYILLA PRIMARY SCHOOL, Selkirk St, North Perth	60 E 5
LA SALLE COLLEGE, La Salle Ave, Middle Swan	50 C 6
LAKE GWELUP PRIMARY SCHOOL, Porter St, Gwelup	45 C 4
LAKE JOONDALUP BAPTIST COLLEGE, Kennedya Dr, Joondalup	19 D 5
LAKE JOONDALUP PRE-SCHOOL, 10 Neville Dr, Wanneroo	20 C 6
LAKE MONGER PRIMARY SCHOOL, Dodd St, Wembley	60 A 6
LAKELAND HIGH SCHOOL, South Lake Dr, South Lake	102 D 7
LANCE HOLT SCHOOL, 10 Henry St, Fremantle	1D B 5
LANDSDALE FARM SCHOOL, Cnr Evandale & Landsdale Rd, Landsdale	32 D 3
LANGFORD ABORIGINAL PRE-SCHOOL, C/- Lot 180 Imber Pl, Langford	94 E 2
LANGFORD EDUCATION SUPPORT CTR, Southgate Rd, Langford	94 E 3
LANGFORD PRIMARY SCHOOL, Southgate Rd, Langford	94 E 3
LATHLAIN PRIMARY SCHOOL, Howick St, Lathlain	74 A 6
LEEDERVILLE PRIMARY SCHOOL, Oxford St, Leederville	60 C 9
LEEMING PRIMARY SCHOOL, Meharry Rd, Leeming	93 A 10
LEEMING SENIOR HIGH SCHOOL, Aulberry Pde, Leeming	92 E 9
LESMURDIE PLAY CENTRE, Gladys Rd, Lesmurdie	87 B 3
LESMURDIE PRIMARY SCHOOL, Sanderson Rd, Lesmurdie	87 C 3
LESMURDIE SENIOR HIGH SCHOOL, Reid Rd, Lesmurdie	87 C 5
LIWARA CATHOLIC SCHOOL, 5 Tuart Rd, Greenwood	31 C 6
LOCKRIDGE CATHOLIC PRIMARY SCHOOL, Cnr Altone Rd & Morley Dr, Kiara	48 E 8
LOCKRIDGE JUNIOR PRIMARY SCHOOL, Rosher Rd, Lockridge	49 A 7
LOCKRIDGE PRIMARY SCHOOL, Rosher Rd, Lockridge	49 A 7
LOCKRIDGE SENIOR HIGH SCHOOL, Cnr Shadwell Ave & Benara Rd, Kiara	48 D 5
LOMBARDY STREET PRE-SCHOOL, Sportsman Pavillion, Woodlands Reserve	59 B 4
LORETO PRIMARY SCHOOL, Webster St, Nedlands	71 D 9
LUMEN CHRISTI COLLEGE, Station St, Martin	96 D 8
LYMBURNER PRIMARY SCHOOL, Lymburner Dr, Hillarys	30 C 2
LYNWOOD PRIMARY SCHOOL, Purley Cr, Lynwood	94 D 1
LYNWOOD SENIOR HIGH SCHOOL, Metcalfe Rd, Lynwood	94 C 2
MACKILLOP CATHOLIC PRIMARY SCHOOL, Verna Rd, Jandakot	102 E 8
MADDINGTON EDUCATION SUPPORT CTR, Albany Hwy, Maddington	96 A 5
MADDINGTON PRE-SCHOOL, 24 Helm St, Maddington	96 B 5
MADDINGTON PRIMARY SCHOOL, Albany Hwy, Maddington	96 A 5
MADDINGTON SENIOR HIGH SCHOOL, Dellar Rd, Maddington	96 C 3
MAIDA VALE PRIMARY SCHOOL, Cnr Kalamunda & Midland Rds, Maida Vale	76 E 1
MAJELLA PRIMARY SCHOOL, 9 Finchley Cr, Balga	46 D 1
MALIBU SCHOOL, Georgetown Dr, Safety Bay	137 B 10
MANDURAH PRIMARY SCHOOL, Hackett St, Mandurah	163 A 10
MANDURAH SENIOR HIGH SCHOOL, Gibla St, Mandurah	163 B 7
MANIANA PRE-SCHOOL, Maniana Rd North, Queens Park	85 B 3
MANNING PRE-SCHOOL, 17 Craigie Cr, Manning	83 A 7
MANNING PRIMARY SCHOOL, Ley St, Manning	83 A 6
MARANATHA CHRISTIAN COMMUNITY SCHOOL, Gnangara Dr, Waikiki	145 D 3
MARANGAROO PRIMARY SCHOOL, Giralt Rd, Marangaroo	32 B 5
MARGARET PRE-SCHOOL, 45 Richmond St, Leederville	60 D 8
MARMION PRIMARY SCHOOL, Telford St, Marmion	30 D 8
MARY'S MOUNT PRIMARY SCHOOL, 47 Davies Cr, Gooseberry Hill	77 C 4
MAYLANDS PRIMARY SCHOOL, Guildford Rd, Maylands	61 D 8
MAZENOD COLLEGE, Gladys Rd, Lesmurdie	87 B 4
MCDOUGALL PARK PRE-SCHOOL, Cnr Henley & Bruce Sts, Como	83 B 4
MEDINA ABORIGINAL PRE-SCHOOL, 13 Leasham Wy, Medina	130 E 6
MEDINA PRIMARY SCHOOL, Medina Ave, Medina	130 E 5
MEL MARIA CATHOLIC PRIMARY SCHOOL, Attadale Annexe, Cnr Davidson & Galloway Sts, Attadale	81 D 9
MEL MARIA CATHOLIC PRIMARY SCHOOL, Myaree Annexe, Evershed St, Myaree	92 A 2
MEL MARIA CATHOLIC PRIMARY SCHOOL, Santa Maria Annexe, 5 Cawston Rd, Attadale	81 C 7
MELVILLE PRIMARY SCHOOL, Kitchener Rd, Melville	91 E 1
MELVILLE SENIOR HIGH SCHOOL, Potts St, Melville	91 D 3
MELVISTA PRE-SCHOOL, Cnr Hackett Rd & Melvista Ave, Nedlands	81 C 1
MERCEDES COLLEGE, Goderich St, Perth	1C A 3
MERCY COLLEGE, Cnr Mirrabooka Ave & Beach Rd, Koondoola	32 E 9
MERCY PRIMARY SCHOOL, Beach Rd, Koondoola	32 E 9
METHODIST LADIES' COLLEGE, 356 Stirling Hwy, Claremont	71 A 10
METRO NORTH WEST S.P.E.R. CENTRE, c/- City Beach Primary School, Marapana Rd, City Beach	58 D 9
MIDDLE SWAN PRE-SCHOOL, 5 Whittome St, Middle Swan	50 D 3
MIDDLE SWAN PRIMARY SCHOOL, Cockman Cro, Middle Swan	50 D 5
MIDLAND CHRISTIAN SCHOOL, Cnr Amherst Rd & Archer St, Midland	50 B 9
MIDLAND PRIMARY SCHOOL, Cnr Morrison Rd & William St, Midland	50 B 7
MIDVALE PRIMARY SCHOOL, Wellaton St, Midvale	50 D 7
MILL POINT PRE-SCHOOL, 14 Labouchere Rd, South Perth	72 E 7
MILLEN PRIMARY SCHOOL, Playfield St, East Victoria Park	84 A 2
MIRRABOOKA PRIMARY SCHOOL, Laythorne St, Nollamara	46 E 6
MIRRABOOKA SENIOR HIGH SCHOOL, Nollamara Ave, Nollamara	46 E 6
MIRRABOOKA SHS ED. SUPPORT CENTRE, Nollamara Ave, Nollamara	46 E 6
MOERLINA SCHOOL, Members Pavillion, Showgrounds, Claremont	71 B 8
MONTESSORI CHILDREN'S CENTRE, 2 Egham St, Victoria Park	73 E 5
MONTESSORI SCHOOL, 18 Montessori Pl, Kingsley	31 D 1
MONTROSE EDUCATION SUPPORT CTR, Stebbing Wy, Girrawheen	32 E 8
MONTROSE PRIMARY SCHOOL, Stebbing Wy, Girrawheen	32 E 7
MORLEY PRIMARY SCHOOL, Wellington Rd, Morley	47 E 9
MORLEY SENIOR HIGH SCHOOL, Bramwell Rd, Noranda	47 C 5
MOSMAN PARK PRIMARY SCHOOL, Victoria St, Mosman Park	80 D 7
MOSMAN PARK SCHOOL FOR THE DEAF, 53 Curtin Ave, Cottesloe	80 C 5
MOUNT HAWTHORN ED. SUPPORT CENTRE, Matlock St, Mount Hawthorn	60 C 5
MOUNT HAWTHORN JNR PRIMARY SCHOOL, Scarborough Beach Rd, Mount Hawthorn	60 C 5
MOUNT HAWTHORN PRIMARY SCHOOL, Matlock St, Mount Hawthorn	60 C 5
MOUNT HELENA PRIMARY SCHOOL, Keane St East, Mount Helena	55 C 5
MOUNT INGLE PRE-SCHOOL, Hamer Pde, Inglewood	61 C 5
MOUNT LAWLEY PRE-SCHOOL, 81 Railway Pde, Mount Lawley	61 C 8
MOUNT LAWLEY PRIMARY SCHOOL, Second Ave, Mount Lawley	61 C 6
MOUNT LAWLEY SENIOR HIGH SCHOOL, Woodsome St, Mount Lawley	61 B 5

Name	Map Ref.
MOUNT PLEASANT PRIMARY SCHOOL, Queens Rd, Mount Pleasant	82 D 9
MULLALOO BEACH PRIMARY SCHOOL, West View Blvd, Mullaloo	23 A 4
MULLALOO HEIGHTS PRIMARY SCHOOL, Charonia Rd, Mullaloo	23 B 4
MULLALOO PRE-SCHOOL, Koorana Rd, Mullaloo	23 B 4
MUNDARING AND DISTRICT PRE-SCHOOL, 79 Jacoby St, Mundaring	68 B 1
MUNDARING CHRISTIAN SCHOOL, 15 Mann St, Mundaring	54 C 10
MUNDARING MONTESSORI SCHOOL, 10 Tee Ave, Mundaring	54 B 10
MUNDARING PRIMARY SCHOOL, Stevens St, Mundaring	54 C 9
MUNDIJONG PRIMARY SCHOOL, Livesey St, Mundijong	143 A 7
MUSLIM COMMUNITY SCHOOL, 17 Tonbridge Wy, Thornlie	95 C 5
NEDLANDS PARK PRE-SCHOOL, Cnr Bruce St & Melvista Ave, Nedlands	81 E 1
NEDLANDS PRIMARY SCHOOL, 35 Kingsway, Nedlands	71 E 9
NEERIGEN BROOK PRIMARY SCHOOL, Seventh Rd, Armadale	116 B 6
NEWBOROUGH PRIMARY SCHOOL, Newborough St, Doubleview	45 A 7
NEWMAN COLLEGE JUNIOR SCHOOL, 216 Empire Ave, Churchlands	59 B 6
NEWMAN COLLEGE, 216 Empire Ave, Churchlands	59 B 6
NEWMAN SIENA COLLEGE, 33 Williamstown Rd, Doubleview	59 B 3
NEWTON PRIMARY SCHOOL, Marvell Ave, Spearwood	101 C 8
NOLLAMARA CHRISTIAN ACADEMY, 148 Hillsborough Dr, Nollamara	46 C 5
NOLLAMARA JUNIOR PRIMARY SCHOOL, 11 Mayfair St, Nollamara	46 C 7
NOLLAMARA PRIMARY SCHOOL, Harrison St, Nollamara	46 C 7
NORANDA PRIMARY SCHOOL, Walmsley Dr, Noranda	48 A 5
NORTH BALGA JUNIOR PRIMARY, Wallington Rd, Balga	32 C 10
NORTH BALGA PRIMARY SCHOOL, Maitland Rd, Balga	32 C 10
NORTH BEACH EDUCATION SUPP. CTR, Cnr North Beach Rd & Groat St, North Beach	44 D 2
NORTH BEACH PRIMARY SCHOOL, Cnr North Beach Rd & Groat St, North Beach	44 D 2
NORTH COTTESLOE PRE-SCHOOL, Cnr Ackland Wy & Marmion St, Cottesloe	70 D 10
NORTH COTTESLOE PRIMARY SCHOOL, 100 Eric St, Cottesloe	80 E 1
NORTH EAST METRO. DISTRICT LANGUAGE DEVELOPMENT CENTRE, 2 Bayview St, Bayswater	62 A 3
NORTH FREMANTLE PRIMARY SCHOOL, John St, North Fremantle	90 D 1
NORTH INNALOO PRIMARY SCHOOL, Ambrose St, Innaloo	45 B 9
NORTH LAKE PRIMARY SCHOOL, Montague Wy, Coolbellup	101 E 1
NORTH LAKE SENIOR HIGH SCHOOL, Torquil Rd, Kardinya	91 E 9
NORTH MANDURAH PRIMARY SCHOOL, Park Rd, Mandurah	163 B 7
NORTH MORLEY PRIMARY SCHOOL, Gordon Rd West, Dianella	47 C 6
NORTH PARMELIA PRIMARY SCHOOL, Durrant Ave, Parmelia	131 C 5
NORTH PERTH PRIMARY SCHOOL, Albert St, North Perth	60 E 7
NORTH WEST METRO DISTRICT LANGUAGE DEVELOPMENT CENTRE, c/- Balcatta Primary School, Main St, Balcatta	46 B 7
NORTH WOODVALE PRIMARY SCHOOL, Chichester Dr, Woodvale	24 B 5
NORTHERN SUBURBS Seventh Day Adventist Primary School, Queensway, Landsdale	26 A 10
NOTRE DAME SCHOOL, 360 Daly St, Cloverdale	74 E 3
OAKFORD PRIMARY SCHOOL, Kargotich Rd, Oakford	125 B 10
OBERTHUR PRIMARY SCHOOL, Nicholls Cr, Bull Creek	93 B 6
OCEAN REEF PRIMARY SCHOOL, Kaufman Ave, Ocean Reef	23 A 1
OCEAN REEF SENIOR HIGH SCHOOL, Venturi Dr, Ocean Reef	19 A 10
ORANA CATHOLIC SCHOOL, Querrin Ave, Willetton	93 E 3
ORANGE GROVE PRIMARY SCHOOL, Boyle La, Orange Grove	96 D 1
ORELIA PRIMARY SCHOOL, Bolton Wy, Orelia	131 A 5
OSBORNE PRIMARY SCHOOL, Albert St, Osborne Park	60 A 1
OUR LADY OF FATIMA SCHOOL, 3 Harris Rd, Palmyra	91 B 1
OUR LADY OF GOOD COUNSEL SCHOOL, Miles St, Karrinyup	45 A 7
OUR LADY OF GRACE SCHOOL, 5 Kitchener St, North Beach	44 C 3
OUR LADY OF LOURDES SCHOOL, 263 Flinders St, Nollamara	46 D 8
OUR LADY OF MERCY PRIMARY SCHOOL, 55 Hudson Ave, Girrawheen	32 C 7
OUR LADY OF MT CARMEL SCHOOL, 82 Collick St, Hilton	91 B 9
OUR LADY'S ASSUMPTION SCHOOL, 356 Grand Pro, Dianella	47 B 10
PADBURY CATHOLIC PRIMARY SCHOOL, O'Leary Rd, Padbury	30 D 2
PADBURY PRE-SCHOOL, Cnr Alexnder & Caley Rds, Padbury	23 D 8
PADBURY PRIMARY SCHOOL, MacDonald Ave, Padbury	23 D 10
PADBURY SENIOR HIGH SCHOOL, Giles Ave, Padbury	23 D 10
PALMYRA PRIMARY SCHOOL, McKimmie Rd, Palmyra	91 B 3
PARKERVILLE PRIMARY SCHOOL, Windoo Rd, Parkerville	53 C 7
PARKWOOD PRIMARY SCHOOL, Zelkova Dr, Lynwood	94 B 2
PENRHOS COLLEGE, 101 Thelma St, Como	83 B 2
PERTH COLLEGE, 31 Lawley Cr, Mount Lawley	61 B 8
PERTH MODERN SENIOR HIGH SCHOOL, Roberts Rd, Subiaco	72 C 1
PHOENIX PRIMARY SCHOOL, Phoenix Rd, Spearwood	101 A 3
PICKERING BROOK PRIMARY SCHOOL, Pickering Brook Rd, Pickering Brook	89 C 10
PINEVIEW PRE-SCHOOL, 30 Mopsa Wy, Coolbellup	91 E 10
PIONEER VILLAGE SCHOOL, C/- Pioneer World, 2 South West Hwy, Armadale	116 E 6
PONDEROSA SCHOOL, (meets at Armadale Recreation Centre) Townley St, Kelmscott	116 C 8
POSEIDON PRIMARY SCHOOL, Poseidon Rd, Heathridge	19 B 10
POYNTER PRIMARY SHOOL, Poynter Drive, Duncraig	30 E 8
PRENDIVILLE CATHOLIC COLLEGE, Prendiville Ave, Ocean Reef	19 A 8
PRESBYTERIAN LADIES' COLLEGE, McNeil St, Peppermint Grove	80 E 2
PRINCESS MARGARET HOSPITAL SCH., Thomas St, Subiaco	72 C 1
QUEEN OF APOSTLES SCHOOL, 108 Tribute St East, Riverton	83 E 9
QUEENS PARK PRIMARY SCHOOL, 202 Treasure Rd, Queens Park	85 A 2
QUINNS ROCKS PRIMARY SCHOOL, Rees Dr, Quinns Rock	10 B 1
QUINTILIAN SCHOOL, 19 Henry St, Shenton Park	72 A 4
REDCLIFFE PRE-SCHOOL, Cnr Greenshields Wy & Morrison St, Redcliffe	62 E 8
REDCLIFFE PRIMARY SCHOOL, Kanowna Ave, Redcliffe	63 A 8
REGENT COLLEGE, 22 Columbo St, Victoria Park	73 D 7
REHOBOTH CHRISTIAN PRIMARY SCHOOL, Armstrong Rd, Wilson	84 B 6
REHOBOTH CHRISTIAN SCHOOL, 94 Kenwick Rd, Kenwick	85 E 10
RICHMOND PRIMARY SCHOOL, Windsor Rd, East Fremantle	90 E 1
RIVERTON PRIMARY SCHOOL, Corinthian Rd, East Riverton	83 E 10
RIVERTON-WILLETTON KINDERGARTEN, 40 Wavel Ave, Riverton	93 D 1
ROCKINGHAM BEACH PRIMARY SCHOOL, Bay View St, Rockingham	136 E 6
ROCKINGHAM EDUCATION SUPPORT CTR, Bay View St, Rockingham	136 E 6
ROCKINGHAM FAMILY SCHOOL, 218 Safety Bay Rd, Safety Bay	136 D 10
ROCKINGHAM SENIOR HIGH SCHOOL, Read St, Rockingham	137 A 6
ROLEYSTONE DISTRICT HIGH SCHOOL, Brooks Rd, Roleystone	108 B 5
ROLEYSTONE PRIMARY SCHOOL, Robin Rd, Roleystone	108 A 7
ROSALIE PRIMARY SCHOOL, Onslow Rd, Shenton Park	71 E 4
ROSSMOYNE PRIMARY SCHOOL, Second Ave, Rossmoyne	93 B 2
ROSSMOYNE SENIOR HIGH SCHOOL, Keith Rd, Rossmoyne	93 B 3
ROSSMOYNE-RIVERTON PRE-SCHOOL, Central Rd, Rossmoyne	93 B 1
ROSTRATA PRIMARY SCHOOL, Rostrata Ave, Willetton	93 E 4
ROYAL PERTH HOSPITAL SCHOOL, Selby St, Shenton Park	71 D 3
SACRED HEART COLLEGE, Hocking Pde, Sorrento	30 B 5
SACRED HEART PRIMARY SCHOOL, 40 Mary St, Highgate	61 B 9
SACRED HEART PRIMARY SCHOOL, Discovery Dr, Thornlie	95 B 8
SACRED HEART SCHOOL, 20 Coolgardie St, Mundaring	68 B 1
SAFETY BAY PRIMARY SCHOOL, Rae Rd, Safety Bay	136 D 9
SAFETY BAY SENIOR HIGH SCHOOL, Malibu Rd, Safety Bay	145 B 1
SAMSON PRIMARY SCHOOL, Lawrence Wy, Samson	91 D 9
SANTA CLARA SCHOOL, 91 Coolgardie St, Bentley	84 B 4
SANTA MARIA COLLEGE, Moreing Rd, Attadale	81 C 7
SAWYERS VALLEY PRIMARY SCHOOL, Railway Tce, Sawyers Valley	69 A 1
SCARBOROUGH PRIMARY SCHOOL, Hinderwell St, Scarborough	44 E 10
SCARBOROUGH SENIOR HIGH SCHOOL, Newborough St, Doubleview	45 A 7
SCHOENSTATT KINDERGARTEN, 55 Tudor Ave South, Riverton	83 E 9
SCOTCH COLLEGE, 76 Shenton Rd, Swanbourne	70 E 9
SEABROOK PRE-SCHOOL, 17 Seabrook St, Dianella	47 C 7
SEAFORTH PRIMARY SCHOOL, Verna St, Gosnells	106 B 2
SEAVIEW PRE-SCHOOL, Cnr Broome & Jarrad Sts, Cottesloe	80 C 3
SERPENTINE PRIMARY SCHOOL, Lefroy St, Serpentine	154 E 4
SERVITE COLLEGE, 134 Cape St, Tuart Hill	60 B 1
SETON CATHOLIC COLLEGE, De Vialar Campus, Marchant Rd, Samson	91 C 9
SETON CATHOLIC COLLEGE, St Brendans Campus, York St, Hilton	91 A 9

Name	Map Ref.
SEVENTH DAY ADVENTIST PRIMARY SCHOOL, 27 Colombo St, Victoria Park	73 D 6
SEVENTH DAY ADVENTIST SCHOOL, 17 First Ave, Bickley	88 C 4
SEVENTH DAY ADVENTIST SCHOOL, Cnr Ninth & Wungong Rds, Wungong	126 C 1
SHELLEY PRE-SCHOOL, 20 Aldam Cr, Shelley	83 D 10
SHELLEY PRIMARY SCHOOL, Monota Ave, Shelley	83 D 10
SHENTON PARK PRE-SCHOOL, 334 Onslow Rd, Shenton Park	71 D 4
SIR DAVID BRAND SCHOOL, 106 Bradford St, Coolbinia	60 E 3
SORRENTO PRIMARY SCHOOL, Elfreda Ave, Sorrento	30 D 6
SOUTH COOGEE PRIMARY SCHOOL, Russell Rd, Munster	111 B 5
SOUTH FREMANTLE SENIOR HIGH SCHOOL, Lefroy Rd, Beaconsfield	90 E 8
SOUTH KENSINGTON SCHOOL, George St, Kensington	73 D 10
SOUTH LAKE PRIMARY SCHOOL, Mason Ct, South Lake	102 C 6
SOUTH PADBURY PRIMARY SCHOOL, Warburton Ave, Padbury	30 D 1
SOUTH PERTH PRIMARY SCHOOL, Forrest St, South Perth	73 A 9
SOUTH TERRACE PRIMARY SCHOOL, Cnr Brennan & Alma Sts, Fremantle	1D C 6
SOUTH THORNLIE PRIMARY SCHOOL, Ovens Rd, Thornlie	95 B 7
SOUTHERN CHRISTIAN ACADEMY, 110 Rockingham Rd, Hamilton Hill	101 A 2
SOUTHWELL PRIMARY SCHOOL, Grandpre Cr, Hamilton Hill	101 B 3
SPEARWOOD ALTERNATIVE SCHOOL, Rockingham Rd, Spearwood	101 B 7
SPEARWOOD PRIMARY SCHOOL, Gerald St, Spearwood	101 B 6
SPEECH & HEARING CENTRE, Dodd Street, Wembley	60 A 6
SPRINGFIELD PRE-PRIMARY CENTRE, Bridgewater Dr, Kallaroo	23 B 7
SPRINGFIELD PRIMARY SCHOOL, Bridgewater Dr, Kallaroo	23 B 7
ST ANDREW'S GREEK ORTHODOX SCHOOL, 75 Gordon Rd West, Dianella	47 C 6
ST ANTHONY'S SCHOOL, 990 Wanneroo Rd, Wanneroo	20 D 7
ST ANTHONY'S SCHOOL, Innamincka Rd, Greenmount	51 B 9
ST AUGUSTINE'S SCHOOL, 34 Gladstone Rd, Rivervale	74 A 4
ST BENEDICT'S SCHOOL, Alness St, Ardross	82 C 7
ST BRIGID'S COLLEGE, 200 Lesmurdie Rd, Lesmurdie	87 C 2
ST BRIGID'S PRIMARY SCHOOL, Glen Rd, Lesmurdie	87 C 1
ST BRIGID'S SCHOOL, Lot 3/4 Toodyay Rd, Middle Swan	50 D 5
ST CLARE'S SCHOOL, 117 Alma Rd, North Perth	60 E 8
ST COLUMBA'S SCHOOL, 27 Forrest St, South Perth	73 A 8
ST COLUMBA'S SCHOOL, 32 Roberts St, Bayswater	62 B 6
ST DENIS' SCHOOL, 157 Powell St, Joondanna	60 D 3
ST DOMINIC'S SCHOOL, 95 Beatrice St, Innaloo	45 B 10
ST FRANCIS XAVIER SCHOOL, Cnr Third Rd & South Western Hwy, Armadale	116 E 7
ST GERARD'S PRIMARY SCHOOL, 31 Changton Wy, Balga	46 D 4
ST HILDA'S ANGLICAN SCHOOL GIRLS, Bay View Tce, Mosman Park	80 E 4
ST JEROME'S SCHOOL, Troode St, Munster	101 B 10
ST JOHN'S SCHOOL, 100 Scarborough Beach Rd, Scarborough	44 E 9
ST JOSEPH'S PRIMARY SCHOOL, 140 Railway Pde, Queens Park	84 E 4
ST JUDE'S CATHOLIC PRIMARY SCHOOL, Barnston Wy, Langford	94 E 3
ST KIERAN PRE-PRIMARY SCHOOL, Waterloo St, Tuart Hill	60 B 1
ST KIERAN PRIMARY SCHOOL, 1 Morgans St, Tuart Hill	60 B 1
ST LAWRENCE SCHOOL, 405 Main St, Balcatta	46 B 6
ST LUKE'S CATHOLIC PRIMARY SCHOOL, 17 Duffy Tce, Woodvale	24 D 9
ST MARGARET'S INDEPENDENT KINDERGARTEN, 58 Tyrell St, Nedlands	71 E 9
ST MARIA GORETTI SCHOOL, 64 Morrison St, Redcliffe	63 A 9
ST MARY'S ANGLICAN GIRLS' SCHOOL, Elliot Rd, Karrinyup	44 D 6
ST MICHAEL'S SCHOOL, 4 James St, Bassendean	63 A 1
ST MUNCHIN'S SCHOOL, 175 Corfield St, Gosnells	106 A 1
ST NORBERT COLLEGE, 135 Treasure Rd, Queens Park	84 E 4
ST PATRICK'S SCHOOL, Point St, Fremantle	1D C 5
ST PAUL'S PRIMARY SCHOOL, Learoyd St, Mount Lawley	61 A 6
ST PETER'S PRIMARY SCHOOL, 169 Salisbury St, Bedford	61 D 3
ST PIUS X SCHOOL, Cloister Ave, Como	83 A 7
ST SIMON PETER CATHOLIC PRIMARY SCHOOL, Prendiville Ave, Ocean Reef	19 A 8
ST STEPHEN'S SCHOOL, Doveridge Dr, Duncraig	31 A 3
ST THOMAS' PRIMARY SCHOOL, 8 Warden St, Claremont	71 B 8
ST VINCENT'S SCHOOL, Pace Rd, Medina	130 E 5
STAR OF THE SEA SCHOOL, Farris St, Rockingham	137 A 6
SUBIACO PRIMARY SCHOOL, Bagot Rd, Subiaco	72 A 2
SUPPORT SERVICES FOR THE VISUALLY IMPAIRED, Sutherland Ave, Dianella	47 A 9
SUTHERLAND EDUCATION SUPPORT CTR, Sutherland Ave, Dianella	47 A 9
SUTHERLAND PRIMARY SCHOOL, Sutherland Ave, Dianella	47 A 9
SWAN CHRISTIAN HIGH SCHOOL, 97 Gt Northern Hwy, Middle Swan	50 D 1
SWAN VIEW PRIMARY SCHOOL, Morrison Rd, Swan View	51 C 7
SWAN VIEW SENIOR HIGH SCHOOL, Salisbury Rd, Swan View	51 B 8
SWAN VIEW-GREENMOUNT PRE-SCHOOL, 80 Salisbury Rd, Swan View	51 C 8
SWANBOURNE PRIMARY SCHOOL, Derby St, Swanbourne	70 E 8
SWANBOURNE SENIOR HIGH SCHOOL, Narla Rd, Swanbourne	70 E 7
SWANNEE NOONGHAS ABORIGINAL PRE-SCHOOL, Cnr Benara & West Swan Rds, Caversham	49 D 5
TAKARI PRIMARY SCHOOL, Rickman St, Balcatta	46 A 4
TEMPLE DAVID KINDERGARTEN, 35 Clifton Cr, Mount Lawley	61 B 7
THE CHILDREN'S MONTESSORI HOUSE 266 Kalamunda Rd, Maida Vale	76 E 2
THE FAMILY PRIMARY SCHOOL, Cnr Herbert Rd & Evans St, Shenton Park	71 E 4
THE JAPANESE SCHOOL IN PERTH, 157 Deanmore Rd, Doubleview	44 E 10
THE NEW SCHOOL, Warwick Centre, 316 Erindale Rd, Warwick	31 E 7
THOMAS SCOTT ANGLICAN COMMUNITY SCHOOL, Blackboy Wy, Morley	48 C 4
THORNLIE CHRISTIAN COLLEGE, Lot 1570 Warton Rd, Southern River	104 E 5
THORNLIE PRIMARY SCHOOL, Thornlie Ave, Thornlie	95 C 4
THORNLIE SENIOR HIGH SCHOOL, Ovens Rd, Thornlie	95 C 7
TRANBY PRIMARY SCHOOL, 99 Acton Ave, Rivervale	74 C 3
TREETOPS MONTESSORI SCHOOL, 12 Beenong Rd, Darlington	66 A 5
TRINITY COLLEGE, Trinity Ave, East Perth	73 C 4
TUART HILL JUNIOR PRIMARY SCHOOL, Cape St, Tuart Hill	60 C 1
TUART HILL PRE-SCHOOL, 194 Royal St, Yokine	46 D 10
TUART HILL PRIMARY SCHOOL, Banksia St, Tuart Hill	60 C 1
TUART SENIOR COLLEGE, Banksia St, Tuart Hill	60 C 2
UPPER SWAN PRIMARY SCHOOL, Great Northern Hwy, Millendon	29 E 5
URSULA FRAYNE CATHOLIC COLLEGE, 15 Duncan St, Victoria Park	73 E 7
URSULA FRAYNE CATHOLIC COLLEGE, Balmoral St, East Victoria Park	84 A 1
VICTORIA PARK PRIMARY SCHOOL, Cargill St, Victoria Park	73 D 6
WADDINGTON PRIMARY SCHOOL, Henniker Way, Koondoola	33 A 8
WALDORF SCHOOL RUDOLF STEINER EDUCATION, Cnr Forrest Rd & Progress Dr, Bibra Lake	102 A 3
WALLISTON PRE-SCHOOL, 12 Grove Rd, Walliston	88 A 2
WALLISTON PRIMARY SCHOOL, Dianella Rd, Walliston	87 E 2
WANNEROO JUNIOR PRIMARY SCHOOL, 18 Church St, Wanneroo	20 C 8
WANNEROO PRIMARY SCHOOL, Wanneroo Rd, Wanneroo	20 D 8
WANNEROO SENIOR HIGH SCHOOL, Quarkum St, Wanneroo	20 E 9
WARNBRO PRE-PRIMARY SCHOOL, Fairmile St, Warnbro	145 D 7
WARNBRO PRIMARY SCHOOL, Axminister Rd, Warnbro	145 D 7
WARRIAPENDI PRIMARY SCHOOL, Redcliffe Ave, Balga	46 D 1
WARRIAPENDI S.P.E.R. CENTRE, Redcliffe Ave, Balga	46 D 1
WARWICK PRIMARY SCHOOL, Ellersdale Ave, Warwick	31 E 8
WARWICK SENIOR HIGH SCHOOL, Erindale Rd, Warwick	31 E 7
WATTLE GROVE PRIMARY SCHOOL, Welshpool Rd, Wattle Grove	86 A 4
WATTLEUP PRIMARY SCHOOL, Hitchcock Pl, Wattleup	121 D 3
WELD SQUARE PRIMARY SCHOOL, Dorking Pl, Morley	48 B 9
WEMBLEY DOWNS PRIMARY SCHOOL, Bournemouth Cr, Wembley Downs	58 E 3
WEMBLEY PRE-SCHOOL, 203 Jersey St, Wembley	59 E 9
WEMBLEY PRIMARY SCHOOL, Cnr Grantham & Alexander Sts, Wembley	59 E 8
WESLEY COLLEGE, 40 Coode St, South Perth	73 A 8
WEST ARMADALE PRE-SCHOOL, 20 Kiama Rd, Armadale	116 B 5
WEST BALCATTA PRIMARY SCHOOL, Cedric St, Balcatta	45 E 5
WEST GREENWOOD E.C.E. CENTRE, Coolibah Dr, Greenwood	31 B 4
WEST GREENWOOD PRIMARY SCHOOL, Coolibah Dr, Greenwood	31 B 4
WEST LEEDERVILLE PRIMARY SCHOOL, Northwood St, Leederville	60 B 9
WEST LEEMING PRIMARY SCHOOL, Westall Tce, Leeming	92 E 8
WEST MIDLAND PRIMARY SCHOOL, Archer St, Midland	50 B 9
WEST MORLEY PRIMARY SCHOOL, Fitzroy St, Dianella	47 D 8
WESTFIELD PARK EDUCATION SUPPORT CENTRE, Cnr Cammillo Rd & Hemingway Dr, Westfield	106 C 7

275

	Map	Ref.

WESTFIELD PARK PRIMARY SCHOOL, Cnr Cammillo Rd & Hemingway Dr, Westfield ... 106 C 7
WESTMINSTER EDUCATION SUPP. CTR, Marloo Rd, Balga .... 46 C 4
WESTMINSTER JNR PRIMARY SCHOOL, Ungaroo Rd, Balga .... 46 C 4
WESTMINSTER PRIMARY SCHOOL, Marloo Rd, Balga .... 46 C 4
WESTVIEW KINDERGARTEN, 144 Westview St, Scarborough .. 44 E 9
WHITE GUM VALLEY PRIMARY SCHOOL, Watkins St, White Gum Valley .... 90 E 6
WHITESIDE PRIMARY SCHOOL, Whiteside St, Cloverdale .... 75 A 5
WHITFORD CATHOLIC PRIMARY SCHOOL, 256 Camberwarra Dr, Craigie .... 23 C 5
WILLAGEE PRIMARY SCHOOL, Drury St, Willagee .... 91 D 4
WILLETTON PRIMARY SCHOOL, Cnr Apsley Rd & Woodpecker Ave, Willetton .... 93 C 4
WILLETTON SENIOR HIGH SCHOOL, Pinetree Gully Rd, Willetton .... 93 C 6
WILSON PRIMARY SCHOOL, Armstrong Rd, Wilson .... 84 B 7
WINTERFOLD PRIMARY SCHOOL, Annie St, Hamilton Hill .... 90 E 9
WINTHROP PRIMARY SCHOOL, Jackson Ave, Winthrop .... 92 C 5
WIRRABIRRA EDUCATION SUPPORT CTR, Cnr Corfield & Jenkinson Sts, Gosnells .... 95 E 9
WIRRABIRRA PRIMARY SCHOOL, Cnr Corfield & Jenkinson Sts, Gosnells ..... 95 E 9
WOODLANDS PRIMARY SCHOOL, Bentwood Ave, Woodlands .... 59 B 3
WOODLUPINE E.C.E. CENTRE, Solandra Wy, Forrestfield .... 76 C 9
WOODLUPINE PRIMARY SCHOOL, Solandra Wy, Forrestfield .... 76 C 9
WOODVALE PRIMARY SCHOOL, Timberlane Dr, Woodvale .... 24 C 7
WOODVALE SENIOR HIGH SCHOOL, Woodvale Dr, Woodvale ...... 24 C 7
W.A. INTERNATIONAL COLLEGE, Cnr Joondalup Dr & Shenton Ave, Joondalup .... 19 D 5
YAGAN PRE-SCHOOL, 10 Poimena Me, Kingsley .... 31 E 3
YALE PRIMARY SCHOOL, Sage Rd, Thornlie .... 95 B 4
YANCHEP DISTRICT HIGH SCHOOL, Lagoon Dr, Yanchep .... 4 C 4
YANGEBUP PRIMARY SCHOOL, Moorhen Dr, Yangebup .... 102 A 9
YARINGA PRE-SCHOOL, Lot 646 Smythe St, Rockingham .... 137 A 4
YELLAGONGA WALDORF PRE-SCHOOL, MacDonald Reserve, Padbury 23 D10
YIDARRA CATHOLIC PRIMARY SCHOOL, Cnr Murdoch Dr & Marsengo Rd, Bateman .... 92 D 6
YOKINE PRE-SCHOOL, 26 Ranger Rd, Yokine .... 60 E 1

YOKINE PRIMARY SCHOOL, Woodrow Ave, Yokine .... 60 E 1

SPECIAL SCHOOLS

BLIND INSTITUTE, Guildford Rd, Maylands ..... 61 D 7
HILLVIEW ADULT SPASTIC CENTRE, Hillview Rd, Mt Lawley ..... 61 B 7
MT LAWLEY RECEPTION HOME SCHOOL, Walcott St, Mt Lawley .... 61 B 9

UNIVERSITIES

CURTIN UNIVERSITY OF TECHNOLOGY, Kent St, Bentley (Facing Map 135) ..... 83 E 4
EDITH COWAN UNIVERSITY - CHURCHLANDS CAMPUS, Pearson St, Churchlands .... 59 C 6
EDITH COWAN UNIVERSITY - CLAREMONT CAMPUS, Goldsworthy Rd, Claremont 71 B10
EDITH COWAN UNIVERSITY - JOONDALUP CAMPUS, Joondalup Dr, Joondalup ...... 19 E 8
EDITH COWAN UNIVERSITY - MOUNT LAWLEY CAMPUS, 2 Bradford St, Menora .... 61 A 5
EDITH COWAN UNIVERSITY - W.A. ACADEMY OF PERFORMING ARTS, located on Mt Lawley Campus .... 61 A 5
MURDOCH UNIVERSITY, South St, Murdoch, (Facing Map 128) .... 92 C 8
THE UNIVERSITY OF WESTERN AUSTRALIA, Mounts Bay Rd, Crawley, (Inset Map 120) .... 72 A 8

FERRY TERMINALS

BARRACK ST, Perth .... 1C E 4
COODE ST, South Perth .... 73 A 7
FREMANTLE, East St, Fremantle .... 90 D 2
HILLARYS BOAT HARBOUR, Sorrento .... 30 A 4
MENDS ST, South Perth .... 72 E 6
WOODBRIDGE, Third Ave, Midland .... 50 A 8

FIRE SERVICES

VOLUNTEER FIRE STATIONS

ARMADALE, Forrest Rd .... 116 D 6
BASSENDEAN, Parker St .... 63 A 2
FALCON, Flavia St .... 162A C 3
GLEN FORREST, Marnie Rd .... 66 D 2
GUILDFORD, Meadow St .... 63 D 1
KALAMUNDA, Central Rd .... 77 D 7
KELMSCOTT, Clifton St .... 106 E 7
KWINANA, Cnr Meares Ave & Chisham Ave .... 131 A 7
MANDURAH, Pinjarra Rd .... 165 A 2
ROCKINGHAM, Hefron St ..... 137 C 8
YANCHEP/TWO ROCKS, Lot 11 Bracknell St, Yanchep .... 4 D 2

W.A. BUSH FIRES BOARD FIRE STATIONS

BALDIVIS, Baldivis Rd .... 147 B 1
BEDFORDALE .... 127 C 1

BUSH FIRES BOARD STATE HEADQUARTERS, 210 Kent St, Kensington .... 83 D 1
BYFORD, Clara St .... 135 D 1
CHIDLOW, Old Northam Rd .... 56 D 1
DARLINGTON, Pine Tce .... 66 A 4
EAST SWAN, Cathedral Ave, Brigadoon .... 168 C 5
FORRESTDALE, Weld St ...... 114 E 6
GLEN FORREST, Marnie Rd .... 66 D 2
GOSNELLS, Canning Park Ave .... 96 A 3
JANDAKOT, Liddelow Rd 113 D10
JARRAHDALE, Wanliss St ..... 152 E 7
KALAMUNDA, Raymond Rd.... 88 A 1
KELMSCOTT, Clifton St .... 106 E 7
KWINANA SOUTH, Barker Rd, Wellard .... 132 C 9
MANDOGALUP, Hope Valley Rd .... 122 D 9
MOUNT HELENA, Chidlow St .... 55 C 5
MUNDARING, Chipper st 54 B10
MUNDIJONG, Cockram St ..... 143 A 8
OAKFORD, Nicholson Rd ..... 124 D 9
PARKERVILLE, Riley Rd .... 53 C 6
QUINNS ROCKS, Gumblossom Wy 10 B10
ROLEYSTONE, Peet Rd .... 107 E 9
SAWYERS VALLEY, Pearce St .... 69 A 1
SERPENTINE, Karnup Rd ..... 154 E 3
SINGLETON, Cavender St ..... 160 D 3
SOUTH COOGEE, Corin Wy, Wattleup .... 121 D 2
STONEVILLE, Bentley St .... 54 B 4
WANNEROO, Wanneroo Rd ... 20 C 6
WEST SWAN, Henley St, Henley Brook 29 B10
WESTFIELD, Brigade Rd ...... 115 D 5

W.A. FIRE BRIGADES BOARD PERMANENT

ARMADALE, Forrest Rd .... 116 D 6
BALCATTA, Delawney St .... 45 E 3
BASSENDEAN, Parker St .... 63 A 2
BEDFORD, Cnr Walter Rd West and The Strand .... 61 D 1
BELMONT, Cnr Belmont Ave and Fulham St .... 74 E 5
CANNING VALE, Lot 206 Catalano St .... 94 A 6
CANNINGTON, George Wy ..... 84 D 6
CLAREMONT, Congdon St 70 E10
DAGLISH, Cnr Selby St and Stubbs Tce .... 71 D 4
FREMANTLE, Phillimore St ..... 1D B 5
KENSINGTON, George St ...... 73 D 9
MADDINGTON, Albany Hwy ..... 96 A 5
MIDLAND, Great Eastern Hwy .... 50 E 9
OSBORNE PARK, Cnr Scarborough Beach Rd and Main St .... 60 B 4
O'CONNOR, Peel Rd .... 91 D 6
PERTH Headquarters, Cnr Hay and Irwin Sts .... 1C A 3
SPEARWOOD, Spearwood Ave .... 101 C 6
WANGARA, Cnr Prindiville Dr & Mackie St .... 24 E 7
WELSHPOOL, Welshpool Rd .... 85 C 3

GOLF COURSES

PRIVATE

CHIDLEY POINT, Mosman Park .... 81 A 7
COTTESLOE, Swanbourne ..... 70 E 6
GOSNELLS, Canning Vale .... 104 D 3
HARTFIELD COUNTRY CLUB, Forrestfield .... 86 C 3
JOONDALUP COUNTRY CLUB, Connolly .... 19 B 7

KWINANA CLUB, Calista .... 130 D 7
LAKE KARRINYUP COUNTRY CLUB, Karrinyup .... 45 B 2
LAKELANDS, Gnangara .... 25 E 2
MANDURAH COUNTRY CLUB, Halls Head .... 164 C 1
MEADOW SPRINGS, Meadow Springs .... 163 D 3
MELVILLE GLADES, Leeming 93 B10
MOUNT LAWLEY, Inglewood .... 61 B 4
MUNDARING, Mundaring ...... 68 B 4
NEDLANDS, Nedlands .... 81 D 1
PICKERING BROOK, Pickering Brook .... 98 E 1
ROCKINGHAM, Cooloongup . 138 A 9
ROYAL FREMANTLE, Fremantle .... 91 A 5
ROYAL PERTH, South Perth ... 72 E 9
SEAVIEW, Cottesloe .... 80 C 3
SERPENTINE, Serpentine .... 154 D 3
SUN CITY COUNTRY CLUB, Yanchep .... 5 A 2
VINES COUNTRY CLUB, Ellenbrook .... 29 C 1
WAGC (Mt Yokine), Yokine 46 E10
WANNEROO, Neerabup .... 16 E 2
WEST AVIAT GOLF CLUB, Perth Airport .... 64 A 5

PUBLIC

ARMADALE, Forrestdale ..... 115 B 8
BAYSWATER, Embleton .... 62 A 2
BURSWOOD PARK, Victoria Park .... 73 D 2
CITY OF PERTH GOLF COMPLEX, Wembley Downs .... 59 A 7
COLLIER PARK, Como .... 83 C 3
FREMANTLE, Fremantle .... 90 E 5
HAMERSLEY, Karrinyup .... 44 E 3
HILLVIEW, Maida Vale .... 64 E 9
LAKE CLAREMONT, Claremont .... 71 A 7
MADDINGTON, Maddington ... 96 D 4
MARANGAROO, Marangaroo .... 32 B 4
MARRI PARK, Casuarina ..... 132 B 4
MAYLANDS, Maylands 62 A10
MELVILLE, Bicton .... 81 B 7
PT WALTER - See Melville
ROSEHILL, South Guildford .... 63 E 2
THE LAKES, Jandakot .... 102 E 5
WHALEBACK, Lynwood .... 94 D 4

GOVERNMENT DEPARTMENTS

COMMONWEALTH

ABORIGINAL DEVELOPMENT COMMISSION, Piccadilly Square, Nash St, East Perth .... 1C A 2
ABORIGINAL & TORRES STRAIT ISLANDER COMMISSION, 256 Adelaide Tce, Perth .... 1C D 1
ADMINISTRATIVE APPEALS TRIBUNAL, Natwest House, 251 Adelaide Tce, Perth. .... 1C A 3
ADMINISTRATIVE SERVICES - AUST. ARCHIVES, 384 Berwick St, E Victoria Pk .... 84 A 2
ADMINISTRATIVE SERVICES - AUST. CONSTRUCTION SERVICES, Sheraton Ct, 207 Adelaide Tce, Perth ...... 1C B 4
ADMINISTRATIVE SERVICES - AUST. GOVT ANALYTICAL LABORATORIES, 3 Clive Rd, Cottesloe 70 E10

Name	Map Ref.
ADMINISTRATIVE SERVICES - AUST. GOVT PUBLISHING SERVICE, Albert Facey House, 469-489 Wellington ST, Perth	1C A 2
ADMINISTRATIVE SERVICES - AUST. PROTECTIVE SERVICES, Perth Airport	63 B 8
ADMINISTRATIVE SERVICES - AUST. SURVEYING & LAND INFO. GROUP(AUSLIG), 2 Hawthorne Pl, Vic. Park	73 E 5
ADMINISTRATIVE SERVICES - AUST. VALUATION OFFICE, 12 St Georges Tce	1C A 3
ADMINISTRATIVE SERVICES - PARLIAMENTARY & MINISTERIAL SERVICES GROUP, 12 St Georges Tce, Perth	1C A 3
ADMINISTRATIVE SERVICES - PROPERTY GROUP, 12 St Georges Tce, Perth	1C A 3
ADMINISTRATIVE SERVICES - PURCHASING & SALES GROUP, 12 St Georges Tce, Perth	1C A 3
ADMINISTRATIVE SERVICES - TRANSPORT & STORAGE GROUP, 113 - 125 Wellington St, East Perth	1C B 3
ADMINSTRATIVE SERVICES - REGIONAL CO-ORDINATOR CORPORATE SUPPORT, Sheraton Ct, 207 Adelaide Tce	1C B 4
AIR FORCE RECRUITING, 256 Adelaide Tce, Perth	1C A 3
ARMY RECRUITING, 256 Adelaide Tce, Perth	1C A 3
ARTS, SPORT, THE ENVIRONMENT, TOURISM & TERRITORIES, Capita Building, 5 Mill St, Perth	1C E 3
ATTORNEY GENERAL, Natwest House, 251 Adelaide Tce, Perth	1C A 3
AUSTRALIA POST, Head Office, G.P.O., 3 Forrest Pl, Perth	1C A 2
AUSTRALIAN AUDIT OFFICE, 44 St Georges Tce, Perth	1C A 3
AUSTRALIAN BROADCASTING CORPORATION, 191 Adelaide Tce, East Perth	1C B 4
AUSTRALIAN BROADCASTING TRIBUNAL, 251 Adelaide Tce, Perth	1C A 3
AUSTRALIAN BUREAU OF STATISTICS, 30 Terrace Rd, East Perth	1C B 4
AUSTRALIAN CONSTRUCTION SERVICES, Sheraton Court, 207 Adelaide Tce, East Perth	1C B 4
AUSTRALIAN CUSTOMS SERVICE, Customs House, 2 Henry St, Fremantle	1D B 5
AUSTRALIAN DAIRY CORPORATION, 14/83 Mill Point Rd, South Perth	72 E 6
AUSTRALIAN FEDERAL POLICE, Sheraton Court, 207 Adelaide Tce, Perth	1C B 4
AUSTRALIAN INDUSTRIAL RELATIONS COMMISSION, 251 Adelaide Tce, Perth	1C A 3
AUSTRALIAN INSTITUTE OF SPORT, "Commonwealth Hockey Stadium", Hayman Rd, Bentley (See enlargement facing Map 135)	83 E 3
AUSTRALIAN NATIONAL RAILWAYS, Suite 3, First Floor, City Arcade Office Tower, 207 Murray St, Perth	1C A 2
AUSTRALIAN TELECOMMUNICATIONS COMMISSION, 80 Stirling St, Perth	1C A 2
AUSTRALIAN TRADE COMMISSION, Quadrant Building, 1 William St, Perth	1C E 3
BANKRUPTCY ADMINISTRATION, Natwest House, 251 Adelaide Tce, Perth	1C A 2
BUREAU OF AIR SAFETY INVESTIGATION, Kalamunda Rd, South Guildford	64 A 6
BUREAU OF METEOROLOGY, 127 Wellington St, Perth	1C B 3
BUREAU OF MINERAL RESOURCES, Observatory, 7 Hodgson St, Mundaring	68 B 1
CAREER REFERENCE CENTRE, Durack Centre, 263 Adelaide Tce, Perth	1C A 3
CIVIL AVIATION AUTHORITY (CAA), 256 Adelaide Tce, Perth	1C A 3
COMCARE, Flr 7, 50 St Georges Tce, Perth	1C A 3
COMMONWEALTH EMPLOYMENT SERVICE - PROFESSIONAL EMPLOYMENT SERVICE, St Martins Tower, 44 St Georges Tce, Perth	1C A 3
COMMONWEALTH EMPLOYMENT SERVICE, 186 St Georges Tce, Perth	1C E 2
COMMONWEALTH EMPLOYMENT SERVICE, Armadale, 412 Commerce Ave	116 D 7
COMMONWEALTH EMPLOYMENT SERVICE, Balcatta, 257 Balcatta Rd	46 A 3
COMMONWEALTH EMPLOYMENT SERVICE, Booragoon, AMP House, Davy St	92 C 1
COMMONWEALTH EMPLOYMENT SERVICE, Cannington, 32 Burton St	84 C 5
COMMONWEALTH EMPLOYMENT SERVICE, Claremont, 33 St Quentin Ave	71 A 9
COMMONWEALTH EMPLOYMENT SERVICE, Cockburn, Cnr Lancaster St & Rockingham Rd, Spearwood	101 B 4
COMMONWEALTH EMPLOYMENT SERVICE, East Perth, 206 Adelaide Tce	1C A 3
COMMONWEALTH EMPLOYMENT SERVICE, Fremantle, 27 - 35 William St	1D C 5
COMMONWEALTH EMPLOYMENT SERVICE, Innaloo, 384 Scarborough Beach Rd	59 C 1
COMMONWEALTH EMPLOYMENT SERVICE, Kwinana, Shop 97 Kwinana Hub Shopping Centre, Gilmore Ave	131 A 7
COMMONWEALTH EMPLOYMENT SERVICE, Maddington, 4 Binley Pl	95 E 5
COMMONWEALTH EMPLOYMENT SERVICE, Mandurah, 39 Pinjarra Rd	164 E 2
COMMONWEALTH EMPLOYMENT SERVICE, Midland, 272 Gt Northern Hwy	50 C 8
COMMONWEALTH EMPLOYMENT SERVICE, Mirrabooka, 6 Ilkeston Pl	46 E 4
COMMONWEALTH EMPLOYMENT SERVICE, Morley, 6 Dewar St	61 E 1
COMMONWEALTH EMPLOYMENT SERVICE, Mt Hawthorn, 363 Oxford St	60 C 6
COMMONWEALTH EMPLOYMENT SERVICE, Rockingham, 23-25 Simpson Ave	137 B 7
COMMONWEALTH EMPLOYMENT SERVICE, Victoria Park, 117-121 Shepperton Rd	73 E 7
COMMONWEALTH GOVERNMENT BOOKSHOP, Albert Facey House, 469 Wellington St, Perth	1C A 2
COMMONWEALTH OMBUDSMAN'S OFFICE, St Martins Tower, 44 St Georges Tce, Perth	1C A 3
COMMONWEALTH PARLIAMENT OFFICES, St Martins Tower, 44 St Georges Tce, Perth	1C A 3
COMMONWEALTH REPORTING SERVICE, Natwest House, 251 Adelaide Tce, Perth	1C A 3
COMMONWEALTH SERUM LABORATORIES, 293 Fitzgerald St, Perth	60 E 9
COMMUNITY EMPLOYMENT PROGRAM, St Martins Tower, 44 St Georges Tce, Perth	1C A 3
COMMUNITY SERVICES & HEALTH, Capita Centre, 197 St Georges Tce, Perth	1C E 3
CSIRO, DIVISION OF WILDLIFE AND ECOLOGY, Clayton Rd, Helena Valley	65 D 5
CSIRO, FLOREAT PARK LABORATORY, Underwood Ave, Floreat	71 B 2
DEFENCE FORCE CAREERS REFERENCE CENTRE, 256 Adelaide Tce, Perth	1C A 3
DEFENCE FORCE OMBUDSMAN, St Martins Tower, 44 St Georges Tce, Perth	1C A 3
DEFENCE HOUSING AUTHORITY, Irwin Barracks, Karrakatta	71 C 5
DEFENCE SERVICE HOMES, 20 Terrace Rd, East Perth	1C B 4
DEFENCE, Regional Offices, 256 Adelaide Tce, Perth	1C A 3
DIRECTOR OF PUBLIC PROSECUTIONS, 256 Adelaide Tce, Perth	1C A 3
ELECTORAL COMMISSION, Australian Electoral Office, 28 Thorogood St, Victoria Park	73 E 5
EMPLOYMENT EDUCATION & TRAINING, Durack Centre, 263 Adelaide Tce, Perth	1C A 3
EXPORT FINANCE AND INSURANCE CORPORATION, Quadrant Building, 1 William St, Perth	1C E 3
FEDERAL COURT OF AUSTRALIA, Natwest House, 251 St Georges Tce, Perth	1C A 3
FINANCE, Eastpoint Plaza, 233 Adelaide Tce, Perth	1C A 4
FIRST HOME OWNERS SCHEME, Capita Building, 1 Mill St, Perth	1C E 3
FOREIGN AFFAIRS & TRADE, St Martins Tower, 44 St Georges Tce, Perth	1C A 3
HIGH COURT OF AUSTRALIA, Supreme Court Bldg, Stirling Gns, Perth	1C A 3
HOUSING LOANS INSURANCE CORP, 77 St Georges Tce, Perth	1C E 3
HUMAN RIGHTS & EQUAL OPPORTUNITY COMMISSION, 5 Mill St, Perth	1C E 3
IMMIGRATION REVIEW TRIBUNAL, 1 Altona St, West Perth	72 C 2
IMMIGRATION, LOCAL GOVT & ETHNIC AFFAIRS, 1240 Hay St, West Perth	72 C 1
INDUSTRIAL RELATIONS, 8th Flr, 190 St Georges Tce, Perth	1C E 3
INDUSTRY RESEARCH & DEVELOPMENT BOARD, 28 The Esplanade, Perth	1C E 3
INDUSTRY, TECHNOLOGY & COMMERCE, 28 The Esplanade, Perth	1C E 3
MEDIBANK - MEDICARE, 93 William St, Perth	1C E 2
MERIT PROTECTION & REVIEW AGENCY PROMOTION APPEAL COMMITTEE, 190 St Georges Tce, Perth	1C E 3
MULTICULTURAL AFFAIRS OFFICE, St Martins Tower, 44 St Georges Tce, Perth	1C A 3
NATIONAL INDUSTRY EXTENSION SERVICE, SGIO Atrium, 170 St Georges Tce, Perth	1C E 3
NATIONAL TRAINING COUNCIL, St Martins Tower, 44 St Georges Tce, Perth	1C A 3
NAVY RECRUITING, 256 Adelaide Tce, Perth	1C A 3
OBSERVATORY GEOPHYSICAL, 7 Hodgson St, Mundaring	68 B 1
OFFICIAL TRUSTEE IN BANKRUPTCY, 251 Adelaide Tce, Perth	1C A 3
OVERSEAS TELECOMMUNICATIONS COMMISSION, 26 St Georges Tce, Perth	1C A 3
PATENT TRADE MARKS & DESIGNS SUB-OFFICE, 233 Adelaide Tce, Perth	1C A 4
PRIMARY INDUSTRIES & ENERGY, Primary Industry House, 239 Adelaide Tce, Perth	1C A 4
PROMOTION APPEAL COMMITTEE, 8th Floor, 190 St Georges Tce, Perth	1C E 3
SOCIAL SECURITY APPEALS TRIBUNAL, Mt Newman House, 200 St Georges Tce	1C E 2

	Map Ref.
SOCIAL SECURITY, Cannington, 13-23 Leila St	84 E 6
SOCIAL SECURITY, Fremantle, 7 Pakenham St	1D C 5
SOCIAL SECURITY, Gosnells, 88 Lissiman St	96 B 8
SOCIAL SECURITY, Innaloo, 384 Scarborough Beach Rd	59 C 1
SOCIAL SECURITY, Mandurah, 15 Pinjarra Rd	164 E 2
SOCIAL SECURITY, Midland, 18 Viveash Rd	50 C 9
SOCIAL SECURITY, Mirrabooka, 22 Chesterfield Rd	46 E 4
SOCIAL SECURITY, Morley, 38 Rudloc Rd	47 E 10
SOCIAL SECURITY, Perth East, 108 Stirling St	1C A 2
SOCIAL SECURITY, Perth West, 647 Wellington St	1C E 2
SOCIAL SECURITY, Rivervale, 2 Hawksburn Rd	74 A 3
SOCIAL SECURITY, Rockingham, Rockingham City Shopping Centre, Simpson Ave	137 B 7
SOCIAL SECURITY, Spearwood, Phoenix Shopping Centre, Lancaster St	101 B 4
SOCIAL SECURITY, State Office, Mt Newman House, 200 St Georges Tce, Perth	1C E 2
SOCIAL SECURITY, Victoria Park, 117-121 Shepperton Rd	73 E 8
TAXATION OFFICE AUSTRALIAN, 1 St Georges Tce, Perth	1C A 3
TRADE PRACTICES COMMISSION, Eastpoint Plaza, 233 Adelaide Tce, Perth	1C A 4
TRANSPORT & COMMUNICATIONS - AVIATION BRANCH, 256 Adelaide Tce, Perth	1C A 3
TRANSPORT & COMMUNICATIONS - COMMUNICATION BRANCH, 200 Adelaide Tce, Perth	1C B 4
TRANSPORT & COMMUNICATIONS - TRANSPORT BRANCH, 200 Adelaide Tce, Perth	1C B 4
VETERANS AFFAIRS, 20 Terrace Rd, East Perth	1C B 4
VETERANS AFFAIRS, Repatriation General Hospital, Monash Ave, Nedlands	71 E 6
VETERANS REVIEW BOARD, 256 Adelaide Tce, Perth	1C A 3
VIETNAM VETERANS COUNSELLING SERVICE, 44 Outram St, West Perth	72 C 2

LOCAL

	Map Ref.
ARMADALE, CITY OF, 145 Jull St, Armadale	116 D 6
BASSENDEAN, TOWN OF, Old Perth Rd, Bassendean	63 A 1
BAYSWATER, CITY OF, Broun Ave, Morley	62 A 2
BELMONT, CITY OF, 215 Wright St, Cloverdale	74 D 4
CANNING, CITY OF, Albany Hwy, Cannington	84 D 6
CLAREMONT, TOWN OF, Stirling Hwy, Claremont	71 A 9
COCKBURN, CITY OF, Coleville Cr, Spearwood	101 B 5
COTTESLOE, TOWN OF, Broome St, Cottesloe	80 C 2
EAST FREMANTLE, TOWN OF, Canning Hwy, East Fremantle	90 D 2

	Map Ref.
FREMANTLE, CITY OF, William St, Fremantle	1D C 5
GOSNELLS, CITY OF, Albany Hwy, Gosnells	96 B 7
KALAMUNDA, SHIRE OF, Railway Rd, Kalamunda	77 D 8
KWINANA, TOWN OF, Cnr Gilmore Ave & Sulphur Rd, Kwinana Town Centre	131 A 6
MANDURAH, CITY OF, Mandurah Tce	162 E 10
MELVILLE, CITY OF, Almondbury Rd, Ardross	82 C 10
MOSMAN PARK, TOWN OF, Memorial Dr, Mosman Park	80 E 5
MUNDARING, SHIRE OF, Great Eastern Hwy, Mundaring	68 A 1
NEDLANDS, CITY OF, 71 Stirling Hwy, Nedlands	71 D 8
PEPPERMINT GROVE, SHIRE OF, Leake St, Peppermint Grove	80 D 3
PERTH, CITY OF, Council House, St Georges Tce, Perth	1C A 3
ROCKINGHAM, CITY OF, Council Ave, Rockingham	137 C 7
SERPENTINE - JARRAHDALE SHIRE OF, Patterson St, Mundijong	143 A 9
SOUTH PERTH, CITY OF, South Tce, South Perth	73 A 10
STIRLING, CITY OF, Civic Pl, Stirling	45 D 8
SUBIACO, CITY OF, Rokeby Rd, Subiaco	72 A 2
SWAN, SHIRE OF, Gt Northern Hwy, Middle Swan	50 D 4
WANNEROO, CITY OF, Shenton Ave, Joondalup	19 E 6

STATE

	Map Ref.
ABORIGINAL AFFAIRS PLANNING AUTHORITY & ABORIGINAL LAND TRUST, Construction House, 35 Havelock St, West Perth	1C D 2
ABORIGINAL LAND TRUST, Construction House, 37 Havelock St, West Perth	1C D 2
AGED OPEN LINE, Alexander Library, James St, Perth	1C A 1
AGED PERSONS BUREAU, Construction House, 37 Havelock St, West Perth	1C D 2
AGRICULTURAL PROTECTION BOARD, Baron-Hay Ct, South Perth	73 D 10
AGRICULTURE DEPARTMENT, 3 Baron-Hay Ct, South Perth	73 D 10
ALCOHOL AND DRUG AUTHORITY, Construction House, 35 Havelock St, West Perth	1C D 2
ANALYST, 125 Hay St, East Perth	73 C 4
ARBITRATION COURT, Supply House, 815 Hay St, Perth	1C E 2
ART GALLERY OF WA, James St, Perth	1C A 2
ARTS (DEPT OF), Alexander Library, James St, Perth	1C A 1
ASTRONOMER, Observatory Bldg, Walnut Rd, Bickley	89 C 4
ATTORNEY GENERAL, Capita Centre, 197 St Georges Tce, Perth	1C E 3
AUDIT, 2 Havelock St, West Perth	1C D 2

	Map Ref.
AUTHORITY FOR THE INTELLECTUALLY HANDICAPPED, Eastern Region, 60 Lord St, Eden Hill	49 B 9
AUTHORITY FOR THE INTELLECTUALLY HANDICAPPED, Irrabeena, 53 Ord St, West Perth	72 C 2
AUTHORITY FOR THE INTELLECTUALLY HANDICAPPED, Northern Region, 124 Dundas Rd, Inglewood	61 C 4
AUTHORITY FOR THE INTELLECTUALLY HANDICAPPED, South Eastern Region, 1275 Albany Hwy, Cannington	84 D 6
AUTHORITY FOR THE INTELLECTUALLY HANDICAPPED, South Western Region, 22 Queen St, Fremantle	1D C 5
BATTERIES, 6th Floor Mineral House, 100 Plain St, East Perth	1C B 4
BUILDING MANAGEMENT AUTHORITY DEPOT, Park Rd, Mandurah	163 C 7
BUILDING MANAGEMENT AUTHORITY, Dumas House, 2 Havelock St, West Perth	1C D 2
BUILDING SOCIETIES REGISTRAR, NZI Securities House, 19 Pier St, Perth	1C A 3
BUSH FIRES BOARD STATE HEADQUARTERS, 201 Kent St, Kensington	83 D 2
CHEST CLINIC, 17 Murray St, Perth	1C A 3
CHILDREN'S COURT, Cnr Bennett & Royal Sts, East Perth	1C B 2
COALMINE WORKERS CLAIMS TRIBUNAL, 8th Floor Mineral House, 100 Plain St, East Perth	1C B 4
COLLECTOR AND ACCOUNTS, Westpac Building, 109 St Georges Tce, Perth	1C E 3
COMMUNICABLE DISEASE CLINIC, 70-72 Murray St, Perth	1C A 3
COMMUNITY SERVICES (DEPT OF), 189 Royal St, East Perth	1C B 2
COMMUNITY SERVICES (DEPT OF), 79 Mandurah Tce, Mandurah	164 E 1
COMMUNITY SKILLS TRAINING CENTRE, Grace Vaughan House, 227 Stubbs Tce, Shenton park	71 D 4
CONSERVATION AND LAND MANAGEMENT, Operations Headquarters, 50 Hayman Rd, Kensington	83 D 2
CONSERVATION AND LAND MANAGEMENT, Policy Directorate, Hackett Dr, Crawley	72 A 10
CONSERVATION AND LAND MANAGEMENT, Wildlife Research Centre, Ocean Reef Rd, Woodvale	24 A 4
CONSUMER AFFAIRS (MINISTRY OF), 251-257 Hay St, East Perth	1C D 1
CORONER'S COURT, Grain Pool Building, 172 St Georges Tce, Perth	1C E 3
CORRECTIVE SERVICES (DEPT OF), 441-5 Murray St, Perth	1C E 2

	Map Ref.
COUNTRY HIGH SCHOOLS HOSTEL AUTHORITY, Hyatt Centre, 87 Adelaide Tce, East Perth	1C B 4
COURT OF PETTY SESSIONS, District Court Building, 30 St Georges Tce, Perth	1C A 3
CRIMINAL INVESTIGATION BRANCH, Curtin House, 60 Beaufort St, Perth	1C A 2
CROWN LAW DEPARTMENT, Administration, Crown Solicitors & Solicitor General, 109 St Georges Tce, Perth	1C E 2
CROWN LAW DEPARTMENT, Attorney General, 197 St Georges Tce, Perth	1C E 3
CROWN LAW DEPARTMENT, Bailiff, Armadale, 64 Attfield St, Maddington	95 E 4
CROWN LAW DEPARTMENT, Bailiff, Fremantle, Crane House, 185 High St	1D C 5
CROWN LAW DEPARTMENT, Bailiff, Midland, 294 Gt Eastern Hwy	50 C 8
CROWN LAW DEPARTMENT, Bailiff, Northern Suburbs, Suite 8, 73 Gibson Ave, Padbury	30 D 1
CROWN LAW DEPARTMENT, Bailiff, Perth, 184 St Georges Tce	1C E 3
CROWN LAW DEPARTMENT, Bailiff, Sheriff's Office, 30 St Georges Tce, Perth	1C A 3
CROWN LAW DEPARTMENT, Coroner's Court, 172 St Georges Tce, Perth	1C E 3
CROWN LAW DEPARTMENT, Court of Petty Sessions, 30 St Georges Tce, Perth	1C A 3
CROWN LAW DEPARTMENT, District Court, 30 St Georges Tce, Perth	1C A 3
CROWN LAW DEPARTMENT, Family Court of W.A., 45 St Georges Tce, Perth	1C E 3
CROWN LAW DEPARTMENT, Local Court - Administration, 30 St Georges Tce, Perth	1C A 3
CROWN LAW DEPARTMENT, Local Court - Courts, 30 St Georges Tce, Perth	1C A 3
CROWN LAW DEPARTMENT, Magistrate's Court, 109 Jull St, Armadale	116 E 6
CROWN LAW DEPARTMENT, Magistrate's Court, 24 Spring Park Rd, Midland	50 B 8
CROWN LAW DEPARTMENT, Magistrate's Court, 45 Henderson St, Fremantle	1D C 5
CROWN LAW DEPARTMENT, Magistrate's Court, Flinders La, Rockingham	137 A 4
CROWN LAW DEPARTMENT, Magistrate's Court, Pinjarra Rd, Mandurah	165 C 2
CROWN LAW DEPARTMENT, Parliamentary Counsel's Office, 40 The Esplanade, Perth	1C E 3

Name	Map Ref.
CROWN LAW DEPARTMENT, Supreme Court, "Stirling Gardens", Barrack St, Perth	1C A 3
DAIRY INDUSTRY AUTHORITY OF WA, 217 Stirling Hwy, Claremont	71 C 8
EGG MARKETING BOARD, 43 McGregor Rd, Palmyra	91 B 4
ELECTORAL, 480 Hay St, Perth	1C A 3
EMPLOYMENT AND TRAINING (DEPT OF), St Georges Centre, 81 St Georges Tce, Perth	1C E 3
ENVIRONMENTAL PROTECTION AUTHORITY, BP House, 1 Mount St, Perth	1C E 2
EQUAL EMPLOYMENT OPPORTUNITY IN PUBLIC EMPLOYMENT DIRECTORATE OF, 5 Mill St, Perth	1C E 3
EXPLOSIVES, Mineral House, 100 Plain St, East Perth	1C B 4
FAMILY COURT OF AUSTRALIA, OFFICE AND COURTS, 45 St Georges Tce, Perth	1C A 3
FINANCE BROKERS SUPERVISORY BOARD, 251-257 Hay St, East Perth	1C B 3
FINANCIAL ASSISTANCE BRANCH, CSA Centre, 445 Hay St, Perth	1C A 3
FIRE BRIGADE'S BOARD, 480 Hay St, Perth	1C A 3
FIREARMS BRANCH, POLICE DEPT, 210 Adelaide Tce, East Perth	1C B 4
FISHERIES, 108 Adelaide Tce, East Perth	1C B 4
FISHERIES, 15 Leslie St, Mandurah	164 E 2
FISHERIES, Cnr Main Tce & Collie St, Fremantle	1D B 6
FREMANTLE PORT AUTHORITY, 1 Cliff St, Fremantle	1D B 5
GAMING DIVISION, Hyatt Centre, 87 Adelaide Tce, East Perth	1C B 4
GEOLOGICAL SURVEY, 100 Plain St, East Perth	1C B 4
GOVT AUCTIONEER, Land Administration, Cathedral Ave, Perth	1C A 3
GOVT CHEMICAL LABS, 125 Hay St, East Perth	73 C 4
GOVT EMPLOYEES HOUSING AUTHORITY, Hyatt Centre, 87 Adelaide Tce, East Perth	1C B 4
GOVT EMPLOYEES STATE SUPERANNUATION BOARD, 10 Kings Park Rd, West Perth	72 C 2
GREYHOUND RACING CONTROL BOARD, Cnr Albany Hwy & Station St, Cannington	84 E 8
HEALTH DEPT OF WESTERN AUSTRALIA, 189 Royal St, East Perth	1C B 2
HEALTH DEPT OF WESTERN AUSTRALIA, Ormsby Tce, (within Community Health Centre) Mandurah	162 E10
HIGHER EDUCATION AUTHORITY, 30 Richardson St, West Perth	72 C 1
HOMESWEST, 99 Plain St, East Perth	1C B 4
INDUSTRIAL COMMISSION, Supply House, 815 Hay St, Perth	1C E 2
INDUSTRIAL LANDS DEVELOPMENT AUTHORITY, 26 St Georges Tce, Perth	1C A 3
INDUSTRIAL RELATIONS, OFFICE OF, 2nd Floor Dumas House, 2 Havelock St, West Perth	1C D 2
INFOLINK GOVERNMENT & COMMUNITY INFORMATION, Alexander Library Building, Perth Cultural Centre, Northbridge	1C A 1
LABORATORY STATE HEALTH, Queen Elizabeth II Medical Centre, Hospital Ave, Nedlands	71 E 6
LAND ADMINISTRATION, Cartographic Services, Jardine House, 184 St Georges Tce, Perth	1C E 3
LAND ADMINISTRATION, Cathedral Ave, Perth	1C A 3
LAND ADMINISTRATION, Geodetic Services, Sterling House, 8 Parliament Pl, West Perth	1C D 2
LAND ADMINISTRATION, Land Titles Division, Law Chambers Bldg, Cnr Hay St & Cathedral Ave, Perth	1C A 3
LAND ADMINISTRATION, Topographic Services, Govt Print Building, Station St, Wembley	60 A10
LAND VALUATION APPEAL TRIBUNAL, Kings Building, 517 Hay Street, Perth	1C A 3
LAND VALUERS LICENSING BOARD, 251-257 Hay St, East Perth	1C B 3
LAW REFORM COMMISSION, St Martins Tower, 40-50 St Georges Tce, Perth	1C A 3
LEGAL AID COMMISSION, Royal Insurance Centre, 105 St Georges Tce, Perth	1C E 3
LIBRARY, James St, Perth	1C A 2
LIBRARY, STATE REFERENCE, James St, Perth	1C A 2
LICENSING COURT, May Holman Centre, 32 St Georges Tce, Perth	1C A 3
LIQUOR LICENSING DIVISION, Hyatt Centre, 87 Adelaide Tce, East Perth	1C B 4
LIQUOR & GAMING BRANCH, Curtin House, 60 Beaufort St, Perth	1C A 2
LOCAL COURT AND CLERK OF COURTS, Central Law Courts Building 30 St Georges Tce, Perth	1C A 3
LOCAL GOVT, May Holman Centre, 32 St Georges Tce, Perth	1C A 3
LOTTERIES COMMISSION, 334 Rokeby Rd, Subiaco	72 A 3
MAILWEST, 311 Hay St, Perth	1C B 3
MAIN ROADS, Cnr Wellington & Plain Sts, East Perth	73 C 3
MARINE AND HARBOURS, 15 Leslie St, Mandurah	164 E 2
MARINE AND HARBOURS, Marine House, 1 Essex St, Fremantle	1D B 6
MARINE LABORATORY, Waterman	30 C10
MEAT MARKETING CORPORATION, 823-827 Wellington St, West Perth	1C D 1
MICROFILM BUREAU, Albert House, 12 Victoria Ave, Perth	1C A 3
MINEROLOGIST, Mineral House, 100 Plain St, East Perth	1C B 4
MINES, Mineral House, 100 Plain St, East Perth	1C B 4
MINISTRY FOR EDUCATION, 151 Royal St, East Perth	1C B 2
MINISTRY OF ECONOMIC DEVELOPMENT & TRADE, SGIO Atrium, 170 St Georges Tce, Perth	1C E 3
NATIONAL TRUST, Old Perth Observatory, 4 Havelock St, West Perth	1C E 2
OCCUPATIONAL HEALTH SAFETY AND WELFARE, Westcentre, 1266 Hay St, West Perth	72 C 1
OFFICE OF EXECUTIVE PERSONNEL, Albert Facey House, 469-489 Wellington St, Perth	1C A 2
OFFICE OF GOVERNMENT ACCOMMODATION, 2 Havelock St, West Perth	1C D 2
OFFICE OF THE FAMILY, 3rd Floor May Holman Centre, 32 St Georges Tce, Perth	1C A 3
PARLIAMENT HOUSE, Harvest Tce, West Perth	1C D 2
PARLIAMENTARY COMMISSIONER OF ADMIN. INVESTIGATIONS, St Martins Tower, 40-50 St Georges Tce, Perth	1C A 3
PASTORAL APPRAISEMENT BOARD, Central Govt Buildings, Barrack St, Perth	1C A 3
PEEL INLET MANAGEMENT AUTHORITY, Sholl House, 21 Sholl St, Mandurah	164 E 1
PERTH ZOOLOGICAL GARDENS, Labouchere Rd, South Perth	72 E 8
PLANNING & URBAN DEVELOPMENT (DEPT OF), Albert Facey House, Cnr Forrest Pl & Wellington St, Perth	1C A 2
POLICE COURTS AND CLERK OF COURTS, FREMANTLE, 45 Henderson St, Fremantle	1D C 5
POLICE COURTS AND CLERK OF COURTS, MIDLAND, 24 Spring Park Rd, Midland	50 B 8
POLICE COURTS AND CLERK OF COURTS, PERTH, Hay St, East Perth	73 C 4
POLICE HEADQUARTERS, 2 Adelaide Tce, East Perth	73 C 4
PREMIER AND CABINET (MINISTRY OF), Capita Centre, 197 St Georges Tce, Perth	1C E 3
PUBLIC SERVICE COMMISSION, Albert Facey House, 469-489 Wellington St, Perth	1C A 2
PUBLIC TRUST, 565 Hay St, Perth	1C A 3
RACING AND GAMING (OFFICE OF), Hyatt Centre, Adelaide Tce, Perth	1C B 4
REAL ESTATE AND SUPERVISORY BOARD, 251 Hay St, East Perth	1C B 3
REDEPLOYMENT & RETRAINING, (OFFICE OF), 81 St Georges Tce, Perth	1C E 3
REGIONAL DEVELOPMENT AND THE NORTH WEST(DEPT OF), Floor 12 May Holman Centre, 32 St Georges Tce, Perth	1C A 3
REGISTRAR GENERAL AND REGISTRY, Oakleigh Bldg, 22 St Georges Tce, Perth	1C A 3
RESOURCES DEVELOPMENT (DEPT OF), Atrium Building, Cnr King St & St Georges Tce, Perth	1C E 3
RURAL ADJUSTMENT & FINANCE CORPORATION, May Holman Centre, 32 St Georges Tce, Perth	1C A 3
RURAL HOUSING AUTHORITY, Kings Building, Adelaide Tce, Perth	1C A 3
RURAL INNOVATION CENTRE, Capita Centre, 197 St Georges Tce, Perth	1C E 3
SECONDARY EDUCATION AUTHORITY, 27 Waters Dr, Osborne Park	59 E 3
SENIORS INFORMATION SERVICE, Construction House, 35 Havelock St, West Perth	1C D 2
SERVICES (DEPT OF) 2 Havelock St, West Perth	1C D 2
SHERIFF'S OFFICE, Supreme Court Bldg, Stirling Gardens, Perth	1C A 3
SMALL BUSINESS DEVELOPMENT CORPORATION, NZI Securities House, 19 Pier St, Perth	1C A 3
SOLICITOR GENERAL, Westpac Building, 109 St Georges Tce, Perth	1C E 3
SPORT AND RECREATION, Perry Lakes Stadium, Floreat	71 B 1
STAMP DUTY, Central Govt Buildings, Cnr Barrack St & St Georges Tce, Perth	1C A 3
STATE EMERGENCY SERVICE 91 Leake St, Belmont	62 D 9
STATE EMERGENCY SERVICE, H.Q., 91 Leake St, Belmont	62 E10
STATE EMERGENCY SERVICE, North Metropolitan Regional Co-ordinator, 7 Lynton St, Mt Hawthorn	60 B 6
STATE ENERGY COMMISSION, Accounts, 365 Wellington St, Perth	1C A 2
STATE ENERGY COMMISSION, Head Office, 363-365 Wellington St, Perth	1C A 2
STATE GOVERNMENT INSURANCE COMMISSION, Atrium Building, Cnr King St & St Georges Tce, Perth	1C E 3
STATE GOVERNMENT INSURANCE COMMISSION, Shop 42, Mandurah Forum, Pinjarra Rd, Mandurah	165 C 2
STATE PLANNING COMMISSION, Albert Facey House, Cnr Forrest Pl & Wellington St, Perth	1C A 2
STATE PRINTING DIVISION, Station St, Wembley	60 A10
STATE SUPPLY DIVISION, Supply House, 815 Hay St, Perth	1C E 2
STATE TAXATION, Central Govt Bldg, Barrack St, Perth	1C A 3
STATESHIPS, Port Beach Rd, North Quay	90 A 4
SUPREME COURT OF WA, Stirling Gardens, Perth	1C A 3

Name	Map Ref.
SWAN RIVER MANAGEMENT AUTHORITY, Jardine House, 184 St Georges Tce, Perth	1C E 3
TAFE COUNSELLING SERVICE, Cable House, 399 Hay St, Perth	1C A 3
TENDER BOARD, Supply House, 815 Hay St, Perth	1C E 2
TOURISM COMMISSION, St Georges Court, 16 St Georges Tce, Perth	1C A 3
TOWN PLANNING APPEALS COMMITTEE, Hyatt Centre, 69 Adelaide Tce, East Perth	1C B 4
TRANSPERTH, Adelaide Tce, Perth	73 C 4
TRANSPORT (DEPT OF), 136 Stirling Hwy, Nedlands	71 C 9
TREASURY, Capita Centre, 197 St Georges Tce, Perth	1C E 3
VALUER GENERAL'S OFFICE, 18 Mount St, Perth	1C D 2
WA HERITAGE COMMITTEE, Jardine House, 184 St Georges Tce, Perth	1C E 3
WA MEAT EXPORT WORKS, Robb Jetty, Hamilton Hill	100 D 3
WA WEEK COUNCIL, 16 St Georges Tce, Perth	1C A 3
WATER AUTHORITY OF WESTERN AUSTRALIA (Perth North Region) - Cnr Shenton Ave & Davidson Tce, Joondalup	19 E 5
WATER AUTHORITY OF WESTERN AUSTRALIA (Perth South Region) - Queensgate Building, Cnr William & Newman Sts, Fremantle	1D C 5
WATER AUTHORITY OF WESTERN AUSTRALIA, 629 Newcastle St, Leederville	60 D 9
WATER POLICE, Harvest Rd, North Fremantle	80 D 10
WATERWAYS COMMISSION, Jardine House, 184 St Georges Tce, Perth	1C E 3
WEIGHTS AND MEASURES, Menzies House, 638 Murray St, Perth	1C D 1
WESTERN AUSTRALIAN INDUSTRIAL RELATIONS COMMISSION, Supply House, 815-823 Hay St, Perth	1C E 2
WESTERN AUSTRALIAN MINT, Hay St, Perth	1C B 3
WESTERN AUSTRALIAN MUSEUM, Francis St, Perth	1C A 2
WESTERN AUSTRALIAN TOURIST CENTRE, Albert Facey House, 469-489 Wellington St, Perth	1C A 2
WESTRAIL, West Pde, East Perth	61 C 10
WORKERS COMPENSATION & REHABILITATION COMMISSION, 1 Bredbook Pl, Shenton Park	71 D 3
WORKERS' COMPENSATION BOARD, 480 Hay St, Perth	1C A 3
ZOOLOGICAL GARDENS BOARD, 20 Labouchere Rd, South Perth	72 E 7

HOMES FOR CHILDREN

Name	Map Ref.
ALLANDALE (Uniting Church), 149 Sussex St, East Victoria Park	83 D 1
BOURKEDALE (Uniting Church), 10 Bourke St, North Perth	60 D 8
CATHERINE McAULEY CENTRE, Station St, Wembley	60 A 9
COLLINS HOUSE (Uniting Church), 41 Woodford St, Mt Lawley	61 B 6
COOINDAH CHILDREN'S HOSTEL (Uniting Church), 24 Queens Cr, Mt Lawley	61 B 8
COTTESLOE GIRLS' HOME, Broome St, Cottesloe	80 C 4
COTTESLOE HOUSE, (Salvation Army), 68 Guildford Rd, Mt Lawley	61 C 9
HOLLYWOOD CHILDREN'S VILLAGE, Karella St, Nedlands	71 E 7
KATUKUTU (Baptist), 28 Alvan St, Mt Lawley	61 B 8
KINGSWAY (Uniting Church), 81 Kingsway, Nedlands	71 E 10
KYEWONG (Baptist), 152 Robert St, Como	82 E 5
LONGMORE REMAND CENTRE, Bentley	83 E 3
MERIBAH CHILDREN'S HOME (Uniting Church), 4 Hillview Tce, St James	84 A 2
MOFFLYN (Uniting Church), 145 Sussex St, East Victoria Park	83 E 1
NGAL-A MOTHERCRAFT CENTRE, 1 Jarrah Rd, Kensington	73 D 10
PARKERVILLE CHILDREN'S HOME, Roland Rd, Parkerville	53 C 4
SISTER KATE'S CHILD AND FAMILY SERVICES, 180 Lawley St, Yokine	60 D 1
SISTER KATE'S CHILD AND FAMILY SERVICES, 190 Treasure Rd, Queens Park	85 A 2
SISTER KATE'S CHILD AND FAMILY SERVICES, 50 Carcoola St, Nollamara	46 C 5
SISTER KATE'S CHILD AND FAMILY SERVICES, Applecross Cottage, 62 Matheson Rd, Applecross	82 B 7
SISTER KATE'S CHILD AND FAMILY SERVICES, Ardross Hostel, 7 Hallin Ct, Ardross	82 C 8
SISTER KATE'S CHILD AND FAMILY SERVICES, Greenmount Hostel, 28 Innamincka Rd, Greenmount	51 C 10
SISTER KATE'S CHILD AND FAMILY SERVICES, Maddington Cottage, 8 Holling St, Maddington	96 B 6
WANSLEA HOME, 80 Railway St, Cottesloe	70 E 10
WARMINDAH CHILDREN'S HOME (Uniting Church), 4 Welshpool Rd, East Victoria Park	84 B 1
WERRIBEE (Uniting Church), 2 Jarrah Rd, East Victoria Park	83 D 1

HOSPITALS

CASUALTY OR EMERGENCY

Name	Map Ref.
FREMANTLE (Tel. 3350111), Alma St, Fremantle	1D C 6
PRINCESS MARGARET HOSPITAL FOR CHILDREN (Tel. 3828222), Roberts Rd, Subiaco (Inset Map 28)	72 C 1
ROCKINGHAM - KWINANA (Tel. 5272777), Elanora Ave, Cooloongup	138 A 8
ROYAL PERTH (Tel. 2242244), Wellington St, Perth (Inset Map 150)	1C A 3
THE QUEEN ELIZABETH II MEDICAL CENTRE (SIR CHARLES GAIRDNER) (Tel. 3893333), Verdun St, Nedlands (Inset Map 149)	71 E 6
WANNEROO (Tel. 4052211), Shenton Ave, Joondalup	19 E 5

PRIVATE

Name	Map Ref.
ATTADALE (Women), 21-31 Hislop Rd, Attadale	81 E 10
BETHESDA, 25 Queenslea Dr, Claremont	71 A 10
BICTON, 220 Preston Point Rd, Bicton	81 B 10
CAMBRIDGE, 178 Cambridge St, Wembley	60 A 10
GLENGARRY, 53 Arnisdale Rd, Duncraig	31 B 6
GOSNELLS FAMILY, Cnr Eudoria St & Hamilton Ct, Gosnells	96 B 10
GREENMOUNT MATERNITY, 20 Coongan Ave, Greenmount	65 B 1
KALEEYA, 15 Wolseley Rd, East Fremantle	90 E 1
MOUNT LAWLEY, 14 Alvan St, Mt Lawley	61 B 8
MOUNT, 150 Mounts Bay Rd, West Perth	1C D 4
NIOLA, 61 Cambridge St, Leederville	60 C 10
SOUTH PERTH COMM., South Tce, South Perth	73 A 10
ST ANNES, Cnr Thirlmere & Ellesmere Rds, Mt Lawley	61 D 9
ST JOHN OF GOD, Cambridge St, Subiaco (Inset Map 27)	60 B 10
ST JOHN OF GOD, Gt Eastern Hwy, Rivervale	74 B 2
ST JOSEPHS, 153 Stock Rd, Bicton	81 C 10
STIRLING COMM., 32 Spencer Ave, Yokine	61 A 2
UNDERCLIFFE, 20 Coongan Ave, Greenmount	65 B 1

PUBLIC

Name	Map Ref.
ARMADALE-KELMSCOTT, Albany Hwy, Armadale	116 E 2
BENTLEY, Mills St, Bentley	84 D 4
FREMANTLE, Alma St, Fremantle	1D C 6
HOLLYWOOD REPATRIATION GENERAL HOSPITAL, Monash Ave, Nedlands	71 E 6
KALAMUNDA DISTRICT COMMUNITY, Elizabeth St, Kalamunda	77 D 5
KING EDWARD MEMORIAL, Bagot Rd, Subiaco	72 A 2
MANDURAH DISTRICT, Lakes Rd, Greenfields	165 E 1
MOUNT HENRY, Cloister Ave, Como	83 A 7
OSBORNE PARK, Osborne Pl, Stirling	45 D 8
PERTH DENTAL, 196 Goderich St, Perth	1C B 3
PRINCESS MARGARET HOSPITAL FOR CHILDREN, Roberts Rd, Subiaco	72 C 1
QUEEN ELIZABETH II MEDICAL CENTRE, Verdun St, Nedlands	71 E 6
ROCKINGHAM - KWINANA, Elanora Dr, Cooloongup	138 A 8
ROYAL PERTH (REHABILITATION), Selby St, Shenton Park	71 D 3
ROYAL PERTH, Wellington St, Perth	1C A 3
SIR CHARLES GAIRDNER, Verdun St, Nedlands	71 E 6
SWAN DISTRICT, Eveline Rd, Middle Swan	50 C 5
WANNEROO DISTRICT, Shenton Ave, Joondalup	19 E 5
WOODSIDE MATERNITY, 18 Dalgety St, East Fremantle	90 E 2

HOTELS, TAVERNS & WINE BARS

Name	Map Ref.
ABERDEEN TAVERN, Northbridge	1C A 1
ACT ONE TAVERN, Entertainment Centre, Perth	1C E 2
ALBION HOTEL, Cottesloe	80 D 2
AMBASSADOR TAVERN, Bassendean	49 A 9
ARCADIA HOTEL, Perth	1C E 1
ARMADALE TAVERN, Armadale	116 D 6
ASCOT AIRPORT INN, Ascot	62 D 8
ASHFIELD TAVERN, Bayswater	62 E 5
ASTORIA BAR & CAFE, Claremont	71 A 9
ATRIUM RESORT HOTEL, Mandurah	162 E 9
ATTFIELD TAVERN, Maddington	95 E 4
BALLAJURA TAVERN, Ballajura	33 B 4
BASSENDEAN HOTEL, Bassendean	63 A 1
BAT N' BALL HOTEL, Lathlain	74 A 4
BAYSWATER HOTEL, Bayswater	62 B 4
BEACONSFIELD TAVERN, Fremantle	90 D 7
BEGA TAVERN, Armadale	116 B 6
BEL EYRE TAVERN, Belmont	62 D 9
BELDON TAVERN, Beldon	23 C 4
BELMONT HOTEL, Cloverdale	74 E 5
BENTLEYS TAVERN, Bentley	84 C 3
BLUE NOTE TAVERN, West Perth	1C D 1
BOATHOUSE TAVERN, Mandurah	164 E 2
BOORAGOON TAVERN, Booragoon	92 C 1
BOULEVARD ALEHOUSE, THE, East Victoria Park	74 A 10
BRADY'S RESORT HOTEL, Mandurah	162 E 10
BRASS MONKEY, THE, Northbridge	1C A 1
BREAKWATER TAVERN, Hillarys Boat Harbour	30 A 4
BREWERY ALEHOUSE, THE, Nedlands	71 C 8
BRIAR PATCH TAVERN, Victoria Park	73 E 6
BRIGHTON HOTEL, Mandurah	164 E 2
BROADWAY TAVERN, Crawley	71 B 1
BROKEN HILL HOTEL, Victoria Park	73 E 7
BULL CREEK TAVERN, Bullcreek	93 A 7

Name	Map Ref.
BURRENDAH TAVERN, Willetton	93 C 6
BURSWOOD RESORT HOTEL, Perth	73 E 4
BYFORD TAVERN & RECEPTION CENTRE, Byford	135 D 2
CAGNEYS ON THE TERRACE, Claremont	71 A 9
CAPTAIN STIRLING HOTEL, Nedlands	71 D 8
CARINE GLADES TAVERN, Duncraig	31 B 9
CARLISLE HOTEL, Carlisle	74 B 8
CARLTON HOTEL, East Perth	1C B 3
CAROUSEL TAVERN, Cannington	84 E 7
CASTLE HOTEL, North Beach	44 C 1
CHARLES HOTEL, North Perth	60 D 4
CHASE'S BAR & BISTRO, Perth	1C A 2
CHATEAU COMMODORE HOTEL, Perth	1C A 3
CHIDLOW INN TAVERN, Chidlow	56 D 1
CHURCHILLS TAVERN & RESTAURANT, Perth	1C A 4
CITY HOTEL, Perth	1C E 2
CIVIC HOTEL, Inglewood	61 D 4
CLAISEBROOK JUNCTION TAVERN, East Perth	1C B 1
CLANCYS TAVERN, Fremantle	1D C 4
CLEOPATRA HOTEL, THE, Fremantle	1D B 5
CLOVERDALE HOTEL, Cloverdale	75 A 3
CLUB CAPRICORN, Yanchep	4 B 1
COBBLERS TAVERN, Falcon	162A C 2
COMMERCIAL HOTEL, Fremantle	1D B 5
COMMERCIAL TAVERN, Midland	50 C 9
COMO HOTEL, Como	73 B 10
CONTACIO INTERNATIONAL MOTOR HOTEL, Trigg	44 C 8
COOLABAH TAVERN, Morley	47 E 10
COOLBELLUP HOTEL, Coolbellup	101 E 1
CORFIELD TAVERN, Gosnells	106 B 2
CORONADO HOTEL, Claremont	71 B 9
CORONATION HOTEL, Queens Park	84 E 4
COTTESLOE BEACH RESORT, Cottesloe	80 C 2
COUNCIL CLUB HOTEL, Midland	50 C 8
COURT HOTEL, Perth	1C A 2
COURTNEYS TAVERN, Perth	1C E 3
CRAIGIE TAVERN, Craigie	23 D 5
DARLING RANGE TAVERN, Bellevue	51 A 9
DAVILAK TAVERN, South Fremantle	90 C 9
DIANELLA HOTEL, Dianella	47 B 9
DIANELLA TAVERN, Dianella	47 C 10
DOOLEYS BAR, Northbridge	1C E 1
DUCK INN WINE BAR, Subiaco	72 A 1
EASTSIDE TAVERN, Maylands	61 E 8
ESPLANADE PLAZA HOTEL, Fremantle	1D B 6
FAIRWAY TAVERN, Wembley Downs	59 A 7
FEDERAL HOTEL, Fremantle	1D C 5
FLOREAT HOTEL, Floreat	59 C 9
FORRESTFIELD TAVERN, Forrestfield	86 D 1
FOXY LADY TAVERN, Perth	1C E 3
FREEWAY HOTEL, South Perth	72 D 6
FREMANTLE HOTEL, Fremantle	1D B 5
GEORGE 'N DRAG'N TAVERN, Safety Bay	136 D 8
GIRRAWHEEN TAVERN, Girrawheen	32 B 6
GLENGARRY TAVERN, Duncraig	31 A 6
GLOBE HOTEL, Perth	1C E 2
GODIVA'S TAVERN, Attadale	81 E 10
GOSNELLS HOTEL, Gosnells	96 B 8
GRAND CENTRAL PRIVATE HOTEL, Perth	1C A 2
GREENWOOD FORREST HOTEL, Greenwood	31 D 6
GROSVENOR HOTEL, Perth	1C B 3
HAMILTON HOTEL, Hamilton Hill	91 A 10
HARBOURSIDE HOTEL, Fremantle	1D C 4
HARE & HOUND TAVERN, Leederville	60 C 10
HENRY AFRICAS WINEHOUSE, Subiaco	72 A 1
HERDSMAN MOTOR HOTEL, Wembley	59 E 7
HICKEYS CINE CELLARS, Perth	1C A 3
HILTON PARK TAVERN, Hilton Park	91 A 7
HIS LORDSHIPS LARDER, Fremantle	1D B 5
HIS MAJESTYS TAVERN, Perth	1C E 2
HOTEL REGATTA, Perth	1C A 3
HUMPHREY'S TAVERN, Koondoola	33 A 8
HURLINGHAM TAVERN, South Perth	73 C 8
HYATT REGENCY HOTEL, East Perth	1C B 4
HYDE PARK, West Perth	60 E 9
INGLEWOOD HOTEL, Inglewood	61 C 6
INNALOO TAVERN, Innaloo	59 C 1
INNTOWN HOTEL, Perth	1C A 3
IRENES PARK TAVERN, East Victoria Park	74 A 10
JARRAHDALE TAVERN, Jarrahdale	152 E 7
JOHN BARLEYCORN HOTEL, Nollamara	46 C 6
JOHN FORREST WILDFLOWER TAVERN, John Forrest National Park	52 C 7
JOONDALUP COUNTRY CLUB TAVERN, Connolly	19 B 7
JUNCTION HOTEL, Midland	50 C 8
KALAMUNDA HOTEL, Kalamunda	77 D 6
KARALEE TAVERN, Como	83 A 2
KARDINYA TAVERN, Kardinya	92 A 8
KARRINYUP TAVERN, Karrinyup	45 A 6
KASTELBETS TAVERN, Osborne Park	59 E 2
KELMSCOTT INN, Kelmscott	106 D 7
KEWDALE HOTEL, Kewdale	75 B 9
KINGS AMBASSADOR HOTEL, Perth	1C A 3
KINGSLEY TAVERN, Kingsley	24 B 10
KINSELLAS TAVERN, Guildford	49 C 10
KNUTSFORD ARMS HOTEL, North Perth	60 E 6
KWINANA LODGE HOTEL, Kwinana	131 A 7
LAKES HOTEL, Bibra Lake	102 E 6
LANGFORD TAVERN, Langford	94 E 2
LANGLEY PLAZA HOTEL, Perth	1C B 4
LAST DROP TAVERN, Kalamunda	77 D 6
LE TRAP BAR & GARDEN, Mt Lawley	61 B 8
LEEDERVILLE HOTEL, Leederville	60 D 9
LEISURE INN, Rockingham	137 B 7
LEOPOLD HOTEL, Bicton	91 B 1
LOMBARDOS FISHING BOAT HARBOUR TAVERN, Fremantle	1D B 6
LYNWOOD ARMS HOTEL, Lynwood	84 D 10
MADDINGTON TAVERN, Maddington	96 C 4
MADORA BAY TAVERN, Madora	160 C 7
MALAGA TAVERN, Malaga	47 D 2
MALTHOUSE TAVERN, Balga	46 C 1
MANNING HOTEL, Manning	83 A 6
MARRI PARK TAVERN, Casuarina	132 B 4
MAYLANDS HOTEL, Maylands	61 E 7
MEDINA TAVERN, Medina	130 E 5
MELBOURNE HOTEL, Perth	1C E 2
METRO INN APARTMENTS, East Perth	73 C 3
METRO INN, THE, South Perth	73 C 8
MIDLAND INN HOTEL, Midland	50 B 8
MILLIGANS BAR, Northbridge	1C E 1
MINDARIE KEYS RESORT HOTEL, Mindarie	14 B 5
MINSKY'S TAVERN, Nedlands	71 E 7
MIRRABOOKA TAVERN, Mirrabooka	46 E 4
MISS MAUD EUROPEAN HOTEL, Perth	1C A 3
MOON & SIXPENCE PUB, Perth	1C E 2
MORLEY PARK HOTEL, Morley	47 E 9
MOUNT HELENA TAVERN, Mount Helena	55 B 6
MOUNT ST INN & TAVERN, Perth	1C D 2
MULLALOO TAVERN, Mullaloo	23 A 6
MUNDARING HOTEL, Mundaring	68 B 1
MUNDIJONG TAVERN, Mundijong	143 A 8
NATIONAL HOTEL, Fremantle	1D B 5
NAVAL BASE HOTEL, Naval Base	121 B 7
NEW BEAUFORT HOTEL, Perth	1C A 1
NEW CANNINGTON HOTEL, Cannington	84 E 8
NEWMARKET INNE, Hamilton Hill	100 D 1
NEWPORT HOTEL, THE, Fremantle	1D B 5
NOOKENBURRA MOTOR HOTEL, Innaloo	59 C 2
NORFOLK SINCE 1887, Fremantle	1D C 6
NORTHBRIDGE HOTEL, Perth	61 A 10
NORTHLANDS TAVERN, Balcatta	46 B 5
NORWOOD HOTEL, East Perth	61 B 10
NOVAKS BAR & GRILL, Perth	1C E 1
OBSERVATION CITY, Scarborough	44 C 9
OCEAN BEACH HOTEL, Cottesloe	80 C 1
OCEAN VIEW TAVERN, Nowergup	11 E 5
OCEANIC HOTEL, Mosman Park	80 D 5
ODIN TAVERN, Balcatta	45 D 3
OGILVIES BAR & RESTAURANT, Mt Pleasant	82 D 6
OLD BRISBANE HOTEL, Perth	61 A 10
ORCHARD HOTEL, Perth	1C E 2
ORIEL BISTRO & BAR, Subiaco	72 A 1
ORIENT HOTEL, Fremantle	1D B 5
OSBORNE PARK HOTEL, Osborne Park	46 B 10
OSCAR'S BAR & TAVERN, East Victoria Park	74 A 9
OXFORD HOTEL, Leederville	60 C 6
OZONE BAR, Northbridge	1C E 1
PADDINGTON ALEHOUSE, Mount Hawthorn	60 C 6
PARKERVILLE TAVERN, Parkerville	53 C 5
PARMELIA HILTON INTERNATIONAL HOTEL	1C E 3
PENINSULA HOTEL, Mandurah	162 E 10
PENINSULA TAVERN, Maylands	61 D 7
PENINSULA & ORIENTAL HOTEL, Fremantle	1D B 5
PERTH AMBASSADOR HOTEL, East Perth	1C B 4
PERTH INTERNATIONAL HOTEL, THE, Perth	1C A 3
PERTH PARKROYAL HOTEL, East Perth	1C B 4
PHOENIX HOTEL, Spearwood	101 B 4
PICCADILLY BAR, Perth	1C B 2
PINE CREEK TAVERN, Forrestfield	76 C 10
PIONEER WORLD HOTEL/MOTEL, Armadale	116 E 6
PLAISTOWES BAR & GRILL, West Perth	60 D 10
PRINCES HOTEL, THE, Perth	1C E 2
QUEENS TAVERN, Highgate	61 B 9
RAFFLES MOTOR HOTEL, Applecross	82 E 5
RAILWAY HOTEL, North Fremantle	90 C 1
RAILWAY HOTEL, Perth	1C A 2
RANGEVIEW HOTEL, Eden Hill	49 A 8
RASCALS TAVERN, Ascot	62 C 10
RED CASTLE MOTOR HOTEL, Lathlain	74 A 4
RHODES HOTEL, South Perth	73 B 8
RIVERTON HOTEL, Lynwood	94 A 1
ROCK INN TAVERN, Karragullen	109 B 6
ROCKINGHAM HOTEL, Rockingham	137 A 4
ROCKINGHAM OCEAN CLIPPER INN, Rockingham	137 A 5
ROKEBYS WINE, Subiaco	72 B 2
ROSE AND CROWN HOTEL MOTEL, Guildford	49 D 10
ROSE HOTEL, North Fremantle	80 C 10
ROSEMOUNT HOTEL, North Perth	60 E 8
ROYAL GEORGE TAVERN, East Fremantle	90 D 2
SAIL & ANCHOR TAVERN, Fremantle	1D C 5
SAN MIGUEL TAVERN, Tuart Hill	60 D 1
SANDRINGHAM HOTEL, Belmont	74 B 2
SANDS MOTOR HOTEL, Scarborough	44 D 10
SASSELLAS TAVERN, City Arcade, Perth	1C A 2
SAVOY HOTEL, Perth	1C A 3
SAWYERS VALLEY TAVERN, Sawyers Valley	69 A 1

281

	Map	Ref.
SEA VIEW TAVERN, South Fremantle	90	C 8
SHAFTESBURY HOTEL, Perth	1C	A 2
SHAFTO TAVERN, Perth	1C	E 2
SHENTON PARK HOTEL, Shenton Park	71	E 3
SHERATON PERTH HOTEL, Perth	1C	B 4
SHIP & DOCK INN, Henderson	110	E 3
SILVER SANDS TAVERN, Silver Sands	163	A 8
SOUTHERN RIVER TAVERN, Gosnells	95	E 4
SPEARWOOD TAVERN, Spearwood	101	B 9
ST GEORGE HOTEL, THE, Innaloo	45	C 8
STEVE'S NEDLANDS PARK TAVERN, Nedlands	71	E10
STIRLING ARMS HOTEL, Guildford	49	D10
STIRLING GREENS TAVERN, Maylands	62	A10
STOCK ROAD MARKETS TAVERN, Bibra Lake	101	D 5
STOCKMAN HOTEL, Midland	50	C 9
STONED CROW WINEHOUSE, North Fremantle	90	C 1
SUBIACO HOTEL, Subiaco	72	A 1
SULLIVANS HOTEL, West Perth	1C	D 4
SUN CITY TAVERN, Two Rocks	2	B 2
SUNDOWNER HOTEL, Balcatta	46	A 2
SUNNYS SHINING ON THE SWAN, East Fremantle	90	D 2
SWAN INNE, North Fremantle	90	C 1
SWANBOURNE HOTEL, Swanbourne	70	E 9
THORNLIE HOTEL, Thornlie	95	C 5
TIBBYS TAVERN, Redcliffe	63	A 7
TOWNHOUSE HOTEL, Perth	1C	E 2
TRACKS TAVERN, Perth	1C	A 2
TRADE WINDS HOTEL, Fremantle	90	D 2
TRANSIT INN HOTEL, Perth	1C	A 3
VALE TAVERN, Swan View	51	B 7
VEGAS HOTEL, North Perth	60	E 7
VICTORIA HOTEL, Subiaco	72	B 1
VICTORIA PARK HOTEL, Victoria Park	73	E 8
VILLAGE PUB, THE, Perth	1C	E 2
WAIKIKI HOTEL MOTEL, Safety Bay	145	A 2
WANGARA TAVERN, Wangara	24	E 7
WANNEROO VILLA TAVERN, Wanneroo	20	D 8
WARNBRO TAVERN, Warnbro	145	C 5
WARWICK HOTEL, Warwick	31	E 8
WATERFORD TAVERN, Karawara	83	D 5
WATTLEUP TAVERN, Wattleup	121	C 2
WEIR HOTEL, Mundaring Weir, (Inset Map 79)		
WEMBLEY HOTEL, Wembley	59	E10
WENTWORTH PLAZA HOTEL, Perth	1C	E 2
WESTFIELD TAVERN, Westfield	106	C 9
WHITE SANDS TAVERN, Scarborough	44	D10
WHITFORD TAVERN, Hillarys	23	C 8
WILLAGEE PARK HOTEL, Willagee	91	C 4
WINDSOR HOTEL, South Perth	72	E 7
WINNING POST TAVERN, Redcliffe	74	E 1

	Map	Ref.
WOODBRIDGE TAVERN, Guildford	49	E10
WOODVALE TAVERN, Woodvale	24	B 5
WYCOMBE COUNTRY CLUB HOTEL, High Wycombe	64	C 8
YANCHEP INN, Yanchep	5	D 2
YE OLDE SERPENTINE INNE TAVERN, Serpentine	154	E 3
ZIGGYS BAR, Perth	1C	A 3

LIBRARIES

	Map	Ref.
ARMADALE, Orchard Ave	116	D 6
BALLAJURA, Cnr Illawarra Cr & Kingfisher Ave	33	E 7
BASSENDEAN MEMORIAL, 46 Old Perth Rd, Bassendean	63	A 1
BATTYE LIBRARY OF WESTERN AUSTRALIAN HISTORY, Alexander Library Building, Cultural Centre, Perth	1C	A 2
BAYSWATER, 25 King William St	62	B 5
BECKENHAM, Streatham St	85	C 8
BELMONT, (Ruth Faulkner) Progress Wy, Cloverdale	74	D 4
BENTLEY, Hedley Pl	84	B 5
BULL CREEK, Cnr Leichardt St & Hassell Cr	92	E 7
CANNING BRIDGE, 2 Kintail Rd, Applecross	82	E 5
CLAREMONT, 308 Stirling Hwy	71	A 9
COOLBELLUP, 90 Cordelia Ave	101	E 2
COTTESLOE, 1 Leake St, Peppermint Grove	80	D 3
DIANELLA, Dianella Plaza Shopping Centre, Waverley St	47	B10
DUNCRAIG, Cnr Warwick Rd & Marmion Ave	30	D 6
FLOREAT, Floreat Forum Shopping Centre, Howtree Pl	59	C 9
FORRESTFIELD, Cnr Salix Way & Strelitzia Ave	76	C 9
FREMANTLE CIVIC LIBRARY, City Offices, 8 William St	1D	C 5
GIRRAWHEEN, 6 Patrick Ct	32	C 7
GOSNELLS, 2240 Albany Hwy	96	C 9
GREENMOUNT, Scott St	65	C 1
GUILDFORD, Cnr James & Meadow Sts	49	D10
HIGH WYCOMBE, Western Ave	64	C 9
INGLEWOOD, Cnr Beaufort St & Ninth Ave	61	D 5
KALAMUNDA, Railway Rd (opp Haynes St)	77	D 6
KARRINYUP, Davenport St	45	A 5
KELMSCOTT, 2817 Albany Hwy	106	D 3
KWINANA, Pace Rd, Medina	130	E 5
LEEDERVILLE, Cnr Loftus & Vincent Sts	60	D 9
LESMURDIE, School/Community Library, Reid Rd	87	C 5
MANDURAH DISTRICT LIBRARY, 331 Pinjarra Rd.	165	C 2
MANNING, Cnr Manning Rd & Goss Ave	83	B 5
MAYLANDS, Cnr Guildford Rd & Eighth Ave	61	E 7
MELVILLE, Civic Square, Almondbury Rd, Ardross	82	C10
MELVILLE, Cnr Stock Rd & Canning Hwy	91	C 1
MIDLAND, Tuohy Gardens	50	C 8
MIRRABOOKA, Mirrabooka Shopping Centre, Chesterfield Rd	47	A 3
MOUNT CLAREMONT, 19 Haldane St	71	A 4

	Map	Ref.
MUNDARING, Nichol St	68	B 1
NEDLANDS, 60 Stirling Hwy	71	D 8
OSBORNE, 11 Royal St, Tuart Hill	46	B10
PERTH, Council House, 27 St Georges Tce	1C	A 3
QUEENS PARK, Cnr Railway Pde & George St	84	E 4
RIVERTON, Cnr High & Riley Rds	94	A 1
ROCKINGHAM, Kent St	137	A 4
ROCKINGHAM, TAFE Public, Simpson Ave	137	D 5
SAFETY BAY, Safety Bay Rd	136	D10
SCARBOROUGH, Gildercliffe St, (south of Scarborough Beach Rd)	45	A 9
SERPENTINE-JARRAHDALE, Patterson St, Mundijong	143	A 9
SOUTH PERTH, Civic Centre, South Tce	73	A10
SPEARWOOD, Coleville Cr	101	B 5
STATE ARCHIVES, Alexander Library Building, Cultural Centre, Perth	1C	A 1
STATE FILM & VIDEO LIBRARY, Alexander Library Building, Cultural Centre, Perth	1C	A 1
STATE MUSIC LIBRARY, Alexander Library Building, Cultural Centre, Perth	1C	A 1
STATE REFERENCE LIBRARY, Alexander Library Building, Cultural Centre, Perth	1C	A 1
SUBIACO, Cnr Rokeby & Bagot Rds	72	A 2
THORNLIE, Cnr Connemara Dr & Culross Ave	95	C 5
VICTORIA PARK, Community/Recreation Centre, Cnr Kent & Gloucester Sts	73	E 9
WANNEROO, Civic Dr	20	D 8
WESTFIELD, Champion Dr, Armadale	116	C 2
WHITFORD, Cnr Marmion & Banks Aves, Hillarys	23	C 8
WILLAGEE, Cnr Winnacott & Archibald Sts	91	D 5
WILLETTON, 39 Burrendah Blvd	93	C 5
WOODVALE LIBRARY, Trappers Dr	24	C 8
YANCHEP-TWO ROCKS, Yanchep Community Recreation Centre, Lisford Ave, Two Rocks	2	C 2

LOCALITIES, POSTCODES & POSTAL DISTRICTS

	Map	Ref.
ALEXANDER HEIGHTS 6064	33	A 4
ALFRED COVE 6154	81	E10
ALKIMOS 6033	8	A 7
ANKETELL 6167	132	B 1
APPLECROSS 6153	82	C 6
ARDROSS 6153	82	C 9
ARMADALE 6112	116	C 4
ASCOT 6104	62	C 9
ASHFIELD 6054	62	E 4
ATTADALE 6156	81	D 8
BALCATTA 6021	45	E 3
BALDIVIS 6171	147	A 6
BALGA 6061	46	C 2
BALLAJURA 6066	33	D 7
BANJUP 6164	113	C 5
BASSENDEAN 6054	63	A 3
BATEMAN 6150	92	D 5
BAYSWATER 6053	62	B 4
BEACONSFIELD 6162	90	D 8

	Map	Ref.
BECKENHAM 6107	85	C 7
BEDFORD 6052	61	D 3
BEDFORDALE 6112	117	C 6
BEECHBORO 6063	48	D 2
BEECHINA 6556	43	D 8
BELDON 6025	23	C 1
BELHUS 6056	29	C 4
BELLEVUE 6056	50	D 9
BELMONT 6104	74	D 2
BENTLEY 6102	84	C 4
BIBRA LAKE 6163	102	B 3
BICKLEY 6076	88	E 3
BICTON 6157	81	B 7
BOORAGOON 6154	92	C 1
BOYA 6056	65	D 4
BRENTWOOD 6153	92	E 2
BRIGADOON 6056	168	A 4
BULL CREEK 6149	93	A 5
BURNS 6028	18	D 1
BUTLER 6032	11	B 4
BYFORD 6201	135	C 2
CALISTA 6167	130	D 8
CANNING MILLS 6111	98	C 6
CANNING VALE 6155	94	C 7
CANNINGTON 6107	84	D 5
CARABOODA 6033	8	D 5
CARDUP 6201	135	C 7
CARINE 6020	31	B10
CARLISLE 6101	74	B 8
CARMEL 6076	88	C 7
CASUARINA 6167	132	B 6
CAVERSHAM 6055	49	D 5
CHIDLOW 6556	42	D 6
CHURCHLANDS 6018	59	B 6
CITY BEACH 6015	58	D 7
CLAREMONT 6010	71	A 7
CLARKSON 6030	14	D 4
CLOVERDALE 6105	74	C 4
COMO 6152	83	B 3
CONNOLLY 6027	19	B 7
COODANUP 6210	165	D 5
COOGEE 6166	100	E 8
COOLBELLUP 6163	101	D 2
COOLBINIA 6050	60	E 3
COOLOONGUP 6168	137	E 9
COTTESLOE 6011	80	C 2
CRAIGIE 6025	23	D 6
CRAWLEY 6009	72	A 9
CULLACABARDEE 6067	33	E 3
CURRAMBINE 6028	19	B 4
DAGLISH 6008	71	E 2
DALKEITH 6009	81	D 2
DARLINGTON 6070	66	B 7
DIANELLA 6062	47	B 8
DOUBLEVIEW 6018	59	A 2
DUDLEY PARK 6210	165	A 6
DUNCRAIG 6023	31	A 6
EAST CANNINGTON 6107	85	B 5
EAST FREMANTLE 6158	90	E 2
EAST PERTH 6004	73	B 2
EAST ROCKINGHAM 6168	137	D 2
EAST VICTORIA PARK 6101	74	A 9
EDEN HILL 6054	49	B 8
EDGEWATER 6027	24	A 2
EGLINTON 6034	5	A 9
ELLENBROOK 6056	29	A 3
EMBLETON 6062	62	A 1
ERSKINE 6210	164	C 7
FALCON 6210	162A	C 1
FERNDALE 6148	84	C 9
FLOREAT 6014	59	C 9
FORRESTDALE 6112	114	D 4
FORRESTFIELD 6058	76	D 7
FREMANTLE 6160	90	D 5
FURNISSDALE 6210	165	E 6
GIDGEGANNUP 6555	40	D 3
GIRRAWHEEN 6064	32	C 7
GLEN FORREST 6071	66	D 5
GLENDALOUGH 6016	60	A 5
GNANGARA 6065	25	E 3
GOLDEN BAY 6174	158	D 6
GOOSEBERRY HILL 6076	77	C 2
GOSNELLS 6110	96	B 9
GREENFIELDS 6210	163	D 7
GREENMOUNT 6056	65	D 1
GREENWOOD 6024	31	C 4

282

Place	Map	Ref.
GUILDFORD 6055	49	E 8
GWELUP 6018	45	C 3
HACKETTS GULLY 6076	79	B 8
HALLS HEAD 6210	164	D 2
HAMERSLEY 6022	31	D10
HAMILTON HILL 6163	101	B 2
HAZELMERE 6055	64	C 3
HEATHRIDGE 6027	23	D 1
HELENA VALLEY 6056	65	B 6
HENDERSON 6166	111	B 8
HENLEY BROOK 6055	28	E 8
HERNE HILL 6056	37	A 4
HIGH WYCOMBE 6057	64	C 8
HIGHGATE 6003	61	B 9
HILLARYS 6025	30	A 1
HILLMAN 6168	137	E 5
HILTON 6163	91	B 8
HOPE VALLEY 6165	121	D 6
HOVEA 6071	53	A 6
HUNTINGDALE 6110	95	D10
ILUKA 6028	18	E 5
INGLEWOOD 6052	61	C 4
INNALOO 6018	45	C10
JANDABUP 6065	21	D 4
JANDAKOT 6164	103	A 4
JARRAHDALE 6203	152	E 6
JINDALEE 6032	10	D 3
JOLIMONT 6014	71	E 1
JOONDALUP 6027	19	D 6
JOONDANNA 6060	60	C 3
KALAMUNDA 6076	77	C 7
KALLAROO 6025	23	B 7
KARAWARA 6152	83	C 5
KARDINYA 6163	92	A 6
KARNUP 6176	157	C10
KARRAGULLEN 6111	109	A 5
KARRAKATTA 6010	71	C 7
KARRINYUP 6018	45	A 5
KELMSCOTT 6111	107	A 6
KENSINGTON 6151	73	C 9
KENWICK 6107	85	E 7
KEWDALE 6105	75	B 8
KIARA 6054	48	E 6
KINGSLEY 6026	31	C 1
KINROSS 6028	19	A 1
KOONDOOLA 6064	33	B 7
KOONGAMIA 6056	65	B 2
KWINANA BEACH 6167	129	E 5
KWINANA TOWN CENTRE 6167	131	A 8
LAKELANDS 6210	161	B 7
LANDSDALE 6065	25	C10
LANGFORD 6147	95	A 2
LATHLAIN 6100	74	A 6
LEDA 6170	130	D 9
LEEDERVILLE 6007	60	C 8
LEEMING 6149	93	B 9
LESMURDIE 6076	87	C 5
LOCKRIDGE 6054	49	A 6
LYNWOOD 6147	94	C 3
MADDINGTON 6109	96	A 3
MADORA 6210	160	D 7
MAHOGANY CREEK 6072	67	D 2
MAIDA VALE 6057	64	E 9
MALAGA 6062	48	B 2
MANDOGALUP 6167	122	D 5
MANDURAH 6210	165	A 2
MANNING 6152	83	B 7
MARANGAROO 6064	32	C 3
MARIGINIUP 6065	21	B 2
MARMION 6020	30	C 2
MARTIN 6110	97	B 8
MAYLANDS 6051	61	E 8
MEADOW SPRINGS 6210	163	D 4
MEDINA 6167	130	C 4
MELVILLE 6156	91	D 2
MENORA 6050	61	A 3
MERRIWA 6030	11	D 8
MIDDLE SWAN 6056	50	C 1
MIDLAND 6056	50	D 4
MIDVALE 6056	50	E 8
MILLENDON 6056	29	D 7
MINDARIE 6030	14	B 4
MIRRABOOKA 6061	47	A 3
MORLEY 6062	48	B 7
MOSMAN PARK 6012	80	D 5
MT CLAREMONT 6010	71	A 3

Place	Map	Ref.
MT HAWTHORN 6016	60	C 5
MT HELENA 6555	55	A 3
MT LAWLEY 6050	61	B 7
MT PLEASANT 6153	82	E 8
MULLALOO 6025	23	A 3
MUNDARING 6073	68	B 3
MUNDIJONG 6202	142	E 6
MUNSTER 6166	111	C 4
MURDOCH 6150	92	C 9
MYAREE 6154	92	A 3
NAVAL BASE 6165	121	B 6
NEDLANDS 6009	71	D 9
NEERABUP 6031	16	B 5
NEWBURN 6104	75	D 5
NOLLAMARA 6061	46	C 6
NORANDA 6062	48	A 4
NORTH BEACH 6020	44	D 2
NORTH FREMANTLE 6159	90	C 1
NORTH LAKE 6163	92	B10
NORTH PERTH 6006	60	E 7
NORTHBRIDGE 6003	72	E 1
NOWERGUP 6032	12	D 4
OAKFORD 6113	124	E 7
OCEAN REEF 6027	23	A 1
ORANGE GROVE 6109	86	D 8
ORELIA 6167	131	A 4
OSBORNE PARK 6017	60	A 2
O'CONNOR 6163	91	C 6
PADBURY 6025	23	D 9
PALMYRA 6157	91	B 3
PARKERVILLE 6553	53	D 5
PARKLANDS 6210	163	E 5
PARMELIA 6167	131	B 8
PAULLS VALLEY 6076	79	A 3
PEEL ESTATE 6167	141	B 6
PEPPERMINT GROVE 6011	80	E 3
PERON 6168	136	C 5
PERTH AIRPORT 6105	63	D 7
PERTH CITY 6000	72	E 2
PICKERING BROOK 6076	89	B 8
PIESSE BROOK 6076	78	B 5
PINJAR 6065	17	D 3
PORT KENNEDY 6169	156	B 5
POSTANS 6167	130	D 2
QUEENS PARK 6107	85	A 3
QUINNS ROCKS 6030	11	A 8
RED HILL 6555	37	E 6
REDCLIFFE 6104	62	E 9
RIVERTON 6148	83	E10
RIVERVALE 6103	74	B 4
ROCKINGHAM 6168	137	B 5
ROLEYSTONE 6111	108	C 9
ROSSMOYNE 6148	93	B 2
SAFETY BAY 6169	136	D 9
SALTER POINT 6152	83	B 8
SAMSON 6163	91	C 8
SAN REMO 6210	163	C 2
SAWYERS VALLEY 6074	69	A 1
SCARBOROUGH 6019	44	B 6
SECRET HARBOUR 6173	158	C 2
SERPENTINE 6205	155	A 6
SHELLEY 6148	83	D 9
SHENTON PARK 6008	71	E 4
SHOALWATER 6169	136	C 8
SILVER SANDS 6210	163	B 5
SINGLETON 6175	160	D 1
SORRENTO 6020	30	B 4
SOUTH FREMANTLE 6162	90	C 8
SOUTH GUILDFORD 6055	63	C 3
SOUTH LAKE 6164	102	D 7
SOUTH PERTH 6151	73	A 9
SOUTHERN RIVER 6110	105	C 6
SPEARWOOD 6163	101	A 6
ST JAMES 6102	84	A 3
STIRLING 6021	45	E 7
STONEVILLE 6554	54	C 5
STRATTON 6056	51	B 3
SUBIACO 6008	72	B 2
SUCCESS 6164	112	D 7
SWAN VIEW 6056	51	D 6
SWANBOURNE 6010	70	D 5
TAMALA PARK 6030	14	C 8
THE LAKES 6556	57	D 7
THE SPECTACLES 6167	131	C 2
THORNLIE 6108	95	B 5
TRIGG 6029	44	D 6

Place	Map	Ref.
TUART HILL 6060	60	B 1
TWO ROCKS 6037	2	D 2
UPPER SWAN 6056	29	D 2
VICTORIA PARK 6100	73	D 7
VIVEASH 6056	50	B 6
WAIKIKI 6169	145	D 3
WALLISTON 6076	88	A 3
WANDI 6167	123	C 5
WANGARA 6065	25	C 3
WANNEROO 6065	20	D 6
WARNBRO 6169	145	D 9
WARWICK 6024	31	D 7
WATERFORD 6152	83	D 5
WATERMAN 6020	30	C10
WATTLE GROVE 6107	86	C 4
WATTLEUP 6166	121	D 2
WELLARD 6170	131	C 9
WELSHPOOL 6106	84	D 1
WEMBLEY 6014	59	E 8
WEMBLEY DOWNS 6019	58	E 4
WEST PERTH 6005	72	C 2
WEST SWAN 6055	35	D 8
WESTFIELD 6112	106	B 6
WHITBY 6202	143	C 4
WHITE GUM VALLEY 6162	90	E 6
WHITEMAN 6068	35	A 4
WILLAGEE 6156	91	D 4
WILLETTON 6155	93	D 4
WILSON 6107	84	B 7
WINTHROP 6150	92	A 4
WOODLANDS 6018	59	C 2
WOODVALE 6026	24	C 8
WOOROLOO 6558	43	D 3
WUNGONG 6112	126	D 3
YANCHEP 6035	5	A 4
YANGEBUP 6164	111	D 1
YOKINE 6060	60	E 2

MOTELS

Name	Map	Ref.
ABERDEEN LODGE (TRAVELLERS HOSTEL), Northbridge	1C	A 1
ADELPHI, THE, West Perth	1C	D 3
AIRWAYS HOTEL APARTMENTS, Perth City	1C	B 4
ANGELO AUTO LODGE, Rivervale	74	A 3
ASTORIA APARTMENTS, West Perth	1C	D 3
ASTRALODGE MOTEL, Beckenham	85	A 9
BEATTY LODGE, North Perth	60	D 9
BEL EYRE MOTEL, Belmont	62	D 9
BLUE BAY MOTEL, Halls Head	162	C 9
BRADY'S RESORT MOTEL, Mandurah	162	E10
BRIGHTON LODGE, Rivervale	74	A 3
CANNING BRIDGE AUTO LODGE, Applecross	82	D 7
CHEVIOT LODGE, Perth City	61	B10
CITY AUTO LODGE, Osborne Park	60	D 9
CITY WATERS LODGE, Perth City	1C	B 4
COMO BEACH MOTEL, Como	82	E 1
CRABSHELL MOTEL, Mandurah	164	E 1
DEVENISH LODGE, East Victoria Park	83	E 1
EASTWAY LODGE, Rivervale	74	A 3
FLAG MOTOR LODGE, Rivervale	74	B 2
FLORINA LODGE, Applecross	82	E 5
FOUNTAIN MOTEL, Wattle Grove	86	A 4
GILDERCLIFFE LODGE, Scarborough	45	A10
GLENVALE LODGE, Rivervale	74	A 3
GREAT EASTERN MOTOR LODGE, Rivervale	74	B 3
HIGHWAY MOTEL, Bentley	84	C 5

Name	Map	Ref.
HOMETEL, West Perth	1C	D 1
HOSPITALITY INN, Bentley	84	C 5
JEWELL HOUSE, Perth City	1C	B 3
KINGS PARK LODGE, Shenton Park	72	A 4
LADYBIRD LODGE, Leederville	60	C 8
LAKESIDE COUNTRY RESORT, Bedfordale	117	B 3
LAKESIDE VILLAS, Mandurah	163	A 9
LINCOLN AUTO LODGE, Perth City	61	A10
LOXTON HOLIDAY FLATS, Mandurah	165	A 2
MANDURAH HOLIDAY VILLAGE, Mandurah	163	A 9
MANDURAH SPINAWAY MOTEL, Mandurah	162	E10
MARACOONDA MOTEL, Redcliffe	62	E 8
MIDLAND MEWS MOTEL, Midland	50	C 9
MOUNTWAY HOLIDAY UNITS, Perth City	1C	D 3
MURRAY LODGE MOTEL, West Perth	72	C 1
OLL'ROY LODGE, Mandurah	165	A 2
PACIFIC MOTEL, Highgate	61	B 9
PARK LODGING HOUSE, THE, Fremantle	1D	C 5
PARKLANE AUTO LODGE, South Perth	73	A 9
PARKSIDE MOTEL, East Perth	1C	B 3
PIONEER WORLD HOTEL/MOTEL, Armadale	116	E 6
ROCKINGHAM OCEAN CLIPPER INN, Rockingham	137	A 5
ROSE & CROWN HOTEL/MOTEL, Guildford	49	D10
SEAPINES HOLIDAY CHALETS, (Cottesloe Beach Resort), Cottesloe	80	C 2
SILVER SANDS TIMESHARE RESORT, Silver Sands	163	A 8
SOUTHWAY LODGE MOTEL, South Perth	73	A 9
SPINDRIFTER HOLIDAY RESORT, Scarborough	44	C10
SURFSIDE HOLIDAY UNITS, Scarborough	44	D10
SWAN VIEW MOTEL, Como	82	B 3
TOORAK LODGE, Rivervale	74	B 3
TOWN LODGE, South Perth	72	E 7
TRAVELLERS REST MOTEL, Mundaring	68	D 1
WAIKIKI HOTEL-MOTEL, Safety Bay	145	A 2
WEST BEACH LAGOON, Scarborough	44	D10
WEST COAST SEAS, Scarborough	44	C 9
WEST POINT COTTAGES, Halls Head	162	C10
WINDSOR LODGE MOTEL, Como	82	E 2
WINDSOR REGENCY LODGE, Rivervale	74	A 3

MUSEUMS & ART GALLERIES

Name	Map	Ref.
ARMY MUSEUM, "Dilhorn", 2 Bulwer St, East Perth	1C	B 1
ART GALLERY OF WESTERN AUSTRALIA, 47 James St, Perth	1C	A 2
AZELIA LEY HOMESTEAD, Azelia Rd, Hamilton Hill	100	E 3
BUCKLAND HILL MILITARY MUSEUM, Somerset Cr, Mosman Park	80	D 7
CITY OF BELMONT MUSEUM, Faulkner Park, Elizabeth St, Belmont	74	D 4

283

Name	Map Ref.
CLAREMONT MUSEUM (Fresh Water Bay Sch.), 66 Victoria Ave, Claremont	81 B 1
ELIZABETHAN VILLAGE, Canns Rd, Armadale	117 B 4
FANNY SAMSON'S COTTAGE MUSEUM, 33 Cliff St, Fremantle	1D B 5
FIRE SAFETY EDUCATION CENTRE & MUSEUM, Cnr Murray & Irwin Sts, Perth	1C A 3
FREMANTLE ART GALLERY, High St, Fremantle	1D B 5
FREMANTLE ARTS CENTRE, 1 Finnerty St, Fremantle	1D C 4
FREMANTLE MUSEUM, Finnerty St, Fremantle	1D C 4
FREMANTLE PRISON MUSEUM, 16 The Terrace, Fremantle	1D C 5
GALLOP HOUSE, Esplanade, Dalkeith	81 E 2
GEOLOGICAL SURVEY MUSEUM (Mineral House) 66 Adelaide Tce, Perth	1C B 4
GLOUCESTER LODGE MUSEUM, Yanchep National Park, Yanchep	5 D 2
GOSNELLS MUSEUM, Homestead Rd, Gosnells	95 E 7
HISTORY HOUSE, Armadale-Kelmscott, Municipal Museum, Jull St, Armadale	116 D 6
IT'S A SMALL WORLD, 12 Parliament Pl, West Perth	1C D 2
KALAMUNDA STATION MUSEUM, Williams Rd, Kalamunda	77 D 6
KELMSCOTT MUSEUM, Kelmscott	106 D 8
KERRYELLES COLLECTORS MUSEUM, Gordon Rd, Parklands	163 E 6
LAW SOCIETY MUSEUM, Supreme Court Gardens, Perth	1C A 3
MEDICAL MUSEUM, Harvey House, Cnr Barker & Railway Rds, Subiaco	72 A 2
MILLER BAKEHOUSE MUSEUM, Baal St, Palmyra	91 B 2
MOUNT FLORA REGIONAL MUSEUM, Elvire St, Waterman	30 C 10
MUSEUM OF CHILDHOOD, 160 Hamersley Rd, Subiaco	72 A 2
MUSEUM OF WESTERN AUSTRALIAN SPORT, Superdrome, Stephenson Ave, Mt Claremont	71 A 2
O'CONNOR MUSEUM, Mundaring Weir, (See Inset Map 79)	
PERTH CULTURAL CENTRE	1C A 2
PIONEER WORLD, Sth Western Hwy, Armadale	116 E 6
POST & TELECOM OPEN AIR MUSEUM, Brisbane St, Perth	61 A 10
RAIL TRANSPORT MUSEUM, Railway Pde, Bassendean	62 E 3
ROCKINGHAM DISTRICT HISTORICAL SOCIETY, Cnr Flinders La & Kent St, Rockingham	137 A 4
ROYAL AUSTRALIAN AIR FORCE ASSOCIATION AVIATION MUSEUM, Bull Creek Dr, Bull Creek	93 A 4
SAILS OF THE CENTURY, 'B' Shed, Victoria Quay, Fremantle	1D B 5
SAMSON HOUSE, Cnr Ellen & Ord Sts, Fremantle	1D C 4
SCITECH DISCOVERY CENTRE, Cnr Railway Pde & Sutherland St, West Perth	1C D 1
SCOUT ASSOCIATION MUSEUM, Baden-Powell House, 581 Murray St, Perth	1C D 2
STIRK COTTAGE, Kalamunda Rd, Kalamunda	77 D 6
STIRLING HOUSE, Royal WA Historical Society Headquarters 49 Broadway, Nedlands	71 E 8
SUBIACO HISTORICAL MUSEUM, adjacent to Council House, Rokeby Rd, Subiaco	72 A 2
SWAN COTTAGE HOMES MUSEUM & ART GALLERY, Pine Ave, Bentley	83 E 3
SWAN - GUILDFORD HISTORICAL MUSEUM, 14 Swan St	49 D 10
THE ENERGY MUSEUM, Cnr Parry & Quarry Sts, Fremantle	1D C 4
THE HALL COLLECTION, 105 Swan St, Guildford	49 D 10
THE OLD MILL, Mill Point Rd, South Perth	72 D 5
THE ROYAL AUSTRALIAN ARTILLERY HISTORICAL SOCIETY MUSEUM, Hobbs Artillery Park, Karrakatta	71 C 5
THE ROYAL PERTH HOSPITAL MUSEUM, Block N, Wellington St, Perth	1C A 3
THE THEATRE COLLECTIONS, His Majestys Theatre, 825 Hay St, Perth	1C E 2
TOM COLLINS HOUSE, 7 Servetus St, Swanbourne	70 E 9
TRANBY HOUSE, National Trust of Australia (WA), Johnson Rd, Maylands	62 B 10
WATERWAY FARM STUDIO, South Western Hwy, Byford	126 D 6
WESTERN AUSTRALIAN MARITIME MUSEUM, Cliff St, Fremantle	1D B 6
WESTERN AUSTRALIAN MUSEUM, Francis St, Perth	1C A 2
WIRELESS HILL TELECOMMUNICATIONS MUSEUM, Wireless Hill Park, Almondbury Rd, Ardross	82 B 10
WOODBRIDGE, National Trust of Australia (WA), Third Ave, West Midland	50 A 8
WOODLOES MUSEUM, 13 Woodloes St, Cannington	84 E 9

NURSING, REST HOMES, HOSTELS & RETIREMENT COMMUNITIES

Name	Map Ref.
ABORIGINAL RIGHTS LEAGUE AUTUMN CENTRE, 340 Guildford Rd, Bayswater	62 A 7
ADELPHI, 29 Neville St, Bayswater	62 B 7
AGMAROY, 115 Leach Hwy, Wilson	84 B 7
AIR FORCE MEMORIAL ESTATE, Bull Creek Dr, Bull Creek	92 E 3
ALFRED CARSON, 30 Bay Rd, Claremont	71 B 10
AMAROO RETIREMENT VILLAGE, 60 Stalker Rd, Gosnells	96 B 9
APPLECROSS NURSING HOME, Riverway, Applecross	82 D 5
ARCHBISHOP GOODY HOSTEL, (Catholic), 29 Goderich St, East Perth	1C B 4
ARMSTRONG HOUSE (Anglican), Headingly Rd, Kalamunda	77 D 6
BARRIDALE LODGE, 89 Barridale Dr, Kingsley	31 C 1
BASSENDEAN NURSING HOME, 27 Hamilton St, Bassendean	63 A 1
BEDBROOK LODGE, Selby St, Shenton Park	71 D 3
BELGRADE PARK, 55 Belgrade Rd, Wanneroo	20 E 8
BELMONT NURSING HOME, 5 Kemp Pl, Rivervale	74 B 3
BELMONT SENIOR CITIZENS CENTRE, Progress Wy, Belmont	74 D 4
BEN RITCHER LODGE, 480 Guildford Rd, Bayswater	62 C 6
BETHESDA DOMINICAN HOSTEL, Williamstown Rd, Doubleview	59 B 3
BRAEMAR COURT (Presbyterian) Cnr Canning Hwy & Stratford St, East Fremantle	91 A 1
BRAEMAR GARDENS LODGE (Presbyterian), 51 Point Walter Rd, Bicton	81 B 9
BRAEMAR, 214 Canning Hwy, East Fremantle	90 E 2
BRAILLE HOSPITAL FOR THE BLIND, 61 Kitchener Ave, Victoria Park	74 A 6
BRAILLE NURSING HOME & ASSOCIATED SERVICES, 61 Kitchener Ave, Victoria Park	74 A 6
CABRINI, 111 Guildford Rd, Maylands	61 D 8
CALLISTEMON COURT, Gilmore Ave, Calista	130 E 8
CAMELIA COURT, Guildford Rd, Bayswater	62 C 6
CARINYA VILLAGE LODGE, 20 Plantation St, Menora	61 A 3
CARINYA VILLAGE, (Churches of Christ), 20 Plantation St, Menora	61 A 3
CARINYA, 41 Bristol Ave, Bicton	81 B 9
CARLISLE COTTAGES, 110 Star St, Carlisle	74 C 8
CARLISLE, 110 Star St, Carlisle	74 C 8
CASSON HOUSE, 2-10 Woodville St, North Perth	60 E 7
CATHERINE McAULEY, 18 Barrett St, Wembley	60 A 9
CHALLENGER LODGE, Read St, Rockingham	137 A 5
CHRYSTAL GARDENS (Uniting Church) Unit 13 Kitchener St, Trigg	44 C 4
CHRYSTAL HALLIDAY (Uniting Church), 61 Jeanes Rd, Karrinyup	44 E 6
CHRYSTAL HALLIDAY (Uniting Church), 61 Jeanes Rd, Karrinyup	44 E 6
CITY OF BAYSWATER AGED PERSONS HOMES, (Mertome Home), Winifred Rd, Bayswater	62 B 4
CLAUDIA HICKS LODGE, (Rowethorpe) Hill View Tce, Bentley	84 A 4
COLLIER PARK RETIREMENT VILLAGE, Saunders St, Como	83 B 3
COMO NURSING HOME, 36-38 Talbot Ave, Como	83 B 3
CONCORDE NURSING HOME, 25 Anstey St, South Perth	73 A 9
CRAIGMONT NURSING HOME, Cnr Third & Riverslea Aves, Maylands	61 D 8
CRAIGVILLE NURSING HOME, Cnr Stock & French Rds, Melville	91 C 1
CRAIGWOOD, 29 Gardner St, Como	82 E 1
CURTIN AGED PERSONS HOME, Stirling Hwy, Mosman Park	80 C 6
DALE COTTAGES, 17 Coombe Ave, Armadale	116 D 8
DEAN LODGE, Bullcreek Dr, Bullcreek	92 E 3
DIANELLA MASONIC VILLAGE, Cnr Cornwall St & Alexander Dr, Dianella	47 A 10
DOROTHY GENDERS VILLAGE, Cnr McCabe & Beagle Sts, Mosman Park	80 E 7
DUNCRAIG RETIREMENT VILLAGE (Catholic), Marmion Ave, Duncraig	30 D 7
ELIMATTA, (Uniting Church), 45 Alexander Dr, Menora	61 A 5
ELLIS MASONIC VILLAGE, Lavinia Cr, Coolbellup	101 E 2
ELLOURA LODGE HOSTEL, (Salvation Army) 31 Williams Rd, Nedlands	71 E 7
EMBLETON, Cnr Broun Ave & Drake St, Embleton	62 A 2
EUROKA VILLAGE (Uniting Church), Cnr Flora Tce and Margaret St, Waterman	30 C 10
FAIRHAVEN HOSTEL, Pinetree Cl, Armadale	116 C 6
FLORENCE HUMMERSTON LODGE & CLEAVER COTTAGE, 67 Cleaver St, West Perth	60 D 9
FRASER HOUSE (Uniting Church), 73 Mill Point Rd, South Perth	72 D 6
FREDERICK GUEST VILLAGE, Gleddon Rd, Bull Creek	93 A 4
FREEMAN NURSING HOME, Bullcreek Rd, Rossmoyne	93 B 3
FREMANTLE NURSING HOME, Cnr Holland & Robinson Sts, East Fremantle	91 A 4
GLENDALOUGH HOSTEL, Rawlins St, Glendalough	60 A 5
GLENDALOUGH, Rawlins St, Glendalough	60 A 5
GOLINE HOUSE, c/- Armadale - Kelmscott Hospital, Albany Hwy, Armadale	116 E 2
GORDON LODGE, Bullcreek Dr, Bullcreek	101 C 3
GRACEWOOD NURSING HOME, 18 Roebuck Dr, Salter Point	83 A 7
GRACEWOOD (Baptist), Cnr Mt Henry Rd & Roebuck Drive, Manning	83 A 7
GREVILLEA HOSTEL, Gilmore Ave, Calista	130 E 8
GWENYFRED NURSING HOME, 62 Gwenyfred Rd, South Perth	73 D 8
HALE HOUSE (Anglican), 37 Waverley Rd, Coolbellup	91 E 10
HALLS HEAD RETIREMENT VILLAGE, Hungerford Ave	164 D 4
HAMERSLEY, 441 Rokeby Rd, Subiaco	72 A 4

Name	Map Ref.
HAMILTON HILL NURSING HOME, 27 Ivermey Rd, Hamilton Hill	101 A 1
HARDEY LODGE, 57 Monmouth St, Mt Lawley	61 A 7
HARDY LODGE (Uniting Church) 57 Monmouth St, Mt Lawley	61 A 7
HARRY HUNTER REHABILITATION CENTRE (Salvation Army), Albany Hwy, Kelmscott	106 E 3
HAWTHORN, 100 Flinders St, Mt Hawthorn	60 C 5
HILLCREST SENIOR CITIZENS RESIDENCE, (Salvation Army), 23 Harvest Rd, Nth Fremantle	80 D 10
HILLCREST, 23 Harvest Rd, North Fremantle	80 D 10
HILLROYD NURSING HOME, 106 Bradford St, Coolbinia	60 E 3
HILLTOP LODGE, (Rowethorpe), Hill View Tce, Bentley (Inset Map 144)	
HILLVIEW NURSING HOME, 21 Angelo St, Armadale	116 C 7
HOLLYWOOD EVENTIDE HOME, (Salvation Army), 31 Williams Rd, Nedlands	71 E 7
HOLLYWOOD SENIOR CITIZENS VILLAGE, (Salvation Army), Monash Ave, Nedlands	71 E 7
HOME OF PEACE, 125 Thomas St, Subiaco	72 B 3
HOME OF PEACE, Walter Rd, Inglewood	61 C 3
HOWARD SOLOMON MASONIC HOSTEL NURSING HOME, 91 Hybanthus Rd, Lynwood	94 C 1
HOWARD SOLOMON NURSING HOME, 91 Hybanthus Rd, Ferndale	94 C 1
HYDE RETIREMENT VILLAGE, 2 James St, Bassendean	63 A 2
IDA MANN HOSTEL, 134 Whatley Cr, Maylands	61 D 7
ILLAWONG VILLAGE HOSTEL, 1 Rodd Pl, Hamilton Hill	101 C 3
ITALIAN COMMUNITY NURSING HOME, 33 Kent Rd, Marangaroo	32 A 5
JACARANDA LODGE, 55 Belgrade Rd, Wanneroo	20 E 8
JALON, 47 Goldsworthy Rd, Claremont	71 B 10
JAMES BROWN HOSTEL (Anglican), 171 Albert St, Osborne Park	46 A 10
JAMES BROWN HOUSE, 171 Albert St, Osborne Park	46 A 10
JAMES T. POLLARD CONVALESCENT HOSPITAL, 19 Market St, Guildford	49 C 10
JE MURRAY HOME, 16 Deerness Wy, Armadale	116 D 8
JOONDANNA HOSTEL, (Church of Christ), 136 Edinboro St, Joondanna	60 C 4
JOONDANNA VILLAGE LODGE, 5-9 Osborne St, Joondanna	60 D 3
JOONDANNA VILLAGE (Churches of Christ) 5-9 Osborne St, Joondanna	60 D 3
JOSEPH COOK HOSTEL, 2 Houtmans Rd, Rossmoyne	93 B 1
KEITH SIMPSON MASONIC VILLAGE, Cnr Renegade Wy & Hepburn Ave, Kingsley	31 D 3
KIMBERLEY NURSING HOME, 78 Kimberley St, Leederville	60 C 9
KINGSLEY RETIREMENT VILLAGE, 186 Twickenham Dr, Kingsley	31 B 1
KOH-I-NOOR, 34-36 Pangbourne St, Wembley	59 E 9
KWINANA NURSING HOME, Lot 643 Gilmore Ave	130 E 8
LADY LAWLEY COTTAGE BY THE SEA, 8 Gibney St, Mosman Park	80 C 5
LAKELAND RETIREMENT VILLAGE, Bibra Dr, Bibra Lake	102 B 5
LAKEVIEW LODGE, 5 Britannia Rd, Leederville	60 C 7
LATHLAIN NURSING HOME, Cnr Star & Archer Sts, Carlisle	74 B 7
LE FANU COURT (Anglican), 5-7 Anstey St, South Perth	73 A 9
LEAWEENA LODGE, Cnr Alfred Rd & Lisle St, Mt Claremont	71 A 6
LEEMING RETIREMENT VILLAGE, Cnr Beckley Ci & Theakeston Grn	92 E 8
LEFROY HOSTEL, (Anglican), 22 Lefroy Rd, Bull Creek	93 B 5
LEIGHTON, 40 Florence St, West Perth	60 E 9
LESLIE A. WATSON NURSING HOME, 18 Roebuck Dr, Salter Point	83 A 7
LISLE LODGE AGED PEOPLES HOME, Cnr Alfred Rd & Lisle St, Mt Claremont	71 A 6
LITTLE SISTERS OF THE POOR, Rawlin St, Glendalough	60 A 5
LUCY CREETH, 92 McCabe St, Mosman Park	80 E 7
MANDURAH NURSING HOME, 164 Hungerford Ave, Halls Head	164 D 3
MANDURAH RETIREMENT LODGE, Third Ave, Mandurah	165 C 3
MANNING BAPTIST HOMES, Roebuck Dr, Como	83 A 8
MANNING SENIOR CITIZENS CENTRE, 3 Downey Dr, Manning	83 A 6
MARIST LODGE (Catholic), 12 Lapage St, Belmont	74 C 1
MARJORIE APPLETON HOUSE (Anglican), Freedman Rd, Menora	61 A 4
MAURICE ZEFFERT MEMORIAL HOME, 91 Woodrow Ave St, Dianella	61 A 1
MAURICE ZEFFERT MEMORIAL HOME, 91 Woodrow Ave, Yokine	61 A 1
MAYFLOWER HOMES, (Uniting Church), 179 Bagot Rd, Subiaco	72 B 2
MCDOUGALL PARK NURSING HOME, 18 Ley St, Como	83 A 5
MEATH HOME, (Anglican), 77 Lynn St, Trigg	44 D 4
MELVISTA NURSING HOME, 20 Betty St, Nedlands	71 C 10
MERCYVILLE, (Catholic), 252 Camberwarra Dr, Craigie	23 C 5
MERTOME HOUSE, 30 Winifred Rd, Bayswater	62 B 4
MIDLAND, 44 John St, Midland	50 C 6
MOLINE HOUSE (Anglican), Cnr Deanmore Rd & Rinaldi Cr, Karrinyup	44 E 7
MON REPOS, 67 Palmerston St, Mosman Park	80 E 6
MONTROSE, 12 Grange St, Claremont	71 A 10
MORLANCOURT LADIES' REST HOME, 13 Teague St, Victoria Park	73 E 6
MOSMAN PARK NURSING HOME, 57 Palmerston St, Mosman Park	80 E 5
MOUNT HAWTHORN BAPTIST CHURCH HOME, Hobart St, Mt Hawthorn	60 D 6
MOUNT HENRY, Cloister Ave, Como	83 A 7
MOUNT SAINT CAMILLUS NURSING HOME, 185 Lewis Rd, Forrestfield	86 E 1
MT ST EMILIES, 75 Kalamunda Rd, Kalamunda	77 C 5
MURLALI LODGE, 25 Mt Henry Rd, Como	83 A 7
MURRAY RIVER NURSING HOME, Cnr Boundary Rd & Coolibah Ave, Mandurah Central	165 B 3
NAZARETH HOUSE, 84 Collick St, Hilton	91 C 9
NAZARETH HOUSE, 84 Collick St, Hilton	91 B 9
NONAREENA, 32 Alexandra Rd, East Fremantle	90 E 2
OCEAN GARDENS RETIREMENT VILLAGE, Kalinda Dr, City Beach	58 E 8
ORELIA HOSTEL, Burke Pl, Orelia	131 B 6
PARRY HOUSE (Anglican), Warlingham Dr, Lesmurdie	87 C 2
PARRY NURSING HOME, 74 Warlingham Walk, Lesmurdie	87 C 2
PENN-ROSE REST HOME, 229 James St, Guildford	49 C 10
PILGRIM HOUSE (Uniting Church), 22 Wolsely Rd, East Fremantle	90 E 1
POLLARD, 19 Market St, Guildford	63 C 1
QUADRIPLEGIC WORKSHOP & HOSTEL, Selby St, Shenton Park	71 D 2
RILEY HOUSE (Anglican), 20 Excelsior St, Shenton Park	71 E 3
RIVERSLEA LODGE (Uniting Church) 100 Guildford Rd, Mount Lawley	61 D 8
ROCKINGHAM NURSING HOME, 14 Langley St, Rockingham	136 E 5
ROWETHORPE NURSING HOME, Hayman Rd, Bentley	84 A 4
ROWETHORPE SETTLEMENT (Uniting Church), Hill View Tce, Bentley (Inset Map 144)	
ROY COLLINS MASONIC VILLAGE, 55 Alexander Drive, Menora	61 A 4
RSL WAR VETERANS' HOME, 51 Alexander Dr, Menora	61 A 4
SACRED HEART CONVENT, 40 Mary St, Highgate	61 B 9
SALVADO VILLA (Catholic), 18 Barrett St, Wembley	60 A 9
SALVATION ARMY VILLAGE HOSPITAL, 31 Williams Rd, Nedlands	71 E 7
SANDSTORM, 44 Whatley Cres, Mt Lawley	61 C 8
SANTRALLA PRIV. NURSING HOME, 16 Duncan St, Victoria Park	73 E 7
SEAFORTH SENIOR CITIZENS CENTRE, 2542 Albany Hwy, Gosnells	106 D 4
SENIOR CITIZENS CENTRE, The Avenue, Midland	50 C 8
SERPENTINE - JARRAHDALE, Lot 105 Gordin Way, Byford	135 C 3
SERVITE VILLA, 184 Edinboro St, Joondanna	60 C 3
SHERWIN LODGE HOMES (Seventh Day Adventist), Bull Creek Rd, Rossmoyne	93 B 3
SHOALWATER NURSING HOME, Cnr Fourth Ave & Coventry Rd, Shoalwater	136 C 8
SILVER CHAIN COTTAGE HOMES, 21 Wright St, Highgate	61 B 10
SILVER CHAIN NURSING ASSOCIATION, Laidlaw St, Hilton	91 C 9
SIR DAVID BRAND CENTRE (Spastic Welfare), 106 Bradford St, Coolbinia	60 E 3
SKYE, 13 Stevens St, Fremantle	1D C 6
SOUTHERN CROSS, 529 Leach Hwy, Bateman	92 D 3
ST CATHERINES HOSTEL, Williamstown Rd, Doubleview	59 B 3
ST CATHERINES, 131 Broadway, Nedlands	71 E 10
ST DAVID'S HOSTEL (Uniting Church), 19 Lawley Cr, Mt Lawley	61 B 7
ST DAVID'S NURSING HOME, 19 Lawley Cr, Mt Lawley	61 B 7
ST FLORENCE, 32 Whatley Cr, Mt Lawley	61 C 8
ST FRANCIS COURT (Anglican), 34 Robinson St, Inglewood	61 C 5
ST FRANCIS NURSING HOME, Cnr Healy & Clara Rds, Hamilton Hill	91 B 10
ST GEORGES NURSING HOME, 20 Pinaster St, Menora	61 A 4
ST IVES RETIREMENT VILLAGE, Rome Rd, Myaree	91 E 1
ST JOHN OF GOD VILLA, McCourt St, Subiaco	60 B 10
ST JOSEPHS, York St, South Perth	73 A 8
ST LUKES NURSING HOME, 429 Rokeby Rd, Subiaco	72 A 3
ST MICHAELS NURSING HOME, 53 Wasley St, North Perth	61 A 8
ST PAULS, 19 Doongalla Rd, Attadale	81 D 8
ST RITAS, 32 Queens Cr, Mt Lawley	61 C 8
ST VINCENTS HOSTEL, 224 Swan St, Guildford	49 C 10
ST VINCENTS, 224 Swan St, Guildford	49 C 10
STAN REILLY FRAIL AGED LODGE, 94 South Tce, Fremantle	1D C 6
SUBIACO NURSING HOME (Uniting Church), 137 Heytesbury Rd, Subiaco	72 A 3
SUNDOWNER HOSTEL, 416 Stirling Hwy, Claremont	80 E 1
SUNNINGDALE REST HOME, 19 Flora Tce, Waterman	30 C 9
SUNSET, Beatrice Rd, Dalkeith	81 D 3
SUNSHINE PARK HOSTEL (CWA), 10 Brady Rd, Lesmurdie	87 B 5

Name	Map	Ref.
SWAN COTTAGE HOMES RETIREMENT VILLAGE, Hill View Tce, Bentley (Inset Map 144)		
TANDARA-NINGANA NURSING HOME, Pine Ave, Swan Cottage Homes, Bentley	83	E 3
TEASDALE MASONIC VILLAGE, 19 Christmas Ave, Orelia	131	A 5
THE AVENUE NURSING HOME, 51-53 Second Ave, Mt Lawley	61	C 7
THOMAS SCOTT HOSTEL, 63 Ypres Rd, Westfield	106	B 9
TORMEY HOUSE, 67 Cleaver St, West Perth	60	D 9
TRINITY LODGE, (Rowethorpe), Hill View Tce, Bentley (Inset Map 144)		
TUOHY MEMORIAL, 22 Morrison Rd, Midland	50	B 8
TWO PINES HOSPITAL, 61 Clarkson Rd, Maylands	74	B 1
UNDERCLIFFE, 482 Great Eastern Hwy, Greenmount	65	B 1
VALENCIA NURSING HOME, Valencia Rd, Carmel	88	D 7
VICTORIA PARK EAST NURSING HOME, Cnr Alday & Burlington Sts, St James	84	B 2
VILLA DALMATIA NURSING HOME, Gorham Wy, Spearwood	101	A 5
VILLA MARIA (Sisters of Mercy), 173 Lesmurdie Rd, Lesmurdie	87	D 1
VILLA MARIA, 173 Lesmurdie Rd, Lesmurdie	87	D 1
VILLA PELLETIER HOSTEL, 48 Ruislip St, Leederville	60	B 9
VILLA PELLETIER, 48 Ruislip St, Leederville	60	B 9
VILLA TERENZIO, Cabrini Rd, Marangaroo	32	A 5
WALRIDGE LODGE, 45 Berkshire Rd, Forrestfield	76	D 8
WAMINDA HOSTEL, (Swan Cottage Homes), Adie Ct, Bentley (Inset Map 144)		
WARWICK NURSING HOME, 98 Ellersdale Ave, Warwick	31	E 8
WARWICK VILLAGE (Churches of Christ) Cnr Ellersdale Ave & Erindale Rd, Warwick	31	E 8
WEARNE HOSTEL, 40 Marine Pde, Cottesloe	80	C 5
WEARNE HOSTEL, Cnr Marine Pde & Warton St, Cottesloe	80	C 5
WEARNE HOUSE (Anglican), 7 Leslie St, Mandurah	164	E 2
WEARNE NURSING HOME, 7 Leslie St, Mandurah Central	164	E 2
WEERONGA HOMES, Cnr Worley & Archibald Sts, Willagee	91	E 5
WESTON LODGE, 31 Williams Rd, Nedlands	71	E 7
WILLIAM BUCKLEY HOSTEL, 60 Stalker Rd, Gosnells	96	B 9
WILSON VILLAGE, Eureka Rd, Wilson	84	A 7
WOODLANDS VILLAGE, 52 Liege St, Woodlands	59	C 2
WOODVILLE HOUSE, 76 Clayton Rd, Helena Valley	65	B 4
WYBALENA, (Baptist), 96 Hobart St, Mt Hawthorn	60	D 6
YALLAMBEE AGED PERSONS HOME, Fenton St, Mundaring	68	B 1

OFF ROAD VEHICLE AREAS

Name	Map	Ref.
AMAROO, Toodyay Rd	38	D 6
CHIDLOW, Old Northam Rd	56	C 3
GNANGARA, Gnangara Rd	27	B 7
MEDINA, Thomas Rd	130	C 3
NOWERGUP, Wattle Ave East	13	B 7
PORT KENNEDY	156	C 4

OVALS, PARKS, RESERVES & LEISURE CENTRES

Name	Map	Ref.
ABBETT PARK, Scarborough	44	D 9
ABRAHAM FRANCE RESERVE, Mandurah	163	A 9
ADDLESTONE RESERVE, Embleton	48	B10
ADVENTURE WORLD Bibra Lake	102	A 4
AGINCOURT RESERVE, Willetton	93	C 5
ALAN ANDERSON PARK, Bickley	88	B 4
ALAN EDWARDS PARK, Kardinya	91	E 8
ALAN MADDEN PARK, Bateman	92	D 7
ALBOURNE PARK, Balga	46	B 2
ALDERBURY RESERVE, Floreat	59	B10
ALEXANDER HEIGHTS PARK, Alexander Heights	33	B 5
ALEXANDER PARK, Menora	61	A 5
ALF BROOKS PARK, Bayswater	62	B 7
ALF CURLEWIS GARDENS, Perth City	1C	E 3
ALFRED POWELL PARK, Cooloongup	137	D 9
ALFRED SKEET OVAL, Forrestdale	114	D 6
ALISON HARRIS PARK, Kardinya	91	E 9
ALLAN HILL PARK, Morley	48	C 7
ALLEN PARK, Swanbourne	70	D 9
ALMA PARK, Fremantle	1D	C 6
ALMERIA PARK, Upper Swan	29	E 1
ANAWIN PARK, Ballajura	33	C 8
ANNING PARK, South Lake	102	D 9
ANNIVERSARY PARK, Rockingham	137	C 8
ANZAC TERRACE RESERVE, Bassendean	49	A10
APEX PARK, Medina	130	C 6
APEX PARK, Mt Pleasant	82	E 6
ARBOR PARK, Morley	48	D 6
ARBUCKLE RESERVE, Innaloo	45	C 8
ARMADALE SETTLERS COMMON, Bedfordale	117	C 8
ARMSTRONG PARK, Huntingdale	95	C 9
ASCOT PARK Redcliffe	63	A10
ASCOT WATER PLAYGROUND Ascot	62	E 8
ASHFIELD RESERVE, Ashfield	62	E 3
ASHINGTON CHATTON RESERVE, Dianella	47	B 9
ATTADALE RESERVE, Attadale	81	D 7
AUBIN PARK, Bibra Lake	102	D 3
AVON VALLEY NATIONAL PARK, Swan Shire (See Inset Map 6)	12	E 1
AXON PARK, Subiaco	72	B 1
A.L. RICHARDSON RESERVE, Ardross	82	C 9
A.P. HINDS PARK, Bayswater	62	C 7
A.S. LUKETINA PARK, Wembley Downs	59	B 5

Name	Map	Ref.
BADEN POWELL RESERVE, Ardross	82	B 8
BAKER SQUARE, Hamilton Hill	101	A 1
BALCATTA RESERVE, Balcatta	45	E 3
BALGA RESERVE, Balga	32	C10
BANDY PARK, Coolbinia	60	D 3
BANJUP MEMORIAL RESERVE, Banjup	113	E 3
BANKS RESERVE, Mt Lawley	61	C10
BARBLETT OVAL, Curtin University, Bentley (Facing Map 135)		
BARDON PARK, Maylands	61	D 8
BARLEE PARK, Mundaring	68	A 3
BARRACUDA PARK, Willetton	93	B 7
BARRIDALE PARK, Kingsley	31	C 2
BARWON PARK, Craigie	23	C 5
BASSENDEAN IMPROVEMENT CENTRE, Bassendean	63	A 1
BASSENDEAN OVAL Bassendean	63	B 1
BASSETT RESERVE, Coolbellup	92	A10
BATEMAN PARK, Brentwood	93	A 3
BATH STREET RESERVE, Maylands	62	A 9
BAVICH PARK, Spearwood	101	B 4
BAY VIEW PARK, Mosman Park	80	E 5
BAYSWATER OVAL Bayswater	62	A 5
BAYSWATER RIVERSIDE GARDENS, Bayswater	62	C 7
BAYVIEW PARK, Ballajura	33	D 6
BEALE PARK, Spearwood	101	B 6
BEASLEY PARK, Leeming	93	B 9
BEATON PARK, Dalkeith	81	E 3
BEATTY PARK, North Perth	60	E 9
BEAUFORT PARK, Bedford	61	E 4
BEDALE PARK, Swan View	51	C 8
BEECROFT PARK, City Beach	58	E 6
BELDON PARK, Beldon	23	C 3
BELL PARK, Rockingham	137	A 4
BELLA CUMMING RESERVE, Mundijong	143	A 5
BELROSE PARK, Kallaroo	23	B 8
BENNETT PARK, Doubleview	59	A 1
BENTLEY PARK, Stoneville	54	B 4
BERNICE HARGRAVE RESERVE, Westfield	106	B10
BERRINGA PARK, Maylands	61	E 9
BERT WRIGHT PARK, Bayswater	62	B 5
BERYL PLACE RESERVE, Mt Pleasant	92	E 1
BEVERLEY - MURCHISON RESERVE, Coolbinia	60	E 3
BICKLEY OUTDOOR RECREATION CENTRE, Harding Rd, Lesmurdie	87	B 9
BICKLEY RECREATION GROUND, Bickley	88	C 4
BILL BENNETT PARK, Applecross	82	C 6
BILL BROWN PARK, Leeming	93	B 8
BILL DIXON PARK, Kardinya	91	D 8
BILL ELLSON RESERVE, Bateman	92	D 4
BILL MCGRATH, RESERVE, Kensington	73	D 9
BILL SHAW RESERVE, Lesmurdie	87	E 3
BINBROOK PARK, Darlington	66	B 4
BINDAREE ROTARY PARK, Kingsley	31	E 2
BINDARING PARK, Bassendean	63	B 3

Name	Map	Ref.
BIRDWOOD SQUARE, Perth	61	A10
BIRRALEE PARK, Innaloo	45	C 9
BISHOP PARK, Spearwood	101	B 8
BLACKALL RESERVE, Greenwood	31	C 5
BLACKBOY HILL COMMEMORATIVE SITE, Greenmount	51	B10
BLACKBOY PARK, Mullaloo	23	A 5
BLACKBURN PARK, South Lake	102	C 7
BLACKMORE PARK, Girrawheen	32	B 8
BLUE GUM RESERVE, Brentwood	92	D 1
BLUE LAKE PARK, Joondalup	19	C 2
BOB BLACKBURN RESERVE, Armadale	116	C 2
BOB GORDON RESERVE, Bull Creek	92	E 6
BODKIN PARK, Waterford	83	C 7
BOLD PARK, City Beach	59	A 8
BOORABILLA PARK, Greenmount	51	D 9
BORRELLO PARK, Roleystone	108	B 8
BORTOLO PARK, Greenfields	163	D10
BOSWORTH RESERVE, Banjup	113	C 4
BOTANIC GARDENS, Perth	72	C 5
BRADEN PARK, Marmion	30	C 8
BRADLEY RESERVE, Innaloo	45	B 9
BRAITHWAITE PARK, Mt Hawthorn	60	C 5
BRAND DRIVE PLAYING FIELDS, Curtin University, Bentley (Facing Map 135)		
BREAR PARK, Mt Lawley	61	C 6
BRECKLER PARK, Dianella	47	A10
BRIAN BURKE RESERVE, Balga	32	C10
BRICKWOOD RESERVE, Byford	135	C 4
BRIDGEWATER RESERVE, Kallaroo	23	C 6
BRIGATTI GARDENS, Highgate	61	B10
BRIGGS PARK, Byford	135	C 3
BROOKSIDE PARK, Parkerville	53	C 6
BROUN PARK, Embleton	48	B10
BROWN PARK, Mosman Park	80	E 6
BROWN PARK, Swan View	51	C 8
BRUCE LEE RESERVE, Beaconsfield	90	E 7
BRYAN GELL RESERVE, Westfield	106	C 9
BRYAN MANWARING RESERVE, Medina	130	D 4
BRYANT PARK, Jandakot	103	A 9
BUCKINGHAM RESERVE, Banjup	113	D 8
BULL CREEK RESERVE, Bull Creek	93	B 3
BUNGAREE OVAL, Rockingham	137	B 8
BUNGENDORE PARK, Bedfordale	117	B10
BUNYA RESERVE, Noranda	47	C 5
BURKINSHAW PARK, Glen Forrest	66	D 2
BURRENDAH RESERVE, Willetton	93	C 5
BURTON PARK, Greenmount	65	E 1
BUTLERS RESERVE, Scarborough	58	E 2
BUTTERWORTH RESERVE, Koondoola	33	A 8
BYFIELD PARK, Parkerville	53	C 5
CABRINI RESERVE, Marangaroo	32	A 5
CAIRNHILL PARK, Greenmount	65	D 1
CALISTA OVAL, Calista	130	E 7

Name	Map	Ref.
CAMBERWARRA RESERVE, Craigie	23	D 7
CAMBERWELL PARK, Balga	46	B 1
CAMFIELD PARK, Greenmount	66	A 1
CANDLEWOOD PARK, Joondalup	19	D 2
CANNING VALE OVAL, Langford	94	D 4
CARATTI PARK, Stirling	45	E 9
CAREEBA PARK, Rockingham	137	D 6
CARLISLE RESERVE, Carlisle	74	D 9
CARMEL RECREATION, Carmel	88	C 6
CARMEL RESERVE, Carmel	88	D 7
CASTLE FUN PARK Halls Head	164	D 4
CASTLECRAG PARK, Kallaroo	23	A 7
CATHERINE POINT RESERVE, Hamilton Hill	100	C 1
CAULFIELD RESERVE, Willetton	93	E 3
CAVERSHAM WILDLIFE PARK & ZOO West Swan	35	D 10
CELEBRATION PARK, Balga	32	A 10
CENTENARY PARK, Belmont	62	D 10
CENTENARY PARK, Wilson	84	A 7
CENTRAL PARK, (Newburn Park), Mandurah	164	E 1
CHALLENGER RESERVE, Manning	83	C 7
CHARLES HOOK PARK, Huntingdale	95	D 8
CHARLES NEWMAN GARDEN, Bayswater	62	C 6
CHARLES PATERSON PARK, Victoria Park	73	D 5
CHARLES RILEY RESERVE, North Beach	44	D 3
CHARLES VERYARD RESERVE, North Perth	60	D 7
CHARNWOOD RESERVE, Two Rocks	2	C 2
CHARONIA RESERVE, Mullaloo	23	B 4
CHIDLEY POINT RESERVE, Mosman Park	81	A 7
CHIDLOW RECREATION GROUND, Chidlow	56	D 2
CHISHAM OVAL, Parmelia	131	B 7
CHRISTCHURCH GRAMMAR PLAYING FIELDS, Mt Claremont	70	E 4
CHRISTOWE PARK, Swan View	51	C 7
CHURCHILL PARK, Rockingham	137	A 4
CHURTON RESERVE, Warwick	31	D 8
CITY BEACH OVAL, City Beach	58	D 9
CITY OF STIRLING SPORTS GROUND, Balcatta	46	A 6
CLAREMONT OVAL Claremont	71	B 8
CLAREMONT PARK, Claremont	71	B 10
CLARKO RESERVE, Trigg	44	C 5
CLARKSON RESERVE, Maylands	74	B 1
CLAUGHTON RESERVE, Bayswater	62	E 7
CLIFF SADLIER V.C. MEMORIAL PARK, Daglish	71	D 2
CLIFTON PARK, Chidlow	56	C 1
CLIFTON RESERVE, Canning Vale	104	A 4
CLYDESDALE PARK, South Perth	73	A 8
COASTAL PARK, Henderson	111	A 10

Name	Map	Ref.
COBB DRABBLE RESERVE, Wembley Downs	58	D 3
COHUNU WILDLIFE SANCTUARY Martin	107	B 3
COKER PARK, Cannington	84	E 5
COLIN VENTNOR RESERVE, Scarborough	58	D 2
COLLEGE PARK, Nedlands	71	C 10
COLLERAN PARK, Booragoon	92	C 1
COLLIER PARK, Swan View	51	B 8
COLLIER RESERVE, Como	83	C 2
COLLINS OVAL, Como	83	C 2
COLLINS PARK, Willetton	93	E 5
COMER RESERVE, Como	82	E 1
COMMONWEALTH HOCKEY STADIUM Curtin University, Bentley, (Facing Map 135)	135	B 9
CONGDON STREET RESERVE, Cottesloe	80	E 2
CONWAY RESERVE, Balcatta	46	B 7
COPLEY PARK, Mt Lawley	61	C 7
CORALBERRY VERBENA RESERVE, Dianella	46	E 5
COTTESLOE OVAL, Cottesloe	80	C 3
COUN SMITH RESERVE, Eden Hill	48	D 9
COWDEN PARK, Leederville	60	B 9
CRACKNELL PARK, Rivervale	74	A 3
CRACOVIA SPORTING CENTRE Beechboro	48	D 1
CRESSWELL PARK, Swanbourne	70	E 8
CREYK PARK, Armadale	116	D 2
CRIMEA PARK, Morley	48	A 7
CROATIA HOUSE SPORTS GROUND, Gwelup	45	C 6
CROSS PARK, Roleystone	107	E 7
DALKEITH OVAL, Dalkeith	81	C 3
DALKEITH RECREATION, Dalkeith	81	C 2
DALMATINAC PARK, Spearwood	101	A 4
DALRYMPLE PARK, Mandurah	164	E 2
DARLINGTON PARK, Darlington	66	A 4
DAVID BEN-GURION PARK, Dianella	61	B 1
DAVID CRUICKSHANK RESERVE, Dalkeith	81	C 3
DAVID VINCENT PARK, Kensington	73	C 9
DAVIES PARK, Maida Vale	76	D 1
DAVILAK OVAL, Hamilton Hill	100	E 2
DAVIS OVAL, Mosman Park	80	D 5
DAWSON PARK, Forrestfield	76	B 7
DE LACY RESERVE, Maylands	62	A 9
DE MARCHI PARK, North Lake	102	A 1
DEANMORE DUKE RESERVE, Karrinyup	44	E 7
DEANMORE SQUARE, Scarborough	44	D 10
DEEP WATER POINT, Mt Pleasant	82	E 8
DEEPDENE PARK, Wattleup	121	D 2
DENIS DE YOUNG RESERVE, Banjup	113	E 9
DES PENMAN MEMORIAL RESERVE, Nollamara	46	C 6
DESCHAMP RESERVE, Noranda	48	A 6
DICK PIERCY PARK, Kardinya	92	A 6
DISBREY PARK, Scarborough	58	E 2
DIXON RESERVE, Hamilton Hill	100	E 1
DIZZYLAMB PARK Karaborup Rd, Carabooda	8	B 5

Name	Map	Ref.
DOG SWAMP, Yokine	60	D 3
DOM SERRA GROVE, Jolimont	71	E 1
DON CUTHBERTSON RESERVE, Cooloongup	137	E 8
DORRIEN GARDENS West Perth	60	E 9
DRAPER PARK, Mahogany Creek	67	C 1
DRAYCOTT PARK, Karrinyup	44	E 5
DUBOVE PARK, Spearwood	101	C 4
DUDLEY HARTREE PARK, Leeming	92	E 8
DUFFIELD RESERVE, Bibra Lake	102	D 3
DURDHAM PARK, Bicton	81	A 9
EAST FREMANTLE OVAL East Fremantle	90	E 3
EATON PARK, Noranda	47	C 4
EDISON STREET RESERVE, Dianella	47	B 7
EDWARDES PARK, Spearwood	101	B 7
EGLINTON AINTREE RESERVE, Hamersley	31	D 10
ELDER PARK, Bellevue	65	A 1
ELIZA CAVE RESERVE, Bibra Lake	102	C 5
ELIZA PARK, Hamilton Hill	101	C 3
ELIZABETH MANION PARK, Bull Creek	93	B 6
ELIZABETHAN VILLAGE Canns Rd, Bedfordale	117	B 4
ELLEN BROOK NATURE RESERVE,	166	A 7
ELSIE AUSTIN RESERVE, Mt Helena	55	B 5
ELSTEAD RESERVE, Morley	48	B 9
EMANDER RESERVE, Dianella	47	C 8
EMBERSON RESERVE, Morley	48	B 7
EMERALD PARK, Edgewater	24	A 2
EMMA TREEBY RESERVE, Banjup	113	C 3
EMMS RESERVE, High Wycombe	64	B 8
EMPIRE AVENUE RESERVE, Wembley Downs	59	A 5
ENRIGHT RESERVE, Hamilton Hill	101	B 1
ERIC SILBERT GARDENS	1C	D 2
ERIC SINGLETON BIRD SANCTUARY, Bayswater	62	C 7
ERN CLARK ATHLETIC CENTRE, Cannington	84	E 6
ERN HALLIDAY RECREATION CAMP, Hillarys	30	A 1
ERN STAPLETON RESERVE, Attadale	81	D 8
ERNEST JOHNSON OVAL, South Perth	73	A 10
ERNEST WILD PARK, Leeming	93	C 8
EROS PLACE RESERVE, San Remo	163	C 1
ESPLANADE RESERVE, THE, Fremantle	1D	B 6
ESPLANADE, THE, Perth	1C	E 3
EVERSDEN RESERVE, Lesmurdie	87	C 1
E.G. SMITH FIELD, Mosman Park	81	A 6
E.J. CHAPMAN PLAYGROUND, East Fremantle	80	E 9
FAIRFAX PARK, Swan View	51	C 7
FALCON OVAL, Falcon	162A	C 2
FALLS PARK, Hovea	53	B 5
FANCOTE PARK, Kelmscott	106	D 7
FAULKNER PARK, Cloverdale	74	D 4
FAULL PARK, Inglewood	61	C 6
FAWELL PARK, Herne Hill	36	D 4
FERNDALE RESERVE, Ferndale	84	C 10

Name	Map	Ref.
FERNHURST CRESCENT RESERVE, Balga	46	D 2
FERRARA RESERVE, Girrawheen	32	D 7
FERRES RESERVE, Bibra Lake	102	C 3
FISH MARKET RESERVE, Guildford	49	B 10
FLEMING RESERVE, High Wycombe	64	B 10
FLETCHER PARK, Carlisle	74	C 7
FLETCHER PARK, Lesmurdie	87	D 1
FLETCHER PARK, Wungong	126	D 2
FLORA TERRACE RESERVE, Lesmurdie	87	D 3
FLOREAT OVAL, Floreat	59	B 9
FLORENCE HUMMERSTON RESERVE, Perth	1C	D 2
FORESHORE 1, Nedlands	81	E 1
FORESHORE 2, Dalkeith	81	E 3
FORREST PARK, Mt Lawley	61	B 9
FORREST RESERVE, Padbury	23	D 9
FORSTER PARK, Cloverdale	75	A 6
FRANK CANN PARK, Kardinya	91	D 8
FRANK GIBSON PARK, Fremantle	90	E 4
FRANKLAND PARK, Wattleup	122	D 3
FRASER PARK, East Victoria Park	84	A 1
FRED JACOBY PARK, Mundaring Weir (Inset Map 79)		
FRED JOHNSON PARK, Bull Creek	93	A 6
FRED JONES RESERVE, Bicton	91	A 1
FREDERICK BALDWIN PARK, Kardinya	91	E 6
FREMANTLE OVAL Fremantle	1D	C 5
FREMANTLE PARK, Fremantle	1D	C 4
FRYE PARK, Kelmscott	106	E 7
F.J. BEALES PARK, Morley	47	E 7
GAIRLOCH RESERVE, Applecross	82	C 6
GALLUCCIO RESERVE, Balga	46	B 4
GARDEN PARK, Wanneroo	21	A 5
GARVEY PARK, Redcliffe	63	A 5
GEMMELL PARK, Bull Creek	92	E 4
GENDERS PARK, Mosman Park	80	E 7
GENEFF PARK, Sorrento	30	B 5
GEO LITHGO RESERVE, Bicton	81	B 10
GEO THOMPSON PARK, Palmyra	91	B 2
GEORGE BURNETT PARK, Karawara	83	C 5
GEORGE FOSTER RESERVE, Golden Bay	158	D 9
GEORGE SEARS PARK, Greenwood	32	A 5
GEORGE SPRIGGS RESERVE, Pickering Brook	88	E 10
GEORGE WELBY PARK, Bateman	92	E 6
GIBBNEY RESERVE, Maylands	62	A 7
GIBBON PARK, Mosman Park	80	C 6
GIBBS PARK, Maddington	96	B 3
GIL CHALWELL RESERVE, Banjup	113	E 6
GILBERT FRASER RESERVE, North Fremantle	90	D 1
GLASSON PARK, East Fremantle	90	D 3
GLEN MIA PARK, South Lake	102	C 8
GLEN PARK, Darlington	66	A 6

287

	Map Ref.
GLENGARRY PARK, Duncraig	31 B 6
GOLDING READ RESERVE, Dianella	47 A 7
GOODCHILD OVAL, Bellevue	64 E 1
GOODCHILD PARK, Hamilton Hill	101 B 2
GOODRIDGE CENTRE Jolimont	71 D 1
GOORALONG PARK, Jarrahdale	152 C 7
GOOSEBERRY HILL NATIONAL PARK Helena Valley	65 C 8
GOOSEBERRY HILL RECREATION RESERVE, Gooseberry Hill	77 D 2
GORDON RESERVE, Dianella	47 B 6
GOSNELLS RECREATION GROUND, Gosnells	96 B 8
GOURLEY PARK, East Fremantle	90 D 1
GRADIENT PARK, Beldon	23 C 5
GRAND PROMENADE RESERVE, Bedford	61 D 3
GRANT MARINE PARK, Cottesloe	70 C 10
GREEN PLACE RESERVE, Mosman Park	81 A 6
GREENMOUNT NATIONAL PARK Greenmount	65 D 2
GREENSLADE RESERVE, Spearwood	101 C 6
GRENVILLE RESERVE, Tuart Hill	60 C 1
GRIMREY PARK, Lockridge	49 B 6
GROVE FARM RESERVE, Ascot	62 C 10
GUMBLOSSOM PARK, Quinns Rocks	10 B 10
GUS WEIMAR PARK, Morley	48 D 7
GWYNNE PARK, Armadale	116 C 8
G.O. EDWARDS PARK, Victoria Park	73 E 5
HAGAN PARK, Munster	101 B 10
HAGART PARK, Lockridge	49 A 5
HAIG PARK, East Perth	73 C 2
HAINSWORTH PARK, Girrawheen	32 D 8
HALE OVAL, Kings Park	72 C 3
HALLIDAY PARK, Bayswater	62 B 4
HALLS PARK, Halls Head	164 E 1
HAMER PARK, Mt Lawley	61 B 5
HARDEY PARK, Rivervale	74 B 2
HARGREAVES PARK, Coolbellup	101 D 1
HAROLD BOAS GARDENS, West Perth	1C D 1
HAROLD FIELD RESERVE, Kardinya	92 A 7
HAROLD ROSSITER PARK, Kensington	73 D 10
HARPER PARK, Midland	50 A 8
HARRY BAILEY PARK, Willagee	91 D 5
HARRY BAKER PARK, Leeming	93 A 9
HARRY BUCKLEY PARK, Bateman	92 D 5
HARRY CLEMENS RESERVE, Myaree	91 E 1
HARRY GOSE RESERVE, Bicton	81 A 10
HARRY McGUIGAN PARK, Medina	130 E 5
HARRY RISEBOROUGH OVAL, Mundaring	54 C 10
HARRY SANDON PARK, Attadale	81 E 9
HARRY WARING MARSUPIAL RESERVE, Wattleup	112 C 9
HARTFIELD PARK, Forrestfield	86 B 1
HARVEY FIELD, Cottesloe	80 C 3

	Map Ref.
HARWOOD PARK, Jandakot	112 D 3
HATFIELD PARK, Booragoon	92 C 2
HAWKER PARK, Warwick	31 C 7
HAWTHORNE PARK, Victoria Park	73 D 8
HEATHRIDGE PARK, Heathridge	23 C 1
HELENA VALLEY RECREATION GROUND, Helena Valley	65 C 4
HENDERSON PARK, Jolimont	59 E 10
HENNESSY PARK, Orelia	131 B 5
HENRY JEFFERY OVAL, East Fremantle	80 E 9
HENRY SUTTON GROVE, Halls Head	164 D 1
HENSMAN PARK, South Perth	73 A 9
HERB ELLIOTT OVAL, Karrinyup	44 D 7
HERDSMAN LAKE WILDLIFE CENTRE, Churchlands	59 D 7
HERDSMAN LAKE, Churchlands	59 D 5
HERITAGE PARK, Balga	32 B 9
HESTER PARK, Langford	85 A 10
HEWETT PARK, Balga	32 B 9
HIGGINS PARK, St. James	84 A 3
HIGHVIEW PARK, Nedlands	71 D 6
HILL PARK, Winthrop	92 B 5
HILLARYS PARK, Hillarys	30 B 2
HILLCREST PARK, Bayswater	62 A 3
HILTON PARK, Hilton	91 A 8
HOBBS PARK, Hamilton Hill	91 C 10
HOLDEN RESERVE, Noranda	47 E 5
HOLDSWORTH PARK, Wattleup	112 A 10
HOLLIS PARK, South Fremantle	90 D 10
HOP BUSH PARK, South Lake	102 C 7
HORRIE LONG RESERVE, Fremantle	90 D 4
HOSSACK RESERVE, Lynwood	94 B 3
HOUGHTON PARK, Bayswater	48 C 10
HUDSON PARK, Girrawheen	32 C 7
HULL PARK, Beechboro	49 A 3
HYDE PARK Perth	61 A 9
INGLEWOOD OVAL Inglewood	61 B 5
ISTED RESERVE, Hamilton Hill	101 B 2
IVORY PARK, Noranda	47 E 4
I.G. HANDCOCK PLAYGROUND, East Fremantle	81 A 9
JABE DODD PARK, Mosman Park	80 E 5
JACK IRELAND PARK, Mandurah	165 C 2
JACK JEFFERY PARK, Kardinya	91 E 9
JACK MANN OVAL, Middle Swan	50 D 3
JACKADDER LAKE, Woodlands	59 C 2
JACKANA PARK, Ballajura	33 E 7
JAMES COOK PARK, Hillarys	23 B 9
JAMES MILLER OVAL, Manning	83 A 6
JAMES OVAL, University of W.A. (Inset Map 120)	72 A 8
JAMES PATERSON PARK, North Lake	92 B 9
JARRAHDALE OVAL, Jarrahdale	153 A 5
JARVIS PARK, Coolbellup	91 D 10
JASON RESERVE, Balcatta	46 B 7
JASPER GREEN RESERVE, Cottesloe	70 E 10

	Map Ref.
JEAN GARVEY PARK, Gosnells	106 A 3
JEFF JOSEPH RESERVE, Applecross	82 C 4
JIM AINSWORTH RESERVE, Ardross	82 C 9
JOE RICE PLAYGROUND, Wembley Downs	59 A 3
JOHN CONNELL RESERVE, Bicton	91 A 1
JOHN CONNELL RESERVE, Leeming	103 C 1
JOHN CREANEY PARK, Bull Creek	93 A 5
JOHN DICKENSON RESERVE, Bicton	91 A 1
JOHN DUNN MEMORIAL PARK, Kelmscott	106 C 10
JOHN D'ORAZIO PARK, Bayswater	62 B 6
JOHN FORREST NATIONAL PARK Swan View	52 B 5
JOHN K. LYON RESERVE, Doubleview	59 A 1
JOHN MOLONEY PARK, Marangaroo	32 C 5
JOHN MORGAN RESERVE, Glen Forrest	66 D 2
JOHN TAYLOR PARK, Parkerville	53 D 5
JOHN TONKIN PARK, East Fremantle	80 D 9
JONES PASKIN RESERVE, Balcatta	46 A 4
JORGENSEN PARK, Kalamunda	77 E 6
JUBILEE PARK, City Beach	58 C 10
JUBILEE RESERVE, Eden Hill	48 E 8
JUDY PANNELL RESERVE, Wilson	84 B 7
JUETT PARK, Winthrop	92 B 4
JUNIPER RESERVE, Duncraig	31 B 8
J. DOLAN RESERVE, East Fremantle	90 D 2
J. MILLAR PARK, Kalamunda	77 E 10
J.H. ABRAHAMS RESERVE, Crawley	72 A 10
KAGOSHIMA PARK, Victoria Park	73 E 4
KALAMUNDA NATIONAL PARK Piesse Brook	78 A 3
KARINGA RESERVE, San Remo	160 C 10
KAROONDA PARK, Booragoon	92 C 2
KARRAGULLEN OVAL, Karragullen	109 A 1
KARRINYUP RECREATION RESERVE, Karrinyup	45 B 6
KATE STREET RESERVE, East Victoria Park	74 A 9
KATICH PARK, Spearwood	101 C 8
KATRINE PARK, Joondalup	19 C 3
KEANES POINT RESERVE, Peppermint Grove	81 A 3
KEEMORE PARK, Balga	46 E 1
KEITH FRAME PARK, Leederville	60 D 9
KELLY PARK, Bassendean	49 B 10
KELLY PARK, Medina	130 C 4
KEN DOUGLAS RESERVE, Mt Pleasant	82 E 10
KEN HURST PARK, Leeming	103 D 1
KING CARNIVAL FAIRGROUND Halls Head	164 D 1
KINGS MEADOW OVAL, Guildford	63 C 1
KINGS PARK Perth	72 B 4
KINGSLEY FAIRBRIDGE RESERVE, Halls Head	162 D 10
KINGSLEY PARK, Kingsley	24 B 10
KINGSWAY RESERVE Landsdale	32 B 2
KITCHENER PARK, Subiaco	72 B 1

	Map Ref.
KOONDOOLA PARK, Koondoola	33 A 7
KORBOSKY PARK, Lockridge	49 A 8
KOSTERA OVAL, Kalamunda	77 D 7
KRAEMER RESERVE, Banjup	113 E 5
KUHL PARK, Westfield	106 B 9
KYILLA PARK, North Perth	60 E 5
LA GRANGE DONGARA RESERVE, Innaloo	45 C 10
LAKE LESCHENAULTIA, Chidlow	42 B 10
LAKE MONGER RESERVE, Wembley	60 A 7
LANGFORD PARK, Jarrahdale	153 A 3
LANGFORD SPORTS CENTRE, Langford	95 A 3
LANGLEY PARK, Perth	1C B 4
LANIUS PARK, Beechboro	49 B 5
LATHLAIN PARK Lathlain	74 A 7
LAURIE STRUTT RESERVE, Waterman	30 C 10
LAWLER PARK, Floreat	71 C 1
LAYMAN PARK, Booragoon	82 D 10
LEE PARK, East Fremantle	91 A 2
LEE RESERVE, Lathlain	74 A 5
LEEDERVILLE OVAL Leederville	60 D 8
LEES PARK, Wattleup	121 D 1
LEMONGRASS PARK, Ballajura	33 C 4
LEN McTAGGART PARK, Coogee	100 E 8
LEN PACKHAM PARK, Coolbellup	101 E 1
LEN SHEARER RESERVE, Booragoon	92 B 2
LEONARD GOOLD PARK, Kardinya	91 E 7
LES LILLEYMAN RESERVE, North Perth	60 D 5
LESMURDIE FALLS NATIONAL PARK Forrestfield	87 A 1
LESMURDIE RECREATION RESERVE, Lesmurdie	86 E 4
LESMURDIE RECREATION RESERVE, Lesmurdie	87 A 5
LEVI PARK, Yangebup	102 A 8
LIDDELL RESERVE, Girrawheen	32 A 7
LILAC HILL PARK, Caversham	49 D 7
LILBURNE RESERVE, Duncraig	30 E 3
LITTLEMORE PARK, Orelia	131 A 4
LLOYD HUGHES PARK, Kelmscott	107 A 9
LLOYD PENN PARK, Koongamia	65 B 2
LOCKE PARK, East Fremantle	90 E 3
LUCIUS PARK, Spearwood	101 A 4
LUCKEN RESERVE, South Lake	102 D 6
LUDERMAN PARK, Noranda	47 C 4
LUISINI PARK, Wangara	24 E 6
LUPINO MEMORIAL PARK, Whitby	143 D 6
MABEL DAVIES PARK, Gosnells	95 D 7
MABEL TALBOT PARK, Jolimont	71 E 1
MACAULAY PARK, Inglewood	61 C 4
MACCABEAN MEMORIAL OVAL, Yokine	61 A 1
MACDONALD RESERVE, Padbury	23 C 10
MACEDONIA PARK, Balcatta	46 A 8
MACFAULL PARK, Spearwood	101 C 5
MACLAGAN PARK, Swanbourne	70 E 8

Name	Map Ref.
MADDINGTON RECREATION, Maddington	96 A 3
MAGNOLIA PARK, Beechboro	48 D 3
MAGUIRE PARK, Beechboro	49 A 4
MAHOGANY PARK, Morley	48 C 5
MAIDA VALE RECREATION RESERVE, Maida Vale	76 E 1
MALABAR PARK, Bibra Lake	101 D 4
MAMILLIUS PARK, Coolbellup	91 E 10
MANAPOURI PARK, Joondalup	19 C 2
MANDOGALUP PIONEER RESERVE, Mandogalup	122 D 9
MANDURAHS FARMWORLD, Lakelands	161 B 8
MANN OVAL, Mosman Park	80 D 5
MANNERS HILL PARK, Peppermint Grove	80 E 4
MANNING PARK, Hamilton Hill	100 E 3
MARAPANA WILDLIFE WORLD Paganoni Rd, Karnup	159 C 8
MARCON PARK, Nollamara	46 C 5
MARGARET HARRISON PARK, Willetton	93 C 2
MARGARET RESERVE, Maylands	61 D 6
MARGUERITE SMITH RESERVE, Attadale	81 D 8
MARKET CITY PARK, Canning Vale	93 E 8
MARKET SQUARE, Subiaco	72 B 1
MARMION MARINE PARK	18 B 10
MARMION RESERVE, Myaree	91 E 2
MARRI RESERVE, Duncraig	30 E 5
MARRIOTT PARK, Boya	65 C 4
MARSHALL PARK, Midland	50 A 8
MARY CARROL PARK, Gosnells	106 C 1
MARY CRESCENT RESERVE, Eden Hill	49 A 8
MASON GARDENS, Dalkeith	81 C 1
MATHER RESERVE, Banjup	113 C 5
MATILDA BAY RESERVE, Crawley	72 A 10
MATILDA BIRKETT RESERVE, Coolbellup	101 E 3
MATT WILLIAMS RESERVE, Balga	46 C 4
MATTHEW STOTT RESERVE, Armadale	116 A 5
MATTHEWS NETBALL CENTRE Jolimont	59 D 10
MAURIE HAMER PARK, Herdsman Lake	59 C 6
MAWSON PARK, Hillarys	23 B 10
MAZZUCCHELLI PARK, Gosnells	96 C 9
MCCABE MEMORIAL PARK, North Fremantle	90 C 1
MCCALLUM PARK, Victoria Park	73 D 6
MCDOUGALL PARK, Como	83 A 5
MCGILLIVRAY OVAL, Mt Claremont	71 B 3
MCKENZIE PARK, High Wycombe	64 D 10
MCLEAN PARK, Floreat	59 B 9
MCLENNAN PARK, Madora	160 C 7
MEARES PARK, Bibra Lake	102 B 6
MEDINA OVAL, Medina	130 E 4
MELENE RESERVE, Duncraig	31 A 4
MELLER PARK, Bibra Lake	102 C 2
MELVILLE RESERVE, Melville	91 C 1
MELVISTA PARK, Nedlands	81 D 1
MEMORIAL GARDENS, Mt Lawley	61 B 7
MEMORIAL GARDENS, Victoria Park	73 E 7
MEMORIAL PARK, Armadale	116 D 6
MEMORIAL PARK, Mosman Park	80 E 5
MENZIES PARK, Mt Hawthorn	60 B 5
MERLIN STREET RESERVE, Falcon	162A E 9
MICK JAHN RESERVE, Alfred Cove	81 E 10
MICK MICHAEL PARK, West Perth	60 E 9
MIDDLETON PARK, Cloverdale	75 B 3
MIDLAND OVAL, Midland	50 C 8
MILES PARK, Cloverdale	74 E 3
MILGAR STREET RESERVE, Mandurah	163 C 8
MILGUN RESERVE, Yangebup	102 A 10
MILLETT PARK, Innaloo	45 B 10
MILLIGAN PARK, Stoneville	54 B 6
MILLINGTON RESERVE, Karrinyup	44 E 6
MILLS PARK, Beckenham	85 D 8
MINIM COVE PARK, Mosman Park	80 E 8
MINNAWARRA PARK, Armadale	116 D 6
MONACO PARK, North Lake	92 A 10
MONTAGUE HILLARY PARK, Leeming	93 A 10
MONTROSE PARK, Girrawheen	32 E 8
MONUMENT PARK, Mosman Park	80 D 6
MOOJEBING RESERVE, Bayswater	62 D 5
MORESBY ST RESERVE, Kensington	73 C 10
MORGAN PARK, Armadale	116 B 6
MORLEY RESERVE, Morley	47 E 9
MORRIS BUZACOTT RESERVE, Kardinya	92 B 7
MORRIS MUNDY RESERVE, Kensington	73 C 9
MORRISON PARK, Midvale	51 A 8
MOSES SAUNDERS PARK, Morley	48 D 7
MOSMAN PARK RESERVE, Mosman Park	80 D 6
MOSS PARK, Winthrop	92 C 5
MRS HERBERTS PARK, Claremont	81 B 1
MUELLER PARK, Subiaco	72 C 1
MUNDARING RECREATION, Mundaring	68 B 3
MUNRO RESERVE, Doubleview	45 A 9
MURDOCH PARK, Murdoch	92 D 7
NALYA PARK, Swan View	51 E 8
NANIKA PARK, Joondalup	19 C 3
NANOVICH PARK, Wanneroo	25 C 2
NASH FIELD, Mosman Park	80 D 6
NEERABUP NATIONAL PARK Nowergup	11 D 3
NEIL HAWKINS PARK, Joondalup	20 A 6
NICHOLSON RESERVE, Yangebup	102 A 9
NOEL KROLL RESERVE, Bull Creek	93 A 7
NORA HUGHES PARK, Morley	61 E 2
NORANDA SPORTING COMPLEX, Noranda	47 E 6
NORM McKENZIE RESERVE, East Fremantle	80 D 9
NORMAN PLAYGROUND, Welshpool	84 B 2
NOWERGUP LAKE FAUNA SANCTUARY, Nowergup	11 D 1
OCEAN REEF PARK, Ocean Reef	23 B 2
OKELY LORRAINE RESERVE, Carine	45 A 1
OLDING PARK, Melville	91 D 3
OLIVES RESERVE, Como	82 E 4
OLLIE WORRELL RESERVE, High Wycombe	64 B 8
ORANGE GROVE OVAL, Orange Grove	96 D 1
ORANGE GROVE PARK, Orange Grove	86 C 8
ORELIA PARK, Orelia	131 A 5
ORMOND BOWYER PARK, Kardinya	91 D 6
OTAGO RESERVE, Craigie	23 D 6
OTTAWA PARK, Beechboro	48 D 3
PACKER PARK, Kenwick	95 C 1
PAGOTTO PARK, Lesmurdie	87 B 2
PALAMINO RESERVE, Forrestdale	115 E 2
PALMERSTON SQUARE, Bassendean	63 B 2
PARIN PARK, Greenwood	32 A 4
PARKERVILLE RECREATION GROUND, Parkerville	53 D 9
PARMELIA PARK, South Fremantle	90 C 9
PARNHAM PARK, Carlisle	74 C 9
PARTRIDGE PARK, Orelia	130 E 3
PATULA PARK, Menora	61 A 4
PEACE MEMORIAL ROSE GARDENS, Nedlands	71 D 9
PEACE PARK, Spearwood	101 A 6
PEELWOOD PARADE RESERVE, Halls Head	164 C 5
PEET PARK, Kewdale	74 C 6
PENISTONE RESERVE, Greenwood	31 E 5
PERCY DOYLE RESERVE, Duncraig	30 E 7
PERENA ROCCHI RESERVE, Yangebup	102 A 10
PERRY LAKES STADIUM Floreat	71 B 1
PERTH OVAL East Perth	1C B 1
PERTH ZOOLOGICAL GARDENS Labouchere Rd, South Perth (Inset Map 100)	72 E 8
PETER BOSCI PARK, Leeming	92 E 9
PETER ELLIS PARK, Leeming	92 E 10
PEXTON MEMORIAL PLAYING FIELDS, South Guildford	64 A 1
PHILLIP JANE PARK, Leeming	93 C 8
PICKERING BROOK RECREATION, Pickering Brook	88 E 10
PICKERING PARK, Bassendean	63 B 3
PINE TREE RESERVE, High Wycombe	64 B 9
PINEY LAKES RESERVE, Winthrop	92 C 4
PIONEER PARK, Bibra Lake	102 A 2
PIONEER PARK, Forrestfield	76 A 9
PIONEER PARK, Gosnells	96 B 8
PIONEER PARK, Mt Helena	55 B 5
PIONEER RESERVE, Fremantle	1D B 5
PIONEER WORLD, Albany Hwy, Armadale	116 E 6
PITTERSEN PARK, Greenmount	65 E 1
PLATTE PARK, Beechboro	48 D 3
POINT RESERVE, Bassendean	63 C 1
POINT RESOLUTION RESERVE, Dalkeith	81 C 4
POINT WALTER RESERVE, Bicton	81 B 6
PORTREE RESERVE, Duncraig	31 A 6
POWELL RESERVE, Coogee	100 E 9
PRENDWICK RESERVE, Willetton	93 E 4
PRIES PARK, Kelmscott	106 E 4
PRINCESS MAY PARK, Fremantle	1D C 4
PROGRESS RESERVE, High Wycombe	64 C 9
PULLMAN PARK, Upper Swan	29 E 4
PUMP STATION PARK, Joondalup	19 D 4
PURLEY PARK, Lynwood	94 D 1
P.J. HANLEY PARK, Leeming	93 C 8
QUARRY PARK, Martin	96 E 10
QUEENS GARDENS East Perth	73 C 4
QUEENS PARK RESERVE, Queens Park	85 A 3
QUEENS SQUARE, Fremantle	1D C 5
RABONE PARK, Boya	65 D 5
RALPH TROTTER PARK, Kardinya	91 E 8
RANGE VIEW PARK, High Wycombe	64 C 10
RANKIN GARDENS, Subiaco	72 A 2
RAPHAEL PARK, Victoria Park	73 D 7
RAY OWEN RESERVE, Lesmurdie	87 C 3
RAY O'CONNOR RESERVE, Karrinyup	45 A 2
READ PARK, Victoria Park	73 E 8
READER RESERVE, Yokine	60 D 2
REG BOND RESERVE, Viveash	50 B 3
REG BOURKE RESERVE, Bull Creek	93 A 4
REG WILLIAMS RESERVE, Armadale	116 B 6
REID OVAL, Forrestfield	86 B 2
REMEMBRANCE PARK, Bedford	61 D 4
RHINE PARK, Swan View	51 C 8
RHODES PARK, Calista	130 E 9
RICHARD ANGELONI PARK, North Lake	92 A 10
RICHARD DIGGINS PARK, Subiaco	72 B 2
RICHARD LEWIS PARK, Bull Creek	93 A 3
RICHARDSON PARK, South Perth	72 E 8
RICHMOND PARK, East Fremantle	90 E 3
RICKMAN BANGALLA RESERVE, Balcatta	46 A 4
RICKMAN DELAWNEY RESERVE, Balcatta	46 B 4
RIDLEY GREEN, Medina	130 D 4
RINALDO RESERVE, Coolbellup	101 E 2
RIVERTON RESERVE, Riverton	94 A 1
ROB CAMPBELL PARK, Bicton	81 A 9
ROBB PARK, Coolbellup	91 D 9
ROBERT HEWSON PARK, High Wycombe	64 D 9
ROBERT SMITH PARK, Kardinya	92 A 3
ROBERT STREET PARK, Winthrop	92 A 3
ROBERT THOMPSON RESERVE, Noranda	47 E 5
ROBERT WEIR PARK, Leeming	92 E 10
ROBERTSBRIDGE RESERVE, Nollamara	46 E 5
ROBERTSON PARK, Perth	60 E 10
ROBIN RESERVE, Sorrento	30 C 6
ROBINSON PARK, Gosnells	106 B 1
ROBINSON RESERVE, Tuart Hill	46 B 10
ROCKINGHAM OVAL, Rockingham	137 A 1
ROGERSON GARDENS, Floreat	71 C 1
RON CARROLL RESERVE, Bull Creek	93 A 5
RON STONE RESERVE, Menora	61 A 5
ROPE WORKS PARK, Mosman Park	80 D 7

Name	Map Ref.
ROSALIE PARK, Shenton Park	72 A 5
ROSE SHANKS RESERVE, Banjup	113 E 3
ROSHER PARK, Lockridge	49 A 7
ROSMEAD PARK, Beechboro	48 D 4
ROSS PARK, Winthrop	92 B 4
ROTARY ADVENTURE PARK, Mandurah	163 B 10
ROTARY PARK, Armadale	116 C 7
ROTARY PARK, Rockingham	136 D 4
ROWE PARK, Claremont	71 B 8
RUSHTON PARK, Kelmscott	106 E 9
RUSHTON PARK Mandurah	165 C 1
RUSSELL SQUARE, Northbridge	1C E 1
RUTTER PARK, Wembley	59 E 9
R.A. COOK RESERVE, Bedford	61 D 1
SACRAMENTO PARK, Beechboro	48 E 3
SAINT ANDREWS PARK, Yanchep	4 E 1
SALATA PARK, Duncraig	30 E 5
SAMUEL CAPHORN RESERVE, Yangebup	102 B 7
SAMUEL RENFREY RESERVE, Mandurah	163 A 9
SANDY BEACH RESERVE, Bassendean	63 A 5
SANTICH PARK, Munster	111 B 1
SAWYERS VALLEY RECREATION, Sawyers Valley	55 A 10
SCARBOROUGH LIONS CLUB RESERVE, Scarborough	58 D 2
SCOTCH COLLEGE PLAYING FIELDS, Swanbourne	71 A 8
SCOTT RESERVE, High Wycombe	64 C 10
SEATON PARK, Lesmurdie	87 D 1
SELBY PARK, Redcliffe	62 E 8
SERPENTINE FALLS NATIONAL PARK, Serpentine	151 E 9
SHALFORD RESERVE, Bayswater	62 C 1
SHANNON BELLET PARK, Leeming	93 D 9
SHEARN MEMORIAL PARK, Maylands	61 D 7
SHELDRAKE RESERVE, Stirling	45 D 6
SHELLEY RESERVE, Shelley	93 C 1
SHELVOCK RESERVE, Koondoola	32 E 6
SHENTON PARK, Shenton Park	71 E 4
SHEOAK PARK, Greenwood	31 C 6
SHEPHERDS BUSH RESERVE, Kingsley	31 C 1
SHIRLEY STRICKLAND OVAL, Ardross	82 C 8
SHOALWATER OVAL, Shoalwater	136 C 8
SHOWGROUND (RAS) Claremont	71 B 7
SIMPSON PARK, Padbury	23 D 9
SINGLETON SPORTING COMPLEX, Singleton	160 D 2
SIR ALBERT JENNINGS PARK, Willetton	93 D 3
SIR FREDERICK SAMSON MEMORIAL RESERVE, Samson	91 D 8
SIR JAMES MITCHELL PARK, South Perth	73 A 7
SKAIFE PARK, Munster	111 E 7
SKEET MEMORIAL PARK, Forrestdale	114 E 6
SLOANS RESERVE, Leda	130 D 10
SMART PARK, Spearwood	101 B 9
SOMERVILLE PARK, Winthrop	92 C 6
SOUTH BEACH RECREATION, South Fremantle	90 C 9
SOUTH COOGEE RESERVE, South Coogee	111 B 5
SOVEREIGN PARK, Willetton	93 C 6
SPEARWOOD SOCCER GROUND, Spearwood	101 B 5
SPENCER RESERVE, Serpentine	154 E 3
SPRINGSIDE PARK, Glen Forrest	66 D 1
SPRINGVALE RESERVE, Warwick	31 D 9
SRDAROV RESERVE, Wattleup	121 C 2
ST JOHNS SQUARE, Fremantle	1D C 5
STAR SWAMP RESERVE, North Beach	44 D 1
STEVENS RESERVE, Fremantle	90 D 6
STEWART PARK, Scarborough	58 E 1
STIRK PARK, Kalamunda	77 D 6
STIRLING GARDENS, Perth	1C A 3
STIRLING SQUARE, Guildford	49 D 10
STOKES PARK, Daglish	71 D 3
STRINGFELLOW PARK, Mosman Park	80 D 7
STRUTT WAY RESERVE, Noranda	47 E 6
STUART PARK, Greenmount	51 B 10
SUBIACO OVAL Subiaco	72 B 1
SUCCESS HILL RESERVE, Bassendean	49 B 10
SUPERDROME Mt Claremont	71 B 2
SUPREME COURT GARDENS Perth	1C A 4
SUTHERLANDS PARK, Huntingdale	105 C 3
SWAN REGIONAL RECREATION PARK Midvale	50 E 6
SWAN VIEW PARK, Swan View	51 B 7
SWANBOURNE RESERVE, Swanbourne	70 C 8
SWEETING RESERVE, Woodlands	59 B 4
SWINGLER PARK, Gosnells	106 A 1
TAYLOR PARK, Caversham	49 D 5
TED CROSS MEMORIAL RESERVE, Balga	46 B 3
TEMPEST PARK, Coolbellup	101 D 2
THOMAS MOORE PARK, Wilson	84 B 6
THOMAS OVAL, Medina	130 D 5
THOMAS PARK, Glen Forrest	66 E 2
THOMSONS LAKE NATURE RESERVE, Banjup	112 B 4
THORBURN PARK, Beechboro	49 A 2
THORNLIE PARK, Thornlie	95 C 3
THORSON PARK, Lockridge	49 B 7
TILLBROOK PARK, Glen Forrest	66 D 3
TOLLINGTON PARK, Kelmscott	106 D 10
TOM BATEMAN SPORTING COMPLEX, Thornlie	94 D 5
TOM WALKER PARK, Sorrento	30 D 5
TOM WRIGHT RESERVE, Carlisle	74 B 7
TOMPKINS PARK, Alfred Cove	82 A 9
TOTTERDELL PARK, West Perth	60 D 10
TREGONNING FIELD (Highview Park) Nedlands	71 D 3
TREVOR GRIBBLE PARK, Bull Creek	93 B 5
TREWIN PARK, Morley	47 D 6
TRINITY PLAYING FIELDS, Waterford	83 C 6
TROY PARK, Attadale	81 E 8
TUART PARK, San Remo	163 C 1
TUOHY GARDENS, Midland	50 C 8
T.J. PERROTT RESERVE, Mosman Park	80 E 7
ULRICH PARK, East Fremantle	90 E 1
UNDERWATER WORLD (Hillarys Boat Harbour) Sorrento	30 A 5
UNIVERSITY PLAYING FIELDS, Murdoch	92 B 9
VELA-LUKA PARK, Spearwood	101 C 7
VELLGROVE RESERVE, Lynwood	94 C 3
VELLGROVE RESERVE, Middle Swan	50 E 3
VELODROME Leederville	60 B 7
VERBENA PARK, Greenmount	65 E 1
VICTOR ADAM PARK, Halls Head	162 D 9
VRANKOVICH RESERVE, Balcatta	45 D 4
WACA OVAL East Perth	73 C 4
WAKE POLA RESERVE, Dianella	47 C 10
WAL HUGHES RESERVE, Attadale	81 D 9
WALLISTON RECREATION, Walliston	88 A 2
WALTER PADBURY PARK, Thornlie	95 B 6
WALTER PARK, Langford	95 A 1
WALTHAM RESERVE, Morley	48 A 7
WALYUNGA NATIONAL PARK Swan Shire (See Inset Map 6)	
WANNEROO SHOWGROUND, Wanneroo	20 D 9
WAR MEMORIAL PARK, Halls Head	164 E 2
WAR MEMORIAL (Monument Hill), Fremantle	90 D 5
WARNBRO SPORTS COMPLEX, Warnbro	145 C 6
WARRANDYTE RESERVE, Craigie	23 E 5
WARTHWYKE PARK, Yangebup	101 D 10
WARWICK SAVAGE PARK, Roleystone	108 C 7
WARWICK WILD PARK, Applecross	82 D 5
WATER TOWER PARK, Joondalup	19 D 3
WATSON OVAL, Spearwood	101 B 7
WATTLE PARK, Morley	48 D 5
WATTON PARK, Swan View	51 C 8
WAUHOP PARK, East Fremantle	80 E 9
WEBBER RESERVE, Willagee	91 C 4
WEDDALL PARK, Lockridge	49 A 6
WELBOURNE PARK, Greenmount	65 C 1
WELD SQUARE, Perth	1C A 1
WELLINGTON SQUARE, East Perth	1C B 3
WELLS PARK, Kwinana Beach	129 D 8
WESLEY PLAYING FIELDS, Como	83 C 2
WESTERN AUSTRALIAN SPORTS CENTRE Mt Claremont	71 B 2
WESTERN ROSELLA BIRD PARK Greenfields	165 E 3
WESTFIELD RESERVE, Westfield	106 C 7
WHITEMAN PARK Youle-Dean Rd, Whiteman	34 D 6
WHYBOURNE PARK, Bellevue	51 A 10
TRINITY PLAYING FIELDS, Waterford	83 C 6
WILD KINGDOM WILDLIFE PARK Two Rocks	3 A 7
WILLETTON RESERVE, Willetton	93 C 3
WILLIAM HALL PARK, Leeming	93 A 8
WILLIAM SKEET OVAL, Forrestdale	114 E 6
WILLIAM TURNER RESERVE, Armadale	116 D 2
WILSON PARK, Rivervale	74 B 5
WILSON PARK, Safety Bay	136 D 10
WILSON PARK, South Fremantle	90 C 10
WILSON PARK, Wilson	84 C 7
WINDEMERE PARK, Joondalup	19 D 1
WINDSOR PARK, South Perth	72 E 7
WINNACOTT RESERVE, Willagee	91 E 4
WINTHROP PARK, Winthrop	92 B 4
WIRELESS HILL PARK, Ardross	82 B 10
WOODCHESTER RESERVE, Nollamara	46 D 8
WOODFORD PARK, Lynwood	94 D 2
WOODLANDS RESERVE, Woodlands	59 B 4
WOODMAN POINT RECREATION CAMP, Munster	110 C 2
WOODMAN POINT RECREATION RESERVE, Munster	110 D 1
WOODVILLE RESERVE, North Perth	60 E 7
WOOLGAR PARK, Lockridge	49 A 6
WORDSWORTH RESERVE, Menora	61 B 2
WOTTON RESERVE, Embleton	48 C 10
WREN PENGUIN RESERVE, Dianella	47 C 7
WRIGHT PARK, Mosman Park	80 D 4
WRIGLEY SEABROOK RESERVE, Dianella	47 C 7
WYONG RESERVE, Bentley	84 B 5
W. WAYMAN RESERVE, East Fremantle	80 E 9
W.A. KITSON RESERVE, East Fremantle	90 D 2
W.N. MALCOLM RESERVE, Melville	91 C 2
YANCHEP NATIONAL PARK Yanchep	5 C 1
YELLAGONGA REGIONAL PARK, Wanneroo	20 B 9
YENNERDIN PARK, Parkerville	53 C 6
YILGARN PARK, Mundaring	68 B 3
YOKINE RESERVE, Menora	61 A 3
YULUMA PARK, Innaloo	45 C 8
ZOOLOGICAL GARDENS Labouchere Rd, South Perth (Inset Map 100)	

POLICE-Stations, Traffic & Licensing Centres

Name	Map Ref.
ACCIDENT INQUIRY SECTION, Wellington St, East Perth	73 C 3
ARMADALE POLICE, Prospect Rd	116 D 6
ARMADALE TRAFFIC, Prospect Rd	116 D 6
BALLAJURA POLICE POST, Ballajura City Shopping Centre, 3 Shearwater Tce	33 E 8
BAYSWATER, 73 Whatley Cr	62 B 5

	Map Ref.
BELMONT, 208 Gt Eastern Hwy	62 D 9
BRENTWOOD, 308 Leach Hwy	92 D 3
CANNINGTON POLICE, Cnr Albany Hwy & Nicholson Rd	85 A 9
CANNINGTON TRAFFIC, Cnr Albany Hwy & Nicholson Rd	85 A 9
CHILD CARE UNIT, 555 Newcastle St, West Perth	60 D10
CITY POLICE STATION, Ground Floor Curtin House, 60 Beaufort St, Northbridge	1C A 2
CLAREMONT, 288 Stirling Hwy	71 B 9
COCKBURN, 392 Rockingham Rd, Spearwood	101 B 8
CORONIAL INQUIRY SECTION, 246 Rokeby Rd, Subiaco	72 A 3
COTTESLOE, Curtin Ave	80 D 3
CRIMINAL INVESTIGATION BRANCH, Curtin House, 60 Beaufort St, Northbridge	1C A 2
EAST PERTH LICENSING, Wickham St	73 C 3
EAST PERTH VEHICLE LICENSING (Inspections only), Bronte St, East Perth	73 C 3
EAST PERTH, POLICE HEADQUARTERS, 2 Adelaide Tce	73 C 4
FEDERATION OF POLICE AND CITIZENS YOUTH CLUBS, Level 2, Hyatt Centre, Adelaide Tce, Perth	1C B 4
FIREARMS BRANCH, 210 Adelaide Tce, Perth	1C B 4
FORRESTFIELD POLICE POST, Shop 26 Forrestfield Forum Shopping Centre, Strelitzia Ave	76 C10
FREMANTLE LICENSING, Forrest St	91 A 4
FREMANTLE POLICE, Henderson St	1D C 5
FREMANTLE TRAFFIC, Henderson St	1D C 5
GOSNELLS, 2291 Albany Hwy	96 C 9
HILTON, 42 Paget St	91 B 8
INGLEWOOD, Eighth Ave	61 D 5
INNALOO, 9 Morris Rd	45 B 8
JOONDALUP POLICE COMPLEX, Shenton Ave	19 E 5
KALAMUNDA LICENSING, 21 Canning Rd	77 D 7
KALAMUNDA POLICE, 31 Canning Rd	77 D 7
KALAMUNDA TRAFFIC, 17 Mead St	77 D 7
KELMSCOTT LICENSING, 2 Gillam Dr	116 C 1
KWINANA POLICE, 23 Pace Rd, Medina	130 E 5
LEEDERVILLE POLICE, 252 Oxford St, Leederville	60 C 8
LOCKRIDGE, 2 Korbosky Rd, Lockridge	49 A 8
MANDURAH LICENSING, Ranceby Ave, Coodanup	165 C 2
MANDURAH POLICE, Cnr Mandurah Bypass & Pinjarra Rd	165 C 3
MANDURAH TRAFFIC, Cnr Mandurah Bypass & Pinjarra Rd	165 C 3
MAYLANDS POLICE, 196 Guildford Rd	61 E 7
MEDINA, KWINANA POLICE, 23 Pace Rd	130 E 5
MIDLAND LICENSING, 11 Victoria St	50 C 8
MIDLAND POLICE, 32 Spring Park Rd	50 B 8

	Map Ref.
MIDLAND TRAFFIC, 32 Spring Park Rd	50 B 8
MIRRABOOKA POLICE POST, Shop 14 Mirrabooka Shopping Centre, Yirragin Dr	47 A 4
MORLEY POLICE, 47 Russell St	47 E10
MT HAWTHORN POLICE, 82 Ellesmere St	60 C 4
MUNDARING LICENSING, 4 Mann St	68 B 1
MUNDARING POLICE, 72 Gt Eastern Hwy	68 B 1
MUNDARING TRAFFIC, 72 Gt Eastern Hwy	68 B 1
MUNDIJONG POLICE, Anstey St	143 A 8
NEDLANDS POLICE, 39 The Avenue	71 E10
NOLLAMARA POLICE, 71 Nollamara Ave	46 D 6
NORTH PERTH POLICE, 81 Angove St	60 E 7
PALMYRA POLICE, 349 Canning Hwy	91 B 1
PERTH CENTRAL POLICE, Hay St, East Perth	73 C 4
PERTH CITY POLICE, William St Bridge, Perth	1C A 2
POLICE HEADQUARTERS, 2 Adelaide Tce, East Perth	73 C 4
POLICE STABLES, Swan Bank Rd, Maylands	74 A 1
POLICE TRAINING ACADEMY, Swan Bank Rd, Maylands	74 A 1
PROPERTY TRACING SECTION, C/- Maylands Academy, Maylands	74 A 1
RECRUITING BRANCH, 190 Hay St, East Perth	1C B 4
ROCKINGHAM LICENSING, Council Ave	137 C 7
ROCKINGHAM POLICE, Smythe St	137 A 4
ROCKINGHAM TRAFFIC, Council Ave	137 C 7
SCARBOROUGH POLICE, 92 Scarborough Beach Rd	44 D 9
SOUTH PERTH POLICE, 1 Mends St	72 E 7
SUBIACO LICENSING, 365 Bagot Rd	72 A 2
SUBIACO POLICE, 365 Bagot Rd	72 A 2
TOWN HALL POLICE POST, Perth Town Hall, Cnr Hay & Barrack Sts, Perth	1C A 3
TRAFFIC BRANCH HEADQUARTERS, Wellington St, East Perth	73 C 3
TWO ROCKS POLICE POST, Shop 15 Two Rocks Marina Shopping Centre, Sovereign Dr	2 B 2
VICTORIA PARK POLICE, 5 Litchfield St	73 E 7
WANNEROO POLICE, 941 Wanneroo Rd	20 D 8
WARWICK LICENSING, 37 Eddington Rd	31 E 7
WARWICK POLICE, 37 Eddington Rd	31 E 7
WARWICK TRAFFIC, 37 Eddington Rd	31 E 7
WATER POLICE, Harvest Road, North Fremantle	80 D10
WELSHPOOL LICENSING, 2-10 Murray Rd	85 B 2
WEMBLEY POLICE, 379 Cambridge St	59 E10

POST OFFICES (Official)

	Map Ref.
APPLECROSS, 776 Canning Hwy	82 C 7
ARMADALE, 234 Jull St	116 D 7
BASSENDEAN, 31 Old Perth Rd	63 A 1
BAYSWATER, 14 King William St	62 B 5
BELMONT, 176 Eastern Hwy	62 C10
BENTLEY, La Plaza Shopping Centre, Albany Hwy	84 C 3
BOORAGOON, Gateway Building, Cnr Davey & Marmion Sts	92 C 1
CANNINGTON, 18 Grose St	84 E 7
CLAREMONT, 2 Bay View Tce	71 A 9
CLOVERDALE, 225 Belmont Ave	74 D 5
COMO, 299 Canning Hwy	83 B 1
COTTESLOE, 543 Stirling Hwy	80 D 3
DIANELLA, Shop 24 Dianella Plaza Shopping Centre, Alexander Dr	47 B10
DOUBLEVIEW, 254 Scarborough Beach Rd	45 B10
EAST PERTH, 249 Hay St	1C B 4
FALCON, Old Coast Rd	162 C 2
FLOREAT FORUM, Shop 23B Floreat Forum Shopping Centre	59 C 9
FREMANTLE, 13 Market St	1D B 5
GOSNELLS, 2244 Albany Hwy	96 C 8
GREENWOOD, Shop 19 Greenwood Village Shopping Centre, Calectasia St	31 D 6
GUILDFORD, 24 Stirling St	49 D10
HAMILTON HILL, 9 Dodd St	91 B10
HILLARYS, Shop 7 Whitford City Shopping Centre, Marmion Ave	23 C 8
INGLEWOOD, 885 Beaufort St	61 D 5
KALAMUNDA, 14 Barber St	77 D 6
KARRINYUP, Shop 5 Karrinyup Shopping Centre, Karrinyup Rd	45 A 6
KELMSCOTT, Shop 12, Kelmscott Plaza, 2883 Albany Hwy	106 D 8
KWINANA, 8 Chisham Ave	131 A 7
LEEDERVILLE, 156 Oxford St	60 C 9
MADDINGTON, Shop 48, Maddington Metro Shopping Centre, Burslem Dr	95 E 4
MANDURAH, Cnr Sholl St & Pinjarra Rd	164 E 2
MAYLANDS, Shop 18, Maylands Shopping Centre, Guildford Rd	61 E 7
MELVILLE, Melville Shopping Centre, 390 Canning Hwy	91 C 1
MIDLAND, 39 Helena St	50 B 8
MIRRABOOKA, 23 Sudbury Pl	47 A 4
MORLEY, 14 Old Collier Rd	47 E10
MOSMAN PARK, 592 Stirling Hwy	80 D 4
MOUNT HAWTHORN, 180 Scarborough Beach Rd	60 C 5
MOUNT LAWLEY, 669 Beaufort St	61 B 8
MUNDARING, 68 Gt Eastern Hwy	68 B 1
NEDLANDS, 35 Stirling Hwy	71 E 8
NORTH BEACH, Shop 7, West Coast Plaza, North Beach Rd	44 C 2
NORTH FREMANTLE, 211 Queen Victoria St	90 C 1
NORTH PERTH, 2A View St	60 E 8
NORTHBRIDGE, 133 Aberdeen St	1C E 1
NORTHLANDS, Shop 7, Northlands Shopping Centre, Cnr Amelia St & Wanneroo Rd, Balcatta	46 B 5
OSBORNE PARK, 213-215 Main St	46 B10

	Map Ref.
PALMYRA, Shop 6, Stammers Arcade, 275 Canning Hwy	91 A 1
PERTH GPO, 3 Forrest Pl	1C A 2
PERTH, 115 Brisbane St	61 A10
PERTH, 144 Stirling St	1C A 2
PERTH, 33 Victoria Sq	1C A 3
PERTH, 62 St Georges Tce	1C A 3
PERTH, Cloisters Square, 863 Hay St	1C E 2
PERTH, Cnr Pier & Wellington Sts	1C A 2
RIVERVALE, 21 Gt Eastern Hwy	74 A 3
ROCKINGHAM BEACH, Cnr Railway Tce & Kent St	137 A 4
ROCKINGHAM, Rockingham City Shopping Centre, Simpson Ave	137 B 7
SCARBOROUGH, 25 Scarborough Beach Rd	44 D10
SOUTH FREMANTLE, 195 Hampton Rd	90 D 8
SOUTH PERTH, 103 Mill Point Rd	72 E 7
SOUTH PERTH, 59 Angelo St	73 A 9
SUBIACO, 164 Rokeby Rd	72 A 2
THORNLIE, Shop 15 Thornlie Square Shopping Centre, Thornlie Ave	95 C 5
TUART HILL, 73 Wanneroo Road	60 C 1
VICTORIA PARK EAST, 879 Albany Hwy	74 A10
VICTORIA PARK, 414 Albany Hwy	73 E 7
WANGARA, 5 Dellamarta Rd	24 E 6
WANNEROO, Shop 7 Wanneroo Villa Shopping Centre	20 D 8
WARWICK, Warwick Grove Shopping Centre, 675 Beach Rd	31 E 8
WEMBLEY, Alexander St	59 E10
WEST LEEDERVILLE, 125 Cambridge St	60 C10
WEST PERTH, 1274 Hay St	72 C 1
WEST PERTH, 468 Newcastle St	60 E10
WILLETTON, 39 Burrendah Blvd	93 C 5

PSYCHIATRIC SERVICES

CLINICS

	Map Ref.
ARMADALE, 3056 Albany Hwy, Armadale	116 E 2
AVRO COMMUNITY HEALTH CENTRE, 2 Nicholson Rd, Subiaco	72 B 3
BENTLEY, 35 Mills St, Bentley	84 D 4
CHILD GUIDANCE, Selby St, Shenton Park	71 D 4
FREMANTLE, Stirling St, Fremantle	1D C 5
HILLVIEW CHILD & ADOLESCENT, Hillview Tce, E Victoria Pk	84 A 1
MULTICULTURAL, 590 Newcastle St, Perth	60 D 9
OSBORNE PARK, Civic Pl, Stirling	45 D 8
SWAN, La Salle Ave, Viveash	50 C 5
WARWICK FAMILY, Erindale Rd, Warwick	31 E 8

EXTENDED CARE UNITS

	Map Ref.
ARMADALE LODGE, C/- Armadale-Kelmscott Hospital, Albany Hwy, Armadale	116 E 2
BENTLEY LODGE, Mills St, Bentley	84 D 4

291

	Map	Ref.
EDEN HILL CLUSTER HOMES, 52 Freeland Way, Eden Hill	48	D 8
MOSS STREET LODGE, 33 Moss St, East Fremantle	90	E 2
OSBORNE LODGE, C/- Osborne Park Hospital, Osborne Pl, Stirling	45	D 8
ROYAL PERTH (REHABILITATION), Selby St, Shenton Park	71	D 3
SELBY LODGE, Lemnos St, Shenton Park	71	D 4
SWAN LODGE, C/- Swan Districts Hospital, Eveline Rd, Middle Swan	50	C 5

HOSPITALS

	Map	Ref.
GRAYLANDS, Brockway Rd, Mt Claremont	71	B 4
HEATHCOTE, 68 Duncraig Rd, Applecross	82	D 4
HILLVIEW TERRACE, (adolescents), Cnr Albany Hwy & Hill View Tce, East Victoria Park	84	B 1
LEMNOS, 227 Stubbs Tce, Shenton Park	71	D 4
STUBBS TERRACE (children), 233 Stubbs Tce, Shenton Park	71	D 4

OTHER FACILITIES

	Map	Ref.
COMMUNITY PSYCHIATRIC DIVISION, 227 Stubbs Tce, Shenton Park	71	D 4
HAWKVALE FARM VILLAGE, Hawkvale Rd, High Wycombe	64	D 8
INDUSTRIAL REHABILITATION DIVISION, Mooro Dr, Mt Claremont	71	B 5
MILDRED CREAK CENTRE (autistic children), Cnr Albany Hwy & Hillview Tce, East Victoria Park	84	B 1
NEUROSCIENCES UNIT, Graylands Hospital, Brockway Rd, Mt Claremont	71	B 4
SOUTH GUILDFORD DAY CENTRE, 144 Queens Rd, South Guildford	63	D 2
WHITBY FALLS HOSTEL, South Western Hwy, Whitby	143	D 7

RACING TRACKS

BMX

	Map	Ref.
ACTION PARK, Victoria Rd, Malaga	48	A 2
COCKBURN, Malabar Wy, Bibra Lake	101	D 4
KALAMUNDA, Ray Owen Reserve, Gladys Rd, Lesmurdie	87	B 3
KELMSCOTT, John Dunn Memorial Park, Third Ave, Kelmscott	106	C 10
KEWDALE, Chisholm Cr, Wattle Grove	85	E 1
MILLS PARK, Mills Park, Brixton St, Beckenham	85	D 8
PEGASUS, Briggs Park, Gordon Wy, Byford	135	C 3
ROCKINGHAM, Cnr Dixon Rd & Dowling St, Rockingham	137	C 5
SOUTH SIDE, Bob Gordon Res, Cnr Benningfield Rd & Parry Ave, Bull Creek	92	E 5
SOUTHERN DISTRICTS, Atkinson Rd, Medina	130	D 5
WANNEROO, Mary St, Wanneroo	25	B 5

	Map	Ref.
WEST SIDE, Balcatta Rd, Balcatta	46	A 3

CAR & MOTORCYCLE

	Map	Ref.
CLAREMONT SPEEDWAY, RAS Showground, Claremont	71	B 8
COCKBURN INTERNATIONAL RACEWAY (GO-KART), Henderson	121	A 1
WANNEROO PARK MOTOR RACING CIRCUIT, Wanneroo	13	B 8

DOG

	Map	Ref.
CANNINGTON CENTRAL GREYHOUND RACING, Cannington	84	E 8
MANDURAH GREYHOUND RACING TRACK, Gordon Rd, Greenfields	163	D 7

HORSE

	Map	Ref.
ASCOT (WATC), Ascot	62	C 8
BELMONT PARK, Rivervale	73	D 1

TROTTING

	Map	Ref.
BYFORD TROTTING COMPLEX, Byford	135	B 1
GLOUCESTER PARK RACEWAY (WATA), East Perth	73	C 3

RAILWAY STATIONS

COUNTRY PASSENGER STATIONS

	Map	Ref.
BYFORD	135	C 2
MUNDIJONG	143	A 8
SERPENTINE	154	E 3

FREIGHT TERMINALS

	Map	Ref.
FORRESTFIELD MARSHALLING YARD	76	A 3
KEWDALE FREIGHT TERMINAL	75	C 9
LEIGHTON MARSHALLING YARD	80	C 8
ROB JETTY MARSHALLING YARD	100	D 2

PERTH - ARMADALE LINE

	Map	Ref.
ARMADALE, Armadale	116	D 7
BECKENHAM, Beckenham	85	B 8
BELMONT PARK, Victoria Park	73	D 1
CANNINGTON, Cannington	85	A 6
CARLISLE, Carlisle	74	B 8
CHALLIS, Kelmscott	116	C 1
CLAISEBROOK, East Perth	73	B 2
GOSNELLS, Gosnells	96	C 9
KELMSCOTT, Kelmscott	106	D 8
KENWICK, Kenwick	95	D 1
LATHLAIN, Lathlain	74	A 7
MADDINGTON, Maddington	95	E 3
McIVER, Perth City	1C	A 2
OATS STREET, Carlisle	74	B 10
QUEENS PARK, Cannington	84	E 4
RIVERVALE, Victoria Park	73	E 4
SEAFORTH, Gosnells	106	D 1
SHERWOOD, Armadale	116	D 3
TREDALE, Armadale	116	D 4
VICTORIA PARK, Lathlain	74	A 6
WELSHPOOL, Bentley	84	C 2

PERTH - FREMANTLE LINE

	Map	Ref.
CITY WEST, West Perth	1C	D 1
CLAREMONT, Claremont	71	A 9
COOGEE, Coogee	100	E 8
COTTESLOE, Cottesloe	80	D 2

	Map	Ref.
DAGLISH, Daglish	71	E 2
ESPLANADE, THE, Fremantle	1C	B 6
FREMANTLE, Fremantle	1C	B 4
GRANT STREET, Cottesloe	70	E 10
KARRAKATTA, Karrakatta	71	C 6
LOCH STREET, Karrakatta	71	C 7
MOSMAN PARK, Mosman Park	80	D 5
NORTH FREMANTLE, North Fremantle	80	C 10
PERTH, Perth City	1C	A 2
ROBB JETTY, Hamilton Hill	100	D 2
SHENTON PARK, Shenton Park	71	D 4
SHOWGROUND, Claremont	71	B 7
SOUTH BEACH, South Fremantle	90	C 10
SUBIACO, Subiaco	72	A 1
SUCCESS HARBOUR, South Fremantle	90	C 8
SWANBOURNE, Claremont	70	E 9
THE ESPLANADE, Fremantle	1C	B 6
VICTORIA STREET, Mosman Park	80	C 6
WEST LEEDERVILLE, Subiaco	60	C 10

PERTH - MIDLAND LINE

	Map	Ref.
ASHFIELD, Ashfield	62	E 3
BASSENDEAN, Bassendean	63	A 1
BAYSWATER, Bayswater	62	B 5
EAST GUILDFORD, Guildford	49	E 10
EAST PERTH TERMINAL, East Perth	61	C 10
EAST PERTH, East Perth	61	C 10
GUILDFORD, Guildford	49	C 10
MAYLANDS, Maylands	61	D 7
MELTHAM, Bayswater	61	E 6
MIDLAND, Midland	50	B 9
MOUNT LAWLEY, Mount Lawley	61	C 8
SUCCESS HILL, Bassendean	49	B 10
WEST MIDLAND, Midland	50	A 9

RUBBISH TIPS & BALING PLANTS

	Map	Ref.
ARMADALE (City), Hopkinson Rd, Forrestdale	125	D 6
ARMADALE (City), Springdale Rd, Roleystone	108	C 3
BASSENDEAN (Town) - see SWAN	12	A 9
BAYSWATER (City) - see SWAN	12	B 9
BAYSWATER (City), Collier Rd, Bayswater	62	C 2
BELMONT (City), Abernethy Rd, Kewdale	75	D 9
CANNING (City), Ranford Rd, Canning Vale	93	E 10
CLAREMONT (Town) - see NEDLANDS	12	B 9
COCKBURN (City), Rockingham Rd, Henderson	111	C 9
COTTESLOE (Town) - see NEDLANDS	12	B 9
EAST FREMANTLE (Town) - see MELVILLE	12	B 9
FREMANTLE (City), Cockburn Rd, Hamilton Hill	100	D 1
GOSNELLS (City), Kelvin Rd, Orange Grove	86	D 8
KALAMUNDA (Shire), Dawson Ave, Forrestfield	76	B 8
KWINANA (Town), Thomas Rd, Kwinana Beach	130	C 3
MELVILLE (City), Dundee St, Leeming	93	C 10
MOSMAN PARK (Town) - see NEDLANDS	12	B 9

	Map	Ref.
MUNDARING (Shire), Elfreda St, Chidlow	56	B 5
NEDLANDS (City), Brockway Rd, Mt Claremont	71	B 3
PEPPERMINT GROVE (Shire) - see NEDLANDS	12	B 9
SERPENTINE-JARRAHDALE, Watkins Rd, Whitby	143	C 9
SOUTH PERTH (City), Thelma St, Como	83	C 2
STIRLING (City), Balcatta Rd, Balcatta	46	A 3
SUBIACO (City) - see NEDLANDS	12	B 9
SWAN (Shire), Toodyay Rd, Red Hill	38	D 6
WANNEROO (City), Marmion Ave, Tamala Park	14	E 8

SCHOOLS (See Education Institutions)

SEA RESCUE GROUP (VOLUNTEER)

	Map	Ref.
COCKBURN, Cnr Cockburn & Redemptora Rds, Henderson	110	E 7
FREMANTLE, Fremantle Sailing Club, Success Boat Harbour, South Fremantle	90	C 8
MANDURAH, Peninsula Ent, Mandurah	162	D 10
ROCKINGHAM, Point Peron Rd, Peron	136	B 4
WHITFORDS, Whitfords Sea Sports Club, Ocean Reef Boat Harbour	18	E 10

SHOPPING CENTRES (Major)

	Map	Ref.
ALINJARRA VILLAGE, Greenpark Rd, Alexander Heights	33	B 5
AMELIA HEIGHTS, Jones St, Balcatta	46	A 4
ARMADALE SHOPPING TOWN, Jull St, Armadale	116	D 7
ARMADALE SQUARE, Cnr Jull St & Third Rd, Armadale	116	D 6
ASHBURTON VILLAGE, Stennett St, Gosnells	106	A 2
BALGA BAZAAR, Cnr Princess Rd & Balga Ave, Balga	46	C 1
BALLAJURA, Cnr Illawarra Cr & Kingfisher Ave	33	E 7
BARBERRY SQUARE, Barber St, Kalamunda	77	D 6
BASSENDEAN SQUARE, Cnr Old Perth Rd & West Rd, Bassendean	63	B 1
BEECHBORO SQUARE, Cnr Altone Rd & Hull Wy, Beechboro	49	A 4
BELMONT FORUM, Cnr Abernethy Rd & Fulham St, Cloverdale	74	E 5
BELMONT VILLAGE, Knutsford Ave, Cloverdale	74	D 5
BIBRA LAKE, Cnr Parkway & Annois Rds, Bibra Lake	102	D 3
BICTON, Cnr Pembroke St & Harris Rd	81	B 9
BOULEVARD PLAZA, Moolanda Blvd, Kingsley	31	D 3
BRENTWOOD, Cranford Ave	92	E 9
BULL CREEK, Cnr South St & Benningfield Rd	92	E 7
BURRENDAH, Apsley Rd & Woodpecker Ave, Willetton	93	C 4

Name	Map Ref.
CARINE GLADES, Cnr Davallia & Beach Rds, Duncraig	31 B 9
CAROUSEL, Albany Hwy, Cannington	84 E 7
CARRAMAR CENTRAL, Cnr Beechboro & Benara Rds, Morley	48 C 5
CENTREPOINT, Cnr Great Eastern Hwy & Helena St, Midland	50 B 8
CHIDLOWS WELL VILLAGE, Thomas St	56 D 2
CITY WEST, Sutherland St, West Perth	60 D10
CLAREMONT, Stirling Hwy	71 A 9
COCKBURN, Cnr Rockingham Rd & Carrington St, Hamilton Hill	101 A 2
CONNOLLY, Country Club Blvd	19 B 8
COOLBELLUP, Cnr Coolbellup & Cordelia Aves	101 E 1
COOLIBAH PLAZA, Cnr Wahroonga Wy & Kanangra Cr, Greenwood	31 B 4
COOLOONGUP, Cnr Ennis Ave & Grange Dr	137 E 8
CORFIELD, Corfield St, Gosnells	106 B 2
CRAIGIE PLAZA, Eddystone Ave, Craigie	23 D 5
CROSSWAYS, Cnr Bagot Rd & Rokeby Rd, Subiaco	72 A 2
DARLING RIDGE CENTRE, Morrison Rd, Swan View	51 B 7
DIANELLA PLAZA, Cnr Alexander Dr & Grand Pro, Dianella	47 B10
DOG SWAMP, Wanneroo Rd, Yokine	60 D 3
DORIC ST, Cnr Weaponess Rd & Doric St, Scarborough	58 E 2
DUNCRAIG, Cnr Marri & Cassinia Rds	30 E 6
EAST FREMANTLE, Canning Hwy	90 D 2
EDEN HILL, Cnr Morley Dr East & Ivanhoe St	49 A 8
EDGEWATER MARKETS, Edgewater Dr, Edgewater	24 B 3
FALCON, Cobblers Rd	162A C 2
FARRINGTON FAYRE, Cnr Farrington & Findlay Rds, Leeming	93 A10
FIELDGATE SQUARE, Cnr Culloton Cr & Lindway St, Balga	32 A 9
FLINDERS SQUARE, Flinders St, Yokine	60 D 3
FLOREAT FORUM, Howtree Pl, Floreat	59 C 9
FOOTHILLS, Cnr Albany Hwy & Dorothy St, Gosnells	96 B 8
FOREST LAKES, Murdoch Rd, Thornlie	95 A 8
FORREST PLAZA, Cnr Forrest & Alexander Rds, Padbury	23 D 9
FORRESTFIELD FORUM, Strelitzia Ave, Forrestfield	76 C10
FORRESTFIELD, Edinburgh Rd	86 D 1
GARDEN CITY, Riseley St, Booragoon	82 C10
GIRRAWHEEN PARK, Marangaroo Dr, Girrawheen	32 B 6
GLEN FORREST, Great Eastern Hwy	66 D 1
GLENDALOUGH, Cnr Jon Sanders Dr & Harborne St	60 A 6
GLENGARRY, Cnr Glengarry Dr & Amisdale Rd, Duncraig	31 A 6
GOLDEN BAY, Cnr Tangadee Rd & Yuin St	158 D 8
GREENWOOD KINGSLEY PLAZA, Cockman Rd, Greenwood	31 E 3
GREENWOOD VILLAGE, Calectasia St, Greenwood	31 D 6
GROVE PLAZA, Stirling Hwy, Peppermint Grove	80 D 3
GWELUP, North Beach Rd	45 C 5
HALLS HEAD SHOPPING VILLAGE, Cnr Glencoe & Peelwood Pdes, Halls Head	164 C 5
HAMILTON HILL, Rockingham Rd	100 E 1
HAMPTON PARK, Paine Rd, Morley	48 B 7
HEATHRIDGE, Cnr Caridean St & Admiral Gr	19 D10
HERDSMAN, Flynn St, Churchlands	59 D 8
HIGH WYCOMBE, Kalamunda Rd	64 C 9
HILTON, Cnr Carrington & South Sts	91 A 7
HOME BASE, Cnr Harborne St & Salvado Rd, Wembley	60 A10
HUNTINGDALE, Cnr Warton Rd & Matilda St	95 C 9
INNALOO SHOPPERS VILLAGE, Cnr Scarborough Beach Rd & Oswald St	59 C 1
INNALOO, Morris Pl, Innaloo	45 C 9
JOONDALUP, Cnr Shenton Ave & Seddon Rd	19 E 5
KALAMUNDA CENTRAL, Cnr Railway Pde & Mead St	77 D 6
KALAMUNDA GLADES, Cnr Canning & Lewis Rds, Kalamunda	77 E 9
KARAWARA, Cnr Manning Rd & Kent St	83 D 5
KARDINYA, Cnr South St & North Lake Rd	92 A 8
KARRINYUP, Cnr Karrinyup Rd & Francis Ave	45 A 6
KELMSCOTT PLAZA, Albany Hwy, Kelmscott	106 D 8
KELMSCOTT VILLAGE, Albany Hwy	106 D 8
KINGSLEY VILLAGE, Kingsley Dr, Kingsley	24 B10
KOONDOOLA PLAZA, Koondoola Ave, Koondoola	32 E 8
KWINANA HUB, Cnr Chisham Ave & Gilmore Ave, Kwinana Town Centre	131 A 7
LA PLAZA, Cnr Albany Hwy & John St, Bentley	84 C 3
LAKELANDS, Cnr Moorhen & Swallow Drs, Yangebup	102 A 9
LANGFORD VILLAGE, Langford Ave, Langford	94 E 2
LESMURDIE, Lesmurdie Rd, Lesmurdie	87 C 2
LILBURNE, Cnr Lilburne & Hilarion Rds, Duncraig	30 E 3
MADDINGTON METRO, Cnr Burslem Dr & Olga Rd	95 E 4
MADDINGTON VILLAGE, Westfield St	96 B 4
MAIDA VALE, Kalamunda Rd, High Wycombe	64 D 9
MANDURAH FORUM, Cnr Pinjarra & Fremantle Rds, Mandurah	165 C 2
MANDURAH PLAZA, Cnr Tuckey St & Mandurah Tce, Mandurah	164 E 1
MARKET CITY, Bannister Rd, Canning Vale	93 E 8
MARMION, Sheppard Wy	30 C 8
MAYLANDS PARK, Guildford Rd, Maylands	61 E 7
MEADOWVALE, Meadowvale Ave, South Perth	73 B 8
MELVILLE, Canning Hwy, Bicton	91 C 1
MIAMI VILLAGE, Old Coast Rd, Falcon	162A C 2
MIDLAND GATE, Brockman Rd, Midland	50 C 8
MIRRABOOKA VILLAGE, Honeywell Blvd	47 A 1
MIRRABOOKA, Yirrigan Dr	47 A 4
MOOLANDA VILLAGE, Cnr Moolanda Blvd & Bargate Way, Kingsley	24 D10
MORLEY, Cnr Old Collier Rd & Walter Rd West	47 E10
MOSMAN PARK, 50 Harvey St	80 D 5
MT CLAREMONT, Cnr Asquith & Strickland Sts	71 A 5
MULLALOO, Cnr Dampier Ave & Koorana Rds	23 B 4
MUNDARING MALL, 53 Great Eastern Hwy, Mundaring	54 B10
NEWBURN, Newburn Rd, High Wycombe	64 C 9
NOLLAMARA, Cnr Nollamara Ave & Hillsborough Dr	46 C 6
NORANDA SQUARE, Cnr Benara Rd & McGilvray Ave, Noranda	47 E 5
NORTHLANDS, Cnr Amelia St & Wanneroo Rd, Balcatta	46 B 5
OCEAN REEF, Venturi Dr	23 A 1
OCEAN VILLAGE, Cnr Hale & Brompton Rds, City Beach	58 D 4
PADBURY, Cnr Warburton & Leichardt Aves	30 D 1
PARKWOOD SQUARE, Cnr Vellgrove & Whaleback Aves, Lynwood	94 C 4
PARRY VILLAGE, Parry Ave, Bull Creek	93 A 5
PHOENIX PARK, Rockingham Rd, Spearwood	101 B 5
PINE GLADES, Wanneroo Rd (opp. Balcatta Rd), Balga	46 B 2
QUINNS ROCKS, Quinns Rd	10 B 1
RIVERTON FORUM, High Rd, Lynwood	94 A 1
ROCKINGHAM CITY, Read St, Rockingham	137 B 7
ROLEYSTONE, Cnr Jarrah & Wygona Rds	108 A 7
ROSSMOYNE, Central Rd	93 B 1
SAMSON, Cnr McCoombe & Petterson Ave	91 D 9
SANDERSON ROAD, Sanderson Rd, Lesmurdie	87 C 4
SCARBOROUGH, Scarborough Beach Rd	44 C10
SHELLEY HUB, Tribute St West, Shelley	83 D10
SOMERVILLE, Cnr Le Souef Dr & McMahon Wy, Kardinya	91 E 6
SORRENTO QUAY, Hillarys Boat Harbour	30 A 4
SOUTH FREMANTLE, Cnr Hampton Rd & Scott St	90 D 9
SOUTH LAKE, Cnr South Lake Dr & Berrigan Dr	102 C 7
SOUTHLANDS, Pinetree Gully Rd, Willetton	93 C 6
SPEARWOOD, Rockingham Rd	101 B 5
SPENCER VILLAGE, Spencer Rd, Thornlie	95 B 3
STIRLING VILLAGE, Cnr Cedric & Sanderling Sts, Stirling	45 E 7
SUBIACO PAVILION MARKETS, Cnr Roberts & Rokeby Rds, Subiaco	72 A 1
SUBIACO VILLAGE, Cnr Hay St & Railway Rd, Subiaco	72 A 1
SUMMERFIELD, Girrawheen Ave, Girrawheen	32 C 7
SWAN CITY, Cnr Sayer St & Great Eastern Hwy, Midland	50 C 8
SWAN VIEW, Marlboro Rd	51 C 8
THE DOWNS, Bournemouth Cr, Wembley Downs	58 E 3
THE MARKET PLACE, Cnr Parkview Dr & Illawarra Cr, Ballajura	33 C 4
THE PARK CENTRE, Albany Hwy, East Vic. Park	74 A10
THE SANDS, Cnr Anstruther Rd & Mandurah Tce, Mandurah	163 A 8
THE VILLAGE, The Boulevard, City Beach	58 E 7
THORNLIE SQUARE, Cnr Spencer Rd & Thornlie Ave, Thornlie	95 C 5
TWO ROCKS VILLAGE, Enterprise Ave, Two Rocks	2 B 1
VICTORIA PARK, Albany Hwy	73 E 7
WANNEROO MARKET, Cnr Prindiville Dr & Ismail St, Wangara	25 A 6
WANNEROO VILLA, Conlan Ave, Wanneroo	20 D 8
WARWICK GROVE, Cnr Beach & Erindale Rds, Warwick	31 E 8
WEST ARMADALE, Girrawheen St, Armadale	116 B 6
WEST COAST PLAZA, Cnr West Coast Hwy & North Beach Rd, North Beach	44 C 2
WESTFIELD, Westfield Rd	106 C 9
WHITFORD CITY, Cnr Marmion & Banks Aves, Hillarys	23 B 8
WINTHROP, Cnr Somerville Blvd & Jackson Ave	92 B 6
WOODLANDS VILLAGE, Cnr Birchwood & Rosewood Aves, Woodlands	59 B 3
WOODVALE, Cnr Trappers & Timberlane Drs	24 B 5

SKATING RINKS

ICE

Name	Map Ref.
ICE WORLD, Yirrigan Dr, Mirrabooka	46 E 4

ROLLER

Name	Map Ref.
ASTROSKATE, Gilmore Ave, Kwinana	130 E 7
CAROUSEL ROLLAWAYS, Cecil Ave, Cannington	84 E 6
KALAMUNDA LEISURE CENTRE, Collins Rd, Kalamunda	77 E 8
MANDURAH SKATE-ARENA, 96 Mandurah Tce, Mandurah	162 E10
ROLLERDROME, 8 Gibberd Rd, Balcatta	45 E 3
ROLLERDROME, 95 Catherine St, Morley	61 E 1
SPEED DOME, Eddie Barron Dr, Middle Swan	50 E 6
WEST COAST ROLLER SKATE, 9 Perilya St, Craigie	23 D 5

SPORTING VENUES (Major)

ATHLETICS

Name	Map Ref.
PERRY LAKES STADIUM, Floreat	71 B 1

BASEBALL

Name	Map Ref.
PARRY FIELD, Ascot	62 C10

BASKETBALL

Name	Map Ref.
HAGAN STADIUM, Hamilton Hill	100 E 1
MIDLAND & DISTRICTS REC. SPORTS CENTRE, Midvale	50 E 7

	Map Ref.
PERRY LAKES STADIUM, Floreat	71 B 1
SUPERDROME, Mt Claremont	71 B 2

CRICKET

WACA OVAL, East Perth	73 C 4

CYCLING

SPEED DOME, Eddie Barron Dr, Middle Swan	50 E 6
VELODROME, Leederville	60 B 7

FOOTBALL

BASSENDEAN OVAL, Bassendean	63 B 1
CLAREMONT OVAL, Claremont	71 B 8
EAST FREMANTLE OVAL, East Fremantle	90 E 3
FREMANTLE OVAL, Fremantle	1D C 6
LATHLAIN PARK, Lathlain	74 A 7
LEEDERVILLE OVAL, Leederville	60 D 8
PERTH OVAL, East Perth	1C B 1
SUBIACO OVAL, Subiaco	72 B 1

HOCKEY

COMMONWEALTH HOCKEY STADIUM, CURTIN UNIVERSITY, Bentley, (Facing Map 135)	

NETBALL

GIBSON PARK, East Fremantle	90 E 4
KINGSWAY RESERVE, Landsdale	32 B 2
MATTHEWS NETBALL CENTRE, Jolimont	59 D10

SOCCER

BAYSWATER OVAL, Bayswater	62 A 5
DORRIEN GARDENS, West Perth	60 E 9
INGLEWOOD OVAL, Inglewood	61 B 5
KINGSWAY RESERVE, Landsdale	32 B 2
MEDINA OVAL, Medina	130 E 4
PERRY LAKES STADIUM, Floreat	71 B 1
VELODROME, Leederville	60 B 7

SQUASH

WA INTERNATIONAL SQUASH CENTRE, CURTIN UNIVERSITY, Bentley, (Facing Map 135)	83 E 4

SWIMMING

BEATTY PARK, North Perth	60 D 9
SUPERDROME, Mt Claremont	71 B 2

TENNIS

ROYAL KING'S PARK, West Perth	72 C 3

WATERPOLO

SUPERDROME, Mt Claremont	71 B 2

SQUASH CENTRES

ARMADALE, 18 Prospect Rd	116 E 6
BALGA, 678 Wanneroo Rd	32 A 9
BASSENDEAN, 85-87 Old Perth Rd	63 B 2
BELMONT, 144 Robinson Ave	74 D 4
BLUE GUM RESERVE, Rountree Rd, Mt Pleasant	92 D 2
BULL CREEK (Healthworld), 77 Wheatley Dr	93 A 6

	Map Ref.
CAMBRIDGE, 292 Cambridge St, Wembley	59 E10
CARINE GLADES, Cnr Beach & Davilia Rds, Carine	31 B 9
CARLISLE, 52 Raleigh St	74 B 8
COCKBURN, 410 Carrington St, Hamilton Hill	101 A 1
DIANELLA, 5 Waverley St	61 C 1
EAST FREMANTLE, 163 Canning Hwy	90 E 2
FLOREAT, 437 Cambridge St	59 D10
GOSNELLS, 68 Wheatley St	96 C 9
HARTFIELD PARK, Hale Rd, Forrestfield	86 B 1
HILTON, 292 South St	91 A 7
HYATT HOTEL, Level 4, Adelaide Tce, East Perth	1C B 4
KALAMUNDA SQUASH & HEALTH ACADEMY, 81 Canning Rd	77 E 8
KARAWARA, 33 Walanna Dr	83 D 5
KELMSCOTT, 2938 Albany Hwy	106 E 9
KENSINGTON, 1 Third Ave	73 C 8
KENWICK, 1609 Albany Hwy, Beckenham	85 C10
KWINANA RECREATION CENTRE, Cnr Chisham & Gilmour Aves	131 A 7
LEEMING, Recreation Centre, Farrington Rd	92 E10
LIONS, Subiaco Football & Sporting Club, Subiaco Rd, Subiaco	60 B10
LORDS INDOOR SPORTS CITY, 588 Hay St, Subiaco	71 E 1
MADDINGTON (Super Squash), 1860 Albany Hwy	95 E 3
MAIDA VALE, 268 Kalamunda Rd	76 E 2
MANDURAH, Mandurah Tce	163 A 9
MANNING, 69 Manning Rd	83 A 6
MARMION, 4 Warburton Ave, Padbury	30 D 2
MAYLANDS, 282 Guildford Rd	61 E 7
MENORA, 344-6 Walcott St, Mt Lawley	60 E 5
MEULEMAN'S, 140 Canning Hwy, South Perth	73 C 9
MIRRABOOKA, Cnr Mirrabooka Ave & Yirrigan Dr	46 E 4
MORLEY, 15 Wellington Rd	47 E 9
MULLALOO, 25 Koorana Rd	23 B 4
MUNDARING, Gt Eastern Hwy	53 E10
MURDOCH UNIVERSITY (Private), South St, Murdoch (Facing Map 128)	92 C 7
NOLLAMARA, 253 Wanneroo Rd	46 C 7
NORTH BEACH, 99 Flora Tce	44 C 1
OXFORD, 337 Oxford St, Leederville	60 C 7
PARK RECREATION CENTRE, Cnr Kent & Gloucester Sts, East Victoria Park	73 E 9
PHOENIX, 66 Phoenix Rd, Hamilton Hill	101 B 4
ROCKINGHAM, Council Ave	137 C 8
ROLEYSTONE (Leisure Sports), 8 Wygonda Rd	108 A 8
ROSSMOYNE, 161 High Rd, Willetton	93 D 1
ROYAL KINGS PARK (Private), Kings Park Rd, West Perth	72 C 3
SCARBOROUGH SPORTSMEN'S CLUB (Private), 75 Deanmore St, Scarborough	44 E 8
SCARBOROUGH, 270 Scarborough Beach Rd, Doubleview	45 B10
SOUTH PERTH, 134 Canning Hwy	73 C 9

	Map Ref.
TERRACE HEALTH CLUB (Private), 4th Floor CTA Building, Entry via Allendale Sq	1C E 3
UNIVERSITY OF W.A. (Private), Mounts Bay Rd, Crawley (Inset Map 120)	
VITAL HEALTH & LEISURE, Cnr Sundercombe St & Scarborough Beach Rd, Osborne Park	59 E 2
W.A. INTERNATIONAL, Curtin University, Kent St, Bentley (Facing Map 135)	
WALTER ROAD, 549 Walter Rd, Bayswater	48 D 9
WEST COAST SQUASH CENTRE, 2 St Leonards St, Mosman Park	80 D 5
WHITFORDS (Healthworld), Cnr Marmion & Whitford Aves, Kallaroo	23 C 8

STATE EMERGENCY SERVICE

ARMADALE, Lot 92 Owen Rd, Kelmscott	116 C 1
BASSENDEAN, Scadden St	62 E 1
BAYSWATER, Cnr Toowong & Hobart Sts	61 E 4
BELMONT, Cnr Fairbrother & Abernethy Rds	74 D 2
CANNING, 1139 Albany Hwy, Bentley	84 C 3
COCKBURN, Kent St, Spearwood	101 A 5
GOSNELLS, Canning Park Ave, Maddington	96 A 3
KALAMUNDA, 31 Canning Rd	77 D 7
MANDURAH, Park Rd	163 C 8
MELVILLE, Almondbury Rd, Wireless Hill Park, Ardross	82 B10
METRO NORTH/SOUTH REGIONAL H.Q., 3-7 Lynton St, Mt Hawthorn	60 B 6
PERTH, 60 Frame Ct	60 D 9
ROCKINGHAM, Shire Depot, Crocker St	137 C 4
SERPENTINE - JARRAHDALE, Cockram St, Mundijong	143 A 9
STATE H.Q. (WASES), 91 Leake St, Belmont	62 E10
STIRLING, (Des Penman Reserve), Carcoola St, Nollamara	46 C 6
SUBIACO, Upham St	59 E10
SWAN, Bishop Rd, Midland	50 D 3
WANNEROO, 15 Winton Rd, Joondalup	19 D 8

SUBURBS (See Localities, Postcodes & Postal Districts)

TENNIS CLUBS & PUBLIC COURTS

PUBLIC COURTS

ARMADALE, Orchard Ave	116 D 6
BALCATTA, Rickman St	46 A 4
BALGA, Camberwell Rd	46 C 1
BUCKLAND HILL, Edwards Pde, Mosman Park	80 D 7
CARINE, Beach Rd	31 B 9
COLLEGE PARK, Princess Rd, Nedlands	71 C10
CRAIGIE, Camberwarra Dr (opposite Eagle St)	23 D 7
DIANELLA, Light St	47 B 7

	Map Ref.
EMERALD PARK, Harvest Lp, Edgewater	24 A 2
FLOREAT WATERS, The Lane	59 C 5
FLOREAT, Shann St	71 C 1
GIBBON STREET, Gibbon St, Mosman Park	80 D 6
GIRRAWHEEN, Hudson Ave	32 C 7
GLENDALOUGH, Jon Sanders Dr	59 E 6
GLENGARRY, Merrick Wy, Duncraig	31 B 6
GREENWOOD, Penistone St	31 E 6
HILLARYS, Fenton St	30 C 1
HOLLYWOOD, Smyth Rd, Nedlands	71 D 6
INGLEWOOD, Walter Rd	61 C 4
INNALOO, Langley Wy	45 C 8
JOONDANNA, Powell St	60 D 3
KINGSLEY, Cherokee Village, Hocking Rd	24 E 9
LATHLAIN PARK, McCartney Cr, Lathlain	74 A 6
LYNWOOD, Purley Cr	94 D 1
MAYLANDS, Peninsula Rd	62 A10
MT LAWLEY, Queens Cr	61 B 7
MULLALOO, Karalundie Wy	23 A 5
MUNDARING, Chipper St	68 B 1
McCALLUM PARK, Garland St, Victoria Park	73 D 6
POINT WALTER RESERVE, Honour Dr, Bicton	81 B 6
ROBERTSON PARK, Fitzgerald St, North Perth	60 E10
SCARBOROUGH (Scarborough High Sch), Newborough St	45 A 7
THORNLIE (Castle Glen Estate), Discovery Dr	95 C 8
WANNEROO COUNTRY CLUB, Crisafulli Ave, Wanneroo	20 D 9
YANCHEP, Yanchep Beach Rd	4 D 3

TENNIS CLUBS

ALEXANDER PARK, Melrose Cr, Mount Lawley	61 A 5
ALLEN PARK, Clement Rd, Swanbourne	70 D 9
APPLECROSS, The Strand	82 C 4
ARMADALE, Gwynne Park, Forrest Rd	116 C 8
BASSENDEAN, behind Bassendean Civic Centre	63 A 1
BAYSWATER, Cnr Garratt Rd & Murray St	62 A 6
BELMONT PARK, Cnr Scott St & Robinson Ave, Cloverdale	75 A 6
BLUE GUM RESERVE, Cnr Rountree & Disney Sts, Mt Pleasant	92 D 2
BULL CREEK, Benningfield Rd	93 A 5
CANNING, Hedley Pl, Bentley	84 B 5
CITY BEACH, Frinton Ave	70 D 1
CLAREMONT, Cnr Claremont Cr & Davies Rd	71 A 8
COCKBURN, Recreation Rd, Hamilton Hill	101 A 2
CORINTHIAN PARK, Cnr Beatrice Ave & Leach Hwy, Shelley	83 C10
COTTESLOE, Cnr Broome & Napier Sts	80 C 1
CURTIN, Curtin University, next to Commonwealth Hockey Stadium, Hayman Rd, Bentley (Facing Map 135)	
DALKEITH, Cnr Beatrice Rd & Victoria Ave	81 C 3
DARLINGTON, Darlington Park, Pine Tce	66 A 4
EAST FREMANTLE, Preston Point Rd	81 A10
FLOREAT PARK, The Boulevard, Floreat	59 D 9

294

	Map	Ref.
FORRESTFIELD, Morrison Rd	86	B 1
FREMANTLE, Cnr Parry & Ellen Sts	1C	C 4
GLEN FORREST, Marnie Rd	66	D 2
GREENMOUNT, Welbourne Park, Scott St	65	C 1
GREENWOOD, Beach Rd, Warwick	31	E 7
HENSMAN PARK, Cnr Coode & Hensman Sts, South Perth	73	A 9
HIGGINS PARK, Playfield St, East Victoria Park	84	A 2
KALAMUNDA, Railway Rd	77	D 7
KARDINYA, Kingston Pl	92	B 7
KELMSCOTT, Kelmscott Recreation Centre, River Rd	106	E 10
KENWICK, Brixton St, Beckenham	85	D 8
KWINANA DISTRICTS, Wallgreen Cr, Calista	130	E 6
LEEDERVILLE, Bourke St	60	C 8
LESMURDIE, Eversden Reserve, Falls Rd	87	C 1
LOTON PARK, Cnr Bulwer & Lord Sts, Perth	1C	B 1
MACCABI, Woodrow Ave, Dianella	61	A 1
MAIDA VALE, Maida Vale Recreation Reserve off Acacia Rd	76	E 1
MANDURAH, Dower St	165	C 1
MANNING, Elderfield Rd, Waterford	83	C 7
MAYLANDS, Clarkson Rd	74	B 1
MELVILLE/PALMYRA, Cnr Princep Rd & Canning Hwy, Melville	91	C 1
MEMORIAL PARK, Cnr Gosnells & Mills Rds, Gosnells	96	B 7
MIDLAND, Sayer St	50	C 8
MOSMAN PARK, McCabe St	80	E 8
MT LAWLEY, Cnr Hamer Pde & Central Ave, Inglewood	61	C 5
NEDLANDS, Cnr Gallop Rd & Bruce St	81	E 1
NOLLAMARA, Kindra Wy	46	C 6
NORANDA, Garson Ct	47	E 5
NORTH BEACH, Wilberforce St	44	D 3
NORTH PERTH, Farmer St	60	E 7
OCEAN RIDGE, Sail Tce, Heathridge	23	C 2
ONSLOW PARK, Onslow Rd, Shenton Park	72	A 4
PEPPERMINT GROVE, Bay View Tce	80	E 4
PICKERING BROOK, Weston Rd	88	E 9
REABOLD, Howtree Pl (opposite Floreat Forum), Floreat	59	C .9
ROCKINGHAM, Wanliss St	137	A 4
ROLEYSTONE, Jarrah Rd	107	E 7
ROYAL KINGS PARK, Kings Park Rd, West Perth	72	C 3
SAFETY BAY, Royal Rd	136	D 10
SCARBOROUGH, Deanmore Rd	44	E 9
SORRENTO, Cnr Warwick & Marmion Rds, Duncraig	30	D 6
SOUTH MANDURAH, Merlin Street Reserve, Falcon	162A	E 9
SOUTH PERTH, Murray St, Como	83	B 3
THORNLIE, Thornlie Ave	95	C 3
UNIVERSITY OF W.A., Hackett Dr, Crawley (Facing Map 120)		
UNIVERSITY OF W.A., McGillivray Oval, Brockway Rd, Mt Claremont	71	B 2
WANNEROO, Elliot Rd	20	E 10

	Map	Ref.
WEMBLEY DOWNS, Cnr Empire Ave & Eltham St	59	A 6
WILLETTON, Burrendah Blvd	93	C 5

THEATRES, CINEMAS & DRIVE-IN CINEMAS

CINEMAS

	Map	Ref.
ASTOR, Mt Lawley	61	B 8
CAROUSEL 8, Carousel Shopping Centre, Cannington	84	E 7
CINECENTRE, Perth	1C	A 3
CINEMA 1, City Arcade, Perth	1C	A 2
CINEMA CITY, Perth	1C	A 3
CYGNET, Como	83	A 1
ESSEX STREET CINEMAS, Fremantle	1D	C 6
FTI, Fremantle	1D	C 4
GREATER UNION 8 CINEMAS, Woodlands	59	C 2
HOYTS CENTRE, St Martins Arcade, Perth	1C	A 3
KIMBERLEY CINEMA, Perth	1C	A 3
LUMIERE, Perth	1C	E 2
NEW OXFORD, Leederville	60	C 9
OMNI, West Perth	60	D 10
PICCADILLY, Hay St Mall, Perth	1C	E 3
PORT, Fremantle	1D	C 4
QUEENSGATE 6 CINEMAS, Fremantle	1D	C 5
SAVOY, Perth	1C	A 3
SWAN PARK CINEMA, Midvale	50	E 7
TOWN, Perth	1C	E 2
VILLAGE, Dalkeith	81	C 2
WINDSOR, Nedlands	71	D 8

DRIVE-IN CINEMAS

	Map	Ref.
GALAXY, Goollelal Dr, Kingsley	24	D 10
HIGHWAY TWIN, Bentley	84	C 5
METRO TWIN, Innaloo	59	C 2

THEATRES

	Map	Ref.
BELVOIR VALLEY AMPHITHEATRE, Millendon	29	D 6
DOLPHIN, University of W.A., Crawley (Inset Map 120)		
ENTERTAINMENT CENTRE, Perth	1C	E 1
GARRICK THEATRE, Guildford	49	D 2
HAYMAN THEATRE, Curtin University, Bentley (Facing Map 135)		
HIS MAJESTYS, Perth	1C	E 2
HOLE IN THE WALL, Subiaco	72	A 2
KADS THEATRE, Kalamunda	77	D 6
MANDURAH LITTLE THEATRE, Mandurah Tce, Mandurah	164	E 2
OCTAGON, University of W.A., Crawley (Inset Map 120)		
PARKERVILLE AMPHITHEATRE, Parkerville	53	A 5
PATCH THEATRE, Victoria Park	73	E 5
PERTH CONCERT HALL, Perth	1C	A 3
PLAYHOUSE THEATRE, Perth	1C	A 3
PRINCESS MAY THEATRE, Fremantle	1D	C 4
REGAL THEATRE, Subiaco	72	A 1
ROLEYSTONE THEATRE, Brookton Hwy, Roleystone	108	A 10

	Map	Ref.
SPARE PARTS PUPPET THEATRE, Fremantle	1D	B 6
STIRLING THEATRE, Cedric St, Stirling	45	E 8
SWY THEATRE, Murray St, Perth	1C	A 3
THE QUARRY AMPHITHEATRE, City Beach	59	A 9

WATER SKIING AREAS

	Map	Ref.
AQUINAS BAY	83	B 9
ASSOCIATION HEADQUARTERS, Heirisson Island	73	C 6
CABLE WATERSKIING, Munster	101	B 10
CANNING RIVER	82	E 9
CHIDLEY POINT	81	A 6
FREEWAY	72	D 7
INSTRUCTION AREA (commercial only)	72	E 5
MANGLES BAY	137	B 1
MULLALOO	22	E 8
POINT WALTER	81	C 6
ROCKINGHAM - SHOALWATER	136	B 6
SAFETY BAY	145	B 8
THE BAMBOOS	81	A 1
WAYLEN BAY (or Frenchmans Bay)	82	C 3
WHITE BEACH	81	B 3
W.A. WATERSKI PARK, Baldivis	139	E 6

WEIGHBRIDGES (Public)

	Map	Ref.
BASSENDEAN, Non Ferral Pty Ltd, Cnr Collier Rd & Jackson St (Capacity 60 tonne)	62	D 2
BAYSWATER Cleanaway, Lot 102 Collier Rd (Capacity 60 tonne)	62	C 2
BAYSWATER, Simsmetal, 15 Mooney St, (Capacity 60 tonne)	62	C 3
BENTLEY, Wesfeeds Pty Ltd, 31 Sevenoaks St, (Capacity 60 tonne)	84	C 2
CANNING VALE, The Shell Company of Australia, Market City Service Station, 280 Bannister Rd, (Capacity 60 tonne)	93	E 8
JANDAKOT, Rustproofers Ltd, 26 Cutler Rd, (Capacity 60 tonne)	103	A 9
KEWDALE, NR & NJ Gardiner & Son, Hardy Rd, (Capacity 60 tonne)	75	E 10
KEWDALE, Westrail, Freight Yards off Kewdale Rd, (Capacity 50 tonne)	75	B 9
MUNDIJONG, Medulla Brook Enterprises, Cnr Sth Western Hwy & Shanley Rd, (Capacity 60 tonne)	151	C 1
OSBORNE PARK, Inghams Enterprises, Baden St, (Capacity 40 tonne)	60	B 3
RED HILL, Swan Shire Council, Regional Refuse Disposal Site, Toodyay Rd, (Capacity 60 tonne)	38	D 5
SPEARWOOD, Simsmetals Pty Ltd, 200 Barrington St (Capacity 50 tonne)	101	E 9
SPEARWOOD, Temple Freights WA, 80 Howson Wy, Bibra Lake (Capacity 85 tonne)	101	D 7
WEST MIDLAND, DL Cowling, Great Eastern Hwy, (Capacity 30 tonne)	50	A 8

WINERIES

	Map	Ref.
AVALON WINES, Glen Forrest	67	A 4
BANARA WINES, Caversham	49	D 5
BARTOLONE WINES, Maddington	96	E 3
BONANNELLA WINES, Wanneroo	20	D 4
CAROSA WINES, Mt Helena	55	D 6
CHIDLOW BROOK VINEYARD, Chidlow	42	C 10
COBANOV WINES, Herne Hill	37	A 5
CORSHAM WINE, Carmel	88	D 6
DARLINGTON ESTATE WINERY, Glen Forrest	66	C 8
FARANDA WINES, Wanneroo	24	E 1
GNANGARA WINES (Evans & Tate), Henley Brook	29	B 8
HAINAULT VINEYARD, Bickley	89	B 3
HENLEY PARK, Henley Brook	29	B 8
HIGHWAY WINES, Middle Swan	36	D 7
HOUGHTON WINES, Middle Swan	36	B 10
IOPPOLO WINES, Wanneroo	20	D 4
JADRAN WINES, Orange Grove	96	E 2
JANE BROOK ESTATE, Middle Swan	51	A 2
LAMONTS WINERY, Millendon	168	B 9
LECKVILLE VINEYARD, Maddington	96	A 4
LITTLE RIVER WINES, Henley Brook	36	B 4
MANN WINERY, Millendon	29	C 7
OLIVE FARM WINES, South Guildford	63	C 4
PAUL CONTI WINES, Woodvale	24	D 6
PEEL ESTATE WINES, Karnup	159	C 4
PIESSE BROOK WINES, Bickley	78	C 10
PINELLI WINES, Caversham	49	B 5
REVELRY WINES, Herne Hill	36	E 5
RIVERSIDE VINEYARD, Bassendean	63	B 4
RIVERVIEW WINES, Henley Brook	36	B 3
SANDALFORD WINES, Caversham	50	A 4
TALIJANCICH WINES, Herne Hill	36	E 2
TWIN HILL WINES, Millendon	29	D 7
VALLEY WINES, Herne Hill	37	B 6
VINDARA WINES, Herne Hill	36	D 6
VINO ITALIA WINES, Middle Swan	37	C 8
VISNICA WINERY, Millendon	29	E 8
WEST SWAN WINES, West Swan	49	E 1
WESTFIELD WINES, Millendon	29	D 7

YACHTING, ROWING & ANGLING CLUBS

	Map	Ref.
AMATEUR ROWING ASSOCIATION OF WA (Inc) (ARAWA)	82	E 6
AUSTRALIAN NATIVES ASSOCIATION ROWING CLUB (ANARC)	82	E 6

Name	Map	Ref.
AUSTRALIAN POWER BOAT ASSOCIATION HEADQUARTERS (APBA)	73	D 4
BELMONT SPORTS & RECREATION CLUB/ANGLING (BS&RC), Cnr Keane St & Abernethy Rd, Belmont	74	E 6
CLAREMONT YACHT CLUB (CYC)	81	A 1
COCKBURN POWER BOATS ASSOCIATION/ANGLING (CPBA/A)	110	D 4
CURTIN UNIVERSITY OF TECHNOLOGY ROWING CLUB (CUBC)	83	C 8
EAST FREMANTLE YACHT CLUB (EFYC)	81	A 9
FREMANTLE ROWING CLUB (FRC)	80	D 9
FREMANTLE SAILING CLUB/ANGLING (FSC/A)	90	C 8
HILLARYS YACHT CLUB/ANGLING (HYC/A)	30	A 3
JERVOISE BAY SAILING CLUB (JBSC)	110	C 2
MANDURAH OFFSHORE FISHING CLUB (MOFC)	162	D 10
MANDURAH YACHT CLUB (MYC), Mandurah Tce	162	D 9
MARINA, Ocean Reef	18	E 10
MARMION ANGLING & AQUATIC CLUB (MAAC)	30	B 7
MAYLANDS YACHT CLUB (MYC)	61	D 9
MOUNTS BAY SAILING CLUB (MBSC)	72	B 10
NEDLANDS YACHT CLUB (NYC)	81	E 2
PERTH DINGHY SAILING CLUB (PDSC)	72	A 8
PERTH FLYING SQUADRON YACHT CLUB (PFSYC)	81	E 3
PERTH ROWING CLUB (CPRC)	82	E 6
ROYAL FRESHWATER BAY YACHT CLUB (RFBYC)	81	A 4
ROYAL PERTH YACHT CLUB (RPYC)	72	B 10
SAFETY BAY YACHT CLUB (SBYC)	144	D 1
SHELLEY SAILING CLUB (SSC)	83	C 8
SOUTH OF PERTH YACHT CLUB (SPYC)	82	D 3
STIRLING GO BOAT CLUB (SGBC)	73	D 4
SUN CITY YACHT CLUB (SCYC), Sun City Marina, Two Rocks	2	B 2
SWAN RIVER ROWING CLUB (SRRC)	82	E 6
SWAN YACHT CLUB (SYC)	80	D 9
THE CRUISING YACHT CLUB (TCYC)	136	C 4
UNIVERSITY OF WESTERN AUSTRALIA BOAT CLUB (UWABC)	72	A 8
WA ROWING CLUB (WARC)	1C	A 4
WA SPEED BOAT CLUB (WASBC)	73	D 4
WANNEROO COUNTRY CLUB/ANGLING (WCC/A), Crisafulli Ave, Wanneroo	20	C 9
WHITFORDS BAY SAILING CLUB (WBSC)	22	E 10
WHITFORDS SEA SPORTS CLUB/ANGLING (WSSC/A)	18	E 10

Y.H.A. HOSTELS

Name	Map	Ref.
BRITANNIA YHA, William St, Perth	1C	A 1
FREMANTLE YHA, 81 Solomon Rd, Fremantle	90	D 6
FREMANTLE YHA, 96-98 Hampton Rd, Fremantle	90	D 6
KALAMUNDA YHA, Mundaring Weir Rd, Bickley	78	C 9
MUNDARING WEIR YHA, (Inset Map 79)		
PERTH CITY YHA, 42-48 Francis St, Perth	1C	A 1
PERTH CITY YHA, 60-62 Newcastle St, East Perth	1C	A 1

TOWN AND SHIRE CAR REGISTRATION NUMBERS
Outside the Metropolitan Area

Where a town council and shire council district bear the same letter, the shire council plates bear a dot between the letters and number. Town councils do not bear a dot between letters and number.

Licence Plate No.	Local Authority
AL	Albany (Shire)
A	Albany (Town)
AK	Armadale-Kelmscott
AS	Ashburton
AU	Augusta-Margaret River
AW	West Arthur
BE	Beverley
BT	Boddington
BD	Boulder
BU	Boyup Brook
B	Bridgetown-Greenbushes
BO	Brookton
BM	Broome
BH	Broomehill
BK	Bruce Rock
BY	Bunbury (Town)
BSN	Busselton
CP	Capel
CA	Carnamah
C	Carnarvon
CV	Chapman Valley
CH	Chittering
CO	Collie
CG	Coolgardie
CW	Coorow
CR	Corrigin
CB	Cranbrook
CN	Cuballing
CD	Cue
CMT	Cunderdin
DL	Dalwallinu
DN	Dandaragan
DA	Dardanup
DE	Denmark
DB	Donnybrook-Balingup
D	Dowerin
DU	Dumbleyung
DS	Dundas
East Pilbara:	
1. EP	Marble Bar
2. EP	Nullagine
E	Esperance
EX	Exmouth

Licence Plate No.	Local Authority
GN	Geraldton (town)
GG	Gingin
GN	Gnowangerup
GO	Goomalling
G	Greenough
HC	Halls Creek
H	Harvey
IR	Irwin
JP	Jerramungup
KM	Kalamunda
KA	Katanning
KMC	Kalgoorlie (town)
KE	Kellerberrin
KT	Kent
KO	Kojonup
KN	Kondinin
KD	Koorda
KU	Kulin
LG	Lake Grace
LA	Laverton
L	Leonora
MM	Mount Marshall
MA	Mount Magnet
MH	Mandurah
WA	Manjimup
MK	Meekatharra
MN	Menzies
MD	Merredin
MI	Mingenew
M	Moora
MO	Morawa
MBL	Mukinbudin
MW	Mullewa
MDG	Mundaring
MU	Murchison
MY	Murray
NP	Nannup
NB	Narembeen
NO	Narrogin (shire)
NGN	Narrogin (town)
N	Northam (shire)
N	Northam (town)
NR	Northampton

Licence Plate No.	Local Authority
NA	Nungarin
PJ	Perenjori
PN	Pingelly
PL	Plantagenet
PH	Port Hedland
Q	Quairading
RA	Ravensthorpe
R	Roebourne
S	Sandstone
SJ	Serpentine-Jarrahdale
SB	Shark Bay
SW	Swan
TA	Tambellup
TN	Tammin
TS	Three Springs
T	Toodyay
KTY	Trayning
GU	Upper Gascoyne
VP	Victoria Plains
W	Wagin
WD	Wandering
WN	Wanneroo
WR	Waroona
KW	West Kimberley (Derby)
WT	Westonia
West Pilbara	
1. WP	Ashburton
2. WP	Tableland
WK	Wickepin
WU	Wiluna
WL	Williams
WO	Woodanilling
WB	Wongan-Ballidu
WM	Wyalkatchem
WY	Wyndham-East Kimberley
YA	Yalgoo
YL	Yilgarn
Y	York

DESCRIPTION OF ROAD SUFFIXES

CULS-DE-SAC

SUFFIXES	ABBREV.	DESCRIPTIONS
CLOSE	CL	A short enclosed roadway.
COURT	CT	A short enclosed roadway.
COURTYARD	CY	An enclosed area.
COVE	CE	A short enclosed roadway.
CROSS	CRO	A roadway forming a "T" or cross.
DALE	DL	A roadway situated between hills.
ELBOW	EL	A roadway containing a sharp bend or turn.
GAP	GP	A roadway that traverses a passage or pass through a ridge or hill.
GARDENS	GNS	A roadway with special plantings of trees, flowers etc. and often leading to a place for public enjoyment.
GLADE	GL	A roadway usually in a valley of trees.
GLEN	GLEN	A roadway usually in a valley of trees.
GREEN	GRN	A roadway often leading to a grassed public recreation area.
GROVE	GR	A roadway which often features a group of trees standing together.
HEIGHTS	HTS	A roadway traversing high ground.
HILL	HL	A roadway going up a natural rise.
LOOKOUT	LKT	A roadway leading to or having a view of fine natural scenery.
MEWS	ME	A roadway having houses grouped around the end.
PLACE	PL	A short sometimes narrow enclosed roadway.
PLAZA	PA	A roadway enclosing the four sides of an area forming a market place or open space.
RETREAT	RT	A roadway forming a place of seclusion.
RISE	RI	A roadway going to a higher place or position.
SQUARE	SQ	A roadway bounding the four sides of an area to be used as open space or a group of buildings.
TOP	TP	A roadway constructed at the highest part of an area.
TOR	TR	A roadway along a rocky height or hillside.
VALE	VL	A roadway along low ground between hills.
VIEW	VW	A roadway commanding a wide panoramic view across surrounding areas.
YARD	YD	A short roadway ending in an enclosed place used for a particular purpose or business.

OPEN ENDED STREETS

SUFFIXES	ABBREV.	DESCRIPTIONS
ALLEY	AL	A usually narrow roadway for people or vehicles in cities and towns. A minor roadway through the centre of city blocks or squares.
ARCADE	AR	A passage having an arched roof, or any covered passageway, especially one with shops along the sides.
AVENUE	AVE	A broad roadway, usually planted on each side with trees.
BOULEVARD	BLVD	A wide roadway, well paved, usually ornamented with trees and grass plots.
BREAK	BK	Vehicular access on a formed or unformed surface which was originally prepared as a firebreak.
BYPASS	BY	An alternative roadway constructed to enable through traffic to avoid congested areas or other obstructions to movement.
CHASE	CH	A roadway leading down to a valley.
CIRCLE	CI	A roadway which forms a circle or part of a circle.
CIRCUIT	CC	A roadway enclosing an area.
CIRCUS	CS	A circular open place where many roadways come together.
CORNER	CNR	A roadway containing a sharp bend or corner.
CRESCENT	CR	A crescent of half mooned shaped roadway.
CREST	CST	A roadway running along the top or summit of a hill.
DIP	DIP	Short roadway through a steep valley or gully.
DRIVE	DR	A wide thoroughfare allowing a steady flow of traffic without many cross streets.
EDGE	ED	A roadway constructed along the edge of a cliff or ridge.
ENTRANCE	ENT	A roadway connecting other roads.
ESPLANADE	ES	A level roadway, often along the seaside or a river.
FAIRWAY	FRY	A short open roadway between other roadways.
FOLLOW	FO	A roadway meandering through wooded or undulating country.
FORMATION	FMN	A formed surface, once a timber railway which now provides vehicular access.
FREEWAY	FWY	An express highway, with limited or controlled access.
HIGHWAY	HWY	A main road or thoroughfare, a main route.
INTERCHANGE	INT	A highway or freeway junction designed so that traffic streams do not intersect.
LANE	LA	A narrow way between walls, buildings etc. a narrow country or city roadway.
LOOP	LP	A roadway that diverges from and rejoins the main thoroughfare.
MALL	ML	A sheltered walk, promenade or shopping precinct.
MEANDER	MR	A sinuous, winding roadway, wandering at random through an area or subdivision.
PARADE	PDE	A public promenade or roadway which has good pedestrian facilities along the side.
PARKWAY	PWY	A roadway through parklands or an open grassland area.
PASS	PS	A roadway connecting major thoroughfares or running through hills.
PATH	PT	A roadway usually used for pedestrian traffic.
PROMENADE	PRO	A roadway like an avenue with plenty of facilities for the public to take a leisurely walk, a public place for walking.
QUAYS	QS	A roadway leading to a landing place alongside or projecting into water.
RAMBLE	RA	A roadway that meanders from place to place.
RIDGE	RGE	A roadway along the top of a hill.
ROAD	RD	A place where one may ride, an open way or public passage for vehicles, persons and animals, a roadway forming a means of communication between one place and another.
ROTARY	RTY	An intersection of two or more carriageways at a common level where all traffic travels around a central island.
ROW	RW	A roadway with a line of professional buildings on either side.
SPUR	SP	A minor roadway running off at less than 45 degrees.
STREET	ST	A public roadway in a town, city or urban area, especially a paved thoroughfare with footpaths and buildings along one or both sides.
TERRACE	TCE	A roadway usually with houses on either side raised above the road level.
TRACK	TK	A roadway with a single carriageway.
TRAIL	TRL	A roadway through a natural bushland region.
TURN	TN	A roadway containing a sharp bend or turn.
VISTA	VS	A road with a view or outlook.
WALK	WK	A thoroughfare with restricted vehicle access used mainly by pedestrians.
WAY	WY	An accessway between two streets.